ROADWATCH

Wherever you're driving, call AA Roadwatch for the latest reports on roadworks and weather. Information is regularly updated throughout the day and night. Save yourself time and frustration— phone before you go . . .

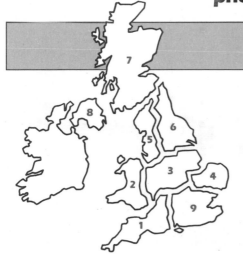

NATIONAL ROADWORKS AND WEATHER

National motorways	0836-401-110
1. West Country	0836-401-111
2. Wales	0836-401-112
3. Midlands	0836-401-113
4. East Anglia	0836-401-114
5. North-west England	0836-401-115
6. North-east England	0836-401-116
7. Scotland	0836-401-117
8. Northern Ireland	0836-401-118
9. South-east England	see below

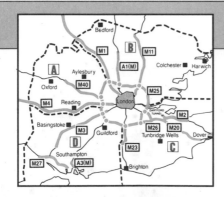

LONDON AND THE SOUTH-EAST— TRAFFIC, ROADWORKS AND WEATHER

Central London (inside North/South Circulars)	0836-401-122
A. Motorways/roads between M4 and M1	0836-401-123
B. Motorways/roads between M1 and Dartford Tunnel	0836-401-124
C. Motorways/roads between Dartford Tunnel and M23	0836-401-125
D. Motorways/roads between M23 and M4	0836-401-126
M25 London Orbital only	0836-401-127
London special events (certain weekends only)	0836-401-128

ROADWATCH

Messages are charged at a rate of 25p per minute cheap rate, 38p per minute at all other times.
Callers pay only for the time they use.

FOR YOUR FREE COPY OF THE FULL AA DIRECTORY OF RECORDED INFORMATION WRITE TO
AA INFORMATION SERVICES (DEPT BRA) CWI, FANUM HOUSE, BASINGSTOKE, HANTS RG21 2EA.

AA

COMPLETE ATLAS OF BRITAIN

12th edition October 1989
11th edition October 1988
10th edition October 1987
9th edition October 1986
Reprinted March 1987
8th edition October 1985
7th edition October 1984
Reprinted May 1985
6th edition March 1984
5th edition January 1983
4th edition October 1981
3rd edition January 1981
2nd edition January 1980
1st edition April 1979

Published by The Automobile Association, Fanum House, Basingstoke, Hampshire RG21 2EA.
ISBN 07495 0001 8

Printed in Spain by Artes Gráficas Toledo, S.A.
D.L.TO:996-1989

The contents of this book are believed correct at the time of printing. Nevertheless, the publisher can accept no responsibility for errors or omissions, or for changes in the details given.

Mapping produced by the Cartographic Department of The Automobile Association. This atlas has been compiled and produced from the Automaps database utilising electronic and computer technology.

The London section is based on Ordnance Survey maps with the permission of the Controller of Her Majesty's Stationery Office. Crown copyright.

Every effort has been made to ensure that the contents of our new database are correct. However, if there are any errors or omissions, please write to the Cartographic Editor, Publishing Division, The Automobile Association, Fanum House, Basingstoke, Hampshire RG21 2EA.

A CIP catalogue record for this book is available from the British Library.

Contents

Using this atlas

Whether you wish to trace the route of the M4 from London to South Wales, find the most direct route from Ipswich to Liverpool, pick your way round Coventry, or need to solve any other journey planning problem the Complete Atlas of Britain is an essential guide.

ROUTE PLANNING
Specially designed route planning maps, showing a basic road network of motorways, primary routes and most A roads, help you plan long distance journeys quickly and easily.

ATLAS
Clear, easy-to-read mapping helps you to plan more detailed journeys, and provides a wealth of information for the motorist. All motorways, primary, A and B roads and unclassified roads are shown. The atlas also identifies those roads outside urban areas which are under construction. Additional features include rivers, lakes and reservoirs, railway lines, interesting places to visit, picnic sites and Tourist Information Centres, and to assist you in estimating journey length, distances are shown in miles between blue marker symbols.

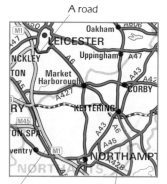

A road
Motorway
Primary routes

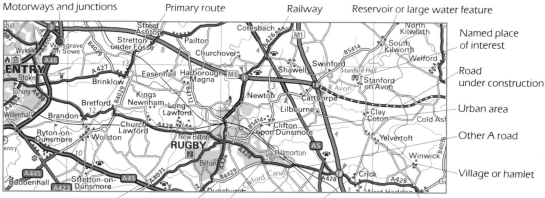

Motorways and junctions
Primary route
Railway
Reservoir or large water feature
Named place of interest
Road under construction
Urban area
Other A road
Village or hamlet
Tourist Information Centre
B road
Mileage
River
Unclassified road

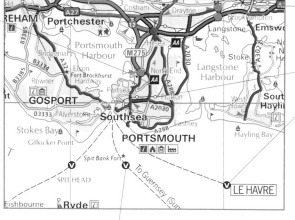

AA Port Service Centre
Level crossing
Railway station
Continental ferry routes
Local ferry route

FERRY AND RAIL ROUTES
Coastal stretches of mapping provide basic off-shore information including ferry routes within Great Britain and to the Continent, to assist you in planning journeys overseas. Throughout the atlas, railway lines with stations and level crossings are shown, to assist with general navigation or rail travel requirements.

MOTORWAYS
The principal motorway maps, arranged in easy-to-follow strip form, highlight junctions, exit signs, service areas, and access on and off the motorway.

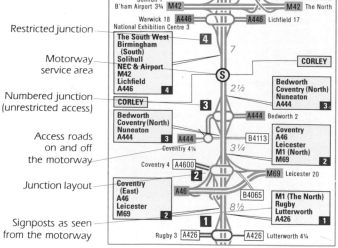

Restricted junction
Motorway service area
Numbered junction (unrestricted access)
Access roads on and off the motorway
Junction layout
Signposts as seen from the motorway

Tourist attraction within urban area
Long distance footpath marked
Place of interest located and named
AA viewpoint
Tourist Information Centre

TOURISM AND LEISURE
Red pictorial symbols and red type, highlight numerous places of interest, catering for every taste. Red symbols within yellow boxes show tourist attractions in towns. Use them to plan days out or places to visit on holiday. Remember to check opening times before you visit to avoid disappointment.

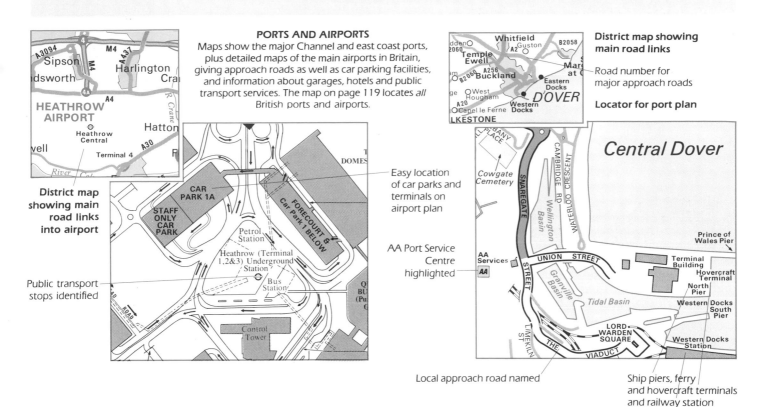

PORTS AND AIRPORTS

Maps show the major Channel and east coast ports, plus detailed maps of the main airports in Britain, giving approach roads as well as car parking facilities, and information about garages, hotels and public transport services. The map on page 119 locates *all* British ports and airports.

District map showing main road links into airport

Public transport stops identified

Easy location of car parks and terminals on airport plan

AA Port Service Centre highlighted

District map showing main road links

Road number for major approach roads

Locator for port plan

Central Dover

Local approach road named

Ship piers, ferry and hovercraft terminals and railway station clearly shown

TOWN PLANS

Up-to-date, fully-indexed town plans show AA recommended roads and other practical information such as one way streets, car parks and restricted roads, making navigation much easier. Area plans show major road networks into and out of the region.

Area map showing main road links and neighbouring towns

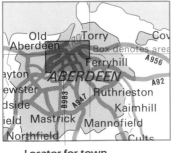

Locator for town plan

AA recommended throughroutes clearly identified

Town parking facilities

Central Aberdeen

Major buildings and places of interest highlighted and named

Street index with every plan

Aberdeen

Abbotsford Lane	C2-D2
Academy Street	C4-D4
Advocates Road	E8
Affleck Street	D3
Albert Quay	E3-F3
Albert Place	A5-A6
Albert Street	A4-A5
Albert Terrace	A4-A5
Albury Place	B2-C2
Albury Road	B2-C2-C3
Albyn Grove	A4

Churches located

Pedestrian areas located

One way streets shown

LONDON

Easy-to-read, fully-indexed street maps of Inner London, including a map of Theatreland, provide a simple guide to finding your way around the city.

Underground railway stations located and named

Major places of tourist interest shown

Open spaces and parks highlighted

Garage parking identified

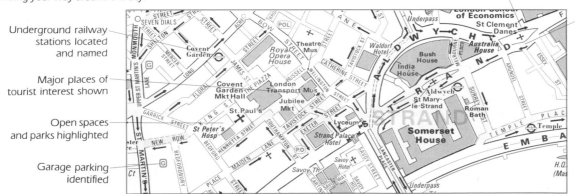

One way systems clearly shown

AA recommended routes for easier navigation

Alphabetical street index

Signs and symbols

To assist you in journey planning and making the most of the comprehensive information contained in this atlas, it helps if you understand the signs on the roads and the symbols used on the maps. The principal benefit of the Department of Transport road signs is that the primary road signs (green) indicate the most straightforward route between one town and another. They do not necessarily indicate the most *direct* route, but it should be remembered that direct routes may not be the quickest, or the easiest to follow.

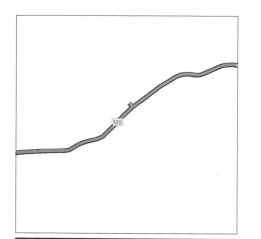

MOTORWAYS

On the map – all motorways are blue. Motorway signposts have white lettering on a blue background. Advance direction signs approaching an interchange generally include the junction number in a black box. On the map, the junction number appears in white on a solid *blue* circle.

A white number on a solid *red* circle indicates restricted access on or off the motorway at that point.

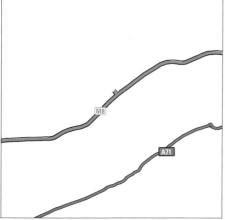

PRIMARY ROUTES

On the map – all the primary routes are green. The signposts on primary roads are also green, with white lettering and yellow numbers. Apart from the motorways, primary routes are the most important traffic routes in both urban and rural areas. They form a network of throughroutes connecting 'primary towns', which are generally places of traffic importance. Primary routes are usually along A roads.

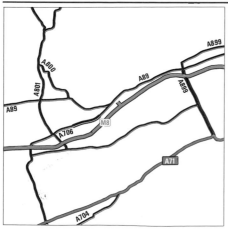
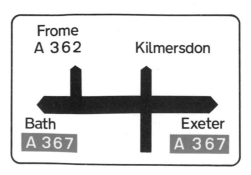

A ROADS

On the map – all A roads are shown in red, unless part of the primary network when they are green. The signposts along these roads have black lettering on a white background. At a junction with a primary route, the primary road number appears yellow in a green box.

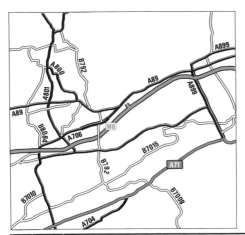

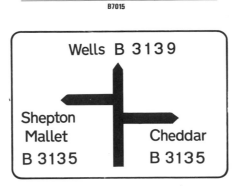

B ROADS
On the map – all B roads not in the primary network are represented in yellow. The signs on B roads are black lettering on a white background, the same as for A roads.

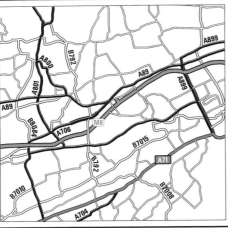

UNCLASSIFIED ROADS
On the map – all unclassified (unnumbered) roads are white. New signposts along unclassified roads are usually of the 'local direction' type. These have black lettering on a white background with a blue border. Many minor roads still have pre-World War II 'finger' post signs.

PLACE NAMES
Throughout the atlas, the size of lettering and its style is an indication of the size and importance of a place or location. This is generally related to population. All places with over 3,000 inhabitants are shown, plus there is a selection of smaller locations which are useful navigation points or possible destinations in some of the more isolated rural areas.

The section of map below highlights the various population categories and explains the difference in the size and style of lettering. The name London is a special category as it has a population in excess of 8 million.

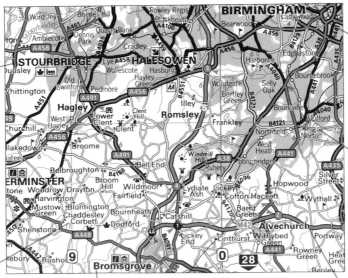

Stourbridge
Places with this style and size of lettering include major towns and cities with populations between 50,000 and 200,000.

Birmingham
Places using this style and size of lettering indicate cities and very large towns with populations between 200,000 and 500,000.

King's Norton
This style and size of lettering is used to show suburban locations within large urban areas. Their population size is included within the 200,000 and 500,000 category.

Chaddesley Corbett
This style and size of lettering is used to show villages and hamlets with less than 3,000 inhabitants. In isolated rural areas in the north a selection of crossroads and farms are shown in slightly smaller lettering – Auchnotteroch

Bromsgrove
Metropolitan Districts, larger market and developing towns with populations between 10,000 and 50,000 are indicated by this size and style of lettering.

Alvechurch
Locations shown in this style and size of lettering are generally small market towns or developing communities situated on the fringes of large urban areas. Their populations vary between 3,000 and 10,000 inhabitants.

Journey planning

Whether you are planning a journey for business or for pleasure, the Complete Atlas will make it much easier. A little preparation can save valuable time.

Alertness
If you are planning a long journey, or just going out for the day, it is essential you set out feeling alert and confident. Tired, frustrated drivers are a potential danger to themselves, to their passengers and to other road users. You will feel more capable of dealing with unexpected situations, and have a more comfortable journey if you plan ahead.

CHECK LIST
On long journeys, in particular, it pays to make a check list of thing to do, even down to cancelling the milk and papers, taking the dog to the kennels, making sandwiches and a thermos, checking the roof rack and locking the door. We all forget something at some time or other! Have you never set off without having to stop just a few miles from home to wonder if you had remembered to turn the gas off?

PREPARATION
How to get there
The special route planning maps will help you to plan a basic route, and the atlas will enable you to make a more detailed one. (Taking a note of road numbers, towns and directions is useful, as this reduces the need to consult the atlas on the way.)

Distance and time
One of the fundamental considerations to be taken into account when planning any journey is how far it is. The mileage chart on the inside back cover will help you estimate the distance and this in turn can help you calculate your journey time. On the atlas, distances between places are indicated as blue numbers between blue arrowheads eg. ◀ 12 ▶ Do not forget to allow extra time for peak hours and holiday weekends.

Motorways
Despite ever-increasing traffic, motorways are still the quickest and most efficient means of travelling across the country. The map on page 108 gives an overall picture of the system, while pages 109 to 118 show the principal motorways.

A Roads
London is the hub for the spokes of roads numbered A1 to A6, and Edinburgh is the hub for the A7, A8 and A9.

Starting with the A1 running north from London, the roads radiate clockwise: the A2 runs generally east, the A3 south-west etc. This system has made the numbering of other roads very simple. Generally, the lower the subsequent number, the closer the road's starting point to London – similarly to Edinburgh.

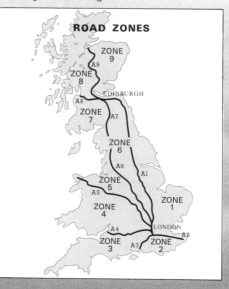

ROAD ZONES

DELAYS AND HOLD-UPS
Radio
Frequent radio bulletins are issued by the BBC and Independent Local radio stations on road conditions, possible hold-ups etc, and these can be of great assistance. By tuning in to the local stations as you pass through the area, you can avoid delays, and prepare yourself to make changes to your route. However, local radio does not yet cover the entire country. For radio frequencies consult the map on the inside back cover.

AA Roadwatch
However, if you require this information *before* setting out, you can call AA Roadwatch. This service provides information (updated every 15 minutes) on major roadworks and weather conditions for the whole country, and can be used as part of your basic journey planning. (See inside front cover.)

Getting the most out of the maps
The mapping contains a wide range of practical information for the motorist. Not only does it show the existing road network, but it also shows new roads which are due to be opened shortly or within approximately the next 12 months. It even indicates where A and B roads are very narrow in the Scottish Highlands. Passing bays are usually provided on these roads at regular intervals.

In addition you can use the atlas to plan trips and days out. Look for the special red tourist symbols and red names. The attractions highlighted in this way range from the cultural and historic – abbeys, museums, stately homes, to the sporting – cricket, golf, gliding, horseracing, and include Tourist Information Centres and AA viewpoints.

You can find any place listed in the index by using the National Grid, which is explained in simple terms below.

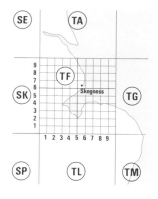

FINDING YOUR PLACE
One of the unique features of AA mapping is the use of the National Grid system.

It covers Britain with an imaginary network of squares, using blue horizontal lines called northings and vertical lines called eastings.

On the atlas pages these lines are numbered along the bottom and up the left hand side.

Each entry in the index is followed by a page number, two letters denoting an area on the map and a 4-figure grid reference. You will not need to use the two letters for simple navigation, but they come in useful if you want to use your map in relation to the rest of the country and other map series.

For quick reference, the 4 figures of the grid reference in the index are arranged so that the 1st and 3rd are larger in size than the 2nd and 4th.

The 1st figure shows which number along the bottom to locate, and the 3rd figure, which number up the left hand side. These will indicate the square in which you will find the place name. However, to pinpoint a place more accurately, you use the 2nd and 4th numbers also. The 2nd will tell you how many imaginary tenths along the bottom line to go from the 1st number, and the 4th will tell you how many tenths up the line to go from the 3rd number.

Where these two lines intersect, you will locate your place. Eg Skegness 51 TF **56**63. Skegness is located on page 51, within grid square 56, in National Grid square TF. Its exact location is **56**63.

If you find you get the numbers confused, it might help if you can imagine entering a house, walking in the door and along a corridor first, and then going up the stairs, then you will remember how to get them in the correct order.

Routeplanner

The Complete Atlas of Britain combines superb mapping with accurate and practical routefinding information which are designed to help you complete a journey as quickly and easily as possible.

PLANNING YOUR ROUTE

The route planning maps on the following pages are an invaluable guide when deciding on a *general route*.

These maps show the principal routes throughout the country and you can use them to plan a *basic route*.

Look for the name of your destination in the index section at the back of the book. The entry is followed by an atlas page number and a National Grid reference.

Turn to the atlas page indicated and use the grid reference to pinpoint the place (see page   for an explanation of how to use the reference).

When you have located it, find the nearest place to it shown on the routeplanner maps.

In the same way, by locating the nearest place to your start point, you can plot the route between the two.

A more detailed route can be worked out from studying the main atlas.

Remember to take a note of road numbers and directions, then you will not need to stop to use the atlas while on the journey.

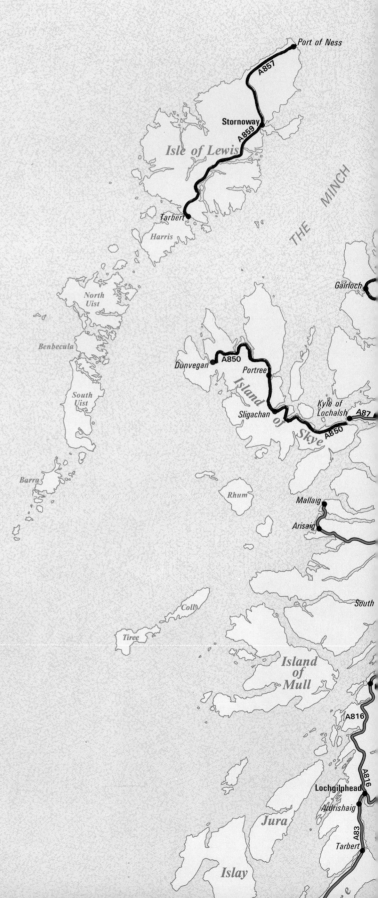

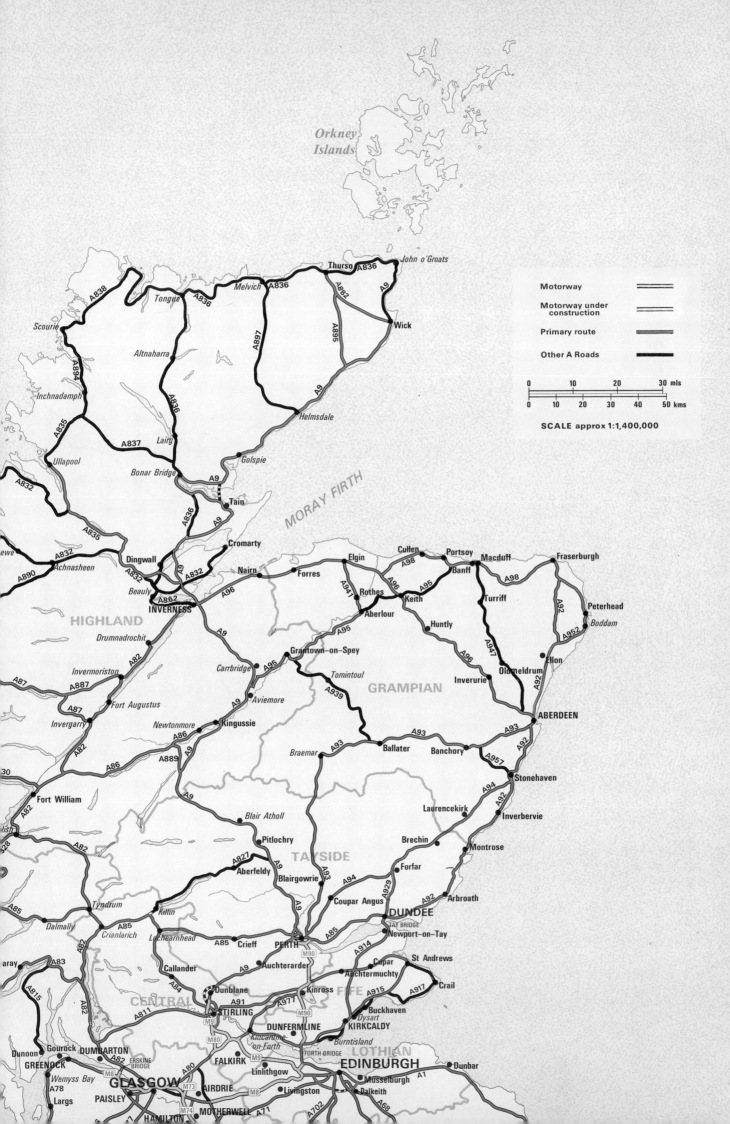

Motorway

Motorway under
construction

Primary route

Other A Roads

SCALE approx 1:1,400,000

Orkney
Islands

John o'Groats
Thurso A836
Melvich A836
A836
Tongue
A838
Scourie
A894
Inchnadamph
A835
A837
Ullapool
A832
Lairg
Altnaharra
A836
A897
A895
A9
Wick
Helmsdale
Golspie
Bonar Bridge
A9
Tain
A836
A9
Cromarty
MORAY FIRTH
ewe
A832
A835
A832
Achnasheen
A890
Dingwall
A862
Beauly
A832
A9
A832
Nairn
Forres
Elgin
Cullen
Portsoy
Macduff
Fraserburgh
A98
A98
Banff
A96
A95
Turriff
A92
Peterhead
A952
Boddam
A947
Ellon
Oldmeldrum
A92
INVERNESS
A941
Rothes
Keith
Aberlour
A95
Huntly
A96
Inverurie
HIGHLAND
Drumnadrochit
A9
A82
Invermoriston
A87
A887
A87
Fort Augustus
Invergarry
A82
Carrbridge
A95
Grantown-on-Spey
Aviemore
Tomintoul
A939
GRAMPIAN
Newtonmore
A86
Kingussie
A889
A86
A9
Braemar
A93
Ballater
Banchory
A93
A957
ABERDEEN
A92
Stonehaven
30
Fort William
A82
A93
Laurencekirk
A94
A92
Inverbervie
A82
Blair Atholl
Brechin
Montrose
ish
A82
Pitlochry
TAYSIDE
A827
Aberfeldy
A9
Blairgowrie
A93
Forfar
A94
A929
Arbroath
A85
Tyndrum
Killin
Coupar Angus
A92
A85
A85
DUNDEE
Dalmally
Crianlarich
Lochearnhead
A85
Crieff
A85
Newport-on-Tay
TAY BRIDGE
aray
A83
Callander
A9
Auchterarder
PERTH
A914
Cupar
St Andrews
A85
A82
A84
Auchtermuchty
A917
Crail
A815
Dunblane
Kinross
A915
Buckhaven
A91
A977
FIFE
Dysart
CENTRAL
M90
Dunoon
Gourock
DUMBARTON
A82
STIRLING
M9
KIRKCALDY
Burntisland
A811
DUNFERMLINE
Kincardine-
on-Forth
M80
FORTH BRIDGE
LOTHIAN
GREENOCK
ERSKINE
BRIDGE
FALKIRK
M9
EDINBURGH
Dunbar
Wemyss Bay
M8
Linlithgow
Livingston
Musselburgh
A1
A78
M73
AIRDRIE
M8
Dalkeith
Largs
GLASGOW
PAISLEY
Crianlarich
A702
A68
HAMILTON
MOTHERWELL
A71
M74

11

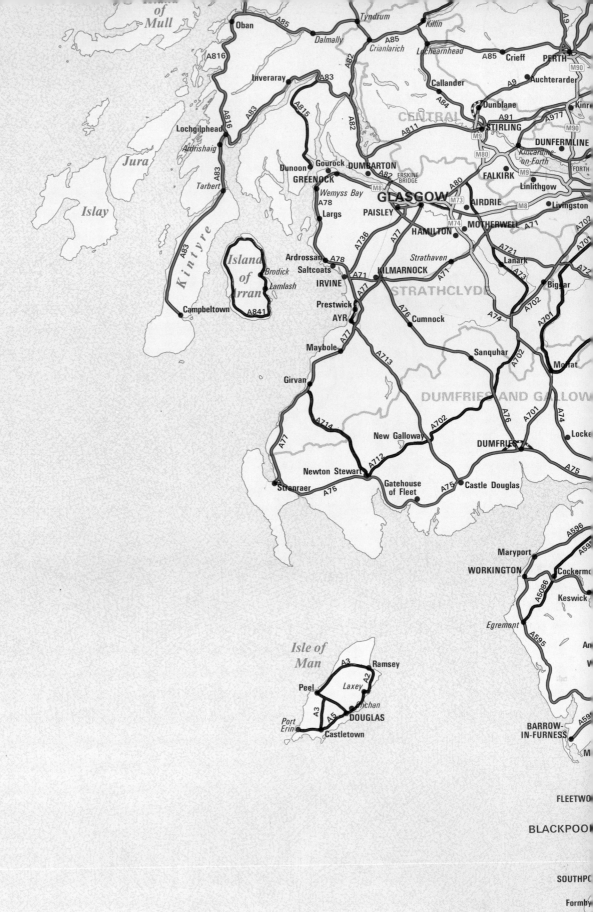

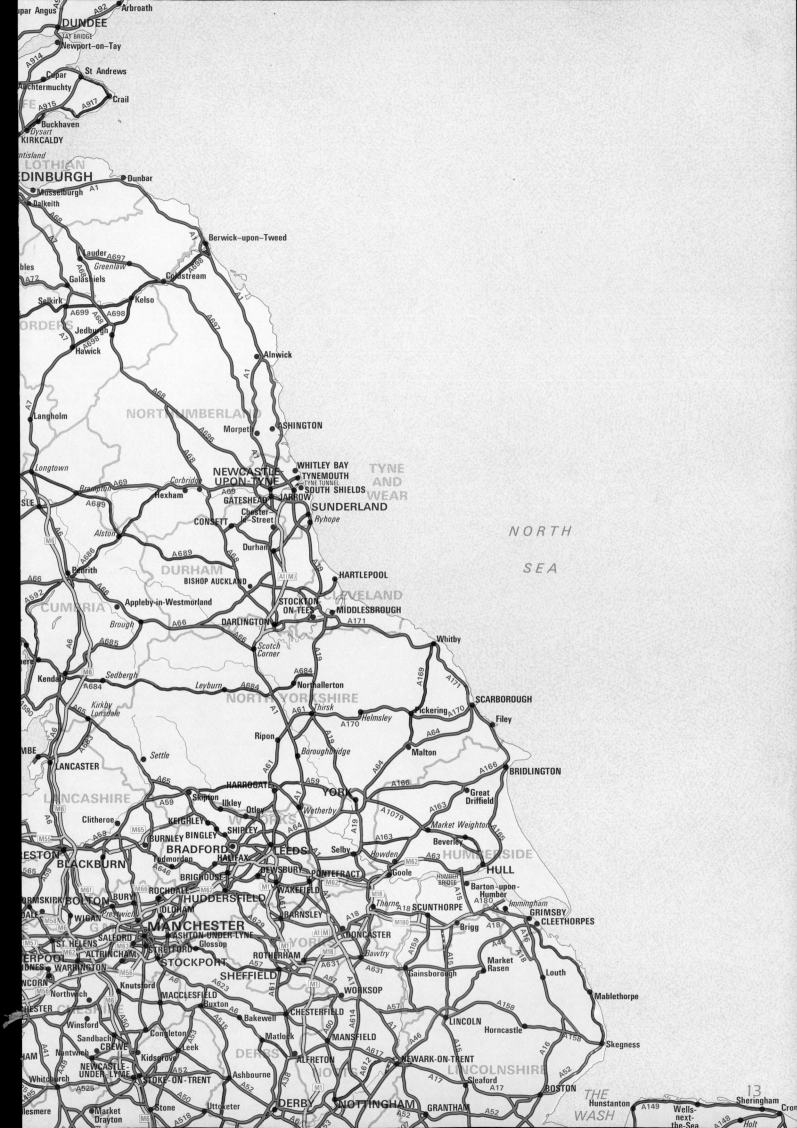

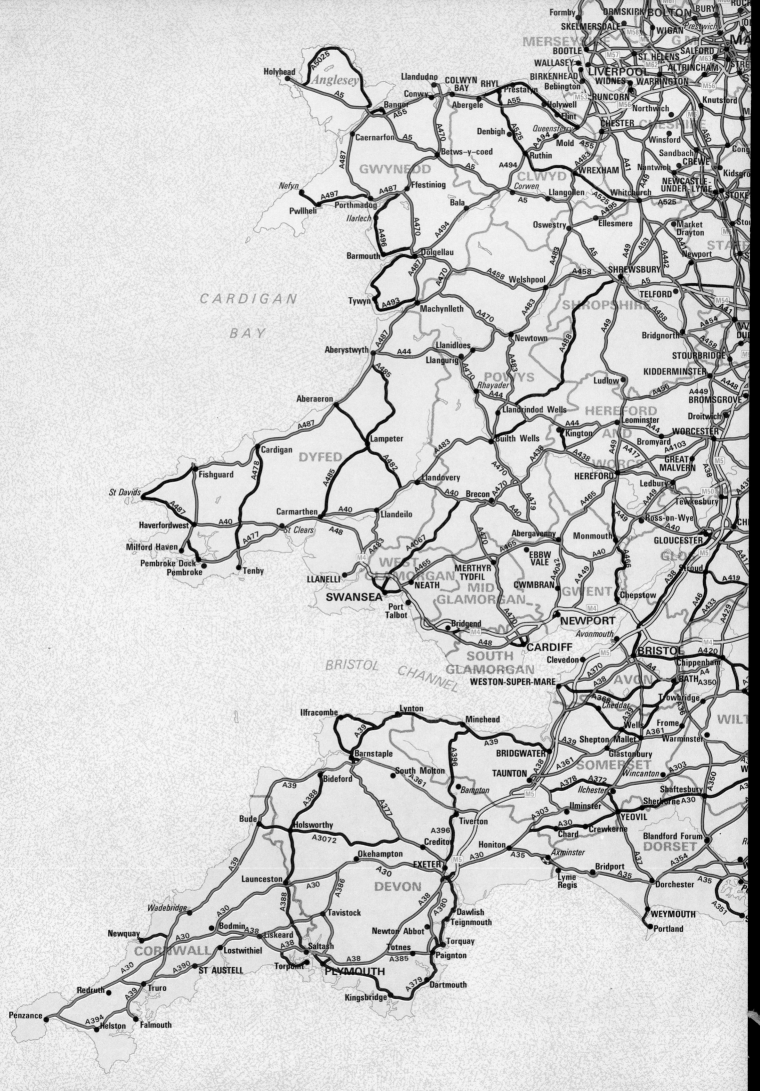

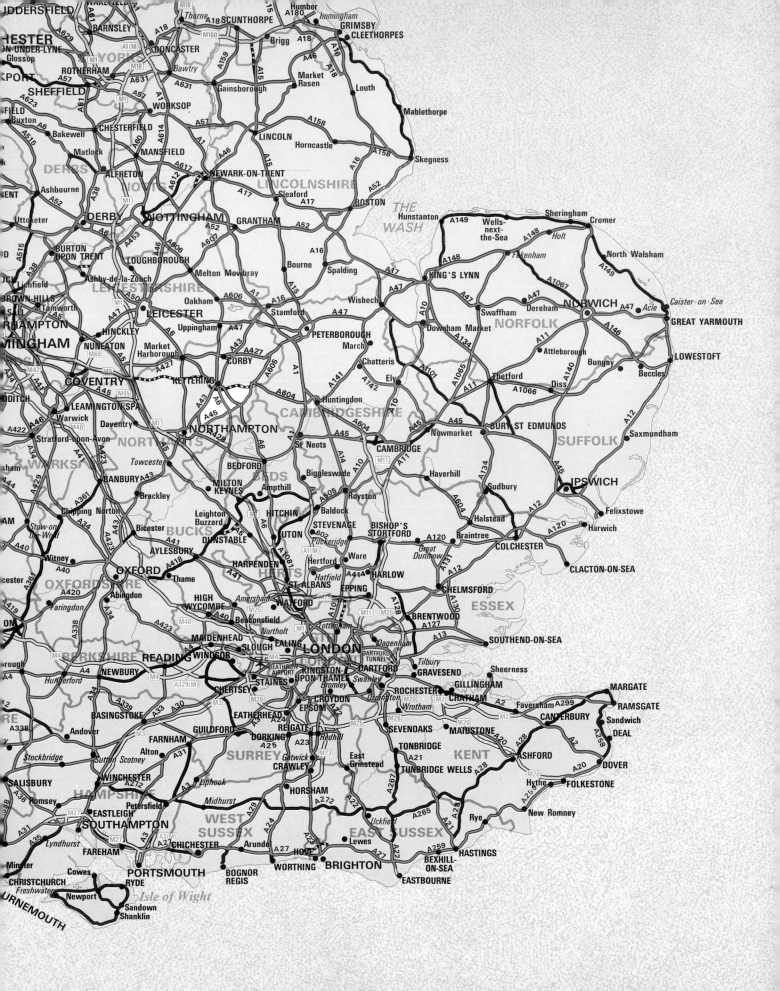

Map symbols

MOTORING INFORMATION : VERKEHRSINFORMATIONEN : INFORMATIONS ROUTIERES

M4 Motorway with number
Autobahn mit Nummer
Autoroute avec numéro

11 Motorway junction with and without number
Anschlußstelle mit/ohne Nummer
Echangeur avec/sans numéro

3 Motorway junction with limited access
Anschlußstelle mit beschränkter Auf- bzw. Abfahrt
Echangeur partiel

S Motorway service area
Tanken und Rasten
Aire de Service

Motorway and junction under construction
Autobahn und Anschlußstelle im Bau
Autoroute et échangeur en construction

A4 Primary route single/dual carriageway
Hauptverbindungsstraße 1 Fahrspur/2 Fahrspuren
Route principale 1 voie/2 voies

A1123 Other A road single/dual carriageway
Andere Straße der Klasse A 1 Fahrspur/2 Fahrspuren
Autre route catégorie A 1 voie/2 voies

B2070 B road single/dual carriageway
Straße der Klasse B 1 Fahrspur/2 Fahrspuren
Route catégorie B 1 voie/2 voies

Unclassified road, single/dual carriageway
Nicht klassifizierte Straße 1 Fahrspur/2 Fahrspuren
Route non classifiée 1 voie/ 2 voies

Road under construction
Straße im Bau
Route en construction

Narrow primary, other A or B road with passing places (Scotland)
enge Hauptverbindungsstraße, 'A' bzw. 'B' Straße mit Ausweichstellen (in Schottland)
Route principale étroite/autre route catégorie A ou B étroite avec places d'évitement (en Ecosse)

Road tunnel
Straßentunnel
Tunnel routier

Steep gradient (arrows point downhill)
Steigung/Gefälle (Pfeile weisen bergab)
Montée/Descente (à la flèche dirigée vers le bas)

Toll Road toll
Straße mit Gebühr
Route à péage

5 Distance in miles between symbols
Entfernungen in Meilen zwischen Zeichen
Distance en milles entre symboles

V Vehicle ferry – Great Britain
Autofähre – Inland
Bac pour automobiles en Grande Bretagne

CHERBOURG V Vehicle ferry – Continental
Autofähre – Ausland
Bac pour automobile – à l'étranger

H Hovercraft ferry
Luftkissenfähre
Aéroglisseur

Airport
Flughafen
Aéroport

H Heliport
Hubschrauberlandungsplatz
Héliport

Railway line/in tunnel
Bahnlinie/im Tunnel
Voie ferrée/sous tunnel

Railway station and level crossing
Bahnhof und Bahnübergang
Gare et passage à niveau

AA AA Centre – full services
AA-Hauptdienststelle
Centre AA principal

AA AA Road Service Centre – limited services
AA-Straßendienststelle – beschränkte Dienstleistungen
Centre-service routier auxiliaire

AA AA Port Services – open as season demands
AA-Hafendienststelle – Öffnungszeiten von Jahreszeit abhängig
AA Centre-service de port – heures d'ouvertures varient selon la saison

AA and RAC telephones
AA bzw. RAC-Telefon
Téléphone AA et RAC

BT telephone in isolated places
Öffentliche Telefonzelle in abgelegenen Gebieten
Téléphone PTT aux endroits isolés

Urban area/village
Stadtgebiet/Dorf
Agglomération/Village

628 Spot height in metres
Höhenangabe in Meters
Altitude en mètres

River, canal, lake
Fluss, Kanal, See
Fleuve, canal, lac

Sandy beach
Sandstrand
Plage de sable

National boundary
Landesgrenze
Frontière nationale

88 Page overlap and number
Hinweiszahlen für die Anschlußkarten
Suite à la page indiquée

TOURIST INFORMATION : FREMDENVERKEHR : RENSEIGNEMENTS TOURISTIQUES

Tourist Information Centre
Informationsbüro
Syndicat d'initiative

Tourist Information Centre (summer only)
Informationsbüro (nur im Sommer)
Syndicat d'initiative (seulement en été)

Abbey, cathedral or priory
Abtei, Dom, Kloster
Abbaye, cathédrale, prieuré

Ruined abbey, cathedral or priory
Abtei-, Dom-, Klosterruine
Abbaye, cathédrale, prieuré en ruines

Castle
Schloss/Burg
Château

Historic house
Historisches Gebäude
Edifice d'intérêt historique

Museum or art gallery
Museum/Kunstgalerie
Musée/galerie d'art

Industrial interest
Von industriellem Interesse
De l'intérêt industriel

Garden
Gartenanlage
Jardin

Arboretum
Arboretum
Arborétum

Country park
Park auf dem Lande
Parc promenade

Theme park
Freizeitpark
Parc d'attractions

Zoo
Tiergarten
Zoo

Wildlife collection – mammals
Tierpark – Säugetiere
Réserve d'animaux sauvages/mammifères

Wildlife collection – birds
Tierpark – Vögel
Réserve Ornithologique

Aquarium
Aquarium
Aquarium

Nature reserve
Naturschutzgebiet
Réserve naturelle

Nature trail
Naturlehrpfad
Sentier de découverte de la nature

Forest drive
Waldstraße
Route forestière

Long distance footpath
Fernwanderweg
Sentier de grande randonnée

Hill fort
Prähistorische Festungsanlage
Colline fortifiée

Roman antiquity
Überreste aus der Römerzeit
Antiquités romaines

Prehistoric monument
Prähistorisches Monument
Monument préhistorique

Battle site with year
Schlachtfeld mit Datum
Champ de bataille et Date

Preserved railway/steam centre
Museumbahn/Dampflokomotivmuseum
Chemin de fer touristique/musée de la vapeur

Cave
Höhle
Grotte

Windmill
Windmühle
Moulin à vent

AA viewpoint
AA-Aussichtspunkt
AA-Panorama

Picnic site
Picknickplatz
Lieu pour pique-nique

Golf course
Golfplatz
Golf

County cricket ground
wichtiger Kricketspielplatz
Terrain de cricket important

Horse racing
Pferderennbahn
Hippodrome

Show jumping/equestrian circuit
Reit-und Springturnier
Saut d'obstacles/circuit equestre

Motor racing circuit
Autorennen
Courses automobiles

Gliding centre
Segelflugplatz
Centre de vol à voile

Coastal launching site
Slipanlage für Boote
Air de mise à l'eau

Ski slope – natural
Skigelände
Piste de ski

Ski slope – artificial
Skigelände – künstlich
Piste de ski artificielle

Other places of interest
Weitere Sehenswürdigkeiten
Autres curiosités

Boxed symbols indicate attractions within urban areas
Das Einrahmen eines Zeichens bedeutet: die Sehenswürdigkeit befindet sich in einem Stadtgebiet
Dans le cas où le symbole est dans une case, la curiosité se trouve dans une localité

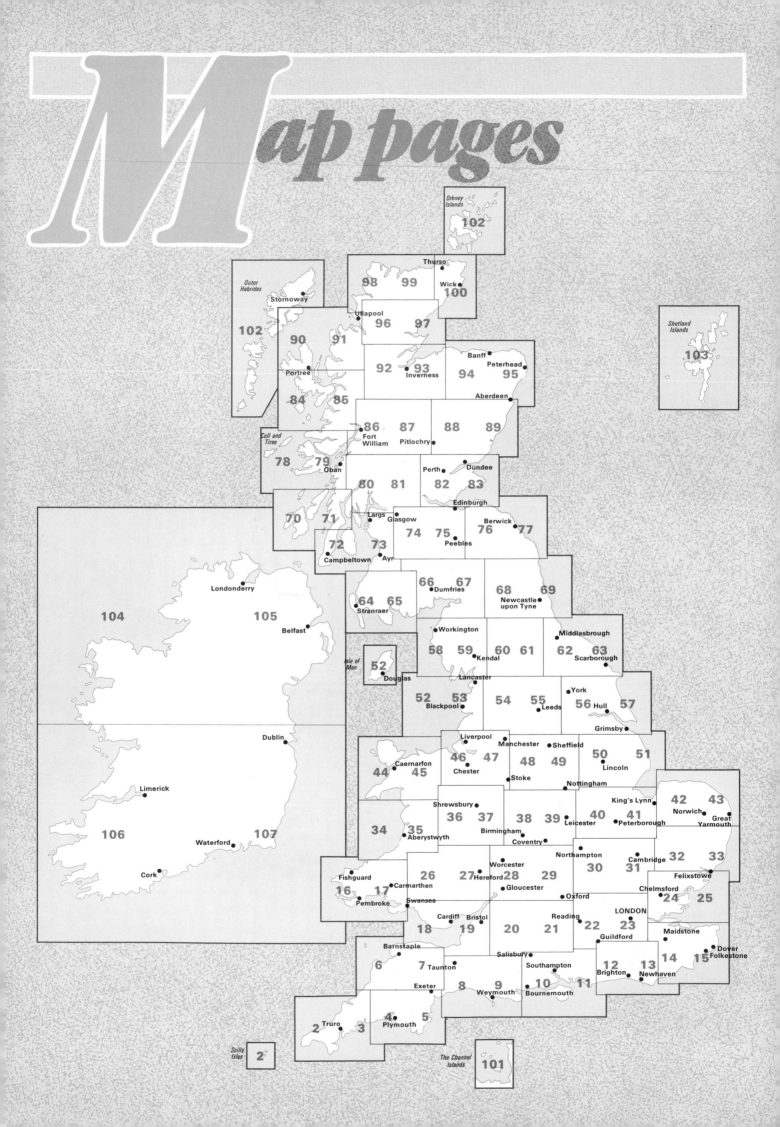

Map pages

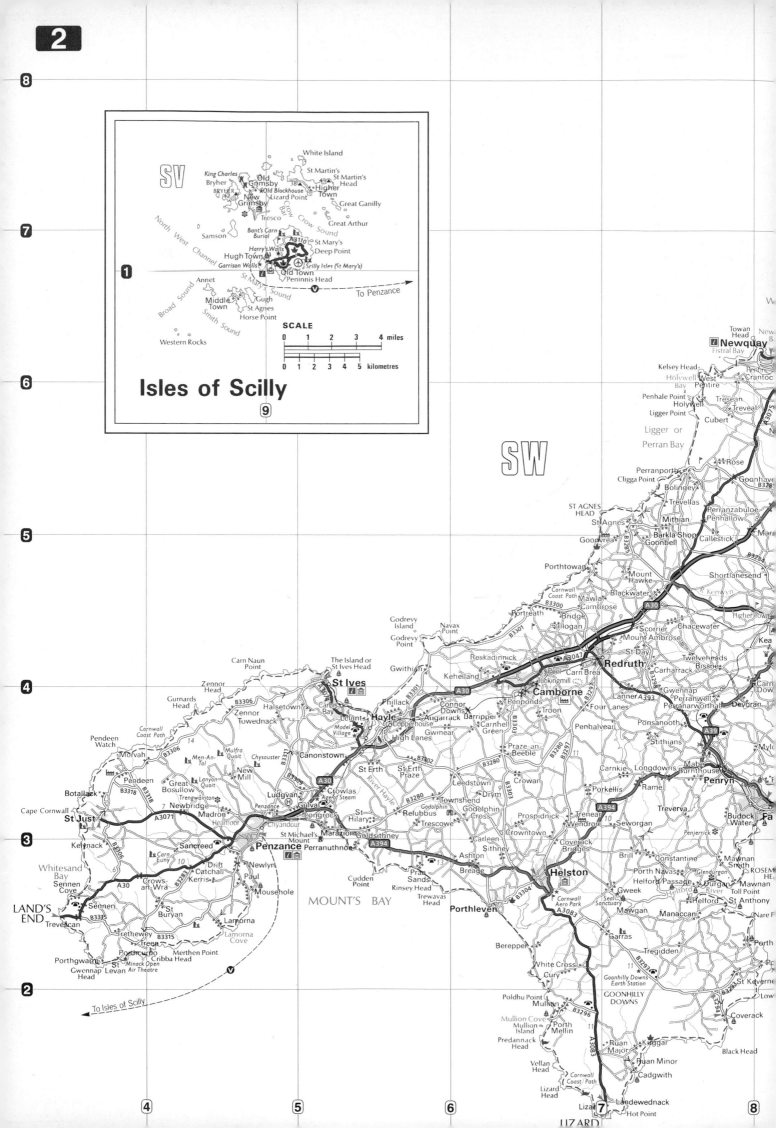

Isles of Scilly

SV

White Island
King Charles
Bryher · Old
BRYHER · Grimsby
Old Blockhouse
St Martin's
St Martin's Head
New Grimsby
Lizard Point
Higher Town
Tresco
Great Ganilly
Great Arthur
Samson
Bant's Carn Burial
St Mary's
Deep Point
Harry's Walls
Hugh Town
Garrison Walls
Scilly Isles (St Mary's)
Old Town
Peninnis Head
St Mary's Sound
To Penzance

North West Channel
Broad Sound
Annet
Middle Town
Gugh
St Agnes
Horse Point
Smith Sound
Western Rocks
Crow Sound

SCALE

0   1   2   3   4 miles

0 1 2 3 4 5 kilometres

Isles of Scilly

⑨

SW

Towan Head
Newquay
Fistral Bay
Kelsey Head
Holywell West Bay · Pentire
Crantock
Penhale Point
Holywell
Ligger Point
Cubert
Ligger or Perran Bay
Tresean · Treveal
Rose
Goonhaven
Perranporth
Cligga Point
Bolingey
Trevellas
Perranzabuloe
Penhallow
ST AGNES HEAD
St Agnes
Mithian
Goonvrea
Barkla Shop
Goonbell
Callestick
Porthtowan
Mount Hawke
Blackwater
Shortlanesend
Cornwall Coast Path
Mawla
Cambrose
Portreath
Bridge
Illogan
Redruth
Chacewater
Godrevy Island
Navax Point
Reskadinnick
Scorrier
Mount Ambrose
St Day
Godrevy Point
Gwithian
Keheland
Pool
Carn Brea
Carharrack
Bissoe
Tuckingmill
Twelveheads
The Island or St Ives Head
Carn Naun Point
Camborne
Gwennap
Lanner A393
Perranwell
Devoran
Zennor Head
St Ives
Phillack
Connor Downs
Penponds
Four Lanes
Perranarworthal
Gurnards Head
Carbis Bay
Lelant
Hayle
Copperhouse
Angarrack
Barripper
Carnhell Green
Troon
Penhalvean
Ponsanooth
Zennor
Halsetown
Towednack
Model Village
High Lanes
Gwinear
Praze-an-Beeble
Carnkie
Longdowns
Cornwall Coast Path
Pendeen Watch
Morvah
Men-An-Tol
Mulfra Quoit
Chysauster
Canonstown
St Erth
St Erth Praze
Leedstown
Drym
Crowan
Porkellis
Rame
Pendeen
Great Bosullow
Lanyon Quoit
New Mill
Ludgvan
Crowlas
River Hayle
Townshend
Godolphin Cross
Prospidnick
Wendron
Seworgan
Botallack
Trengwainton
Age of Steam
St Hilary
Trescowe
Godolphin
Treverva
Budock Water
Cape Cornwall
Newbridge
Madron
Penzance
Guival
Longrock
Relubbus
Carleen
Crowntown
Coverack Bridges
Penjerrick
St Just
Heamoor
Chyandour
Marazion
Goldsithney
Ashton
Sithney
Brill
Kelynack
Sancreed
Penzance
Perranuthnoe
Breage
Helston
Porth Navas
Constantine
Mawnan Smith
Carn Euny
St Michael's Mount
Praa Sands
Helford Passage
Durgan
Glendurgan
Mawnan
Whitesand Bay
Drift
Newlyn
Cudden Point
Rinsey Head
Trewavas Head
White Cross
Cornwall Aero Park
Gweek
Helford
St Anthony
Sennen Cove
Crows-an-Wra
Kerris
Paul
Mousehole
MOUNT'S BAY
Porthleven
Seal Sanctuary
Mawgan
Manaccan
Sennen
St Buryan
Lamorna
Cury
Garras
Tregidden
LAND'S END
Trevescan
Tretheway
Treen
Lamorna Cove
Poldhu Point
Mullion
Goonhilly Downs Earth Station
Porthcurno
Merthen Point
Cribba Head
To Isles of Scilly
Mullion Cove
Mullion Island
Porth Mellin
GOONHILLY DOWNS
Porthgwarra
Gwennap Head
St Levan
Minack Open Air Theatre
Predannack Head
Ruan Major
Kuggar
Black Head
Vellan Head
Ruan Minor
Cadgwith
Coverack
Lizard Head
Cornwall Coast Path
Lizard
Landewednack
Hot Point
LIZARD

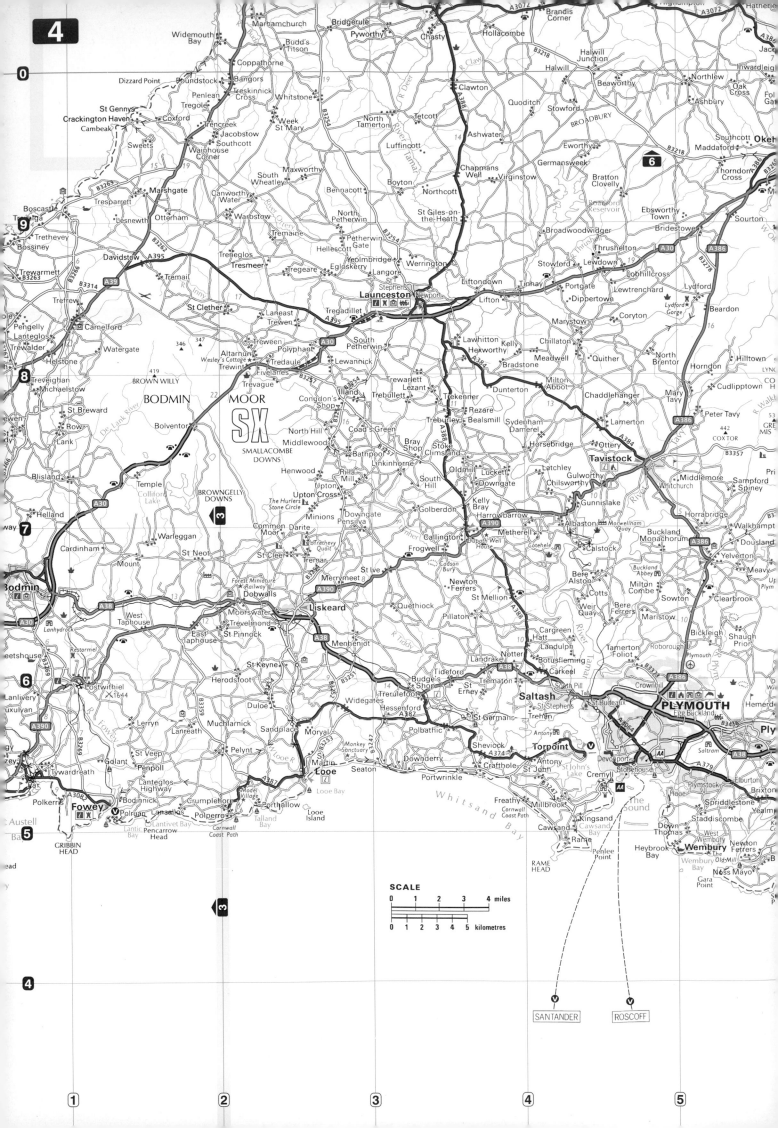

6

LUNDY ISLAND
142
Marisco
Surf Point
North West Point

SCALE
0 1 2 3 4 miles
0 1 2 3 4 5 kilometres

BARNSTAPLE
OR
BIDEFORD BAY

Ilfracombe
Hele Bay
Water Mouth
Combe Martin Bay
Watermouth
Combe Martin
Bull Point
Rockham Bay
Lee Bay
Slade
Hele
Hele Mill
Chambercombe Manor
Berrynarbor
Morte Point
Mortehoe
Lee
West Down
Bittadon
East Down
Woolacombe
Trimstone
North Buckland
Higher Muddiford
Milltown
Muddiford
Loxhore Cott
Morte Bay
Baggy Point
Georgeham
Winsham
Marwood
Boode
Marwood Hill
Guineaford
Kingsheanton
Shirwell
Shirwell Cross
Croyde Bay
Darracott
Knowle
Croyde
Saunton
Heanton Punchardon
Ashford
Northleigh
Braunton
Wrafton
Bradiford
Pilton
Goodleigh
River Taw
Barnstaple
Newport
Landkey Town
Bishop's Tawton
Swimbridge
New
Landkey
Tawstock
St John's Chapel
Hannaford
Appledore
Instow
Horwood
Harracott
Herner
Cobbaton
Northam
Tapeley Park
Westleigh
Newton Tracey
Hiscott
Ensis
Chapelton
Chittle
Westward Ho!
Eastleigh
Bideford
Alverdiscott
Yarnscombe
Atherington
HARTLAND POINT
Shipload Bay
Titchberry
Damehole Point
Brownsham
Somerset and North Devon Coast Path
Clovelly
Buck's Mills
Abbotsham
Ford
Landcross
Huntshaw
High Bickington
Hartland Quay
Hartland
Stoke
Fairy Cross
Horns Cross
Woodtown
Littleham
Saltrens
Weare Giffard
Spekes Mill Mouth
Philham
Buck's Cross
Goldworthy
Parkham
Buckland Brewer
Monkleigh
Roborough
Woolfardisworthy
Frithelstock
Great Torrington
St Giles in the Wood
Hardisworthy
Frithelstock Stone
Rosemoor
Kingscott
Welcombe
Darracott
Ashmansworthy
West Putford
East Putford
Langtree
Little Torrington
Beaford
Riddlecot
East Youlstone
Dinworthy
Haytown
Bulkworthy
Stibb Cross
Peters Marland
Winswell
Dolton
Morwenstow
Higher Sharpnose Point
Shop
West Youlstone
Bradworthy
Upper Tamar Reservoir
Abbots Bickington
Newton St Petrock
Merton
Huish
Dowland
Lower Sharpnose Point
Kilkhampton
Alfardisworthy
Sutcombe
Venngreen
Milton Damerel
North Town
Petrockstowe
Iddesleigh
Steeple Point
Sutcombemill
River Waldon
Thornbury
Shebbear
Buckland Filleigh
Barwick
Sandy Mouth
Stibb
Holsworthy Beacon
Bradford
Meeth
Northcott Mouth
Poughill
Dunsdon
Holsworthy
Little Lashbrook
Cookbury
Hole
Sheepwash
R Torridge
Monkokehampton
Splatt
Bude
Flexbury
Grimscott
Kingford
Chilsworthy
Black Torrington
Highampton
Hatherleigh
Honey
Bude Bay
Stratton
Launcells
Pancrasweek
Holsworthy
Brandis Corner
Exbo
Marhamchurch
Budd's Titson
Bridgerule
Pyworthy
Chasty
Hollacombe
Halwill Junction
Northlew
Jacobstowe
Widemouth Bay
Coppathorne
Halwill
wardleigh
Dizzard Point
Poundstock
Bangors
Treskinnick Cross
Whitstone
R Claw
Clawton
Beaworthy
Oak Cross
Folly Gate
St Gennys
Penlean
Tregole
North Tamerton
Tetcott
Quoditch
Stowford
BROADBURY
Ashbury
Brightley
ckington Haven
Coxford
Trencreek
Week St Mary
Luffincott
Ashwater
Eworthy
Maddaford
Southcott
Okehampton
Cambeak
Jacobstow
Southcott
Germansweek
Sweets
Warehouse Corner
South Wheatley
Maxworthy
Boyton
Chapmans Well
Virginstow
Bratton Clovelly
Thorndon Cross
Meldon
Marshgate
Canworthy Water
Bennacott
Northcott
St Giles-on-the-Heath
Bradford Reservoir
Ebsworthy Town
YES TOR 618
Tresparrett
Warbstow
North Petherwin
Broadwoodwidger
Sourton
HIGH WILLHAYS
W Okement River
Lesnewth
Otterham
Tremaine
Petherwin Gate
Thrushelton
Bridestowe
GREAT KNESET
Davidstow
Tremail
Tresmeer
Tregeare
Hellescott
Yeolmbridge
Egloskerry
Langore
Werrington
Stowford
Lewdown
Lobhillcross
Lewtrenchard
Lydford
Lydford Gorge
Beardon
SX
Tremail
Laneast
Tregadillet
Launceston
Newports
St Stephens
Lifton
Tinhay
Liftondown
Portgate
Coryton
St Clether
St Clether
Lifton
Dippertown

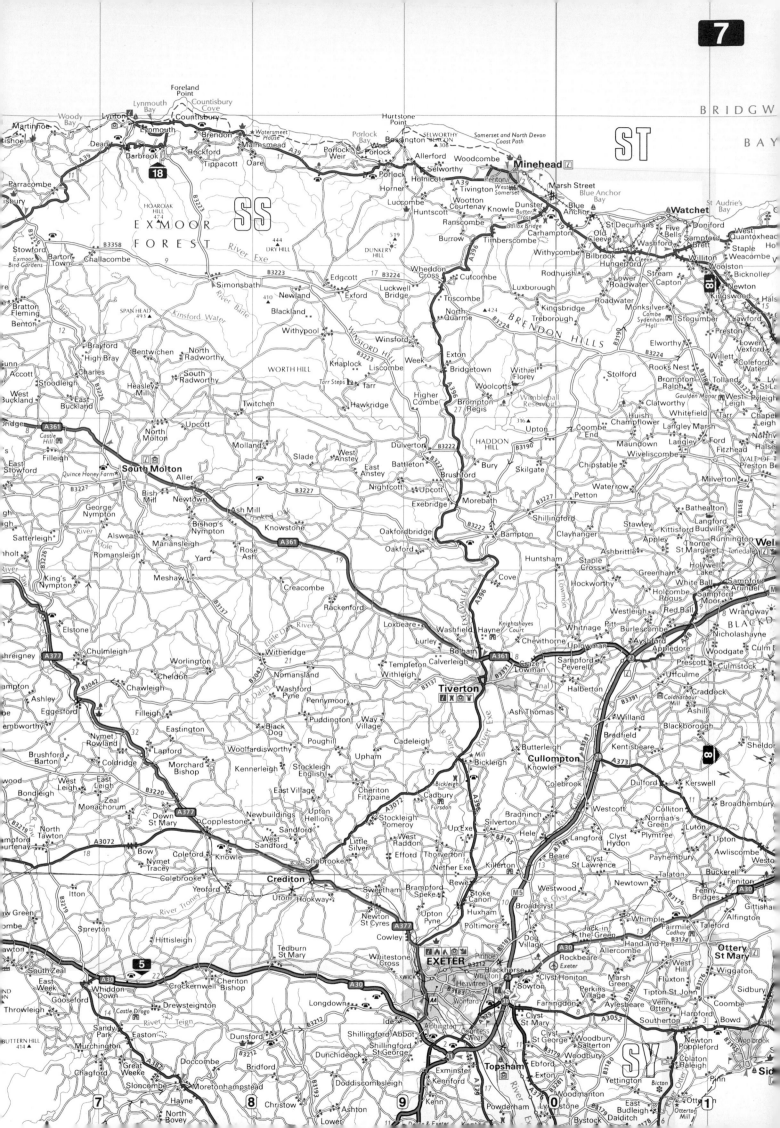

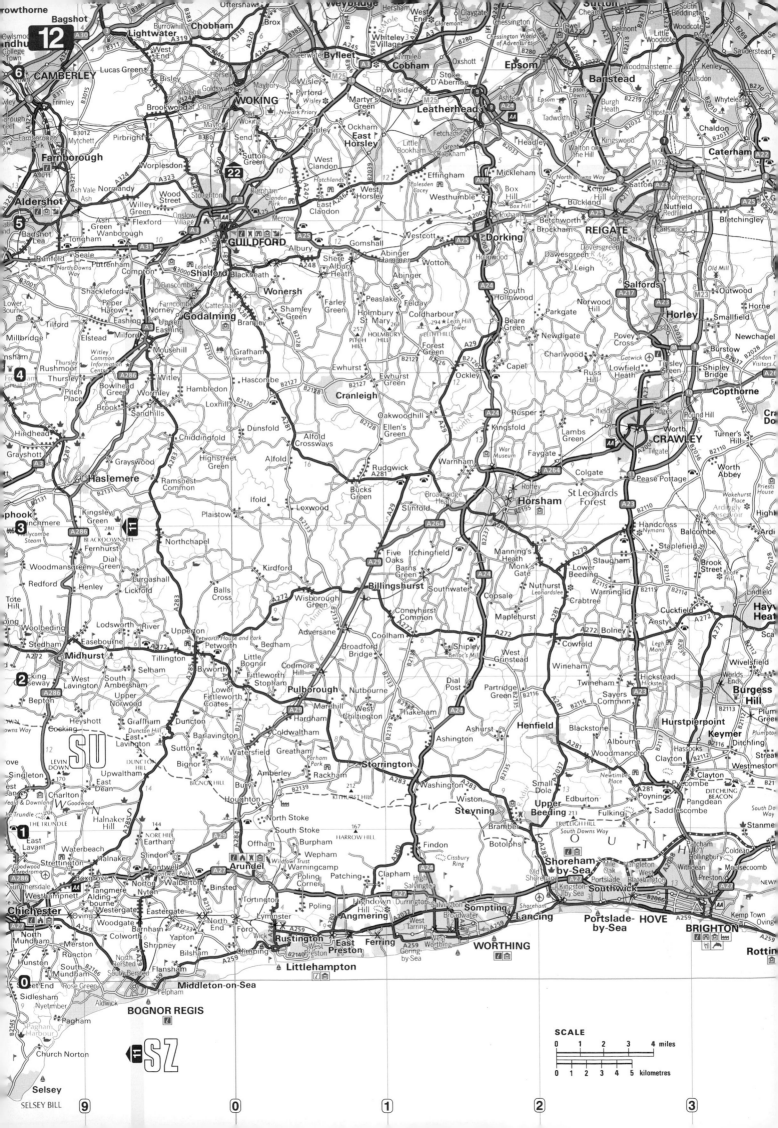

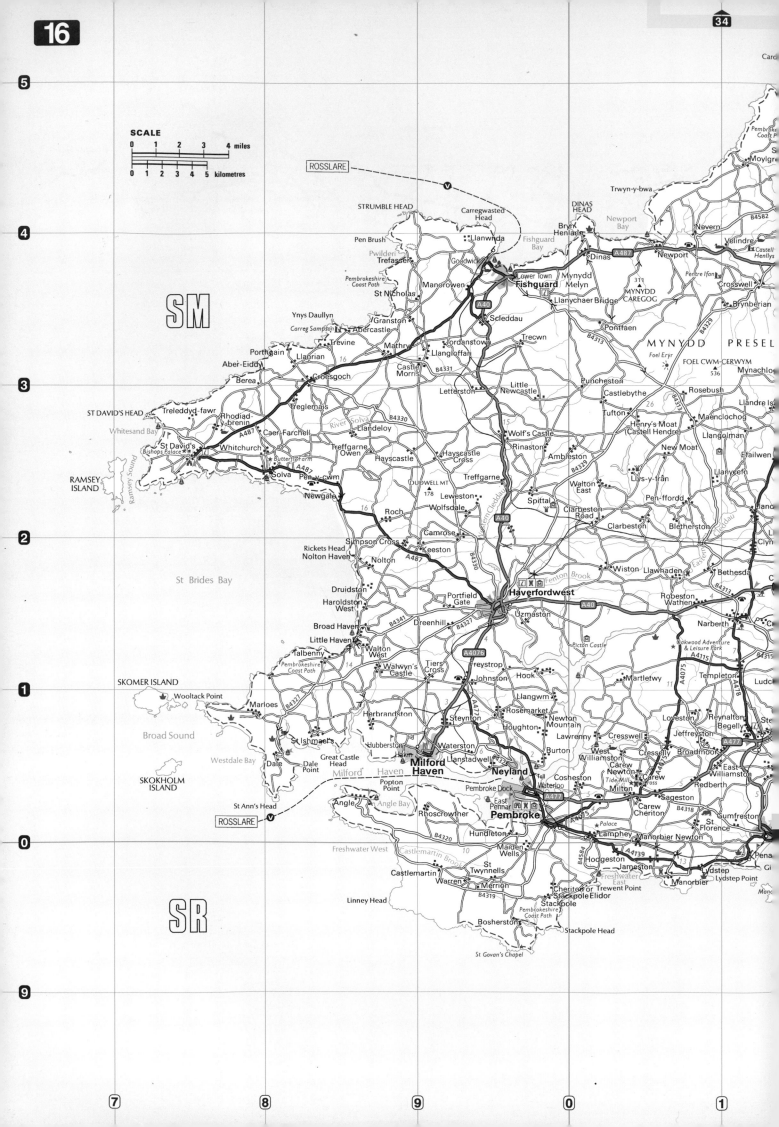

5

SCALE

0   1   2   3   4 miles
0 1 2 3 4 5 kilometres

ROSSLARE

STRUMBLE HEAD
Carregwasted Head
Pen Brush
Llanwnda
Fishguard Bay
DINAS HEAD
Bryn Henllan
Newport Bay
B4582
Trwyn-y-bwa
Nevern
Moylgr
Pembroke Coast P

4

SM

Pwilderi
Trefasser
Pembrokeshire Coast Path
St Nicholas
Granston
Ynys Daullyn
Carreg Sampson
Abercastle
Porthgain
Trevine
Mathry
Llanrian
Berea
16
Croesgoch
Aber-Eiddy

Goodwick
Lower Town
Manorowen
Fishguard
Scleddau
A40
Llanychaer Bridge
Jordanstown
Llangloffan
Castle Morris
B4331
Letterston
Mynydd Melyn
MYNYDD CAREGOG
311
Pontfaen
Trecwn
Little Newcastle
B4313
MYNYDD PRESEL
Foel Eryr
FOEL CWM-CERWYM
536
Dinas
A487
Newport
Crosswell
Pentre Ifan
Brynberian
Castell Henllys
Velindre
Mynachlo
Mynachlo

3

ST DAVID'S HEAD
Treleddyd-fawr
Whitesand Bay
Rhodiad-y-brenin
Caer-Farchell
A487
Treglemais
River Solva
Llandeloy
Treffgarne Owen
Hayscastle
Hayscastle Cross
B4330

RAMSEY ISLAND
St David's
Bishops Palace
Whitchurch
Butterfly Farm
A487
Solva
Pen-y-cwm
Newgale
16
Roch
DUDWELL MT
178
Lewenston
Wolfsdale
Treffgarne
Walton East
Spittal
A40
Clarbeston Road
Clarbeston
Bletherston

Punchcheston
Castlebythe
Tufton
26
Henry's Moat (Castell Hendre)
New Moat
Ambleston
B4329
Rosebush
Llandre Is
Maenclochog
Llangolman
Efailwen
Llanycefn
Llano
Clyn
C

2

St Brides Bay
Rickets Head
Nolton Haven
Simpson Cross
Camrose
Keeston
A487
Nolton
B4330
Druidston
Haroldston West
Portfield Gate
Dreenhill
B4327
Uzmaston
B4341
Wiston
Llawhaden
Bethesda
Fenton Brook
HAVERFORDWEST
A40
7
Robeston Wathen
4
Narberth
B4313
C

1

SKOMER ISLAND
Wooltack Point
Marloes
B4327
Herbrandston
Broad Haven
Little Haven
Talbenny
Pembrokeshire Coast Path
14
Walton West
Walwyn's Castle
Tiers Cross
Johnston
A4076
Freystrop
Hook
Llangwm
Rosemarket
Martletwy
11
A4075
Templeton
Ludc
Broad Sound
3
Steynton
A477
Houghton
Newton Mountain
Lawrenny
Cresswell
Loveston
Jeffreyston
Reynalton
Begelly
A477
Ste
A418
Cresselly
Broadmoor

0

St Ishmael's
Great Castle Head
Dale
Dale Point
Milford Haven
Popton Point
Westdale Bay
SKOKHOLM ISLAND
St Ann's Head
ROSSLARE
Angle
Angle Bay
Rhoscrowther
B4320
Hundleton
MILFORD HAVEN
Hakin
Hubberston
Waterston
Llanstadwell
Neyland
Toll
Waterloo
Pembroke Dock
A477
East Pennar
PEMBROKE
Palace
Lamphey
6
Burton
West Williamston
Carew Newton
Tide Mill
Carew
Cosheston
Milton
Carew Cheriton
B4318
Sageston
5
Redberth
Gumfreston
St Florence
East Williamston
Pena

9

Freshwater West
Castlemartin
Castlemartin Brook
Warren
Maiden Wells
St Twynnells
Merrion
B4319
Linney Head
Hodgeston
Jamiston
Freshwater East
A4139
13
Cheriton or Trewent Point
Stackpole Elidor
Stackpole
Pembrokeshire Coast Path
Bosherston
Stackpole Head
St Govan's Chapel
B4584
Manorbier Newton
Manorbier
Lydstep
Lydstep Point
Gi
Monk

SR

7   8   9   0   1

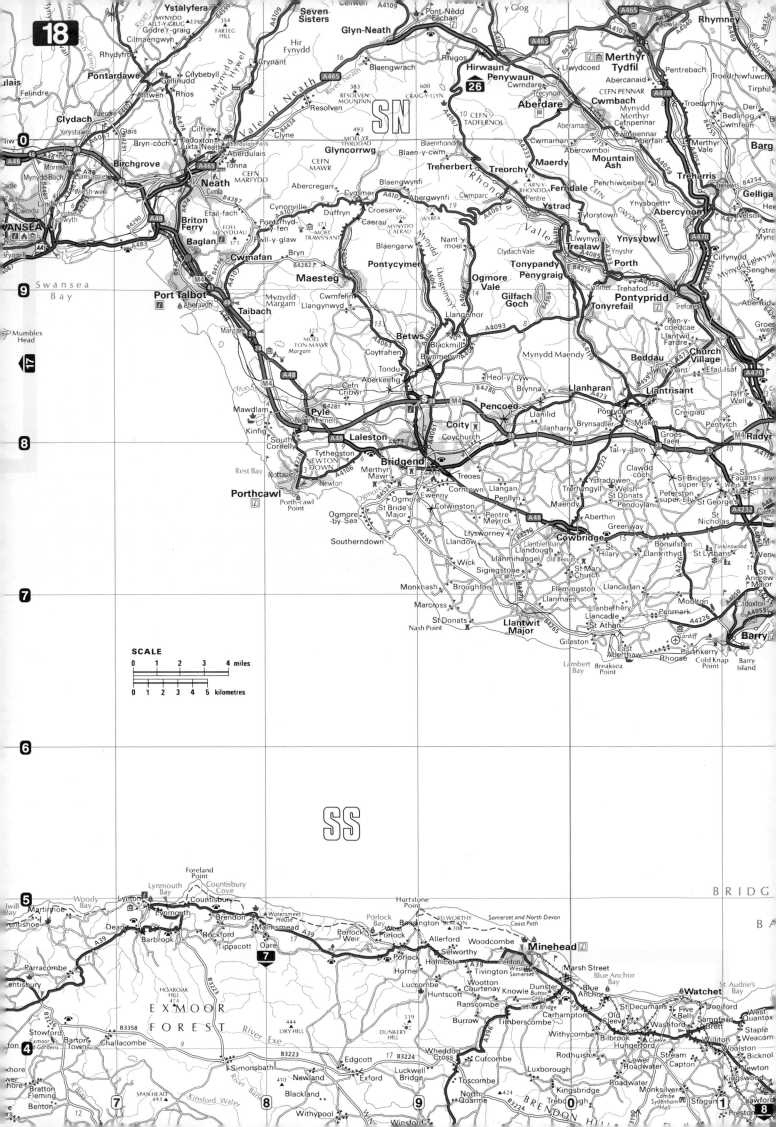

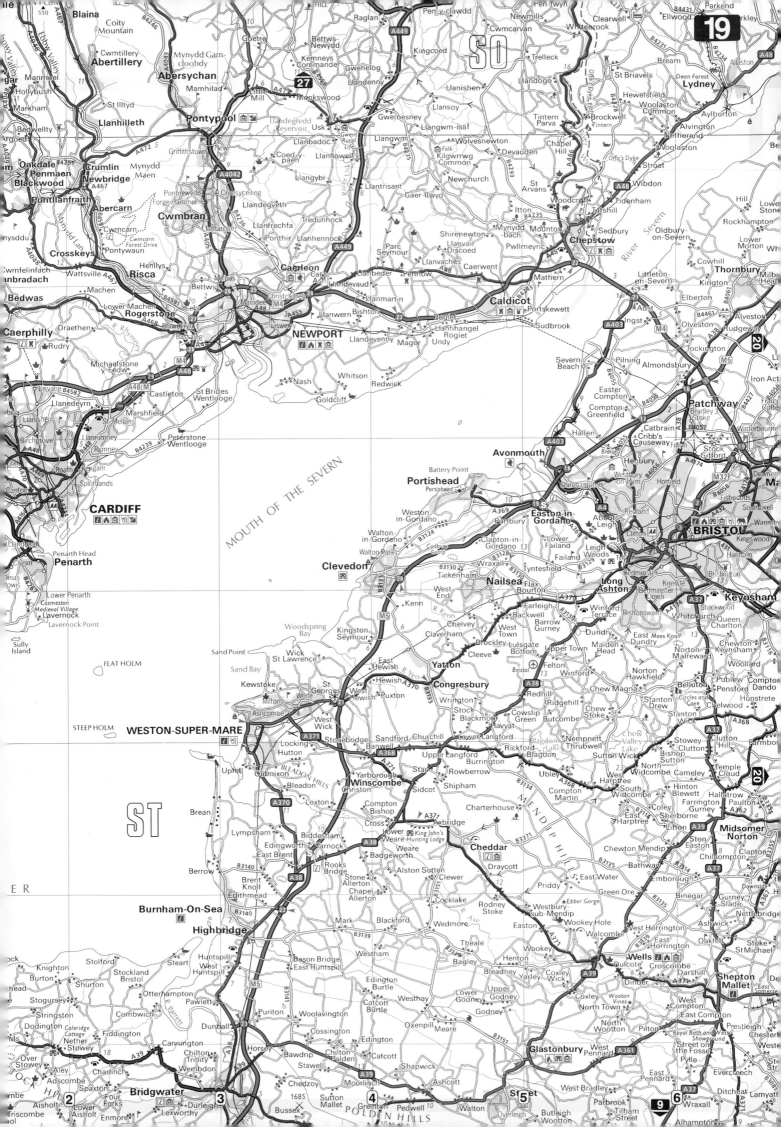

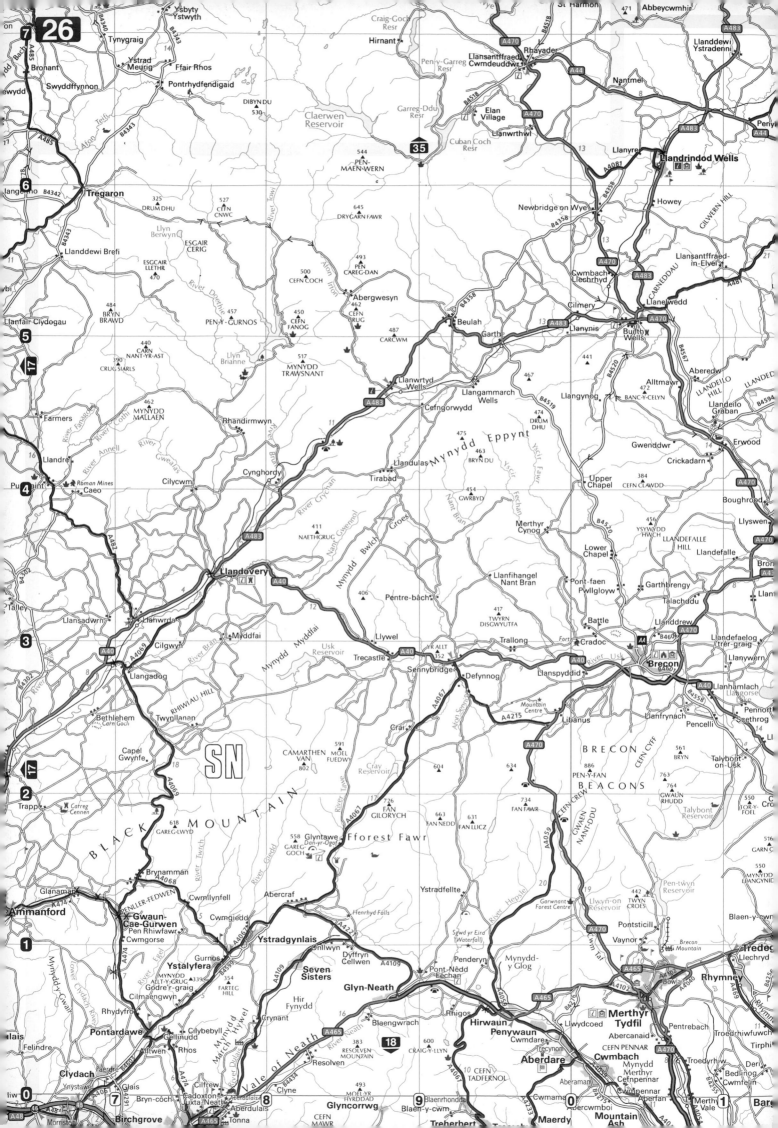

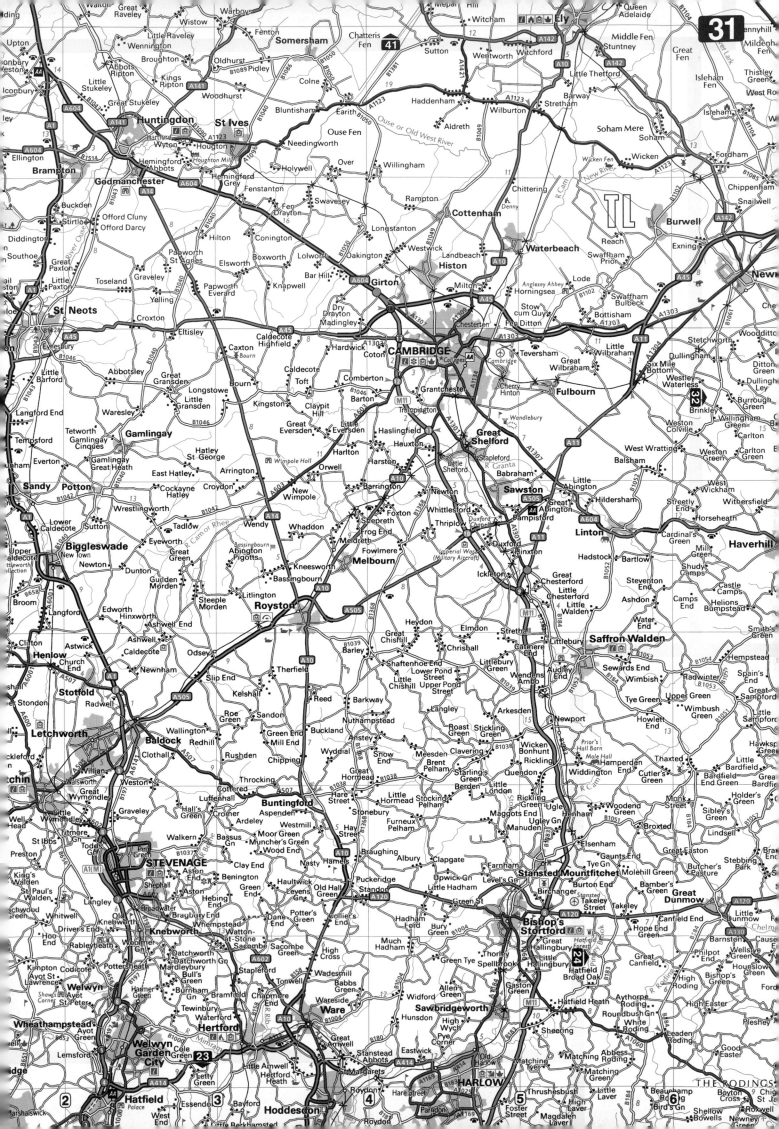

Aberdaron Llanfaelrhys
Porth
Ysgo
Aberdaron
Bay
rth Neigwl
Bwlchtocyn
Porth
Ceiriad
St Tudwal's
Island East
St Tudwal's
Island West

St Mary's
BARDSEY
ISLAND
rdsey Sound

Shell Island
Maes Artro
Tourist Village
Dyffryn
Ardudwy
Llanddwywe

2

Ba
Barmouth
Bay

SCALE

| 0 | 1 | 2 | 3 | 4 miles |

| 0 | 1 | 2 | 3 | 4 | 5 kilometres |

1

Llang
Rhosle
Ll
Aber
Dysynni

SH

Tywyn

0

C A R D I G A N

B A Y

9

Clarach Bay

Aberystwyth

8

SN

Blaenplwyf

A487

16 Llanddeiniol

7

Llanrhystud

Llansantffraid
Llanon

B4337

Joppa

Nebo

Aberarth

A487

Aberaeron

B4577

B4576

Cilcennin

6

New Quay
Maen-y-groes
Llanina
Gilfachrheda
Oakford
Llwyncelyn

Afon Aeron

B4337

B

Cross
Inn
Nanternis
B4342
Llanarth
A487
Dihewyd
B4339
Ystrad
Aeron
Trefilan
Talsarn

Ynys-Lochtyn
Llwyndafydd
Caerwedros

Llan nog
Pontgarreg

Mydroilyn

Temple Bar

B4337

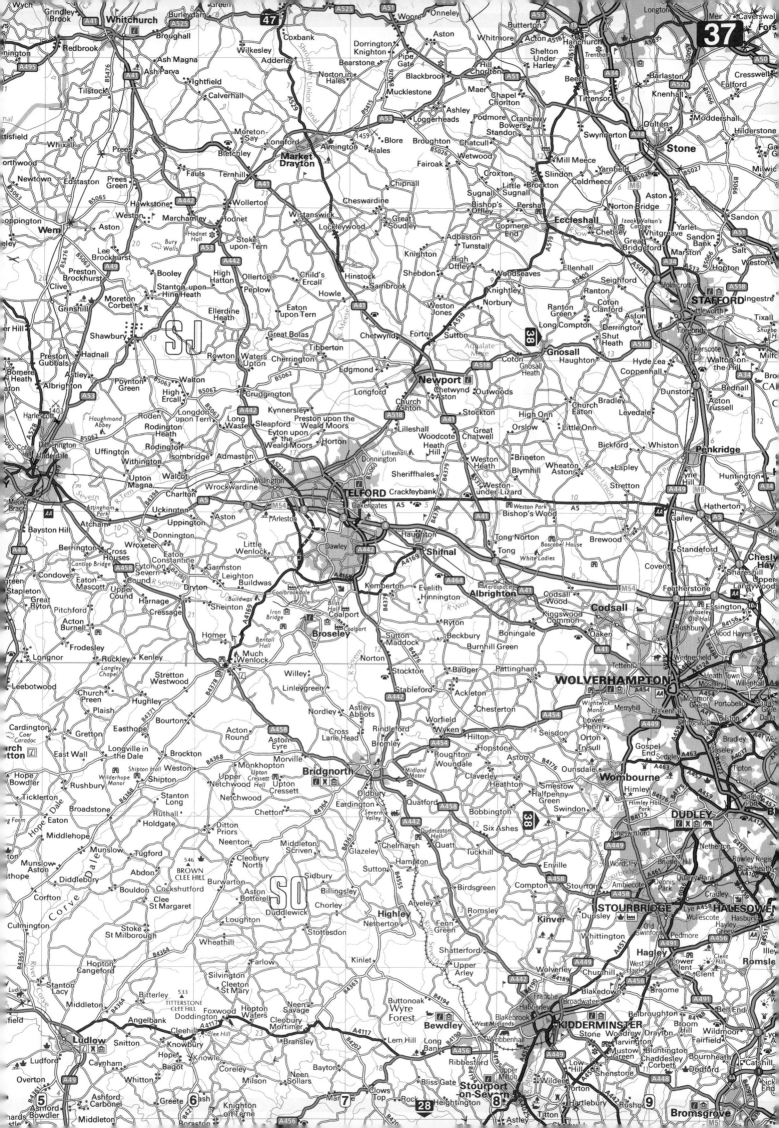

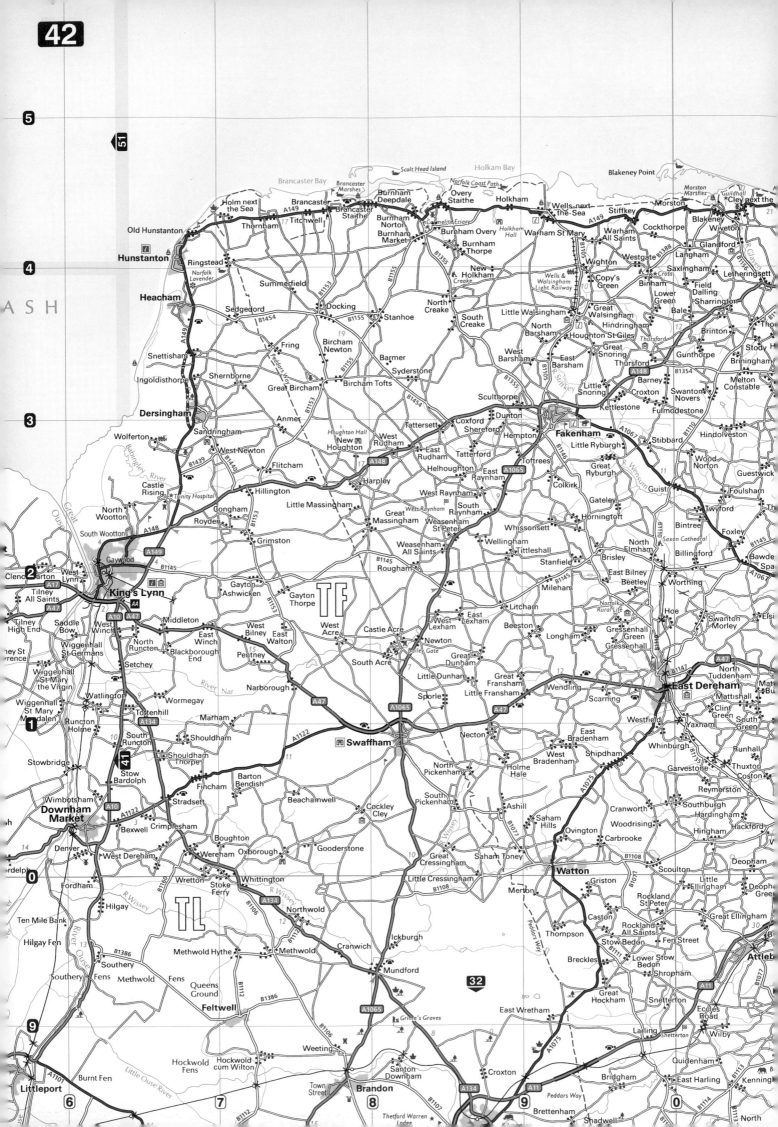

SCALE

0 1 2 3 4 miles
0 1 2 3 4 5 kilometres

Sheringham   West Runton   East Runton
Weybourne
Kelling   Upper Sheringham   Beeston Regis
Bodham Street
Cromer
Overstrand
Sidestrand
West Beckham   East Beckham   Felbrigg   Crossdale Street
Gresham   Metton   Felbrigg Hall   Northrepps   Trimingham
Baconsthorpe   Sustead   Roughton   Southrepps   Gimingham
Plumstead   Thurgarton   Hanworth   Mundesley
Edgefield Green   Matlaske   Thorpe Market   Lower Street   Knapton   Paston
Little Barningham   Wickmere   Erpingham   Suffield   Trunch   Bacton
Saxthorpe   Calthorpe   Colby   Bradfield   Antingham   Edingthorpe   Walcott
Mannington Hall   Itteringham   Ingworth   Banningham   Swafield   Edingthorpe Green   Witton   Ridlington   Happisburgh
Oulton   Blickling   North Walsham   Whimpwell Green
Heydon   Aylsham   Burgh next Aylsham   Meeting House Hill   Honing   Lessingham   Happisburgh Common   Hempstead
Sall   Marsham   Felmingham   Briggate   East Ruston   Ingham Corner   Sea Palling   Waxham
Cawston   Reepham   Brampton   Tuttington   Worstead   Dilham   Stalham   Ingham   Calthorpe Street   Hickling
Eastgate   Buxton Heath   Oxnead   Lamas   Market Street   Smallburgh   Sutton   Hickling Green   Horsey
Whitwell Street   Brandiston   Buxton   Stratton Strawless   Neatishead   Wood Street   Horsey Windpump
Alderford   Swannington   Felthorpe   Hevingham   Horstead   Coltishall   Tunstead   Catfield   Hickling Broad   Winterton-on-Sea
Morton   Upgate   Hainford   Belaugh   Hoveton   Ludham   Potter Heigham   Hemsby Hole
Attlebridge   Frettenham   Wroxham   Upper Street   Bastwick   Martham   Hemsby   Scratby
Weston Longville   Horsford   Newton St Faith   Horning   Repps   Rollesby   Ormesby St Michael   California
Ringland   Crostwick   Upper Street   Thurne   Clippesby   Burgh St Margaret   Ormesby St Margaret
Honingham   Taverham   Horsham St Faith   Spixworth   Woodbastwick   Ranworth   Pilson Green   Billockby   Thrigby   Filby   Mautby   Caister-on-Sea
Easton   Drayton   Crostwick   Rackheath   Salhouse   Cargate Green   West End   West Caister
Colton   Hellesdon   New Costessey   New Rackheath   Panxworth   South Walsham   Upton   Stokesby   Runham
Marlingford   Costessey   Sprowston   Thorpe End   Hemblington   Acle   Great Yarmouth
Barford   Bawburgh   Colney   Little Plumstead   Burlingham Green   Damgate   Southtown
Eaton   Thorpe St Andrew   Great Plumstead   North Burlingham   Lingwood   Beighton   Moulton St Mary   Burgh Castle
High Green   Little Melton   Cringleford   Norwich   Witton   Blofield   Tunstall   Halvergate   Berney Arms   Bradwell   Gorleston on Sea
Hethersett   Keswick   Trowse Newton   Postwick   Strumpshaw   South Burlingham   Freethorpe   Wickhampton   Belton
Ketteringham   Caistor St Edmund   Kirby Bedon   Surlingham   Buckenham   Freethorpe Common   Pettits Crafts
Swardeston   Framingham Pigot   Bramerton   Hassingham   Cantley   Limpenhoe   Reedham
Wymondham   Mulbarton   Dunston   Armingham   Hellington   Rockland St Mary   Claxton   Langley Street   Fritton
East Carleton   Swainsthorpe   Framingham Earl   Yelverton   Ashby St Mary   Carleton St Peter   Hardley Street   Chedgrave   Haddiscoe   Hopton on Sea
Bracon Ash   Upper Stoke   East Poringland   Bergh Apton   Thurton   Norton Subcourse   St Olaves   Lound
Silfield   Wreningham   Hawes Green   Stoke Holy Cross   Howe   Brooke   Mundham   Loddon   Thurlton   Herringfleet   Corton
Ashwellthorpe   Newton Flotman   Saxlingham Thorpe   Shotesham   Seething   Hales   Thurlton   Somerleyton   Blundeston
Spooner Row   Fundenhall   Hapton   Flordon   Saxlingham Nethergate   Thwaite St Mary   Kirby Cane   Raveningham   Pleasurewood Hills
Tacolneston   Low Tharston   Tasburgh   Saxlingham Green   Kirstead Green   Woodton   Kirby Row   Toft Monks   Wheatacre   Oulton
Bunwell Street   Forncett St Mary   Upper Tasburgh   Hempnall   Hedenham   Maypole Green   Stockton   Oulton Broad
Bunwell   Forncett End   Tharston   Hempnall Green   Ellingham   Aldeby   Burgh St Peter   Lowestoft
Aslacton   Forncett St Peter   Stratton St Michael   Topcroft   Kirby Row   Gillingham   Corton
New Buckenham   Tibenham   Morningthorpe   Fritton   Topcroft Street   Ditchingham   Broome   Geldeston   Worlingham
Wacton   Great Moulton   Shelton   Bungay   Shipmeadow   Beccles   Barnby   Carlton Colville
High Common   Long Stratton   Hardwick   Denton   Mettingham   Barsham   North Cove   Gisleham
Tivetshall St Margaret   Colegate End   Earsham   Ringsfield   Mutford   Black Street
Tivetshall St Mary   Pulham Market   The Otter Trust   Alburgh   Flixton   Ringsfield Corner   Hulver Street   Rushmere   Kessingland
Gissing   Pulham St Mary   Homersfield   Ilketshall St Andrew   Sotterly   Henstead
Garlic Street   Redenhall   St Margaret South Elmham   Ilketshall St Margaret   Redisham   Shadingfield   Benacre Ness
Starston   Wortwell   St Cross   St Michael   Wrentham

A148   A149   A1082   A151   A140   A1145   B1436   A149   B1159   B1150   A1062   A1064   A143   A146   A12   A11   A47   A140   A1151   B1108   B1113   B1135   B1332   A144   B1062   B1074   A145   A1117   B1127

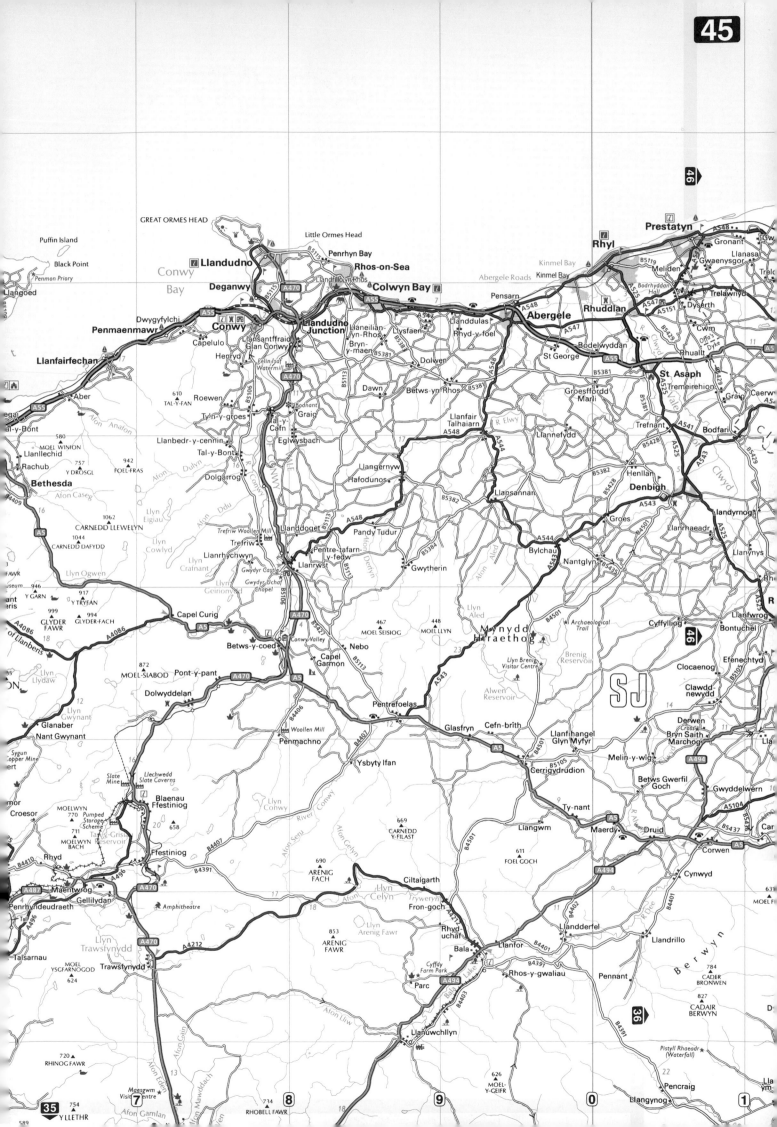

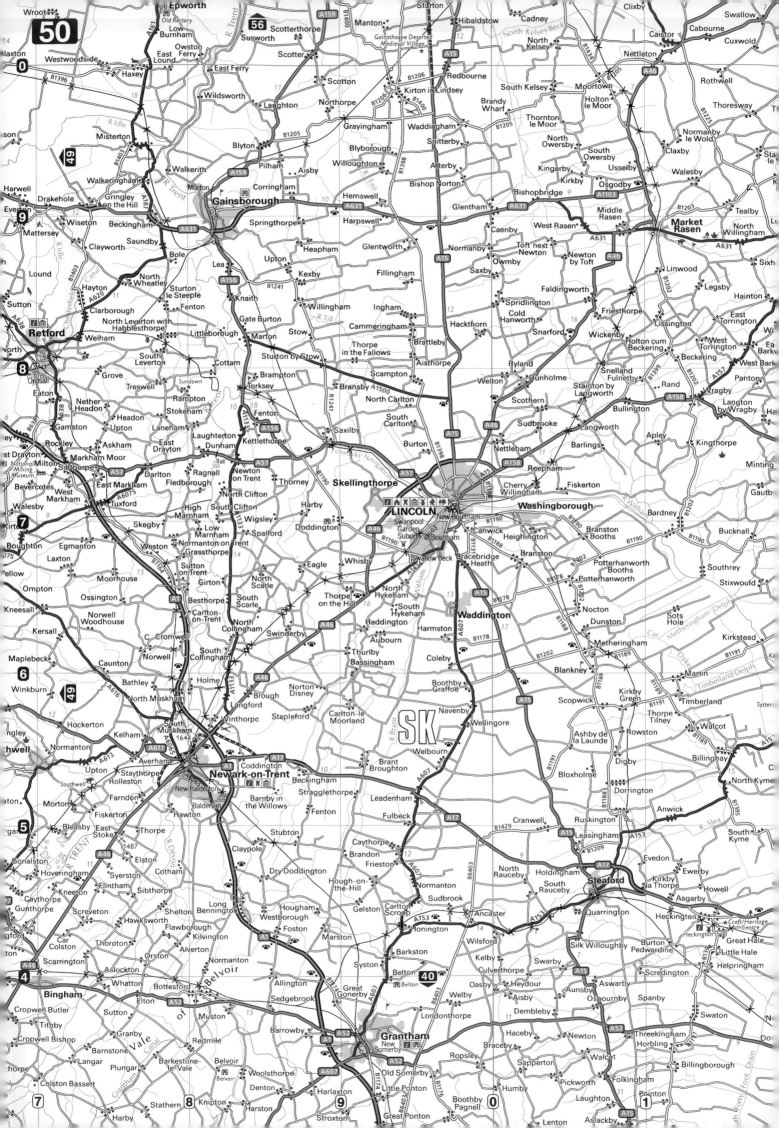

Isle of Man

SCALE

0 1 2 3 4 miles

0 1 2 3 4 5 kilometres

NX

POINT OF AYRE

Rue Point
Knock'e Doonee
Boat Burial

The Lhen

Bride

A10

A16

A19

A17

Andreas

A10

5

Point Cranstal
(Shellag Point)

Jurby Head
Jurby

A10

A14

A9

Sandygate

St Jude's

Ballachurry
Fort

A13

A17

Rural Life

A13

Ramsey Bay

Curraghs

Sulby

Sulby R.

A3

Ramsey

Ballaugh

A3

Cronk
Sumark

Lezayre

A2

Maughold
Maughold
Head
Port Mooar

Orrisdale Head

A14

A18

TT Circuit

A15

Cashtal Lajer

Block Eary

561
NORTH
BARRULE

Ballafayle

Kirkmichael

TT Circuit

620
SNAEFELL

7

462
SLIEAU LHEAN

A15

Cashtal yn Ard

A23

A4

488

Corvalley
Coich

The
Bungalow

Snaefell
Mountain

Laxey R.

Laxey
Wheel

Dhoon Bay

A9

A30

Peel

St Patrick's Isle

Giant's
Grave

R Nebb

B10

A2

Laxey

Contrary Head

Corrin's
Folly

A20

487
COLDEN

Dhoon

King Orry's
Grave

Patrick

Tynwald Hill

A1

Port y Candas

B22

Laxey Head

A30

St John's

TT Circuit

479
SLIEAU RUY

Millenium
Way

A18

B12

Laxey Bay

Glen Maye

R Dhoo

A1

A23

B20

Cloven Stones

To Belfast (Summer Only)

Clay Head

Crosby

Dalby

Foxdale

A4

A24

A26

Union
Mills

A7

Norse
Houses

Castleward

Strang

A2

A1

Onchan

Onchan Head

To Stranraer (Summer Only)

A27

Round
Table

16

483
SOUTH
BARRULE

A36

B39

Ballanicholas
Fort

A35

A5

A5

DOUGLAS
Douglas Bay

V

V

To Heysham

Niarbyl Bay

Brooghl
Fort

A25

A3

AA

Douglas
Head

V

To Fleetwood (Summer Only)

Freshwick Bay

St Mark's

A5

10

Ballakelly

Isle of Man
Steam

Port Soderick

V

To Liverpool (Summer Only)

Grenaby

A25

Cronk ny Merriu

Santon Head

Bradda Head

Milners
Tower

Colby

A5

Arbory

Rushen

Arragon Circles

Cass ny Hawin

Ballasalla

SC

Port Erin

Corvalie

A7

5

Isle of Man (Ronaldsway)

V

Meayl Circle

Castletown

Port St
Mary

Derbyhaven

Cregneish

A31

A3

Close ny Chollagh

Langness
Point

Hango
Hill

Castletown
Bay

Derby Fort

Derby Round Tower

Calf of Man

Calf Sound

Spanish
Head

Dreswick Point

Caigher
Point

DUBLIN
Summer Only

V

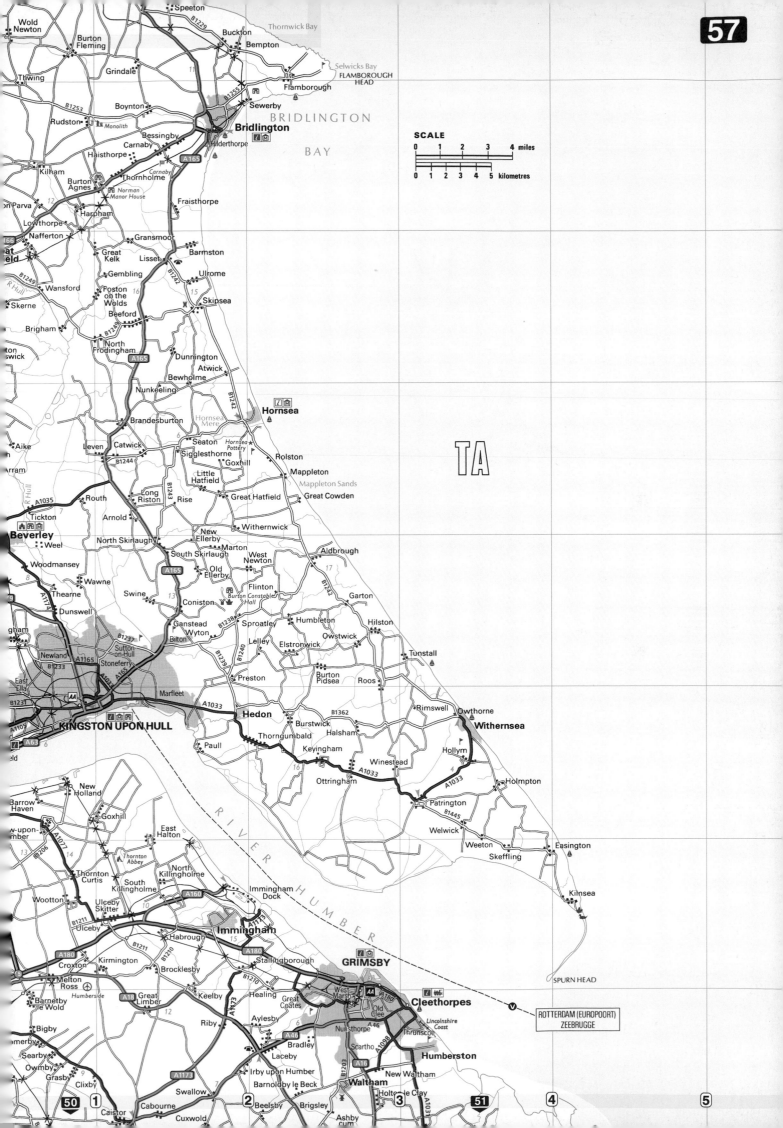

SCALE

0 1 2 3 4 miles

0 1 2 3 4 5 kilometres

Wold Newton
Speeton
B1229
Buckton
Bempton
Thornwick Bay
Burton Fleming
Grindale
Thwing
B1253
Boynton
Flamborough
Selwicks Bay
FLAMBOROUGH HEAD
Rudston
Monolith
Bessingby
Sewerby
BRIDLINGTON
Kilham
Carnaby
Bridlington
Haisthorpe
Thornholme
Hilderthorpe
A165
BAY
Burton Agnes
Norman Manor House
Carnaby
on Parva
Lowthorpe
Harpham
Fraisthorpe
Nafferton
B1249
Gransmoor
Barmston
B1242
Great Kelk
Lisset
Ulrome
Wansford
Gembling
Skipsea
Skerne
Foston on the Wolds
Beeford
Brigham
North Frodingham
A165
Dunnington
Atwick
Bewholme
Nunkeeling
B1242
Leven
Brandesburton
Hornsea Mere
HORNSEA
Catwick
Seaton
Hornsea Pottery
Aike
Sigglesthorne
Goxhill
Rolston
arram
B1244
Little Hatfield
Mappleton
Routh
Long Riston
B1243
Rise
Great Hatfield
Mappleton Sands
A1035
Tickton
Arnold
Withernwick
Great Cowden
Beverley
Weel
North Skirlaugh
New Ellerby
Woodmansey
Marton
West Newton
Aldbrough
East Ella
Wawne
South Skirlaugh
A165
Old Ellerby
B1242
Thearne
Swine
Flinton
Garton
Dunswell
Coniston
Burton Constable Hall
Sproatley
Humbleton
Hilston
Ganstead
Wyton
Lelley
Owstwick
A1165
Bilton
B1238
Elstronwick
Tunstall
Newland
Sutton on Hull
B1240
B1239
Stoneferry
Preston
Burton Pidsea
Roos
Marfleet
A1033
Hedon
Rimswell
Owthorne
KINGSTON UPON HULL
Burstwick
B1362
Withernsea
A63
Paull
Thorngumbald
Halsham
Hollym
Keyingham
Winestead
A1033
Holmpton
Ottringham
A1033
Patrington
B1445
New Holland
Welwick
Barrow Haven
Goxhill
Weeton
Easington
w-upon-umber
East Halton
Skeffling
A1077
Thornton Abbey
Kilnsea
Wootton
North Killingholme
Thornton Curtis
South Killingholme
B1211
Ulceby Skitter
A160
Immingham Dock
Ulceby
RIVER HUMBER
B1211
Habrough
Immingham
A180
A180
Croxton
Kirmington
Brocklesby
Stallingborough
GRIMSBY
Melton Ross
B1120
Keelby
B1210
Healing
West Marsh
AA
Barnetby le Wold
A18
Great Limber
A73
Great Coates
Old Clee
Cleethorpes
Bigby
Riby
Aylesby
Lincolnshire Coast
Humberside
A46
Nunsthorpe
Thrunscoe
Searby
Bradley
Scartho
Humberston
Owmby
Irby upon Humber
A1098
Grasby
A1173
Swallow
Barnoldby le Beck
New Waltham
Clixby
Cabourne
Beelsby
Brigsley
Waltham
A16
Holton le Clay
A1031
Caistor
Cuxwold
Ashby cum

SPURN HEAD

ROTTERDAM (EUROPOORT) ZEEBRUGGE

TA

50 1   2   3   51   4   5

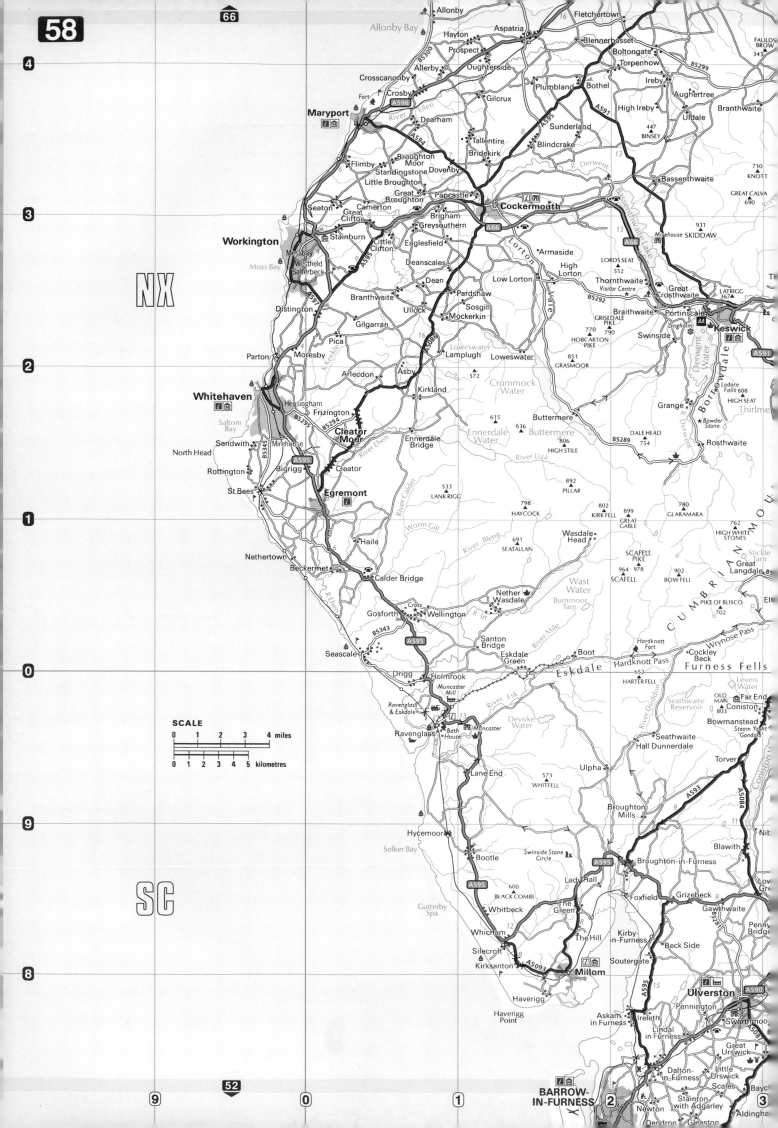

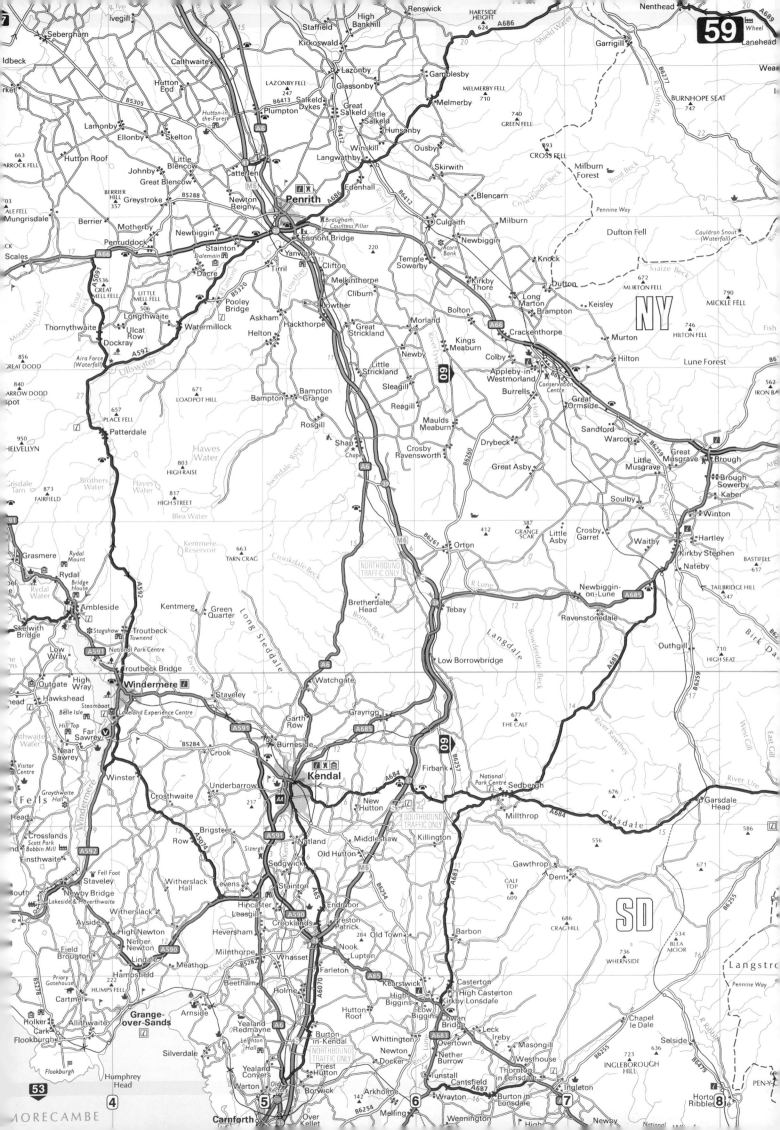

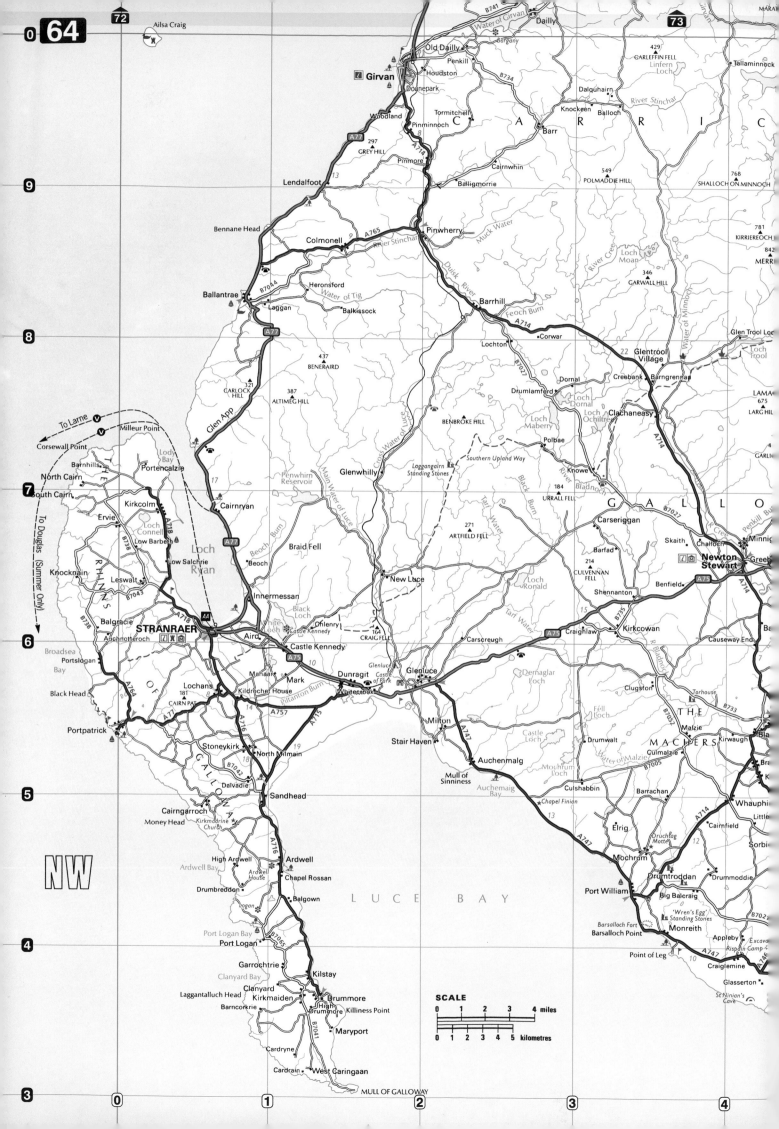

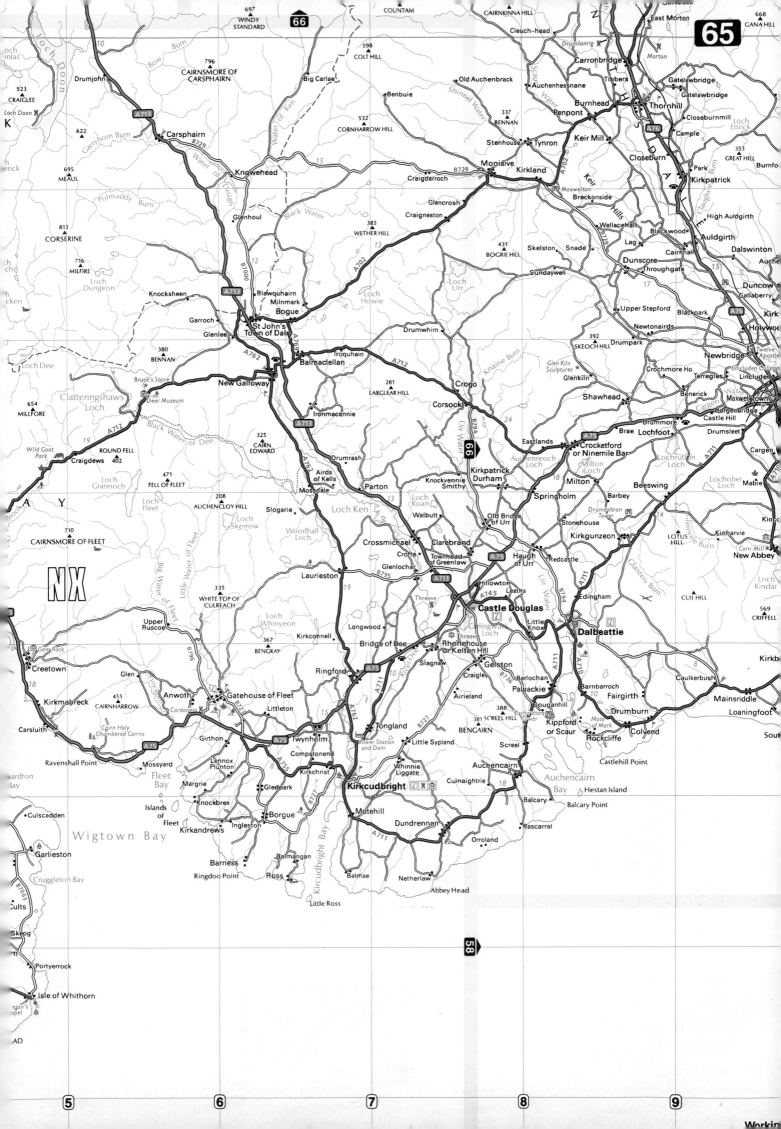

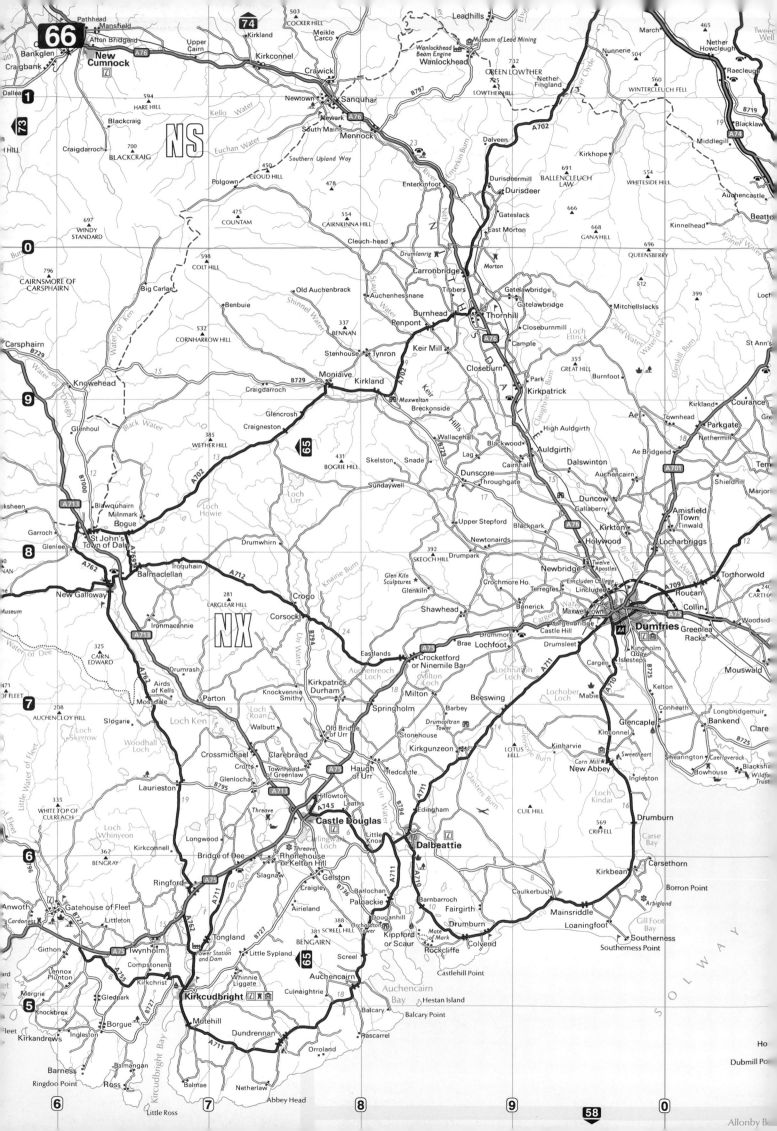

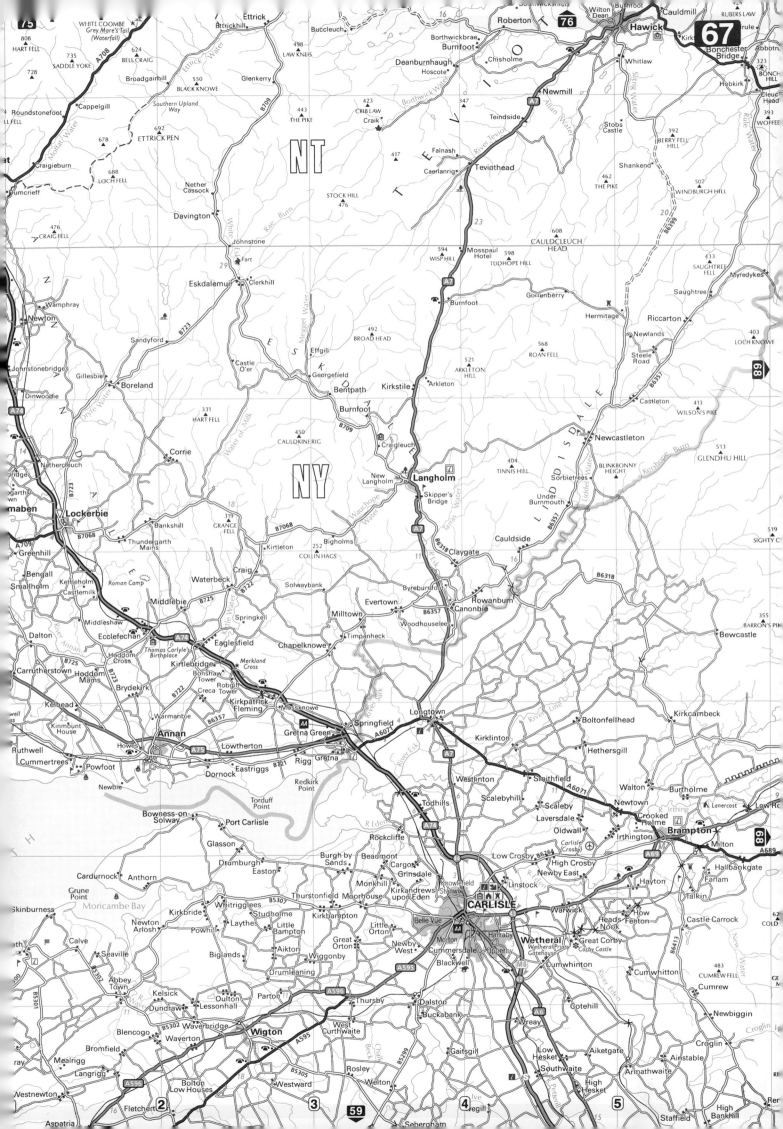

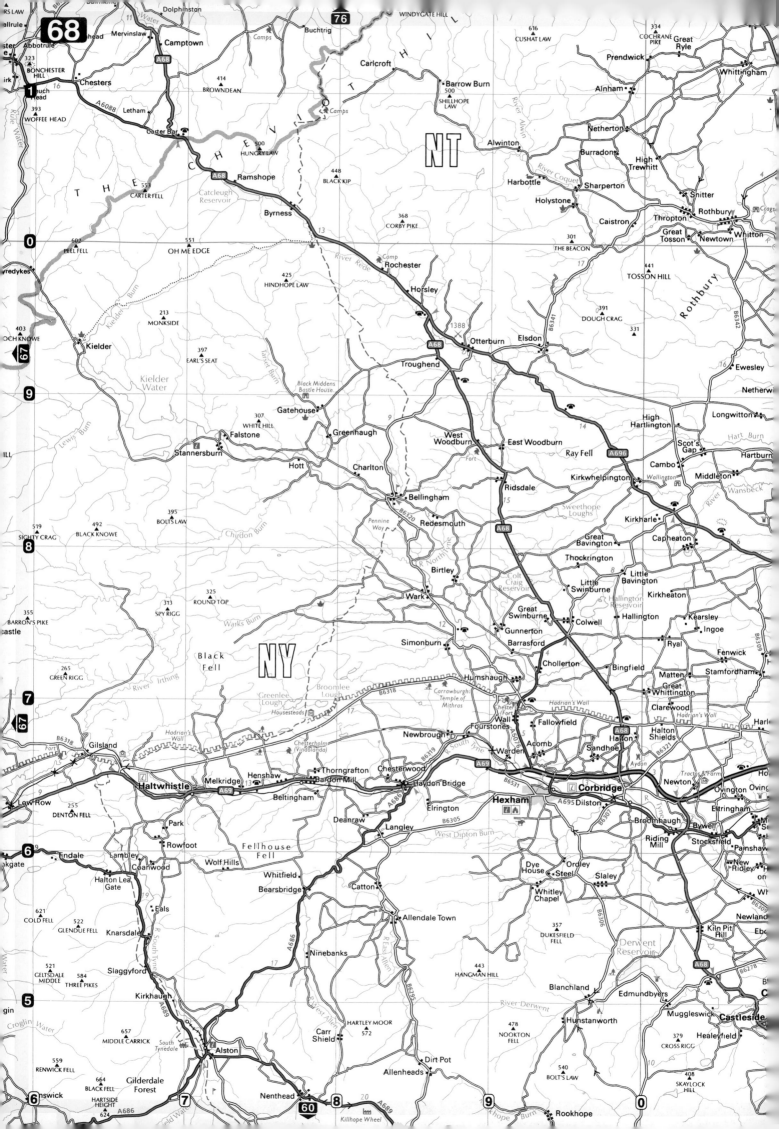

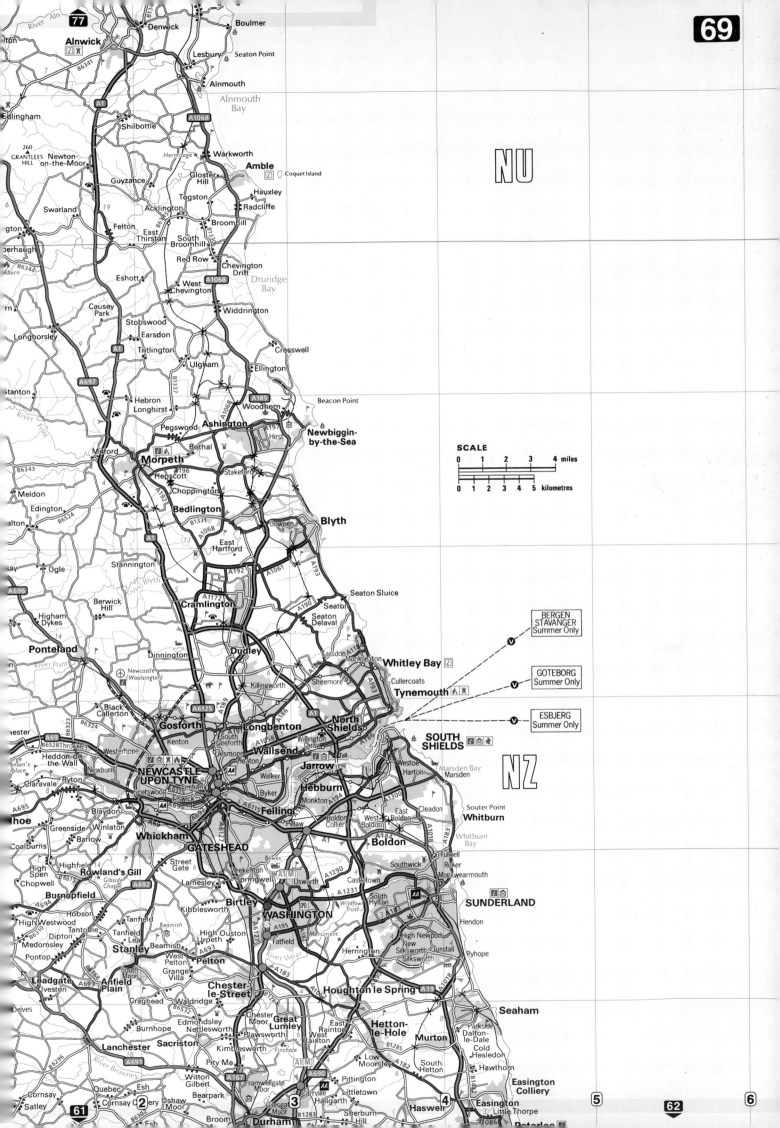

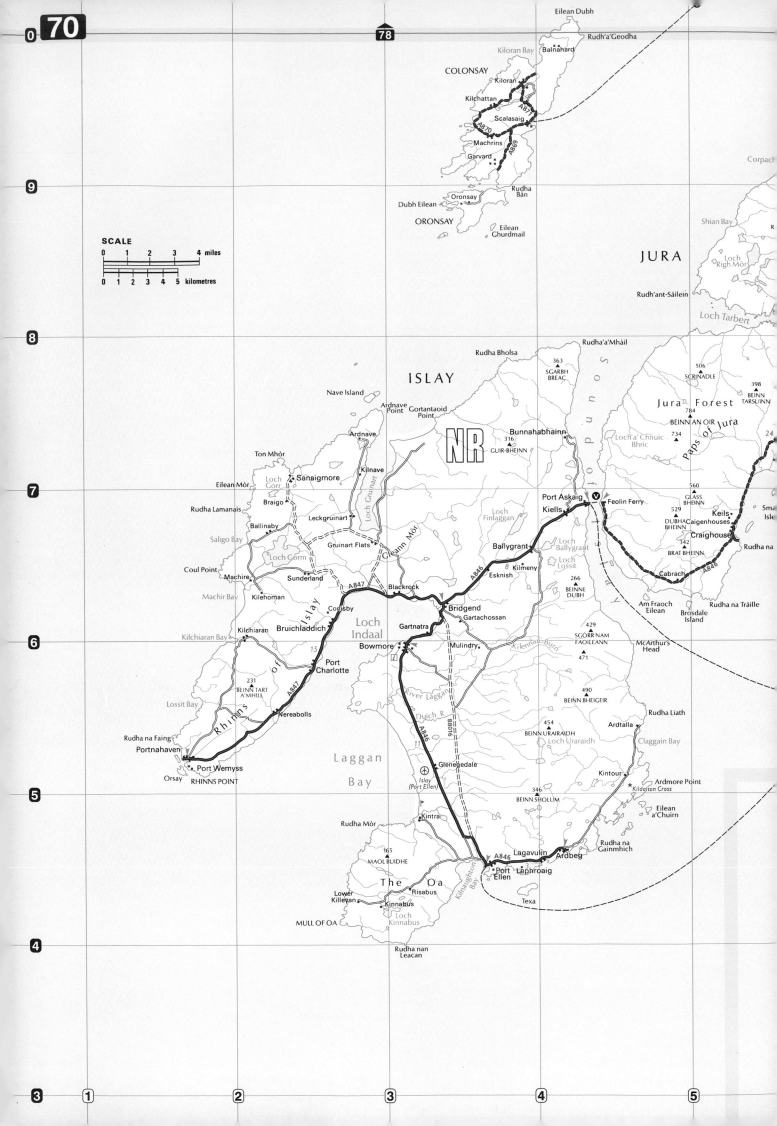

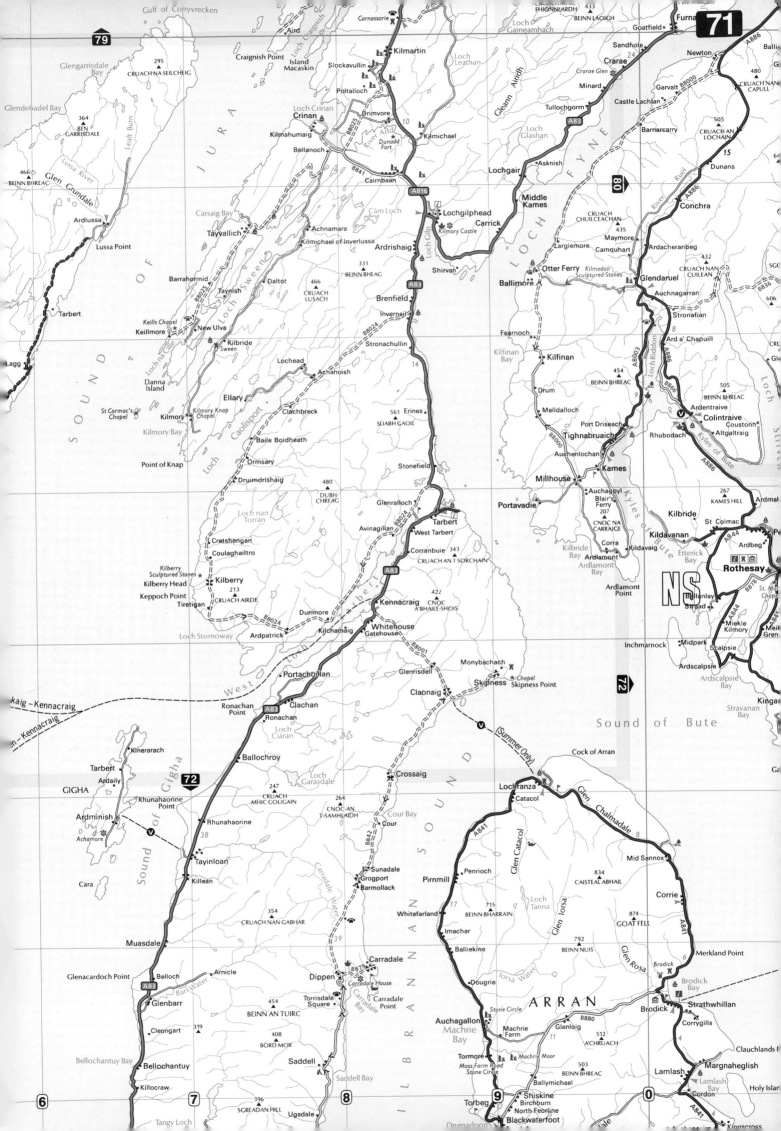

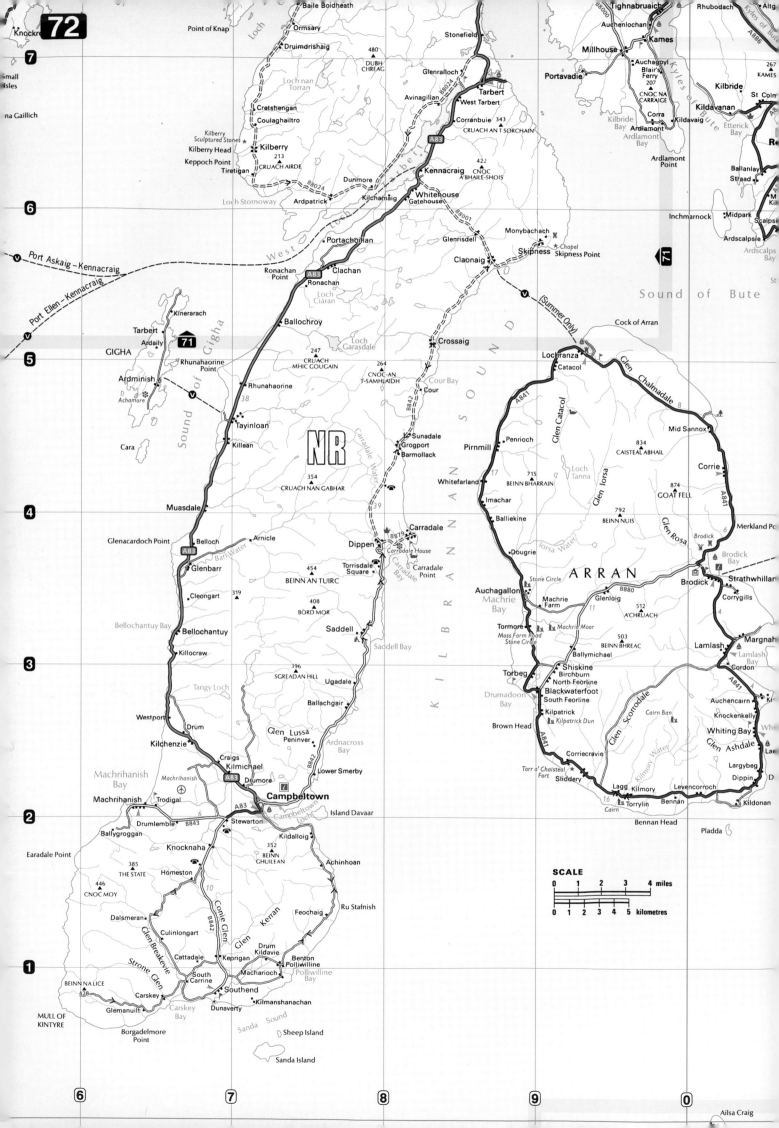

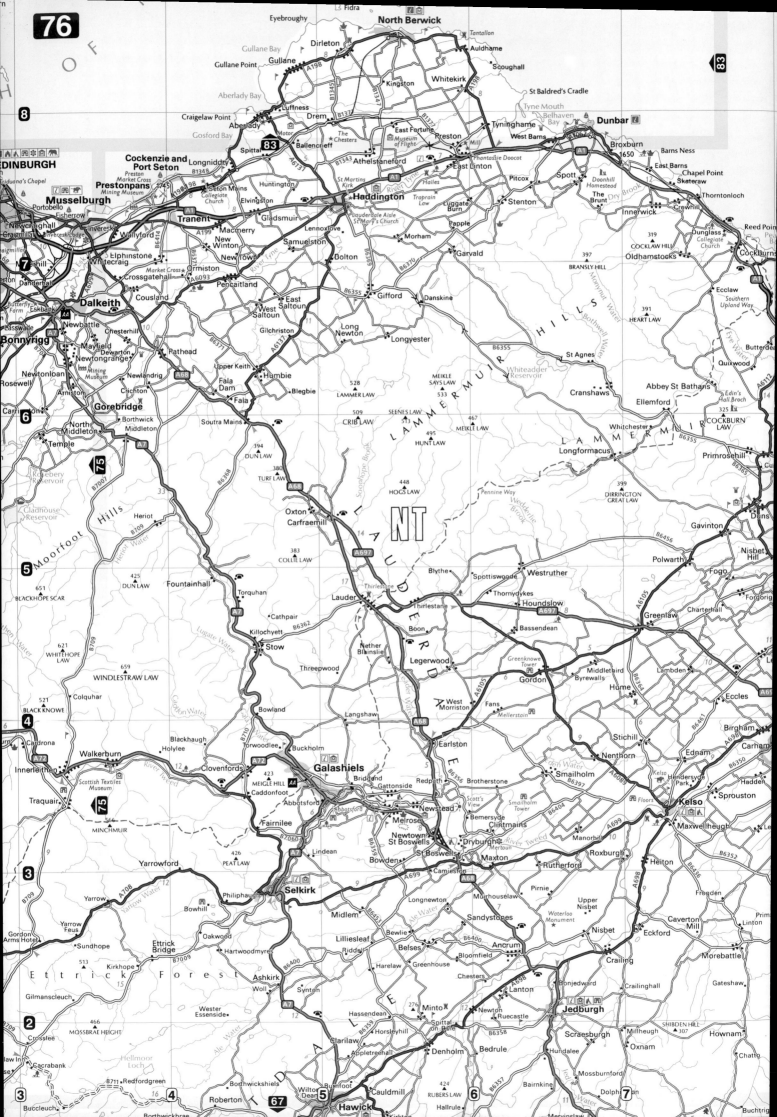

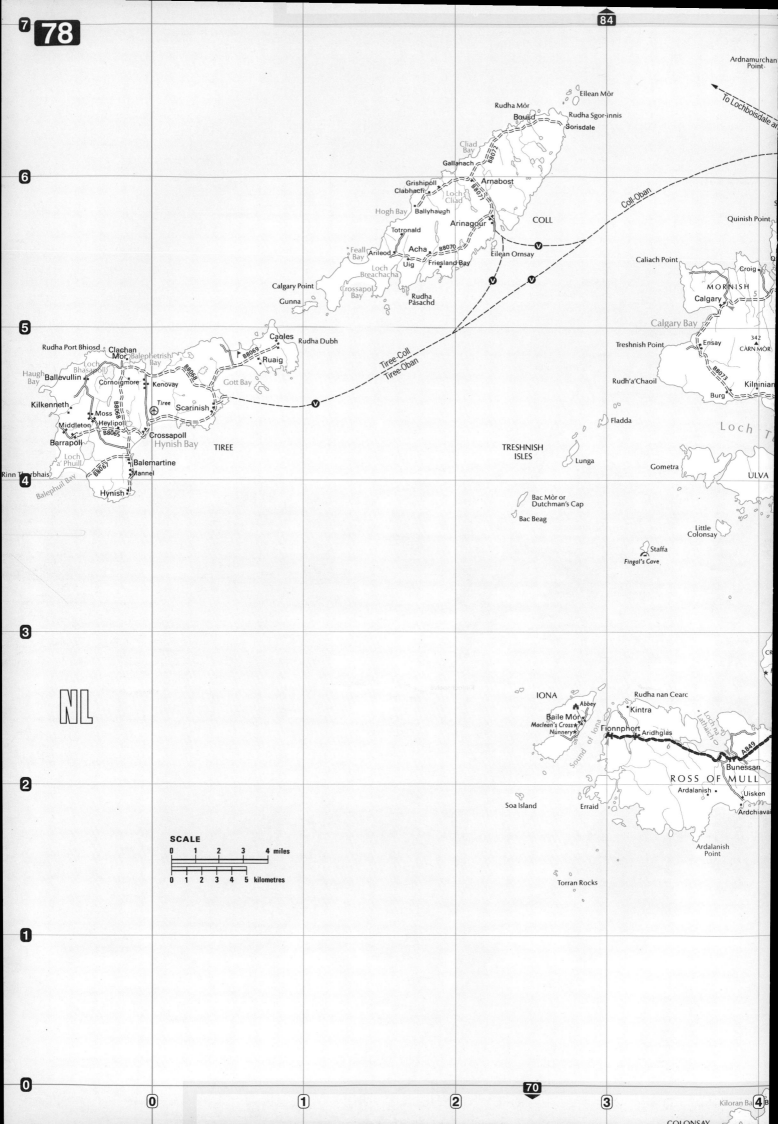

Ardnamurchan Point

To Lochboisdale an

Eilean Mòr

Rudha Mòr

Bousd

Rudha Sgor-innis

Sorisdale

Cliad Bay

Gallanach

B8071

6

Grishipoll

Clabhach

Arnabost

Loch Cliad

B8071

Hogh Bay

Ballyhaugh

Totronald

Arinagour

COLL

Quinish Point

Coll-Oban

Feall Bay

Arileod

Acha

B8070

Friesland Bay

Eilean Ornsay

V

Caliach Point

Croig

MORNISH

Uig

Loch Breachacha

Calgary Point

Crossapol Bay

Rudha Pàsachd

V

V

Calgary

Gunna

Tiree-Coll

Tiree-Oban

Calgary Bay

5

Rudha Port Bhiosd

Clachan Mòr

Caoles

Rudha Dubh

Balephetrish Bay

Treshnish Point

Ensay

342
CÀRN MÒR

Loch Bhasapoll

B8069

Ruaig

Haugh Bay

Ballevullin

Cornaigmore

Kenovay

Gott Bay

B8068

Tiree

Rudh'a'Chaoil

B8073

Kilkenneth

Moss

Heylipoll

Scarinish

Burg

Kilninian

Middleton

B8068

B8065

Crossapoll

TRESHNISH
ISLES

Fladda

Loch T

Barrapol

Hynish Bay

TIREE

Lunga

Gometra

ULVA

Balemartine

4

Rinn Thorbhais

Loch a' Phuill

B8067

Mannel

Bac Mòr or
Dutchman's Cap

Balephuill Bay

Hynish

Bac Beag

Little
Colonsay

Staffa

Fingal's Cave

3

NL

IONA

Rudha nan Cearc

CR

Abbey

Baile Mòr

Kintra

Maclean's Cross

Nunnery

Fionnphort

Aridhglas

Loch na Làthaich

A849

B

Sound of Iona

Bunessan

ROSS OF MULL

2

Ardalanish

Uisken

Soa Island

Erraid

Ardchiavai

Ardalanish
Point

SCALE

| 0 | 1 | 2 | 3 | 4 miles |

| 0 | 1 | 2 | 3 | 4 | 5 kilometres |

Torran Rocks

1

0

0   1   2   3   4

Kiloran Ba

COLONSAY

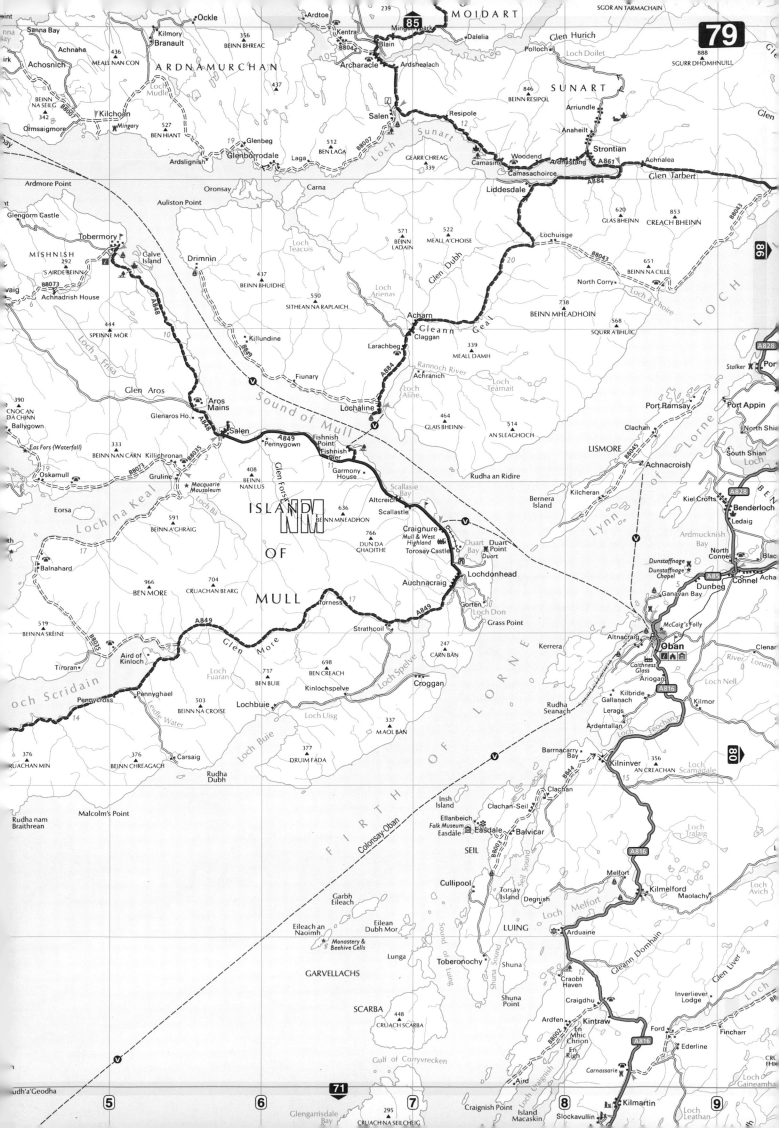

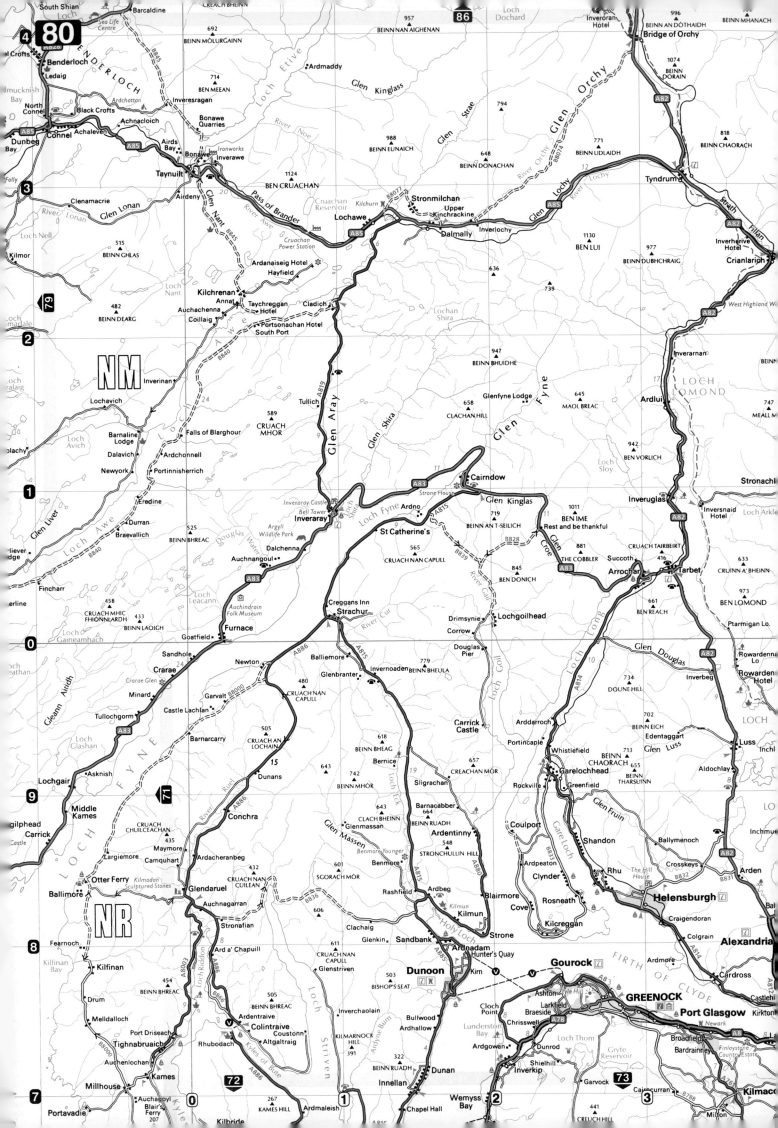

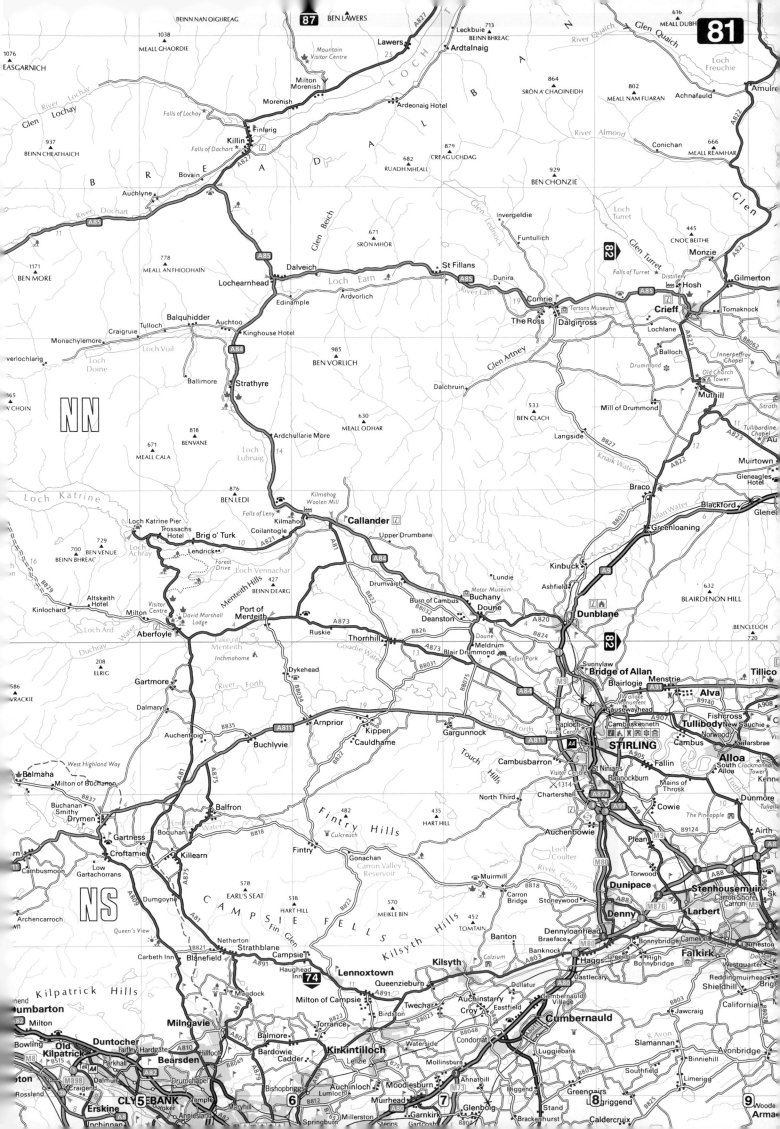

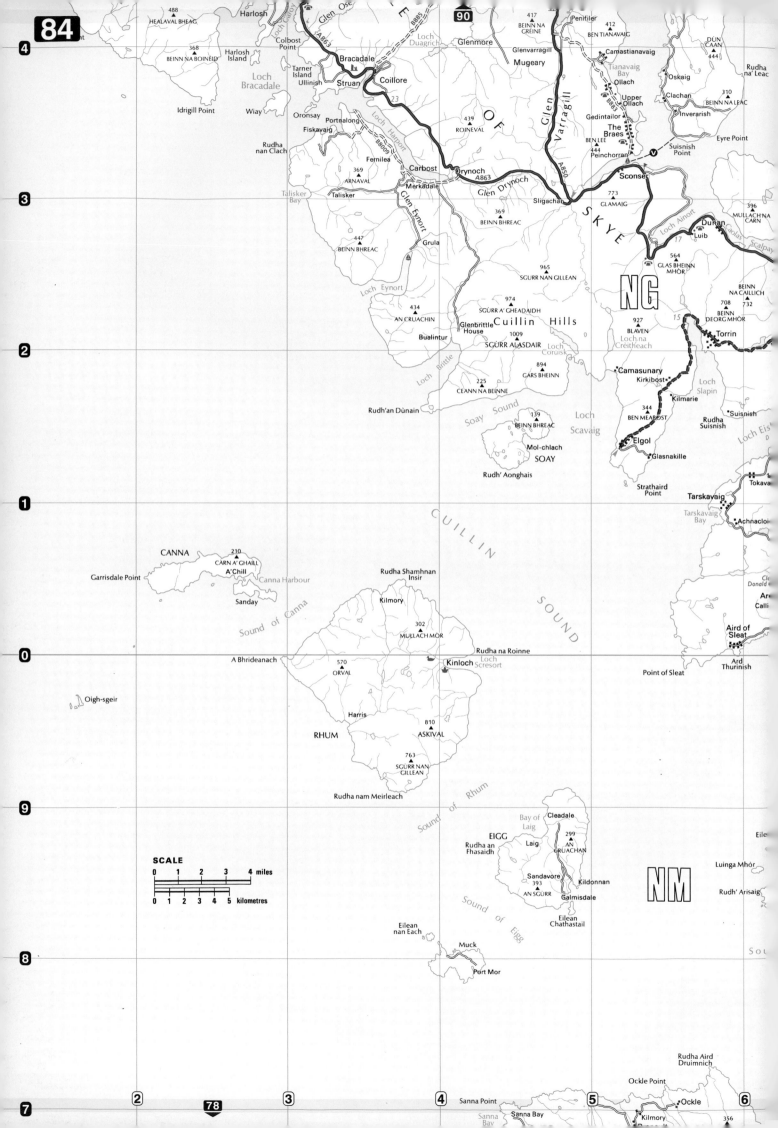

SCALE

0 1 2 3   4 miles

0 1 2 3 4 5 kilometres

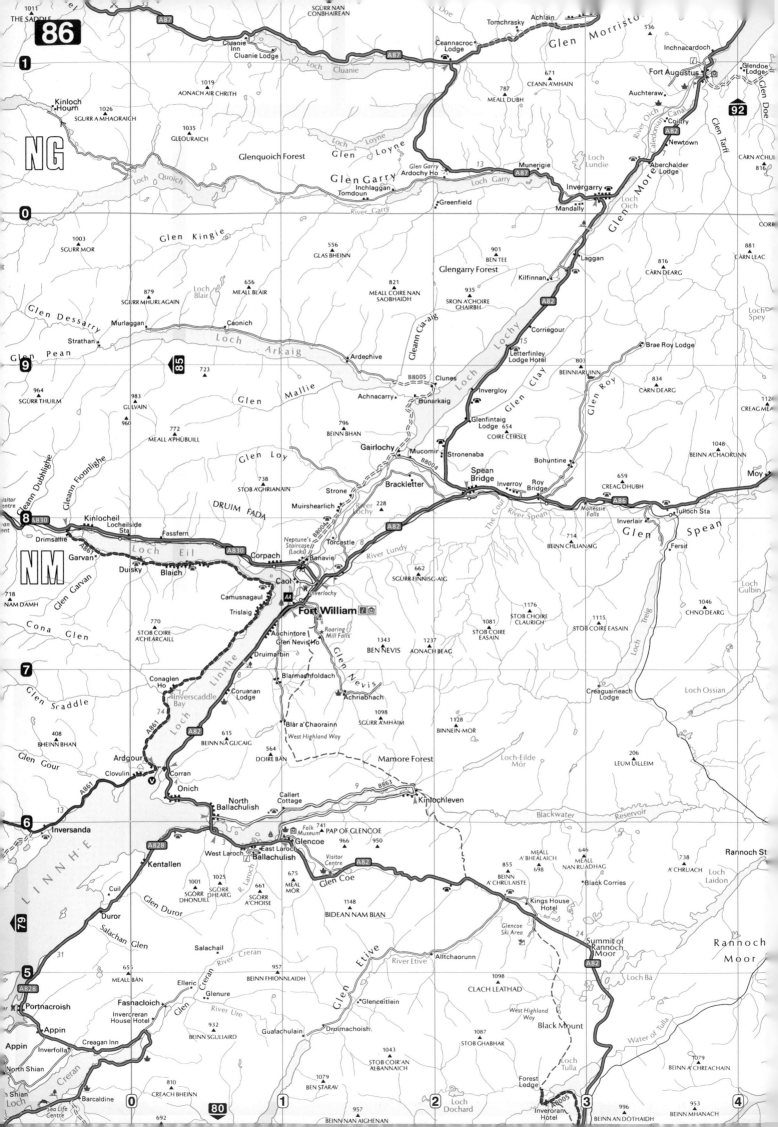

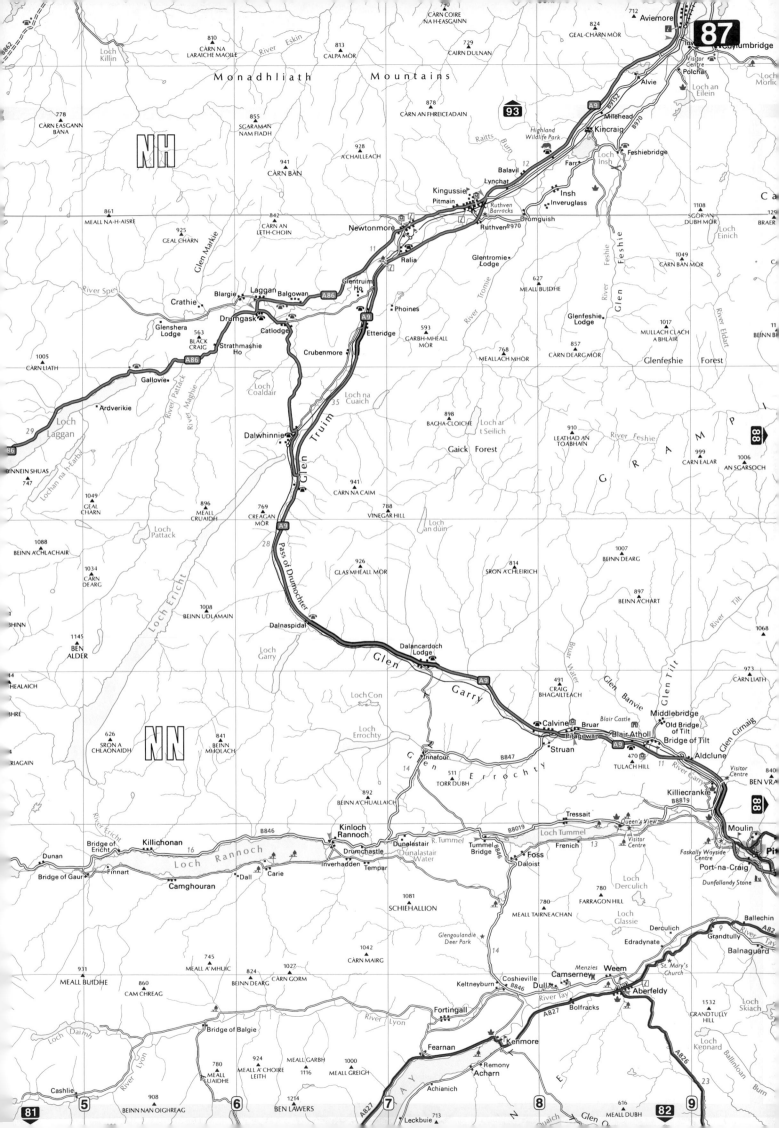

1

0

9

8

7

6

5

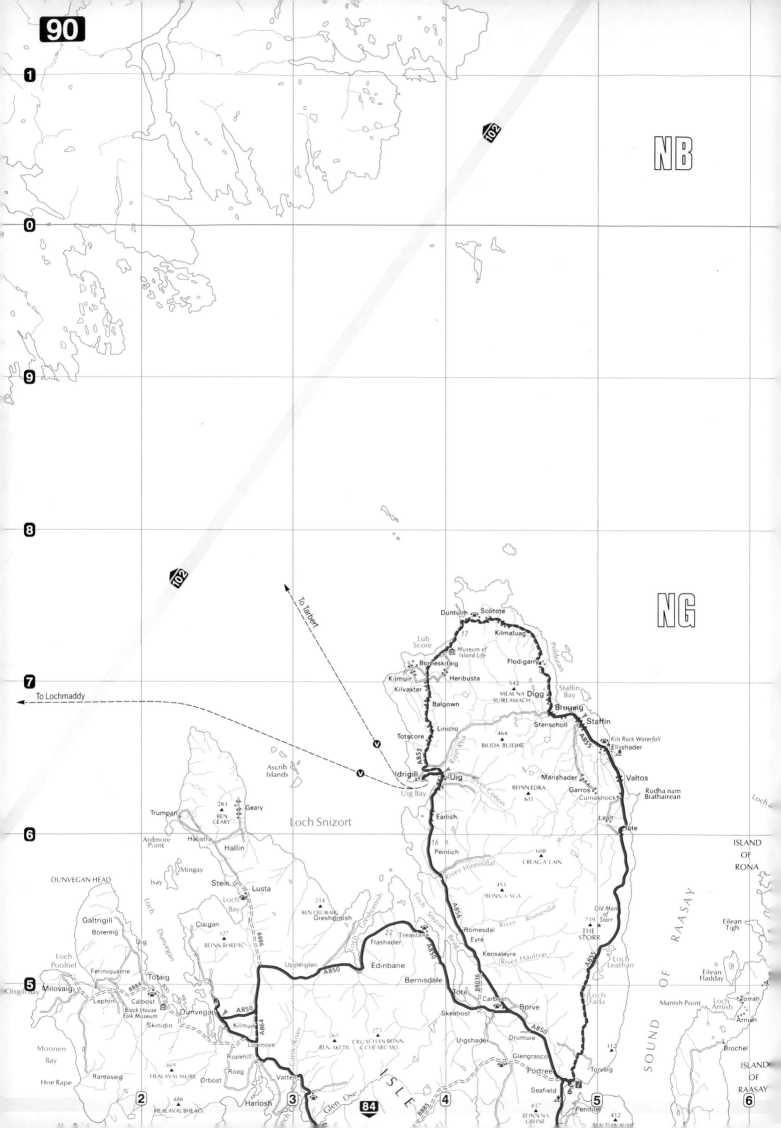

NG

ISLAND OF RONA

SOUND OF RAASAY

ISLAND OF RAASAY

To Tarbert

To Lochmaddy

Duntulm   Solitote
                    Kilmaluag
Lùb Score   Museum of Island Life
Borneskitaig   Flodigarry
Kilmuir   Heribusta
Kilvaxter   542   Poldorais
Balgown   MEAL NA   Digg
            SUIREAMACH
Linicro   464   Broguig   Staffin Bay
Totscore   BIODA BUIDHE   Stenscholl   Staffin
                    A855
Idrigill   River Rha   Kilt Rock Waterfall
Uig   Ellishader
Uig Bay   River Conon   Marishader   Valtos
            BEINN EDRA   Garros
            611   Culnaknock   Rudha nam Brathairean
Earlish
                Lealt
                    Tote
16   Peinlich   608
            CREAG A'LAIN
A856   River Hinnisdal   BEINN A'SGA   Old Man of Storr   Eilean Tigh
                    451   719
                    THE STORR   Loch Leathan
                River Romesdal
        Romesdal   Loch Fada   Eilean Fladday
        Eyre
        Kensaleyre   Loch Arnish
        River Haulton   Manish Point
                    Torran
                    312   Arnish
Drumuie
Uigshader   Glengrasco   Brochel
            Portree
            Torvaig
            Seafield   Penifiler
            417
            BEINN NA   412
            GRÈINE

Loch Snizort

Trumpan   283
        BEN GEARY   Geary
Ardmore Point   Halistra
        Hallin
DUNVEGAN HEAD   Isay   Mingay
        Stein   Lusta
Galtrigill   Loch Bay
Boreraig   Claigan
        Uig   137   214
        BEINN BHREAC   BEN DIUBAIG   Greshornish   Loch Greshornish
Loch Pooltiel   Feriniquarrie   Upperglen   22   Treaslane
Oisgill Bay   Milovaig   A850   Flashader
        Lephin   Totaig   Edinbane   A850
        Calbost   Bernisdale   B8036
        Black House   Tote   Carbost   Borve
        Folk Museum   Skeabost
Moonen Bay   Dunvegan   A850
        Kilmuir   A850
        Lonmore   271   Drumuie
        Rockhill   CRUACHAN BEINN
Hoe Rape   Ramasaig   265   A'CHEARCAILL
        469   Roag   Caroy River
        HEALAVAL MORE   Vatten
        Orbost   Glen Ose
        488   Harlosh
        HEALAVAL BHEAG

ISLE

2   3   84   4   5   6

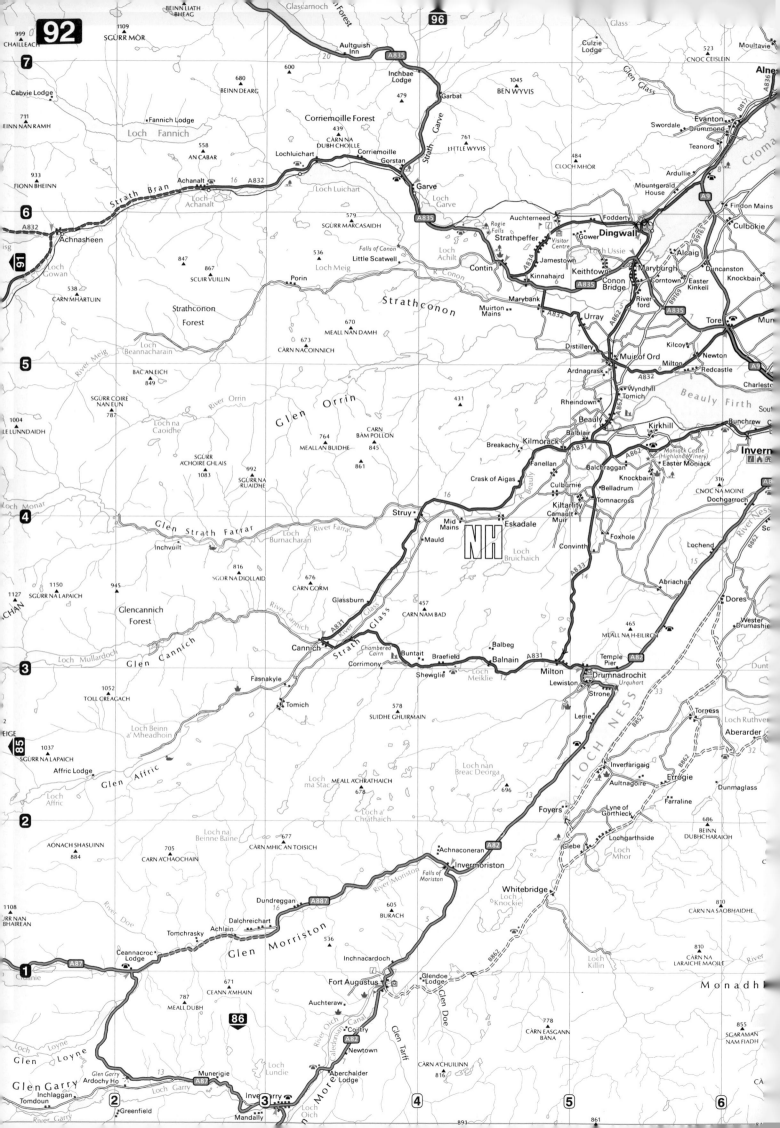

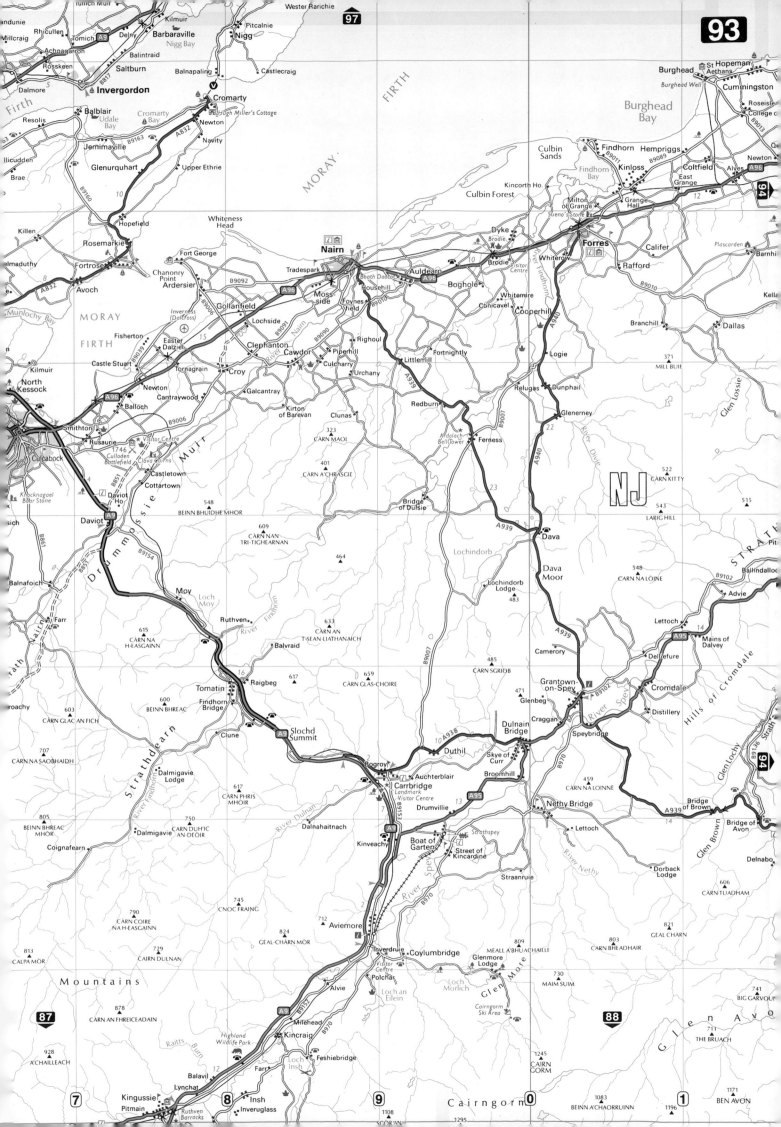

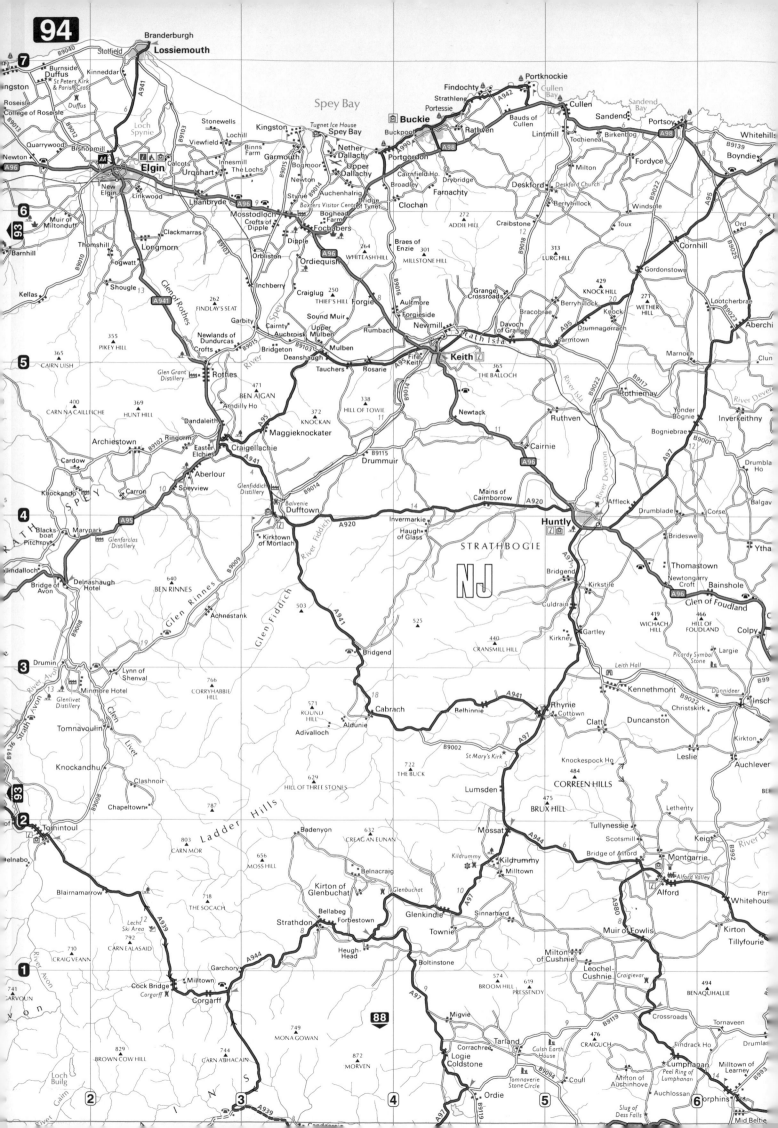

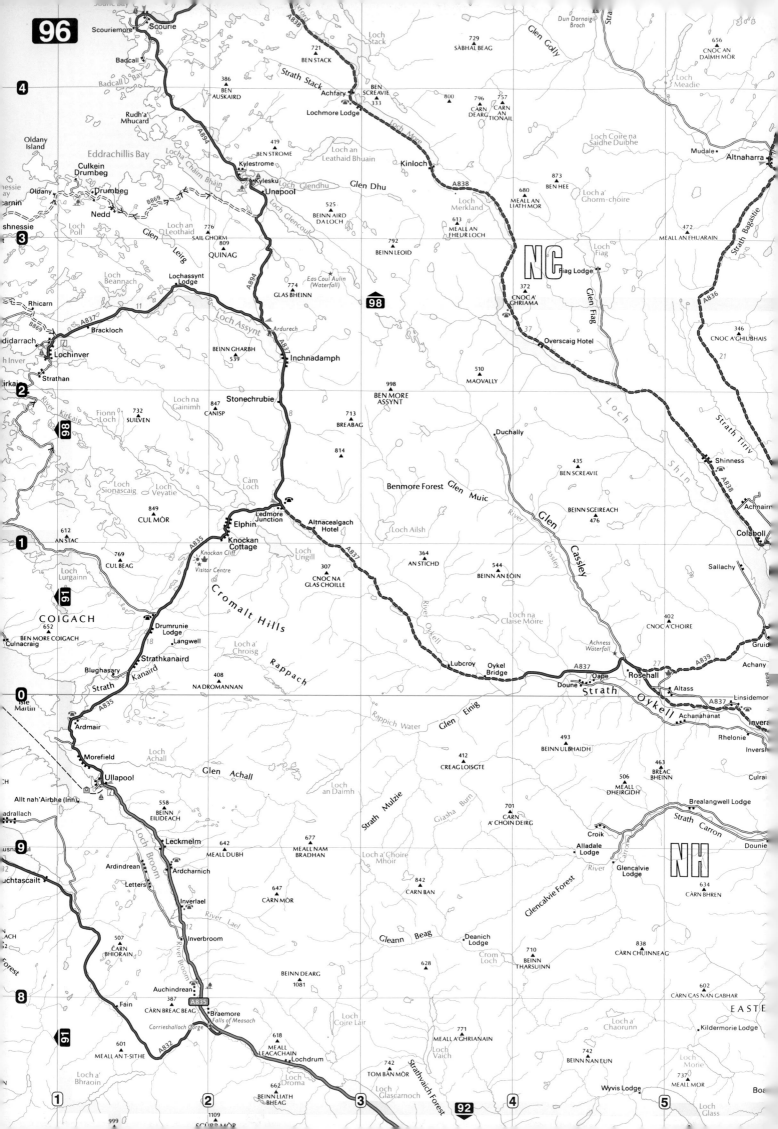

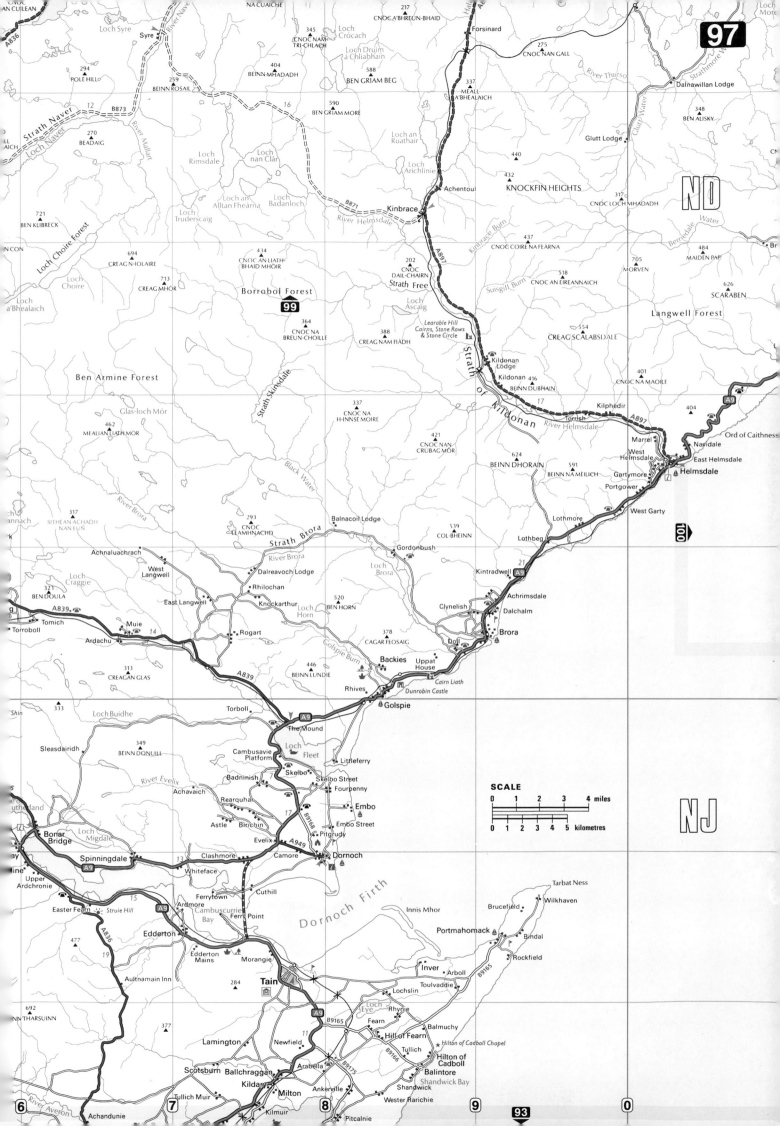

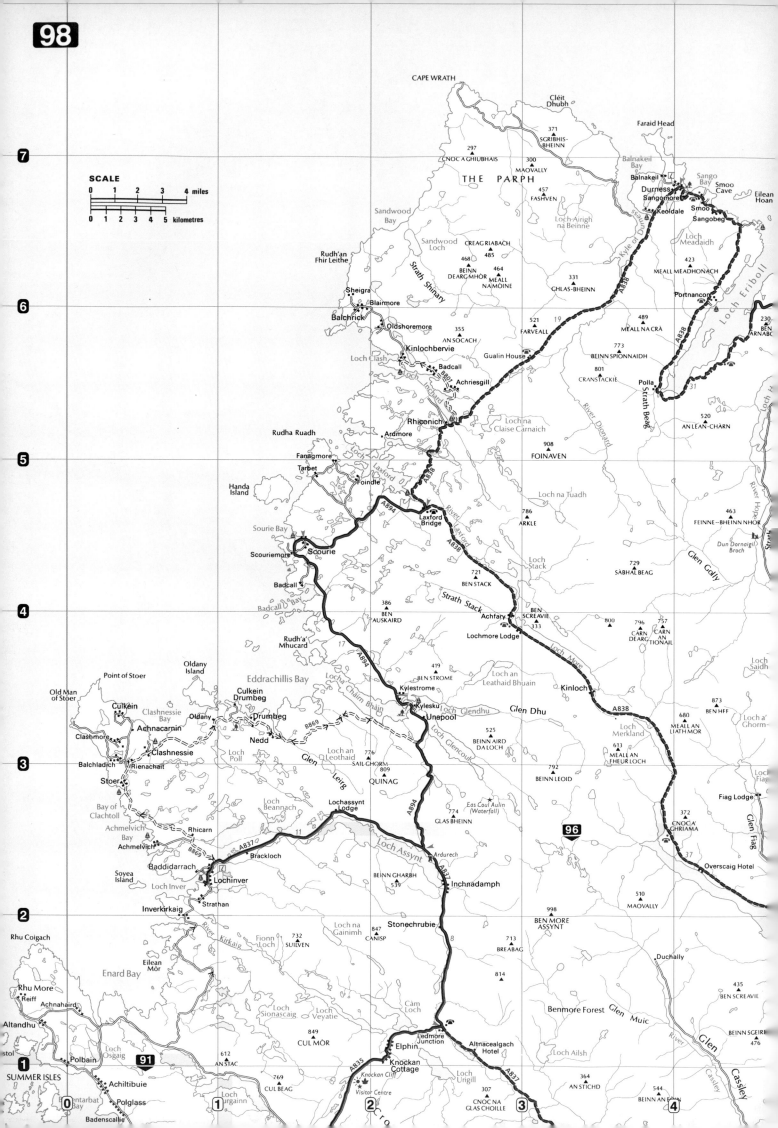

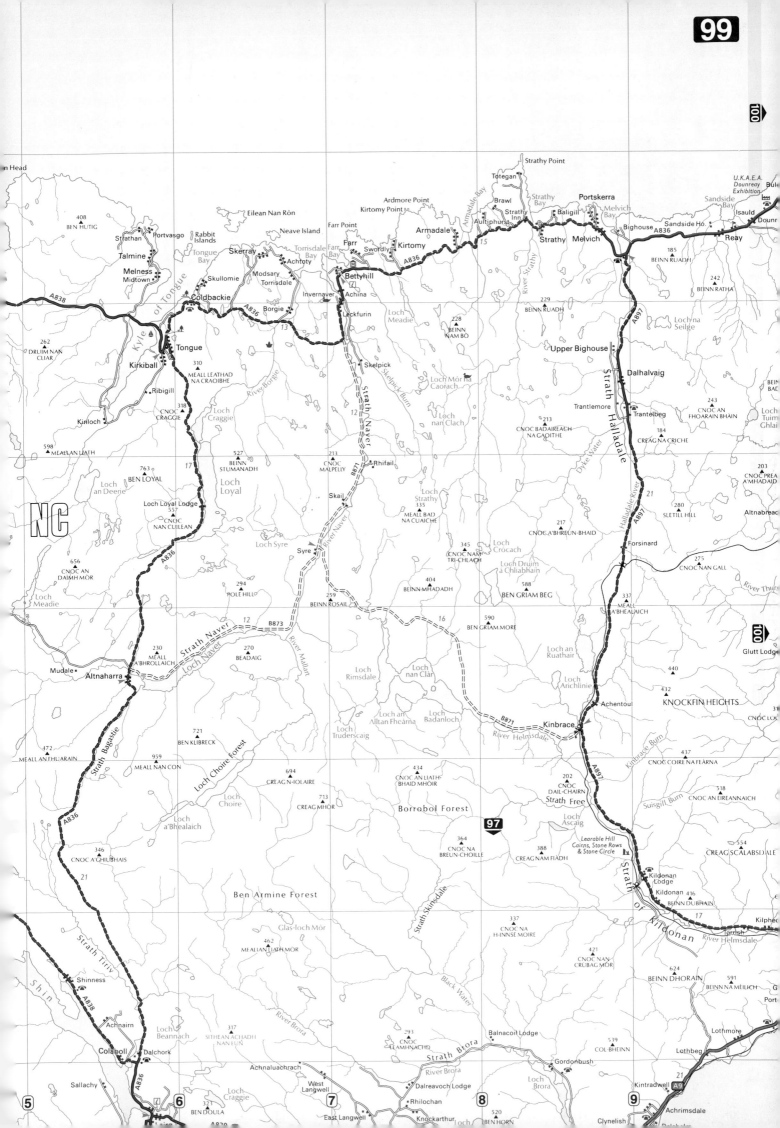

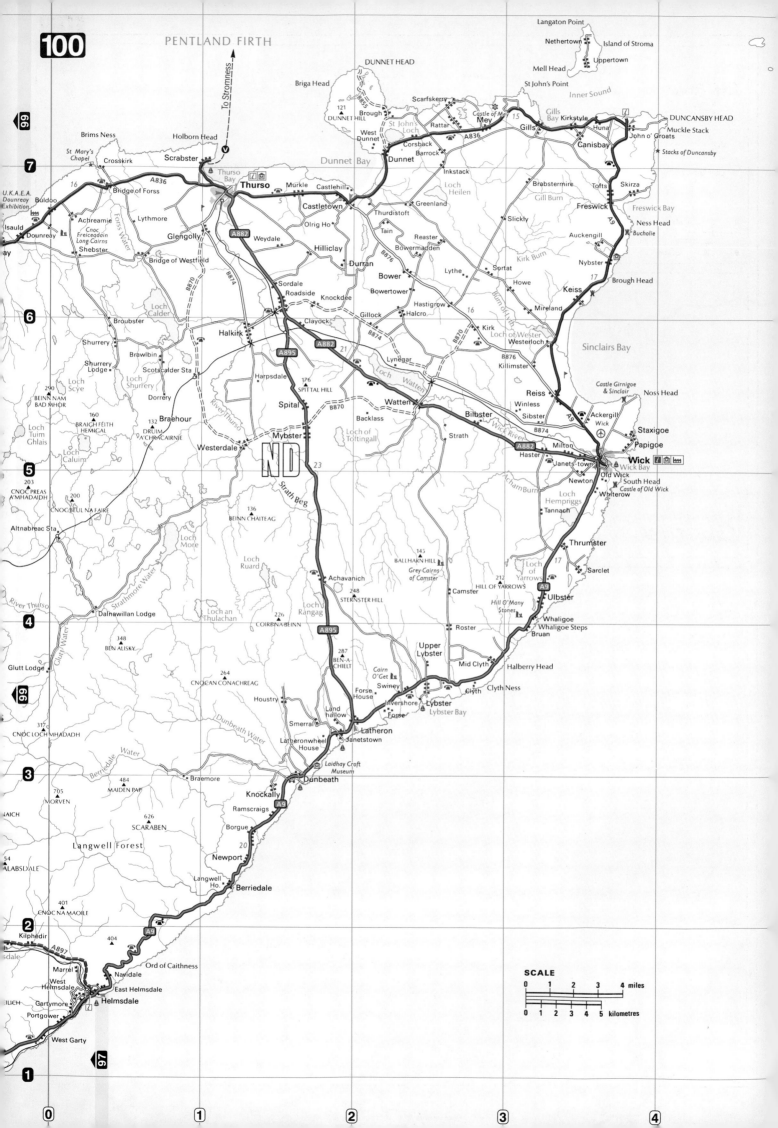

PENTLAND FIRTH

To Stromness →

66

7

Langaton Point
Netherton
Island of Stroma
Mell Head
Uppertown
St John's Point
Inner Sound
DUNNET HEAD
Briga Head
Scarfskerry
121
Brough
DUNNET HILL
St John's
Loch
Rattar
Castle of Mey
Mey 15
Gills Kirkstyle
Huna
DUNCANSBY HEAD
West
Dunnet
Corsback
A836
Gills
Canisby
John o' Groats
Muckle Stack
Brims Ness
Holborn Head
Barrock
Stacks of Duncansby
St Mary's
Chapel
Crosskirk
Scrabster
Dunnet Bay
Dunnet
Inkstack
Thurso Bay
Thurso
Murkle
Castlehill
Greenland
Brabstermire
Tofts
Skirza
A836
16
Bridge of Forss
Castletown
Thurdistoft
Tain
Slickly
Freswick
Freswick Bay
U.K.A.E.A.
Dounreay
Exhibition
Buldoo
Achreamie
Cnoc Freiceadain
Long Cairns
Lythmore
Glengolly
A882
Weydale
Olrig Ho
Reaster
Bowermadden
A9
Ness Head
Bucholie
Isauld
Dounreay
Shebster
Bridge of Westfield
Hilliclay
Durran
Bower
Lythe
Sortat
Howe
Auckengill
Nybster
Brough Head
Keiss
Forss Water
B870
B874
Sordale
Roadside
Knockdee
Bowertower
Hastigrow
Halcro
Kirk Burn
Mireland
6
Loch
Calder
Broubster
Clayock
Gillock
16
Loch of Wester
Westerloch
Sinclairs Bay
Shurrery
Brawlin
Halkirk
B874
Kirk
Sibster
Reiss
Castle Girnigoe
& Sinclair
Noss Head
Shurrery
Lodge
Scotscalder Sta
A895
A882
21
Harpsdale
Lynegar
B876
Killimster
290
BEINN
NAM
BAD MHOR
160
BRAIGH FEITH
HEMIGAL
132
DRUIM
A'CHRACAIRNIE
Braehour
Dorrery
Loch Scye
Loch Shurrery
176
SPITTAL HILL
Spital
Loch Watten
Watten
Winless
Ackergill
Wick
Staxigoe
Papigoe
Loch
Tuim
Ghlais
Loch
Caluim
Westerdale
River Thurso
Mybster
ND
B870
Backlass
Bilbster
Strath
A882
Milton
Haster
Janets-town
Wick
Wick Bay
5
203
CNOC PREAS
A'MHADAIDH
200
CNOC BEUL NA FAIRE
Loch of
Toftingall
23
Loch More
Newton
Old Wick
Castle of Old Wick
Whiterow
South Head
Altnabreac Sta
136
BEINN CHAITEAG
226
COIRENA-BEINN
Strath Beg
Acharn Burn
Loch
Hempriggs
Tannach
River Thurso
4
Dalnawillan Lodge
Loch an
Thulachan
A895
Loch
Ruard
145
BALLHARN HILL
Grey Cairns
of Camster
Thrumster
348
BEN ALISKY
Loch
Rangag
Achavanich
248
STERNSTER HILL
Camster
212
HILL OF YARROWS
Loch of
Yarrows
17
Sarclet
Glutt Lodge
264
CNOCAN CONACHREAG
287
BEN-A-CHIELT
Cairn
O'Get
Hill O' Many
Stones
A9
Ulbster
66
Houstry
Upper
Lybster
Mid Clyth
Halberry Head
317
CNOC LOCH MHADADH
Smerral
Land
hallow
Forse
House
Swiney
Clyth
Clyth Ness
Whaligoe
Whaligoe Steps
Bruan
Laversh ore
Forse
Lybster
Lybster Bay
Dunbeath Water
Latheronwheel
House
Latheron
Janetstown
Berriedale Water
3
Braemore
Laidhay Croft
Museum
484
MAIDEN PAP
Dunbeath
705
MORVEN
Knockally
A9
Ramscraigs
626
SCARABEN
Borgue
20
Langwell Forest
Newport
54
ALABSDALE
Langwell
Ho.
Berriedale
401
CNOC NA MAOILE
2
Kilphedir
404
A9
A897
Ord of Caithness
Marrel
Navidale
West
Helmsdale
East Helmsdale
Gartymore
Helmsdale
Portgower
97
West Garty
1

SCALE
0 1 2 3 4 miles
0 1 2 3 4 5 kilometres

0 1 2 3 4

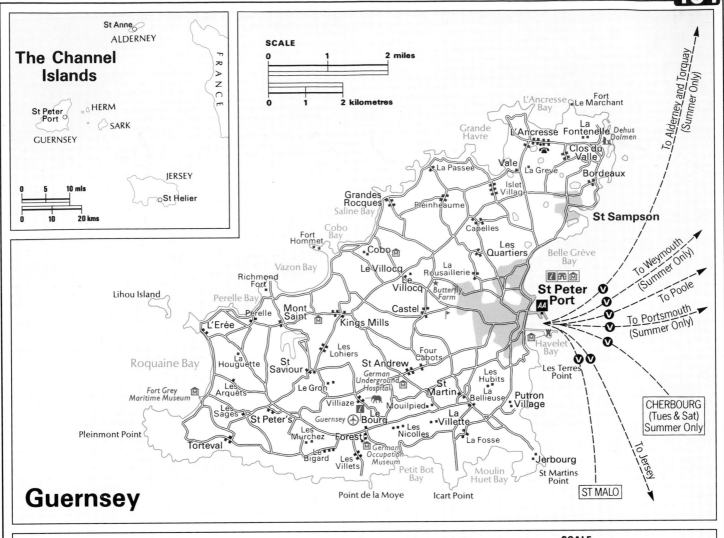

The Channel Islands

St Anne
ALDERNEY

FRANCE

St Peter
Port ○ ◇ HERM
◇ SARK
GUERNSEY

JERSEY
○ St Helier

SCALE
0 _____ 5 _____ 10 mls
0 _____ 10 _____ 20 kms

SCALE
0 _____ 1 _____ 2 miles
0 _____ 1 _____ 2 kilometres

To Alderney and Torquay
(Summer Only)

L'Ancresse
Bay
Fort
Le Marchant
Grande
Havre
L'Ancresse Fontenelle La
Clos du
Valle
Dehus
Dolmen
Vale
La Grève
Bordeaux
La Passee
Islet
Village
St Sampson

Grandes
Rocques
Saline Bay
Pleinheaume
Capelles
Les
Quartiers
Belle Grève
Bay
To Weymouth
(Summer Only)

Fort
Hommet
Cobo
Bay
Cobo
La
Rousaillerie
St Peter
Port
To Poole

Vazon Bay
Le Villocq
Le
Villocq
Butterfly
Farm
AA
To Portsmouth
(Summer Only)

Richmond
Fort
Castel
Havelet
Bay

Lihou Island
Perelle Bay
Perelle
Mont
Saint
Kings Mills
Les
Lohiers
Four
Cabots
Les Terres
Point

L'Erée
La
Houguette
St
Saviour
St Andrew
Les
Hubits
La
Bellieuse
Putron
Village
CHERBOURG
(Tues & Sat)
Summer Only

Roquaine Bay
Les
Arquets
Le Gron
German
Underground
Hospital
St
Martin

Fort Grey
Maritime Museum
Les
Sages
St Peter's
Villiaze
Le
Bourg
Mouilpied
La
Villette
To Jersey

Pleinmont Point
Torteval
Les
Murchez
Forest
Les
Nicolles
La Fosse

Le
Bigard
Les
Villets
German
Occupation
Museum
Jerbourg

Point de la Moye
Petit Bot
Bay
Icart Point
Moulin
Huet Bay
St Martins
Point
ST MALO

Guernsey

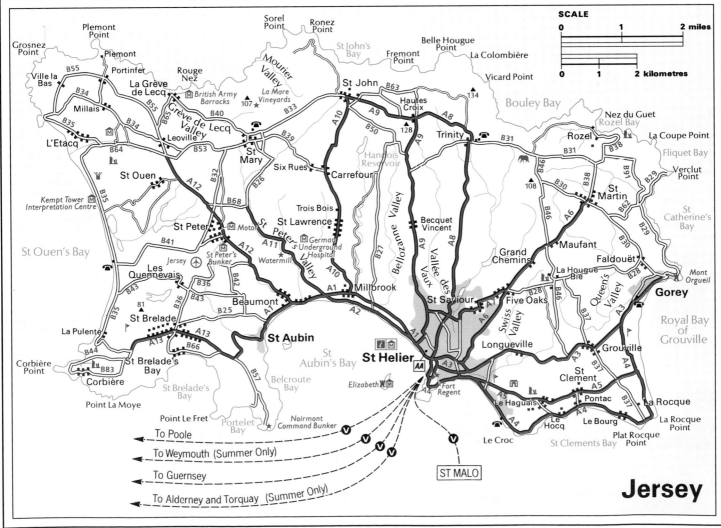

SCALE
0 _____ 1 _____ 2 miles
0 _____ 1 _____ 2 kilometres

Plemont
Point
Sorel
Point
Ronez
Point
Belle Hougue
Point
La Colombière

Grosnez
Point
Plemont
St John's
Bay
Fremont
Point
Vicard Point
Bouley Bay

Ville la
Bas
B55
Portinfer
Rouge
Nez
Mourier
Valley
St John
B63
Hautes
Croix
A8
Nez du Guet
Rozel Bay

B34
La Grève
de Lecq
British Army
Barracks
107
La Mare
Vineyards
A10
A9
128
A9
Trinity
B31
Rozel
La Coupe Point

Millais
B34
B55
Grève de Lecq
Valley
B40
B33
B50
B31
Fliquet Bay
Verclut
Point

B35
B64
Leoville
B39
St
Mary
Six Rues
Hautois
Reservoir
108
St
Martin
B38
B91
B29

L'Etacq
B53
B26
Carrefour
B46
A6
B62
St
Catherine's
Bay

St Ouen
A12
B32
B68
Trois Bois
Bellozanne Valley
Becquet
Vincent
A8
Grand
Chemins
Maufant
B46
Queen's
Valley
A3

Kempt Tower
Interpretation Centre
B35
St Peter
Motor
St Lawrence
B27
A9
Vallée des Vaux
Faldouët
B28
Mont
Orgueil

St Peter's Bunker
German
Underground
Hospital
La Hougue
Bie
B30
Gorey

Jersey
St Ouen's Bay
Les
Quennevais
B36
B42
Watermill
A11
A10
Five Oaks
A1
B46
Grouville
Royal Bay
of Grouville

B43
B41
Beaumont
A1
Millbrook
St Saviour
Swiss Valley
Longueville
A3

La Pulente
B44
81
St Brelade
B25
A13
A2
St Helier
AA
A6
A7
St Clement
A5
La Rocque

Corbière
Point
B83
St Brelade's
Bay
B66
St Aubin
St Aubin's Bay
Elizabeth
Fort
Regent
A3
Le Haguais
Pontac
B37
La Rocque
Point

Corbière
St Brelade's
Bay
B57
Belcroute
Bay
Noirmont
Command Bunker
A4
Le Hocq
Le Bourg
Plat Rocque
Point

Point La Moye
Point Le Fret
Portelet
Bay
To Poole
To Weymouth (Summer Only)
To Guernsey
To Alderney and Torquay (Summer Only)
Le Croc
St Clements Bay
ST MALO

Jersey

Outer Hebrides

THE WESTERN ISLES

The Western Isles, na h-Eileanan Siar, stretch for 130 miles along the edge of the Atlantic, fringed on the west by mile after mile of clean, sandy beaches. The islands have a distinctive culture and Gaelic is the first language of the majority of islanders. Roadside placename signs are all in Gaelic, except in Stornoway (Steornabhagh) on Lewis, and Benbecula (Beinn na Faoghla), where they are bilingual.

Although one island, Lewis (north) and Harris (south) are very different. Lewis is lowlying and covered with bleak peat moors, whereas Harris is rocky and mountainous, with fertile green 'machair' land to the west.

North Uist, Benbecula and South Uist offer beaches and lowlying 'machair' to the west and mountains and moorland to the east, while Barra has a rocky, broken east coast and fine-sand bays on the west, rising to a summit at Heaval.

Ferry Services

Lewis is linked by ferry to the mainland at Ullapool, with daily sailings (except Sun). Harris is linked to Skye at Uig, and North Uist at Lochmaddy in a triangular service. North Uist is served from Uig and Tarbert (Harris), also in a triangular service. South Uist is served from Oban (mainland), as is Barra, with the ferry arriving at Castlebay.

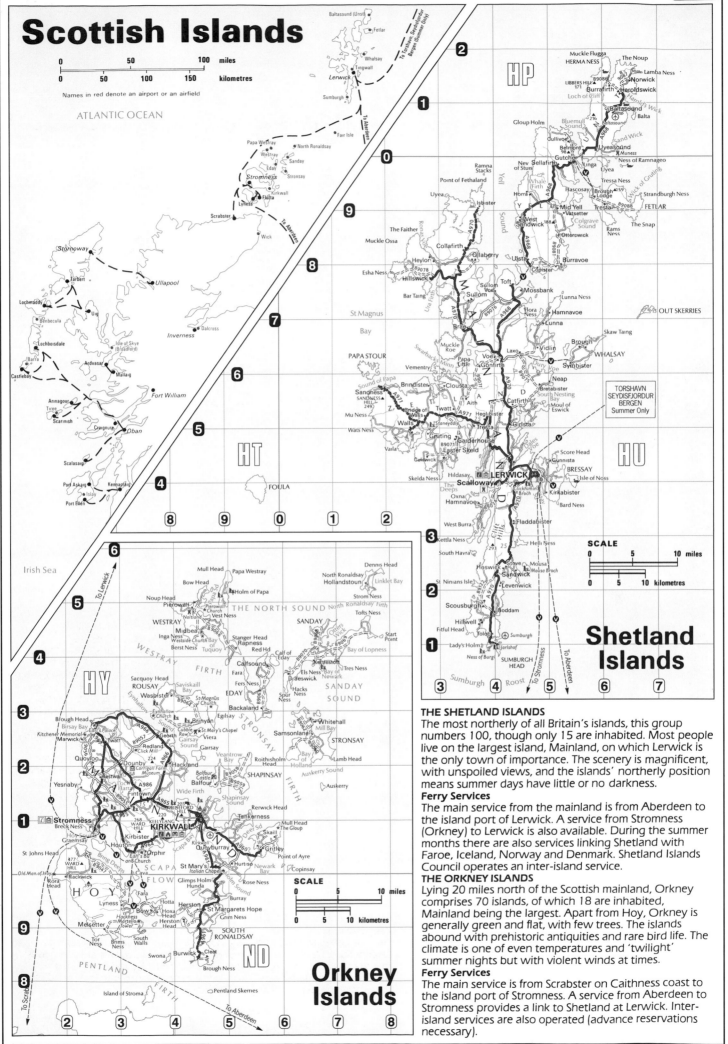

Scottish Islands

50 100 miles
50 100 150 kilometres

Names in red denote an airport or an airfield

ATLANTIC OCEAN

Shetland Islands

Orkney Islands

TORSHAVN
SEYDISFJORDUR
BERGEN
Summer Only

THE SHETLAND ISLANDS

The most northerly of all Britain's islands, this group numbers 100, though only 15 are inhabited. Most people live on the largest island, Mainland, on which Lerwick is the only town of importance. The scenery is magnificent, with unspoiled views, and the islands' northerly position means summer days have little or no darkness.

Ferry Services

The main service from the mainland is from Aberdeen to the island port of Lerwick. A service from Stromness (Orkney) to Lerwick is also available. During the summer months there are also services linking Shetland with Faroe, Iceland, Norway and Denmark. Shetland Islands Council operates an inter-island service.

THE ORKNEY ISLANDS

Lying 20 miles north of the Scottish mainland, Orkney comprises 70 islands, of which 18 are inhabited, Mainland being the largest. Apart from Hoy, Orkney is generally green and flat, with few trees. The islands abound with prehistoric antiquities and rare bird life. The climate is one of even temperatures and 'twilight' summer nights but with violent winds at times.

Ferry Services

The main service is from Scrabster on Caithness coast to the island port of Stromness. A service from Aberdeen to Stromness provides a link to Shetland at Lerwick. Inter-island services are also operated (advance reservations necessary).

Ireland

Abbeydorney G2
Abbeyfeale G2
Abbeyleix G4
Adamstown G4
Adare G2
Adrigole H2
Ahascragh F3
Ahoghill D5
Allihies H1
Anascaul H1
Annalong E5
Annestown H4
Antrim D5
Ardagh G2
Ardara D3
Ardcath F5
Ardee E4
Ardfert G2
Ardfinnan G3
Ardglass E5
Ardgroom H1
Arklow G5
Arless G4
Armagh D4
Armoy C5
Arthurstown H4
Arvagh E4
Ashbourne F4
Ashford F5
Askeaton G2
Athboy E4
Athea G2
Athenry F3
Athleague F3
Athlone F3
Athy F4
Augher D4
Aughnacloy D4
Aughrim G5
Avoca G5

Bailieborough E4
Balbriggan F5
Balla E2
Ballacolla G4
Ballaghaderreen E3
Ballina G3
Ballina E2
Ballinafad E3
Ballinagh E4
Ballinakill G4
Ballinalee E3
Ballinamallard D4
Ballinamore F3
Ballinamore E3
Ballinascarty H2
Ballindine E2
Ballineen H2
Ballingarry G3
Ballingarry G2
Ballingeary H2
(Beal Atha an Ghaorfthaidh)
Ballinhassig H3
Ballinlough E3
Ballinrobe E2
Ballinspittle H2
Ballintober E3
Ballintra D3
Ballivor F4
Ballon G4
Ballybaun F3
Ballybay E4
Ballybofey D3
Ballybunion G2
Ballycanew G5
Ballycarry D5
Ballycastle D2
Ballycastle C5
Ballyclare D5
Ballyconneely F1
Ballycotton H3
Ballycumber F3
Ballydehob J2
Ballydesmond H2
Ballyduff H3
Ballyduff G2
Ballyfarnan E3
Ballygalley D5
Ballygar F3
Ballygawley D4
Ballyhaise E3
Ballyhale G4
Ballyhaunis E3
Ballyhean E2
Ballyheige G1
Ballyjamesduff E4
Ballykeeran F3
Ballylanders G3
Ballylongford G2
Ballylooby G3
Ballylynan G4
Ballymahon F3
Ballymakeery H2
Ballymaloe H3
Ballymena D5
Ballymoe E3
Ballymoney C4
Ballymore F3
Ballymore Eustace F4
Ballymote E3
Ballynahinch D5
Ballynure D5

Ballyragget G4
Ballyroan G4
Ballyronan D4
Ballysadare E3
Ballyshannon D3
Ballyvaughan F2
Ballywalter D5
Balrothery F5
Baltimore J2
Baltinglass G4
Banagher F3
Banbridge D5
Bandon H2
Bangor D5
Bangor Erris E2
Bansha G3
Banteer H2
Bantry H2
Barryporeen H3
Beaufort H2
Belcoo D3
Belfast D5
Belgooly H3
Bellaghy D4
Belleek D3
Belmullet D2
(Beal an Mhuirhead)
Belturbet E4
Benburb D4
Bennetsbridge G4
Beragh D4
Birr F3
Blacklion D3
Blackwater G5
Blarney H3
Blessington F4
Boherbue H2
Borris G4
Borris-in-Ossory G3
Borrisokane F3
Borrisoleigh G3
Boyle E3
Bracknagh F4
Bray F5
Bridgetown H4
Brittas F4
Broadford G3
Broadford G2
Broughshane D5
Bruff G3
Bruree G3
Bunclody G4
Buncrana C4
Bundoran D3
Bunnahowen D2
Bunnyconnellan E2
Bushmills C4
Butler's Bridge E4
Buttevant G3

Cadamstown F3
Caherconlish G3
Caherdaniel H1
Cahir G3
Cahirciveen H1
Caledon D4
Callan G4
Caltra F3
Camolin G4
Camp G1
Cappagh White G3
Cappamore G3
Cappoquin H3
Carlanstown E4
Carlingford E5
Carlow G4
Carndonagh C4
Carnew G5
Carnlough D5
Carracastle E3
Carrick D3
(An Charraig)
Carrickfergus D5
Carrickmacross E4
Carrickmore D4
Carrick-on-Shannon E3
Carrick -on-Suir G4
Carrigahorig F3
Carrigaline H3
Carrigallen E3
Carriganimmy H2
Carrigans C4
Carrigtohill H3
Carrowkeel C4
Carryduff D5
Cashel G3
Cashel E2
Castlebar E2
Castlebellingham E5
Castleblayney E4
Castlebridge G4
Castlecomer G4
Castle Cove H1
Castlederg D4
Castledermot F4
Castleisland G2
Castlemaine H2
Castlemartyr H3
Castleplunkett E3
Castlepollard E4
Castlerea E3
Castlerock C4
Castleshane E4
Castletown F4
Castletownbere H1

Castletownroche H3
Castletownshend J2
Castlewellan E5
Causeway G2
Cavan E4
Ceanannus Mor (Kells) E4
Celbridge F4
Charlestown E3
Clady D4
Clane F4
Clara F3
Clarecastle G2
Claremorris E2
Clarinbridge F2
Clashmore H3
Claudy D4
Cliffony D3
Clogan F3
Clogh G4
Clogheen H3
Clogher D4
Clohamon G4
Clonakilty H2
Clonard F4
Clonaslee F4
Clonbulloge F4
Clonbur (An Fhairche) E2
Clondalkin F4
Clones E4
Clonmany C4
Clonmel G3
Clonmellon E4
Clonmore G3
Clonony F3
Clonoulty G3
Clonroche G4
Clontibret E4
Cloonbannin H2
Cloondara E3
Cloonkeen H2
Cloonlara G3
Clough D5
Cloughjordan F3
Cloyne H3
Coagh D4
Coalisland D4
Cobh H3
Coleraine C4
Collinstown E4
Collon E4
Colooney G3
Comber D5
Conna H3
Cookstown D4
Coole E4
Cooraclare G2
Cootehill E4
Cork H3
Cork Airport H3
Cornamona F2
Corofin F2
Courtmacsherry H2
Courtown Harbour G5
Craigavon D5
Craughwell F3
Creggs E3
Cresslough C3
Croagh G2
Crolly (Croithli) C3
Crookedwood E4
Crookhaven J1
Crookstown H2
Croom G2
Crossakeel E4
Cross Barry H2
Crosshaven H3
Crossmaglen E4
Crossmolina E2
Crumlin D5
Crusheen F2
Culdaff C4
Culleybackey D5
Curracloe G4
Curraghboy F3
Curry E3

Daingean F4
Delvin E4
Derrygonnelly D3
Derrylin E4
Dervock C4
Dingle (An Daingean) H1
Doagh D5
Donaghadee D5
Donaghmore G3
Donegal D3
Doneraile H3
Doonbeg G2
Douglad H3
Downpatrick D5
Dowra E3
Draperstown D4
Drimoleague H2
Dripsey H3
Drogheda E5
Droichead Nua F4
(Newbridge)
Dromahair D3
Dromcolliher G2
Dromore D5
Dromore D4
Dromore West D2
Drum E4
Drumconrath E4
Drumkeeran E3
Drumlish E3
Drumod E3
Drumquin D3
Drumshanbo E3
Drumsna E3
Duagh G2
Dublin F5
Duleek E4
Dunboyne F4
Duncormick H4
Dundalk E5
Dunderrow H2
Dundrum E5
Dunfanaghy C3
Dungannon D4
Dungarvan H3
Dungarvan G4
Dungiven C4
Dungloe C3
Dungourney H3
Dunhill D3
Dun Laoghaire F5
Dunlavin F4
Dunleer E4
Dunloy C5
Dunmanway H2
Dunmore E3
Dunmore East H4
Dunmurry D5
Dunshauglin F4
Durrow G4
Durrus H2

Eaky D2
Edenderry F4
Edgeworthstown E3
Eglinton C4
Elphin E3
Emyvale D4
Enfield F4
Ennis F2
Enniscorthy G4
Enniscrone D2
Enniskean H2
Enniskillen D4
Ennistymon F2
Eyrecourt F3

Farnaght E3
Farranfore H2
Feakle F3
Fenagh E3
Fermoy H3
Ferns G4
Fethard H4
Fethard G3
Finnea E4
Fintona D4
Fivemiletown D4
Fontstown F4
Foulksmills G4
Foxford E2
Foynes G2
Freemount G2
Frenchpark E3
Freshford G4
Fuerty E3

Galbally G3
Galway F2
Garrison D3
Garvagh C4
Geashill F4
Gilford D5
Glandore J2
Glanmire H3
Glanworth H3
Glaslough D4
Glassan F3
Glenamaddy E3
Glenarm C5
Glenavy D5
Glenbeigh H1
Glencolumbkille C3
(Gleann Cholm Cille)
Glendalough F5
Glenealy G5
Glenfarne D3
Glengarriff H2
Glenties D3
Glenville H3
Glin G2
Glinsk F2
(Glinsce)
Golden G3
Goleen J1
Goresbridge G4
Gorey G5

Gort F2
Gortin D4
Gowran G4
Graiguenamanagh G4
Grallagh E3
Granard E3
Grange D3
Greencastle E5
Greyabbey D5
Greystones F5
Gulladuff D4

Hacketstown G4
Headford F2
Herbertstown G3
Hillsborough D5
Hilltown E5
Hospital G3
Holycross G3
Holywood D5
Howth F5

Inch H1
Inchigeelagh H2
Inishannon H2

Johnstown G3

Kanturk H2
Keadue E3
Keady E4
Keel E1
Keenagh E3
Kells D5
Kenmare H2
Kesh D3
Kilbeggan F4
Kilberry E4
Kilbrittain H2
Kilcar D3
(Cill Charthaigh)
Kilcock F4
Kilcolgan F2
Kilconnell F3
Kilconnell F2
Kilcoole F5
Kilcormac F3
Kilcullen F4
Kilcurry E4
Kildare F4
Kildavin G4
Kildorrery H3
Kildress D4
Kilfenora F2
Kilfinnane G3
Kilgarvan H2
Kilkee G2
Kilkeel E5
Kilkelly E2
Kilkenny G4
Kilkieran F2
(Cill Ciarain)
Kilkinlea G2
Kill H4
Killadysert G2
Killala D2
Killaloe G3
Killarney H2
Killashandra E4
Killashee E3
Killeagh H3
Killeigh F4
Killenaule G3
Killimer G2
Killimor F3
Killiney F5
Killinick H4
Killorglin H1
Killough E5
Killucan F4
Killybegs D3
Killyleagh D5
Kilmacanoge F5
Kilmacrenan C3
Kilmacthomas H4
Kilmaganny G4
Kilmaine E2
Kilmallock G3
Kilmanagh G4
Kilmanahan G3
Kilmeaden H4
Kilmeage F4
Kilmeedy G2
Kilmichael H2
Kilmore Quay H4
Kilnaleck E4
Kilrea C4
Kilrush G2
Kilsheelan G3
Kiltealy G4
Kiltegan G4
Kiltimagh E2
Kiltoom F3
Kingscourt E4

Kinlough D3
Kinnegad F4
Kinnitty F3
Kinsale H3
Kinvarra F2
Kircubbin D5
Knock E2
Knockcroghery E3
Knocklofty G3
Knockmahon H4
Knocktopher G4

Lahinch F2
Lanesborough E3
Laragh F5
Lauragh H1
Laurencetown F3
Leap J2
Leenane E2
Leighlinbridge G4
Leitrim E3
Leixlip F4
Lemybrien H3
Letterfrack E2
Letterkenny C3
Lifford D4
Limavady C4
Limerick G3
Lisbellaw D4
Lisburn D5
Liscarroll G2
Lisdoonvarna F2
Lismore H3
Lisnaskea D4
Lisryan E4
Listowel G2
Loghill G2
Londonderry C4
Longford E3
Loughbrickland D5
Loughgall D4
Loughglinn E3
Loughrea F3
Louisburgh E2
Lucan F4
Lurgan D5
Lusk F5

Macroom H2
Maghera E5
Maghera D4
Magherafelt D4
Maguiresbridge D4
Malahide F5
Malin C4
Malin More D3
Mallow H2
Manorhamilton D3
Markethill D4
Maynooth F4
Maze D5
Middletown D4
Midleton H3
Milford E4
Millstreet H2
Milltown H2
Milltown Malbay G2
Mitchelstown H3
Moate F3
Mohill E3
Molls Cap H2
Monaghan E4
Monasterevin F4
Moneygall G3
Moneymore D4
Monivea F3
Mooncoin H4
Moorfields D5
Mount Bellew F3
Mount Charles D3
Mountmellick F4
Mountrath F4
Mountshannon F3
Mourne Abbey H3
Moville C4
Moy D4
Moylett E4
Moynalty E4
Moyvore F3
Muckross H2
Muff C4
Muine Bheag G4
Mullabohy H4
Mullagh F4
Mullinavat G4
Mullingar F4
Myshall G4

Naas F4
Nad H2
Naul F5
Navan E4
Neale E2
Nenagh G3

Newbliss E4
Newcastle E5
Newcastle West G2
Newinn G3
Newmarket E2
Newmarket-on-Fergus G2
Newport E2
Newport E2
New Ross G4
Newry E5
Newtown G4
Newtownabbey D5
Newtownards D5
Newtown Butler E4
Newtown Forbes E3
Newtownhamilton E4
Newtown Mount Kennedy F5
Newtownstewart D4
Nobber E4

Oilgate G4
Oldcastle E4
Omagh D4
Omeath E5
Oola G3
Oranmore F2
Oughterard F2
Ovens H3

Pallasgreen G3
Parknasilla H1
Partry E2
Passage East H4
Passage West H3
Patrickswell G2
Paulstown G4
Pettigo D3
Plumbridge D4
Pomeroy D4
Portadown D4
Portaferry D5
Portarlington F4
Portavogie D5
Portglenone D5
Port Laoise F4
Portmarnock F5
Portrane F5
Portroe G3
Portrush C4
Portstewart C4
Portumna F3
Poyntzpass D5

Raharney F4
Randalstown D5
Rasharkin C4
Rathangen F4
Rathcoole F5
Rathcormack H3
Rathdowney G4
Rathdrum G5
Rathfriland D5
Rathkeale G2
Rath Luric G2
(Charleville)
Rathmelton C4
Rathmolyon F4
Rathmore H2
Rathmullan C4
Rathnew F5
Rathowen E4
Rathvilty G4
Ratoath F4
Ray C4
Ring H3
(An Rinn)
Ringaskiddy H3
Riverstown F3
Rockcorry E4
Roosky E3
Rosapenna C3
Rosebercon G4
Roscommon E3
Roscrea F3
Ross Carberry J2
Rosscor D3
Rosses Point D3
Rosslare Harbour H4
Rosslea E4
Rostrevor E5
Roundstone F2
Roundwood F5
Rush F5

St Johnstown C4
Saintfield D5
Sallins F4
Scarriff G3
Scartaglen H2
Scarva D5
Schull J2
Scramoge E3
Scribbagh D3
Seskinore D4
Shanagolden G2
Shannon Airport G2
Shannonbridge F3
Shercock E4
Shillelagh G4
Shinrone F3
Shrule E2
Silvermines G3
Sion Mills D4
Sixmilebridge G2
Skerries F5
Skibbereen J2
Slane E4
Sligo D3
Smithborough E4
Sneem H1
Spiddal F2
(An Spideal)
Sporthouse Cross Roads H4
Stewartstown D4
Stonyford G4
Strabane D4
Stradbally F4
Stradone E4
Strandhill D3
Strangford D5
Stranorlar D3
Stratford F4
Strokestown E3
Summerhill F4
Swanlinbar E3
Swatragh D4
Swinford E3
Swords F5

Taghmon G4
Tagoat H4
Tahilla H1
Tallaght F5
Tallow H3
Tallowbridge H3
Tandragee D5
Tang F3
Tarbert G2
Templemore G3
Templepatrick D5
Templetouhy G3
Termonfeckin E5
Thomas Street F3
Thomastown G4
Thurles G3

Timahoe F4
Timoleague H2
Tinahely G5
Tipperary G3
Tobercurry E3
Tobermore D4
Togher F3
Toomyvara G3
Toormore J1
Tralee G2
Tramore H4
Trim F4
Tuam F3
Tuamgraney G3
Tulla G2
Tullamore F4
Tullow G4
Tulsk E3
Turlough G2
Tyholland D4
Tyrrellspass F4

Urlingford G3

Virginia E4
Waddington H4
Warrenpoint E5
Waterford H4
Watergrasshill H3
Waterville H1
Westport E2
Wexford G4
Whitegate H3
Whitehead D5
Wicklow F5
Woodenbridge G5
Woodford F3

Youghal H3

C

D

E

1

2

Aran Island

Rossan Point
Malin More
Glencolumbkille (Gleann Cholm Cille)
Glencolumbkille Folk Museum
1972
SLIEVE LEAGUE
Kilcar (Cill Charthaigh)
Carrick (An Cha...)
St John's Poi...

Inishmurray

Erris Head
Broad Haven
Downpatrick Head
Ballycastle
Killala Bay
Easky
Dromore West
Strandhill
Sligo Bay
Rosses Point
Lissadell House
Grange

Belmullet (Béal an Mhuirhead)
Bunnahowen
Inishkea
Duvillaun More
Blacksod Bay
2204
SLIEVE MORE
Keel
Achill Head
Achill Island
Bangor Erris
Carrowmore Lough
Crossmolina
Killala
Enniscrone
Ballina
Connaught Regional Airport
Colloney
Bunnyconnellan
Tobercurry
Curry
Charlestown
Carracastle
Ballaghade...
2369
2646
NEPHIN
Foxford
Swinford
Kilkelly
Frenchpark
Clare
Lough Feeagh
Newport
Clew Bay
Westport
Castlebar
Turlough
Ballyhean
Balla
Kiltimagh
OX MTS

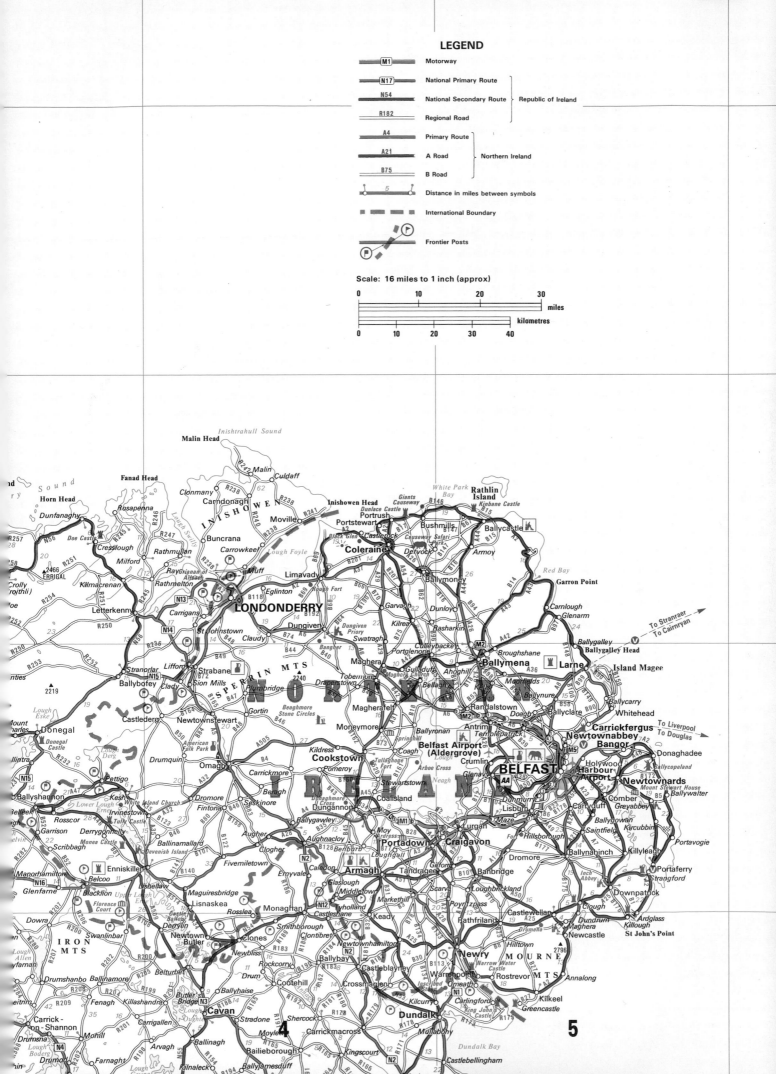

LEGEND

M1	Motorway
N17	National Primary Route
N54	National Secondary Route
R182	Regional Road
A4	Primary Route
A21	A Road
B75	B Road

Republic of Ireland

Northern Ireland

5 — Distance in miles between symbols

— International Boundary

Frontier Posts

Scale: 16 miles to 1 inch (approx)

miles
0   10   20   30

kilometres
0   10   20   30   40

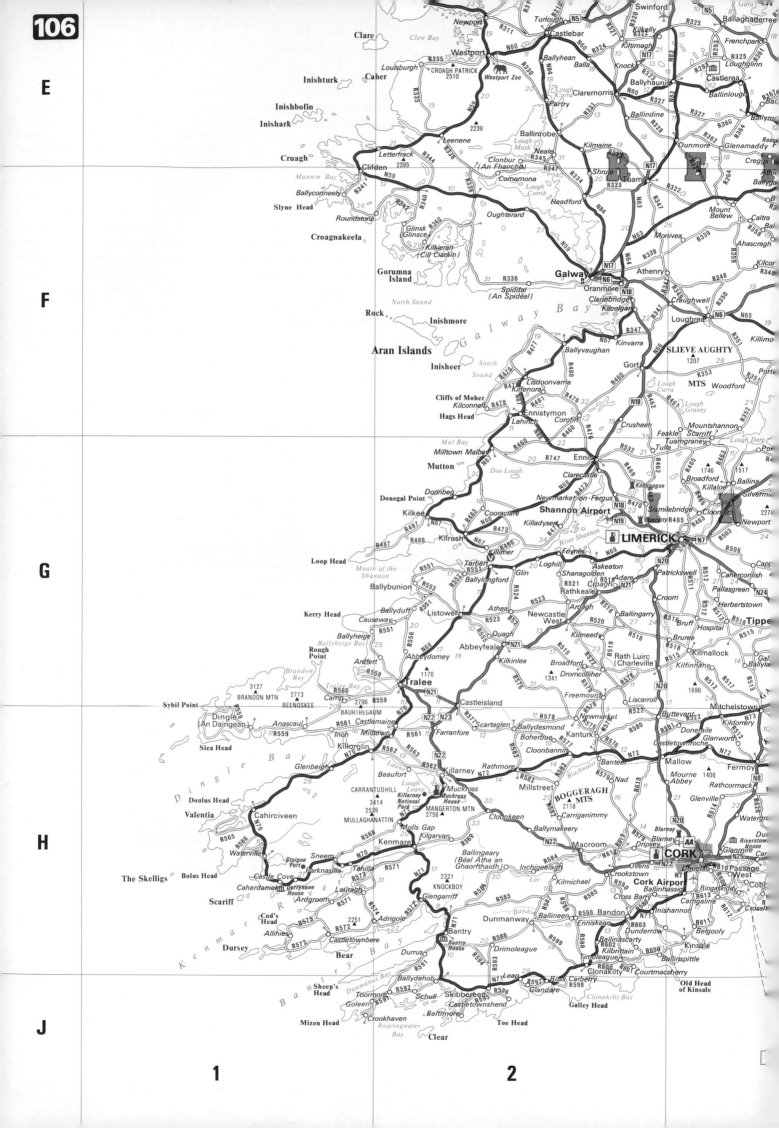

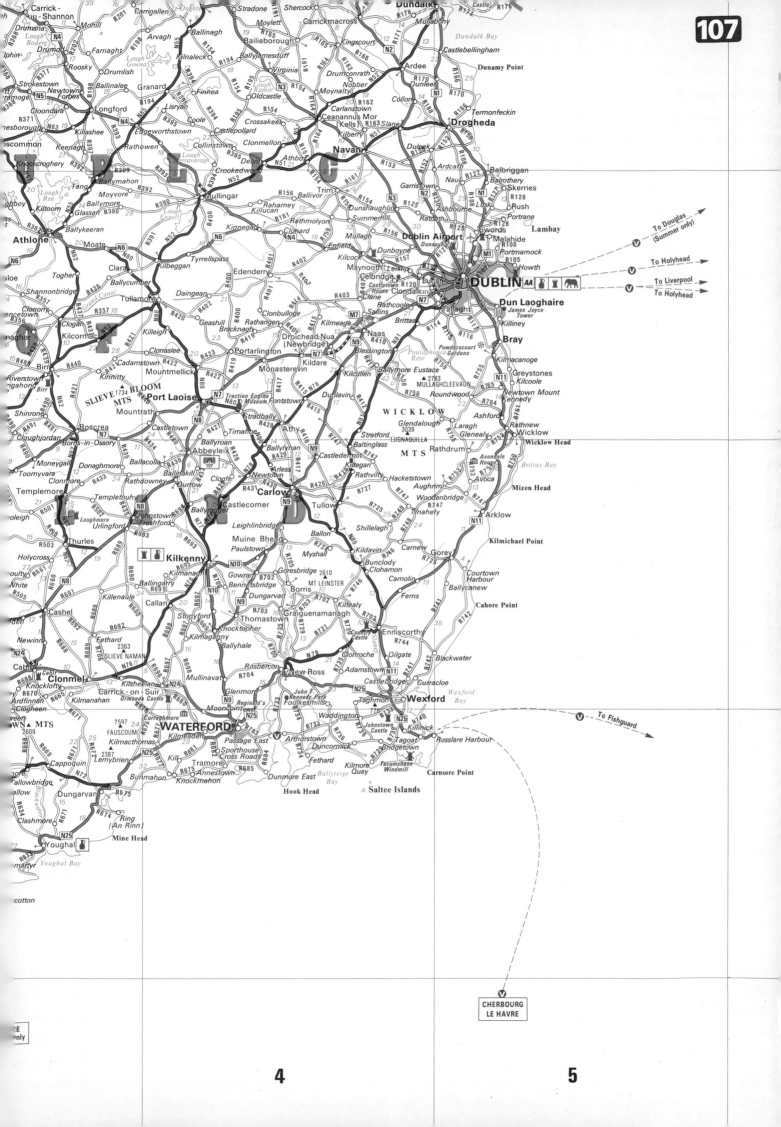

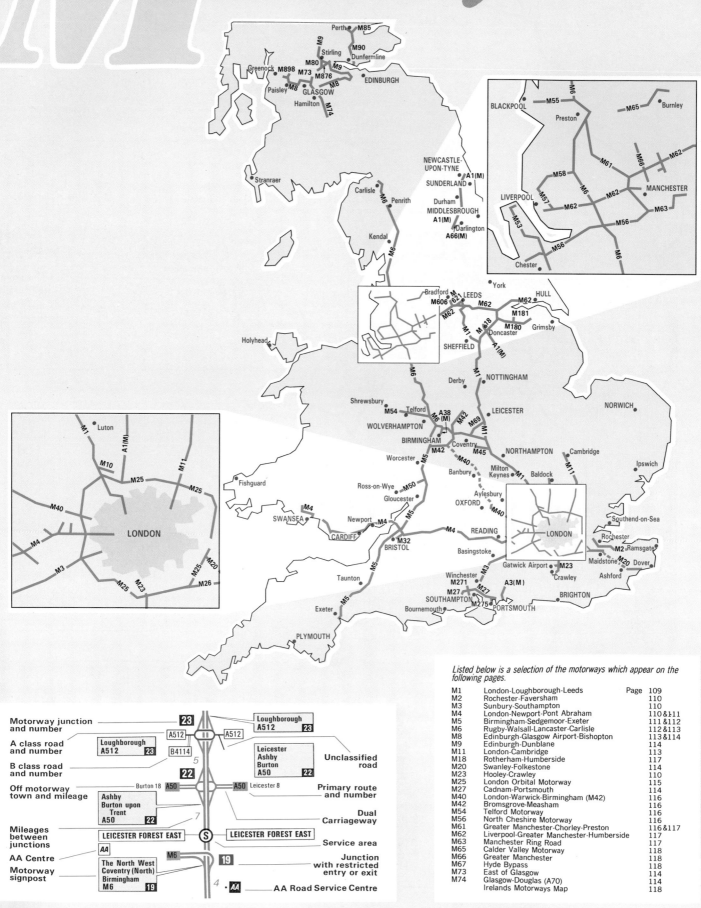

Motorways

Motorway junction and number

A class road and number — Loughborough A512 23

B class road and number — B4114

Off motorway town and mileage — Burton 18

Mileages between junctions

AA Centre

Motorway signpost — The North West Coventry (North) Birmingham M6 19

Loughborough A512 23

A512 | A512

Leicester Ashby Burton A50 22 — **Unclassified road**

A50 Leicester 8 — **Primary route and number**

— **Dual Carriageway**

Ashby Burton upon Trent A50 22

LEICESTER FOREST EAST (S) LEICESTER FOREST EAST — **Service area**

Junction with restricted entry or exit

AA — **AA Road Service Centre**

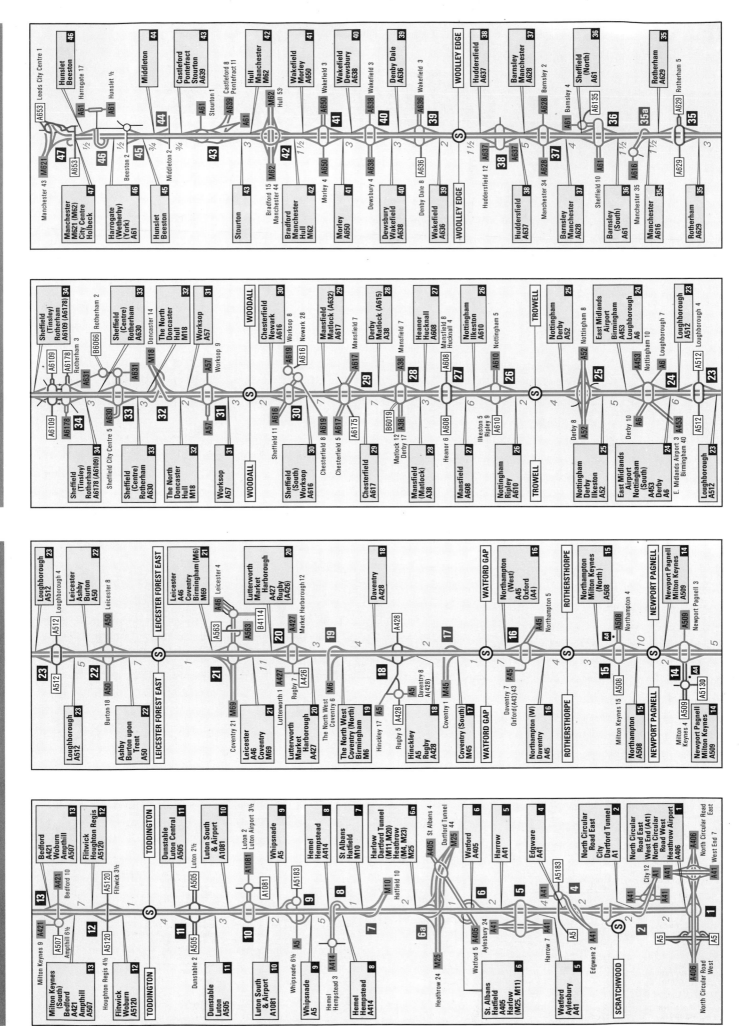

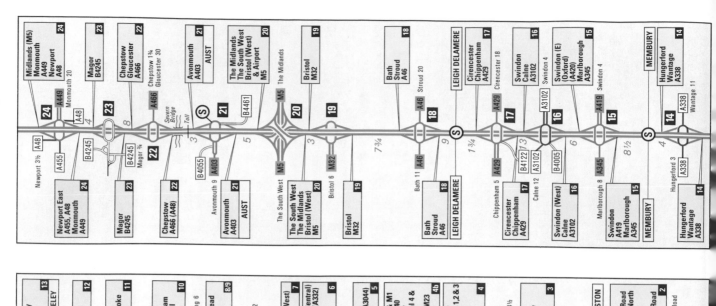

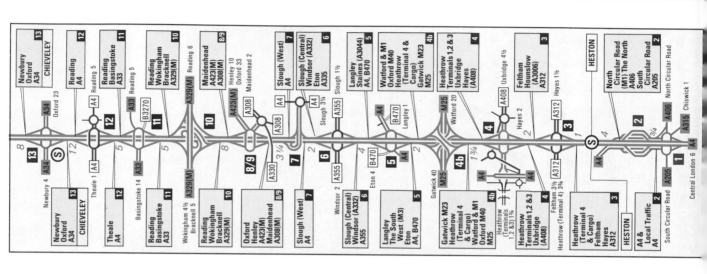

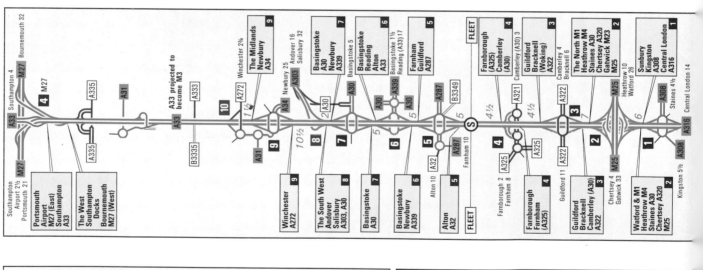

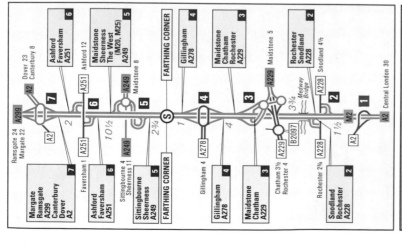

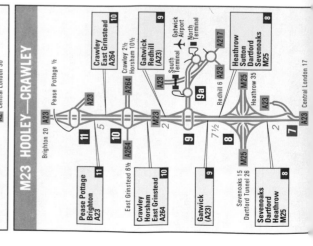

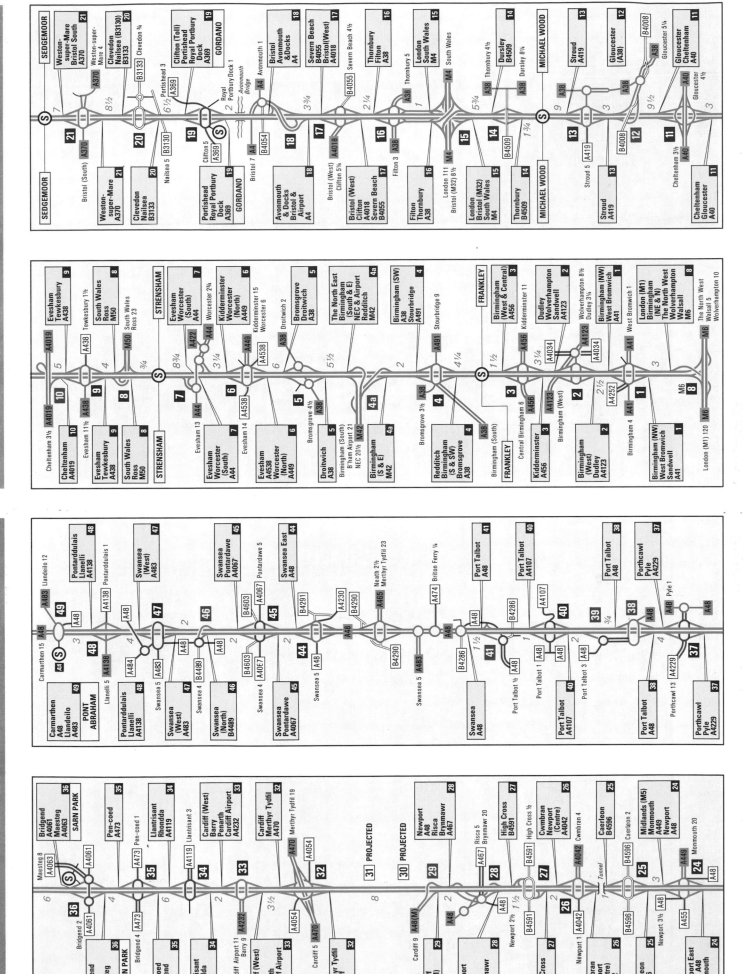

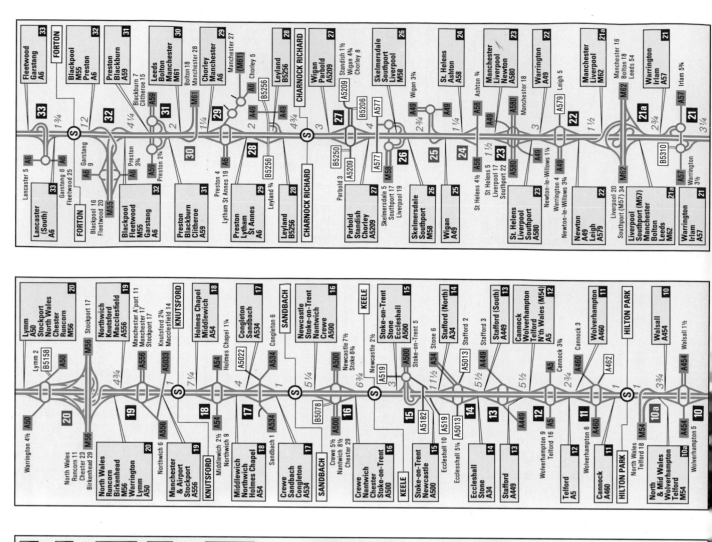

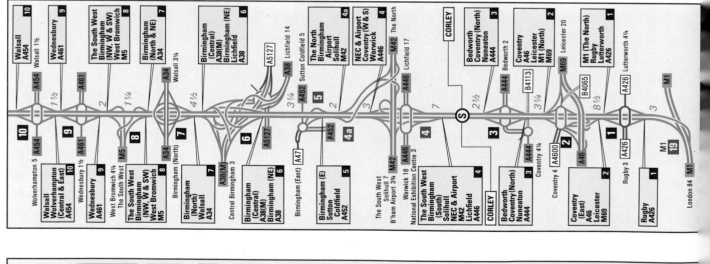

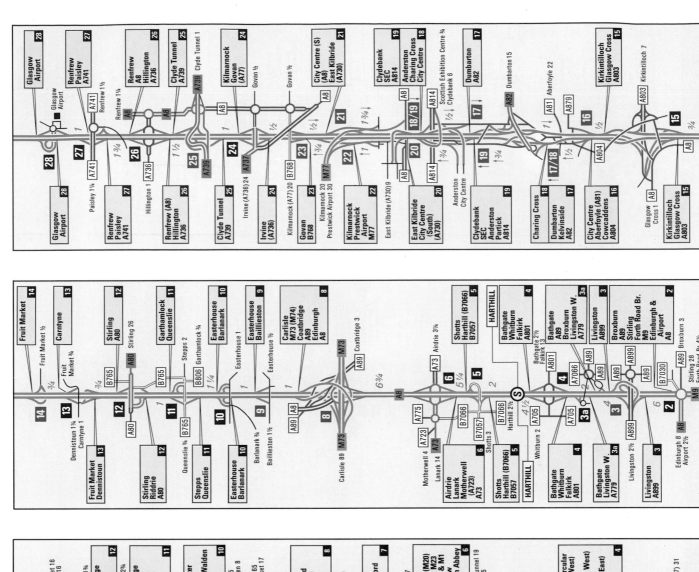

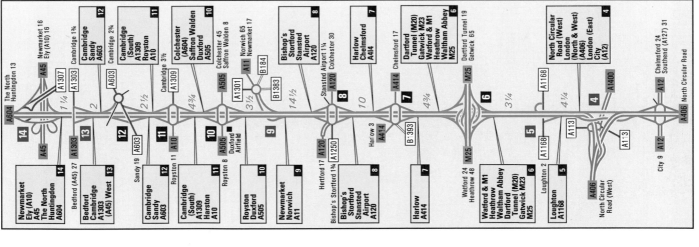

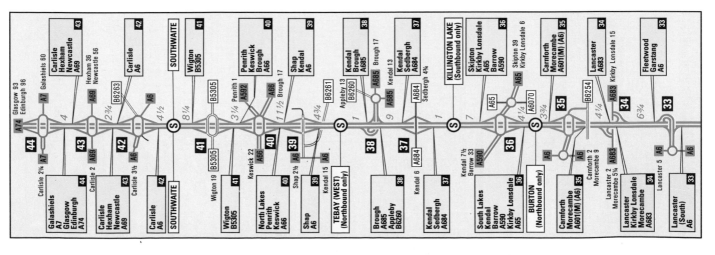

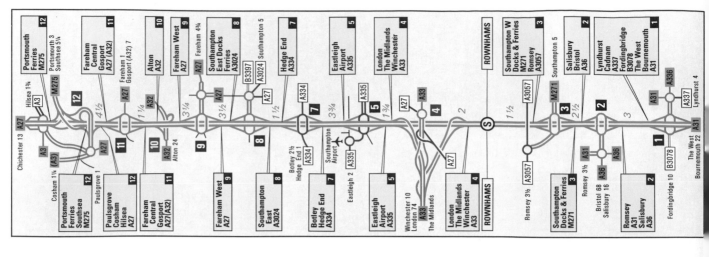

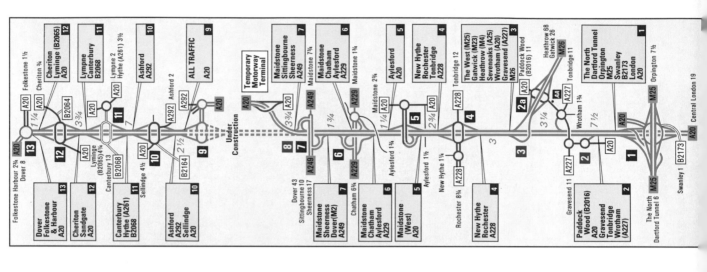

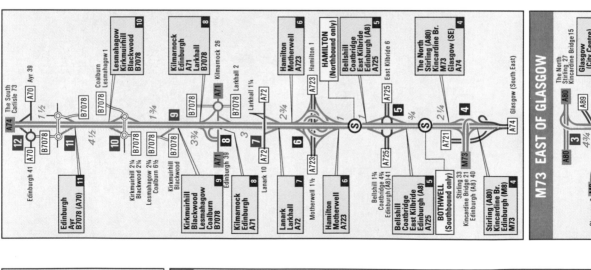

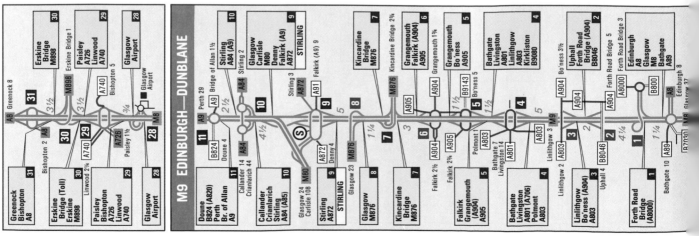

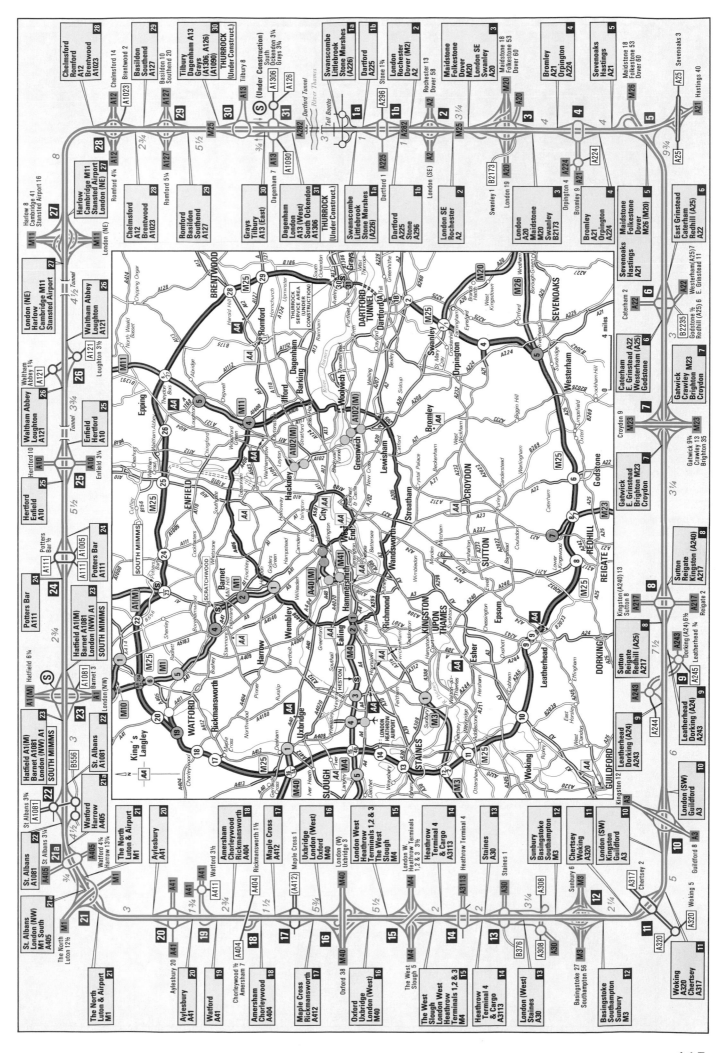

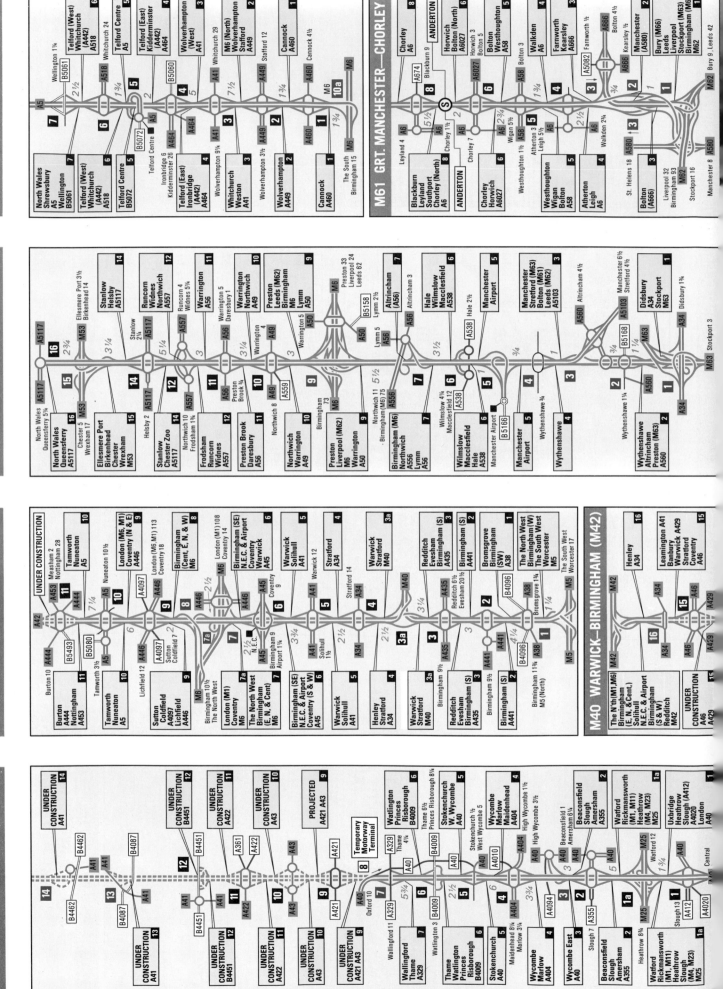

M54 TELFORD MOTORWAY

M56 NORTH CHESHIRE MOTORWAY

M61 GRT. MANCHESTER—CHORLEY

M42 BROMSGROVE—MEASHAM

M40 WARWICK—BIRMINGHAM (M42)

M40 LONDON—WARWICK

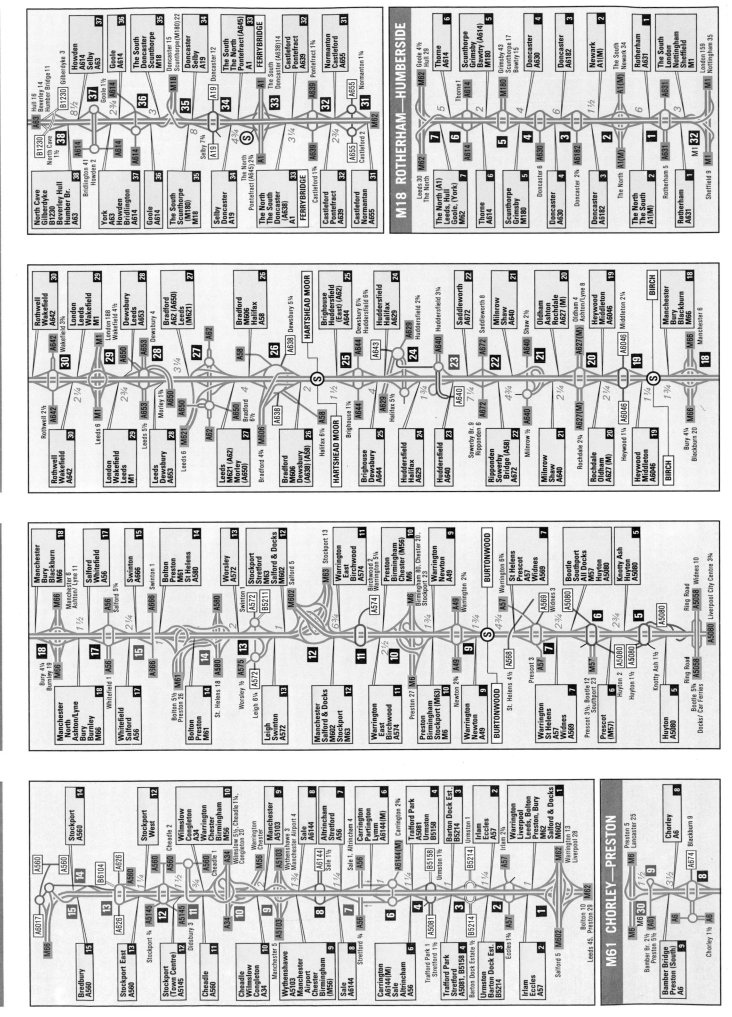

M18 ROTHERHAM—HUMBERSIDE

M61 CHORLEY—PRESTON

MOTORWAYS IN IRELAND

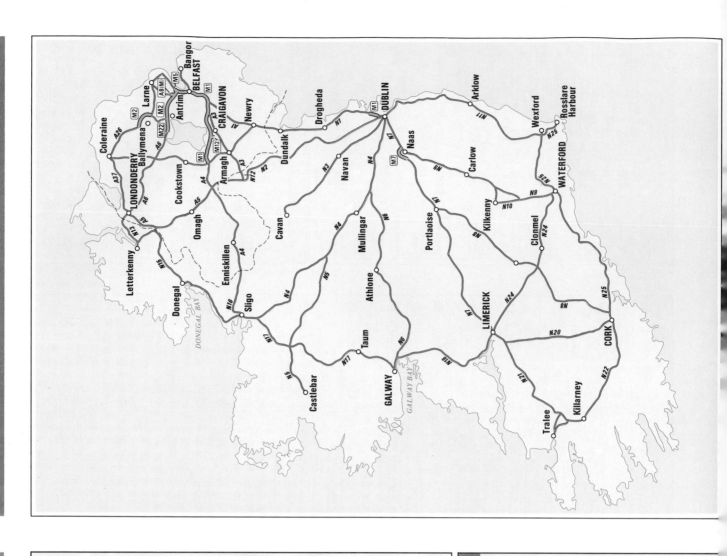

M66 GREATER MANCHESTER

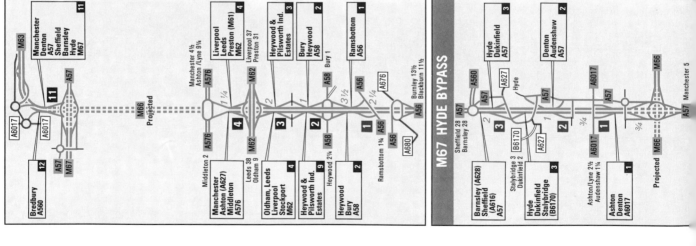

M67 HYDE BYPASS

M65 CALDER VALLEY MOTORWAY

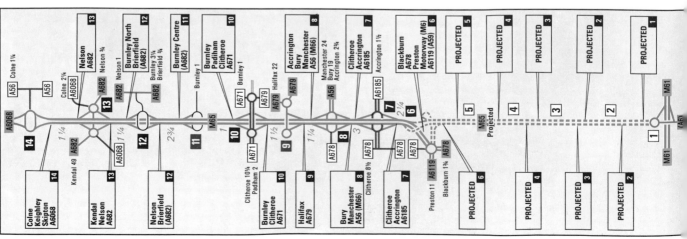

118

Ports and airports

MANCHESTER _____ International airports

LUTON _____ Airports with regular scheduled services abroad

Lydd _____ Other airports and airfields

DOVER _____ Major ports

Weymouth _____ Ports with summer services only

Detailed location plans are included on the following pages for those ports and airports named with capital letters on this map

Military airfields are not shown on this map. Ports and airports on the Channel Islands and the Scottish Islands are located within the main atlas section.

Wick
Stornoway
Benbecula
Barra
Isle of Skye
Inverness
Aberdeen
Aberdeen
Tiree
Dundee
Islay
GLASGOW
EDINBURGH
Machrihanish
Prestwick
Londonderry
Stranraer
Cairnryan
Newcastle-upon-Tyne
Newcastle-upon-Tyne
Larne
Carlisle
Belfast
Belfast
Belfast Harbour
Teesside
Isle of Man
Barrow-in-Furness
Heysham
Fleetwood
Leeds/Bradford
HULL
Blackpool
Dublin
Liverpool
Humberside
Dublin
MANCHESTER
Holyhead
Liverpool
Dun Laoghaire
East Midlands
Norwich
Rosslare
BIRMINGHAM
Cambridge
Ipswich
Fishguard
Cranfield
FELIXSTOWE
LUTON
London Stanstead
HARWICH
Pembroke Dock
Hatfield
Southend
Cardiff
London-City
Sheerness
Bristol
LONDON HEATHROW
Biggin Hill
Ramsgate
DOVER
Southampton
LONDON GATWICK
Lydd
FOLKESTONE
Exeter
Bournemouth
Shoreham
St Mawgan
Plymouth
Portsmouth
NEWHAVEN
Penzance (Heliport)
Plymouth
Torquay
Weymouth
Poole

119

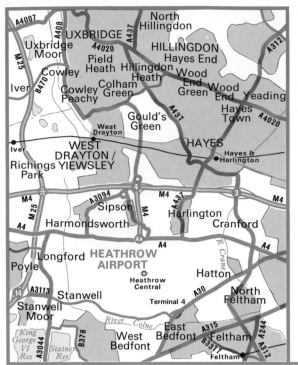

HEATHROW AIRPORT Tel: 01-759 4321 (Airport Information)

Heathrow, one of the world's busiest international airports, lies sixteen miles west of London. The airport is situated on the Piccadilly Underground line at Heathrow Central station. It is also served by local bus and long distance coach services. For short-term parking, multi-storey car parks are sited at each of the passenger terminals Tel: 01-745 7160 (terminals 1, 2, 3) & 01-759 4931 (terminal 4). Charges for the long-term car parks on the northern perimeter road are designed to encourage their use for a stay in excess of four hours. A free coach takes passengers to and from the terminals. Commercial garages offering long-term parking facilities within easy reach of the airport include: Airways Garage Ltd. Tel: 01-759 9661/4; Quo-Vadis Airport Parking Tel: 01-759 2778;

Cranford Parking Tel: 01-759 9661; Flyaway Car Storage Tel: 01-759 1567 or 2020; Kenning Car Hire Tel: 01-759 9701; and National Car Parks Tel: 01-759 9878. Car Hire: Avis Rent-A-Car Tel: 01-897 9321; Budget Rent-A-Car Tel: 01-759 2216; Godfrey Davis Europcar Tel: 01-897 0811/5; Guy Salmon Tel: 01-897 0541; Hertz Rent-A-Car Tel: 01-897 3347; and Kenning Car Hire Tel: 01-759 9701. The 4-star hotels in the area are The Excelsior Tel: 01-759 6611; the Heathrow Penta Tel: 01-897 6363; the Holiday Inn Tel: (0895) 445555 and the Sheraton-Heathrow Tel: 01-759 2424. The 3-star hotels are the Berkeley Arms Tel: 01-897 2121; the Ariel Tel: 01-759 2552; the Post House Tel: 01-759 2323; and the Skyway Tel: 01-759 6311.

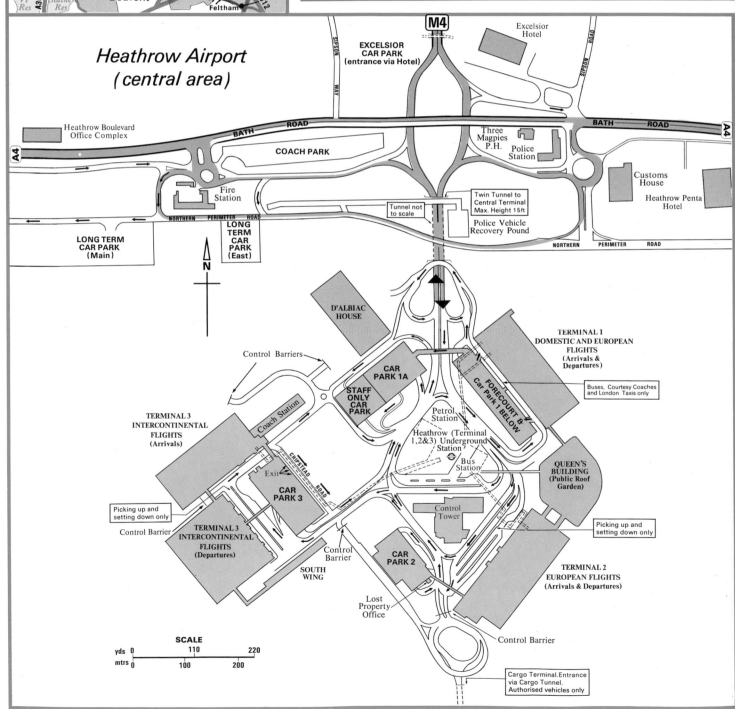

Heathrow Airport (central area)

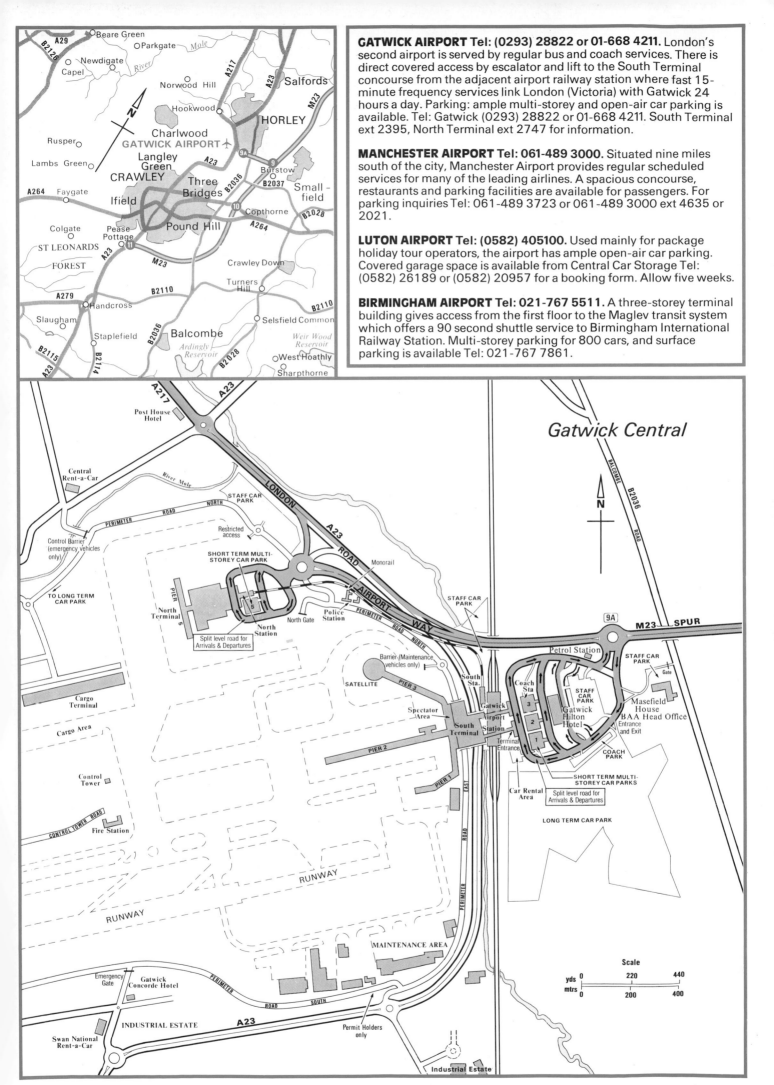

GATWICK AIRPORT Tel: (0293) 28822 or 01-668 4211. London's second airport is served by regular bus and coach services. There is direct covered access by escalator and lift to the South Terminal concourse from the adjacent airport railway station where fast 15-minute frequency services link London (Victoria) with Gatwick 24 hours a day. Parking: ample multi-storey and open-air car parking is available. Tel: Gatwick (0293) 28822 or 01-668 4211. South Terminal ext 2395, North Terminal ext 2747 for information.

MANCHESTER AIRPORT Tel: 061-489 3000. Situated nine miles south of the city, Manchester Airport provides regular scheduled services for many of the leading airlines. A spacious concourse, restaurants and parking facilities are available for passengers. For parking inquiries Tel: 061-489 3723 or 061-489 3000 ext 4635 or 2021.

LUTON AIRPORT Tel: (0582) 405100. Used mainly for package holiday tour operators, the airport has ample open-air car parking. Covered garage space is available from Central Car Storage Tel: (0582) 26189 or (0582) 20957 for a booking form. Allow five weeks.

BIRMINGHAM AIRPORT Tel: 021-767 5511. A three-storey terminal building gives access from the first floor to the Maglev transit system which offers a 90 second shuttle service to Birmingham International Railway Station. Multi-storey parking for 800 cars, and surface parking is available Tel: 021-767 7861.

Gatwick Central

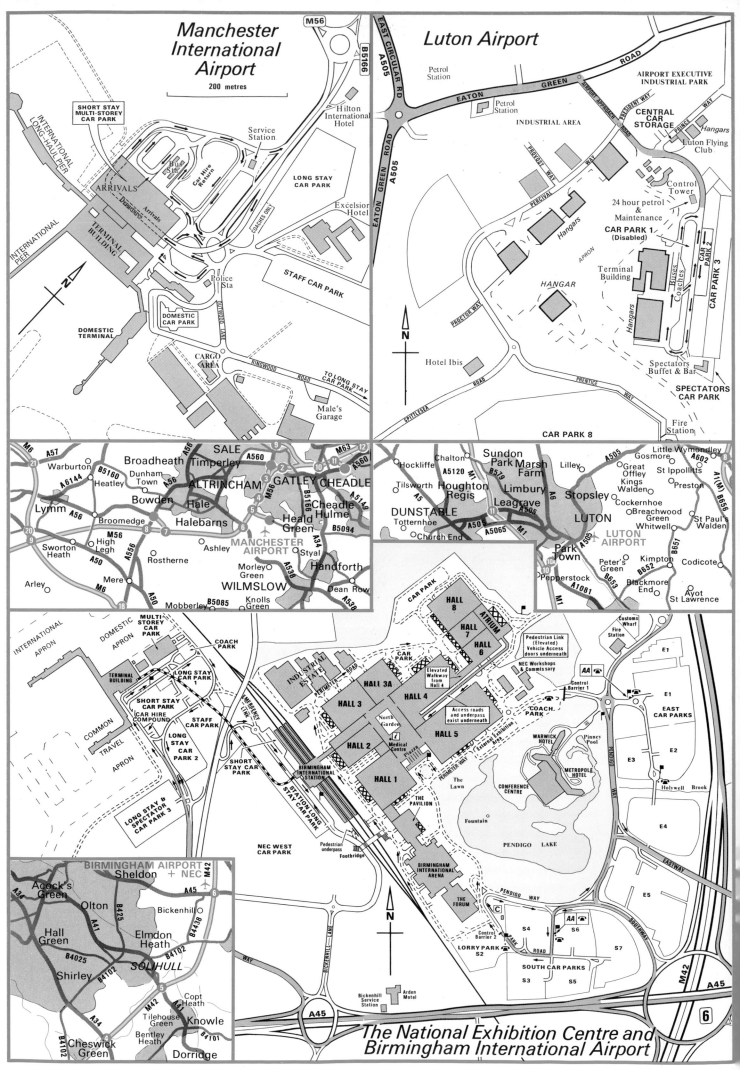

Manchester International Airport

200 metres

SHORT STAY MULTI-STOREY CAR PARK

INTERNATIONAL LONG-HAUL PIER

ARRIVALS

Departures

Arrivals

TERMINAL BUILDING

Bus Sta

Car Hire Return

Service Station

Hilton International Hotel

LONG STAY CAR PARK

COACHES ONLY

Excelsior Hotel

INTERNATIONAL PIER

N

Police Sta

DOMESTIC TERMINAL

DOMESTIC CAR PARK

STAFF CAR PARK

RINGWOOD ROAD

OULTWOOD LANE

CARGO AREA

TO LONG STAY CAR PARK

Male's Garage

Luton Airport

EAST CIRCULAR RD

EATON GREEN ROAD

A505

Petrol Station

Petrol Station

INDUSTRIAL AREA

EATON GREEN ROAD

AIRPORT APPROACH ROAD

PRESIDENT WAY

AIRPORT EXECUTIVE INDUSTRIAL PARK

CENTRAL CAR STORAGE

PRINCE WAY

Hangars

Luton Flying Club

Control Tower

PROVOST WAY

PERCIVAL WAY

Hangars

APRON

24 hour petrol & Maintenance

CAR PARK 1 (Disabled)

Terminal Building

HANGAR

Buses Coaches

CAR PARK 2

CAR PARK 3

N

PROCTOR WAY

Hotel Ibis

Hangars

SPITTLESEA ROAD

PRENTICE WAY

Spectators Buffet & Bar

SPECTATORS CAR PARK

Fire Station

CAR PARK 8

M6 A57 A560 SALE M63
21 A560 9 11 12
Warburton B5160 Broadheath Timperley 3 2 10 M63 A560 8
Heatley Dunham Town A56 ALTRINCHAM GATLEY CHEADLE
A6144 Bowden 4 M56
Lymm A56 Hale Cheadle Hulme
Broomedge Halebarns 5 B5166
20 8 7 6 Heald A514
9 Sworton High Green B5094
Heath Legh A556 MANCHESTER
Mere AIRPORT Styal A34
Arley Rostherne Ashley
M6 Morley A538
18 Mobberley B5085 Green Handforth
Knolls WILMSLOW A538
Green Dean Row

Hockliffe Chalton Sundon Lilley A505 Little Wymondley
Park Marsh Gosmore A602 8
Tilsworth A5120 B579 Farm Great St Ippollitts
Houghton Offley Preston A1(M) B656
DUNSTABLE A5 Regis Limbury A6 Kings Cockernhoe
Totternhoe Leagrave Stopsley Walden Breachwood
11 A505 Whitwell Green St Paul's
Church End A5065 M1 LUTON Walden
A505 LUTON B651
Park AIRPORT
10A Town A505 Peter's Kimpton
10 Green Codicote
Pepperstock A1081 B652 B653 Blackmore Ayot
M1 End St Lawrence

The National Exhibition Centre and Birmingham International Airport

INTERNATIONAL APRON

DOMESTIC APRON

MULTI-STOREY CAR PARK

COACH PARK

CAR PARK

HALL 8

ATRIUM

HALL 7

HALL 6

Customs Wharf

Fire Station

TERMINAL BUILDING

LONG STAY CAR PARK 1

SHORT STAY CAR PARK

CAR HIRE COMPOUND

STAFF CAR PARK

COMMON TRAVEL APRON

LONG STAY CAR PARK 2

SHORT STAY CAR PARK

LONG STAY & SPECTATOR CAR PARK 3

NEC WEST CAR PARK

INDUSTRIAL ESTATE

PERIMETER ROAD

EMERGENCY LTWY

HALL 3A

HALL 3

HALL 2

HALL 1

North Garden

Medical Centre

Plaza

Pedestrian Link (Elevated) Vehicle Access doors underneath

NEC Workshops & Commissary

Elevated Walkway from Hall 4

HALL 4

Access roads and underpass exist underneath

HALL 5

Control Barrier 1

COACH PARK

AA

E1

E1

EAST CAR PARKS

E2

WARWICK HOTEL

Pinney Pool

METROPOLE HOTEL

E3

Holywell Brook

THE PAVILION

PERIMETER WAY

External Exhibition Area

The Lawn

CONFERENCE CENTRE

PENDIGO WAY

E4

BIRMINGHAM INTERNATIONAL STATION

STATION LONG STAY CAR PARK

Pedestrian underpass

Footbridge

BIRMINGHAM INTERNATIONAL ARENA

N

Fountain

PENDIGO LAKE

E5

THE FORUM

PENDIGO WAY

C

Control Barrier 2

S4

S6

AA

EASTWAY

BICKENHILL LANE

A45

Bickenhill Service Station

Arden Motel

LORRY PARK S2

PARK ROAD

S3

SOUTH CAR PARKS

S5

S7

M42

A45

6

BIRMINGHAM AIRPORT + NEC

Acock's Green

A34

Olton

B425

Sheldon

A45

M42

6

Bickenhill

B4438

Hall Green

A41

Elmdon Heath

B4102

Shirley

B4025

B4102

SOLIHULL

WAY

5

Copt Heath

M42

Tilehouse Green

A34

B4102

Cheswick Green

Bentley Heath

Knowle

B4101

Dorridge

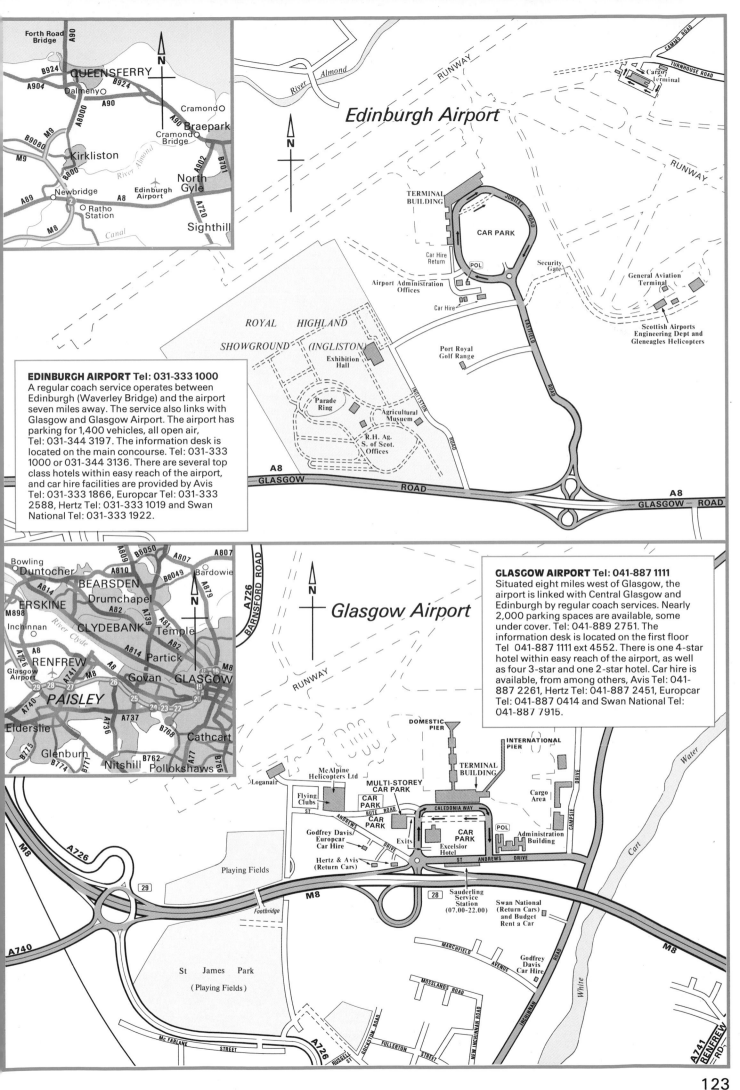

Edinburgh Airport

EDINBURGH AIRPORT Tel: 031-333 1000
A regular coach service operates between
Edinburgh (Waverley Bridge) and the airport
seven miles away. The service also links with
Glasgow and Glasgow Airport. The airport has
parking for 1,400 vehicles, all open air,
Tel: 031-344 3197. The information desk is
located on the main concourse. Tel: 031-333
1000 or 031-344 3136. There are several top
class hotels within easy reach of the airport,
and car hire facilities are provided by Avis
Tel: 031-333 1866, Europcar Tel: 031-333
2588, Hertz Tel: 031-333 1019 and Swan
National Tel: 031-333 1922.

Glasgow Airport

GLASGOW AIRPORT Tel: 041-887 1111
Situated eight miles west of Glasgow, the
airport is linked with Central Glasgow and
Edinburgh by regular coach services. Nearly
2,000 parking spaces are available, some
under cover. Tel: 041-889 2751. The
information desk is located on the first floor
Tel 041-887 1111 ext 4552. There is one 4-star
hotel within easy reach of the airport, as well
as four 3-star and one 2-star hotel. Car hire is
available, from among others, Avis Tel: 041-
887 2261, Hertz Tel: 041-887 2451, Europcar
Tel: 041-887 0414 and Swan National Tel:
041-887 7915.

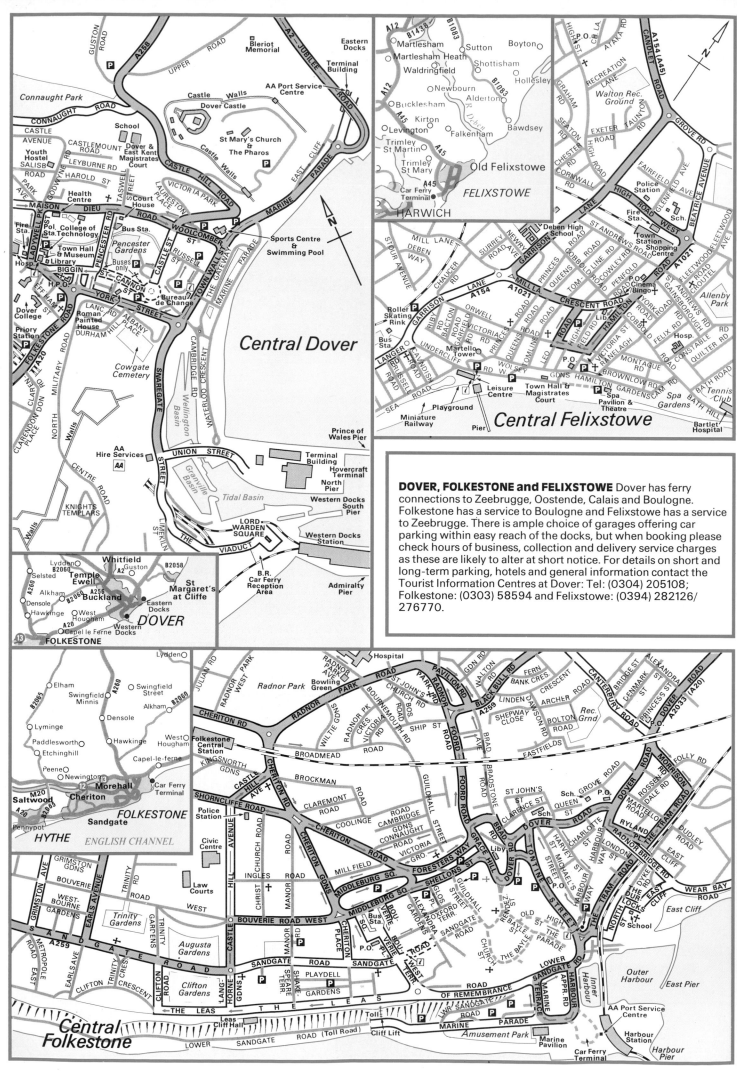

Central Dover

Connaught Park
Guston Road
A258
Upper Road
A2 Jubilee Road
Bleriot Memorial
Eastern Docks
Terminal Building
Castle Walls
Dover Castle
AA Port Service Centre
School
Castle Hill Road
St Mary's Church & The Pharos
Castle Walls
Connaught Road
Castle Avenue
Castlemount Road
Youth Hostel SALISB Road
Leyburne Rd
Harold St
Park Ave
Godwyne Rd
Victoria Park
East Cliff
Marine Parade
Health Centre
Maison Dieu
Taswell St
Court House
Laureston Place
Woolcomber St
Marine Parade
Sports Centre & Swimming Pool
Fire Sta.
Pol. Sta.
College of Technology
Bus Sta.
Pencester Gardens
Castle St
Russell St
Town Hall & Museum
Library
Biggin
Cannon St
Buses only
The Gateway
Town Wall St
Hosp.
H.P.O.
York Street
Bureau de Change
Dover College
Lanc Rd
Albany Place
Durham Hill
Roman Painted House
Folkestone Road A20
Military Road
Cambridge Rd
Waterloo Crescent
Priory Station
Cowgate Cemetery
Wellington Basin
Central Dover
North Military Road
Clarendon Place
Centre Road
Snargate Street
Union Street
Granville Basin
AA Hire Services
Tidal Basin
Prince of Wales Pier
Terminal Building
Hovercraft Terminal
North Pier
Western Docks South Pier
Knights Templars
Limekiln St
The Viaduct
Lord Warden Square
Western Docks Station
B.R. Car Ferry Reception Area
Admiralty Pier

FELIXSTOWE
A12 B1438 B1083
Martlesham
Sutton
Boyton
Martlesham Heath
Shottisham
Waldringfield
Hollesley
A12
Newbourn
Alderton
Bucklesham
B1083
Kirton
Bawdsey
Levington
Falkenham
Trimley St Martin
A45
Trimley St Mary
Old Felixstowe
A45
FELIXSTOWE
Car Ferry Terminal
HARWICH

Central Felixstowe
A154/A45
Candle St
P.O. LA.
High St
Ataka Rd
Recreation Lane
Graham Rd
Walton Rec. Ground
Seaton Rd
Exeter Road
Grove Rd
Chester Lane
Cornwall Rd
High Road
Fairfield Ave
Glenfield Ave
Beatrice Avenue
Police Station
Fire Sta.
Sch.
Town Station Shopping Centre
Mill Lane
Deben High School
St Andrews Road
Fleetwood Road
Garrison Lane
Surrey Rd
Newry Ave
Cobbold Road
St Andrews Rd
Gainsborough Rd
Chaucer Rd
Princes Road
Queens Road
Tom. Rd
Cowley Rd
Penfold Rd
Allenby Park
A154
A1021
Crescent Road
High Rd
Hamilton St
Felix Rd
Roller Skating Rink
Riby Rd
Orwell Rd
Bacton Rd
Garfield Rd
Victoria Rd
Queens Road
Leo Rd
Field Rd
Victoria St
Ranelagh Rd
Constable Rd
Quilter Rd
Bus Sta.
Langer Rd
Cavendish Rd
Undercliff
Wolsey Gdns
Montague Rd
Bath Road
Martello Tower
Russell Rd
Brownlow Rd
Hamilton Gardens
Spa Bath Hill
Tennis Club
Sea
Leisure Centre
Town Hall & Magistrates Court
Spa Pavilion & Theatre
Spa Gardens
Playground
Central Felixstowe
Miniature Railway
Pier
Bartlet Hospital

DOVER, FOLKESTONE and FELIXSTOWE Dover has ferry connections to Zeebrugge, Oostende, Calais and Boulogne. Folkestone has a service to Boulogne and Felixstowe has a service to Zeebrugge. There is ample choice of garages offering car parking within easy reach of the docks, but when booking please check hours of business, collection and delivery service charges as these are likely to alter at short notice. For details on short and long-term parking, hotels and general information contact the Tourist Information Centres at Dover: Tel: (0304) 205108; Folkestone: (0303) 58594 and Felixstowe: (0394) 282126/ 276770.

DOVER
Lydden
Whitfield
B2058
Temple Ewell
Guston
B2060
Selsted
A2
A260
Alkham
B2060
Buckland
A256
Densole
West Hougham
Eastern Docks
St Margaret's at Cliffe
Hawkinge
Western Docks
Capel le Ferne
13
FOLKESTONE
A20

Central Folkestone
Lydden
Radnor Park West
Hospital
Elham
A260
Swingfield Street
Radnor Park Ave
Radnor Park
Bowling Green
Pavilion Rd
Gdn Rd
Walton Rd
Black Bull Rd
Fern Rd
Alexandra St
Bridge St
Swingfield Minnis
B2060
Alkham
Radnor Park
Bank Cres.
Crescent
Linden Rd
Archer Rd
Denmark St
Canterbury Road
Cheriton Rd
Radnor Pk Cres
Church Bos
Victoria Rd
Bournemouth Rd
Ship St
Shepway Close
Dawson Rd
Bolton Road
Rec. Grnd
Dover Rd A2033 (A20)
Lyminge
Densole
Julian Rd
Wiltie Gdns
Broadmead
Eastfields
Paddlesworth
Hawkinge
West Hougham
Folkestone Central Station
Kingsnorth Gdns
Castle Hill Ave
Brockman Rd
Guildhall Street
St John's St
Clarence St
Princess St
Folly Rd
Etchinghill
Capel-le-ferne
Shorncliffe Road
Claremont Road
Coolinge Rd
Cambridge Gdns
Connaught Rd
St Michael's St
Grove Road
Peene
Newington
13
Morehall
Cheriton
Police Station
Church Road
Cheriton Gdns
Mill Field
Victoria Gro
Foresters Way
Guildhall St
Harvey St
Charlotte St
Morrison Rd
Rossendale Rd
Dale Rd
Saltwood
Cheriton
Civic Centre
Hill Avenue
Ingles Road
Cheriton Road
Middleburg Sq
Bus Sta.
Glos St
Oxford Terr
London St
Ryland Place
Dudley Rd
M20
B2065
Law Courts
Christ Church
Manor Rd
Victoria Rd
Sandgate Rd
Bouverie Rd
Middleburg Sq
Sandgate Rd
Harbour Way
The Tram Road
Radnor Bridge Rd
East Cliff
A259
FOLKESTONE
Sandgate
Trinity Gdns
West Rd
Playdell Gdns
The Bayle
Rendez'vous St
Old High St
Bayle Parade
North Locks
Wear Bay Road
Pennypot
HYTHE
Trinity Rd
Augusta Gardens
Shakespeare Terr
Bouverie Rd West
P.O.
Church St
Sandgate Rd
Marine Terrace
The Durlocks
East Cliff
ENGLISH CHANNEL
Grimston Ave
Grimston Gdns
West-bourne Gardens
Earls Ave
Trinity Gardens
Clifton Gardens
Langhorne Gdns
Sandgate Rd
Speare Terr
Playdell Gdns
Road of Remembrance
Marine Parade
Outer Harbour
East Pier
Sandgate Road
Metropole Road East
Earls Ave
Clifton Crescent
The Leas
Leas Cliff Hall
The Leas
Toll
Cliff Lift
Lwr Sandgate Road
Marine Parade
Amusement Park
AA Port Service Centre
Inner Harbour
A259
Central Folkestone
Lower Sandgate Road (Toll Road)
Marine Pavilion
Car Ferry Terminal
Harbour Station
Harbour Pier

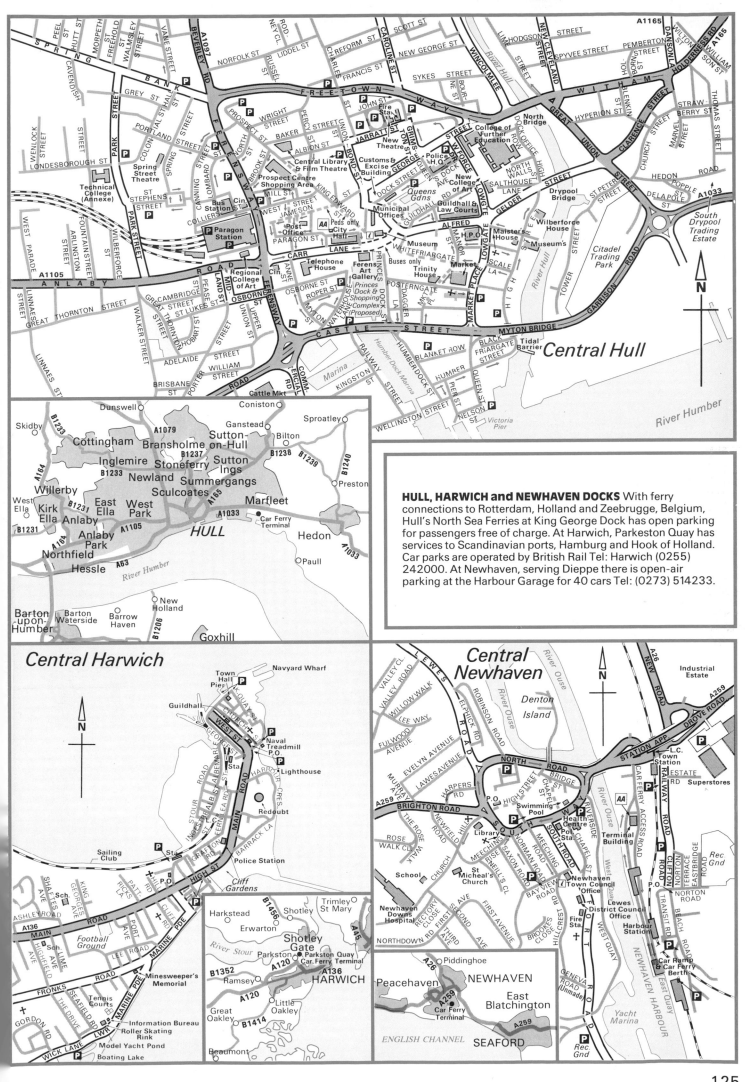

Central Hull

HULL, HARWICH and NEWHAVEN DOCKS With ferry connections to Rotterdam, Holland and Zeebrugge, Belgium, Hull's North Sea Ferries at King George Dock has open parking for passengers free of charge. At Harwich, Parkeston Quay has services to Scandinavian ports, Hamburg and Hook of Holland. Car parks are operated by British Rail Tel: Harwich (0255) 242000. At Newhaven, serving Dieppe there is open-air parking at the Harbour Garage for 40 cars Tel: (0273) 514233.

Central Harwich

Central Newhaven

Town plans

127

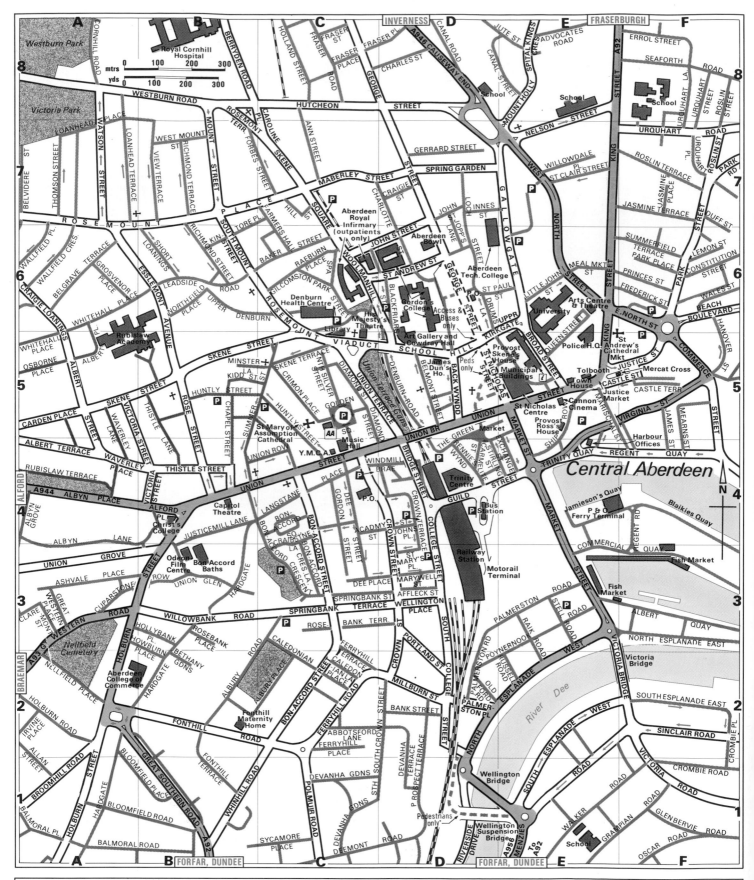

Aberdeen

Granite gives Aberdeen its especial character; but this is not to say that the city is a grim or a grey place, the granites used are of many hues – white, blue, pink and grey. Although the most imposing buildings date from the 19th century, granite has been used to dramatic effect since at least as early as the 15th century. From that time dates St Machar's Cathedral, originally founded in AD580,

but rebuilt several times, especially after a devasting fire started on the orders of Edward III of England in 1336. St Machar's is in Old Aberdeen, traditionally the ecclesiastical and educational hub of the city, while 'New' Aberdeen (actually no newer) has always been the commercial centre. Even that definition is deceptive, for although Old Aberdeen has King's College, founded in 1494, New Aberdeen has Marischal College, founded almost exactly a century later (but rebuilt in 1844)

and every bit as distinguished as a seat of learning. Both establishments functioned as independent universities until they were merged in 1860 to form Aberdeen University. The North Sea oil boom has brought many changes to the city, some of which threatened its character. But even though high-rise buildings are now common, the stately façades, towers and pillars of granite still reign supreme and Union Street remains one of the best thoroughfares in Britain.

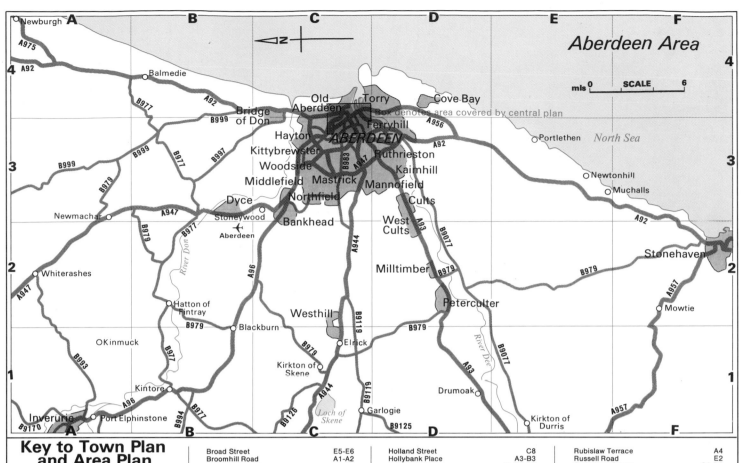

Key to Town Plan and Area Plan

Town Plan
A A Recommended roads
Other roads
Restricted roads
Buildings of interest — Cinema
Car Parks — P
Parks and open spaces
One Way Streets
Churches — +

Area Plan
A roads
B roads
Locations — Hattoncrook O
Urban area

Street Index with Grid Reference

Aberdeen

Abbotsford Lane	C2-D2
Academy Street	C4-D4
Advocates Road	E8
Affleck Street	D3
Albert Quay	E3-F3
Albert Place	A5-A6
Albert Street	A4-A5
Albert Terrace	A4-A5
Albury Place	B2-C2
Albury Road	B2-C2-C3
Albyn Grove	A4
Albyn Lane	A4-A3-B3-B4
Albyn Place	A4-B4
Alford Place	B4
Allan Street	A1-A2
Ann Street	C7-C8
Ashvale Place	A3-B3
Back Wynd	D5
Baker Street	B6-C6
Balmoral Place	A1
Balmoral Road	A1-B1
Bank Street	D2
Beach Boulevard	F6
Belgrave Terrace	A6
Belmont Street	D5
Belvidere Street	A7
Berryden Road	B8-C8
Bethany Gardens	B2
Blackfriars Street	D6
Bloomfield Place	A2-A1-B1
Bloomfield Road	A1-B1
Bon-Accord Crescent	B4-C4-C3
Bon-Accord Crescent Lane	C3-C4
Bon-Accord Square	C4
Bon-Accord Street	C2-C3-C4
Bridge Place	D4

Broad Street	E5-E6
Broomhill Road	A1-A2
Caledonian Lane	C2
Caledonian Place	C2-C3
Canal Road	D8
Canal Street	D8-E8
Carden Place	A5
Carmelite Street	D4
Caroline Place	B8-B7-C7-C8
Castle Street	E5-F5
Castle Terrace	F5
Causeway End	D8
Chapel Street	B4-B5
Charles Street	C8-D8
Charlotte Street	C7-D7-D6
Claremont Street	A3
College Street	D3-D4
Commerce Street	F4-F5
Commercial Quay	E3-F3
Constitution Street	F6
Cornhill Road	A8
Craibstone Lane	C3-C4
Craigie Loanings	A5-A6
Craigie Street	D7
Crimon Street	C5
Crombie Place	F1-F2
Crombie Road	F1
Crown Street	D2-D3-D4-C4
Crown Terrace	D3-D4
Cuparstone Row	A3-B3
Dee Place	C3-D3
Dee Street	C3-C4
Deemont road	C1-D1
Denburn Road	D5
Devanha Gardens	C1
Devanha Terrace	D1-D2
Diamond Street	C4-D4-C5
Drum's Lane	D6
Duff Street	F6-F7
East North Street	E6-F6
Errol Street	F8
Esslemont Avenue	A6-B6-B5
Exchange Street	E4-E5
Farmers Hill	C6-C7
Ferryhill Place	C2
Ferryhill Road	C2-D2
Ferryhill Terrace	C2-D2
Fonthill Road	A2-B2-C2
Fonthill Terrace	B1-B2
Forbes Street	B7-C7
Fraser Place	C8-D8
Fraser Road	C8
Fraser Street	C8
Frederick Street	E6-F6
Gallowgate	D7-E7-E6
George Street	C8-D8-D7-D6-D5
Gerrard Street	D7
Gilcomston Park	C6
Glenbervie Road	F1
Golden Square	C5
Gordon Street	C3-C4
Grampian Road	E1-F1
Great Southern Road	A1-B2-B1
Great Western Place	A3
Great Western Road	A2-A3
Grosvenor Place	A6
Guild Street	D4-E4
Hanover Street	F5
Hardgate	A1-A2-B2-B3-B4
Hill Street	C7
Holburn Road	A2
Holburn Street	A1-A2-A3-B3-B4

Holland Street	C8
Hollybank Place	A3-B3
Howburn Place	A3-B3-B2
Huntly Street	B5-C5-C4
Hutcheon Street	B8-C8-D8
Innes Street	D7-E7
Irvine Place	A2
Jasmine Place	F7
Jasmine Terrace	E7-F7
John Street	C6-D6-D7
Jopp's Lane	D6-D7
Justice Street	E5-F5-F6
Justice Mill Lane	B3-B4
Jute Street	D8-E8
Kidd Street	B5-C5
King Street	E5-E6-E7-E8-F8
Kintore Place	B6-B7-C7
Langstone Place	C4
Leadside Road	B6
Lemon Street	F6
Little John Street	E6
Loanhead Place	A7-A8-B8
Loanhead Terrace	A7
Loch Street	D6-D7
Maberley Street	C7-D7
Marischal Street	E5-F5-F4
Market Street	E3-E4-F5
Marywell Street	D3
Meal Market Street	E6
Mearns Street	F4-F5
Menzies Road	E1-E2-F2
Millburn Street	D2
Minster Holly	B5-C5
Mount Holly	E7-E8
Mount Street	B7-B8
Nellfield Place	A2
Nelson Street	E7-E8
North Esplanade East	E3-F3
North Esplanade West	D1-D2-E2-E3
North Silver Street	C5
Northfield Place	B6
Old Ford Road	D2
Osborne Place	A5
Oscar Road	F1
Palmerston Place	D2
Palmerston Road	D2-D3-E3
Park Place	F6
Park Road	F7
Park Street	F6-F7
Polmuir Road	C1-C2
Portland Street	D2-D3
Poynernook Road	D2-E2-E3
Princes Street	E6-F6
Prospect Terrace	D1-D2
Queen Street	E5-E6
Raeburn Place	C6
Raik Road	E2-E3
Regent Road	F3-F4
Regent Quay	E5-F5
Rennies Wyndd	D4
Richmond Street	B6-B7
Richmond Terrace	B7
Riverside Drive	D1
Rose Street	B4-B5
Rosebank Place	B3
Rosebank Terrace	C3-D3
Rosemount Place	A7-A6-B6-B7-C7
Rosemount Terrace	B7-B8
Rosemount Viaduct	B6-C6-C5
Roslin Street	F7-F8
Roslin Terrace	E7-F7

Rubislaw Terrace	A4
Russell Road	E2
St Andrew Street	C6-D6
St Clair Street	E7
St John's Place	D4
St Mary's Place	D3
St Nicholas Street	D5-E5
St Paul Street	D6-E6
School Hill	D5
Seaforth Road	F8
Ship Row	E4-E5
Short Loanings	B6
Sinclair Road	F2
Skene Square	C6-C7
Skene Street	A5-B5-C5
Skene Terrace	C5
South College Street	D2-D3
South Crown Street	C1-D1-D2
South Esplanade East	F2
South Esplanade West	E1-E2
South Mount Street	B6-B7
Spa Street	C6
Spital Kings Crescent	E8
Spring Garden	D7
Spring Bank Street	C3-D3
Spring Bank Terrace	C3-D3
Stell Road	E3
Stirling Street	D4-E4
Summer Street	B4-B5-C5
Summerfield Terrace	E6-F6
Sycamore Place	B1-C1
The Green	D4-D5
Thistle Lane	B4-B5
Thistle Street	B4
Thomson Street	A7
Trinity Quay	E4
Upper Denburn	B6-C6
Upper Kirkgate	D5-D6-E5-E6
Urquhart Lane	F7-F8
Urquhart Place	F7
Urquhart Road	F7
Urquhart Street	F7-F8
Union Bridge	D4-D5
Union Glen	B3
Union Grove	A3-B3
Union Row	B4-C4
Union Street	B4-C4-D4-D5-E5
Union Terrace	C5-D5
Victoria Bridge	E3-E2-F2
Victoria Road	F1-F2
Victoria Street	A5-B4-B5
View Terrace	B7
Virginia Street	E5-F5
Wales Street	F6
Walker Road	E1-F1
Wallfield Crescent	A6
Wallfield Place	A6-A7
Watson Street	A7-A8
Waverley Lane	A4-A5
Waverley Place	A4-B4
Wellington Place	D3
West Mount Street	B7
West North Street	E6-E7-E8
Westburn Road	A8-B8
Whinhill Road	B1-C1-C2
Whitehall Place	A5-A6-B6
Willow Bank Road	B3-C3
Willowdale Place	E7
Windmill Brae	C4-D4
Woolmanhill	C6-D6-D5

129

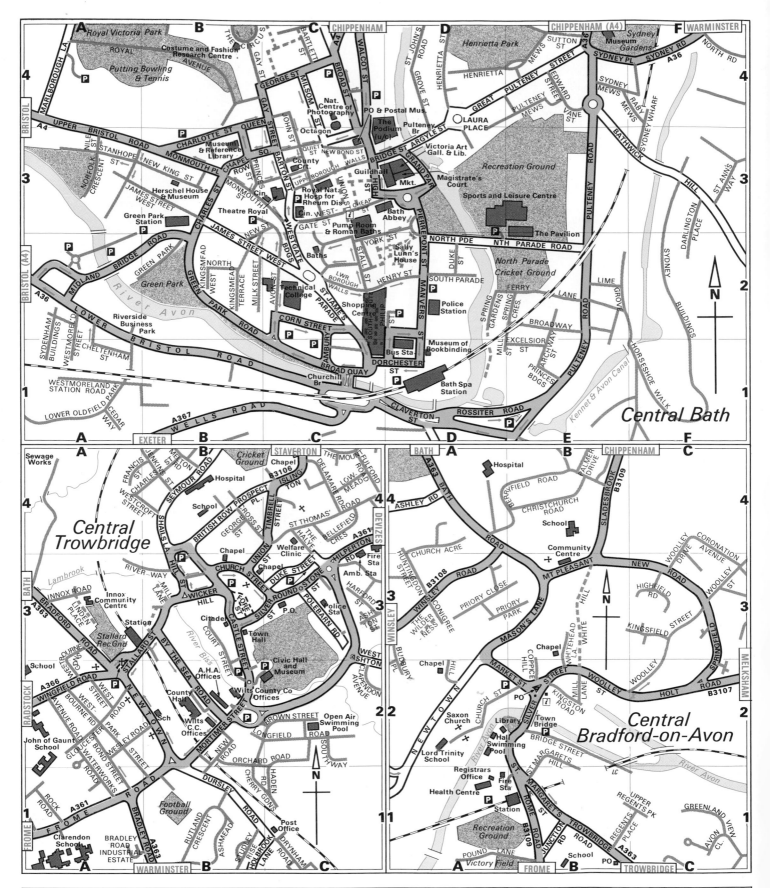

Bath

This unique city combines Britain's most impressive collection of Roman relics with the country's finest Georgian townscape. Its attraction to Romans and fashionable 18th-century society alike was its mineral springs, which are still seen by thousands of tourists who visit the Roman Baths every year. They are now the centre-piece of a Roman museum, where exhibits give a vivid impression of life 2000 years ago. The adjacent Pump Room to which the waters were piped for drinking was a focal point of social life in 18th- and 19th-century Bath.

The Georgian age of elegance also saw the building of Bath's perfectly proportioned streets, terraces and crescents. The finest examples are Queen Square, the Circus, and Royal Crescent, all built of golden local stone. Overlooking the Avon from the west is the great tower of Bath Abbey – sometimes called the "Lantern of the West" because of its large and numerous windows.

Bath has much to delight the museum-lover. Near the abbey, in York Street, is the Burrows Toy Museum – a treasure-trove of playthings spanning two centuries.

The Assembly Rooms in Bennett Street, very much a part of the social scene in Georgian Bath, are now the home of the Museum of Costume with displays illustrating fashion through the ages.

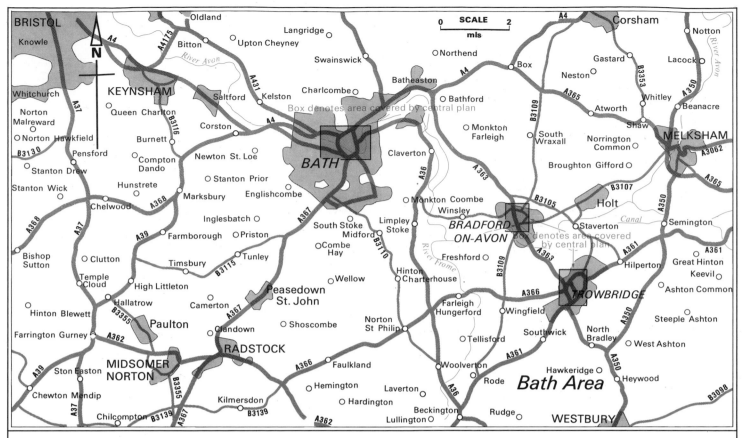

Key to Town Plan and Area Plan

Town Plan

A A Recommended roads	
Other roads	
Restricted roads	
Buildings of interest	Library
Car Parks	P
Parks and open spaces	
Churches	†

Area Plan

A roads	
B roads	
Locations	Box O
Urban Area	

Street Index with Grid Reference

Central Bath

Ambury	C1-C2
Archway Street	E1-E2
Argyle Street	D3-D4
Avon Street	C2
Bartlett Street	C4
Barton Street	C3
Bathwick Hill	E3-F3
Bridge Street	C3-D3
Broadway	E2
Broad Street	C3-C4
Broad Quay	C1
Chapel Row	D3
Charles Street	B2-B3
Charlotte Street	B3-B4
Cheap Street	C3
Cheltenham Street	A1
Claverton Street	C1-D1
Corn Street	C2
Darlington Place	F2-F3
Dorchester Street	C1-D1
Duke Street	D2
Edward Street	E4
Excelsior Street	E1
Ferry Lane	D2-E2
Gay Street	B4-C4-C3

George Street	B4-C4
Grand Parade	D3
Great Pulteney Street	D4-E4
Green Park	A2-B2
Green Park Road	B1-B2-C2-C1
Grove Street	D3-D4
Henrietta Mews	D4-E4
Henrietta Street	D4
Henry Street	C2-D2
High Street	C3
Horseshoe Walk	F1
James Street West	A3-B3-B2-C2
John Street	C3-C4
Kingsmead North	B2
Kingsmead Terrace	B2
Kingsmead West	B2
Laura Place	D3-D4
Lime Grove	E2-F2-F1
Lower Bristol Road	A2-A1-B1-C1
Lower Borough Walls	C2
Lower Oldfield Park	A1
Manvers Street	D1-D2
Marlborough Lane	A4
Midland Bridge Road	A2-B2-B3
Milk Street	B2
Mill Street	D1
Milsom Street	C3-C4
Monmouth Place	B3
Monmouth Street	B3-C3
New Street	B2-B3-C3
New Bond Street	C3
New King Street	A3-B3
Nile Street	A3
Norfolk Crescent	A3
North Parade	D2
North Parade Road	D2-E2
North Road	F4
Philip Street	C1-C2-D2
Pierrepont Street	E1
Princes Buildings	E1
Princes Street	B3
Pulteney Mews	E4
Pulteney Road	E1-E2-E3-E4
Queen Square	B3-B4-C4-C3
Quiet Street	C3
Raby Mews	E4-F4
Rossiter Road	D1-E1
Royal Avenue	A4-B4
St Ann's Way	F3
St Jame's Parade	C2
St John's Road	D4r
Southgate	C1-C2
South Parade	D2
Spring Crescent	E2
Spring Gardens	D2
Stall Street	C2-C3
Stanhope Street	A3
Sutton Street	E4
Sydenham Buildings	A1-A2
Sydney Buildings	F1-F2-F3
Sydney Mews	E4-F4
Sydney Place	E4-F4
Sydney Road	F4
Sydney Wharf	F3-F4
The Circus	B4
Union Street	C3
Upper Borough Walls	C3
Upper Bristol Road	A4-A3-B3

Vane Street	E4
Walcot Street	C3-C4
Wells Road	A1-B1-C1
Westgate Buildings	C2-C3
Westgate Street	C3
Westmoreland Station Road	A1
Westmoreland Street	A1
York Street	C2-D2-D3

Trowbridge

Ashmead	D1
Ashton Street	C3
Avenue Road	A2
Bellefield Crescent	C4
Bond Street	A1-A2
Bradford Road	A2-A3
Bradley Road	A1-B1
British Row	B4
Brown Street	B2-C2
Bythesea Road	B2-B3
Castle Street	B2-B3
Charles Street	A4-B4
Cherry Gardens	B1-C1
Church Street	D3-C3
Clapendon Avenue	C2
Court Street	B2-B3
Cross Street	B4-C4
Delamare Road	C4
Dynham Road	C1
Duke Street	C3-C4
Dursley Road	B1-C1
Fore Street	B3
Francis Street	A4-B4
Frome Road	A1-B1
Fulford Road	C4
George Street	B4
Gloucester Road	A2
Haden Road	C1
Harford Street	C3
Hill Street	B3
Hilperton Road	C3-C4
Holbrook Lane	B1-C1
Innox Road	A3
Islington	C4
Jenkins Street	A4-B4
Linden Place	A3
Longfield Road	B2-C2
Lowmead	C4
Melton Road	B4
Mill Lane	B3
Mortimer Street	B2
New Road	B1-B2
Newtown	aA2-B2
Orchard Road	B1-B2-C2-C1
Park Street	A2-A1-B1
Polebarn Road	C3
Prospect Place	D4-C4
River Way	A3-B3
Rock Road	A1
Roundstone Street	C3
Rutland Crescent	B1
St Thomas' Road	C4
Seymour Road	B4
Shails Lane	B3-B4
Silver Street	B3-C3

Southway	C2
Stallard Street	A2-A3-B3
Studley Rise	B1
The Hayle	C4
The Mount	C4
Timbrell Street	C4
Union Street	B3-B4-C4-C3
Waterworks Road	A1-A2
Wesley Road	A2-B2
West Street	A2
West Ashton	C2-C3
Westbourne Gardens	A2-A3
Westbourne Road	A2
Westcroft Street	A4-B4
Wicker Hill	B3
Wingfield Road	A2

Bradford-upon-Avon

Ashley Road	A4
Avon Close	C1
Bath Road	A3-A4-B4-B3
Berryfield Road	A4-B4
Bridge Street	B2
Christchurch Road	B4
Christchurch Road	B4
Church Acre	A4
Church Street	A2-B2
Conigre Hill	A2-A3
Coppice Hill	B2-B3
Coronation Avenue	C3-C4
Greenland View	C1
Highfield Road	C3
Holt Road	B2-C2
Huntingdon Street	A3
Kingston Road	B2
Junction Road	B1
Market Street	A2-B2
Masons Lane	A3-B3
Mill Lane	B2
Mount Pleasant	B3
Newtown	A1-A2-A3
New Road	B3-C3
Palmer Drive	B4
Pound Lane	A1-B1
Priory Close	A3-B3
Priory Park	A3-B3
Regents Place	B1-C1
Rome Road	B1
St Margaret's Place	B1-B2
St Margaret's Street	B1-C2
Silver Street	B2
Sladesbrook	B3-B4
Springfield	C2-C3
The Wilderness	A3
Trowbridge Road	B1
Upper Regents Park	B1-C1
White Hill	B2-B3
Whitehead Lane	B2-B3
Winsley Road	A3-A4
Woolley Drive	C3-C4
Woolley Street	C2-C3

HTT

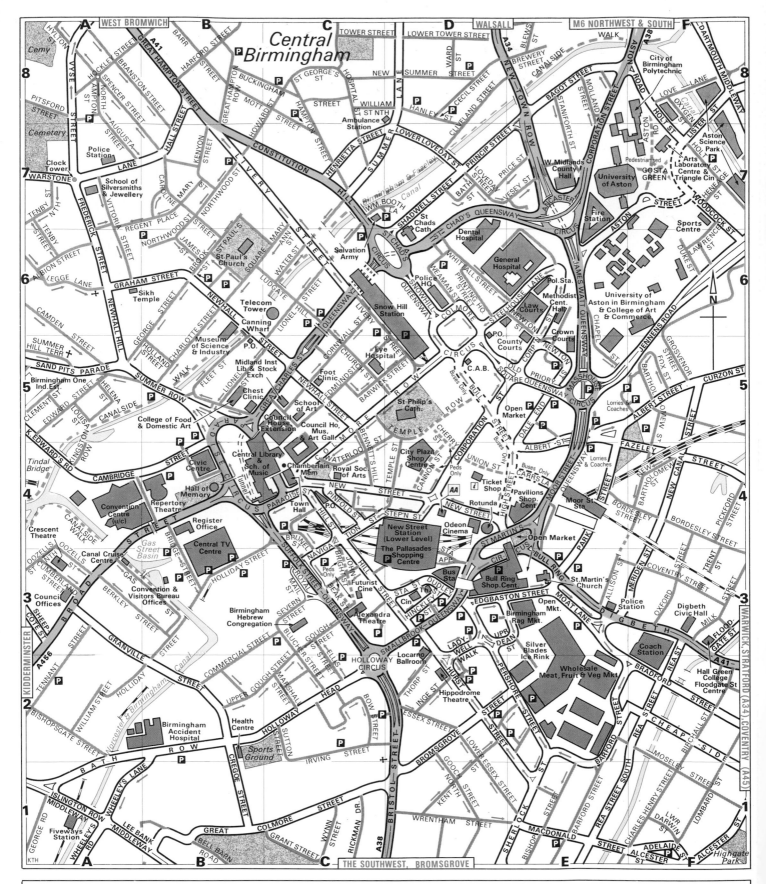

Birmingham

It is very difficult to visualise Birmingham as it was before it began the growth which eventually made it the second-largest city in England. When the Romans were in Britain it was little more than a staging post on Icknield Street. Throughout medieval times it was a sleepy agricultural centre in the middle of a heavily-forested region. Timbered houses clustered together round a green that was

eventually to be called the Bull Ring. But by the 16th century, although still a tiny and unimportant village by today's standards, it had begun to gain a reputation as a manufacturing centre. Tens of thousands of sword blades were made here during the Civil War. Throughout the 18th century more and more land was built on. In 1770 the Birmingham Canal was completed, making trade very much easier and increasing the town's development dramatically. All of that pales into near

insignificance compared with what happened in the 19th century. Birmingham was not represented in Parliament until 1832 and had no town council until 1838. Yet by 1889 it had already been made a city, and after only another 20 years it had become the second largest city in England. Many of Birmingham's most imposing public buildings date from the 19th century, when the city was growing so rapidly. Surprisingly, the city has more miles of waterway than Venice.

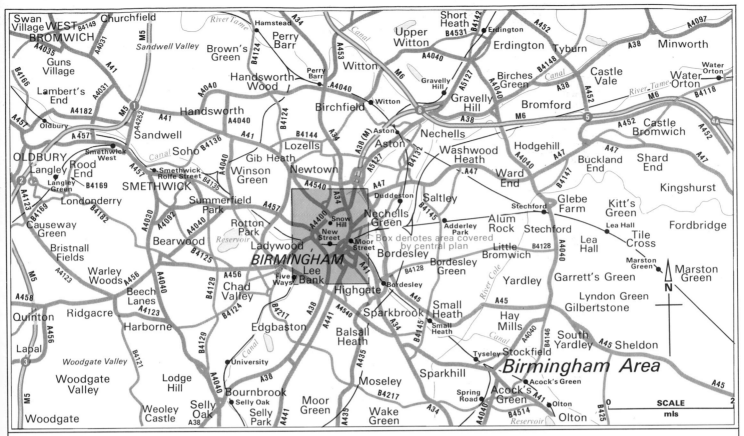

Key to Town Plan and Area Plan

Town Plan

AA Recommended roads	
Restricted roads	
Other roads	
Buildings of interest	Station
One Way Streets	←
Car Parks	P
Parks and open spaces	
Churches	†

Area Plan

A roads	
B roads	
Locations	Meer End ○
Urban area	

Street Index with Grid Reference

Birmingham

Adelaide Street	F1
Albert Street	E4-E5-F5
Albion Street	A6
Alcester Street	F1
Allison Street	E3
Aston Road	F8-E8-F8-F7
Aston Street	E6-E7-F7
Augusta Street	A7-A8
Bagot Street	E8
Barford Street	E1-E2-F2
Barr Street	B8
Bartholomew Street	F4-F5
Barwick Street	C5-D5
Bath Row	A1-A2-B2
Bath Street	D7
Beak Street	C3
Bell Barn Road	B1
Bennett's Hill	C4-C5
Berkley Street	A3-B3
Birchall Street	F1-F2
Bishop Street	E1
Bishopsgate Street	A2
Blews Street	E8
Blucher Street	C2-C3
Bordesley Street	E4-F4-F3
Bow Street	C2
Bradford Street	E3-E2-F2
Branston Street	A8-B8-B7
Brewery Street	E8
Bridge Street	B3-B4
Bristol Street	C1-D1-D2-C2
Broad Street	A2-A3-A4-B4
Bromsgrove Street	D1-D2-E2
Brook Street	B6
Brunel Street	C3-C4
Buckingham Street	B8-C8
Bull Ring	E3
Bull Street	D5-E5-E4

Cambridge Street	A4-B4-B5
Camden Street	A5-A6
Cannon Street	D4
Caroline Street	B6-B7
Carrs Lane	E4
Cecil Street	D8
Chapel Street	E5-E6
Charles Henry Street	F1
Charlotte Street	B5-B6
Cheapside	F1-F2
Cherry Street	D4-D5
Church Street	C6-C5-D5
Clement Street	A5
Cliveland Street	D7-D8-E8
Colmore Circus	D5-D6
Colmore Row	C4-C5-D5
Commercial Street	B2-B3-C3
Constitution Hill	B7-C7
Cornwall Street	C5-C6
Corporation Street	D4-D5-E5-E6-E7-E8-F8
Coventry Street	E3-F3
Cregoe Street	B1-B2
Cumberland Street	A3
Curzon Street	F5
Dale End	E4-E5
Dartmouth Middleway	E3-F3
Digbeth	D3
Dudley Street	D3
Duke Street	F6
Edgbaston Street	D3-E3
Edmund Street	C5-D5
Edward Street	A5
Ellis Street	C2-C3
Essex Street	D2
Fazeley Street	E5-E4-F4
Fleet Street	B5
Floodgate Street	F3
Fox Street	F5
Frederick Street	A6-A7
Gas Street	A3-B3
George Road	A1
George Street	A5-B5-B6
Gooch Street North	D1-D2
Gosta Green	F7
Gough Street	C3
Graham Street	A6-B6
Grant Street	C1
Granville Street	A3-A2-B2
Great Charles St Queensway	B5-C5-C6
Great Colmore Street	B1-C1-D1
Great Hampton Row	B8
Great Hampton Street	A8-B8
Grosvenor Street	F5-F6
Hall Street	B7-B8
Hampton Street	C7-C8
Harford Street	B8
Hanley Street	D7-D8
Helena Street	A5
Heneage Street	F7
Henrietta Street	C7-D7
High Street	D4-E4
Hill Street	C4-C3-D3
Hinckley Street	D3
Hockley Street	A8-B8
Holland Street	B5
Holliday Street	A2-B2-B3-C3-C4
Holloway Circus	C2-C3-D3-D2
Holloway Head	B2-C2
Holt Street	F7-F8
Hospital Street	C7-C8
Howard Street	B7-C7-C8
Hurst Street	D3-D2-E2-E1

Hylton Street	A8
Inge Street	D2
Irving Street	C2-D2
Islington Row Middleway	A1
James Street	B6
James Watt Queensway	E5-E6
Jennens Road	E5-F5-F6
John Bright Street	C3-C4
Kent Street	D1-D2
Kenyon Street	B7
King Edward's Road	A4-A5
Kingston Row	A4
Ladywell Walk	D2-D3
Lancaster Circus	E6-E7
Lawrence Street	F6-F7
Lee Bank Middleway	A1-B1
Legge Lane	A6
Lionel Street	B5-C5-C6
Lister Street	F7-F8
Livery Street	B7-C7-C6-D6-D5
Lombard Street	F1-F2
Louisa Street	A5
Love Lane	F8
Loveday Street	D7
Lower Darwin Street	F1
Lower Essex Street	D2-D1-E1
Lower Loveday Street	D7
Lower Tower Street	D8
Ludgate Hill	B6-C6
Macdonald Street	E1-F1
Marshall Street	C2
Mary Street	B7
Mary Ann Street	C6-C7
Masshouse Circus	E5
Meriden Street	E3-F3
Milk Street	F3
Moat Lane	E3
Molland Street	E8
Moor Street Queensway	E4-E5
Moseley Street	E2-F2-F1
Mott Street	B8-C8-C7
Navigation Street	C3-C4
New Street	C4-D4
New Bartholomew Street	F4
New Canal Street	F4-F5
Newhall Hill	A5-A6
Newhall Street	B6-B5-C5
New Summer Street	C8-D8
Newton Street	E5
New Town Row	D8-E8-E7
Northampton Street	A8
Northwood Street	B6-B7
Old Square	D5-E5
Oozells Street	A3-A4
Oozells Street North	A3-A4
Oxford Street	F3-F4
Oxygen Street	F7-F8
Paradise Circus	B4-B5
Paradise Street	C4
Park Street	E3-E4
Pershore Street	D3-D2-E2
Pickford Street	F4
Pinfold Street	C4
Pitsford Street	A8
Price Street	D7-E7
Princip Street	D7-E7-E8
Printing House Street	D6
Priory Queensway	E5
Rea Street	E2-F2-F3
Rea Street South	E1-F1-F2
Regent Place	A7-B7
Rickman Drive	C1

Royal Mail Street	C3
St Chad's Circus	C7-C6-D6
St Chad's Queensway	D6-D7-E7
St George's Street	C8
St Martin's Circus	D3-D4-E4-E3
St Paul's Square	B7-B6-C6
Sand Pits Parade	A5
Severn Street	C3
Shadwell Street	D6-D7
Sheepcote Street	A3
Sherlock Street	D1-E1-E2
Smallbrook Queensway	C3-D3
Snow Hill Queensway	D6
Spencer Street	A8-A7-B7
Staniforth Street	E7-E8
Station Approach	D3
Station Street	D3
Steelhouse Lane	D6-E6
Stephenson Street	C4-D4
Suffolk Street Queensway	B4-C4-C3
Summer Hill Terrace	A5
Summer Row	A5-B5
Summer Lane	C7-D7-D8
Sutton Street	C2
Temple Row	C5-D5
Temple Street	D4-D5
Tenby Street	A6-A7
Tenby Street North	A7
Tennant Street	A2-A3
Thorp Street	D2-D3
Tower Street	C8-D8
Trent Street	F3-F4
Union Street	D4
Upper Dean Street	D3-E3
Upper Gough Street	B2-C2-C3
Vesey Street	D7-E7
Vittoria Street	A6-A7
Vyse Street	A7-A8
Ward Street	D8
Warstone Lane	A7-B7
Water Street	C6
Waterloo Street	C4-C5-D5
Weaman Street	D6
Wheeley's Lane	A1-B1-B2
Wheeley's Road	A1
Whittall Street	D6-E6
William Booth Lane	C7-D7
William Street	A2
William Street North	C8-D8
Woodcock Street	F6-F7
Wrentham Street	D1-E1
Wynn Street	C1

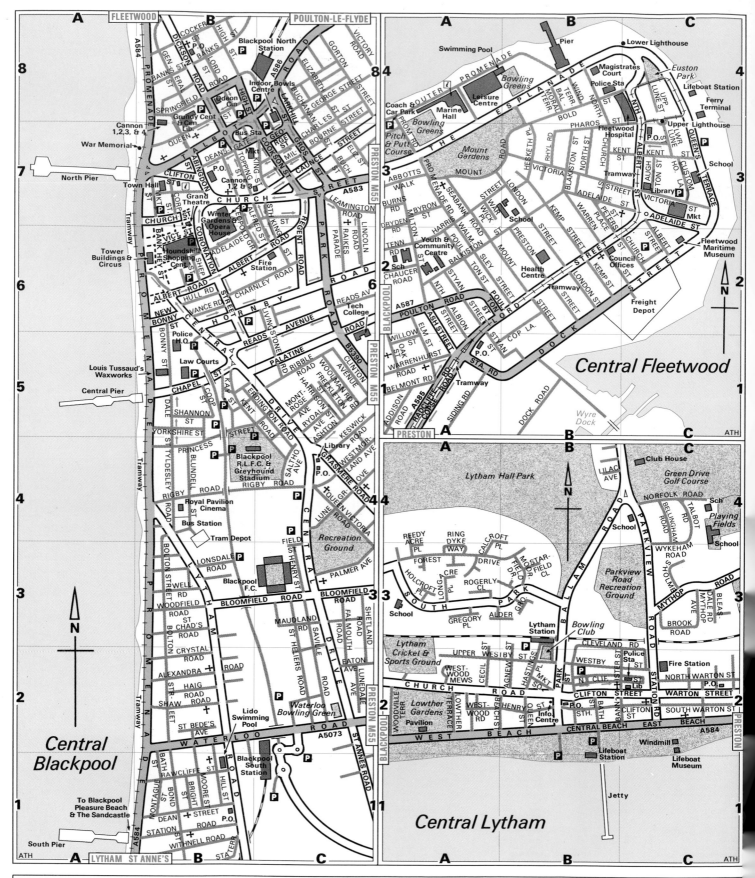

Blackpool

No seaside resort is regarded with greater affection than Blackpool. It is still the place where millions of North Country folk spend their holidays; its famous illuminations draw visitors from all over the world. It provides every conceivable kind of traditional holiday entertainment, and in greater abundance than any other seaside resort in Britain. The famous tower – built in the 1890s as a replica of the Eiffel Tower – the three piers, seven miles of promenade, five miles of illuminations, countless guesthouses, huge numbers of pubs, shops, restaurants and cafes play host to eight million visitors a year.

At the base of the tower is a huge entertainment complex that includes a ballroom, a circus and an aquarium. Other 19th-century landmarks are North Pier and Central Pier, the great Winter Gardens and Opera House and the famous trams that still run along the promenade – the only electric trams still operating in Britain. The most glittering part of modern Blackpool is the famous Golden Mile, packed with amusements, novelty shops and snack stalls. Every autumn it becomes part of the country's most extravagant light show – the illuminations – when the promenade is ablaze with neon representations of anything and everything from moon rockets to the Muppets. Autumn is also the time when Blackpool is a traditional venue for political party conferences.

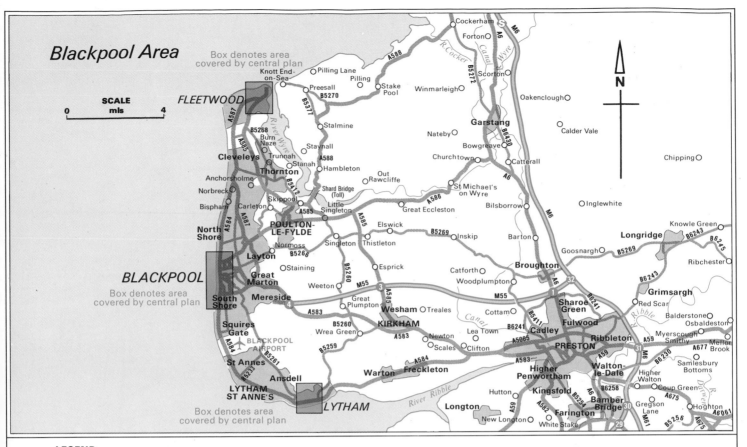

Blackpool Area

Box denotes area covered by central plan

SCALE
mls
0   4

FLEETWOOD

BLACKPOOL

Box denotes area covered by central plan

Box denotes area covered by central plan   LYTHAM

LEGEND

Town Plan

AA Recommended roads	
Restricted roads	- - -
Other roads	
Buildings of interest	Hall
Car parks	P
Parks and open spaces	

Area Plan

A roads	
B roads	
Locations	Trunnah O
Urban area	

Street Index with Grid Reference

Blackpool

Abingdon Street	B7
Adelaide Street	B6-B7-C7
Albert Road	B6-C6
Alexandra Road	B2
Alfred Street	B7-C7-C6
Ashton Road	C4-C5
Bank Hey Street	B6-B7
Banks Street	B8
Bath Street	B1-B2
Bloomfield Road	B3-C3
Blundell Street	B4
Bolton Street	B2-B3-B4
Bond Street	B1-B2
Bonny Street	B5-B6
Bright Street	B1
Buchanan Street	C7-C8
Caunce Street	C7-C8
Central Drive	B6-B5-C5-C4-C3-C2
Chapel Street	B5
Charles Street	C7-C8
Charnley Road	B6-C6
Church Street	B7-C7
Clifton Street	B7
Clinton Avenue	C5
Cocker Street	B8
Cookson Street	B8-B7-C7
Coop Street	B5
Coronation Street	B5-B6-B7
Corporation Street	B7
Crystal Road	B2

Dale Street	B4-B5
Deansgate	B7-C7
Dean Street	B1
Dickson Road	B7-B8
Eaton Avenue	C2
Erdington Road	B5-C5-C4
Elizabeth Street	C7-C8
Falmouth Road	C2-C3
Field Street	C3
Freckleton Street	C5
General Street	B8
George Street	C7-C8
Gorton Street	C8
Grasmere Road	C4
Grosvenor Street	C7
Haig Road	B2
Harrison Street	C5
Henry Street	C3
High Street	B8
Hill Street	B1
Hornby Road	B6-C6
Hull Road	B6
Kay Street	B5
Kent Road	B5-C5-C4
Keswick Road	C4-C5
King Street	C7
Larkhill Street	C8
Leamington Road	C7
Leopold Grove	B7-B6-C6
Lincoln Road	C6-C7
Livingstone Road	C5-C6
Lonsdale Road	B3
Lord Street	B8
Lune Grove	C4
Lunedale Avenue	C2
Lytham Road	B1-B2-B3-B4
Market Street	B7
Maudland Road	B3-C3
Milbourne Street	C7-C8
Montague Street	B1
Montrose Avenue	B5-C5
Moore Street	B1
New Bonny Street	B5-B6
Palatine Road	B5-C5-C6
Palmer Avenue	C3
Park Road	C5-C6-C7
Princes Street	B4-B5-C5
Promenade	B1-B2-B3-B4-B5-B6-A6-A7-B7-B8
Queen Street	B7-B8
Queen Victoria Road	C3-C4
Raikes Parade	C6-C7
Rawcliffe Street	B1
Reads Avenue	B5-C5-C6
Regent Road	C6-C7
Ribble Road	C5
Rigby Road	B4-C4
Rydal Avenue	C5
St Annes Road	C1-C2
St Bede's Avenue	B2
St Chad's Road	B3
St Heliers Road	C2-C3
Salthouse Avenue	C4
Saville Road	C2-C3
Shannon Street	B5
Shaw Road	B2
Sheppard Street	B6
Shetland Road	C2-C3
South King Street	C6-C7
Springfield Road	B8

Station Road	B1
Station Terrace	B1
Talbot Road	B7-B8-C8
Topping Street	B7
Tyldesley Road	B4
Vance Road	B6
Victoria Street	B6
Victory Road	C8
Waterloo Road	B2-C2
Wellington Road	B3
Westmorland Avenue	C4
Withnell Road	B1
Woodfield Road	B3
Woolman Road	C5
Yorkshire Street	B5

Fleetwood

Abbots Walk	A3
Adelaide Street	B3-C3-C2
Addison Road	A1
Albert Street	C2-C3
Ash Street	A1-A2
Aughton Street	C3
Balmoral Terrace	B4
Belmont Road	A1
Blakiston Street	A2-B2-B3
Bold Street	B4-C4
Burns Road	A3
Byron Street	A3
Chaucer Road	A2
Church Street	C2
Cop Lane	A1-B1-B2
Copse Road	A1
Custom House Lane	C3
Dock Road	B1
Dock Street	B1-B2-C2
Dryden Road	A2-A3
Elm Street	A1-A2
Harris Street	A2-A3-B3
Hesketh Place	B3
Kemp Street	B2-B3
Kent Street	B3-C3
London Street	B2-B3
Lord Street	A1-A2-B2-C2-C3
Lower Lune Street	C3
Milton Street	A2-A3
Mount Road	A3-B3
Mount Street	A2-B2
North Albert Street	C3-C4
North Albion Street	A1-A2
North Church Street	B3-B4
North Street	B3
Oak Street	A1
Outer Promenade	A4-B4
Pharos Street	B3-C3-C4
Poulton Road	A2
Poulton Street	A2
Preston Street	B2
Promenade Road	A3-A4
Queen's Terrace	C3-C4
Radcliffe Road	A1
Rhyl Street	B3
St Peters Place	B2-B3
Seabank Road	A2-A3

Siding Road	A1
Station Road	A1
Styan Street	A2-A1-B1
Tennyson Road	A2
The Esplanade	A3-A4-B4
Upper Lune Street	C4
Victoria Street	B3-C3
Walmsley Street	A3-A2-B2
Warrenhurst Road	A1
Warren Street	B3-B2-C2
Warwick Place	A3
Willow Street	A1
Windsor Terrace	B4

Lytham

Agnew Street	B2-B3
Alder Grove	A3-B3
Ballam Road	B2-B3-B4-C4
Bath Street	B2
Beach Street	B2
Bellingham Road	C4
Bleasdale Road	C3
Brook Road	C3
Calcroft Place	A3-B4
Cecil Street	A2-A3
Central Beach	B2-C2
Church Road	A2-B2
Cleveland Road	B3-C3
Clifton Street	B2-C2
East Beach	C2
Forest Drive	A3-B3
Gregory Place	A3
Hastings Place	B2-B3
Henry Street	B2
Holcroft Place	A3
Lilac Avenue	B4
Longacre Place	A3
Lowther Terrace	A2
Market Square	B2
Moorfield Drive	B3
Mythop Avenue	C3
Mythop Road	C3
Norfolk Road	C4
North Clifton Street	B2-C2
North Warton Street	C2
Park Street	B2
Parkview Road	C2-C3-C4
Queen Street	B2
Reedy Acre Place	A3-A4
Ring Dyke Way	A3
Rogerly Close	A3
South Clifton Street	B2-C2
South-Holme	C3
South Park	A3-B3
South Warton Street	C2
Starfield Close	B3
Station Road	C2
Talbot Road	C4
Upper Westby Street	A2-B2
Warton Street	C2
West Beach	A2-B2
Westby Street	B2-C2
Westwood Mews	A2
Westwood Road	A2

Woodville Terrace	A2
Wykeham Road	C3-C4

ATH

Street Index with Grid Reference

Bournemouth

Albert Road	C3-D3
Avenue Road	B3-C3
Bath Road	D2-E2-E3-E4-F4
Beacon Road	C1
Bodorgan Road	C4
Bourne Avenue	B3-C3
Bradbourne Road	B3
Braidley Road	B3-B4
Branksome Wood Gardens	A4
Branksome Wood Road	A4
Cambridge Road	A2-A3
Central Drive	B4
Chine Crescent	A1
Chine Crescent Road	A1-A2
Christchurch Road	F4
Commercial Road	B2
Cotlands Road	F4
Cranbourne Road	B2-C2
Crescent Road	A3-B3
Cumnor Road	E4
Dean Park Crescent	C4-D4
Dean Park Road	C4
Durley Chine Road	A1-A2
Durley Chine Road South	A1
Durley Gardens	A1-A2
Durley Road	A1-A2-B1
Durrant Road	B4
East Overcliff Drive	E2-F2-F3
Exeter Crescent	C2
Exeter Park Road	C2-D2
Exeter Road	C2-D2
Fir Vale Road	D3-D4
Gervis Place	C3-D3
Gervis Road	E3-F3
Glenfern Road	D3-E3-E4
Grove Road	E3-F3
Hahnemann Road	A1-B1-B2
Hinton Road	D2-D3-E2
Holdenhurst Road	F4
Kensington Drive	A4
Kerley Road	C1
Lansdowne Road	E4-F4
Lorne Park Road	E4
Madeira Road	D4-E4
Marlborough Road	A2
Meyrick Road	F3-F4
Norwich Avenue	A2
Norwich Avenue West	A3
Norwich Road	A2-B2
Old Christchurch Road	D3-D4-E4-F4
Orchard Street	C2-C3
Parsonage Road	D3-E3
Poole Hill	A2-B2
Poole Road	A2
Post Office Road	C3
Priory Road	C1-C2
Purbeck Road	B2
Richmond Gardens	C4
Richmond Hill	C3-C4
Richmond Hill Drive	C4
Russell Cotes Road	E2
Somerville Road	A2
St Michael's Road	B2-B1-C1
St Peter's Road	D3-E3
St Stephen's Road	B3-B4-C4-C3
St Stephen's Way	E4
Stafford Road	E4
Suffolk Road	A3-B3
Surrey Road	A3
Terrace Road	B2-C2
The Triangle	B2-B3
Tregonwell Road	B2-C2-C1
Trinity Road	E4
Undercliffe Drive	D1-D2-E1-E2-F2
Upper Hinton Road	D2-D3-E2
Upper Norwich Road	A2-B2
Upper Terrace Road	B2-C2
Wessex Way	A3-A4-B4-C4-D4-E4
West Cliff Gardens	B1
West Cliff Promenade	B1-C1-D1-C1
West Cliff Road	A1-B1
Westhill Road	A2-B2-B1
Westover Road	D2-D3
West Promenade	C1-D1
Wimborne Road	C4
Wootton Gardens	E3-E4
Wootton Mount	E4
Yelverton Road	C3-D3

Christchurch

Albion Road	A4
Arcadia Road	A4
Arthur Road	B3
Avenue Road	A3-B3-B4
Avon Road West	A3-A4-B4
Bargates	B2-B3
Barrack Road	A4-A3-B2-B3
Beaconsfield Road	B2-B3
Bridge Street	C2
Bronte Avenue	B4
Canberra Road	A4
Castle Street	B2-C2
Christchurch By-Pass	B2-C2-C3
Clarendon Road	A3-B3
Douglas Avenue	A2-B2
Endfield Road	A4
Fairfield	B3
Fairfield Drive	A2
Fairmile Road	A4-B4-B3
Flambard Avenue	B4
Gardner Road	A3-A4
Gleadows Avenue	A2-B2
Grove Road East	A3-B3
Grove Road West	A3
High Street	B2
Iford Lane	A1
Jumpers Avenue	A4
Jumpers Road	A3-A4-B4
Kings Avenue	A2-B2
Manor Road	B2
Milhams Street	B2-C2
Mill Road	B3-B4
Portfield Road	A3-B3
Queens Avenue	B1
Quay Road	B1
River Lea Road	B2
Soapers Lane	B1
Saxonbury Road	A1
St John's Road	A2
St Margarets Avenue	B1
Sopers Lane	B1-B2
South View Road	A1-B1
Stony Lane	C4-C3-C2
Stour Road	B3-B2-A1-A2
Stourbank Road	B2
The Grove	A4
Tuckton Road	A1
Twynham Avenue	B2-B3
Walcott Avenue	A4-B4
Waterloo Place	C2
Wickfield Avenue	B1-B2
Wick Lane	A1-B1-B2
Willow Drive	A1-B1
Willow Way	A1-B1
Windsor Road	A3

Poole

Ballard Road	B1-C1
Church Street	A1
Dear Hay Lane	A2-B2
Denmark Road	C3
East Quay Road	B1
East Street	B1
Elizabeth Road	C3
Emerson Road	B1-B2
Esplanade	B3
Garland Road	C4
Green Road	B2-B1-C1
Heckford Road	C3-C4
High Street	A1-B1-B2
Hill Street	B2
Johns Road	C3-C4
Jolliffe Road	C4
Kingland Road	B2-C2
Kingston Road	C3-C4
Lagland Street	B1-B2
Longfleet Road	C3
Maple Road	C3-C4
Mount Pleasant Road	C2-C3
Newfoundland Drive	C1
New Orchard	A1-A2
North Street	B2
Old Orchard	B1
Parkstone Road	C1-C2
Perry Gardens	R1
Poole Bridge	A1
Sandbourne Road	C4
St Mary's Road	C3
Seldown Lane	C2-C3
Shaftesbury Road	C3
Skinner Street	B1
South Road	B2
Stanley Road	B1
Sterte Avenue	A4-B4
Sterte Road	B2-B3-B4
Stokes Avenue	B4-C4
Strand Street	A1-B1
Tatnam Road	B4-C4
The Quay	A1-B1
Towngate Bridge	B2-B3
West Quay Road	A1-A2-B2
West Street	A1-A2-B2
Wimborne Road	B3-C3-C4

Swanage

Argyle Road	A2
Atlantic Road	A1-B1
Battlemead	B4
Beach Gardens	B4
Bon Accord Road	B1
Broad Road	C1
Cauldron Avenue	B4
Cauldron Barn Road	A4-B4
Cauldron Crescent	A4
Church Hill	A2
Clifton Road	B4
Cluny Crescent	B1-C1
Court Hill	A2
Court Road	A2
Cowlease	A1-A2
Cranborne Road	B2
De Moulham Road	B3-B4
D'uberville Drive	A4-B4
Eldon Terrace	B2
Encombe Road	C1
Exeter Road	B1-C1
Gannets Park	B3
Gilbert Road	A2-B2
Gordon Road	B1
Grosvenor Road	C1
Hanbury Road	A2
High Street	A2-B3
Ilminster Road	B2-B3
Institute Road	B2-B2
Kings Road	A2-B2
Kings Road East	B2
Kings Road West	A2
Locarno Road	A2
Manor Road	B1-C1
Manwell Drive	A1
Manwell Road	A1
Mariners Drive	A1
Marshall Row	C1
Mount Pleasant Lane	B1-B2
Mountscar	A1
Newton Road	B1
Northbrook Road	A2-A3-B3-B4
Osborne Road	A1
Park Road	C1
Princess Road	A2
Prospect Crescent	A3
Peveril Heights	C1
Peveril Point Road	C1
Priests Road	C1
Queens Mead	B1
Queens Road	A1-B1-C1
Rabling Road	A3-B3
Rempstone Road	B2-B3
Richmond Road	A1
St Vast's Road	B1
Sentry Road	C1
Seymer Road	C1
Shore Road	B3-B4
Springfield Road	B2
Stafford Road	B1-B2
Station Road	B2
Sunridge Close	B1
Taunton Road	C1
The Parade	C2
Townsend Road	A1
Ulwell Road	B4
Victoria Avenue	A3-B3
Vivian Park	B4
Walrond Road	A3-B3

Central Swanage

STUDLAND, BOURNEMOUTH

SWANAGE BAY

Road Closed: 11am-7pm between 15th May and 30th Sept.

LEGEND

AA Recommended roads	
Other roads	
Restricted roads	
Buildings of interest	Sta
AA Centre	AA
Churches	+
Car parks	P
One Way streets	
Parks and open spaces	

Bournemouth

Until the beginning of the 19th-century the landscape was open heath. Bournemouth's rise began in Victorian times when the idea of seaside holidays was very new. In the next 50 years it had become a major resort. Holidaymakers today enjoy miles of sandy beaches, a mild climate and beautiful setting, along with a tremendous variety of amenities, including some of the best shopping in the south. Entertainments range from variety shows, cinemas, opera and the world famous Bournemouth Symphony Orchestra.

Christchurch is situated at the confluence of the rivers Avon and Stour which flow into Christchurch Harbour at Mudeford. The Priory Church dominates the town with its many attractive walks and old buildings.

Poole is famous for the large natural harbour and Poole Quay with its unique historical interest. The Maritime Museum illustrates the town's associations with the sea since prehistoric times and the famous Poole Pottery offers guided tours of its workshops with exhibits of pottery past and present.

Swanage is one of Dorset's most popular holiday resorts that has still retained much of its Victorian influence. Dramatic coastal scenery with cliff top walks and many places of interest are within easy reach.

136

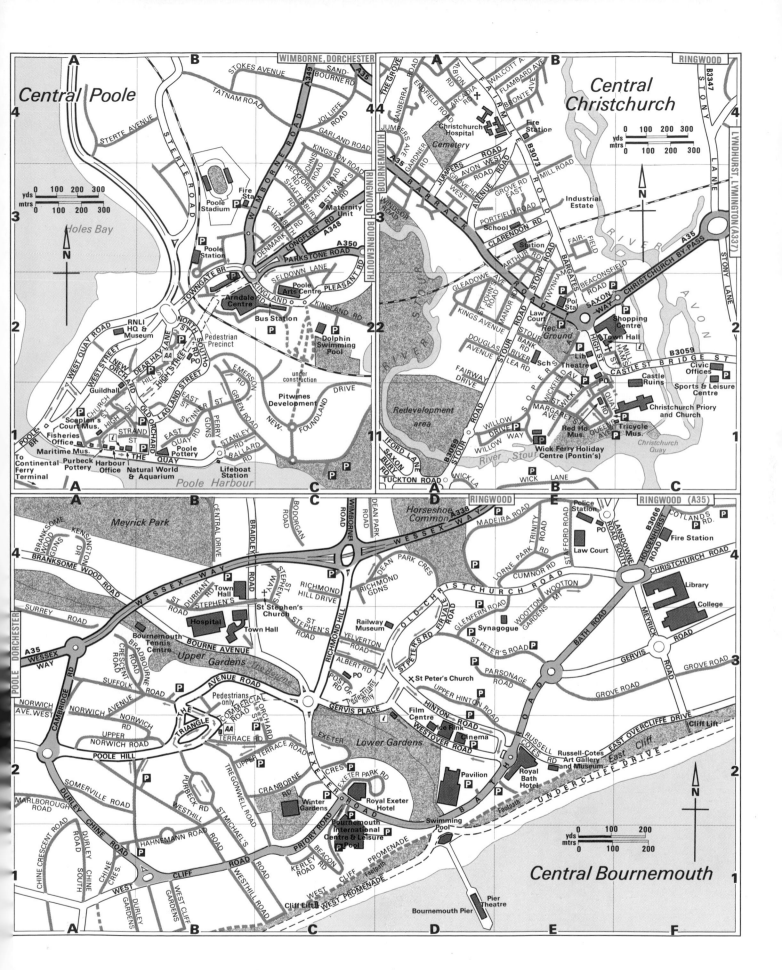

BOURNEMOUTH
The pier, safe sea-bathing, golden sands facing south and sheltered by steep cliffs, and plenty of amenities for the holiday maker make Bournemouth one of the most popular resorts on the south coast of England.

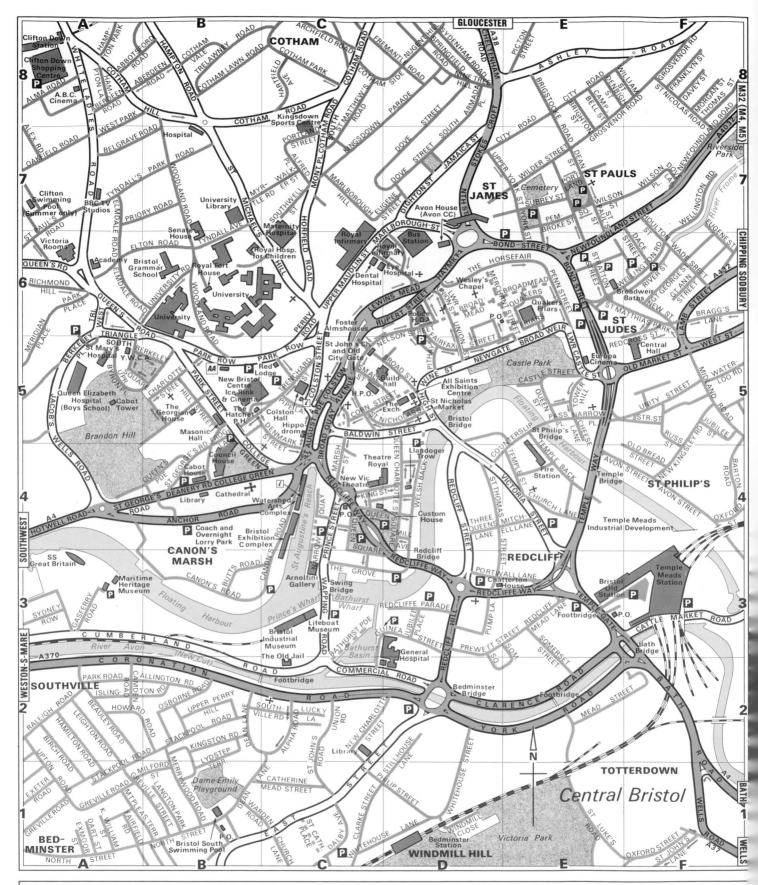

Bristol

One of Britain's most historic seaports, Bristol retains many of its visible links with the past, despite terrible damage inflicted during bombing raids in World War II. Most imposing is the cathedral, founded as an abbey church in 1140. Perhaps even more famous than the cathedral is the Church of St Mary Redcliffe. Ranking among the finest churches in the country, it owes much of its splendour to 14th- and 15th-century merchants who bestowed huge sums of money on it.

The merchant families brought wealth to the whole of Bristol, and their trading links with the world are continued in today's modern aerospace and technological industries. Much of the best of Bristol can be seen in the area of the Floating Harbour – an arm of the Avon. Several of the old warehouses have been converted into museums, galleries and exhibition centres. Among them are genuinely picturesque old pubs, the best-known of which is the Llandoger Trow. It is a timbered 17th-century house, the finest of its kind in Bristol. Further up the same street – King Street – is the Theatre Royal, built in 1766 and the oldest theatre in the country. In Corn Street, the heart of the business area, is a magnificent 18th-century corn exchange. In front of it are the four pillars known as the 'nails', on which merchants used to make cash transactions, hence 'to pay on the nail'.

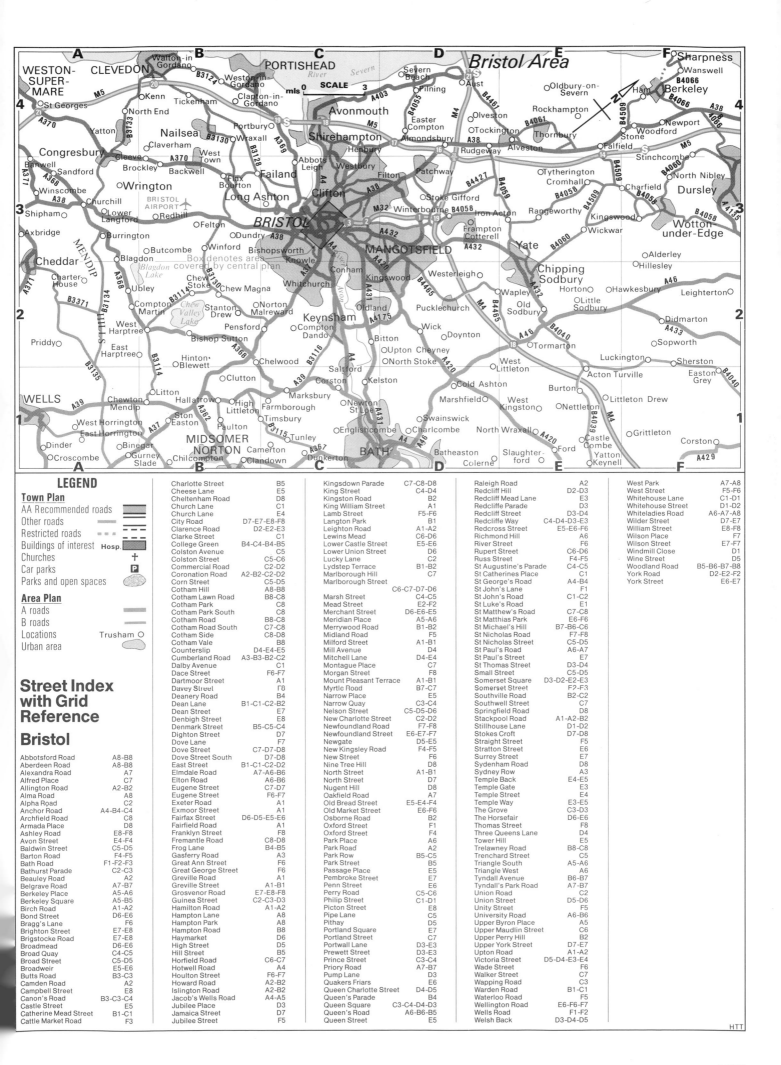

Bristol Area

WESTON-SUPER-MARE · CLEVEDON · PORTISHEAD · Bristol Area · Sharpness

LEGEND

Town Plan

AA Recommended roads	▅▅▅
Other roads	▅▅
Restricted roads	▄ ▄ ▄
Buildings of interest	Hosp. ▇
Churches	†
Car parks	P
Parks and open spaces	◯

Area Plan

A roads	▅▅
B roads	▅▅
Locations	Trusham ◯
Urban area	◯

Street Index with Grid Reference

Bristol

Street	Grid
Abbotsford Road	A8-B8
Aberdeen Road	A8-B8
Alexandra Road	A7
Alfred Place	C7
Allington Road	A2-B2
Alma Road	A8
Alpha Road	C2
Anchor Road	A4-B4-C4
Archfield Road	C8
Armada Place	D8
Ashley Road	E8-F8
Avon Street	E4-F4
Baldwin Street	C5-D5
Barton Road	F4-F5
Bath Road	F1-F2-F3
Bathurst Parade	C2-C3
Beauley Road	A2
Belgrave Road	A7-B7
Berkeley Place	A5-A6
Berkeley Square	A5-B5
Birch Road	A1-A2
Bond Street	D6-E6
Bragg's Lane	F6
Brighton Street	E7-E8
Brigstocke Road	E7-E8
Broadmead	D6-E6
Broad Quay	C4-C5
Broad Street	C5-D5
Broadweir	E5-E6
Butts Road	B3-C3
Camden Road	A2
Campbell Street	D8
Canon's Road	B3-C3-C4
Castle Street	E5
Catherine Mead Street	B1-C1
Cattle Market Road	F3
Charlotte Street	B5
Cheese Lane	E5
Cheltenham Road	D8
Church Lane	C1
Church Lane	E4
City Road	D7-E7-E8-F8
Clarence Road	D2-E2-E3
Clarke Street	C1
College Green	B4-C4-B4-B5
Colston Avenue	C5
Colston Street	C5-C6
Commercial Road	D2-D2
Coronation Road	A2-B2-C2-D2
Corn Street	C5-D5
Cotham Hill	A8-B8
Cotham Lawn Road	B8-C8
Cotham Park	C8
Cotham Park South	C8
Cotham Road	B8-C8
Cotham Road South	C7-C8
Cotham Side	C8-D8
Cotham Vale	B8
Counterslip	D4-E4-E5
Cumberland Road	A3-B3-B2-C2
Dalby Avenue	C1
Dace Street	F6-F7
Dartmoor Street	A1
Davey Street	F8
Deanery Road	B4
Dean Lane	B1-C1-C2-B2
Dean Street	E7
Denbigh Street	E8
Denmark Street	B5-C5-C4
Dighton Street	D7
Dove Lane	F7
Dove Street	C7-D7-D8
Dove Street South	D7-D8
East Street	B1-C1-C2-D2
Elmdale Road	A7-A6-B6
Elton Road	A6-B6
Eugene Street	C7-D7
Eugene Street	F6-F7
Exeter Road	A1
Exmoor Street	A1
Fairfax Street	D6-D5-E5-E6
Fairfield Road	A1
Franklyn Street	F8
Fremantle Road	C8-D8
Frog Lane	B4-B5
Gasferry Road	A3
Great Ann Street	F6
Great George Street	F6
Greville Road	A1
Greville Street	A1-B1
Grosvenor Road	E7-E8-F8
Guinea Street	C2-C3-D3
Hamilton Road	A1-A2
Hampton Lane	A8
Hampton Park	A8
Hampton Road	B8
Haymarket	D6
High Street	D5
Hill Street	B5
Horfield Road	C6-C7
Hotwell Road	A4
Houlton Street	F6-F7
Howard Road	A2-B2
Islington Road	A2-B2
Jacob's Wells Road	A4-A5
Jubilee Place	D3
Jamaica Street	D7
Jubilee Street	F5
Kingsdown Parade	C7-C8-D8
King Street	C4-D4
Kingston Road	B2
King William Street	A1
Lamb Street	F5-F6
Langton Park	B1
Leighton Road	A1-A2
Lewins Mead	C6-D6
Lower Castle Street	E5-E6
Lower Union Street	D6
Lucky Lane	C2
Lydstep Terrace	B1-B2
Marlborough Hill	C7
Marlborough Street	C6-C7-D7-D6
Marsh Street	C4-C5
Mead Street	E2-F2
Merchant Street	D6-E6-E5
Meridian Place	A5-A6
Merrywood Road	B1-B2
Midland Road	F5
Milford Street	A1-B1
Mill Avenue	D4
Mitchell Lane	D4-E4
Montague Place	C7
Morgan Street	F8
Mount Pleasant Terrace	A1-B1
Myrtle Road	B7-C7
Narrow Place	E5
Narrow Quay	C3-C4
Nelson Street	C5-D5-D6
New Charlotte Street	C2-D2
Newfoundland Road	F7-F8
Newfoundland Street	E6-E7-F7
Newgate	D5-E5
New Kingsley Road	F4-F5
New Street	F6
Nine Tree Hill	D8
North Street	A1-B1
North Street	D7
Nugent Hill	A7
Oakfield Road	A7
Old Bread Street	E5-E4-F4
Old Market Street	E6-F6
Osborne Road	B2
Oxford Street	F1
Oxford Street	F4
Park Place	A6
Park Road	A2
Park Row	B5-C5
Park Street	B5
Passage Place	E5
Pembroke Street	E7
Penn Street	E6
Perry Road	C5-C6
Philip Street	C1-D1
Picton Street	E8
Pipe Lane	C5
Pithay	D5
Portland Square	E7
Portland Street	C7
Portwall Lane	D3-E3
Prewett Street	D3-E3
Prince Street	C3-C4
Priory Road	A7-B7
Pump Lane	D3
Quakers Friars	E6
Queen Charlotte Street	D4-D5
Queen's Parade	B4
Queen Square	C3-C4-D4-D3
Queen's Road	A6-B6-B5
Queen Street	E5
Raleigh Road	A2
Redcliff Hill	D2-D3
Redcliff Mead Lane	E3
Redcliffe Parade	D3
Redcliff Street	D3-D4
Redcliffe Way	C4-D4-D3-E3
Redcross Street	E5-E6-F6
Richmond Hill	A6
River Street	F6
Rupert Street	C6-D6
Russ Street	F4-F5
St Augustine's Parade	C4-C5
St Catherines Place	C1
St George's Road	A4-B4
St John's Lane	F1
St John's Road	C1-C2
St Luke's Road	E1
St Matthew's Road	C7-C8
St Matthias Park	E6-F6
St Michael's Hill	B7-B6-C6
St Nicholas Road	F7-F8
St Nicholas Street	C5-D5
St Paul's Road	A6-A7
St Paul's Street	E7
St Thomas Street	D3-D4
Small Street	C5-D5
Somerset Square	D3-D2-E2-E3
Somerset Street	F2-F3
Southville Road	B2-C2
Southwell Street	C7
Springfield Road	D8
Stackpool Road	A1-A2-B2
Stillhouse Lane	D1-D2
Stokes Croft	D7-D8
Straight Street	F5
Stratton Street	E6
Surrey Street	E7
Sydenham Road	D8
Sydney Row	A3
Temple Back	E4-E5
Temple Gate	E3
Temple Street	E4
Temple Way	E3-E5
The Grove	C3-D3
The Horsefair	D6-E6
Thomas Street	F8
Three Queens Lane	D4
Tower Hill	E5
Trelawney Road	B8-C8
Trenchard Street	C5
Triangle South	A5-A6
Triangle West	A6
Tyndall Avenue	B6-B7
Tyndall's Park Road	A7-B7
Union Road	C2
Union Street	D5-D6
Unity Street	F5
University Road	A6-B6
Upper Byron Place	A5
Upper Maudlin Street	C6
Upper Perry Hill	B2
Upper York Street	D7-E7
Upton Road	A1-A2
Victoria Street	D5-D4-E3-E4
Wade Street	F6
Walker Street	C7
Wapping Road	C3
Warden Road	B1-C1
Waterloo Road	F5
Wellington Road	E6-F6-F7
Wells Road	F1-F2
Welsh Back	D3-D4-D5
West Park	A7-A8
West Street	F5-F6
Whitehouse Lane	C1-D1
Whitehouse Street	D1-D2
Whiteladies Road	A6-A7-A8
Wilder Street	D7-E7
William Street	E8-F8
Wilson Place	F7
Wilson Street	E7-F7
Windmill Close	D1
Wine Street	D5
Woodland Road	B5-B6-B7-B8
York Road	D2-E2-F2
York Street	E6-E7

HTT

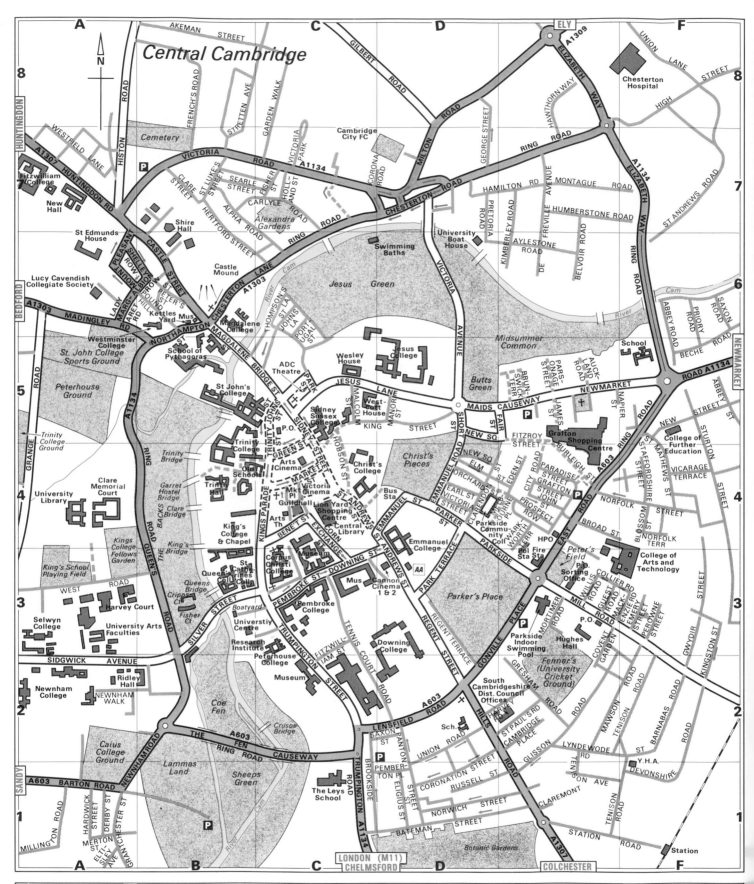

Central Cambridge

Cambridge

Few views in England, perhaps even in Europe, are as memorable as that from Cambridge's Backs towards the colleges. Dominating the scene, in every sense, is King's College Chapel. One of the finest Gothic buildings anywhere, it was built in three stages from 1446 to 1515.

No one would dispute that the chapel is Cambridge's masterpiece, but there are dozens of buildings here that would be the finest in any other town or city. Most are colleges, or are attached to colleges, and it is the university which permeates every aspect of Cambridge's landscape and life. In all there are 33 university colleges in the city, and nearly all have buildings and features of great interest. Guided tours of the colleges are available.

Cambridge can provide a complete history of English architecture. The oldest surviving building is the tower of St Benet's Church dating back to before the Norman Conquest, and its most famous church is the Church of the Holy Sepulchre, one of only four round churches of its kind.

Of the many notable museums in Cambridge, the Fitzwilliam Museum contains some of the best collections of ceramics, paintings, coins, medals and Egyptian, Greek and Roman antiquities outside London.

Huntingdon and Ely are both within easy driving distance of Cambridge.

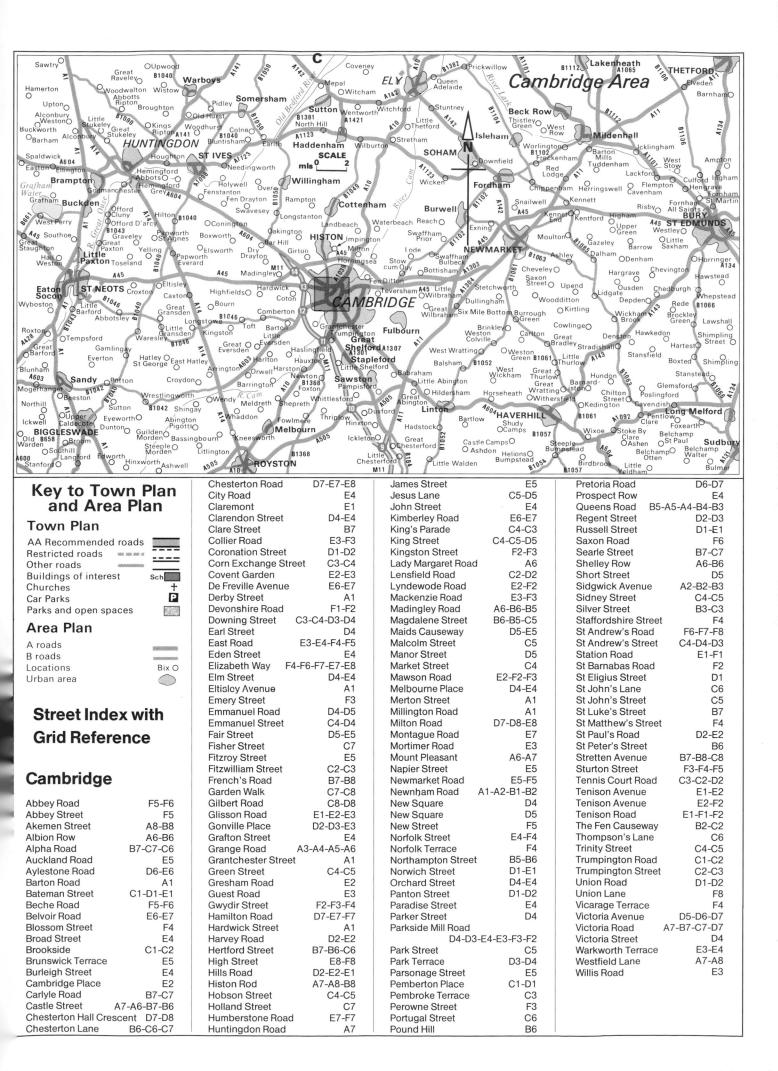

Key to Town Plan and Area Plan

Town Plan

AA Recommended roads
Restricted roads
Other roads
Buildings of interest — Sch
Churches — +
Car Parks — P
Parks and open spaces

Area Plan

A roads
B roads
Locations — Bix ○
Urban area

Street Index with Grid Reference

Cambridge

Abbey Road	F5-F6
Abbey Street	F5
Akemen Street	A8-B8
Albion Row	A6-B6
Alpha Road	B7-C7-C6
Auckland Road	E5
Aylestone Road	D6-E6
Barton Road	A1
Bateman Street	C1-D1-E1
Beche Road	F5-F6
Belvoir Road	E6-E7
Blossom Street	F4
Broad Street	E4
Brookside	C1-C2
Brunswick Terrace	E5
Burleigh Street	E4
Cambridge Place	E2
Carlyle Road	B7-C7
Castle Street	A7-A6-B7-B6
Chesterton Hall Crescent	D7-D8
Chesterton Lane	B6-C6-C7
Chesterton Road	D7-E7-E8
City Road	E4
Claremont	E1
Clarendon Street	D4-E4
Clare Street	B7
Collier Road	E3-F3
Coronation Street	D1-D2
Corn Exchange Street	C3-C4
Covent Garden	E2-E3
De Freville Avenue	E6-E7
Derby Street	A1
Devonshire Road	F1-F2
Downing Street	C3-C4-D3-D4
Earl Street	D4
East Road	E3-E4-F4-F5
Eden Street	E4
Elizabeth Way	F4-F6-F7-E7-E8
Elm Street	D4-E4
Eltisley Avenue	A1
Emery Street	F3
Emmanuel Road	D4-D5
Emmanuel Street	C4-D4
Fair Street	D5-E5
Fisher Street	C7
Fitzroy Street	E5
Fitzwilliam Street	C2-C3
French's Road	B7-B8
Garden Walk	C7-C8
Gilbert Road	C8-D8
Glisson Road	E1-E2-E3
Gonville Place	D2-D3-E3
Grafton Street	E4
Grange Road	A3-A4-A5-A6
Grantchester Street	A1
Green Street	C4-C5
Gresham Road	E2
Guest Road	E3
Gwydir Street	F2-F3-F4
Hamilton Road	D7-E7-F7
Hardwick Street	A1
Harvey Road	D2-E2
Hertford Street	B7-B6-C6
High Street	E8-F8
Hills Road	D2-E2-E1
Histon Rod	A7-A8-B8
Hobson Street	C4-C5
Holland Street	C7
Humberstone Road	E7-F7
Huntingdon Road	A7
James Street	E5
Jesus Lane	C5-D5
John Street	E4
Kimberley Road	E6-E7
King's Parade	C4-C3
King Street	C4-C5-D5
Kingston Street	F2-F3
Lady Margaret Road	A6
Lensfield Road	C2-D2
Lyndewode Road	E2-F2
Mackenzie Road	E3-F3
Madingley Road	A6-B6-B5
Magdalene Street	B6-B5-C5
Maids Causeway	D5-E5
Malcolm Street	C5
Manor Street	D5
Market Street	C4
Mawson Road	E2-F2-F3
Melbourne Place	D4-E4
Merton Street	A1
Millington Road	A1
Milton Road	D7-D8-E8
Montague Road	E7
Mortimer Road	E3
Mount Pleasant	A6-A7
Napier Street	E5
Newmarket Road	E5-F5
Newnham Road	A1-A2-B1-B2
New Square	D4
New Square	D5
New Street	F5
Norfolk Street	E4-F4
Norfolk Terrace	F4
Northampton Street	B5-B6
Norwich Street	D1-E1
Orchard Street	D4-E4
Panton Street	D1-D2
Paradise Street	E4
Parker Street	D4
Parkside Mill Road	D4-D3-E4-E3-F3-F2
Park Street	C5
Park Terrace	D3-D4
Parsonage Street	E5
Pemberton Place	C1-D1
Pembroke Terrace	C3
Perowne Street	F3
Portugal Street	C6
Pound Hill	B6
Pretoria Road	D6-D7
Prospect Row	E4
Queens Road	B5-A5-A4-B4-B3
Regent Street	D2-D3
Russell Street	D1-E1
Saxon Road	F6
Searle Street	B7-C7
Shelley Row	A6-B6
Short Street	D5
Sidgwick Avenue	A2-B2-B3
Sidney Street	C4-C5
Silver Street	B3-C3
Staffordshire Street	F4
St Andrew's Road	F6-F7-F8
St Andrew's Street	C4-D4-D3
Station Road	E1-F1
St Barnabas Road	F2
St Eligius Street	D1
St John's Lane	C6
St John's Street	C5
St Luke's Street	B7
St Matthew's Street	F4
St Paul's Road	D2-E2
St Peter's Street	B6
Stretten Avenue	B7-B8-C8
Sturton Street	F3-F4-F5
Tennis Court Road	C3-C2-D2
Tenison Avenue	E1-E2
Tenison Avenue	E2-F2
Tenison Road	E1-F1-F2
The Fen Causeway	B2-C2
Thompson's Lane	C6
Trinity Street	C4-C5
Trumpington Road	C1-C2
Trumpington Street	C2-C3
Union Road	D1-D2
Union Lane	E7
Vicarage Terrace	F4
Victoria Avenue	D5-D6-D7
Victoria Road	A7-B7-C7-D7
Victoria Street	D4
Warkworth Terrace	E3-E4
Westfield Lane	A7-A8
Willis Road	E3

141

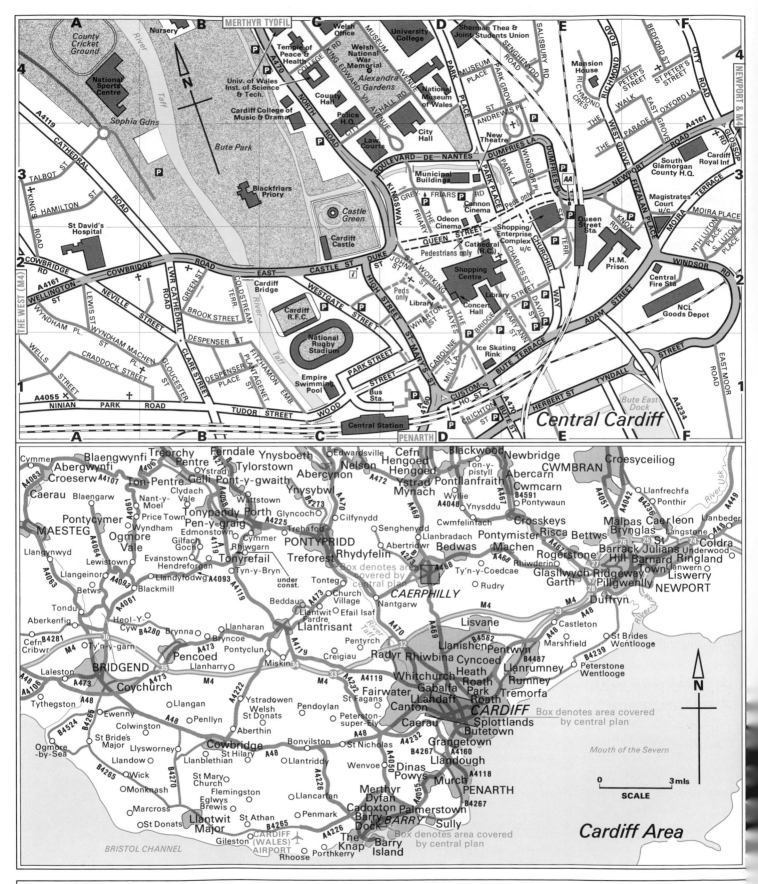

Central Cardiff

Cardiff Area

Cardiff

Strategically important to both the Romans and the Normans, Cardiff slipped from prominence in medieval times and remained a quiet market town in a remote area until it was transformed – almost overnight – by the effects of the Industrial Revolution. The valleys of South Wales were a principal source of iron and coal – raw materials which helped to change the shape and course of

the 19th-century world. Cardiff became a teeming export centre; by the end of the 19th century it was the largest coal-exporting city in the world.

Close to the castle – an exciting place with features from Roman times to the 19th century – is the city's civic centre – a fine concourse of buildings dating largely from the early part of the 20th century. Among them is the National Museum of Wales – a superb collection of art and antiquities from Wales and around the world.

Barry has sandy beaches, landscaped gardens and parks, entertainment arcades and funfairs. Like Cardiff it grew as a result of the demand for coal and steel, but now its dock complex is involved in the petrochemical and oil industries.

Caerphilly is famous for two things – a castle and cheese. The cheese is no longer made here, but the 13th-century castle, slighted by Cromwell, still looms above its moat. No castle in Britain – except Windsor – is larger.

142

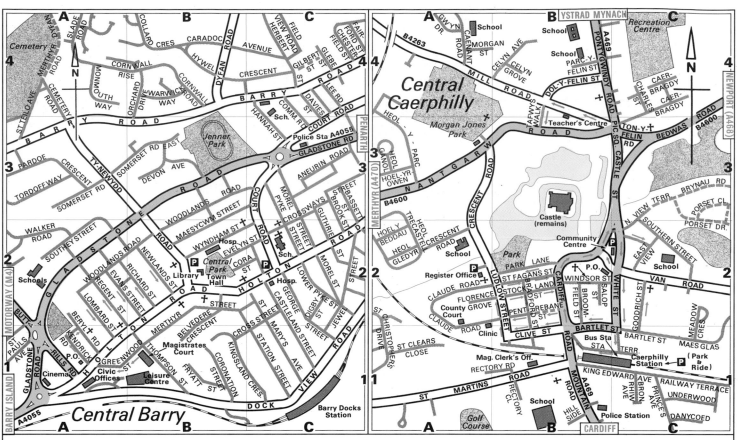

Central Barry / Central Caerphilly (maps)

LEGEND

Town Plan

AA recommended route
Restricted roads
Other roads
Buildings of interest — Cinema 🎦
Car parks — 🅿
Parks and open spaces — ▲
One way streets — ⌐

Area Plan

A roads
B roads
Locations — Glyncoch ○
Urban area

Street Index with Grid Reference

Cardiff

Street	Grid
Adam Street	E1-E2-F2
Bedford Street	F4
Boulevard de Nantes	C3-D3
Bridge Street	D1-D2-E2
Brook Street	B2
Bute Street	D1-E1
Bute Terrace	D1-E1
Caroline Street	D1
Castle Street	C2
Cathedral Street	A4-A3-B3-B2-A2
Charles Street	D2-E2
Churchill Way	E2-E3
City Hall Road	C3-C4-D4
City Road	F4
Clare Street	B1
Coldstream Terrace	B2
College Road	C4
Cowbridge Road	A2
Cowbridge Road East	A2-B2-C2
Craddock Street	A1-B1
Crichton Street	D1
Customhouse Street	D1
David Street	E2
Despenser Place	B1
Despenser Street	B1
Duke Street	C2-D2
Dumfries Lane	D3-E3
Dumfries Place	E3
East Grove	F4-F3
East Moor Road	F1
Fitzalan Place	F3-F2
Fitzhamon Embankment	B1-C1
Glossop Road	F3
Gloucester Street	B1
Green Street	B2
Greyfriars Road	D3
Hamilton Street	A3
Herbert Street	E1
High Street	C2-D2
King Edward VII Avenue	C4-D4-D3-C3
King's Road	A2-A3
Kingsway	C3-D3-D2
Knox Road	E3-F3-F2
Lewis Street	A2
Lower Cathedral Road	B1-B2
Machen Place	A1-B1
Mary Ann Street	E1-E2
Mill Lane	D1
Moira Place	F3
Moira Terrace	F2-F3
Museum Avenue	C4-D4
Museum Place	D4
Neville Street	A2-B2-B1
Newport Road	E3-F3-F4
Ninian Park Road	A1-B1
North Luton Place	F2-F3
North Road	B4-C4-C3
Oxford Lane	F4
Park Grove	D4-E4
Park Lane	D3-E3
Park Place	D4-D3-E3
Park Street	C1-D1
Plantagenet Street	B1-C1
Queen Street	D2-D3
Richmond Crescent	E4
Richmond Road	E4
St Andrew's Place	D4-E4
St John Street	D2
St Mary's Street	D1-D2
St Peter's Street	E4-F4
Salisbury Road	E4
Senghenydd Road	D4-E4
South Luton Place	F2-F3
Station Terrace	E2-E3
The Friary	D2-D3
The Hayes	D1-D2
The Parade	E3-F3-F4
The Walk	E3-E4-F4
Talbot Street	A3
Tudor Street	B1-C1
Tyndall Street	E1-F1
Wellington Street	A2
Wells Street	A1
Westgate Street	C2-D2-D1
West Grove	E4-E3-F3
Wharton Street	D2
Windsor Place	E3
Windsor Road	F2
Wood Street	C1-D1
Working Street	D2
Wyndham Place	A2
Wyndham Street	A1-A2

Barry

Street	Grid
Aneurin Road	C3
Barry Road	A3-A4-B3-B4-C4
Bassett Street	C2-C3
Belvedere Crescent	B1-B2
Beryl Road	A1-A2
Brook Street	C2-C3
Buttrills Road	A1-A2
Caradoc Avenue	B4-C4
Castleland Street	C1-C2
Cemetery Road	A3-A4
Chesterfield Street	C4
Collard Crescent	B4
Commercial Road	C3-C4
Cora Street	B2-C2
Cornwall Rise	A3-A4
Cornwall Road	B4
Coronation Street	B1
Cross Street	B1-C1-C2
Crossways Street	C2-C3
Court Road	C2-C3-C4
Davies Street	C3-C4
Devon Avenue	B3
Digby Street	C2
Dock View Road	B1-C1-C2
Dyfan Road	B4
Evans Street	A2-B2
Evelyn Street	B2-C2
Fairford Street	C4
Field View Road	C4
Fryatt Street	B1
George Street	C1-C2
Gilbert Street	C4
Gladstone Road	A1-A2-B2-B3-C3
Glebe Street	C4
Greenwood Street	A1-B1
Guthrie Street	C3-C2
Hannah Street	C4-C3
Herbert Street	C3
Holton Road	A1-B1-B2-C2
Hywel Crescent	B4-C4
Jewel Street	C1-C2
Kendrick Road	A1
Kingsland Crescent	B1-C1
Lee Road	C4
Lombard Street	A1-A2
Lower Pyke Street	C2
Maesycwm Street	B2-B3-C3
Merthyr Dyfan Road	A4
Merthyr Street	B1-B2-C2
Monmouth Way	A4
Morel Street	C2-C3
Newlands Street	B2
Orchard Drive	B3-B4
Pardoe Crescent	A3
Pyke Street	C3-C2
Regent Street	A2-B2
Richard Street	A2-B2
St Mary's Avenue	C1-C2
St Pauls Avenue	A1
St Teilo Avenue	A3-A4
Slade Road	A4
Somerset Road	A3
Somerset Road East	A3-B3
Southey Street	A2-A3
Station Street	C1
Thompson Street	B1
Tordoff Way	A3
Ty-Newydd Road	A3-B3-B2
Walker Road	A2
Warwick Way	B4
Woodlands Road	A2-B2-B3-C3
Wyndham Street	B2-C2

Caerphilly

Street	Grid
Bartlet Street	B2-B1-C1
Bedwas Road	C3-C4
Bradford Street	B1-B2
Broomfield Street	B2
Bronrhiw Avenue	C1
Brynau Road	C3
Caenant Road	A4
Caer Bragdy	C4
Cardiff Road	B1-B2
Castle Street	C3
Celyn Avenue	B4
Celyn Grove	B4
Charles Street	C4
Claude Road	A1-A2-B2
Clive Street	B1-B2
Crescent Rod	A2-A3-B3
Danycoed	C1
Dol-y-Felen Street	B4
East View	C2
Florence Grove	A2-B2
Goodrich Street	C1-C2
Gwyn Drive	A4
Heol Ganol	A3
Heol Gledyr	A2
Heol Trecastell	A2-A3
Hillside	B1
Heol y Beddau	A2
Heol-yr-Owen	A3
King Edward Avenue	B1-C1
Ludlow Street	A2-B2-B1
Maes Glas	C1
Meadow Crescent	C1-C2
Mill Road	A4-B4-B3
Morgan Street	A4-B4
Mountain Road	B1
Nantgarw Road	A3-B3
North View Terrace	C2-C3
Parc-y-Felin Street	B4
Park Lane	B2
Pentrebone Street	B2
Piccadilly Square	C3
Pontygwindy Road	B4-C4
Porset Close	C3
Porset Drive	C2-C3
Prince's Avenue	C1
Railway Terrace	C1
Rectory Road	A1-B1
Rectory Close	B1
St Christopher's Drive	A1-A2
St Clears Close	A1
St Fagans Street	B2
St Martins Road	A1-B1
Salop Street	B2
Southern Street	C2-C3
Station Terrace	B1-C1
Stockland Street	B2
Tafwy Walk	B3-B4
Ton-y-Felin Road	C3
Underwood	C1
Van Road	C2
White Street	C2
Windsor Street	B2

LTH

143

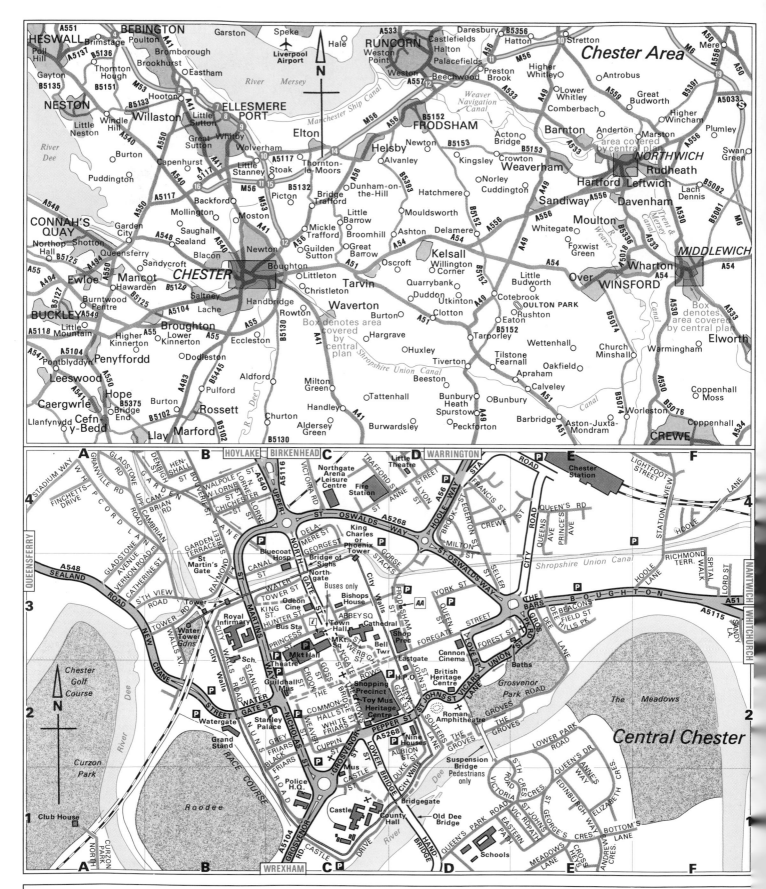

Chester

Chester is the only English city to have preserved the complete circuit of its Roman and medieval walls. On the west side, the top of the walls is now at pavement level, but on the other three sides the walk along the ramparts is remarkable. Two of the old watchtowers contain small museums: the Water Tower, built to protect the old river port, displays relics of medieval Chester; King Charles's Tower, from which Charles I watched the defeat of the Royalist army at the Battle of Rowton Moor in 1645, portrays Chester's role in the Civil War.

Looking down from the top of the Eastgate, crowned with the ornate and gaily-coloured Jubilee Clock erected in 1897, the view down the main street, the old Roman *Via Principalis*, reveals a dazzling display of the black-and-white timbered buildings for which Chester is famous. One of these, Providence House, bears the inscription 'God's Providence is Mine Inheritance', carved in thanks for sparing the survivors of the plague of 1647 that ravaged the city.

On either side of Eastgate, Watergate and Bridge Street are the Rows, a feature unique to Chester, and dating back at least to the 13th century. These covered galleries of shops, raised up at first-floor level, protected pedestrians from weather and traffic. Chester's magnificent cathedral has beautifully carved choir stalls.

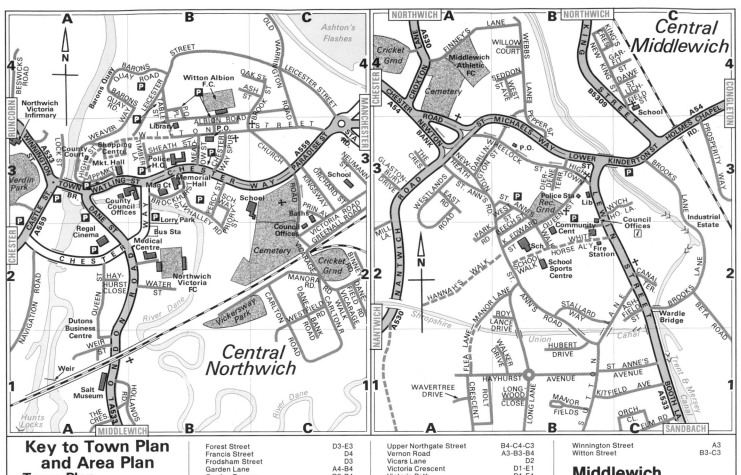

Key to Town Plan and Area Plan

Town Plan

AA Recommended roads	
Other roads	
Restricted roads	
Buildings of interest	College
AA Service Centre	AA
Car Parks	P
Parks and open spaces	
Churches	+

Area Plan

A roads	
B roads	
Locations	DuddonO
Urban area	
Locks	

Street Index with Grid Reference

Chester

Abbey Square	C3
Albion Street	D2
Andrews Crescent	E1
Anne's Way	E2-E1
Beaconsfield Street	E3
Black Friars	C1-C2
Bottom's Lane	E1-F1
Boughton	E3-F3
Bouverie Street	B4
Bridge Street	C2
Brook Street	D4
Cambrian Road	A4-B4
Canal Street	B3-C3
Castle Drive	C1
Castle Street	C1
Catherine Street	A3-B3
Chichester Street	B4-C4
City Road	E3-E4
City Walls Road	B3-B2
Commonhall Street	C2
Crewe Street	D4-E4
Crook Street	C2
Cross Heys	E1
Cuppin Street	C2
Curzon Park North	A1
Dee Hills Park	E3
Dee Lane	E3
Delamere Street	C4
Denbigh Street	B4
Duke Street	D1-D2
Eastern Path	D1-E1
Edinburgh Way	E1
Egerton Street	D4
Elizabeth Crescent	E1-E2
Finchetts Drive	A4
Foregate Street	D3

Forest Street	D3-E3
Francis Street	D4
Frodsham Street	D3
Garden Lane	A4-B4
Garden Terrace	B3-B4
George Street	C3-C4
Gladstone Avenue	A3-A4
Gladstone Road	A4
Gorse Stacks	C4-C3-D3
Goss Street	C2
Granville Road	A4
Grey Friars	C2
Grosvenor Park Road	E3
Grosvenor Road	C1
Grosvenor Street	C1-C2
Groves Road	D2-E2
Handbridge	D1
Henshall Street	B4
Hoole Lane	F3-F4
Hoole Way	D4
Hunter Street	B3-C3
King Street	B3-C3
Lightfoot Street	E4-F4
Lord Street	F3
Lorne Street	B4
Lower Bridge Street	C2-C1-D1
Lower Park Road	D2-E2
Love Street	D3
Lyon Street	D4
Meadows Lane	E1
Milton Street	D4
New Crane Street	A3-B3-B2
Newgate Street	D2
Nicholas Street	C2-C1
Northgate Street	C3-C2
North Lorne Street	B4
Nuns Road	B2-B1-C1
Pepper Street	C2-D2
Princess Street	C3
Prince's Avenue	E4
Queens Avenue	E4
Queen's Drive	E1-E2
Queen's Park Road	D1-E1
Queen's Road	E4
Queen Street	D3
Raymond Street	B3-B4
Richmond Terrace	F4
St Anne Street	C4-D4
St Georges Crescent	E1
St Johns Road	E1
St Johns Street	D2
St John Street	D3-D2
St Martins Way	B4-B3-C3-B2-C2
St Oswalds Way	C4-D4-D3
St Werburgh Street	C3
Sealand Road	A3
Sellier Street	D3
Souters Lane	D2
South Crescent Road	D2-E2-E1
South View Road	A3-B3
Spittal Walk	F4-F3
Stadium Way	A4
Stanley Street	B2
Station Road	D4-E4
Station View	F4
The Bars	E3
The Groves	D2-E2
The Rows	C2
Tower Road	B3
Trafford Street	C4-D4
Union Street	D2-D3-E3
Upper Cambrian Road	A4-B4-B3

Upper Northgate Street	B4-C4-C3
Vernon Road	A3-B3-B4
Vicars Lane	D2
Victoria Crescent	D1-E1
Victoria Path	D1-E1
Victoria's Road	C4
Walls Avenue	B3-B2
Walpole Street	B4
Watergate Street	B2-C2
Water Tower Street	B3-C3
Weaver Street	C2
West Lorne Street	B4
White Friars	C2
Whipcord Lane	A4-B4
York Street	D3

Northwich

Albion Road	B3
Apple Market	A3
Ash Street	B4-C4
Barons Quay Road	A4-B4
Beswicks Road	A4
Binney Road	C2
Brockhurst Street	B3
Brook Street	B3-C3-C4
Carlton Road	C2-C1
Castle Street	A2-A3
Chester Way	A2-B2-B3-C3
Chester Way Spur	B3
Church Road	C3
Danebank Road	C2-C1
Danefield Road	C2
Dane Street	A3-A2
Greenall Road	C2-C3
Hayhurst Close	A2
High Street	A3
Hollands Road	A1-B1
Kingsway	C3
Leicester Street	B3-B4
Lock Street	A3
London Road	A1-A2-B2
Manora Road	C2
Meadow Street	B3
Navigation Road	A1-A2
Neumann Street	C3
Oak Street	B4-C4
Old Warrington Road	C4-C3
Orchard Street	C3
Paradise Street	C3
Percy Street	B3
Post Office Place	B4-B3
Princes Avenue	C3
Priory Street	B2-B3
Queen Street	A2
School Way	B3
Sheath Street	B3
Station Road	C3
The Crescent	A1
Tabley Street	B4-B3
Timber Lane	B3
Town Bridge	A3
Vicarage Road	C2
Vicarage Walk	C2
Victoria Road	C2-C3
Water Street	B2
Watling Street	A3-B3
Weaver Way	A3-B3-B4
Weir Street	A1
Wesley Place	C3
Westfield Road	C2
Whalley Road	B3-B2

Winnington Street	A3
Witton Street	B3-C3

Middlewich

Ashfield Street	C2
Beech Road	B2-B3
Beta Road	C2-C1
Booth Lane	C1
Brooks Lane	C3-C2
Canal Terrace	C2
Chester Road	A4-A3
Croxton Lane	A4
Darlington Street	A3-B3
Dawe Street	C4
Dierdene Terrace	B3
East Road	A3
Elm Road	C1
Finney's Lane	A4-B4
Flea Lane	A1
Garfit Street	B4-C4
Glastonbury Drive	A3
Hannah's Walk	A2-B2
Hauhurst Avenue	A1-B1
High Town	B3
Holmes Chapel Road	C3-C4
Hubert Drive	B1
Kinderton Street	B3-C3
King Edward Street	B2
King's Crescent	B4-C4
King Street	B4-C4-C3
Kittfield Avenue	B1-C1
Lewin Street	B3-B2-C2-C1
Lichfield Street	C4
Long Lane	B1
Longwood Close	B2
Lower Street	B3
Manor Fields	B1
Manor Lane	A2-B2
Mill Lane	A2
Nantwich Road	A1-A2-A3
New King Street	B4-C4
Newton Bank	A4-A3
Newton Heath	A3
Orchard Close	C1
Park Road	A2-B2
Pepper Street	B4-B3
Prosperity Way	C3
Queen Street	B2-B3
Rolt Crescent	A1-B1
Roy Lance Drive	B2
St Anne's Avenue	B1-C1
St Ann's Road	A3-B3-B2-B1
St Ann's Walk	B2-B3
St Michaels Way	A3-B3
School Walk	B2
Seddon Street	B4
Southway	B3
Stallard Way	B2
Sutton Lane	B1-B2-C2
The Crescent	A3
Walker Drive	B1
Wavertree Drive	A1
Webbs Lane	B4
West Avenue	B4
Westlands Road	A3-A2
West Street	B3
Wheelock Street	A3-B3
White Horse Alley	B2
Willow Court	B4
Wych House Lane	B3-C3

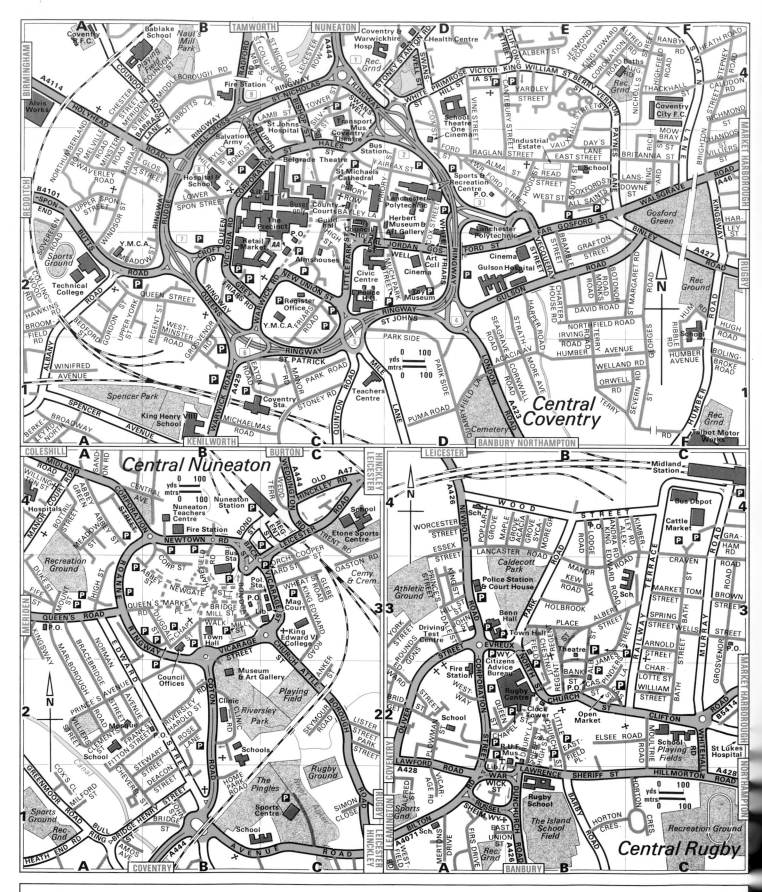

Coventry

Few British towns were as battered by the Blitz as Coventry. A raid in November 1940 flattened most of the city and left the lovely cathedral church a gaunt shell with only the tower and spire still standing. Rebuilding started almost immediately. Symbolising the creation of the new from the ashes of the old is Sir Basil Spence's cathedral, completed in 1962 beside the bombed ruins.

A few medieval buildings have survived intact in the city. St Mary's Guildhall is a finely restored 14th-century building with an attractive minstrels' gallery. Whitefriars Monastery now serves as a local museum. The Herbert Art Gallery and Museum has several collections. Coventry is an important manufacturing centre – most notably for cars – and it is also a university city with the fine campus of the University of Warwick some four miles from the centre.

Nuneaton is an industrial town to the north of Coventry with two distinguished old churches – St Nicholas' and St Mary's. Like Coventry it was badly damaged in the war and its centre has been rebuilt.

Rugby was no more than a sleepy market town until the arrival of the railway. Of course it did have the famous Rugby School, founded in 1567 and one of the country's foremost educational establishments. The railway brought industry – still the town's mainstay.

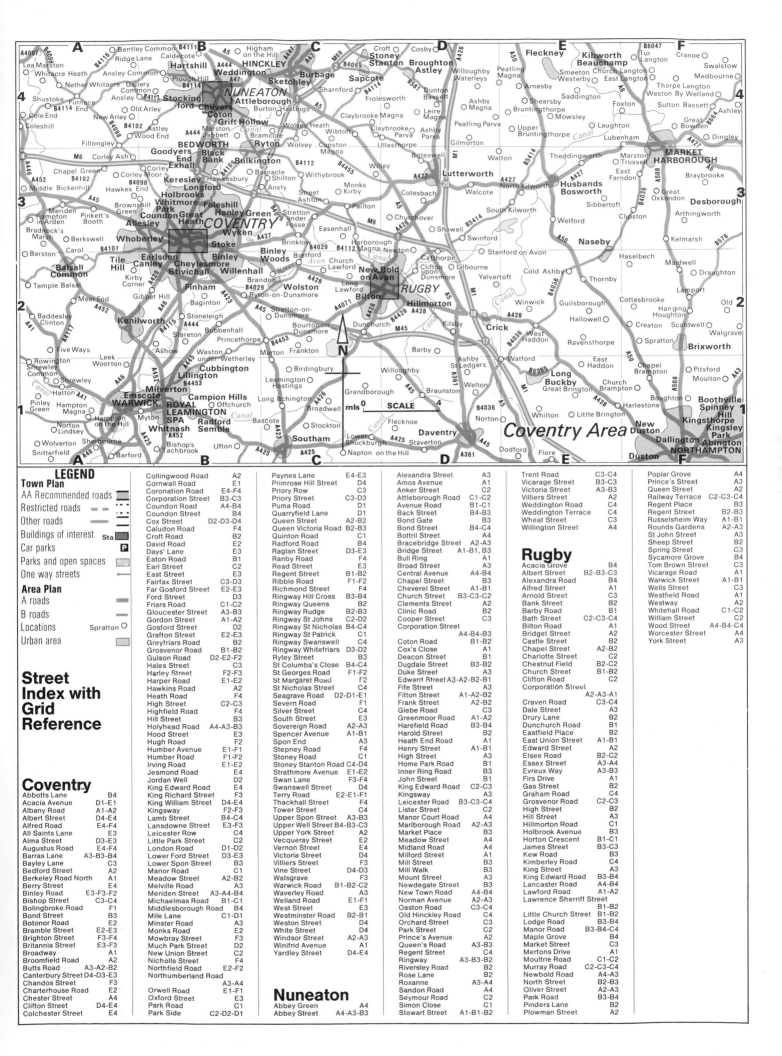

LEGEND

Town Plan

AA Recommended roads	
Restricted roads	
Other roads	
Buildings of interest	Sta.
Car parks	P
Parks and open spaces	
One way streets	

Area Plan

A roads	
B roads	
Locations	Spratton O
Urban area	

Street Index with Grid Reference

Coventry

Abbotts Lane	B4
Acacia Avenue	D1-E1
Albany Road	A1-A2
Albert Street	D4-E4
Alfred Road	E4-F4
All Saints Lane	E3
Alma Street	D3-E3
Augustus Road	E4-F4
Barras Lane	A3-B3-B4
Bayley Lane	C3
Bedford Street	E4
Berkeley Road North	A1
Berry Street	E4
Binley Road	E3-F3-F2
Bishop Street	C3-C4
Bolingbroke Road	F1
Bond Street	B3
Botonor Road	E2
Bramble Street	E2-E3
Brighton Street	F3-F4
Britannia Street	E3-F3
Broadway	A1
Broomfield Road	A2
Butts Road	A3-A2-B2
Canterbury Street	D4-D3-E3
Chandos Street	F3
Charterhouse Road	E2
Chester Street	A3
Clifton Street	D4-E4
Colchester Street	E4
Collingwood Road	A2
Cornwall Road	E1
Coronation Road	E4-F4
Corporation Street	B3-C3
Coundon Road	A4-B4
Coundon Street	B4
Cox Street	D2-D3-D4
Caludon Road	F4
Croft Road	B2
David Road	E2
Days' Lane	E3
Eaton Road	B1
Earl Street	C2
East Street	E3
Fairfax Street	C3-D3
Far Gosford Street	E2-E3
Ford Street	D3
Friars Road	C1-C2
Gloucester Street	A3-B3
Gordon Street	A1-A2
Gosford Street	D2
Grafton Street	E2-E3
Greyfriars Road	B2
Grosvenor Road	B1-B2
Gulson Road	D2-E2-F2
Hales Street	C3
Harley Street	F2-F3
Harper Road	E1-E2
Hawkins Road	A2
Heath Road	F4
High Street	C2-C3
Highfield Road	F4
Hill Street	B3
Holyhead Road	A4-A3-B3
Hood Street	E3
Hugh Road	F2
Humber Avenue	E1-F1
Humber Road	F1-F2
Irving Road	E1-E2
Jesmond Road	E4
Jordan Well	D2
King Edward Road	E4
King Richard Street	F3
King William Street	D4-E4
Kingsway	F2-F3
Lamb Street	B4-C4
Lansdowne Street	E3-F3
Leicester Row	C4
Little Park Street	C2
London Road	D1-D2
Lower Ford Street	D3-E3
Lower Spon Street	B3
Manor Road	C1
Meadow Street	A2-B2
Melville Road	A3
Meriden Street	A3-A4-B4
Michaelmas Road	B1-C1
Middlesborough Road	B4
Mile Lane	C1-D1
Minster Road	A3
Monks Road	E2
Mowbray Street	F3
Much Park Street	D2
New Union Street	C2
Nicholls Street	F4
Northfield Road	E2-F2
Northumberland Road	A3-A4
Orwell Road	E1-F1
Oxford Street	E3
Park Road	C1
Park Side	C2-D2-D1

Paynes Lane	E4-E3
Primrose Hill Street	D4
Priory Row	C3
Priory Street	C3-D3
Puma Road	D1
Quarryfield Lane	D1
Queen Street	A2-B2
Queen Victoria Road	B2-B3
Quinton Road	C1
Radford Road	B4
Raglan Street	D3-E3
Ranby Road	F4
Read Street	E4
Regent Street	B1-B2
Ribble Road	F1-F2
Richmond Street	F4
Ringway Hill Cross	B3-B4
Ringway Queens	B2
Ringway Rudge	B2-B3
Ringway St Johns	C2-D2
Ringway St Nicholas	B4-C4
Ringway St Patrick	C1
Ringway Swanswell	C4
Ringway Whitefriars	D3-D2
Ryley Street	B3
St Columba's Close	B4-C4
St Georges Road	F1-F2
St Margaret Road	F2
St Nicholas Street	A3
Seagrave Road	D2-D1-E1
Severn Road	F1
Silver Street	C4
South Street	E3
Sovereign Road	A2-A3
Spencer Avenue	A1-B1
Spon End	A3
Stepney Road	F4
Stoney Road	C1
Stoney Stanton Road	C4-D4
Strathmore Avenue	E1-E2
Swan Lane	F3-F4
Swanswell Street	D4
Terry Road	E2-E1-F1
Thackhall Street	F4
Tower Street	C4
Upper Spon Street	A3-B3
Upper Well Street	B4-B3-C3
Upper York Street	A2
Vecqueray Street	E2
Vernon Street	E4
Victoria Street	D4
Villiers Street	F3
Vine Street	D4-D3
Walsgrave	F3
Warwick Road	B1-B2-C2
Waverley Road	A3
Welland Road	E1-F1
West Street	E3
Westminster Road	B2-B1
Weston Street	D4
White Street	D4
Windsor Street	A2-A3
Winifrid Avenue	A1
Yardley Street	D4-E4

Nuneaton

Abbey Green	A4
Abbey Street	A4-A3-B3
Alexandra Street	A3
Amos Avenue	A1
Anker Street	C2
Attleborough Road	C1-C2
Avenue Road	B1-C1
Back Street	B4-B3
Bond Gate	B3
Bond Street	B4-C4
Bottril Road	A3
Bracebridge Street	A2-A3
Bridge Street	A1-B1, B3
Bull Ring	A1
Broad Street	A3
Central Avenue	A4-B4
Chapel Street	B3
Cheverel Street	A1-B1
Church Street	B3-C3-C2
Clements Street	A2
Clinic Road	B2
Cooper Street	C3
Corporation Street	A4-B4-B3
Coton Road	B1-B2
Cox's Close	A1
Deacon Street	B1
Dugdale Street	B3-B2
Duke Street	A3
Edward Street	A3-A2-B2-B1
Fife Street	A2
Fitton Street	A1-A2-B2
Frank Street	A2-B2
Glebe Road	C3
Greenmoor Road	A1-A2
Harefield Road	B3-B4
Harold Street	B2
Heath End Road	A1
Henry Street	A1-B1
High Street	A3
Home Park Road	B1
Inner Ring Road	B3
John Street	B1
King Edward Road	C2-C3
Kingsway	A3
Leicester Road	B3-C3-C4
Lister Street	C2
Manor Court Road	A4
Marlborough Road	A2-A3
Market Place	B3
Meadow Street	A4
Midland Road	A4
Milford Street	A1
Mill Street	B3
Mill Walk	B3
Mount Street	A3
Newdegate Street	B3
New Town Road	A4-B4
Norman Avenue	A1
Oaston Road	C3-C4
Old Hinckley Road	C4
Orchard Street	C3
Park Street	C2
Prince's Avenue	A2
Queen's Road	A3-B3
Regent Street	C3
Ringway	A3-B3-B2
Riversley Road	B2
Rose Lane	B2
Roxanne	A3-A4
Sandon Road	A4
Seymour Road	C2
Simon Close	C1
Stewart Street	A1-B1-B2

Trent Road	C3-C4
Vicarage Street	B3-C3
Victoria Street	A3-B3
Villiers Street	A2
Weddington Road	C4
Weddington Terrace	C4
Wheat Street	C3
Willington Street	A4

Rugby

Acacia Grove	B4
Albert Street	B2-B3-C3
Alexandra Road	B4
Alfred Street	A1
Arnold Street	C3
Bank Street	B2
Barby Road	B1
Bath Street	C2-C3-C4
Bilton Road	A1
Bridget Street	A2
Castle Street	B2
Chapel Street	A2-B2
Charlotte Street	C2
Chestnut Field	B2-C2
Church Street	B1-B2
Clifton Road	C2
Corporation Street	A2-A3-A1
Craven Road	C3-C4
Dale Street	A3
Drury Lane	B2
Dunchurch Road	B1
Eastfield Place	B2
East Union Street	A1-B1
Edward Street	A2
Elsee Road	B2-C2
Essex Street	A3-A4
Evreux Way	A3-B3
Firs Drive	A1
Gas Street	B2
Graham Road	C4
Grosvenor Road	C2-C3
High Street	B2
Hill Street	A3
Hillmorton Road	C1
Holbrook Avenue	B3
Horton Crescent	B1-C1
James Street	B3-C3
Kew Road	B1
Kimberley Road	C4
King Street	B3
King Edward Road	B3-B4
Lancaster Road	A4-B4
Lawford Road	A1-A2
Lawrence Sherriff Street	B1-B2
Little Church Street	B1-B2
Lodge Road	B3-B4
Manor Road	B3-B4-C4
Maple Grove	B4
Market Street	C3
Mertons Drive	A1
Moultrie Road	C1-C2
Murray Road	C2-C3-C4
Newbold Road	A4-A3
North Street	B2-B3
Oliver Street	A2-A3
Park Road	B3-B4
Pinders Lane	B2
Plowman Street	A2

Poplar Grove	A4
Prince's Street	A3
Queen Street	A2
Railway Terrace	C2-C3-C4
Regent Place	B3
Regent Street	B2-B3
Russelsheim Way	A1-B1
Rounds Gardens	A2-A3
St John Street	A3
Sheep Street	B2
Spring Street	C3
Sycamore Grove	B4
Tom Brown Street	C3
Vicarage Road	A1
Warwick Street	A1-B1
Wells Street	C3
Westfield Road	A1
Westway	A2
Whitehall Road	C1-C2
William Street	C2
Wood Street	A4-B4-C4
Worcester Street	A4
York Street	A3

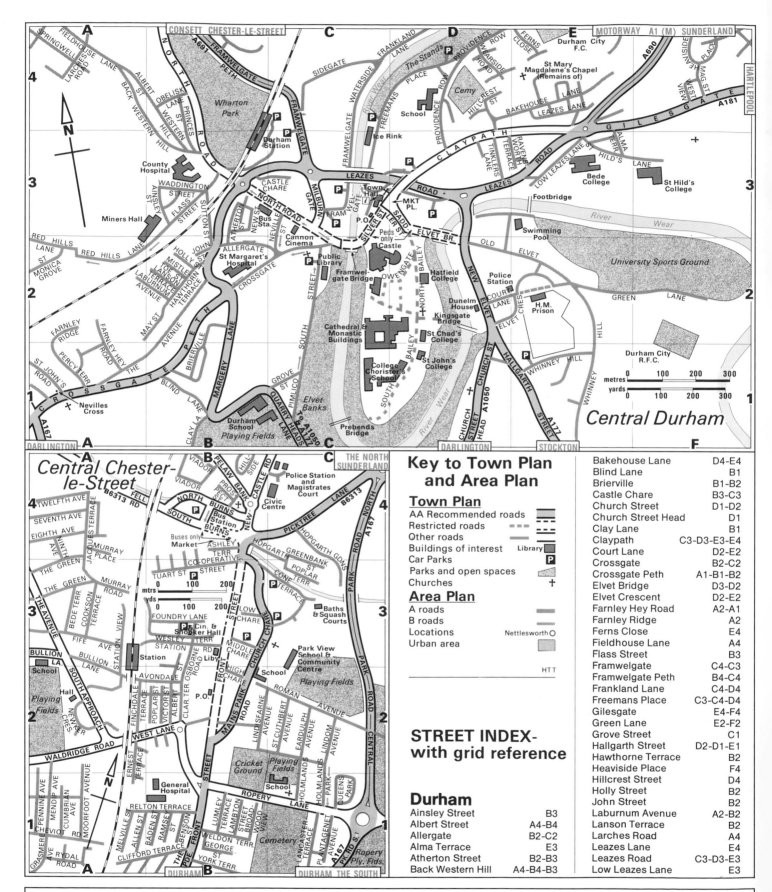

Central Durham

Central Chester-le-Street

THE NORTH
SUNDERLAND

DARLINGTON
DURHAM
DURHAM THE SOUTH

Key to Town Plan and Area Plan

Town Plan
AA Recommended roads
Restricted roads
Other roads
Buildings of interest — Library
Car Parks — P
Parks and open spaces
Churches — +

Area Plan
A roads
B roads
Locations — Nettlesworth O
Urban area

HTT

STREET INDEX- with grid reference

Durham

Durham

The castle and the cathedral stand side by side high above the city like sentinels, dramatically symbolising the military and religious power Durham wielded in the past. Its origins date from about 995 when the remains of St Cuthbert arrived from Lindisfarne and his shrine was a popular centre of pilgrimage. Soon after that early fortifications were built, later replaced by a stone castle which became the residence of the Prince-Bishops of Durham – powerful feudal rulers appointed by the King. Today the city's university, the oldest in England after Oxford and Cambridge, occupies the castle and most of the buildings around peaceful, secluded Palace Green. The splendid Norman cathedral, sited on the other side of the Green, is considered to be one of the finest in Europe. Its combination of strength and size, tempered with grace and beauty, is awe-inspiring.

Under the shadow of these giants the old city streets, known as vennels, ramble down the bluff past the 17th-century Bishop Cosin's House and the old grammar school, to the thickly-wooded banks of the Wear. Here three historic bridges link the city's heart with the pleasant Georgian suburbs on the other side of the river.

Although Durham is not an industrial city, it has become the venue for the North-East miners' annual Gala Day in July.

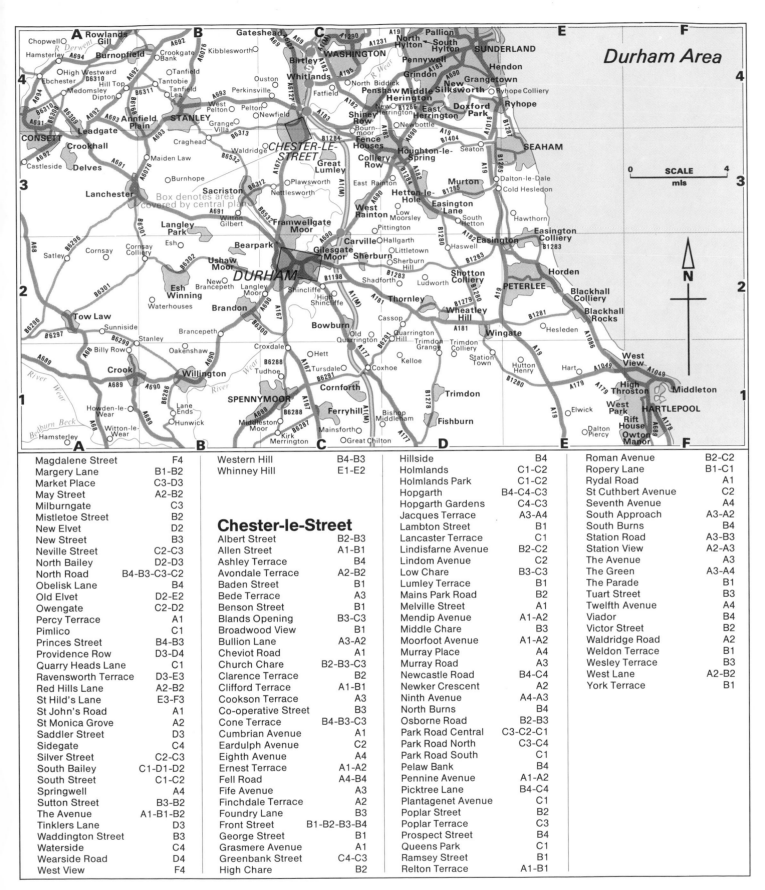

Durham Area

DURHAM
High above the wooded banks of the River Wear, Durham's castle and cathedral crown the steep hill on which the city is built. They share the site with several of the university's attractive old buildings.

149

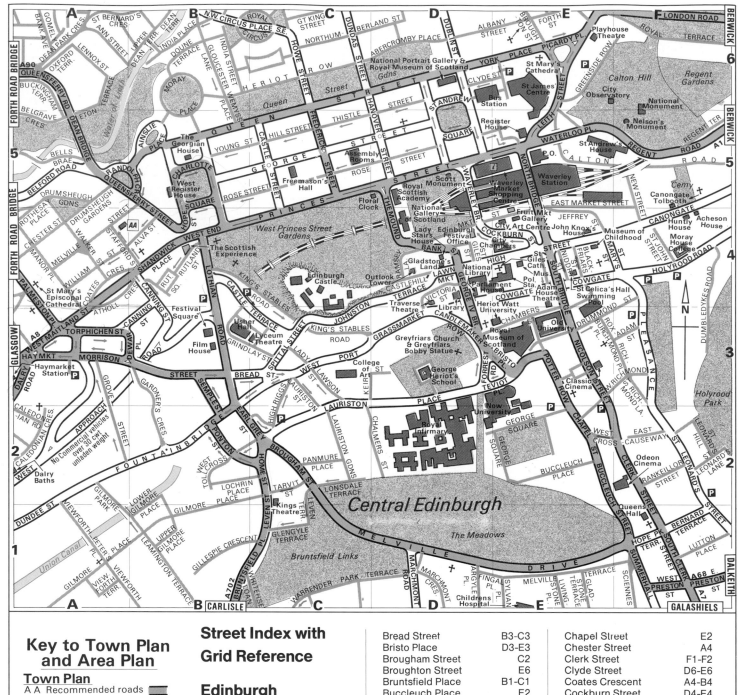

Key to Town Plan and Area Plan

Town Plan
A A Recommended roads
Other roads
Restricted roads
Buildings of intrest   Gallery
Car Parks   P
Parks and open spaces
A A Service Centre   AA
Churches   †

Area Plan
A roads
B roads
Locations   Newcraighall O
Urban area

Street Index with Grid Reference

Edinburgh

Abercromby Place	C6-D6
Adam Street	F3
Ainslie Place	B5
Albany Street	D6-E6
Alva Street	A4-B4
Ann Street	A6
Argyle Place	D1
Athol Crescent	A3-A4-B4
Bank Street	D4
Belford Road	A5
Belgrave Crescent	A5
Bells Brae	A5
Bernard Terrace	F1
Blackfriars Street	E4

Bread Street	B3-C3
Bristo Place	D3-E3
Brougham Street	C2
Broughton Street	E6
Bruntsfield Place	B1-C1
Buccleuch Place	E2
Buccleuch Street	E2-F2-F1
Buckingham Terrace	A5-A6
Caledonian Crescent	A2
Caledonian Road	A2
Calton Road	E5-F5
Candlemaker Row	D3
Canning Street	A3-B3-B4
Canongate	E4-F4-F5
Castle Hill	D4
Castle Street	C5
Castle Terrace	B4-B3-C3
Chalmers Street	C2-D2
Chambers Street	D3-E3
Charlotte Square	B4-B5

Chapel Street	E2
Chester Street	A4
Clerk Street	F1-F2
Clyde Street	D6-E6
Coates Crescent	A4-B4
Cockburn Street	D4-E4
Comely Bank Avenue	A6
Cowgate	D4-E4-F4
Dalry Road	A3
Dean Bridge	A5
Dean Park Crescent	A6
Dean Terrace	B6
Dewar Place	A3-B3
Doune Terrace	B6
Drummond Street	E3-F3-F4
Drumsheugh Gardens	A4-A5
Dublin Street	D6
Dumbiedykes Road	F3-F4
Dundas Street	C6
Dundee Street	A1-A2

Edinburgh

Scotland's ancient capital, dubbed the "Athens of the North", is one of the most splendid cities in the whole of Europe. Its buildings, its history and its cultural life give it an international importance which is celebrated every year in its world-famous festival. The whole city is overshadowed by the craggy castle which seems to grow out of the rock itself. There has been a fortress here since the 7th century and most of the great figures of Scottish history have been associated with it. The old town grew up around the base of Castle Rock within the boundaries of the defensive King's Wall and, unable to spread outwards, grew upwards in a maze of tenements. However, during the 18th century new prosperity from the shipping trade resulted in the building of the New Town and the regular, spacious layout of the Georgian development makes a striking contrast with the old hotch-potch of streets. Princes Street is the main east-west thoroughfare with excellent shops on one side and Princes Street Gardens with their famous floral clock on the south side.

As befits such a splendid capital city there are numerous museums and art galleries packed with priceless treasures. Among these are the famous picture gallery in 16th-century Holyroodhouse, the present Royal Palace, and the fascinating and unusual Museum of Childhood.

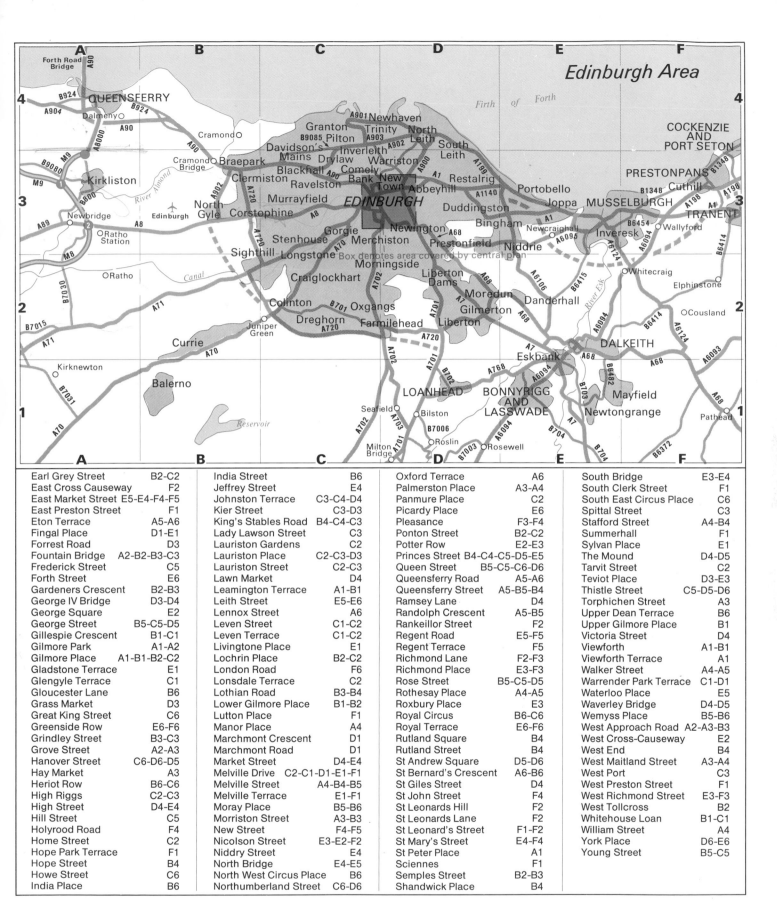

Edinburgh Area

EDINBURGH
Holyrood Palace orginated as a guest house for the Abbey of Holyrood in the 16th century, but most of the present building was built for Charles II. Mary Queen of Scots was one of its most famous inhabitants.

151

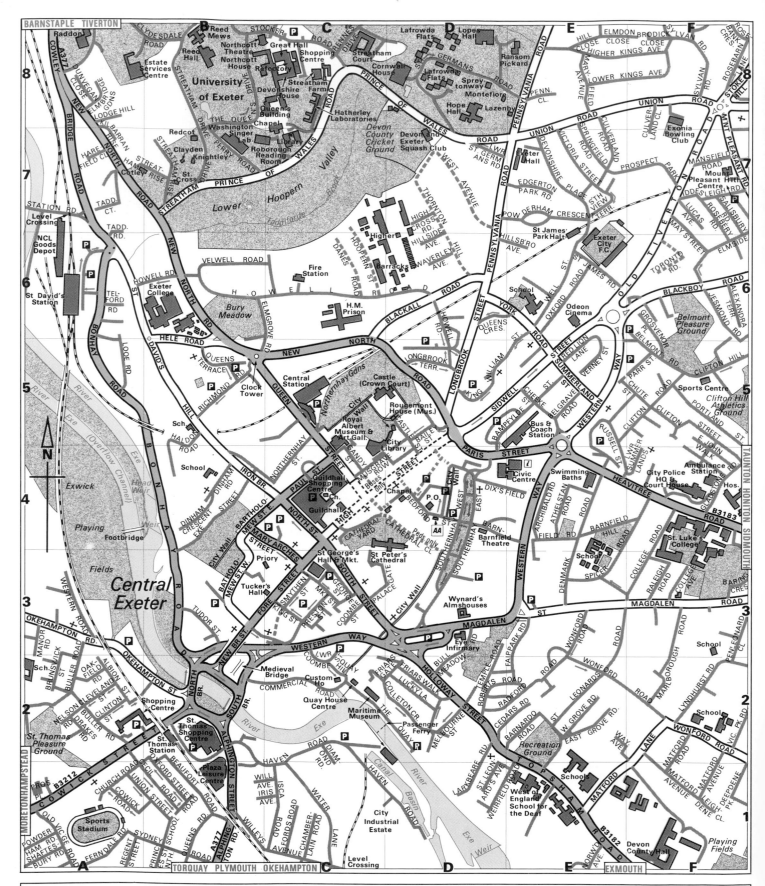

Exeter

The cathedral is Exeter's greatest treasure. Founded in 1050, but rebuilt by the Normans during the 12th century and again at the end of the 13th century, it has many beautiful and outstanding features – especially the exquisite rib-vaulting of the nave. Most remarkable, perhaps, is the fact that it still stood after virtually everything around it was flattened during the bombing raids in World War II.

There are still plenty of reminders of Old Exeter; Roman and medieval walls encircle parts of the city; 14th-century underground passages can be explored; the Guildhall is 15th-century; and Sir Francis Drake is said to have met his explorer companions at Mol's Coffee House. Of the city's ancient churches, the most interesting are St Mary Steps, St Mary Arches and St Martin's. The extensive Maritime Museum has over 100 boats from all over the world. Other museums include the

Rougemont House, the Devonshire Regiment and the Royal Albert Memorial Museum and Art Gallery.

Exmouth has a near-perfect position at the mouth of the Exe estuary. On one side it has expanses of sandy beach, on another a wide estuary alive with wildfowl and small boats, while inland is beautiful Devon countryside.

Honiton is famous for traditional hand-made lace and pottery which can still be bought in the busy town.

152

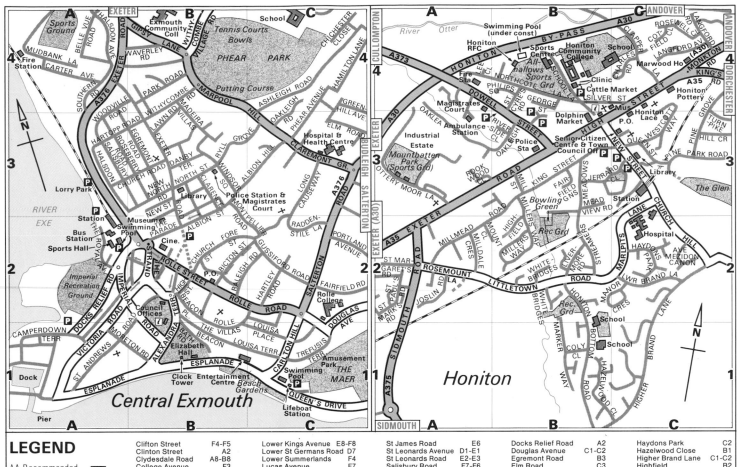

LEGEND

AA Recommended roads
Other roads
Restricted roads
Buildings of interest
Churches +
Car parks P
Parks, open spaces
One way streets ←

Street Index with Grid Reference

Exeter

Albion Street	A2
Alexandra Terrace	F6
Alphington Road	B1
Alphington Street	B1-B2
Archibald Road	E4
Athelstan Road	E4
Bailey Street	D5
Bampfylde Street	D4-D5-E5
Baring Crescent	F3
Barnado Road	E2
Barnfield Hill	E4-F4
Barnfield Road	D4-E4
Bartholomew Street East	B4-C4
Bartholomew Street West	B3
Bedford Street	D4
Belgrave Road	E5
Belmont Road	F6-F5
Blackall Road	C6-D6
Blackboy Road	F5
Bonhay Road	A5-B4-B3
Brodick Close	F8
Brunswick Street	A2
Buller Road	A2-A3
Bull Meadow Road	D2
Castle Street	D5
Cathedral Close	D4
Cathedral Yard	C4
Cecil Road	A1-B1
Cedars Road	E2
Chamberlain Road	C1
Cheeke Street	E5
Church Road	A1-A2-B2
Chute Street	E5-F5
Clevedon Street	A2
Clifton Hill	F5
Clifton Road	E5-F5
Clifton Street	F4-F5
Clinton Street	A2
Clydesdale Road	A8-B8
College Avenue	F3
College Road	F3-F4
Colleton Crescent	C2-D2
Commercial Road	B2-C2
Coombe Street	C3
Cowick Road	A1
Cowick Street	A1-A2-B2
Cowley Bridge Road	A6-A7-A8
Culverland Close	F7-F8
Culverland Road	E7-E8
Danes Road	C6
Deepdene Park	F1
Denmark Road	F3-F4
Devonshire Place	E7
Diamond Road	C2-C1
Dineham Crescent	B4
Dinham Road	B4
Dix's Field	D4
Drakes Road	A2
East John Walk	F4-F5
Dunvegan Close	A8
East Grove Road	E2
Edgerton Park Road	E7
Elmbridge Gardens	A8
Elmdon Close	E8-F8
Elmgrove Road	B6-C6-B5
Elmside	F6
Exe Street	B4
Fairpark Road	E2-E3
Ferndale Road	A1
Fords Road	C1
Fore Street	B3-C3
Friars Gate	C2-D2
Friars Walk	D2
Gandy Street	C4
George Street	C3
Gladstone Road	F4
Grosvenor Place	F6
Haldon Road	B4-B5
Harefield Close	A7
Haven Road	C1-C2-D1
Heavitree Road	E4-F4
Hele Road	B6-B5
Highcross Road	D7
Higher Kings Avenue	E8-F8
High Street	C4-D4-D5
Hill Close	F8
Hillsborough Avenue	D6-E6
Hillside Avenue	D6
Holloway Street	D2
Hoopern Street	C6-C7
Howell Road	A6-D6
Iddesleigh Road	F7
Iris Avenue	B1-C1
Iron Bridge	B4-C4
Isca Road	D2-E2
Jesmond Road	F6-F5-F6
Kilbarran Rise	A7-A8
King Street	C3
King William Street	D5-E5-E6
Larkbeare Road	D1-D2
Leighdene Close	F1
Lodge Hill	A8
Longbrook Street	D5-D6
Longbrook Terrace	D5
Looe Road	A5-A6
Lower Coombe Street	C2
Lower Kings Avenue	E8-F8
Lower St Germans Road	D7
Lower Summerlands	F4
Lucas Avenue	F7
Lucky Lane	D2
Lyndhurst Road	F2
Magdalen Road	E3-F3
Magdalen Street	D3-E3
Manor Road	A3
Mansfield Road	F7
Market Street	C4
Marlborough Road	F2-F3
Mary Arches Street	B4-C3
Maryfield Avenue	E8
Matford Avenue	F2-F1-F2
Matford Lane	E1-F1-F2
Matford Road	F1-F2
May Street	F7-F6
Melbourne Street	D2
Mount Pleasant Road	F8-F7
Musgrave Row	C4-C5
Nelson Road	A2
New Bridge Street	B2-B3
New North Road	A7-B6-C6-D5
North Bridge	B2
Northernhay Street	C4-C5
North Street	C4
Norwood Avenue	E1
Oakfield Road	A2
Oakhampton Street	A2-B2
Okehampton Road	A3-A2-B2
Old Tiverton Road	E6-F7
Old Vicarage Road	A1
Oxford Road	E6
Oxford Street	B1-B2
Palace Gate	C3-D3
Paris Street	D5-D4-E4
Parr Street	F5
Paul Street	C4
Penleonard Close	F3
Pennsylvania Close	E8
Pennsylvania Road	D6-E8
Perry Road	B7
Portland Street	F5
Powderham Crescent	D7-E7
Powderham Road	A1
Preston Street	C3
Prince of Wales Road	B7-C8-D7
Princes Street North	B1
Prospect Park	E7-F7
Prospect Place	A1
Quay Hill	C2
Queens Crescent	D6
Queens Road	B1
Queen Street	B5-C5-C4
Queens Terrace	B5
Radford Road	D2-E2
Raleigh Road	F3
Red Lion Lane	E5
Regent Street	A1
Rennes Drive	C8
Richmond Road	B5
Roberts Road	D2-E2
Rosebank Crescent	F8
Rosebarn Lane	F8
Rosebery Road	F6-F7
Russell Street	E5
St David's Hill	A6-B5
St Germans Road	D8-E8

St James Road	E6
St Leonards Avenue	D1-E1
St Leonards Road	E2-E3
Salisbury Road	F7-F6
School Road	B1
Shaftesbury Road	A1
Sidwell Street	D5-E5-E6
Smythen Street	C3
South Bridge	B2
South Street	D3
South View Terrace	E7
Spicer Road	E3-E4-F4
Springfield Road	E8-E7
Station Road	A7
Stocker Road	B8-C8
Stoke Hill	F8
Streatham Drive	B7-B8
Streatham Rise	A7-B7
Summerland Street	E5
Sydney Road	A1-B1
Sylvan Road	F8
Taddiforde Court	A7
Taddiforde Road	A6-A7
Telford Road	A6
Temple Road	D2-D3
The Quay	C2-D2
The Queen's Drive	B8
Thornton Hill	D7-D6
Topsham Road	E2-E1-F1
Toronto Road	F6
Tudor Street	B3
Union Road	E7-E8-F8
Union Street	A1-B1
Velwell Road	B6-C6
Verney Street	E5
Victoria Park Road	F2
Victoria Street	E7
Water Lane	C1
Waverley Avenue	C6
Way Avenue	C2
Weirfield Road	D1-E1
Well Street	E6
West Avenue	D7
Western Road	A3
Western Way	E3-E5, C3
West Grove Road	E2
Willeys Avenue	B1-C1
Williams Avenue	B1-C1
Wonford Road	E3-E2-F2
York Road	D6-E6-E5

Exmouth

Albion Hill	B3-C3
Albion Street	B2-B3
Alexandra Terrace	B1-B2
Ashleigh Road	C4
Bath Road	B1-B2
Beacon Place	B2
Belle View Road	A4
Bicton Street	B2-C2
Camperdown Terrace	A1
Carter Avenue	A4
Carlton Hill	C1-C2
Church Road	A3-B3
Claremont Grove	C3
Clarence Road	B3
Danby Terrace	B3

Docks Relief Road	A2
Douglas Avenue	C1-C2
Egremont Road	B3
Elm Road	C3
Esplanade	A1-B1-C1
Exeter Road	B3-A4
Fairfield Road	C2
Fore Street	B2-C2
Gipsy Lane	A4-B4
Green Hill Avenue	C3-C4
Gussiford Road	C2
Halsdon Avenue	A4
Hamilton Lane	C4
Hartley Road	C2
Hartopp Road	A3-B3
Halsdon Road	A3
High Street	B2
Imperial Road	A2-B1
Lawn Road	B3
Long Causeway	C3
Louisa Place	B1-C1
Louisa Terrace	B1-C1
Lyndhurst Road	A4-B4
Madeira Villas	B3-B4
Marpool Hill	B4-C3
Montpellier Road	B3-B2-C2
Moreton Road	A1-B1
Mudbank Lane	A4
New North Road	B3
New Street	B3
North Street	B3
Oakleigh Road	C3-C4
Park Road	B4
Phear Avenue	C3-C4
Portland Avenue	C2
Queens Drive	C1
Raddenstile Lane	C2
Raleigh Road	B2-C2
Rolle Road	B2-C2
Rolle Street	B2
Rolle Villas	B1-B2
Roseberry Road	A3-B3
Ryll Grove	B3-C3
St Andrews Road	A1-B1-B2
Salisbury Road	A3-B3
Salterton Road	C2-C3
Southern Road	A4
The Beacon	B1-B2
The Parade	B2
The Strand	B2
The Royal Avenue	A2
Trefusis Terrace	C1
Victoria Road	A1-A2-B2
Waverley Road	B4
Windsor Square	B3
Withycombe Road	B3-B4
Withycombe Village Road	B4
Woodville Road	A3-A4-B4

Honiton

Avenue Mezidon-Canon	C2
Charles Road	C4
Church Hill	C2-C3
Clapper Lane	C4
Coly Close	B1
Cotfield Close	C4
Dowell Street	A4-B3
Exeter Road	A2-B3
Fairfield Gardens	B3
George Street	B4
Haydons Park	C2
Hazelwood Close	B1
Higher Brand Lane	C1-C2
Highfield	B2
High Street	B3-C4
Hill Crescent	C3
Honiton Bottom Road	B1-B2
Honiton By-Pass	A4-B4
Jerrard Close	B3-C3
Jerrard Crescent	C3
Joslin Road	A2
King's Road	C4
Kings Street	B3
Langford Avenue	C4
Langford Road	C4
Lee Close	A4
Littledown Road	A2
Livermore Road	B2
Lower Brand Lane	C2
Manor Crescent	B2-C2
Marker Way	B1
Marlpits Lane	C2
Mead View Road	B3
Milldale Crescent	A2
Millers Way	B2-B3
Millmead Road	A2-B3
Mill Street	B3
Monkton Road	C4
Mount Close	A2
New Street	C3
Northcote Lane	B4
Oaklea	A3
Oakleigh	B3
Ottery Moor Lane	A3
Philips Square	B4
Pine Grove	C3-C4
Pine Park Road	C3
Queen Street	C3
Riverside Close	B3
Rookwood Close	A3
Rosemount Lane	A2
Rosewell Close	C4
St Cyre's Road	B4
St Margaret's Road	A2
St Mark's Road	A2
St Paul's Road	A2
School Lane	B4
Sidmouth Road	A1-A2
Silver Street	B4-C4
Streamers Meadows	B2-B3
Turnpike	C3
Westcott Way	C3
Whitebridges	B2

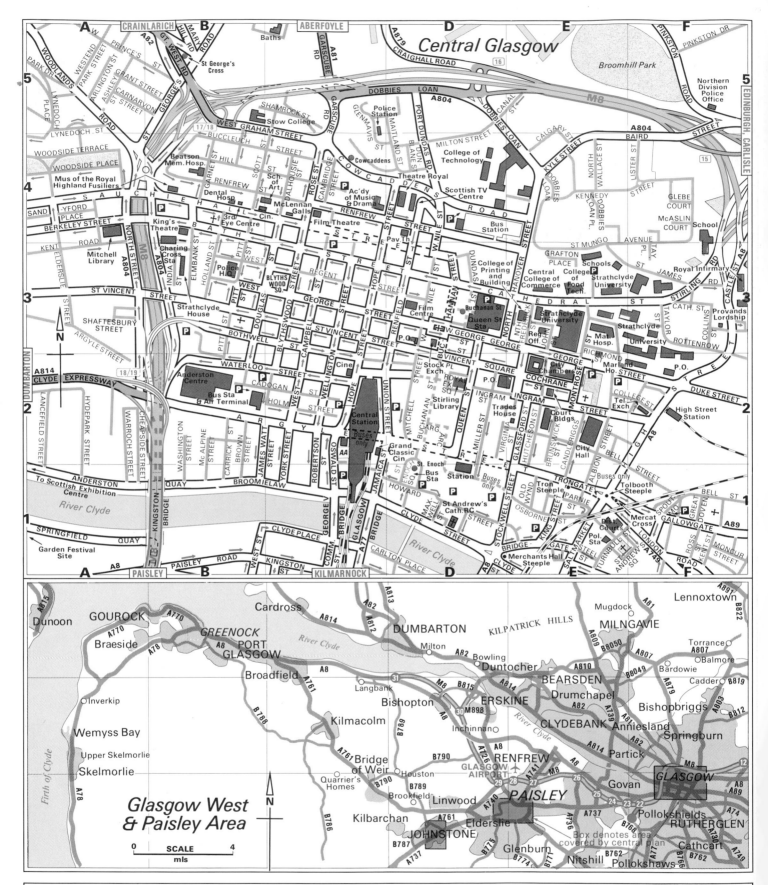

Glasgow

Although much of Glasgow is distinctly Victorian in character, its roots go back very many centuries. Best link with the past is the cathedral; founded in the 6th century, it has features from many succeeding centuries, including an exceptional 13th-century crypt. Nearby is Provand's Lordship, the city's oldest house. It dates from 1471 and is now a museum. Two much larger museums are to

be found a little out of the centre – the Art Gallery and Museum contains one of the finest collections of paintings in Britain, while the Hunterian Museum, attached to the University, covers geology, archaeology, ethnography and more general subjects. On Glasgow Green is People's Palace – a museum of city life. Most imposing of the Victorian buildings are the City Chambers and City Hall which was built in 1841 as a concert hall but now houses the Scottish National Orchestra.

Paisley is famous for the lovely fabric pattern to which it gives its name. It was taken from fabrics brought from the Near East in the early 19th century, and its manufacture, along with the production of thread, is still important. Coats Observatory is one of the best-equipped in the country.

Johnstone grew rapidly as a planned industrial town in the 19th century, but suffered from the effects of the Industrial Revolution. Today, engineering is the main industry.

154

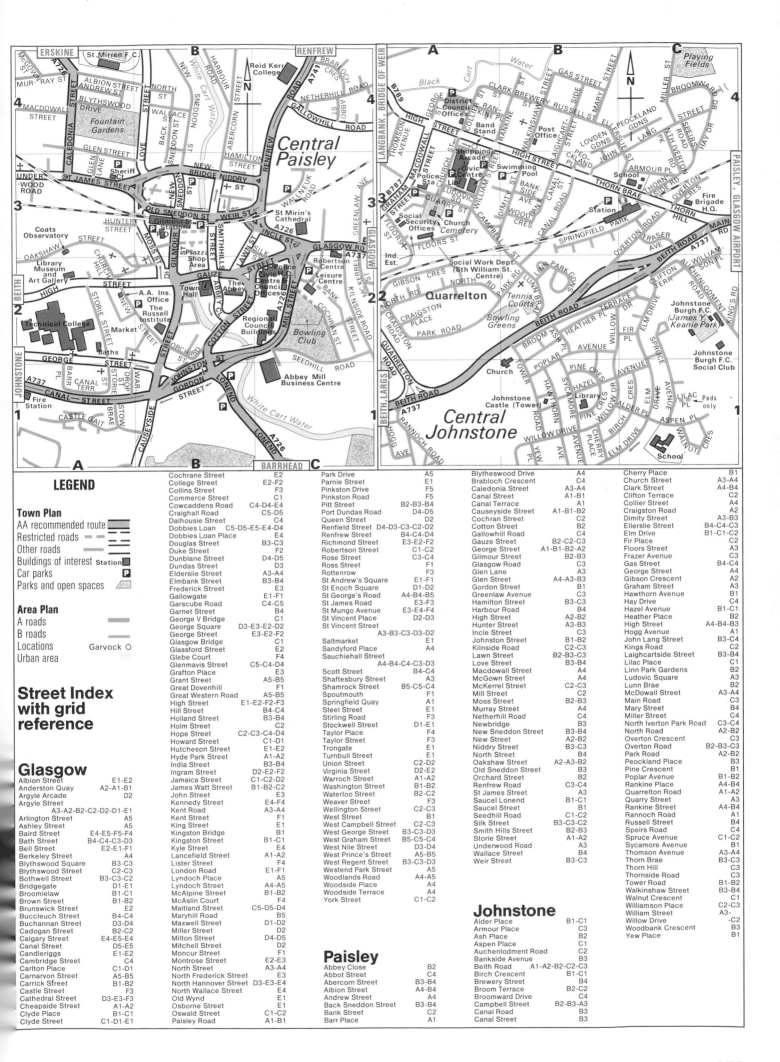

LEGEND

Town Plan

AA recommended route	
Restricted roads	
Other roads	
Buildings of interest	Station ▨
Car parks	P
Parks and open spaces	

Area Plan

A roads	
B roads	
Locations	Garvock O
Urban area	

Street Index with grid reference

Glasgow

Albion Street	E1-E2
Anderston Quay	A2-A1-B1
Argyle Arcade	D2
Argyle Street	A3-A2-B2-C2-D2-D1-E1
Arlington Street	A5
Ashley Street	A5
Baird Street	E4-E5-F5-F4
Bath Street	B4-C4-C3-D3
Bell Street	E2-E1-F1
Berkeley Street	A4
Blythswood Square	B3-C3
Blythswood Street	C2-C3
Bothwell Street	B3-C3-C2
Bridgegate	D1-E1
Broomielaw	B1-C1
Brown Street	B1-B2
Brunswick Street	E2
Buccleuch Street	B4-C4
Buchannan Street	D3-D4
Cadogan Street	B2-C2
Calgary Street	E4-E5-E4
Canal Street	D5-E5
Candleriggs	E1-E2
Cambridge Street	C4
Carlton Place	C1-D1
Carnarvon Street	A5-B5
Carrick Street	B1-B2
Castle Street	F3
Cathedral Street	D3-E3-F3
Cheapside Street	A1-A2
Clyde Place	B1-C1
Clyde Street	C1-D1-E1
Cochrane Street	E2
College Street	E2-F2
Collins Street	F3
Commerce Street	C1
Cowcaddens Road	C4-D4-E4
Craighall Road	C5-D5
Dalhousie Street	C4
Dobbies Loan	C5-D5-E5-E4-D4
Dobbies Loan Place	E4
Douglas Street	B3-C3
Duke Street	F2
Dunblane Street	D4-D5
Dundas Street	D3
Elderslie Street	A3-A4
Elmbank Street	B3-B4
Frederick Street	E3
Gallowgate	E1-F1
Garscube Road	C4-C5
Garnet Street	B4
George V Bridge	C1
George Square	D3-E3-E2-D2
George Street	E3-E2-F2
Glasgow Bridge	C1
Glassford Street	E2
Glebe Court	F4
Glenmavis Street	C5-C4-D4
Grafton Place	E3
Grant Street	A5-B5
Great Dovenhill	F1
Great Western Road	A5
High Street	E1-E2-F2-F3
Hill Street	B4-C4
Holland Street	B3-B4
Holm Street	C2
Hope Street	C2-C3-C4-D4
Howard Street	C1-D1
Hutcheson Street	E1-E2
Hyde Park Street	A1-A2
India Street	A4
Ingram Street	D2-E2-F2
Jamaica Street	C1-C2-D2
James Watt Street	B1-B2-C2
John Street	E3
Kennedy Street	E4-F4
Kent Road	A3-A4
Kent Street	F1
King Street	E1
Kingston Bridge	B1
Kingston Street	B1-C1
Kyle Street	E4
Lancefield Street	A1-A2
Lister Street	F4
London Road	E1-F1
Lyndoch Place	A5
Lyndoch Street	A4-A5
McAlpine Street	B1-B2
McAslin Court	F4
Maitland Street	C5-D5-D4
Maryhill Road	B5
Maxwell Street	D1-D2
Miller Street	D2
Milton Street	D4-D5
Mitchell Street	D2
Moncur Street	F1
Montrose Street	E2-E3
North Street	A3-A4
North Frederick Street	E3
North Hannover Street	D3-E3-E4
North Wallace Street	E4
Old Wynd	E1
Osborne Street	E1
Oswald Street	C1-C2
Paisley Road	A1-B1
Park Drive	A5
Parnie Street	E1
Pinkston Drive	F5
Pinkston Road	F5
Pitt Street	B2-B3-B4
Port Dundas Road	D4-D5
Queen Street	D2
Renfield Street	D4-D3-C3-C2-D2
Renfrew Street	B4-C4-D4
Richmond Street	E3-E2-F2
Robertson Street	C1-C2
Rose Street	C3-C4
Ross Street	F1
Rottenrow	F3
St Andrew's Square	E1-F1
St Enoch Square	D1-D2
St George's Road	A4-B4-B5
St James Road	E3-F3
St Mungo Avenue	E3-E4-F4
St Vincent Place	D2-D3
St Vincent Street	A3-B3-C3-D3-D2
Saltmarket	E1
Sandyford Place	A4
Sauchiehall Street	A4-B4-C4-C3-D3
Scott Street	B4-C4
Shaftesbury Street	A3
Shamrock Street	B5-C5-C4
Spoutmouth	F1
Springfield Quay	A1
Steel Street	E1
Stirling Road	F3
Stockwell Street	D1-E1
Taylor Place	F4
Taylor Street	F3
Trongate	E1
Turnbull Street	E1
Union Street	C2-D2
Virginia Street	D2-E2
Warroch Street	A1-A2
Washington Street	B1-B2
Waterloo Street	B2-C2
Weaver Street	F3
Wellington Street	C2-C3
West Street	B1
West Campbell Street	C2-C3
West George Street	B3-C3-D3
West Graham Street	B5-C5-C4
West Nile Street	D3-D4
West Prince's Street	A5-B5
West Regent Street	B3-C3-D3
Westend Park Street	A5
Woodlands Road	A4-A5
Woodside Place	A4
Woodside Terrace	A4
York Street	C1-C2

Paisley

Abbey Close	B2
Abbot Street	C4
Abercorn Street	B3-B4
Albion Street	A4-B4
Andrew Street	A4
Back Sneddon Street	B3-B4
Bank Street	C2
Barr Place	A1
Blytheswood Drive	A4
Brabloch Crescent	C4
Caledonia Street	A3-A4
Canal Street	A1-B1
Canal Terrace	A1
Causeyside Street	A1-B1-B2
Cochran Street	C2
Cotton Street	B2
Gauze Street	B2-C2-C3
George Street	A1-B1-B2-A2
Gilmour Street	B2-B3
Glasgow Road	C3
Glen Lane	A3
Glen Street	A4-A3-B3
Gordon Street	B1
Greenlaw Avenue	C3
Hamilton Street	B3-C3
Harbour Road	B4
High Street	A2-B2
Hunter Street	A3-B3
Incle Street	C3
Johnston Street	B1-B2
Kilnside Road	C2-C3
Lawn Street	B2-B3-C3
Love Street	B3-B4
Macdowall Street	A4
McGown Street	A4
McKerrel Street	C2-C3
Mill Street	C2
Moss Street	B2-B3
Murray Street	A4
Netherhill Road	C4
Newbridge	B3
New Sneddon Street	B3-B4
New Street	A2-B2
Niddry Street	B3-C3
North Street	B4
Oakshaw Street	A2-A3-B2
Old Sneddon Street	B3
Orchard Street	B2
Renfrew Road	C3-C4
St James Street	A3
Saucel Lonend	B1-C1
Saucel Street	B1
Seedhill Road	C1-C2
Silk Street	B3-C3-C2
Smith Hills Street	B2-B3
Storie Street	A1-A2
Underwood Road	A3
Wallace Street	B4
Weir Street	B3-C3

Johnstone

Alder Place	B1-C1
Armour Place	C3
Ash Place	B2
Aspen Place	C1
Auchenlodment Road	C2
Bankside Avenue	B3
Beith Road	A1-A2-B2-C2-C3
Birch Crescent	B1-C1
Brewery Street	B4
Broom Terrace	B2-C2
Broomward Drive	C4
Campbell Street	B2-B3-A3
Canal Road	B3
Canal Street	B3
Cherry Place	B1
Church Street	A3-A4
Clark Street	A4-B4
Clifton Terrace	C2
Collier Street	A4
Craigston Road	A2
Dimity Street	A3-B3
Ellerslie Street	B4-C4-C3
Elm Drive	B1-C1-C2
Fir Place	C2
Floors Street	A3
Frazer Avenue	C3
Gas Street	B4-C4
George Street	A4
Gibson Crescent	A2
Graham Street	A3
Hawthorn Avenue	B1
Hay Drive	C4
Hazel Avenue	B1-C1
Heather Place	B2
High Street	A4-B4-B3
Hogg Avenue	A1
John Lang Street	B3-C3
Kings Road	C2
Laighcartside Street	B3-B4
Lilac Place	C1
Linn Park Gardens	B2
Ludovic Square	A3
Lunn Brae	B2
McDowall Street	A3-A4
Main Road	C3
Mary Street	B4
Miller Street	C4
North Iverton Park Road	C3-C4
North Road	A2-B2
Overton Crescent	C3
Overton Road	B2-B3-C3
Park Road	A2-B2
Peockland Place	B3
Pine Crescent	B1
Poplar Avenue	B1-B2
Quarrelton Road	A1-A2
Quarry Street	A3
Rankine Place	A4-B4
Rankine Street	A4-B4
Rannoch Road	A1
Russell Street	B4
Speirs Road	C4
Spruce Avenue	C1-C2
Sycamore Avenue	B1
Thomson Avenue	A3-A4
Thorn Brae	B3-C3
Thorn Hill	C3
Thornside Road	C3
Tower Road	B1-B2
Walkinshaw Street	B3-B4
Walnut Crescent	C1
Williamson Place	C2-C3
William Street	A3-C2
Willow Drive	B3
Woodbank Crescent	B3
Yew Place	B1

155

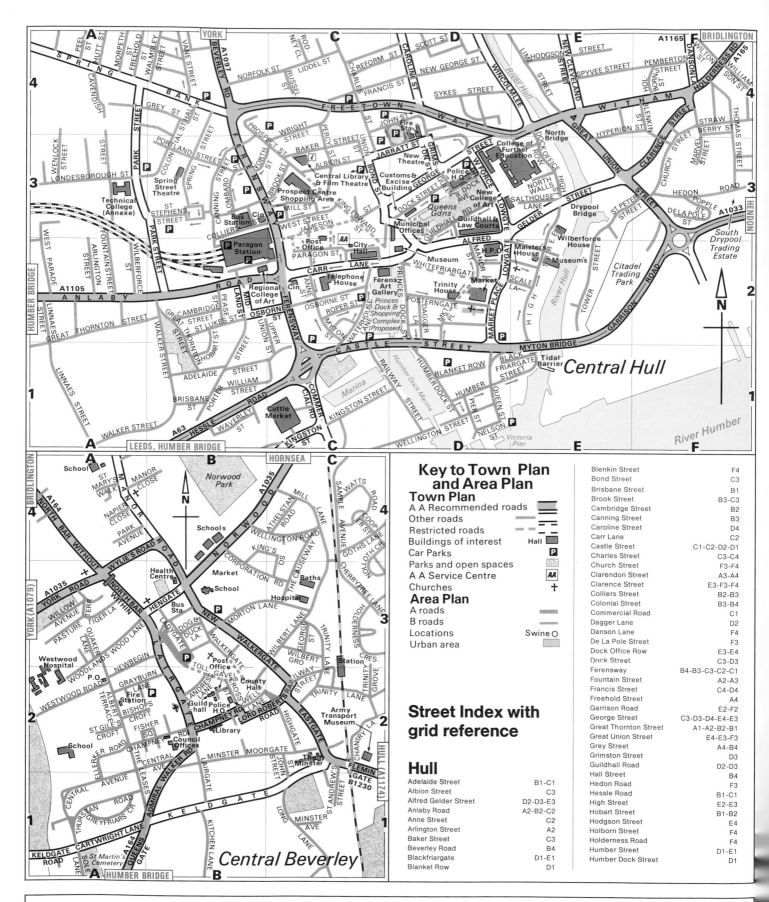

Key to Town Plan and Area Plan

Town Plan
A A Recommended roads	
Other roads	
Restricted roads	
Buildings of interest	Hall
Car Parks	P
Parks and open spaces	
A A Service Centre	AA
Churches	+

Area Plan
A roads	
B roads	
Locations	Swine O
Urban area	

Street Index with grid reference

Hull
Adelaide Street	B1-C1
Albion Street	C3
Alfred Gelder Street	D2-D3-E3
Anlaby Road	A2-B2-C2
Anne Street	C2
Arlington Street	A2
Baker Street	C3
Beverley Road	B4
Blackfriargate	D1-E1
Blanket Row	D1

Blenkin Street	F4
Bond Street	C3
Brisbane Street	B1
Brook Street	B3-C3
Cambridge Street	B2
Canning Street	B3
Caroline Street	D4
Carr Lane	C2
Castle Street	C1-C2-D2-D1
Charles Street	C3-C4
Church Street	F3-F4
Clarendon Street	A3-A4
Clarence Street	E3-F3-F4
Colliers Street	B2-B3
Colonial Street	B3-B4
Commercial Road	C1
Dagger Lane	D2
Danson Lane	F4
De La Pole Street	F3
Dock Office Row	E3-E4
Dock Street	C3-D3
Ferensway	B4-B3-C3-C2-C1
Fountain Street	A2-A3
Francis Street	C4-D4
Freehold Street	A4
Garrison Road	E2-F2
George Street	C3-D3-D4-E4-E3
Great Thornton Street	A1-A2-B2-B1
Great Union Street	E4-E3-F3
Grey Street	A4-B4
Grimston Street	D3
Guildhall Road	D2-D3
Hall Street	B4
Hedon Road	F3
Hessle Road	B1-C1
High Street	E2-E3
Hobart Street	B1-B2
Hodgson Street	E4
Holborn Street	F4
Holderness Road	F4
Humber Street	D1-E1
Humber Dock Street	D1

Hull

Officially Kingston-upon-Hull, this ancient port was specially laid out with new docks in 1293, on the decree of Edward I, and echoes of the town's past can be seen in the Town Docks Museum. The docks and the fishing industry are synonymous with Hull – it has Britain's busiest deep-sea fishing port – although flour-milling, vegetable oil extraction and petrochemical production are also important. The centre of Hull consists of broad streets and spacious squares and parks, such as Queen's Gardens, laid out on the site of what used to be Queen's Dock. The older part of the town which lies south-east of here between the docks and the River Hull is full of character, with a number of Georgian buildings and places of interest.

Beverley is one of England's most distinguished towns. Between its two principal buildings – the famous Minster and St Mary's Church – are medieval streets and pleasing market squares graced by redbrick Georgian houses built by the landed gentry of the East Riding during the town's heyday as a fashionable resort. The Minster's twin towers soar above the rooftops of the town as a constant reminder that here is one of the most beautiful pieces of Gothic architecture in Europe. The wealth of beauty and detail throughout is immense, but carving in both stone and wood is one of its most outstanding features.

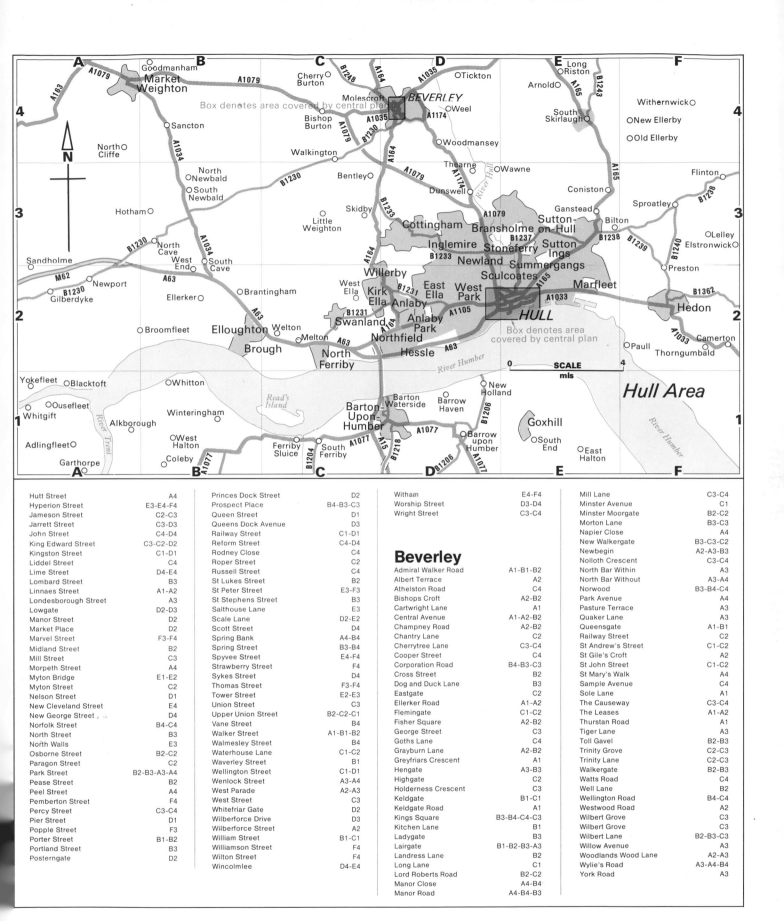

Hull Area

Box denotes area covered by central plan

SCALE mls 0 ... 4

Schemes to cross the Humber estuary were first discussed over 100 years ago, but it was not until 1981 that the mammoth project was sucessfully completed. At 4626ft, the Humber Bridge has the longest main span in the world.

Hutt Street	A4
Hyperion Street	E3-E4-F4
Jameson Street	C2-C3
Jarrett Street	C3-D3
John Street	C4-D4
King Edward Street	C3-C2-D2
Kingston Street	C1-D1
Liddel Street	C4
Lime Street	D4-E4
Lombard Street	B3
Linnaes Street	A1-A2
Londesborough Street	A3
Lowgate	D2-D3
Manor Street	D2
Market Place	D2
Marvel Street	F3-F4
Midland Street	B2
Mill Street	C3
Morpeth Street	A4
Myton Bridge	E1-E2
Myton Street	C2
Nelson Street	D1
New Cleveland Street	E4
New George Street	D4
Norfolk Street	B4-C4
North Street	B3
North Walls	E3
Osborne Street	B2-C2
Paragon Street	C2
Park Street	B2-B3-A3-A4
Pease Street	B2
Peel Street	A4
Pemberton Street	F4
Percy Street	C3-C4
Pier Street	D1
Popple Street	F3
Porter Street	B1-B2
Portland Street	B3
Posterngate	D2

Princes Dock Street	D2
Prospect Place	B4-B3-C3
Queen Street	D1
Queens Dock Avenue	D3
Railway Street	C1-D1
Reform Street	C4-D4
Rodney Close	C4
Roper Street	C2
Russell Street	C4
St Lukes Street	B2
St Peter Street	E3-F3
St Stephens Street	B3
Salthouse Lane	E3
Scale Lane	D2-E2
Scott Street	D4
Spring Bank	A4-B4
Spring Street	B3-B4
Spyvee Street	E4-F4
Strawberry Street	F4
Sykes Street	D4
Thomas Street	F3-F4
Tower Street	E2-E3
Union Street	C3
Upper Union Street	B2-C2-C1
Vane Street	B4
Walker Street	A1-B1-B2
Walmesley Street	B4
Waterhouse Lane	C1-C2
Waverley Street	B1
Wellington Street	C1-D1
Wenlock Street	A3-A4
West Parade	A2-A3
West Street	C3
Whitefriar Gate	D2
Wilberforce Drive	D3
Wilberforce Street	A2
William Street	B1-C1
Williamson Street	F4
Wilton Street	F4
Wincolmlee	D4-E4

Witham	E4-F4
Worship Street	D3-D4
Wright Street	C3-C4

Beverley

Admiral Walker Road	A1-B1-B2
Albert Terrace	A2
Athelston Road	C4
Bishops Croft	A2-B2
Cartwright Lane	A1
Central Avenue	A1-A2-B2
Champney Road	A2-B2
Chantry Lane	C2
Cherrytree Lane	C3-C4
Cooper Street	C4
Corporation Road	B4-B3-C3
Cross Street	B2
Dog and Duck Lane	B3
Eastgate	C2
Ellerker Road	A1-A2
Flemingate	C1-C2
Fisher Square	A2-B2
George Street	C3
Goths Lane	C4
Grayburn Lane	A2-B2
Greyfriars Crescent	A1
Hengate	A3-B3
Highgate	C2
Holderness Crescent	C3
Keldgate	B1-C1
Keldgate Road	A1
Kings Square	B3-B4-C4-C3
Kitchen Lane	B1
Ladygate	B3
Lairgate	B1-B2-B3-A3
Landress Lane	B2
Long Lane	C1
Lord Roberts Road	B2-C2
Manor Close	A4-B4
Manor Road	A4-B4-B3

Mill Lane	C3-C4
Minster Avenue	C1
Minster Moorgate	B2-C2
Morton Lane	B3-C3
Napier Close	A4
New Walkergate	B3-C3-C2
Newbegin	A2-A3-B3
Nolloth Crescent	C3-C4
North Bar Within	A3
North Bar Without	A3-A4
Norwood	B3-B4-C4
Park Avenue	A4
Pasture Terrace	A3
Quaker Lane	A3
Queensgate	A1-B1
Railway Street	C2
St Andrew's Street	C1-C2
St Gile's Croft	A2
St John Street	C1-C2
St Mary's Walk	A4
Sample Avenue	C4
Sole Lane	A1
The Causeway	C3-C4
The Leases	A1-A2
Thurstan Road	A1
Tiger Lane	A3
Toll Gavel	B2-B3
Trinity Grove	C2-C3
Trinity Lane	C2-C3
Walkergate	B2-B3
Watts Road	C4
Well Lane	B2
Wellington Road	B4-C4
Westwood Road	A2
Wilbert Grove	C3
Wilbert Grove	C3
Wilbert Lane	B2-B3-C3
Willow Avenue	A3
Woodlands Wood Lane	A2-A3
Wylie's Road	A3-A4-B4
York Road	A3

HULL

157

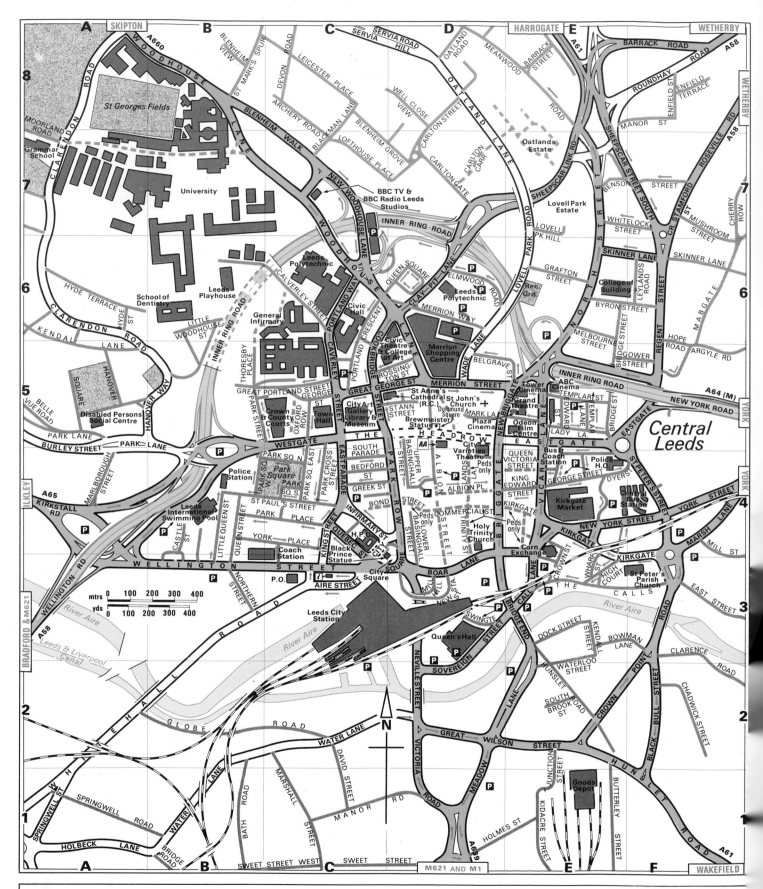

Leeds

In the centre of Leeds is its town hall – a monumental piece of architecture with a 225ft clock-tower. It was opened by Queen Victoria in 1858, and has been a kind of mascot for the city ever since. It exudes civic pride; such buildings could only have been created in the heyday of Victorian prosperity and confidence. Leeds' staple industry has always been the wool trade, but it only became a boom town towards the end of the 18th century, when textile mills were introduced. Today, the wool trade and ready-made clothing (Mr Hepworth and Mr Burton began their work here) are still important, though industries like paper, leather, furniture and electrical equipment are prominent.

Across Calverley Street from the town hall is the City Art Gallery, Library and Museum. Its collections include sculpture by Henry Moore, who was a student at Leeds School of Art. Nearby is the Headrow, Leeds' foremost shopping thoroughfare. On it is the City Varieties Theatre, venue for many years of the famous television programme 'The Good Old Days'. Off the Headrow are several shopping arcades, of which Leeds has many handsome examples. Leeds has a good number of interesting churches; perhaps the finest is St John's, unusual in that it dates from 1634, a time when few churches were built.

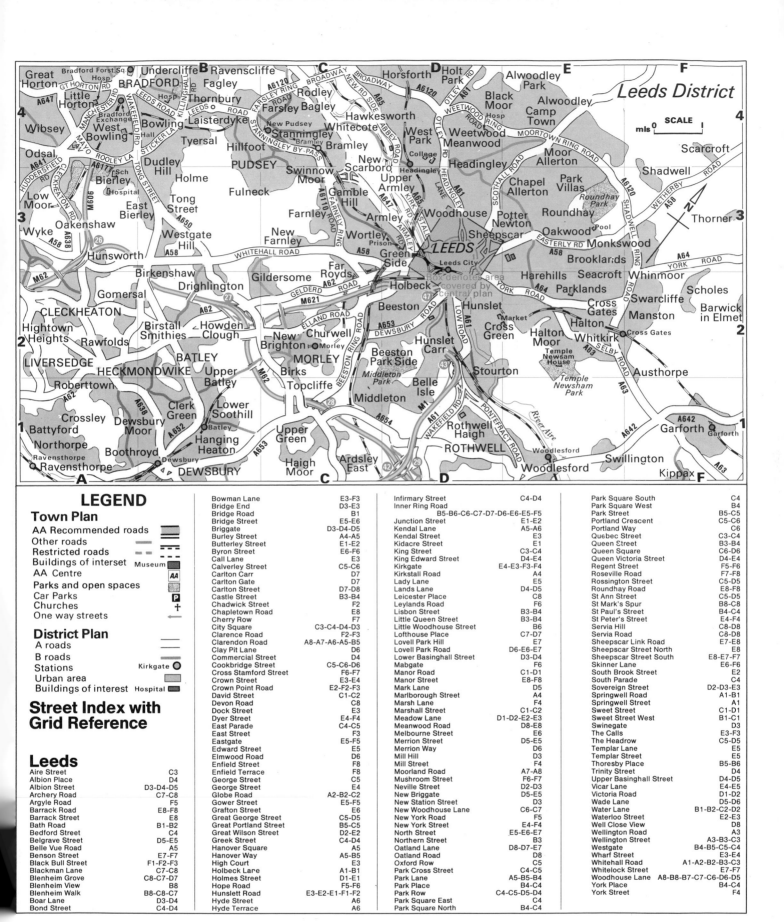

Leeds District

SCALE mls 0 1

Box denotes area covered by central plan

LEGEND

Town Plan

AA Recommended roads	▬▬
Other roads	══
Restricted roads	▬ ▬
Buildings of interset	Museum ■
AA Centre	AA
Parks and open spaces	▓
Car Parks	P
Churches	†
One way streets	←

District Plan

A roads	──
B roads	──
Stations	Kirkgate ○
Urban area	▓
Buildings of interest	Hospital ■

Street Index with Grid Reference

Leeds

Aire Street	C3	Bowman Lane	E3-F3	Infirmary Street	C4-D4	Park Square South	C4
Albion Place	D4	Bridge End	D3-E3	Inner Ring Road		Park Square West	B4
Albion Street	D3-D4-D5	Bridge Road	B1		B5-B6-C6-C7-D7-D6-E6-E5-F5	Park Street	B5-C5
Archery Road	C7-C8	Bridge Street	E5-E6	Junction Street	E1-E2	Portland Crescent	C5-C6
Argyle Road	F5	Briggate	D3-D4-D5	Kendal Lane	A5-A6	Portland Way	C6
Barrack Road	E8-F8	Burley Street	A4-A5	Kendal Street	E3	Quebec Street	C3-C4
Barrack Street	E8	Butterley Street	E1-E2	Kidacre Street	E1	Queen Street	B3-B4
Bath Road	B1-B2	Byron Street	E6-F6	King Street	C3-C4	Queen Square	C6-D6
Bedford Street	C4	Call Lane	E3	King Edward Street	D4-E4	Queen Victoria Street	D4-E4
Belgrave Street	D5-E5	Calverley Street	C5-C6	Kirkgate	E4-E3-F3-F4	Regent Street	F5-F6
Belle Vue Road	A5	Carlton Carr	D7	Kirkstall Road	A4	Roseville Road	F7-F8
Benson Street	E7-F7	Carlton Gate	D7	Lady Lane	E5	Rossington Street	C5-D5
Black Bull Street	F1-F2-F3	Carlton Street	D7-D8	Lands Lane	D4-D5	Roundhay Road	E8-F8
Blackman Lane	C7-C8	Castle Street	B3-B4	Leicester Place	C8	St Ann Street	C5-D5
Blenheim Grove	C8-C7-D7	Chadwick Street	F2	Leylands Road	F6	St Mark's Spur	B8-C8
Blenheim View	B8	Chapeltown Road	E8	Lisbon Street	B3-B4	St Paul's Street	B4-C4
Blenheim Walk	B8-C8-C7	Cherry Row	F7	Little Queen Street	B3-B4	St Peter's Street	E4-E5
Boar Lane	D3-D4	City Square	C3-C4-D4-D3	Little Woodhouse Street	B6	Servia Hill	C8-D8
Bond Street	C4-D4	Clarence Road	F2-F3	Lofthouse Place	C7-D7	Servia Road	C8-D8
		Clarendon Road	A8-A7-A6-A5-B5	Lovell Park Hill	E7	Sheepscar Link Road	E7-E8
		Clay Pit Lane	D6	Lovell Park Road	D6-E6-E7	Sheepscar Street North	E8
		Commercial Street	D4	Lower Basinghall Street	D3-D4	Sheepscar Street South	E8-E7-F7
		Cookbridge Street	C5-C6-D6	Mabgate	F6	Skinner Lane	E6-F6
		Cross Stamford Street	F6-F7	Manor Road	C1-D1	South Brook Street	E2
		Crown Street	E3-E4	Manor Street	E8-F8	South Parade	C4
		Crown Point Road	E2-F2-F3	Mark Lane	D5	Sovereign Street	D2-D3-E3
		David Street	C1-C2	Marlborough Street	A4	Springhall Road	A1-B1
		Devon Road	C8	Marsh Lane	F4	Springwell Street	A1
		Dock Street	E3	Marshall Street	C1-C2	Sweet Street	C1-D1
		Dyer Street	E4-F4	Meadow Lane	D1-D2-E2-E3	Sweet Street West	B1-C1
		East Parade	C4-C5	Meanwood Road	D8-E8	Swinegate	D3
		East Street	F3	Melbourne Street	E6	The Calls	E3-F3
		Eastgate	E5-F5	Merrion Street	D5-E5	The Headrow	C5-D5
		Edward Street	E5	Merrion Way	D6	Templar Lane	E5
		Elmwood Road	D6	Mill Hill	D3	Templar Street	E5
		Enfield Street	F8	Mill Street	F4	Thoresby Place	B5-B6
		Enfield Terrace	F8	Moorland Road	A7-A8	Trinity Street	D4
		George Street	C5	Mushroom Street	F6-F7	Upper Basinghall Street	D4-D5
		George Street	E4	Neville Street	D2-D3	Vicar Lane	E4-E5
		Globe Road	A2-B2-C2	New Briggate	D5-E5	Victoria Road	D1-D2
		Gower Street	E5-F5	New Station Street	D3	Wade Lane	D5-D6
		Grafton Street	E5	New Woodhouse Lane	C6-C7	Water Lane	B1-B2-C2-D2
		Great George Street	C5-D5	New York Road	F5	Waterloo Street	E2-E3
		Great Portland Street	B5-C5	New York Street	E4-F4	Well Close View	D8
		Great Wilson Street	D2-E2	North Street	E5-E6-E7	Wellington Road	A3
		Greek Street	C4-D4	Northern Street	B3	Wellington Street	A3-B3-C3
		Hanover Square	A5	Oatland Lane	D8-D7-E7	Westgate	B4-B5-C5-C4
		Hanover Way	A5-B5	Oatland Road	D8	Wharf Street	E3-E4
		High Court	E3	Oxford Row	C5	Whitehall Road	A1-A2-B2-B3-C3
		Holbeck Lare	A1-B1	Park Cross Street	C4-C5	Whitelock Street	E7-F7
		Holmes Street	D1-E1	Park Lane	A5-B5-B4	Woodhouse Lane	A8-B8-B7-C7-C6-D6-D5
		Hope Road	F5-F6	Park Place	B4-C4	York Place	B4-C4
		Hunslet Road	E3-E2-E1-F1-F2	Park Row	C4-C5-D5-D4	York Street	F4
		Hyde Street	A6	Park Square East	C4		
		Hyde Terrace	A6	Park Square North	B4-C4		

LEEDS

Offices now occupy the handsome twin-towered Civic Hall which stands in Calverley Street in front of the new buildings of Leeds Polytechnic. This area of the city – the commercial centre – has been extensively redeveloped

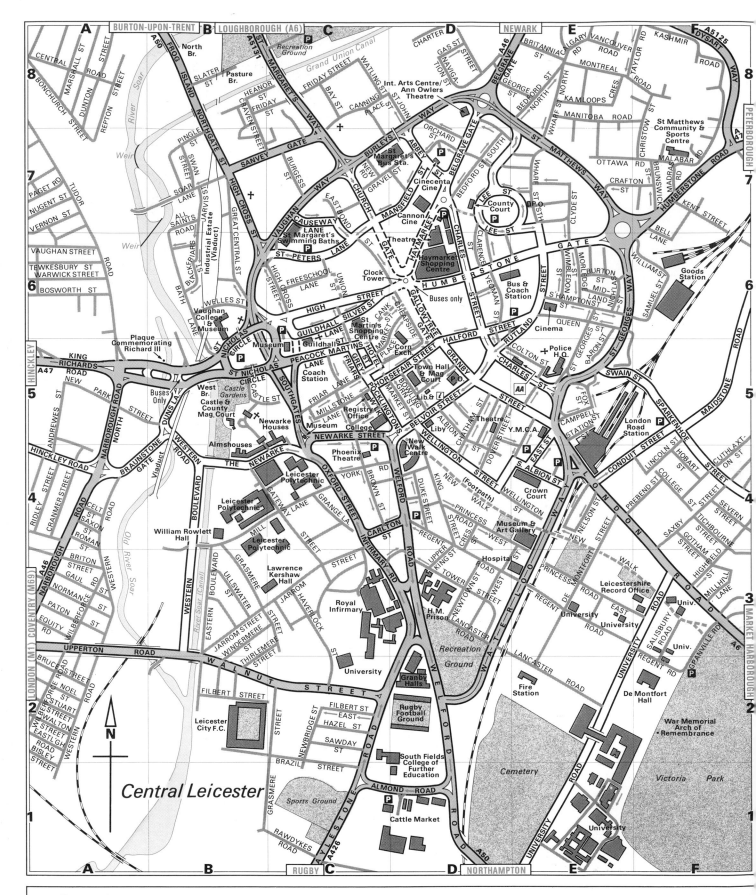

Leicester

A regional capital in Roman times, Leicester has retained many buildings from its eventful and distinguished past. Today the city is a thriving modern place, a centre for industry and commerce, serving much of the Midlands. Among the most outstanding monuments from the past is the Jewry Wall, a great bastion of Roman masonry. Close by are remains of the Roman baths and

several other contemporary buildings. Attached is a museum covering all periods from prehistoric times to 1500. Numerous other museums include the Wygston's House Museum of Costume, with displays covering the period 1769 to 1924; Newarke House, with collections showing changing social conditions in Leicester through four hundred years; and Leicestershire Museum and Art Gallery, with collections of drawings, paintings, ceramics, geology and natural history.

The medieval Guildhall has many features of interest, including a great hall, library and police cells. Leicester's castle, although remodelled in the 17th century, retains a 12th-century great hall. The Church of St Mary de Castro, across the road from the castle, has features going back at least as far as Norman times; while St Nicholas's Church is even older, with Roman and Saxon foundations. St Martin's Cathedral dates mainly from the 13th to 15th centuries and has a notable Bishop's throne.

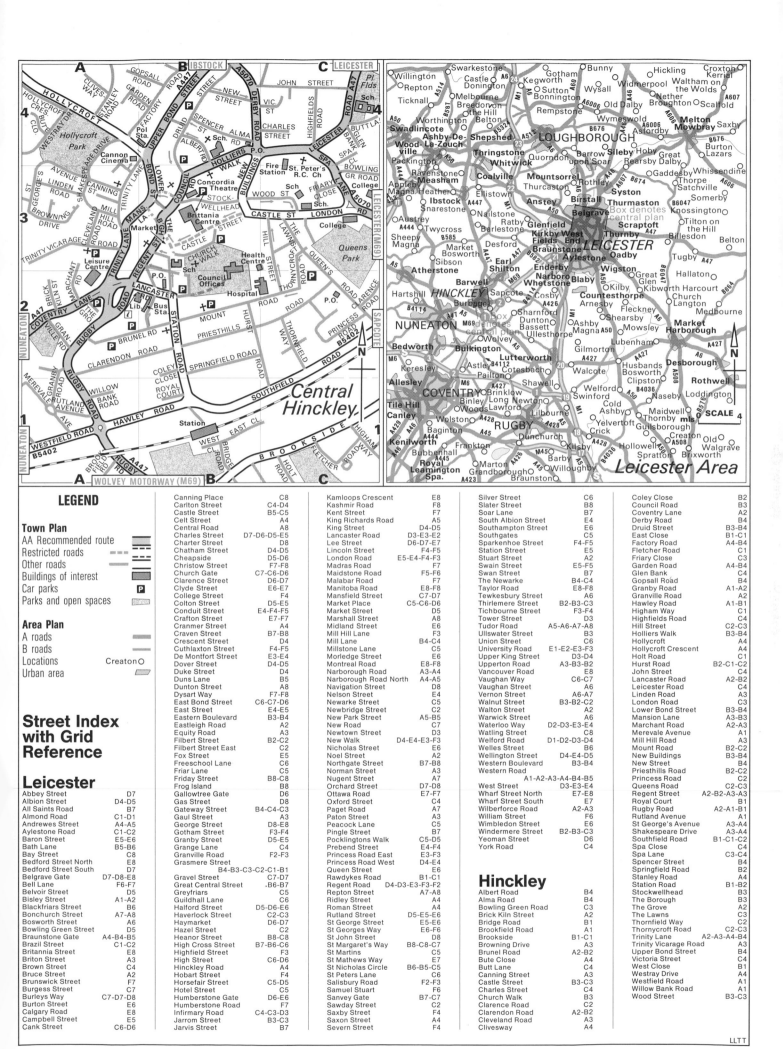

LEGEND

Town Plan

AA Recommended route
Restricted roads
Other roads
Buildings of interest
Car parks　[P]
Parks and open spaces　[P]

Area Plan

A roads
B roads
Locations　　Creaton o
Urban area

Street Index with Grid Reference

Leicester

Abbey Street	D7
Albion Street	D4-D5
All Saints Road	B7
Almond Road	C1-D1
Andrewes Street	A4-A5
Aylestone Road	C1-C2
Baron Street	E5-E6
Bath Lane	B5-B6
Bay Street	C8
Bedford Street North	E8
Bedford Street South	D7
Belgrave Gate	D7-D8-E8
Bell Lane	F6-F7
Belvoir Street	D5
Bisley Street	A1-A2
Blackfriars Street	B6
Bonchurch Street	A7-A8
Bosworth Street	A6
Bowling Green Street	D5
Braunstone Gate	A4-B4-B5
Brazil Street	C1-C2
Britannia Street	E8
Briton Street	A3
Brown Street	C4
Bruce Street	A2
Brunswick Street	F7
Burgess Street	C7
Burleys Way	C7-D7-D8
Burton Street	E6
Calgary Road	E8
Campbell Street	E5
Cank Street	C6-D6
Canning Place	C8
Carlton Street	C4-D4
Castle Street	B5-C5
Celt Street	A4
Central Road	A8
Charles Street	D7-D6-D5-E5
Charter Street	D8
Chatham Street	D4-D5
Cheapside	D5-D6
Christow Street	F7-F8
Church Gate	C7-C6-D6
Clarence Street	D6-D7
Clyde Street	E6-E7
College Street	F4
Colton Street	D5-E5
Conduit Street	E4-F4-F5
Crafton Street	E7-F7
Cranmer Street	A4
Craven Street	B7-B8
Crescent Street	D4
Cuthlaxton Street	F4-F5
De Montfort Street	E3-E4
Dover Street	D4-D5
Duke Street	D4
Duns Lane	B5
Dunton Street	A8
Dysart Way	F7-F8
East Bond Street	C6-C7-D6
East Street	E4-E5
Eastern Boulevard	B3-B4
Eastleigh Road	A2
Equity Road	A3
Filbert Street	B2-C2
Filbert Street East	C2
Fox Street	E5
Freeschool Lane	C5
Friar Lane	C5
Friday Street	B8-C8
Frog Island	B8
Gallowtree Gate	D6
Gas Street	D8
Gateway Street	B4-C4-C3
Gaul Street	A3
George Street	D8-E8
Gotham Street	F3-F4
Granby Street	D5-E5
Grange Lane	C4
Granville Road	F2-F3
Grasmere Street	B4-B3-C3-C2-C1-B1
Gravel Street	C7-D7
Great Central Street	.B6-B7
Greyfriars	C5
Guildhall Lane	C5
Halford Street	D5-D6-E6
Haverlock Street	C2-C3
Haymarket	D6-D7
Hazel Street	C2
Heanor Street	B8-C8
High Cross Street	B7-B6-C6
Highfield Street	F3
High Street	C6-D6
Hinckley Road	A4
Hobart Street	F4
Horsefair Street	C5-D5
Hotel Street	C5
Humberstone Gate	D6-E6
Humberstone Road	F7
Infirmary Road	C4-C3-D3
Jarrom Street	B3-C3
Jarvis Street	B7
Kamloops Crescent	E8
Kashmir Road	F8
Kent Street	F7
King Richards Road	A5
King Street	D4-D5
Lancaster Road	D3-E3-E2
Lee Street	D6-D7-E7
Lincoln Street	F4-F5
London Road	E5-E4-F4-F3
Madras Road	F7
Maidstone Road	F5-F6
Malabar Road	F7
Manitoba Road	E8-F8
Mansfield Street	C7-D7
Market Place	C5-C6-D6
Market Street	D5
Marshall Street	A8
Midland Street	E6
Mill Hill Lane	F3
Mill Lane	B4-C4
Millstone Lane	C5
Morledge Street	E6
Montreal Road	E8-F8
Narborough Road	A3-A4
Narborough Road North	A4-A5
Navigation Street	D8
Nelson Street	E4
Newarke Street	C5
Newbridge Street	C2
New Park Street	A5-B5
New Road	C7
Newtown Street	D3
New Walk	D4-E4-E3-F3
Nicholas Street	E6
Noel Street	A2
Northgate Street	B7-B8
Norman Street	A3
Nugent Street	A7
Orchard Street	D7-D8
Ottawa Road	E7-F7
Oxford Street	C4
Paget Road	A7
Paton Street	A3
Peacock Lane	C5
Pingle Street	B7
Pocklingtons Walk	C5-D5
Prebend Street	E4-F4
Princess Road East	E3-F3
Princess Road West	D4-E4
Queen Street	E6
Rawdykes Road	B1-C1
Regent Road	D4-D3-E3-F3-F2
Repton Street	A7-A8
Ridley Street	A4
Roman Street	A4
Rutland Street	D5-E5-E6
St George Street	E5-E6
St Georges Way	E6-F6
St John Street	D8
St Margaret's Way	B8-C8-C7
St Martins	C5
St Mathews Way	E7
St Nicholas Circle	B6-B5-C5
St Peters Lane	C5
Salisbury Road	F2-F3
Samuel Stuart	F6
Sanvey Gate	B7-C7
Sawday Street	C2
Saxby Street	F4
Saxon Street	A4
Severn Street	F4
Silver Street	C6
Slater Street	B8
Soar Lane	B7
South Albion Street	E4
Southampton Street	E6
Southgates	C5
Sparkenhoe Street	F4-F5
Station Street	E5
Stuart Street	A2
Swain Street	E5-F5
Swan Street	B7
The Newarke	B4-C4
Taylor Road	E8-F8
Tewkesbury Street	A6
Thirlemere Street	B2-B3-C3
Tichbourne Street	F3-F4
Tower Street	D3
Tudor Road	A5-A6-A7-A8
Ullswater Street	B3
Union Street	C6
University Road	E1-E2-E3-F3
Upper King Street	D3-D4
Upperton Road	A3-B3-B2
Vancouver Road	E8
Vaughan Way	C6-C7
Vaughan Street	A6
Vernon Street	A6-A7
Walnut Street	B3-B2-C2
Walton Street	A2
Warwick Street	A6
Waterloo Way	D2-D3-E3-E4
Watling Street	C8
Welford Road	D1-D2-D3-D4
Welles Street	B6
Wellington Street	D4-E4-D5
Western Boulevard	B3-B4
Western Road	A1-A2-A3-A4-B4-B5
West Street	D3-E3-E4
Wharf Street North	E7-E8
Wharf Street South	E7
Wilberforce Road	A2-A3
William Street	F6
Wimbledon Street	E6
Windermere Street	B2-B3-C3
Yeoman Street	D6
York Road	C4

Hinckley

Albert Road	B4
Alma Road	B4
Bowling Green Road	C3
Brick Kiln Street	A2
Bridge Road	B1
Brookfield Road	A1
Brookside	B1-C1
Browning Drive	A3
Brunel Road	A2-B2
Bute Close	A4
Butt Lane	C4
Canning Street	A3
Castle Street	B3-C3
Charles Street	C4
Church Walk	B3
Clarence Road	C2
Clarendon Road	A2-B2
Cleveland Road	A3
Clivesway	A4
Coley Close	B2
Council Road	B3
Coventry Lane	A2
Derby Road	B3
Druid Street	B3-B4
East Close	B1-C1
Factory Road	A4-B4
Fletcher Road	C1
Friary Close	C3
Garden Road	A4-B4
Glen Bank	C4
Gopsall Road	B3
Granby Road	A1-A2
Granville Road	A2
Hawley Road	A1-B1
Higham Way	C1
Highfields Road	C1
Hill Street	C2-C3
Holliers Walk	B3-B4
Hollycroft	A4
Hollycroft Crescent	A4
Holt Road	C1
Hurst Road	B2-C1-C2
John Street	C4
Lancaster Road	A2-B2
Leicester Road	C4
Linden Road	A3
London Road	C3
Lower Bond Street	B3-B4
Mansion Lane	A3-B3
Marchant Road	A2-A3
Merevale Avenue	A1
Mill Hill Road	A3
Mount Road	B2-C2
New Buildings	B3-B4
New Street	B4
Priesthills Road	B2-C2
Princess Road	C2
Queens Road	C2-C3
Regent Street	A2-B2-A3-A3
Royal Court	B1
Rugby Road	A2-A1-B1
Rutland Avenue	A1
St George's Avenue	A3-A4
Shakespeare Drive	A4
Southfield Road	B1-C1-C2
Spa Close	C4
Spa Lane	C3-C4
Spencer Street	B4
Springfield Road	B2
Stanley Road	A4
Station Road	B1-B2
Stockwellhead	B3
The Borough	B3
The Grove	A2
The Lawns	C3
Thornfield Way	C2
Thornycroft Road	C2-C3
Trinity Lane	A2-A3-A4-B4
Trinity Vicarage Road	A3
Upper Bond Street	B4
Victoria Street	C4
West Close	B1
Westray Drive	A4
Westfield Road	A1
Willow Bank Road	A1
Wood Street	B3-C3

LLTT

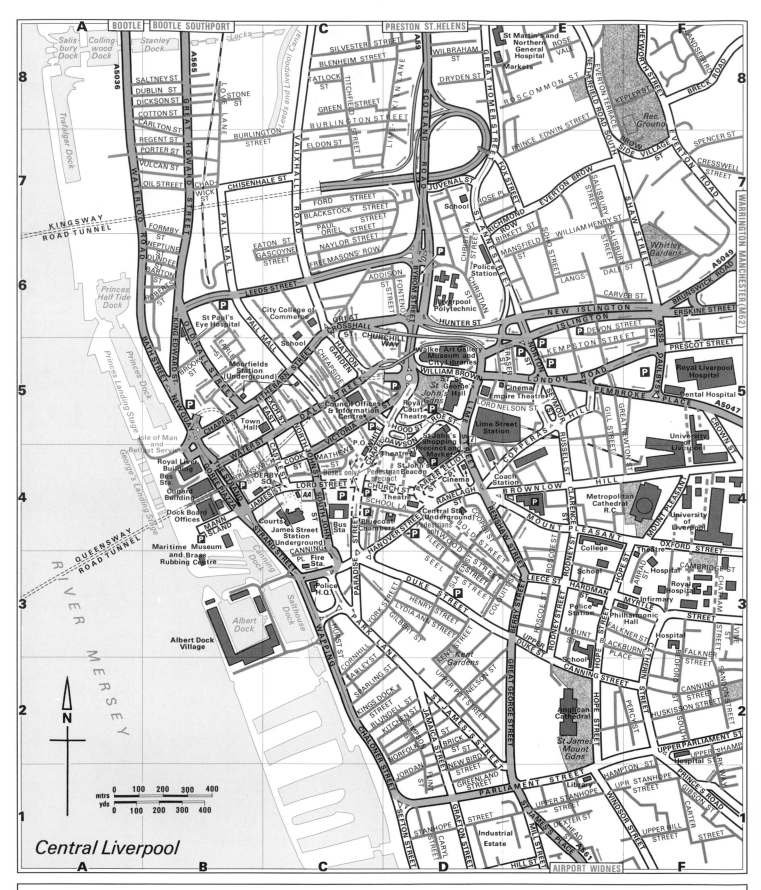

Liverpool

Although its dock area has been much reduced, Liverpool was at one time second only to London in pre-eminence as a port. Formerly the centrepiece of the docks area are three monumental buildings – the Dock Board Offices, built in 1907 with a huge copper-covered dome; the Cunard Building, dating from 1912 and decorated with an abundance of ornamental carving; and best-known of all, the world-famous Royal Liver Building, with the two 'liver birds' crowning its twin cupolas.

Some of the city's best industrial buildings have fallen into disuse in recent years, and have been preserved as monuments of the industrial age. One has become a maritime museum housing full-sized craft and a workshop where maritime crafts are demonstrated. Other museums and galleries include the Walker Art Gallery, with excellent collections of European painting and sculpture; Liverpool City Libraries, one of the oldest and largest public libraries in Britain, with a vast collection of books and manuscripts; and Bluecoat Chambers, a Queen Anne building now used as a gallery and concert hall. Liverpool has two outstanding cathedrals: the Roman Catholic, completed in 1967 in an uncompromising controversial style; and the Protestant, constructed in the great tradition of Gothic architecture, but begun in 1904 and only recently completed.

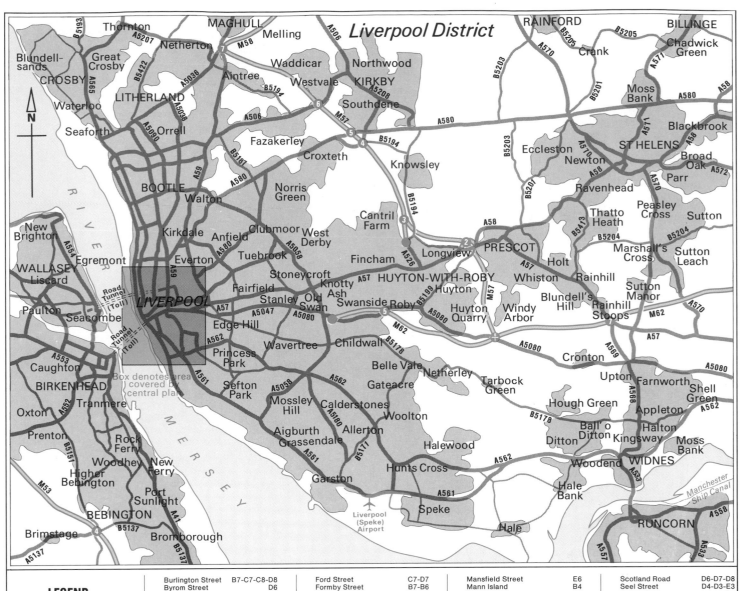

Liverpool District

LEGEND

Town Plan
AA recommended route
Restricted roads
Other roads
Buildings of interest
Car parks
Parks and open spaces
AA Centre

Area Plan
A roads
B roads
Urban area

Street Index with Grid Reference

Liverpool

Street	Grid
Addison Street	C6-D6
Arrad Street	F3-F4-F3
Barton Street	B6
Bath Street	A6-B6-B5
Bedford Street South	F2-F3
Berry Street	E3
Birkett Street	D6-E6-E7
Blackburne Place	E3-F3
Blackstock Street	C7-D7
Blenheim Street	C8-D8
Blundell Street	C2-D2
Bold Street	D4-D3-E3
Breck Road	F8
Brick Street	D2
Brook Street	B5
Brownlow Hill	D4-E4-F4
Brow Side	E7-F7
Brunswick Road	F6
Brunswick Street	B4-C4

Street	Grid
Burlington Street	B7-C7-C8-D8
Byrom Street	D6
Cambridge Street	F3
Canning Place	C3
Canning Street	E2-F2
Carlton Street	A8-B8-B7
Carter Street	F1
Carver Street	E6-F6
Caryl Street	D1
Castle Street	C4-C5
Cathrin Street	F2-F3
Chadwick Street	B7
Chaloner Street	C2-C1-D1-D2
Chatham Street	F3
Chapel Street	B5
Cheapside	C5
Chisenhale Street	B7-C7
Christian Street	D6
Christian Street	D6-D7
Churchill Way	C6-D6-D5
Church Street	C4-D4
Clarence Street	E4
Colquitt Street	D3-E3
Cook Street	C4
Cooper Street	D4-D3-E3
Copperas Hill	D4-E4-E5
Cornhill	C2-C3
Cotton Street	A8-B8
Cresswell Street	F7
Crown Street	F4-F5
Dale Street	C5
Daulby Street	F5
Dawson Street	D5-D4
Derby Square	C4
Devon Street	E6-F6
Dexter Street	E1
Dickson Street	A8-B8
Dryden Street	D8
Dublin Street	A8-B8
Duke Street	C3-D3-E3
Dundee Street	B6
Earle Street	B5
Eaton Street	B6-C6
Eldon Street	C7
Elliot Street	D4
Erskine Street	F6
Everton Brow	E7
Everton Road	F7-F8
Everton Terrace	E8-E7-F7
Exchange Street East	B5-C5
Falkner Street	F2-F3
Falkner Street	E3-F3
Fleet Street	D3-D4
Flint Street	D1
Fontenoy Street	D6

Street	Grid
Ford Street	C7-D7
Formby Street	B7-B6
Fox Street	D7-E7
Fraser Street	E5
Freemasons' Row	C6-D6
Gascoyne Street	B6-C6
Gibson Street	F1
Gilbert Street	D3
Gill Street	E4-E5
Goree Piazza	B4
Grafton Street	D1
Great Crosshall Street	C6
Great George Street	E1-E2-E3
Great Homer Street	D7-D8
Great Howard Street	B6-B7-B8
Great Newton Street	E5-E4-F4
Greenland Street	D1
Green Street	C8-D8
Hampton Street	E1-F1
Hanover Street	C3-C4-D4
Hardman Street	E3
Hatton Garden	C5-C6
Head Street	E1
Henry Street	D3
Heyworth Street	F8
Hill Street	D1-E1
Hood Street	D5
Hope Street	E2-E3-F3-F4
Hunter Street	D6
Hurst Street	C2-C3
Huskisson Street	F2
Islington	E6-F6
Jamaica Street	D1-D2
James Street	B4-C4
Jordan Street	D1-D2
Juvenal Street	D7
Kempston Street	E5-F5-F6
Kent Street	D2-D3
Kepler Street	E8-F8
Kings Dock Street	C2-D2
King Edward Street	B5-B6
Kingsway Road Tunnel	A6-A7-B7-C7
Kitchen Street	C2-D2
Landseer Road	F8
Langsdale Street	E6-F6
Leece Street	E3
Leeds Street	B6-C6-D6
Limekiln Lane	C7-D7-D8
Lime Street	D4-D5
London Road	D5-E5-F5
Lord Nelson Street	D5-E5
Lord Street	C4
Love Lane	B7-B8
Lydia Ann Street	D3

Street	Grid
Mansfield Street	E6
Mann Island	B4
Mathews Street	C4
Mill Street	E1
Moss Street	F5-F6
Mount Pleasant	F4
Mount Street	E3
Myrtle Street	E3-F3
Naylor Street	C6-D6
Nelson Street	D2-D3-E3
Neptune Street	B6
Netherfield Road South	E8-E7
New Bird Street	D1-D2
New Islington	E6-F6
New Quay	B5
North John Street	C4-C5
Norton Street	E5
Oil Street	A7-B7
Old Hall Street	B5-B6
Oriel Street	C6-C7-D7
Oxford Street	F3-F4
Pall Mall	B7-B6-C6-B5-C5
Paradise Street	C3-C4
Parker Street	D4
Park Lane	C3-D3-D2
Park Way	F1-F2
Parliament Street	D1-E1-E2
Paul Street	C7-D7
Pembroke Place	E5-F5
Percy Street	E2-F2
Porter Street	A7-B7
Prescot Street	F5-F6
Prince Edwin Street	E7-E8
Prince's Road	F1-F2
Queensway Road Tunnel	A3-A4-B4-C4-C5
Ranelagh Street	D4
Regent Street	A7-B7
Renshaw Street	D4-E4-E3
Richmond Row	D7-E7
Roberts Street	B6
Rodney Street	E3-E4
Roe Street	D5
Roscoe Street	E3-E4
Roscommon Street	D8-E8
Rose Place	D7-E7
Rose Vale	E8
Russell Street	E4-E5
St Anne Street	D7-D6-E6
St James's Place	E1
St James's Street	D2-D1-E1
Salisbury Street	E7-E6-F6
Saltney Street	A8-B8
Sandon Street	F2
School Lane	C4-D4

Street	Grid
Scotland Road	D6-D7-D8
Seel Street	D4-D3-E3
Sefton Street	D1
Seymour Street	E5
Shaw Street	E7-F7-F6
Silvester Street	C8-D8
Simpson Street	D1-D2
Slater Street	D3-D4
Soho Street	E6-E7
South John Street	C4
Sparling Street	C2-D2
Spencer Street	F7
Stanhope Street	D1-E1
Stone Street	B8
Strand Street	B4-C4-C3
Tabley Street	C2-C3-D3
Tatlock Street	C8
Titchfield Street	C7-C8
Tithebarn Street	B5-C5-C6
The Strand	B4
Upper Duke Street	E3
Upper Hampton Street	F2
Upper Hill Street	E1-F1
Upper Parliament Street	F2
Upper Pitt Street	D2
Upper Stanhope Street	F1-F2
Upper Stanhope Street	E1-F1
Vauxhall Road	C6-C7-C8
Victoria Street	C4-C5-D5
Village Street	F7
Vine Street	F3
Vulcan Street	A7-B7
Wapping	C2-C3
Waterloo Road	A8-A7-B7-A6-B6
Water Street	B4-B5-C5
Whitechapel	C4-C5-D5
Wilbraham Street	D8
William Brown Street	D5
William Henry Street	E6-E7-F7
Windsor Street	E1-F1
Wood Street	D4-D3-E3
York Street	C3-D3

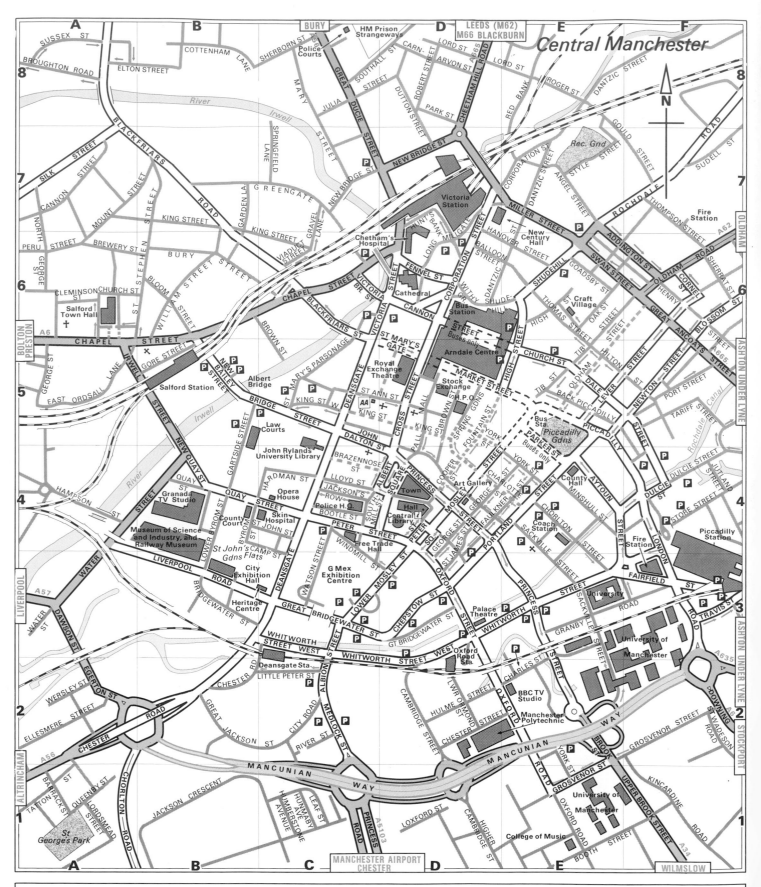

Manchester

The gigantic conurbation called Greater Manchester covers a staggering 60 square miles, reinforcing Manchester's claim to be Britain's second city. Commerce and industry are vital aspects of the city's character, but it is also an important cultural centre – the Halle Orchestra has its home at the Free Trade Hall (a venue for many concerts besides classical music), there are several theatres, a library (the John Rylands) which houses one of the most important collections of books in the world, and a number of museums and galleries, including the Whitworth Gallery with its lovely watercolours.

Like many great cities it suffered badly during the bombing raids of World War II, but some older buildings remain, including the town hall, a huge building designed in Gothic style by Alfred Waterhouse and opened in 1877. Manchester Cathedral dates mainly from the 15th century and is noted for its fine tower and outstanding carved woodwork. Nearby is Chetham's Hospital, also 15th-century and now housing a music school. Much new development has taken place, and more is planned. Shopping precincts cater for the vast population, and huge hotels have provided services up to international standards. On the edge of the city is the Belle Vue centre, a large entertainments complex including concert and exhibition facilities, and a speedway stadium.

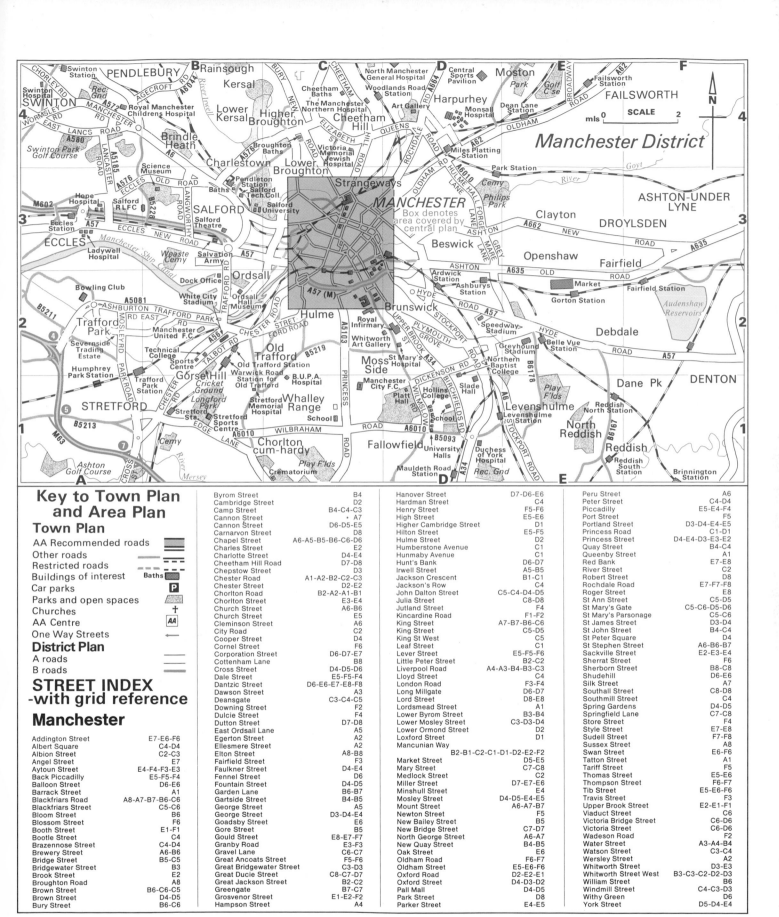

Key to Town Plan and Area Plan

Town Plan

AA Recommended roads	
Other roads	
Restricted roads	
Buildings of interest	Baths
Car parks	P
Parks and open spaces	
Churches	†
AA Centre	AA
One Way Streets	←

District Plan

A roads	
B roads	

STREET INDEX
-with grid reference

Manchester

Addington Street	E7-E6-F6
Albert Square	C4-D4
Albion Street	C2-C3
Angel Street	E7
Aytoun Street	E4-F4-F3-E3
Back Piccadilly	E5-F5-F4
Balloon Street	D6-E6
Barrack Street	A1
Blackfriars Road	A8-A7-B7-B6-C6
Blackfriars Street	C5-C6
Bloom Street	B6
Blossom Street	F6
Booth Street	E1-F1
Bootle Street	C4
Brazennose Street	C4-D4
Brewery Street	A6-B6
Bridge Street	B5-C5
Bridgewater Street	B3
Brook Street	E2
Broughton Road	A8
Brown Street	B6-C6-C5
Brown Street	D4-D5
Bury Street	B6-C6

Byrom Street	B4
Cambridge Street	D2
Camp Street	B4-C4-C3
Cannon Street	• A7
Cannon Street	D6-D5-E5
Carnarvon Street	D8
Chapel Street	A6-A5-B5-B6-C6-D6
Charles Street	E2
Charlotte Street	D4-E4
Cheetham Hill Road	D7-D8
Chepstow Street	D3
Chester Road	A1-A2-B2-C2-C3
Chester Street	B2-A2-A1-B1
Chorlton Road	E3-E4
Chorlton Street	A6-B6
Church Street	E5
Church Street	A6
Cleminson Street	C2
City Road	D4
Cooper Street	F6
Cornel Street	D6-D7-E7
Corporation Street	B8
Cottenham Lane	D4-D5-D6
Cross Street	D6-E6-E7-E8-F8
Dale Street	A3
Dantzic Street	F4
Dawson Street	C3-C4-C5
Deansgate	F2
Downing Street	F4
Dulcie Street	D7-D8
Dutton Street	A5
East Ordsall Lane	A2
Egerton Street	A2
Ellesmere Street	A8-B8
Elton Street	D4-E4
Fairfield Street	F3
Faulkner Street	D6
Fennel Street	D4-D5
Fountain Street	B6-B7
Garden Lane	B4-B5
Gartside Street	D3-D4-E4
George Street	E6
George Street	A5
Goadsby Street	B5
Gore Street	E8-E7-F7
Gould Street	C6-C7
Granby Road	C3-D3
Gravel Lane	B2-C2
Great Ancoats Street	C3-D3
Great Bridgewater Street	B2-C2
Great Ducie Street	B7-C7
Great Jackson Street	E1-E2-F2
Greengate	A4
Grosvenor Street	
Hampson Street	

Hanover Street	D7-D6-E6
Hardman Street	C4
Henry Street	F5-F6
High Street	E5-E6
Higher Cambridge Street	D1
Hilton Street	E5-F5
Hulme Street	D2
Humberstone Avenue	C1
Hunmaby Avenue	C4
Hunt's Bank	D6-D7
Irwell Street	A5-B5
Jackson Crescent	B1-C1
Jackson's Row	C4
John Dalton Street	C5-C4-D4-D5
Julia Street	C8-D8
Jutland Street	F4
Kincardine Road	F1-F2
King Street	A7-B7-B6-C6
King Street	C5-D5
King St West	C5
Leaf Street	C1
Lever Street	E5-F5-F6
Little Peter Street	B2-C2
Liverpool Road	A4-A3-B4-B3-C3
Lloyd Street	C4
London Road	F3-F4
Long Millgate	D6-D7
Lord Street	D8-E8
Lordsmead Street	A1
Lower Byrom Street	B3-B4
Lower Mosley Street	C3-D3-D4
Lower Ormond Street	D2
Loxford Street	D1
Mancunian Way	
	B2-B1-C2-C1-D1-D2-E2-F2
Market Street	D5-E5
Mary Street	C7-C8
Medlock Street	C2
Miller Street	D7-E7-E6
Minshull Street	E4
Mosley Street	D4-D5-E4-E5
Mount Street	A6-A7-B7
Newton Street	F5
New Bailey Street	B5
New Bridge Street	C7-D7
North George Street	A6-A7
New Quay Street	B4-B5
Oak Street	E6
Oldham Road	F6-F7
Oldham Street	E5-E6-F6
Oxford Road	D2-E2-E1
Oxford Street	D4-D3-D2
Pall Mall	D4-D5
Park Street	D8
Parker Street	E4-E5

Peru Street	A6
Peter Street	C4-D4
Piccadilly	E5-E4-F4
Port Street	F5
Portland Street	D3-D4-E4-E5
Princess Road	C1-D1
Princess Street	D4-E4-D3-E3-E2
Quay Street	B4-C4
Queenby Street	A1
Red Bank	E7-E8
River Street	C2
Robert Street	D8
Rochdale Road	E7-F7-F8
Roger Street	E8
St Ann Street	C5-D5
St Mary's Gate	C5-C6-D5-D6
St Mary's Parsonage	C5-C6
St James Street	D3-D4
St John Street	B4-C4
St Peter Square	D4
St Stephen Street	A6-B6-B7
Sackville Street	E2-E3-E4
Sherrat Street	F6
Sherborn Street	B8-C8
Shudehill	D6-E6
Silk Street	A7
Southall Street	C8-D8
Southmill Street	C4
Spring Gardens	D4-D5
Springfield Lane	C7-C8
Store Street	F4
Style Street	E7-E8
Sudell Street	F7-F8
Sussex Street	A8
Swan Street	E6-F6
Tatton Street	A1
Tariff Street	F5
Thomas Street	E5-E6
Thompson Street	F6-F7
Tib Street	E5-E6-F6
Travis Street	F3
Upper Brook Street	E2-E1-F1
Viaduct Street	C6
Victoria Bridge Street	C6-D6
Victoria Street	C6-D6
Wadeson Road	F2
Water Street	A3-A4-B4
Watson Street	C3-C4
Wersley Street	A2
Whitworth Street	D3-E3
Whitworth Street West	B3-C3-C2-D2-D3
William Street	B6
Windmill Street	C4-C3-D3
Withy Green	D6
York Street	D5-D4-E4

MANCHESTER
The Barton Swing Bridge carries the Bridgewater Canal over the Manchester Ship Canal, which links Manchester with the sea nearly 40 miles away. Completed in 1894, the canal is navigable by vessels up to 15,000 tons.

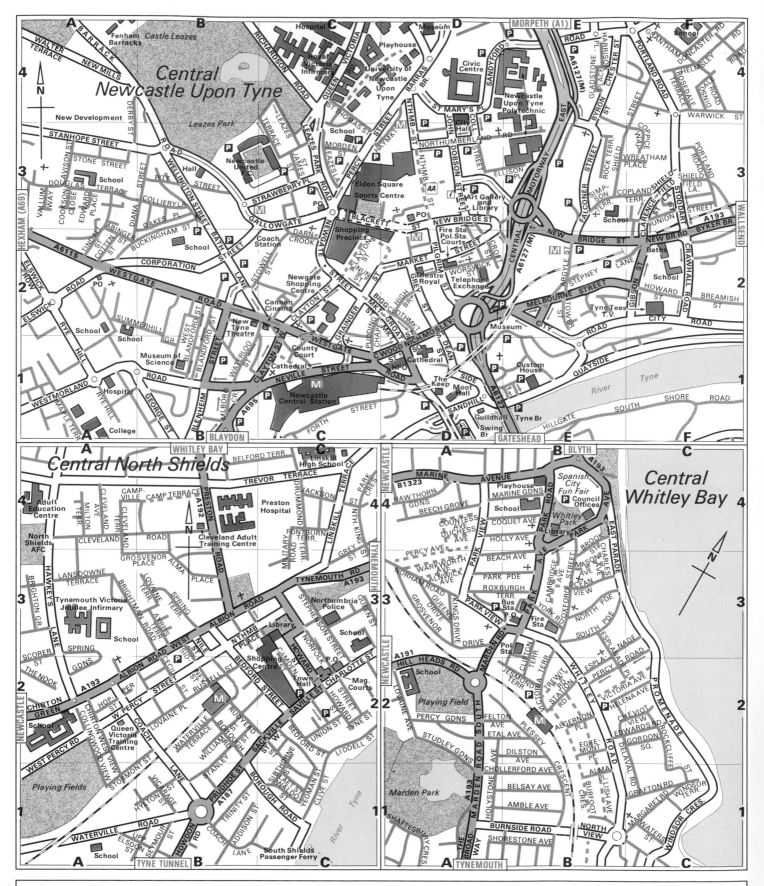

Newcastle

Six bridges span the Tyne at Newcastle; they all help to create a striking scene, but the most impressive is the High Level Bridge, built by Robert Stephenson in 1845-49 and consisting of two levels, one for the railway and one for the road. It is from the river that some of the best views of the city can be obtained. Grey Street is Newcastle's most handsome thoroughfare. It dates from the time, between 1835 and 1840, when much of this part of the city was replanned and rebuilt. Elegant façades curve up to Grey's Monument. Close to the Monument is the Eldon Centre, combining sports facilities and shopping centre to form an integrated complex which is one of the largest of its kind in Europe. Newcastle has many museums. The industrial background of the city is traced in the Museum of Science and Engineering, while the Laing Art Gallery and Museum covers painting, costumes and local domestic history. The Hancock Museum has an exceptional natural history collection and the John George Joicey Museum has period displays in a 17th-century almshouse. In Black Gate is one of Britain's most unusual museums – a collection of over 100 sets of bagpipes. Within the University precincts are three further museums. Of the city's open spaces, Town Moor is the largest. At nearly 1,000 acres it is big enough to feel genuinely wild.

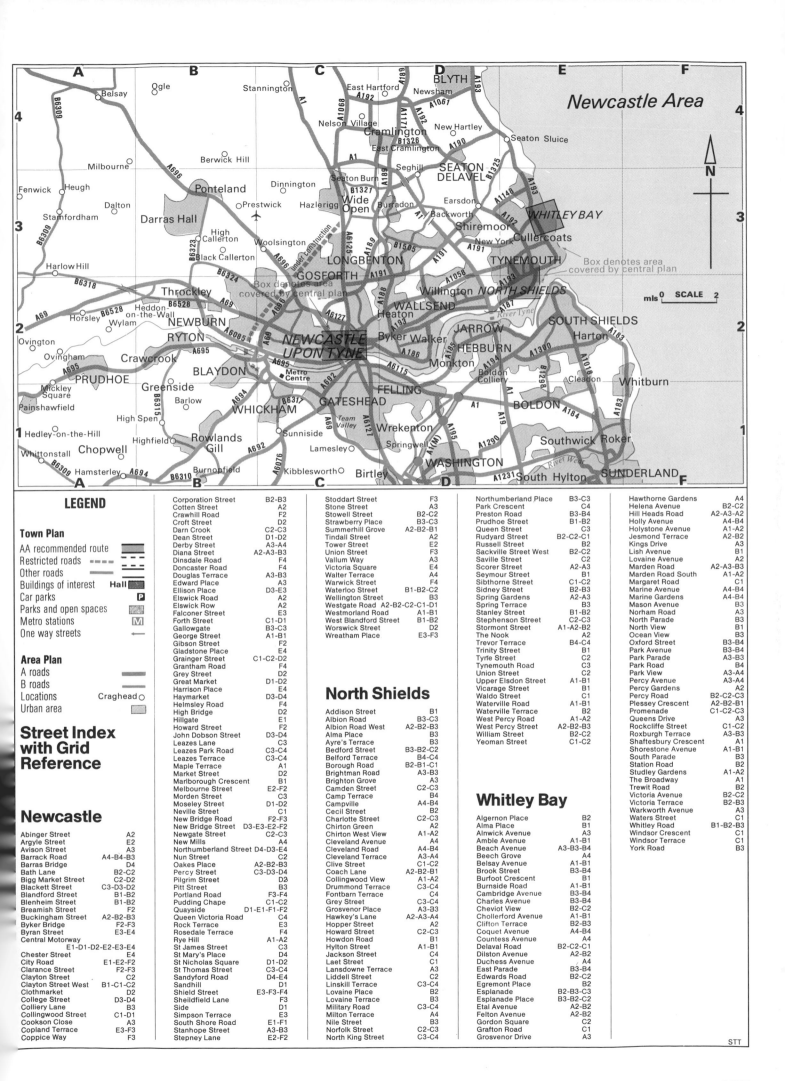

LEGEND

Town Plan

AA recommended route
Restricted roads
Other roads
Buildings of interest — Hall
Car parks — P
Parks and open spaces
Metro stations — M
One way streets

Area Plan

A roads
B roads
Locations — Craghead
Urban area

Street Index with Grid Reference

Newcastle

Abinger Street	A2
Argyle Street	E2
Avison Street	A3
Barrack Road	A4-B4-B3
Barras Bridge	D4
Bath Lane	B2-C2
Bigg Market Street	C2-D2
Blackett Street	C3-D3-D2
Blandford Street	B1-B2
Blenheim Street	B1-B2
Breamish Street	F2
Buckingham Street	A2-B2-B3
Byker Bridge	F2-F3
Byron Street	E3-E4
Central Motorway	E1-D1-D2-E2-E3-E4
Chester Street	E4
City Road	E1-E2-F2
Clarance Street	F2-F3
Clayton Street	C2
Clayton Street West	B1-C1-C2
Clothmarket	D2
College Street	D3-D4
Colliery Lane	B3
Collingwood Street	C1-D1
Cookson Close	A3
Copland Terrace	E3-F3
Coppice Way	F3
Corporation Street	B2-B3
Cotten Street	A2
Crawhill Road	F2
Croft Street	D2
Darn Crook	C2-C3
Dean Street	D1-D2
Derby Street	A3-A4
Diana Street	A2-A3-B3
Dinsdale Road	F4
Doncaster Road	F4
Douglas Terrace	A3-B3
Edward Place	A3
Ellison Place	D3-E3
Elswick Place	A2
Elswick Row	A2
Falconer Street	E3
Forth Street	C1-D1
Gallowgate	B3-C3
George Street	A1-B1
Gibson Street	F2
Gladstone Place	E4
Grainger Street	C1-C2-D2
Grantham Road	F4
Grey Street	D2
Great Market	D1-D2
Harrison Place	E4
Haymarket	D3-D4
Helmsley Road	F4
High Bridge	D2
Hillgate	E1
Howard Street	F2
John Dobson Street	D3-D4
Leazes Lane	C3
Leazes Park Road	C3-C4
Leazes Terrace	C3-C4
Maple Terrace	A1
Market Street	D2
Marlborough Crescent	B1
Melbourne Street	E2-F2
Morden Street	C3
Moseley Street	D1-D2
Neville Street	C1
New Bridge Road	F2-F3
New Bridge Street	D3-E3-E2-F2
Newgate Street	C2-C3
New Mills	A4
Northumberland Street	D4-D3-E4
Nun Street	C2
Oakes Place	A2-B2-B3
Percy Street	C3-D3-D4
Pilgrim Street	D2
Pitt Street	B3
Portland Road	F3-F4
Pudding Chape	C1-C2
Quayside	D1-E1-F1-F2
Queen Victoria Road	C4
Rock Terrace	E3
Rosedale Terrace	F4
Rye Hill	A1-A2
St James Street	C3
St Mary's Place	D4
St Nicholas Square	D1-D2
St Thomas Street	C3-C4
Sandyford Road	D4-E4
Sandhill	D1
Shield Street	E3-F3-F4
Sheildfield Lane	F3
Side	D1
Simpson Terrace	E3
South Shore Road	E1-F1
Stanhope Street	A3-B3
Stepney Lane	E2-F2
Stoddart Street	F3
Stone Street	A3
Stowell Street	B2-C2
Strawberry Place	B3-C3
Summerhill Grove	A2-B2-B1
Tindall Street	A2
Tower Street	E2
Union Street	F3
Vallum Way	A3
Victoria Square	E4
Walter Terrace	A4
Warwick Street	F4
Waterloo Street	B1-B2-C2
Westmorland Road	A1-B1
West Blandford Street	B1-B2
Worswick Street	D2
Wreatham Place	E3-F3

North Shields

Addison Street	B1
Albion Road	B3-C3
Albion Road West	A2-B2-B3
Alma Place	B3
Ayre's Terrace	B3
Bedford Street	B3-B2-C2
Belford Terrace	B4-C4
Borough Road	B2-B1-C1
Brightman Road	A3-B3
Brighton Grove	A3
Camden Street	C2-C3
Camp Terrace	B4
Campville	A4-B4
Cecil Street	B2
Charlotte Street	C2-C3
Chirton Green	A2
Chirton West View	A1-A2
Cleveland Avenue	A4
Cleveland Road	A4-B4
Cleveland Terrace	A3-A4
Clive Street	C1-C2
Coach Lane	A2-B2-B1
Collingwood View	A1-A2
Drummond Terrace	C3-C4
Fontbarn Terrace	C4
Grey Street	C3-C4
Grosvenor Place	A3-B3
Hawkey's Lane	A2-A3-A4
Hopper Street	A2
Howard Street	C2-C3
Howdon Road	B1
Hylton Street	A1-B1
Jackson Street	C4
Laet Street	C1
Lansdowne Terrace	A3
Liddell Street	C2
Linskill Terrace	C3-C4
Lovaine Place	B2
Lovaine Terrace	B3
Military Road	C3-C4
Milton Terrace	A4
Nile Street	B3
Norfolk Street	C2-C3
North King Street	C3-C4
Northumberland Place	B3-C3
Park Crescent	C4
Preston Road	B3-B4
Prudhoe Street	B1-B2
Queen Street	C3
Rudyard Street	B2-C2-C1
Russell Street	B2
Sackville Street West	B2-C2
Saville Street	C2
Scorer Street	A2-A3
Seymour Street	B1
Sibthorne Street	C1-C2
Sidney Street	B2-B3
Spring Gardens	A2-A3
Spring Terrace	B3
Stanley Street	B1-B2
Stephenson Street	C2-C3
Stormont Street	A1-A2-B2
The Nook	A2
Trevor Terrace	B4-C4
Trinity Street	B1
Tyrle Street	C2
Tynemouth Road	C3
Union Street	C2
Upper Elsdon Street	A1-B1
Vicarage Street	B1
Waldo Street	C1
Waterville Road	A1-B1
Waterville Terrace	B2
West Percy Road	A1-A2
West Percy Street	A2-B2-B3
William Street	B2-C2
Yeoman Street	C1-C2

Whitley Bay

Algernon Place	B2
Alma Place	B1
Alnwick Avenue	A3
Amble Avenue	A1-B1
Beach Avenue	A3-B3-B4
Beech Grove	A4
Belsay Avenue	A1-B1
Brook Street	B3-B4
Burfoot Crescent	B1
Burnside Road	A1-B1
Cambridge Avenue	B3-B4
Charles Avenue	B3-B4
Cheviot View	B2-C2
Chollerford Avenue	A1-B1
Clifton Terrace	B2-B3
Coquet Avenue	A4-B4
Countess Avenue	A4
Delaval Road	B2-C2-C1
Dilston Avenue	A2-B2
Duchess Avenue	A4
East Parade	B3-B4
Edwards Road	B2-C2
Egremont Place	B2
Esplanade	B2-B3-B3
Esplanade Place	B3-B2-C2
Etal Avenue	A2-B2
Felton Avenue	A2-B2
Gordon Square	C2
Grafton Road	C1
Grosvenor Drive	A3
Hawthorne Gardens	A4
Helena Avenue	B2-C2
Hill Heads Road	A2-A3-A2
Holly Avenue	A4-B4
Holystone Avenue	A1-A2
Jesmond Terrace	A2-B2
Kings Drive	A3
Lish Avenue	B1
Lovaine Avenue	A2
Marden Road	A2-A3-B3
Marden Road South	A1-A2
Margaret Road	C1
Marine Avenue	A4-B4
Marine Gardens	A4-B4
Mason Avenue	B3
Norham Road	A3
North Parade	B3
North View	B1
Ocean View	B3
Oxford Street	B3-B4
Park Avenue	B3-B4
Park Parade	A3-B3
Park Road	B4
Park View	A3-A4
Percy Avenue	A3-A4
Percy Gardens	A2
Percy Road	B2-C2-C3
Plessey Crescent	A2-B2-B1
Promenade	C1-C2-C3
Queens Drive	A3
Rockcliffe Street	C1-C2
Roxburgh Terrace	A3-B3
Shaftesbury Crescent	A1
Shorestone Avenue	A1-B1
South Parade	B3
Station Road	B2
Studley Gardens	A1-A2
The Broadway	A1
Trewit Road	B2
Victoria Avenue	B2-C2
Victoria Terrace	B2-B3
Warkworth Avenue	A3
Waters Street	C1
Whitley Road	B1-B2-B3
Windsor Crescent	C1
Windsor Terrace	C1
York Road	B3

STT

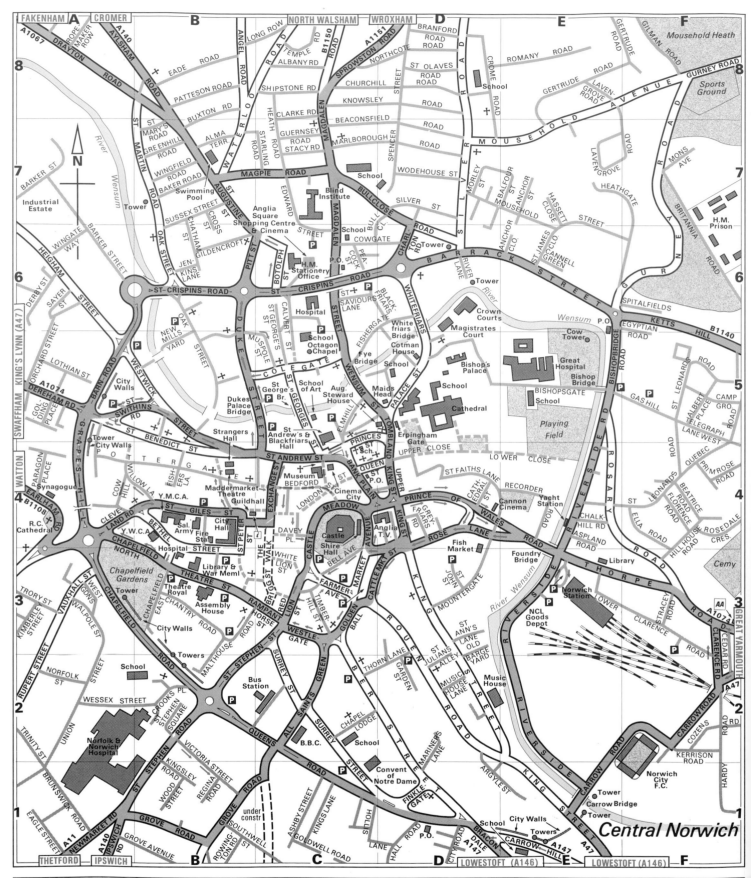

Norwich

Fortunately the heart has not been ripped out of Norwich to make way for some bland precinct, so its ancient character has been preserved. Narrow alleys run between the streets – sometimes opening out into quiet courtyards, sometimes into thoroughfares packed with people, sometimes into lanes which seem quite deserted. It is a unique place, with something of interest on every corner.

The cathedral was founded in 1096 by the city's first bishop, Herbert de Losinga. Among its most notable features are the nave, with its huge pillars, the bishop's throne (a Saxon survival unique in Europe) and the cloisters with their matchless collection of roof bosses. Across the city is the great stone keep of the castle, set on a mound and dominating all around it. It dates from Norman times, but was refaced in 1834. The keep now forms part of Norwich Castle Museum – an extensive and fascinating collection. Other museums are Bridewell Museum – collections relating to local crafts and industries within a 14th-century building – and Strangers' Hall, a genuinely 'old world' house, rambling and full of surprises, both in its tumble of rooms and in the things which they contain. Especially picturesque parts of the city are Elm Hill – a street of ancient houses; Tombland – with two gateways into the Cathedral Close; and Pull's Ferry – a watergate by the river.

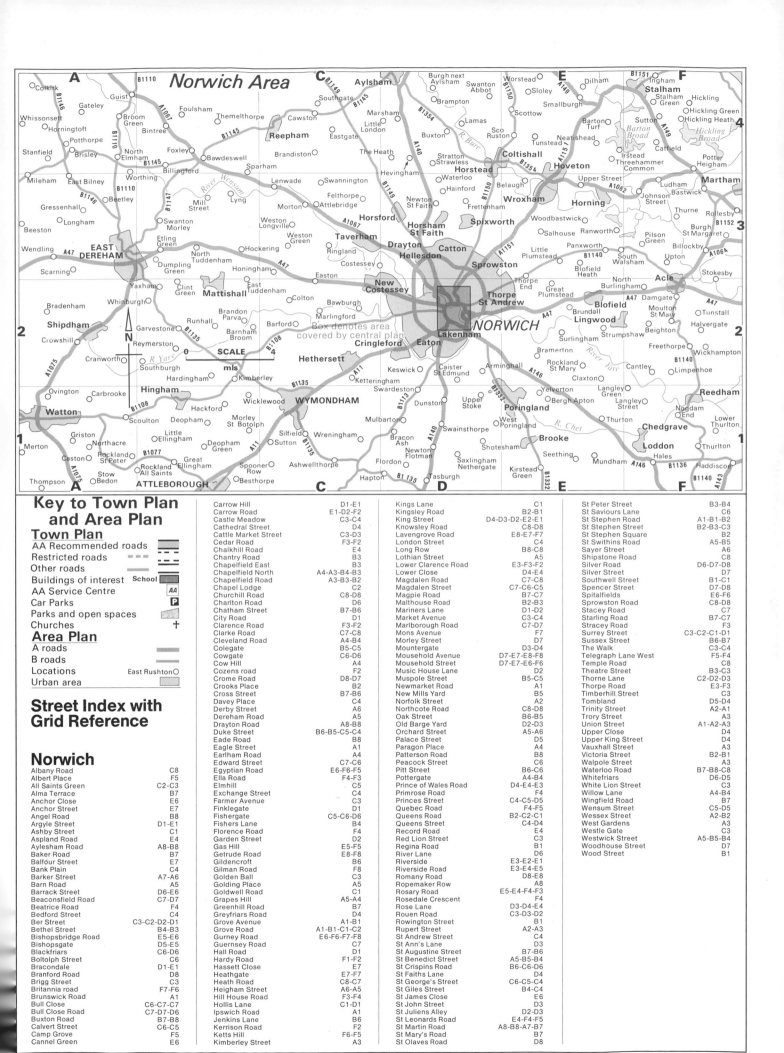

Norwich Area

Key to Town Plan and Area Plan

Town Plan
- AA Recommended roads
- Restricted roads
- Other roads
- Buildings of interest — School
- AA Service Centre — AA
- Car Parks — P
- Parks and open spaces
- Churches — †

Area Plan
- A roads
- B roads
- Locations — East Rushton○
- Urban area

Street Index with Grid Reference

Norwich

Street	Grid Ref
Albany Road	C8
Albert Place	F5
All Saints Green	C2-C3
Alma Terrace	B7
Anchor Close	E6
Anchor Street	E7
Angel Road	B8
Argyle Street	D1-E1
Ashby Street	C1
Aspland Road	E4
Aylesham Road	A8-B8
Baker Road	B7
Balfour Street	E7
Bank Plain	C4
Barker Street	A7-A6
Barn Road	A5
Barrack Street	D6-E6
Beaconsfield Road	C7-D7
Beatrice Road	F4
Bedford Street	C4
Ber Street	C3-C2-D2-D1
Bethel Street	B4-B3
Bishopsbridge Road	E5-E6
Bishopsgate	D5-E5
Blackfriars	C6-D6
Boltolph Street	C6
Bracondale	D1-E1
Branford Road	D8
Brigg Street	C3
Britannia road	F7-F6
Brunswick Road	A1
Bull Close	C6-C7-C7
Bull Close Road	C7-D7-D6
Buxton Road	B7-B8
Calvert Street	C6-C5
Camp Grove	F5
Cannel Green	E6

Street	Grid Ref
Carrow Hill	D1-E1
Carrow Road	E1-D2-F2
Castle Meadow	C3-C4
Cathedral Street	D4
Cattle Market Street	C3-D3
Cedar Road	F3-F2
Chalkhill Road	E4
Chantry Road	B3
Chapelfield East	B3
Chapelfield North	A4-A3-B4-B3
Chapelfield Road	A3-B3-B2
Chapel Lodge	C2
Churchill Road	C8-D8
Charlton Road	D6
Chatham Street	B7-B6
City Road	D1
Clarence Road	F3-F2
Clarke Road	C7-C8
Cleveland Road	A4-B4
Colegate	B5-C5
Cowgate	C6-D6
Cow Hill	A4
Cozens road	F2
Crome Road	D8-D7
Crooks Place	B2
Cross Street	B7-B6
Davey Place	C4
Derby Street	A6
Dereham Road	A5
Drayton Road	A8-B8
Duke Street	B6-B5-C5-C4
Eade Road	B8
Eagle Street	A1
Earlham Road	A4
Edward Street	C7-C6
Egyptian Road	E6-F6-F5
Ella Road	F4-F3
Elmhill	C5
Exchange Street	C4
Farmer Avenue	C3
Finklegate	D1
Fishergate	C5-C6-D6
Fishers Lane	B4
Florence Road	F4
Garden Street	D2
Gas Hill	E5-F5
Getrude Road	E8-F8
Gildencroft	B6
Gilman Road	F8
Golden Ball	C3
Golding Place	A5
Goldwell Road	C1
Grapes Hill	A5-A4
Greenhill Road	B7
Greyfriars Road	D4
Grove Avenue	A1-B1
Grove Road	A1-B1-C1-C2
Gurney Road	E6-F6-F7-F8
Guernsey Road	C7
Hall Road	D1
Hardy Road	F1-F2
Hassett Close	E7
Heathgate	E7-F7
Heath Road	C8-C7
Heigham Street	A6-A5
Hill House Road	F3-F4
Hollis Lane	C1-D1
Ipswich Road	A1
Jenkins Lane	B6
Kerrison Road	F2
Ketts Hill	F6-F5
Kimberley Street	A3

Street	Grid Ref
Kings Lane	C1
Kingsley Road	B2-B1
King Street	D4-D3-D2-E2-E1
Knowsley Road	C8-D8
Lavengrove Road	E8-E7-F7
London Street	C4
Long Row	B8-C8
Lothian Street	A5
Lower Clarence Road	E3-F3-F2
Lower Close	D4-E4
Magdalen Road	C7-C8
Magdalen Street	C7-C6-C5
Magpie Road	B7-C7
Malthouse Road	B2-B3
Mariners Lane	D1-D2
Market Avenue	C3-C4
Marlborough Road	C7-D7
Mons Avenue	F7
Morley Street	D7
Mountergate	D3-D4
Mousehold Avenue	D7-E7-E8-F8
Mousehold Street	D7-E7-E6-F6
Music House Lane	D2
Muspole Street	B5-C5
Newmarket Road	A1
New Mills Yard	B5
Norfolk Street	A2
Northcote Road	C8-D8
Oak Street	B6-B5
Old Barge Yard	D2-D3
Orchard Street	A5-A6
Palace Street	D5
Paragon Place	A4
Patterson Road	B8
Peacock Street	C5
Pitt Street	B6-C6
Pottergate	A4-B4
Prince of Wales Road	D4-E4-E3
Primrose Road	F4
Princes Street	C4-C5-D5
Quebec Road	F4-F5
Queens Road	B2-C2-C1
Queens Street	C4-D4
Record Road	E4
Red Lion Street	C3
Regina Road	B1
River Lane	D6
Riverside	E3-E2-E1
Riverside Road	E3-E4-E5
Romany Road	D8-E8
Ropemaker Row	A8
Rosary Road	E5-E4-F4-F3
Rosedale Crescent	F4
Rose Lane	D3-D4-E4
Rouen Road	C3-D3-D2
Rowington Street	B1
Rupert Street	A2-A3
St Andrew Street	C4
St Ann's Lane	D3
St Augustine Street	B7-B6
St Benedict Street	A5-B5-B4
St Crispins Road	B6-C6-D6
St Faiths Lane	D4
St George's Street	C6-C5-C4
St Giles Street	B4-C4
St James Close	E6
St John Street	D3
St Juliens Alley	D2-D3
St Leonards Road	E4-F4-F5
St Martin Road	A8-B8-A7-B7
St Mary's Road	B7
St Olaves Road	D8

Street	Grid Ref
St Peter Street	B3-B4
St Saviours Lane	C6
St Stephen Road	A1-B1-B2
St Stephen Street	B2-B3-C3
St Stephen Square	B2
St Swithins Road	A5-B5
Sayer Street	A6
Shipstone Road	C8
Silver Road	D6-D7-D8
Silver Street	D7
Southwell Street	B1-C1
Spencer Street	D7-D8
Spitalfields	E6-F6
Sprowston Road	C8-D8
Stacey Road	C7
Starling Road	B7-C7
Stracey Road	F3
Surrey Street	C3-C2-C1-D1
Sussex Street	B6-B7
The Walk	C3-C4
Telegraph Lane West	F5-F4
Temple Road	C8
Theatre Street	B3-C3
Thorne Lane	C2-D2-D3
Thorpe Road	E3-F3
Timberhill Street	C3
Tombland	D5-D4
Trinity Street	A2-A1
Trory Street	A3
Union Street	A1-A2-A3
Upper Close	D4
Upper King Street	D4
Vauxhall Street	A3
Victoria Street	B2-B1
Walpole Street	A3
Waterloo Road	B7-B8-C8
Whitefriars	D6-D5
White Lion Street	C3
Willow Lane	A4-B4
Wingfield Road	B7
Wensum Street	C5-D5
Wessex Street	A2-B2
West Gardens	A3
Westle Gate	C3
Westwick Street	A5-B5-B4
Woodhouse Street	D7
Wood Street	B1

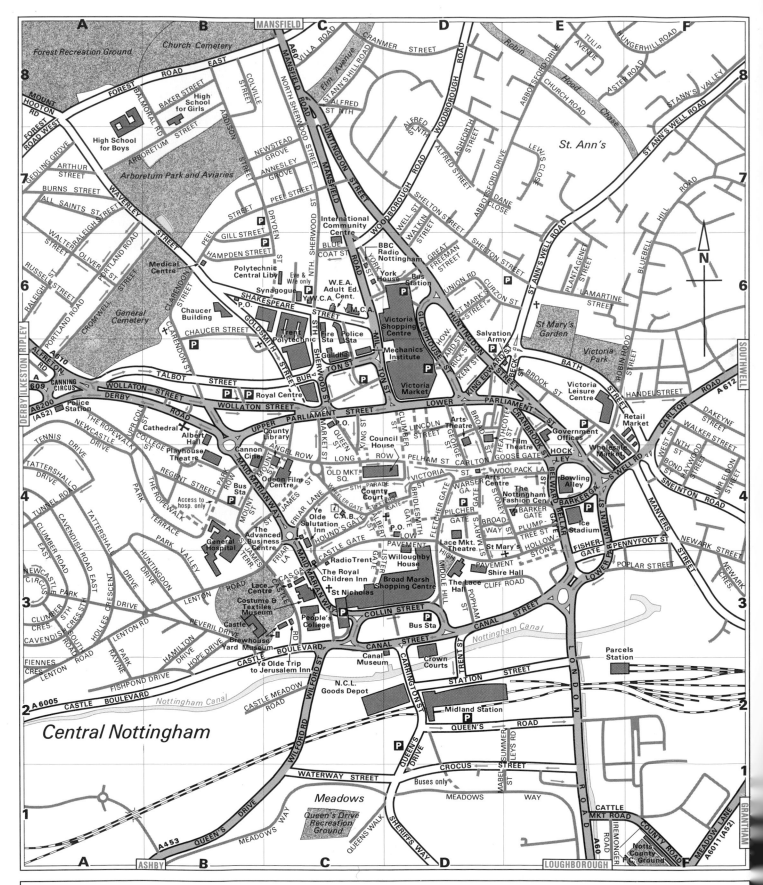

Nottingham

Hosiery and lace were the foundations upon which Nottingham's prosperity was built. The stockings came first – a knitting machine for these had been invented by a Nottinghamshire man as early as 1589 – but a machine called a 'tickler', which enabled simple patterns to be created in the stocking fabric, prompted the development of machine-made lace. The earliest fabric was produced in 1768, and an example from not much later than that is kept in the city's Castlegate Costume and Textile Museum. In fact, the entire history of lacemaking is beautifully explained in this converted row of Georgian terraces. The Industrial Museum at Wollaton Park has many other machines and exhibits tracing the development of the knitting industry, as well as displays on the other industries which have brought wealth to the city – tobacco, pharmaceuticals, engineering and printing. At Wollaton Hall is a natural history museum, while nearer the centre are the Canal Museum and the Brewhouse Yard Museum, a marvellous collection which shows items from daily life in the city up to the present day. Nottingham is not complete without mention of Robin Hood, the partly mythical figure whose statue is in the castle grounds. Although the castle itself has Norman foundations, the present structure is largely Victorian. It is now a museum.

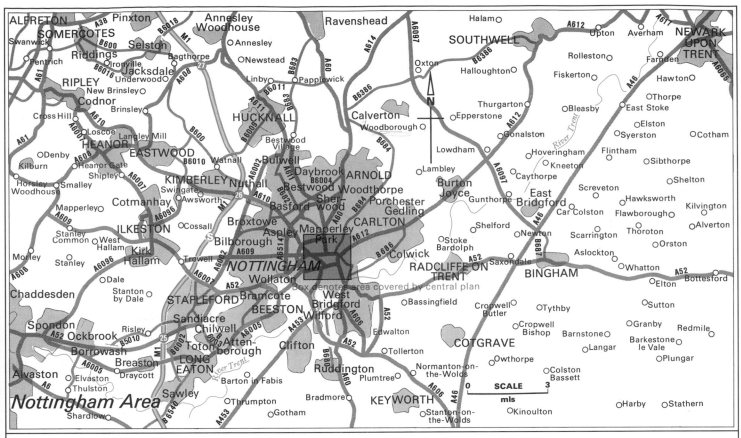

Nottingham Area

Key to Town Plan and Area Plan
Town Plan
AA Recommended roads
Restricted roads
Other roads
Buildings of interest — Theatre
Car Parks — P
Parks and open spaces
Churches — †
One Way Streets — →

Area Plan
A roads
B roads
Locations — Bagthorpe○
Urban area

Street Index with Grid Reference

Nottingham

LBTT

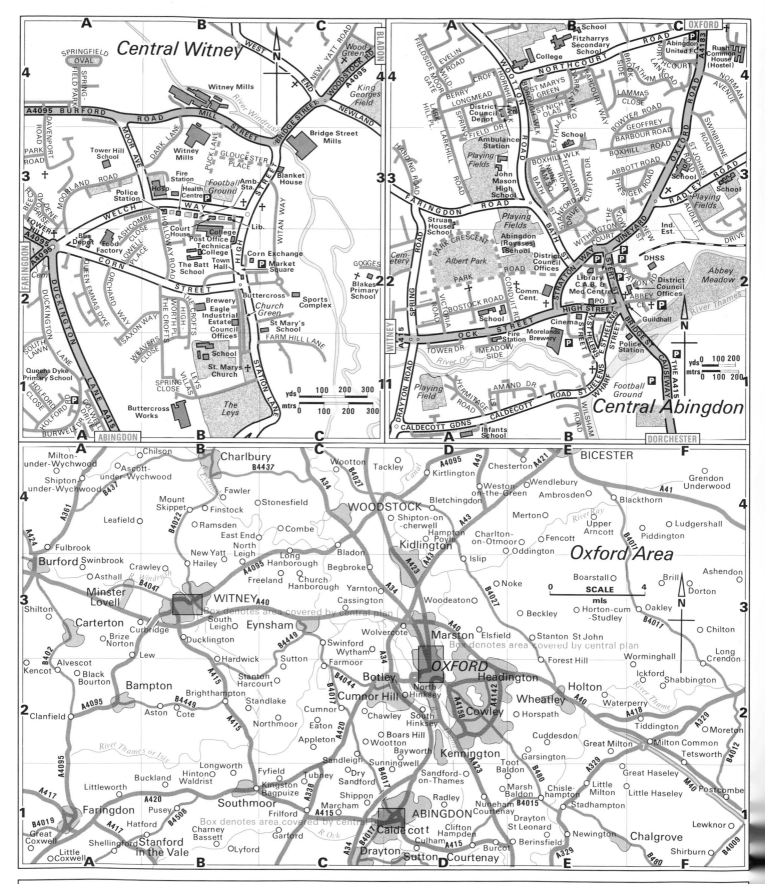

Central Witney

A4 · A B C

Springfield Oval / Spring Field Park

WEST END · NEW YATT ROAD · BLADON · WOODSTOCK RD

Witney Mills

King Georges Field

A4095 BURFORD ROAD · MILL STREET · BRIDGE STREET · NEWLAND

River Windrush

Witney Mills

Bridge Street Mills

Park Road · Davenport Road · Moor Ave · Dark Lane · Puck Lane · Gloucester Place

Tower Hill School

Fire Station · Blanket House

Moorland Road · Witney Mills · Football Ground · Amb. Sta.

Tower Hill · A4095 · Police Station · Hosp · Health Centre

Welch Way · Ashcombe Close · Holloway Road · Court House · Post Office · Technical College · College · Lib.

Witan Way

Corn Exchange

Beech Crt Rise · Dene Rise · Faringdon · A4095

Bus Depot · Food Factory · Lowell Place · The Batt School · Town Hall · Market Square

Cem · Duckington · Queen Emmas Dyke · Orchard Way · Corn Street · High · Worth Pl · The Crofts · High St · Station Street · Buttercross · Sports Complex · Gogges · Blakes Primary School

South Lawn · Saxon Way · Weavers Close · The Crofts · Brewery Eagle Industrial Estate Council Offices · St Mary's School · Church Green

Queens Dyke Primary School · School · St. Marys Church · Farm Hill Lane · Leys Villas · Spring Close

Holford Close · Holford · Colwell Drive · A415 · Burwell Dr · Buttercross Works · The Leys

ABINGDON

yds 0 100 200 300
mtrs 0 100 200 300

Central Abingdon

A B C · OXFORD · A4183

Fieldside · Evelin Road · Wild Road · School · Fitzharrys School · College · Abingdon United FC · Rush Common House (Hostel)

Moor Gate · Croft · Berry Longmead · Hill Pl · Larkhill · Spring · NORTHCOURT · Wootton Road · Harcourt Way · Brotan Rd · Northcourt Side · Norman Avenue

District Council Depot · Ambulance Station · Boxhill Wlk · St Marys Green · St Nicholas · Clifton Dr · Lammas Close · Bower Road · Geoffrey · Barbour Road · Boxhill Road · Abbott Road · Swinburne

Faringdon Road · Playing Fields · John Mason High School · Lenthall Rd · Bath St · Stanford Drive · Thesiger Road · Oxford Road · St Johns Road · Radley Road · School · School · Playing Fields

Struan House School · Playing Fields · Abingdon (Roysses) School · Withington Court · Vineyard · New Cut · Ind. Est.

Spring Road · Cemetery · PARK CRESCENT · Albert Park · ROAD · CONDUIT ROAD · District Council Offices · Stratton Way · Library C.A.B. & Med Centre · Abbey · CL · District Council Offices · Abbey Meadow

Witney · A415 · Victoria Road · Bostock Road · School · Comm. Cent. · OCK STREET · HIGH STREET · PO · St Helens · Guildhall · River Thames

Drayton Road · Tower Dr · Meadow Side · River Ock · Fire Station · Morelands Brewery · Cinema · Bridge St · Police Station · Wharf · Causeway · THE A415

Playing Field · Hermitage Road · AMAND DR · CALDECOTT ROAD · WILSHAM ROAD · Football Ground

N · yds 0 100 200
mtrs 0 100 200

CALDECOTT GDNS · Infants School · Caldecott Road · DORCHESTER

Oxford Area

A B C D E F · BICESTER

Milton-under-Wychwood · Chilson · Charlbury · Wootton · Tackley · A4095 · Chesterton · A421 · Grendon Underwood

Ascott-under-Wychwood · B4437 · B4027 · Kirtlington · Weston-on-the-Green · Wendlebury · Ambrosden · Blackthorn · A41

Shipton-under-Wychwood · B437 · Fawler · A34 · Bletchingdon · River Ray · Upper Arncott · Piddington · Ludgershall

Mount Skippet · Finstock · Stonesfield · WOODSTOCK · Shipton-on-cherwell · Hampton Poyle · Charlton-on-Otmoor · Fencott · Oddington · B4011

Leafield · B4022 · Ramsden · Combe · Kidlington · A423 · Islip · Oxford Area

A424 · Fulbrook · East End · North Leigh · Long Hanborough · Bladon · Woodeaton · Boarstall · Brill · Ashendon

A361 · Burford · Swinbrook · New Yatt · A4095 · Begbroke · A34 · Noke · SCALE · Horton-cum-Studley · Oakley · Dorton · Chilton

Shilton · Crawley · Hailey · Freeland · Church Hanborough · Yarnton · Cassington · Beckley · B4017

Minster Lovell · R. Windrush · B4047 · WITNEY A40 · South Leigh · Eynsham · Wolvercote · Marston · Elsfield · Stanton St John · Worminghall · Long Crendon

Carterton · Curbridge · Ducklington · B4449 · Swinford Wytham · Farmoor · A34 · OXFORD · Headington · Forest Hill · Ickford · Shabbington

B402 · Brize Norton · Lew · Hardwick · Sutton · North Hinksey · Botley · Cowley · Wheatley · A40 · Waterperry · A418

Alvescot · Black Bourton · Bampton · Brighthampton · Stanton Harcourt · B4044 · Cumnor Hill · South Hinksey · A4158 · A4142 · Horspath · Cuddesdon · Tiddington · A329 · Moreton

Kencot · Clanfield · A4095 · Aston · Cote · Standlake · A415 · Northmoor · Cumnor · Chawley · Eaton · Boars Hill · Wootton · Bayworth · Kennington · A423 · Toot Baldon · Garsington · Great Milton · Milton Common · Tetsworth · A4012

Longworth · Fyfield · Tubney · Dry Sandford · Sandleigh · Sunningwell · Sandford-on-Thames · Marsh Baldon · Chislehampton · Little Milton · Great Haseley · Postcombe · M40

A4095 · Buckland · Hinton Waldrist · Kingston Bagpuize · A338 · Shippon · Radley · Nuneham Courtenay · B4015 · Stadhampton · Little Haseley · Lewknor · A40

A417 · Littleworth · Frilford · A415 · Marcham · ABINGDON · Drayton St Leonard · Newington · Chalgrove · B4009

Faringdon · Pusey · A420 · Hatford · B4508 · Charney Bassett · Southmoor · Garford · Caldecott · Clifton Hampden · Culham · Berinsfield · A329 · Shirburn · B480

B4019 · Great Coxwell · Little Coxwell · Shellingford · Stanford in the Vale · Lyford · R Ock · Drayton · Sutton Courtenay · Burcot · A415

mls · 0 4

Box denotes area covered by central plan

Oxford

From Carfax (at the centre of the city) round to Magdalen Bridge stretches High Street, one of England's best and most interesting thoroughfares. Shops rub shoulders with churches and colleges, alleyways lead to ancient inns and to a large covered market, and little streets lead to views of some of the finest architecture to be seen anywhere. Catte Street, beside St Mary's Church (whose lovely tower gives a panoramic view of Oxford), opens out into Radcliffe Square, dominated by the Radcliffe Camera, a great round structure built in 1749. Close by is the Bodleian Library, one of the finest collections of books and manuscripts in the world. All around are ancient college buildings. Close to Magdalen Bridge is Magdalen College, founded in 1448 and certainly not to be missed. Across the High Street are the Botanical Gardens, founded in 1621 and the oldest such foundation in England. Footpaths lead through Christ Church Meadow to Christ Church College and the cathedral. Tom Tower is the college's most notable feature; the cathedral is actually its chapel and is the smallest cathedral in England. Among much else not to be missed in Oxford is the Ashmolean Museum, whose vast collections of precious and beautiful objects from all over the world repay many hours of study; perhaps the loveliest treasure is the 9th-century Alfred Jewel.

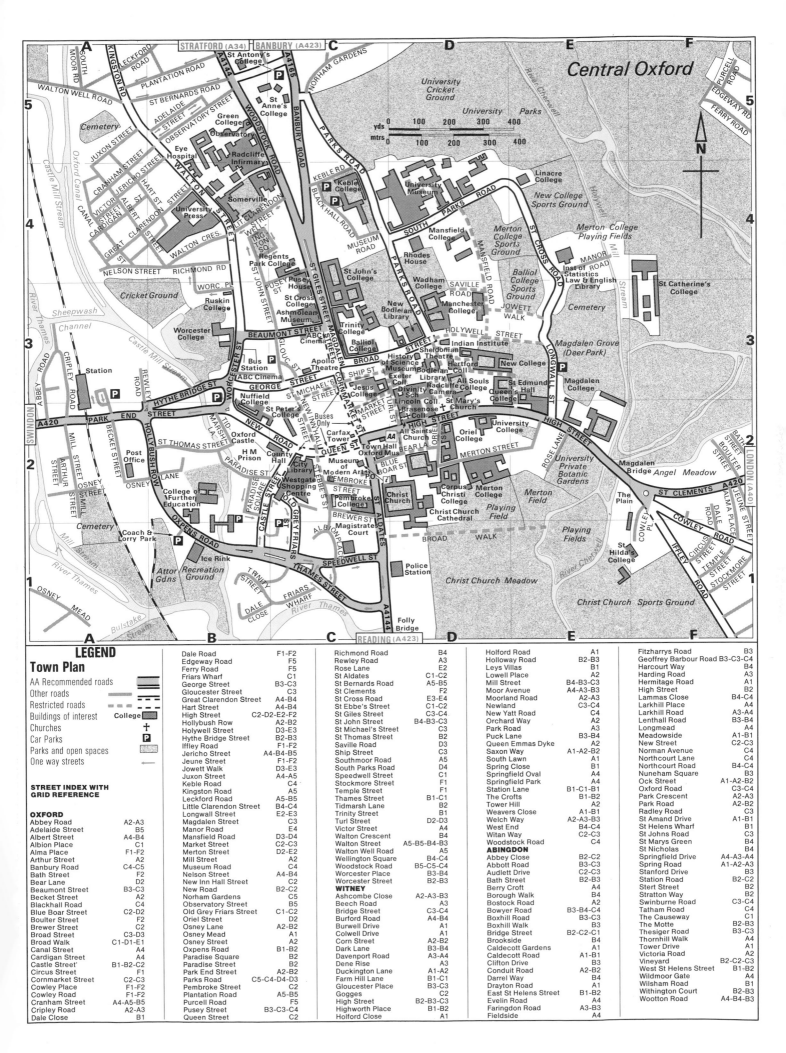

Central Oxford

STRATFORD (A34) BANBURY (A423)

READING (A423)

LEGEND

Town Plan

AA Recommended roads	
Other roads	
Restricted roads	
Buildings of interest	College
Churches	†
Car Parks	P
Parks and open spaces	
One way streets	→

STREET INDEX WITH GRID REFERENCE

OXFORD

Abbey Road	A2-A3
Adelaide Street	B5
Albert Street	A4-B4
Albion Place	C1
Alma Place	F1-F2
Arthur Street	A2
Banbury Road	C4-C5
Bath Street	F2
Bear Lane	D2
Beaumont Street	B3-C3
Becket Street	A2
Blackhall Road	C4
Blue Boar Street	C2-D2
Boulter Street	F2
Brewer Street	C2
Broad Street	C3-D3
Broad Walk	C1-D1-E1
Canal Street	A4
Cardigan Street	A4
Castle Street	B1-B2-C2
Circus Street	F1
Cornmarket Street	C2-C3
Cowley Place	F1-F2
Cowley Road	F1-F2
Cranham Street	A4-A5-B5
Cripley Road	A2-A3
Dale Close	B1

Dale Road	F1-F2
Edgeway Road	F5
Ferry Road	F5
Friars Wharf	C1
George Street	B3-C3
Gloucester Street	C3
Great Clarendon Street	A4-B4
Hart Street	A4-B4
High Street	C2-D2-E2-F2
Hollybush Row	A2-B2
Holywell Street	D3-E3
Hythe Bridge Street	B2-B3
Iffley Road	F1-F2
Jericho Street	A4-B4-B5
Jeune Street	F1-F2
Jowett Walk	D3-E3
Juxon Street	A4-A5
Keble Road	C4
Kingston Road	A5
Leckford Road	A5-B5
Little Clarendon Street	B4-C4
Longwall Street	E2-E3
Magdalen Street	C3
Manor Road	E4
Mansfield Road	D3-D4
Market Street	C2-C3
Merton Street	D2-E2
Mill Street	A2
Museum Road	C4
Nelson Street	A4-B4
New Inn Hall Street	C2
New Road	B2-C2
Norham Gardens	C5
Observatory Street	B5
Old Grey Friars Street	C1-C2
Oriel Street	D2
Osney Lane	A2-B2
Osney Mead	A1
Osney Street	A2
Oxpens Road	B1-B2
Paradise Square	B2
Paradise Street	B2
Park End Street	A2-B2
Parks Road	C5-C4-D4-D3
Pembroke Street	C2
Plantation Road	A5-B5
Purcell Road	F5
Pusey Street	B3-C3-C4
Queen Street	C2

Richmond Road	B4
Rewley Road	A3
Rose Lane	E2
St Aldates	C1-C2
St Bernards Road	A5-B5
St Clements	F2
St Cross Road	E3-E4
St Ebbe's Street	C1-C2
St Giles Street	C3-C4
St John Street	B4-B3-C3
St Michael's Street	C3
St Thomas Street	B2
Saville Road	D3
Ship Street	C3
Southmoor Road	A5
South Parks Road	D4
Speedwell Street	C1
Stockmore Street	F1
Temple Street	F1
Thames Street	B1-C1
Tidmarsh Lane	B2
Trinity Street	B1
Turl Street	D2-D3
Victor Street	A4
Walton Crescent	B4
Walton Street	A5-B5-B4-B3
Walton Well Road	A5
Wellington Square	B4-C4
Woodstock Road	B5-C5-C4
Worcester Place	B3-B4
Worcester Street	B2-B3

WITNEY

Ashcombe Close	A2-A3-B3
Beech Road	A3
Bridge Street	C3-C4
Burford Road	A4-B4
Burwell Drive	A1
Colwell Drive	A1
Corn Street	A2-B2
Dark Lane	B3-B4
Davenport Road	A3-A4
Dene Rise	A3
Duckington Lane	A1-A2
Farm Hill Lane	B1-C1
Gloucester Place	B3-C3
Gogges	C2
High Street	B2-B3-C3
Highworth Place	B1-B2
Holford Close	A1

Holford Road	A1
Holloway Road	B2-B3
Leys Villas	B1
Lowell Place	A2
Mill Street	B4-B3-C3
Moor Avenue	A4-A3-B3
Moorland Road	A2-A3
Newland	C3-C4
New Yatt Road	C4
Orchard Way	A2
Park Road	A3
Puck Lane	B3-B4
Queen Emmas Dyke	A2
Saxon Way	A1-A2-B2
South Lawn	A1
Spring Close	B1
Springfield Oval	A4
Springfield Park	A4
Station Lane	B1-C1-B1
The Crofts	B1-B2
Tower Hill	A2
Weavers Close	A1-B1
Welch Way	A2-A3-B3
West End	B4-C4
Witan Way	C2-C3
Woodstock Road	C4

ABINGDON

Abbey Close	B2-C2
Abbott Road	B3-C3
Audlett Drive	C2-C3
Bath Street	B2-B3
Berry Croft	A4
Borough Walk	B4
Bostock Road	B4
Bowyer Road	B3-B4-C4
Boxhill Road	B3-C3
Boxhill Walk	B3
Bridge Street	B2-C2-C1
Brookside	B4
Caldecott Gardens	A1
Caldecott Road	A1-B1
Clifton Drive	B3
Conduit Road	A2-B2
Darrel Way	B4
Drayton Road	A1
East St Helens Street	B1-B2
Evelin Road	A4
Faringdon Road	A3-B3
Fieldside	A4

Fitzharrys Road	B3
Geoffrey Barbour Road	B3-C3-C4
Harcourt Way	B4
Harding Road	A3
Hermitage Road	A1
High Street	B2
Lammas Close	B4-C4
Larkhill Place	A4
Larkhill Road	A3-A4
Lenthall Road	B3-B4
Longmead	A4
Meadowside	A1-B1
New Street	C2-C3
Norman Avenue	C4
Northcourt Lane	C4
Northcourt Road	B4-C4
Nuneham Square	B3
Ock Street	A1-A2-B2
Oxford Road	C3-C4
Park Crescent	A2-A3
Park Road	A2-B2
Radley Road	C3
St Amand Drive	A1-B1
St Helens Wharf	B1
St Johns Road	C3
St Marys Green	B4
St Nicholas	
Springfield Drive	A4-A3-A4
Spring Road	A1-A2-A3
Stanford Drive	B3
Station Road	B2-C2
Stert Street	B2
Stratton Way	B2
Swinburne Road	C3-C4
Tatham Road	C4
The Causeway	C1
The Motte	B2-B3
Thesiger Road	B3-C3
Thornhill Walk	A4
Tower Drive	A1
Victoria Road	A2
Vineyard	B2-C2-C3
West St Helens Street	B1-B2
Wildmoor Gate	A4
Wilsham Road	B1
Withington Court	B2-B3
Wootton Road	A4-B4-B3

173

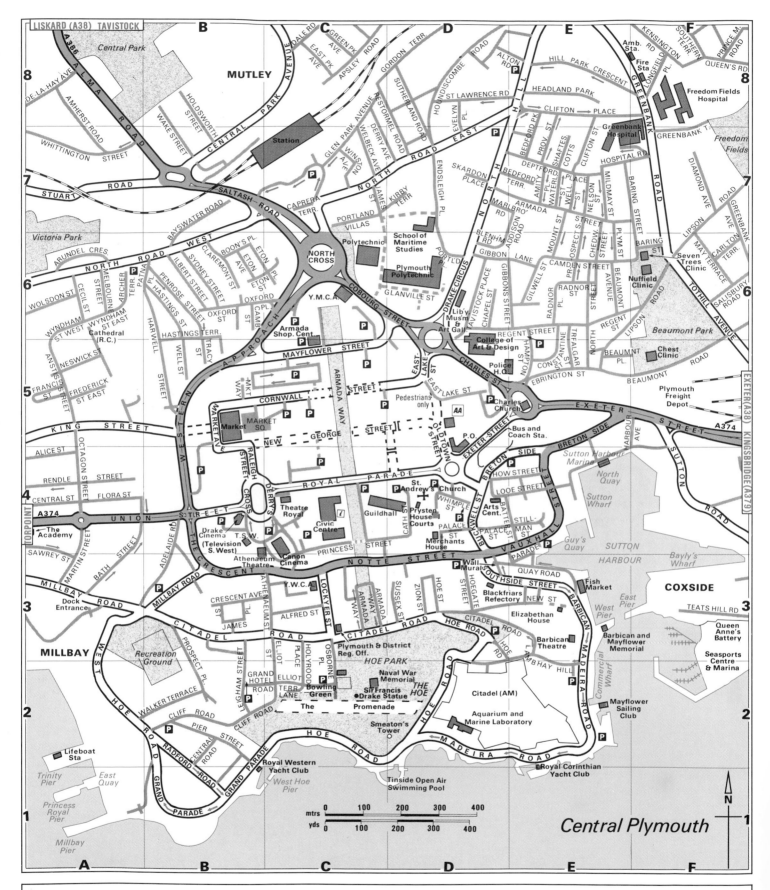

Plymouth

Ships, sailors and the sea permeate every aspect of Plymouth's life and history. Its superb natural harbour – Plymouth Sound – has ensured its importance as a port, yachting centre and naval base (latterly at Devonport) over many centuries. Sir Francis Drake is undoubtedly the city's most famous sailor. His statue stands on the Hoe – where he really did play bowls before tackling the Spanish Armada. Also on the Hoe are Smeaton's Tower, which once formed the upper part of the third Eddystone Lighthouse, and the impressive Royal Naval War Memorial. Just east of the Hoe is the Royal Citadel, an imposing fortress built in 1666 by order of Charles II. North is Sutton Harbour, perhaps the most atmospheric part of Plymouth. Here fishing boats bob up and down in a harbour whose quays are lined with attractive old houses, inns and warehouses. One of the memorials on Mayflower Quay just outside the harbour commemorates the sailing of the *Mayflower* from here in 1620. Plymouth's shopping centre is one of the finest of its kind, and was built after the old centre was badly damaged in World War II. Nearby is the 200ft-high tower of the impressive modern Civic Centre. Some buildings escaped destruction, including the Elizabethan House and the 500-year-old Prysten House. Next door is St Andrew's Church, with stained glass by John Piper.

174

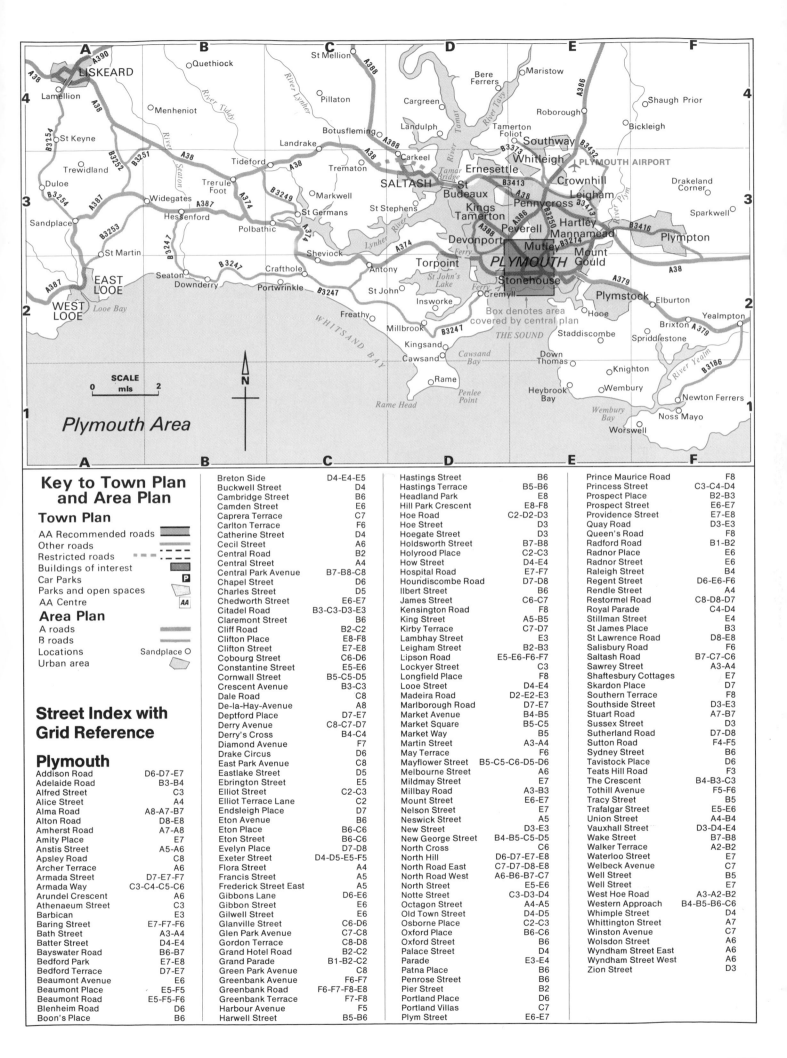

Plymouth Area

SCALE
mls
0   2

N

Key to Town Plan and Area Plan

Town Plan

AA Recommended roads
Other roads
Restricted roads
Buildings of interest
Car Parks   P
Parks and open spaces
AA Centre   AA

Area Plan

A roads
B roads
Locations   Sandplace O
Urban area

Street Index with Grid Reference

Plymouth

Addison Road	D6-D7-E7
Adelaide Road	B3-B4
Alfred Street	C3
Alice Street	A4
Alma Road	A8-A7-B7
Alton Road	D8-E8
Amherst Road	A7-A8
Amity Place	E7
Anstis Street	A5-A6
Apsley Road	C8
Archer Terrace	A6
Armada Street	D7-E7-F7
Armada Way	C3-C4-C5-C6
Arundel Crescent	A6
Athenaeum Street	C3
Barbican	E3
Baring Street	E7-F7-F6
Bath Street	A3-A4
Batter Street	D4-E4
Bayswater Road	B6-B7
Bedford Park	E7-E8
Bedford Terrace	D7-E7
Beaumont Avenue	E6
Beaumont Place	E5-F5
Beaumont Road	E5-F5-F6
Blenheim Road	D6
Boon's Place	B6

Breton Side	D4-E4-E5
Buckwell Street	D4
Cambridge Street	B6
Camden Street	E6
Caprera Terrace	C7
Carlton Terrace	F6
Catherine Street	D4
Cecil Street	A6
Central Road	B2
Central Street	A4
Central Park Avenue	B7-B8-C8
Chapel Street	D6
Charles Street	D5
Chedworth Street	E6-E7
Citadel Road	B3-C3-D3-E3
Claremont Street	B6
Cliff Road	B2-C2
Clifton Place	E8-F8
Clifton Street	E7-E8
Cobourg Street	C6-D6
Constantine Street	E5-E6
Cornwall Street	B5-C5-D5
Crescent Avenue	B3-C3
Dale Road	C8
De-la-Hay-Avenue	A8
Deptford Place	D7-E7
Derry Avenue	C8-C7-D7
Derry's Cross	B4-C4
Diamond Avenue	F7
Drake Circus	D6
East Park Avenue	C8
Eastlake Street	D5
Ebrington Street	E5
Elliot Street	C2-C3
Elliot Terrace Lane	C2
Endsleigh Place	D7
Eton Avenue	B6
Eton Place	B6-C6
Eton Street	B6-C6
Evelyn Place	D7-D8
Exeter Street	D4-D5-E5-F5
Flora Street	A4
Francis Street	A5
Frederick Street East	A5
Gibbons Lane	D6-E6
Gibbon Street	E6
Gilwell Street	E6
Glanville Street	C6-D6
Glen Park Avenue	C7-C8
Gordon Terrace	C8-D8
Grand Hotel Road	B2-C2
Grand Parade	B1-B2-C2
Green Park Avenue	C8
Greenbank Avenue	F6-F7
Greenbank Road	F6-F7-F8-E8
Greenbank Terrace	F7-F8
Harbour Avenue	F5
Harwell Street	B5-B6

Hastings Street	B6
Hastings Terrace	B5-B6
Headland Park	E8
Hill Park Crescent	E8-F8
Hoe Road	C2-D2-D3
Hoe Street	D3
Hoegate Street	D3
Holdsworth Street	B7-B8
Holyrood Place	C2-C3
How Street	D4-E4
Hospital Road	E7-F7
Houndiscombe Road	D7-D8
Ilbert Street	B6
James Street	C6-C7
Kensington Road	F8
King Street	A5-B5
Kirby Terrace	C7-D7
Lambhay Street	E3
Leigham Street	B2-B3
Lipson Road	E5-E6-F6-F7
Lockyer Street	C3
Longfield Place	F8
Looe Street	D4-E4
Madeira Road	D2-E2-E3
Marlborough Road	D7-E7
Market Avenue	B4-B5
Market Square	B5-C5
Market Way	B5
Martin Street	A3-A4
May Terrace	F6
Mayflower Street	B5-C5-C6-D5-D6
Melbourne Street	A6
Mildmay Street	E7
Millbay Road	A3-B3
Mount Street	E6-E7
Nelson Street	E7
Neswick Street	A5
New Street	D3-E3
New George Street	B4-B5-C5-D5
North Cross	C6
North Hill	D6-D7-E7-E8
North Road East	C7-D7-D8-E8
North Road West	A6-B6-B7-C7
North Street	E5-E6
Notte Street	C3-D3-D4
Octagon Street	A4-A5
Old Town Street	D4-D5
Osborne Place	C2-C3
Oxford Place	B6-C6
Oxford Street	B6
Palace Street	D4
Parade	E3-E4
Patna Place	B6
Penrose Street	B6
Pier Street	B2
Portland Place	D6
Portland Villas	C7
Plym Street	E6-E7

Prince Maurice Road	F8
Princess Street	C3-C4-D4
Prospect Place	B2-B3
Prospect Street	E6-E7
Providence Street	E7-E8
Quay Road	D3-E3
Queen's Road	F8
Radford Road	B1-B2
Radnor Place	E6
Radnor Street	E6
Raleigh Street	B4
Regent Street	D6-E6-F6
Rendle Street	A4
Restormel Road	C8-D8-D7
Royal Parade	C4-D4
Stillman Street	E4
St James Place	B3
St Lawrence Road	D8-E8
Salisbury Road	F6
Saltash Road	B7-C7-C6
Sawrey Street	A3-A4
Shaftesbury Cottages	E7
Skardon Place	D7
Southern Terrace	F8
Southside Street	D3-E3
Stuart Road	A7-B7
Sussex Street	D3
Sutherland Road	D7-D8
Sutton Road	F4-F5
Sydney Street	B6
Tavistock Place	D6
Teats Hill Road	F3
The Crescent	B4-B3-C3
Tothill Avenue	F5-F6
Tracy Street	B5
Trafalgar Street	E5-E6
Union Street	A4-B4
Vauxhall Street	D3-D4-E4
Wake Street	B7-B8
Walker Terrace	A2-B2
Waterloo Street	E7
Welbeck Avenue	C7
Well Street	B5
Well Street	B5
West Hoe Road	A3-A2-B2
Western Approach	B4-B5-B6-C6
Whimple Street	D4
Whittington Street	A7
Winston Avenue	C7
Wolsdon Street	A6
Wyndham Street East	A6
Wyndham Street West	A6
Zion Street	D3

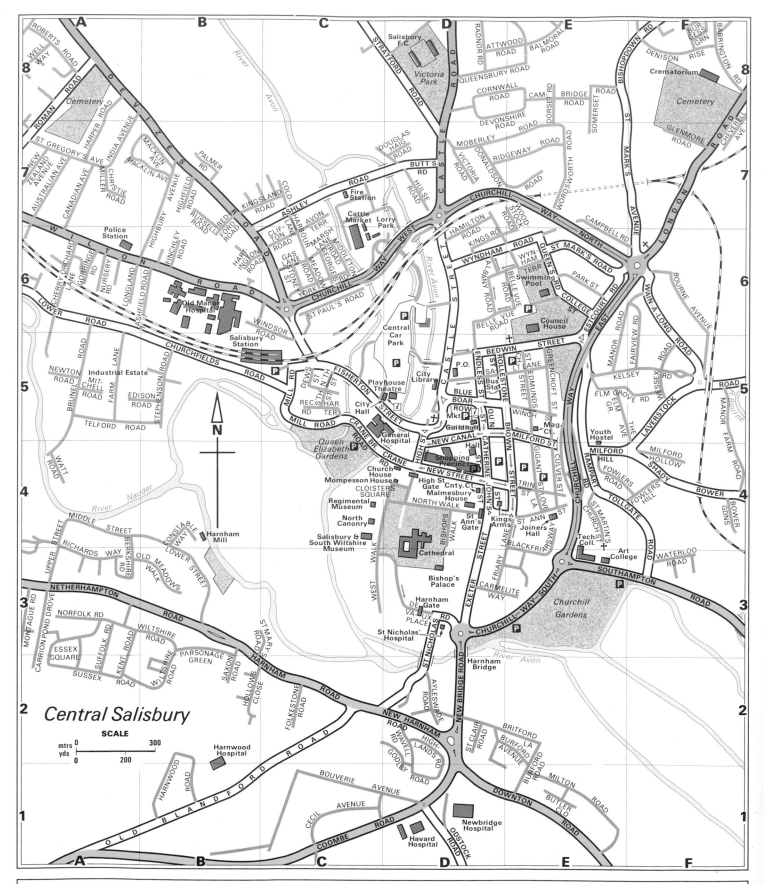

Salisbury

Its attractive site where the waters of the Avon and Nadder meet, its beautiful cathedral and its unspoilt centre put Salisbury among England's finest cities. In 1220 the people of the original settlement at Old Sarum, two miles to the north, moved down to the plain and laid the first stone of the cathedral. Within 38 years its was completed and the result is a superb example of Early English architecture.

The cloisters are the largest in England and the spire the tallest in Britain. All the houses within the Cathedral Close were built for cathedral functionaries, and although many have Georgian façades, most date back to the 13th century. Mompesson House is one of the handsome mansions here and as it belongs to the National Trust, its equally fine interior can be seen. Another building houses the Museum of the Duke of Edinburgh's Royal Regiment. At one time, relations

between the clergy and the citizens of Salisbury were not always harmonious, so the former built a protective wall around the Close.

The streets of the modern city follow the medieval grid pattern of squares, or 'chequers', and the tightly-packed houses provide a very pleasing townscape. Salisbury was granted its first charter in 1227 and flourished as a market and wool centre; there is still a twice-weekly market in the spacious square.

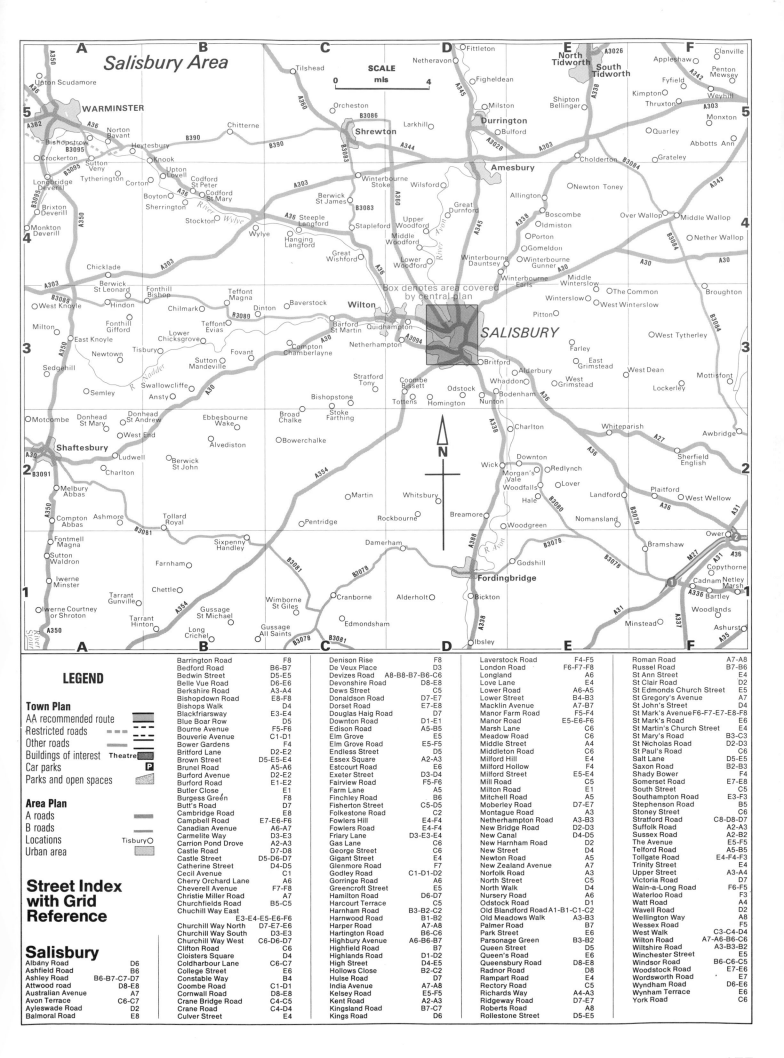

Salisbury Area

SCALE
0 mls 4

Box denotes area covered by central plan

SALISBURY

N

LEGEND

Town Plan
AA recommended route
Restricted roads
Other roads
Buildings of interest — Theatre
Car parks — P
Parks and open spaces

Area Plan
A roads
B roads
Locations — Tisbury○
Urban area

Street Index with Grid Reference

Salisbury

Albany Road	D6
Ashfield Road	B6
Ashley Road	B6-B7-C7-D7
Attwood road	D8-E8
Australian Avenue	A7
Avon Terrace	C6-C7
Ayleswade Road	D2
Balmoral Road	E8
Barrington Road	F8
Bedford Road	B6-B7
Bedwin Street	D5-E5
Belle Vue Road	D6-E6
Berkshire Road	A3-A4
Bishopdown Road	E8-F8
Bishops Walk	D4
Blackfriarsway	E3-E4
Blue Boar Row	D5
Bourne Avenue	F5-F6
Bouverie Avenue	C1-D1
Bower Gardens	F4
Britford Lane	D2-E2
Brown Street	D5-E5-E4
Brunel Road	A5-A6
Burford Avenue	D2-E2
Burford Road	E1-E2
Butler Close	E1
Burgess Green	F8
Butt's Road	D7
Cambridge Road	E8
Campbell Road	E7-E6-F6
Canadian Avenue	A6-A7
Carmelite Way	D3-E3
Carrion Pond Drove	A2-A3
Castle Road	D7-D8
Castle Street	D5-D6-D7
Catherine Street	D4-D5
Cecil Avenue	C1
Cherry Orchard Lane	A6
Cheverell Avenue	F7-F8
Christie Miller Road	A7
Churchfields Road	B5-C5
Churchill Way East	E3-E4-E5-E6-F6
Churchill Way North	D7-E7-E6
Churchill Way South	D3-E3
Churchill Way West	C6-D6-D7
Clifton Road	C6
Cloisters Square	D4
Coldharbour Lane	C6-C7
College Street	E6
Constable Way	B4
Coombe Road	C1-D1
Cornwall Road	D8-E8
Crane Bridge Road	C4-C5
Crane Road	C4-D4
Culver Street	E4
Denison Rise	F8
De Veux Place	D3
Devizes Road	A8-B8-B7-B6-C6
Devonshire Road	D8-E8
Dews Street	C5
Donaldson Road	D7-E7
Dorset Road	E7-E8
Douglas Haig Road	D7
Downton Road	D1-E1
Edison Road	A5-B5
Elm Grove	E5
Elm Grove Road	E5-F5
Endless Street	D5
Essex Square	A2-A3
Estcourt Road	E6
Exeter Street	D3-D4
Fairview Road	F5-F6
Farm Lane	A5
Finchley Road	B6
Fisherton Street	C5-D5
Folkestone Road	C2
Fowlers Hill	E4-F4
Fowlers Road	E4-F4
Friary Lane	D3-E3-E4
Gas Lane	C6
George Street	C6
Gigant Street	E4
Glenmore Road	F7
Godley Road	C1-D1-D2
Gorringe Road	A6
Greencroft Street	E5
Hamilton Road	D6-D7
Harcourt Terrace	C5
Harnham Road	B3-B2-C2
Harnwood Road	B1-B2
Harper Road	A7-A8
Hartington Road	B6-C6
Highbury Avenue	A6-B6-B7
Highfield Road	B7
Highlands Road	D1-D2
High Street	D4-E5
Hollows Close	B2-C2
Hulse Road	D7
India Avenue	A7-A8
Kelsey Road	E5-F5
Kent Road	A2-A3
Kingsland Road	B7-C7
Kings Road	D6
Laverstock Road	F4-F5
London Road	F6-F7-F8
Longland	A6
Love Lane	E4
Lower Road	A6-A5
Lower Street	B4-B3
Macklin Road	A7-B7
Manor Farm Road	F5-F4
Manor Road	E5-E6-F6
Marsh Lane	C6
Meadow Road	C6
Middle Street	A5
Middleton Road	C6
Milford Hill	E4
Milford Hollow	F4
Milford Street	E5-E4
Mill Road	C5
Milton Road	E1
Mitchell Road	A5
Moberley Road	D7-E7
Montague Road	A3
Netherhampton Road	A3-B3
New Bridge Road	D2-D3
New Canal	D4-D5
New Harnham Road	D2
New Street	D4
Newton Road	A5
New Zealand Avenue	A7
Norfolk Road	A3
North Street	C5
North Walk	A6
Nursery Road	A6
Odstock Road	D1
Old Blandford Road	A1-B1-C1-C2
Old Meadows Walk	A3-B3
Palmer Road	B7
Park Street	E6
Parsonage Green	B3-B2
Queen Street	D5
Queen's Road	E6
Queensbury Road	D8-E8
Radnor Road	D8
Rampart Road	E4
Rectory Road	C5
Richards Way	A4-A3
Ridgeway Road	D7-E7
Roberts Road	A8
Rollestone Street	D5-E5
Roman Road	A7-A8
Russel Road	B7-B6
St Ann Street	E4
St Clair Road	D2
St Edmonds Church Street	E5
St Gregory's Avenue	A7
St John's Street	D4
St Mark's Avenue	F6-F7-E7-E8-F8
St Mark's Road	E6
St Martin's Church Street	E4
St Mary's Road	B3-C3
St Nicholas Road	D2-D3
St Paul's Road	C6
Salt Lane	D5-E5
Saxon Road	B2-B3
Shady Bower	E4
Somerset Road	E7-E8
South Street	C5
Southampton Road	E3-F3
Stephenson Road	B5
Stoney Street	C6
Stratford Road	C8-D8-D7
Suffolk Road	A2-A3
Sussex Road	A2-B2
The Avenue	E5-F5
Telford Road	A5-B5
Tollgate Road	E4-F4-F3
Trinity Street	E4
Upper Street	A3-A4
Victoria Road	D7
Wain-a-Long Road	F6-F5
Waterloo Road	F3
Watt Road	A4
Wavell Road	D2
Wellington Way	A8
Wessex Road	F5
West Walk	C3-C4-D4
Wilton Road	A7-A6-B6-C6
Wiltshire Road	A3-B3-B2
Winchester Street	E5
Windsor Road	B6-C6-C5
Woodstock Road	E7-E6
Wordsworth Road	E7
Wyndham Road	D6-E6
Wynham Terrace	E6
York Road	C6

177

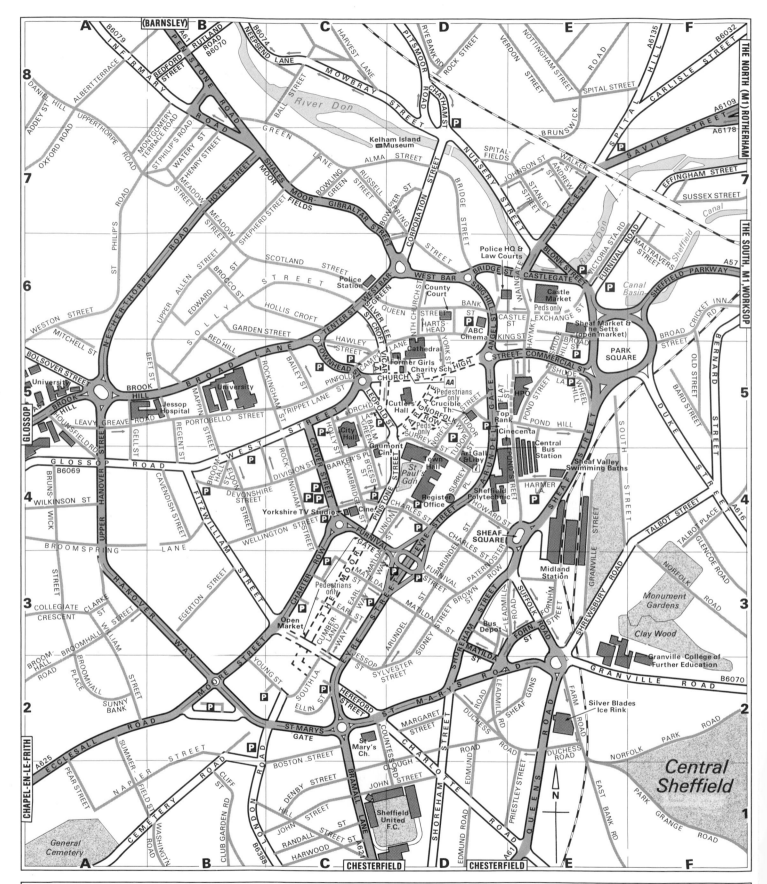

Sheffield

Cutlery – which has made the name of Sheffield famous throughout the world – has been manufactured here since at least as early as the time of Chaucer. The god of blacksmiths, Vulcan, is the symbol of the city's industry, and he crowns the town hall, which was opened in 1897 by Queen Victoria. At the centre of the industry, however, is Cutlers' Hall, the headquarters of the Company of Cutlers. This society was founded in 1624 and has the right to grant trade marks to articles of a sufficiently high standard. In the hall is the company's collection of silver, with examples of craftsmanship dating back every year to 1773. A really large collection of cutlery is kept in the city museum. Steel production, a vital component of the industry, was greatly improved when the crucible process was invented here in 1740. At Abbeydale Industrial Hamlet, 3½ miles south-west of the city centre, is a complete restored site open as a museum and showing 18th-century methods of steel production. Sheffield's centre, transformed since World War II, is one of the finest and most modern in Europe. There are no soot-grimed industrial eyesores here, for the city has stringent pollution controls and its buildings are carefully planned and set within excellent landscaping projects. Many parks are set in and around the city, and the Pennines are within easy reach.

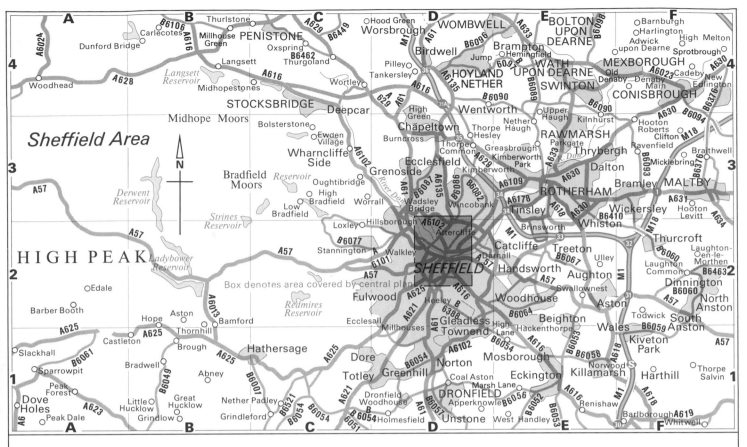

Sheffield Area

HIGH PEAK

Box denotes area covered by central plan

SHEFFIELD

LEGEND

Town Plan
AA Recommended roads	═══
Other roads	- - -
Restricted roads	░░░
Buildings of interest	▦
AA Centre	AA
Car Parks	P
Parks and open spaces	▱

Area Plan
A roads	──
B roads	──
Locations	Oakworth ○
Urban area	◹

Street Index with grid reference

Sheffield

Street	Grid
Addey Street	A7-A8
Albert Terrace	A8
Alma Street	C7 D7
Andrew Street	E7
Angel Street	D5-D6
Arundel Gate	D4-D5
Arundel Street	C2-D2-D3-D4
Bailey Street	C5
Ball Street	C8
Balm Green	C4-C5
Bank Street	D6
Bard Street	F5
Barker's Pool	C4-C5-D5
Bedford Street	B8
Beet Street	B5
Bernard Street	F4-F5-F6
Blonk Street	E6
Bolsover Street	A5
Boston Street	C1-C2
Bower Street	C7-D7
Bowling Green	C7
Bramall Lane	C1-C2
Bridge Street	D7-D6-E6
Broad Lane	B5-C5-C6
Broad Street	E6-F5-F6
Brocco Street	B6
Brook Hill	A5-B5
Broomhall Place	A2
Broomhall Road	A2
Broomhall Street	A2-A3-B4
Broomspring Lane	A4-B4
Brown Street	D3
Brunswick Street	A3-A4
Brunswick Road	E7-E8
Burgess Street	C4
Cambridge Street	C4
Campo Lane	C5-D5-D6
Carlisle Street	F8
Carver Street	C4-C5
Castle Street	D6-E6
Castlegate	E6
Cavendish Street	B4
Cemetery Road	A1-B1-B2
Charles Street	D3-D4
Charlotte Road	C2-D2-D1-E1
Charter Row	C3-C4
Chatham Street	D7-D8
Church Street	C5-D5
Clarke Street	A3
Cliff Street	B1
Clough Road	C1-D1-D2
Club Garden Road	B1
Collegiate Crescent	A3
Commercial Street	E5
Corporation Street	D6-D7
Countess Road	C2-D2-D1
Cricket Inn Road	F6
Cumberland Way	C3
Daniel Hill	A8
Denby Street	C1
Devonshire Street	B4-C4
Division Street	C4
Duchess Road	D2-E2
Duke Street	F4-F5
Earl Street	C3
Earl Way	C3
East Bank Road	E1-E2
Ecclesall Road	A1-A2-B2
Edmund Road	D1-D2
Edward Street	B6
Effingham Street	F7
Egerton Street	B3
Eldon Street	B4
Ellin Street	C2
Eyre Street	C2-C3-D3-D4
Exchange Street	E6
Fargate	D5
Farm Road	E2
Fitzwilliam Street	B4-B3-C3
Flat Street	E5
Fornham Street	E3
Furnival Gate	C3-C4-D3-D4
Furnival Road	E6-F6-F7
Furnival Street	D3
Garden Street	B6-C6-C5
Gell Street	A4-A5
Gibraltar Street	C7-C6-D6
Glencoe Road	F3-F4
Glossop Road	A4-B4
Granville Road	E2-F2
Granville Street	E3-E4
Green Lane	B8-C8-C7
Hanover Way	A3-B3-B2
Harmer Lane	E4
Hartshead	D6
Harwood Street	C1
Harvest Lane	C8
Hawley Street	C5
Haymarket	E5-E6
Henry Street	B7
Hereford Street	C2
High Street	D5-E5
Hill Street	B1-C1
Hollis Croft	B6-C6
Holly Street	C4-C5
Hounsfield Road	A4-A5
Howard Street	D4-E4
Hoyle Street	B7
Infirmary Road	A8-B8 B7
Jessop Street	C2
John Street	C1-D1
Johnson Street	D7-E7
King Street	D5-E5-E6
Leadmill Road	D2-D3-E3
Leavy Greave Road	A5-B5
Lee Croft	C5-C6
Leopold Street	C5-D5
London Road	C1-B1-B2-C2
Maltravers Street	F6
Mappin Street	B4-B5
Margaret Street	D2
Matilda Street	C3-D3-D2
Matilda Way	C3
Meadow Street	B6-B7
Mitchell Street	A5-A6
Montgomery Terrace Road	A7-B7-B8
Moorfields	C7
Moore Street	B2-B3-C3
Mowbray Street	C8-D8-D7
Napier Street	A1-B1-B2
Neepsend Lane	B8-C8
Netherthorpe Road	A5-A6-B6-B7
Norfolk Park Road	E1-E2-F2
Norfolk Road	F3-F4
Norfolk Row	D5
Norfolk Street	D4-D5
North Church Street	D6
Nottingham Street	E8
Nursery Street	D7-E7-E6
Old Street	F5-F6
Orchard Lane	C5
Oxford Road	A7-A8
Park Grange Road	E1-F1
Park Square	E5-E6-F6-F5
Paternoster Row	D3-D4-E4
Pear Street	A1
Penistone Road	B7-B8
Pinfold Street	C5
Pinstone Street	C4-D4-D5
Pitsmoor Road	D8
Pond Hill	E5
Pond Street	E4-E5
Portobello Street	B5-C5
Priestley Street	D1-E1-E2
Queen Street	C6-D6
Queen's Road	E1-E2
Randall Street	C1
Red Hill	B5-B6
Regent Street	B4-B5
Rock Street	D8
Rockingham Street	B5-C5-C4
Russell Street	C7
Rutland Road	B8
Rye Bank Road	D8
St Mary's Gate	C2
St Mary's Road	C2-D2-E2
St Philip's Road	A6-A7-B7-B8
Savile Street	E7-F7-F8
Scotland Street	B6-C6
Shales Moor	B7-C7
Sheaf Gardens	D2-E2
Sheaf Street	E4-E5
Sheffield Parkway	F6
Shepherd Street	B6-B7-C7
Shoreham Street	D1-D2-D3-E3
Shrewsbury Road	E3-E4-F3-F4
Shude Lane	E5
Shude Hill	E5-E6
Sidney Street	D3
Silver Street	C6
Snig Hill	D6
Solly Street	B5-B6-C6
South Lane	C2
South Street	E4-E5
Spital Hill	E7-E8-F8
Spital Street	E8-F8
Spitalfields	D7-E7
Spring Street	D6-D7
Stanley Street	E7
Suffolk Road	E3
Summerfield Street	A2-A1-B1
Sunny Bank	A2
Surrey Place	D4
Surrey Street	D4-D5
Sussex Street	F7
Sylvester Street	C2-D2
Talbot Place	F4
Talbot Street	F4
Tenter Street	C6
The Moor	C3-C4
Townhead Street	C5
Trippet Lane	C5
Tudor Street	D4-D5
Tudor Way	D5
Union Street	C4-D4
Upper Allen Street	B6
Upper Hanover Street	A3-A4-A5
Upperthorpe Road	A7-A8
Verdon Street	D8-E8
Vicar Lane	C5-D5
Victoria Station Road	E6-E7-F7
Waingate	E6
Walker Street	E7
Washington Road	B1
Watery Street	B7-B8
Wellington Street	B4-C4
West Bar	D6
West Bar Green	C6-D6
West Street	B4-B5-C5
Weston Street	A5-A6
Wheel Hill	E5
Wicker	E6-E7
Wilkinson Street	A4
William Street	A2-A3
York Street	D5-D6
Young Street	B2-C2

179

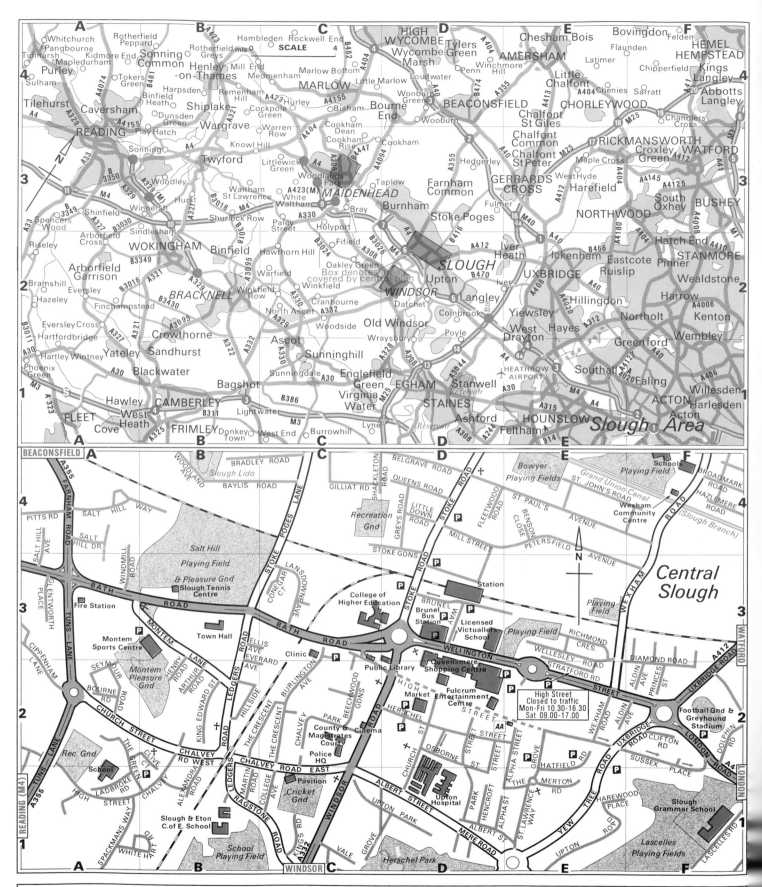

Slough

The town is something of a non-starter as far as architectural beauty or historical interest is concerned. However, it is a good shopping centre and has plenty of sports and leisure facilities.

Windsor The distinctive outline of the castle's towers and battlements above the Thames completely dominates the town. First built by the Normans to guard the approaches to London, it has been altered and added to at different times by various kings, but Henry III and Edward III contributed most to its present haphazard shape. The State Apartments are magnificent, as is St George's Chapel, with its superb fan-vaulted ceiling. Queen Mary's Dolls House is an exquisite model house of the 1920s, complete down to the last detail. The town itself, squeezed between the castle walls and the river, has several attractive streets graced with fine buildings. One 17th-century colonnaded building by Sir Christopher Wren contains a small museum of local interest, and a fairly new attraction is the Madame Tussaud's Royalty and Railways Exhibition.

Maidenhead used to be an important stage-post on the London to Bath road and is now a prosperous Thameside residential town. Oldfield House, near the ancient bridge designed by Brunel, contains the Henry Reitlinger Bequest Museum, specialising in glass and ceramics.

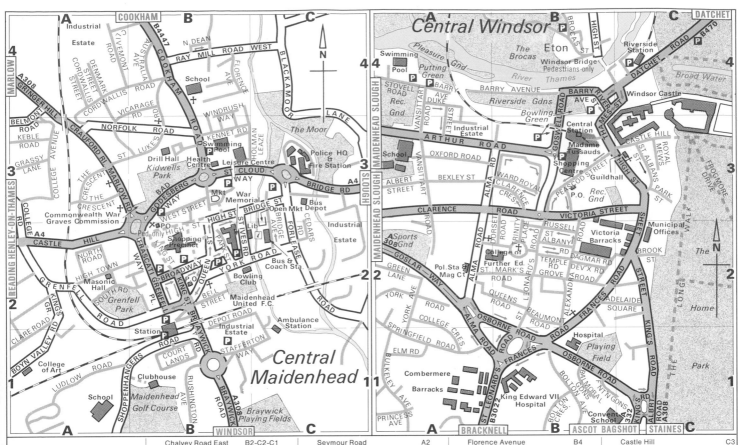

LEGEND

Town Plan

AA recommended route	
Restricted roads	
Other roads	
Buildings of interest	Station ▼
Car parks	P
Parks and open spaces	
One way streets	→

Area Plan

A roads	
B roads	
Locations	Hightown○
Urban area	

Street Index with Grid Reference

Slough

Albert Street	C1-D1-E1
Aldin Avenue	E2-F2
Alexandra Road	B1-B2
Alpha Street	D1-E1-E2
Arthur Road	B2
Bath Road	A3-B3-C3
Baylis Road	B4-C4
Beechwood Gardens	C2
Belgrave Road	D4
Benson Close	E4
Bourne Road	A2
Bradley Road	B4-C4
Broadmark Road	F4
Brunel Way	D3
Burlington Avenue	C2-C3
Chalvey Park	C2

Chalvey Road East	B2-C2-C1
Chalvey Road West	B2
Church Street	A2-B2
Church Street	D1-D2
Cippenham Lane	A2-A3
Clifton Road	F2
Clive Court	A2-B2-B1
College Avenue	C1
Conegar Court	C3
Diamond Road	E3-F3-F2
Dolphin Road	F2
Ellis Avenue	B3-C3
Everard Avenue	B3-B2-C2
Farnham Road	A3-A4
Fleetwood Road	D4
Gilliat Road	C4
Glentworth Place	A3
Greys Road	D4
Harewood Place	E1
Hatfield Road	E1-E2
Hazlemere Road	F4
Hencroft Street	D1-D2
Henry Road	B2-B3
Herschel Street	D2-E2
High Street	D2-E2
High Street Chalvey	A2-A1-B1-B2
Hillside	B2
King Edward Street	B2
Kings Road	C1
Ladbroke Road	A1
Landsdowne Avenue	C3
Lascelles Road	F1
Ledgers Road	B1-B2-B3
Little Down Road	D4
London Road	F1-F2
Martin Road	B1
Mere Road	D1
Merton Road	E1
Mill Street	D4
Montem Lane	A3-B3-B2
Osborne Street	D1-D2
Park Street	D1-D2
Petersfield Avenue	E4-E3-F3
Pitts Road	A4
Princes Street	F2
Queens Road	D4
Ragstone Road	B1-C1
Richmond Crescent	E3
St John's Road	E4-F4
St Lawrence Way	E1
St Paul's Avenue	D4-E4-F4
Salt Hill Avenue	A3-A4
Salt Hill Drive	A4
Salt Hill Way	A4-B4
Shackleton Road	C4

Seymour Road	A2
Spackmans Way	A1
Stoke Gardens	C4-D4
Stoke Road	D3-D4
Stoke Poges Lane	B3-C3-C4
Stratford Road	E2-E3
Sussex Place	E2-F2-F1
The Crescent	B2-C2
The Green	A2-A1-B1
The Grove	E1-E2
Tuns Lane	A1-A2-A3
Upton Park	C1-D1
Upton Road	E1
Uxbridge Road	E2-F2-F3
Vale Grove	C1-D1
Wellesley Road	E3
Wellington Street	
	D2-D3-E3-E2-F2
Wexham Road	E2-E3-F3-F4
White Hart Road	A1-B1
Windmill Road	A3-A4
Windsor Road	C1-C2-D2-D3
Woodland Avenue	B4
Yew Tree Road	E1-E2

Maidenhead

Australia Avenue	B4
Bad Godesberg Way	B3
Bell Street	B2
Belmont Road	A3-A4
Blackamoor Lane	C3-C4
Boyn Valley Road	A1-A2
Braywick Road	B1-B2
Bridge Avenue	C2-C3
Bridge Road	C3
Bridge Street	B3-C3
Broadway	B2
Castle Hill	A2
Cedars Road	C2-C3
Clare Road	A1-A2
Clivemont Road	A4-B4
College Avenue	A3
College Road	A2-A3
Cookham Road	B3-B4
Cordwallis Road	A3-A4-B4
Cordwallis Street	A4
Court Lands	B1
Crauford Rise	A3
Denmark Street	A4
Depot Road	B1-B2-C2
Forlease Road	C2-C3

Florence Avenue	B4
Frascati Way	B2
Grassy Lane	A3
Grenfell Place	B2
Grenfell Road	A2-B2
Gringer Hill	A4
High Street	B2-B3
High Town	A2-B2
Holman Leaze	B3-C3
Keble Road	A3
Kennet Road	B3
King's Grove	A2
King Street	B2
Ludlow Road	A1
Marlow Road	A3-B3
Norfolk Road	A3-B3
North Dean	A4
North Road	A2
Park Street	B2
Queen Street	B2-B3
Ray Mill Road West	B4-C4
Rushington Avenue	B1
St Cloud Way	B3-C3
St Ives' Road	B2
St Luke's Road	A3-B3-B4
Shoppenhangers Road	A1-B1
South Road	A2-B2
Stafferton Way	B1-C1
The Crescent	A3
Vicarage Road	A3-A4-B4
West Street	B3
Windrush Way	B3-B4
York Road	B2-C2

Windsor

Adelaide Square	B2-C2
Albany Road	B2
Albert Road	C1
Albert Street	A3
Alexandra Road	B2-B3
Alma Road	B3-A3-A2-A1-B1
Arthur Road	A3-B3
Balmoral Gardens	B1
Barry Avenue	A4-B4
Beaumont Road	B2
Bexley Street	A3
Bolton Avenue	B1
Bolton Crescent	B1
Brocas Street	B4
Brook Street	C2
Bulkeley Avenue	A1

Castle Hill	C3
Clarence Crescent	B3
Clarence Road	A3-B3
College Crescent	A1-A2
Dagmar Road	B2
Datchet Road	B4-C4
Devereux Road	B3
Dorset Road	B2-B3
Duke Street	A3-A4
Elm Road	A1
Fountain Gardens	B1
Frances Road	B1-B2-C2
Frogmore Drive	C3
Goslar Way	A2
Goswell Road	B3-B4
Green Lane	B2
Grove Road	B2
High Street	B4
High Street	B3-C3
King's Road	C1-C2
Osborne Road	A2-B2-B1-C1
Oxford Road	A3
Park Street	C3
Peascod Street	B3
Princess Avenue	A1
Queens Road	A2-B2
River Street	B4
Royal Mews	C3
Russell Street	B2
St Albans Street	C3
St Leonard's Road	A1-B1-B2
St Mark's Road	A2-B2
Sheet Street	C2-C3
Springfield Road	A1-A2
Stovell Road	A4
Temple Road	B2
Thames Street	B3-B4-C4
The Long Walk	C1-C2-C3
Trinity Place	B2-B3
Vansittart Road	A2-A3-A4
Victoria Street	B3-C3
Ward Royal	B3
York Avenue	A1-A2
York Road	A2

SLOUGH
Salt Hill Park in the centre of Slough features a bowling green, tennis courts and a children's play area, as well as pleasant walks through landscaped gardens. This is one of several recreational areas scattered throughout the town.

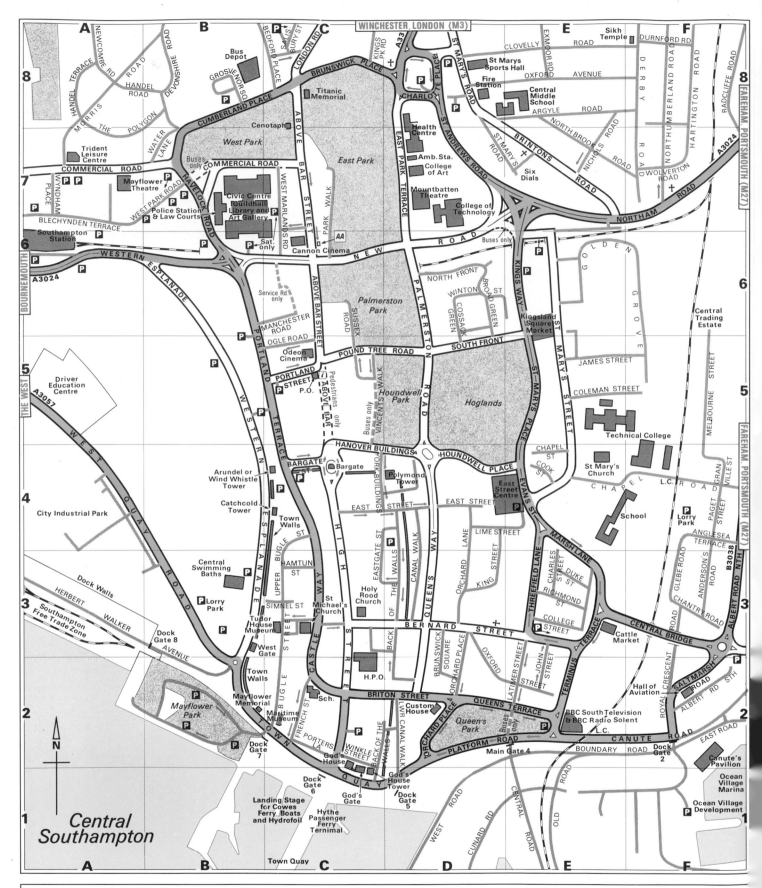

Southampton

In the days of the great ocean-going liners, Southampton was Britain's premier passenger port. Today container traffic is more important, but cruise liners still berth there. A unique double tide caused by the Solent waters, and protection from the open sea by the Isle of Wight, has meant that Southampton has always been a superb and important port. Like many great cities it was devastated by bombing raids during World War II. However, enough survives to make the city a fascinating place to explore. Outstanding are the town walls, which stand to their original height in some places, especially along Western Esplanade. The main landward entrance to the walled town was the Bargate – a superb medieval gateway with a Guildhall (now a museum) on its upper floor. The best place to appreciate old Southampton is in and around St Michael's Square. Here is St Michael's Church, oldest in the city and founded in 1070. Opposite is Tudor House Museum, a lovely gabled building housing much of interest. Down Bugle Street are old houses, with the town walls, pierced by the 13th-century West Gate, away to the right. At the corner of Bugle Street is the Wool House Maritime Museum, contained in a 14th-century warehouse. On the quayside is God's House Tower, part of the town's defences and now an archaeological museum.

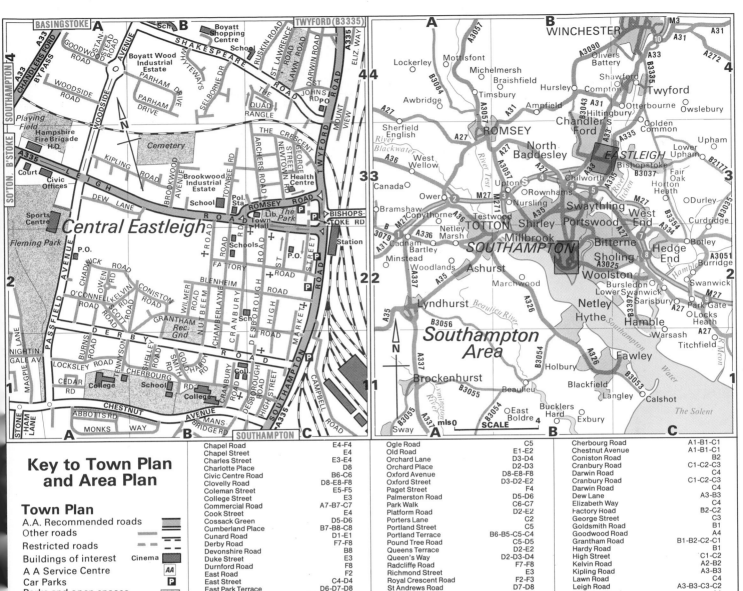

Key to Town Plan and Area Plan

Town Plan

A.A. Recommended roads	
Other roads	
Restricted roads	
Buildings of interest	Cinema
A A Service Centre	AA
Car Parks	P
Parks and open spaces	
One way streets	→

Area Plan

A roads	
B roads	
Locations	Ower ○
Urban Area	

SOUTHAMPTON

Above Bar	C5
Above Bar Street	C5-C6-C7-C8
Albert Road North	F3-F4
Albert Road South	F2
Anderson's Road	F4
Anglesea Terrace	F4
Argyle Road	D8-E8-F8
Back of the Walls	C1-C2-D2-D3-D4
Bargate Street	C4
Bedford Place	B8-C8
Bernard Street	C3-D3-E3
Blechynden Terrace	A7
Boundary Road	E2-F2
Briton Street	C2-D2
Britons Road	D8-E8-E7
Broad Green	D6
Brunswick Place	C8-D8
Brunswick Square	D2-D3
Bugle Street	C2-C3
Canal Walk	D3-D4
Canute Road	E2-F2
Castle Way	C2-C3-C4
Central Bridge	E3-F3
Central Road	E1-E2
Chantry Road	F3
Chapel Road	E4-F4
Chapel Street	E4
Charles Street	E3-E4
Charlotte Place	D8
Civic Centre Road	B6-C6
Clovelly Road	D8-E8-F8
Coleman Street	E5-F5
College Street	E3
Commercial Road	A7-B7-C7
Cook Street	E4
Cossack Green	D5-D6
Cumberland Place	B7-B8-C8
Cunard Road	D1-E1
Derby Road	F7-F8
Devonshire Road	B8
Duke Street	E3
Durnford Road	F8
East Road	C4-D4
East Street	C4
East Park Terrace	D6-D7-D8
Eastgate Street	D3-C3-C4-D4
Evans Street	E4
Exmoor Road	E8
French Street	C2
Glebe Road	F3-F4
Golden Grove	E6-F6-F5
Granville Street	F4
Grosvenor Square	B8
Hamtun Street	C3
Handel Road	A8-B8
Handel Terrace	A8
Hanover Buildings	C5-C4-D4
Hartington Road	F7-F8
Havelock Road	B6-B7
Herbert Walker Avenue	A3-B3-B2
High Street	C2-C3-C4
Houndwell Place	D4-E4
James Street	E5-F5
John Street	E2-E3
Kings Way	E6-E7
King Street	D3-D4
Kings Park Road	C8
Latimer Street	E2-E3
Lime Street	D4-E4
London Road	C8
Lower Canal Walk	D1-D2
Manchester Street	B6-C6
Marsh Lane	E3-E4
Melbourne Street	F4-F5-F6
Morris Road	A7-A8-B8
New Road	C6-D6-D7
Newcombe Road	A8
Nichols Road	E7-E8
North Brook Road	E8-E7-F7
North Front	D6
Northam Road	E7-F7
Northumberland Road	F7-F8
Ogle Road	C5
Old Road	E1-E2
Orchard Lane	D3-D4
Orchard Place	D2-D3
Oxford Avenue	D8-E8-F8
Oxford Street	D3-D2-E2
Paget Street	F4
Palmerston Road	D5-D6
Park Walk	C6-C7
Platform Road	D2-E2
Porters Lane	C2
Portland Street	C5
Portland Terrace	B6-B5-C5-C4
Pound Tree Road	C5-D5
Queens Terrace	D2-E2
Queen's Way	D2-D3-D4
Radcliffe Road	F7-F8
Richmond Street	E3
Royal Crescent Road	F2-F3
St Andrews Road	D7-D8
St Mary's Place	E4-E5
St Mary's Road	D8-D7-E7
St Mary's Street	E4-E5-E6
Salisbury Street	C8
Saltmarsh Road	F2-F3
Simnel Street	C3
South Front	D5-E5-E6-D6
Sussex Road	C5-C6
The Polygon	A8-A7-B7-B8
Terminus Terrace	E2-E3
Threefield Lane	E2-E3
Town Quay	B2-C2-C1-D1
Upper Bugle Street	C3-C4
Vincents Walk	C5
West Marlands Road	C6-C7
West Road	D1-D2-E2
West Park Road	A7-B7
West Quay Road	A4-A5-B2-B3-B4
Western Esplanade	B2-B3-B4-B5-B6-A6
Winkle Street	C1-C2
Winton Street	D6-E6
Wolverton Road	F7
Wyndham Place	A7
York Buildings	C4-D4

EASTLEIGH

Abbotts Road	A1
Archers Road	C3
Blenheim Road	B2-C2
Bishopstoke Road	C3
Brookwood Avenue	B3
Burns Road	A1
Campbell Road	C1
Cedar Road	A1
Chadwick Road	A2-B2
Chamberlayne Road	B1-B2-B3
Chandlers Ford By-pass	A4
Cherbourg Road	A1-B1-C1
Chestnut Avenue	A1-B1-C1
Coniston Road	B2
Cranbury Road	C1-C2-C3
Darwin Road	C4
Cranbury Road	C1-C2-C3
Darwin Road	C4
Dew Lane	A3-B3
Elizabeth Way	C4
Factory Road	B2-C2
George Street	C3
Goldsmith Road	B1
Goodwood Road	B1
Grantham Road	B1-B2-C2-C1
Hardy Road	B1
High Street	C1-C2
Kelvin Road	A2-B2
Kipling Road	A3-B3
Lawn Road	C4
Leigh Road	A3-B3-C3-C2
Locksley Road	A1
Magpie Lane	A1-A2
Mansbridge Road	B1
Market Street	C1-C2-C3
Monks Way	A1-B1
Mount View	C3-C4
Newtown Road	C3
Nightingale Avenue	A1
Nutbeem Road	B1-B2-B3
O'Connell Road	A2
Owen Road	A2
Parham Drive	A4-B4
Passfield Avenue	A1-A2-A3
Romsey Road	B3-C3
Ruskin Road	C4
Stanstead Road	A4
Stoneham Lane	A1
St John's Road	C4
St Lawrence Road	C4
Scott Road	A2
Selborne Drive	B4
Shakespeare Road	B4-C4
Shelley Road	B1
Southampton Road	C1-C2
The Crescent	C3
The Quadrangle	C4
Tennyson Road	A1-A2-B2
Toynbee Road	B3
Twyford Road	C3-C4
Whyteways	B4
Wilmer Road	B2
Woodside Avenue	A3-A4-B4
Woodside Road	A4

SOUTHAMPTON
Although liners still use Southampton's docks which handled all the great ocean-going passenger ships before the age of air travel replaced sea travel, the port is chiefly used by commercial traffic today.

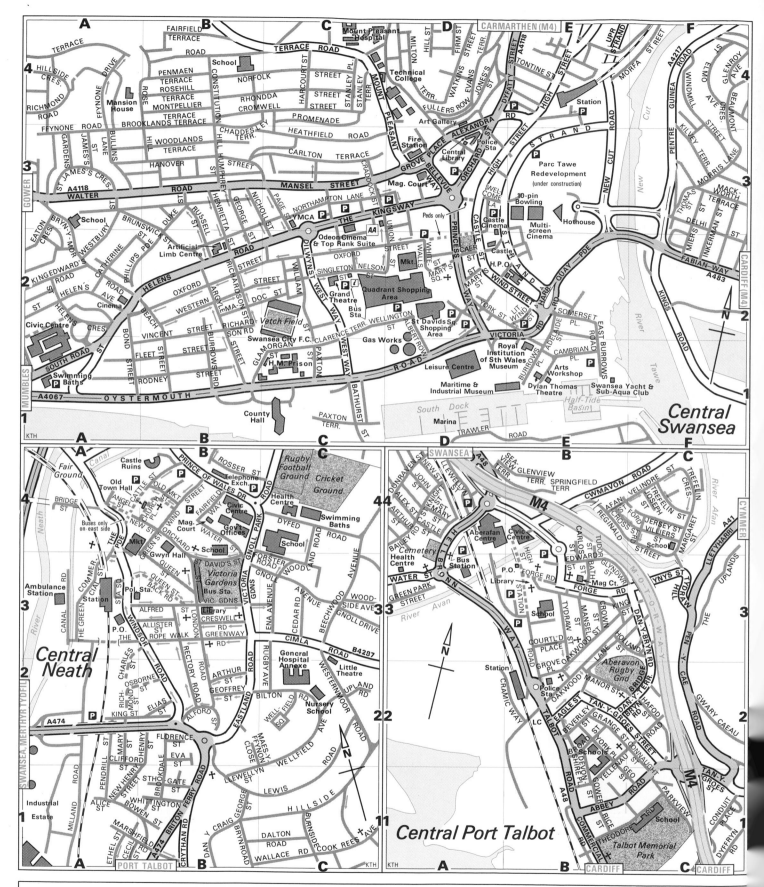

Central Swansea

Central Neath

Central Port Talbot

Swansea

Like nearly all the towns in the valleys and along the coast of Glamorgan, Swansea grew at an amazing speed during the Industrial Revolution. Ironworks, non-ferrous metal smelting works and mills and factories of every kind were built to produce the goods which were exported from the city's docks. There had been a settlement here from very early times – the city's name is derived from Sweyn's Ea – Ea means island, and Sweyn was a Viking pirate who had a base here. Heavy industry is still pre-eminent in the area, but commerce is of increasing importance and the university exerts a strong influence. Hundreds of acres of parkland and open space lie in and around the city, and just to the west is the Gower, one of the most beautiful areas of Wales. The history of Swansea is traced in the Maritime, Industrial and Royal Institution of South Wales Museums, while the Glynn Vivian Art Gallery contains notable paintings and porcelain.

Neath and **Port Talbot** are, like Swansea, dominated by heavy industry. Neath was once a Roman station, and later had a castle and an abbey, ruins of which can still be seen. Port Talbot has been an industrial centre since 1770, when a copper-smelting works was built. Steelworks and petrochemical works stretch for miles around Swansea Bay.

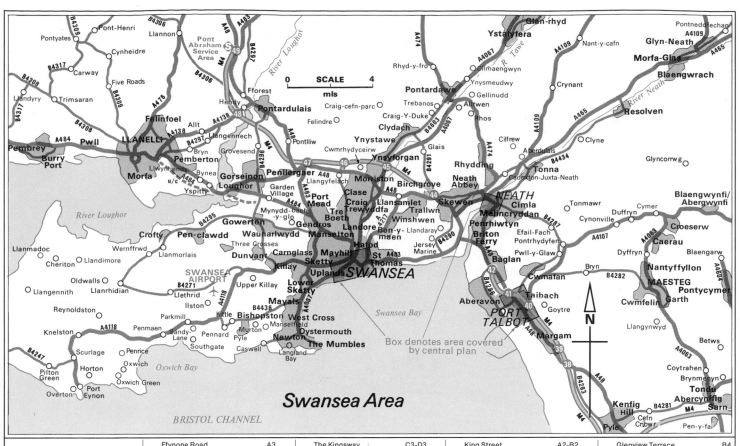

Swansea Area

BRISTOL CHANNEL

Box denotes area covered by central plan

LEGEND

Town Plan

AA Recommended roads	
Other roads	
Restricted roads	
Buildings of interest	
Car parks	P
Parks and open spaces	
One way streets	←

Area Plan

A roads	
B roads	
Locations	Bishopston O
Urban area	

Street Index with Grid Reference

Swansea

Adelaide Street	E1-E2
Albert Row	D1-D2
Alexandra Road	D3-D4-E4
Argyle Street	B1-B2
Bathurst Street	C1
Beach Street	A2-B2-B1
Beaumont Crescent	F3-F4
Bellevue Way	D3
Bond Street	A1-A2
Brooklands Terrace	A3-B3-B4
Brunswick Street	A3-B3-B2
Bryn-y-mor Road	A2-A3
Bullins Lane	A3
Burrows Place	E1
Burrows Road	B1-B2
Caer Street	D2
Cambrian Place	E1
Carlton Terrace	B3-C3
Castle Street	D2-D3
Catherine Street	A2-B2
Chaddesley Terrace	B3-B4
Clarence Terrace	C1-C2
Constitution Hill	B3-B4
Craddock Street	C3
Cromwell Street	B4-C4
Delhi Street	F2-F3
Dilwyn Street	C2
Duke Street	B2-B3
Dyfatty Street	D4-E4
East Burrows Road	E1-E2
Eaton Crescent	A2-A3
Evans Terrace	D4
Fabian Way	E2-E3-F3-F2
Fairfield Terrace	B4
Ffynone Drive	A3-A4

Ffynone Road	A3
Firm Street	D4
Fleet Street	A1-B1
Fullers Row	D4
George Street	B2-B3
Glamorgan Street	B1-C1
Glenroy Avenue	F4
Grove Place	D3
Hanover Street	A3-B3-C3
Harbour Road	E2
Harcourt Street	C4
Heathfield Road	C3
Henrietta Street	B2-B3
High Street	D3-E3-E4
Hill Street	D4
Hillside Crescent	A4
Humphrey Street	B3
Inkerman Street	F2-F3
Jones's Street	D4
Kilvey Terrace	F3-F4
King Edward's Road	A2
Kings Road	F1-F2
Little Wind Street	E2
Mackworth Terrace	F3
Madoc Street	B2-C2
Mansel Street	B3-C3-D3
Miers Street	F2-F3
Milton Terrace	D4
Montpellier Terrace	B4
Morfa Street	E4-F4
Morris Lane	F3
Mount Pleasant	C4-D4-D3
Nelson Street	C2
New Cut Road	E3-E4
Nicholl Street	B3-C3-C2
Norfolk Street	B4-C4
Northampton Lane	C3-D3
Orchard Street	D3-D4
Oxford Street	A2-B2-C2-D2
Oystermouth Road	A1-B1-C1-D1-D2
Page Street	C3
Paxton Street	C1
Paxton Terrace	C1
Penmaen Terrace	B4
Pentre Guinea Road	F2-F3-F4
Phillips Parade	A2-B2
Princess Way	D2-D3
Promenade	C4
Quay Parade	E2
Rhondda Street	B4-C4
Richardson Road	B2
Richardson Street	B2
Richmond Road	A4
Rodney Street	A1-B1
Rose Hill	A4-B4-B3
Rosehill Terrace	B4
Russell Street	B2-B3
St Elmo Avenue	F4
St Helen's Avenue	A2
St Helens Crescent	A2
St Helens Road	A1-A2-B2-C2
St James's Crescent	A3
St James's Gardens	A3
St Mary's Square	D2
St Mary's Street	D2
Singleton Street	C2
Somerset Place	E2
South Road	A1
Stanley Place	C4
Stanley Terrace	C4
Strand	E2-D2-D3-E3-E4
Terrace Road	A4-B4-C4

The Kingsway	C3-D3
Thomas Street	F3
Tontine Street	E4
Trawler Road	D1
Union Street	C3-D3-D2
Upper Strand	E4
Victoria Road	D2-E2
Vincent Street	A1-B1-B2
Walter Road	A3-B3
Watkins Street	D4
Welcome Lane	D3
Wellington Street	D3
West Way	C1-C2
Westbury Street	A2-A3
Western Street	B2-C2
Whitewalls	D2
William Street	C2
Wind Street	D2-E2
Windmill Street	F3-F4
Woodlands Terrace	A3-B3
York Street	D2-E2

Neath

Alford Street	B2
Alfred Street	A3-B3
Alice Street	A1
Allister Street	A3-B3
Angel Street	A4
Arthur Street	B2
Beechwood Avenue	C3-C4
Bilton Road	B2-C2
Bowen Street	A1-B1
Bridge Street	A4
Briton Ferry Road	B1-B2
Brookdale Street	B1-B2
Bryn Road	B1
Burnside	C1
Canal Road	A3-A4
Cattle Street	A4-B4
Cecil Street	A1
Cedar Road	C2
Charles Street	A2-A3-B3
Church Place	A4-B4
Cimla Road	B3-C3-C2
Clifford Street	A2-B2
Commercial Street	A3
Cook Rees Avenue	C1
Creswell Road	B3
Croft Road	A4
Crytham Road	B1
Dalton Road	B1-C1
Dan Y Craig	B1
Dyfed Road	C4
Eastland Road	B2-B3
Elias Street	B2
Ena Avenue	C3
Ethel Street	A1
Eva Street	B2
Fairfield Way	B4
Florence Street	B2
Forster Road	B4-C4-C3
Geoffrey Street	B2
George Street	B1
Gnoll Avenue	B3-C3
Gnoll Drive	C3
Gnoll Park Road	B4-C4
Green Street	A3-B3-B4
Greenway Road	B3
Henry Street	B2
Hillside	B1-C1-C2

King Street	A2-B2
Lewis Road	B2-B1-C1-C2
Llewellyn Street	B1
London Road	B2-B3
Maes-y-ffrynon Close	B2
Marshfield Road	A1-B1
Mary Street	A2
Milland Road	A1
New Street	A4-B4
New Henry Street	A1-B1
Old Market Street	B4
Orchard Street	B3-B4
Osborne Street	A2-B2
Pendrill Street	A1-A2
Prince of Wales Drive	B4
Queen Street	B3
Queen Street Back Road	A3-B3
Rectory Road	B2-B3
Richmond Street	A2
Rosser Street	B4-C4
Rugby Avenue	C2-C3
Russell Street	A4-B4
St Davids Street	B3
Southgate Street	B1
Station Square	A3
The Green	A3
The Parade	A4
The Rope Walk	A3-B3
Upland Road	C2
Victoria Gardens	B3
Wallace Road	B1-C1
Water Street	B3-B4
Wellfield Avenue	C1-C2
Wellfield Square	C2
Westernmoor Road	C2-C3
Whittington Street	B1
Windsor Road	A3-B3-B2
Wind Street	B4
Woodland Road	C3-C4
Woodside Avenue	C3

Port Talbot

Abbey Road	B1-C1-C2
Afan Street	B4
Alexander Street	A4
Arthur Street	A4
Bailey Road	A4
Bath Street	B3
Beverley Street	B2
Bridge Terrace	C2
Broad Street	B2
Carlos Street	B3-B4
Castle Street	A4
Commercial Road	B1
Conduit Place	C1
Connaught Street	C1-C2
Courtland Place	B3
Cramic Way	B1-B2
Cross Street	B4-C4
Crown Street	B3
Cwmavon Road	B4-C4
Dan-y-Bryn Road	B2-C2-C3
Devonshire Place	B1-B2
Dunraven Street	A4
Dyffryn Road	C1
Eagle Street	B2
Edward Street	B3
Ford Road	B4-C4
Forge Road	B3
George Street	B2-B1-C1

Glenview Terrace	B4
Glyndawr Street	B3-C3
Gower Street	B1
Grange Street	B2-C2
Green Park Street	A3
Grove Place	B2
Gwary Caeau	C2
Hafod Street	C2
Heilbronn Way	A4-A3-B3-B2
High Street	B3-B4
Holland Street	B3-C3
Jersey Street	C4
John Street	A4
Joseph Street	C4
King Street	B3-C3
Lletyharri	C3-C4
Llewellyn Street	A4
Manor Street	B2-C2
Mansel Street	B3
Margaret Street	C4
New Street	A4
Oakwood Lane	B2-B3
Oakwood Street	B2-B3
Parkview	C1
Pen-y-cae Road	C1-C2-C3
Reginald Street	B4-C4-C3
Rice Street	B1
St Mary Street	A4
St Knight Street	A4
Seaview Terrace	A4-B4
Springfield Terrace	A4-B4
Station Road	B2-B3
Talbot Road	B1-B2
Tan-y-groes Street	B2-B2-C1
Tellenau Road	B1-B2-C2
The Uplands	C3-C4
Theodore Road	B1-C1
Trefelin Crescent	C4
Trefelin Street	C4
Tudor Street	B3-B4
Tyndraw Hill	C3
Tyndraw Street	B3
Velindre Street	B4-C4
Villiers Street	C4
Water Street	A3
Ynys Street	C3
York Place	B2

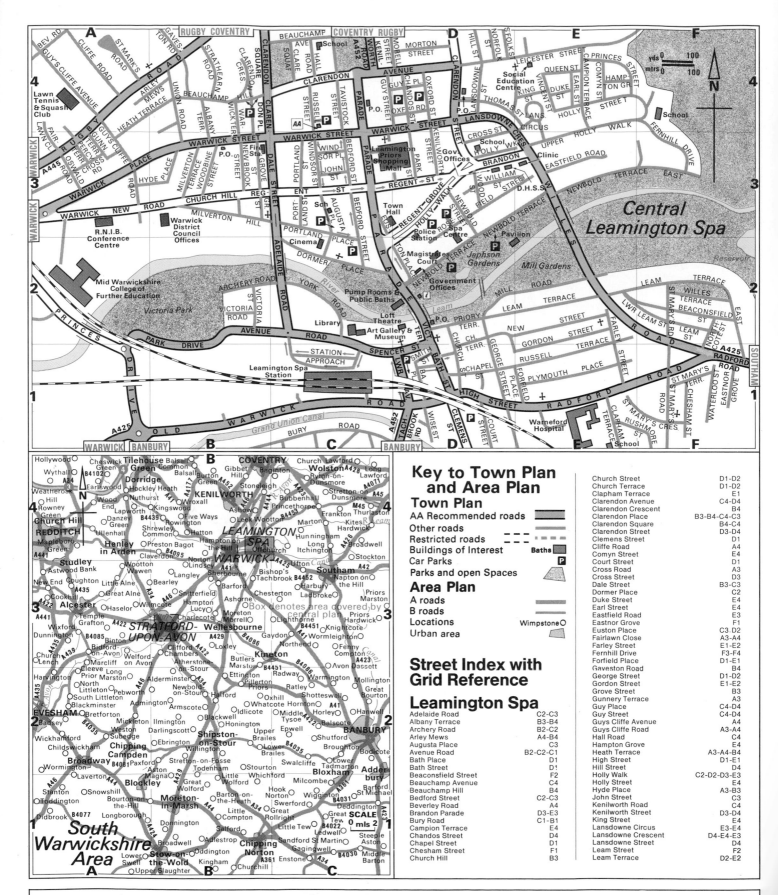

Key to Town Plan and Area Plan

Town Plan

AA Recommended roads
Other roads
Restricted roads
Buildings of Interest — Baths
Car Parks — P
Parks and open Spaces

Area Plan

A roads
B roads
Locations — Wimpstone○
Urban area

Street Index with Grid Reference

Leamington Spa

Adelaide Road	C2-C3
Albany Terrace	B3-B4
Archery Road	B2-C2
Arley Mews	A4-B4
Augusta Place	D1
Avenue Road	B2-C2-C1
Bath Place	D1
Bath Street	D1
Beaconsfield Street	F2
Beauchamp Avenue	C4
Beauchamp Hill	B4
Bedford Street	C2-C3
Beverley Road	A4
Brandon Parade	D3-E3
Bury Road	C1-B1
Campion Terrace	E4
Chandos Street	D4
Chapel Street	D1
Chesham Street	F1
Church Hill	B3
Church Street	D1-D2
Church Terrace	D1-D2
Clapham Terrace	E1
Clarendon Avenue	C4-D4
Clarendon Crescent	B4
Clarendon Place	B3-B4-C4-C3
Clarendon Square	B4-C4
Clarendon Street	D3-D4
Clemens Street	D1
Cliffe Road	A4
Comyn Street	E4
Court Street	D1
Cross Road	A3
Cross Street	D3
Dale Street	B3-C3
Dormer Place	C2
Duke Street	E4
Earl Street	E4
Eastfield Road	E3
Eastnor Grove	F1
Euston Place	C3.D2
Fairlawn Close	A3-A4
Farley Street	E1-E2
Fernhill Drive	F3-F4
Forfield Place	D1-E1
Gaveston Road	B4
George Street	D1-D2
Gordon Street	E1-E2
Grove Street	B3
Gunnery Terrace	A3
Guy Place	C4-D4
Guy Street	C4-D4
Guys Cliffe Avenue	A4
Guys Cliffe Road	A3-A4
Hall Road	C4
Hampton Grove	E4
Heath Terrace	A3-A4-B4
High Street	D1-E1
Hill Street	D4
Holly Walk	C2-D2-D3-E3
Holly Street	E3
Hyde Place	A3-B3
John Street	C3
Kenilworth Road	C4
Kenilworth Street	D3-D4
King Street	E4
Lansdowne Circus	E3-E4
Lansdowne Crescent	D4-E4-E3
Lansdowne Street	D4
Leam Street	F2
Leam Terrace	D2-E2

Warwick

The old county town of the shire, Warwick lies in the shadow of its massive, historic castle which occupies the rocky ridge above the River Avon. Thomas Beauchamp and his son built the huge towers and curtain walls in the 14th century, but it was the Jacobean holders of the earldom, the Grevilles, who transformed the medieval stronghold into a nobleman's residence. In 1694, the heart of the town was almost completely destroyed by fire and the few medieval buildings that survived lie on the outskirts of the present 18th-century centre. Of these Oken House, now a doll museum, and Lord Leycester's Hospital, almshouses dating back to the 14th century, are particularly striking.

Stratford-upon-Avon, as the birthplace of William Shakespeare, England's most famous poet and playwright, is second only to London as a tourist attraction. This charming old market town is a living memorial to him; his plays are performed in the Royal Shakespeare Theatre which dominates the river bank, a waxwork museum specialises in scenes from his works, and his childhood home in Henley Street is a museum.

Leamington Spa, an inland spa on the River Leam, gained the prefix 'Royal' after Queen Victoria had visited it in 1838, and the town has been a fashionable health resort ever since.

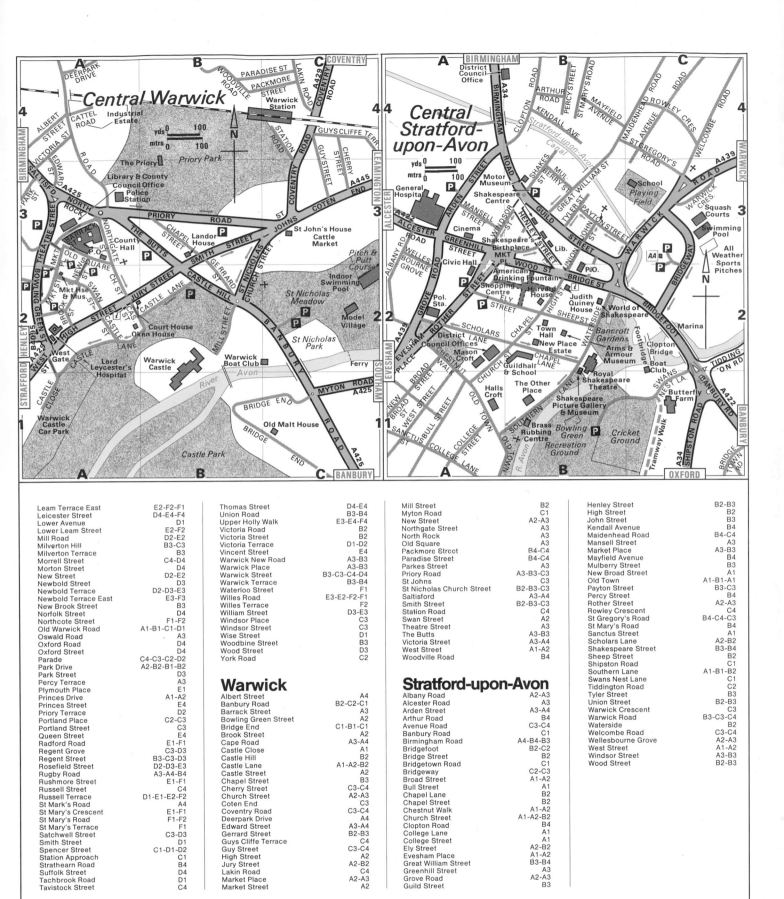

Central Warwick

COVENTRY

yds 0 — 100
mtrs 0 — 100

Central Stratford-upon-Avon

BIRMINGHAM

yds 0 — 100
mtrs 0 — 100

WARWICK

Leam Terrace East	E2-F2-F1
Leicester Street	D4-E4-F4
Lower Avenue	D1
Lower Leam Street	E2-F2
Mill Road	D2-E2
Milverton Hill	B3-C3
Milverton Terrace	B3
Morrell Street	C4-D4
Morton Street	D4
New Street	D2-E2
Newbold Street	D3
Newbold Terrace	D2-D3-E3
Newbold Terrace East	E3-F3
New Brook Street	B3
Norfolk Street	D4
Northcote Street	F1-F2
Old Warwick Road	A1-B1-C1-D1
Oswald Road	D4
Oxford Road	D4
Oxford Street	D4
Parade	C4-C3-C2-D2
Park Drive	A2-B2-B1-B2
Park Street	D3
Percy Terrace	A3
Plymouth Place	E1
Princes Drive	A1-A2
Princes Street	E4
Priory Terrace	D2
Portland Place	C2-C3
Portland Street	C3
Queen Street	E4
Radford Road	E1-F1
Regent Grove	C3-D3
Regent Street	B3-C3-D3
Rosefield Street	D2-D3-E3
Rugby Road	A3-A4-B4
Rushmore Street	E1-F1
Russell Street	C4
Russell Terrace	D1-E1-E2-F2
St Mark's Road	A4
St Mary's Crescent	E1-F1
St Mary's Road	F1-F2
St Mary's Terrace	F1
Satchwell Street	C3-D3
Smith Street	D1
Spencer Street	C1-D1-D2
Station Approach	C1
Strathearn Road	B4
Suffolk Street	D4
Tachbrook Road	D1
Tavistock Street	C4

Thomas Street	D4-E4
Union Road	B3-B4
Upper Holly Walk	E3-E4-F4
Victoria Road	B2
Victoria Street	B2
Victoria Terrace	D1-D2
Vincent Street	E4
Warwick New Road	A3-B3
Warwick Place	A3-B3
Warwick Street	B3-C3-C4-D4
Warwick Terrace	B3-B4
Waterloo Street	F1
Willes Road	E3-E2-F2-F1
Willes Terrace	F2
William Street	D3-E3
Windsor Place	C3
Windsor Street	C3
Wise Street	D1
Woodbine Street	B3
Wood Street	D3
York Road	C2

Warwick

Albert Street	A4
Banbury Road	B2-C2-C1
Barrack Street	A3
Bowling Green Street	A2
Bridge End	C1-B1-C1
Brook Street	C1
Cape Road	A3-A4
Castle Close	A1
Castle Hill	B2
Castle Lane	A1-A2-B2
Castle Street	B2
Chapel Street	B3
Cherry Street	C3-C4
Church Street	A2-A3
Coten End	C3
Coventry Road	C3-C4
Deerpark Drive	A4
Edward Street	A3-A4
Gerrard Street	B2-B3
Guys Cliffe Terrace	C4
Guy Street	C3-C4
High Street	A2
Jury Street	A2-B2
Lakin Road	C4
Market Place	A2-A3
Market Street	A2

STRATFORD-UPON-AVON / Warwick index (continued)

Mill Street	B2
Myton Road	C1
New Street	A2-A3
Northgate Street	A3
North Rock	A3
Old Square	A3
Packmore Street	B4-C4
Paradise Street	B4-C4
Parkes Street	A3
Priory Road	A3-B3-C3
St Johns	C3
St Nicholas Church Street	B2-B3-C3
Saltisford	A3-A4
Smith Street	B2-B3-C3
Station Road	C4
Swan Street	A2
Theatre Street	A3
The Butts	A3-B3
Victoria Street	A3-A4
West Street	A1-A2
Woodville Road	B4

Stratford-upon-Avon

Albany Road	A2-A3
Alcester Road	A3
Arden Street	A3-A4
Arthur Street	B4
Avenue Road	C3-C4
Banbury Road	C1
Birmingham Road	A4-B4-B3
Bridgefoot	B2-C2
Bridge Street	B2
Bridgetown Road	C1
Bridgeway	C2-C3
Broad Street	A1-A2
Bull Street	A1
Chapel Lane	B2
Chapel Street	B2
Chestnut Walk	A1-A2
Church Street	A1-A2-B2
Clopton Road	B4
College Lane	A1
College Street	A1
Ely Street	A2-B2
Evesham Place	A1-A2
Great William Street	B3-B4
Greenhill Street	A3
Grove Road	A2-A3
Guild Street	B3

Henley Street	B2-B3
High Street	B2
John Street	B3
Kendall Avenue	B4
Maidenhead Road	B4-C4
Mansell Street	A3
Market Place	A3-B3
Mayfield Avenue	B4
Mulberry Street	B3
New Broad Street	A1
Old Town	A1-B1-A1
Payton Street	B3-C3
Percy Street	B4
Rother Street	A2-A3
Rowley Crescent	C4
St Gregory's Road	B4-C4-C3
St Mary's Road	B4
Sanctus Street	A1
Scholars Lane	A2-B2
Shakespeare Street	B3-B4
Sheep Street	B2
Shipston Road	C1
Southern Lane	A1-B1-B2
Swans Nest Lane	C1
Tiddington Road	C2
Tyler Street	B3
Union Street	B2-B3
Warwick Crescent	C3
Warwick Road	B3-C3-C4
Waterside	B2
Welcombe Road	C3-C4
Wellesbourne Grove	A2-A3
West Street	A1-A2
Windsor Street	A3-B3
Wood Street	B2-B3

WARWICK
These pretty brick and timbered cottages standing in the shadow of the great medieval towers of Warwick Castle are among the few buildings in the town that survived a devastating fire in the late 17th century.

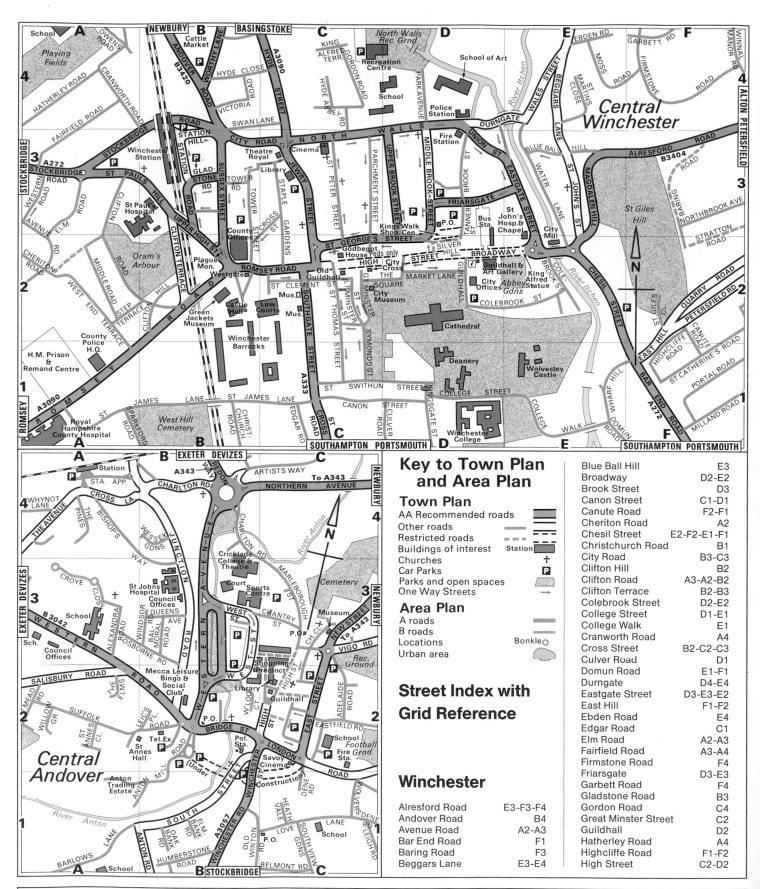

Key to Town Plan and Area Plan

Town Plan

AA Recommended roads	
Other roads	
Restricted roads	
Buildings of interest	Station
Churches	✝
Car Parks	P
Parks and open spaces	
One Way Streets	→

Area Plan

A roads	
B roads	
Locations	Bonkle○
Urban area	

Street Index with Grid Reference

Winchester

Alresford Road	E3-F3-F4
Andover Road	B4
Avenue Road	A2-A3
Bar End Road	F1
Baring Road	F3
Beggars Lane	E3-E4
Blue Ball Hill	E3
Broadway	D2-E2
Brook Street	D3
Canon Street	C1-D1
Canute Road	F2-F1
Cheriton Road	A2
Chesil Street	E2-F2-E1-F1
Christchurch Road	B1
City Road	B3-C3
Clifton Hill	B2
Clifton Road	A3-A2-B2
Clifton Terrace	B2-B3
Colebrook Street	D2-E2
College Street	D1-E1
College Walk	E1
Cranworth Road	A4
Cross Street	B2-C2-C3
Culver Road	D1
Domun Road	E1-F1
Durngate	D4-E4
Eastgate Street	D3-E3-E2
East Hill	F1-F2
Ebden Road	E4
Edgar Road	C1
Elm Road	A2-A3
Fairfield Road	A3-A4
Firmstone Road	F4
Friarsgate	D3-E3
Garbett Road	F4
Gladstone Road	B3
Gordon Road	C4
Great Minster Street	C2
Guildhall	D2
Hatherley Road	A4
Highcliffe Road	F1-F2
High Street	C2-D2

Winchester

King Alfred designated Winchester capital of England, a status it retained until after the Norman Conquest. Although gradually eclipsed by London, the city maintained close links with the Crown until the reign of Charles II.

Tucked away unobtrusively in the heart of Winchester is the impressive cathedral which encompasses Norman, and all the later Gothic styles of architecture. William of Wykeham was a bishop here in the 14th century and it was he who founded Winchester College, one of the oldest and most famous public schools in England. The buildings lie just outside the peaceful, shady Close where Pilgrims' Hall can be visited. Nearby are the Bishop's Palace and remains of Wolvesley Castle, one of Winchester's two Norman castles. Of the other, only the Great Hall, just outside the Westgate, survives. Here hangs the 14th-century Round Table associated with the legend of King Arthur.

The streets of the city, which cover a remarkably small area, are lined with many charming old buildings of different periods. A walk along the pedestrianised High Street takes you past the former Guildhall – now a bank – and the old Butter Cross, into the Broadway where a statue of King Alfred stands near the River Itchen. A delightful path follows the river alongside the remnants of the old city walls.

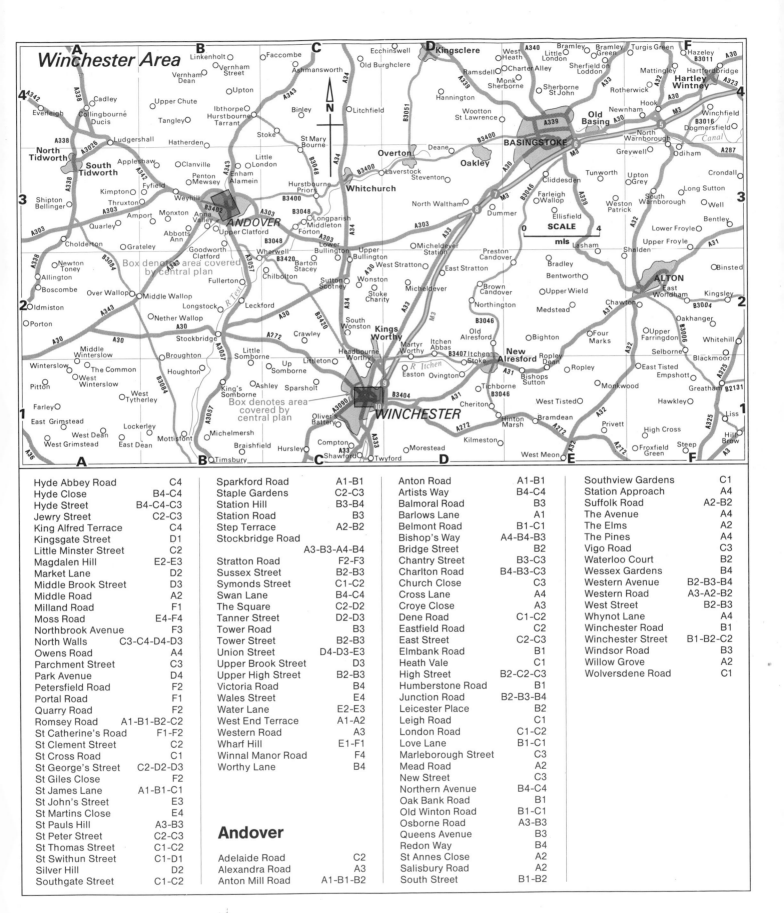

Winchester Area

Hyde Abbey Road	C4
Hyde Close	B4-C4
Hyde Street	B4-C4-C3
Jewry Street	C2-C3
King Alfred Terrace	C4
Kingsgate Street	D1
Little Minster Street	C2
Magdalen Hill	E2-E3
Market Lane	D2
Middle Brook Street	D3
Middle Road	A2
Milland Road	F1
Moss Road	E4-F4
Northbrook Avenue	F3
North Walls	C3-C4-D4-D3
Owens Road	A4
Parchment Street	C3
Park Avenue	D4
Petersfield Road	F2
Portal Road	F1
Quarry Road	F2
Romsey Road	A1-B1-B2-C2
St Catherine's Road	F1-F2
St Clement Street	C2
St Cross Road	C1
St George's Street	C2-D2-D3
St Giles Close	F2
St James Lane	A1-B1-C1
St John's Street	E3
St Martins Close	E4
St Pauls Hill	A3-B3
St Peter Street	C2-C3
St Thomas Street	C1-C2
St Swithun Street	C1-D1
Silver Hill	D2
Southgate Street	C1-C2

Sparkford Road	A1-B1
Staple Gardens	C2-C3
Station Hill	B3-B4
Station Road	B3
Step Terrace	A2-B2
Stockbridge Road	A3-B3-A4-B4
Stratton Road	F2-F3
Sussex Street	B2-B3
Symonds Street	C1-C2
Swan Lane	B4-C4
The Square	C2-D2
Tanner Street	D2-D3
Tower Road	B3
Tower Street	B2-B3
Union Street	D4-D3-E3
Upper Brook Street	D3
Upper High Street	B2-B3
Victoria Road	B4
Wales Street	E4
Water Lane	E2-E3
West End Terrace	A1-A2
Western Road	A3
Wharf Hill	E1-F1
Winnal Manor Road	F4
Worthy Lane	B4

Andover

Adelaide Road	C2
Alexandra Road	A3
Anton Mill Road	A1-B1-B2

Anton Road	A1-B1
Artists Way	B4-C4
Balmoral Road	B3
Barlows Lane	A1
Belmont Road	B1-C1
Bishop's Way	A4-B4-B3
Bridge Street	B2
Chantry Street	B3-C3
Charlton Road	B4-B3-C3
Church Close	C3
Cross Lane	A4
Croye Close	A3
Dene Road	C1-C2
Eastfield Road	C2
East Street	C2-C3
Elmbank Road	B1
Heath Vale	C1
High Street	B2-C2-C3
Humberstone Road	B1
Junction Road	B2-B3-B4
Leicester Place	B2
Leigh Road	C1
London Road	C1-C2
Love Lane	B1-C1
Marleborough Street	C3
Mead Road	A2
New Street	C3
Northern Avenue	B4-C4
Oak Bank Road	B1
Old Winton Road	B1-C1
Osborne Road	A3-B3
Queens Avenue	B3
Redon Way	B4
St Annes Close	A2
Salisbury Road	A2
South Street	B1-B2

Southview Gardens	C1
Station Approach	A4
Suffolk Road	A2-B2
The Avenue	A4
The Elms	A2
The Pines	A4
Vigo Road	C3
Waterloo Court	B2
Wessex Gardens	B4
Western Avenue	B2-B3-B4
Western Road	A3-A2-B2
West Street	B2-B3
Whynot Lane	A4
Winchester Road	B1
Winchester Street	B1-B2-C2
Windsor Road	B3
Willow Grove	A2
Wolversdene Road	C1

WINCHESTER
Standing on the site of the old Hall of Court in the Broadway is the city's Guildhall. Built in 1873, its style was influenced by Northampton Town Hall. It is now a centre for culture and the arts.

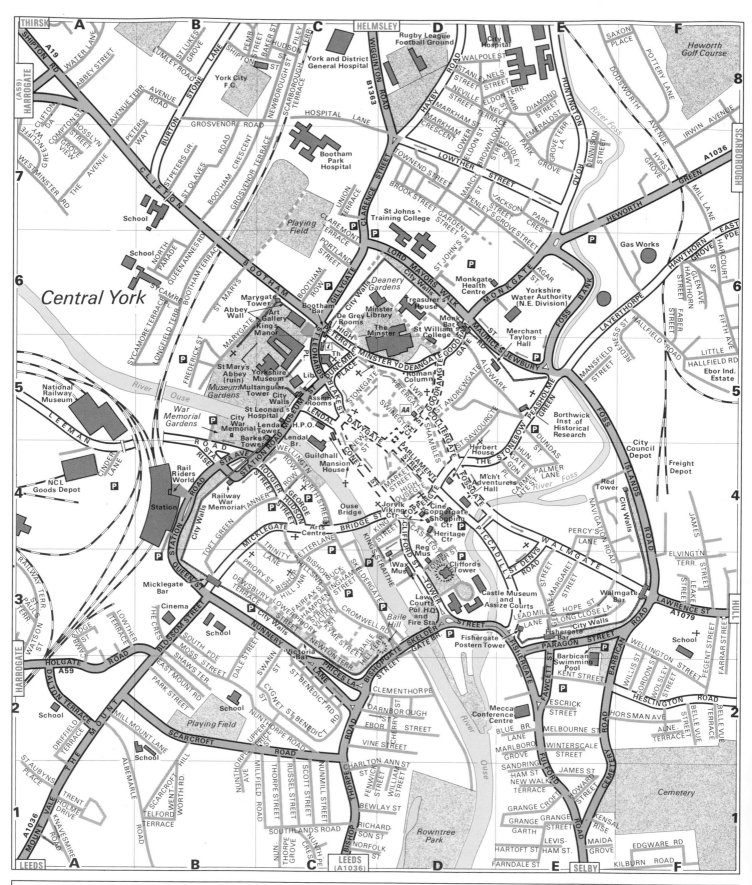

York

York Minster, unquestionably the city's outstanding glory, is considered to be one of the greatest cathedral churches in Europe. It is especially famous for its lovely windows which contain more than half the medieval stained glass in England.

Great medieval walls enclose the historic city centre and their three-mile circuit offers magnificent views of the Minster, York's numerous fine buildings, churches and the River Ouse. The ancient streets consist of a maze of alleys and lanes, some of them so narrow that the overhanging upper storeys of the houses almost touch. The most famous of these picturesque streets is The Shambles, formerly the butchers' quarter of the city, but now colonised by antique and tourist shops. York flourished throughout Tudor, Georgian and Victorian times and handsome buildings from these periods also feature throughout the city.

The Castle Museum gives a fascinating picture of York as it used to be and the Heritage Centre interprets the social and architectural history of the city. Other places of exceptional note in this city of riches include the Merchant Adventurer's Hall; the Treasurer's House, now owned by the National Trust and filled with fine paintings and furniture; the Jorvik Viking Centre, where there is an exciting restoration of the original Viking settlement at York, and the National Railway Museum.

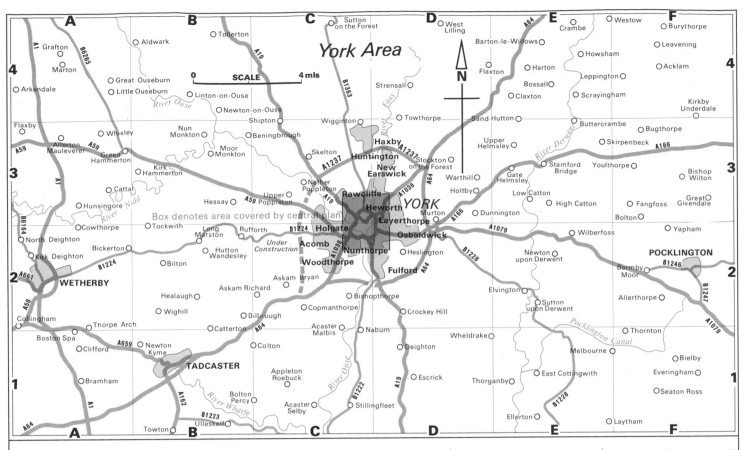

York Area

SCALE 0 ——— 4 mls

N

Box denotes area covered by central plan

Key to Town Plan and Area Plan

Town Plan

AA Recommended roads
Other roads
Restricted roads
Buildings of interest   Station
Churches
Car Parks
Parks and open spaces
AA Service Centre

Area Plan

A roads
B roads
Locations   Fangfoss○
Urban area

Street Index with Grid Reference

York

Abbey Street	A8
Agar Street	E6
Albemarle Road	A2-A1-B1
Aldwark	D5-E5
Alne Terrace	F2
Amber Street	E8
Ann Street	D1
Avenue Road	B8
Avenue Terrace	A7-A8-B8
Baile Hill Terrace	C2-C3-D3
Baker Street	C8
Barbican Road	E2-F2-F3-E3
Belle Vue Street	F2
Belle Vue Terrace	F2
Bewlay Street	C1-D1
Bishopgate Street	C2-D2-D3
Bishophill Junior	C3
Bishophill Senior	C3
Bishop Thorpe Road	C1-C2
Blake Street	C5
Blossom Street	B2-B3
Blue Bridge Lane	E2
Bootham	B6-C6
Bootham Crescent	B7-C7-C8
Bootham Row	C6
Bootham Terrace	B6
Bridge Street	C4-D4
Brook Street	D7
Brownlow Street	D7-E7-E8
Buckingham Street	C3
Burton Stone Lane	B7-B8
Cambridge Street	A2-A3
Carmelite Street	D4-E4
Castlegate	D3-D4
Cemetery Road	E1-E2
Charlton Street	C1-D1
Cherry Street	D5
Church Street	D5
Cinder Lane	A4
Claremont Terrace	C6-C7
Clarence Street	C6-C7-D7
Clementhorpe	C2-D2
Clifford Street	D3-D4
Clifton	A8-A7-B7
Clifton Dale	A7-A8
Colliergate	D4-D5
Compton Street	A7-A8
Coppergate	D4
Cromwell Road	C3-D3
Cygnet Street	C2
Dale Street	B2-B3
Dalton Terrace	A2
Darnborough Street	C2-D2
Davygate	C5-C4-D4-D5
Deangate	D5
Dennison Street	E7
Dewsbury Terrace	B3-C3
Diamond Street	E8
Dodsworth Avenue	E8-F8-F7
Driffield Terrace	A2
Dudley Street	D7-E7
Duncombe Place	C5
Dundas Street	E4-E5
East Parade	F6-F7
East Mount Road	B2
Ebor Street	C2-D2
Edgware Road	F1
Eldon Terrace	D8-E8
Elvington Terrace	F3
Emerald Street	E7-E8
Escrick Street	E2
Faber Street	F6
Fairfax Street	C3
Farndale Street	E1
Farrar Street	F2-F3
Fawcett Street	E2-E3
Fenwick Street	C1-D1
Fetter Lane	C3-C4
Fifth Avenue	F5-F6
Filey Terrace	C8
Fishergate	E2-E3
Foss Bank	E5-E6
Fossgate	D4
Foss Islands Road	E4-E5-F5-F4
Frederick Street	B5
Fulford Road	E1-E2
Garden Street	D7
George Hudson Street	C4
George Street	E3-E4
Gillygate	C6
Glen Avenue	F6
Goodramgate	D5-D6
Gordon Street	F2
Grange Croft	E1
Grange Garth	E1

Grange Street	E1
Greencliffe Way	A7-A8
Grosvenor Road	B8-C8
Grosvenor Terrace	B6-B7-C7-C8
Grove Terrace Lane	E7-E8
Grove View	A7
Hallfield Road	F5-F6
Hampden Street	C3
Harcourt Street	F6
Harloft Street	E1
Hawthorn Grove	F6
Hawthorne Street	F6
Haxby Road	D7-D8
Heslington Road	E2-F2
Heworth Green	E6-E7-F7
High Ousegate	D4
High Petergate	C5-C6
Holgate Road	A2-A3-B3
Hope Street	E2-F2
Horsman Avenue	E2-F2
Hospital Lane	C8
Howard Street	E1
Hudson Street	C8
Hungate	E4
Huntington Road	E6-E7-E8
Hyrst Grove	F7
Irwin Avenue	F7-F8
Jackson Street	D7-E7
James Street	E1
James Street	F3-F4
Jewbury	E5
Kensal Rise	E1
Kent Street	E2
Kilburn Road	E1-F1
Kings Straithe	C4-D4-D3
King Street	C4-D4
Knavesmire Road	A1
Kyme Street	C3
Lawrence Street	F3
Layerthorpe	E5-E6-F6
Lead Mill Lane	E3
Leake Street	F3
Leeman Road	A5-A4-B5-B4
Lendal Coney Street	C5-C4-D4
Levisham Street	E1
Little Hallfield Road	F5
Long Close Lane	E3-F3
Longfield Terrace	B5-B6
Lord Mayors Walk	C6-D6
Love Lane	A1-A2
Lower Eldon Street	D7
Lower Petergate	D5
Lower Priory Street	C3
Lowther Street	D7-E7
Lowther Terrace	A3
Maida Grove	E1
Mansfield Street	E5
March Street	D7
Margaret Street	E3
Market Street	D4
Markham Crescent	D7-D8
Markham Street	D7-D8
Marlborough Grove	E2
Marygate	B5-B6-C6
Melbourne Street	E2
Micklegate	B3-B4-C4
Millfield Road	C1-C2
Mill Lane	F7
Mill Mount Lane	A2-B2

Minster Yard	C5-D5
Monkgate	D6-E6
Moss Street	B2-B3
Mount Vale	A1
Museum Street	C5
Navigation Road	E4-E3-F3
Nelson Street	D8-E8
Neville Street	D8
Neville Terrace	D8-E8
Newborough Street	C8
New Street	C4-C5
Newton Terrace	C2-C3
New Walk Terrace	E1
Norfolk Street	C1-D1
North Parade	B6
North Street	C4
Nunmill Street	C1-C2
Nunnery Lane	B3-C3-C2
Nunthorpe Avenue	B1-B2
Nunthorpe Grove	C1
Nunthorpe Road	B2-C2
Palmer Lane	E4
Paragon Street	E3-F3
Park Crescent	E7
Park Grove	E7-E8
Park Street	B2
Parliament Street	D4-D5
Peasholme Green	E5
Pembroke Street	B8
Penley's Grove Street	D7-E7-E6
Percy's Lane	E4
Peters Way	A7-B7-B8
Piccadilly	D4-D3-E3-E4
Portland Street	C6
Pottery Lane	F8
Prices Lane	C2
Priory Street	B3-C3
Queen Annes Road	B6
Queen Street	B3
Railway Terrace	A3
Redness Street	F5-F6
Regent Street	F2-F3
Richardson Street	C1-D1
Rosslyn Street	A7
Rougier Street	C4
Russel Street	C1-C2
St Andrewgate	D5
St Aubyns Place	A1
St Benedict Road	C2
St Denys Road	E3-E4
St Johns Street	D6-D7
St Leonards Place	D5-D6
St Lukes Grove	B8
St Marys	B6
St Maurices	D6-D5-E5
St Olaves Road	B7-B8
St Pauls Terrace	A3
St Peters Grove	B7
St Saviourgate	D4-D5-E5
Sandringham Street	E1
Saxon Place	E8-F8
Scarborough Terrace	C8
Scarcroft Hill	B1-B2
Scarcroft Road	A2-B2-C2-C1
Scott Street	C1-C2
Shambles	D4-D5
Shaws Terrace	B2-B3
Shipton Road	A8
Shipton Street	B8-C8
Skeldergate	C4-C3-D3

Skeldergate Bridge	D3
South Esplanade	D3
Southlands Road	C1
South Parade	B2-B3
Stanley Street	D8
Station Avenue	B4
Station Rise	B4
Station Road	B3-B4-C4-C5
Stonegate	C5-D5
Swann Street	C9
Swinegate	D5
Sycamore Place	B6
Sycamore Terrace	A5-B5-B6
Tanner Row	B4-C4
Telford Terrace	B1
The Avenue	A7
The Crescent	B3
The Mount	A1-A2-B2
The Stonebow	D4-E4-E5-D5
Thorpe Street	C1-C2
Toft Green	B3-B4
Tower Street	D4-D3-E3
Townend Street	D7
Trent Holme Drive	A1
Trinity Lane	C3-C4
Union Terrace	C7
Upper Price Street	B2-C2
Victor Street	C3
Vine Street	C2-D2
Walmgate	D4-E4-E3-F3
Walpole Street	D8-E8
Water Lane	A8
Watson Street	A2-A3
Wellington Row	C4
Wellington Street	F2-F3
Wentworth Road	B1
Westminster Road	A7
William Street	D1
Willis Street	F2-F3
Winterscale Street	E2
Wolsley Street	F2

191

London

Key to Inner London Maps

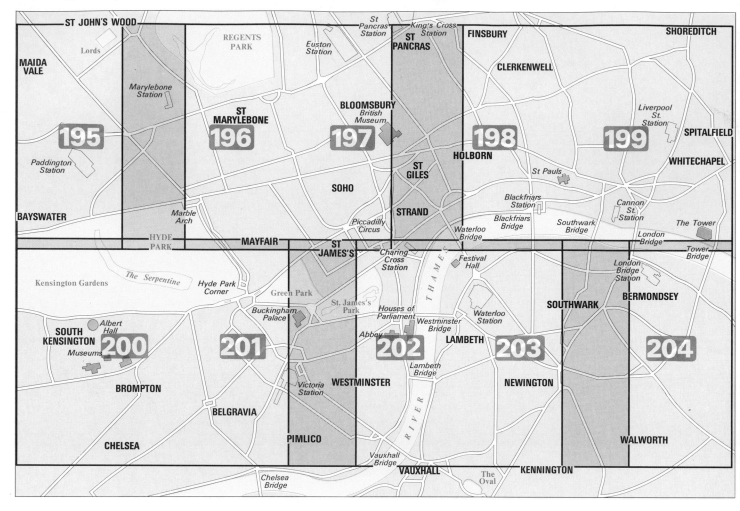

```
0        110      220           440            660 yards
0        100      200           400            600 metres
Scale: seven inches to one mile
```

Map Symbols

Symbol		Symbol	
Motorway	≡≡≡	Hospital	Ⓗ
One-way street	←	Post office	P.O
No vehicular access	‖—‖	Church or religious centre	†
Traffic roundabout	⟳	Water feature	*Thames*
Banned turn	↗	Park or open space	◯
Parking	Ⓟ	Place of interest	*Museum*
Garage parking	Ⓖ	AA Service centre	**AA**
British Rail station	Euston Station	District name	**STRAND**
London Transport station	Holborn ⊖	Overlap extent and number of continuing page	▲198
Police station	POL		

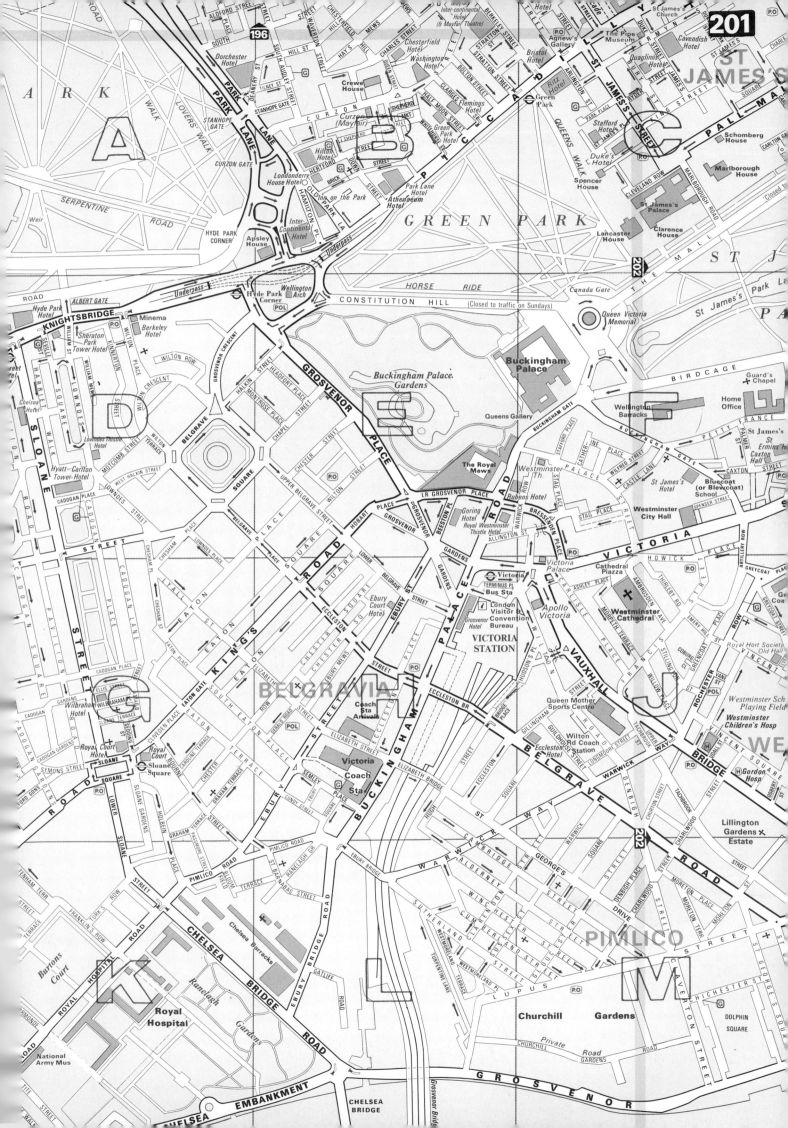

Theatreland

London is the world centre of the performing arts. In addition to the National Theatre and the Royal Shakespeare Company, there are over 40 commercial theatres in the West End. Centring on Shaftesbury Avenue and the Covent Garden area, the map highlights these theatres in red.
Below are the addresses and telephone numbers for the theatres shown. Dial 01 (071 after 6 May 1990) before the telephone number if ringing from outside London.

Theatres

Adelphi, The Strand, WC2 Tel: 836 7611
Albery, St Martin's Lane, WC2 Tel: 867 1115
Aldwych, Aldwych, WC2 Tel: 836 6404
Ambassadors, West Street, WC2 Tel: 836 6111/2
Apollo, Shaftesbury Avenue, W1 Tel: 437 2663

Arts (Theatre Club), Great Newport Street, WC2 Tel: 836 2132
Astoria, Charing Cross Road WC2 Tel: 434 0403
Cambridge, Earlham Street, WC2 Tel: 379 5299
Coliseum, St Martins Lane, WC2 Tel: 836 3161
Comedy, Panton Street, SW1 Tel: 930 2578
Criterion, Piccadilly, W1 Tel: 867 1117
Donmar Warehouse, Earlham Street, WC2 Tel: 240 8230
Duchess, Catherine Street, WC2 Tel: 836 1134
Duke of York's, St Martin's Lane, WC2 Tel: 836 5122
Fortune, Russell Street, WC2 Tel: 836 2238
Garrick, Charing Cross Road, WC2 Tel: 379 6107
Globe, Shaftesbury Avenue, W1 Tel: 437 3667
Her Majesty's, Haymarket, SW1 Tel: 839 2244
Institute of Contemporary Arts, The Mall, SW1 Tel: 930 0493
Lyric, Shaftesbury Avenue, W1 Tel: 437 3686
New London, Parker Street, WC2 Tel: 405 0072
Palace, Shaftesbury Avenue, W1 Tel: 434 0909
Phoenix, Charing Cross Road, WC2 Tel: 836 2294
Players, Villiers Street, WC2 Tel: 839 1134
Playhouse, Northumberland Avenue, WC2 Tel: 839 4401

Prince Edward, Old Compton Street, W1 Tel: 734 8951
Prince of Wales, Coventry Street, W1 Tel: 839 5972
Queen's, Shaftesbury Avenue, W1 Tel: 734 1166
Royal Opera House, Covent Garden, WC2 Tel: 240 1066
Royalty, Portugal Street, WC2 Tel: 831 0660
Savoy, Strand, WC2 Tel: 836 8888
Shaftesbury, Shaftesbury Avenue, WC2 Tel: 379 5399
St Martin's, West Street, WC2 Tel: 836 1443
Strand, Aldwych, WC2 Tel: 836 2660
Theatre Royal (Drury Lane), Catherine Street, WC2 Tel: 836 8108
Theatre Royal, (Haymarket), SW1 Tel: 930 9832
Unicorn, Great Newport Street, WC2 Tel: 836 3334
Vaudeville, Strand, WC2 Tel: 836 9987
Whitehall, Whitehall, SW1 Tel: 867 1119
Wyndham's, Charing Cross Road, WC2 Tel: 867 1116

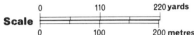

Scale
0   110   220 yards
0   100   200 metres

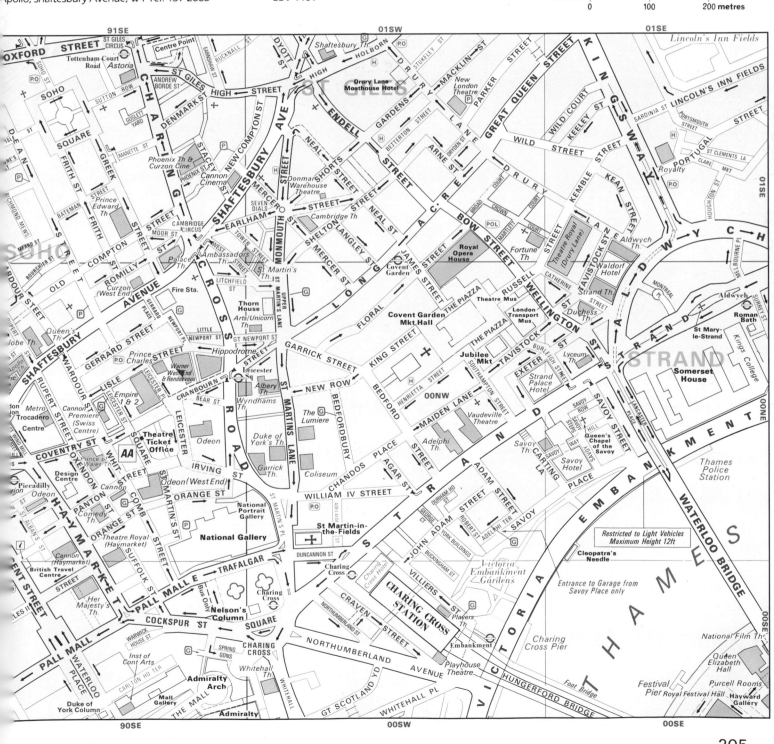

London street index

This map employs an arbitrary system of grid reference. Pages are identified by numbers and divided into twelve squares. Each square contains a blue letter; all references give the page number first, followed by the letter of the square in which a particular street can be found. Reference for Exhibition Road is *200*E, meaning that the relevant map is on page *200* and that the street appears in the square designated E.

Index to atlas

All towns and villages are included in this index.

To locate a place in the atlas, first look up the name of the town or village required in the index. Turn to the page number indicated in **bold** type, and find the location using the last four numbers. Taking Hythe *Kent* .... **15** TR1634 as our example, take the first **bold** figure of the reference, **1**, which refers to the number along the bottom of the page. The second figure, 6, tells you the distance to move in tenths to the right of this numbered line. A vertical line through this point is the first half of the reference. The third, **bold** figure, **3**, refers to the number on the lefthand side of the page. Finally, the fourth figure, 4, indicates the distance to move in tenths above this numbered line. A horizontal line drawn through this point to intersect with the first line gives the precise location of the place in question.

Allbrook Hants ... 10 SU4521
Allen's Green Herts ... 31 TL4516
Allendale Town Nthumb ... 68 NY8455
Allenheads Nthumb ... 68 NY8645
Allensford Dur ... 68 NZ0750
Allensmore H & W ... 27 SO4635
Allenton Derbys ... 39 SK3732
Aller Devon ... 7 SS7625
Aller Somset ... 8 ST4029
Allerby Cumb ... 66 NY0839
Allercombe Devon ... 7 SY0494
Allerford Somset ... 18 SS9047
Allerston N York ... 63 SE8782
Allerthorpe Humb ... 56 SE7847
Allerton Mersyd ... 46 SJ3987
Allerton W York ... 55 SE1234
Allerton Bywater W York ... 55 SE4127
Allerton Mauleverer N York ... 55 SE4458
Allesley W Mids ... 39 SP2980
Allestree Derbys ... 49 SK3439
Allexton Leics ... 40 SK8100
Allgreave Ches ... 48 SJ9767
Allhallows Kent ... 24 TQ8377
Alligin Shuas Highld ... 91 NG8358
Allington Dorset ... 8 SY4693
Allington Kent ... 14 TQ7557
Allington Lincs ... 50 SK8540
Allington Wilts ... 20 ST8975
Allington Wilts ... 20 SU0663
Allithwaite Cumb ... 10 SD2039
Alllen End Warwks ... 38 SP1696
Alloa Cent ... 82 NS8893
Allonby Cumb ... 66 NY0843
Alloway Strath ... 73 NS3318
Allowenshay Somset ... 8 ST3913
Allt Na h'Airbhe (Inn) Highld ... 96 NH1193
Alltchaorunn Highld ... 86 NN1951
Alltmawr Powys ... 26 SO0746
Alltwalis Dyfed ... 17 SN4431
Alltwen W Glam ... 18 SN7303
Alltyblaca Dyfed ... 17 SN5245
Allweston Dorset ... 9 ST6614
Almeley H & W ... 27 SO3351
Almeley Wooton H & W ... 27 SO3352
Almer Dorset ... 9 SY9098
Almholme S York ... 56 SE5008
Almington Staffs ... 37 SJ7034
Alminstone Cross Devon ... 6 SS3420
Almondbank Tays ... 82 NO0625
Almondbury W York ... 55 SE1615
Almondsbury Avon ... 19 ST6083
Alness Highld ... 97 NH6599
Alnham Nthumb ... 68 NT9810
Alnmouth Nthumb ... 69 NU2410
Alnwick Nthumb ... 69 NU1813
Alperton Gt Lon ... 23 TQ1884
Alphamstone Essex ... 24 TL8835
Alpheton Suffk ... 32 TL8850
Alphington Devon ... 5 SX9090
Alport Derbys ... 48 SK2264
Alresford Essex ... 25 TM0721
Alrewas Staffs ... 38 SK1715
Alsager Ches ... 47 SJ7955
Alsagers Bank Staffs ... 47 SJ8048
Alshot Somset ... 18 ST1936
Alsop en le Dale Derbys ... 48 SK1655
Alston Devon ... 8 ST3002
Alston Sutton Somset ... 19 ST4151
Alstone Gloucs ... 28 SO9832
Alstone Somset ... 19 ST3147
Alstone Green Staffs ... 38 SJ8618
Alstonefield Staffs ... 48 SK1355
Alswear Devon ... 7 SS7222
Altandhu Highld ... 98 NB9812
Altarnun Cnwll ... 4 SX2281
Altass Highld ... 96 NC5000
Altcreich Strath ... 79 NM6939
Altgaltraig Strath ... 80 NS0473
Altham Lancs ... 54 SD7733
Althorne Essex ... 24 TQ9199
Althorpe Humb ... 56 SE8309
Altnabreac Station Highld ... 100 ND0045
Altnacealgach Hotel Highld ... 96 NC2810
Altnacraig Strath ... 79 NM8429
Altnaharra Highld ... 99 NC5635
Altofts W York ... 55 SE3723
Alton Derbys ... 49 SK3664
Alton Hants ... 11 SU7139
Alton Staffs ... 48 SK0742
Alton Barnes Wilts ... 20 SU1062
Alton Pancras Dorset ... 9 ST6902
Alton Priors Wilts ... 20 SU1062
Altrincham Gt Man ... 47 SJ7687
Alva Cent ... 82 NS8897
Alvanley Ches ... 46 SJ4974
Alvaston Derbys ... 39 SK3833
Alvechurch H & W ... 38 SO9372
Alvecote Warwks ... 39 SK2404
Alvediston Wilts ... 9 ST9723
Alverdiscott Devon ... 6 SS5225
Alverstoke Hants ... 11 SZ6098
Alverstone IOW ... 11 SZ5785
Alverthorpe W York ... 55 SE3121
Alverton Notts ... 50 SK7942
Alves Gramp ... 93 NJ1362
Alvescot Oxon ... 29 SP2704
Alveston Avon ... 19 ST6387
Alveston Avon ... 19 ST6388
Alveston Warwks ... 29 SP2256
Alvie Highld ... 93 NH8609
Alvingham Lincs ... 51 TF3691
Alvington Gloucs ... 19 SO6000
Alwalton Cambs ... 40 TL1396
Alwinton Nthumb ... 68 NT9106
Alwoodley W York ... 55 SE2840
Alwoodley Gates W York ... 55 SE3141
Alyth Tays ... 88 NO2448
Amberley Gloucs ... 20 SO8401
Amberley W Susx ... 12 TQ0313
Amble Nthumb ... 69 NU2604
Amblecote W Mids ... 38 SO8985
Ambler Thorn W York ... 55 SE0929
Ambleside Cumb ... 59 NY3704
Ambleston Dyfed ... 16 SN0026
Ambrosden Oxon ... 29 SP6019
Amcotts Humb ... 56 SE8514
Amersham Bucks ... 22 SU9597
Amesbury Wilts ... 20 SU1541
Amhuinnsuidhe W Isls ... 102 NB0408
Amisfield Town D & G ... 66 NY0082
Amlwch Gwynd ... 44 SH4492
Ammanford Dyfed ... 17 SN6212
Amotherby N York ... 63 SE7473
Ampleforth N York ... 62 SE5878
Amney Crucis Gloucs ... 20 SP0602
Ampney St. Mary Gloucs ... 20 SP0802
Ampney St. Peter Gloucs ... 20 SP0801
Amport Hants ... 21 SU2944
Amport Hants ... 21 SU3044
Ampthill Beds ... 30 TL0337
Ampton Suffk ... 32 TL8671
Amroth Dyfed ... 17 SN1608
Amwell Herts ... 31 TL1613
Anaheilt Highld ... 79 NM8162
Ancaster Lincs ... 50 SK9843
Anchor Shrops ... 36 SO1784
Ancroft Nthumb ... 77 NU0045
Ancrum Border ... 76 NT6224
Anderby Lincs ... 51 TF5275
Andersfield Somset ... 8 ST2333
Anderson Dorset ... 9 SY8797
Andover Hants ... 21 SU3645
Andoversford Gloucs ... 28 SP0219
Andreas IOM ... 52 SC4199
Anerley Gt Lon ... 23 TQ3369
Anfield Mersyd ... 46 SJ3692
Angarrack Cnwll ... 2 SW5838
Angelbank Shrops ... 37 SO5776
Angersleigh Somset ... 8 ST1918
Angle Dyfed ... 16 SM8603
Angmering W Susx ... 12 TQ0604
Angram N York ... 55 SE5248
Ankerville Highld ... 97 NH8174
Ankle Hill Leics ... 40 SK7518
Anlaby Humb ... 56 TA0352
Anmer Norfk ... 42 TF7429

Anmore Hants ... 11 SU6711
Anna Valley Hants ... 21 SU3443
Annan D & G ... 67 NY1966
Annat Highld ... 91 NG8954
Annat Strath ... 80 NN0322
Annathill Strath ... 74 NS7270
Annbank Strath ... 73 NS4023
Annesley Woodhouse Notts ... 49 SK4953
Annesley Notts ... 49 SK5153
Annfield Plain Dur ... 68 NZ1751
Anniesland Strath ... 74 NS5368
Annscroft Shrops ... 36 SJ4508
Ansdell Lancs ... 53 SD3428
Ansford Somset ... 8 ST6432
Ansley Warwks ... 39 SP3091
Anslow Staffs ... 39 SK1924
Anslow Gate Staffs ... 39 SK2125
Anstey Herts ... 31 TL4033
Anstey Leics ... 39 SK5408
Anston S York ... 49 SK5184
Anstruther Fife ... 83 NO5703
Anstruther Easter Fife ... 83 NO5704
Ansty W Susx ... 12 TQ2923
Ansty Warwks ... 39 SP4083
Ansty Wilts ... 9 ST9526
Ansty Cross Dorset ... 9 ST7603
Anthill Common Hants ... 11 SU6412
Anthorn Cumb ... 67 NY1958
Antingham Norfk ... 43 TG2533
Antony Cnwll ... 4 SX3954
Antony M Glam ... 18 SX4054
Antrobus Ches ... 47 SJ6480
Anwick Lincs ... 50 TF1150
Anwoth D & G ... 65 NX5856
Aperfield Gt Lon ... 23 TQ4158
Apes Dale H & W ... 38 SO9973
Aperthorpe Nhants ... 40 TL0295
Apley Lincs ... 50 TF1075
Apperknowle Derbys ... 49 SK3878
Apperley Gloucs ... 28 SO8628
Appersett N York ... 60 SD8590
Appin Strath ... 86 NM9346
Appin House Gramp ... 95 NJ9549
Appleby Humb ... 56 SE9414
Appleby Magna Leics ... 39 SK3009
Appleby Parva Leics ... 39 SK3008
Appleby-in-Westmorland Cumb ... 60 NY6820
Applecross Highld ... 91 NG7144
Appledore Devon ... 6 SS4630
Appledore Devon ... 7 ST0614
Appledore Kent ... 14 TQ9529
Appledore Oxon ... 21 SU5293
Applegarth Town D & G ... 67 NY1084
Appleshaw Hants ... 21 SU3048
Appleton Ches ... 46 SJ5186
Appleton Oxon ... 21 SP4401
Appleton Roebuck N York ... 56 SE5542
Appleton Thorn Ches ... 47 SJ6483
Appleton Wiske N York ... 62 NZ3904
Appleton-le-Moors N York ... 63 SE7387
Appleton-le-Street N York ... 63 SE7373
Appletreehall Border ... 76 NT5117
Appletreewick N York ... 55 SE0560
Appley Somset ... 7 ST0721
Appley Bridge Lancs ... 53 SD5209
Apse Heath IOW ... 11 SZ5683
Apsley End Beds ... 30 TL1232
Apuldram W Susx ... 11 SU8403
Arabella Highld ... 97 NH7975
Arbeadie Gramp ... 89 NO6996
Arbirlot Tays ... 83 NO6040
Arboll Highld ... 97 NH8782
Arborfield Berks ... 22 SU7567
Arborfield Cross Berks ... 22 SU7666
Arbory IOM ... 52 SC2470
Arbourthorpe S York ... 49 SK3685
Arbroath Tays ... 89 NO6441
Arbuthnott Gramp ... 89 NO8074
Arcadia Kent ... 14 TQ8736
Archaracle Highld ... 79 NM6767
Archdeacon Newton Dur ... 61 NZ2517
Archiestown Gramp ... 94 NJ2344
Arclid Green Ches ... 47 SJ7962
Ard a'Chapuill Strath ... 80 NS0179
Ardachu Highld ... 97 NC6603
Ardaily Strath ... 72 NR6450
Ardalanish Strath ... 78 NM3619
Ardanaiseig Strath ... 80 NN0824
Ardaneaskan Highld ... 85 NG8335
Ardarroch Highld ... 85 NG8339
Ardarroch Strath ... 80 NS2394
Ardbeg Strath ... 70 NR4146
Ardbeg Strath ... 72 NS0766
Ardbeg Strath ... 80 NS1583
Ardcharnich Highld ... 96 NH1788
Ardchiavaig Strath ... 78 NM3818
Ardchonnel Strath ... 80 NM9812
Ardchullarie More Cent ... 81 NN5813
Ardchyle Cent ... 81 NN5229
Ardechive Highld ... 86 NN1490
Ardeer Strath ... 73 NS2740
Ardeley Herts ... 31 TL3027
Ardelve Highld ... 85 NG8727
Arden Strath ... 80 NS3684
Ardens Grafton Warwks ... 28 SP1154
Ardentinny Strath ... 80 NS1887
Ardeonaig Cent ... 81 NN6635
Ardersier Highld ... 93 NH7854
Ardessie Highld ... 96 NH0689
Ardfern Strath ... 79 NM8004
Ardgartan Strath ... 80 NN2703
Ardgay Highld ... 97 NH5990
Ardgour Highld ... 86 NN0163
Ardgowan Strath ... 80 NS2073
Ardhallow Strath ... 80 NS1574
Ardhasig W Isls ... 90 NB1303
Ardheslaig Highld ... 91 NG7855
Ardindrean Highld ... 96 NH1588
Ardingly W Susx ... 12 TQ3429
Ardington Oxon ... 21 SU4388
Ardivachar W Isls ... 102 NF7445
Ardlamont House Strath ... 71 NR9865
Ardleigh Essex ... 25 TM0529
Ardleigh Heath Essex ... 25 TM0430
Ardler Tays ... 88 NO2642
Ardley Oxon ... 29 SP5427
Ardley End Essex ... 31 TL5214
Ardlui Strath ... 80 NN3115
Ardlussa Strath ... 71 NR6487
Ardmaddy Strath ... 80 NN0837
Ardmair Highld ... 96 NH1198
Ardmaleish Strath ... 72 NS0768
Ardmay Strath ... 80 NN2802
Ardminish Strath ... 72 NR6448
Ardmolich Highld ... 85 NM7171
Ardmore Highld ... 98 NC2151
Ardmore Highld ... 97 NH7086
Ardmore Strath ... 80 NS3178
Ardnadam Strath ... 80 NS1780
Ardnagrask Highld ... 92 NH5249
Ardnarff Highld ... 85 NG8935
Ardnastang Highld ... 79 NM8061
Ardnave Strath ... 70 NR2873
Ardochrig Strath ... 74 NS6346
Ardochy House Highld ... 86 NH3002
Ardpatrick Strath ... 71 NR7660
Ardpeaton Strath ... 80 NS2185
Ardrishaig Strath ... 71 NR8585
Ardroil W Isls ... 102 NB0432
Ardroscadale Strath ... 72 NS0558
Ardrossan Strath ... 73 NS2342
Ardshealach Highld ... 79 NM6867
Ardsley East W York ... 55 SE3024
Ardslignish Highld ... 79 NM5661
Ardtalnaig Tays ... 81 NN7039
Ardtoe Highld ... 79 NM6270
Ardullie Highld ... 92 NH5862
Ardvaine Strath ... 79 NM7910
Ardvasar Highld ... 85 NG6304
Ardverikie Highld ... 87 NN5087
Ardvorlich Tays ... 81 NN6322
Ardvourlie W Isls ... 90 NB1911
Ardwell D & G ... 64 NX1045
Ardwick Gt Man ... 47 SJ8597
Arford Hants ... 11 SU8236
Argoed Gwent ... 19 SO1700

Argoed Shrops ... 36 SJ3221
Argoed Mill Powys ... 26 SN9962
Argos Hill E Susx ... 13 TQ5628
Aribruach W Isls ... 102 NB2518
Aridhglas Strath ... 78 NM3123
Arileod Highld ... 78 NM1665
Arinacrinachd Highld ... 91 NG7458
Arinagour Strath ... 79 NM8627
Arisaig Highld ... 85 NM6686
Arisaig House Highld ... 85 NM6984
Arivruaich W Isls ... 90 NB2417
Arkendale N York ... 55 SE3861
Arkesden Essex ... 31 TL4834
Arkholme Lancs ... 54 SD5871
Arkleton D & G ... 67 NY3791
Arkley Gt Lon ... 23 TQ2295
Arksey S York ... 56 SE5707
Arksey S York ... 56 SE5807
Arkwright Town Derbys ... 49 SK4270
Arle Gloucs ... 28 SO9223
Arlecdon Cumb ... 58 NY0419
Arleston Shrops ... 37 SJ6610
Arley Ches ... 47 SJ6780
Arley Warwks ... 39 SP2890
Arlingham Gloucs ... 28 SO7010
Arlington Devon ... 6 SS6140
Arlington E Susx ... 13 TQ5407
Arlington Beccott Devon ... 6 SS6240
Armadale Highld ... 99 NC7864
Armadale Loth ... 75 NS9368
Armadale Castle Highld ... 84 NG6304
Armadale Cumb ... 66 NY1527
Armathwaite Cumb ... 67 NY5046
Arminghall Norfk ... 43 TG2504
Armitage Staffs ... 38 SK0816
Armitage Bridge W York ... 55 SE1313
Armley W York ... 55 SE2733
Armston Nhants ... 40 TL0686
Armthorpe S York ... 56 SE6205
Arnabost Strath ... 78 NM2159
Arnburn Strath ... 80 NS3588
Arncliffe N York ... 54 SD9371
Arncroach Fife ... 83 NO5105
Arndilly House Gramp ... 94 NJ2847
Arne Dorset ... 9 SY9788
Arnesby Leics ... 39 SP6192
Arnfield Derbys ... 48 SK0198
Arngask Tays ... 82 NO1411
Arnicle Strath ... 72 NR7138
Arnisdale Highld ... 85 NG8410
Arnish Highld ... 90 NG5948
Arnol W Isls ... 102 NB3148
Arnold Humb ... 57 TA1241
Arnold Notts ... 49 SK5845
Arnprior Cent ... 81 NS6194
Arnside Cumb ... 59 SD4578
Aros Mains Strath ... 79 NM5645
Arotalla Strath ... 70 NR3654
Arrad Foot Cumb ... 58 SD3080
Arram Humb ... 56 TA0344
Arrathorne N York ... 61 SE2093
Arreton IOW ... 11 SZ5386
Arrington Cambs ... 31 TL3250
Arriundle Highld ... 79 NM8264
Arrochar Strath ... 80 NN3004
Arrow Warwks ... 28 SP0857
Artafallie Highld ... 92 NH6349
Arthington W York ... 55 SE2644
Arthingworth Nhants ... 40 SP7581
Arthrath Gramp ... 95 NJ9636
Artrochie Gramp ... 95 NK0032
Arundel W Susx ... 12 TQ0107
Asby Cumb ... 58 NY0620
Ascog Strath ... 73 NS1062
Ascot Berks ... 22 SU9268
Ascott-under-Whychwood Oxon ... 29 SP3018
Asenby N York ... 62 SE3975
Asfordby Leics ... 40 SK7018
Asfordby Hill Leics ... 40 SK7219
Asgarby Lincs ... 50 TF1145
Asgarby Lincs ... 51 TF3366
Ash Kent ... 14 TQ6064
Ash Kent ... 15 TR2858
Ash Somset ... 8 ST4720
Ash Surrey ... 22 SU8950
Ash Bullayne Devon ... 7 SS7704
Ash Green Surrey ... 22 SU9049
Ash Green Warwks ... 39 SP3385
Ash Magna Shrops ... 37 SJ5739
Ash Mill Devon ... 7 SS7823
Ash Parva Shrops ... 37 SJ5739
Ash Priors Somset ... 8 ST1529
Ash Street Suffk ... 32 TM0146
Ash Thomas Devon ... 7 ST0010
Ash Vale Surrey ... 22 SU8952
Ashampstead Berks ... 21 SU5676
Ashampstead Green Berks ... 21 SU5677
Ashbocking Suffk ... 33 TM1754
Ashbocking Green Suffk ... 33 TM1854
Ashbourne Derbys ... 48 SK1846
Ashbourne Green Derbys ... 48 SK1947
Ashbrittle Somset ... 7 ST0521
Ashburton Devon ... 5 SX7569
Ashbury Devon ... 6 SX5097
Ashby Humb ... 56 SE9008
Ashby Folville Leics ... 40 SK7012
Ashby Magna Leics ... 39 SP5690
Ashby Parva Leics ... 39 SP5288
Ashby Puerorum Lincs ... 51 TF3271
Ashby St. Ledgers Nhants ... 29 SP5768
Ashby St. Mary Norfk ... 43 TG3202
Ashby by Partney Lincs ... 51 TF4266
Ashby cum Fenby Humb ... 51 TA2500
Ashby de la Launde Lincs ... 50 TF0555
Ashby-de-la-Zouch Leics ... 39 SK3516
Aschurch Gloucs ... 28 SO9233
Ascombe Avon ... 19 ST3361
Ascott Somset ... 19 ST3436
Ascott Corner Somset ... 19 ST4539
Asculme Devon ... 8 ST1415
Ashdon Essex ... 31 TL5842
Asheldham Essex ... 25 TL9701
Ashen Essex ... 32 TL7442
Ashendon Bucks ... 30 SP7014
Asheridge Bucks ... 22 SP9304
Ashfield Cent ... 81 NN7803
Ashfield Suffk ... 33 TM2162
Ashfield Green Suffk ... 33 TL7656
Ashford Derbys ... 48 SK1969
Ashford Devon ... 6 SS5335
Ashford Devon ... 6 SX6848
Ashford Kent ... 15 TR0142
Ashford Surrey ... 22 TQ0771
Ashford Bowdler Shrops ... 27 SO5070
Ashford Carbonel Shrops ... 27 SO5270
Ashford Hill Hants ... 21 SU5662
Ashgill Strath ... 74 NS7850
Ashill Devon ... 7 ST0811
Ashill Norfk ... 42 TF8804
Ashill Somset ... 8 ST3217
Ashingdon Essex ... 24 TQ8693
Ashington Nthumb ... 69 NZ2787
Ashington Somset ... 8 ST5621
Ashington W Susx ... 12 TQ1315
Ashkirk Border ... 76 NT4722
Ashleworth Gloucs ... 28 SO8125
Ashleworth Quay Gloucs ... 28 SO8125
Ashley Cambs ... 32 TL6961
Ashley Ches ... 47 SJ7784
Ashley Devon ... 7 SS6411
Ashley Gloucs ... 20 ST9394
Ashley Hants ... 10 SU3831
Ashley Hants ... 10 SZ2595
Ashley Kent ... 15 TR3048
Ashley Nhants ... 40 SP7990
Ashley Staffs ... 37 SJ7536
Ashley Green Bucks ... 22 SP9705
Ashmansworth Hants ... 21 SU4157
Ashmansworthy Devon ... 6 SS3317
Ashmore Dorset ... 9 ST9117
Ashmore Green Berks ... 21 SU5069
Ashover Derbys ... 49 SK3463
Ashow Warwks ... 29 SP3170

Ashperton H & W ... 27 SO6441
Ashprington Devon ... 5 SX8157
Ashreigney Devon ... 6 SS6213
Ashtead Surrey ... 23 TQ1858
Ashton Ches ... 46 SJ5069
Ashton Devon ... 5 SX8584
Ashton H & W ... 27 SO5164
Ashton Hants ... 11 SU5519
Ashton Nhants ... 30 SP7649
Ashton Nhants ... 40 TL0588
Ashton Somset ... 8 ST4149
Ashton Common Wilts ... 20 ST8958
Ashton Keynes Wilts ... 20 SU0494
Ashton under Hill H & W ... 28 SO9938
Ashton-under-Lyne Gt Man ... 48 SJ9399
Ashurst Hants ... 10 SU3310
Ashurst Kent ... 13 TQ5138
Ashurst W Susx ... 12 TQ1716
Ashurstwood W Susx ... 13 TQ4136
Ashwater Devon ... 6 SX3895
Ashwell Herts ... 31 TL2639
Ashwell Leics ... 40 SK8613
Ashwell End Herts ... 31 TL2540
Ashwellthorpe Norfk ... 43 TM1497
Ashwick Somset ... 19 ST6447
Ashwicken Norfk ... 42 TF7018
Askam in Furness Cumb ... 58 SD2177
Askern S York ... 56 SE5613
Askerswell Dorset ... 8 SY5292
Askett Bucks ... 22 SP8105
Askham Cumb ... 59 NY5123
Askham Notts ... 50 SK7374
Askham Bryan N York ... 56 SE5548
Askham Richard N York ... 56 SE5347
Asknish Strath ... 71 NR9391
Askrigg N York ... 61 SD9490
Askwith N York ... 55 SE1648
Aslackby Lincs ... 40 TF0830
Aslockton Notts ... 50 SK7440
Asney Somset ... 8 ST4636
Aspatria Cumb ... 58 NY1442
Aspenden Herts ... 31 TL3528
Aspley Guise Beds ... 30 SP9335
Aspley Heath Beds ... 30 SP9334
Aspull Gt Man ... 47 SD6108
Aspull Common Gt Man ... 47 SJ6498
Asselby Humb ... 56 SE7127
Assington Suffk ... 25 TL9338
Assington Green Suffk ... 32 TL7751
Astbury Ches ... 47 SJ8461
Astcote Nhants ... 30 SP6753
Asterby Lincs ... 51 TF2678
Asterley Shrops ... 36 SJ3707
Asterton Shrops ... 36 SO3991
Asthall Oxon ... 29 SP2811
Astle Highld ... 97 NH7391
Astley H & W ... 28 SO7867
Astley Shrops ... 37 SJ5319
Astley Warwks ... 39 SP3189
Astley Abbots Shrops ... 37 SO7196
Astley Bridge Gt Man ... 54 SD7111
Aston Berks ... 22 SU7884
Aston Ches ... 47 SJ6146
Aston Ches ... 47 SJ5578
Aston Clwyd ... 46 SJ3067
Aston H & W ... 36 SO4671
Aston Herts ... 31 TL2722
Aston Oxon ... 21 SP3403
Aston S York ... 49 SK4685
Aston Shrops ... 37 SJ5328
Aston Shrops ... 37 SJ6109
Aston Staffs ... 37 SJ7541
Aston Staffs ... 38 SJ9131
Aston Abbotts Bucks ... 30 SP8419
Aston Botterell Shrops ... 37 SO6384
Aston Cantlow Warwks ... 28 SP1360
Aston Clinton Bucks ... 30 SP8812
Aston Crews H & W ... 28 SO6723
Aston End Herts ... 31 TL2724
Aston Eyre Shrops ... 37 SO6594
Aston Fields H & W ... 28 SO9669
Aston Flamville Leics ... 39 SP4692
Aston Heath Ches ... 47 SJ5679
Aston Ingham H & W ... 28 SO6823
Aston Magna Gloucs ... 29 SP1935
Aston Pigott Shrops ... 36 SJ3306
Aston Rogers Shrops ... 36 SJ3406
Aston Rowant Oxon ... 22 SU7299
Aston Somerville H & W ... 28 SP0438
Aston Subedge Gloucs ... 28 SP1341
Aston Tirrold Oxon ... 21 SU5586
Aston Upthorpe Oxon ... 21 SU5586
Aston juxta Mondrum Ches ... 47 SJ6457
Aston le Walls Nhants ... 29 SP4950
Aston on Clun Shrops ... 36 SO3982
Aston-in-Makerfield Gt Man ... 47 SJ5799
Aston-on-Trent Derbys ... 39 SK4129
Astwick Beds ... 31 TL2139
Astwith Derbys ... 49 SK4364
Astwood Bucks ... 30 SP9547
Astwood H & W ... 28 SO9365
Astwood Bank H & W ... 28 SP0462
Aswarby Lincs ... 40 TF0639
Aswardby Lincs ... 51 TF3770
Atch Lench H & W ... 28 SP0350
Atcham Shrops ... 37 SJ5409
Athelhampton Dorset ... 9 SY7694
Athelington Suffk ... 33 TM2171
Athelney Somset ... 8 ST3428
Athelstaneford Loth ... 76 NT5377
Atherington Devon ... 6 SS5923
Atherstone Somset ... 8 ST3816
Atherstone Warwks ... 39 SP3097
Atherstone on Stour Warwks ... 29 SP2050
Atherton Gt Man ... 47 SD6703
Atlow Derbys ... 48 SK2348
Attadale Highld ... 85 NG9238
Attenborough Notts ... 39 SK5134
Atterby Lincs ... 50 SK9893
Attercliffe S York ... 49 SK3788
Atterton Leics ... 39 SP3598
Attleborough Norfk ... 42 TM0495
Attleborough Warwks ... 39 SP3790
Attlebridge Norfk ... 43 TG1317
Attleton Green Suffk ... 32 TL7464
Attonburn Border ... 76 NT8122
Atwick Humb ... 57 TA1850
Atworth Wilts ... 20 ST8565
Auburn Lincs ... 50 SK9262
Auchachenna Strath ... 80 NN0221
Auchagallon Strath ... 72 NR8934
Auchagoyl Strath ... 71 NR9669
Auchavan Tays ... 88 NJ8932
Auchbraad Gramp ... 89 NO7278
Auchenblae Gramp ... 89 NO7278
Auchenbowie Cent ... 81 NS7988
Auchencairn D & G ... 66 NX7951
Auchencairn D & G ... 66 NX9885
Auchencarroch Strath ... 81 NS4182
Auchencastle D & G ... 66 NT0603
Auchencrow Border ... 77 NT8560
Auchendinny Loth ... 75 NT2561
Auchengray Strath ... 75 NS9954
Auchenhalrig Gramp ... 94 NJ3761
Auchenheath Strath ... 74 NS8043
Auchenhessnane D & G ... 66 NX8096
Auchenlochan Strath ... 71 NR9772
Auchenmade Strath ... 73 NS3548
Auchenmalg D & G ... 64 NX2352
Auchentiber Strath ... 73 NS3647
Auchintroig Cent ... 81 NS5493
Auchindrain Strath ... 80 NN0303
Auchindrean Highld ... 96 NH1980
Auchininna Gramp ... 94 NJ6656
Auchinleck Strath ... 74 NS5521
Auchinloch Strath ... 74 NS6570
Auchinstarry Strath ... 74 NS7176
Auchintore Highld ... 86 NN0972
Auchiries Gramp ... 95 NK0737
Auchlee Gramp ... 89 NO8996
Auchleven Gramp ... 94 NJ6224
Auchlochan Strath ... 74 NS7937
Auchlossan Gramp ... 89 NJ5701
Auchlyne Cent ... 81 NN5029
Auchlyne Cent ... 81 NN5129
Auchmacoy Gramp ... 95 NJ9931

Name	Pg	Grid
Auchmillan *Strath*	74	NS5129
Auchmithie *Tays*	89	NO6743
Auchmuirbridge *Fife*	82	NO2101
Auchnacraig *Strath*	79	NM7283
Auchnacree *Tays*	89	NO4663
Auchnagarron *Strath*	80	NS0082
Auchnagatt *Gramp*	95	NJ9241
Auchnangoul *Strath*	80	NN0605
Auchronie *Tays*	88	NO4480
Auchtascailt *Highld*	91	NH0987
Auchterarder *Tays*	82	NN9412
Auchteraw *Highld*	92	NH3507
Auchterblair *Highld*	93	NH9222
Auchtercairn *Highld*	91	NG8077
Auchterhouse *Tays*	83	NO3337
Auchterless *Gramp*	95	NJ7141
Auchtermuchty *Fife*	83	NO2311
Auchterneed *Highld*	92	NH4859
Auchtertool *Fife*	82	NT2190
Auchtertyre *Highld*	85	NG8327
Auchtoo *Cent*	81	NN5520
Auckengill *Highld*	100	ND3664
Auckley *S York*	49	SE6501
Audenshaw *Gt Man*	48	SJ9197
Audlem *Ches*	47	SJ6543
Audley *Staffs*	47	SJ7950
Audley End *Essex*	31	TL5237
Audley End *Essex*	31	TL8037
Audley End *Suffk*	32	TL8553
Aughertree *Cumb*	85	NY2538
Aughton *Humb*	56	SE7038
Aughton *Humb*	53	SO3950
Aughton *Lancs*	53	SD5467
Aughton *Lancs*	53	SK4586
Aughton *S York*	49	SK4586
Aughton *Wilts*	21	SU2356
Aughton Park *Lancs*	46	SD4006
Auldallan *Tays*	88	NO3158
Auldearn *Highld*	93	NH9155
Aulden *H & W*	27	SO4654
Auldgirth *D & G*	66	NX9186
Auldhame *Loth*	83	NT5984
Auldhouse *Strath*	74	NS6250
Ault Hucknall *Derbys*	49	SK4665
Ault-a-Chruinn *Highld*	85	NG9420
Aultbea *Highld*	91	NG8789
Aultgrishan *Highld*	91	NG7485
Aultguish Inn *Highld*	92	NH3570
Aultiphurst *Highld*	99	NC8065
Aultmore *Gramp*	94	NJ4053
Aultnagoire *Highld*	92	NH5423
Aultnamain Inn *Highld*	97	NH6681
Aunsby *Lincs*	40	TF0438
Aust *Avon*	19	ST5789
Austerfield *Notts*	49	SK6594
Austonley *W York*	55	SE1207
Austrey *Warwks*	39	SK2906
Austwick *N York*	54	SD7668
Authorpe *Lincs*	51	TF3980
Avebury *Wilts*	20	SU1069
Aveley *Essex*	24	TQ5680
Avening *Gloucs*	20	ST8897
Averham *Notts*	50	SK7654
Aveton Gifford *Devon*	5	SX6947
Aviemore *Highld*	93	NH8913
Avinagillan *Strath*	71	NR8367
Avington *Berks*	21	SU3767
Avoch *Highld*	93	NH6955
Avon *Dorset*	10	SZ1498
Avon Dassett *Warwks*	29	SP4150
Avonbridge *Cent*	75	NS9172
Avonmouth *Avon*	19	ST5177
Avonmouth *Avon*	19	ST5278
Avonwick *Devon*	5	SX7158
Awkley *Avon*	19	ST5885
Awliscombe *Devon*	8	ST1301
Awre *Gloucs*	28	SO7008
Awsworth *Notts*	49	SK4844
Axbridge *Somset*	19	ST4354
Axford *Hants*	21	SU6043
Axford *Wilts*	21	SU2370
Axminster *Devon*	8	SY2998
Axmouth *Devon*	8	SY2591
Aycliffe *Dur*	61	NZ2822
Aylburton *Gloucs*	19	SO6101
Aylesbeare *Devon*	5	SY0391
Aylesbury *Bucks*	30	SP8214
Aylesby *Humb*	57	TA2007
Aylesford *Kent*	14	TQ7359
Aylesham *Kent*	15	TR2352
Aylestone *Leics*	39	SK5700
Aylestone Park *Leics*	39	SK5801
Aylmerton *Norfk*	43	TG1839
Aylsham *Norfk*	43	TG1926
Aylton *H & W*	27	SO6537
Aylworth *Gloucs*	28	SP1021
Aymestrey *H & W*	27	SO4265
Aynho *Nhants*	29	SP5133
Ayot Green *Herts*	31	TL2214
Ayot St. Lawrence *Herts*	31	TL1916
Ayot St. Peter *Herts*	31	TL2115
Ayr *Strath*	73	NS3321
Aysgarth *N York*	61	SE0088
Ayshford *Devon*	7	ST0415
Ayside *Cumb*	59	SD3983
Ayston *Leics*	40	SK8601
Aythorpe Roding *Essex*	24	TL5815
Ayton *Border*	77	NT9261
Azerley *N York*	61	SE2574

B

Name	Pg	Grid
Babbacombe *Devon*	5	SX9265
Babbinswood *Shrops*	36	SJ3330
Babbs Green *Herts*	31	TL3916
Babcary *Somset*	8	ST5628
Babel Green *Suffk*	32	TL7348
Babeny *Devon*	5	SX6774
Babraham *Cambs*	31	TL5150
Babworth *Notts*	49	SK6880
Bache *Shrops*	37	SO4782
Bachelor Bump *E Susx*	14	TQ8312
Back of Keppoch *Highld*	85	NM6587
Backaland *Ork*	103	HY6530
Backfolds *Gramp*	95	NK0252
Backford *Ches*	46	SJ4071
Backhill of Trustach *Gramp*	89	NO6397
Backies *Highld*	97	NC8302
Backlass *Highld*	100	ND2053
Backwell *Avon*	19	ST4968
Bacon End *Essex*	24	TL6018
Bacon's End *W Mids*	38	SP1887
Baconsthorpe *Norfk*	43	TG1237
Bacton *H & W*	27	SO3732
Bacton *Norfk*	43	TG3433
Bacton *Suffk*	32	TM0567
Badachro *Highld*	91	NG7873
Badavanich *Highld*	91	NH1058
Badbury *Wilts*	20	SU1980
Badby *Nhants*	29	SP5559
Badcall *Highld*	98	NC1541
Badcall *Highld*	98	NC2455
Badcaul *Highld*	91	NH0291
Baddesley Clinton *Warwks*	39	SP2071
Baddesley Ensor *Warwks*	39	SP2798
Baddidarroch *Highld*	98	NC0822
Badenscallie *Highld*	91	NC0306
Badenscoth *Gramp*	95	NJ7038
Badenyon *Gramp*	94	NJ3319
Badgall *Cnwll*	4	SX2386
Badger *Shrops*	37	SO7699
Badgeworth *Gloucs*	28	SO9019
Badgworth *Somset*	19	ST3952
Badicaul *Highld*	85	NG7528
Badingham *Suffk*	33	TM3068
Badlesmere *Kent*	15	TR0153
Badlieu *Border*	75	NT0518
Badluarach *Highld*	91	NG9994
Badninish *Highld*	97	NH7594
Badrallach *Highld*	91	NH0691
Badsey *H & W*	28	SP0743

Name	Pg	Grid
Badshot Lea *Surrey*	22	SU8648
Badsworth *W York*	55	SE4614
Badwell Ash *Suffk*	32	TL9069
Bag Enderby *Lincs*	51	TF3573
Bagber *Dorset*	9	ST7513
Bagby *N York*	62	SE4680
Bage The *H & W*	27	SO3243
Bagendon *Gloucs*	28	SP0006
Baggrow *Cumb*	58	NY1742
Baginton *Warwks*	39	SP3474
Baglan *W Glam*	18	SS7492
Bagley *Shrops*	36	SJ4027
Bagley *Somset*	19	ST4745
Bagmore *Hants*	22	SU6645
Bagnall *Staffs*	48	SJ9250
Bagot *Shrops*	37	SO5973
Bagshot *Surrey*	22	SU9063
Bagshot *Wilts*	20	ST6987
Bagstone *Avon*	20	ST6987
Bagthorpe *Notts*	49	SK4751
Bagworth *Leics*	39	SK4408
Bagwy Llydiart *H & W*	27	SO4426
Baildon *W York*	55	SE1539
Baildon Green *W York*	55	SE1439
Baile Mor *Strath*	78	NM2824
Baileyhead *Cumb*	67	NY5181
Baillieston *Strath*	74	NS6763
Bainshole *Gramp*	94	NH8519
Bainbridge *N York*	61	SD9390
Bainshole *Gramp*	94	NJ6035
Bainton *Cambs*	40	TF0906
Bainton *Humb*	56	SE9652
Baintown *Fife*	83	NO3503
Bairnkine *Border*	76	NT6515
Bakewell *Derbys*	48	SK2168
Bala *Gwynd*	45	SH9236
Balallan *W Isls*	102	NB2720
Balavil *Highld*	87	NH7902
Balbeg *Highld*	92	NH4431
Balbeggie *Tays*	82	NO1629
Balblair *Highld*	92	NH5145
Balblair *Highld*	93	NH7066
Balby *S York*	49	SE6800
Balchladich *Highld*	98	NC0330
Balchraggan *Highld*	92	NH5343
Balchrick *Highld*	98	NC1959
Balcombe *W Susx*	12	TQ3130
Balcomie Links *Fife*	83	NO6209
Balcurvie *Fife*	83	NO3401
Baldersby *N York*	62	SE3578
Baldersby St. James *N York*	62	SE3676
Balderstone *Lancs*	54	SD6332
Balderton *Leics*	50	SK8151
Baldinnie *Fife*	83	NO4211
Baldinnies *Tays*	82	NO0217
Baldock *Herts*	31	TL2434
Baldovie *Tays*	83	NO4533
Baldshaw *E Susx*	14	TQ8013
Baldwin's Gate *Staffs*	37	SJ7940
Bale *Norfk*	42	TG0136
Baledgarno *Tays*	83	NO2730
Balemartine *Strath*	78	NL9841
Balerno *Loth*	75	NT1666
Balfarg *Fife*	83	NO2803
Balfield *Tays*	89	NO5468
Balfour *Ork*	103	HY4716
Balfron *Cent*	81	NS5488
Balgarva *W Isls*	102	NF7647
Balgaveny *Gramp*	94	NJ6540
Balgavies *Tays*	89	NO5451
Balgedie *Tays*	82	NO1604
Balgonar *Fife*	82	NT0293
Balgowan *Highld*	87	NN6494
Balgown *D & G*	64	NX1142
Balgown *Highld*	90	NG3868
Balgracie *D & G*	64	NW9761
Balgray *Tays*	83	NO4038
Balhalgardy *Gramp*	95	NJ7623
Balham *Gt Lon*	23	TQ2873
Balhary *Tays*	88	NO2446
Balholme *Tays*	82	NO1436
Baligill *Highld*	99	NC8565
Balintore *Highld*	97	NH8675
Balintore *Tays*	88	NO2859
Balintraid *Highld*	93	NH7370
Balivanich *W Isls*	102	NF7755
Balk *N York*	62	SE4781
Balkeerie *Tays*	88	NO3344
Balkholme *Humb*	56	SE7828
Balkissock *Strath*	64	NX1482
Ball Haye Green *Staffs*	48	SJ9857
Ball Hill *Hants*	21	SU4263
Ballabeg *IOM*	52	SC2470
Ballacannell *IOM*	52	SC4382
Ballacarnane Beg *IOM*	52	SC3088
Ballachgair *Strath*	72	NR7727
Ballajora *IOM*	52	SC4790
Ballantrae *Strath*	64	NX0882
Ballasalla *IOM*	52	SC2870
Ballasalla *IOM*	52	SC3497
Ballater *Gramp*	88	NO3795
Ballaugh *IOM*	52	SC3493
Ballchraggan *Highld*	97	NH7675
Ballechin *Tays*	87	NN9353
Ballencrieff *Loth*	83	NT4878
Ballevullin *Strath*	78	NL9546
Ballidon *Derbys*	48	SK2054
Balliekine *Strath*	72	NR8739
Balliemore *Strath*	80	NS1099
Ballig *IOM*	52	SC2882
Balligmorrie *Strath*	64	NX2290
Ballimore *Cent*	81	NN5317
Ballimore *Strath*	71	NR9283
Ballinaby *Strath*	70	NR2267
Ballindalloch *Gramp*	94	NJ1636
Ballindean *Tays*	83	NO2529
Ballingdon *Essex*	32	TL8840
Ballingham *H & W*	27	SO5731
Ballingry *Fife*	82	NT1797
Ballinluig *Tays*	88	NN9752
Ballinshoe *Tays*	88	NO4153
Ballintuim *Tays*	88	NO1055
Balloch *Highld*	93	NH7246
Balloch *Strath*	74	NS3295
Balloch *Tays*	82	NN8419
Ballochroy *Strath*	71	NR7352
Ballogie *Gramp*	89	NO5795
Balls Cross *W Susx*	12	SU9826
Balls Green *E Susx*	13	TQ4936
Ballygown *Strath*	79	NM4343
Ballygrant *Strath*	70	NR3966
Ballygroggan *Strath*	72	NR6219
Ballyhaugh *Strath*	78	NM1758
Ballymenoch *Strath*	80	NS3086
Ballymichael *Strath*	72	NR9932
Balmacara *Highld*	85	NG8028
Balmaclellan *D & G*	65	NX6579
Balmacneil *Tays*	88	NN9750
Balmae *D & G*	65	NX6845
Balmaha *Cent*	81	NS4290
Balmalcolm *Fife*	83	NO3208
Balmedie *Gramp*	95	NJ9618
Balmerino *Fife*	83	NO3524
Balmore *Highld*	74	NS5973
Balmuchy *Highld*	97	NH8678
Balmuir *Tays*	89	NO5648
Balmule *Fife*	82	NT2088
Balmullo *Fife*	83	NO4320
Balnaboth *Tays*	88	NO3166
Balnacoil Lodge *Highld*	97	NC8011
Balnacra *Highld*	91	NG9746
Balnacroft *Gramp*	88	NO2894
Balnafoich *Highld*	93	NH6835
Balnaguard *Tays*	87	NN9451
Balnahard *Strath*	79	NM4534
Balnahard *Strath*	70	NR4199
Balnain *Highld*	92	NH4430
Balnakeil *Highld*	98	NC3968
Balnapaling *Highld*	93	NH7969
Balquharn *Tays*	82	NO0235
Balquhidder *Cent*	81	NN5320
Balruddery House *Tays*	83	NO3132
Balsall *W Mids*	39	SP2376
Balsall Common *W Mids*	39	SP2477
Balsall Heath *W Mids*	38	SP0784
Balscote *Oxon*	29	SP3941
Balsham *Cambs*	31	TL5850
Baltasound *Shet*	103	HP6208

Name	Pg	Grid
Balterley *Staffs*	47	SJ7550
Baltersan *D & G*	64	NX4261
Balthangie *Gramp*	95	NJ8351
Baltonsborough *Somset*	8	ST6434
Balvarran *Tays*	86	NN0761
Balvicar *Strath*	79	NM7616
Balvraid *Highld*	85	NG8416
Balvraid *Highld*	93	NH8231
Bamber Bridge *Lancs*	53	SD5625
Bamber's Green *Essex*	24	TL5722
Bamburgh *Nthumb*	77	NU1735
Bamff *Tays*	88	NO2251
Bamford *Derbys*	48	SK2083
Bampton *Cumb*	59	NY5118
Bampton *Devon*	7	SS9522
Bampton *Oxon*	21	SP3103
Bampton Grange *Cumb*	59	NY5218
Banavie *Highld*	86	NN1177
Banbury *Oxon*	29	SP4540
Banc-y-ffordd *Dyfed*	17	SN4137
Bancffosfelem *Dyfed*	17	SN4811
Banchory *Gramp*	89	NO6995
Banchory-Devenick *Gramp*	89	NJ9101
Bancycapel *Dyfed*	17	SN4315
Bancyfelin *Dyfed*	17	SN3218
Bandirran *Tays*	82	NO2030
Bandrake Head *Cumb*	59	NY3187
Banff *Gramp*	95	NJ6864
Bangor *Gwynd*	44	SH5872
Bangor *Gwynd*	44	SH5872
Bangor-is-y-coed *Clwyd*	46	SJ3945
Bangors *Cnwll*	6	SX2099
Bangrove *Suffk*	32	TL9463
Banham *Norfk*	32	TM0688
Bank *Hants*	10	SU2807
Bank *Hants*	10	SU2807
Bank Ground *Cumb*	67	NY3196
Bankend *D & G*	66	NY0268
Bankend *Strath*	74	NS8033
Bankfoot *Tays*	82	NO0635
Bankglen *Strath*	66	NS5912
Bankhead *Gramp*	89	NJ8910
Bankhead *Strath*	73	NS3739
Banknock *Cent*	81	NS7779
Banks *Lancs*	53	SD3820
Bankshill *D & G*	67	NY1982
Banningham *Norfk*	43	TG2129
Bannister Green *Essex*	24	TL6921
Bannockburn *Cent*	82	NS8190
Banstead *Surrey*	23	TQ2559
Bantham *Devon*	5	SX6643
Banton *Strath*	81	NS7480
Banwell *Avon*	19	ST3959
Bapchild *Kent*	14	TQ9263
Bapton *Wilts*	20	ST9938
Bar Hill *Cambs*	31	TL3863
Barassie *Strath*	73	NS3232
Barbaraville *Highld*	93	NH7472
Barber Green *Cumb*	67	NY3982
Barbey *D & G*	73	NS4317
Barbieston *Strath*	73	NS4317
Barbon *Cumb*	60	SD6282
Barbrook House *Strath*	79	NM8206
Barby *Nhants*	29	SP5470
Barcaldine *Strath*	86	NM9641
Barcheston *Warwks*	29	SP2639
Barcombe *E Susx*	13	TQ4214
Barden *N York*	61	SE1493
Barden Park *Kent*	13	TQ5746
Bardfield End Green *Essex*	24	TL6231
Bardfield Saling *Essex*	24	TL6826
Bardney *Lincs*	50	TF1169
Bardowie *Strath*	39	SK4412
Bardrainney *Strath*	74	NS5873
Bardsea *Cumb*	80	NS3372
Bardsey *W York*	58	SD2974
Bardwell *Suffk*	55	SE3643
Bare *Lancs*	32	TL9473
Barfad *D & G*	53	SD4464
Barford *Norfk*	64	NX3266
Barford *Warwks*	43	TG1107
Barford St. John *Oxon*	29	SP2760
Barford St. Martin *Wilts*	29	SP4333
Barford St. Michael *Oxon*	10	SU0531
Barfreston *Kent*	29	SP4332
Bargate *Derbys*	15	TR2650
Bargeddie *Strath*	49	SK3646
Bargoed *M Glam*	74	NS6865
Bargrennan *D & G*	36	SO1599
Barham *Cambs*	64	NX3577
Barham *Suffk*	33	TL1375
Barholm *Lincs*	33	TM1451
Barkby *Leics*	40	TF0810
Barkby Thorpe *Leics*	39	SK6309
Barkestone-le-Vale *Leics*	39	SK6309
Barkham *Berks*	40	SK7734
Barking *Gt Lon*	22	SU7766
Barking *Suffk*	23	TQ4484
Barking Tye *Suffk*	32	TM0753
Barkingside *Gt Lon*	32	TM0652
Barkisland *W York*	23	TQ4488
Barkla Shop *Cnwll*	55	SE0519
Barkston *Lincs*	2	SW7350
Barkston *N York*	50	SK9341
Barkway *Herts*	55	SE4936
Barlanark *Strath*	31	TL3835
Barlaston *Staffs*	48	SJB938
Barlavington *W Susx*	12	SU9716
Barlborough *Derbys*	49	SK4777
Barlby *N York*	56	SE6334
Barlestone *Leics*	39	SK4205
Barley *Herts*	31	TL4038
Barley *Lancs*	54	SD8240
Barley Hole *S York*	49	SK3696
Barleycroft *Herts*	31	TL4327
Barleythorpe *Leics*	40	SK8409
Barling *Essex*	25	TQ9389
Barlings *Lincs*	50	TF0774
Barlow *N York*	49	SK3474
Barlow *N York*	56	SE6428
Barlow *T & W*	69	NZ1561
Barmby Moor *Humb*	56	SE7748
Barmer *Norfk*	42	TF8133
Barmollack *Strath*	72	NR8144
Barmouth *Gwynd*	35	SH6115
Barmpton *Dur*	62	NZ3118
Barmston *Humb*	57	TA1659
Barnacabber *Strath*	80	NS1788
Barnacarry *Strath*	80	NS0093
Barnack *Cambs*	40	TF0705
Barnaline *Strath*	80	NN9613
Barnard Castle *Dur*	61	NZ0516
Barnardiston *Suffk*	32	TL7148
Barnburgh *S York*	55	SE4803
Barnby *Suffk*	33	TM4789
Barnby Dun *S York*	56	SE6109
Barnby Moor *Notts*	49	SK6684
Barnby in the Willows *Notts*	50	SK8552
Barnes *Gt Lon*	23	TQ2276
Barnes Street *Kent*	13	TQ6447
Barnet *Gt Lon*	23	TQ2496
Barnetby le Wold *Humb*	57	TA0509
Barney *Norfk*	42	TF9932
Barnham *Suffk*	32	TL8779
Barnham Broom *Norfk*	42	TG0807
Barnhead *Tays*	89	NO6657
Barnhill *Ches*	46	SJ4854
Barnhill *Gramp*	93	NJ1457
Barnhill *Tays*	40	NO4731
Barnhills *D & G*	64	NW9871
Barningham *Dur*	61	NZ0810
Barningham *Suffk*	32	TL9676
Barnmoor Green *Warwks*	29	SP1865
Barnoldby le Beck *Humb*	51	TA2302
Barnoldswick *Lancs*	54	SD8746
Barns Green *W Susx*	12	TQ1227
Barnsley *Gloucs*	28	SP0705
Barnsley *S York*	55	SE3406
Barnsley *Shrops*	37	SO7593
Barnsole *Kent*	15	TR2756
Barnstaple *Devon*	6	SS5533
Barnston *Essex*	24	TL6419
Barnston *Mersyd*	46	SJ2883
Barnstone *Notts*	40	SK7335
Barnt Green *H & W*	38	SP0173
Barnton *Ches*	47	SJ6375
Barnton *Loth*	75	NT1975

Name	Pg	Grid
Barnwell All Saints *Nhants*	40	TL0584
Barnwell St. Andrew *Nhants*	40	TL0585
Barnwood *Gloucs*	28	SO8518
Barons Wood *Devon*	7	SS6903
Barr *Strath*	64	NX2794
Barrahormid *Strath*	71	NR7183
Barrapoll *Strath*	78	NL9542
Barravullin *Strath*	79	NM8207
Barregarrow *IOM*	52	SC3288
Barrets Green *Ches*	47	SJ5859
Barrhead *Strath*	74	NS4958
Barrhill *Strath*	64	NX2382
Barrington *Cambs*	31	TL3848
Barrington *Somset*	8	ST3918
Barripper *Cnwll*	2	SW6338
Barrmill *Strath*	73	NS3651
Barrock *Highld*	100	ND2571
Barrow *Gloucs*	28	SO8824
Barrow *Lancs*	54	SD7338
Barrow *Leics*	40	SK8815
Barrow *Somset*	9	ST7231
Barrow *Suffk*	32	TL7663
Barrow Burn *Nthumb*	68	NT8610
Barrow Common *Somset*	19	ST5467
Barrow Gurney *Avon*	19	ST5268
Barrow Haven *Humb*	57	TA0622
Barrow Hill *Derbys*	49	SK4375
Barrow upon Soar *Leics*	39	SK5717
Barrow upon Trent *Derbys*	39	SK3528
Barrow-in-Furness *Cumb*	53	SD1971
Barrow-upon-Humber *Humb*	57	TA0720
Barrowby *Lincs*	40	SK8736
Barrowden *Leics*	40	SK9400
Barrowford *Lancs*	54	SD8539
Barry *S Glam*	18	ST1268
Barry *Tays*	83	NO5334
Barsby *Leics*	40	SK6911
Barsham *Suffk*	33	TM3989
Barskimmings *Strath*	73	NS4825
Barston *W Mids*	39	SP2078
Bartestree *H & W*	27	SO5640
Barthol Chapel *Gramp*	95	NJ8134
Bartholomew Green *Essex*	24	TL7221
Barthomley *Ches*	47	SJ7652
Bartley *Hants*	10	SU3012
Bartley Green *W Mids*	38	SP0081
Bartlow *Cambs*	31	TL5845
Barton *Cambs*	31	TL3956
Barton *Ches*	46	SJ4454
Barton *Devon*	5	SX9067
Barton *Gloucs*	28	SP0925
Barton *Lancs*	53	SD3509
Barton *Lancs*	53	SD5137
Barton *N York*	61	NZ2308
Barton *Oxon*	29	SP5408
Barton Bendish *Norfk*	42	TF7105
Barton End *Gloucs*	20	ST8497
Barton Hartshorn *Bucks*	29	SP6430
Barton Mills *Suffk*	32	TL7273
Barton St. David *Somset*	8	ST5431
Barton Stacey *Hants*	21	SU4341
Barton Town *Devon*	6	SS6840
Barton Waterside *Humb*	56	TA0222
Barton in Fabis *Notts*	39	SK5232
Barton in the Beans *Leics*	39	SK3906
Barton in the Clay *Beds*	30	TL0831
Barton on Sea *Hants*	10	SZ2493
Barton upon Irwell *Gt Man*	47	SJ7698
Barton-Upon-Humber *Humb*	57	TA0022
Barton-le-Street *N York*	63	SE7274
Barton-le-Willows *N York*	56	SE7163
Barton-on-the-Heath *Warwks*	29	SP2532
Barton-under-Needwood *Staffs*	38	SK1818
Barugh Green *S York*	55	SE3106
Barvas *W Isls*	102	NB3649
Barway *Cambs*	31	TL5475
Barwell *Leics*	39	SP4496
Barwick *Devon*	6	SS5907
Barwick *Somset*	8	ST5513
Barwick in Elmet *W York*	55	SE3937
Baschurch *Shrops*	36	SJ4221
Bascote *Warwks*	29	SP4063
Bashall Eaves *Lancs*	54	SD6943
Basildon *Berks*	21	SU6078
Basildon *Essex*	24	TQ7189
Basingstoke *Hants*	21	SU6352
Baslow *Derbys*	48	SK2572
Bason Bridge *Somset*	19	ST3445
Bassaleg *Gwent*	19	ST2787
Bassendean *Border*	76	NT6245
Bassenthwaite *Cumb*	58	NY2332
Bassett *Hants*	10	SU4116
Bassingbourn *Cambs*	31	TL3343
Bassingham *Lincs*	50	SK9059
Bassingham *Lincs*	50	SK9160
Bassingthorpe *Leics*	40	SK9628
Bassus Green *Herts*	31	TL3025
Baston *Lincs*	40	TF1114
Bastwick *Norfk*	43	TG4217
Batchworth *Herts*	22	TQ0694
Batcombe *Somset*	9	ST6838
Batcombe *Dorset*	8	ST6104
Bath *Avon*	20	ST7464
Bath Side *Essex*	25	TM2532
Bathampton *Avon*	20	ST7765
Bathealton *Somset*	7	ST0724
Batheaston *Avon*	20	ST7767
Bathford *Avon*	20	ST7966
Bathgate *Loth*	75	NS9768
Bathley *Notts*	50	SK7759
Bathpool *Cnwll*	4	SX2874
Bathpool *Somset*	8	ST2526
Bathville *Loth*	75	NS9367
Bathway *Somset*	19	ST5952
Batley *W York*	55	SE2424
Batsford *Gloucs*	29	SP1834
Batsworthy *Devon*	7	SS8119
Battersby *N York*	62	NZ5907
Battersea *Gt Lon*	23	TQ2776
Battisborough Cross *Devon*	5	SX6048
Battisford Tye *Suffk*	32	TM0354
Battle *E Susx*	14	TQ7415
Battle *Powys*	26	SO0131
Battledykes *Tays*	89	NO4555
Battlesbridge *Essex*	24	TQ7894
Battleton *Somset*	7	SS9127
Battramsley Cross *Hants*	10	SZ3198
Bauds of Cullen *Gramp*	94	NJ4766
Baughton *H & W*	28	SO8742
Baughurst *Hants*	21	SU5860
Baulds *Gramp*	89	NO6093
Baulking *Oxon*	21	SU3190
Baumber *Lincs*	51	TF2174
Baunton *H & W*	28	SP0004
Baverstock *Wilts*	20	SU0231
Bawburgh *Norfk*	43	TG1508
Bawdeswell *Norfk*	42	TG0420
Bawdrip *Somset*	8	ST3339
Bawdrip *Somset*	8	ST3339
Bawdsey *Suffk*	33	TM3440
Bawsey *Norfk*	49	SK6592
Baxenden *Lancs*	54	SD7726
Baxterley *Warwks*	39	SP2896
Bayble *W Isls*	102	NB5231
Baybridge *Hants*	11	SU5223
Baycliff *Cumb*	53	SD2872
Baydon *Wilts*	21	SU2777
Bayford *Herts*	23	TL3108
Bayford *Somset*	9	ST7229
Bayhead *W Isls*	102	NF7468
Bayles *Cumb*	68	NY7044
Baylham *Suffk*	33	TM1051
Baynard's Green *Oxon*	29	SP5529
Baysham *H & W*	27	SO5627
Baythorne End *Essex*	32	TL7242
Bayton *H & W*	37	SO6973
Bayton Common *H & W*	37	SO7172
Bayworth *Oxon*	21	SP4901
Beach *Avon*	20	ST7070
Beachampton *Bucks*	30	SP7736
Beachamwell *Norfk*	42	TF7505
Beachley *Gloucs*	19	ST5491
Beacon *Devon*	8	ST1705
Beacon End *Essex*	25	TL9524
Beacon's Bottom *Bucks*	22	SU7895

Place	County	Sheet	Grid ref
Beaconsfield	Bucks	22	SU9490
Beacontree	Gt Lon	23	TQ4786
Beadlam	N York	62	SE6584
Beadlow	Beds	30	TL1038
Beadnell	Nthumb	77	NU2229
Beaford	Devon	6	SS5515
Beal	N York	55	SE5325
Beal	Nthumb	77	NU0642
Bealsmill	Cnwll	4	SX3677
Beam Hall	N York	39	SK2326
Beaminster	Dorset	8	ST4801
Beamish	Dur	69	NZ2253
Beamsley	N York	55	SE0752
Beanacre	Wilts	20	ST9066
Beanley	Nthumb	77	NU0618
Beara Charter Barton	Devon	6	SS5238
Beardon	Devon	4	SX5184
Beare Green	Surrey	12	TQ1742
Bearley	Warwks	29	SP1860
Bearpark	Dur	69	NZ2343
Bearsbridge	Nthumb	68	NY7857
Bearsden	Strath	74	NS5372
Bearstone	Shrops	37	SJ7239
Bearwood	W Mids	38	SP0286
Beattock	D & G	66	NT0702
Beauchamp Roding	Essex	24	TL5809
Beaufort	Gwent	27	SO1611
Beaulieu	Hants	10	SU3602
Beauly	Highld	92	NH5246
Beaumaris	Gwynd	44	SH6076
Beaumont	Cumb	67	NY3459
Beaumont	Essex	25	TM1625
Beaumont	Jersey	101	SV0000
Beausale	Warwks	29	SP2470
Beauworth	Hants	11	SU5726
Beaworthy	Devon	6	SX4699
Beazley End	Essex	24	TL7429
Bebington	Mersyd	46	SJ3383
Beccles	Suffk	33	TM4290
Becconsall	Lancs	53	SD4523
Beck Hole	N York	63	NZ8102
Beck Row	Suffk	32	TL6977
Beck Side	Cumb	58	SD2382
Beckbury	Shrops	37	SJ7601
Beckenham	Gt Lon	23	TQ3769
Beckering	Lincs	50	TF1180
Beckermet	Cumb	58	NY0206
Beckfoot	Cumb	67	NY0949
Beckford	H & W	28	SO9735
Beckhampton	Wilts	20	SU0868
Beckingham	Lincs	50	SK8753
Beckingham	Notts	50	SK7889
Beckington	Somset	20	ST7951
Beckley	Shrops	36	SO3977
Beckley	E Susx	14	TQ8523
Beckley	Hants	10	SZ2297
Beckley	Oxon	29	SP5611
Beckton	Gt Lon	23	TQ4381
Beckwithshaw	N York	55	SE2653
Bedale	N York	61	SE2687
Bedchester	Dorset	9	ST8517
Beddau	M Glam	18	ST0585
Beddgelert	Gwynd	44	SH5848
Beddingham	E Susx	13	TQ4407
Beddington	Gt Lon	23	TQ3065
Beddington Corner	Gt Lon	23	TQ2866
Bedfield	Suffk	33	TM2266
Bedford	Beds	30	TL0449
Bedham	W Susx	12	TQ0122
Bedhampton	Hants	11	SU6906
Bedingfield	Suffk	33	TM1768
Bedingfield Street	Suffk	33	TM1767
Bedlam	N York	55	SE2661
Bedlam Lane	Kent	14	TQ8845
Bedlington	T & W	69	NZ2581
Bedlinog	M Glam	18	SO0901
Bedminster	Avon	19	ST5771
Bedminster Down	Avon	19	ST5770
Bedmond	Herts	22	TL0903
Bednall	Staffs	38	SJ9517
Bedrule	Border	76	NT6017
Bedstone	Shrops	36	SO3776
Bedwas	M Glam	19	ST1789
Bedwellty	Gwent	19	SO1600
Bedworth	Warwks	39	SP3687
Beeby	Leics	39	SK6608
Beech	Hants	11	SU6938
Beech	Staffs	38	SJ8538
Beech Hill	Berks	22	SU6964
Beechingstoke	Wilts	20	SU0859
Beedon	Berks	21	SU4877
Beedon Hill	Berks	21	SU4877
Beeford	Humb	57	TA1253
Beeley	Derbys	49	SK2667
Beelsby	Humb	51	TA2001
Beenham	Berks	21	SU5868
Beer	Devon	8	SY2289
Beer	Somset	8	ST4031
Beer Hackett	Dorset	9	ST5911
Beercrocombe	Somset	8	ST3220
Beesands	Devon	5	SX8140
Beesby	Lincs	51	TF4680
Beeson	Devon	5	SX8140
Beeston	Beds	31	TL1648
Beeston	Ches	47	SJ5458
Beeston	Norfk	42	TF9015
Beeston	Notts	39	SK5336
Beeston	N York	55	SE2930
Beeston Regis	Norfk	43	TG1742
Beeswing	D & G	66	NX8969
Beetham	Cumb	59	SD4979
Beetham	Somset	8	ST2712
Beetley	Norfk	42	TF9718
Begbroke	Oxon	29	SP4613
Begelly	Dyfed	16	SN1107
Beggarinton Hill	W York	55	SE2824
Beguildy	Powys	36	SO1979
Beighton	Norfk	43	TG3808
Beighton	S York	49	SK4483
Beighton Hill	Derbys	49	SK2951
Bein Inn	Tays	82	NO1613
Beith	Strath	73	NS3553
Bekesbourne	Kent	15	TR1955
Belaugh	Norfk	43	TG2818
Belbroughton	H & W	38	SO9277
Belchalwell	Dorset	9	ST7909
Belchalwell Street	Dorset	9	ST7908
Belchamp Otten	Essex	32	TL8041
Belchamp Walter	Essex	32	TL8240
Belchford	Lincs	51	TF2975
Belgrave	Leics	39	SK5906
Belhelvie	Gramp	95	NJ9417
Belhinnie	Gramp	94	NJ4627
Bell Busk	N York	54	SD9056
Bell Heath	H & W	38	SO9577
Bell Hill	Hants	11	SU7424
Bell o' th'Hill	Ches	46	SJ5245
Bellabeg	Gramp	94	NJ3513
Belladrum	Highld	92	NH5142
Bellanoch	Strath	71	NR7992
Bellaty	Tays	88	NO2359
Belle Vue	Cumb	58	NY1232
Belle Vue	W York	67	NY3756
Belleau	Lincs	51	TF4078
Bellerby	N York	61	SE1192
Bellfield	Strath	74	NS8234
Bellfield	Strath	75	NS9620
Bellingdon	Bucks	22	SP9405
Bellingham	Nthumb	68	NY8383
Belloch	Strath	80	NR3738
Bellochantuy	Strath	72	NR6632
Bellows Cross	Dorset	10	SU0613
Bellside	Strath	74	NS8058
Bellsmyre	Strath	80	NS4076
Bellsquarry	Loth	75	NT0465
Belluton	Avon	19	ST6164
Belmaduthy	Highld	92	NH6456
Belmesthorpe	Leics	40	TF0410
Belmont	Gt Lon	23	TQ2562
Belmont	Lancs	54	SD6715
Belmont	Shet	103	HP5600
Belmont	Strath	73	NS3520
Belnacraig	Gramp	94	NJ3716
Belper	Derbys	49	SK3447
Belper Lane End	Derbys	49	SK3349
Belph	Notts	62	SE5475
Belsay	Nthumb	68	NZ0978
Belses	Border	76	NT5725
Belsford	Devon	5	SX7659
Belsize	Herts	22	TL0301
Belstead	Suffk	33	TM1241
Belstone	Devon	5	SX6193
Belstone Corner	Devon	6	SX6298
Belthorn	Lancs	54	SD7124
Beltinge	Kent	15	TR1967
Beltingham	Nthumb	68	NY7863
Beltoft	Humb	56	SE8006
Belton	Leics	39	SK4420
Belton	Lincs	40	SK8101
Belton	Lincs	40	SK9339
Belton	Norfk	43	TG4802
Belvedere	Gt Lon	23	TQ4978
Belvoir	Leics	40	SK8133
Bembridge	IOW	11	SZ6488
Bemersyde	Border	76	NT5933
Bemerton	Wilts	10	SU1230
Bempton	Humb	57	TA1972
Ben Rhydding	W York	55	SE1448
Benacre	Suffk	33	TM5184
Benbuie	D & G	65	NX7196
Benderloch	Strath	86	NM9038
Benenden	Kent	14	TQ8033
Benfield	D & G	64	NX3764
Benfieldside	Dur	68	NZ0952
Bengall	D & G	67	NY1178
Bengeworth	H & W	28	SP0443
Benhall Green	Suffk	33	TM3961
Benhall Street	Suffk	33	TM3561
Benholm	Gramp	89	NO8069
Beningborough	N York	55	SE5257
Benington	Herts	31	TL2923
Benington	Lincs	51	TF3946
Benllech	Gwynd	44	SH5182
Benmore	Cent	81	NN4125
Benmore	Strath	86	NS1385
Bennacott	Cnwll	4	SX2992
Bennan	Strath	72	NR9921
Bennett End	Bucks	22	SU7897
Benniworth	Lincs	51	TF2081
Benover	Kent	14	TQ7048
Benson	Oxon	21	SU6291
Benthoul	Gramp	89	NJ8003
Bentley	Hants	22	SU7844
Bentley	Humb	56	TA0135
Bentley	S York	56	SE5605
Bentley	Suffk	25	TM1238
Bentley	Warwks	39	SP2895
Bentley Heath	W Mids	38	SP1676
Bentley Rise	S York	56	SE5605
Benton	Devon	7	SS6536
Benton Polliwilline	Strath	72	NR7310
Bentpath	D & G	67	NY3190
Bentwichen	Devon	7	SS7334
Bentworth	Hants	11	SU6640
Benvie	Tays	83	NO3231
Benville	Dorset	8	ST5403
Beoch	D & G	41	TL3490
Beoley	H & W	28	SP0669
Beoraidbeg	Highld	85	NM6793
Bepton	W Susx	11	SU8518
Berden	Essex	31	TL4629
Bere Alston	Devon	4	SX4466
Bere Ferrers	Devon	4	SX4563
Bere Regis	Dorset	9	SY8494
Berea	Dyfed	16	SM7930
Bergh Apton	Norfk	43	TG3000
Berhill	Somset	8	ST4435
Berinsfield	Oxon	21	SU5696
Berkeley	Gloucs	20	ST6899
Berkeley Road	Gloucs	20	ST7299
Berkhamsted	Herts	22	SP9907
Berkley	Somset	20	ST8049
Berkswell	W Mids	39	SP2479
Bermondsey	Gt Lon	23	TQ3479
Bernera	Highld	85	NG8021
Bernice	Strath	80	NS1391
Bernisdale	Highld	90	NG4050
Berrick Prior	Oxon	21	SU6294
Berrick Salome	Oxon	21	SU6293
Berriedale	Highld	100	ND1222
Berrier	Cumb	59	NY3929
Berriew	Powys	36	SJ1801
Berrington	H & W	27	SO5767
Berrington	Shrops	37	SJ5207
Berrington Green	H & W	27	SO5866
Berrow	Somset	19	ST2952
Berry Brow	W York	55	SE1514
Berry Head	Devon	5	SX9456
Berry Hill	Gloucs	27	SO5712
Berry Pomeroy	Devon	5	SX8261
Berry's Green	Gt Lon	23	TQ4358
Berryhillock	Gramp	94	NJ5054
Berryhillock	Gramp	94	NJ5060
Berrynarbor	Devon	6	SS5546
Bersham	Clwyd	46	SJ3048
Berwick	E Susx	13	TQ5105
Berwick Bassett	Wilts	20	SU0973
Berwick Hill	Nthumb	69	NZ1775
Berwick St. James	Wilts	20	SU0739
Berwick St. John	Wilts	9	ST9421
Berwick St. Leonard	Wilts	9	ST9233
Berwick-upon-Tweed	Nthumb	77	NT9953
Bescaby	Leics	40	SK8126
Bescar	Cumb	53	SD3913
Besford	H & W	28	SO9145
Bessacarr	S York	56	SE6101
Bessels Leigh	Oxon	21	SP4501
Bessingby	Humb	57	TA1565
Bessingham	Norfk	43	TG1636
Bestbeech Hill	E Susx	13	TQ6131
Besthorpe	Norfk	42	TM0595
Besthorpe	Notts	50	SK8264
Beswick	Humb	56	TA0148
Betchcott	Shrops	36	SO4399
Betchworth	Surrey	12	TQ2150
Bethel	Gwynd	44	SH3970
Bethel	Gwynd	44	SH5265
Bethersden	Kent	14	TQ9240
Bethesda	Dyfed	16	SN0918
Bethesda	Gwynd	44	SH6266
Bethlehem	Dyfed	26	SN6825
Bethnal Green	Gt Lon	23	TQ3482
Betley	Staffs	47	SJ7548
Betsham	Kent	14	TQ6071
Betteshanger	Kent	15	TR3152
Bettiscombe	Dorset	8	SY3999
Bettiscombe	Dorset	8	SY3999
Bettisfield	Clwyd	36	SJ4635
Betton	Shrops	37	SJ6937
Betton Strange	Shrops	37	SJ5109
Bettws	Gwent	19	ST2990
Bettws Bledrws	Dyfed	17	SN5952
Bettws Cedewain	Powys	36	SO1296
Bettws Evan	Dyfed	17	SN3047
Bettws Gwerfil Goch	Clwyd	45	SJ0346
Bettws Malpas	Gwent	19	ST3090
Bettws-Newydd	Gwent	27	SO3606
Bettyhill	Highld	99	NC7061
Betws	M Glam	18	SS9086
Betws-y-coed	Gwynd	45	SH7956
Betws-yn-Rhos	Clwyd	45	SH9073
Beulah	Dyfed	17	SN2846
Beulah	Powys	26	SN9251
Bevendean	E Susx	12	TQ3406
Bevercotes	Notts	49	SK6972
Beverley	Humb	56	TA0339
Beverston	Gloucs	20	ST8693
Bewcastle	Cumb	67	NY5674
Bewdley	H & W	37	SO7875
Bewerley	N York	55	SE1564
Bewholme	Humb	57	TA1649
Bewlie	Border	76	NT5626
Bexhill	E Susx	14	TQ7407
Bexley	Gt Lon	23	TQ4973
Bexleyheath	Gt Lon	23	TQ4875
Bexwell	Norfk	41	TF6303
Beyton	Suffk	32	TL9363
Beyton Green	Suffk	32	TL9363
Bibury	Gloucs	28	SP1106
Bicester	Oxon	29	SP5822
Bickenhill	W Mids	38	SP1882
Bicker	Lincs	41	TF2237
Bickerstaffe	Lancs	46	SD4404
Bickerton	N York	55	SE4450
Bickford	Staffs	38	SJ8814
Bickleigh	Devon	4	SX5262
Bickleigh	Devon	7	SS9407
Bickleton	Devon	6	SS5031
Bickley	Ches	47	SJ5448
Bickley	Gt Lon	23	TQ4268
Bickley Moss	Ches	47	SJ5449
Bicknacre	Essex	24	TL7802
Bicknoller	Somset	18	ST1039
Bicknor	Kent	14	TQ8658
Bickton	H & W	37	SO6371
Bicton	Shrops	36	SO2983
Bicton	Shrops	36	SJ4415
Bidborough	Kent	13	TQ5643
Bidden	Hants	22	SU7049
Biddenden	Kent	14	TQ8538
Biddenham	Beds	30	TL0250
Biddestone	Wilts	20	ST8673
Biddisham	Somset	19	ST3853
Biddlesden	Bucks	29	SP6340
Biddulph	Staffs	47	SJ8857
Bideford	Devon	6	SS4426
Bidford-on-Avon	Warwks	28	SP1052
Bielby	Humb	56	SE7843
Bieldside	Gramp	89	NJ8702
Bierley	IOW	11	SZ5178
Bierton	Bucks	30	SP8315
Big Corlae	D & G	65	NX6897
Big Sand	Highld	91	NG7579
Bigbury	Devon	5	SX6646
Bigby	Lincs	57	TA0507
Biggar	Strath	75	NT0437
Biggin	Derbys	48	SK1559
Biggin	Derbys	48	SK2549
Biggin	N York	55	SE5434
Biggin Hill	Gt Lon	23	TQ4159
Biggleswade	Beds	31	TL1944
Bigholms	D & G	67	NY3181
Bighouse	Highld	99	NC8964
Bighton	Hants	11	SU6134
Biglands	Cumb	67	NY2553
Bignor	W Susx	12	SU9814
Bigrigg	Cumb	58	NY0013
Bilborough	Notts	49	SK5241
Bilbrook	Somset	7	ST0341
Bilbrough	N York	55	SE5246
Bilbster	Highld	100	ND2853
Bildershaw	Dur	61	NZ2024
Bildeston	Suffk	32	TL9949
Billacott	Cnwll	4	SX2691
Billericay	Essex	24	TQ6794
Billesdon	Leics	40	SK7202
Billesley	Warwks	28	SP1456
Billingborough	Lincs	40	TF1134
Billinge	Mersyd	46	SD5200
Billingford	Norfk	42	TG0120
Billingford	Norfk	33	TM1678
Billingham	Cleve	62	NZ4624
Billinghay	Lincs	50	TF1554
Billingley	S York	55	SE4304
Billingsley	Shrops	37	SO7085
Billington	Beds	30	SP9422
Billington	Lancs	54	SD7235
Billockby	Norfk	43	TG4313
Billy Row	Dur	61	NZ1637
Bilsborrow	Lancs	53	SD5139
Bilsby	Lincs	51	TF4776
Bilsham	W Susx	12	SU9702
Bilsington	Kent	15	TR0434
Bilston	Loth	75	NT2664
Bilston	W Mids	38	SO9596
Bilstone	Leics	39	SK3605
Bilton	Humb	57	TA1532
Bilton	N York	55	SE4749
Bilton	N York	55	SE4749
Bilton	Nthumb	69	NU2211
Bilton	Warwks	39	SP4873
Binbrook	Lincs	51	TF2093
Binchester Blocks	Dur	61	NZ2231
Bincombe	Dorset	9	SY6884
Bindal	Highld	97	NH9284
Binegar	Somset	19	ST6149
Binfield	Berks	22	SU8471
Binfield Heath	Oxon	22	SU7477
Bingfield	Nthumb	68	NY9772
Bingham	Notts	49	SK7039
Bingham's Melcombe	Dorset	9	ST7701
Bingley	W York	55	SE1039
Binham	Norfk	42	TF9839
Binley	Hants	21	SU4153
Binley	W Mids	39	SP3778
Binnegar	Dorset	9	SY8887
Binniehill	Cent	74	NS8572
Binns Farm	Gramp	94	NJ3164
Binscombe	Surrey	12	SU9746
Binstead	Hants	11	SU7741
Binsted	W Susx	12	SU9806
Binton	Warwks	28	SP1454
Bintree	Norfk	42	TG0123
Binweston	Shrops	36	SJ3004
Birch Cross	Staffs	38	SK1230
Birch Green	Essex	25	TL9418
Birch Hill	Ches	46	SJ5273
Birch Vale	Derbys	48	SK0286
Bircham Newton	Norfk	42	TF7734
Bircham Tofts	Norfk	42	TF7732
Birchanger	Essex	31	TL5122
Bircher	H & W	27	SO4765
Bircher	H & W	27	SO4765
Birchfield	W Mids	38	SP0690
Birchgrove	E Susx	13	TQ4029
Birchgrove	S Glam	19	ST1679
Birchgrove	W Glam	18	SS7098
Birchington	Kent	15	TR3069
Birchley Heath	Warwks	39	SP2994
Birchmoor Green	Beds	30	SP9434
Birchover	Derbys	48	SK2462
Birchwood	Somset	8	ST2414
Birdbrook	Essex	32	TL7041
Birdforth	N York	62	SE4875
Birdham	W Susx	11	SU8200
Birdingbury	Warwks	29	SP4368
Birdlip	Gloucs	28	SO9214
Birdoswald	Cumb	68	NY6266
Birds Edge	W York	48	SE2000
Birds Green	Essex	24	TL5809
Birdsall	N York	56	SE8165
Birdsgreen	Shrops	37	SO7785
Birdsmoorgate	Dorset	8	ST3900
Birdston	Strath	74	NS6575
Birdwood	Gloucs	28	SO7318
Birgham	Border	76	NT7939
Birichin	Highld	97	NH7592
Birkacre	Lancs	53	SD5715
Birkby	N York	62	NZ3202
Birkdale	Mersyd	53	SD3215
Birkenbog	Gramp	94	NJ5365
Birkenhead	Mersyd	46	SJ3288
Birkenhills	Gramp	95	NJ7445
Birkenshaw	W York	55	SE2028
Birkhall	Gramp	88	NO3493
Birkhill	D & G	75	NT2015
Birkhill & Muirkill	Tays	88	NO3343
Birkholme	Lincs	40	SK9723
Birley	H & W	27	SO4553
Birley Carr	S York	49	SK3391
Birling	Kent	14	TF6280
Birling	Nthumb	69	NU2406
Birlingham	H & W	28	SO9343
Birmingham	W Mids	38	SP0787
Birnam	Tays	88	NO0041
Birness	Gramp	95	NJ9933
Birse	Gramp	89	NO5596
Birsemore	Gramp	89	NO5290
Birstall	Leics	39	SK5909
Birstall Smithies	W York	55	SE2226
Birstwith	N York	55	SE2359
Birtley	H & W	27	SO3669
Birtley	Nthumb	68	NY8778
Birtley	T & W	69	NZ2756
Birts Street	H & W	28	SO7836
Bisbrooke	Leics	40	SP8899
Biscathorpe	Lincs	51	TF2284
Biscovey	Cnwll	3	SX0553
Bish Mill	Devon	7	SS7425
Bisham	Berks	22	SU8485
Bishampton	H & W	28	SO9851
Bishop Auckland	Dur	61	NZ2029
Bishop Burton	Humb	56	SE9839
Bishop Middleham	Dur	62	NZ3231
Bishop Monkton	N York	55	SE3366
Bishop Norton	Lincs	50	SK9892
Bishop Sutton	Avon	19	ST5859
Bishop Thornton	N York	55	SE2663
Bishop Wilton	Humb	56	SE7955
Bishop's Castle	Shrops	36	SO3288
Bishop's Cleeve	Gloucs	28	SO9527
Bishop's Frome	H & W	28	SO6648
Bishop's Green	Essex	24	TL6217
Bishop's Green	Hants	21	SU5062
Bishop's Itchington	Warwks	29	SP3857
Bishop's Norton	Gloucs	28	SO8424
Bishop's Nympton	Devon	7	SS7523
Bishop's Stortford	Herts	31	TL4821
Bishop's Sutton	Hants	11	SU6031
Bishop's Tachbrook	Warwks	29	SP3161
Bishop's Tawton	Devon	6	SS5630
Bishop's Waltham	Hants	11	SU5517
Bishop's Wood	Staffs	38	SJ8309
Bishop's Caundle	Dorset	9	ST6913
Bishopbridge	Lincs	50	TF0391
Bishopbriggs	Strath	74	NS6070
Bishopmill	Gramp	94	NJ2164
Bishops Cannings	Wilts	20	SU0364
Bishops Hull	Somset	8	ST2024
Bishops Lydeard	Somset	8	ST1729
Bishopsbourne	Kent	15	TR1852
Bishopsteignton	Devon	5	SX9173
Bishopstoke	Hants	10	SU4619
Bishopstone	Bucks	22	SP8010
Bishopstone	E Susx	13	TQ4701
Bishopstone	H & W	27	SO4143
Bishopstone	Wilts	23	TQ2068
Bishopstone	Wilts	10	SU0625
Bishopstrow	Wilts	20	ST8943
Bishopswood	Somset	8	ST2612
Bishopsworth	Avon	19	ST5768
Bishopthorpe	N York	56	SE5947
Bishopton	Dur	62	NZ3621
Bishopton	Strath	81	NS4371
Bishton	Gwent	19	ST3887
Bisley	Gloucs	28	SO9005
Bisley	Surrey	22	SU9559
Bissoe	Cnwll	2	SW7741
Bisterne	Hants	10	SU1401
Bitchfield	Lincs	40	SK9228
Bittaford	Devon	5	SX6657
Bittering	Norfk	42	TF9317
Bitterlees	Cumb	67	NY1252
Bitterley	Shrops	37	SO5677
Bitterne	Hants	10	SU4513
Bitteswell	Leics	39	SP5385
Bitton	Avon	20	ST6869
Bix	Oxon	22	SU7285
Blaby	Leics	39	SP5697
Black Bourton	Oxon	29	SP2804
Black Callerton	T & W	69	NZ1769
Black Corries	Highld	86	NN2956
Black Crofts	Strath	80	NM9234
Black Cross	Cnwll	3	SW9160
Black Dog	Devon	7	SS8009
Black Heddon	Nthumb	68	NZ0776
Black Notley	Essex	24	TL7621
Black Street	Suffk	33	TM5186
Black Tar	Dyfed	16	SM9909
Black Torrington	Devon	6	SS4605
Black Torrington	Devon	6	SS4605
Blackadder	Border	77	NT8452
Blackawton	Devon	5	SX8050
Blackborough	Devon	7	ST0909
Blackborough End	Norfk	42	TF6614
Blackboys	E Susx	13	TQ5220
Blackbrook	Derbys	49	SK3347
Blackbrook	Staffs	37	SJ7639
Blackburn	Gramp	89	NJ8212
Blackburn	Lancs	54	SD6827
Blackburn	Loth	75	NS9865
Blackcraig	Strath	66	NS6308
Blackdog	Gramp	95	NJ9514
Blackdown	Devon	4	SX5079
Blackdown	Dorset	8	ST3903
Blackenhall Heath	W Mids	38	SK0001
Blacker	S York	55	SE3309
Blacker Hill	S York	55	SE3602
Blackfield	Hants	10	SU4402
Blackford	Cumb	67	NY3962
Blackford	Somset	19	ST4147
Blackford	Somset	9	ST6526
Blackford	Tays	82	NN8908
Blackfordby	Leics	39	SK3318
Blackhall Colliery	Dur	62	NZ4539
Blackhaugh	Border	76	NT4238
Blackheath	Gt Lon	23	TQ3876
Blackheath	Suffk	33	TM4275
Blackheath	Surrey	12	TQ0346
Blackheath	W Mids	38	SO9786
Blackhill	Dur	68	NZ0852
Blackhill	Gramp	95	NK0039
Blackhill	Gramp	95	NK0755
Blackhill of Clackriach	Gramp	95	NJ9236
Blackhorse	Devon	5	SX9893
Blackland	Somset	7	SS8336
Blacklaw	D & G	66	NT0408
Blackley	Gt Man	47	SD8502
Blacklunans	Tays	88	NO1560
Blackmarstone	H & W	27	SO5038
Blackmill	M Glam	18	SS9386
Blackmoor	Avon	19	ST4461
Blackmoor	Hants	11	SU7833
Blackmoor Gate	Devon	7	SS6443
Blackmoorfoot	W York	55	SE0913
Blackmore	Essex	24	TL6002
Blackmore End	Essex	24	TL7430
Blackness	Loth	82	NT0579
Blacknest	Berks	22	SU9568
Blacknest	Hants	11	SU7941
Blacko	Lancs	54	SD8541
Blackpark	D & G	64	NX8181
Blackpill	W Glam	17	SS6190
Blackpool	Lancs	53	SD3036
Blackpool Gate	Cumb	67	NY5378
Blackridge	Loth	74	NS8967
Blackrock	Cnwll	2	SW6035
Blackrock	Gwent	19	SO5188
Blackrod	Gt Man	54	SD6111
Blacks Boat	Gramp	94	NJ1838
Blackshaw	D & G	67	NY0465
Blackshaw Head	W York	54	SD9527
Blacksnape	Lancs	54	SD7121
Blackshaw	W Susx	12	TQ2416
Blackthorn	Oxon	29	SP6219
Blackthorpe	Suffk	32	TL9063
Blacktoft	Humb	56	SE8324
Blacktop	Gramp	89	NJ8604
Blackwall	Derbys	49	SK2348
Blackwater	Cnwll	2	SW7346
Blackwater	Hants	22	SU8559
Blackwater	IOW	11	SZ5086
Blackwater	Somset	8	ST2615
Blackwaterfoot	Strath	72	NR9028
Blackwell	Cumb	67	NY4053
Blackwell	Derbys	48	SK1272
Blackwell	Derbys	49	SK4458
Blackwell	Warwks	29	SP2443
Blackwood	D & G	66	NX9087
Blackwood	Gwent	19	ST1797
Blackwood	Strath	74	NS7844
Blacon	Ches	46	SJ3868
Bladnoch	D & G	64	NX4254
Bladon	Oxon	29	SP4414
Bladon	Somset	8	ST4220

Place	Page	Grid Ref
Blaen-y-Coed *Dyfed*	17	SN3427
Blaen-y-cwm *Gwent*	26	SO1311
Blaen-y-cwm *M Glam*	18	SS9298
Blaenannerch *Dyfed*	17	SN2449
Blaenau Ffestiniog *Gwynd*	45	SH7045
Blaenavon *Gwent*	27	SO2509
Blaenawey *Gwent*	27	SO2919
Blaenffos *Dyfed*	17	SN1937
Blaengarw *M Glam*	18	SS9092
Blaengeuffardd *Dyfed*	35	SN6379
Blaengwrach *W Glam*	26	SN8605
Blaengwynfi *W Glam*	18	SS8996
Blaenpennal *Dyfed*	35	SN6264
Blaenplwyf *Dyfed*	34	SN5775
Blaenporth *Dyfed*	17	SN2648
Blaenrhondda *M Glam*	18	SS9299
Blaenwaun *Dyfed*	17	SN2327
Blagdon *Avon*	19	ST5059
Blagdon *Devon*	5	SX8561
Blagdon *Somset*	8	ST2117
Blagdon Hill *Somset*	8	ST2117
Blaguegate *Lancs*	46	SD4506
Blaich *Highld*	86	NN0476
Blaina *Gwent*	79	NM6769
Blair Atholl *Tays*	87	NN8765
Blair Drummond *Cent*	81	NS7399
Blairgowrie *Tays*	88	NO1745
Blairingone *Fife*	82	NS9896
Blairlogie *Cent*	82	NS8396
Blairmore *Highld*	98	NC1960
Blairmore *Strath*	80	NS1983
Blairnamarrow *Gramp*	94	NJ2015
Blairs Ferry *Strath*	71	NR9869
Blaisdon *Gloucs*	28	SO7017
Blake End *Essex*	24	TL7023
Blakebrook *H & W*	37	SO8177
Blakedown *H & W*	38	SO8878
Blakeley Lane *Staffs*	48	SJ9747
Blakemere *Ches*	47	SJ5571
Blakemere *H & W*	27	SO3640
Blakemore *Devon*	5	SX7759
Blakeney *Gloucs*	28	SO6707
Blakeney *Norfk*	42	TG0243
Blakenhall *Ches*	47	SJ7247
Blakenhall *W Mids*	38	SO9197
Blakesley *Nhants*	29	SP6250
Blanchland *Nthumb*	68	NY9650
Bland Hill *N York*	55	SE2053
Blandford Camp *Dorset*	9	ST9108
Blandford Forum *Dorset*	9	ST8806
Blandford St. Mary *Dorset*	9	ST8805
Blankney *Lincs*	50	TF0660
Blantyre *Strath*	74	NS6657
Blar a' Chaorainn *Highld*	86	NN1066
Blargie *Highld*	87	NN6094
Blarmachfoldach *Highld*	86	NN0969
Blashford *Hants*	10	SU1406
Blaston *Leics*	40	SP8095
Blatherwycke *Nhants*	40	SP9795
Blawith *Cumb*	58	SD2888
Blawquhairn *D & G*	65	NX6282
Blaxhall *Suffk*	33	TM3657
Blaxton *S York*	49	SE6600
Blaydon *T & W*	69	NZ1863
Bleadney *Somset*	19	ST4845
Bleadon *Somset*	19	ST3456
Bleak Street *Somset*	9	ST7531
Blean *Kent*	15	TR1260
Bleasby *Lincs*	49	SK7149
Bleasdale *Lancs*	53	SD5745
Blebocraigs *Fife*	83	NO4215
Bleddfa *Powys*	27	SO2168
Bledington *Gloucs*	29	SP2422
Bledlow *Bucks*	22	SP7702
Bledlow Ridge *Bucks*	22	SU7997
Blegbie *Loth*	76	NT4861
Blencarn *Cumb*	60	NY6331
Blencogo *Cumb*	67	NY1947
Blendworth *Hants*	11	SU7113
Bletchingley *Surrey*	12	TQ3250
Bletchingley *Surrey*	30	SP8633
Bletchley *Bucks*	37	SJ6233
Bletchley *Shrops*	16	SN0721
Bletherston *Dyfed*	30	TL0258
Bletsoe *Beds*	21	SU5385
Blewbury *Oxon*	43	TG1728
Blickling *Norfk*	49	SK5986
Blidworth *Notts*	49	SK5954
Blidworth Bottoms *Notts*	12	TQ3645
Blindley Heath *Surrey*	37	SO7472
Bliss Gate *H & W*	10	SU1713
Blissford *Hants*	30	SP7253
Blisworth *Nhants*	38	SK0819
Blithbury *Staffs*	32	TM0179
Blo Norton *Nthumb*	28	SP1634
Blockley *Gloucs*	43	TG3309
Blofield *Norfk*	76	NT5824
Bloomfield *Border*	37	SJ7234
Blore *Staffs*	48	SK1349
Blore *Staffs*	38	SK0832
Blounts Green *Staffs*	29	SP4235
Bloxham *Oxon*	38	SJ9002
Bloxwith *W Mids*	55	SE1655
Blubberhouses *N York*	3	SW9158
Blue Anchor *Cnwll*	7	ST0243
Blue Anchor *Somset*	14	TQ7462
Blue Bell Hill *Kent*	96	NC1301
Blughasary *Highld*	46	SJ3099
Blundellsands *Mersyd*	43	TM5197
Blunderston *Suffk*	30	TL1551
Blunham *Beds*	20	SU1389
Blunsdon St. Andrew *Wilts*	38	SO8974
Bluntington *H & W*	31	TL3674
Bluntisham *Cambs*	4	SX3462
Blunts *Cnwll*	48	SJ8942
Blurton *Staffs*	50	SK9394
Blyborough *Lincs*	33	TM4276
Blyford *Suffk*	37	SJ8112
Blymhill *Staffs*	49	SK6287
Blyth *Notts*	69	NZ3181
Blyth *Nthumb*	75	NT1345
Blyth Bridge *Border*	33	TM4575
Blythburgh *Suffk*	76	NT8849
Blythe *Border*	48	SJ9541
Blythe Bridge *Staffs*	48	SJ9541
Blythe Bridge *Staffs*	50	SK8594
Blyton *Lincs*	82	NT0081
Bo'Ness *Cent*	83	NO5614
Boarhills *Fife*	11	SU6008
Boarhunt *Hants*	28	SP6214
Boarstall *Bucks*	93	NH9319
Boat of Garten *Highld*	96	NH5774
Boath *Highld*	14	TQ8865
Bobbing *Kent*	37	SO8190
Bobbington *Staffs*	2	SW6820
Bochym *Cnwll*	24	TL7624
Bocking *Essex*	24	TL7626
Bocking Churchstreet *Essex*	95	NK1342
Boddam *Gramp*	103	HU3915
Boddam *Shet*	89	NO7153
Boddin *Tays*	28	SO8925
Boddington *Gloucs*	44	SH3380
Bodedern *Gwynd*	45	SJ0075
Bodelwyddan *Clwyd*	45	SJ0075
Bodelwyddan *Clwyd*	27	SO5361
Bodenham *H & W*	10	SU1626
Bodenham *Wilts*	27	SO5450
Bodenham Moor *H & W*	44	SH3990
Bodewryd *Gwynd*	46	SJ0970
Bodfari *Clwyd*	44	SH4276
Bodffordd *Gwynd*	44	SH3237
Bodham Street *Norfk*	43	TG1240
Bodiam *E Susx*	14	TQ7825
Bodicote *Oxon*	29	SP4538
Bodinnick *Cnwll*	3	SX1352
Bodior *Gwynd*	44	SH2876
Bodle Street Green *E Susx*	13	TQ6514
Bodmin *Cnwll*	3	SX0767
Bodney *Norfk*	42	TL8398
Bodorgan *Gwynd*	44	SH3867
Bodsham Green *Kent*	15	TR1045
Bodwen *Cnwll*	3	SX0360
Bogallan *Highld*	92	NH6350
Bogbrae *Gramp*	95	NK0335
Boghall *Loth*	75	NS9868
Boghall *Loth*	75	NT2465
Boghead *Strath*	74	NS7742

Place	Page	Grid Ref
Boghead Farm *Gramp*	94	NJ3559
Boghole *Highld*	93	NH9655
Bogmoor *Gramp*	94	NJ3563
Bogmuir *Gramp*	89	NO6571
Bognie Brae *Gramp*	94	NJ5945
Bognor Regis *W Susx*	11	SZ9399
Bogroy *Highld*	93	NH9023
Bogue *D & G*	65	NX6481
Bohortha *Cnwll*	3	SW8632
Bohuntine *Highld*	86	NN2883
Bolam *Dur*	61	NZ1922
Bolberry *Devon*	5	SX6939
Boldmere *W Mids*	38	SP1194
Boldon *T & W*	69	NZ3461
Boldon Colliery *T & W*	69	NZ3462
Boldron *Dur*	61	NZ0314
Bole *Notts*	50	SK7987
Bolehill *Derbys*	49	SK2955
Bolfracks *Tays*	87	NN8248
Bolham *Devon*	7	SS9514
Bolham Water *Devon*	8	ST1612
Bolingey *Cnwll*	2	SW7653
Bollington *Ches*	47	SJ7286
Bollington *Ches*	48	SJ9377
Bolney *W Susx*	12	TQ2622
Bolnhurst *Beds*	30	TL0859
Bolshan *Tays*	89	NO6252
Bolsover *Derbys*	49	SK4770
Bolsterstone *S York*	49	SK2698
Bolstone *H & W*	27	SO5532
Bolt Head *Devon*	5	SX7236
Bolt Tail *Devon*	5	SX6639
Boltby *N York*	62	SE4886
Bolton *Cumb*	60	NY6323
Bolton *Gt Man*	52	SD7109
Bolton *Humb*	56	SE7752
Bolton *Loth*	76	NT5070
Bolton *Nthumb*	68	NU1013
Bolton Abbey *N York*	55	SE0754
Bolton Percy *N York*	56	SE5341
Bolton Town End *Lancs*	53	SD4767
Bolton Upon Dearne *S York*	49	SE4502
Bolton by Bowland *Lancs*	54	SD7849
Bolton-on-Swale *N York*	61	SE2699
Boltonfellend *Cumb*	67	NY4768
Boltongate *Cumb*	58	NY2240
Bolventor *Cnwll*	3	SX1876
Bomere Heath *Shrops*	37	SJ4719
Bon-y-Maen *W Glam*	18	SS6895
Bonar Bridge *Highld*	97	NH6191
Bonawe *Strath*	80	NN0141
Bonawe Quarries *Strath*	80	NN0033
Bonby *Humb*	56	TA0015
Boncath *Dyfed*	17	SN2038
Bonchester Bridge *Border*	67	NT5812
Bondleigh *Devon*	7	SS6504
Bonds *Lancs*	53	SD4945
Bonehill *D & G*	66	NX9076
Boney Hay *Staffs*	38	SK0510
Bonhill *Strath*	80	NS3979
Boningale *Shrops*	38	SJ8202
Bonjedward *Border*	76	NT6522
Bonkle *Strath*	74	NS8457
Bonnington *Kent*	15	TR0535
Bonnington *Loth*	75	NT1269
Bonnington *Tays*	83	NO5740
Bonnybridge *Cent*	82	NS8280
Bonnykelly *Gramp*	95	NJ8663
Bonnyrigg *Loth*	75	NT3065
Bonnyton *Tays*	83	NO3338
Bont-Dolgadfan *Powys*	35	SH8800
Bontddu *Gwynd*	35	SH6719
Bontnewydd *Dyfed*	35	SN6185
Bontnewydd *Gwynd*	44	SH4859
Bontuchel *Clwyd*	46	SJ0857
Bonvilston *S Glam*	18	ST0673
Boode *Devon*	6	SS5038
Booham *Devon*	5	SX8952
Booker *Bucks*	22	SU8391
Booley *Shrops*	37	SJ5725
Boon *Border*	47	SJ8050
Boosbeck *Cleve*	62	NZ6616
Boose's Green *Essex*	24	TL8531
Boot *Cumb*	58	NY1701
Booth *W York*	55	SE0427
Boothby Graffoe *Lincs*	50	SK8859
Boothby Pagnell *Lincs*	40	SK9730
Bootle *Cumb*	58	SD1088
Bootle *Mersyd*	46	SJ3495
Bootle Station *Cumb*	58	SD0989
Boquhan *Cent*	81	NS5387
Boraston *Shrops*	27	SO6169
Bordeaux *Jersey*	101	SV0000
Boyden Gate *Kent*	15	TR2265
Bordon *Hants*	11	SU7935
Boreham *Essex*	24	TL7610
Boreham *Wilts*	20	ST8944
Boreham Street *E Susx*	14	TQ6611
Borehamwood *Herts*	23	TQ1996
Boreland *D & G*	67	NY1790
Boreraig *Highld*	90	NG1853
Borestone *Devon*	5	SX7753
Borgie *Highld*	99	NC6759
Borgue *D & G*	65	NX6248
Borgue *Highld*	100	ND1326
Borley Green *Essex*	32	TL8543
Borneskitaig *Highld*	90	NG3771
Borness *D & G*	65	NX6145
Borough Green *Kent*	14	TQ6057
Boroughbridge *N York*	55	SE3966
Borrowash *Derbys*	39	SK4134
Borrowby *N York*	62	SE4289
Borrowdale Hotel *Cumb*	58	NY2618
Borrowstoun *Cent*	82	NS9980
Borstal *Kent*	14	TQ7366
Borth *Dyfed*	34	SN6090
Borth-y-Gest *Gwynd*	44	SH5637
Borthwick *Loth*	76	NT3659
Borthwickbrae *Border*	67	NT4113
Borthwickshiels *Border*	76	NT4315
Borve *Highld*	90	NG4448
Borve *W Isls*	102	NB4057
Borve *W Isls*	102	NF6501
Borve *W Isls*	102	NF9181
Borwick *Lancs*	59	SD5273
Borwick Lodge *Cumb*	67	NY3499
Bosbury *H & W*	28	SO6943
Boscarne *Cnwll*	3	SX0367
Boscastle *Cnwll*	4	SX0990
Boscombe *Dorset*	10	SZ1191
Boscombe *Wilts*	10	SU2038
Bosham *W Susx*	11	SU8004
Bosherton *Dyfed*	16	SR8694
Boskennal *Cnwll*	2	SW4323
Bosley *Ches*	48	SJ9165
Bosoughan *Cnwll*	3	SW8760
Bossall *N York*	56	SE7160
Bossiney *Cnwll*	4	SX0688
Bossingham *Kent*	15	TR1549
Bossington *Somset*	18	SS8947
Bostock Green *Ches*	47	SJ6769
Boston *Lincs*	51	TF3243
Boston Spa *W York*	55	SE4245
Boswinger *Cnwll*	3	SW9941
Botany Bay *Gt Lon*	23	TQ2999
Botesdale *Suffk*	32	TM0576
Bothal *Nthumb*	69	NZ2386
Bothampstead *Berks*	21	SU5076
Bothamsall *Notts*	49	SK6773
Bothel *Cumb*	58	NY1838
Bothwell *Strath*	74	NS7058
Botley *Bucks*	22	SP9802
Botley *Hants*	11	SU5113
Botley *Oxon*	29	SP4806
Botolph Claydon *Bucks*	30	SP7324
Botolphs *W Susx*	12	TQ1909
Bottesford *Humb*	56	SE8907
Bottesford *Leics*	40	SK8038
Bottisham *Cambs*	31	TL5480
Bottomcraig *Fife*	83	NO3724
Bottoms *W York*	54	SD9321
Botusfleming *Cnwll*	4	SX4060
Botwnnog *Gwynd*	44	SH2631
Bough Beech *Kent*	13	TQ4847
Boughrood *Powys*	26	SO1239
Boughton *Cambs*	31	TL1965
Boughton *Nhants*	30	SP7565
Boughton *Norfk*	42	TF7002
Boughton *Notts*	49	SK6768

Place	Page	Grid Ref
Boughton Aluph *Kent*	15	TR0348
Boughton Green *Kent*	14	TQ7651
Boughton Lees *Kent*	15	TR0246
Boughton Malherbe *Kent*	14	TQ8849
Boughton Monchelsea *Kent*	14	TQ7749
Boughton Street *Kent*	15	TR0559
Boulder Clough *W York*	55	SE0324
Bouley Bay *Jersey*	101	SV0000
Boulmer *Nthumb*	69	NU2614
Boultham *Lincs*	50	SK9568
Boulton Low Houses *Cumb*	67	NY2344
Bourn *Cambs*	31	TL3256
Bourne *Devon*	7	SS6514
Bourne *Lincs*	40	TF0920
Bourne End *Beds*	30	SP9644
Bourne End *Bucks*	30	TL0260
Bourne End *Bucks*	22	SU8987
Bourne End *Herts*	22	TL0206
Bournebridge *Essex*	23	TQ5094
Bournheath *W Mids*	38	SO9482
Bournemouth *Dorset*	10	SZ0991
Bournes Green *Gloucs*	24	TQ9186
Bournheath *H & W*	38	SO9474
Bournstream *Gloucs*	20	ST7594
Bournville *W Mids*	38	SP0481
Bourton *Dorset*	9	ST7630
Bourton *Oxon*	21	SU2386
Bourton *Shrops*	37	SO5996
Bourton *Wilts*	20	SU0464
Bourton on Dunsmore *Warwks*	29	SP4370
Bourton-on-the- Hill *Gloucs*	29	SP1732
Bourton-on-the-Water *Gloucs*	28	SP1620
Bousd *Strath*	78	NM2563
Bouth *Cumb*	59	SD3385
Bouthwaite *N York*	55	SE1171
Bovain *Cent*	81	NN5430
Boveridge *Dorset*	10	SU0615
Bovey Tracey *Devon*	5	SX8178
Bovingdon *Herts*	22	TL0103
Bovinger *Essex*	31	TL5215
Bow *Devon*	5	SX8156
Bow *Ork*	103	ND3693
Bow Brickhill *Bucks*	30	SP9034
Bow End *Cumb*	67	NY2674
Bow Fife *Fife*	83	NO3212
Bow Street *Dyfed*	35	SN6285
Bowbridge *Gloucs*	28	SO8605
Bowburn *Dur*	61	NZ3038
Bowcombe *IOW*	10	SZ4786
Bowd *Devon*	8	SY1190
Bowden *Border*	76	NT5530
Bowden Hill *Wilts*	20	ST3967
Bowdon *Gt Man*	47	SJ7686
Bower *Highld*	100	ND2362
Bower House Tye *Suffk*	32	TL9941
Bower's Row *W York*	55	SE4027
Bowerchalke *Wilts*	9	SU0122
Bowermadden *Highld*	100	ND2464
Bowers *Staffs*	37	SJ8135
Bowers Gifford *Essex*	24	TQ7588
Bowershall *Fife*	82	NT0991
Bowertower *Highld*	100	ND2361
Bowes *Dur*	61	NY9913
Bowgreave *Lancs*	53	SD4943
Bowhill *Border*	76	NT4227
Bowland *Border*	76	NT4540
Bowley *H & W*	27	SO5452
Bowlhead Green *Surrey*	11	SU9138
Bowling *Strath*	81	NS4373
Bowling *W York*	55	SE1731
Bowling Bank *Clwyd*	46	SJ3949
Bowling Green *H & W*	28	SO8151
Bowmanstead *Cumb*	58	SD3096
Bowmore *Strath*	70	NR3159
Bowness-on-Solway *Cumb*	67	NY2262
Bowsden *Nthumb*	77	NT9941
Box *Gloucs*	20	SO8600
Box Hill *Surrey*	12	TQ2051
Boxbush *Gloucs*	28	SO7412
Boxford *Berks*	21	SU4271
Boxford *Suffk*	32	TL9640
Boxgrove *W Susx*	11	SU9007
Boxholme *Lincs*	50	TF0663
Boxley *Kent*	14	TQ7758
Boxmoor *Herts*	22	TL0406
Boxted *Essex*	25	TL9933
Boxted *Suffk*	32	TL8251
Boxted Cross *Essex*	25	TM0032
Boxted Heath *Essex*	25	TM0031
Boxworth *Cambs*	31	TL3464
Boylestone *Derbys*	28	SK1835
Boyndie *Gramp*	94	NJ6463
Boyndlie *Gramp*	95	NJ9162
Boynton *Humb*	57	TA1368
Boys Hill *Dorset*	9	ST6709
Boysack *Tays*	89	NO6249
Boyton *Cnwll*	4	SX3192
Boyton *Suffk*	33	TM3747
Boyton *Wilts*	20	ST9539
Boyton Cross *Essex*	24	TL6409
Boyton End *Suffk*	32	TL7244
Bozeat *Nhants*	30	SP9058
Braaid *IOM*	52	SC3176
Brabourne *Kent*	15	TR1041
Brabourne Lees *Kent*	15	TR0840
Brabstermire *Highld*	100	ND3169
Bracadale *Highld*	84	NG3538
Braceborough *Lincs*	40	TF0713
Bracebridge Heath *Lincs*	50	SK9867
Braceby *Lincs*	40	TF0135
Bracewell *Lancs*	54	SD8648
Brackenfield *Derbys*	49	SK3759
Brackenhurst *Strath*	74	NS7468
Brackenthwaite *Cumb*	58	NY1522
Brackletter *Highld*	86	NN1882
Brackley *Nhants*	29	SP5837
Brackloch *Highld*	96	NC1224
Bracknell *Berks*	22	SU8669
Braco *Tays*	82	NN8309
Bracon Ash *Norfk*	43	TM1899
Bracora *Highld*	85	NM7192
Bracorina *Highld*	85	NM7292
Bradbourne *Derbys*	48	SK2052
Bradbury *Dur*	62	NZ3128
Bradda *IOM*	52	SC1970
Bradden *Nhants*	29	SP6448
Bradenham *Bucks*	22	SU8297
Bradenstoke *Wilts*	20	SU0079
Bradfield *Devon*	7	ST0509
Bradfield *Essex*	25	TM1430
Bradfield *S York*	43	TG2633
Bradfield Combust *Suffk*	32	TL8957
Bradfield Green *Ches*	47	SJ6859
Bradfield Heath *Essex*	25	TM1430
Bradfield St. Clare *Suffk*	32	TL9158
Bradfield St. George *Suffk*	32	TL9060
Bradford *Devon*	6	SS4207
Bradford *W York*	55	SE1633
Bradford Abbas *Dorset*	9	ST5814
Bradford Leigh *Wilts*	20	ST8362
Bradford Peverell *Dorset*	9	SY6593
Bradford-on Avon *Wilts*	20	ST8260
Bradford-on-Tone *Somset*	8	ST1722
Brading *IOW*	11	SZ6087
Bradley *Derbys*	48	SK2246
Bradley *H & W*	28	SO8860
Bradley *Hants*	21	SU6341
Bradley *Humb*	57	TA2406
Bradley *Staffs*	38	SJ8717
Bradley *W Mids*	38	SO9595
Bradley Green *Ches*	46	SJ5046
Bradley Green *H & W*	28	SO9862
Bradley Stoke *Avon*	19	ST6081
Bradley in the Moors *Staffs*	48	SK0541
Bradmore *Notts*	39	SK5831
Bradnich *Devon*	7	SS9903
Bradnop *Staffs*	48	SK0155
Bradpole *Dorset*	8	SY4794
Bradshaw *W York*	55	SE0729
Bradstone *Devon*	4	SX3880
Bradwall Green *Ches*	47	SJ7663
Bradwell *Bucks*	30	SP8340
Bradwell *Norfk*	43	TG5003

Place	Page	Grid Ref
Bradwell Waterside *Essex*	25	TL9907
Bradwell-on-Sea *Essex*	25	TM0007
Bradworthy *Devon*	6	SS3213
Brae *D & G*	66	NX8674
Brae *Highld*	93	NH6662
Brae *Shet*	103	HU3568
Brae Roy Lodge *Highld*	86	NN3391
Braeface *Central*	81	NS7880
Braefield *Highld*	92	NH4130
Braegrum *Tays*	82	NO0025
Braehead *D & G*	64	NX4252
Braehead *Strath*	75	NS9550
Braehead *Tays*	89	NO6952
Braehour *Highld*	100	ND0953
Braelangwell Lodge *Highld*	96	NH5192
Braemar *Gramp*	88	NO1591
Braemore *Highld*	96	NH2078
Braemore *Highld*	100	ND0829
Braes The *Highld*	84	NG5234
Braes of Coul *Tays*	88	NO2857
Braes of Enzie *Gramp*	94	NJ3957
Braeside *Strath*	80	NS2375
Braeswick *Ork*	103	HY6037
Braevallich *Strath*	80	NM9507
Brafferton *Dur*	61	NZ2921
Brafferton *N York*	55	SE4370
Brafield-on-the-Green *Nhants*	30	SP8258
Bragar *W Isls*	102	NB2847
Bragbury End *Herts*	31	TL2621
Brahen Hill *W York*	55	SE4317
Braidwood *Strath*	74	NS8448
Braigo *Strath*	70	NR2369
Brailsford Green *Derbys*	48	SK2641
Brain's Green *Gloucs*	28	SO6608
Braintree *Essex*	24	TL7523
Braiseworth *Suffk*	33	TM1372
Braishfield *Hants*	10	SU3725
Braithwaite *Cumb*	58	NY2323
Braithwaite *N York*	55	SE0341
Braithwaite *W York*	55	SE0341
Braithwell *S York*	49	SK5394
Bramber *W Susx*	12	TQ1811
Bramcote *Warwks*	39	SP4088
Bramcote *Warwks*	11	SU6128
Bramerton *Norfk*	43	TG2904
Bramfield *Herts*	31	TL2915
Bramfield *Suffk*	33	TM4074
Bramford *Suffk*	33	TM1246
Bramhall *Gt Man*	48	SJ8984
Bramham *W York*	55	SE4242
Bramhope *W York*	55	SE2443
Bramley *Derbys*	49	SK3979
Bramley *Hants*	21	SU6559
Bramley *S York*	49	SK4892
Bramley *Surrey*	12	TQ0044
Bramley *W York*	55	SE2435
Bramley Corner *Hants*	21	SU6359
Bramleyhead *N York*	55	SE5218
Bramling *Kent*	15	TR2256
Brampford Speke *Devon*	7	SX9298
Brampton *Cambs*	31	TL2170
Brampton *Cumb*	60	NY6723
Brampton *Cumb*	67	NY5361
Brampton *Lincs*	50	SK8479
Brampton *Norfk*	43	TG2223
Brampton *S York*	49	SE4101
Brampton *Suffk*	33	TM4381
Brampton Abbotts *H & W*	27	SO6026
Brampton Ash *Nhants*	40	SP7987
Brampton Bryan *H & W*	36	SO3672
Brampton-en-le-Morthen *S York*	49	SK4888
Bramshall *Staffs*	38	SK0633
Bramshaw *Hants*	10	SU2615
Bramshott *Hants*	11	SU8432
Bramwell *Somset*	8	ST4229
Bran End *Essex*	24	TL6525
Branault *Highld*	79	NM5269
Brancaster *Norfk*	42	TF7743
Brancaster Staithe *Norfk*	42	TF7944
Brancepeth *Dur*	61	NZ2237
Branch End *Nthumb*	68	NZ0662
Branchill *Gramp*	93	NJ0852
Brand End *Lincs*	51	TF3844
Branderburgh *Gramp*	94	NJ2371
Brandesburton *Humb*	57	TA1147
Brandeston *Suffk*	33	TM2460
Brandis Corner *Devon*	6	SS4104
Brandiston *Norfk*	43	TG1421
Brandon *Dur*	61	NZ2439
Brandon *Lincs*	50	SK9048
Brandon *Suffk*	32	TL7886
Brandon *Warwks*	39	SP4176
Brandon Bank *Cambs*	41	TL6289
Brandon Parva *Norfk*	42	TG0708
Brandsby *N York*	56	SE5872
Brandy Wharf *Lincs*	50	TF0196
Branksome *Dorset*	9	SZ0393
Brankstone Park *Dorset*	10	SZ0590
Bransbury *Hants*	21	SU4242
Bransby *Lincs*	50	SK8979
Branscombe *Devon*	8	SY1988
Bransford *H & W*	28	SO7952
Bransgore *Hants*	10	SZ1897
Bransley *Shrops*	37	SO6575
Branston *Leics*	40	SK8129
Branston *Lincs*	50	TF0166
Branston *Staffs*	39	SK2221
Branston Booths *Lincs*	50	TF0669
Branstone *IOW*	11	SZ5583
Brant Broughton *Lincs*	50	SK9854
Brantham *Suffk*	25	TM1134
Branthwaite *Cumb*	58	NY0525
Branthwaite *Cumb*	58	NY2937
Brantingham *Humb*	56	SE9429
Branton *Nthumb*	77	NU0416
Branton *S York*	49	SE6401
Branton Green *N York*	55	SE4462
Branxton *Nthumb*	77	NT8937
Brassington *Derbys*	48	SK2354
Brasted *Kent*	23	TQ4855
Brasted Chart *Gt Lon*	13	TQ4653
Brathens *Gramp*	89	NO6798
Bratoft *Lincs*	51	TF4764
Brattleby *Lincs*	50	SK9481
Bratton *Shrops*	37	SJ6314
Bratton *Somset*	7	SS9546
Bratton Clovelly *Devon*	4	SX4691
Bratton Clovelly *Devon*	4	SX4691
Bratton Fleming *Devon*	6	SS6437
Bratton Seymour *Somset*	9	ST6729
Braughing *Herts*	31	TL3925
Braunston *Leics*	40	SK8306
Braunston *Nhants*	29	SP5466
Braunstone *Leics*	39	SK5602
Braunton *Devon*	6	SS4836
Brawby *N York*	63	SE7378
Brawl *Highld*	99	NC8166
Brawlbin *Highld*	100	ND0757
Bray *Berks*	22	SU9079
Bray Shop *Cnwll*	4	SX3374
Braybrooke *Nhants*	40	SP7684
Braydon *Wilts*	20	SU0588
Brayford *Devon*	7	SS6934
Braystones *Cumb*	58	NY0106
Braythorn *N York*	55	SE2449
Brayton *N York*	56	SE6030
Braywick *Berks*	22	SU8979
Braywoodside *Berks*	22	SU8976
Breaclete *W Isls*	102	NB1537
Breadsall *Derbys*	49	SK3639
Breadstone *Gloucs*	20	SO7000
Breage *Cnwll*	2	SW6128
Breakachy *Highld*	92	NH4644
Bream *Gloucs*	27	SO5905
Bream's Meend *Gloucs*	10	SU1617
Brean *Somset*	19	ST2955
Brearley *W York*	55	SE0226
Brearton *N York*	55	SE3260
Breascete *W Isls*	102	NB2135
Breaston *Derbys*	39	SK4633
Brechfa *Dyfed*	17	SN5230
Brechin *Tays*	89	NO6060
Breckles *Norfk*	42	TL9594
Breckonside *D & G*	66	NX8489
Breckrey *Highld*	90	NG5061

Brecon Powys	26	SO0428
Bredbury Gt Man	48	SJ9291
Bredenbury H & W	27	SO6056
Bredfield Suffk	33	TM2753
Bredgar Kent	14	TQ8860
Bredhurst Kent	14	TQ7962
Bredon H & W	28	SO9236
Bredon's Hardwick H & W	28	SO9135
Bredon's Norton H & W	28	SO9339
Bredwardine H & W	27	SO3344
Bredon on the Hill Leics	39	SK4022
Breich Loth	75	NS9560
Breightmet Gt Man	54	SD7409
Breighton Humb	56	SE7033
Breinton H & W	27	SO4739
Bremhill Wilts	20	ST9873
Bremley Devon	7	SS8128
Brenchley Kent	14	TQ6741
Brendon Devon	18	SS7648
Brenfield Strath	71	NR8482
Brenish W Isls	102	NA9926
Brent Eleigh Suffk	32	TL9448
Brent Knoll Somset	19	ST3350
Brent Knoll Somset	19	ST3350
Brent Mill Devon	5	SX7059
Brent Pelham Herts	31	TL4330
Brentford Gt Lon	23	TQ1777
Brentingby Leics	40	SK7818
Brentwood Essex	24	TQ5993
Brenzett Kent	15	TR0027
Brenzett Green Kent	15	TR0028
Brereton Green Ches	47	SJ7764
Bressingham Norfk	32	TM0780
Bressingham Common Norfk	33	TM0982
Bretabister Shet	103	HU4857
Bretby Derbys	39	SK2923
Bretford Warwks	39	SP4377
Bretforton H & W	28	SP0944
Bretherton Lancs	53	SD4720
Brettenham Norfk	32	TL9383
Brettenham Suffk	32	TL9654
Bretton Clwyd	46	SJ3564
Brewhouse D & G	66	NY0165
Brewood Staffs	38	SJ8808
Brgoed M Glam	19	ST1599
Briantspuddle Dorset	9	SY8193
Brick Houses S York	49	SK3081
Bricket Wood Herts	22	TL1302
Bricklehampton H & W	28	SO9842
Bride IOM	52	NX4501
Bridekirk Cumb	58	NY1133
Bridestowe Devon	4	SX5189
Brideswell Gramp	94	NJ5739
Bridford Devon	5	SX8186
Bridge Cnwll	2	SW6744
Bridge Kent	15	TR1854
Bridge End Devon	5	SX7046
Bridge End Nthumb	68	NY8965
Bridge End Surrey	22	TQ0767
Bridge Fields Leics	39	SK4927
Bridge Hewick N York	55	SE3370
Bridge Reeve Devon	7	SS6613
Bridge Sollers H & W	27	SO4142
Bridge Street Suffk	32	TL8749
Bridge Trafford Ches	46	SJ4571
Bridge of Alford Gramp	94	NJ5617
Bridge of Avon Gramp	94	NJ1835
Bridge of Balgie Tays	87	NN5746
Bridge of Brewlands Tays	88	NO1961
Bridge of Brown Highld	93	NJ1120
Bridge of Cally Tays	88	NO1451
Bridge of Canny Gramp	89	NO6597
Bridge of Craigisla Tays	88	NO2553
Bridge of Dee D & G	65	NX7360
Bridge of Don D & G	95	NJ9409
Bridge of Dulsie Highld	93	NH9341
Bridge of Dye Gramp	89	NO6586
Bridge of Earn Tays	82	NO1318
Bridge of Ericht Tays	87	NN5258
Bridge of Feugh Gramp	89	NO7095
Bridge of Forss Highld	100	ND0068
Bridge of Gairn Gramp	88	NO3597
Bridge of Gaur Tays	87	NN5056
Bridge of Orchy Strath	80	NN2939
Bridge of Tilt Tays	87	NN8765
Bridge of Tynet Gramp	94	NJ3862
Bridge of Walls Shet	103	HU2651
Bridge of Weir Strath	73	NS3865
Bridge of Westfield Highld	100	ND0664
Bridgehampton Somset	8	ST5624
Bridgehouse Gate N York	55	SE1565
Bridgemary Hants	11	SU5803
Bridgend Border	76	NT5235
Bridgend D & G	66	NT0708
Bridgend Devon	4	SX5547
Bridgend Fife	83	NO3911
Bridgend Gramp	94	NJ3731
Bridgend Gramp	94	NJ5135
Bridgend Gramp	95	NJ7249
Bridgend Loth	75	NT0475
Bridgend M Glam	18	SS9079
Bridgend Strath	70	NR3362
Bridgend Tays	82	NO1224
Bridgend Tays	89	NO5368
Bridgend of Lintrathen Tays	88	NO2854
Bridgerule Devon	6	SS2703
Bridgeton Gramp	94	NJ3251
Bridgetown Devon	5	SX3489
Bridgetown Somset	7	SS9233
Bridgeyate Avon	20	ST6873
Bridgham Norfk	32	TL9686
Bridgnorth Shrops	37	SO7193
Bridgwater Somset	19	ST3037
Bridlington Humb	57	TA1766
Bridport Dorset	8	SY4692
Bridstow H & W	27	SO5824
Brierfield Lancs	54	SD8436
Brierley Gloucs	27	SO6215
Brierley S York	55	SE4011
Brierley Hill W Mids	38	SO9187
Brierton Cleve	62	NZ4729
Brig o'Turk Cent	81	NN5306
Brigg Humb	56	TA0007
Brigg of Blair Gramp	89	NO8899
Briggate Norfk	43	TG3127
Briggswath N York	63	NZ8608
Brigham Cumb	58	NY0830
Brigham Cumb	57	TA0753
Brigham Humb	57	TA0853
Brighouse W York	55	SE1423
Brighstone IOW	10	SZ4282
Brightgate Derbys	49	SP3803
Brightholmlee Derbys	49	SK2995
Brightley Devon	6	SX5997
Brightlingsea Essex	25	TM0817
Brighton E Susx	12	TQ3105
Brighton le Sands Mersyd	46	SJ3199
Brightons Cent	75	NS9277
Brightwalton Berks	21	SU4279
Brightwell Oxon	21	SU5790
Brightwell Suffk	33	TM2543
Brightwell Baldwin Oxon	21	SU6595
Brightwell Upperton Oxon	21	SU6594
Brigland Hall Cumb	67	NY3683
Brignall Dur	61	NZ0712
Brigsley Humb	51	TA2501
Brigsteer Cumb	59	SD4889
Brigstock Nhants	40	SP9485
Brill Bucks	29	SP6513
Brilley H & W	27	SO2648
Brilley Cross H & W	27	SO2648
Brimfield Cross H & W	27	SO5368
Brimington Derbys	49	SK4073
Brimley Devon	5	SX7977
Brimpsfield Gloucs	28	SO9312
Brimpton Berks	21	SU5564
Brimscombe Gloucs	20	SO8602
Brimstage Mersyd	46	SJ3082
Brincliffe S York	49	SK3284
Brind Humb	56	SE7430
Brindham Somset	19	ST5140
Brindister Shet	103	HU2857
Brindle Lancs	54	SD6024
Brineton Staffs	37	SJ8013
Bringhurst Leics	40	SP8492
Brington Cambs	30	TL0875
Briningham Norfk	42	TG0434
Brinkely Notts	49	SK7152

Brinkhill Lincs	51	TF3773
Brinkley Cambs	32	TL6254
Brinklow Warwks	39	SP4379
Brinkworth Wilts	20	SU0184
Brinscall Lancs	54	SD6221
Brinscombe Somset	19	ST4252
Brinsley Notts	49	SK4649
Brinton Norfk	42	TG0335
Brisco Norfk	29	SK4649
Brinyan Ork	103	HY4327
Brisley Norfk	42	TF9421
Brislington Avon	19	ST6170
Brissenden Green Kent	14	TQ9339
Bristol Avon	19	ST5873
Briston Norfk	42	TG0632
Britford Wilts	10	SU1628
Brithdir Gwynd	35	SH7618
Brithdir M Glam	18	SO1401
British Legion Village Kent	14	TQ7257
Briton Ferry W Glam	18	SS7494
Britwell Salome Oxon	22	SU6792
Brixham Devon	5	SX9255
Brixton Devon	4	SX5452
Brixton Gt Lon	23	TQ3175
Brixton Deverill Wilts	20	ST8638
Brixworth Nhants	30	SP7470
Brize Norton Oxon	29	SP2907
Broad Alley H & W	28	SO8867
Broad Blunsdon Wilts	20	SU1490
Broad Campden Gloucs	28	SP1537
Broad Carr W York	55	SE0919
Broad Chalke Wilts	9	SU0325
Broad Clough Lancs	54	SD8624
Broad Green Cambs	32	TL6960
Broad Green Essex	24	TL8823
Broad Green H & W	28	SO7756
Broad Green Suffk	32	TL7859
Broad Haven Dyfed	16	SM8613
Broad Hinton Wilts	20	SU1076
Broad Laying Hants	21	SU4362
Broad Marston H & W	28	SP1446
Broad Oak E Susx	14	TQ8219
Broad Oak H & W	27	SO4821
Broad Oak Mersyd	46	SJ5395
Broad Street E Susx	14	TQ8616
Broad Street Kent	14	TQ8356
Broad Street Kent	15	TR1139
Broad Street Wilts	20	SU1158
Broad Street Green Essex	24	TL8610
Broad Town Wilts	20	SU0877
Broad's Green Essex	24	TL6912
Broadbottom Derbys	48	SJ9993
Broadbridge W Susx	11	SU8105
Broadbridge Heath W Susx	12	TQ1431
Broadclyst Devon	7	SX9897
Broadfield Strath	80	NS3273
Broadford Highld	85	NG6423
Broadford Bridge W Susx	12	TQ0921
Broadgairhill Border	67	NT2010
Broadgate Lincs	41	TF3609
Broadgrass Green Suffk	32	TL9763
Broadhaugh Border	77	NT8655
Broadheath Gt Man	47	SJ7689
Broadhembury Devon	8	ST1004
Broadhempston Devon	5	SX8066
Broadland Row E Susx	14	TQ8319
Broadley Lancs	54	SD8316
Broadmayne Dorset	9	SY7286
Broadmoor Dyfed	16	SN0906
Broadoak Dorset	8	SY4496
Broadoak E Susx	13	TQ6022
Broadoak Kent	15	TR1761
Broadstairs Kent	15	TR3967
Broadstone Dorset	9	SZ0095
Broadstone Gwent	19	SO5002
Broadstone Shrops	37	SO5489
Broadwas H & W	28	SO7559
Broadwas H & W	28	SO7655
Broadwater Herts	31	TL2422
Broadwater W Susx	12	TQ1504
Broadwaters H & W	38	SO8478
Broadway Dyfed	17	SN3808
Broadway H & W	28	SP0937
Broadway Somset	8	ST3215
Broadwell Gloucs	29	SP2027
Broadwell Oxon	21	SP2503
Broadwell Warwks	29	SP4565
Broadwindsor Dorset	8	ST4302
Broadwood-Kelly Devon	6	SS6105
Broadwoodwidger Devon	4	SX4089
Brochel Highld	90	NG5846
Brockbridge Hants	11	SU6118
Brockdish Norfk	33	TM2179
Brockenhurst Hants	10	SU2902
Brockenhurst Hants	10	SU3002
Brocketsbrae Strath	74	NS8240
Brockford Street Suffk	33	TM1167
Brockhall Nhants	29	SP6362
Brockham Surrey	12	TQ1949
Brockhampton Gloucs	28	SO9425
Brockhampton Gloucs	28	SP0322
Brockhampton Hants	11	SU7106
Brockholes W York	55	SE1511
Brockhurst Warwks	39	SP4683
Brocklebank Cumb	67	NY3043
Brocklesby Lincs	57	TA1311
Brockley Avon	19	ST4667
Brockley Suffk	32	TL8371
Brockley Green Suffk	32	TL7247
Brockley Green Suffk	32	TL8254
Brockleymoor Cumb	67	NY4957
Brockmoor W Mids	38	SO9187
Brockton Shrops	36	SJ3104
Brockton Shrops	36	SO3285
Brockton Shrops	37	SJ7203
Brockton Shrops	37	SO5794
Brockton Staffs	37	SJ8131
Brockwell Gwent	19	SO5301
Brockworth Gloucs	28	SO8916
Brocton Staffs	38	SJ9619
Brodick Strath	72	NS0135
Brodie Gramp	93	NH9757
Brodsworth S York	55	SE5007
Brogaig Highld	90	NG4768
Brokenborough Wilts	20	ST9189
Brokerswood Wilts	20	ST8352
Bromborough Mersyd	46	SJ3582
Brome Suffk	33	TM1376
Brome Street Suffk	33	TM1576
Bromeswell Suffk	33	TM3050
Bromfield Cumb	67	NY1746
Bromfield Shrops	37	SO4877
Bromham Beds	30	TL0051
Bromham Wilts	20	ST9665
Bromley Gt Lon	23	TQ4069
Bromley Shrops	37	SO7395
Bromlow Shrops	36	SJ3201
Brompton Kent	14	TQ7668
Brompton Kent	14	TQ7668
Brompton N York	62	SE3796
Brompton N York	63	SE9482
Brompton Ralph Somset	7	ST0832
Brompton Regis Somset	7	SS9531
Brompton-on-Swale N York	61	SE2199
Bromsash H & W	27	SO6523
Bromsberrow Gloucs	28	SO7434
Bromsberrow Heath Gloucs	28	SO7332
Bromsgrove H & W	28	SO9570
Bromyard H & W	27	SO6554
Bronaber Gwynd	45	SH7132
Bronant Dyfed	35	SN6467
Brongest Dyfed	17	SN3245
Bronington Clwyd	37	SJ4839
Bronllys Powys	26	SO1434
Bronwydd Arms Dyfed	17	SN4124
Brongarth Shrops	36	SJ2637
Brook Hants	10	SU2713
Brook Hants	10	SU2713
Brook Hants	10	SU3428
Brook IOW	10	SZ3983
Brook Kent	15	TR0644
Brook Surrey	11	SU9338
Brook Surrey	12	TQ0646
Brook End Bucks	30	SP9144
Brook End Cambs	30	TL0875
Brook End Staffs	38	SK0714
Brook Hill Hants	10	SU2714
Brook Hill Hants	10	SU2714
Brook Street Essex	24	TQ5792

Brook Street Kent	14	TQ9334
Brook Street Kent	32	TL8348
Brook Street W Susx	12	TQ3026
Brooke Leics	40	SK8405
Brooke Norfk	43	TM2999
Brookfield Strath	73	NS4164
Brookhampton Oxon	21	SU6098
Brookhampton Somset	9	ST6327
Brookhouse Lancs	53	SD5464
Brookhouse S York	49	SK5188
Brookhouse Green Ches	47	SJ8161
Brookhouses Derbys	48	SK0389
Brookland Kent	15	TQ9926
Brooklands Gt Man	47	SJ7890
Brookmans Park Herts	23	TL2404
Brooks End Kent	23	TQ2967
Brooks Green W Susx	12	TQ1225
Brooksby Leics	39	SK6716
Brookthorpe Gloucs	28	SO8312
Brookwood Surrey	22	SU9557
Broom Beds	31	TL1742
Broom S York	49	SK4491
Broom Warwks	28	SP0953
Broom Green Norfk	42	TF9924
Broom Hill H & W	38	SO9275
Broom Hill S York	49	SE4102
Broom Street Kent	15	TR0462
Broom of Dalreoch Tays	82	NO0017
Broome's Green H & W	28	SO7133
Broome H & W	38	SO9078
Broome Norfk	33	TM3591
Broome Shrops	36	SO3981
Broomedge Ches	47	SJ6985
Broomer's Corner W Susx	12	TQ1221
Broomfield Essex	24	TL7011
Broomfield Kent	14	TQ8362
Broomfield Kent	15	TR1966
Broomfield Somset	8	ST2221
Broomfleet Humb	56	SE8727
Broomhaugh Nthumb	68	NZ0261
Broomhill Highld	93	NH9922
Broomhill Nthumb	69	NU2401
Broomhill Green Ches	47	SJ6247
Brora Highld	97	NC9104
Broseley Shrops	37	SJ6701
Brotherlee Dur	60	NY9237
Brotherstone Border	76	NT6145
Brothertoft Lincs	51	TF2746
Brotherton N York	55	SE4825
Brotton Cleve	62	NZ6819
Broubster Highld	100	ND0359
Brough Cumb	60	NY7914
Brough Highld	100	ND2273
Brough Notts	50	SE9326
Brough Notts	50	SK8458
Brough Shet	103	HU5564
Brough Lodge Shet	103	HU5892
Brough Sowerby Cumb	60	NY7912
Broughall Shrops	37	SJ5741
Broughton Border	75	NT1136
Broughton Bucks	30	SP8939
Broughton Cambs	31	TL2877
Broughton Clwyd	46	SJ3363
Broughton Gt Man	47	SD8201
Broughton Hants	10	SU3032
Broughton Humb	56	SE9508
Broughton Lancs	53	SD5234
Broughton N York	54	SD9451
Broughton N York	63	SE7673
Broughton Nhants	30	SP8375
Broughton Oxon	29	SP4238
Broughton S Glam	18	SS9271
Broughton S York	57	SJ7634
Broughton Astley Leics	39	SP5292
Broughton Gifford Wilts	20	ST8763
Broughton Green H & W	28	SO9561
Broughton Hackett H & W	28	SO9254
Broughton Mills Cumb	58	SD2290
Broughton Moor Cumb	58	NY0533
Broughton Poggs Oxon	21	SP2303
Broughton Tower Cumb	67	NY2188
Broughty Ferry Tays	83	NO4630
Brown Candover Hants	11	SU5739
Brown Edge Staffs	48	SJ9053
Brown Street Suffk	32	TM0664
Brown's Green W Mids	38	SP0491
Brownheath Shrops	36	SJ4629
Brownhill Gramp	95	NJ8640
Brownhills Fife	83	NO6215
Brownhills W Mids	38	SK0405
Browninghall Green Hants	21	SU5859
Brownmuir Gramp	89	NO7377
Brownsham Devon	6	SS2826
Brownston Devon	5	SX6952
Brox N York	22	TQ0263
Broxa N York	63	SE9491
Broxbourne Herts	23	TL3607
Broxburn Loth	75	NT0872
Broxburn Loth	76	NT6977
Broxted Essex	24	TL5727
Broxwood H & W	27	SO3654
Bruan Highld	100	ND3139
Bruar Tays	87	NN8266
Brucefield Highld	97	NH9386
Bruchag Strath	73	NS1157
Brue W Isls	102	NB3349
Bruernish W Isls	102	NF7102
Bruisyard Suffk	33	TM3266
Bruisyard Street Suffk	33	TM3365
Brumby Humb	56	SE8009
Brund Staffs	48	SK1061
Brundall Norfk	43	TG3208
Brundish Suffk	33	TM2669
Brundish Street Suffk	33	TM2671
Brunnian Cnwll	2	SW5036
Bruno Derbys	48	SK1061
Bruntingthorpe Leics	39	SP6090
Brunton Fife	83	NO3220
Brunton Nthumb	77	NU2024
Brushford Somset	7	SS9225
Brushford Barton Devon	7	SS6707
Brushy by Sands Cumb	9	ST6834
Bryan's Green H & W	28	SO8868
Branston Dorset	9	ST8706
Bryant's Bottom Bucks	22	SU8599
Brympton Somset	8	ST5115
Bryn W Glam	18	SS8192
Bryn Du Gwynd	44	SH3472
Bryn Gates Lancs	47	SD5901
Bryn Saith Marchog Clwyd	46	SD0750
Bryn-Mawr Gwynd	44	SH2433
Bryn-henllan Dyfed	16	SN0139
Bryn-y-maen Clwyd	45	SH8376
Brynamman Dyfed	26	SN7114
Brynberian Dyfed	16	SN1035
Bryncir Gwynd	44	SH4641
Bryncroes Gwynd	44	SH2931
Bryncrug Gwynd	34	SH6003
Bryneglwys Clwyd	46	SJ1447
Brynford Clwyd	46	SJ1772
Bryngwran Gwynd	44	SH3477
Bryngwyn Gwent	27	SO3809
Bryngwyn Powys	27	SO1849
Brynhoffnant Dyfed	17	SN3351
Bryning Lancs	53	SD4030
Brynithel Gwent	19	SO2101
Brynmawr Gwent	27	SO1911
Brynmenyn M Glam	18	SS9085
Brynna M Glam	18	SS9883
Brynrefail Gwynd	44	SH4786
Brynsadler M Glam	18	ST0280
Brynsiencyn Gwynd	44	SH4867
Bualintur Highld	84	NG4010
Bubbenhall Warwks	39	SP3672
Bubwith Humb	56	SE7136
Buccleuch Border	67	NT3214
Buchanan Smithy Cent	81	NS4689
Buchanhaven Gramp	95	NK1247
Buchanty Tays	82	NN9328
Buchany Cent	81	NN7102
Buchlyvie Cent	81	NS5793
Buchtrig Border	68	NT7714
Buck's Cross Devon	6	SS3523
Buck's Mills Devon	6	SS3523

Buckden Cambs	31	TL1967
Buckden N York	61	SD9477
Buckenham Norfk	43	TG3506
Buckerell Devon	8	ST1200
Buckfast Devon	5	SX7366
Buckfastleigh Devon	5	SX7366
Buckfastleigh Devon	5	SX7466
Buckhaven Fife	83	NT3598
Buckholt Gwent	27	SO5016
Buckhorn Weston Dorset	9	ST7524
Buckhurst Hill Essex	23	TQ4194
Buckie Gramp	94	NJ4265
Buckingham Bucks	30	SP6933
Buckland Bucks	30	SP8812
Buckland Devon	5	SX6743
Buckland Gloucs	28	SP0836
Buckland Herts	31	TL3533
Buckland Kent	15	TR3042
Buckland Oxon	21	SU3497
Buckland Surrey	12	TQ2250
Buckland Brewer Devon	6	SS4120
Buckland Common Bucks	22	SP9307
Buckland Dinham Somset	20	ST7550
Buckland Filleigh Devon	6	SS4609
Buckland Monachorum Devon	4	SX4868
Buckland Newton Dorset	9	ST6805
Buckland Ripers Dorset	9	SY6482
Buckland St. James Suffk	8	ST2713
Buckland in the Moor Devon	5	SX7273
Buckland-Tout-Saints Devon	5	SX7546
Bucklebury Berks	21	SU5570
Buckleheads Tays	83	NO4636
Bucklers Hard Hants	10	SU4000
Bucklesham Suffk	33	TM2442
Buckley Clwyd	46	SJ2864
Buckley Green Warwks	28	SP1667
Buckley Mountain Clwyd	46	SJ2865
Bucklow Hill Ches	47	SJ7383
Buckminster Leics	40	SK8722
Bucknall Lincs	50	TF1668
Bucknall Staffs	48	SJ9047
Bucknell Oxon	29	SP5626
Bucknell Shrops	36	SO3574
Buckpool Gramp	94	NJ4265
Bucks Green W Susx	12	TQ0732
Bucks Horn Oak Hants	11	SU8041
Bucksburn Gramp	95	NJ8909
Buckton Humb	57	TA1872
Buckton Nthumb	77	NU0838
Buckworth Cambs	30	TL1476
Budbrooke Warwks	29	SP2665
Budby Notts	49	SK6169
Budd's Titson Cnwll	6	SS2401
Buddon Tays	83	NO5232
Bude Cnwll	6	SS2006
Budge's Shop Cnwll	4	SX3259
Budlake Devon	7	SS9700
Budleigh Salterton Devon	5	SY0682
Budock Water Cnwll	2	SW7832
Buerton Ches	47	SJ6843
Bugbrooke Nhants	29	SP6757
Bugley Dorset	9	ST7822
Bugthorpe Humb	56	SE7757
Buildwas Shrops	37	SJ6304
Builth Road Powys	26	SO0253
Builth Wells Powys	26	SO0350
Bulbridge Wilts	10	SU0930
Buldoo Highld	100	NU0067
Bulford Wilts	20	SU1643
Bulkeley Ches	46	SJ5254
Bulkington Warwks	39	SP3986
Bulkington Wilts	20	ST9458
Bulkworthy Devon	6	SS3914
Bull's Green Herts	31	TL2717
Bullbrook Berks	22	SU8869
Bullington Hants	21	SU4541
Bullington Lincs	50	TF0977
Bullington End Bucks	30	SP8144
Bullwood Strath	80	NS1675
Bulmer Essex	32	TL8440
Bulmer N York	56	SE6967
Bulmer Tye Essex	32	TL8439
Bulphan Essex	24	TQ6386
Bulstrode Herts	22	TL0303
Bulval Cnwll	2	SW4831
Bulwark Gramp	95	NJ9345
Bulwell Notts	49	SK5345
Bulwick Nhants	40	SP9694
Bumble's Green Essex	23	TL4004
Bunacaimb Highld	85	NM6588
Bunarkaig Highld	86	NN1888
Bunbury Ches	47	SJ5658
Bunchrew Highld	92	NH6446
Bundalloch Highld	85	NG8927
Bunessan Strath	78	NM3821
Bungay Suffk	33	TM3389
Bunnahabhain Strath	70	NR4173
Bunny Notts	39	SK5829
Buntait Highld	92	NH4030
Buntingford Herts	31	TL3629
Bunwell Norfk	33	TM1292
Bunwell Street Norfk	43	TM1194
Burbage Leics	39	SP4492
Burbage Wilts	21	SU2261
Burcombe Wilts	10	SU0630
Burcot Oxon	21	SU5595
Burcote Shrops	30	SP8723
Bures Suffk	24	TL9034
Burford H & W	27	SO6868
Burford Oxon	29	SP2411
Burg Strath	78	NM3845
Burgates Hants	11	SU7728
Burgess Hill W Susx	12	TQ3118
Burgh Suffk	33	TM2351
Burgh Castle Norfk	43	TG4805
Burgh Heath Surrey	23	TQ2457
Burgh Hill E Susx	14	TQ7227
Burgh Le Marsh Lincs	51	TF4965
Burgh St. Margaret Norfk	43	TG4413
Burgh St. Peter Norfk	43	TM4693
Burgh by Sands Cumb	67	NY3259
Burgh next Aylsham Norfk	43	TG2125
Burghclere Hants	21	SU4761
Burghead Gramp	93	NJ1168
Burghfield Berks	22	SU6668
Burghfield Common Berks	21	SU6566
Burghill H & W	27	SO4744
Burghwallis S York	56	SE5311
Burghwallis S York	56	SE5312
Burham Kent	14	TQ7262
Buriton Hants	11	SU7320
Burland Ches	47	SJ6153
Burlawn Cnwll	3	SW9970
Burleigh Berks	22	SU9069
Burleigh Gloucs	20	SO8601
Burlescombe Devon	7	ST0716
Burleston Dorset	9	SY7794
Burley Hants	10	SU2103
Burley Leics	40	SK8810
Burley Street Hants	10	SU2004
Burley Gate H & W	27	SO5947
Burley Wood Head W York	55	SE1544
Burley in Wharfedale W York	55	SE1646
Burleydam Ches	37	SJ6042
Burlingham Green Norfk	43	TG3611
Burlington Shrops	37	SJ7511
Burlton Shrops	36	SJ4526
Burmarsh Warwks	29	SP2638
Burn Cross S York	56	SK5928
Burn Cross S York	49	SK3495
Burn of Cambus Cent	81	NN7103
Burnage Gt Man	47	SJ8692
Burnaston Derbys	39	SK2832
Burnby Humb	56	SE8346
Burneside Cumb	59	SD5095
Burneston N York	61	SE3084
Burnett Avon	20	ST6665
Burnfoot Border	76	NT5116
Burnfoot D & G	66	NX9791
Burnfoot D & G	67	NY3388
Burnfoot D & G	67	NY3886
Burnfoot Tays	82	NN9904
Burnham Bucks	22	SU9382
Burnham Humb	57	TA0517

Burnham Deepdale Norfk 42 TF8044
Burnham Green Herts 31 TL2616
Burnham Market Norfk 42 TF8342
Burnham Norton Norfk 42 TF8243
Burnham Overy Norfk 42 TF8442
Burnham Thorpe Norfk 42 TF8541
Burnham-on-Crouch Essex 25 TQ9496
Burnham-on-Sea Somset 19 ST3049
Burnhaven Gramp 95 NK1244
Burnhead D & G 66 NX8695
Burnhervie Gramp 95 NJ7319
Burnhill Green Staffs 37 SJ7800
Burnhope Dur 69 NZ1948
Burnhouse Strath 73 NS3850
Burniston N York 63 TA0193
Burnley Lancs 54 SD8432
Burnmouth Border 77 NT9560
Burnopfield Dur 69 NZ1756
Burnsall N York 55 SE0361
Burnside Fife 75 NT0575
Burnside Fife 82 NO1608
Burnside Gramp 94 NJ1669
Burnside Tays 88 NO4259
Burnside Tays 89 NO5050
Burnside of Duntrune Tays 83 NO4434
Burnt Heath Essex 25 TM0628
Burnt Hill Berks 21 SU5774
Burnt Yates N York 55 SE2461
Burntisland Fife 83 NT2385
Burnworthy Somset 8 ST1915
Burpham Surrey 12 TQ0151
Burpham W Susx 12 TQ0408
Burradon Nthumb 68 NT9806
Burrafirth Shet 103 HP6113
Burraton Cnwll 4 SX4167
Burraton Devon 5 SX6152
Burravoe Shet 103 HU5279
Burrells Cumb 60 NY6718
Burrelton Tays 82 NO2037
Burridge Devon 8 ST3106
Burridge Hants 11 SU5110
Burrill N York 61 SE2386
Burringham Humb 56 SE8309
Burrington Avon 19 ST4769
Burrington Devon 7 SS6316
Burrington H & W 36 SO4472
Burrough End Cambs 32 TL6256
Burrough Green Cambs 32 TL6355
Burrough on the Hill Leics 40 SK7510
Burrow Somset 7 SS9342
Burrow Bridge Somset 8 ST3530
Burrowhill Surrey 22 SU9763
Burry W Glam 17 SS4596
Burry Port Dyfed 17 SN4400
Burrygreen W Glam 17 SS4591
Burscough Lancs 53 SD4310
Burscough Bridge Lancs 53 SD4412
Bursea Humb 56 SE8033
Bursledon Hants 10 SU4809
Burslem Staffs 47 SJ8749
Burstall Suffk 33 TM1044
Burstock Dorset 8 ST4202
Burston Devon 7 SS7102
Burston Norfk 33 TM1383
Burstwick Humb 57 TA2228
Burtersett N York 54 SD8989
Burtholme Cumb 67 NY5463
Burthorpe Green Suffk 32 TL7764
Burtle Hill Somset 19 ST3943
Burtoft Lincs 41 TF2635
Burton Ches 46 SJ3174
Burton Ches 46 SJ5063
Burton Cumb 59 SD5276
Burton Dorset 9 SY6892
Burton Dorset 10 SZ1794
Burton Dyfed 16 SM9805
Burton Lincs 50 SK9574
Burton Somset 19 ST1944
Burton Wilts 20 ST8179
Burton Agnes Humb 57 TA1063
Burton Bradstock Dorset 8 SY4889
Burton Coggles Lincs 40 SK9725
Burton Dassett Warwks 29 SP3951
Burton End Essex 31 TL5323
Burton Fleming Humb 57 TA0872
Burton Green Warwks 39 SP4190
Burton Joyce Notts 49 SK6443
Burton Latimer Nhants 30 SP9074
Burton Lazars Leics 40 SK7716
Burton Leonard N York 55 SE3263
Burton Overy Leics 39 SP6798
Burton Pedwardine Lincs 50 TF1142
Burton Pidsea Humb 57 TA2431
Burton Salmon N York 55 SE4827
Burton in Lonsdale N York 54 SD6572
Burton on the Wolds Leics 39 SK5921
Burton upon Stather Humb 56 SE8617
Burton upon Trent Staffs 39 SK2423
Burton's Green Essex 24 TL8327
Burton-in-Lonsdale N York 54 SD6572
Burtonwood Ches 47 SJ5692
Burwardsley Ches 46 SJ5156
Burwarton Shrops 37 SO6185
Burwash E Susx 14 TQ6724
Burwash Common E Susx 13 TQ6423
Burwash Weald E Susx 13 TQ6523
Burwell Cambs 31 TL5866
Burwell Lincs 51 TF3579
Burwen Gwynd 44 SH4293
Burwick Ork 103 ND4384
Bury Cambs 41 TL2883
Bury Gt Man 54 SD8111
Bury Somset 7 SS9427
Bury W Susx 12 TQ0113
Bury End Bucks 22 SU9597
Bury St. Edmunds Suffk 32 TL8564
Burythorpe N York 56 SE7964
Busby Strath 74 NS5756
Buscot Wilts 21 SU2298
Bush Gramp 89 NO7565
Bush Bank H & W 27 SO4551
Bush Hill Park Gt Lon 23 TQ3395
Bushbury W Mids 38 SJ9202
Bushby Leics 39 SK6504
Bushey Herts 22 TQ1395
Bushey Heath Herts 22 TQ1494
Bushley H & W 28 SO8734
Bushton Wilts 20 SU0677
Buslingthorpe Lincs 50 TF0885
Bussex Somset 8 ST3435
Butcher's Cross E Susx 13 TQ5525
Butcher's Pasture Essex 24 TL6024
Butchers Row W Susx 12 TQ1720
Butcombe Avon 19 ST5162
Butleigh Somset 8 ST5233
Butleigh Wootton Somset 8 ST5034
Butlers Marston Warwks 29 SP3150
Butley Suffk 33 TM3751
Butt Green Ches 47 SJ6751
Buttercrambe N York 56 SE7358
Butterdean Border 76 NT7964
Butterknowle Dur 61 NZ1025
Butterleigh Devon 7 SS9708
Buttermere Cumb 58 NY1726
Buttermere Wilts 21 SU3361
Buttershaw W York 55 SE1330
Butterstone Tays 88 NO0645
Butterton Staffs 38 SJ8242
Butterton Staffs 48 SK0756
Butterwick Dur 62 NZ3829
Butterwick Lincs 51 TF3827
Butterwick N York 63 SE7377
Butterwick N York 56 SE9871
Buttington Powys 36 SJ2508
Buttonoak Shrops 37 SO7578
Buttsash Hants 10 SU4205
Buxhall Suffk 32 TM0057
Buxted E Susx 13 TQ4923
Buxton Derbys 48 SK0673
Buxton Norfk 43 TG2322
Buxton Heath Norfk 43 TG1821
Bwlch Powys 27 SO1522
Bwlch-y-cibau Powys 36 SJ1717
Bwlch-y-ffrid Powys 36 SO0795
Bwlch-y-groes Dyfed 17 SN2436
Bwlch-y-sarnau Powys 36 SO0374
Bwlchgwyn Clwyd 46 SJ2653
Bwlchllan Dyfed 34 SN5758

Bwlchymyrdd W Glam 17 SS5798
Byers Garth Dur 62 NZ3141
Byers Green Dur 61 NZ2233
Byfield Nhants 29 SP5153
Byfleet Surrey 22 TQ0661
Byford H & W 27 SO3942
Byker T & W 69 NZ2764
Bylchau Clwyd 45 SH9762
Byre Burnfoot D & G 67 NY3877
Byrewalls Border 76 NT6643
Byrness Nthumb 68 NT7602
Bystock Devon 5 SY0283
Bythorn Cambs 30 TL0575
Byton H & W 27 SO3764
Bywell Nthumb 68 NZ0461
Byworth W Susx 12 SU9820

C

Cabourne Lincs 50 TA1401
Cabrach Gramp 94 NJ3826
Cabrach Strath 70 NR4964
Cabus Lancs 53 SD4948
Cabvie Lodge Highld 92 NH1567
Cackle Street E Susx 14 TQ8219
Cacrabank Border 75 NT3017
Cadbury Devon 7 SS9105
Cadder Strath 74 NS6172
Caddington Beds 30 TL0619
Caddonfoot Border 76 NT4535
Cade Street E Susx 13 TQ6021
Cadeby Leics 39 SK4202
Cadeby S York 49 SE5100
Cadeleigh Devon 7 SS9107
Cadgwith Cnwll 2 SW7214
Cadham Fife 83 NO2802
Cadishead Gt Man 47 SJ7191
Cadle W Glam 17 SS6296
Cadley Wilts 21 SU2066
Cadley Wilts 21 SU2454
Cadmore End Bucks 22 SU7892
Cadnam Hants 10 SU2913
Cadney Humb 56 TA0103
Cadoxton S Glam 18 ST1269
Cadoxton Juxta-Neath W Glam 18 SS7598
Caeathro Gwynd 44 SH5061
Caenby Lincs 50 TF0089
Caeo Dyfed 26 SN6739
Caer Farchell Dyfed 16 SM7927
Caerau M Glam 18 SS8694
Caerau S Glam 18 ST1375
Caergeiliog Gwynd 44 SH3178
Caergwrle Clwyd 46 SJ3057
Caerlanrig Border 67 NT3904
Caerleon Gwent 19 ST3491
Caernarfon Gwynd 44 SH4862
Caerphilly M Glam 19 ST1587
Caerphilly M Glam 19 ST1598
Caersws Powys 36 SO0392
Caerwedros Dyfed 34 SN3755
Caerwent Gwent 19 ST4790
Caerwys Clwyd 46 SJ1272
Cairnbaan Strath 71 NR8390
Cairnbrogie Gramp 95 NJ8527
Cairnbulg Gramp 95 NK0365
Cairncross Border 77 NT8963
Cairncurran Strath 73 NS3170
Cairndow Strath 80 NN1810
Cairneyhill Fife 82 NT0486
Cairnfield House Gramp 94 NJ4162
Cairngarroch D & G 64 NX0649
Cairngrassie Gramp 89 NO9095
Cairnie Gramp 94 NJ4844
Cairnorrie Gramp 95 NJ8641
Cairnryan D & G 64 NX0668
Cairnty Auchroisk Gramp 94 NJ3351
Cairnwhin Strath 66 NX2491
Caistor Lincs 50 TA1101
Caister-on-Sea Norfk 43 TG5212
Caistor St. Edmund Norfk 43 TG2303
Caistron Nthumb 68 NT9901
Cake Street Norfk 32 TM0790
Calais Street Suffk 32 TL9740
Calbost Highld 90 NG2148
Calbourne IOW 10 SZ4286
Calceby Lincs 51 TF3877
Calcot Clwyd 46 SJ1775
Calcot Gloucs 28 SP0910
Calcot Row Berks 22 SU6771
Calcots Gramp 94 NJ2563
Calcott Shrops 36 SJ4414
Caldecote Cambs 31 TL1488
Caldecote Cambs 31 TL3456
Caldecote Herts 31 TL2338
Caldecote Highfields Cambs 31 TL3559
Caldecott Leics 40 SP8693
Caldecott Nhants 30 SP8668
Caldecott Oxon 21 SU4996
Calder Bridge Cumb 58 NY0306
Calder Grove W York 55 SE3016
Calder Vale Lancs 53 SD5345
Calderbank Strath 74 NS7663
Caldercruix Strath 74 NS8167
Caldermill Strath 74 NS6642
Caldermore Gt Man 54 SD9316
Caldicot Gwent 19 ST4888
Caldwell N York 61 NZ1613
Calfsound Ork 103 HY5738
Calgary Strath 78 NM3751
Califer Gramp 93 NJ0857
California Cent 74 NS9076
California Derbys 39 SK3335
California Norfk 43 TG5114
Calke Derbys 39 SK3722
Callander Cent 81 NN6208
Callanish W Isls 102 NB2133
Callert Cottage Highld 86 NN1060
Callestick Cnwll 2 SW7750
Calligarry Highld 84 NG6203
Callington Cnwll 4 SX3669
Callow H & W 27 SO4934
Callow End H & W 28 SO8349
Callow Hill H & W 28 SO9164
Callow Hill Wilts 20 SU0385
Callows Grave H & W 27 SO5966
Calmore Hants 10 SU3314
Calmsden Gloucs 28 SP0508
Calne Wilts 20 ST9971
Calshot Hants 10 SU4701
Calstock Cnwll 4 SX4368
Calthorpe Norfk 43 TG1831
Calthorpe Street Norfk 43 TG4025
Calthwaite Cumb 59 NY4640
Calton N York 54 SD9259
Calton Staffs 48 SK1050
Calton Green Staffs 48 SK1050
Calveley Ches 47 SJ5958
Calver Derbys 48 SK2474
Calverhall Shrops 37 SJ6037
Calverleigh Devon 7 SS9214
Calverton Bucks 30 SP7938
Calverton Notts 49 SK6149
Calvine Tays 87 NN8065
Calzeat Border 75 NT1135
Cam Gloucs 20 ST7599
Camas - luinie Highld 85 NG9428
Camasachoirce Highld 79 NM7660
Camascross Highld 85 NG6911
Camasine Highld 79 NM7561
Camastianavaig Highld 84 NG5118
Camasunary Highld 84 NG5118
Camault Muir Highld 92 NH5040
Camb Shet 103 HU4980
Camber E Susx 14 TQ9618
Camberley Surrey 22 SU8860
Camberwell Gt Lon 23 TQ3276
Camblesforth N York 56 SE6425
Cambo Nthumb 68 NZ0285
Camborne Cnwll 2 SW6440

Cambridge Cambs 31 TL4558
Cambridge Gloucs 20 SO7403
Cambrose Cnwll 2 SW6845
Cambus Cent 82 NS8593
Cambus O' May Gramp 88 NO4198
Cambusavie Platform Highld 97 NH7696
Cambusbarron Cent 81 NS7792
Cambuskenneth Cent 81 NS8094
Cambusmoon Strath 81 NS4285
Cambuswallace Strath 75 NT0438
Camden Town Gt Lon 23 TQ2784
Cameley Avon 19 ST6157
Camelford Cnwll 3 SX1083
Camelon Cent 82 NS8680
Camer's Green H & W 28 SO7735
Camerory Highld 93 NJ0131
Camerton Avon 20 ST6857
Camerton Cumb 58 NY0431
Camghouran Tays 87 NN5556
Cammachmore Gramp 89 NO9195
Cammeringham Lincs 50 SK9482
Camore Highld 97 NH7889
Campbeltown Strath 72 NR7120
Cample D & G 66 NX8993
Campmuir Tays 82 NO2137
Camps Loth 75 NT0968
Camps End Cambs 31 TL6142
Campsall S York 56 SE5313
Campsea Ashe Suffk 33 TM3356
Campsie Strath 81 NS6179
Campton Beds 30 TL1238
Campton Beds 30 TL1238
Camptown Border 68 NT6813
Camquhart Strath 80 NR9985
Camrose Dyfed 16 SM9220
Camserney Tays 87 NN8149
Camster Highld 100 ND2642
Camusnagaul Highld 86 NN0874
Camusnagaul Highld 91 NH0589
Camusteel Highld 91 NG7042
Camusterrach Highld 85 NG7141
Canada Hants 10 SU2817
Canada Hants 10 SU2818
Canadacraig Gramp 88 NO3499
Candlesby Lincs 51 TF4567
Candyburn Strath 75 NT0741
Cane End Oxon 22 SU6779
Canewdon Essex 24 TQ9094
Canfield End Essex 24 TL5821
Canford Bottom Dorset 9 SU0300
Canford Cliffs Dorset 10 SZ0689
Canford Magna Dorset 9 SZ0398
Canhams Green Suffk 32 TM0565
Canisbay Highld 100 ND3472
Canley W Mids 39 SP3077
Cann Dorset 9 ST8723
Cannich Highld 92 NH3331
Cannington Somset 19 ST2539
Cannock Staffs 38 SJ9810
Cannon Bridge H & W 27 SO4340
Canon Frome H & W 27 SO6543
Canon Pyon H & W 27 SO4548
Canonbie D & G 67 NY3976
Canons Ashby Nhants 29 SP5750
Canonstown Cnwll 2 SW5335
Canterbury Kent 15 TR1457
Cantley Norfk 43 TG3804
Cantley S York 49 SE6202
Canton S Glam 19 ST1676
Cantraywood Highld 93 NH7847
Cantsfield Lancs 54 SD6172
Canvey Island Essex 24 TQ7983
Canwick Lincs 50 SK9869
Canworthy Water Cnwll 4 SX2291
Caol Highld 86 NN1075
Caoles Highld 78 NM0848
Caonich Highld 86 NN0692
Capel Kent 13 TQ6344
Capel Surrey 12 TQ1740
Capel Bangor Dyfed 35 SN6580
Capel Betws Lleucu Dyfed 34 SN6058
Capel Coch Gwynd 44 SH4582
Capel Curig Gwynd 45 SH7258
Capel Dewi Dyfed 17 SN4720
Capel Dewi Dyfed 17 SN4542
Capel Garmon Gwynd 45 SH8155
Capel Green Suffk 33 TM3749
Capel Gwyn Gwynd 44 SH3575
Capel Gwynfe Dyfed 26 SN7222
Capel Hendre Dyfed 17 SN5911
Capel Iwan Dyfed 17 SN2836
Capel Mawr Gwynd 44 SH4171
Capel Seion Dyfed 35 SN6379
Capel St. Andrews Suffk 33 TM3748
Capel St. Mary Suffk 25 TM0838
Capel le Ferne Kent 15 TR2439
Capel-Dewi Dyfed 35 SN6282
Capelles Guern 101 SV0000
Capelulo Gwynd 45 SH7476
Capelulo Gwynd 45 SH7476
Capenhurst Ches 46 SJ3673
Capernwray Lancs 53 SD5372
Capheaton Nthumb 68 NZ0380
Caplaw Strath 73 NS4458
Capon's Green Suffk 33 TM2867
Cappelgill D & G 67 NT1409
Cappercleuch Border 75 NT2423
Capton Devon 5 SX8353
Capton Somset 7 ST0739
Caputh Tays 82 NO0840
Car Colston Notts 49 SK7242
Carbeth Inn Cent 81 NS5279
Carbis Cnwll 2 SW9999
Carbis Bay Cnwll 2 SW5238
Carbost Highld 84 NG3732
Carbost Highld 90 NG4248
Carbrook S York 49 SK3889
Carbrooke Norfk 42 TF9502
Carburton Notts 49 SK6173
Carcary Tays 89 NO6455
Cardenden Fife 82 NT2195
Cardiff S Glam 19 ST1876
Cardigan Dyfed 17 SN1846
Cardinal's Green Cambs 31 TL6147
Cardington Beds 30 TL0847
Cardington Shrops 37 SO5095
Cardinham Cnwll 3 SX1268
Cardow Gramp 94 NJ1943
Cardrona Border 75 NT3038
Cardross Strath 80 NS3477
Cardurnock Cumb 67 NY1758
Careby Lincs 40 TF0216
Careston Tays 89 NO5260
Carew Dyfed 16 SN0404
Carew Cheriton Dyfed 16 SN0402
Carew Newton Dyfed 16 SN0404
Carey H & W 27 SO5730
Carfin Strath 74 NS7759
Carfraemill Border 76 NT5053
Cargate Green Norfk 43 TG3913
Cargen D & G 66 NX9672
Cargenbridge D & G 66 NX9275
Cargill Tays 82 NO1536
Cargo Cumb 67 NY3659
Cargreen Cnwll 4 SX4262
Cargurrel Cnwll 3 SW8837
Carham Nthumb 76 NT7938
Carhampton Somset 7 ST0042
Carharrack Cnwll 2 SW7341
Carie Tays 87 NN6257
Carie Tays 87 NN6437
Carinish W Isls 102 NF8159
Carisbrooke IOW 10 SZ4888
Cark Cumb 59 SD3676
Carkeel Cnwll 4 SX4060
Carland Cross Cnwll 2 SW8454
Carlby Lincs 61 NZ2116
Carlby Lincs 40 TF0514
Carlcroft Nthumb 68 NT8311
Carleen Cnwll 2 SW6130
Carleton Cumb 67 NY4253
Carleton Cumb 59 NY5330
Carleton N York 54 SD9749
Carleton Forehoe Norfk 43 TG0905
Carleton Rode Norfk 33 TM1193
Carleton St. Peter Norfk 43 TG3402
Carlin How Cleve 62 NZ7018
Carlincraig Gramp 95 NJ6743

Carlingcott Avon 20 ST6958
Carlisle Cumb 67 NY3955
Carloggas Cnwll 3 SW8765
Carlops Border 75 NT1656
Carloway W Isls 102 NB2042
Carlton Beds 30 SP9555
Carlton Cambs 32 TL6452
Carlton Cleve 62 NZ3921
Carlton Leics 39 SK3905
Carlton N York 56 SE6423
Carlton N York 56 SE6423
Carlton N York 62 NZ5004
Carlton Notts 61 SE6086
Carlton S York 49 SK6041
Carlton S York 55 SE3610
Carlton Suffk 33 TM3864
Carlton W York 55 SE3327
Carlton Colville Suffk 33 TM5190
Carlton Curlieu Leics 40 SP6997
Carlton Green Cambs 32 TL6451
Carlton Husthwaite N York 62 SE4976
Carlton Miniott N York 62 SE3980
Carlton Scroop Lincs 50 SK9445
Carlton in Lindrick Notts 49 SK5984
Carlton-le-Moorland Lincs 50 SK9058
Carlton-on-Trent Notts 50 SK7963
Carluke Strath 74 NS8450
Carmacoup Strath 74 NS7927
Carmarthen Dyfed 17 SN4020
Carmel Dyfed 17 SN5816
Carmel Gwynd 44 SH3882
Carmel Gwynd 44 SH4954
Carminowe Cnwll 2 SW6624
Carmunnock Strath 74 NS5957
Carmyle Strath 74 NS6462
Carmyllie Tays 89 NO5542
Carn Brea Cnwll 2 SW6841
Carn-Gorm Highld 85 NG9520
Carnaby Humb 57 TA1465
Carnach W Isls 90 NG2297
Carnan W Isls 102 NF8143
Carnbee Fife 83 NO5206
Carnbo Tays 82 NO0503
Carndu Highld 85 NG8927
Carnduff Strath 74 NS6646
Carnell Strath 73 NS4731
Carnforth Lancs 53 SD4970
Carnhell Green Cnwll 2 SW6137
Carnie Gramp 89 NJ8005
Carnkie Cnwll 2 SW7134
Carno Powys 35 SN9696
Carnock Fife 82 NT0489
Carnon Downs Cnwll 2 SW7940
Carnousie Gramp 94 NJ6650
Carnoustie Tays 83 NO5534
Carnwath Strath 75 NS9746
Carol Green W Mids 39 SP2577
Carpalla Cnwll 3 SW9654
Carperby N York 61 SE0089
Carr S York 49 SK5091
Carr Gate W York 55 SE3024
Carr Shield Nthumb 68 NY8047
Carr Vale Derbys 49 SK4670
Carradale Strath 72 NR8138
Carragrich W Isls 90 NG2098
Carrbridge Highld 93 NH9022
Carrefour Jersey 101 SV0000
Carreglefn Gwynd 44 SH3889
Carrhouse Humb 56 SE7706
Carrick Fife 83 NO4422
Carrick Dur 71 NR9187
Carrick Castle Strath 80 NS1994
Carriden Cent 82 NT0281
Carrington Gt Man 47 SJ7492
Carrington Loth 75 NT3160
Carrington Moss Gt Man 47 SJ7592
Carrosh Nmery Cnwll 3 SX0188
Carrog Clwyd 45 SH7548
Carron Cent 82 NS8882
Carron Gramp 94 NJ2241
Carron Highld 93 NJ1234
Carron Bridge Cent 81 NS7483
Carronbridge D & G 66 NX8698
Carronshore Cent 82 NS8983
Carruth House Strath 73 NS3566
Carrutherstown D & G 67 NY1071
Carrville Dur 69 NZ3243
Carsaig Strath 79 NM5421
Carscreugh D & G 64 NX2260
Carse Gray Tays 88 NO4553
Carseriggen D & G 64 NX3197
Carsethorn D & G 66 NX9959
Carshalton Gt Lon 23 TQ2764
Carsie Tays 88 NO1742
Carsington Derbys 48 SK2553
Carskiey Strath 72 NR6508
Carsphairn D & G 65 NS5693
Carstairs Strath 75 NS9346
Carstairs Junction Strath 75 NS9545
Carswell Marsh Oxon 21 SU3298
Carter Bar Border 68 NT6907
Carters Green Essex 23 TL5111
Carterton Oxon 29 SP2706
Carterway Heads Nthumb 68 NZ0552
Carthew Cnwll 3 SX0086
Carthorpe N York 62 SE3083
Cartland Strath 74 NS8646
Cartledge Derbys 49 SK3477
Cartmel Cumb 59 SD3778
Carway Dyfed 17 SN4606
Carwinley Cumb 67 NY4073
Cashe's Green Gloucs 28 SO8305
Cashlie Tays 87 NN4942
Cashmoor Dorset 9 ST9813
Cassington Oxon 29 SP4511
Cassop Colliery Dur 62 NZ3438
Castel Guern 101 SV0000
Castellau M Glam 18 ST0687
Casterton Cumb 60 SD6279
Casterton Lancs 60 SD6279
Castle Gwynd 45 SH7669
Castle Acre Norfk 42 TF8115
Castle Ashby Nhants 30 SP8659
Castle Bolton N York 61 SE0391
Castle Bromwich W Mids 38 SP1489
Castle Bytham Lincs 40 SK9818
Castle Caereinion Powys 36 SJ1605
Castle Camps Cambs 32 TL6342
Castle Carrock Cumb 67 NY5455
Castle Cary Somset 9 ST6332
Castle Combe Wilts 20 ST8477
Castle Donington Leics 39 SK4427
Castle Douglas D & G 65 NX7662
Castle Eaton Wilts 20 SU1495
Castle Eden Dur 62 NZ4338
Castle End Cambs 40 TF1208
Castle Frome H & W 28 SO6645
Castle Green Cumb 59 SD5391
Castle Gresley Derbys 39 SK2717
Castle Hedingham Essex 24 TL7835
Castle Hill Suffk 33 TM1446
Castle Howard N York 56 SE7069
Castle Inn Cumb 59 NY2233
Castle Kennedy D & G 64 NX1059
Castle Lachlan Strath 80 NS0195
Castle O'er D & G 67 NY2492
Castle Pulverbatch Shrops 36 SJ4202
Castle Rising Norfk 42 TF6624
Castle Stuart Highld 93 NH7349
Castlebay W Isls 102 NL6698
Castlebythe Dyfed 16 SN0229
Castlecary Strath 81 NS7878
Castlecraig Highld 93 NH8289
Castleford W York 55 SE4225
Castlehill Border 75 NT2135
Castlehill Highld 100 ND1968
Castlehill Strath 74 NS8452
Castlemartin Dyfed 16 SR9198
Castlemilk D & G 67 NY1577
Castlemilk Strath 74 NS6059
Castleside Dur 62 NZ0748
Castlethorpe Bucks 30 SP7944
Castlethorpe Humb 56 SE9807
Castleton Border 67 NY5190
Castleton Derbys 48 SK1582
Castleton Gt Man 54 SD8810
Castleton Gwent 19 ST2583

Castleton N York	62	NZ6808
Castleton Strath	71	NR8884
Castletown Highld	93	NH7442
Castletown Highld	100	ND1967
Castletown IOM	52	SC2667
Castley N York	69	NS2358
Castley T & W	55	SE2645
Caston Norfk	42	TL9597
Castor Cambs	40	TL1298
Cat & Fiddle Inn Derbys	48	SK0072
Cat's Ash Gwent	19	ST3790
Catacol Strath	71	NR9149
Catcliffe S York	49	SK4288
Catcomb Wilts	20	SU0076
Catcott Somset	19	ST3939
Catcott Burtle Somset	19	ST4043
Caterham Surrey	23	TQ3455
Catfield Norfk	43	TG3821
Catfirth Shet	103	HU4354
Catford Gt Lon	23	TQ3772
Catforth Lancs	53	SD4735
Cath Pair Border	76	NT4646
Cathcart Strath	74	NS5860
Cathedine Powys	26	SO1425
Catherington Hants	11	SU6914
Catherston Leweston Dorset	8	SY3694
Catisfield Hants	11	SU5406
Catlodge Highld	87	NN6392
Catlowdy Cumb	67	NY4677
Catmere End Essex	31	TL4939
Catmore Berks	21	SU4580
Caton Lancs	53	SD5364
Caton Green Lancs	53	SD5564
Catrine Strath	74	NS5225
Catsfield E Susx	14	TQ7213
Catsham Somset	8	ST5534
Catshill H & W	38	SO9673
Cattadale Strath	72	NR6710
Cattal N York	55	SE4454
Cattawade Suffk	25	TM1033
Catterall Lancs	53	SD5042
Catterick N York	61	SE2397
Catterlen Cumb	59	NY4833
Catterton N York	55	SE5145
Catteshall Surrey	12	SU9844
Catthorpe Leics	39	SP5578
Cattistock Dorset	9	SY5999
Catton Cumb	68	NY8257
Catton N York	62	SE3678
Catton Norfk	43	TG2312
Catwick Humb	57	TA1245
Catworth Cambs	30	TL0973
Caudle Green Gloucs	28	SO9410
Caulcott Oxon	29	SP5024
Cauldhame Cent	81	NS6493
Cauldmill Border	76	NT5315
Cauldon Staffs	48	SK0749
Cauldside D & G	67	NY4480
Caulkerbush D & G	66	NX8357
Caundle Marsh Dorset	9	ST6713
Caunton Notts	50	SK7460
Causeway End D & G	64	NX4260
Causewayend Strath	75	NT0336
Causewayhead Cent	81	NS8095
Causey Park Nthumb	69	NZ1794
Causeyend Gramp	95	NJ9419
Caute Devon	6	SS4310
Cautley Cumb	60	SD6994
Cavendish Suffk	32	TL8046
Cavenham Suffk	32	TL7669
Caversfield Oxon	29	SP5825
Caversham Berks	22	SU7274
Caverswall Staffs	48	SJ9542
Caverton Mill Border	76	NT7425
Cavil Humb	56	SE7630
Cawdor Highld	93	NH8450
Cawood N York	56	SE5737
Cawsand Cnwll	4	SX4350
Cawston Norfk	43	TG1323
Cawthorne S York	55	SE2807
Caxton Cambs	31	TL3058
Caxton End Cambs	31	TL2759
Caynham Shrops	37	SO5573
Caythorpe Lincs	50	SK9348
Caythorpe Notts	49	SK6845
Cayton N York	63	TA0583
Ceannacroc Lodge Highld	92	NH3211
Cefn Gwent	19	ST2788
Cefn Cribwr M Glam	18	SS8582
Cefn Mably M Glam	19	ST2284
Cefn-brith Clwyd	45	SH9350
Cefn-mawr Clwyd	36	SJ2842
Cefneithin Dyfed	17	SN5514
Cefngorwydd Powys	26	SN9045
Cellarhead Staffs	48	SJ9547
Cemaes Gwynd	44	SH3793
Cemmaes Powys	35	SH8406
Cemmaes Powys	35	SH8406
Cemmaes Road Powys	35	SH8104
Cenarth Dyfed	17	SN2641
Cennin Gwynd	44	SH4645
Ceres Fife	83	NO4011
Cerne Abbas Dorset	9	ST6601
Cerney Wick Gloucs	20	SU0796
Cerrigceinwen Gwynd	44	SH4274
Cerrigydrudion Clwyd	45	SH9548
Ceunant Gwynd	44	SH5361
Chaceley Gloucs	28	SO8530
Chacewater Cnwll	2	SW7444
Chackmore Bucks	30	SP6835
Chacombe Nhants	29	SP4943
Chadbury H & W	28	SP0146
Chadderton Gt Man	54	SD9204
Chadderton Fold Gt Man	54	SD9006
Chaddesden Derbys	49	SK3737
Chaddesley Corbett H & W	38	SO8973
Chaddlehanger Devon	4	SX4678
Chaddleworth Berks	21	SU4177
Chadlington Oxon	29	SP3222
Chadshunt Warwks	29	SP3552
Chadwell Leics	40	SK7824
Chadwell End Beds	30	TL0865
Chadwell Heath Gt Lon	23	TQ4888
Chadwell St. Mary Essex	24	TQ6478
Chadwick H & W	28	SO8369
Chadwick End W Mids	39	SP2073
Chaffcombe Somset	8	ST3510
Chagford Devon	5	SX7087
Chailey E Susx	13	TQ3919
Chainbridge Cambs	41	TL4299
Chainhurst Kent	14	TQ7248
Chaldon Surrey	23	TQ3055
Chaldon Herring or East Chaldon Dorset	9	SY7983
Chale IOW	10	SZ4877
Chale Green IOW	10	SZ4879
Chalfont Common Bucks	22	TQ0092
Chalfont St. Giles Bucks	22	SU9893
Chalfont St. Peter Bucks	22	TQ0090
Chalford Gloucs	20	SO8902
Chalford Oxon	20	SP7101
Chalgrave Beds	30	TL0127
Chalgrove Oxon	21	SU6396
Chalk Kent	14	TQ6773
Chalkwell Kent	14	TQ8963
Challaborough Devon	5	SX6545
Challacombe Devon	7	SS6941
Challoch D & G	64	NX3867
Challock Lees Kent	15	TR0050
Chalmington Dorset	9	ST5901
Chalton Beds	30	TL0326
Chalton Hants	11	SU7316
Chalvey Berks	22	SU9679
Chalvington E Susx	13	TQ5109
Chandler's Cross Herts	22	TQ0698
Chandler's Ford Hants	10	SU4320
Channel's Green Beds	30	TL1057
Chantry Suffk	33	TM1443
Chapel Fife	83	NT2593
Chapel Allerton Somset	19	ST4050
Chapel Allerton W York	55	SE3037
Chapel Amble Cnwll	3	SW9975
Chapel Brampton Nhants	30	SP7266

Chapel Chorlton Staffs	37	SJ8137
Chapel End Beds	30	TL1057
Chapel End Cambs	40	TL1282
Chapel Green Warwks	29	SP4660
Chapel Haddlesey N York	56	SE5826
Chapel Hall Strath	73	NS1368
Chapel Hill Gramp	95	NK0635
Chapel Hill Gwent	19	SO5300
Chapel Hill Lincs	51	TF2054
Chapel Hill N York	55	SE3346
Chapel Lawn Shrops	36	SO3176
Chapel Le Dale N York	60	SD7377
Chapel Leigh Somset	8	ST1222
Chapel Row Berks	21	SU5669
Chapel St. Leonards Lincs	51	TF5572
Chapel Stile Cumb	58	NY3205
Chapel of Garioch Gramp	95	NJ7124
Chapel-en-le-Frith Derbys	48	SK0580
Chapelend Way Essex	32	TL7139
Chapelhall Strath	74	NS7862
Chapelhill Tays	82	NO0030
Chapelhope Border	67	NT2308
Chapelknowe D & G	67	NY3173
Chapelton Devon	6	SS5826
Chapelton Strath	74	NS6848
Chapelton Tays	89	NO6247
Chapeltown Lancs	54	SD7315
Chapeltown S York	49	SK3596
Chapmans Well Devon	4	SX3592
Chapmanslade Wilts	20	ST8247
Chapmore End Herts	31	TL3216
Chappel Essex	24	TL8928
Charaton M Glam	4	SX3169
Chard Somset	8	ST3208
Chard Junction Somset	8	ST3404
Chardleigh Green Somset	8	ST3110
Chardstock Devon	8	ST3004
Charfield Avon	20	ST7292
Charing Kent	14	TQ9549
Charing Heath Kent	14	TQ9249
Charingworth Gloucs	29	SP1939
Charlbury Oxon	29	SP3519
Charlcombe Avon	20	ST7467
Charlcutt Wilts	20	ST9875
Charlecote Warwks	29	SP2656
Charles Devon	7	SS6832
Charles Tye Suffk	32	TM0252
Charleston Tays	88	NO3845
Charlestown Cnwll	3	SX0351
Charlestown Fife	82	NT0683
Charlestown Gramp	89	NJ9300
Charlestown Gt Man	47	SD8100
Charlestown Highld	91	NG8174
Charlestown Highld	92	NH6448
Charlestown W York	54	SD9726
Charlestown W York	55	SE1938
Charlinch Somset	19	ST2338
Charlton Gt Lon	23	TQ4277
Charlton Nhants	29	SP5236
Charlton Nthumb	68	NY8184
Charlton Oxon	21	SU4088
Charlton Shrops	37	SJ5911
Charlton Somset	19	ST2827
Charlton Somset	19	ST6242
Charlton W Susx	11	SU8812
Charlton Wilts	20	ST9688
Charlton Wilts	9	ST9021
Charlton Wilts	20	SU1155
Charlton Wilts	10	SU1723
Charlton Abbots Gloucs	28	SP0324
Charlton Adam Somset	8	ST5328
Charlton Horethorne Somset	9	ST6623
Charlton Kings Gloucs	28	SO9620
Charlton Mackrell Somset	8	ST5228
Charlton Marshall Dorset	9	ST8903
Charlton Musgrove Somset	9	ST7229
Charlton on the Hill Dorset	9	ST8903
Charlton-on-Otmoor Oxon	29	SP5616
Charlwood Hants	11	SU6731
Charlwood Surrey	12	TQ2441
Charminster Dorset	9	SY6792
Charmouth Dorset	8	SY3693
Charndon Bucks	30	SP6724
Charney Bassett Oxon	21	SU3894
Charnock Richard Lancs	53	SD5615
Charsfield Suffk	33	TM2556
Chart Sutton Kent	14	TQ8049
Charter Alley Hants	21	SU5957
Charterhall Border	76	NT7647
Charterhouse Somset	19	ST4955
Chartershall Cent	81	NS7990
Chartham Kent	15	TR1054
Chartham Hatch Kent	15	TR1056
Chartridge Bucks	22	SP9303
Charwelton Nhants	29	SP5355
Chase Terrace Staffs	38	SK0409
Chastleton Oxon	29	SP2429
Chatburn Lancs	54	SD7644
Chatcull Staffs	37	SJ7934
Chatham Gwent	19	ST2189
Chatham Kent	14	TQ7567
Chatham Green Essex	24	TL7115
Chathill Nthumb	77	NU1827
Chattenden Kent	14	TQ7572
Chatteris Cambs	41	TL3985
Chattisham Suffk	33	TM0942
Chatto Border	76	NT7717
Chatton Nthumb	77	NU0528
Chawleigh Devon	7	SS7112
Chawton Hants	11	SU7037
Cheadle Gt Man	47	SJ8688
Cheadle Staffs	48	SK0043
Cheadle Hulme Gt Man	47	SJ8786
Cheam Gt Lon	23	TQ2563
Chearsley Bucks	22	SP7110
Checkendon Oxon	22	SU6683
Checkley Ches	47	SJ7346
Checkley Staffs	48	SK0237
Chedburgh Suffk	32	TL7957
Cheddar Somset	19	ST4553
Cheddington Bucks	30	SP9217
Cheddleton Staffs	48	SJ9752
Cheddon Fitzpaine Somset	8	ST2327
Chedglow Wilts	20	ST9492
Chedgrave Norfk	43	TM3699
Chedington Dorset	8	ST4805
Chediston Suffk	33	TM3577
Chedworth Gloucs	28	SP0511
Chedzoy Somset	19	ST3337
Cheeseman's Green Kent	15	TR0238
Cheetham Hill Gt Man	47	SD8301
Cheetwood Gt Man	47	SJ8399
Cheldon Devon	7	SS7313
Chelford Ches	47	SJ8174
Chellington Beds	30	SP9555
Chelmarsh Shrops	37	SO7288
Chelmorton Derbys	48	SK1169
Chelmsford Essex	24	TL7007
Chelmsley Wood W Mids	38	SP1886
Chelsea Gt Lon	23	TQ2778
Chelsfield Gt Lon	23	TQ4864
Chelsworth Suffk	32	TL9748
Cheltenham Gloucs	28	SO9422
Chelveston Nhants	30	SP9969
Chelvey Avon	19	ST4668
Chelwood Avon	19	ST6361
Chelwood Gate E Susx	13	TQ4130
Chelworth Lower Green Wilts	20	SU0892
Chelworth Upper Green Wilts	20	SU0892
Cheney Longville Shrops	36	SO4288
Chenies Bucks	22	TQ0198
Chepstow Gwent	19	ST5393
Cherhill Wilts	20	SU0370
Cherington Gloucs	20	ST9098
Cherington Warwks	29	SP2936
Cheriton Devon	7	SS7346
Cheriton Devon	8	ST1001
Cheriton Kent	15	TR2037
Cheriton W Glam	17	SS4593
Cheriton Bishop Devon	5	SX7793
Cheriton Fitzpaine Devon	7	SS8606
Cherrington or Stackpole Elidor Dyfed	16	SR9997
Cherrington Shrops	37	SJ6619
Cherry Burton Humb	56	SE9842
Cherry Hinton Cambs	31	TL4856
Cherry Orchard H & W	28	SO8553
Cherry Willingham Lincs	50	TF0372

Cherry Willingham Lincs	50	TF0372
Chertsey Surrey	22	TQ0466
Cheselbourne Dorset	9	SY7699
Chesham Bucks	22	SP9601
Chesham Bois Bucks	22	SU9699
Cheshunt Herts	23	TL3502
Cheslyn Hay Staffs	38	SJ9707
Chessetts Wood Warwks	38	SP1873
Chessington Surrey	23	TQ1863
Chester Ches	46	SJ4066
Chester Moor Dur	69	NZ2649
Chester-le-Street T & W	69	NZ2751
Chesterblade Somset	20	ST6641
Chesterfield Derbys	49	SK3871
Chesterfield Staffs	38	SK1005
Chesters Border	76	NT3765
Chesters Border	76	NT6022
Chesters Border	68	NT6210
Chesterton Cambs	31	TL4660
Chesterton Cambs	40	TL1295
Chesterton Gloucs	20	SP0200
Chesterton Oxon	29	SP5621
Chesterton Shrops	37	SO7697
Chesterton Green Warwks	29	SP3558
Chesterwood Nthumb	68	NY8365
Chestfield Kent	15	TR1365
Chestnut Street Kent	14	TQ8862
Cheston Devon	5	SX6758
Cheswardine Shrops	37	SJ7130
Cheswick Nthumb	77	NU0346
Chetnole Dorset	9	ST6008
Chettiscombe Devon	7	SS9614
Chettisham Cambs	41	TL5483
Chettle Dorset	9	ST9513
Chetton Shrops	37	SO6690
Chetwode Bucks	29	SP6429
Chetwynd Shrops	37	SJ7321
Chetwynd Aston Shrops	37	SJ7517
Cheveley Cambs	32	TL6861
Chevening Kent	23	TQ4857
Cheverton IOW	10	SZ4584
Chevington Suffk	32	TL7860
Chevington Drift Nthumb	69	NZ2598
Chevithorne Devon	7	SS9715
Chew Magna Avon	19	ST5763
Chew Stoke Avon	19	ST5561
Chewton Keynsham Avon	19	ST6566
Chewton Mendip Somset	19	ST5952
Chicheley Bucks	30	SP9046
Chichester W Susx	11	SU8604
Chickerell Dorset	9	SY6480
Chicklade Wilts	9	ST9134
Chidden Hants	11	SU6517
Chiddingfold Surrey	12	SU9635
Chiddingly E Susx	13	TQ5414
Chiddingstone Kent	13	TQ5045
Chiddingstone Causeway Kent	13	TQ5146
Chideock Dorset	8	SY4292
Chidham W Susx	11	SU7903
Chidswell W York	55	SE2623
Chieveley Berks	21	SU4773
Chignall Smealy Essex	24	TL6611
Chignall St. James Essex	24	TL6610
Chigwell Essex	23	TQ4494
Chigwell Row Essex	23	TQ4693
Chilbolton Hants	10	SU3939
Chilcomb Hants	10	SU5028
Chilcombe Dorset	8	SY5291
Chilcompton Somset	19	ST6452
Chilcote Leics	39	SK2811
Child Okeford Dorset	9	ST8312
Child's Ercall Shrops	37	SJ6625
Childer Thornton Ches	46	SJ3677
Childrey Oxon	21	SU3887
Childswickham H & W	28	SP0738
Childwall Mersyd	46	SJ4189
Childwick Bury Herts	22	TL1410
Chilfrome Dorset	9	SY5898
Chilgrove W Susx	11	SU8314
Chilham Kent	15	TR0653
Chilla Devon	6	SS4402
Chillaton Devon	4	SX4382
Chillenden Kent	15	TR2653
Chillerton IOW	10	SZ4984
Chillesford Suffk	33	TM3852
Chillingham Nthumb	77	NU0525
Chillington Devon	5	SX7942
Chillington Somset	8	ST3811
Chilmark Wilts	9	ST9632
Chilmington Green Kent	15	TQ9740
Chilson Oxon	29	SP3119
Chilsworthy Cnwll	4	SX4172
Chilsworthy Devon	6	SS3206
Chilthorne Domer Somset	8	ST5219
Chiltington E Susx	13	TQ3815
Chilton Bucks	22	SP6811
Chilton Oxon	21	SU4885
Chilton Suffk	32	TL8942
Chilton Candover Hants	21	SU5940
Chilton Cantelo Somset	8	ST5622
Chilton Foliat Wilts	21	SU3170
Chilton Polden Somset	19	ST3739
Chilton Street Suffk	32	TL7547
Chilton Trinity Somset	19	ST2939
Chilworth Hants	10	SU4118
Chilworth Surrey	12	TQ0247
Chimney Oxon	21	SP3501
Chineham Hants	21	SU6554
Chingford Gt Lon	23	TQ3894
Chinley Derbys	48	SK0482
Chinnor Oxon	22	SP7501
Chipnall Shrops	37	SJ7231
Chippenham Bucks	22	SU9480
Chippenham Cambs	32	TL6669
Chippenham Wilts	20	ST9273
Chipperfield Herts	22	TL0401
Chipping Herts	31	TL3532
Chipping Lancs	54	SD6243
Chipping Campden Gloucs	28	SP1539
Chipping Norton Oxon	29	SP3127
Chipping Ongar Essex	24	TL5503
Chipping Sodbury Avon	20	ST7281
Chipping Warden Nhants	29	SP4948
Chipstable Somset	7	ST0427
Chipstead Kent	23	TQ5056
Chipstead Surrey	23	TQ2757
Chirbury Shrops	36	SO2698
Chirk Clwyd	36	SJ2938
Chirnside Border	77	NT8756
Chirnsidebridge Border	77	NT8556
Chirton Wilts	20	SU0757
Chisbury Wilts	21	SU2766
Chiselborough Somset	8	ST4614
Chiseldon Wilts	21	SU1879
Chisholme Border	67	NT4112
Chislehampton Oxon	21	SU5999
Chislehurst Gt Lon	23	TQ4470
Chislet Kent	15	TR2264
Chisley W York	54	SE0028
Chiswellgreen Herts	22	TL1304
Chiswick Gt Lon	23	TQ2078
Chisworth Derbys	48	SJ9991
Chisworth Derbys	48	SJ9991
Chithurst W Susx	11	SU8423
Chittering Cambs	31	TL4969
Chitterne Wilts	20	ST9943
Chittlehamholt Devon	7	SS6421
Chittlehampton Devon	7	SS6325
Chittlehampton Devon	7	SS6325
Chittoe Wilts	20	ST9566
Chivelstone Devon	5	SX7838
Chivelstone Devon	5	SX7838
Chlenry D & G	64	NX1261
Chobham Surrey	22	SU9762
Cholderton Wilts	21	SU2242
Cholesbury Bucks	22	SP9307
Chollerton Nthumb	68	NY9372
Cholstrey H & W	27	SO4859
Chop Lane Devon	58	SE5599
Chop Gate N York	62	SE5699
Choppington T & W	69	NZ2484
Chopwell T & W	69	NZ1158
Chorley Ches	46	SJ5751
Chorley Lancs	54	SD5817
Chorley Shrops	37	SO6983
Chorley Staffs	38	SK0711
Chorleywood Herts	22	TQ0396
Chorleywood West Herts	22	TQ0296
Chorlton Ches	47	SJ7250

Chorlton Lane Ches	46	SJ4548
Chorlton-cum-Hardy Gt Man	47	SJ8193
Choulton Shrops	36	SO3788
Chowley Ches	46	SJ4756
Chrishall Essex	31	TL4439
Chriswell Strath	80	NS2274
Christchurch Cambs	41	TL4996
Christchurch Dorset	10	SZ1593
Christchurch Gloucs	27	SO5713
Christchurch Gwent	19	ST3489
Christian Malford Wilts	20	ST9678
Christleton Ches	46	SJ4465
Christmas Common Oxon	22	SU7193
Christon Avon	19	ST3956
Christon Bank Nthumb	77	NU2123
Christow Devon	5	SX8385
Christkirk Gramp	94	NJ6027
Chudleigh Devon	5	SX8679
Chudleigh Knighton Devon	5	SX8477
Chulmleigh Devon	7	SS6814
Chunal Derbys	48	SK0391
Church Lancs	54	SD7429
Church Ashton Shrops	37	SJ7317
Church Brampton Nhants	30	SP7165
Church Broughton Derbys	39	SK2033
Church Crookham Hants	22	SU8152
Church End Beds	30	TL0334
Church End Beds	31	TL1937
Church End Beds	30	TL0458
Church End Beds	30	TL1059
Church End Cambs	41	TF3909
Church End Cambs	30	TL0093
Church End Cambs	41	TL2083
Church End Essex	24	TL6323
Church End Essex	24	TL7228
Church End Essex	24	TL7416
Church End Gt Lon	23	TQ2490
Church End Hants	22	SU6756
Church End Herts	31	TL4422
Church End Lincs	51	TF4195
Church End Warwks	39	SP2892
Church Enstone Oxon	29	SP3725
Church Fenton N York	55	SE5136
Church Green Devon	8	SY1796
Church Hanborough Oxon	29	SP4212
Church Hill Ches	47	SJ6466
Church Hill Staffs	38	SK0012
Church Houses N York	62	SE6697
Church Knowle Dorset	9	SY9481
Church Langton Leics	40	SP7293
Church Lawford Warwks	39	SP4576
Church Lawton Staffs	47	SJ8255
Church Leigh Staffs	38	SK0235
Church Lench H & W	28	SP0251
Church Mayfield Staffs	48	SK1544
Church Minshull Ches	47	SJ6660
Church Norton W Susx	11	SZ8695
Church Preen Shrops	37	SO5498
Church Pulverbatch Shrops	36	SJ4303
Church Stoke Powys	36	SO2694
Church Stowe Nhants	29	SP6357
Church Street Kent	14	TQ7174
Church Stretton Shrops	36	SO4593
Church Town Humb	56	SE7806
Church Village M Glam	18	ST0886
Church Warsop Notts	49	SK5666
Churcham Gloucs	28	SO7618
Churchbridge Staffs	38	SJ9808
Churchdown Gloucs	28	SO8819
Churchend Essex	25	TR0093
Churchill Avon	19	ST4359
Churchill Devon	8	ST2901
Churchill H & W	28	SO8263
Churchill H & W	38	SO8879
Churchill Oxon	29	SP2824
Churchill Green Avon	19	ST3460
Churchingford Devon	8	ST2112
Churchover Warwks	39	SP5180
Churchstow Devon	5	SX7145
Churchthorpe Lincs	51	TF3297
Churchtown Cumb	59	NY3242
Churchtown Derbys	49	SK2663
Churchtown IOM	52	SC4294
Churchtown Lancs	53	SD4843
Churnsike Lodge Nthumb	68	NY6777
Churston Ferrers Devon	5	SX9056
Churt Surrey	11	SU8538
Churton Ches	46	SJ4156
Churwell W York	55	SE2729
Chute Lodge Wilts	21	SU3151
Chwilog Gwynd	44	SH4338
Chyanvounder Cnwll	2	SW6522
Cilcain Clwyd	46	SJ1765
Cilcennin Dyfed	34	SN5160
Cilcewydd Powys	36	SJ2204
Cilfrew W Glam	18	SN7700
Cilfynydd M Glam	18	ST0892
Cilgerran Dyfed	17	SN1943
Cilgwrn Dyfed	26	SN7429
Ciliau-Aeron Dyfed	34	SN5058
Cilmaengwn W Glam	26	SN7406
Cilmery Powys	26	SO0051
Cilmery Powys	26	SO0051
Cilrhedyn Dyfed	17	SN2835
Cilsan Dyfed	17	SN5922
Ciltalgarth Gwynd	45	SH8840
Cilycwm Dyfed	26	SN7540
Cinderford Gloucs	18	SS7696
Cinderford Gloucs	27	SO6513
Cirencester Gloucs	20	SP0201
Citadilla N York	61	NZ2200
Clabhach Strath	78	NM1858
Clachaig Strath	80	NS1181
Clachan Highld	84	NG5436
Clachan Highld	91	NR7656
Clachan Strath	79	NM7819
Clachan Strath	79	NM8843
Clachan Strath	84	NN1812
Clachan W Isls	102	NF7746
Clachan W Isls	102	NF8163
Clachan Mor Strath	78	NL9847
Clachan-Seil Strath	79	NM7718
Clachanmore D & G	64	NX3575
Clachbreck Strath	71	NR7675
Clachnaharry Highld	92	NH6446
Clackavoid Tays	88	NO1463
Clackmannan Cent	82	NS9191
Clackmarrass Gramp	94	NJ2458
Clacton-on-Sea Essex	25	TM1715
Cladich Strath	80	NN0921
Cladswell H & W	28	SP0458
Claggan Highld	79	NM6649
Claigan Highld	90	NG2354
Clandown Avon	20	ST6955
Clanfield Hants	11	SU6916
Clanfield Oxon	21	SP2801
Clanville Hants	21	SU3148
Clanville Somset	9	ST6232
Clanyard D & G	64	NX1037
Claonaig Strath	71	NR8656
Clapgate Herts	31	TL4424
Clapham Beds	30	TL0352
Clapham Gt Lon	23	TQ2875
Clapham N York	54	SD7469
Clapham W Susx	12	TQ0906
Clapton Somset	8	ST4006
Clapton Somset	19	ST6453
Clapton Somset	20	ST6852
Clapton-in-Gordano Avon	19	ST4773
Clapton-on-the-Hill Gloucs	28	SP1617
Claravale T & W	69	NZ1361
Clarbeston Dyfed	16	SN0421
Clarbeston Road Dyfed	16	SN0121
Clarborough Notts	50	SK7383
Clare Suffk	32	TL7745
Clarebrand D & G	65	NX7666
Clarencefield D & G	67	NY0968
Clarewood Nthumb	68	NZ0169
Clarilaw Border	76	NT5218
Clarken Green Hants	11	SU5631
Clarkston Strath	74	NS5757
Clashmore Highld	98	NC0331
Clashmore Highld	97	NH7489
Clashnessie Highld	98	NC0530
Clashnoir Gramp	94	NJ2222
Clathy Tays	75	NS9920
Clathymore Tays	82	NO0121

Place	Sheet	Grid
Clatt Gramp	94	NJ5326
Clatter Powys	35	SN9994
Clatworthy Somset	7	ST0530
Claughton Lancs	53	SD5342
Claughton Lancs	53	SD5666
Claughton Mersyd	46	SJ3088
Claverham Warwks	29	SP1965
Claverham Avon	19	ST4566
Clavering Essex	31	TL4731
Claverley Shrops	37	SO7993
Claverton Avon	20	ST7864
Clawdd-coch S Glam	18	ST0577
Clawdd-newydd Clwyd	46	SJ0852
Clawton Devon	6	SX3599
Claxby Lincs	50	TF1194
Claxton N York	56	SE6959
Claxton N York	56	SE6960
Clay Coton Nhants	39	SP5977
Clay Cross Derbys	49	SK3963
Clay End Herts	31	TL3024
Claybrooke Magna Leics	39	SP4988
Claydon Oxon	29	SP4549
Claydon Suffk	33	TM1349
Claygate D & G	67	NY3979
Claygate Kent	14	TQ7144
Claygate Surrey	22	TQ1563
Clayhanger Devon	7	ST0222
Clayhidon Devon	8	ST1615
Clayhill E Susx	14	TQ8323
Clayhill Hants	10	SU3007
Clayock Highld	100	ND1659
Claypits Gloucs	20	SO7606
Claypole Lincs	50	SK8449
Clayton S York	55	SE4507
Clayton W Susx	12	TQ2914
Clayton W York	55	SE1131
Clayton West W York	55	SE2511
Clayton-le-Moors Lancs	54	SD7530
Clayton-le-Woods Lancs	53	SD5622
Clayworth Notts	49	SK7288
Cleadale Highld	84	NM4789
Cleadon T & W	69	NZ3862
Clearbrook Devon	4	SX5265
Clearwell Gloucs	27	SO5608
Cleasby N York	61	NZ2412
Cleat Ork	103	ND4584
Cleatlam Dur	61	NZ1118
Cleator Cumb	58	NY0123
Cleator Moor Cumb	58	NY0125
Cleckheaton W York	55	SE1825
Clee St. Margaret Shrops	37	SO5684
Cleehill Shrops	37	SO5975
Cleekhimin Strath	74	NS7658
Cleethorpes Humb	57	TA3008
Cleeton St. Mary Shrops	37	SO6178
Cleeve Avon	19	ST4666
Cleeve Oxon	21	SU6081
Cleeve Hill Gloucs	28	SO9827
Cleeve Prior H & W	28	SP0849
Clehonger H & W	27	SO4637
Cleish Tays	82	NT0998
Cleland Strath	74	NS7958
Clement Street Kent	14	TQ5671
Clenamacrie Strath	80	NM9228
Clenchwarton Norfk	41	TF5920
Clent H & W	38	SO9279
Clenterty Gramp	95	NJ7760
Cleobury Mortimer Shrops	37	SO6775
Cleobury North Shrops	37	SO6287
Cleongart Strath	72	NR6734
Clephanton Highld	93	NH8150
Cleuch Head Border	67	NT5910
Cleuch-head D & G	66	NS8200
Clevancy Wilts	20	SU0575
Clevedon Avon	19	ST4071
Cleveleys Lancs	53	SD3143
Cleverton Wilts	20	ST9785
Clewer Somset	19	ST4351
Cley next the Sea Norfk	42	TG0444
Cliburn Cumb	59	NY5724
Cliddesden Hants	21	SU6349
Cliff Warwks	39	SP2198
Cliff End E Susx	14	TQ8813
Cliffe Dur	61	NZ2015
Cliffe N York	56	SE6631
Clifford W York	27	SO2445
Clifford W York	55	SE4244
Clifford Chambers Warwks	29	SP1952
Clifford's Mesne Gloucs	28	SO7023
Clifton Avon	19	ST5774
Clifton Beds	31	TL1639
Clifton Cumb	59	NY5326
Clifton Derbys	48	SK1644
Clifton H & W	28	SO8446
Clifton Lancs	53	SD4630
Clifton N York	56	SE5953
Clifton Notts	39	SK5434
Clifton Oxon	29	SP4931
Clifton S York	49	SK5196
Clifton W York	55	SE1622
Clifton W York	55	SE1948
Clifton Campville Staffs	39	SK2510
Clifton Hampden Oxon	21	SU5495
Clifton Reynes Bucks	30	SP9051
Clifton upon Dunsmore Warwks	39	SP5376
Clifton upon Teme H & W	28	SO7161
Cliftonville Kent	15	TR3771
Climping W Susx	12	TQ0002
Clink Somset	20	ST7848
Clint N York	55	SE2559
Clint Green Norfk	42	TG0211
Clinterty Gramp	95	NJ8311
Clintmains Border	76	NT6132
Clippesby Norfk	43	TG4214
Clipsham Leics	40	SK9616
Clipston Nhants	40	SP7181
Clipston Notts	39	SK6333
Clipstone Beds	30	SP9426
Clipstone Notts	49	SK6064
Clitheroe Lancs	54	SD7441
Clive Shrops	37	SJ5124
Cloatley Wilts	20	ST9890
Clocaenog Clwyd	46	SJ0854
Cloch Mhor Highld	92	NH5063
Clochan Gramp	89	NJ4060
Clochtow Tays	89	NO4852
Clock H & W	27	SO3227
Clola Gramp	95	NK0043
Clophill Beds	30	TL0838
Clopton Nhants	40	TL0680
Clopton Suffk	33	TM2253
Clopton Corner Suffk	33	TM2254
Clopton Green Suffk	32	TL8759
Clos du Valle Guern	101	SV0000
Closeburn D & G	66	NX8992
Closeburnmill D & G	66	NX9094
Closworth Somset	8	ST5610
Clothall Herts	31	TL2731
Clotton Ches	46	SJ5264
Clough Foot W York	54	SD9123
Clough Head Staffs	48	SJ9864
Cloughton N York	63	TA0094
Clousta Shet	103	HU3157
Clova Tays	88	NO3273
Clovelly Cross Devon	6	SS3123
Clovenfords Border	76	NT4536
Clovulin Highld	86	NN0063
Clow Bridge Lancs	54	SD8228
Clowne Derbys	49	SK4875
Clows Top H & W	37	SO7171
Cluanie Inn Highld	85	NH0711
Cluanie Lodge Highld	85	NH0910
Clun Shrops	36	SO3081
Clunas Highld	93	NH8846
Clunbury Shrops	36	SO3780
Clune Highld	93	NH7925
Clunes Highld	86	NN2088
Clungunford Shrops	36	SO4078
Clunie Gramp	94	NJ6450
Clunie Tays	88	NO1043
Clunton Shrops	36	SO3381
Clutton Avon	19	ST6159
Clutton Ches	46	SJ4654
Clutton Hill Avon	19	ST6359
Clydach Gwent	27	SO2013
Clydach W Glam	18	SN6801
Clydach Vale M Glam	18	SS9792
Clydebank Strath	74	NS5069
Clydey Dyfed	17	SN2535
Clyffe Pypard Wilts	20	SU0776
Clynder Strath	80	NS2484
Clynderwen Dyfed	16	SN1219
Clyne W Glam	18	SN8000
Clynnog-fawr Gwynd	44	SH4149
Clyro Powys	27	SO2143
Clyst Honiton Devon	5	SX9893
Clyst Hydon Devon	7	ST0301
Clyst St. George Devon	5	SX9888
Clyst St. Lawrence Devon	7	ST0200
Clyst St. Mary Devon	5	SX9790
Clyth Highld	100	ND2836
Cnwch Coch Dyfed	35	SN6775
Coad's Green Cnwll	4	SX2976
Coalbrookdale Shrops	37	SJ6603
Coalburn Strath	74	NS8134
Coalburns T & W	69	NZ1261
Coaley Gloucs	20	SO7701
Coalhill Essex	24	TQ7598
Coalpit Heath Avon	20	ST6781
Coalport Shrops	37	SJ6902
Coalsnaughton Cent	82	NS9295
Coaltown of Balgonie Fife	83	NT3099
Coaltown of Wemyss Fife	83	NT3295
Coalville Leics	39	SK4214
Coanwood Nthumb	68	NY6759
Coat Somset	8	ST4520
Coatbridge Strath	74	NS7365
Coatdyke Strath	74	NS7465
Coate Wilts	20	SU0461
Coate Wilts	21	SU1783
Coates Cambs	41	TL3097
Coates Gloucs	20	SO9700
Coates W Susx	12	SU9917
Cobbaton Devon	6	SS6116
Coberley Gloucs	28	SO9616
Cobham Kent	14	TQ6768
Cobham Surrey	22	TQ1060
Cobnash H & W	27	SO4560
Cobo Guern	101	SV0000
Cobridge Staffs	47	SJ8748
Coburby Gramp	95	NJ9164
Cock Bridge Gramp	94	NJ2508
Cock Clarks Essex	24	TL8103
Cock Green Essex	24	TL6920
Cock Marling E Susx	14	TQ8719
Cockayne N York	62	SE6298
Cockayne Hatley Beds	31	TL2549
Cockburnspath Border	76	NT7770
Cockenzie and Port Seton Loth	76	NT4075
Cockerham Lancs	53	SD4651
Cockermouth Cumb	58	NY1230
Cockernhoe Green Herts	30	TL1223
Cockett W Glam	17	SS6394
Cockfield Dur	61	NZ1224
Cockfield Suffk	32	TL9054
Cockfosters Gt Lon	23	TQ2796
Cocking W Susx	11	SU8717
Cocking Causeway W Susx	11	SU8819
Cockington Devon	5	SX8964
Cocklake Somset	19	ST4349
Cockley Beck Cumb	58	NY2501
Cockley Cley Norfk	42	TF7904
Cockpole Green Berks	22	SU7981
Cockshutford Shrops	37	SO5885
Cockshutt Shrops	36	SJ4328
Cockthorpe Norfk	42	TF9842
Cockwood Devon	5	SX9780
Cockwood Somset	8	ST2223
Coddenham Suffk	33	TM1354
Coddington H & W	28	SO7142
Coddington Notts	50	SK8354
Codford St. Mary Wilts	20	ST9739
Codford St. Peter Wilts	20	ST9640
Codicote Herts	31	TL2118
Codmore Hill W Susx	12	TQ0520
Codnor Derbys	49	SK4149
Codrington Avon	20	ST7278
Codsall Staffs	38	SJ8603
Codsall Wood Staffs	38	SJ8405
Coed-y-paen Gwent	19	ST3398
Coed Talon Clwyd	46	SJ2658
Coedana Gwynd	44	SH4381
Coffinswell Devon	5	SX8868
Coffle End Beds	30	TL0059
Cofnpennar Gwent	27	SO3006
Cofton Hackett H & W	38	SP0075
Cogan S Glam	19	ST1772
Cogenhoe Nhants	30	SP8260
Coggeshall Essex	24	TL8522
Coignafearn Highld	93	NH7011
Coilacriech Gramp	88	NO3296
Coilantogle Cent	81	NN5907
Coillaig Strath	80	NN0120
Coillore Highld	84	NG3538
Coiltry Highld	86	NH3506
Coity M Glam	18	SS9281
Colaboll Highld	96	NC5610
Colan Cnwll	3	SW8661
Colaton Raleigh Devon	5	SY0787
Colburn N York	61	SE1999
Colby Cumb	60	NY6620
Colby IOM	52	SC2370
Colby Norfk	43	TG2231
Colchester Essex	25	TL9926
Cold Ash Berks	21	SU5169
Cold Ashby Nhants	39	SP6576
Cold Ashton Avon	20	ST7472
Cold Aston Gloucs	28	SP1219
Cold Brayfield Bucks	30	SP9252
Cold Hanworth Lincs	50	TF0383
Cold Harbour Herts	30	TL1415
Cold Harbour Wilts	20	ST8646
Cold Hatton Shrops	37	SJ6121
Cold Hesledon Dur	69	NZ4146
Cold Hiendly W York	55	SE3114
Cold Higham Nhants	30	SP6653
Cold Kirby N York	62	SE5384
Cold Norton Essex	24	TL8500
Cold Overton Leics	40	SK8110
Coldbackie Highld	99	NC6160
Coldbeck Cumb	60	NY7104
Coldean E Susx	12	TQ3308
Coldeast Devon	5	SX8274
Colden W York	54	SD9628
Colden Common Hants	10	SU4822
Coldfair Green Suffk	33	TM4361
Coldham Cambs	41	TF4302
Coldharbour Devon	7	ST0612
Coldharbour Surrey	12	TQ1443
Coldingham Border	77	NT9065
Coldmeece Staffs	38	SJ8532
Coldred Kent	15	TR2747
Coldridge Devon	7	SS6907
Coldstone Kent	23	TQ5061
Coldstream Border	77	NT8439
Coldwaltham W Susx	12	TQ0216
Coldwell H & W	27	SO4535
Coldwells Gramp	95	NJ9538
Coldwells Gramp	95	NK1039
Cole Somset	9	ST6633
Cole Green Herts	23	TL2911
Cole Green Herts	31	TL4330
Cole Henley Hants	21	SU4751
Cole's Cross Devon	5	SX7747
Colebatch Shrops	36	SO3187
Colebrook Devon	7	ST0006
Colebrooke Devon	7	SX7799
Coleby Humb	56	SE8919
Coleby Lincs	50	SK9760
Coleford Devon	7	SS7701
Coleford Gloucs	27	SO5710
Coleford Somset	20	ST6848
Coleford Water Somset	8	ST1234
Colegate End Norfk	33	TM1988
Coleman's Hatch E Susx	13	TQ4533
Colemere Shrops	36	SJ4232
Colemore Hants	11	SU7030
Colemore Green Shrops	37	SO7097
Colenden Tays	82	NO1029
Coleorton Leics	39	SK3917
Colerne Wilts	20	ST8171
Colesbourne Gloucs	28	SP0013
Coleshill Bucks	22	SU9495
Coleshill Oxon	21	SU2393
Coley Avon	19	ST5855
Colgate W Susx	12	TQ2332
Colgrain Strath	80	NS3280
Colinsburgh Fife	83	NO4703
Colinton Loth	75	NT2268
Colintraive Strath	80	NS0374
Colkirk Norfk	42	TF9126
Coll W Isls	102	NB4539
Collace Tays	82	NO2032
Collafirth Shet	103	HU3482
Collaton Devon	5	SX7338
Collaton St. Mary Devon	5	SX8660
College Green Somset	19	ST5736
College Town Berks	22	SU8560
College of Roseisle Gramp	93	NJ1466
Collessie Fife	83	NO2813
Collier Row Gt Lon	23	TQ4991
Collier Street Kent	14	TQ7145
Collier's End Herts	31	TL3720
Collier's Green Kent	14	TQ7822
Colliers Green Kent	14	TQ7439
Colliery Row T & W	69	NZ3349
Collieston Gramp	95	NK0328
Collin D & G	66	NY0276
Collingbourne Ducis Wilts	21	SU2453
Collingbourne Kingston Wilts	21	SU2455
Collingham W York	55	SE3845
Collington H & W	27	SO6460
Collingtree Nhants	30	SP7555
Collins Green Ches	47	SJ5694
Colliston Tays	89	NO6045
Colliton Devon	7	ST0900
Collyweston Nhants	40	SK9902
Colmonell Strath	64	NX1485
Coln Rogers Gloucs	28	SP0809
Coln St. Aldwyns Gloucs	28	SP1405
Coln St. Dennis Gloucs	28	SP0811
Colne Cambs	31	TL3776
Colne Lancs	54	SD8940
Colne Engaine Essex	24	TL8530
Colney Norfk	43	TG1807
Colney Heath Herts	23	TL2005
Colney Street Herts	22	TL1502
Colpy Gramp	94	NJ6432
Colquhar Border	76	NT3341
Colsterworth Lincs	40	SK9324
Colston Bassett Notts	40	SK7033
Colt Hill Hants	22	SU7451
Colt's Hill Kent	13	TQ6443
Coltfield Gramp	93	NJ1163
Coltishall Norfk	43	TG2619
Colton Cumb	58	SD3186
Colton N York	56	SE5444
Colton Norfk	43	TG1009
Colton Staffs	38	SK0520
Colton W York	55	SE3732
Colva Powys	27	SO1952
Colvend D & G	66	NX8654
Colwall Green H & W	28	SO7441
Colwall Stone H & W	28	SO7542
Colwell Nthumb	68	NY9575
Colwich Staffs	38	SK0121
Colwinston S Glam	18	SS9375
Colworth W Susx	11	SU9102
Colwyn Bay Clwyd	45	SH8479
Colyford Devon	8	SY2492
Colyton Devon	8	SY2493
Combe Berks	21	SU3760
Combe Devon	5	SX8448
Combe Devon	5	SX9173
Combe H & W	27	SO3463
Combe Oxon	29	SP4116
Combe Almer Dorset	9	SY9497
Combe Fishacre Devon	5	SX8465
Combe Florey Somset	8	ST1531
Combe Hay Avon	20	ST7359
Combe Martin Devon	6	SS5846
Combe Moor H & W	27	SO3663
Combe Raleigh Devon	8	ST1502
Combe St. Nicholas Somset	8	ST3011
Combebow Devon	5	SX4888
Combeinteignhead Devon	5	SX9071
Comberbach Ches	47	SJ6477
Comberford Staffs	39	SK1907
Comberton Cambs	31	TL3856
Comberton H & W	27	SO4968
Combrook Warwks	29	SP3051
Combs Derbys	48	SK0478
Combs Suffk	32	TM0456
Combs Ford Suffk	32	TM0557
Combwich Somset	8	ST2522
Comedivock Cumb	67	NY3449
Comers Gramp	95	NJ6707
Comhampton H & W	28	SO8366
Commercial Dyfed	16	SN1416
Commins Coch Powys	35	SH8403
Common Moor Cnwll	4	SX2469
Common The Wilts	10	SU2432
Commondale N York	62	NZ6610
Commonside Ches	47	SJ5573
Compstall Gt Man	48	SJ9690
Compton Berks	21	SU5280
Compton Devon	5	SX8664
Compton Hants	10	SU3529
Compton Hants	10	SU4625
Compton Staffs	38	SO8285
Compton Surrey	12	SU9547
Compton W Susx	11	SU7714
Compton Abbas Dorset	9	ST8718
Compton Bassett Wilts	20	SU0372
Compton Beauchamp Oxon	21	SU2886
Compton Bishop Somset	19	ST3955
Compton Chamberlayne Wilts	9	SU0229
Compton Dando Avon	19	ST6464
Compton Dundon Somset	8	ST4933
Compton Durville Somset	8	ST4117
Compton Greenfield Avon	19	ST5682
Compton Martin Avon	19	ST5456
Compton Pauncefoot Somset	9	ST6425
Compton Valence Dorset	9	SY5993
Comrie Fife	82	NT0289
Comrie Tays	81	NN7722
Conaglen House Highld	86	NN0268
Concraigie Tays	88	NO0844
Conder Green Lancs	53	SD4655
Conderton H & W	28	SO9637
Condicote Gloucs	28	SP1528
Condorrat Strath	74	NS7373
Condover Shrops	37	SJ4906
Coney Hill Gloucs	28	SO8516
Coney Weston Suffk	32	TL9578
Coneyhurst Common W Susx	12	TQ1024
Coneysthorpe N York	56	SE7171
Congdon's Shop Cnwll	4	SX2778
Congerstone Leics	39	SK3605
Congham Norfk	42	TF7123
Congleton Ches	47	SJ8563
Congresbury Avon	19	ST4563
Congreve Staffs	38	SJ8914
Conicavel Gramp	93	NH9853
Conichan Tays	82	NN8432
Coningsby Lincs	51	TF2258
Conington Cambs	40	TL1886
Conington Cambs	31	TL3266
Conisbrough S York	49	SK5098
Conisby Strath	70	NR2661
Conisholme Lincs	51	TF3995
Coniston Cumb	58	SD3097
Coniston Humb	57	TA1535
Coniston Cold N York	54	SD9054
Conistone N York	55	SD9867
Connah's Quay Clwyd	46	SJ2969
Connel Strath	80	NM9133
Connel Park Strath	66	NS6012
Connor Downs Cnwll	2	SW5939
Conon Bridge Highld	92	NH5455
Cononley N York	54	SD9847
Consall Staffs	38	SJ9748
Consett Dur	69	NZ1150
Constable Burton N York	61	SE1690
Constable Lee Lancs	54	SD8123
Constantine Cnwll	2	SW7329
Contin Highld	92	NH4586
Convinth Highld	92	NH5138
Conwy Gwynd	45	SH7777
Conyer's Green Suffk	32	TL8867
Cooden E Susx	14	TQ7107
Coodham Strath	73	NS3932
Cooil IOM	52	SC3475
Cook's Green Essex	25	TM1819
Cookbury Devon	6	SS4005
Cookbury Wick Devon	6	SS3805
Cookham Berks	22	SU8985
Cookham Dean Berks	22	SU8685
Cookham Rise Berks	22	SU8885
Cookhill Warwks	28	SP0558
Cookley Suffk	33	TM3475
Cookley Green Oxon	22	SU6990
Cookney Gramp	89	NO8693
Cooks Green Suffk	32	TL9853
Cooksmill Green Essex	24	TL6306
Cookson Green Ches	47	SJ5774
Coolham W Susx	12	TQ1222
Cooling Kent	14	TQ7575
Coombe Cnwll	3	SW9551
Coombe Devon	7	SS9725
Coombe Devon	5	SX8384
Coombe Gloucs	20	ST7693
Coombe Devon	7	SY1092
Coombe Cnwll	6	SS2006
Coombe Bissett Wilts	10	SU1026
Coombe Cellars Devon	5	SX9072
Coombe Cross Hants	11	SU6621
Coombe End Somset	7	ST0329
Coombe Hill Gloucs	28	SO8827
Coombe Keynes Dorset	9	SY8484
Coombe Street Somset	9	ST7531
Coombes W Susx	12	TQ1908
Coombeswood W Mids	38	SO9685
Cooperhill Gramp	93	NH9953
Coopersale Common Essex	23	TL4702
Coopersale Street Essex	23	TL4701
Cop Street Kent	23	TQ2960
Copford Green Essex	24	TL9222
Copgrove N York	55	SE3463
Copister Shet	103	HU4878
Cople Beds	30	TL1048
Copley Dur	61	NZ0825
Copmanthorpe N York	56	SE5646
Copmere End Staffs	37	SJ8029
Copp Lancs	53	SD4239
Copathorne Cnwll	6	SS2000
Coppenhall Staffs	38	SJ9019
Copperhouse Cnwll	2	SW5738
Coppicegate Shrops	37	SO7380
Coppingford Cambs	40	TL1680
Copplestone Devon	7	SS7702
Coppull Lancs	53	SD5614
Copsale W Susx	12	TQ1724
Copston Magna Warwks	39	SP4588
Copt Heath W Mids	38	SP1778
Copt Hewick N York	55	SE3471
Copthall Green Essex	23	TL4200
Copthorne W Susx	12	TQ3139
Copy's Green Norfk	42	TF9439
Copythorne Hants	10	SU3014
Corbets Tay Gt Lon	23	TQ5685
Corbiere Jersey	101	SV0000
Corbridge Nthumb	68	NY9964
Corby Nhants	40	SP8988
Corby Glen Lincs	40	SK9925
Cordon Strath	72	NS0230
Cordwell Unthank Derbys	48	SK2076
Coreley Shrops	37	SO6273
Cores End Bucks	22	SU9087
Corfe Somset	8	ST2319
Corfe Castle Dorset	9	SY9681
Corfe Mullen Dorset	9	SY9798
Corfton Shrops	37	SO4985
Corgarff Gramp	94	NJ2708
Corhampton Hants	11	SU6120
Corley Warwks	39	SP3085
Corley Ash Warwks	39	SP2986
Corley Moor Warwks	39	SP2885
Cormuir Tays	88	NO3066
Cornabus Strath	70	NR3346
Cornard Tye Suffk	32	TL9041
Corndon Devon	5	SX6885
Cornelly M Glam	18	SS8281
Cornforth Dur	62	NZ3134
Cornheath D & G	66	NX9969
Cornhill Gramp	94	NJ5858
Cornhill-on-Tweed Nthumb	77	NT8639
Cornholme W York	54	SD9126
Cornoigmore Strath	78	NL9546
Cornsay Dur	69	NZ1443
Cornsay Colliery Dur	69	NZ1643
Corntown Highld	92	NH5556
Corntown M Glam	18	SS9177
Cornwell Oxon	29	SP2727
Cornwood Devon	5	SX6059
Cornworthy Devon	5	SX8255
Corpach Highld	86	NN0976
Corpusty Norfk	43	TG1130
Corra Strath	71	NR9765
Corrachree Gramp	89	NJ4604
Corran Highld	86	NN0263
Corranbuie Strath	71	NR8465
Corrie D & G	67	NY2086
Corrie Strath	72	NS0242
Corriecravie Strath	72	NR9223
Corriegour Highld	86	NN2692
Corriemoille Highld	92	NH3663
Corrimony Highld	92	NH3730
Corringham Essex	24	TQ7083
Corringham Lincs	50	SK8691
Corris Gwynd	35	SH7507
Corris Uchaf Gwynd	35	SH7408
Corrow Strath	80	NN1800
Corry Highld	85	NG6424
Corrygills Strath	72	NS0335
Corsback Highld	100	ND2372
Corscombe Devon	6	SX6290
Corscombe Dorset	8	ST5105
Corse Gloucs	28	SO7926
Corse Gramp	94	NJ6040
Corse Lawn Gloucs	28	SO8330
Corsham Wilts	20	ST8670
Corsindae Gramp	95	NJ6808
Corsley Wilts	20	ST8246
Corsley Heath Wilts	20	ST8245
Corsock D & G	65	NX7675
Corston Avon	20	ST6965
Corston Wilts	20	ST9283
Corstorphine Loth	75	NT1972
Cortachy Tays	88	NO3959
Corton Suffk	43	TM5497
Corton Wilts	20	ST9340
Corton Denham Somset	9	ST6322
Coruanan Lodge Highld	86	NN0668
Corvallie IOM	52	SC1968
Corwar Strath	64	NX2780
Corwen Clwyd	46	SJ0743
Coryton Devon	4	SX4583
Coryton Essex	24	TQ7482
Cosby Leics	39	SP5495
Coseley W Mids	38	SO9494
Cosgrove Nhants	30	SP7942
Cosham Hants	11	SU6605
Cosheston Dyfed	16	SN0003
Coshieville Tays	87	NN7749
Cossall Marsh Notts	49	SK4842
Cossington Leics	39	SK6013
Cossington Somset	19	ST3540
Costessey Norfk	43	TG1712
Costock Leics	39	SK5726
Coston Leics	40	SK8422
Coston Norfk	42	TG0506
Cote Oxon	21	SP3502
Cote Somset	19	ST3544
Cotebrook Ches	47	SJ5765
Cotehill Cumb	59	NY4650
Cotes Cumb	59	SD4886
Cotes Leics	39	SK5520
Cotes Staffs	38	SJ8434
Cotesbach Leics	39	SP5382
Cotgrave Notts	39	SK6435
Cotham Notts	50	SK7947
Cotherstone Dur	61	NZ0119
Cothill Oxon	21	SU4699
Cotleigh Devon	8	ST2002
Cotmanhay Derbys	49	SK4643
Coton Cambs	31	TL4058

Coton *Nhants* 30 SP6771
Coton *Staffs* 37 SJ8120
Coton *Staffs* 38 SK1805
Coton Clanford *Staffs* 38 SJ8723
Coton Hayes *Staffs* 38 SJ9832
Coton Hill *Shrops* 37 SJ4913
Coton Park *Derbys* 39 SK2717
Coton in the Clay *Staffs* 38 SK1629
Coton in the Elms *Derbys* 39 SK2415
Cott *Devon* 5 SX7861
Cottage End *Hants* 21 SU4143
Cottam *Lancs* 53 SD5032
Cottam *Notts* 50 SK8179
Cottartown *Highld* 93 NH7442
Cottenham *Cambs* 31 TL4467
Cottered *Herts* 31 TL3129
Cotterstock *Nhants* 40 TL0490
Cottesbrooke *Nhants* 30 SP7173
Cottesmore *Leics* 40 SK9013
Cottingham *Humb* 57 TA0532
Cottingham *Nhants* 40 SP8490
Cottingley *W York* 55 SE1139
Cottisford *Oxon* 29 SP5831
Coton *Suffk* 32 TM0767
Cotton Tree *Lancs* 54 SD9040
Cottown *Gramp* 94 NJ5026
Cottown *Gramp* 95 NJ7715
Cottown *Gramp* 95 NJ8140
Cotts *Devon* 4 SX4365
Coughton *Warwks* 28 SP0860
Coulaghailtro *Strath* 71 NR7165
Coulags *Highld* 91 NG9645
Coulderton *Cumb* 58 NX9809
Coull *Gramp* 89 NJ5102
Coulport *Strath* 80 NS2187
Coulsdon *Gt Lon* 23 TQ2959
Coulter *Strath* 75 NT0234
Coulton *N York* 62 SE6373
Coultra *Fife* 83 NO3523
Cound *Shrops* 37 SJ5505
Coundon *Dur* 61 NZ2429
Coundon Grange *Dur* 61 NZ2328
Countersett *N York* 60 SD9187
Countess Wear *Devon* 5 SX9489
Countesthorpe *Leics* 39 SP5896
Countisbury *Devon* 7 SS7449
Coupar Angus *Tays* 82 NO2239
Coupland *Cumb* 60 NY7018
Coupland *Nthumb* 77 NT9331
Cour *Strath* 72 NR8248
Courance *D & G* 66 NY0590
Court Henry *Dyfed* 17 SN5522
Courteachan *Highld* 85 NM6897
Courteenhall *Nhants* 30 SP7653
Courtsend *Essex* 25 TR0293
Courtway *Somset* 8 ST2033
Cousland *Loth* 76 NT3768
Cousley Wood *E Susx* 13 TQ6433
Coustonn *Strath* 80 NS0774
Cove *Devon* 7 SS9519
Cove *Hants* 22 SU8555
Cove *Highld* 91 NG8090
Cove *Strath* 80 NS2282
Cove Bay *Gramp* 89 NJ9501
Cove Bottom *Suffk* 33 TM4980
Covehithe *Suffk* 33 TM5282
Coven *Staffs* 38 SJ9006
Coveney *Cambs* 41 TL4882
Covenham St. Bartholomew *Lincs* .. 51 TF3395
Covenham St. Mary *Lincs* 51 TF3394
Coventry *W Mids* 39 SP3379
Coverack Bridges *Cnwll* 2 SW6630
Coverham *N York* 61 SE1086
Covington *Cambs* 30 TL0570
Cow Honeybourne *H & W* 28 SP1143
Cowan Bridge *Lancs* 60 SD6376
Cowbeech *E Susx* 13 TQ6114
Cowbit *Lincs* 41 TF2518
Cowbridge *S Glam* 18 SS9974
Cowdale *Derbys* 48 SK0872
Cowden *Kent* 13 TQ4640
Cowdenbeath *Fife* 82 NT1691
Cowdenburn *Border* 75 NT2052
Cowers Lane *Derbys* 49 SK3046
Cowes *IOW* 10 SZ4995
Cowesby *N York* 62 SE4689
Cowesfield Green *Wilts* 10 SU2623
Cowfold *W Susx* 12 TQ2122
Cowgill *Cumb* 60 SD7586
Cowhill *Avon* 19 ST6191
Cowie *Cent* 82 NS8389
Cowley *Derbys* 49 SK3377
Cowley *Devon* 7 SX9095
Cowley *Gloucs* 28 SO9614
Cowley *Gt Lon* 22 TQ0582
Cowley *Oxon* 29 SP5404
Cowling *Lancs* 54 SD5917
Cowling *N York* 54 SD9643
Cowling *N York* 61 SE2387
Cowlinge *Suffk* 32 TL7154
Cowpen *Nthumb* 69 NZ2981
Cowplain *Hants* 11 SU6911
Cowshill *Dur* 60 NY8540
Cowslip Green *Avon* 19 ST4862
Cowthorpe *N York* 55 SE4252
Cowton *Somset* 8 ST1919
Coxbank *Ches* 37 SJ6541
Coxbench *Derbys* 49 SK3743
Coxford *Cnwll* 6 SX1696
Coxford *Norfk* 42 TF8529
Coxheath *Kent* 14 TQ7451
Coxhoe *Dur* 62 NZ3235
Coxley *Somset* 19 ST5343
Coxley Wick *Somset* 19 ST5244
Coxtie Green *Essex* 24 TQ5696
Coxwold *N York* 62 SE5377
Coychurch *M Glam* 18 SS9379
Coylton *Strath* 73 NS4219
Coylumbridge *Highld* 93 NH9110
Coytrahen *M Glam* 18 SS8985
Crab Orchard *Dorset* 10 SU0806
Crabadon *Devon* 5 SX7655
Crabbs Cross *H & W* 28 SP0465
Crabtree *W Susx* 12 TQ2225
Crackenthorpe *Cumb* 60 NY6622
Crackington Haven *Cnwll* 6 SX1496
Cracklleybank *Shrops* 37 SJ7611
Crackpot *N York* 61 SD9696
Cracoe *N York* 54 SD9760
Craddock *Devon* 7 ST0812
Craddock *Devon* 7 ST0812
Cradle End *Herts* 31 TL4621
Cradley *H & W* 28 SO7347
Cradley *W Mids* 38 SO9484
Cradoc *Powys* 26 SO0130
Crafthole *Cnwll* 4 SX3654
Crafton *Bucks* 30 SP8819
Cragabus *Strath* 70 NR3245
Cragg *W York* 55 SE0023
Craggan *Highld* 93 NJ0226
Craghead *Dur* 69 NZ2150
Crai *Powys* 26 SN8924
Craibstone *Gramp* 94 NJ4959
Craibstone *Gramp* 95 NJ8710
Craichie *Tays* 89 NO5047
Craig *D & G* 67 NX2678
Craig Llangiwg *W Glam* 26 SN7304
Craigburn *Border* 75 NT2354
Craigdam *Gramp* 95 NJ8430
Craigdarroch *D & G* 65 NX7391
Craigdarroch *Strath* 65 NS6306
Craigdews *D & G* 65 NX5072
Craigdhu *Strath* 79 NM8205
Craigearn *Gramp* 95 NJ7214
Craigellachie *Gramp* 94 NJ2844
Craigend *Strath* 73 NS4670
Craigend *Strath* 82 NO1120
Craigend *Tays* 82 NS3181
Craigengillan *Strath* 73 NS4702
Craigenhouses *Strath* 70 NR5267
Craighat *Cent* 81 NS4984
Craighlaw *D & G* 64 NX3061
Craighleuch *D & G* 67 NY3487
Craigie *Strath* 73 NS4232
Craigie *Tays* 82 NO1143
Craigieburn *D & G* 67 NT1105
Craigiefold *Gramp* 95 NJ9265
Craiglockhart *Fife* 75 NT2271

Craiglug *Gramp* 94 NJ3354
Craigmillar *Loth* 75 NT3071
Craigneston *D & G* 65 NX7588
Craigneuk *Strath* 74 NS7656
Craigo *Tays* 89 NO6864
Craigrothie *Fife* 83 NO3810
Craigruie *Cent* 81 NN4920
Craigton *Gramp* 89 NJ8301
Craigton *Strath* 74 NS4954
Craigton *Tays* 88 NO3280
Craigton *Tays* 83 NO8138
Craik *Border* 67 NT3408
Crail *Fife* 83 NO6107
Crailing *Border* 76 NT6824
Crailinghall *Border* 76 NT6922
Crakehall *N York* 62 SE2489
Crambe *N York* 56 SE7364
Cramlington *Nthumb* 69 NZ2676
Cramond *Loth* 75 NT1976
Cramond Bridge *Loth* 75 NT1775
Cranage *Ches* 47 SJ7568
Cranberry *Staffs* 38 SJ8235
Cranborne *Dorset* 10 SU0513
Cranbrook *Devon* 5 SX7488
Cranfield *Beds* 30 SP9542
Cranford *Gt Lon* 22 TQ1077
Cranford St. Andrew *Nhants* 30 SP9277
Cranford St. John *Nhants* 30 SP9276
Cranham *Gloucs* 28 SO8913
Cranhill *Warwks* 28 SP1253
Crank *Mersyd* 46 SJ5099
Cranleigh *Surrey* 12 TQ0639
Cranmer Green *Suffk* 32 TM0271
Cranmore *Somset* 20 ST6843
Cranoe *Leics* 40 SP7695
Cransford *Suffk* 33 TM3164
Cranshaws *Border* 76 NT6861
Cranswick *Humb* 56 TA0252
Crantock *Cnwll* 2 SW7960
Cranwell *Lincs* 50 TF0349
Cranwich *Norfk* 42 TL7795
Cranworth *Norfk* 42 TF9804
Crarae *Strath* 71 NR9897
Crask of Aigas *Highld* 92 NH4642
Craster *Nthumb* 77 NU2520
Craswall *H & W* 27 SO2735
Cratfield *Suffk* 33 TM3175
Crathes *Gramp* 89 NO7596
Crathie *Gramp* 88 NO2695
Crathie *Highld* 87 NN5794
Crathorne *N York* 62 NZ4407
Craven Arms *Shrops* 36 SO4382
Crawford *Lancs* 46 SD5003
Crawford *Strath* 75 NS9520
Crawfordjohn *Strath* 74 NS8824
Crawick *D & G* 66 NS7811
Crawley *Hants* 10 SU4234
Crawley *Oxon* 29 SP3412
Crawley *W Susx* 12 TQ2636
Crawley Down *W Susx* 12 TQ3437
Crawleyside *Dur* 61 NY9840
Crawton *Gramp* 89 NO8779
Cray *N York* 61 SD9479
Crayke *N York* 56 SE5670
Crays Hill *Essex* 24 TQ7192
Craze Lowman *Devon* 7 SS9814
Creacombe *Devon* 7 SS8119
Creagan Inn *Strath* 86 NM9744
Creagorry *W Isls* 102 NF7948
Creaguaineach Lodge *Highld* 86 NN3068
Creaton *Nhants* 30 SP7071
Creca *D & G* 67 NY2270
Credenhill *H & W* 27 SO4543
Crediton *Devon* 7 SS8300
Creebank *D & G* 64 NX3477
Creech Heathfield *Somset* 8 ST2827
Creech St. Michael *Somset* 8 ST2725
Creed *Cnwll* 3 SW9347
Creedy Park *Devon* 7 SS8302
Creekmouth *Gt Lon* 23 TQ4581
Creeton *Lincs* 40 TF0120
Creetown *D & G* 65 NX4758
Creggans Hotel *Strath* 80 NN0902
Cregneish *IOM* 52 SC1967
Creich *Fife* 83 NO3221
Creigiau *M Glam* 18 ST0781
Cremyll *Cnwll* 4 SX4553
Cressage *Shrops* 37 SJ5904
Cressbrook *Derbys* 48 SK1673
Cresselly *Dyfed* 16 SN0606
Cressex *Bucks* 22 SU8392
Cressing *Essex* 24 TL7920
Cresswell *Dyfed* 16 SN0506
Cresswell *Nthumb* 69 NZ2993
Cresswell *Staffs* 38 SJ9739
Creswell *Derbys* 49 SK5274
Cretingham *Suffk* 33 TM2260
Cretshengan *Strath* 71 NR7166
Crew Green *Powys* 36 SJ3215
Crewe *Ches* 46 SJ4253
Crewe *Ches* 47 SJ7055
Crewe Green *Ches* 47 SJ7285
Crewkerne *Somset* 8 ST4409
Crews Hill Station *Herts* 23 TL3190
Crewton *Derbys* 39 SK3733
Crianlarich *Strath* 80 NN3825
Cribb's Causeway *Avon* 19 ST5780
Cribyn *Dyfed* 17 SN5251
Criccieth *Gwynd* 44 SH4938
Crich *Derbys* 49 SK3554
Crich Carr *Derbys* 49 SK3554
Crich Common *Derbys* 49 SK3553
Crichton *Loth* 76 NT3862
Crick *Nhants* 39 SP5972
Crickadarn *Powys* 26 SO0942
Cricket St. Thomas *Somset* 8 ST3708
Crickheath *Shrops* 36 SJ2923
Crickhowell *Powys* 27 SO2118
Cricklade *Wilts* 20 SU0993
Cricklewood *Gt Lon* 23 TQ2385
Cridling Stubbs *N York* 55 SE5221
Crieff *Tays* 82 NN8621
Criggion *Powys* 36 SJ2915
Crigglestone *W York* 55 SK3690
Crimond *Gramp* 95 NK0656
Crimonmogate *Gramp* 95 NK0358
Crimplesham *Norfk* 42 TF6503
Crimscote *Warwks* 29 SP2347
Crinan *Strath* 71 NR7894
Crindledyke *Strath* 74 NS8356
Cringleford *Norfk* 43 TG1905
Cringles *N York* 55 SE0448
Crinow *Dyfed* 16 SN1214
Cripplestyle *Dorset* 10 SU0912
Crizeley *H & W* 27 SO4432
Croachy *Highld* 93 NH6527
Croasdale *Cumb* 58 NY0917
Crochmore House *D & G* 66 NX8977
Crockenhill *Kent* 23 TQ5067
Crocker End *Oxon* 22 SU7086
Crockerhill *W Susx* 11 SU9207
Crockernwell *Devon* 5 SX7592
Crockerton *Wilts* 20 ST8642
Crockham Hill *Kent* 13 TQ4450
Crockhurst Street *Kent* 13 TQ6235
Croes-lan *Dyfed* 17 SN3844
Croeserw *W Glam* 18 SS8795
Croesgoch *Dyfed* 16 SM8330
Croesor *Gwynd* 45 SH6344
Croesyceiliog *Dyfed* 17 SN4016
Croesyceiliog *Gwent* 19 ST3096
Croesywaun *Gwynd* 44 SH5159
Croft *Leics* 39 SP5195
Croft *Lincs* 51 TF5162
Croftamie *Cent* 81 NS4786
Crofton *Devon* 5 SX9680
Crofton *Wilts* 21 SU2662
Crofts *Gramp* 94 NJ2856
Crofts of Dipple *Gramp* 94 NJ3258
Crofts of Savoch *Gramp* 95 NK0460
Crofty *W Glam* 17 SS5295
Croggan *Strath* 79 NM7027
Croglin *Cumb* 67 NY5747
Crogo *D & G* 65 NX7576
Croick *Highld* 96 NH4591
Croig *Strath* 78 NM3953

Cromarty *Highld* 93 NH7867
Crombie *Fife* 82 NT0584
Cromdale *Highld* 93 NJ0728
Cromer *Herts* 41 TL2980
Cromer *Norfk* 43 TG2242
Cromford *Derbys* 49 SK2956
Cromhall *Avon* 20 ST6990
Cromore *W Isls* 102 NB4021
Cromwell *Notts* 50 SK7761
Cronberry *Strath* 74 NS6022
Crondall *Hants* 22 SU7948
Cronk The *IOM* 52 SC3495
Cronk-y-Voddy *IOM* 52 SC3086
Cronton *Mersyd* 46 SJ4988
Crook *Cumb* 59 SD4695
Crook *Dur* 61 NZ1635
Crook of Devon *Tays* 82 NO0300
Crooked Holme *Cumb* 67 NY5162
Crooked Soley *Wilts* 19 ST3172
Crookedholm *Strath* 73 NS4537
Crookes *S York* 49 SK3288
Crookham *Berks* 21 SU5364
Crookham *Nthumb* 77 NT9138
Crookham Village *Hants* 22 SU7952
Crooklands *Cumb* 59 SD5383
Cropredy *Oxon* 29 SP4646
Cropston *Leics* 39 SK5511
Cropthorne *H & W* 28 SO9944
Cropton *N York* 63 SE7589
Cropwell Bishop *Notts* 39 SK6835
Cropwell Butler *Notts* 49 SK6837
Crosbie *Strath* 73 NS2149
Crosby *Cumb* 59 NY0738
Crosby *Humb* 56 SE8912
Crosby *IOM* 52 SC3279
Crosby *Mersyd* 46 SJ3198
Crosby Garrett *Cumb* 60 NY7309
Crosby Ravensworth *Cumb* 60 NY6214
Croscombe *Somset* 19 ST5844
Cross *Somset* 19 ST4154
Cross Coombe *Cnwll* 2 SW7351
Cross End *Essex* 24 TL8634
Cross Flatts *W York* 55 SE1040
Cross Gates *W York* 55 SE3534
Cross Green *Devon* 4 SX3888
Cross Green *Suffk* 32 TL8353
Cross Green *Suffk* 32 TL8965
Cross Green *Suffk* 32 TL8953
Cross Hands *Dyfed* 17 SN5612
Cross Houses *Shrops* 37 SJ5307
Cross Inn *Dyfed* 26 SN7725
Cross Inn *Dyfed* 34 SN3957
Cross Inn *Dyfed* 34 SN5463
Cross Inn *M Glam* 18 ST0583
Cross Lane *IOW* 11 SZ6090
Cross Lane Head *Shrops* 37 SO7095
Cross Lanes *Cnwll* 2 SW6921
Cross Lanes *Cnwll* 2 SW7642
Cross Lanes *N York* 55 SE5264
Cross Roads *Devon* 4 SX4586
Cross Street *Suffk* 33 TM1876
Cross Town *Ches* 47 SJ7578
Cross Ways *Dorset* 9 SY7688
Cross in Hand *E Susx* 13 TQ5521
Cross o' th' hands *Derbys* 49 SK2846
Cross of Jackston *Gramp* 95 NJ7432
Cross-at-Hand *Kent* 14 TQ7846
Crossaig *Strath* 72 NR8351
Crossapol *Strath* 78 NL9943
Crossbost *W Isls* 102 NB3924
Crosscanonby *Cumb* 58 NY0739
Crossdale Street *Norfk* 43 TG2239
Crossford *Fife* 82 NT0786
Crossford *Strath* 74 NS8246
Crossgatehall *Loth* 76 NT3688
Crossgates *Fife* 82 NT1488
Crossgates *Powys* 26 SO0865
Crossgates *Strath* 73 NS3744
Crossgill *Lancs* 53 SD5563
Crosshands *Strath* 73 NS4830
Crosshill *Fife* 82 NT1796
Crosshill *Strath* 73 NS3206
Crosshouse *Strath* 73 NS3938
Crosskeys *Gwent* 19 ST7292
Crosskeys *Strath* 80 NS3385
Crosskirk *Highld* 100 ND0369
Crossland Edge *W York* 55 SE1212
Crosslands *Cumb* 67 NY3489
Crosslee *Border* 75 NT3018
Crossmichael *D & G* 65 NX7367
Crossroads *Gramp* 94 NJ5607
Crossroads *Gramp* 89 NO7594
Crosston *Tays* 89 NO5256
Crossway *Powys* 26 SO0558
Crossway Green *H & W* 28 SO8368
Crosswell *Dyfed* 16 SN1236
Crosthwaite *Cumb* 59 SD4391
Croston *Lancs* 53 SD4918
Crostwick *Norfk* 43 TG2515
Crouch *Kent* 15 TR0458
Crouch End *Gt Lon* 23 TQ3088
Croucheston *Wilts* 10 SU0425
Croughton *Nhants* 29 SP5433
Crovie *Gramp* 95 NJ8065
Crow Edge *S York* 55 SE1804
Crow Street *Essex* 24 TQ5796
Crowan *Cnwll* 2 SW6434
Crowborough *E Susx* 13 TQ5131
Crowcombe *Somset* 18 ST1336
Crowdicote *Derbys* 48 SK1065
Crowdleham *Kent* 14 TQ5688
Crowell *Oxon* 22 SU7499
Crowfield *Suffk* 33 TM1557
Crowhill *Loth* 76 NT7374
Crowhurst *E Susx* 14 TQ7512
Crowhurst *Surrey* 13 TQ3847
Crowhurst Lane End *Surrey* 13 TQ3847
Crowland *Lincs* 41 TF2410
Crowland *Suffk* 32 TM0170
Crowlas *Cnwll* 2 SW5133
Crowle *H & W* 28 SO9256
Crowle *Humb* 56 SE7712
Crowle Green *H & W* 28 SO9256
Crowmarsh Gifford *Oxon* 21 SU6189
Crown Corner *Suffk* 33 TM2570
Crownhill *Devon* 4 SX4857
Crownpits *Surrey* 12 SU9743
Crownthorpe *Norfk* 42 TG0803
Crowntown *Cnwll* 2 SW6331
Crows-an-Wra *Cnwll* 2 SW3927
Crowshill *Norfk* 42 TF9406
Crowsnest *Shrops* 36 SJ3701
Crowthorne *Berks* 22 SU8464
Croxdale *Dur* 61 NZ2636
Croxden *Staffs* 48 SK0639
Croxley Green *Herts* 22 TQ0795
Croxton *Cambs* 31 TL2460
Croxton *Humb* 57 TA0912
Croxton *Norfk* 32 TL8786
Croxton *Norfk* 42 TF9831
Croxton Kerrial *Leics* 40 SK8329
Croxtonbank *Staffs* 37 SJ7832
Croy *Highld* 93 NH7949
Croy *Strath* 74 NS7275
Croyde *Devon* 6 SS4439
Croydon *Cambs* 31 TL3149
Croydon *Gt Lon* 23 TQ3265
Crubenmore *Highld* 87 NN6790
Cruckmeole *Shrops* 36 SJ4309
Cruckton *Shrops* 36 SJ4310
Cruden Bay *Gramp* 95 NK0836
Crudgington *Shrops* 37 SJ6318
Crudwell *Wilts* 20 ST9592
Crug-y-byddar *Powys* 36 SO1682
Crulivig *W Isls* 102 NB1733
Crumplehorn *Cnwll* 4 SX2051
Crumpsall *Gt Man* 47 SD8402
Crunanne *Border* 76 NT8053
Crundale *Kent* 15 TR0749
Crunwear *Dyfed* 17 SN1810
Crux Easton *Hants* 21 SU4256
Crwbin *Dyfed* 17 SN4713
Cryers Hill *Bucks* 22 SU8797
Crymmych *Dyfed* 17 SN1833
Crynant *Dyfed* 26 SN7904
Crystal Palace *Gt Lon* 23 TQ3371
Cuaig *Highld* 91 NG7057

Cubbington *Warwks* 29 SP3468
Cubert *Cnwll* 2 SW7857
Cublington *Bucks* 30 SP8422
Cublington *H & W* 27 SO3938
Cuckfield *W Susx* 12 TQ3025
Cucklington *Somset* 9 ST7527
Cuckney *Notts* 49 SK6571
Cuckoo's Nest *Ches* 46 SJ3759
Cuddesdon *Oxon* 21 SP5903
Cuddington *Bucks* 22 SP7311
Cuddington *Ches* 47 SJ5971
Cuddington Heath *Ches* 46 SJ4747
Cudham *Gt Lon* 23 TQ4459
Cudliptown *Devon* 4 SX5279
Cudworth *S York* 55 SE3808
Cudworth *Somset* 8 ST3810
Cuerdley Cross *Ches* 47 SJ5487
Cuffley *Herts* 23 TL3003
Culbo *Highld* 92 NH6461
Culbokie *Highld* 92 NH6059
Culburnie *Highld* 92 NH4941
Culcabock *Highld* 93 NH6844
Culcharry *Highld* 93 NH8650
Culcheth *Ches* 47 SJ6694
Culdrain *Gramp* 94 NJ5135
Culduie *Highld* 91 NG7140
Culford *Suffk* 32 TL8370
Culgaith *Cumb* 59 NY6029
Culham *Oxon* 21 SU5095
Culinlongart *Strath* 72 NR6511
Culkein *Highld* 98 NC0333
Culkein Drumbeg *Highld* 98 NC1133
Culkerton *Gloucs* 20 ST9395
Cullen *Gramp* 94 NJ5167
Cullercoats *T & W* 69 NZ3671
Cullerlie *Gramp* 89 NJ7603
Cullicudden *Highld* 92 NH6463
Cullingworth *W York* 55 SE0636
Cullipool *Strath* 79 NM7313
Cullompton *Devon* 103 HP5402
Cullompton *Devon* 7 ST0207
Culm Davy *Devon* 8 ST1215
Culmalzie *D & G* 64 NX3752
Culmington *Shrops* 37 SO4982
Culmstock *Devon* 8 ST1013
Culnacraig *Highld* 91 NC0603
Culnaknock *Highld* 90 NG5263
Culpho *Suffk* 33 TM2149
Culrain *Highld* 96 NH5794
Culross *Fife* 82 NS9886
Culroy *Strath* 73 NS3114
Culshabbin *D & G* 64 NX3050
Culswick *Shet* 103 HU2745
Cultercullen *Gramp* 95 NJ9223
Cults *D & G* 65 NX4643
Cults *Gramp* 89 NJ8903
Culverlane *Devon* 5 SX7460
Culverstone Green *Kent* 14 TQ6362
Culverthorpe *Lincs* 50 TF0240
Culworth *Nhants* 29 SP5446
Culzie Lodge *Highld* 92 NH5171
Cumbernauld *Strath* 74 NS7674
Cumberworth *Lincs* 51 TF5073
Cuminestown *Gramp* 95 NJ8050
Cummersdale *Cumb* 67 NY3953
Cummertrees *D & G* 67 NY1366
Cummingston *Gramp* 93 NJ1368
Cumnor *Oxon* 29 SP4504
Cumrew *Cumb* 67 NY5450
Cumwhinton *Cumb* 67 NY4552
Cumwhitton *Cumb* 67 NY5052
Cundall *N York* 55 SE4272
Cunninghamhead *Strath* 73 NS3741
Cupar *Fife* 83 NO3714
Cupar Muir *Fife* 83 NO3313
Curbar *Derbys* 48 SK2574
Curbridge *Hants* 11 SU5211
Curbridge *Oxon* 29 SP3208
Curdridge *Hants* 11 SU5313
Curdworth *Warwks* 38 SP1892
Curland *Somset* 8 ST2716
Currarie *Strath* 64 NX1691
Curridge *Berks* 21 SU4972
Currie *Loth* 75 NT1867
Curry Mallet *Somset* 8 ST3221
Curry Rivel *Somset* 8 ST3824
Curtisden Green *Kent* 14 TQ7440
Curtisknowle *Devon* 5 SX7353
Cury *Cnwll* 2 SW6721
Cusop *H & W* 27 SO2441
Cutcombe *Somset* 7 SS9239
Cuthill *Highld* 97 NH7587
Cutler's Green *Essex* 24 TL5930
Cutnall Green *H & W* 28 SO8868
Cutsdean *Gloucs* 28 SP0831
Cutthorpe *Derbys* 49 SK3473
Cuxham *Oxon* 22 SU6695
Cuxton *Kent* 14 TQ7066
Cuxton *Kent* 14 TQ7066
Cuxwold *Lincs* 50 TA1701
Cwm *Clwyd* 45 SJ0677
Cwm *W Glam* 18 SS6895
Cwm Morgan *Dyfed* 17 SN2933
Cwm-Crownon *Powys* 26 SO1419
Cwm-Llinau *Powys* 35 SH8408
Cwm-celyn *Gwent* 27 SO2008
Cwm-y-glo *Gwynd* 44 SH5562
Cwmafan *W Glam* 18 SS7791
Cwmaman *M Glam* 18 ST0090
Cwmann *Dyfed* 17 SN5847
Cwmbach *Dyfed* 17 SN2526
Cwmbach *M Glam* 18 SO0201
Cwmbach *Powys* 27 SO1639
Cwmbach Llechryd *Powys* 26 SO0254
Cwmbran *Gwent* 19 ST2994
Cwmcarn *Gwent* 19 ST2293
Cwmcarvan *Gwent* 27 SO4707
Cwmcoy *Dyfed* 17 SN2942
Cwmdare *M Glam* 18 SN9803
Cwmdu *Dyfed* 17 SO1823
Cwmdu *M Glam* 17 SS8494
Cwmduad *Dyfed* 17 SN3731
Cwmfelin *M Glam* 18 SS8689
Cwmfelin *M Glam* 18 SO0901
Cwmfelin Boeth *Dyfed* 17 SN1919
Cwmfelin Mynach *Dyfed* 17 SN2324
Cwmfelinfach *Gwent* 19 ST1891
Cwmffrwd *Dyfed* 17 SN4217
Cwmgiedd *Powys* 26 SN7911
Cwmgorse *W Glam* 26 SN7010
Cwmgwili *Dyfed* 17 SN5710
Cwmhiraeth *Dyfed* 17 SN3438
Cwmllynfell *Dyfed* 26 SN7412
Cwmparc *M Glam* 18 SS9495
Cwmpengraig *Dyfed* 17 SN3436
Cwmpennar *M Glam* 18 SO0400
Cwmrhos *Powys* 17 SN1824
Cwmsychpant *Dyfed* 17 SN4746
Cwmtillery *Gwent* 27 SO2105
Cwmtwrch Uchaf *Dyfed* 26 SN7874
Cwrt-newydd *Dyfed* 17 SN4847
Cyffylliog *Clwyd* 45 SJ0557
Cylibebyll *W Glam* 26 SN7404
Cymmer *M Glam* 18 ST0290
Cymmer *W Glam* 18 SS8696
Cynghardy *Dyfed* 26 SN8040
Cynonville *W Glam* 18 SS8395
Cynwyd *Clwyd* 36 SJ0541
Cynwyl Elfed *Dyfed* 17 SN3727

D

Daccombe *Devon* 5 SX9068
Dacre *Cumb* 59 NY4526
Dacre *N York* 55 SE1960
Dacre Banks *N York* 55 SE1962
Daddry Shield *Dur* 60 NY8937
Dadford *Bucks* 30 SP6638
Dadlington *Leics* 39 SP4098

Dagenham Gt Lon 23 TQ5084
Daglingworth Gloucs 28 SO9905
Dagnall Bucks 30 SP9916
Dailly Strath 73 NS2701
Dainton Devon 5 SX8486
Dairsie Fife 83 NO4117
Daivaich Strath 80 NM9612
Dalbeattie D & G 66 NX8361
Dalblair Strath 74 NS6419
Dalbog Tays 83 NO5871
Dalby IOM 52 SC2178
Dalby N York 62 SE6370
Dalcapon Tays 88 NN9754
Dalchalm Highld 97 NC9105
Dalchenna Strath 80 NN0706
Dalchork Highld 96 NC5710
Dalchreichart Highld 92 NH2912
Dalchriun Tays 81 NN7116
Dalcrue Tays 82 NO0417
Dalderby Lincs 51 TF2465
Dalditch Devon 3 SX0483
Dale Derbys 49 SK4338
Dale Dyfed 16 SM8005
Dale End N York 55 SD9646
Dale Head Cumb 59 NY4316
Dalelia Highld 79 NM7369
Dalgarven Strath 73 NS2846
Dalgety Bay Fife 82 NT1683
Dalgig Strath 73 NS5513
Dalginross Tays 81 NN7721
Dalguise Tays 88 NN9047
Dalhalvaig Highld 99 NC8954
Dalham Suffk 32 TL7261
Daliburgh W Isls 102 NF7421
Dalkeith Loth 75 NT3367
Dallas Gramp 93 NJ1252
Dalleagles Strath 73 NS5610
Dallinghoo Suffk 33 TM2655
Dallington E Susx 13 TQ6519
Dallington Nhants 30 SP7261
Dalmally Strath 80 NN1527
Dalmarnock Tays 75 NS5945
Dalmary Cent 81 NS5195
Dalmellington Strath 73 NS4706
Dalmeny Loth 75 NT1477
Dalmigavie Highld 93 NH7319
Dalmigavie Lodge Highld 93 NH7523
Dalmore Highld 93 NH6668
Dalnacardoch Lodge Tays 87 NN7270
Dalnaspidal Tays 87 NN6473
Dalnawillan Lodge Highld 100 ND0240
Daloist Tays 87 NN7857
Dalqueich Tays 82 NO0704
Dalquhairn Strath 64 NX3296
Dalreavoch Lodge Highld 97 NC7508
Dalry Strath 73 NS2949
Dalserf Strath 74 NS7950
Dalsmeran Strath 72 NR6413
Dalston Cumb 67 NY3650
Dalston Gt Lon 23 TQ3384
Dalswinton D & G 66 NX9385
Dalton D & G 67 NY1173
Dalton N York 61 NZ1108
Dalton N York 62 SE4376
Dalton Nthumb 68 NZ1172
Dalton Magna S York 49 SK4693
Dalton Piercy Clevel 62 NZ4631
Dalton in Furness Cumb 58 SD2273
Dalton-le-Dale Dur 69 NZ4047
Dalton-on-Tees N York 61 NZ2907
Daltot Strath 71 NR7583
Dalveich Cent 81 NN6124
Dalwhinnie Highld 87 NN6385
Dalwood Devon 8 ST2400
Damgate Norfk 43 TG4009
Danbury Essex 24 TL7805
Danby N York 62 NZ7008
Danby Wiske N York 62 SE3398
Dandaleith Gramp 94 NJ2845
Danderhall Loth 75 NT3069
Dane End Herts 31 TL3321
Dane Hills Leics 39 SK5605
Dane Street Kent 15 TR0552
Danebridge Ches 48 SJ9665
Danegate E Susx 13 TQ5634
Danehill E Susx 13 TQ4027
Danesford Shrops 37 SO7391
Danesmoor Derbys 49 SK4263
Danshillack Gramp 95 NJ7157
Danskine Loth 76 NT5667
Danthorpe Humb 57 TA2732
Darenth Kent 23 TQ5571
Daresbury Ches 47 SJ5882
Darfield S York 55 SE4104
Dargate Kent 15 TR0761
Darite Cnwll 4 SX2569
Darlaston W Mids 38 SO9796
Darlaston Green W Mids 38 SO9797
Darley N York 55 SE2059
Darley Abbey Derbys 49 SK3538
Darley Bridge Derbys 49 SK2661
Darley Green Warwks 38 SP1874
Darley Head N York 55 SE1959
Darleyhall Herts 30 TL1422
Darlingscott Warwks 29 SP2342
Darlington Dur 61 NZ2914
Darlton Notts 50 SK7773
Darowen Powys 35 SH8301
Darra Gramp 95 NJ7447
Darracott Cnwll 3 SX2712
Darracott Devon 6 SS2317
Darracott Devon 6 SS4739
Darrington W York 55 SE4919
Darsham Suffk 33 TM4170
Dartford Kent 23 TQ5474
Dartington Devon 5 SX7862
Dartmouth Devon 5 SX8751
Darton S York 55 SE3110
Darvel Strath 74 NS5637
Darwen Lancs 54 SD6922
Datchet Berks 22 SU9877
Datchworth Herts 31 TL2619
Datchworth Green Herts 31 TL2618
Daubhill Gt Man 47 SD7007
Dauntsey Wilts 20 ST9782
Dauntsey Green Wilts 20 ST9982
Dava Highld 93 NJ0138
Davenham Ches 47 SJ6571
Daventry Nhants 29 SP5762
David Street Kent 14 TQ6466
Davidson's Mains Loth 75 NT2175
Davidstow Cnwll 4 SX1587
Davington D & G 67 NT2302
Davington Hill Kent 15 TR0161
Daviot Gramp 95 NJ7528
Daviot Highld 93 NH7239
Daviot House Highld 93 NH7240
Davis Street Berks 22 SU7872
Davoch of Grange Gramp 94 NJ4851
Dawesgreen Surrey 12 TQ2147
Dawley Shrops 37 SJ6807
Dawlish Devon 5 SX9676
Dawlish Warren Devon 5 SX9778
Dawn Clwyd 45 SH8672
Daws Green Somset 8 ST2021
Daybrook Notts 49 SK5745
Daylesford Gloucs 29 SP2425
Deal Kent 15 TR3752
Dean Cumb 58 NY0725
Dean Devon 5 SX7364
Dean Devon 18 SS7048
Dean Hants 10 SU4431
Dean Hants 11 SU5619
Dean Lancs 54 SD8526
Dean Oxon 29 SP3422
Dean Somset 20 ST6743
Dean Bottom Kent 14 TQ5868
Dean Court Devon 29 SP4705
Dean Cross Devon 6 SS5042
Dean End Dorset 9 ST9617
Dean Prior Devon 5 SX7363
Dean Street Kent 14 TQ7451
Deanburnhaugh Border 67 NT3912
Deancombe Devon 5 SX7264
Deane Gt Man 47 SD6907
Deane Hants 21 SU5450

Deanhead W York 55 SE0415
Deanich Lodge Highld 96 NH3683
Deanland Dorset 9 ST9918
Deanraw Nthumb 68 NY8162
Deanscale Cumb 58 NY0926
Deanshanger Nhants 30 SP7639
Deanshaugh Gramp 94 NJ3550
Deanston Cent 81 NN7101
Debach Suffk 33 TM2454
Debden Cross Essex 24 TL5731
Debden Green Essex 23 TQ4398
Debenham Suffk 33 TM1763
Deblin's Green H & W 28 SO8149
Dechmont Loth 75 NT0470
Dechmont Road Loth 75 NT0269
Deddington Oxon 29 SP4631
Dedham Essex 25 TM0533
Dedworth Berks 22 SU9476
Deebank Gramp 89 NO6994
Deene Nhants 40 SP9492
Deenethorpe Nhants 40 SP9591
Deepdale Cumb 60 SD7284
Deepdale N York 60 SD8989
Deeping Gate Lincs 40 TF1509
Deeping St. James Lincs 41 TF1609
Deeping St. Nicholas Lincs 41 TF2115
Deerhurst Gloucs 28 SO8729
Defford H & W 28 SO9143
Defynnog Powys 26 SN9227
Deganwy Gwynd 45 SH7779
Degnish Strath 79 NM7812
Deighton N York 62 NZ2801
Deighton N York 56 SE6244
Deiniolen Gwynd 44 SH5863
Delabole Cnwll 4 SX0683
Delamere Ches 47 SJ5668
Delfrigs Gramp 95 NJ9620
Dell Quay W Susx 11 SU8302
Delliefure Highld 93 NJ0731
Delnashaugh Hotel Gramp 94 NJ1835
Delnato Gramp 93 NJ1517
Delny Highld 93 NH7372
Delves Dur 69 NZ1149
Delvine Tays 82 NO1240
Dembleby Lincs 40 TF0437
Denaby S York 49 SK4899
Denbigh Clwyd 45 SJ0566
Denbrae Fife 83 NO3818
Denbury Devon 5 SX8268
Denby Derbys 49 SK3946
Denby Dale W York 55 SE2208
Denchworth Oxon 21 SU3891
Dendron Cumb 53 SD2470
Denfield Strath 75 NS9517
Denford Nhants 30 SP9976
Dengie Essex 25 TL9802
Denham Suffk 33 TM1974
Denham Bucks 22 TQ0487
Denham Suffk 32 TL7561
Denham End Suffk 32 TL7683
Denham Green Bucks 22 TQ0388
Denhead Fife 83 NO4613
Denhead Gramp 95 NJ9952
Denhead of Gray Tays 83 NO3431
Denhead of Gray Tays 83 NO3531
Denholm Border 76 NT5718
Denholme W York 55 SE0734
Denmead Hants 11 SU6512
Denmore Gramp 95 NJ9411
Dennis Park W Mids 38 SO9585
Denny Cent 81 NS8082
Dennyloanhead Cent 82 NS8180
Denside Gramp 89 NO8095
Densole Kent 15 TR2141
Denston Suffk 32 TL7652
Denstone Staffs 48 SK0940
Denstroude Kent 15 TR1061
Dent Cumb 60 SD7087
Dent-de-Lion Kent 15 TR3269
Denton Cambs 40 TL1487
Denton Dur 61 NZ2118
Denton E Susx 13 TQ4502
Denton Gt Man 48 SJ9295
Denton Kent 15 TR2147
Denton Lincs 40 SK8632
Denton N York 55 SE1448
Denton Nhants 30 SP8358
Denton Norfk 41 TM2888
Denver Norfk 41 TF6101
Denwick Nthumb 69 NU2014
Deopham Norfk 42 TG0500
Deopham Green Norfk 42 TM0499
Deptford Gt Lon 23 TQ3777
Deptford Wilts 20 SU0038
Derby Derbys 49 SK3536
Derbyhaven IOM 52 SC2867
Derculich Tays 87 NN8852
Deri M Glam 18 SO1201
Derringstone Kent 15 TR2049
Derrington Staffs 38 SJ8922
Derriton Devon 6 SS3303
Derry Hill Wilts 20 ST9670
Derrythorpe Humb 56 SE8208
Dersingham Norfk 42 TF6830
Dervaig Strath 79 NM4352
Derwen Clwyd 46 SJ0750
Derwenlas Powys 35 SN7298
Desborough Nhants 40 SP8083
Desford Leics 39 SK4703
Deskford Gramp 94 NJ5061
Detling Kent 14 TQ7958
Devauden Gwent 19 ST4898
Devil's Bridge Dyfed 35 SN7477
Devizes Wilts 20 SU0061
Devonport Devon 4 SX4554
Devonside Cent 82 NS9296
Devoran Cnwll 2 SW7939
Dewarton Loth 76 NT3763
Dewlish Dorset 9 SY7798
Dewsbury W York 55 SE2422
Deytheur Powys 36 SJ2417
Dhoon IOM 52 SC3784
Dhoor IOM 52 SC4396
Dhowin IOM 52 NX4101
Dial A Von 19 ST5367
Dial Green W Susx 11 SU9227
Dial Post W Susx 12 TQ1519
Dibden Hants 10 SU4108
Dibden Purlieu Hants 10 SU4106
Dickens Heath W Mids 38 SP1076
Dickleburgh Norfk 33 TM1682
Didbrook Gloucs 28 SP0531
Didcot Oxon 21 SU5190
Diddlebury Shrops 37 SO5085
Didling W Susx 11 SU8318
Didmarton Gloucs 20 ST8287
Didsbury Gt Man 47 SJ8392
Digby Lincs 50 TF0854
Digg Highld 90 NG4669
Diggle Gt Man 48 SD9808
Digmore Lancs 46 SD4805
Digswell Water Herts 31 TL2414
Dihewyd Dyfed 34 SN4855
Dilham Norfk 43 TG3325
Dilhorne Staffs 48 SJ9743
Dillington Cambs 30 TL1365
Dilston Nthumb 68 NY9763
Dilton Wilts 20 ST8548
Dilton Marsh Wilts 20 ST8449
Dilwyn H & W 27 SO4154
Dinas Cnwll 3 SW9174
Dinas Dyfed 16 SN0139
Dinas Gwynd 44 SH2732
Dinas Dinlle Gwynd 44 SH4356
Dinas Powis S Glam 19 ST1571
Dinas-Mawddwy Gwynd 35 SH8615
Dinder Somset 19 ST5744
Dinedor H & W 27 SO5336
Dingle Mersyd 46 SJ3687
Dingley Nhants 40 SP7787
Dingwall Highld 92 NH5458
Dinnet Gramp 88 NO4598
Dinnington S York 49 SK5386
Dinnington Somset 8 ST4012
Dinnington T & W 69 NZ2073
Dinorwic Gwynd 44 SH5961
Dinton Bucks 22 SP7611
Dinton Wilts 9 SU0131
Dinwoodie D & G 67 NY1090

Dinworthy Devon 6 SS3015
Dipford Somset 8 ST2022
Dippen Strath 72 NR7937
Dippertown Devon 4 SX4385
Dippin Strath 72 NS0422
Dipple Gramp 94 NJ3258
Dipple Strath 73 NS2002
Diptford Devon 5 SX7256
Dipton Dur 69 NZ1554
Dirleton Loth 83 NT5184
Dirt Pot Nthumb 68 NY8546
Diseworth Leics 39 SK4524
Dishforth N York 62 SE3873
Diss Norfk 33 TM1180
Distillery Highld 92 NH5150
Distillery Highld 93 NJ0727
Distington Cumb 58 NY0023
Ditchampton Wilts 10 SU0831
Ditchburn Nthumb 77 NU1320
Ditchingham Norfk 33 TM3391
Ditchling E Susx 12 TQ3215
Ditteridge Wilts 20 ST8169
Dittisham Devon 5 SX8684
Ditton Ches 46 SJ4986
Ditton Kent 14 TQ7158
Ditton Green Cambs 32 TL6558
Ditton Priors Shrops 37 SO6089
Dixton Gloucs 28 SO9830
Dixton Gwent 27 SO5113
Dobcross St Man 54 SD9906
Dobwalls Cnwll 4 SX2165
Doccombe Devon 5 SX7786
Dochgarroch Highld 92 NH6241
Docker Lancs 59 SD5774
Docking Norfk 42 TF7636
Docklow H & W 27 SO5587
Dockray Cumb 59 NY3921
Dodd's Green Ches 47 SJ6043
Doddinghurst Essex 24 TQ5999
Doddington Cambs 41 TL4090
Doddington Kent 14 TQ9357
Doddington Lincs 50 SK9070
Doddington Nthumb 77 NT9932
Doddington Shrops 37 SO6176
Doddiscombsleigh Devon 5 SX8586
Dodford H & W 38 SO9373
Dodford Nhants 29 SP6160
Dodington Avon 20 ST7580
Dodleston Ches 46 SJ3661
Dodside Strath 74 NS5053
Dodworth S York 55 SE3105
Dodworth Bottom S York 55 SE3205
Dodworth Green S York 55 SE3103
Doe Lea Derbys 49 SK4566
Dog Village Devon 7 SX9896
Dogdyke Lincs 51 TF2055
Dogmersfield Hants 22 SU7852
Dogridge Wilts 20 SU0787
Dolanog Powys 36 SJ0612
Dolau Powys 26 SO1367
Dolbenmaen Gwynd 44 SH5043
Dolcombe Devon 5 SX7786
Dolfor Powys 36 SO1087
Dolgarrog Gwynd 45 SH7767
Dolgellau Gwynd 35 SH7217
Dolgoch Gwynd 35 SH6404
Doll Highld 97 NC8803
Dollar Cent 82 NS9698
Dollarbeg Cent 82 NS9796
Dollarfield Cent 82 NS9697
Dollwen Dyfed 35 SN6981
Dolphin Clwyd 46 SJ1973
Dolphinholme Lancs 53 SD5263
Dolphinstone Border 76 NT6815
Dolphinton Strath 75 NT1046
Dolton Devon 6 SS5712
Dolwen Clwyd 45 SH8874
Dolwyddelan Gwynd 45 SH7352
Domgay Powys 36 SJ2819
Doncaster S York 56 SE5803
Doncaster Carr S York 49 SE5901
Donhead St. Mary Wilts 9 ST9024
Donibristle Fife 82 NT1688
Donington Lincs 41 TF2035
Donington on Bain Lincs 51 TF2382
Donington Leics 39 SK3114
Donkey Street Kent 15 TR1233
Donkey Town Surrey 22 SU9460
Donnington Berks 21 SU4668
Donnington Gloucs 29 SP1928
Donnington Shrops 37 SJ5808
Donnington W Susx 11 SU8502
Donnington Wood Shrops 37 SJ7012
Donyatt Somset 8 ST3313
Doomsday Green W Susx 12 TQ1930
Doon Castle Strath 65 NX4895
Doonfoot Strath 73 NS3219
Doonholm Strath 73 NS3317
Dorback Lodge Highld 93 NJ0716
Dorchester Dorset 9 SY6990
Dorchester Oxon 21 SU5794
Dordon Warwks 39 SK2600
Dore S York 49 SK3081
Dores Highld 92 NH5934
Dorking Surrey 12 TQ1649
Dorking Tye Suffk 32 TL9257
Dorlin House Highld 85 NM6471
Dormans Land Surrey 13 TQ4041
Dormans Park Surrey 13 TQ3940
Dormington H & W 27 SO5840
Dormston H & W 28 SO9857
Dornal Strath 64 NX3077
Dorney Berks 22 SU9378
Dornie Highld 85 NG8826
Dornoch Highld 97 NH7989
Dornock D & G 67 NY2366
Dorrery Highld 100 ND0755
Dorridge W Mids 38 SP1775
Dorrington Lincs 50 TF0852
Dorrington Shrops 37 SJ4703
Dorsington Warwks 28 SP1349
Dorstone H & W 27 SO3141
Dorton Bucks 30 SP6714
Douglas IOM 52 SC3876
Douglas Strath 74 NS8330
Douglas Castle Strath 74 NS8431
Douglas Hill Gwynd 44 SH6065
Douglas Pier Strath 80 NS1999
Douglas Water Strath 74 NS8736
Douglas West Strath 74 NS8231
Douglas and Angus Tays 83 NO4233
Douglastown Tays 88 NO4147
Dougrie Strath 72 NR8837
Dounby Ork 103 HY2920
Doune Cent 81 NN7201
Doune Highld 96 NC4400
Dounepark Strath 64 NX1897
Dounie Highld 96 NH5690
Dounreay Highld 100 NC9965
Dousland Devon 4 SX5368
Dove Holes Derbys 48 SK0778
Dovenby Cumb 58 NY0933
Dovercourt Essex 25 TM2531
Doverdale H & W 28 SO8666
Doveridge Derbys 38 SK1134
Doversgreen Surrey 12 TQ2548
Dowally Tays 88 NO0048
Dowdeswell Gloucs 28 SP0019
Dowlais M Glam 18 SO0607
Dowland Devon 6 SS5610
Dowlish Wake Somset 8 ST3712
Down Ampney Gloucs 20 SU0997
Down Hatherley Gloucs 28 SO8622
Down St. Mary Devon 7 SS7404
Down Thomas Devon 4 SX5050
Downderry Cnwll 4 SX3153
Downe Gt Lon 23 TQ4361
Downend Avon 19 ST6577
Downend Gloucs 20 ST8398
Downgate Cnwll 4 SX2871
Downgate Cnwll 4 SX3773
Downham Cambs 41 TL5284
Downham Essex 24 TQ7296

Downham Gt Lon 23 TQ3871
Downham Lancs 54 SD7844
Downham Market Norfk 41 TF6003
Downhead Somset 8 ST5625
Downhead Somset 20 ST5945
Downhill Tays 82 NO0930
Downholme N York 61 SE1197
Downies Gramp 89 NO9294
Downley Bucks 22 SU8495
Downside Surrey 22 TQ1088
Downton Hants 10 SZ2693
Downton Wilts 10 SU1721
Downton on the Rock H & W 36 SO4273
Dowsby Lincs 40 TF1129
Doxey Staffs 38 SJ9023
Doynton Avon 20 ST7173
Draethen M Glam 19 ST2287
Draffan Strath 74 NS7945
Draicie Hole Notts 49 SK7090
Drakeland Corner Devon 4 SX5758
Drakemyre Strath 73 NS2950
Drakes Broughton H & W 28 SO9248
Drakewalls Cnwll 4 SX4271
Draughton N York 55 SE0352
Draughton Nhants 30 SP7676
Drax N York 56 SE6726
Drax Hales N York 56 SE6726
Draycote Warwks 29 SP4570
Draycott Derbys 39 SK4433
Draycott Gloucs 29 SP1835
Draycott Shrops 37 SO8192
Draycott Somset 37 ST4751
Draycott in the Clay Staffs 38 SK1528
Draycott in the Moors Staffs 48 SJ9840
Drayford Devon 7 SS7913
Drayton H & W 38 SO9076
Drayton Hants 11 SU6705
Drayton Leics 40 SP8392
Drayton Norfk 43 TG1833
Drayton Oxon 29 SP4241
Drayton Oxon 21 SU4794
Drayton Somset 8 ST4024
Drayton Bassett Staffs 39 SK1900
Drayton Beauchamp Bucks 22 SP9011
Drayton Parslow Bucks 30 SP8428
Drayton St. Leonard Oxon 21 SU5996
Dreenhill Dyfed 16 SM9214
Drefach Dyfed 17 SN3538
Drefach Dyfed 17 SN5213
Drefach Dyfed 17 SN5045
Dreghorn Strath 73 NS3538
Drellingore Kent 15 TR2141
Drem Loth 83 NT5079
Drewsteignton Devon 5 SX7391
Driby Lincs 51 TF3784
Driffield Gloucs 20 SU0799
Driffield Cross Roads Gloucs 20 SU0699
Drift Cnwll 2 SW4328
Drigg Cumb 58 SD0699
Drighlington W York 55 SE2229
Drimnin Highld 79 NM6554
Drimpton Dorset 8 ST4104
Drimsallie Highld 85 NM9578
Drimsynie Strath 80 NN1901
Drimvore Strath 71 NR8394
Dringhouses N York 56 SE5849
Drinkstone Suffk 32 TL9661
Drinkstone Green Suffk 32 TL9660
Drinsey Nook Notts 50 SK8673
Driver's End Herts 31 TL2220
Drointon Staffs 38 SK0226
Droitwich Spa H & W 28 SO8963
Dron Tays 82 NO1416
Dronfield Derbys 49 SK3578
Dronfield Woodhouse Derbys 49 SK3278
Drongan Strath 73 NS4519
Dronley Tays 83 NO3435
Droop Dorset 9 ST7908
Dropping Well S York 49 SK3993
Droxford Hants 11 SU6018
Droylsden Gt Man 48 SJ9098
Druid Clwyd 45 SJ0443
Druidale IOM 52 SC3688
Druids Heath W Mids 38 SK0601
Druidston Dyfed 16 SM8716
Druimachoish Highld 86 NN1246
Druimarbin Highld 86 NN0870
Druimdrishaig Strath 71 NR7370
Druimindarroch Highld 85 NM6884
Drum Strath 72 NR6625
Drum Strath 71 NR9276
Drum Tays 82 NO0400
Drum Kildavie Strath 72 NR7210
Drumalbin Strath 74 NS9038
Drumbeg Highld 98 NC1232
Drumblade Gramp 94 NJ5840
Drumblair House Gramp 94 NJ6343
Drumbuie Highld 85 NG7730
Drumburgh Cumb 67 NY2659
Drumburn D & G 66 NX8855
Drumburn D & G 66 NX9762
Drumchapel Strath 74 NS5270
Drumchastle Tays 87 NN6858
Drumclog Strath 74 NS6439
Drumeldrie Fife 83 NO4403
Drumelzier Border 75 NT1334
Drumfearn Highld 85 NG6716
Drumfrennie Gramp 89 NO7298
Drumgask Highld 87 NN6193
Drumguish Highld 87 NN7900
Drumhead Gramp 89 NO6092
Drumin Gramp 94 NJ1830
Drumjohn D & G 65 NX5297
Drumlamford Strath 64 NX2876
Drumlasie Gramp 89 NJ6405
Drumleaning Cumb 67 NY2751
Drumlemble Strath 72 NR6651
Drumlithie Gramp 89 NO7880
Drummoddie D & G 64 NX3945
Drummond Highld 92 NH6065
Drummore D & G 64 NX1336
Drummore D & G 66 NX9075
Drummuir Gramp 94 NJ3844
Drumnadrochit Highld 92 NH5029
Drumnagorrach Gramp 94 NJ5252
Drumore D & G 72 NR7022
Drumpark D & G 66 NX8780
Drumrash D & G 65 NX6871
Drumrunie Lodge Highld 96 NC1604
Drumshang Strath 73 NS2514
Drumsleet D & G 66 NX9474
Drumstinchall D & G 66 NX3644
Drumuie Highld 90 NG4546
Drumuillie Highld 93 NH9420
Drumvaich Cent 81 NN6703
Drumwhirn D & G 65 NX7480
Drunzie Tays 82 NO1308
Dry Doddington Lincs 50 SK8546
Dry Drayton Cambs 31 TL3962
Dry Sandford Oxon 21 SP4900
Drybeck Cumb 60 NY6615
Drybridge Gramp 94 NJ4362
Drybridge Strath 73 NS3536
Drybrook Gloucs 27 SO6417
Dryhope Border 75 NT2622
Dryhope Border 75 NT2624
Drym Cnwll 2 SW6233
Drymen Cent 81 NS5905
Drymuir Gramp 95 NJ9146
Drynoch Highld 84 NG4031
Dryslwyn Dyfed 17 SN5505
Dryton Shrops 37 SJ5905
Duachy Strath 79 NM7963
Duchally Highld 96 NC3817
Duck End Essex 24 TL6833
Duckington Ches 46 SJ4951
Ducklington Oxon 29 SP3507
Duddenhoe End Essex 31 TL4636
Duddingston Loth 75 NT3072
Duddington Nhants 40 SK9800
Duddlestone Somset 8 ST2321
Duddlewick Shrops 37 SO6583
Duddo Nthumb 77 NT9342
Duddon Ches 46 SJ5164
Dudleston Shrops 36 SJ3438
Dudley T & W 69 NZ2673
Dudley W Mids 38 SO9490
Dudley Port W Mids 38 SO9691
Dudsbury Dorset 10 SZ0898

Place	Sheet	Grid
Duffield Derbys	49	SK3443
Duffryn M Glam	18	SS8495
Dufftown Gramp	94	NJ3240
Duffus Gramp	94	NJ1668
Dufton Cumb	60	NY6825
Duggleby N York	56	SE8767
Duirinish Highld	85	NG7831
Duisdalemore Highld	85	NG6913
Duisky Highld	85	NN0076
Duke Street Suffk	32	TM0842
Dukinfield Gt Man	48	SJ9497
Dulcote Somset	19	ST5644
Dulford Devon	7	ST0606
Dull Tays	87	NN8049
Dullatur Strath	74	NS7476
Dullingham Cambs	32	TL6357
Dullingham Ley Cambs	32	TL6456
Dulnain Bridge Highld	93	NH9924
Duloe Beds	30	TL1560
Duloe Cnwll	4	SX2358
Dulverton Somset	7	SS9127
Dulwich Gt Lon	23	TQ3373
Dumbarton Strath	80	NS3975
Dumbleton Gloucs	28	SP0136
Dumcrieff D & G	67	NT1104
Dumfries D & G	66	NX9776
Dumgoyne Cent	81	NS5283
Dummer Hants	21	SU5846
Dumpton Kent	15	TR3866
Dun Tays	89	NO6660
Dunalastair Tays	87	NN7159
Dunan Highld	84	NG5828
Dunan Strath	80	NS1571
Dunan Tays	87	NN4757
Dunans Strath	80	NS0491
Dunaverty Strath	72	NR6807
Dunavourd Tays	75	NS9657
Dunball Somset	19	ST3041
Dunbar Loth	81	NT6778
Dunbau Somset	19	ST3140
Dunbeath Highld	100	ND1630
Dunbeg Strath	79	NM8833
Dunblane Cent	81	NN7801
Dunbog Fife	83	NO2817
Dunbridge Hants	10	SU3126
Duncanston Gramp	94	NJ5726
Duncanston Highld	92	NH5956
Dunchideock Devon	5	SX8787
Dunchurch Warwks	39	SP4871
Duncow D & G	66	NX9683
Duncrievie Tays	82	NO1309
Duncton W Susx	12	SU9617
Dundee Tays	83	NO4030
Dundon Somset	8	ST4732
Dundonald Strath	73	NS3634
Dundonnell Highld	91	NH0886
Dundreggan Highld	92	NH3214
Dundrennan D & G	65	NX7447
Dundry Avon	19	ST5566
Dunecht Gramp	95	NJ7509
Dunfermline Fife	82	NT0987
Dunfield Gloucs	20	SU1497
Dungavel Strath	74	NS6637
Dunglass Loth	76	NT7671
Dungworth S York	49	SK2889
Dunham Notts	50	SK8174
Dunham Town Gt Man	47	SJ7387
Dunham Woodhouses Gt Man	47	SJ7287
Dunham-on-the-Hill Ches	46	SJ4772
Dunhampton H & W	28	SO8466
Dunholme Lincs	50	TF0279
Dunino Fife	83	NO5311
Dunipace Cent	81	NS8083
Dunira Tays	81	NN7323
Dunk's Green Kent	13	TQ6152
Dunkeld Tays	88	NO0242
Dunkerton Avon	20	ST7159
Dunkeswell Devon	8	ST1407
Dunkeswick W York	55	SE3047
Dunkirk Avon	20	ST7886
Dunkirk Kent	15	TR0759
Dunlappie Tays	89	NO5867
Dunley H & W	28	SO7869
Dunlop Strath	73	NS4049
Dunmaglass Highld	92	NH6922
Dunmore Cent	82	NS8989
Dunmore Strath	71	NR7961
Dunnet Highld	100	ND2171
Dunnichen Tays	89	NO5048
Dunning Tays	82	NO0114
Dunnington Humb	57	TA1551
Dunnington N York	56	SE6652
Dunnington Warwks	28	SP0653
Dunnockshaw Lancs	54	SD8227
Dunoon Strath	80	NS1777
Dunphail Gramp	93	NJ0148
Dunragit D & G	64	NX1557
Dunrod Strath	80	NS2273
Duns Border	76	NT7853
Duns Tew Oxon	29	SP4528
Dunsby Lincs	40	TF1026
Dunscore D & G	66	NX8684
Dunsdale Cleve	62	NZ6019
Dunsden Green Oxon	22	SU7377
Dunsdon Devon	6	SS3008
Dunsfold Surrey	12	TQ0036
Dunsford Devon	5	SX8189
Dunshelt Fife	83	NO2410
Dunshillock Gramp	95	NJ9848
Dunsley N York	63	NZ8511
Dunsley Staffs	38	SO8583
Dunsmore Bucks	22	SP8605
Dunsop Bridge Lancs	54	SD6650
Dunstable Beds	30	TL0122
Dunstall Staffs	39	SK1920
Dunstan Nthumb	77	NU2420
Dunster Somset	7	SS9943
Dunston Lincs	50	TF0663
Dunston Norfk	43	TG2202
Dunston Staffs	38	SJ9217
Dunston T & W	69	NZ2262
Dunston Heath Staffs	38	SJ9117
Dunstone Devon	5	SX5951
Dunstone Devon	5	SX7175
Dunswell Humb	57	TA0736
Dunsyre Strath	75	NT0748
Dunterton Devon	4	SX3779
Duntisbourne Abbots Gloucs	28	SO9607
Duntisbourne Rouse Gloucs	28	SO9805
Duntocher Strath	74	NS4973
Dunton Beds	31	TL2244
Dunton Bucks	30	SP8224
Dunton Norfk	42	TF8830
Dunton Bassett Leics	39	SP5490
Dunton Green Kent	23	TQ5157
Duntulm Highld	90	NG4174
Dunure Strath	73	NS2515
Dunvant W Glam	17	SS5993
Dunvegan Highld	90	NG2548
Duran Cnwll	2	SW7727
Durdar Dur	61	NZ2742
Durisdeer D & G	66	NS8903
Durisdeermill D & G	66	NS8804
Durkar W York	55	SE3117
Durleigh Somset	19	ST2736
Durley Hants	11	SU5116
Durley Wilts	21	SU2364
Durley Street Hants	11	SU5217
Durlock Kent	15	TR2758
Durlock Kent	15	TR3164
Durmgley Tays	88	NO4250
Durnamuck Highld	91	NH0192
Durness Highld	98	NC4067
Durno Gramp	95	NJ7128
Duror Highld	86	NM9754
Durran Highld	100	ND1963
Durran Strath	80	NM9607
Durrington W Susx	12	TQ1105
Durrington Wilts	20	SU1544
Dursley Gloucs	20	ST7597
Dursley Cross Gloucs	28	SO6920
Durston Somset	8	ST2828
Durweston Dorset	9	ST8508
Duston Nhants	30	SP7261
Duthil Highld	93	NH9324
Dutlas Powys	27	SO2077
Dutson M Glam	4	SX3486
Dutton Ches	47	SJ5779
Duxford Cambs	31	TL4846
Duxford Oxon	21	SU3699
Dwygyfylchi Gwynd	45	SH7376
Dwygyfylchi Gwynd	45	SH7377
Dwyran Gwynd	44	SH4466
Dyce Gramp	95	NJ8812
Dye House Nthumb	68	NY9458
Dyer's End Essex	24	TL7238
Dyfatty Dyfed	17	SN4501
Dyffryn Ardudwy Gwynd	34	SH5822
Dyffryn Ceidrych Dyfed	26	SN7025
Dyffryn Cellwn W Glam	26	SN8510
Dyke Gramp	93	NH9858
Dyke Lincs	40	TF1022
Dykehead Cent	81	NS5997
Dykehead Strath	74	NS8659
Dykehead Tays	88	NO2453
Dykehead Tays	88	NO3860
Dykelands Gramp	89	NO7068
Dykends Tays	88	NO2557
Dykeside Gramp	95	NJ7243
Dymchurch Kent	15	TR1029
Dymock Gloucs	28	SO6931
Dyrham Avon	20	ST7375
Dysart Fife	83	NT3093
Dyserth Clwyd	45	SJ0579

E

Place	Sheet	Grid
Eagland Hill Lancs	53	SD4345
Eagle Lincs	50	SK8767
Eaglescliffe Cleve	62	NZ4215
Eaglesfield Cumb	58	NY0928
Eaglesfield D & G	67	NY2374
Eaglesham Strath	74	NS5751
Eagley Gt Man	54	SD7112
Eakring Notts	49	SK6762
Ealand Humb	56	SE7811
Ealing Gt Lon	23	TQ1780
Eals Nthumb	68	NY6756
Eamont Bridge Cumb	59	NY5228
Earby Lancs	54	SD9046
Eardington Shrops	37	SO7290
Eardisland H & W	27	SO4158
Eardisley H & W	27	SO3149
Eardiston H & W	28	SO6968
Eardiston Shrops	36	SJ3725
Earith Cambs	31	TL3875
Earl Shilton Leics	39	SP4697
Earl Soham Suffk	33	TM2363
Earl Sterndale Derbys	48	SK0967
Earl's Croome H & W	28	SO8642
Earlestown Mersyd	47	SJ5795
Earley Berks	22	SU7472
Earlham Norfk	43	TG2008
Earlish Highld	90	NG3961
Earls Barton Nhants	30	SP8563
Earls Colne Essex	24	TL8528
Earls Com H & W	28	SO9559
Earlsdon W Mids	39	SP3278
Earlsferry Fife	83	NO4800
Earlsfield Gt Lon	23	TQ2673
Earlsford Gramp	95	NJ8334
Earlsheaton W York	55	SE2621
Earlston Border	76	NT5738
Earlston Strath	73	NS4035
Earlswood Surrey	12	TQ2849
Earlswood W Mids	38	SO8995
Earlswood Warwks	38	SP1174
Earlswood Common Gwent	19	ST4595
Earnley W Susx	11	SZ8197
Earsdon Nthumb	69	NZ1993
Earsdon T & W	69	NZ3272
Earsham Norfk	33	TM3289
Eartham W Susx	11	SU9309
Easby N York	62	NZ5708
Easebourne W Susx	11	SU8922
Easenhall Warwks	39	SP4679
Eashing Surrey	12	SU9443
Easington Bucks	22	SP6810
Easington Cleve	63	NZ7417
Easington Dur	69	NZ4143
Easington Humb	57	TA3919
Easington Oxon	21	SU6597
Easington Colliery Dur	69	NZ4344
Easingwold N York	55	SE5269
Eassie and Nevay Tays	88	NO3344
East Aberthaw S Glam	18	ST0366
East Allington Devon	5	SX7648
East Anstey Devon	7	SS8626
East Anton Hants	21	SU3647
East Appleton N York	61	SE2395
East Ashley IOW	11	SZ5888
East Ashling W Susx	11	SU8207
East Aston Hants	21	SU4345
East Ayton N York	63	SE9985
East Bank Gwent	27	SO2106
East Barkwith Lincs	50	TF1681
East Barming Kent	14	TQ7254
East Barnby N York	63	NZ8212
East Barnet Gt Lon	23	TQ2794
East Barns Loth	76	NT7176
East Barsham Norfk	42	TF9134
East Beckham Norfk	43	TG1639
East Bedfont Gt Lon	22	TQ0873
East Bergholt Suffk	25	TM0734
East Bilney Norfk	42	TF9519
East Blanerne Border	77	NT8457
East Blatchington E Susx	13	TQ4800
East Bloxworth Dorset	9	SY8994
East Boldon T & W	69	NZ3761
East Boldre Hants	10	SU3700
East Bower Somset	19	ST3137
East Bradenham Norfk	42	TF9308
East Brent Somset	19	ST3452
East Bridgford Notts	49	SK6943
East Buckland Devon	7	SS6731
East Budleigh Devon	5	SY0684
East Butterwick Humb	56	SE8306
East Calder Loth	75	NT0867
East Carleton Norfk	43	TG1702
East Carlton Nhants	40	SP8389
East Carlton W York	55	SE2243
East Challow Oxon	21	SU3888
East Charleton Devon	5	SX7642
East Chelborough Dorset	8	ST5405
East Chiltington E Susx	13	TQ3715
East Chinnock Somset	8	ST4913
East Cholderton Hants	21	SU2945
East Clandon Surrey	12	TQ0651
East Claydon Bucks	30	SP7325
East Coker Somset	8	ST5412
East Combe Somset	8	ST1631
East Compton Somset	19	ST6141
East Cornworthy Devon	5	SX8455
East Cottingwith Humb	56	SE7042
East Coulston Wilts	20	ST9454
East Cowes IOW	10	SZ5065
East Cowick Humb	56	SE6621
East Cowton N York	62	NZ3103
East Cranmore Somset	20	ST6743
East Creech Dorset	9	SY9282
East Dean Gloucs	27	SO6520
East Dean Hants	10	SU2626
East Dean Hants	10	SU2726
East Dean W Susx	11	SU9013
East Dereham Norfk	42	TF9913
East Down Devon	6	SS6041
East Drayton Notts	50	SK7775
East Dulwich Gt Lon	23	TQ3375
East Dundry Avon	19	ST5766
East Ella Humb	57	TA0529
East End Hants	24	SU4160
East End Hants	10	SZ3697
East End Humb	57	TA1930
East End Humb	57	TA2727
East End Kent	14	TQ8335
East End Oxon	29	SP3914
East End Somset	20	ST6746
East Everleigh Wilts	21	SU2053
East Farleigh Kent	14	TQ7353
East Farndon Nhants	40	SP7184
East Ferry Lincs	50	SK8199
East Flexford Surrey	12	SU9448
East Fortune Loth	83	NT5579
East Garforth W York	55	SE4133
East Garston Berks	21	SU3576
East Goscote Leics	39	SK6413
East Grafton Wilts	21	SU2560
East Grange Gramp	93	NJ0691
East Grimstead Wilts	10	SU2227
East Grinstead W Susx	13	TQ3938
East Guldeford E Susx	14	TQ9321
East Haddon Nhants	30	SP6668
East Hagbourne Oxon	21	SU5388
East Halton Humb	57	TA1319
East Ham Gt Lon	23	TQ4283
East Hanney Oxon	21	SU4193
East Hanningfield Essex	24	TL7701
East Hardwick W York	55	SE4616
East Harling Norfk	32	TL9986
East Harlsey N York	62	SE4299
East Harnham Wilts	10	SU1428
East Harptree Avon	19	ST5655
East Hartburn Cleve	62	NZ4117
East Hartford Nthumb	69	NZ2679
East Harting W Susx	11	SU8019
East Hatch Wilts	9	ST9228
East Hatley Cambs	31	TL2850
East Hauxwell N York	61	SE1693
East Haven Tays	83	NO5836
East Heath Berks	22	SU6967
East Heckington Lincs	50	TF1944
East Hedleyhope Dur	61	NZ1540
East Helmsdale Highld	97	ND0315
East Hendred Oxon	21	SU4588
East Herrington T & W	69	NZ3453
East Heslerton N York	63	SE9276
East Hewish Avon	19	ST3964
East Hoathly E Susx	13	TQ5216
East Holme Dorset	9	SY8986
East Horndon Essex	24	TQ6389
East Horrington Somset	19	ST5846
East Horsley Surrey	12	TQ0953
East Horton Nthumb	77	NU0331
East Howe Dorset	10	SZ0795
East Huntington N York	56	SE6155
East Hyde Beds	30	TL1217
East Ilkerton Devon	7	SS7146
East Ilsley Berks	21	SU4980
East Keal Lincs	51	TF3764
East Kennett Wilts	20	SU1167
East Keswick W York	55	SE3544
East Kilbride Strath	74	NS6354
East Kimber Devon	4	SX4989
East Kirkby Lincs	51	TF3362
East Knighton Dorset	9	SY8185
East Knoyle Wilts	9	ST8830
East Kyloe Nthumb	77	NU0639
East Lambrook Somset	8	ST4319
East Langdon Kent	15	TR3346
East Langton Leics	40	SP7292
East Langwell Highld	97	NC7206
East Laroch Highld	86	NN0858
East Lavant W Susx	11	SU8608
East Lavington W Susx	12	SU9416
East Layton N York	61	NZ1609
East Leake Notts	39	SK5526
East Leigh Devon	5	SX7657
East Leigh Devon	7	SS6905
East Lexham Norfk	42	TF8617
East Linton Loth	76	NT5877
East Lockinge Oxon	21	SU4287
East Lound Humb	50	SK7899
East Lulworth Dorset	9	SY8581
East Lutton N York	56	SE9469
East Lydford Somset	8	ST5731
East Mains Gramp	89	NO6797
East Malling Kent	14	TQ7057
East Marden W Susx	11	SU8014
East Markham Notts	50	SK7472
East Martin Hants	10	SU0719
East Marton N York	54	SD9051
East Meon Hants	11	SU6822
East Mersea Essex	25	TM0514
East Molesey Surrey	22	TQ1467
East Morden Dorset	9	SY9194
East Morton D & G	66	NS8801
East Norton Leics	40	SK7800
East Ogwell Devon	5	SX8370
East Orchard Dorset	9	ST8317
East Ord Nthumb	77	NT9751
East Parley Dorset	10	SZ1098
East Pennar Dyfed	16	SM9602
East Pennard Somset	19	ST5937
East Perry Cambs	30	TL1467
East Plean Cent	82	NS8387
East Poringland Norfk	43	TG2701
East Portlemouth Devon	5	SX7438
East Prawle Devon	5	SX7736
East Preston W Susx	12	TQ0702
East Pulham Dorset	9	ST7109
East Putford Devon	6	SS3616
East Quantoxhead Somset	18	ST1343
East Rainton T & W	69	NZ3347
East Ravendale Lincs	51	TF2399
East Raynham Norfk	42	TF8825
East Rigton W York	55	SE3743
East Rounton N York	62	NZ4203
East Rudham Norfk	42	TF8328
East Runton Norfk	43	TG1942
East Ruston Norfk	43	TG3427
East Saltoun Loth	76	NT4767
East Sheen Gt Lon	23	TQ2075
East Shefford Berks	21	SU3974
East Stoke Dorset	9	SY8787
East Stoke Notts	50	SK7549
East Stour Dorset	9	ST8022
East Stourmouth Kent	15	TR2662
East Stowford Devon	7	SS6326
East Stratton Hants	21	SU5440
East Sutton Kent	14	TQ8249
East Taphouse Cnwll	3	SX1863
East Thirston Nthumb	61	NZ1900
East Tilbury Essex	24	TQ6877
East Tisted Hants	11	SU7032
East Torrington Lincs	50	TF1483
East Tuddenham Norfk	42	TG0811
East Tytherley Hants	10	SU2929
East Tytherley Hants	10	SU2929
East Tytherton Wilts	20	ST9674
East Village Devon	7	SS8405
East Wall Shrops	37	SO5293
East Walton Norfk	42	TF7416
East Water Somset	19	ST5251
East Week Devon	5	SX6692
East Wellow Hants	10	SU3020
East Wemyss Fife	83	NT3497
East Whitburn Loth	75	NS9665
East Wickham Gt Lon	23	TQ4576
East Williamston Dyfed	16	SN0905
East Winch Norfk	42	TF6916
East Winterslow Wilts	10	SU2434
East Wittering W Susx	11	SZ7996
East Witton N York	61	SE1486
East Woodburn Nthumb	68	NY9086
East Woodhay Hants	21	SU4061
East Woodlands Somset	20	ST7843
East Worldham Hants	11	SU7438
East Wretham Norfk	32	TL9190
East Youlstone Devon	6	SS2715
Eastbourne Dur	61	NZ3013
Eastbridge Suffk	33	TM4566
Eastburn W York	55	SE0144
Eastbury Berks	21	SU3477
Eastbury Gt Lon	22	TQ1092
Eastbury Herts	22	TQ1092
Eastby N York	54	SE0154
Eastchurch Kent	15	TQ9871
Eastcombe Gloucs	28	SO8804
Eastcote Gt Lon	22	TQ1088
Eastcote W Mids	39	SP1979
Eastcott Cnwll	6	SS2515
Eastcott Wilts	20	SU0255
Eastcourt Wilts	20	ST9792
Eastcourt Wilts	20	SU2361
Eastend Essex	25	TQ9492
Eastend Essex	25	TQ9492
Eastend Strath	75	NS9437
Easter Balmoral Gramp	88	NO2694
Easter Compton Avon	19	ST5782
Easter Dalziel Highld	93	NH7550
Easter Fearn Highld	97	NH6486
Easter Howgate Tays	75	NT2463
Easter Kinkell Highld	92	NH5755
Easter Lednathie Tays	88	NO3463
Easter Moniack Highld	92	NH5543
Easter Ord Gramp	89	NJ3904
Easter Pitkierie Fife	83	NO5606
Easter Sheld Shet	103	HU3144
Eastergate W Susx	12	SU9405
Easterhouse Strath	74	NS6765
Eastern Green W Mids	39	SP2879
Easterton Wilts	20	SU0154
Eastertown Somset	19	ST3454
Eastertown Strath	74	NS8620
Eastfield Cent	74	NS9574
Eastfield Strath	74	NS7575
Eastgate Dur	61	NY9538
Eastgate Norfk	43	TG1423
Easthampstead Berks	22	SU8667
Easthampton H & W	27	SO4063
Easthope Shrops	37	SO5695
Easthorpe Essex	24	TL9121
Easthorpe Notts	49	SK7053
Easthouses Loth	7	SS7409
Eastington Gloucs	28	SP1213
Eastington Gloucs	28	SO7705
Eastlands D & G	66	NX8172
Eastleach Martin Gloucs	29	SP2005
Eastleach Turville Gloucs	29	SP1905
Eastleigh Devon	6	SS4827
Eastleigh Hants	10	SU4519
Eastling Kent	15	TQ9656
Eastney Hants	11	SZ6698
Eastnor H & W	28	SO7337
Eastoft Humb	56	SE8016
Easton Berks	21	SU4271
Easton Cambs	30	TL1371
Easton Cumb	67	NY2759
Easton Devon	5	SX7288
Easton Hants	11	SU5132
Easton IOW	10	SZ3486
Easton Lincs	40	SK9326
Easton Norfk	43	TG1310
Easton Somset	19	ST5147
Easton Suffk	33	TM2858
Easton Wilts	20	ST8970
Easton Grey Wilts	20	ST8787
Easton Maudit Nhants	30	SP8858
Easton Royal Wilts	21	SU2060
Easton on the Hill Nhants	40	TF0104
Easton-in-Gordano Avon	19	ST5175
Eastpeek Devon	6	SX3494
Eastrea Cambs	41	TL2997
Eastriggs D & G	67	NY2465
Eastrington Humb	56	SE7929
Eastrop Wilts	21	SU2092
Eastry Kent	15	TR3055
Eastville Lincs	51	TF4056
Eastwell Leics	40	SK7728
Eastwick Herts	23	TL4311
Eastwood Essex	24	TQ8688
Eastwood Notts	49	SK4646
Eastwood W York	54	SD9727
Eathorpe Warwks	29	SP3969
Eaton Ches	47	SJ5763
Eaton Ches	47	SJ8765
Eaton Leics	40	SK7928
Eaton Norfk	43	TG2006
Eaton Notts	49	SK7077
Eaton Oxon	21	SP4403
Eaton Shrops	37	SO5090
Eaton Bray Beds	30	SP9620
Eaton Constantine Shrops	37	SJ5906
Eaton Green Beds	30	SP9621
Eaton Hastings Oxon	21	SU2698
Eaton Mascott Shrops	37	SJ5305
Eaton Socon Beds	31	TL1659
Eaton upon Tern Shrops	37	SJ6523
Eaves Brow Ches	47	SJ6493
Ebberston N York	63	SE8982
Ebbesborne Wake Wilts	9	ST9824
Ebbw Vale Gwent	27	SO1609
Ebbw Vale Gwent	19	ST2094
Ebchester Dur	68	NZ1055
Ebford Devon	5	SX9887
Ebley Gloucs	28	SO8205
Ebnal Ches	46	SJ4948
Ebrington Gloucs	29	SP1840
Ebsworthy Town Devon	4	SX5090
Ebworth Turbary Humb	56	SE7604
Ecchinswell Hants	21	SU5059
Ecclaw Loth	76	NT7568
Ecclefechan D & G	67	NY1974
Eccles Border	76	NT7641
Eccles Gt Man	47	SJ7798
Eccles Road Norfk	32	TM0190
Ecclesfield S York	49	SK3393
Ecclesgreig Gramp	89	NO7365
Eccleshall S York	49	SK3184
Eccleshall Staffs	38	SJ8329
Eccleshill W York	55	SE1736
Ecclesmachan Loth	75	NT0673
Eccleston Ches	46	SJ4162
Eccleston Lancs	53	SD5217
Eccleston Mersyd	46	SJ4895
Echt Gramp	89	NJ7405
Eckford Border	76	NT7026
Eckington Derbys	49	SK4279
Eckington H & W	28	SO9241
Ecton Nhants	30	SP8263
Edale Derbys	48	SK1285
Edburton W Susx	12	TQ2311
Edderton Highld	97	NH7084
Edderton Mains Highld	97	NH7183
Eddington Kent	15	TR1767
Eddleston Border	75	NT2447
Eddlewood Strath	74	NS7153
Eden Mount Cumb	59	SD4078
Edenbridge Kent	13	TQ4446
Edenfield Lancs	54	SD8019
Edenhall Cumb	59	NY5632
Edenham Lincs	40	TF0621
Edensor Derbys	48	SK2469
Edentaggart Strath	80	NS3293
Edenthorpe S York	56	SE6206
Ederline Strath	79	NM8702
Edern Gwynd	44	SH2739
Edgarley Somset	19	ST5138
Edgbaston W Mids	38	SP0684
Edgcombe Cnwll	2	SW7233
Edgcott Bucks	30	SP6722
Edgcott Somset	7	SS8438
Edge Gloucs	28	SO8409
Edge Shrops	36	SJ3909
Edgefield Norfk	43	TG0934
Edgefield Green Norfk	43	TG0934
Edgeside Lancs	54	SD8322
Edgeworth Gloucs	28	SO9406
Edgmond Shrops	37	SJ7119
Edgton Shrops	36	SO3886
Edgware Gt Lon	23	TQ1991
Edgworth Lancs	54	SD7416
Edinample Strath	81	NN6022
Edinbane Highld	90	NG3451
Edinburgh Loth	75	NT2573
Edingale Staffs	39	SK2112
Edingley Notts	49	SK6655
Edingthorpe Norfk	43	TG3132
Edingthorpe Green Norfk	43	TG3131
Edington Border	77	NT8956
Edington Nthumb	69	NZ1582
Edington Somset	19	ST3940
Edington Wilts	20	ST9252
Edington Burtle Somset	19	ST3943
Edingworth Somset	19	ST3553
Edith Weston Leics	40	SK9205
Edithmead Somset	19	ST3249
Edlesborough Bucks	30	SP9719
Edlingham Nthumb	69	NU1109
Edlington Lincs	51	TF2371

Place	County	Page	Grid
Edmondsham	Dorset	10	SU0611
Edmondsley	Dur	69	NZ2349
Edmondthorpe	Leics	40	SK8517
Edmonton	Cnwll	3	SW9672
Edmonton	Gt Lon	23	TQ3492
Edmondbyers	Dur	68	NZ0150
Ednam	Border	76	NT7337
Edradynate	Tays	87	NN8851
Edrom	Border	77	NT8255
Edstone	Warwks	38	SP1962
Edwinstowe	Notts	49	SK6266
Edworth	Beds	31	TL2241
Edwyn Ralph	H & W	27	SO6457
Edzell	Tays	89	NO5968
Efail Isaf	M Glam	18	ST0884
Efail-fach	W Glam	18	SS7895
Efailnewydd	Gwynd	44	SH3536
Efailwen	Dyfed	16	SN1325
Efenechtyd	Clwyd	46	SJ1155
Effgill	D & G	67	NY3092
Effingham	Surrey	12	TQ1253
Efflinch	Staffs	39	SK1917
Efford	Devon	7	SS8901
Egbury	Hants	21	SU4452
Egerton	Gt Man	54	SD7014
Egerton	Kent	14	TQ9047
Eggesford	Devon	7	SS6810
Eggington	Beds	30	SP9525
Egginton	Derbys	39	SK2628
Egglescliffe	Cleve	62	NZ4113
Eggleston	Dur	61	NY9923
Egham	Surrey	22	TQ0171
Eginswell	Devon	5	SX8865
Egleton	Leics	40	SK8707
Eglingham	Nthumb	77	NU1019
Egloshayle	Cnwll	3	SX0072
Egloskerry	Cnwll	4	SX2786
Eglwys Cross	Clwyd	37	SJ4741
Eglwys-Brewis	S Glam	18	ST0069
Eglwysbach	Gwynd	45	SH8070
Eglwysfach	Dyfed	35	SN6896
Eglwyswrw	Dyfed	16	SN1438
Egmanton	Notts	50	SK7368
Egremont	Cumb	58	NY0110
Egremont	Mersyd	46	SJ3192
Egton	N York	63	NZ8006
Egton Bridge	N York	63	NZ8005
Eight Ash Green	Essex	25	TL9425
Eilanreach	Highld	85	NG8017
Elan Village	Powys	35	SN9364
Elberton	Avon	19	ST6088
Elbridge	W Susx	11	SU9102
Elburton	Devon	4	SX5353
Elcombe	Wilts	20	SU1280
Eldersfield	H & W	28	SO7931
Elderslie	Strath	73	NS4463
Eldon	Dur	61	NZ2328
Eldroth	N York	54	SD7665
Elfhill	Gramp	89	NO8085
Elford	Staffs	38	SK1810
Elgin	Gramp	94	NJ2162
Elgol	Highld	84	NG5214
Elham	Kent	15	TR1744
Elie	Fife	83	NO4900
Eling	Hants	10	SU3612
Elishader	Highld	90	NG5065
Elkesley	Notts	49	SK6875
Elkstone	Gloucs	28	SO9612
Ella	Gramp	94	NJ6459
Ellanbeich	Strath	79	NM7417
Elland	W York	55	SE1020
Elland Lower Edge	W York	55	SE1121
Ellary	Strath	71	NR7476
Ellastone	Staffs	48	SK1143
Ellel	Lancs	53	SD4856
Ellemford	Border	76	NT7260
Ellen's Green	Surrey	12	TQ0935
Ellenborough	Cumb	58	NY0535
Ellenhall	Staffs	38	SJ8426
Ellerbeck	N York	62	SE4396
Ellerby	N York	63	NZ7914
Ellerdine Heath	Shrops	37	SJ6122
Elleric	Strath	86	NN0348
Ellerker	Humb	56	SE9229
Ellerton	Humb	56	SE7039
Ellerton	N York	61	SE2497
Ellerton	Shrops	37	SJ7126
Ellesborough	Bucks	22	SP8306
Ellesmere	Shrops	36	SJ3934
Ellesmere Port	Ches	46	SJ4076
Ellingham	Norfk	33	TM3592
Ellingham	Nthumb	77	NU1725
Ellingstring	N York	61	SE1783
Ellington	Cambs	31	TL1671
Ellington	Nthumb	69	NZ2791
Ellington	Nthumb	69	NZ2791
Ellington Thorpe	Cambs	31	TL1670
Elliots Green	Somset	20	ST7945
Ellisfield	Hants	21	SU6346
Ellistown	Leics	39	SK4311
Ellon	Gramp	95	NJ9530
Ellon Brook	Gt Man	47	SD7201
Ellonby	Cumb	59	NY4235
Elloughton	Humb	56	SE9428
Ellwood	Gloucs	27	SO5908
Elm Park	Gt Lon	23	TQ5385
Elmbridge	H & W	28	SO9068
Elmdon	Essex	31	TL4639
Elmdon	W Mids	38	SP1783
Elmer	W Susx	12	SU9800
Elmers End	Gt Lon	23	TQ3668
Elmesthorpe	Leics	39	SP4696
Elmhurst	Staffs	38	SK1112
Elmley Castle	H & W	28	SO9841
Elmley Lovett	H & W	28	SO8769
Elmore	Gloucs	28	SO7815
Elmore Back	Gloucs	28	SO7616
Elmsett	Suffk	32	TM0546
Elmstead Market	Essex	25	TM0624
Elmstead Row	Essex	25	TM0622
Elmsted Court	Kent	15	TR1144
Elmstone	Kent	15	TR2660
Elmstone Hardwicke	Gloucs	28	SO9226
Elmswell	Humb	56	SE9958
Elmswell	Suffk	32	TL9964
Elmton	Derbys	49	SK5073
Elphin	Highld	96	NC2111
Elphinstone	Loth	76	NT3970
Elrick	Gramp	89	NJ8206
Elrig	D & G	64	NX3247
Elrington	Nthumb	68	NY8663
Elsdon	H & W	27	SO3154
Elsdon	Nthumb	68	NY9393
Elsecar	S York	49	SE3800
Elsenham	Essex	31	TL5326
Elsfield	Oxon	29	SP5310
Elsham	Humb	56	TA0312
Elsick House	Gramp	89	NO8994
Elsing	Norfk	42	TG0517
Elslack	N York	54	SD9349
Elson	Hants	11	SU6001
Elsrickle	Strath	75	NT0643
Elstead	Surrey	11	SU9043
Elsted	W Susx	11	SU8119
Elston	Notts	50	SK7647
Elstone	Devon	7	SS6716
Elstow	Beds	30	TL0547
Elstree	Herts	23	TQ1895
Elstree	Herts	23	TQ1895
Elstronwick	Humb	57	TA2232
Elswick	Lancs	53	SD4238
Elswick	T & W	69	NZ2263
Elsworth	Cambs	31	TL3163
Elterwater	Cumb	58	NY3204
Eltham	Gt Lon	23	TQ4274
Elton	Ches	46	SJ4575
Elton	Cleve	62	NZ4017
Elton	Derbys	48	SK2261
Elton	H & W	27	SO4570
Elton	Notts	40	SK7638
Elton Green	Ches	46	SJ4575
Eltringham	Nthumb	68	NZ0762
Elvaston	Derbys	39	SK4132
Elveden	Suffk	32	TL8180
Elvingston	Loth	76	NT4674
Elvington	Kent	15	TR2750
Elvington	N York	56	SE6947
Elwick	Cleve	62	NZ4532
Elwick	Nthumb	77	NU1137
Elworth	Ches	47	SJ7361
Elworthy	Somset	7	ST0835
Ely	Cambs	31	TL6480
Ely	S Glam	18	ST1476
Emberton	Bucks	30	SP8849
Embleton	Cumb	58	NY1639
Embleton	Nthumb	77	NU2322
Embo	Highld	97	NH8192
Embo Street	Highld	97	NH8091
Emborough	Somset	19	ST6151
Embsay	N York	54	SE0053
Emery Down	Hants	10	SU2808
Emery Down	Hants	10	SU2808
Emley	W York	55	SE2413
Emmett Carr	Derbys	49	SK4477
Emmington	Oxon	22	SP7402
Emneth	Cambs	41	TF4807
Emneth Hungate	Norfk	41	TF5107
Empingham	Leics	40	SK9508
Empshott	Hants	11	SU7531
Emsworth	Hants	11	SU7405
Enaclete	W Isls	102	NB1228
Enborne	Berks	21	SU4365
Enborne Row	Hants	21	SU4463
Encombe	Dorset	9	SY9478
End Moor	Cumb	59	SD5484
Enderby	Leics	39	SP5399
Endon Bank	Staffs	48	SJ9253
Enfield	Gt Lon	23	TQ3597
Enfield Lock	Gt Lon	23	TQ3698
Enfield Wash	Gt Lon	23	TQ3598
Engine Common	Avon	20	ST6984
Englefield	Berks	21	SU6272
Englefield Green	Surrey	22	SU9971
Englesea-brook	Ches	47	SJ7551
English Bicknor	Gloucs	27	SO5815
English Frankton	Shrops	36	SJ4529
Englishcombe	Avon	20	ST7162
Enham-Alamein	Hants	21	SU3649
Enmore	Somset	8	ST2335
Enmore Green	Dorset	9	ST8523
Ennerdale Bridge	Cumb	58	NY0615
Enochdhu	Tays	88	NO0662
Ensay	Strath	78	NM3648
Ensbury	Dorset	10	SZ0896
Ensdon	Shrops	36	SJ4016
Ensis	Devon	6	SS5626
Enstone	Oxon	29	SP3724
Enterkinfoot	D & G	66	NS8504
Enville	Staffs	38	SO8286
Enys	Cnwll	2	SW7936
Epney	Gloucs	28	SO7611
Epperstone	Notts	49	SK6548
Epping	Essex	23	TL4602
Epping Green	Essex	23	TL4305
Epping Green	Herts	23	TL2906
Epping Upland	Essex	23	TL4404
Eppleby	N York	61	NZ1713
Epsom	Surrey	23	TQ2160
Epwell	Oxon	29	SP3540
Epworth	Humb	56	SE7803
Erbistock	Clwyd	36	SJ3541
Erbusaig	Highld	85	NG7629
Erchless Castle	Highld	92	NH4540
Erdington	W Mids	38	SP1191
Eridge Green	E Susx	13	TQ5535
Erines	Strath	71	NR8575
Eriswell	Suffk	32	TL7278
Erith	Gt Lon	23	TQ5177
Erlestoke	Wilts	20	ST9853
Ermington	Devon	5	SX6353
Erpingham	Norfk	43	TG1931
Erriottwood	Kent	14	TQ9359
Errogie	Highld	92	NH5622
Errol	Tays	83	NO2422
Ersary	W Isls	102	NF7100
Erskine	Strath	81	NS4771
Ervie	D & G	64	NW9968
Erwarton	Suffk	25	TM2234
Erwood	Powys	26	SO0943
Erwood	Powys	26	SO1042
Eryholme	N York	62	NZ3200
Eryrys	Clwyd	46	SJ2057
Escomb	Dur	61	NZ1830
Escrick	N York	56	SE6242
Esgair	Dyfed	17	SN3729
Esgairgeiliog	Powys	35	SH7606
Esh	Dur	69	NZ1944
Esh Winning	Dur	61	NZ1942
Esher	Surrey	22	TQ1364
Eshott	Nthumb	69	NZ2097
Eskadale	Highld	92	NH4539
Eskbank	Loth	75	NT3266
Eskdale Green	Cumb	58	NY1400
Eskdalemuir	D & G	67	NY2597
Esknish	Strath	70	NR3664
Esprick	Lancs	53	SD4036
Essendine	Leics	40	TF0412
Essendon	Herts	23	TL2708
Essich	Highld	92	NH6439
Essington	Staffs	38	SJ9603
Esslemont	Gramp	95	NJ9239
Esthorpe	Lincs	40	TF0623
Eston	Cleve	62	NZ5519
Etal	Nthumb	77	NT9339
Etchilhampton	Wilts	20	SU0460
Etchingham	E Susx	14	TQ7126
Etchinghill	Kent	15	TR1639
Etchinghill	Staffs	38	SK0218
Etloe	Gloucs	28	SO6705
Eton	Berks	22	SU9478
Eton Wick	Berks	22	SU9478
Etruria	Staffs	47	SJ8647
Etteridge	Highld	87	NN6892
Ettersgill	Dur	60	NY8829
Ettiley Heath	Ches	47	SJ7360
Ettingshall	W Mids	38	SO9396
Ettington	Warwks	29	SP2649
Etton	Cambs	40	TF1306
Etton	Humb	56	SE9743
Etton	Humb	56	SE9743
Ettrick	Border	67	NT2714
Ettrick Bridge	Border	76	NT3824
Ettrick Hill	Border	67	NT2614
Etwall	Derbys	39	SK2631
Eudon George	Shrops	37	SO6889
Euston	Suffk	32	TL8979
Euximoor Drove	Cambs	41	TL4798
Euxton	Lancs	53	SD5519
Evanton	Highld	92	NH6066
Evedon	Lincs	50	TF0947
Evelith	Shrops	37	SJ7405
Evelix	Highld	97	NH7790
Evenjobb	Powys	27	SO2662
Evenley	Oxon	29	SP5834
Evenlode	Gloucs	29	SP2229
Evercreech	Somset	19	ST6438
Everingham	Humb	56	SE8042
Everleigh	Wilts	21	SU1953
Eversholt	Beds	30	SP9833
Evershot	Dorset	8	ST5704
Eversley	Hants	22	SU7762
Eversley Cross	Hants	22	SU7961
Everthorpe	Humb	56	SE9031
Everton	Beds	31	TL2051
Everton	Hants	10	SZ2993
Everton	Mersyd	46	SJ3491
Everton	Notts	49	SK6891
Evertown	D & G	67	NY3576
Evesbatch	H & W	28	SO6848
Evesham	H & W	28	SP0343
Evington	Leics	39	SK6203
Ewden Village	S York	49	SK2796
Ewdness	Shrops	37	SO7398
Ewell	Surrey	23	TQ2262
Ewell Minnis	Kent	15	TR2643
Ewelme	Oxon	21	SU6491
Ewen	Gloucs	20	SU0097
Ewenny	M Glam	18	SS9077
Ewerby	Lincs	50	TF1247
Ewesley	Nthumb	68	NZ0592
Ewhurst	E Susx	14	TQ7924
Ewhurst	Surrey	12	TQ0940
Ewhurst Green	Surrey	12	TQ0939
Ewloe	Clwyd	46	SJ3066
Eworthy	Devon	6	SX4494
Ewshot	Hants	22	SU8149
Ewyas Harold	H & W	27	SO3828
Exbourne	Devon	6	SS6002
Exbury	Hants	10	SU4200
Exebridge	Somset	7	SS9324
Exelby	N York	61	SE2986
Exeter	Devon	5	SX9292
Exford	Somset	7	SS8538
Exfordsgreen	Shrops	36	SJ4505
Exhall	Warwks	28	SP1055
Exhall	Warwks	29	SP3485
Exlade Street	Oxon	21	SU6581
Exminster	Devon	5	SX9487
Exmouth	Devon	5	SY0080
Exning	Cambs	32	TL6265
Exted	Kent	15	TR1644
Exton	Devon	5	SX9886
Exton	Hants	11	SU6121
Exton	Leics	40	SK9211
Exton	Somset	7	SS9233
Exwick	Devon	5	SX9193
Eyam	Derbys	48	SK2176
Eydon	Nhants	29	SP5450
Eye	Cambs	41	TF2202
Eye	H & W	27	SO4964
Eye	Suffk	33	TM1473
Eye Green	Cambs	41	TF2203
Eyemouth	Border	77	NT9464
Eyeworth	Beds	31	TL2545
Eyhorne Street	Kent	14	TQ8354
Eyke	Suffk	33	TM3151
Eynesbury	Beds	31	TL1859
Eynsford	Kent	23	TQ5465
Eynsham	Oxon	29	SP4309
Eype	Dorset	8	SY4491
Eyre	Highld	90	NG4152
Eythorne	Kent	15	TR2849
Eyton	H & W	27	SO4761
Eyton	Shrops	36	SJ3714
Eyton	Shrops	36	SO3787
Eyton	Shrops	36	SJ4423
Eyton on Severn	Shrops	37	SJ5806
Eyton upon the Weald Moor Shrops		37	SJ6514

F

Faccombe	Hants	21	SU3958
Faceby	N York	62	NZ4902
Fachwen	Powys	36	SJ0316
Faddiley	Ches	47	SJ5852
Fadmoor	N York	62	SE6789
Failand	Avon	19	ST5171
Failford	Strath	73	NS4626
Failsworth	Gt Man	48	SD8901
Fain	Highld	96	NH1379
Fair Oak	Hants	10	SU4918
Fair Oak Green	Hants	22	SU6660
Fairbourne	Gwynd	35	SH6113
Fairburn	N York	55	SE4727
Fairfield	Derbys	48	SK0674
Fairfield	H & W	38	SO9475
Fairford	Gloucs	20	SP1501
Fairgirth	D & G	66	NX8756
Fairhaven	Lancs	53	SD3228
Fairlie	Strath	73	NS2154
Fairlight	E Susx	14	TQ8511
Fairmile	Devon	7	SY0997
Fairmile	Surrey	22	TQ1161
Fairnilee	Border	76	NT4532
Fairoak	Staffs	37	SJ7632
Fairseat	Kent	14	TQ6261
Fairstead	Essex	24	TL7616
Fairwarp	E Susx	13	TQ4626
Fairwater	S Glam	18	ST1477
Fairy Cross	Devon	6	SS4024
Fakenham	Norfk	42	TF9229
Fakenham Magna	Suffk	32	TL9076
Fala	Loth	76	NT4461
Fala Dam	Loth	76	NT4361
Faldingworth	Lincs	50	TF0684
Faldouet	Jersey	101	SV0000
Falfield	Gloucs	20	ST6893
Falkenham	Suffk	33	TM2939
Falkirk	Cent	82	NS8880
Falkland	Fife	83	NO2507
Fallin	Cent	82	NS8391
Falloden	Nthumb	77	NU1922
Fallowfield	Gt Man	47	SJ8594
Fallowfield	Nthumb	68	NY9268
Falls of Blarghour	Strath	80	NM9913
Falmer	E Susx	12	TQ3509
Falmouth	Cnwll	2	SW8032
Falnash	Border	67	NT3906
Falsgrave	N York	63	TA0287
Falstone	Nthumb	68	NY7287
Fambridge Station	Essex	24	TQ8698
Fanagmore	Highld	98	NC1750
Fanellan	Highld	92	NH4842
Fangdale Beck	N York	62	SE5694
Fangfoss	Humb	56	SE7653
Fanmore	Strath	78	NM4144
Fannich Lodge	Highld	92	NH2266
Fans	Border	76	NT6140
Far Bletchley	Bucks	30	SP8533
Far Cotton	Nhants	30	SP7459
Far End	Cumb	58	NY3098
Far Forest	H & W	37	SO7274
Far Green	Gloucs	20	SO7700
Far Moor	Gt Man	46	SD5204
Far Oakridge	Gloucs	20	SO9203
Far Sawrey	Cumb	59	SD3795
Far Thorpe	Lincs	51	TF2673
Farcet	Cambs	41	TL2094
Fareham	Hants	11	SU5806
Farewell	Staffs	38	SK0811
Faringdon	Oxon	21	SU2895
Farkhill	Tays	82	NO0435
Farlam	Cumb	67	NY5558
Farleigh	Avon	19	ST4969
Farleigh	Surrey	23	TQ3760
Farleigh Hungerford	Somset	20	ST7957
Farleigh Wallop	Hants	21	SU6246
Farlesthorpe	Lincs	51	TF4774
Farleton	Cumb	59	SD5380
Farleton	Lancs	53	SD5767
Farley	Staffs	48	SK0644
Farley	Wilts	10	SU2229
Farley Green	Suffk	32	TL7353
Farley Green	Surrey	12	TQ0545
Farley Hill	Berks	22	SU7564
Farleys End	Gloucs	28	SO7615
Farlington	N York	56	SE6160
Farlow	Shrops	37	SO6380
Farmborough	Avon	19	ST6560
Farmcote	Gloucs	28	SP0629
Farmcote	Shrops	37	SO7892
Farmers	Dyfed	17	SN6444
Farmington	Gloucs	28	SP1315
Farmoor	Oxon	29	SP4506
Farms Common	Cnwll	2	SW6734
Farnham	Gramp	94	NJ5051
Farnachty	Gramp	94	NJ4651
Farnborough	Berks	21	SU4381
Farnborough	Gt Lon	23	TQ4564
Farnborough	Hants	22	SU8753
Farnborough	Warwks	29	SP4349
Farnborough	Warwks	29	SP4349
Farnborough Park	Hants	22	SU8755
Farnborough Street	Hants	22	SU8656
Farncombe	Surrey	12	SU9745
Farndish	Beds	30	SP9263
Farndon	Ches	46	SJ4154
Farndon	Notts	50	SK7651
Farnell	Tays	89	NO6255
Farnham	Dorset	9	ST9514
Farnham	Essex	31	TL4724
Farnham	N York	55	SE3460
Farnham	Suffk	33	TM3660
Farnham	Surrey	22	SU8446
Farnham Common	Bucks	22	SU9585
Farnham Royal	Bucks	22	SU9583
Farningham	Kent	23	TQ5467
Farnley	N York	55	SE2543
Farnley	W York	55	SE2332
Farnley Tyas	W York	55	SE1612
Farnsfield	Notts	49	SK6456
Farnworth	Ches	46	SJ5187
Farnworth	Gt Man	47	SD7306
Farr	Highld	93	NH6833
Farr	Highld	88	NH8203
Farr	Highld	99	NC7163
Farraline	Highld	92	NH5621
Farringdon	Devon	5	SY0191
Farrington Gurney	Avon	19	ST6255
Farthinghoe	Nhants	29	SP5339
Farthingstone	Nhants	29	SP6154
Fartown	W York	55	SE1518
Fartown	W York	55	SE2232
Farway	Devon	8	SY1895
Fasnacloich	Strath	86	NN0247
Fasnakyle	Highld	92	NH3128
Fasque	Gramp	89	NO6575
Fassfern	Highld	86	NN0278
Fatfield	T & W	69	NZ2954
Faulkbourne	Essex	24	TL7917
Faulkland	Somset	20	ST7354
Fauls	Shrops	37	SJ5932
Faversham	Kent	15	TR0161
Fawdington	N York	55	SE4372
Fawdon	Nthumb	77	NU0315
Fawkham Green	Kent	23	TQ5865
Fawler	Oxon	29	SP3717
Fawley	Berks	21	SU3981
Fawley	Bucks	22	SU7586
Fawley	Hants	10	SU4503
Fawley Chapel	H & W	27	SO5829
Fawnog	Clwyd	46	SJ2466
Faxfleet	Humb	56	SE8624
Faygate	W Susx	12	TQ2134
Fazakerley	Mersyd	46	SJ3797
Fazeley	Staffs	39	SK2001
Fearby	N York	61	SE1981
Fearn	Highld	97	NH8377
Fearnan	Tays	87	NN7244
Fearnbeg	Highld	91	NG7359
Fearnmore	Highld	91	NG7260
Fearnoch	Strath	71	NR9279
Featherstone	Staffs	38	SJ9305
Featherstone	W York	55	SE4221
Feckenham	H & W	28	SP0162
Feddarate	Gramp	95	NJ8949
Feering	Essex	24	TL8720
Feetham	N York	61	SD9898
Feindside	Border	67	NT4408
Felbridge	Surrey	13	TQ3739
Felbrigg	Norfk	43	TG2039
Felcourt	Surrey	13	TQ3841
Felday	Surrey	12	TQ1144
Felin Fach	Dyfed	17	SN5255
Felin Gwm Uchaf	Dyfed	17	SN4034
Felin-gwm Uchaf	Dyfed	17	SN5024
Felindre	Dyfed	17	SN5521
Felindre	Powys	17	SN1723
Felindre	Powys	36	SO1681
Felingwm Isaf	Dyfed	17	SN5023
Felixkirk	N York	62	SE4684
Felixstowe	Suffk	25	TM3035
Felixstoweferry	Suffk	25	TM3237
Felkirk	W York	55	SE3812
Felling	T & W	69	NZ2761
Felmersham	Beds	30	SP9957
Felmingham	Norfk	43	TG2529
Felpham	W Susx	12	SZ9599
Felsham	Suffk	32	TL9457
Felsted	Essex	24	TL6720
Feltham	Gt Lon	22	TQ1073
Felthamhill	Gt Lon	22	TQ0971
Felthorpe	Norfk	43	TG1618
Felton	Avon	19	ST5165
Felton	H & W	27	SO5748
Felton	Nthumb	69	NU1800
Felton Butler	Shrops	36	SJ3917
Feltwell	Norfk	32	TL7190
Fen Ditton	Cambs	31	TL4860
Fen Drayton	Cambs	31	TL3368
Fen Street	Norfk	32	TL9899
Fence	S York	49	SK4485
Fencote	N York	61	SE2893
Fencott	Oxon	29	SP5716
Fendike Corner	Lincs	51	TF4560
Fenham	Nthumb	68	NU0800
Feniscowles	Lancs	54	SD6425
Feniton	Devon	8	SY1199
Fenn Green	Shrops	37	SO7783
Fenn Street	Kent	14	TQ7975
Fenny Bentley	Derbys	48	SK1750
Fenny Bridges	Devon	5	SY1198
Fenny Compton	Warwks	29	SP4151
Fenny Drayton	Leics	39	SP3597
Fenny Stratford	Bucks	30	SP8834
Fenstead End	Suffk	32	TL8050
Fenton	Cambs	41	TL3279
Fenton	Lincs	50	SK8476
Fenton	Lincs	50	SK8751
Fenton	Notts	49	SK7984
Fenton	Staffs	48	SJ8944
Fenton Town	Nthumb	77	NT9734
Fenwick	Nthumb	68	NZ0572
Fenwick	Nthumb	77	NU0640
Fenwick	S York	56	SE5916
Fenwick	Strath	73	NS4643
Feock	Cnwll	2	SW8238
Feolin Ferry	Strath	70	NR4469
Feriniquarrie	Highld	90	NG1750
Fern	Tays	89	NO4861
Ferndale	M Glam	18	SS9996
Ferndown	Dorset	10	SU0700
Ferness	Highld	93	NH9645
Fernham	Oxon	21	SU2991
Fernhill Heath	H & W	28	SO8859
Fernhurst	W Susx	11	SU8928
Fernie	Fife	83	NO3115
Ferniegair	Strath	74	NS7354
Fernilea	Highld	84	NG3732
Fernilee	Derbys	48	SK0178
Ferrensby	N York	55	SE3760
Ferrindonald	Highld	84	NG6008
Ferring	W Susx	12	TQ0902
Ferry Point	Highld	97	NH7385
Ferryden	Tays	89	NO7156
Ferryhill	Dur	61	NZ2932
Ferryside	Dyfed	17	SN3610
Ferrytown	Highld	97	NH7387
Fersfield	Norfk	32	TM0683
Fetcham	Surrey	22	TQ1455
Fettercairn	Gramp	89	NO6573
Fetterangus	Gramp	95	NJ9850
Feus	Border	83	NO3533
Fewcott	Oxon	29	SP5228
Fewston	N York	55	SE1954
Ffair Rhos	Dyfed	35	SN7368
Ffairfach	Dyfed	17	SN6220
Ffestiniog	Gwynd	45	SH7042
Fforest	Dyfed	17	SN5804
Fforest Fach	W Glam	18	SS6295
Ffostrasol	Dyfed	17	SN3747
Ffridd Uchaf	Gwynd	44	SH5751
Ffrith	Clwyd	46	SJ2855
Ffrwdgrech	Powys	26	SO0227
Ffynnondewi	Dyfed	17	SN3853
Fiag Lodge	Highld	98	NC4528
Fickleshole	Surrey	23	TQ3860
Fiddes	Gramp	89	NO8080
Fiddington	Gloucs	28	SO9231
Fiddington	Somset	19	ST2140
Fiddleford	Dorset	9	ST8013
Fiddlers Green	Cnwll	2	SW8254
Field	Staffs	38	SK0233
Field Broughton	Cumb	59	SD3881
Field Dalling	Norfk	42	TG0039
Field Head	Leics	39	SK4909
Fife Keith	Gramp	94	NJ4250
Fifehead Magdalen	Dorset	9	ST7721
Fifehead Neville	Dorset	9	ST7610

Place	Pg	Grid ref
Fifehead St. Quinton *Dorset*	9	ST7710
Fifield *Berks*	22	SU9076
Fifield *Oxon*	29	SP2318
Figheldean *Wilts*	20	SU1547
Filby *Norfk*	43	TG4613
Filey *N York*	63	TA1180
Filgrave *Bucks*	30	SP8648
Filkins *Oxon*	29	SP2304
Filleigh *Devon*	7	SS6628
Filleigh *Devon*	7	SS7410
Fillingham *Lincs*	50	SK9485
Fillongley *Warwks*	39	SP2887
Filton *Avon*	19	ST6079
Fimber *Humb*	56	SE8960
Finavon *Tays*	89	NO4956
Fincham *Norfk*	42	TF6806
Finchampstead *Berks*	22	SU7963
Fincharr *Strath*	79	NM9003
Finchdean *Hants*	11	SU7312
Finchingfield *Essex*	24	TL6832
Finchley *Gt Lon*	23	TQ2690
Find O' Gask *Tays*	82	NO0019
Findern *Derbys*	39	SK3030
Findhorn *Gramp*	93	NJ0463
Findhorn Bridge *Highld*	93	NH8027
Findochty *Gramp*	94	NJ4667
Findon *Gramp*	89	NO9397
Findon *W Susx*	12	TQ1208
Findon Mains *Highld*	92	NH6060
Findrack House *Gramp*	89	NJ6004
Finedon *Nhants*	30	SP9172
Fingal Street *Suffk*	33	TM2270
Fingask *Gramp*	95	NJ7827
Fingask *Tays*	82	NO1619
Fingest *Bucks*	22	SU7791
Finghall *N York*	61	SE1789
Fingland *D & G*	74	NS7517
Fingringhoe *Essex*	25	TM0320
Finkle Street *S York*	49	SK3099
Finlarig *Cent*	81	NN5733
Finmere *Oxon*	29	SP6333
Finnart *Tays*	87	NN5157
Finningham *Suffk*	32	TM0669
Finningley *Notts*	49	SK6699
Finsbay *W Isls*	102	NG0786
Finstall *H & W*	28	SO9870
Finstock *Oxon*	29	SP3816
Finstown *Ork*	103	HY3514
Fintry *Cent*	81	NS6186
Fintry *Gramp*	95	NJ7554
Finzean *Gramp*	89	NO5993
Fionnphort *Strath*	78	NM3023
Fir Tree *Dur*	61	NZ1434
Firbank *Cumb*	60	SD6293
Firbeck *S York*	49	SK5688
Firby *N York*	61	SE2686
Firby *N York*	56	SE7466
Firsby *Lincs*	51	TF4562
Fishbourne *IOW*	11	SZ5592
Fishbourne *W Susx*	11	SU8304
Fishburn *Dur*	62	NZ3632
Fishcross *Cent*	82	NS8895
Fisher *W Susx*	11	SU8700
Fisher's Pond *Hants*	10	SU4820
Fisherford *Gramp*	95	NJ6735
Fisherrow *Loth*	75	NT3472
Fisherstreet *W Susx*	12	SU9531
Fisherton *Highld*	93	NH7451
Fisherton *Strath*	73	NS2717
Fisherton de la Mere *Wilts*	20	ST9938
Fishery Estate *Berks*	22	SU8980
Fishguard *Dyfed*	16	SM9637
Fishlake *S York*	56	SE6513
Fishnish Pier *Strath*	79	NM6542
Fishponds *Avon*	19	ST6375
Fishtoft *Lincs*	51	TF3642
Fishtoft Drove *Lincs*	51	TF3148
Fishtown of Usan *Tays*	89	NO7254
Fishwick *Border*	77	NT9151
Fishwick *Lancs*	53	SD5529
Fiskavaig *Highld*	84	NG3334
Fiskerton *Lincs*	50	TF0472
Fiskerton *Notts*	50	SK7351
Fittleworth *W Susx*	12	TQ0119
Fitz *Shrops*	36	SJ4418
Fitzhead *Somset*	8	ST1228
Fitzwilliam *W York*	55	SE4115
Fiunary *Highld*	79	NM6246
Five Ash Down *E Susx*	13	TQ4724
Five Bells *Somset*	7	ST0642
Five Oak Green *Kent*	13	TQ6445
Five Oaks *Jersey*	101	SV0000
Five Oaks *W Susx*	12	TQ0928
Fivecrosses *Ches*	46	SJ5376
Fivehead *Somset*	8	ST3522
Fivelanes *Cnwll*	4	SX2280
Flack's Heath *Bucks*	22	SU8990
Fladbury *H & W*	28	SO9946
Fladdabister *Shet*	103	HU4332
Flagg *Derbys*	48	SK1368
Flamborough *Humb*	57	TA2270
Flamstead *Herts*	30	TL0714
Flansham *W Susx*	12	SU9601
Flanshaw *W York*	55	SE3020
Flasby *N York*	54	SD9456
Flash *Staffs*	48	SK0267
Flashader *Highld*	90	NG3453
Flatt *Strath*	74	NS6551
Flaunden *Herts*	22	TL0100
Flawborough *Notts*	50	SK7842
Flawith *N York*	55	SE4865
Flax Bourton *Avon*	19	ST5069
Flaxby *N York*	55	SE3957
Flaxley *Gloucs*	28	SO6815
Flaxmere *Ches*	47	SJ5672
Flaxpool *Somset*	8	ST1435
Flaxton *N York*	56	SE6762
Fleckney *Leics*	39	SP6493
Flecknoe *Warwks*	29	SP5163
Fledborough *Notts*	50	SK8072
Fleet *Dorset*	9	SY6380
Fleet *Hants*	22	SU8053
Fleet *Lincs*	41	TF3923
Fleet Hargate *Lincs*	41	TF3924
Fleetwood *Lancs*	53	SD3348
Flemington *S Glam*	18	ST0170
Flemington *Strath*	74	NS6559
Flempton *Suffk*	32	TL8169
Fletching *E Susx*	13	TQ4223
Fleur-de-lis *M Glam*	36	SO1596
Flexbury *Cnwll*	6	SS2107
Flexford *Surrey*	22	SU9350
Flimby *Cumb*	60	NY0233
Flimwell *E Susx*	14	TQ7131
Flint *Clwyd*	46	SJ2472
Flintham *Notts*	50	SK7445
Flinton *Humb*	57	TA2136
Flitcham *Norfk*	42	TF7326
Flitton *Beds*	30	TL0535
Flixborough *Humb*	56	SE8715
Flixborough Stather *Humb*	56	SE8614
Flixton *N York*	63	TA0479
Flixton *Suffk*	33	TM3186
Flockton Green *W York*	55	SE2514
Flodda *W Isls*	102	NF8455
Flodigarry *Highld*	90	NG4671
Flookburgh *Cumb*	59	SD3675
Flordon *Norfk*	43	TM1897
Flore *Nhants*	29	SP6460
Flotton *Suffk*	32	TM0847
Flushdyke *W York*	55	SE2821
Fluxton *Devon*	8	SY0892
Flyford Flavell *H & W*	28	SO9854
Fobbing *Essex*	24	TQ7184
Fochabers *Gramp*	94	NJ3458
Fockerby *Humb*	56	SE8519
Fodderty *Highld*	92	NH5159
Foddington *Somset*	8	ST5829
Foel *Powys*	35	SH9911
Foel y Dyffryn *M Glam*	18	SS8594
Foelgastell *Dyfed*	17	SN5415
Foffarty *Tays*	88	NO4145
Foggathorpe *Humb*	56	SE7537
Fogo *Border*	77	NT7749
Fogwatt *Gramp*	94	NJ2356
Foindle *Highld*	98	NC1948
Folda *Tays*	88	NO1963
Fole *Staffs*	48	SK0437
Foleshill *W Mids*	39	SP3582
Folke *Dorset*	9	ST6513
Folkestone *Kent*	15	TR2336
Folkingham *Lincs*	40	TF0733
Folkington *E Susx*	13	TQ5603
Folksworth *Cambs*	40	TL1489
Folkton *N York*	63	TA0579
Folla Rule *Gramp*	95	NJ7332
Follifoot *N York*	55	SE3452
Folly Gate *Devon*	6	SX5797
Font-y-gary *S Glam*	18	ST0566
Fonthill Bishop *Wilts*	9	ST9332
Fonthill Gifford *Wilts*	9	ST9231
Fontmell Magna *Dorset*	9	ST8616
Fontmell Parva *Dorset*	9	ST8214
Fontwell *W Susx*	12	SU9507
Foolow *Derbys*	48	SK1976
Foord *Kent*	15	TR2236
Footbridge *Cumb*	94	NJ3613
Forbestown *Gramp*	94	NJ3613
Forcett *N York*	61	NZ1712
Ford *Bucks*	22	SP7709
Ford *Derbys*	49	SK4080
Ford *Devon*	5	SX6150
Ford *Devon*	5	SX7945
Ford *Devon*	5	SS4024
Ford *Gloucs*	28	SP0829
Ford *Nthumb*	77	NT9437
Ford *Somset*	7	ST0928
Ford *Somset*	19	ST5853
Ford *Staffs*	48	SK0653
Ford *Strath*	79	NM8603
Ford *W Susx*	12	TQ0003
Ford *Wilts*	20	ST8475
Ford Barton *Devon*	7	SS9118
Ford End *Essex*	24	TL6716
Ford Street *Somset*	8	ST1518
Forda *Devon*	4	SX5391
Fordcombe *Kent*	13	TQ5240
Fordell *Fife*	82	NT1588
Forden *Powys*	36	SJ2201
Forder *Devon*	5	SX6789
Forder Green *Devon*	5	SX7867
Fordham *Cambs*	32	TL6370
Fordham *Essex*	25	TL9328
Fordham *Norfk*	41	TL6199
Fordingbridge *Hants*	10	SU1413
Fordon *Humb*	63	TA0475
Fordoun *Gramp*	89	NO7475
Fordton *Devon*	7	SX8298
Fordwells *Oxon*	29	SP3014
Fordwich *Kent*	15	TR1859
Fordyce *Gramp*	94	NJ5563
Forebridge *Staffs*	38	SJ9222
Foremark *Derbys*	39	SK3326
Forest *Dur*	60	NY8629
Forest *Guern*	101	SV0000
Forest Becks *Lancs*	54	SD7851
Forest Gate *Gt Lon*	23	TQ4085
Forest Green *Surrey*	12	TQ1241
Forest Hill *Gt Lon*	23	TQ3671
Forest Hill *Oxon*	29	SP5807
Forest Lane Head *N York*	55	SE3356
Forest Lodge *Strath*	86	NN2642
Forest Mill *Cent*	82	NS9694
Forest Moor *N York*	55	SE2256
Forestfield *Strath*	74	NS8566
Forestside *W Susx*	11	SU7512
Forfar *Tays*	88	NO4550
Forgandenny *Tays*	82	NO0818
Forge-Hammer *Gwent*	19	ST2895
Forgie *Gramp*	94	NJ3854
Forgieside *Gramp*	94	NJ4053
Forgorig *Border*	76	NT7748
Formby *Mersyd*	46	SD3007
Forncett End *Norfk*	33	TM1494
Forncett St. Mary *Norfk*	43	TM1694
Forncett St. Peter *Norfk*	43	TM1693
Forneth *Tays*	88	NO1044
Fornham All Saints *Suffk*	32	TL8367
Fornham St. Martin *Suffk*	32	TL8567
Fornside *Cumb*	58	NY3230
Forrabury *Cnwll*	93	NJ0358
Forsbrook *Staffs*	48	SJ9641
Forse *Highld*	100	ND2234
Forse House *Highld*	100	ND2135
Forsinard *Highld*	99	NC8943
Fort Augustus *Highld*	92	NH3709
Fort George *Highld*	93	NH7656
Fort Hommet *Guern*	101	SV0000
Fort William *Highld*	86	NN1074
Fort le Marchant *Guern*	101	SV0000
Forter *Tays*	88	NO1864
Fortescue *Devon*	8	SY1388
Forteviot *Tays*	82	NO0517
Forth *Strath*	75	NS9453
Forthampton *Gloucs*	28	SO8532
Fortingall *Tays*	87	NN7447
Fortnighty *Highld*	93	NH9350
Forton *Hants*	21	SU4243
Forton *Lancs*	53	SD4851
Forton *Shrops*	36	SJ4216
Forton *Somset*	8	ST3306
Forton *Staffs*	37	SJ7521
Fortrose *Highld*	93	NH7256
Fortuneswell *Dorset*	9	SY6873
Forty Hill *Gt Lon*	23	TQ3398
Forward Green *Suffk*	33	TM1060
Fosbury *Wilts*	21	SU3157
Foscot *Oxon*	29	SP2421
Fosdyke *Lincs*	41	TF3133
Fosdyke Bridge *Lincs*	41	TF3132
Foss *Tays*	87	NN7958
Foss-y-ffin *Dyfed*	34	SN4460
Fossebridge *Gloucs*	28	SP0811
Foster Street *Essex*	23	TL4709
Foston *Derbys*	38	SK1831
Foston *Leics*	39	SP6094
Foston *Lincs*	50	SK8542
Foston *N York*	56	SE6965
Foston on the Wolds *Humb*	57	TA1055
Fotherby *Lincs*	51	TF3191
Fotheringhay *Nhants*	40	TL0593
Fotrie *Gramp*	94	NJ6645
Foul End *Warwks*	39	SP2494
Foul Mile *E Susx*	13	TQ6115
Foulden *Border*	77	NT9256
Foulridge *Lancs*	54	SD8942
Foulsham *Norfk*	42	TG0325
Fountainhall *Border*	76	NT4349
Four Ashes *Suffk*	32	TM0070
Four Crosses *Powys*	36	SJ2618
Four Elms *Kent*	13	TQ4648
Four Foot *Somset*	8	ST5733
Four Forks *Somset*	19	ST2336
Four Gates *Gt Man*	47	SD6507
Four Gotes *Cambs*	41	TF4516
Four Lane Ends *Ches*	47	SJ5661
Four Lanes *Cnwll*	2	SW6838
Four Marks *Hants*	11	SU6634
Four Mile Bridge *Gwynd*	44	SH2778
Four Oaks *W Mids*	39	SP2480
Four Points *Berks*	21	SU5579
Four Roads *Dyfed*	17	SN4409
Four Shire Stone *Warwks*	29	SP2332
Four Throws *Kent*	14	TQ7729
Four cabots *Guern*	101	SV0000
Fourpenny *Highld*	97	NH8094
Fourstones *Nthumb*	68	NY8867
Fovant *Wilts*	9	SU0028
Foveran *Gramp*	95	NJ9824
Fowey *Cnwll*	3	SX1251
Fowley Common *Ches*	47	SJ6796
Fowlhall *Kent*	14	TQ6946
Fowlis *Tays*	83	NO3233
Fowlis Wester *Tays*	82	NN9324
Fowlmere *Cambs*	31	TL4245
Fownhope *H & W*	27	SO5834
Fox Corner *Surrey*	22	SU9655
Fox House Inn *S York*	49	SK2680
Foxbar *Strath*	73	NS4561
Foxcote *Somset*	20	ST7155
Foxdale *IOM*	52	SC2778
Foxearth *Essex*	32	TL8344
Foxendown *Kent*	11	TQ6666
Foxfield *Cumb*	58	SD2085
Foxhole *Highld*	92	NH5239
Foxholes *N York*	63	TA0173
Foxley *Norfk*	42	TG0321
Foxley *Wilts*	20	ST8985
Foxt *Staffs*	48	SK0348
Foxton *Cambs*	31	TL4148
Foxton *Leics*	40	SP7089
Foxton *Dur*	62	SE4295
Foxwood *Shrops*	37	SO6276
Foy *H & W*	27	SO5928
Foyers *Highld*	92	NH4921
Foynesfield *Highld*	93	NH8855
Fraddon *Cnwll*	3	SW9158
Fradley *Staffs*	38	SK1513
Fradswell *Staffs*	38	SJ9931
Fraisthorpe *Humb*	57	TA1661
Framfield *E Susx*	13	TQ4920
Framingham Earl *Norfk*	43	TG2702
Framingham Pigot *Norfk*	43	TG2703
Framlingham *Suffk*	33	TM2863
Frampton *Dorset*	9	SY6294
Frampton *Lincs*	41	TF3239
Frampton Cotterell *Avon*	20	ST6682
Frampton Mansell *Gloucs*	20	SO9202
Frampton West End *Lincs*	51	TF2941
Frampton on Severn *Gloucs*	28	SO7407
Framsden *Suffk*	33	TM1959
Franwellgate Moor *Dur*	62	NZ2644
Frances Green *Lancs*	54	SD6236
Franche *H & W*	37	SO8178
Frankaborough *Devon*	4	SX3992
Frankby *Mersyd*	46	SJ2486
Frankley *H & W*	38	SO9980
Frankton *Warwks*	29	SP4270
Frant *E Susx*	13	TQ5835
Fraserburgh *Gramp*	95	NJ9966
Frating *Essex*	25	TM0822
Frating Green *Essex*	25	TM0923
Fratton *Hants*	11	SU6500
Freathy *Cnwll*	4	SX3952
Freckenham *Suffk*	32	TL6672
Freckleton *Lancs*	53	SD4329
Freebirch *Derbys*	49	SK3173
Freeby *Leics*	40	SK8020
Freefolk *Hants*	21	SU4848
Freeland *Oxon*	29	SP4112
Freethorpe *Norfk*	43	TG4005
Freethorpe Common *Norfk*	43	TG4004
Freiston *Lincs*	51	TF3743
Fremington *Devon*	6	SS5132
French Street *Kent*	13	TQ4652
Frenich *Tays*	87	NN8258
Frensham *Surrey*	11	SU8441
Freshfield *Mersyd*	46	SD2908
Freshiebridge *Highld*	87	NH8504
Freshwater *IOW*	10	SZ3487
Fressingfield *Suffk*	33	TM2677
Freston *Suffk*	33	TM1739
Freswick *Highld*	100	ND3667
Fretherne *Gloucs*	28	SO7210
Frettenham *Norfk*	43	TG2417
Freuchie *Fife*	83	NO2806
Freystrop *Dyfed*	16	SM8511
Friar Waddon *Dorset*	9	SY6485
Friar's Hill *N York*	63	SE7385
Friday Bridge *Cambs*	41	TF4605
Friday Street *Suffk*	33	TM3352
Friday Street *Suffk*	33	TM3760
Fridaythorpe *Humb*	56	SE8759
Fridaythorpe *Humb*	56	SE8759
Friern Barnet *Gt Lon*	23	TQ2892
Friesland Bay *Strath*	78	NM1954
Friesthorpe *Lincs*	50	TF0683
Frieston *Lincs*	50	SK9347
Frieth *Bucks*	22	SU7990
Friezeland *Notts*	49	SK4750
Frilford *Oxon*	21	SU4497
Frilsham *Berks*	21	SU5473
Frimley *Surrey*	22	SU8758
Frindsbury *Kent*	14	TQ7369
Fring *Norfk*	42	TF7334
Fringford *Oxon*	29	SP6029
Frinsted *Kent*	14	TQ8957
Frinton-on-Sea *Essex*	25	TM2320
Friockheim *Tays*	89	NO5949
Friog *Gwynd*	35	SH6111
Frisby on the Wreake *Leics*	40	SK6917
Friskney *Lincs*	51	TF4655
Friston *Suffk*	33	TM4160
Fritham *Hants*	10	SU2413
Frithelstock *Devon*	6	SS4619
Frithelstock Stone *Devon*	6	SS4518
Frithville *Lincs*	51	TF3150
Frittenden *Kent*	14	TQ8140
Frittiscombe *Devon*	5	SX8043
Fritton *Norfk*	43	TG4700
Fritton *Norfk*	43	TM2293
Fritwell *Oxon*	29	SP5229
Frizinghall *W York*	55	SE1436
Frizington *Cumb*	58	NY0316
Frocester *Gloucs*	20	SO7803
Frodesley *Shrops*	37	SJ5101
Frodsham *Ches*	46	SJ5177
Frog End *Cambs*	31	TL3946
Frog Pool *H & W*	28	SO8065
Frogbury *Devon*	7	SS6606
Frogden *Border*	76	NT7628
Froggatt *Derbys*	48	SK2476
Froghall *Staffs*	48	SK0247
Frogmore *Devon*	5	SX7742
Frognall *Lincs*	40	TF1610
Frolesworth *Leics*	39	SP5090
Frome *Somset*	20	ST7747
Frome St. Quinton *Dorset*	9	ST5902
Fromes Hill *H & W*	28	SO6846
Fron *Gwynd*	44	SH5055
Fron *Powys*	36	SJ2303
Fron Cysyllte *Clwyd*	36	SJ2740
Fron-isaf *Clwyd*	36	SJ2740
Fron-goch *Gwynd*	45	SH9039
Frostenden *Suffk*	33	TM4881
Frosterley *Dur*	61	NZ0237
Froxfield *Wilts*	21	SU2968
Froxfield Green *Hants*	11	SU7025
Fryern Hill *Hants*	10	SU4321
Fryerning *Essex*	24	TL6300
Fulbeck *Lincs*	50	SK9449
Fulbourn *Cambs*	31	TL5256
Fulbrook *Oxon*	29	SP2513
Fulflood *Hants*	10	SU4730
Fulford *N York*	56	SE6149
Fulford *Somset*	8	ST2129
Fulford *Staffs*	38	SJ9537
Fulham *Gt Lon*	23	TQ2576
Fulham *Gt Lon*	12	TQ2411
Full Sutton *Humb*	56	SE7455
Fullabrook *Devon*	6	SS5240
Fullarton *Strath*	73	NS3238
Fuller Street *Essex*	24	TL7416
Fullerton *Hants*	10	SU3739
Fulletby *Lincs*	51	TF2973
Fullready *Warwks*	29	SP2846
Fullwood *Strath*	73	NS4450
Fulmer *Bucks*	22	SU9985
Fulmodeston *Norfk*	42	TF9931
Fulnetby *Lincs*	50	TF0979
Fulwell *Oxon*	29	SP3723
Fulwell *T & W*	69	NZ3959
Fulwood *Lancs*	53	SD5431
Fulwood *S York*	49	SK3085
Fundenhall *Norfk*	43	TM1596
Funtington *W Susx*	11	SU8008
Funtley *Hants*	11	SU5608
Funtullich *Cent*	81	NN7526
Furley *Devon*	8	ST2704
Furnace *Dyfed*	17	SN5001
Furnace *Strath*	80	NN0200
Furnace End *Warwks*	39	SP2491
Furnace Vale *Derbys*	48	SK0083
Furzehill *Dorset*	9	SU0002
Furzehills *Lincs*	51	TF2572
Furzley *Hants*	10	SU2816
Furzley *Hants*	10	SU2816
Fyfield *Essex*	24	TL5707
Fyfield *Hants*	21	SU2946
Fyfield *Hants*	21	SU2946
Fyfield *Oxon*	21	SU4298
Fyfield *Wilts*	20	SU1468
Fyfield *Wilts*	21	SU1760
Fyfield Wick *Oxon*	21	SU4196
Fylingthorpe *N York*	63	NZ9404
Fyning *W Susx*	11	SU8124
Fyvie *Gramp*	95	NJ7637

G

Place	Pg	Grid ref
Gabroc Hill *Strath*	73	NS4551
Gaddesby *Leics*	39	SK6813
Gaddesden Row *Herts*	30	TL0512
Gadfa *Gwynd*	44	SH4589
Gadgirth *Strath*	73	NS4022
Gaer *Powys*	27	SO1721
Gaer-llwyd *Gwent*	19	ST4496
Gaerwen *Gwynd*	44	SH4871
Gailes *Strath*	73	NS3235
Gailey *Staffs*	38	SJ9110
Gainford *Dur*	61	NZ1716
Gainsborough *Lincs*	50	SK8189
Gainsford End *Essex*	24	TL7335
Gairloch *Highld*	91	NG8076
Gairlochy *Highld*	86	NN1784
Gairney Bank *Tays*	82	NT1299
Gairneybridge *Tays*	82	NT1397
Gaisby *W York*	55	SE1536
Gaisland *Cent*	81	NS5590
Gaitsgill *Cumb*	67	NY3847
Galashiels *Border*	76	NT4936
Galby *Leics*	40	SK6900
Galcantray *Highld*	93	NH8147
Galgate *Lancs*	53	SD4855
Galhampton *Somset*	9	ST6329
Gallaberry *D & G*	66	NX9682
Gallanach *Strath*	78	NM2160
Gallanach *Strath*	79	NM8326
Gallatown *Fife*	83	NT2994
Galley Common *Warwks*	39	SP3192
Galleywood *Essex*	24	TL7003
Gallovie *Highld*	87	NN5589
Gallowfauld *Tays*	88	NO4342
Gallowhill *Tays*	82	NO1635
Gallows Green *Essex*	32	TL9246
Gallows Green *H & W*	28	SO3963
Gallows Green *Staffs*	48	SK0741
Galltair *Highld*	85	NG8120
Gallypot Street *E Susx*	13	TQ4635
Galmisdale *Highld*	84	NM4784
Galmpton *Devon*	5	SX6940
Galmpton *Devon*	5	SX8856
Galphay *N York*	55	SE2572
Galston *Strath*	74	NS5036
Galton *Dorset*	9	SY7785
Galtrigill *Highld*	90	NG1864
Gambles Green *Essex*	24	TL7615
Gamblesby *Cumb*	59	NY6039
Gambling *Humb*	57	TA1057
Gamlingay *Cambs*	31	TL2452
Gamlingay Great Heath *Beds*	31	TL2151
Gamrie *Gramp*	95	NJ7962
Gamston *Notts*	49	SK7076
Ganavan Bay *Strath*	79	NM8832
Ganllwyd *Gwynd*	35	SH7224
Gannachy *Tays*	89	NO5970
Ganstead *Humb*	57	TA1434
Ganthorpe *N York*	56	SE6870
Ganton *N York*	63	SE8977
Ganwick Corner *Herts*	23	TQ2599
Garbat *Highld*	92	NH4188
Garbity *Gramp*	94	NJ3163
Garboldisham *Norfk*	32	TM0081
Garchory *Gramp*	94	NJ2909
Garden Village *Derbys*	49	SK2698
Gardeners Green *Berks*	22	SU8266
Gardenstown *Gramp*	95	NJ7964
Garderhouse *Shet*	103	HU3347
Gare Hill *Somset*	20	ST7840
Garelochhead *Strath*	80	NS2491
Garenin *W Isls*	102	NB1944
Garford *Oxon*	21	SU4296
Garforth *W York*	55	SE4033
Gargrave *N York*	54	SD9354
Gargunnock *Cent*	81	NS7094
Garlandhaves *Devon*	8	ST1716
Garlic Street *Norfk*	33	TM2183
Garlieston *D & G*	65	NX4746
Garlinge *Kent*	15	TR3369
Garlinge Green *Kent*	15	TR1152
Garlogie *Gramp*	89	NJ7805
Garmondsway *Dur*	62	NJ0852
Garmony House *Strath*	79	NM6640
Garmouth *Gramp*	94	NJ3364
Garmston *Shrops*	37	SJ6006
Garn *Gwynd*	44	SH2734
Garn-Dolbenmaen *Gwynd*	44	SH4944
Garnant *Dyfed*	17	SN6713
Garnett Bridge *Cumb*	59	SD5298
Garnkirk *Strath*	74	NS6368
Garnlydan *Gwent*	27	SO1612
Garnoch *Highld*	85	NM8696
Garrabost *W Isls*	102	NB5133
Garrallan *Strath*	74	NS5418
Garraron *Strath*	2	SW7023
Garreg *Gwynd*	45	SH6141
Gargill *Cumb*	60	NY7441
Garrochty *D & G*	65	NX5981
Garrochtie *D & G*	64	NX1038
Garrochty *Strath*	73	NS0953
Garros *Highld*	90	NG4963
Garsdale Head *Cumb*	60	SD7892
Garsdon *Wilts*	20	ST9887
Garshall Green *Staffs*	38	SJ9634
Garsington *Oxon*	21	SP5802
Garstang *Lancs*	53	SD4945
Garston *Herts*	22	TL1100
Garston *Mersyd*	46	SJ4084
Gartachoisan *Strath*	70	NR3461
Gartcosh *Strath*	74	NS6968
Garth *Clwyd*	36	SJ2542
Garth *Powys*	26	SN9549
Garth Penrhyncoch *Dyfed*	35	SN6484
Garth Row *Cumb*	59	SD5297
Garthbrengy *Powys*	26	SO0433
Garthorpe *Humb*	56	SE8419
Garthorpe *Leics*	40	SK8320
Gartly *Gramp*	94	NJ5232
Gartmore *Cent*	81	NS5297
Gartmore *Cent*	81	NS5297
Gartnatra *Strath*	70	NR3260
Gartness *Cent*	81	NS5086
Gartness *N York*	54	NS7864
Gartocharn *Strath*	81	NS4286
Garton *Humb*	57	TA2635
Garton End *Cambs*	40	TF1909
Garton-on-the-Wolds *Humb*	56	SE9759
Gartsherrie *Strath*	74	NS7265
Gartymore *Highld*	97	ND0114
Garvald *Loth*	76	NT5870
Garvan *Highld*	80	NM9779
Garvard *Strath*	70	NR3691
Garve *Highld*	92	NH3961
Garvestone *Norfk*	42	TG0207
Garvock *Strath*	73	NS2570
Garway *H & W*	27	SO4622
Garynahine *W Isls*	102	NB2331
Gasper *Wilts*	9	ST7533
Gass *Strath*	73	NS4105
Gastard *Wilts*	20	ST8868
Gasthorpe *Norfk*	32	TL9781
Gatcombe *IOW*	10	SZ4885
Gate Burton *Lincs*	50	SK8382
Gate Helmsley *N York*	56	SE6855
Gateforth *N York*	55	SE5628
Gatehead *Strath*	73	NS3936
Gatehouse *Nthumb*	68	NY7989
Gatehouse of Fleet *D & G*	65	NX6056
Gatelawbridge *D & G*	66	NX8996

Place	Pg	Grid
Gatelawbridge D & G	66	NX9096
Gateley Norfk	42	TF9624
Gatenby N York	62	SE3287
Gatesgarth Cumb	58	NY1925
Gateshaw Border	76	NT7722
Gateshead T & W	69	NZ2562
Gateside Fife	82	NO1609
Gateside Strath	73	NS3653
Gateside Strath	73	NS4858
Gateside Tays	88	NO4344
Gateslack D & G	66	NS8902
Gatley Gt Man	47	SJ8488
Gattonside Border	76	NT5435
Gauldry Fife	83	NO3723
Gauldswell Tays	88	NO2151
Gaunt's End Essex	24	TL5525
Gautby Lincs	50	TF1772
Gavinton Border	76	NT7652
Gawcott Bucks	30	SP6831
Gawsworth Ches	48	SJ8969
Gawthrop Cumb	60	SD6987
Gawthwaite Cumb	58	SD2784
Gaydon Warwks	29	SP3654
Gayhurst Bucks	30	SP8446
Gayle N York	60	SD8688
Gayles N York	61	NZ1207
Gayton Nhants	30	SP7054
Gayton Norfk	42	TF7219
Gayton Staffs	38	SJ9828
Gayton Thorpe Norfk	42	TF7418
Gayton le Marsh Lincs	51	TF4284
Gaywood Norfk	41	TF6320
Gazeley Suffk	32	TL7264
Geary Highld	90	NG2661
Gedding Suffk	32	TL9458
Geddinge Kent	15	TR2346
Geddington Nhants	40	SP8983
Gedintailor Highld	84	NG5235
Gedling Notts	49	SK6142
Gedney Lincs	41	TF4024
Gedney Broadgate Lincs	41	TF4022
Gedney Drove End Lincs	41	TF4629
Gedney Dyke Lincs	41	TF4126
Gedney Hill Lincs	41	TF3311
Geldeston Norfk	33	TM3991
Gelli Gwent	19	ST2793
Gelli Gynan Clwyd	46	SJ1854
Gellideg M Glam	26	SO0207
Gellifor Clwyd	46	SJ1262
Gelligaer M Glam	18	ST1397
Gelligroes Gwent	19	ST1794
Gellilydan Gwynd	45	SH6839
Gellinudd W Glam	18	SN7303
Gellinudd W Glam	26	SN7304
Gellyburn Tays	82	NO0939
Gellywen Dyfed	17	SN2723
Gelston D & G	66	NX7758
Gelston Lincs	50	SK9145
Gentleshaw Staffs	38	SK0511
George Green Bucks	22	TQ0081
George Nympton Devon	7	SS7023
Georgefield D & G	67	NY3091
Georgeham Devon	6	SS4639
Georgetown Gwent	27	SO1508
Georth Ork	103	HY3626
Germansweek Devon	6	SX4394
Gerrans Cnwll	3	SW8735
Gerrards Cross Bucks	22	TQ0088
Gerrick Cleve	62	NZ7012
Geshader W Isls	102	NB1131
Gestingthorpe Essex	24	TL8138
Geuffordd Powys	36	SJ2114
Gibraltar Lincs	51	TF5558
Gibsmere Notts	49	SK7248
Giddy Green Dorset	9	SY8286
Gidea Park Gt Lon	23	TQ5290
Gidleigh Devon	5	SX6788
Giffnock Strath	74	NS5658
Gifford Loth	76	NT5368
Giffordtown Fife	83	NO2811
Giggleswick N York	54	SD8163
Gilberdyke Humb	56	SE8329
Gilbert Street Hants	11	SU6532
Gilbert's Cross Staffs	37	SO8186
Gilbert's End H & W	28	SO8242
Gilchriston Loth	76	NT4865
Gilcrux Cumb	58	NY1138
Gildersome W York	55	SE2429
Gildingwells S York	49	SK5685
Gilesgate Moor Dur	69	NZ2943
Gileston S Glam	18	ST0167
Gilfach M Glam	19	ST1598
Gilfach Goch M Glam	18	SS9890
Gilfachrheda Dyfed	34	SN4159
Gilgarran Cumb	58	NY0323
Gillamoor N York	62	SE6890
Gillesbie D & G	67	NY1691
Gilling N York	61	NZ1805
Gilling East N York	62	SE6176
Gillingham Dorset	9	ST8026
Gillingham Kent	14	TQ7768
Gillingham Norfk	33	TM4191
Gillock Highld	100	ND2159
Gills Highld	100	ND3272
Gilmanscleuch Border	75	NT3321
Gilmerton Loth	75	NT2968
Gilmerton Tays	82	NN8823
Gilmonby Dur	61	NY9912
Gilmorton Leics	39	SP5787
Gilsland Nthumb	68	NY6366
Gilson Warwks	38	SP1890
Gilstead W York	55	SE1131
Gilwern Gwent	27	SO2414
Gimingham Norfk	43	TG2836
Gipping Suffk	32	TM0763
Gipsey Bridge Lincs	51	TF2849
Girdle Toll Strath	73	NS3440
Girlsta Shet	103	HU4250
Girsby Cleve	62	NZ3508
Girton Cambs	31	TL4262
Girvan Strath	64	NX1897
Gisburn Lancs	54	SD8248
Gisleham Suffk	33	TM5188
Gislingham Suffk	32	TM0771
Gissing Norfk	33	TM1485
Gittisham Devon	8	SY1398
Gladestry Powys	27	SO2355
Gladsmuir Loth	76	NT4573
Glais W Glam	18	SN7000
Glaisdale N York	63	NZ7705
Glamis Tays	88	NO3846
Glan-y-don Clwyd	46	SJ1679
Glan-y-llyn M Glam	18	ST1184
Glanafon Dyfed	16	SM9517
Glanaman Dyfed	26	SN6713
Glandford Norfk	42	TG0441
Glandwr Dyfed	17	SN1928
Glangrwyne Powys	27	SO2316
Glanllynfi M Glam	18	SS8690
Glanton Nthumb	68	NU0714
Glanvilles Wootton Dorset	9	ST6708
Glapthorn Nhants	40	TL0290
Glapwell Derbys	49	SK4766
Glasbury Powys	27	SO1739
Glascoed Gwent	19	SO3201
Glascwm Powys	27	SO1552
Glasfryn Clwyd	45	SH9250
Glasgow Strath	74	NS5865
Glasinfryn Gwynd	44	SH5868
Glaslaw Gramp	89	NO8585
Glasnacardoch Bay Highld	85	NM6795
Glasnakille Highld	84	NG5513
Glassburn Highld	92	NH3634
Glassel Gramp	89	NO6599
Glassford Strath	74	NS7247
Glasshouse Gloucs	28	SO7021
Glasshouses N York	55	SE1764
Glasson Cumb	67	NY2560
Glasson Lancs	53	SD4456
Glassonby Cumb	59	NY5738
Glasterlaw Tays	89	NO5951
Glaston Leics	40	SK8900
Glastonbury Somset	19	ST4938
Glatton Cambs	40	TL1586
Glazebury Ches	47	SJ6797
Glazeley Shrops	37	SO7088
Gleaston Cumb	53	SD2570
Gledhow W York	55	SE3137
Gleding Notts	39	SK5132
Gledrid Shrops	36	SJ2936
Glehearn Tays	82	NO1016
Glemanault Strath	72	NR6407
Glemsford Suffk	32	TL8348
Glen Auldyn IOM	52	SC4393
Glen Clunie Lodge Gramp	88	NO1383
Glen Nevis House Highld	86	NN1272
Glen Parva Leics	39	SP5798
Glen Trool Lodge D & G	64	NX4080
Glen Village Cent	82	NS8878
Glen Vine IOM	52	SC3378
Glen of Foudland Gramp	84	NJ6035
Glenancross Highld	85	NM6691
Glenaros House Strath	79	NM5544
Glenbarr Strath	72	NR6736
Glenbeg Highld	79	NM5862
Glenbervie Gramp	89	NO7680
Glenboig Strath	74	NS7269
Glenborrodale Highld	79	NM6061
Glenbranter Strath	80	NS1197
Glenbreck Border	75	NT0521
Glenbrittle House Highld	84	NG4121
Glenbuck Strath	74	NS7429
Glencally Tays	88	NO3562
Glencaple D & G	66	NX9968
Glencarron Lodge Highld	91	NH0650
Glencarse Tays	82	NO1922
Glenceitlein Highld	86	NN1548
Glencoe Highld	86	NN1058
Glencothe Border	75	NT0929
Glencraig Fife	82	NT1894
Glencrosh D & G	65	NX7689
Glendaruel Strath	80	NR9983
Glendevon Tays	82	NN9904
Glendoe Lodge Highld	87	NH4009
Glendoick Tays	82	NO2022
Glenduckie Fife	83	NO2818
Gleneagles Tays	82	NN9209
Glenegedale Strath	70	NR3351
Glenelg Highld	85	NG8119
Glenerney Gramp	93	NJ0146
Glenfarg Tays	82	NO1310
Glenfeshie Lodge Highld	87	NN8493
Glenfield Leics	39	SK5306
Glenfinnan Highld	85	NM8980
Glenfinntaig Lodge Highld	86	NN2286
Glenfoot Tays	82	NO1815
Glenfyne Lodge Strath	80	NN2215
Glengarnock Strath	73	NS3252
Glengolly Highld	100	ND1065
Glengorm Castle Strath	79	NM4357
Glengrasco Highld	90	NG4444
Glenholm Border	75	NT1033
Glenhoul D & G	65	NX6187
Glenkerry Border	67	NT2711
Glenkiln D & G	66	NX8477
Glenkin Strath	80	NS1280
Glenkindie Gramp	84	NJ4314
Glenlee D & G	65	NX6080
Glenlochar D & G	65	NX7364
Glenloig Strath	72	NR9435
Glenluce D & G	64	NX1957
Glenmallan Strath	80	NS2595
Glenmark Tays	88	NO4283
Glenmassan Strath	80	NS1087
Glenmaye IOM	52	SC2380
Glenmore Highld	84	NG4340
Glenmore Strath	79	NM8412
Glenmore Lodge Highld	93	NH9709
Glenmuirshaw Strath	74	NS6920
Glenquiech Tays	88	NO4286
Glenralloch Strath	71	NR8659
Glenrisdell Strath	71	NR8658
Glenrothes Fife	83	NO2700
Glenshero Lodge Highld	87	NN5593
Glenstriven Strath	80	NS0878
Glentham Lincs	50	TF0090
Glentromie Lodge Highld	87	NN7897
Glentrool Village D & G	64	NX3578
Glentruim House Highld	87	NN6894
Glentworth Lincs	50	SK9488
Glenuig Highld	85	NM6676
Glenure Strath	86	NN0448
Glenurquhart Highld	93	NH7462
Glenvarragill Highld	84	NG4739
Glenwhilly D & G	64	NX1771
Glespin Strath	74	NS8128
Glewstone H & W	27	SO5521
Glinton Cambs	40	TF1505
Glooston Leics	40	SP7595
Glossop Derbys	48	SK0493
Gloster Hill Nthumb	69	NU2504
Gloucester Gloucs	28	SO8318
Glover's Hill Staffs	38	SK0416
Glusburn N York	55	SE0344
Glutt Lodge Highld	100	ND0036
Gluvian Cnwll	3	SW9164
Glympton Oxon	29	SP4221
Glyn Ceiriog Clwyd	36	SJ2038
Glyn-Neath W Glam	26	SN8806
Glynarthen Dyfed	17	SN3148
Glyncoch M Glam	18	ST0792
Glyncorrwg W Glam	18	SS8799
Glynde E Susx	13	TQ4509
Glyndyfrdwy Clwyd	36	SJ1442
Glynogwr M Glam	18	SS9585
Glyntawe Powys	26	SN8416
Glynteg Dyfed	17	SN3638
Gnosall Staffs	38	SJ8220
Gnosall Heath Staffs	38	SJ8220
Goadby Leics	40	SP7598
Goadby Marwood Leics	40	SK7826
Goatacre Wilts	20	SU0176
Goathill Dorset	9	ST6717
Goathland N York	63	NZ8301
Goathurst Somset	8	ST2534
Goathurst Common Kent	13	TQ4952
Gobowen Shrops	36	SJ3033
Godalming Surrey	12	SU9743
Goddard's Green Kent	14	TQ8134
Godmanchester Cambs	31	TL2470
Godmanstone Dorset	9	SY6697
Godmersham Kent	15	TR0550
Godney Somset	19	ST4842
Godolphin Cross Cnwll	2	SW6031
Godre'r-graig W Glam	26	SN7506
Godshill Hants	10	SU1714
Godshill IOW	11	SZ5281
Godstone Staffs	38	SK0134
Godstone Surrey	12	TQ3551
Goetre Gwent	27	SO3206
Goff's Oak Herts	23	TL3203
Gogar Loth	75	NT1672
Goginan Dyfed	35	SN6881
Golan Gwynd	44	SH5242
Golant Cnwll	3	SX1254
Golborne Gt Man	47	SJ6097
Golcar W York	55	SE0915
Goldcliff Gwent	19	ST3683
Golden Green Kent	13	TQ6348
Golders Green Gt Lon	23	TQ2487
Goldhanger Essex	24	TL9009
Goldington Beds	30	TL0750
Goldsborough N York	55	SE3856
Goldsborough N York	63	NZ8314
Goldsithney Cnwll	2	SW5430
Goldsworth Surrey	22	SU9958
Goldthorpe S York	55	SE4604
Goldworthy Devon	6	SS3923
Gollanfield Highld	93	NH8053
Gollinglith Foot N York	61	SE1480
Golsoncott Somset	7	ST0338
Golspie Highld	97	NH8300
Gomeldon Wilts	10	SU1936
Gomshall Surrey	12	TQ0847
Gonachan Cent	81	NS6386
Gonfirth Shet	103	HU3761
Good Easter Essex	24	TL6212
Gooderstone Norfk	42	TF7602
Goodleigh Devon	6	SS6034
Goodmanham Humb	56	SE8842
Goodnestone Kent	15	TR0461
Goodnestone Kent	15	TR2554
Goodrich H & W	27	SO5719
Goodrich Cross H & W	27	SO5619
Goodrington Devon	5	SX8958
Goodshaw Fold Lancs	54	SD8026
Goodstone Devon	5	SX7971
Goodwick Dyfed	16	SM9438
Goodworth Clatford Hants	21	SU3642
Goole Humb	56	SE7423
Goonbell Cnwll	2	SW7249
Goonhavern Cnwll	2	SW7853
Goonvrea Cnwll	2	SW7149
Goose Green Avon	20	ST6774
Goose Green Essex	25	TM1425
Goose Green Essex	25	TM1425
Goosecruives Gramp	89	NO7583
Gooseford Devon	5	SX6892
Goosetrey Ches	47	SJ7770
Goosey Oxon	21	SU3591
Goosnargh Lancs	53	SD5536
Gordon Border	76	NT6443
Gordon Arms Hotel Border	75	NT3125
Gordonbush Highld	97	NC8409
Gordonstown Gramp	94	NJ5656
Gordonstown Gramp	95	NJ7138
Gore Powys	27	SO2658
Gore Street Kent	23	TQ2765
Gorebridge Loth	75	NT3461
Gorey Jersey	101	SV0000
Goring Oxon	21	SU6080
Goring-by-Sea W Susx	12	TQ1102
Gorleston on Sea Norfk	43	TG5204
Gorrachie Gramp	95	NJ7358
Gorran Churchtown Cnwll	3	SW9942
Gorran Haven Cnwll	3	SX0141
Gorran High Lanes Cnwll	3	SW9843
Gorrenberry Border	67	NY4699
Gorse Hill Wilts	20	SU1586
Gorsedd Clwyd	46	SJ1576
Gorseinon W Glam	17	SS5998
Gorsgoch Dyfed	17	SN4850
Gorslas Dyfed	17	SN5713
Gorsley Gloucs	28	SO6925
Gorst Hill H & W	37	SO7473
Gorstan Highld	92	NH3863
Gorstello Ches	46	SJ3562
Gorsty Common H & W	27	SO4437
Gorsty Common H & W	27	SO4537
Gorsty Hill Staffs	38	SK1029
Gorten Strath	79	NM7432
Gorton Gt Man	47	SJ8896
Gosbeck Suffk	33	TM1555
Gosberton Lincs	41	TF2331
Gosfield Essex	24	TL7829
Gosforth Cumb	58	NY0603
Gosforth T & W	69	NZ2467
Gosling Street Somset	8	ST5633
Gospel End Staffs	38	SO8993
Gospel Green W Susx	11	SU9331
Gosport Hants	11	SZ6199
Goswick Nthumb	77	NU0645
Gotham Notts	39	SK5330
Gotherington Gloucs	28	SO9629
Gotton Somset	8	ST2428
Goudhurst Kent	14	TQ7237
Goulceby Lincs	51	TF2579
Gourdas Gramp	95	NJ7741
Gourdie Tays	83	NO3532
Gourdon Gramp	89	NO8271
Gourock Strath	80	NS2477
Govan Strath	74	NS5465
Goveton Devon	5	SX7546
Govilon Gwent	27	SO2614
Gowdall Humb	56	SE6122
Gower Highld	92	NH5058
Gowerton W Glam	17	SS5896
Gowkhall Fife	82	NT0589
Goxhill Humb	57	TA1021
Goxhill Humb	57	TA1844
Graffham W Susx	11	SU9217
Grafham Cambs	31	TL1669
Grafham Surrey	12	TQ0241
Grafton H & W	28	SO9837
Grafton H & W	27	SO5761
Grafton N York	55	SE4163
Grafton Oxon	21	SP2600
Grafton Shrops	36	SJ4319
Grafton Flyford H & W	28	SO9656
Grafton Regis Nhants	30	SP7546
Grafton Underwood Nhants	40	SP9280
Grafty Green Kent	14	TQ8748
Graig Clwyd	46	SJ0872
Graig Clwyd	45	SH8071
Graig-fechan Clwyd	46	SJ1454
Grains Kent	14	TQ8876
Grains o'the Beck Bridge Dur	60	NY8621
Grainsby Lincs	51	TF2799
Grainthorpe Lincs	51	TF3896
Gramisdale W Isls	102	NF8155
Grampound Cnwll	3	SW9348
Grampound Road Cnwll	3	SW9150
Gramsdale W Isls	102	NF8255
Granborough Bucks	30	SP7625
Granby Notts	40	SK7536
Grand Chemins Jersey	101	SV0000
Grandborough Warwks	29	SP4967
Grandes Rocques Guern	101	SV0000
Grandtully Tays	87	NN9153
Grange Cumb	58	NY2517
Grange Kent	14	TQ7968
Grange Tays	83	NO2625
Grange Crossroads Gramp	94	NJ4754
Grange Hall Gramp	93	NJ0660
Grange Hill Gt Lon	23	TQ4492
Grange Lindores Fife	83	NO2516
Grange Moor W York	55	SE2216
Grange Villa Dur	69	NZ2352
Grangehall Strath	75	NS9642
Grangemill Derbys	48	SK2457
Grangemouth Cent	82	NS9282
Grangepans Cent	82	NT0181
Gransmoor Humb	57	TA1259
Granston Dyfed	16	SM8934
Grantchester Cambs	31	TL4355
Grantham Lincs	40	SK9135
Grantown-on-Spey Highld	93	NJ0328
Grantsfield H & W	27	SO5360
Grantshouse Border	76	NT8165
Grappenhall Ches	47	SJ6486
Grasby Lincs	57	TA0804
Grasmere Cumb	59	NY3307
Grassendale Mersyd	46	SJ3985
Grassington N York	54	SE0063
Grassmoor Derbys	49	SK4067
Grassthorpe Notts	50	SK7967
Grateley Hants	21	SU2741
Graveley Cambs	31	TL2564
Graveley Herts	31	TL2327
Gravelly Bank Shrops	36	SJ3600
Graveney Kent	15	TR0562
Gravesend Kent	14	TQ6474
Gravir W Isls	90	NB3715
Grayingham Lincs	50	SK9396
Grayrigg Cumb	59	SD5796
Grays Essex	24	TQ6177
Grayshott Hants	11	SU8735
Grayswood Surrey	11	SU9134
Grazeley Berks	22	SU6966
Grazies Hill Oxon	22	SU6980
Greasbrough S York	49	SK4195
Greasby Mersyd	46	SJ2587
Greasley Notts	49	SK4947
Great Abington Cambs	31	TL5348
Great Addington Nhants	30	SP9675
Great Alne Warwks	28	SP1259
Great Altcar Lancs	46	SD3306
Great Amwell Herts	31	TL3712
Great Asby Cumb	60	NY6713
Great Ashfield Suffk	32	TL9967
Great Ayton N York	62	NZ5510
Great Baddow Essex	24	TL7305
Great Badminton Avon	20	ST8082
Great Bardfield Essex	24	TL6730
Great Barford Beds	31	TL1352
Great Barrington Gloucs	29	SP2013
Great Barrow Ches	46	SJ4768
Great Barton Suffk	32	TL8967
Great Barugh N York	63	SE7478
Great Bavington Nthumb	68	NY9880
Great Bealings Suffk	33	TM2349
Great Bedwyn Wilts	21	SU2764
Great Bentley Essex	25	TM1021
Great Billing Nhants	30	SP8162
Great Bircham Norfk	42	TF7732
Great Blakenham Suffk	33	TM1150
Great Bookham Surrey	22	TQ1354
Great Bosullow Cnwll	2	SW4133
Great Bourton Oxon	29	SP4546
Great Bowden Leics	40	SP7488
Great Bradley Suffk	32	TL6753
Great Braxted Essex	24	TL8614
Great Bricett Suffk	32	TM0350
Great Brickhill Bucks	30	SP9030
Great Bridge W Mids	38	SO9792
Great Bridgeford Staffs	38	SJ8827
Great Brington Nhants	30	SP6665
Great Bromley Essex	25	TM0826
Great Broughton Cumb	58	NY0731
Great Broughton N York	62	NZ5405
Great Budworth Ches	47	SJ6677
Great Burdon Dur	62	NZ3116
Great Burstead Essex	24	TQ6892
Great Busby N York	62	NZ5205
Great Canfield Essex	24	TL5918
Great Carlton Lincs	51	TF4085
Great Casterton Leics	40	TF0009
Great Chart Kent	15	TQ9741
Great Chatfield Wilts	20	ST8663
Great Chatwell Staffs	37	SJ7914
Great Chell Staffs	47	SJ8752
Great Chesterford Essex	31	TL5042
Great Cheverell Wilts	20	ST9858
Great Chishill Cambs	31	TL4238
Great Clacton Essex	25	TM1716
Great Cliffe W York	55	SE3015
Great Clifton Cumb	58	NY0429
Great Coates Humb	57	TA2309
Great Comberton H & W	28	SO9542
Great Corby Cumb	67	NY4754
Great Cornard Suffk	32	TL8840
Great Cowden Humb	57	TA2342
Great Coxwell Oxon	21	SU2693
Great Cressingham Norfk	42	TF8501
Great Crosthwaite Cumb	58	NY2624
Great Cubley Derbys	48	SK1638
Great Dalby Leics	40	SK7414
Great Doddington Nhants	30	SP8864
Great Driffield Humb	56	TA0257
Great Dunham Norfk	42	TF8714
Great Dunmow Essex	24	TL6222
Great Durnford Wilts	10	SU1338
Great Easton Essex	24	TL6025
Great Easton Leics	40	SP8493
Great Eccleston Lancs	53	SD4240
Great Ellingham Norfk	42	TM0196
Great Elm Somset	20	ST7449
Great Englebourne Devon	5	SX7756
Great Everdon Nhants	29	SP5957
Great Eversden Cambs	31	TL3653
Great Finborough Suffk	32	TM0158
Great Fransham Norfk	42	TF8913
Great Gaddesden Herts	22	TL0211
Great Gidding Cambs	40	TL1183
Great Givendale Humb	56	SE8153
Great Glemham Suffk	33	TM3361
Great Glen Leics	39	SP6597
Great Gonerby Lincs	40	SK8938
Great Gransden Cambs	31	TL2655
Great Green Cambs	31	TL2844
Great Green Suffk	32	TL9196
Great Green Suffk	33	TL9365
Great Habton N York	63	SE7576
Great Hale Lincs	50	TF1442
Great Hallingbury Essex	31	TL5119
Great Hanwood Shrops	36	SJ4409
Great Harrowden Nhants	30	SP8770
Great Harwood Lancs	54	SD7332
Great Haseley Oxon	21	SP6401
Great Hatfield Humb	57	TA1842
Great Haywood Staffs	38	SJ9922
Great Heck N York	56	SE5921
Great Henny Essex	24	TL8637
Great Hinton Wilts	20	ST9058
Great Hockham Norfk	32	TL9592
Great Holland Essex	25	TM2019
Great Horkesley Essex	25	TL9731
Great Hormead Herts	31	TL4030
Great Horton W York	55	SE1411
Great Horwood Bucks	30	SP7731
Great Houghton Nhants	30	SP7958
Great Houghton S York	55	SE4206
Great Hucklow Derbys	48	SK1777
Great Kelk Humb	57	TA1058
Great Kimble Bucks	22	SP8206
Great Kingshill Bucks	22	SU8797
Great Langdale Cumb	58	NY2906
Great Langton N York	61	SE2996
Great Leighs Essex	24	TL7217
Great Limber Lincs	57	TA1308
Great Linford Bucks	30	SP8542
Great Livermere Suffk	32	TL8871
Great Longstone Derbys	48	SK1971
Great Lumley T & W	69	NZ2949
Great Malvern H & W	28	SO7845
Great Maplestead Essex	24	TL8134
Great Marton Lancs	53	SD3235
Great Massingham Norfk	42	TF7923
Great Milton Oxon	21	SP6202
Great Missenden Bucks	22	SP8901
Great Mitton Lancs	54	SD7138
Great Mongeham Kent	15	TR3551
Great Moulton Norfk	33	TM1690
Great Munden Herts	31	TL3524
Great Ness Shrops	36	SJ3919
Great Oak Gwent	27	SO3809
Great Oakley Essex	25	TM1927
Great Oakley Nhants	40	SP8686
Great Offley Herts	30	TL1427
Great Ormside Cumb	60	NY7017
Great Orton Cumb	67	NY2554
Great Ouseburn N York	55	SE4461
Great Oxendon Nhants	40	SP7383
Great Oxney Green Essex	24	TL6606
Great Pattenden Kent	14	TQ7345
Great Paxton Cambs	31	TL2063
Great Plumpton Lancs	53	SD3833
Great Plumstead Norfk	43	TG3010
Great Ponton Lincs	40	SK9230
Great Preston W York	55	SE4029
Great Raveley Cambs	41	TL2581
Great Rissington Gloucs	29	SP1917
Great Rollright Oxon	29	SP3231
Great Ryburgh Norfk	42	TF9527
Great Ryle Nthumb	68	NU0212
Great Saling Essex	24	TL7026
Great Salkeld Cumb	59	NY5436
Great Sampford Essex	24	TL6435
Great Saughall Ches	46	SJ3669
Great Shefford Berks	21	SU3875
Great Shelford Cambs	31	TL4652
Great Smeaton N York	62	NZ3404
Great Snoring Norfk	42	TF9434
Great Somerford Wilts	20	ST9682
Great Soudley Shrops	37	SJ7229
Great Stainton Dur	62	NZ3322
Great Stambridge Essex	24	TQ8992
Great Staughton Cambs	30	TL1264
Great Steeping Lincs	51	TF4364
Great Stoke Avon	19	ST6280
Great Strickland Cumb	59	NY5522
Great Stukeley Cambs	31	TL2274
Great Sturton Lincs	51	TF2176
Great Swinburne Nthumb	68	NY9375
Great Tew Oxon	29	SP3929
Great Tey Essex	24	TL8925
Great Torrington Devon	6	SS4919
Great Tosson Nthumb	68	NU0200
Great Totham Essex	24	TL8611
Great Totham Essex	24	TL8713
Great Wakering Essex	24	TQ9487
Great Waldingfield Suffk	32	TL9144
Great Walsingham Norfk	42	TF9437
Great Waltham Essex	24	TL6913
Great Warley Essex	24	TQ5890

Great Washbourne Gloucs	28	SO9834
Great Weeke Devon	5	SX7187
Great Weldon Nhants	40	SP9289
Great Wenham Suffk	25	TM0738
Great Whittington Nthumb	68	NZ0070
Great Wigborough Essex	25	TL9615
Great Wilbraham Cambs	31	TL5557
Great Wishford Wilts	10	SU0835
Great Witcombe Gloucs	28	SO9114
Great Witley H & W	28	SO7566
Great Wolford Warwks	29	SP2534
Great Wratting Essex	32	TL6848
Great Wymondley Herts	31	TL2128
Great Wyrley Staffs	38	SJ9907
Great Yarmouth Norfk	43	TG5207
Great Yeldham Essex	24	TL7638
Greatford Lincs	40	TF0811
Greatgate Staffs	48	SK0540
Greatham Cleve	62	NZ4927
Greatham Hants	11	SU7730
Greatham Hants	12	TQ0415
Greatstone-on-Sea Kent	15	TR0822
Greatworth Nhants	29	SP5542
Green Bank Cumb	67	NY3780
Green Cross Surrey	11	SU8634
Green End Herts	31	TL3333
Green End Herts	31	SP2686
Green Hammerton N York	55	SE4656
Green Heath Staffs	38	SJ9913
Green Hill Nthumb	68	NY8647
Green Moor S York	49	SK2899
Green Ore Somset	19	ST5749
Green Quarter Cumb	59	NY4603
Green Street H & W	28	SO8749
Green Street Herts	23	TQ1998
Green Street Herts	31	TL4521
Green Street Green Kent	14	TQ5870
Green The Cumb	58	SD1784
Green Tye Herts	31	TL4418
green end Herts	31	TL3122
Greenburn Loth	75	NS9360
Greenfield Beds	30	TL0534
Greenfield Clwyd	46	SJ1977
Greenfield Highld	86	NH2000
Greenfield Strath	80	NS2490
Greenford Gt Lon	22	TQ1482
Greengairs Strath	74	NS7870
Greenhalgh Lancs	53	SD4035
Greenham Somset	7	ST0719
Greenhaugh Nthumb	68	NY7987
Greenhill Cent	82	NS8279
Greenhill D & G	67	NY1079
Greenhill Kent	15	TR1666
Greenhill S York	49	SK3481
Greenhill Strath	75	NS9333
Greenhithe Kent	14	TQ5875
Greenholm Strath	74	NS5437
Greenhouse Border	76	NT5624
Greenhow Hill N York	55	SE1164
Greenland Highld	100	ND2367
Greenland S York	49	SK3988
Greenlaw Border	76	NT7146
Greenlea D & G	66	NY0375
Greenloaning Tays	82	NN8307
Greenmount Gt Man	54	SD7714
Greenock Strath	80	NS2776
Greenodd Cumb	58	SD3182
Greens Norton Nhants	30	SP6649
Greenside T & W	69	NZ1362
Greenside W York	55	SE1616
Greenstead Essex	25	TM0125
Greenstead Green Essex	24	TL8227
Greensted Essex	23	TL5303
Greenstreet Green Suffk	32	TM0450
Greenway Gloucs	28	SO7032
Greenway S Glam	18	ST0574
Greenwich Gt Lon	23	TQ3877
Greet Gloucs	28	SP0230
Greete Shrops	37	SO5771
Greetham Leics	40	SK9214
Greetham Lincs	51	TF3070
Greetland W York	55	SE0821
Greinton Somset	19	ST4136
Grenaby IOM	52	SC2672
Grendon Nhants	30	SP8760
Grendon Warwks	39	SP2799
Grendon Underwood Bucks	30	SP6820
Grenofen Devon	4	SX5671
Grenoside S York	49	SK3394
Gresford Clwyd	46	SJ3454
Gresham Norfk	43	TG1638
Greshornish Highld	90	NG3454
Gressenhall Norfk	42	TF9615
Gressenhall Green Norfk	42	TF9616
Gressingham Lancs	53	SD5769
Grestey Green Ches	47	SJ7054
Greta Bridge Dur	61	NZ0813
Gretna D & G	67	NY3167
Gretna Green D & G	67	NY3268
Gretton Gloucs	28	SP0030
Gretton Nhants	40	SP8994
Gretton Shrops	37	SO5195
Grewelthorpe N York	55	SE2376
Grey Friars Suffk	33	TM4770
Grey's Green Oxon	22	SU7183
Greyrigg D & G	66	NY0889
Greysouthen Cumb	58	NY0729
Greysouthen Cumb	58	NY0629
Greystoke Cumb	59	NY4330
Greystone Tays	89	NO5343
Greywell Hants	22	SU7151
Gribb Dorset	8	ST3703
Griff Warwks	39	SP3689
Griffithstown Gwent	19	ST2999
Grigghall Cumb	59	SD4691
Grimeford Village Lancs	54	SD6112
Grimley H & W	28	SO8360
Grimmet Strath	73	NS3210
Grimoldby Lincs	51	TF3988
Grimpo Shrops	36	SJ3526
Grimsargh Lancs	54	SD5834
Grimsby Humb	57	TA2710
Grimscote Nhants	29	SP6553
Grimscott Cnwll	6	SS2607
Grimshader W Isls	102	NB4026
Grimsthorpe Lincs	40	TF0422
Grimston Leics	39	SK6821
Grimston Norfk	42	TF7222
Grimston Hill Notts	49	SK6865
Grimstone End Suffk	32	TL9368
Grindale Humb	57	TA1271
Grindleford Derbys	48	SK2477
Grindleton Lancs	54	SD7545
Grindley Brook Shrops	37	SJ5242
Grindlow Derbys	48	SK1878
Grindon Staffs	48	SK0854
Gringley on the Hill Notts	50	SK7390
Grinsdale Cumb	67	NY3758
Grinshill Shrops	37	SJ5223
Grinton N York	60	SE0498
Grishipoll Strath	78	NM1959
Grisling Common E Susx	13	TQ4422
Gristhorpe N York	63	TA0881
Griston Norfk	42	TL9499
Gritley Ork	103	HY5604
Grittenham Wilts	20	SU0382
Grittleton Wilts	20	ST8580
Grizebeck Cumb	58	SD2384
Grizedale Cumb	59	SD3394
Groby Leics	39	SK5207
Groes Clwyd	45	SJ0064
Groes W Glam	18	SS7986
Groes-Wen M Glam	18	ST1286
Groes-faen M Glam	18	ST0680
Groesffordd Gwynd	44	SH2739
Groesffordd Marli Clwyd	45	SJ0073
Grogport Strath	72	NR8044
Gronant Clwyd	46	SJ0883
Groom's Hill H & W	28	SO9164
Groombridge E Susx	13	TQ5337
Grosebay W Isls	90	NG1592
Grosmont Gwent	27	SO4024
Grosmont N York	63	NZ8305
Grossington Gloucs	20	SO7302
Grouville Jersey	101	SV0000
Grove Notts	50	SK7379
Grove Oxon	21	SU4090

Grove Green Kent	14	TQ7856
Grove Park Gt Lon	23	TQ4072
Gravesend Avon	19	ST6489
Grovesend W Glam	17	SN5900
Gruids Highld	96	NC5603
Gruinard Highld	91	NG9489
Gruinart Flats Strath	70	NR2866
Grula Highld	84	NG3826
Gruline Strath	79	NM5440
Grundisburgh Suffk	33	TM2251
Gruting Shet	103	HU2849
Gualachulain Highld	86	NN1145
Gualin House Highld	98	NC3056
Guardbridge Fife	83	NO4518
Guarlford H & W	28	SO8145
Guay Tays	89	NO9949
Guestling Green E Susx	14	TQ8513
Guestling Thorn E Susx	14	TQ8516
Guestwick Norfk	42	TG0627
Guide Lancs	54	SD7025
Guide Bridge Gt Man	45	SH9297
Guilden Down Shrops	36	SO3083
Guilden Morden Cambs	31	TL2744
Guilden Sutton Ches	46	SJ4468
Guildford Surrey	12	SU9949
Guildstead Kent	14	TQ8262
Guildtown Tays	82	NO1331
Guilsfield Strath	73	NS3610
Guilsborough Nhants	30	SP6772
Guilsfield Powys	36	SJ2211
Guisborough Cleve	62	NZ6115
Guiseley W York	55	SE1942
Guist Norfk	42	TF9925
Guiting Power Gloucs	28	SP0924
Gullane Loth	83	NT4882
Gulling Green Suffk	32	TL8356
Gulworthy Devon	4	SX4572
Gumfreston Dyfed	16	SN1101
Gumley Leics	39	SP6890
Gun Hill E Susx	13	TQ5614
Gunby Humb	56	SE7135
Gunby Lincs	40	SK9121
Gunby Lincs	51	TF4667
Gundleton Hants	11	SU6133
Gunn Devon	7	SS6333
Gunnerside N York	61	SD9598
Gunnerton Nthumb	68	NY9074
Gunness Humb	56	SE8411
Gunnislake Devon	4	SX4371
Gunnista Shet	103	HU5043
Gunthorpe Cambs	40	TF1803
Gunthorpe Norfk	42	TG0134
Gunthorpe Notts	49	SK6844
Gunville IOW	10	SZ4889
Gupworthy Somset	7	SS9735
Gurnard IOW	10	SZ4795
Gurnett Ches	48	SJ9271
Gurney Slade Somset	19	ST6249
Gurnos W Glam	26	SN7709
Gussage All Saints Dorset	9	SU0010
Gussage St. Michael Dorset	9	ST9811
Guston Kent	15	TR3244
Gutcher Shet	103	HU5499
Guthrie Tays	89	NO5650
Guyhirn Cambs	41	TF4003
Guyhirn Gull Cambs	41	TF3903
Guyzance Nthumb	69	NU2104
Gwaenysgor Clwyd	46	SJ0780
Gwalchmai Gwynd	44	SH3876
Gwaun-Cae-Gurwen W Glam	26	SN7011
Gwbert-on-Sea Dyfed	17	SN1649
Gwealavallan Cnwll	2	SW5942
Gweek Cnwll	2	SW7026
Gwenddwr Powys	26	SO0643
Gwendreath Cnwll	2	SW7216
Gwennap Cnwll	2	SW7340
Gwern-y-Steeple S Glam	18	ST0775
Gwernesney Gwent	19	SO4101
Gwernogle Dyfed	17	SN5334
Gwernymynydd Clwyd	46	SJ2162
Gwinear Cnwll	2	SW5937
Gwithian Cnwll	2	SW5841
Gwredog Gwynd	44	SH4086
Gwyddelwern Clwyd	46	SJ0746
Gwyddgrug Dyfed	17	SN4635
Gwytherin Clwyd	45	SH8761

H

Habberley H & W	37	SO8176
Habberley Shrops	36	SJ3903
Habergham Lancs	54	SD8033
Habertoft Lincs	51	TF5069
Habrough Humb	57	TA1413
Haccombe Devon	5	SX8970
Hacconby Lincs	40	TF1025
Haceby Lincs	40	TF0236
Hacheston Suffk	33	TM3059
Hackenthorpe S York	49	SK4183
Hackford Norfk	42	TG0502
Hackforth N York	61	SE2493
Hackland Ork	103	HY3920
Hackleton Nhants	30	SP8055
Hacklinge Kent	15	TR3454
Hackness N York	63	SE9790
Hackney Gt Lon	23	TQ3484
Hackthorn Lincs	50	SK9982
Hackthorpe Cumb	59	NY5323
Hadden Border	76	NT7836
Haddenham Bucks	22	SP7308
Haddenham Cambs	31	TL4675
Haddington Lincs	50	SK9163
Haddington Loth	76	NT5173
Haddiscoe Norfk	43	TM4497
Haddo Gramp	95	NJ8337
Haddon Cambs	40	TL1392
Hadham Ford Herts	31	TL4321
Hadleigh Essex	24	TQ8187
Hadleigh Suffk	32	TM0242
Hadley H & W	28	SO8664
Hadley Shrops	37	SJ6712
Hadley Wood Gt Lon	23	TQ2698
Hadlow Kent	13	TQ6350
Hadlow Down E Susx	13	TQ5324
Hadnall Shrops	37	SJ5220
Hadstock Essex	31	TL5644
Hadzor H & W	28	SO9162
Hafodunos Clwyd	45	SH8667
Hafodyrynys Gwent	19	ST2299
Hafodyrynys Gwent	19	ST2499
Haggbeck Cumb	67	NY4774
Haggerston Nthumb	77	NU0443
Haggington Hill Devon	6	SS5647
Haggs Cent	81	NS7979
Hagley H & W	27	SO5641
Hagley H & W	38	SO9181
Hagworthingham Lincs	51	TF3469
Hail Weston Cambs	31	TL1662
Haile Cumb	58	NY0308
Hailsham E Susx	13	TQ5909
Hainault Gt Lon	23	TQ4591
Hanford Norfk	43	TG2318
Hainton Lincs	50	TF1784
Hainworth W York	55	SE0639
Haisthorpe Humb	57	TA1264
Hakin Dyfed	16	SM8905
Halam Notts	50	SK6754
Halbeath Fife	82	NT1289
Halberton Devon	7	ST0012
Halcro Highld	100	ND2360
Hale Ches	46	SJ4782
Hale Cumb	59	SD5078
Hale Gt Man	47	SJ7786
Hale Hants	10	SU1919
Hale Somset	9	ST7527
Hale Surrey	22	SU8448
Hale Bank Ches	46	SJ4884
Hale Green E Susx	13	TQ5514
Hale Street Kent	14	TQ6749
Hales Norfk	43	TM3897

Hales Staffs	37	SJ7134
Hales Place Kent	15	TR1459
Halesowen W Mids	38	SO9683
Halesworth Suffk	33	TM3877
Halford Shrops	36	SO4383
Halford Warwks	29	SP2545
Halfpenny Green Staffs	38	SO8291
Halfway Powys	26	SN8332
Halfway Bridge W Susx	11	SU9322
Halfway House Shrops	36	SJ3411
Halfway Houses Kent	14	TQ9372
Halifax W York	55	SE0925
Halistra Highld	90	NG2459
Halket Strath	73	NS4252
Halkirk Highld	100	ND1359
Halkyn Clwyd	46	SJ2171
Hall Strath	73	NS4154
Hall Cliffe W York	55	SE2918
Hall Dunnerdale Cumb	58	SD2195
Hall End Beds	30	TL0045
Hall Green W Mids	38	SP1181
Hall's Green Herts	31	TL2728
Halland E Susx	13	TQ4916
Hallaton Leics	40	SP7896
Hallatrow Avon	19	ST6356
Hallbankgate Cumb	67	NY5859
Hallen Avon	19	ST5480
Hallfield Gate Derbys	49	SK3958
Hallgarth Dur	69	NZ3343
Hallin Highld	90	NG2558
Halling Kent	14	TQ7063
Hallington Lincs	51	TF3085
Hallington Nthumb	68	NY9875
Hallins Derbys	49	SK3371
Halliwell Gt Man	54	SD6910
Halloughton Notts	49	SK6951
Hallow H & W	28	SO8258
Hallrule Border	67	NT5914
Hallsands Devon	5	SX8138
Hallthwaites Cumb	58	SD1785
Hallworthy Cnwll	4	SX1887
Hallyne Border	75	NT1940
Halmer End Staffs	47	SJ7949
Halmond's Frome H & W	28	SO6647
Halmore Gloucs	20	SO6902
Halnaker W Susx	11	SU9008
Halsall Lancs	53	SD3710
Halse Nhants	29	SP5640
Halse Somset	8	ST1327
Halse Somset	8	ST1428
Halsetown Cnwll	2	SW5038
Halstead Essex	24	TL8130
Halstead Kent	23	TQ4961
Halstead Leics	40	SK7505
Halstock Dorset	8	ST5308
Halsway Somset	18	ST1338
Haltham Lincs	51	TF2463
Halton Bucks	22	SP8710
Halton Clwyd	36	SJ3039
Halton Lancs	53	SD5064
Halton Nthumb	68	NY9967
Halton W York	55	SE3533
Halton East N York	55	SD0454
Halton Gill N York	60	SD8876
Halton Lea Gate Nthumb	68	NY6458
Halton Shields Nthumb	68	NZ0168
Halton West N York	54	SD8454
Haltwhistle Nthumb	68	NY7064
Halvergate Norfk	43	TG4207
Halwell Devon	5	SX7753
Halwill Devon	6	SX4299
Halwill Devon	6	SX4392
Halwill Junction Devon	6	SS4400
Halwill Junction Devon	6	SX4599
Ham Devon	8	ST2301
Ham Gloucs	20	ST6898
Ham Gt Lon	23	TQ1772
Ham Kent	15	TR3354
Ham Somset	8	ST2825
Ham Wilts	21	SU3262
Ham Street Somset	8	ST5534
Hamble Hants	10	SU4806
Hambleden Bucks	22	SU7886
Hambledon Hants	11	SU6415
Hambledon Surrey	11	SU9638
Hambleton Lancs	53	SD3742
Hambleton N York	56	SE5430
Hambridge Somset	8	ST3921
Hambrook Avon	19	ST6378
Hambrook W Susx	11	SU7806
Hamels Herts	31	TL3724
Hameringham Lincs	51	TF3067
Hamerton Cambs	40	TL1379
Hamilton Strath	74	NS7255
Hamlet Dorset	9	ST5908
Hamlins E Susx	13	TQ5909
Hammerpot W Susx	12	TQ0705
Hammersmith Gt Lon	23	TQ2378
Hammerwich Staffs	38	SK0607
Hammond Street Herts	23	TL3004
Hammoon Dorset	9	ST8114
Hamnavoe Shet	103	HU3735
Hamnavoe Shet	103	HU4971
Hampden Park E Susx	13	TQ6002
Hampden Row Bucks	22	SP8501
Hampden End Essex	24	TL5730
Hampnett Gloucs	28	SP0915
Hampole S York	55	SE5510
Hampreston Dorset	10	SZ0598
Hampsfield Cumb	59	SD4080
Hampstead Gt Lon	23	TQ2685
Hampstead Norrey's Berks	21	SU5276
Hampsthwaite N York	55	SE2558
Hampt M Glam	4	SX3974
Hampton Devon	6	SX2696
Hampton Gt Lon	22	TQ1369
Hampton H & W	28	SP0243
Hampton Kent	15	TR1568
Hampton Wilts	21	SU1892
Hampton Bishop H & W	27	SO5537
Hampton Heath Ches	46	SJ5149
Hampton Loade Shrops	37	SO7486
Hampton Lovett H & W	28	SO8865
Hampton Lucy Warwks	29	SP2557
Hampton Poyle Oxon	29	SP5015
Hampton Wick Gt Lon	23	TQ1769
Hampton in Arden W Mids	39	SP2081
Hampton on the Hill Warwks	29	SP2564
Hamptworth Wilts	10	SU2419
Hamsey E Susx	13	TQ4012
Hamsey Green Gt Lon	23	TQ3760
Hamstall Ridware Staffs	38	SK1019
Hamstead Marshall Berks	21	SU4165
Hamsterley Dur	61	NZ1131
Hamsterley Dur	69	NZ1156
Hamstreet Kent	15	TR0034
Hamworthy Dorset	9	SY9990
Hanbury H & W	28	SO9664
Hanbury Staffs	38	SK1727
Hanchurch Staffs	38	SJ8441
Hand and Pen Devon	7	SY0495
Handbridge Ches	46	SJ4065
Handcross W Susx	12	TQ2629
Handley Ches	46	SJ4657
Handley Derbys	49	SK3761
Handley Green Essex	24	TL6601
Handsacre Staffs	38	SK0916
Handsworth S York	49	SK4186
Handsworth W Mids	38	SP0589
Handy Cross Bucks	22	SU8490
Hanford Dorset	9	ST8410
Hanford Staffs	38	SJ8642
Hanging Langford Wilts	20	SU0237
Hangleton E Susx	12	TQ2607
Hanham Avon	19	ST6372
Hankelow Ches	47	SJ6745
Hankerton Wilts	20	ST9690
Hankham E Susx	13	TQ6207
Hanley Staffs	47	SJ8847
Hanley Child H & W	27	SO6565
Hanley Swan H & W	28	SO8143
Hanley William H & W	27	SO6766
Hanlith N York	54	SD8960
Hanmer Clwyd	36	SJ4540
Hannaford Devon	6	SS6029
Hannington Hants	21	SU5455
Hannington Nhants	30	SP8170
Hannington Wilts	21	SU1793

Hannington Wick Wilts	21	SU1795
Hanslope Bucks	30	SP8046
Hantlorpe Lincs	40	TF0823
Hanwell Gt Lon	22	TQ1579
Hanwell Oxon	29	SP4343
Hanworth Gt Lon	22	TQ1271
Hanworth Norfk	43	TG1935
Happendon Strath	74	NS8533
Happisburgh Norfk	43	TG3831
Happisburgh Common Norfk	43	TG3729
Hapsford Ches	46	SJ4774
Hapton Lancs	54	SD7931
Hapton Norfk	43	TM1796
Harberton Devon	5	SX7758
Harbertonford Devon	5	SX7856
Harbledown Kent	15	TR1357
Harborne W Mids	38	SP0284
Harborough Magna Warwks	39	SP4778
Harborough Parva Warwks	39	SP4778
Harbottle Nthumb	68	NT9304
Harbours Hill H & W	28	SO9566
Harbridge Hants	10	SU1409
Harbridge Green Hants	10	SU1411
Harburn Loth	75	NT0462
Harbury Warwks	29	SP3760
Harby Leics	40	SK7431
Harby Notts	50	SK8770
Harcombe Devon	5	SX8881
Harcombe Devon	8	SY1590
Harcombe Bottom Devon	8	SY3395
Harden W Mids	38	SK0101
Harden W York	55	SE0838
Hardenhuish Wilts	20	ST9074
Hardgate Gramp	89	NJ7901
Hardgate Strath	74	NS5073
Hardham W Susx	12	TQ0317
Hardingham Norfk	42	TG0403
Hardingstone Nhants	30	SP7657
Hardington Somset	20	ST7452
Hardington Mandeville Somset	8	ST5111
Hardington Marsh Somset	8	ST5009
Hardington Moor Somset	8	ST5212
Hardisworthy Devon	3	SX2320
Hardley Hants	10	SU4205
Hardley Street Norfk	43	TG3801
Hardraw N York	60	SD8691
Hardstoft Derbys	49	SK4463
Hardway Hants	11	SU6101
Hardway Somset	9	ST7134
Hardwick Bucks	30	SP8019
Hardwick Cambs	31	TL3788
Hardwick Nhants	30	SP8469
Hardwick Norfk	33	TM2290
Hardwick Oxon	29	SP3706
Hardwick Oxon	29	SP5729
Hardwicke Gloucs	28	SO7912
Hardwicke Gloucs	28	SO9027
Hardy's Green Essex	25	TL9320
Hare Croft W York	55	SE0835
Hare Green Essex	25	TM1025
Hare Hatch Berks	22	SU8077
Hareby Lincs	51	TF3365
Harefield Gt Lon	22	TQ0590
Harehill Derbys	38	SK1735
Harehills W York	55	SE3135
Harelaw Border	76	NT5323
Harelaw Dur	69	NZ1552
Hareplain Kent	14	TQ8140
Haresceugh Cumb	68	NY6043
Harescombe Gloucs	28	SO8310
Harestield Gloucs	28	SO8110
Harestock Hants	10	SU4631
Harewood W York	55	SE3245
Harewood End H & W	27	SO5227
Harford Devon	5	SX6359
Hargate Norfk	33	TM1291
Hargatewall Derbys	48	SK1274
Hargrave Ches	46	SJ4862
Hargrave Nhants	30	TL0370
Hargrave Green Suffk	32	TL7759
Harkstead Suffk	25	TM1834
Harlaston Staffs	39	SK2110
Harlaxton Lincs	40	SK8832
Harlech Gwynd	44	SH5831
Harlescott Shrops	37	SJ5115
Harlesden Gt Lon	23	TQ2383
Harlesthorpe Derbys	49	SK4976
Harleston Devon	5	SX7945
Harleston Norfk	33	TM2483
Harleston Suffk	32	TM0160
Harlestone Nhants	30	SP7064
Harley S York	49	SK3698
Harleyholm Strath	75	NS9238
Harlington Beds	30	TL0330
Harlington Gt Lon	22	TQ0877
Harlington S York	49	SE4802
Harlosh Highld	84	NG2441
Harlow Essex	23	TL4711
Harlow Hill Nthumb	68	NZ0768
Harlthorpe Humb	56	SE7337
Harlton Cambs	31	TL3852
Harlyn Bay Cnwll	3	SW8775
Harman's Cross Dorset	9	SY9880
Harmby N York	61	SE1289
Harmer Green Herts	31	TL2515
Harmer Hill Shrops	37	SJ4822
Harmston Lincs	50	SK9762
Harnage Shrops	37	SJ5604
Harnhill Gloucs	20	SP0600
Harold Hill Gt Lon	23	TQ5392
Harold Wood Gt Lon	24	TQ5590
Haroldston West Dyfed	16	SM8615
Haroldswick Shet	103	HP6312
Harome N York	62	SE6481
Harpenden Herts	30	TL1314
Harpford Devon	8	SY0890
Harpham Humb	57	TA0961
Harpley H & W	28	SO6861
Harpley Norfk	42	TF7825
Harpole Nhants	30	SP6961
Harpsdale Highld	100	ND1385
Harpsden Oxon	22	SU7580
Harpswell Lincs	50	SK9389
Harpurhey Gt Man	47	SD8501
Harraby Cumb	67	NY4154
Harracott Devon	6	SS5627
Harrapool Highld	85	NG6522
Harrietfield Tays	82	NN9829
Harrietsham Kent	14	TQ8652
Harringay Gt Lon	23	TQ3188
Harrington Cumb	58	NX9926
Harrington H & W	38	SO8774
Harrington Lincs	51	TF3671
Harrington Nhants	30	SP7780
Harringworth Nhants	40	SP9197
Harris Highld	88	NO3396
Harriseahead Staffs	47	SJ8656
Harriston Cumb	58	NY1641
Harrogate N York	55	SE3055
Harrold Beds	30	SP9456
Harrop Dale Gt Man	54	SE0008
Harrow Gt Lon	22	TQ1588
Harrow Green Suffk	32	TL8654
Harrow Weald Gt Lon	22	TQ1591
Harrow on the Hill Gt Lon	22	TQ1587
Harrowbarrow Cnwll	4	SX3969
Harrowden Beds	30	TL0646
Harsgeir W Isls	102	NB1040
Harston Cambs	31	TL4250
Harston Leics	40	SK8331
Harswell Humb	56	SE8240
Hart Cleve	62	NZ4734
Hartburn Nthumb	68	NZ0886
Hartest Suffk	32	TL8352
Hartford Cambs	31	TL2572
Hartford Ches	47	SJ6372
Hartford Somset	7	SS9629
Hartford End Essex	24	TL6817
Hartfordbridge Hants	22	SU7757
Hartforth N York	61	NZ1606
Harthill Ches	46	SJ4955
Harthill Loth	74	NS9064
Harthill S York	49	SK4980
Hartington Derbys	48	SK1260
Hartland Devon	6	SS2624

Place		
Hillend *Fife*	82	NT1483
Hillend *Loth*	75	NT2566
Hillend *Strath*	74	NS8267
Hillend *W Glam*	17	SS4291
Hillesden *Bucks*	30	SP6828
Hillesley *Avon*	20	ST7689
Hillfarrance *Somset*	8	ST1624
Hillfoot *Strath*	74	NS5472
Hillhead *Devon*	5	SX9053
Hillhead *Strath*	75	NS9840
Hillhead of Cocklaw *Gramp*	95	NK0844
Hilliclay *Highld*	100	ND1764
Hillingdon *Gt Lon*	22	TQ0783
Hillington *Norfk*	42	TF7225
Hillington *Strath*	74	NS5164
Hillmorton *Warwks*	39	SP5373
Hillowton *D & G*	66	NX7763
Hillpound *Hants*	11	SU5815
Hills Town *Derbys*	49	SK4869
Hillside *Gramp*	89	NO9197
Hillside *T & W*	89	NO7060
Hillstreet *Hants*	10	SU3416
Hillswick *Shet*	103	HU2877
Hilltown *Devon*	4	SX5380
Hillwell *Shet*	103	HU3714
Hilmarton *Wilts*	20	SU0175
Hilperton *Wilts*	20	ST8759
Hilsea *Hants*	11	SU6503
Hilston *Humb*	57	TA2833
Hiltingbury *Hants*	10	SU4222
Hilton *Border*	77	NT8750
Hilton *Cambs*	31	TL2966
Hilton *Cleve*	62	NZ4611
Hilton *Cumb*	60	NY7320
Hilton *Derbys*	39	SK2430
Hilton *Dorset*	9	ST7802
Hilton *Dur*	61	NZ1621
Hilton *Shrops*	37	SO7795
Hilton of Cadboll *Highld*	97	NH8776
Himbleton *H & W*	28	SO9458
Himley *Staffs*	38	SO8891
Hinckley *Leics*	39	SP4294
Hinderclay *Suffk*	32	TM0276
Hinderwell *N York*	63	NZ7916
Hindhead *Surrey*	11	SU8835
Hindle Fold *Lancs*	54	SD7332
Hindley *Gt Man*	47	SD6204
Hindlip *H & W*	28	SO8758
Hindolveston *Norfk*	42	TG0329
Hindon *Wilts*	9	ST9032
Hindringham *Norfk*	42	TF9836
Hingham *Norfk*	42	TG0202
Hinnington *Shrops*	37	SJ7404
Hinstock *Shrops*	37	SJ6926
Hintlesham *Suffk*	32	TM0843
Hinton *Avon*	20	ST7376
Hinton *H & W*	27	SO3338
Hinton *Hants*	10	SZ2095
Hinton *Shrops*	36	SJ4008
Hinton Admiral *Hants*	11	SZ2196
Hinton Ampner *Hants*	11	SU5927
Hinton Blewett *Somset*	19	ST5956
Hinton Charterhouse *Avon*	20	ST7758
Hinton Marsh *Hants*	11	SU5927
Hinton Martell *Dorset*	9	SU0106
Hinton Parva *Wilts*	21	SU2283
Hinton St. George *Somset*	8	ST4212
Hinton St. Mary *Dorset*	9	ST7816
Hinton Waldrist *Oxon*	21	SU3789
Hinton on the Green *H & W*	28	SP0244
Hinton-in-the-Hedges *Nhants*	29	SP5636
Hints *Staffs*	38	SK1503
Hinwick *Beds*	30	SP9361
Hinxhill *Kent*	15	TR0442
Hinxton *Cambs*	31	TL4945
Hinxton *Cambs*	31	TL4945
Hinxworth *Herts*	31	TL2340
Hipperholme *W York*	55	SE1225
Hipswell *N York*	61	SE1798
Hirn *Gramp*	89	NJ7200
Hirnant *Powys*	36	SN8869
Hirnant *Powys*	36	SJ0423
Hirst *Nthumb*	69	NZ2787
Hirst Courtney *N York*	56	SE6124
Hirwaun *M Glam*	26	SN9605
Hiscott *Devon*	6	SS5426
Histon *Cambs*	31	TL4363
Hitcham *Suffk*	32	TL9851
Hitcham Causeway *Suffk*	32	TL9852
Hitcham Street *Suffk*	32	TL9851
Hitchin *Herts*	31	TL1829
Hither Green *Gt Lon*	23	TQ3874
Hittisleigh Cross *Devon*	7	SX7394
Hive *Humb*	56	SE8230
Hixon *Staffs*	38	SK0025
Hoaden *Kent*	15	TR2659
Hoaldalbert *Gwent*	27	SO3923
Hoar Cross *Staffs*	38	SK1323
Hoarwithy *H & W*	27	SO5429
Hoath *Kent*	15	TR2064
Hobarris *Shrops*	36	SO3178
Hobkirk *Border*	67	NT5811
Hobson *Dur*	69	NZ1755
Hoby *Leics*	39	SK6617
Hoccum *Shrops*	37	SO7393
Hockering *Norfk*	42	TG0713
Hockerton *Notts*	49	SK7156
Hockley *Essex*	24	TQ8392
Hockley Heath *W Mids*	38	SP1572
Hockliffe *Beds*	30	SP9726
Hockwold cum Wilton *Norfk*	32	TL7288
Hockworthy *Devon*	7	ST0319
Hoddesdon *Herts*	23	TL3708
Hoddleston *Lancs*	54	SD7122
Hoddom Cross *D & G*	67	NY1873
Hoddom Mains *D & G*	67	NY1572
Hodgeston *Dyfed*	16	SS0399
Hodnet *Shrops*	37	SJ6128
Hodsall Street *Kent*	14	TQ6263
Hodsock *Notts*	49	SK6185
Hodson *Wilts*	21	SU1787
Hodthorpe *Derbys*	49	SK5376
Hoe *Norfk*	42	TF9916
Hog Hill *E Susx*	14	TQ8816
Hogben's Hill *Kent*	15	TR0356
Hoggeston *Bucks*	30	SP8024
Hoghton *Lancs*	54	SD6125
Hognaston *Derbys*	48	SK2350
Hogrill's End *Warwks*	39	SP2292
Hogsthorpe *Lincs*	51	TF5372
Holbeach *Lincs*	41	TF3624
Holbeach Clough *Lincs*	41	TF3427
Holbeach Drove *Lincs*	41	TF3212
Holbeach Hurn *Lincs*	41	TF3926
Holbeach St. Johns *Lincs*	41	TF3518
Holbeach St. Mark's *Lincs*	41	TF3731
Holbeach St. Matthew *Lincs*	41	TF4132
Holbeck *Notts*	49	SK5473
Holbeck Woodhouse *Notts*	49	SK5373
Holberrow Green *H & W*	28	SP0259
Holborn *Gt Lon*	23	TQ3181
Holbrook *Derbys*	49	SK3644
Holbrook *S York*	49	SK4581
Holbrook *Suffk*	25	TM1736
Holbrook Moor *Derbys*	49	SK3645
Holbury *Hants*	10	SU4303
Holcombe *Devon*	5	SX9574
Holcombe *Somset*	20	ST6649
Holcombe Burnell Barton *Devon*	5	SX8591
Holcombe Rogus *Devon*	7	ST0519
Holcot *Nhants*	30	SP7969
Holden *Lancs*	54	SD8833
Holden *Lancs*	54	SD7749
Holdenby *Nhants*	30	SP6967
Holder's Green *Essex*	24	TL6329
Holdgate *Shrops*	37	SO5689
Holdingham *Lincs*	50	TF0547
Holditch *Dorset*	8	ST3402
Hole Street *W Susx*	12	TQ1414
Holehouse *Derbys*	48	SK0092
Holford *Somset*	19	ST1541
Holgate *N York*	56	SE5851
Holker *Cumb*	59	SD3677
Holkham *Norfk*	42	TF8944
Hollacombe *Devon*	6	SS3733
Hollacombe *Devon*	7	SS8000
Holland Fen *Lincs*	51	TF2349
Holland-on-Sea *Essex*	25	TM1916
Hollandstoun *Ork*	103	HY7553
Hollesley *Suffk*	33	TM3544
Hollicombe *Devon*	5	SX8763
Hollingbourne *Kent*	14	TQ8455
Hollingbury *E Susx*	12	TQ0107
Hollingthorpe *W York*	55	SE3832
Hollington *Bucks*	30	SP8727
Hollington *Derbys*	48	SK2239
Hollington *Staffs*	48	SK0539
Hollingworth *Gt Man*	48	SK0096
Hollins End *S York*	49	SK3883
Hollins Green *Ches*	47	SJ6990
Hollinsclough *Staffs*	48	SK0666
Hollinswood *Shrops*	37	SJ7009
Hollinwood *Derbys*	49	SJ5236
Hollingrove *E Susx*	14	TQ6821
Hollocombe *Devon*	7	SS6311
Holloway *Derbys*	49	SK3256
Holloway *Gt Lon*	23	TQ3086
Hollowell *Nhants*	30	SP6972
Hollowmoor Heath *Ches*	46	SJ4868
Hollybush *Gwent*	19	SO1603
Hollybush *H & W*	28	SO7636
Hollybush *Strath*	73	NS3915
Hollym *Humb*	57	TA3425
Holmbridge *W York*	55	SE1106
Holmbury St. Mary *Surrey*	12	TQ1144
Holmbush *Cnwll*	3	SX0352
Holmcroft *Staffs*	38	SJ9125
Holme *Cambs*	40	TL1987
Holme *Cumb*	59	SD5278
Holme *Humb*	56	SE9106
Holme *N York*	62	SE3582
Holme *Notts*	50	SK8059
Holme *W York*	55	SE1005
Holme Chapel *Lancs*	54	SD8728
Holme Green *N York*	56	SE5541
Holme Hale *Norfk*	42	TF8807
Holme Lacy *H & W*	27	SO5535
Holme Marsh *H & W*	27	SO3454
Holme Pierrepont *Notts*	49	SK6238
Holme Street *Cumb*	67	NY1047
Holme next the Sea *Norfk*	42	TF7043
Holme on the Wolds *Humb*	56	SE9646
Holme upon Spalding Moor *Humb*	56	SE8138
Holmer *H & W*	27	SO5042
Holmer Green *Bucks*	22	SU9097
Holmes Chapel *Ches*	47	SJ7667
Holmes Hill *E Susx*	13	TQ5313
Holmesfield *Derbys*	49	SK3277
Holmeswood *Lancs*	53	SD4316
Holmethorpe *Surrey*	12	TQ2851
Holmewood *Derbys*	49	SK4365
Holmfirth *W York*	55	SE1408
Holmhead *Strath*	74	NS5620
Holmpton *Humb*	57	TA3623
Holmrook *Cumb*	58	SD0799
Holmsey Green *Suffk*	32	TL6977
Holmwood *Surrey*	12	TQ1647
Holne *Devon*	5	SX7069
Holnest *Dorset*	9	ST6509
Holnicote *Somset*	7	SS9146
Holsworthy *Devon*	6	SS3403
Holsworthy Beacon *Devon*	6	SS3508
Holt *Clwyd*	46	SJ4053
Holt *Dorset*	9	SU0203
Holt *H & W*	28	SO8262
Holt *Norfk*	42	TG0838
Holt *Wilts*	20	ST8661
Holt End *H & W*	28	SP0769
Holt Green *Lancs*	46	SD3905
Holt Heath *H & W*	28	SO8163
Holtby *N York*	56	SE6754
Holton *Oxon*	29	SP6006
Holton *Oxon*	29	SP6006
Holton *Somset*	9	ST6826
Holton *Suffk*	33	TM4077
Holton Heath *Dorset*	9	SY9491
Holton St. Mary *Suffk*	25	TM0537
Holton cum Beckering *Lincs*	50	TF1181
Holton le Clay *Lincs*	51	TA2802
Holton le Moor *Lincs*	50	TF0797
Holwell *Dorset*	9	ST7011
Holwell *Herts*	31	TL1633
Holwell *Leics*	40	SK7323
Holwell *Oxon*	29	SP2309
Holwick *Dur*	60	NY9126
Holy Cross *H & W*	38	SO9256
Holy Island *Nthumb*	77	NU1241
Holybourne *Hants*	11	SU7340
Holyhead *Gwynd*	44	SH2482
Holylee *Border*	83	NT3978
Holymoorside *Derbys*	49	SK3368
Holystone *Nthumb*	68	NT9502
Holytown *Strath*	74	NS7660
Holywell *Cambs*	31	TL3370
Holywell *Clwyd*	46	SJ1875
Holywell *Cnwll*	2	SW7658
Holywell *Dorset*	9	ST5964
Holywell Green *W York*	55	SE0819
Holywell Lake *Somset*	8	ST1020
Holywell Row *Suffk*	32	TL7077
Holywood *D & G*	66	NX9480
Homer *Shrops*	37	SJ6101
Homer Green *Mersyd*	46	SD3402
Homersfield *Suffk*	33	TM2885
Homeston *Strath*	72	NR6716
Homington *Wilts*	10	SU1226
Honey Tye *Suffk*	25	TL9535
Honeybourne *H & W*	28	SP1144
Honeychurch *Devon*	6	SS6203
Honeystreet *Wilts*	20	SU1061
Honiley *Warwks*	39	SP2472
Honing *Norfk*	43	TG3227
Honingham *Norfk*	43	TG1011
Honington *Lincs*	50	SK9443
Honington *Suffk*	32	TL9174
Honington *Warwks*	29	SP2642
Honiton *Devon*	8	ST1600
Honley *W York*	55	SE1311
Hoo *Kent*	23	TQ2964
Hoo *Kent*	14	TQ7872
Hoo End *Herts*	31	TL1820
Hoo Green *Ches*	47	SJ7182
Hooe *Devon*	4	SX4952
Hooe *E Susx*	14	TQ6809
Hooe Common *E Susx*	14	TQ6910
Hoohill *Lancs*	53	SD3237
Hook *Cambs*	41	TL4393
Hook *Dyfed*	16	SM9811
Hook *Hants*	22	SU7254
Hook *Humb*	56	SE7525
Hook *Kent*	14	TQ6171
Hook *Surrey*	23	TQ1664
Hook *Wilts*	20	SU0784
Hook Green *Kent*	13	TQ6535
Hook Norton *Oxon*	29	SP3533
Hookagate *Shrops*	36	SJ4508
Hooke *Dorset*	8	ST5300
Hookway *Devon*	7	SX8598
Hooton Levitt *S York*	49	SK5291
Hooton Pagnell *S York*	55	SE4808
Hooton Roberts *S York*	49	SK4897
Hope *Clwyd*	46	SJ3158
Hope *Derbys*	48	SK1783
Hope *Devon*	5	SX6740
Hope *Shrops*	37	SO5974
Hope *Staffs*	48	SK1254
Hope Bowdler *Shrops*	37	SO4792
Hope End Green *Essex*	24	TL5720
Hope Mansell *H & W*	27	SO6219
Hope under Dinmore *H & W*	27	SO5052
Hopefield *Highld*	93	NH7359
Hopehouse *Border*	75	NT2916
Hopeman *Gramp*	93	NJ1469
Hopes Nose *Devon*	5	SX9563
Hopesay *Shrops*	36	SO3983
Hopperton *N York*	55	SE4258
Hopstone *Shrops*	37	SO7894
Hopton *Derbys*	49	SK2653
Hopton *Staffs*	38	SJ9426
Hopton *Suffk*	32	TL9979
Hopton Cangeford *Shrops*	37	SO5480
Hopton Castle *Shrops*	36	SO3678
Hopton Wafers *Shrops*	37	SO6376
Hopton on Sea *Norfk*	43	TG5300
Hoptonheath *Shrops*	36	SO3877
Hopwas *Staffs*	38	SK1705
Hopwood *H & W*	38	SP0375
Horam *E Susx*	13	TQ5717
Horbling *Lincs*	40	TF1135
Horbury *W York*	55	SE2918
Horderley *Shrops*	36	SO4087
Hordle *Hants*	10	SZ2795
Hordley *Shrops*	36	SJ3731
Horeb *Dyfed*	17	SN4905
Horfield *Avon*	19	ST5877
Horham *Suffk*	33	TM2072
Horkesley Green *Essex*	25	TL9832
Horkesley Heath *Essex*	25	TL9829
Horkstow *Humb*	56	SE9817
Horkstow *Humb*	56	SE9818
Horley *Oxon*	29	SP4144
Horley *Surrey*	12	TQ2843
Hornby *Lancs*	54	SD5868
Hornby *N York*	62	NZ3605
Hornby *N York*	61	SE2293
Horncastle *Lincs*	51	TF2669
Hornchurch *Gt Lon*	23	TQ5387
Horncliffe *Nthumb*	77	NT9249
Horndean *Border*	77	NT9049
Horndean *Hants*	11	SU7013
Horndon *Devon*	4	SX5080
Horndon on the Hill *Essex*	24	TQ6783
Horne *Surrey*	12	TQ3344
Horner *Somset*	7	SS9045
Horners Green *Suffk*	32	TL9641
Horning *Norfk*	43	TG3417
Horninghold *Leics*	40	SP8097
Horninglow *Staffs*	39	SK2425
Horningsea *Cambs*	31	TL4962
Horningtoft *Norfk*	42	TF9323
Horns Cross *Devon*	6	SS3623
Hornsby *Cumb*	67	NY5050
Hornsea *Humb*	57	TA1947
Hornsey *Gt Lon*	23	TQ3089
Hornton *Oxon*	29	SP3945
Horra *Shet*	103	HU4693
Horrabridge *Devon*	4	SX5170
Horridge *Devon*	5	SX7674
Horringer *Suffk*	32	TL8261
Horrocksford *Lancs*	54	SD7543
Horsebridge *Devon*	4	SX4074
Horsebridge *E Susx*	13	TQ5810
Horsebridge *E Susx*	13	TQ5811
Horsebridge *Hants*	10	SU3430
Horseheath *Cambs*	31	TL6147
Horsehouse *N York*	61	SE0480
Horsell *Surrey*	22	TQ0059
Horseman's Green *Clwyd*	36	SJ4441
Horsenden *Bucks*	22	SP7902
Horsepath *Oxon*	29	SP5704
Horseshoes *Wilts*	20	ST9159
Horsford *Norfk*	43	TG1916
Horsforth *W York*	55	SE2337
Horsham *H & W*	28	SO7358
Horsham *W Susx*	12	TQ1730
Horsham St. Faith *Norfk*	43	TG2114
Horsington *Lincs*	50	TF1868
Horsington *Somset*	9	ST7023
Horsley *Gloucs*	20	ST8397
Horsley *Nthumb*	68	NY8496
Horsley *Nthumb*	68	NZ0965
Horsley Woodhouse *Derbys*	49	SK3945
Horsleycross Street *Essex*	25	TM1228
Horsleyhill *Border*	76	NT5319
Horsmonden *Kent*	14	TQ7040
Horstead *Norfk*	43	TG2619
Horsted Keynes *W Susx*	13	TQ3828
Horton *Avon*	20	ST7584
Horton *Berks*	22	TQ0175
Horton *Bucks*	30	SP9219
Horton *Dorset*	9	SU0307
Horton *Gt Lon*	31	TL1962
Horton *Lancs*	54	SD8550
Horton *Nhants*	30	SP8154
Horton *Shrops*	37	SJ6814
Horton *Somset*	8	ST3214
Horton *Staffs*	48	SJ9457
Horton *W Glam*	17	SS4785
Horton *Wilts*	20	SU0463
Horton Green *Ches*	46	SJ4549
Horton Heath *Hants*	10	SU4917
Horton Kirby *Kent*	14	TQ5668
Horton in Ribblesdale *N York*	54	SD8172
Horton-cum-Studley *Oxon*	29	SP5912
Horwich *Gt Man*	54	SD6311
Horwood *Devon*	6	SS5027
Hoscar *Lancs*	53	SD4711
Hoscote *Border*	67	NT3911
Hose *Leics*	40	SK7329
Hoses *Cumb*	58	SD2393
Hosh *Tays*	82	NN8523
Hoswick *Shet*	103	HU4123
Hotham *Humb*	56	SE8934
Hothfield *Kent*	15	TQ9644
Hoton *Leics*	39	SK5722
Hott *Nthumb*	67	NY7785
Houdston *Strath*	64	NX2097
Hough *Ches*	47	SJ7151
Hough Green *Ches*	46	SJ4886
Hough-on-the-Hill *Lincs*	50	SK9246
Hougham *Lincs*	50	SK8844
Hougharry *W Isls*	102	NF7071
Houghton *Cambs*	31	TL2872
Houghton *Dyfed*	16	SM9807
Houghton *Hants*	10	SU3432
Houghton *W Susx*	12	TQ0111
Houghton Conquest *Beds*	30	TL0441
Houghton Green *E Susx*	14	TQ9222
Houghton Regis *Beds*	30	TL0123
Houghton St. Giles *Norfk*	42	TF9235
Houghton le Spring *T & W*	69	NZ3350
Houghton on the Hill *Leics*	39	SK6703
Hound Green *Hants*	22	SU7259
Houndslow *Border*	76	NT6847
Houndwood *Border*	77	NT8463
Hounslow *Gt Lon*	22	TQ1375
Hounslow Green *Essex*	24	TL6518
Househill *Highld*	93	NH8855
Houses Hill *W York*	55	SE1916
Housieside *Gramp*	89	NS9406
Houston *Strath*	73	NS4067
Houstry *Highld*	100	ND1535
Houton *Ork*	103	HY3104
Hove *E Susx*	12	TQ2804
Hoveringham *Notts*	49	SK6946
Hoveton *Norfk*	43	TG3018
Hovingham *N York*	62	SE6675
How *Cumb*	67	NY5056
How Caple *H & W*	27	SO6030
Howden *Humb*	56	SE7428
Howden-le-Wear *Dur*	61	NZ1633
Howe *Cumb*	59	SD4588
Howe *Highld*	100	ND3061
Howe *N York*	62	SE3580
Howe *Norfk*	43	TM2799
Howe Green *Essex*	24	TL7503
Howe Street *Essex*	24	TL6914
Howe Street *Essex*	24	TL6934
Howe of Teuchar *Gramp*	95	NJ7946
Howegreen *Essex*	24	TL8301
Howell *Lincs*	50	TF1346
Howes *D & G*	67	NY1867
Howgate *Loth*	75	NT2457
Howick *Nthumb*	77	NU2417
Howle *Dur*	61	NZ0925
Howle *Shrops*	37	SJ6823
Howle Hill *H & W*	27	SO6020
Howlett End *Essex*	24	TL5834
Howley *Somset*	8	ST2609
Howmore *W Isls*	102	NF7636
Hownam *Border*	76	NT7719
Howrigg *Cumb*	67	NY3247
Howsham *Humb*	56	TA0404
Howsham *N York*	56	SE7362
Howt Green *Kent*	14	TQ8964
Howtel *Nthumb*	77	NT8934
Howwood *Strath*	73	NS3960
Hoxne *Suffk*	33	TM1877
Hoylake *Mersyd*	46	SJ2189
Hoyland Common *S York*	49	SE3600
Hoyland Nether *S York*	49	SE3600
Hoyland Swaine *S York*	55	SE2604
Hubberston *Dyfed*	16	SM8806
Huby *N York*	55	SE2747
Huby *N York*	56	SE5665
Hucclecote *Gloucs*	28	SO8717
Hucking *Kent*	14	TQ8458
Hucknall *Notts*	49	SK5349
Huddersfield *W York*	55	SE1416
Huddington *H & W*	28	SO9457
Hudscott *Devon*	7	SS6525
Hudswell *N York*	61	NZ1400
Huggate *Humb*	56	SE8855
Hugh Town *IOS*	2	SV9010
Hughenden Valley *Bucks*	22	SU8597
Hughley *Shrops*	37	SO5698
Huish *Devon*	6	SS5311
Huish *Wilts*	20	SU1463
Huish Champflower *Somset*	7	ST0429
Huish Episcopi *Somset*	8	ST4226
Hulcott *Bucks*	30	SP8516
Hulham *Devon*	5	SX0182
Hulland *Derbys*	48	SK2446
Hulland Ward *Derbys*	48	SK2547
Hullavington *Wilts*	20	ST8982
Hullbridge *Essex*	24	TQ8095
Hulme *Gt Man*	47	SJ8396
Hulme *Staffs*	48	SJ9345
Hulme End *Staffs*	48	SK1059
Hulme Walfield *Ches*	47	SJ8465
Hulver Street *Suffk*	33	TM4686
Hulverstone *IOW*	10	SZ3984
Humber Court *H & W*	27	SO5356
Humberston *Humb*	57	TA3105
Humberstone *Leics*	39	SK6305
Humbie *Loth*	76	NT4662
Humbleton *Humb*	57	TA2234
Humby *Lincs*	40	TF0032
Hume *Border*	76	NT7041
Humshaugh *Nthumb*	68	NY9171
Huna *Highld*	100	ND3573
Huncote *Leics*	39	SP5197
Hundalee *Border*	76	NT6418
Hundall *Derbys*	49	SK3877
Hunderthwaite *Dur*	61	NY9821
Hundleby *Lincs*	51	TF3866
Hundleton *Dyfed*	16	SM9600
Hundred End *Lancs*	53	SD4122
Hungarton *Leics*	40	SK6907
Hungerford *Berks*	21	SU3368
Hungerford *Somset*	7	ST0440
Hungerford Newtown *Berks*	21	SU3571
Hungerstone *H & W*	27	SO4435
Hungryhatton *Shrops*	37	SJ6726
Hunmanby *N York*	63	TA0977
Hunningham *Warwks*	29	SP3768
Hunny Hill *IOW*	10	SZ4989
Hunsdon *Herts*	31	TL4114
Hunsingore *N York*	55	SE4253
Hunslet *W York*	55	SE3130
Hunsonby *Cumb*	59	NY5835
Hunstanton *Norfk*	42	TF6740
Hunstanworth *Dur*	68	NY9448
Hunston *Suffk*	32	TL9768
Hunston *W Susx*	11	SU8601
Hunstrete *Avon*	19	ST6662
Hunsworth *W York*	55	SE1827
Hunters Quay *Strath*	80	NS1879
Hunthill Lodge *Tays*	89	NO4771
Huntingdon *Cambs*	31	TL2471
Huntingdon *N York*	27	SO2553
Huntingfield *Suffk*	33	TM3374
Huntingford *Dorset*	9	ST8129
Huntington *H & W*	27	SO4174
Huntington *N York*	56	SE6156
Huntington *N York*	56	SE6156
Huntington *Staffs*	38	SJ9713
Huntingtower *Tays*	82	NO0725
Huntley *Gloucs*	28	SO7219
Huntly *Gramp*	94	NJ5339
Hunton *Hants*	21	SU4640
Hunton *Kent*	14	TQ7149
Hunton *N York*	61	SE1892
Hunton Bridge *Herts*	22	TL0900
Huntscott *Somset*	7	SS9244
Huntsham *Devon*	7	ST0020
Huntshaw *Devon*	6	SS5023
Huntspill *Somset*	19	ST3045
Huntstile *Somset*	8	ST2633
Huntworth *Somset*	8	ST3134
Huntworth *Somset*	8	ST3134
Hunwick *Dur*	61	NZ1832
Hunworth *Norfk*	42	TG0635
Hurdcott *Wilts*	10	SU1633
Hurdsfield *Ches*	48	SJ9274
Hurley *Warwks*	39	SP2495
Hurley Bottom *Berks*	22	SU8283
Hurley Common *Warwks*	39	SP2496
Hurlford *Strath*	73	NS4536
Hurlston Green *Lancs*	53	SD4011
Hurn *Dorset*	10	SZ1296
Hurn's Head *Lincs*	51	TF4248
Hursebridge *Shrops*	36	SJ3606
Hursley *Hants*	10	SU4225
Hurst *Berks*	22	SU7973
Hurst Green *E Susx*	14	TQ7327
Hurst Green *Lancs*	54	TQ0916
Hurst Green *Lancs*	54	SD6838
Hurst Green *Surrey*	13	TQ3951
Hurst Hill *W Mids*	38	SO9394
Hurst Wickham *W Susx*	12	TQ2916
Hurstbourne Priors *Hants*	21	SU4346
Hurstbourne Tarrant *Hants*	21	SU3853
Hurstley *H & W*	27	SO3548
Hurstwood *Lancs*	54	SD8831
Hurtiso *Ork*	103	HY5001
Hurtmore *Surrey*	12	SU9545
Hurworth-on-Tees *Dur*	61	NZ3010
Husabost *Highld*	90	NG2051
Husbands Bosworth *Leics*	39	SP6484
Husborne Crawley *Beds*	30	SP9535
Husinish *W Isls*	102	NA9812
Husthwaite *N York*	62	SE5175
Hut Green *Kent*	56	SE5623
Huthwaite *Notts*	49	SK4659
Huttoft *Lincs*	51	TF5176
Hutton *Avon*	19	ST3458
Hutton *Border*	77	NT9053
Hutton *Essex*	24	TQ6395
Hutton *Humb*	56	TA0253
Hutton *Lancs*	53	SD4926
Hutton Bonville *N York*	62	NZ3300
Hutton Buscel *N York*	63	SE9784
Hutton Conyers *N York*	62	SE3273
Hutton End *Cumb*	59	NY4538
Hutton Henry *Dur*	62	NZ4236
Hutton Lowcross *Cleve*	62	NZ5913
Hutton Magna *Dur*	61	NZ1212
Hutton Mulgrave *N York*	63	NZ8310
Hutton Roof *Cumb*	59	SD5777
Hutton Roof *Cumb*	59	NY3734
Hutton Rudby *N York*	62	NZ4606
Hutton Sessay *N York*	62	SE4776
Hutton Wandesley *N York*	55	SE5050
Hutton-le-Hole *N York*	62	SE7090
Huxham *Devon*	7	SX9497
Huxley *Ches*	46	SJ5161
Huyton *Mersyd*	46	SJ4490
Hycemoor *Cumb*	58	SD0989
Hyde *Gt Man*	48	SJ9494
Hyde End *Berks*	21	SU6266
Hyde End *Berks*	21	SP9300
Hyde Heath *Bucks*	22	SP9300
Hyde Lea *Staffs*	38	SJ9020
Hydestile *Surrey*	12	SU9740
Hynish *Strath*	78	NL9839
Hyssington *Powys*	36	SO3194
Hythe *Hants*	10	SU4207
Hythe *Kent*	15	TR1834
Hythe End *Berks*	22	TQ0172

I

Ibberton Dorset	9	ST7807
Ible Derbys	48	SK2457
Ibsley Hants	10	SU1509
Ibstock Leics	39	SK4010
Ibstone Bucks	22	SU7593
Ibthorpe Hants	21	SU3753
Iburndale N York	63	NZ8707
Ibworth Hants	21	SU5654
Ickburgh Norfk	42	TL8195
Ickenham Gt Lon	22	TQ0886
Ickford Bucks	29	SP6407
Ickham Kent	15	TR2158
Ickleford Herts	31	TL1831
Icklesham E Susx	14	TQ8716
Ickleton Cambs	31	TL4943
Icklingham Suffk	32	TL7772
Ickornshaw N York	54	SD9643
Ickwell Green Beds	30	TL1545
Icomb Gloucs	29	SP2122
Idbury Oxon	29	SP2320
Iddesleigh Devon	6	SS5708
Ide Devon	5	SX8990
Ide Hill Kent	13	TQ4851
Ideford Devon	5	SX8977
Iden E Susx	14	TQ9123
Iden Green Kent	14	TQ7437
Iden Green Kent	14	TQ8031
Idle W York	55	SE1737
Idless Cnwll	2	SW8247
Idlicote Warwks	29	SP2844
Idmiston Wilts	10	SU1937
Idridgehay Derbys	49	SK2849
Idrigill Highld	90	NG3863
Idstone Oxon	21	SU2584
Idvies Tays	89	NO5347
Iffley Oxon	21	SP5303
Ifield W Susx	12	TQ2537
Iford Dorset	10	SZ1493
Iford E Susx	13	TQ4007
Ifton Gwent	19	ST4688
Ifton Heath Shrops	36	SJ3337
Ightfield Shrops	37	SJ5938
Iken Suffk	33	TM4156
Ilam Staffs	48	SK1350
Ilchester Somset	8	ST5222
Ilderton Nthumb	77	NU0121
Ilford Gt Lon	23	TQ4486
Ilfracombe Devon	6	SS5147
Ilkeston Derbys	49	SK4642
Ilketshall St. Andrew Suffk	33	TM3887
Ilketshall St. Margaret Suffk	33	TM3485
Ilkley W York	55	SE1147
Illey W Mids	38	SO9881
Illston on the Hill Leics	40	SP7099
Ilmer Bucks	22	SP7605
Ilmington Warwks	29	SP2143
Ilsington Devon	5	SX7876
Ilston W Glam	17	SS5590
Ilton N York	61	SE1878
Ilton Somset	8	ST3517
Imachar Strath	72	NR8640
Immingham Humb	57	TA1714
Immingham Dock Humb	57	TA1916
Ince Ches		SJ4576
Ince Blundell Mersyd	46	SD3203
Ince-in-Makerfield Gt Man	47	SD5904
Inchbae Lodge Highld	92	NH4069
Inchbare Tays	89	NO6065
Inchberry Gramp	94	NJ3055
Inchinnan Strath	73	NS4868
Inchlaggan Highld	86	NH1801
Inchmagranachan Tays	88	NO0044
Inchmichael Tays	83	NO2425
Inchnacardoch Highld	92	NH3810
Inchnadamph Highld	96	NC2522
Inchture Tays	83	NO2728
Inchvuilt Highld	92	NH2438
Inchyra Tays	82	NO1820
Indian Queens Cnwll	3	SW9159
Ingatestone Essex	24	TQ6499
Ingbirchworth S York	55	SE2205
Ingestre Staffs	38	SJ9724
Ingham Lincs	50	SK9483
Ingham Norfk	43	TG3926
Ingham Suffk	32	TL8570
Ingham Corner Norfk	43	TG3927
Ingleby Derbys	39	SK3426
Ingleby Arncliffe N York	62	NZ4400
Ingleby Greenhow N York	62	NZ5806
Ingleigh Green Devon	6	SS6007
Inglesbatch Avon	20	ST7061
Inglesham Wilts	21	SU2098
Ingleston D & G	66	NX9765
Ingleton Dur	61	NZ1720
Ingleton N York	54	SD6972
Inglewhite Lancs	53	SD5440
Ingliston Tays	68	NO4248
Ingoe Nthumb		NZ0374
Ingoldisthorpe Norfk	42	TF6832
Ingoldmells Lincs	51	TF5668
Ingoldsby Lincs	40	TF0130
Ingon Warwks	29	SP2158
Ingram Nthumb	77	NU0116
Ingrow W York	55	SE0539
Ingst Avon	19	ST5887
Ingst Avon	19	ST5887
Ingthorpe Leics	40	SK9908
Ingworth Norfk	43	TG1929
Inkberrow H & W	28	SP0157
Inkerman Dur	61	NZ1140
Inkhorn Gramp	95	NJ9239
Inkpen Berks	21	SU3664
Inkstack Highld	100	ND2570
Innellan Strath	73	NS1470
Innerleithen Border	75	NT3336
Innerleven Fife	83	NO3700
Innermessan D & G	64	NX0863
Innerwick Loth	76	NT7273
Innesmill Gramp	94	NJ2863
Insch Gramp	94	NJ6328
Insh Highld	87	NH8101
Inskip Lancs	53	SD4637
Instow Devon	6	SS4730
Insworke Cnwll	4	SX4252
Intake S York	49	SK3884
Intake S York	49	SK5891
Inver Gramp	88	NO2393
Inver Highld	97	NH8682
Inver Tays	88	NO0142
Inver-Boyndie Gramp	94	NJ6664
Inverailort Highld	85	NM7681
Inverallligin Highld	91	NG8454
Inverallochy Gramp	95	NK0464
Inveran Highld	96	NH5797
Inveraray Strath	80	NN0908
Inverarish Highld	84	NG5535
Inverarity Tays	88	NO4544
Inverarnan Cent	80	NN3218
Inveravon Cent	82	NS5979
Inverawe Strath	80	NN0231
Inverbervie Gramp	89	NO8372
Inverbroom Highld	96	NH1883
Inverchaolain Strath	80	NS0975
Invercreran House Hotel Strath	80	NN0147
Inverdruie Highld	93	NH8910
Inveresk Loth	75	NT3571
Inveresragan Strath	80	NM9935
Inverey Gramp	88	NO0889
Inverfarigaig Highld	92	NH5223
Inverfolla Strath	86	NM9544
Invergarry Highld	86	NH3101
Invergloy Highld	86	NN2288
Invergordon Highld	93	NH7068
Invergowrie Tays	83	NO3430
Inverguseran Highld	85	NG7407
Inverhadden Tays	87	NN6757

Inverherive Cent	80	NN3626
Inverie Highld	85	NG7600
Inverinan Strath	80	NM9917
Inverinate Highld	85	NG9221
Inverkeilor Tays	89	NO6649
Inverkeithing Fife	82	NT1383
Inverkeithny Gramp	94	NJ6246
Inverkip Strath	80	NS2071
Inverkirkaig Highld	98	NC0819
Inverlael Highld	96	NH1886
Inverlair Highld	86	NN3379
Inverliever Lodge Strath	79	NM8905
Inverlochlarig Cent	81	NN4318
Inverlochy Strath	80	NN1927
Invermarkie Gramp	94	NJ4239
Invermoriston Highld	92	NH4217
Invernaver Highld	99	NC7060
Inverneg Strath	80	NS3497
Inverneil Strath	71	NR8481
Inverness Highld	93	NH6645
Invernoaden Strath	80	NS1297
Inveroran Hotel Strath	86	NN2274
Inverquharity Tays	88	NO4057
Inverquhomery Gramp	95	NK0246
Inverroy Highld	86	NN2581
Inversanda Highld	86	NM9459
Invershiel Highld	85	NG9319
Invershin Highld	96	NH5796
Invershore Highld	100	ND2435
Inversnaid Cent	80	NN3408
Inveruglas Strath	95	NK0947
Inverugie Gramp	80	NN3109
Inveruglas Strath	87	NH8000
Inverurie Gramp	95	NJ7721
Inwardleigh Devon	6	SX5699
Inworth Essex	24	TL8718
Iping W Susx	11	SU8522
Ipplepen Devon	5	SX8366
Ipsden Oxon	21	SU6285
Ipstones Staffs	48	SK0249
Ipswich Suffk	33	TM1644
Irby Mersyd	46	SJ2584
Irby in the Marsh Lincs	51	TF4763
Irby upon Humber Humb	57	TA1904
Irchester Nhants	30	SP9265
Ireby Cumb	58	NY2338
Ireby Lancs	60	SD6575
Ireland Beds	30	TL1341
Ireland's Cross Shrops	37	SJ7341
Ireleth Cumb	58	SD2277
Ireshopeburn Dur	60	NY8638
Ireton Wood Derbys	49	SK2847
Irlam Gt Man	47	SJ7294
Irnham Lincs	40	TF0226
Iron Acton Avon	20	ST6783
Iron Bridge Cambs	41	TL4897
Ironmacannie D & G	65	NX6675
Irons Bottom Surrey	12	TQ2546
Ironville Derbys	49	SK4351
Irstead Norfk	43	TG3620
Irthington Cumb	67	NY4961
Irthlingborough Nhants	30	SP9470
Irton N York	63	TA0184
Irvine Strath	73	NS3239
Isauld Highld	99	NC9865
Isbister Shet	103	HU3790
Isfield E Susx	13	TQ4417
Isham Nhants	30	SP8873
Isington Hants	11	SU7742
Islandpool H & W	38	SO8680
Isle Abbotts Somset	8	ST3520
Isle Brewers Somset	8	ST3621
Isle of Whithorn D & G	65	NX4736
Isleham Cambs	32	TL6474
Isleornsay Highld	85	NG6912
Islet Village Guern	101	SV0000
Isley Walton Leics	39	SK4225
Islington Gt Lon	23	TQ3184
Islip Nhants	30	SP9879
Islip Oxon	29	SP5214
Islivig W Isls	102	NA9927
Isombridge Shrops	37	SJ6113
Istead Rise Kent	14	TQ6369
Itchen Abbas Hants	11	SU5332
Itchen Stoke Hants	11	SU5532
Itchingfield W Susx	12	TQ1328
Itteringham Norfk	43	TG1430
Itton Devon	7	SX6898
Itton Gwent	19	ST4995
Itton Common Gwent	19	ST4895
Ivegill Cumb	67	NY4143
Iver Bucks	22	TQ0381
Iver Heath Bucks	22	TQ0283
Iveston Dur	69	NZ1350
Ivinghoe Bucks	30	SP9416
Ivinghoe Aston Bucks	30	SP9517
Ivington Green H & W	27	SO4756
Ivington Green H & W	27	SO4655
Ivington Green H & W	27	SO4656
Ivy Hatch Kent	14	TQ5854
Ivybridge Devon	5	SX6356
Ivychurch Kent	15	TR0227
Iwade Kent	14	TQ8967
Iwerne Courney Dorset	9	ST8512
Iwerne Minster Dorset	9	ST8614
Ixworth Suffk	32	TL9370
Ixworth Thorpe Suffk	32	TL9173

J

Jack-in-the-Green Devon	7	SY0195
Jackson Bridge W York	55	SE1606
Jackton Strath	74	NS5952
Jacobstow Cnwll	6	SX1995
Jacobstowe Devon	6	SS5801
Jameston Dyfed	16	SS0599
Jamestown Highld	92	NH4756
Jamestown Strath	80	NS3981
Janets-town Highld	100	ND3551
Janetstown Highld	100	ND1932
Jardine Hall D & G	67	NY1088
Jarrow T & W	69	NZ3065
Jasper's Green Essex	24	TL7226
Jawcraig Cent	74	NS8475
Jaywick Essex	25	TM1513
Jedburgh Border	76	NT6420
Jeffreyston Dyfed	16	SN0806
Jemimaville Highld	93	NH7165
Jerbourg Guern	101	3V0000
Jesmond T & W	69	NZ2566
Jevington E Susx	13	TQ5601
Jockey End Herts	30	TL0413
John O'Groats Highld	100	ND3872
Johnby Cumb	59	NY4333
Johnshaven Gramp	89	NO7967
Johnston Dyfed	16	SM9310
Johnston D & G	67	NT1400
Johnstone Strath	73	NS4263
Johnstonebridge D & G	67	NY1092
Joppa Dyfed	34	SN5666
Joppa Strath	73	NS4119
Jordanston Dyfed	16	SM9232
Jump S York	49	SK3581
Juniper Green Loth	49	SE3701
Jurby IOM	75	NT1968
	52	SC3598

K

Kaber Cumb	60	NY7911
Kaimes Loth	75	NT2768
Kalnalkill Highld	91	NG6955
Kames Strath	80	ND3461
Kames Strath	71	NR9771
Kames Strath	79	NM8211
Kea Cnwll	2	SW8142
Keal Cotes Lincs	51	TF3661
Kearby Town End N York	55	SE3446
Kearnsey Kent	15	TR2844
Kearsley Gt Man	47	SD7504
Kearstwick Cumb	59	SD6079
Kedington Suffk	32	TL7046
Kedleston Derbys	49	SK3041
Keelby Lincs	57	TA1610
Keele Staffs	47	SJ8045
Keele University Staffs	47	SJ8145
Keelham W York	55	SE0732
Keeston Dyfed	16	SM9019
Keevil Wilts	20	ST9157
Kegworth Leics	39	SK4826
Keig Gramp	94	NJ6119
Keighley W York	55	SE0641
Keilarsbrae Cent	82	NS8993
Keillmore Strath	71	NR6880
Keillour Tays	82	NN9725
Keiloch Gramp	88	NO1891
Keils Strath	70	NR5268
Keinton Mandeville Somset	8	ST5430
Keir Mill D & G	66	NX8593
Keisley Cumb	60	NY7124
Keiss Highld	100	ND3461
Keith Gramp	94	NJ4250
Keithick Tays	82	NO2038
Keithock Tays	89	NO6063
Keithtown Gramp	92	NH5256
Kelbrook Lancs	54	SD9044
Kelburn Strath	73	NS2156
Kelby Lincs	50	TF0041
Keld N York	60	NY8901
Kelfield N York	56	SE5938
Kelham Notts	50	SK7755
Kelhead D & G	67	NY1469
Kellacott Devon	4	SX4089
Kellas Gramp	94	NJ1654
Kellas Tays	83	NO4535
Kellaton Devon	5	SX8039
Kelling Norfk	43	TG0942
Kellington N York	56	SE5524
Kelloe Dur	62	NZ3436
Kelly Devon	4	SX3981
Kelly Bray Cnwll	4	SX3571
Kelmarsh Nhants	40	SP7379
Kelmscot Oxon	21	SU2499
Kelsale Suffk	33	TM3865
Kelsall Ches	46	SJ5268
Kelshall Herts	31	TL3236
Kelsick Cumb	67	NY1950
Kelso Border	76	NT7234
Kelstedge Derbys	51	TF2489
Kelstern Lincs	51	TF2489
Kelston Avon	20	ST7067
Keltneyburn Tays	87	NN7749
Kelton D & G	66	NX9970
Kelty Fife	82	NT1494
Kelvedon Essex	24	TL8619
Kelvedon Hatch Essex	24	TQ5698
Kelynack Cnwll	2	SW3729
Kemback Fife	83	NO4115
Kemberton Shrops	37	SJ7204
Kemble Wilts	20	ST9897
Kemerton H & W	28	SO9437
Kemnay Gramp	95	NJ7316
Kemneys Commander Gwent	27	SO3404
Kemp Town E Susx	12	TQ3303
Kempley Gloucs	28	SO6729
Kempley Green Gloucs	28	SO6728
Kempsey H & W	28	SO8549
Kempsford Gloucs	20	SU1597
Kempshott Hants	21	SU6050
Kempston Beds	30	TL0347
Kempton Shrops	36	SO3682
Kemsing Kent	23	TQ5558
Kenardington Kent	15	TQ9732
Kenchester H & W	27	SO4342
Kencot Oxon	29	SP2504
Kendal Cumb	59	SD5192
Kenfig M Glam	18	SS8081
Kenilworth Warwks	39	SP2971
Kenley Gt Lon	23	TQ3260
Kenley Shrops	37	SJ5600
Kenmore Highld	91	NG7557
Kenmore Tays	87	NN7745
Kenn Avon	19	ST4269
Kenn Devon	5	SX9285
Kennacley W Isls	90	NG1794
Kennacraig Strath	71	NR8262
Kenneggy Cnwll	2	SW5629
Kennerleigh Devon	7	SS8107
Kennessee Green Mersyd	46	SD3801
Kennet Cent	82	NS9291
Kennethmont Gramp	94	NJ5428
Kennett Cambs	32	TL7068
Kennford Devon	5	SX9186
Kenninghall Norfk	32	TM0386
Kennington Kent	15	TR0245
Kennington Oxon	21	SP5101
Kennoway Fife	83	NO3502
Kenny Somset	8	ST3118
Kennyhill Suffk	32	TL6680
Kennythorpe N York	56	SE7865
Kenovay Strath	78	NL9946
Kensaleyre Highld	90	NG4251
Kensington Gt Lon	23	TQ2579
Kensworth Beds	30	TL0319
Kensworth Common Beds	30	TL0318
Kent's Green Gloucs	28	SO7423
Kentallen Highld	86	NN0057
Kentchurch H & W	27	SO4125
Kentford Suffk	32	TL7066
Kentisbeare Devon	7	ST0608
Kentisbury Devon	6	SS6244
Kentish Town Gt Lon	23	TQ2984
Kentmere Cumb	59	NY4504
Kenton Devon	5	SX9583
Kenton Gt Lon	22	TQ1788
Kenton Suffk	33	TM1965
Kenton T & W	69	NZ2267
Kentra Highld	79	NM6569
Kents Bank Cumb	59	SD3976
Kenwyn Cnwll	2	SW8145
Keoldale Highld	98	NC3866
Keppoch Highld	85	NG8924
Keprigan Strath	72	NR6810
Kepwick N York	62	SE4690
Keresley W Mids	39	SP3182
Keresley Green Warwks	39	SP3184
Kernborough Devon	5	SX7940
Kerridge Ches	48	SJ9377
Kerridge-end Ches	48	SJ9476
Kerris Cnwll	2	SW4427
Kerry Powys	36	SO1490
Kerry's Gate H & W	27	SO3933
Kerrycroy Strath	73	NS1061
Kersall Notts	49	SK7162
Kersbrook Devon	5	SY0683
Kersey Suffk	32	TM0044
Kershader W Isls	102	NB3419
Kersoe H & W	28	SO9939
Kerswell Devon	7	ST0806
Kerswell Green H & W	28	SO8646
Kesgrave Suffk	33	TM2245
Kessingland Suffk	33	TM5286
Kestle Cnwll	3	SW9845
Kestle Mill Cnwll	3	SW8459
Keston Gt Lon	23	TQ4164
Keswick Cumb	58	NY2623

Keswick Norfk	43	TG2004
Ketsby Lincs	51	TF3676
Kettering Nhants	30	SP8678
Ketteringham Norfk	43	TG1603
Kettins Tays	83	NO2339
Kettlebaston Suffk	32	TL9650
Kettlebridge Fife	83	NO3007
Kettleburgh Suffk	33	TM2660
Kettleshulme Ches	48	SJ9879
Kettlesing N York	55	SE2155
Kettlesing Bottom N York	55	SE2257
Kettlestoft Ork	103	HY6538
Kettlestone Norfk	42	TF9631
Kettlethorpe Lincs	50	SK8475
Kettlewell N York	55	SD9772
Ketton Leics	40	SK9804
Kew Gt Lon	23	TQ1877
Kexbrough S York	55	SE2909
Kexby Lincs	50	SK8785
Kexby N York	56	SE7050
Key Green Ches	48	SJ8963
Key Street Kent	14	TQ8964
Keyham Leics	39	SK6706
Keyhaven Hants	10	SZ3091
Keyingham Humb	57	TA2425
Keymer W Susx	12	TQ3115
Keynsham Avon	19	ST6568
Keysoe Beds	30	TL0861
Keysoe Row Beds	30	TL0475
Keyston Notts	39	SK6130
Keyworth Notts	39	SK6130
Kibbear Somset	8	ST2122
Kibblesworth T & W	69	NZ2456
Kibworth Beauchamp Leics	39	SP6893
Kibworth Harcourt Leics	39	SP6894
Kidbrooke Gt Lon	23	TQ4076
Kidderminster H & W	38	SO8376
Kiddington Oxon	29	SP4913
Kidmore End Oxon	22	SU6979
Kidwelly Dyfed	17	SN4006
Kiel Crofts Strath	79	NM9039
Kielder Nthumb	68	NY6293
Kiells Strath	82	NS9290
Kilbagie Cent	85	NG6506
Kilbeg Highld	71	NR7164
Kilberry Strath	73	NS3154
Kilbirnie Strath	84	NG5820
Kilbride Highld	71	NR7229
Kilbride Strath	79	NS0367
Kilbride Strath	79	NM8525
Kilbride W Isls	102	NF7514
Kilburn Derbys	49	SK3845
Kilburn Gt Lon	23	TQ2483
Kilburn N York	62	SE5179
Kilby Leics	39	SP6295
Kilchamaig Strath	71	NR8060
Kilchattan Strath	70	NR3795
Kilchattan Strath	73	NS1054
Kilchenzie Strath	72	NR6724
Kilcheran Strath	79	NM8238
Kilchiaran Strath	70	NR2060
Kilchoan Highld	79	NM4964
Kilchrenan Strath	80	NN0322
Kilconquhar Fife	83	NO4802
Kilcot Gloucs	28	SO6925
Kilcoy Highld	92	NH5751
Kilcreggan Strath	80	NS2380
Kildale N York	62	NZ6009
Kildalloig Strath	72	NR7518
Kildary Highld	97	NH7674
Kildavanan Strath	72	NS0266
Kildermorie Lodge Highld	96	NH5277
Kildonan Highld	97	NC9120
Kildonan Strath	72	NS0321
Kildonan Lodge Highld	97	NH9018
Kildonnan Highld	84	NM4985
Kildrummy Gramp	94	NJ4617
Kidwick N York	54	SE0046
Kilehoman Strath	70	NR2163
Kilfinan Strath	71	NR9378
Kilfinnan Highld	86	NN2795
Kilgetty Dyfed	16	SN1207
Kilgrammie Strath	73	NS2602
Kilgwrrwg Common Gwent	19	ST4798
Kilham Humb	57	TA0664
Kilkenneth Strath	78	NL9444
Kilkerran Strath	73	NS3003
Kilkhampton Cnwll	6	SS2511
Killay W Glam	17	SS6092
Killean Strath	72	NR6944
Killearn Cent	81	NS5286
Killen Highld	92	NH6758
Killerby Dur	61	NZ1919
Killerton Devon	7	SS9700
Killichonan Tays	87	NR5458
Killichronan Strath	79	NM5441
Killiecrankie Tays	87	NN9162
Killilan Highld	85	NG9430
Killimster Highld	100	ND3156
Killin Cent	81	NN5733
Killinghall N York	55	SE2858
Killington Cumb	59	SD6188
Killingworth T & W	69	NZ2870
Killochonochan Strath	71	NR8395
Killochyett Border	76	NT4545
Killocraw Strath	72	NR6530
Killundine Highld	79	NM5849
Kilmacolm Strath	73	NS3569
Kilmahog Cent	81	NN6108
Kilmahumaig Strath	71	NR7893
Kilmaluag Highld	90	NG4373
Kilmansharachan Strath	72	NR7107
Kilmany Fife	83	NO3821
Kilmarie Highld	84	NG5517
Kilmarnock Strath	73	NS4238
Kilmartin Strath	71	NR8398
Kilmaurs Strath	73	NS4141
Kilmelford Strath	79	NM8512
Kilmeny Strath	70	NR3865
Kilmersdon Somset	8	ST6952
Kilmeston Hants	11	SU5926
Kilmichael Glassary Strath	71	NR8593
Kilmichael of Inverlussa Strath	71	NR7786
Kilmington Devon	8	SY2798
Kilmington Wilts	20	ST7736
Kilmington Common Wilts	20	ST7736
Kilmington Street Wilts	9	ST7835
Kilmorack Highld	92	NM8825
Kilmore Highld	85	NG6507
Kilmory Highld	79	NM6863
Kilmory Strath	84	NR3603
Kilmory Strath	71	NR7075
Kilmuir Highld	90	NG2547
Kilmuir Highld	93	SD3770
Kilmuir Highld	97	NH6749
Kilmuir Highld	93	NH7573
Kilmun Strath	80	NS1781
Kiln Green Berks	22	SU8178
Kiln Pit Hill Nthumb	68	NZ0354
Kilnave Strath	70	NR2871
Kilndown Kent	14	TQ7035
Kilninian Strath	78	NM3946
Kilninver Strath	79	NM8221
Kilnsea Humb	57	TA4015
Kilnsey N York	54	SD9767
Kilnwick Humb	56	SE9949
Kiloran Strath	70	NR3996
Kilpeck H & W	27	SO4430
Kilpheder W Isls	102	NF7419
Kilphedir Highld	97	NC9818
Kilpin Humb	56	SE7726
Kilrenny Fife	83	SP5671
Kilsby Nhants	39	NO2125
Kilspindie Tays	64	NX1238
Kilstay D & G	81	NS7178
Kilsyth Strath	62	NZ7018
Kiltarlity Highld	19	ST1644
Kilton Cleve	62	NZ6917
Kilton Thorpe Cleve	90	NG3869
Kilvaxter Highld	8	ST1443
Kilve Somset	50	SK8042
Kilvington Notts	73	TQ0904
Kilwinning Strath	42	TG0700
Kimberley Norfk	49	SK4944
Kimberley Notts	49	SK4092
Kimberworth S York		

Kimblesworth Dur	69	NZ2547
Kimbolton Cambs	30	TL0967
Kimbolton H & W	27	SO5261
Kimcote Leics	39	SP5886
Kimmeridge Dorset	9	SY9179
Kimpton Hants	21	SU2746
Kimpton Hants	21	SU2746
Kimpton Herts	31	TL1718
Kimworthy Devon	6	SS3012
Kinaird Tays	83	NO2428
Kinbrace Highld	99	NC8631
Kinbuck Cent	81	NN7905
Kincaple Fife	83	NO4618
Kincardine Fife	82	NS8387
Kincardine Highld	97	NH6089
Kincardine O'Neil Tays	89	NO5999
Kinclaven Tays	82	NO1538
Kincorth Gramp	89	NJ9403
Kincorth House Gramp	93	NJ0161
Kincraig Highld	87	NH8305
Kincraigie Tays	88	NN9849
Kindallachan Tays	88	NN9950
Kinerarach Strath	71	NR6653
Kineton Gloucs	28	SP0926
Kineton Warwks	29	SP3351
Kinfauns Tays	82	NO1622
King's Bromley Staffs	38	SK1216
King's Cliffe Nhants	40	TL0097
King's Coughton Warwks	28	SP0859
King's Heath W Mids	38	SP0781
King's Lynn Norfk	41	TF6220
King's Mills Guern	101	SV0000
King's Newton Derbys	39	SK3926
King's Norton Leics	39	SK6800
King's Norton W Mids	38	SP0579
King's Nympton Devon	7	SS6819
King's Pyon H & W	27	SO4350
King's Somborne Hants	10	SU3631
King's Stag Dorset	9	ST7210
King's Stanley Gloucs	20	SO8103
King's Sutton Oxon	29	SP5036
King's Walden Herts	31	TL1623
Kingarth Strath	73	NS0956
Kingarvie D & G	66	NX9266
Kingcausie Gramp	89	NO8699
Kingcoed Gwent	27	SO4205
Kingerby Lincs	50	TF0593
Kingford Devon	6	SS2806
Kingham Oxon	29	SP2523
Kingholm Quay D & G	66	NX9773
Kinglassie Loth	83	NT2398
Kingoldrum Tays	88	NO3355
Kingoodie Tays	83	NO3329
Kings Caple H & W	27	SO5528
Kings House Hotel Highld	86	NN2554
Kings Langley Herts	22	TL0702
Kings Meaburn Cumb	59	NY6121
Kings Muir Border	75	NT2539
Kings Newnham Warwks	39	SP4577
Kings Ripton Cambs	31	TL2576
Kings Weston Avon	19	ST5477
Kings Worthy Hants	10	SU4933
Kingsand Cnwll	4	SX4350
Kingsbarns Fife	83	NO5912
Kingsbridge Devon	5	SX7344
Kingsbridge Somset	7	SS9837
Kingsbury Gt Lon	23	TQ1988
Kingsbury Warwks	39	SP2196
Kingsbury Episcopi Somset	8	ST4320
Kingsclere Hants	21	SU5258
Kingscote Gloucs	20	ST8196
Kingscott Devon	6	SS5318
Kingscross Strath	72	NS0528
Kingsdon Somset	8	ST5126
Kingsdown Kent	15	TR3748
Kingsdown Wilts	20	SU1688
Kingseat Fife	82	NT1290
Kingsey Bucks	22	SP7406
Kingsfold W Susx	12	TQ1636
Kingsford H & W	38	SO8281
Kingsford Strath	73	NS4447
Kingsgate Kent	15	TR3970
Kingshall Street Suffk	32	TL9161
Kingshouse Cent	81	NN5620
Kingshurst W Mids	38	SP1788
Kingside Hill Cumb	67	NY1651
Kingskerswell Devon	5	SX8767
Kingskettle Fife	83	NO3008
Kingsland H & W	27	SO4461
Kingsley Ches	47	SJ5574
Kingsley Hants	11	SU7838
Kingsley Staffs	48	SK0147
Kingsley Green W Susx	11	SU8930
Kingsley Park Nhants	30	SP7762
Kingsmuir Fife	83	NO5308
Kingsmuir Tays	89	NO4849
Kingsnorth Kent	15	TR0039
Kingsteignton Devon	5	SX8773
Kingsthorne H & W	27	SO4931
Kingsthorpe Nhants	30	SP7563
Kingston Cambs	31	TL3455
Kingston Devon	5	SX6347
Kingston Devon	4	SX0687
Kingston Dorset	9	ST7509
Kingston Dorset	9	SY9579
Kingston Gramp	94	NJ3365
Kingston IOW	10	SZ4781
Kingston Kent	15	TR1950
Kingston Loth	83	NT5482
Kingston M Glam	4	SX3078
Kingston W Susx	12	TQ0801
Kingston Bagpuize Oxon	21	SU4098
Kingston Blount Oxon	22	SU7399
Kingston Deverill Wilts	20	ST8436
Kingston Lisle Oxon	21	SU3287
Kingston Russell Dorset	9	SY5891
Kingston Seymour Avon	19	ST4066
Kingston St. Mary Somset	8	ST2229
Kingston by Sea W Susx	12	TQ2205
Kingston near Lewes E Susx	13	TQ3908
Kingston on Soar Notts	39	SK5027
Kingston upon Hull Humb	57	TA0929
Kingston upon Thames Gt Lon	23	TQ1869
Kingstone H & W	27	SO4235
Kingstone Oxon	21	SU2685
Kingstone Somset	8	ST3713
Kingstone Staffs	38	SK0529
Kingswear Devon	5	SX8851
Kingswells Gramp	89	NJ8606
Kingswells Strath	74	NS5047
Kingswinford W Mids	38	SO8888
Kingswood Avon	19	ST6473
Kingswood Bucks	22	SP6619
Kingswood Gloucs	20	ST7491
Kingswood Powys	36	SJ2402
Kingswood Somset	8	ST1035
Kingswood Surrey	23	TQ2455
Kingswood Warwks	39	SP1971
Kingswood Common Staffs	38	SJ8302
Kingthorpe Lincs	50	TF1275
Kington Avon	19	ST6190
Kington H & W	27	SO2956
Kington H & W	28	SO9955
Kington Langley Wilts	20	ST9276
Kington Magna Dorset	9	ST7622
Kington St. Michael Wilts	20	ST9077
Kingussie Highld	87	NH7500
Kingweston Somset	8	ST5230
Kinharrachie Gramp	95	NJ9231
Kinkell Bridge Tays	82	NN9316
Kinknockie Gramp	95	NK0041
Kinleith Loth	41	NT1866
Kinlet Shrops	37	SO7280
Kinloch Highld	84	NM4099
Kinloch Highld	98	NC3434
Kinloch Highld	99	NC5552
Kinloch Tays	88	NO1544
Kinloch Tays	88	NO2644
Kinloch Hourn Highld	85	NG9407
Kinloch Rannoch Tays	87	NN6658
Kinlochard Cent	81	NN4502
Kinlochbervie Highld	98	NC2256
Kinlocheil Highld	85	NM9779
Kinlochewe Highld	91	NH0262
Kinlochleven Highld	86	NN1861
Kinlochmoidart Highld	85	NM7172
Kinlochnanuagh Highld	85	NM7384
Kinlochspelve Strath	79	NM6526
Kinloss Gramp	93	NJ0661

Kinmel Bay Clwyd	45	SH9880
Kinmount House D & G	67	NY1468
Kinmuck Gramp	95	NJ8119
Kinmundy Gramp	95	NJ8817
Kinnadie Gramp	95	NJ9743
Kinnahaird Highld	92	NH4755
Kinnaird Castle Tays	75	NS9559
Kinneddar Gramp	89	NO6357
Kineff Gramp	94	NJ2269
Kinnelhead D & G	89	NO8574
Kinnell Tays	66	NT0201
Kinnerley Shrops	89	NO6150
Kinnersley H & W	36	SJ3321
Kinnersley H & W	27	SO8743
Kinnerton Powys	27	SO3449
Kinnesswood Tays	27	SO2463
Kinninvie Dur	82	NO1702
Kinnordy Tays	61	NZ0521
Kinoulton Notts	88	NO3655
Kinross Tays	39	SK6730
Kinrossie Tays	82	NO1202
Kinsey Heath Ches	82	NO1832
Kinsham H & W	49	SK6642
Kinsham H & W	28	SO9335
Kinsley W York	27	SO3665
Kinson Dorset	55	SE4114
Kintbury Berks	10	SZ0696
Kintillo Tays	21	SU3866
Kinton H & W	82	NO1317
Kinton Shrops	36	SO4174
Kintore Gramp	36	SJ3619
Kintour Strath	95	NJ7916
Kintradwell Highld	70	NR4551
Kintraw Strath	78	NM3125
Kinveachy Highld	97	NC9208
Kinver Staffs	79	NM8204
Kiplin N York	93	NH9018
Kippax W York	38	SO8483
Kippen Cent	61	SE2796
Kippford or Scaur D & G	55	SE4130
Kipping's Cross Kent	81	NS8594
Kirbister Ork	66	NX8355
Kirby Bedon Norfk	13	TQ6440
Kirby Bellars Leics	103	HY3607
Kirby Cane Norfk	43	TG2705
Kirby Cross Essex	40	SK7117
Kirby Fields Leics	43	TM3794
Kirby Grindalythe N York	25	TM2121
Kirby Hill N York	39	SK5303
Kirby Hill N York	66	SE9067
Kirby Knowle N York	61	NZ1306
Kirby Misperton N York	55	SE3968
Kirby Muxloe Leics	62	SE4687
Kirby Row Norfk	66	SE7779
Kirby Sigston N York	39	SK5104
Kirby Underdale Humb	33	TM3792
Kirby Wiske N York	62	SE4194
Kirby le Soken Essex	56	SE8058
Kirdford W Susx	62	SE3784
Kirivick W Isls	25	TM2122
Kirk Highld	12	TQ0126
Kirk Bramwith S York	102	NB2041
Kirk Deighton N York	100	ND2859
Kirk Ella Humb	56	SE6111
Kirk Hallam Derbys	55	SE3950
Kirk Hammerton N York	56	TA0229
Kirk Haugh Nthumb	49	SK4540
Kirk Ireton Derbys	55	SE4655
Kirk Langley Derbys	68	NY6950
Kirk Merrington Dur	49	SK2650
Kirk Sandall S York	48	SK2838
Kirk Smeaton N York	61	NZ2631
Kirk Yetholm Border	56	SE6108
Kirk of Shotts Strath	55	SE5116
Kirkabister Shet	77	NT8228
Kirkandrews upon Eden Cumb	74	NS8462
Kirkbampton Cumb	103	HU4938
Kirkbean D & G	67	NY3558
Kirkbride Cumb	67	NY3057
Kirkbuddo Tays	66	NX9859
Kirkburn Border	67	NY2356
Kirkburn Humb	89	NO5043
Kirkburton W York	75	NT2938
Kirkby Lincs	56	SE9855
Kirkby Mersyd	55	SE1912
Kirkby N York	50	TF0692
Kirkby Fleetham N York	46	SJ4099
Kirkby Green Lincs	62	NZ5305
Kirkby Lonsdale Cumb	61	SE2894
Kirkby Malham N York	50	TF0857
Kirkby Mallory Leics	59	SD6178
Kirkby Malzeard N York	54	SD8960
Kirkby Overblow N York	39	SK4500
Kirkby Stephen Cumb	61	SE2374
Kirkby Underwood Lincs	55	SE3249
Kirkby Wharf N York	60	NY7708
Kirkby Woodhouse Notts	40	TF0727
Kirkby in Ashfield Notts	55	SE5041
Kirkby in Furness Cumb	49	SK5065
Kirkby la Thorpe Lincs	49	SK5056
Kirkby on Bain Lincs	67	NY2282
Kirkbymoorside N York	50	TF0946
Kirkcaldy Fife	51	TF2462
Kirkcambeck Cumb	62	SE6986
Kirkcolm D & G	83	NT2892
Kirkconnel D & G	67	NY5368
Kirkconnell D & G	64	NX0268
Kirkconnell D & G	66	NX9868
Kirkcowan D & G	66	NS7312
Kirkcudbright D & G	65	NX6760
Kirkdale Mersyd	64	NX3260
Kirkfieldbank Strath	65	NX6851
Kirkgunzeon D & G	32	SJ3493
Kirkham Lancs	74	NS8643
Kirkham N York	66	NX6666
Kirkhamgate W York	53	SD4232
Kirkharle Nthumb	56	SE7365
Kirkheaton Nthumb	55	SE2922
Kirkheaton W York	68	NZ0182
Kirkhill Highld	68	NZ0177
Kirkhope Border	55	SE1818
Kirkhope Strath	92	NH5545
Kirkhouse Cumb	76	NT3723
Kirkibost Highld	75	NS9606
Kirkibost W Isls	67	NY5659
Kirkinch Tays	59	NC5956
Kirkinner D & G	56	NG5418
Kirkintilloch Strath	102	NB1835
Kirkland Cumb	88	NO3044
Kirkland D & G	64	NX4251
Kirkland D & G	74	NS6573
Kirkland D & G	58	NY0718
Kirklevington Cleve	66	NX8190
Kirkley Suffk	66	NY0389
Kirkleyditch Ches	66	NS7214
Kirklington N York	72	NZ4309
Kirklington Notts	33	TM5391
Kirklinton Cumb	47	SJ8778
Kirkliston Loth	58	SE3181
Kirkmabreck D & G	49	SK6757
Kirkmaiden D & G	67	NY4367
Kirkmichael IOM	75	NT1274
Kirkmichael Strath	64	NX4756
Kirkmichael Tays	52	SC3190
Kirkmuirhill Strath	73	NS3408
Kirknewton Loth	88	NO0759
Kirknewton Nthumb	74	NS7842
Kirknewton Nthumb	75	NT1166
Kirkney Gramp	77	NT9130
Kirkoswald Cumb	77	NT9330
Kirkoswald Strath	94	NJ5132
Kirkpatrick Durham D & G	59	NY5541
Kirkpatrick-Fleming D & G	73	NS2407
Kirksanton Cumb	66	NX7870
Kirkstall W York	67	NY2770
Kirkstile D & G	58	SD1380
Kirkstone Pass Inn Cumb	55	SE2635
Kirkstyle Highld	67	NY3690
Kirkthorpe W York	59	NY4108
Kirkton Border	100	ND3472
Kirkton D & G	55	SE3621
Kirkton D & G	67	NT5413
Kirkton Fife	66	NX9781
Kirkton Gramp	83	NO3625
Kirkton Gramp	94	NJ6112
Kirkton Gramp	94	NJ6425
Kirkton Gramp	95	NJ8243

Kirkton Highld	85	NG8227
Kirkton Highld	85	NG9141
Kirkton Strath	73	NS1654
Kirkton Tays	82	NN9618
Kirkton Manor Border	75	NT2238
Kirkton of Airlie Tays	88	NO3151
Kirkton of Auchterhouse Tays	83	NO3438
Kirkton of Barevan Highld	93	NH8347
Kirkton of Collace Tays	82	NO1932
Kirkton of Craig Tays	89	NO6956
Kirkton of Durris Gramp	89	NO7796
Kirkton of Glenbuchat Gramp	94	NJ3715
Kirkton of Glenisla Tays	88	NO2160
Kirkton of Logie Buchan Gramp	95	NJ9829
Kirkton of Menmuir Tays	89	NO5564
Kirkton of Monikie Tays	83	NO5138
Kirkton of Rayne Gramp	95	NJ6930
Kirkton of Skene Gramp	95	NJ8007
Kirkton of Tealing Tays	83	NO4038
Kirktown Gramp	95	NJ9965
Kirktown of Alvah Gramp	94	NJ6760
Kirktown of Bourtie Gramp	95	NJ8025
Kirktown of Fetteresso Gramp	89	NO8486
Kirktown of Mortlach Gramp	94	NJ3138
Kirktown of Slains Gramp	95	NK0429
Kirkwall Ork	103	HY4410
Kirkwhelpington Nthumb	68	NY9984
Kirmington Humb	57	TA1011
Kirmond le Mire Lincs	50	TF1892
Kirn Strath	80	NS1978
Kirstead Green Norfk	43	TM2997
Kirtlebridge D & G	67	NY2372
Kirtleton D & G	67	NY2780
Kirtling Cambs	32	TL6857
Kirtling Green Suffk	32	TL6856
Kirtlington Oxon	29	SP4919
Kirtomy Highld	99	NC7463
Kirton Lincs	41	TF3038
Kirton Notts	49	SK6869
Kirton Suffk	33	TM2740
Kirton End Lincs	51	TF2840
Kirton Holme Lincs	51	TF2641
Kirton in Lindsey Lincs	51	SK9398
Kirton of Culsalmond Gramp	94	NJ6532
Kirton of Strathmartime Tays	83	NO3735
Kirtonhill Strath	80	NS3875
Kislingbury Nhants	30	SP6959
Kittisford Somset	7	ST0822
Kittybrewster Gramp	95	NJ9207
Kivernoll H & W	27	SO4632
Knaith Lincs	50	SK8284
Knap Corner Dorset	9	ST8023
Knaphill Surrey	22	SU8658
Knapp Somset	8	ST3025
Knapp Hill Hants	10	SU4023
Knapton N York	56	SE5652
Knapton N York	63	SE8776
Knapwell Cambs	31	TL3362
Knaresborough N York	55	SE3557
Knarsdale Nthumb	68	NY6754
Knaven Gramp	95	NJ8943
Knayton N York	62	SE4387
Knebworth Herts	31	TL2520
Knedlington Humb	56	SE7326
Kneesall Notts	49	SK7064
Kneesworth Cambs	31	TL3444
Kneeton Notts	49	SK7146
Knelston W Glam	33	SS4689
Knenhall Staffs	48	SJ9237
Knightcote Warwks	29	SP3954
Knightley Staffs	37	SJ8125
Knighton Devon	4	SX5249
Knighton Dorset	9	ST6111
Knighton Leics	39	SK6001
Knighton Powys	36	SO2872
Knighton Somset	19	ST1944
Knighton Staffs	37	SJ7240
Knighton Staffs	37	SJ7527
Knighton on Teme H & W	27	SO6369
Knightwick H & W	28	SO7355
Knill H & W	27	SO2960
Knipton Leics	40	SK8231
Kniveton Derbys	48	SK2050
Knock Cumb	60	NY6727
Knock Gramp	94	NJ5452
Knock Highld	85	NG6709
Knock W Isls	102	NB4931
Knock Castle Strath	73	NS1963
Knockally Highld	100	ND1429
Knockan Highld	96	NC2110
Knockandhu Gramp	94	NJ2023
Knockando Gramp	93	NJ1941
Knockarthur Highld	97	NC7506
Knockbain Highld	92	NH6543
Knockbain Highld	92	NH6256
Knockdee Highld	100	ND1760
Knockdolian Strath	64	NX1285
Knockeen Strath	20	ST8388
Knockenkelly Strath	64	NX3195
Knockentiber Strath	72	NS0427
Knockespoch House Gramp	73	NS4039
Knockholt Kent	94	NJ5423
Knockholt Pound Kent	23	TQ4658
Knockin Shrops	23	TQ4859
Knockinlaw Strath	36	SJ3322
Knocknaha Strath	73	NS4239
Knocknain Strath	72	NR6818
Knockrome Strath	64	NW9765
Knocksharry IOM	78	NR8571
Knocksheen D & G	52	SC2785
Knockvennie Smithy D & G	65	NX5882
Knodishall Suffk	65	NX7571
Knole Somset	33	TM4062
Knolls Green Ches	8	ST4825
Knook Wilts	23	SJ3739
Knossington Leics	20	ST9341
Knott End-on-Sea Lancs	40	SK8008
Knotting Beds	53	SD3548
Knotting Green Beds	30	TL0063
Knottingley W York	30	TL0062
Knowbury Shrops	55	SE5023
Knowe D & G	37	SO5675
Knowehead D & G	64	NX3171
Knowesgate Nthumb	65	NX6090
Knoweside Strath	89	NY9885
Knowl Hill Berks	73	NS2513
Knowle Avon	22	SU8279
Knowle Devon	19	ST6070
Knowle Devon	6	SS4938
Knowle Devon	7	SS7801
Knowle Devon	7	ST0006
Knowle Devon	7	ST0006
Knowle Shrops	5	SY0482
Knowle W Mids	37	SO5974
Knowle Green Lancs	38	SP1876
Knowle St. Giles Somset	54	SD6338
Knowlton Kent	8	ST3411
Knowsley Mersyd	15	TR2853
Knowstone Devon	46	SJ4395
Knox N York	7	SS8323
Knox Bridge Kent	55	SE2958
Knox Bridge Kent	14	TQ7841
Knucklas Powys	14	TQ7840
Knuston Nhants	36	SO2574
Knutsford Ches	30	SP9266
Krumlin W York	47	SJ7578
Kuggar Cnwll	55	SE0518
Kyle of Lochalsh Highld	2	SW7627
Kyleakin Highld	85	NG7526
Kylerhea Highld	85	NG7526
Kylesku Highld	85	NG7820
Kylesmorar Highld	98	NC2233
Kylestrome Highld	85	NM8093
Kymin Gwent	98	NC2234
Kynnersley Shrops	27	SO5212
Kyre Park H & W	37	SJ6716
	27	SO6264

L'Ancress Guern	101	SV0000
L'Eree Guern	101	SV0000
L'Etacq Jersey	101	SV0000
Little Cheverell Wilts	20	ST9853
La Beilleuse Guern	101	SV0000
La Fontenelle Guern	101	SV0000
La Fosse Guern	101	SV0000
La Greve Guern	101	SV0000
La Greve de Lecq Jersey	101	SV0000
La Hougette Guern	101	SV0000
La Hougue Bie Jersey	101	SV0000
La Passee Guern	101	SV0000
La Pulente Jersey	101	SV0000
La Rocque Jersey	101	SV0000
La Rousaillerie Guern	101	SV0000
La Villette Guern	101	SV0000
La Villocq Guern	101	SV0000
Labbacott Devon	6	SS4220
Laceby Humb	57	TA2106
Lacey Green Bucks	22	SP8200
Lach Dennis Ches	47	SJ7071
Lackford Suffk	32	TL7970
Lackford Green Suffk	32	TL7971
Ladbroke Warwks	29	SP4158
Ladderedge Staffs	48	SJ9654
Laddingford Kent	14	TQ6948
Ladock Cnwll	3	SW8950
Lady Hall Cumb	58	SD1986
Ladybank Fife	83	NO3009
Ladycross Cnwll	4	SX3288
Ladykirk Border	77	NT8847
Ladykirk Ho Border	77	NT8845
Ladywood H & W	28	SO8761
Ladywood W Mids	38	SP0586
Lag D & G	66	NX8786
Laga Highld	79	NM6360
Lagavulin Strath	70	NR4045
Lagg Strath	71	NR5978
Lagg Strath	72	NR9521
Laggan Highld	86	NN2997
Laggan Highld	87	NN6194
Laggan Strath	64	NX1082
Laig Highld	91	NG8992
Laigh Highld	84	NM4687
Laigh Church Strath	73	NS4647
Laigh Fenwick Strath	73	NS4542
Laigh Glenmuir Strath	74	NS6120
Laighstonehall Strath	74	NS7054
Laindon Essex	24	TQ6789
Lair Highld	91	NH0148
Lairg Highld	96	NC5806
Laisterdyke W York	55	SE1832
Lake Devon	6	SS4321
Lake Devon	4	SX5388
Lake IOW	11	SZ5983
Lake Wilts	10	SU1239
Lakenheath Suffk	32	TL7182
Lakesend Norfk	41	TL5196
Laleston M Glam	18	SS8779
Lamarsh Essex	24	TL8835
Lamas Norfk	43	TG2423
Lambden Border	76	NT7443
Lamberhurst Kent	14	TQ6735
Lamberhurst Down Kent	14	TQ6735
Lamberton Border	77	NT9658
Lambfair Green Suffk	32	TL7154
Lambfell Moar IOM	52	SC2984
Lambley Notts	49	SK6345
Lambley Nthumb	68	NY6659
Lambourn Berks	21	SU3278
Lambourne End Essex	23	TQ4794
Lambs Green W Susx	12	TQ2136
Lamellion Cnwll	4	SX2460
Lamerton Devon	4	SX4476
Lamesley T & W	69	NZ2557
Lamington Highld	97	NH7477
Lamington Strath	75	NS9731
Lamlash Strath	72	NS0231
Lamonby Cumb	59	NY4136
Lamorick Cnwll	3	SX0364
Lamorna Cnwll	2	SW4424
Lamorran Cnwll	3	SW8741
Lampen Cnwll	3	SX1867
Lampeter Dyfed	17	SN5748
Lampeter-Velfrey Dyfed	16	SN1514
Lamphey Dyfed	16	SN0100
Lamplugh Cumb	58	NY0820
Lamport Nhants	30	SP7574
Lamyatt Somset	9	ST6535
Lanark Strath	74	NS8843
Lancaster Lancs	53	SD4761
Lanchester Dur	69	NZ1647
Lancing W Susx	12	TQ1804
Land-hallow Highld	100	ND1833
Landbeach Cambs	31	TL4765
Landcross Devon	6	SS4523
Landerberry Gramp	89	NJ7404
Landewednack Cnwll	2	SW7012
Landford Wilts	10	SU2519
Landford Wilts	10	SU2519
Landford Manor Wilts	10	SU2620
Landimore W Glam	17	SS4693
Landkey Town Devon	6	SS5930
Landore W Glam	18	SS6695
Landrake Cnwll	4	SX3760
Landscove Devon	5	SX7766
Landulph Cnwll	4	SX4262
Landywood Staffs	38	SJ9806
Lane End Bucks	22	SU8090
Lane End Cnwll	47	SX6990
Lane End Cnwll	3	SX0369
Lane End Cumb	58	SD1093
Lane End Wilts	20	ST8145
Lane Ends Derbys	39	SK2334
Lane Ends Dur	61	NZ1933
Lane Green W Mids	38	SJ8802
Lane Head Dur	61	NZ1211
Lane Head W Mids	38	SO9799
Laneham Notts	50	SK8076
Lanes Cnwll	3	SW9040
Langaller Somset	8	ST2626
Langar Notts	40	SK7234
Langbank Strath	80	NS3873
Langbar N York	55	SE0951
Langbaurgh N York	62	NZ5611
Langcliffe N York	54	SD8264
Langdale End N York	63	SE9391
Langdyke Fife	83	NO3304
Langenhoe Essex	25	TM0018
Langford Avon	19	ST4561
Langford Beds	31	TL1841
Langford Devon	7	ST0203
Langford Essex	24	TL8309
Langford Notts	50	SK8258
Langford Oxon	21	SP2402
Langford Budville Somset	8	ST1122
Langford End Beds	31	TL1653
Langham Dorset	9	ST0302
Langham Essex	25	TM0333
Langham Leics	40	SK8411
Langham Norfk	42	TG0041
Langham Suffk	32	TL9770
Langho Lancs	54	SD7034
Langholm D & G	67	NY3684
Langley Berks	22	TQ0178
Langley Essex	31	TL4334
Langley Gloucs	28	SP0128
Langley Hants	10	SU4401
Langley Herts	31	TL2122
Langley Nthumb	68	NY8361
Langley Somset	7	ST0828
Langley W Susx	11	SU8029
Langley Warwks	39	SP1965
Langley Burrell Wilts	20	ST9375
Langley Common Derbys	49	SK2938
Langley, Green Essex	24	TL8822
Langley Green Warwks	29	SP1962
Langley Marsh Somset	7	ST0729

Place	Page	Grid
Langley Moor *Dur*	61	NZ2440
Langley Park *Dur*	69	NZ2144
Langley Street *Norfk*	43	TG3601
Langleybury *Herts*	22	TL0700
Langney *E Susx*	13	TQ6302
Langold *Notts*	49	SK5886
Langore *Cnwll*	4	SX2886
Langore *Cnwll*	4	SX3086
Langport *Somset*	8	ST4226
Langrick *Lincs*	51	TF2648
Langridge *Avon*	20	ST7469
Langrigg *Cumb*	67	NY1645
Langrish *Hants*	11	SU7023
Langsett *S York*	48	SE2100
Langshaw *Border*	76	NT5139
Langside *Tays*	81	NN7913
Langstone *Gwent*	19	ST3789
Langstone *Hants*	11	SU7105
Langthorne *N York*	61	SE2491
Langthorpe *N York*	55	SE3867
Langthwaite *N York*	61	NZ0001
Langtoft *Humb*	56	TA0166
Langtoft *Lincs*	40	TF1212
Langton *Dur*	61	NZ1719
Langton *Lincs*	51	TF2368
Langton *Lincs*	51	TF3970
Langton *N York*	56	SE7967
Langton Green *Kent*	13	TQ5439
Langton Green *Kent*	13	TQ5439
Langton Herring *Dorset*	9	SY6182
Langton by Wragby *Lincs*	50	TF1476
Langtree *Devon*	6	SS4515
Langtree Week *Devon*	6	SS4705
Langwathby *Cumb*	59	NY5733
Langwell *Highld*	96	NC1703
Langwell House *Highld*	100	ND1122
Langworth *Lincs*	50	TF0676
Langworthy *Devon*	6	SX4895
Lank *Cnwll*	3	SX0975
Lanlivery *Cnwll*	3	SX0759
Lanner *Cnwll*	2	SW7139
Lanreath *Cnwll*	3	SX1857
Lansallos *Cnwll*	3	SX1751
Lanteglos *Cnwll*	3	SX0882
Lanteglos Highway *Cnwll*	3	SX1453
Lantilio-Crossenny *Gwent*	27	SO3914
Lanton *Border*	76	NT6122
Lanton *Nthumb*	77	NT9231
Lapford *Devon*	7	SS7308
Laphroaig *Strath*	70	NR3845
Lapley *Staffs*	38	SJ8713
Lapworth *Warwks*	38	SP1671
Larachbeg *Highld*	79	NM6948
Larbert *Cent*	82	NS8582
Largie *Gramp*	94	NJ6131
Largiemore *Strath*	71	NR9486
Largoward *Fife*	83	NO4607
Largs *Strath*	73	NS2059
Largybeg *Strath*	72	NS0423
Largymore *Strath*	72	NS0424
Larkfield *Kent*	14	TQ7058
Larkfield *Strath*	80	NS2376
Larkhall *Strath*	74	NS7651
Larkhill *Wilts*	20	SU1243
Larling *Norfk*	32	TL9889
Larrick *Cnwll*	4	SX3078
Larriston *Border*	67	NY5494
Lartington *Dur*	61	NZ0117
Lasham *Hants*	11	SU6742
Lask Edge *Staffs*	48	SJ9156
Lassodie *Fife*	82	NT1292
Lastingham *N York*	63	SE7290
Latchingdon and Snoreham *Essex*	24	TL8800
Latchley *Cnwll*	4	SX4173
Latebrook *Staffs*	47	SJ8453
Lathbury *Bucks*	30	SP8744
Latheron *Highld*	100	ND2033
Latheronwheel House *Highld*	100	ND1832
Lathones *Fife*	83	NO4708
Latimer *Bucks*	22	TQ0199
Latteridge *Avon*	20	ST6684
Lattiford *Somset*	9	ST6926
Latton *Wilts*	20	SU0995
Lauder *Border*	76	NT5347
Laugharne *Dyfed*	17	SN3011
Laughterton *Lincs*	50	SK8375
Laughton *E Susx*	13	TQ4913
Laughton *Leics*	39	SP6688
Laughton *Lincs*	40	TF0731
Laughton *Lincs*	49	SK8497
Laughton-en-le-Morthen *S York*	49	SK5188
Launcells *Cnwll*	6	SS2405
Launceston *Cnwll*	4	SX3384
Launton *Oxon*	29	SP6022
Laurencekirk *Gramp*	89	NO7171
Laurieston *Cent*	82	NS9179
Laurieston *D & G*	65	NX6864
Lavenden *Bucks*	30	SP9153
Lavenham *Suffk*	32	TL9149
Lavernock *S Glam*	19	ST1868
Laversdale *Cumb*	67	NY4762
Laverstock *Wilts*	10	SU1530
Laverstoke *Hants*	21	SU4948
Laverton *Gloucs*	28	SP0735
Laverton *N York*	61	SE2273
Laverton *Somset*	20	ST7753
Lavister *Clwyd*	46	SJ3758
Law *Strath*	74	NS8152
Law Hill *Strath*	74	NS8251
Lawers *Tays*	81	NN6739
Lawers *Tays*	81	NN7923
Lawford *Essex*	25	TM0831
Lawford *Somset*	18	ST1437
Lawgrove *Tays*	82	NO0926
Lawhitton *Cnwll*	4	SX3582
Lawkland *N York*	54	SD7766
Lawkland Green *N York*	54	SD7865
Lawnhead *Staffs*	38	SJ8224
Lawrence End *Herts*	30	TL1419
Lawrenny *Dyfed*	16	SN0107
Lawshall *Suffk*	32	TL8654
Laxay *W Isls*	102	NB3321
Laxdale *W Isls*	102	NB4234
Laxey *IOM*	52	SC4384
Laxfield *Suffk*	33	TM2972
Laxford Bridge *Highld*	98	NC2346
Laxo *Shet*	103	HU4463
Laxton *Humb*	56	SE7825
Laxton *Nhants*	40	SP9596
Laxton *Notts*	49	SK7266
Layer Breton *Essex*	25	TL9418
Layer Marney *Essex*	24	TL9217
Layer-de-la-Haye *Essex*	25	TL9620
Laymore *Dorset*	8	ST3804
Laysters Pole *H & W*	27	SO5563
Laytham *Humb*	56	SE7439
Laythes *Cumb*	67	NY2455
Lazonby *Cumb*	67	NY5449
Le Bigard *Guern*	101	SV0000
Le Bourg *Guern*	101	SV0000
Le Bron *Guern*	101	SV0000
Le Haquais *Jersey*	101	SV0000
Le Hocq *Jersey*	101	SV0000
Le Villocq *Guern*	101	SV0000
Lea *Derbys*	49	SK3257
Lea *H & W*	27	SO6521
Lea *Lincs*	50	SK8286
Lea *Shrops*	36	SO3589
Lea *Wilts*	20	ST9586
Lea Marston *Warwks*	39	SP2093
Leachkin *Highld*	92	NH6445
Leadburn *Loth*	75	NT2365
Leadenham *Lincs*	50	SK9452
Leadgate *Cumb*	68	NY7043
Leadgate *Dur*	69	NZ1251
Leadhills *Strath*	74	NS8815
Leafield *Oxon*	29	SP3115
Leagrave *Beds*	30	TL0523
Leahead *Ches*	47	SJ6964
Leaholm Side *N York*	63	NZ7607
Leake Common Side *Lincs*	51	TF3952
Lealt *Highld*	90	NG5060
Leamington Hastings *Warwks*	39	SP4467
Leargybreck *Strath*	70	NR5371
Leasgill *Cumb*	59	SD4984
Leasingham *Lincs*	50	TF0548
Leasingthorne *Dur*	61	NZ2530
Leatherhead *Surrey*	23	TQ1656
Leathley *N York*	55	SE2346
Leaths *D & G*	66	NX7863
Leaton *Shrops*	36	SJ4618
Leaveland *Kent*	15	TR0053
Leavenheath *Suffk*	25	TL9537
Leavening *N York*	56	SE7863
Leaves Green *Gt Lon*	23	TQ4161
Lebberston *N York*	63	TA0782
Lechampstead Thicket *Berks*	21	SU4276
Lechlade *Wilts*	21	SU2199
Leck *Lancs*	60	SD6476
Leckford *Hants*	10	SU3737
Leckfurin *Highld*	99	NC7059
Leckgruinart *Strath*	70	NR2768
Leckhampstead *Berks*	21	SU4375
Leckhampstead *Bucks*	30	SP7237
Leckhampton *Gloucs*	28	SO9419
Leckhamstead *Bucks*	30	SP7237
Leckmelm *Highld*	96	NH1790
Leconfield *Humb*	56	TA0143
Ledaig *Strath*	79	NM9037
Ledburn *Bucks*	30	SP9021
Ledbury *H & W*	28	SO7037
Ledgemoor *H & W*	27	SO4150
Ledmore Junction *Highld*	96	NC2412
Ledsham *W York*	55	SE4529
Ledston *W York*	55	SE4328
Ledwell *Oxon*	29	SP4128
Lee *Devon*	6	SS4846
Lee *Gt Lon*	23	TQ3875
Lee *Strath*	78	NM4022
Lee Brockhurst *Shrops*	37	SJ5427
Lee Chapel *Essex*	24	TQ6987
Lee Clump *Bucks*	22	SP9004
Lee Common *Bucks*	22	SP9003
Lee Green *Ches*	47	SJ6662
Lee Mill *Devon*	5	SX5855
Lee-on-the-Solent *Hants*	11	SU5600
Leebotwood *Shrops*	37	SO4798
Leece *Cumb*	53	SD2469
Leeds *Kent*	14	TQ8253
Leeds *W York*	55	SE3034
Leedstown *Cnwll*	2	SW6034
Leek Wootton *Warwks*	29	SP2968
Leeming *N York*	61	SE2989
Leeming Bar *N York*	61	SE2889
Lees *Derbys*	49	SK2637
Lees *Gt Man*	54	SD9504
Lees *Gt Man*	54	SD9504
Lees Green *Derbys*	48	SK2637
Leesthorpe *Leics*	40	SK7813
Leetown *Tays*	82	NO2121
Leftwich *Ches*	47	SJ6672
Legbourne *Lincs*	51	TF3684
Legerwood *Border*	76	NT5843
Legsby *Lincs*	50	TF1385
Leicester *Leics*	39	SK5804
Leicester Forest East *Leics*	39	SK5303
Leigh *Devon*	7	SS9115
Leigh *Dorset*	9	ST6108
Leigh *Gloucs*	28	SO8626
Leigh *H & W*	28	SO7853
Leigh *Kent*	13	TQ5446
Leigh *Mersyd*	47	SJ6599
Leigh *Surrey*	12	TQ2246
Leigh *Wilts*	20	SU0692
Leigh Beck *Essex*	24	TQ8183
Leigh Delamere *Wilts*	20	ST8879
Leigh Green *Kent*	14	TQ9033
Leigh Knoweglass *Strath*	74	NS6350
Leigh Sinton *H & W*	28	SO7750
Leigh Woods *Avon*	19	ST5572
Leigh upon Mendip *Somset*	20	ST6846
Leigh-on-Sea *Essex*	24	TQ8286
Leighterton *Gloucs*	20	ST8290
Leighton *Powys*	36	SJ2406
Leighton *Shrops*	37	SJ6105
Leighton Bromswold *Cambs*	30	TL1175
Leighton Buzzard *Beds*	30	SP9225
Leinthall Earls *H & W*	27	SO4467
Leinthall Starkes *H & W*	27	SO4369
Leintwardine *H & W*	36	SO4074
Leire *Leics*	39	SP5290
Leiston *Suffk*	33	TM4462
Leitfie *Tays*	88	NO2545
Leith *Loth*	75	NT2676
Leitholm *Border*	76	NT7944
Lelant *Cnwll*	2	SW5437
Lelley *Humb*	57	TA2032
Lempitlaw *Border*	76	NT7832
Lemreway *W Isls*	102	NB3711
Lemsford *Herts*	31	TL2212
Lenchwick *H & W*	28	SP0347
Lendalfoot *Strath*	64	NX1390
Lendrick *Cent*	81	NN5506
Lendrum Terrace *Gramp*	95	NK1141
Lenham *Kent*	14	TQ8952
Lenie *Highld*	92	NH5126
Lennel *Border*	77	NT8540
Lennoxlove *Loth*	76	NT5172
Lennoxtown *Strath*	74	NS6277
Lenton *Lincs*	40	TF0230
Lenzie *Strath*	74	NS6572
Leochel-Cushnie *Gramp*	94	NJ5210
Leominster *H & W*	27	SO4958
Leonard Stanley *Gloucs*	20	SO8003
Leorin *Strath*	70	NR3548
Lepe *Hants*	10	SZ4598
Lephin *Highld*	90	NG1749
Lephinchapel *Strath*	71	NR9690
Lephinmore *Strath*	71	NR9892
Leppington *N York*	56	SE7661
Lepton *W York*	55	SE2015
Lerags *Strath*	79	NM8324
Lerryn *Cnwll*	3	SX1457
Lerwick *Shet*	103	HU4741
Les Arquets *Guern*	101	SV0000
Les Hubits *Guern*	101	SV0000
Les Lohiers *Guern*	101	SV0000
Les Murchez *Guern*	101	SV0000
Les Nicolles *Guern*	101	SV0000
Les Quartiers *Guern*	101	SV0000
Les Quennevais *Jersey*	101	SV0000
Les Sages *Guern*	101	SV0000
Les Villets *Guern*	101	SV0000
Lesbury *Nthumb*	69	NU2312
Leslie *Fife*	83	NO2501
Leslie *Gramp*	94	NJ5924
Lesmahagow *Strath*	74	NS8139
Lesnewth *Cnwll*	4	SX1390
Lessingham *Norfk*	43	TG3928
Lessonhall *Cumb*	67	NY2249
Leswalt *D & G*	64	NX0164
Letchmore Heath *Herts*	22	TQ1597
Letchworth *Herts*	31	TL2232
Letcombe Bassett *Oxon*	21	SU3785
Letcombe Regis *Oxon*	21	SU3786
Letham *Border*	68	NT6708
Letham *Fife*	83	NO3014
Letham *Tays*	89	NO5348
Letham Grange *Tays*	89	NO6345
Lethenty *Gramp*	95	NJ8140
Letheringham *Suffk*	33	TM2757
Letheringsett *Norfk*	42	TG0639
Lett's Green *Kent*	23	TQ4558
Letterfearn *Highld*	91	NG8823
Letterfinlay Lodge Hotel *Highld*	91	NN2591
Lettermorar *Highld*	85	NM7389
Letters *Highld*	96	NH1687
Lettershaw *Strath*	74	NS8920
Letterston *Dyfed*	16	SM9429
Lettoch *Highld*	93	NJ0219
Lettoch *Highld*	93	NJ0932
Letton *H & W*	27	SO3346
Letty Green *Herts*	23	TL2810
Letwell *S York*	49	SK5587
Leuchars *Fife*	83	NO4521
Leurbost *W Isls*	102	NB3725
Levedale *Staffs*	38	SJ9016
Level's Green *Essex*	31	TL4724
Leven *Fife*	83	NO3800
Leven *Humb*	57	TA1045
Levencorroch *Strath*	72	NS0021
Levens Green *Herts*	31	TL3522
Levenshulme *Gt Man*	47	SJ8794
Levenwick *Shet*	103	HU4021
Leverburgh *W Isls*	102	NG0186
Leverington *Cambs*	41	TF4411
Leverstock Green *Herts*	22	TL0806
Leverton *Lincs*	51	TF3947
Levington *Suffk*	25	TM2339
Levisham *N York*	63	SE8390
Lew *Oxon*	29	SP3206
Lew Middleton *Nthumb*	77	NU1036
Lewannick *Cnwll*	4	SX2780
Lewdown *Devon*	4	SX4486
Lewes *E Susx*	13	TQ4110
Leweston *Dyfed*	16	SM9422
Lewisham *Gt Lon*	23	TQ3774
Lewiston *Highld*	92	NH5129
Lewknor *Oxon*	22	SU7197
Lewson Street *Kent*	15	TQ9661
Lewtrenchard *Devon*	4	SX4686
Lexworthy *Somset*	8	ST2535
Leybourne *Kent*	14	TQ6858
Leyburn *N York*	61	SE1190
Leygreen *Herts*	31	TL1624
Leyland *Lancs*	53	SD5422
Leylodge *Gramp*	95	NJ7613
Leys *Gramp*	95	NK0052
Leys *Tays*	83	NO2537
Leys of Cossans *Tays*	88	NO3849
Leysdown-on-Sea *Kent*	15	TR0370
Leysmill *Tays*	89	NO6047
Leyton *Gt Lon*	23	TQ3886
Leytonstone *Gt Lon*	23	TQ3987
Lezant *Cnwll*	4	SX3379
Lezayre *IOM*	52	SC4294
Lhanbryde *Gramp*	94	NJ2761
Lhen The *IOM*	52	NX3801
Libberton *Strath*	75	NS9843
Liberton *Loth*	75	NT2769
Lichfield *Staffs*	38	SK1109
Lickey *H & W*	38	SO9975
Lickey End *H & W*	38	SO9772
Lickfold *W Susx*	11	SU9226
Liddesdale *Highld*	79	NM7759
Liddington *Wilts*	21	SU2081
Lidgate *Suffk*	32	TL7258
Lidlington *Beds*	30	SP9839
Lienassie *Highld*	85	NG9621
Liff *Tays*	83	NO3332
Lifford *W Mids*	38	SP0580
Lifton *Devon*	4	SX3885
Liftondown *Devon*	4	SX3685
Lighthorne *Warwks*	29	SP3355
Lightwater *Surrey*	22	SU9362
Lightwood Green *Ches*	49	SK6342
Lilbourne *Nhants*	39	SP5677
Lilleshall *Shrops*	37	SJ7315
Lilley *Herts*	30	TL1226
Lilliesleaf *Border*	76	NT5325
Lillingstone Dayrell *Bucks*	30	SP7039
Lillingstone Lovell *Bucks*	30	SP7140
Lillington *Dorset*	9	ST6212
Lilstock *Somset*	19	ST1644
Limbury *Beds*	30	TL0724
Lime Street *H & W*	28	SO8130
Limefield *Gt Man*	54	SD8013
Limekilnburn *Strath*	74	NS7050
Limekilns *Fife*	82	NT0883
Limerigg *Cent*	74	NS8570
Limerstone *IOW*	10	SZ4482
Limington *Somset*	8	ST5422
Limmerhaugh *Strath*	74	NS6127
Limpenhoe *Norfk*	43	TG3903
Limpley Stoke *Wilts*	20	ST7760
Limpsfield *Surrey*	13	TQ4053
Linby *Notts*	49	SK5351
Linchmere *W Susx*	11	SU8731
Lincoln *Lincs*	50	SK9771
Lincomb *H & W*	28	SO8269
Lincombe *Devon*	5	SX7340
Lincombe *Devon*	5	SX7458
Lindal in Furness *Cumb*	58	SD2475
Lindale *Cumb*	59	SD4180
Lindean *Border*	76	NT4931
Lindfield *W Susx*	12	TQ3425
Lindford *Hants*	11	SU8036
Lindley Magna *Lincs*	50	TF1988
Lindley Green *N York*	55	SE2248
Lindores *Fife*	83	NO2617
Lindridge *H & W*	28	SO6769
Lindsell *Essex*	24	TL6427
Lindsey *Suffk*	32	TL9745
Lindsey Tye *Suffk*	32	TL9845
Linford *Hants*	10	SU1707
Lingague *IOM*	52	SC2172
Lingdale *Cleve*	62	NZ6716
Lingen *H & W*	27	SO3667
Lingfield *Surrey*	13	TQ3843
Lingfield Common *Surrey*	13	TQ3844
Lingley Green *Ches*	47	SJ5589
Lingwood *Norfk*	43	TG3608
Liniclet *W Isls*	102	NF7949
Linicro *Highld*	90	NG3967
Linkend *H & W*	28	SO8231
Linkenholt *Hants*	21	SU3658
Linkhill *Kent*	14	TQ8128
Linkinhorne *Cnwll*	4	SX3173
Linktown *Fife*	83	NT2890
Linkwood *Gramp*	94	NJ2361
Linley *Shrops*	36	SO3592
Linley Green *H & W*	28	SO6953
Linleygreen *Shrops*	37	SO6898
Linlithgow *Loth*	75	NS9977
Linnels Bridge *Nthumb*	68	NY9562
Linsidemore *Highld*	96	NH5499
Linslade *Beds*	30	SP9125
Linstead Parva *Suffk*	33	TM3377
Linstock *Cumb*	67	NY4258
Linthurst *H & W*	38	SO9972
Linthwaite *W York*	55	SE0913
Linthwaite *W York*	55	SE1014
Lintlaw *Border*	77	NT8258
Lintmill *Gramp*	94	NJ5165
Linton *Border*	76	NT7726
Linton *Cambs*	31	TL5646
Linton *Derbys*	39	SK2716
Linton *Gloucs*	28	SO7918
Linton *H & W*	28	SO6625
Linton *Kent*	14	TQ7550
Linton *N York*	55	SD9962
Linton *N York*	55	SE3846
Linton Hill *Gloucs*	28	SO6624
Linton-on-Ouse *N York*	55	SE4860
Linwood *Lincs*	50	TF1186
Linwood *Strath*	73	NS4464
Lionel *W Isls*	102	NB5263
Liphook *Hants*	11	SU8431
Liscard *Mersyd*	46	SJ2991
Liscombe *Devon*	7	SS8732
Liskeard *Cnwll*	4	SX2564
Liss *Hants*	11	SU7727
Liss Forest *Hants*	11	SU7829
Lissett *Humb*	57	TA1458
Lissington *Lincs*	50	TF1083
Lisvane *S Glam*	19	ST1983
Liswerry *Gwent*	19	ST3487
Litcham *Norfk*	42	TF8817
Litchard *M Glam*	18	SS9182
Litchborough *Nhants*	29	SP6354
Litchfield *Hants*	21	SU4653
Litherland *Mersyd*	46	SJ3397
Litlington *Cambs*	31	TL3142
Litlington *E Susx*	13	TQ5201
Little Abington *Cambs*	31	TL5349
Little Almshoe *Herts*	31	TL2025
Little Alne *Warwks*	28	SP1461
Little Amwell *Herts*	23	TL3511
Little Asby *Cumb*	60	NY6909
Little Aston *Staffs*	38	SK0900
Little Atherfield *IOW*	10	SZ4680
Little Ayton *N York*	62	NZ5610
Little Baddow *Essex*	24	TL7708
Little Badminton *Avon*	20	ST8084
Little Bampton *Cumb*	67	NY2755
Little Bardfield *Essex*	24	TL6531
Little Barford *Beds*	31	TL1756
Little Barningham *Norfk*	43	TG1333
Little Barrington *Gloucs*	29	SP2012
Little Barrow *Ches*	46	SJ4770
Little Barugh *N York*	63	SE7579
Little Bavington *Nthumb*	68	NY9978
Little Bedwyn *Wilts*	21	SU2966
Little Bentley *Essex*	25	TM1125
Little Berkhamsted *Herts*	23	TL2907
Little Billing *Nhants*	30	SP8061
Little Billington *Beds*	30	SP9322
Little Birch *H & W*	27	SO5130
Little Blakenham *Suffk*	33	TM1049
Little Blencow *Cumb*	59	NY4532
Little Bognor *W Susx*	12	TQ0020
Little Bolehill *Derbys*	49	SK2954
Little Bookham *Surrey*	22	TQ1254
Little Bourton *Oxon*	29	SP4543
Little Bradley *Suffk*	32	TL6852
Little Brampton *Shrops*	36	SO3681
Little Braxted *Essex*	24	TL8314
Little Brechin *Tays*	89	NO5862
Little Brickhill *Bucks*	30	SP9032
Little Brington *Nhants*	30	SP6663
Little Bromley *Essex*	25	TM0928
Little Budworth *Ches*	47	SJ6065
Little Burstead *Essex*	24	TQ6692
Little Bytham *Lincs*	40	TF0118
Little Carlton *Lincs*	51	TF3985
Little Casterton *Leics*	40	TF0109
Little Catwick *Humb*	57	TA1444
Little Cawthorpe *Lincs*	51	TF3583
Little Chalfont *Bucks*	22	SU9997
Little Chart *Kent*	14	TQ9446
Little Chesterford *Essex*	31	TL5141
Little Chishill *Cambs*	31	TL4237
Little Clacton *Essex*	25	TM1618
Little Clanfield *Oxon*	21	SP2701
Little Clifton *Cumb*	58	NY0528
Little Comberton *H & W*	28	SO9643
Little Common *E Susx*	14	TQ7108
Little Comp *Kent*	14	TQ6357
Little Compton *Warwks*	29	SP2530
Little Cornard *Suffk*	32	TL9039
Little Cowarne *H & W*	27	SO6051
Little Coxwell *Oxon*	21	SU2893
Little Crakehall *N York*	61	SE2490
Little Cransley *Nhants*	30	SP8376
Little Creaton *Nhants*	30	SP7171
Little Cressingham *Norfk*	42	TF8700
Little Crosby *Mersyd*	46	SD3201
Little Cubley *Derbys*	48	SK1537
Little Dalby *Leics*	40	SK7714
Little Dens *Gramp*	95	NK0643
Little Dewchurch *H & W*	27	SO5231
Little Ditton *Cambs*	32	TL6658
Little Driffield *Humb*	56	TA0058
Little Dunham *Norfk*	42	TF8612
Little Dunkeld *Tays*	88	NO0342
Little Dunmow *Essex*	24	TL6521
Little Durnford *Wilts*	10	SU1334
Little Easton *Essex*	24	TL6023
Little Eaton *Derbys*	49	SK3641
Little Ellingham *Norfk*	42	TM0099
Little Elm *Somset*	20	ST7246
Little Eversden *Cambs*	31	TL3753
Little Faringdon *S York*	21	SP2201
Little Fencote *N York*	61	SE2793
Little Fenton *N York*	55	SE5135
Little Fransham *Norfk*	42	TF9011
Little Gaddesden *Herts*	22	SP9913
Little Glemham *Suffk*	33	TM3458
Little Gorsley *H & W*	28	SO6824
Little Gransden *Cambs*	31	TL2755
Little Green *Somset*	20	ST7248
Little Grimsby *Lincs*	51	TF3291
Little Hadham *Herts*	31	TL4322
Little Hale *Lincs*	51	TF1441
Little Hallam *Derbys*	49	SK4640
Little Hanford *Dorset*	9	ST8311
Little Harrowden *Nhants*	30	SP8771
Little Haseley *Oxon*	21	SP6400
Little Hatfield *Humb*	57	TA1743
Little Haven *Dyfed*	16	SM8513
Little Hay *Staffs*	38	SK1202
Little Haywood *Staffs*	38	SK0021
Little Heath *Berks*	22	SU6537
Little Heath *W Mids*	39	SP3482
Little Hereford *H & W*	27	SO5568
Little Horkesley *Essex*	25	TL9632
Little Hormead *Herts*	31	TL4028
Little Horsted *E Susx*	13	TQ4718
Little Horton *W York*	55	SE1531
Little Horwood *Bucks*	30	SP7930
Little Houghton *Nhants*	30	SP8059
Little Houghton *S York*	55	SE4205
Little Hucklow *Derbys*	48	SK1678
Little Hutton *N York*	62	SE4576
Little Irchester *Nhants*	30	SP9066
Little Keyford *Somset*	20	ST7746
Little Kimble *Bucks*	22	SP8207
Little Kineton *Warwks*	29	SP3350
Little Kingshill *Bucks*	22	SU8999
Little Knox *D & G*	66	NX8060
Little Langdale *Cumb*	58	NY3103
Little Langford *Wilts*	10	SU0436
Little Lashbrook *Devon*	6	SS4007
Little Laver *Essex*	23	TL5409
Little Leigh *Ches*	47	SJ6175
Little Leighs *Essex*	24	TL7117
Little Lever *Gt Man*	47	SD7507
Little Linford *Bucks*	30	SP8434
Little Load *Somset*	8	ST4624
Little London *E Susx*	13	TQ5720
Little London *Essex*	31	TL4729
Little London *Essex*	24	TL6835
Little London *Hants*	21	SU3749
Little London *Hants*	10	SU6259
Little London *Lincs*	51	TF3375
Little London *Norfk*	43	TF5620
Little London *Powys*	36	SO0489
Little Longstone *Derbys*	48	SK1871
Little Malvern *H & W*	28	SO7740
Little Maplestead *Essex*	24	TL8234
Little Marcle *H & W*	28	SO6736
Little Marlow *Bucks*	22	SU8787
Little Massingham *Norfk*	42	TF7924
Little Melton *Norfk*	43	TG1607
Little Mill *Gwent*	19	SO3203
Little Milton *Oxon*	21	SP6100
Little Missenden *Bucks*	22	SU9298
Little Mongham *Kent*	15	TR3351
Little Musgrave *Cumb*	60	NY7613
Little Ness *Shrops*	36	SJ4019
Little Neston *Ches*	46	SJ3076
Little Newcastle *Dyfed*	16	SM9829
Little Newsham *Dur*	61	NZ1217
Little Norton *Somset*	8	ST4815
Little Norton *Staffs*	38	SK0208
Little Oakley *Essex*	25	TM2129
Little Oakley *Nhants*	40	SP8985
Little Offley *Herts*	30	TL1228
Little Onn *Staffs*	38	SJ8315
Little Orton *Cumb*	67	NY3555
Little Oxendon *Nhants*	40	SP7184
Little Packington *Warwks*	39	SP2184
Little Paxton *Cambs*	31	TL1862
Little Petherick *Cnwll*	3	SW9172
Little Plumstead *Norfk*	43	TG3112
Little Ponton *Lincs*	40	SK9232
Little Preston *Nhants*	29	SP5854
Little Preston *W York*	55	SE3830
Little Ribston *N York*	55	SE3853
Little Rissington *Gloucs*	29	SP1819
Little Rollright *Oxon*	29	SP2930
Little Rowsley *Derbys*	48	SK2566
Little Ryburgh *Norfk*	42	TF9628
Little Ryton *Shrops*	37	SJ4803
Little Salkeld *Cumb*	59	NY5636
Little Sampford *Essex*	24	TL6533
Little Saughall *Ches*	46	SJ3769
Little Saxham *Suffk*	32	TL8063
Little Scatwell *Highld*	92	NH3856
Little Shelford *Cambs*	31	TL4551
Little Silver *Devon*	7	SS8601
Little Singleton *Lancs*	53	SD3739

Place	Sheet	Grid
Little Skipwith N York	56	SE6538
Little Smeaton N York	55	SE6217
Little Snoring Norfk	42	TF9532
Little Sodbury Avon	20	ST7583
Little Somborne Hants	10	SU3832
Little Somerford Wilts	20	ST9684
Little Soudley Shrops	37	SJ7128
Little Stainton Dur	62	NZ3420
Little Staughton Beds	30	TL1062
Little Steeping Lincs	51	TF4362
Little Stonham Suffk	33	TM1160
Little Stretton Leics	39	SK6600
Little Stretton Shrops	36	SO4492
Little Strickland Cumb	59	NY5619
Little Stukeley Cambs	31	TL2175
Little Sugnall Staffs	37	SJ8031
Little Tew Oxon	29	SP3828
Little Tey Essex	24	TL8923
Little Thetford Cambs	31	TL5376
Little Thirkleby N York	62	SE4778
Little Thorpe Dur	62	NZ4242
Little Thurlow Green Suffk	32	TL6851
Little Thurrock Essex	24	TQ6277
Little Torrington Devon	6	SS4916
Little Totham Essex	24	TL8912
Little Town Lancs	54	SD6635
Little Urswick Cumb	67	NY2673
Little Wakering Essex	25	TQ9388
Little Walden Essex	31	TL5541
Little Waldingfield Suffk	32	TL9245
Little Walsingham Norfk	42	TF9336
Little Waltham Essex	24	TL7013
Little Washbourne Gloucs	28	SO9833
Little Weighton Humb	56	SE9833
Little Weldon Nhants	40	SP9289
Little Wenham Suffk	32	TL8960
Little Wenham Suffk	32	TM0039
Little Wenlock Shrops	37	SJ6407
Little Weston Somset	8	ST6125
Little Whitefield IOW	11	SZ5989
Little Wilbraham Cambs	31	TL5458
Little Witcombe Gloucs	28	SO9115
Little Witley H & W	28	SO7864
Little Wittenham Oxon	21	SU5693
Little Wolford Warwks	29	SP2635
Little Woodcote Surrey	23	TQ2861
Little Wratting Suffk	32	TL6847
Little Wymington Beds	30	SP9565
Little Wymondley Herts	31	TL2127
Little Wyrley Staffs	38	SK0105
Little Yeldham Essex	32	TL7839
Littlebeck N York	63	NZ8704
Littleborough Notts	50	SK8282
Littlebourne Kent	15	TR2057
Littlebredy Dorset	9	SY5888
Littlebury Essex	31	TL5139
Littlebury Green Essex	31	TL4938
Littlecott Wilts	20	SU1451
Littledean Gloucs	28	SO6713
Littledown Hants	21	SU3558
Littleferry Highld	97	NH8095
Littleham Devon	6	SS4323
Littleham Devon	5	SY0281
Littlehampton W Susx	12	TQ0202
Littlehempston Devon	5	SX8162
Littlemill Gramp	88	NO3295
Littlemill Highld	93	NH9150
Littlemill Strath	73	NS4515
Littlemore Oxon	21	SP5302
Littleover Derbys	39	SK3234
Littleport Cambs	41	TL5686
Littlestone-on-Sea Kent	15	TR0824
Littlethorpe Leics	39	SP5496
Littlethorpe N York	55	SE3268
Littleton Avon	19	ST5564
Littleton Ches	46	SJ4466
Littleton Hants	10	SU4532
Littleton Somset	8	ST4830
Littleton Surrey	22	TQ0668
Littleton Drew Wilts	20	ST8380
Littleton Pannell Wilts	20	ST9954
Littleton-on-Severn Avon	19	ST5990
Littletown Dur	69	NZ3343
Littlewick Green Berks	22	SU8379
Littlewindsor Dorset	8	ST4303
Littleworth H & W	28	SO8850
Littleworth Oxon	21	SU3197
Littleworth Staffs	38	SJ9323
Littleworth Staffs	38	SK0112
Litley Green Essex	24	TL6917
Litton Derbys	48	SK1675
Litton N York	54	SD9074
Litton Somset	19	ST5954
Litton Cheney Dorset	8	SY5490
Liverpool Mersyd	46	SJ3490
Liverton Cleve	63	NZ7115
Liverton Devon	5	SX8075
Liverton Street Kent	14	TQ8749
Livingston Loth	75	NT0668
Livingston Village Loth	75	NT0366
Lixton Devon	5	SX6950
Lizard Cnwll	2	SW7012
Llaingoch Gwynd	44	SH2282
Llanaelhaearn Gwynd	44	SH3844
Llanafan Dyfed	35	SN6872
Llanafan-fechan Powys	26	SN9650
Llanallgo Gwynd	44	SH5085
Llanarmon Dyffryn Ceiriog Clwyd	36	SJ1532
Llanarmon-yn-Ial Clwyd	46	SJ1956
Llanarth Dyfed	34	SN4257
Llanarth Gwent	27	SO3710
Llanarthney Dyfed	17	SN5320
Llanasa Clwyd	46	SJ1081
Llanbabo Gwynd	44	SH3786
Llanbadarn Fawr Dyfed	34	SN6080
Llanbadarn Fynydd Powys	36	SO0977
Llanbadoc Gwent	19	ST3799
Llanbeder Gwent	19	ST3890
Llanbedr Gwynd	44	SH5826
Llanbedr Powys	27	SO2320
Llanbedr Powys	27	SO1346
Llanbedr-Dyffryn-Clwyd Clwyd	46	SJ1459
Llanbedrgoch Gwynd	44	SH5180
Llanbedrog Gwynd	44	SH3231
Llanberis Gwynd	44	SH5760
Llanbethery S Glam	18	ST0369
Llanbister Powys	36	SO1073
Llanblethian S Glam	18	SS9873
Llanboidy Dyfed	17	SN2123
Llanbradach M Glam	18	ST1490
Llancadle S Glam	18	ST0368
Llancarfan S Glam	18	ST0570
Llancloudy H & W	27	SO4920
Llandaff S Glam	19	ST1578
Llandanwg Gwynd	44	SH5728
Llanddaniel Fab Gwynd	44	SH4970
Llanddarog Dyfed	17	SN5016
Llanddeiniol Dyfed	34	SN5572
Llanddeiniolen Gwynd	44	SH5465
Llandderfel Gwynd	45	SH9837
Llanddeusant Gwynd	44	SH3485
Llanddewi W Glam	17	SS4685
Llanddewi Brefi Dyfed	26	SN6655
Llanddewi Rhydderch Gwent	27	SO3513
Llanddewi Velfrey Dyfed	16	SN1416
Llanddewi Ystradenni Powys	26	SO1068
Llanddoget Gwynd	45	SH8063
Llanddona Gwynd	44	SH5779
Llanddowror Dyfed	17	SN2514
Llanddrew Powys	26	SO0530
Llanddulas Clwyd	45	SH9078
Llanddyfnan Gwynd	44	SH5078
Llandefaelogtre-graig Powys	26	SO1229
Llandefalle Powys	26	SO1035
Llandegai Gwynd	44	SH5971
Llandegfan Gwynd	44	SH5674
Llandegfan Gwynd	44	SH5674
Llandegla Clwyd	46	SJ1952
Llandegley Powys	26	SO1463
Llandegveth Gwent	19	ST3395
Llandegwning Gwynd	44	SH2630
Llandeilo Dyfed	17	SN6322
Llandeilo Graban Powys	26	SO0944
Llandeloy Dyfed	16	SM8526
Llandenny Gwent	27	SO4104
Llandenny Walks Gwent	19	SO4003
Llandevaud Gwent	19	ST4090
Llandevenny Gwent	19	ST4186
Llandinam Powys	35	SO0288
Llandissilio Dyfed	16	SN1221
Llandogo Gwent	19	SO5203
Llandough S Glam	18	SS9972
Llandough S Glam	19	ST1673
Llandovery Dyfed	26	SN7634
Llandow S Glam	18	SS9473
Llandre Gwynd	35	SN6286
Llandre Dyfed	26	SN6741
Llandre Isaf Dyfed	16	SN1328
Llandrillo Dyfed	16	SJ0337
Llandrillo-yn-Rhos Clwyd	45	SH8380
Llandrindod Wells Powys	26	SO0561
Llandrinio Powys	36	SJ2817
Llandudno Gwynd	45	SH7882
Llandudno Junction Gwynd	45	SH7977
Llandudwen Gwynd	44	SH2736
Llandulas Powys	26	SN8841
Llandwrog Gwynd	44	SH4556
Llandybie Dyfed	17	SN6215
Llandyfaelog Dyfed	17	SN4111
Llandyfriog Dyfed	17	SN3341
Llandygwydd Dyfed	17	SN2443
Llandyssil Powys	36	SO1995
Llandysul Dyfed	17	SN4140
Llanedeyrn S Glam	19	ST2182
Llanegryn Gwynd	34	SH5905
Llanegryn Gwynd	34	SH6005
Llanegwad Dyfed	17	SN5121
Llaneilian Gwynd	44	SH4692
Llanelian-yn-Rhos Clwyd	45	SH8676
Llanelidan Clwyd	46	SJ1150
Llanelieu Powys	27	SO1834
Llanelli Dyfed	17	SN5000
Llanelltyd Gwynd	35	SH7119
Llanelwedd Powys	26	SO0451
Llanenddwyn Gwynd	44	SH5823
Llanengan Gwynd	44	SH2926
Llanerch Powys	36	SO3094
Llanerchymedd Gwynd	44	SH4184
Llanerfyl Powys	36	SJ0309
Llanfachraeth Gwynd	44	SH3182
Llanfachreth Gwynd	35	SH7522
Llanfaelog Gwynd	44	SH3373
Llanfaelrhys Gwynd	44	SH2227
Llanfaenor Gwent	27	SO4217
Llanfaethlu Gwynd	44	SH3186
Llanfair Gwynd	44	SH5729
Llanfair H & W	27	SO2444
Llanfair Caereinion Powys	36	SJ1006
Llanfair Clydogau Dyfed	17	SN6251
Llanfair Dyffryn Clwyd Clwyd	46	SJ1355
Llanfair Kilgeddin Gwent	27	SO3407
Llanfair P G Gwynd	44	SH5371
Llanfair Talhaiarn Clwyd	45	SH9269
Llanfair Waterdine Shrops	36	SO2376
Llanfair-is-gaer Gwynd	44	SH5267
Llanfair-y-Cwmmwd Gwynd	44	SH4466
Llanfair-yn-Neubwll Gwynd	44	SH3077
Llanfairfechan Gwynd	45	SH6874
Llanfairynghornwy Gwynd	44	SH3290
Llanfallteg Dyfed	17	SN1520
Llanfallteg West Dyfed	16	SN1419
Llanfaredd M Glam	26	SO0651
Llanfarian Dyfed	34	SN5977
Llanfechain Powys	36	SJ1820
Llanfechelli Gwynd	44	SH3691
Llanfendigaid Gwynd	34	SH5605
Llanferres Clwyd	46	SJ1960
Llanfflewyn Gwynd	44	SH3689
Llanfihangel Glyn Myfyr Clwyd	45	SH9849
Llanfihangel Nant Bran Powys	26	SN9434
Llanfihangel Rhydithon Powys	27	SO1566
Llanfihangel Rogiet Gwent	19	ST4487
Llanfihangel ar-Arth Dyfed	17	SN4539
Llanfihangel yn Nhowyn Gwynd	44	SH3277
Llanfihangel-nant-Melan Powys	27	SO1858
Llanfihangel-uwch-Gwili Dyfed	17	SN4923
Llanfihangel-y-Creuddyn Dyfed	35	SN6675
Llanfihangel-y-pennant Gwynd	44	SH5245
Llanfihangel-y-traethau Gwynd	44	SH5935
Llanfihangel-yng-Ngwynfa Powys	36	SJ0816
Llanfilo Powys	26	SO1132
Llanfoist Gwent	27	SO2813
Llanfor Gwynd	45	SH9336
Llanfrechfa Gwent	19	ST3293
Llanfrynach Powys	26	SO0725
Llanfwrog Clwyd	46	SJ1157
Llanfwrog Gwynd	44	SH3083
Llanfyllin Powys	36	SJ1419
Llanfynydd Clwyd	46	SJ2756
Llanfynydd Dyfed	17	SN5527
Llanfyrnach Dyfed	17	SN2231
Llangadfan Powys	35	SJ0111
Llangadog Dyfed	26	SN7028
Llangadwaladr Clwyd	46	SH3869
Llangaffo Gwynd	44	SH4468
Llangammarch Wells Powys	26	SN9347
Llangan S Glam	18	SS9577
Llangarron H & W	27	SO5220
Llangathen Dyfed	17	SN5822
Llangattock Powys	26	SO2117
Llangattock Lingoed Gwent	27	SO3620
Llangedwyn Clwyd	36	SJ1824
Llangefni Gwynd	44	SH4675
Llangeinor M Glam	18	SS9187
Llangeinwen Gwynd	44	SH4465
Llangeitho Dyfed	35	SN6259
Llangeler Dyfed	17	SN3739
Llangelynin Gwynd	34	SH5707
Llangendeirne Dyfed	17	SN4514
Llangennech Dyfed	17	SN5601
Llangenny Powys	27	SO2418
Llangernyw Clwyd	45	SH8767
Llangian Gwynd	44	SH2928
Llangloffan Dyfed	16	SM9032
Llanglydwen Dyfed	17	SN1827
Llangoed Gwynd	44	SH6079
Llangoedmor Dyfed	17	SN1945
Llangollen Clwyd	36	SJ2141
Llangolman Dyfed	16	SN1127
Llangorse Powys	26	SO1327
Llangower Gwynd	45	SH9032
Llangranog Dyfed	34	SN3154
Llangristolus Gwynd	44	SH4373
Llangrove H & W	27	SO5219
Llangunllo Powys	36	SO2171
Llangunnor Dyfed	17	SN4320
Llangurig Powys	35	SN9080
Llangwm Clwyd	45	SH9644
Llangwm Gwent	19	ST4299
Llangwm-isaf Gwent	19	SO4300
Llangwnnadl Clwyd	46	SJ1266
Llangwyryfon Dyfed	34	SN5970
Llangybi Dyfed	17	SN6053
Llangybi Gwent	19	ST3797
Llangybi Gwynd	44	SH4240
Llangynhafal Clwyd	46	SJ1263
Llangynidr Powys	27	SO1519
Llangynin Dyfed	17	SN2519
Llangynog Dyfed	17	SN3314
Llangynog Powys	35	SO0145
Llangynog Powys	36	SJ0526
Llangynwyd M Glam	18	SS8588
Llangynwyd M Glam	18	SS8988
Llanhamlach Powys	26	SO0926
Llanharan M Glam	18	ST0083
Llanharry M Glam	18	ST0080
Llanhennock Gwent	19	ST3592
Llanhilleth Gwent	19	SO2100
Llanidloes Powys	35	SN9584
Llaniestyn Gwynd	44	SH2633
Llanigon Powys	27	SO2139
Llanilar Dyfed	35	SN6275
Llanilid M Glam	18	SS9781
Llanina Dyfed	34	SN4059
Llanishen Gwent	19	SO4703
Llanishen S Glam	19	ST1781
Llanllechid Gwynd	45	SH6268
Llanllowell Gwent	19	ST3998
Llanllugan Powys	36	SJ0502
Llanllwch Dyfed	17	SN3818
Llanllwchaiarn Powys	36	SO1292
Llanllwni Dyfed	17	SN4741
Llanllyfni Gwynd	44	SH4651
Llanmadoc W Glam	17	SS4493
Llanmaes S Glam	18	SS9869
Llanmartin Gwent	19	ST3989
Llanmerewig Powys	36	SO1593
Llanmihangel S Glam	18	SS9872
Llanmiloe Dyfed	17	SN2508
Llanmorlais W Glam	17	SS5294
Llannefydd Clwyd	45	SH9870
Llannon Dyfed	17	SN5308
Llannor Gwynd	44	SH3537
Llanon Dyfed	34	SN5166
Llanover Gwent	27	SO3109
Llanpumsaint Dyfed	17	SN4229
Llanrhaeadr Clwyd	46	SJ0763
Llanrhaeadr-ym-Mochnant Clwyd	36	SJ1226
Llanrhidian W Glam	17	SS4992
Llanrhos Gwynd	45	SH7880
Llanrhychwyn Gwynd	45	SH7761
Llanrhyddlad Gwynd	44	SH3389
Llanrhystud Dyfed	34	SN5369
Llanrian Dyfed	16	SM8131
Llanrothal H & W	27	SO4618
Llanrothal H & W	27	SO4718
Llanrug Gwynd	44	SH5363
Llanrumney S Glam	19	ST2280
Llanrwst Gwynd	45	SH7961
Llansadurnen Dyfed	17	SN2810
Llansadwrn Dyfed	26	SN6931
Llansadwrn Gwynd	44	SH5575
Llansamlet W Glam	18	SS6897
Llansannan Clwyd	45	SH9365
Llansantffraed Powys	26	SO1223
Llansantffraed-Cwmdeuddwr Powys	35	SN9667
Llansantffraed-in-Elvel Powys	26	SO0954
Llansantffraid Clwyd	34	SN5167
Llansantffraid Glan Conwy Gwynd	45	SH8075
Llansantffraid-ym-Mechain Powys	36	SJ2220
Llansawel Dyfed	17	SN6136
Llansilin Clwyd	36	SJ2128
Llansoy Gwent	19	SO4402
Llanspyddid Powys	26	SO0128
Llanstadwell Dyfed	16	SM9505
Llanstephan Dyfed	17	SN3511
Llantarnam Gwent	19	ST3093
Llanteg Dyfed	17	SN1810
Llanthewy Skirrid Gwent	27	SO3416
Llanthony Gwent	27	SO2827
Llantilio Pertholey Gwent	27	SO3116
Llantrisant Gwent	19	ST3997
Llantrisant Gwynd	44	SH3683
Llantrisant M Glam	18	ST0483
Llantrithyd S Glam	18	ST0472
Llantwit Fardre M Glam	18	ST0886
Llantwit Major S Glam	18	SS9668
Llanuwchllyn Gwynd	45	SH8730
Llanvaches Gwent	19	ST4391
Llanvair Discoed Gwent	19	ST4492
Llanvapley Gwent	27	SO3614
Llanvetherine Gwent	27	SO3617
Llanvihangel Crucorney Gwent	27	SO3220
Llanwddyn Powys	35	SJ0219
Llanwenog Dyfed	17	SN4945
Llanwinio Dyfed	17	SN2626
Llanwnda Dyfed	16	SM9339
Llanwnda Gwynd	44	SH4758
Llanwnnen Dyfed	17	SN5347
Llanwnog Powys	35	SO0293
Llanwrda Dyfed	26	SN7131
Llanwrin Powys	35	SH7803
Llanwrthwl Powys	26	SN9763
Llanwrtyd Wells Powys	26	SN8846
Llanwyddelan Powys	36	SJ0801
Llanyblodwel Shrops	36	SJ2423
Llanybri Dyfed	17	SN3312
Llanybydder Dyfed	17	SN5244
Llanycefn Dyfed	16	SN0923
Llanychaer Bridge Dyfed	16	SM9835
Llanymawddwy Gwynd	35	SH9019
Llanymynech Shrops	36	SJ2620
Llanynghenedl Gwynd	44	SH3181
Llanynis Powys	26	SN9950
Llanynys Clwyd	46	SJ1062
Llanyre Powys	26	SO0462
Llanystumdwy Gwynd	44	SH4738
Llanywern Powys	26	SO1028
Llawhaden Dyfed	16	SN0717
Llawryglyn Powys	35	SN9291
Llay Clwyd	46	SJ3355
Llechcynfarwy Gwynd	44	SH3881
Llechryd Dyfed	17	SN2243
Llechryd M Glam	26	SO1009
Lledrod Dyfed	35	SN6470
Llidiart-y-parc Clwyd	46	SJ1243
Llithfaen Gwynd	44	SH3542
Llowes Powys	27	SO1941
Llwydcoed M Glam	26	SN9904
Llwydiarth Powys	36	SJ0315
Llwyncelyn Dyfed	34	SN4459
Llwyndafydd Dyfed	34	SN3755
Llwynderw Powys	36	SJ2004
Llwyngwril Gwynd	34	SH5909
Llwynmawr Clwyd	36	SJ2237
Llwynypia M Glam	18	SS9993
Llyn-y-pandy Clwyd	46	SJ2065
Llynclys Shrops	36	SJ2823
Llysfaen Gwynd	45	SH4178
Llys-y-fran Dyfed	16	SN0424
Llysfaen Clwyd	45	SH8977
Llyswen Dyfed	34	SN4561
Llyswen Powys	26	SO1337
Llysworney S Glam	18	SS9674
Llywel Powys	26	SN8730
Loan Cent	75	NS9675
Loanhead Loth	75	NT2865
Loaningfoot D & G	66	NX9656
Loans Strath	73	NS3431
Lobb Devon	6	SS4637
Lobhillcross Devon	4	SX4686
Loceport W Isls	102	NF8563
Loch Katrine Pier Cent	81	NN4907
Loch Loyal Lodge Highld	99	NC6146
Loch Maree Hotel Highld	91	NG9668
Loch Skipport W Isls	102	NF8238
Lochailort Highld	85	NM7682
Lochans D & G	64	NX0656
Lochassynt Lodge Highld	96	NC1727
Lochavich Strath	80	NM9415
Lochawe Strath	80	NN1227
Lochboisdale W Isls	102	NF7820
Lochbuie Strath	79	NM6125
Lochcarron Highld	85	NG8939
Lochdochart House Cent	81	NN4327
Lochdrum Highld	96	NH2585
Lochearnhead Cent	81	NN5823
Lochee Tays	83	NO3731
Locheilside Station Highld	85	NM9978
Lochend Highld	92	NH5937
Locherben D & G	66	NX9797
Lochfoot D & G	66	NX8973
Lochgair Strath	71	NR9290
Lochgarthside Highld	92	NH5219
Lochgelly Fife	82	NT1893
Lochgilphead Strath	71	NR8688
Lochgoilhead Strath	80	NN2001
Lochieheads Fife	83	NO2513
Lochill Gramp	94	NJ2964
Lochindorb Lodge Highld	93	NH9635
Lochinver Highld	98	NC0922
Lochlane Tays	82	NN8320
Lochluichart Highld	92	NH3363
Lochmaben D & G	66	NY0882
Lochmaddy W Isls	102	NF9169
Lochore Fife	82	NT1896
Lochranza Strath	72	NR9350
Lochside Gramp	89	NO7364
Lochside Highld	93	NH8152
Lochslin Highld	97	NH8481
Lochton Strath	64	NX2659
Lochty Fife	83	NO5208
Lochty Tays	89	NO5362
Lochuisge Highld	79	NM7956
Lochwinnoch Strath	73	NS3558
Lochwood D & G	66	NY0896
Lochwood Strath	74	NS6966
Lockengate Cnwll	3	SO5361
Lockerbie D & G	67	NY1381
Lockeridge Wilts	20	SU1467
Lockerley Hants	10	SU2925
Lockerley Hants	10	SU3026
Locking Avon	19	ST3659
Lockington Humb	56	SE9947
Lockleywood Shrops	37	SJ6928
Lockmaddy W Isls	102	NF9168
Locksbottom Gt Lon	23	TQ4265
Lockton N York	63	SE8490
Loddington Leics	40	SK7902
Loddington Nhants	30	SP8178
Loddiswell Devon	5	SX7148
Loddon Norfk	43	TM3698
Lode Cambs	31	TL5362
Lode Heath W Mids	38	SP1580
Loders Dorset	8	SY4994
Lodsworth W Susx	11	SU9223
Lofthouse N York	61	SE1073
Lofthouse W York	55	SE3325
Loftus Cleve	63	NZ7118
Logan Strath	74	NS5820
Loganlea Loth	75	NS9762
Loggerheads Staffs	37	SJ7336
Logie Fife	83	NO4020
Logie Gramp	93	NJ0150
Logie Tays	89	NO6963
Logie Coldstone Gramp	88	NJ4304
Logie Pert Tays	89	NO6664
Logierait Tays	88	NN9752
Login Dyfed	17	SN1623
Lolworth Cambs	31	TL3664
Lonbain Highld	91	NG6852
Londesborough Humb	56	SE8645
London Gt Lon	23	TQ2980
London Apprentice Cnwll	3	SX0050
London Colney Herts	23	TL1803
London End Nhants	30	SP8565
Londonderry N York	61	SE3087
Londonthorpe Lincs	40	SK9537
Londubh Highld	91	NG8680
Long Ashton Avon	19	ST5470
Long Bank H & W	37	SO7974
Long Bennington Lincs	50	SK8344
Long Bredy Dorset	8	SY5690
Long Buckby Nhants	29	SP6367
Long Cause Devon	5	SX7461
Long Clawson Leics	40	SK7222
Long Compton Staffs	38	SJ8522
Long Compton Warwks	29	SP2832
Long Crendon Bucks	22	SP6908
Long Crichel Dorset	9	ST9710
Long Ditton Surrey	23	TQ1766
Long Drax N York	56	SE6828
Long Duckmanton Derbys	49	SK4471
Long Eaton Derbys	39	SK4933
Long Green Ches	46	SJ4170
Long Green H & W	28	SO8433
Long Hedges Lincs	51	TF3546
Long Itchington Warwks	29	SP4165
Long Lane Shrops	37	SJ6315
Long Lawford Warwks	39	SP4776
Long Load Somset	8	ST4623
Long Marston Herts	30	SP8915
Long Marston N York	55	SE5051
Long Marston Warwks	28	SP1548
Long Marton Cumb	60	NY6624
Long Meadowend Shrops	36	SO4081
Long Melford Suffk	32	TL8645
Long Newton Gloucs	20	ST9092
Long Newton Loth	76	NT5164
Long Preston N York	54	SD8358
Long Riston Humb	57	TA1242
Long Sight Gt Man	54	SD9207
Long Stratton Norfk	33	TM1992
Long Street Bucks	30	SP7947
Long Sutton Hants	22	SU7347
Long Sutton Lincs	41	TF4322
Long Sutton Somset	8	ST4625
Long Thurlow Suffk	32	TM0168
Long Waste Shrops	37	SJ6115
Long Whatton Leics	39	SK4723
Long Wittenham Oxon	21	SU5493
Longbenton T & W	69	NZ2768
Longborough Gloucs	29	SP1729
Longbridge W Mids	38	SP0177
Longbridgemuir D & G	66	NY0669
Longburgh Cumb	67	NY3159
Longburton Dorset	9	ST6412
Longcliffe Derbys	48	SK2255
Longcombe Devon	5	SX8359
Longcot Oxon	21	SU2790
Longden Shrops	36	SJ4406
Longden Common Shrops	36	SJ4404
Longdon H & W	28	SO8336
Longdon Green Staffs	38	SK0813
Longdon upon Tern Shrops	37	SJ6116
Longdown Devon	5	SX8691
Longdowns Cnwll	2	SW7434
Longfield Kent	14	TQ6069
Longford Derbys	48	SK2137
Longford Gloucs	28	SO8320
Longford Kent	23	TQ5156
Longford Shrops	37	SJ6434
Longford Shrops	37	SJ7218
Longforgan Tays	83	NO2929
Longformacus Border	76	NT6957
Longframlington Nthumb	69	NU1201
Longham Dorset	10	SZ0697
Longham Norfk	42	TF9415
Longhill Gramp	95	NJ9953
Longhirst Nthumb	69	NZ2289
Longhope Gloucs	28	SO6819
Longhorsley Nthumb	69	NZ1494
Longhoughton Nthumb	77	NU2415
Longlane Derbys	48	SK2538
Longlevens Gloucs	28	SO8519
Longleys Tays	88	NO2643
Longmanhill Gramp	95	NJ7462
Longmoor Camp Hants	11	SU7931
Longmorn Gramp	94	NJ2358
Longnewton Border	76	NT5822
Longney Gloucs	28	SO7612
Longniddry Loth	76	NT4476
Longnor Shrops	37	SJ4800
Longnor Staffs	48	SK0865
Longparish Hants	21	SU4344
Longpark Cumb	67	NY4261
Longridge Lancs	54	SD6037
Longridge Loth	75	NS9562
Longriggend Strath	74	NS8270
Longrock Cnwll	2	SW4931
Longshaw Common Gt Man	46	SD5202
Longside Gramp	95	NK0347
Longsleddale Cumb	59	NY4902
Longstanton Cambs	31	TL3966
Longstock Hants	10	SU3836
Longstone Wells Devon	7	SS7634
Longstowe Cambs	31	TL3054
Longstreet Wilts	20	SU1451
Longthorpe Cambs	40	TL1698
Longthwaite Cumb	59	NY4323
Longton Lancs	54	SD4825
Longton Staffs	48	SJ9143
Longtown Cumb	67	NY3768
Longtown H & W	27	SO3129
Longueville Jersey	101	SV0000
Longville in the Dale Shrops	37	SO5494
Longwick Bucks	22	SP7805
Longwitton Nthumb	68	NZ0788
Longwood D & G	65	NX7061
Longwood House Hants	11	SU5424
Longworth Oxon	21	SU3899
Longyester Loth	76	NT5465
Lonmay Gramp	95	NK0159
Lonmore Highld	90	NG2546
Looe Cnwll	4	SX2553
Loose Kent	14	TQ7552
Loosley Row Bucks	22	SP8100
Lootcherbrae Gramp	94	NJ6053
Lopcombe Corner Wilts	10	SU2435
Lopen Somset	8	ST4214
Lornty Tays	88	NO1746
Loscoe Derbys	49	SK4247
Loscombe Dorset	8	SY4998
Losonford Warwks	29	SP1867
Lossiemouth Gramp	94	NJ2370
Lostock Gralam Ches	47	SJ6973
Lostock Green Ches	47	SJ6973
Lostwithiel Cnwll	3	SX1059

Place	Page	Grid Ref
Lothbeg Highld	97	NC9410
Lothersdale N York	54	SD9646
Lothmore Highld	97	NC9611
Loudwater Bucks	22	SU8990
Loughborough Leics	39	SK5319
Loughton Bucks	30	SP8337
Loughton Essex	23	TQ4296
Loughton Shrops	37	SO6183
Lound Lincs	40	TF0618
Lound Suffk	43	TM5099
Lounston Devon	5	SX7874
Lount Leics	39	SK3819
Louth Lincs	51	TF3287
Lovaton Devon	4	SX5466
Love Clough Lancs	54	SD8127
Lovedean Hants	11	SU6812
Loversall S York	49	SK5798
Loveston Dyfed	16	SN0808
Lovington Somset	9	ST5931
Low Ackworth W York	55	SE4517
Low Barbeth D & G	64	NX0166
Low Bell End N York	63	SE7196
Low Borrowbridge Cumb	59	NY6101
Low Bradfield S York	48	SK2691
Low Bradley N York	54	SE0048
Low Brunton Nthumb	68	NY9269
Low Burnham Humb	50	SE7702
Low Catton Humb	56	SE7053
Low Crosby Cumb	67	NY4459
Low Dinsdale Dur	62	NZ3411
Low Eggborough N York	55	SE5523
Low Ellington N York	61	SE1983
Low Fremington N York	61	SE0398
Low Gartachorrans Cent	81	NS4685
Low Gate Nthumb	68	NY9064
Low Grantley N York	55	SE2370
Low Ham Somset	8	ST4329
Low Harrogate N York	55	SE2855
Low Hawsker N York	63	NZ9207
Low Hesket Cumb	67	NY4646
Low Hutton N York	56	SE7567
Low Leighton Derbys	48	SK0085
Low Lorton Cumb	58	NY1525
Low Marnham Notts	50	SK8069
Low Mill N York	62	SE6795
Low Moor Lancs	54	SD7341
Low Moor W York	55	SE1629
Low Moorsley T & W	69	NZ3346
Low Mowthorpe N York	56	SE9066
Low Row Cumb	67	NY1945
Low Row Cumb	67	NY5863
Low Row N York	61	SD9897
Low Salchrie D & G	64	NX0365
Low Salter Lancs	54	SD6063
Low Santon Humb	56	SE9312
Low Street Essex	24	TQ6677
Low Tharston Norfk	43	TM1895
Low Valleyfield Fife	82	NT0086
Low Wood Cumb	67	NY3483
Low Worsall N York	62	NZ3909
Low Wray Cumb	59	NY3731
Lowbands H & W	28	SO7803
Lowdham Notts	49	SK6646
Lower Aisholt Somset	8	ST2035
Lower Apperley Gloucs	28	SO8527
Lower Assendon Oxon	22	SU7484
Lower Bartle Lancs	53	SD4933
Lower Beeding W Susx	12	TQ2227
Lower Benefield Nhants	40	SP9888
Lower Bentham N York	54	SD6469
Lower Bentley H & W	28	SO9865
Lower Boddington Nhants	29	SP4851
Lower Boscaswell Cnwll	22	SW3834
Lower Bourne Surrey	22	SU8444
Lower Brailes Warwks	29	SP3139
Lower Braodheath H & W	28	SO8057
Lower Breakish Highld	85	NG6723
Lower Bullingham H & W	27	SO5038
Lower Bullingham H & W	27	SO5137
Lower Burgate Hants	10	SU1515
Lower Burrowton Devon	5	SY0096
Lower Caldecote Beds	31	TL1746
Lower Cam Gloucs	20	SO7400
Lower Catesby Nhants	29	SP5159
Lower Chapel Powys	26	SO0235
Lower Chicksgrove Wilts	9	ST9730
Lower Chute Wilts	21	SU3153
Lower Clapton Gt Lon	23	TQ3486
Lower Clent H & W	38	SO9279
Lower Crossings Derbys	48	SK0480
Lower Cumberworth W York	55	SE2209
Lower Dalveen D & G	66	NS8807
Lower Dean Beds	30	TL0569
Lower Denby W York	55	SE2307
Lower Diabaig Highld	91	NG7960
Lower Dicker E Susx	13	TQ5511
Lower Down Shrops	36	SO3384
Lower Dunsforth N York	55	SE4464
Lower Egleton H & W	27	SO6245
Lower End Bucks	30	SP9237
Lower Exbury Hants	10	SZ4298
Lower Eythorne Kent	15	TR2749
Lower Failand Avon	19	ST5173
Lower Farringdon Hants	11	SU7035
Lower Feltham Gt Lon	22	TQ0972
Lower Fittleworth W Susx	12	TQ0118
Lower Froyle Hants	22	SU7644
Lower Gabwell Devon	5	SX9169
Lower Gledfield Highld	96	NH6590
Lower Godney Somset	19	ST4742
Lower Gravenhurst Beds	30	TL1034
Lower Green Gt Man	47	SJ7099
Lower Green Herts	31	TL4232
Lower Green Kent	13	TQ5640
Lower Green Kent	13	TQ6341
Lower Green Suffk	32	TL7465
Lower Grove Common H & W	27	SO5525
Lower Hacheston Suffk	33	TM3157
Lower Halliford Surrey	22	TQ0867
Lower Halstow Kent	14	TQ8567
Lower Hamworthy Dorset	9	SY9990
Lower Hardres Kent	15	TR1453
Lower Hartwell Bucks	30	SP7912
Lower Hawthwaite Cumb	67	NY2189
Lower Hergest H & W	27	SO2755
Lower Heyford Oxon	29	SP4824
Lower Holbrook Suffk	25	TM1835
Lower Irlam Gt Man	47	SJ7193
Lower Kilburn Derbys	49	SK3745
Lower Kilkeyan Strath	70	NR2743
Lower Kinnerton Ches	46	SJ3462
Lower Largo Fife	83	NO4102
Lower Leigh Staffs	38	SK0136
Lower Lovacott Devon	6	SS5326
Lower Loxhore Devon	6	SS6137
Lower Lydbrook Gloucs	27	SO5916
Lower Lye H & W	27	SO4067
Lower Machen Gwent	19	ST2288
Lower Mannington Dorset	10	SU0705
Lower Marston Somset	20	ST7643
Lower Meend Gloucs	27	SO5504
Lower Middleton Cheney Nhants	29	SP5041
Lower Milton Somset	19	ST5446
Lower Moor W Mids	28	SO9747
Lower Morton Avon	19	ST6492
Lower Nazeing Essex	23	TL3906
Lower Norton Warwks	29	SP2364
Lower Nyland Dorset	9	ST7421
Lower Penarth S Glam	19	ST1869
Lower Penn Staffs	38	SO8796
Lower Pond Street Essex	31	TL4637
Lower Quinton Warwks	29	SP1847
Lower Raydon Suffk	25	TM0338
Lower Roadwater Somset	7	ST0139
Lower Shelton Beds	30	SP9942
Lower Shiplake Oxon	22	SU7679
Lower Shuckburgh Warwks	29	SP4862
Lower Slaughter Gloucs	28	SP1622
Lower Smerlay Strath	72	NR7522
Lower Standen Kent	15	TR2340
Lower Stanton St. Quintin Wilts	20	ST9180
Lower Stoke Kent	14	TQ8375
Lower Stone Gloucs	20	ST6794
Lower Stow Bedon Norfk	42	TL9694
Lower Street Dorset	9	SY8399
Lower Street E Susx	14	TQ7012
Lower Street Norfk	43	TG2635
Lower Street Suffk	32	TL7852
Lower Street Suffk	33	TM1052
Lower Sundon Beds	30	TL0526
Lower Swanwick Hants	10	SU4909
Lower Swell Gloucs	29	SP1725
Lower Tean Staffs	48	SK0138
Lower Town Devon	5	SX7172
Lower Town Dyfed	16	SM9637
Lower Tysoe Warwks	29	SP3445
Lower Ufford Suffk	33	TM2952
Lower Upcott Devon	5	SX8880
Lower Upham Hants	11	SU5219
Lower Vexford Somset	8	ST1135
Lower Westmancote H & W	28	SO9337
Lower Whatley Somset	20	ST7347
Lower Whitley Ches	47	SJ6179
Lower Wick Gloucs	20	ST7196
Lower Wield Hants	21	SU6340
Lower Willingdon E Susx	13	TQ5803
Lower Winchendon Bucks	30	SP7312
Lower Woodford Wilts	10	SU1334
Lower Wraxall Dorset	8	ST5700
Lowertown Devon	4	SX4584
Lowesby Leics	40	SK7207
Lowestoft Suffk	43	TM5493
Loweswater Cumb	58	NY1420
Lowfield Heath W Susx	12	TQ2740
Lowgill Cumb	60	SD6297
Lowgill Cumb	54	SD2985
Lowick Nhants	40	SP9881
Lowick Nthumb	77	NU0139
Lowick Bridge Cumb	67	NY2886
Lowick Green Cumb	67	NY3085
Lowtherton D & G	67	NY2566
Lowthorpe Humb	57	TA0860
Loxbeare Devon	7	SS9116
Loxhill Surrey	12	TQ0038
Loxhore Devon	6	SS6138
Loxhore Cott Devon	6	SS6138
Loxley Warwks	29	SP2552
Loxton Avon	19	ST3755
Loxwood W Susx	12	TQ0331
Lubcroy Highld	96	NC0502
Lubenham Nhants	40	SP7087
Lucas Green Surrey	22	SU9460
Luccombe Somset	7	SS9144
Luccombe Village IOW	11	SZ5880
Lucker Nthumb	77	NU1530
Luckett Cnwll	4	SX3873
Lucking Street Essex	24	TL8134
Luckington Wilts	20	ST8383
Lucklawhill Fife	83	NO4221
Luckwell Bridge Somset	7	SS9038
Lucton H & W	27	SO4364
Ludag W Isls	102	NF7714
Ludborough Lincs	51	TF2995
Ludbrook Devon	5	SX6654
Ludchurch Dyfed	16	SN1411
Luddenden W York	55	SE0426
Luddenden Foot W York	55	SE0325
Luddenham Court Kent	15	TQ9962
Luddesdown Kent	14	TQ6766
Luddington Humb	56	SE8216
Luddington Warwks	28	SP1652
Luddington in the Brook Nhants	40	TL1083
Ludford Lincs	51	TF1989
Ludford Shrops	37	SO5174
Ludgershall Bucks	29	SP6517
Ludgershall Wilts	21	SU2650
Ludgershall Wilts	21	SU2650
Ludgvan Cnwll	2	SW5033
Ludham Norfk	43	TG3818
Ludlow Shrops	37	SO5175
Ludney Somset	8	ST3812
Ludwell Wilts	9	ST9122
Ludworth Dur	62	NZ3641
Luffenhall Herts	31	TL2928
Luffincott Devon	6	SX3394
Lufflands Devon	6	SS3209
Luffness Loth	83	NT4780
Lugar Strath	74	NS5821
Luggate Burn Loth	76	NT6074
Luggiebank Strath	74	NS7672
Lugton Strath	73	NS4152
Lugwardine H & W	27	SO5540
Luib Highld	84	NG5627
Lulham H & W	27	SO4141
Lullington Derbys	39	SK2513
Lullington Somset	20	ST7851
Lulsgate Bottom Avon	19	ST5165
Lulsley H & W	28	SO7455
Lumb Lancs	54	SD8324
Lumb W York	55	SE0321
Lumbutts W York	55	SD9528
Lumby N York	55	SE4830
Lumloch Strath	74	NS6370
Lumphanan Gramp	89	NJ5804
Lumphinnans Fife	82	NT1692
Lumsden Gramp	94	NJ4722
Lunan Tays	89	NO6851
Lunanhead Tays	89	NO4752
Luncarty Tays	82	NO0929
Lund Humb	56	SE9647
Lund N York	56	SE6532
Lundie Cent	81	NN7304
Lundie Tays	83	NO2836
Lundin Links Fife	83	NO4002
Lunna Shet	103	HU4869
Lunsford Kent	14	TQ6959
Lunsford's Cross E Susx	14	TQ7210
Lunt Mersyd	46	SD3402
Luppitt Devon	8	ST1606
Lupridge Devon	5	SX7153
Lupset W York	55	SE3119
Lupton Cumb	59	SD5581
Lurgashall W Susx	11	SU9327
Lurley Devon	7	SS9214
Lusby Lincs	51	TF3367
Luscombe Devon	5	SX7957
Luskentyre W Isls	102	NG0699
Luss Strath	80	NS3692
Lusta Highld	90	NG2756
Lustleigh Devon	5	SX7881
Luston H & W	27	SO4863
Luthermuir Gramp	89	NO6568
Luthrie Fife	83	NO3319
Lutley W Mids	38	SO9483
Luton Beds	30	TL0921
Luton Devon	5	SX9076
Luton Devon	7	ST0802
Luton Kent	14	TQ7766
Lutterworth Leics	39	SP5484
Lutton Devon	5	SX5959
Lutton Lincs	41	TF4325
Lutton Nhants	40	TL1187
Lutworthy Devon	7	SS7615
Luxborough Somset	7	SS9738
Luxulyan Cnwll	3	SX0458
Luzley Gt Man	48	SD9601
Lybster Highld	100	ND2435
Lydbury North Shrops	36	SO3486
Lydd Kent	15	TR0420
Lydden Kent	15	TR2645
Lydden Kent	15	TR3567
Lyddington Leics	40	SP8797
Lyde Green Hants	22	SU7057
Lydeard St. Lawrence Somset	8	ST1232
Lydford Devon	4	SX5084
Lydford on Fosse Somset	8	ST5630
Lydgate Gt Man	54	SD9526
Lydgate W York	55	SD9225
Lydham Shrops	36	SO3391
Lydiard Millicent Wilts	20	SU0986
Lydiard Tregoze Wilts	20	SU1085
Lydiate Mersyd	46	SD3604
Lydiate Ash H & W	38	SO9775
Lydlinch Dorset	9	ST7413
Lydney Gloucs	19	SO6303
Lydstep Dyfed	16	SS0898
Lye W Mids	38	SO9284
Lye Green E Susx	13	TQ5034
Lye Green Warwks	29	SP1965
Lye's Green Wilts	20	ST8246
Lyford Oxon	21	SU3994
Lymbridge Green Kent	15	TR1244
Lyme Border	75	NT2041
Lyme Regis Dorset	8	SY3492
Lymington Hants	10	SZ3295
Lyminster W Susx	12	TQ0204
Lymm Ches	47	SJ6887
Lympne Kent	15	TR1135
Lympstone Devon	5	SX9984
Lynch Green Norfk	43	TG1505
Lynchat Highld	87	NH7801
Lyndhurst Hants	10	SU2907
Lyndon Leics	40	SK9004
Lyne Surrey	22	TQ0166
Lyne Down H & W	27	SO6530
Lyne Hill Staffs	38	SJ9212
Lyne of Gorthleck Highld	92	NH5420
Lyne of Skene Gramp	95	NJ7610
Lyneal Shrops	36	SJ4433
Lynegar Highld	100	ND2256
Lyneham Oxon	29	SP2720
Lyneham Wilts	20	SU0278
Lyness Ork	103	ND3094
Lyng Norfk	42	TG0717
Lyng Somset	8	ST3328
Lynmouth Devon	18	SS7249
Lynn Staffs	46	SO0804
Lynn of Shenval Gramp	94	NJ2129
Lynsted Kent	14	TQ9460
Lynton Devon	18	SS7149
Lyon's Gate Dorset	9	ST6605
Lyonshall H & W	27	SO3355
Lytchett Matravers Dorset	9	SY9495
Lytham Lancs	53	SD3627
Lytham St. Anne's Lancs	53	SD3427
Lythe H & W	100	ND2762
Lythe N York	63	NZ8413
Lythmore Highld	100	ND0566

M

Place	Page	Grid Ref
Maaruig W Isls	90	NB1906
Mabe Burnthouse Cnwll	2	SW7634
Mabie D & G	66	NX9570
Mablethorpe Lincs	51	TF5085
Macclesfield Ches	48	SJ9173
Macclesfield Forest Ches	48	SJ9772
Macduff Gramp	95	NJ7064
Macharioch Strath	72	NR7309
Machen M Glam	19	ST2189
Machire Strath	70	NR2064
Machrihanish Strath	72	NR6320
Machrins Strath	70	NR3693
Machynlleth Powys	35	SH7400
Machynys Dyfed	17	SS5198
Mackworth Derbys	49	SK3137
Macmerry Loth	76	NT4372
Maddaford Devon	6	SX5495
Madderty Tays	82	NN9522
Maddington Wilts	20	SU0643
Maddiston Cent	75	NS9476
Madeley Staffs	47	SJ7744
Madingley Cambs	31	TL3960
Madley H & W	27	SO4238
Madresfield H & W	28	SO8047
Madron Cnwll	2	SW4532
Maen-y-groes Dyfed	34	SN3858
Maenclochog Dyfed	16	SN0827
Maendy S Glam	18	ST0076
Maentwrog Gwynd	45	SH6640
Maer Staffs	37	SJ7938
Maerdy Clwyd	35	SJ0144
Maerdy M Glam	18	SS9798
Maes-glas Gwent	19	ST2986
Maes-y-cwmmer M Glam	19	ST1794
Maesbrook Shrops	36	SJ3021
Maesbury Marsh Shrops	36	SJ3125
Maesllyn Dyfed	17	SN3644
Maesmynis Powys	26	SO0147
Maesteg M Glam	18	SS8590
Maesybont Dyfed	17	SN5616
Maesycwmmer M Glam	19	ST1594
Magdalen Laver Essex	23	TL5108
Maggieknockater Gramp	94	NJ3145
Maggots End Essex	31	TL4727
Magham Down E Susx	13	TQ6011
Maghull Mersyd	46	SD3703
Magor Gwent	19	ST4287
Mahaar D & G	64	NX1058
Maiden Bradley Wilts	20	ST7938
Maiden Head Avon	19	ST5666
Maiden Newton Dorset	9	SY5997
Maiden Wells Dyfed	16	SR9799
Maidencombe Devon	5	SX9268
Maidenhayne Devon	8	SY2795
Maidenhead Berks	22	SU8980
Maidens Strath	73	NS2107
Maidenwell Lincs	51	TF3179
Maidford Nhants	29	SP6052
Maids Moreton Bucks	30	SP7035
Maidstone Kent	14	TQ7555
Maidwell Nhants	30	SP7476
Maindee Gwent	19	ST3288
Mains of Allardice Gramp	89	NO8375
Mains of Bainakettle Gramp	89	NO6274
Mains of Cairnbarrow Gramp	94	NJ4640
Mains of Dalvey Highld	93	NJ1031
Mains of Dillavaird Gramp	89	NO7482
Mains of Haulkerton Gramp	89	NO7172
Mains of Throsk Cent	82	NS8690
Mainsforth Dur	62	NZ3131
Mainsriddle D & G	66	NX9557
Mainstone Shrops	36	SO2787
Maisemore Gloucs	28	SO8121
Makeney Derbys	49	SK3544
Malborough Devon	5	SX7039
Malden Surrey	23	TQ2175
Maldon Essex	24	TL8507
Malham N York	54	SD9062
Maligar Highld	85	NM6796
Mallaig Highld	85	NM6897
Mallaigvaig Highld	85	NM6897
Malleny Mills Loth	75	NT1665
Malltraeth Gwynd	44	SH4069
Mallwyd Gwynd	35	SH8612
Malmesbury Wilts	20	ST9387
Malmsmead Somset	18	SS7947
Malpas Ches	46	SJ4847
Malpas Cnwll	2	SW8442
Malpas Gwent	19	ST3090
Malshanger House Hants	21	SU5652
Maltby Cleve	62	NZ4613
Maltby Lincs	51	TF3083
Maltby S York	49	SK5392
Maltby le Marsh Lincs	51	TF4681
Malting Green Essex	25	TL9720
Maltman's Hill Kent	14	TQ9043
Malton N York	56	SE7871
Malvern Link H & W	28	SO7847
Malvern Wells H & W	28	SO7742
Mamble H & W	37	SO6971
Mamhilad Gwent	19	SO3003
Manaccan Cnwll	2	SW7625
Manafon Powys	36	SJ1102
Manaton Devon	5	SX7581
Manby Lincs	51	TF3986
Mancetter Warwks	39	SP3296
Manchester Gt Man	47	SJ8497
Mandally Highld	86	NH2900
Manea Cambs	41	TL4789
Maneight Strath	73	NS5409
Maney W Mids	39	SP1295
Manfield N York	61	NZ2213
Mangersta W Isls	102	NB0131
Mangotsfield Avon	20	ST6676
Mangrove End Herts	31	TL1223
Manish W Isls	102	NA9513
Manish W Isls	90	NG1089
Mankinholes W York	54	SD9623
Manley Ches	46	SJ5071
Manmoel Gwent	19	SO1803
Manning's Heath W Susx	12	TQ2028
Manningford Bohune Wilts	20	SU1457
Manningford Bruce Wilts	20	SU1359
Manningham W York	55	SE1435
Mannington Dorset	10	SU0605
Manningtree Essex	25	TM1032
Mannofield Gramp	89	NJ9204
Manor Park Gt Lon	23	TQ4286
Manorbier Dyfed	16	SS0697
Manorbier Newton Dyfed	16	SN0400
Manorhill Border	76	NT6632
Manorowen Dyfed	16	SM9336
Mansell Gamage H & W	27	SO3944
Mansell Lacy H & W	27	SO4245
Mansfield Strath	66	NS6214
Mansfield Notts	49	SK5361
Mansfield Woodhouse Notts	49	SK5363
Mansriggs Cumb	58	SD2880
Manston Dorset	9	ST8115
Manston W York	55	SE3634
Manswood Dorset	9	ST9708
Manthorpe Lincs	40	SK9227
Manthorpe Lincs	40	TF0715
Manton Humb	56	SE9302
Manton Leics	40	SK8704
Manuden Essex	31	TL4926
Maolachy Strath	79	NM8912
Maperton Somset	9	ST6726
Maple Cross Herts	22	TQ0382
Maplebeck Notts	50	SK7160
Mapledurham Oxon	22	SU6776
Mapledurwell Hants	22	SU6851
Maplehurst W Susx	12	TQ1824
Maplescombe Kent	14	TQ5664
Mapleton Derbys	48	SK1648
Mapperley Derbys	49	SK4343
Mapperley Park Notts	49	SK5742
Mapperton Dorset	8	SY5099
Mappleborough Green Warwks	28	SP0866
Mappleton Humb	57	TA2243
Marazanvose Cnwll	2	SW8050
Marazion Cnwll	2	SW5130
March Cambs	41	TL4297
March Strath	66	NS9914
Marcham Oxon	21	SU4596
Marchamley Shrops	37	SJ5929
Marchington Staffs	38	SK1330
Marchros Gwynd	44	SH3126
Marchwiel Clwyd	46	SJ3547
Marchwood Hants	10	SU3910
Marcross S Glam	18	SS9269
Marden H & W	27	SO5146
Marden Kent	14	TQ7444
Marden Wilts	20	SU0857
Marden Beech Kent	14	TQ7343
Marden Thorn Kent	14	TQ7643
Mardleybury Herts	31	TL2618
Mardy Gwent	27	SO3015
Mare Green Somset	8	ST3326
Mareham le Fen Lincs	51	TF2761
Mareham on the Hill Lincs	51	TF2867
Marehay Derbys	49	SK3948
Marehill W Susx	12	TQ0618
Maresfield E Susx	13	TQ4624
Marfleet Humb	57	TA1329
Marford Clwyd	46	SJ3635
Margam W Glam	18	SS7887
Margaret Marsh Dorset	9	ST8218
Margaretting Essex	24	TL6701
Margaretting Tye Essex	24	TL6801
Margate Kent	15	TR3571
Marganaglish Strath	72	NS0322
Margrove Park Cleve	62	NZ6515
Marham Norfk	42	TF7110
Marhamchurch Cnwll	6	SS2203
Marholm Cambs	40	TF1402
Mariansleigh Devon	7	SS7422
Marine Town Kent	14	TQ9274
Marishader Highld	90	NG4963
Maristow Devon	4	SX4764
Marjoriebanks D & G	66	NY0883
Mark D & G	64	NX1158
Mark Somset	19	ST3747
Mark Cross E Susx	13	TQ5010
Mark Cross E Susx	13	TQ5831
Mark's Corner IOW	10	SZ4792
Markbeech Kent	13	TQ4742
Markby Lincs	51	TF4878
Markeaton Derbys	49	SK3337
Market Bosworth Leics	39	SK4003
Market Deeping Lincs	40	TF1310
Market Drayton Shrops	37	SJ6734
Market Harborough Leics	40	SP7387
Market Lavington Wilts	20	SU0154
Market Overton Leics	40	SK8816
Market Rasen Lincs	50	TF1089
Market Stainton Lincs	51	TF2279
Market Street Norfk	43	TG2921
Market Weston Suffk	32	TL9877
Market Weighton Humb	56	SE8741
Markfield Leics	39	SK4810
Markham Gwent	19	SO1601
Markham Moor Notts	50	SK7274
Markinch Fife	83	NO2901
Markington N York	55	SE2864
Marks Tey Essex	24	TL9023
Marksbury Avon	20	ST6662
Markshall Essex	24	TL8425
Markwell Cnwll	4	SX3658
Markyate Herts	30	TL0616
Marlborough Wilts	21	SU1869
Marlbrook H & W	27	SO5054
Marlcliff Warwks	28	SP0950
Marldon Devon	5	SX8663
Marlesford Suffk	33	TM3258
Marley Kent	15	TR1750
Marley Kent	15	TR3352
Marley Green Ches	47	SJ5745
Marlingford Norfk	43	TG1309
Marloes Dyfed	16	SM7908
Marlow Bucks	22	SU8486
Marlpit Hill Kent	13	TQ4447
Marnhull Dorset	9	ST7718
Marnoch Gramp	94	NJ5950
Marple Gt Man	48	SJ9588
Marple Bridge Gt Man	48	SJ9789
Marr S York	55	SE5105
Marrel Highld	97	ND0117
Marrick N York	61	SE0798
Marros Dyfed	16	SN2009
Marsden T & W	69	NZ4064
Marsden W York	55	SE0411
Marsh W York	55	SE0236
Marsh Baldon Oxon	21	SU5699
Marsh Gibbon Bucks	29	SP6422
Marsh Green Devon	5	SY0493
Marsh Green Kent	13	TQ4344
Marsh Green Staffs	47	SJ8859
Marsh Lane Derbys	49	SK4079
Marsh Street Somset	7	SS9944
Marshalswick Herts	31	TL1608
Marsham Norfk	43	TG1924
Marshborough Kent	15	TR2958
Marshbrook Shrops	36	SO4489
Marshchapel Lincs	51	TF3599
Marshfield Avon	20	ST7773
Marshfield Gwent	19	ST2582
Marshgate Cnwll	6	SX1592
Marshland St. James Norfk	41	TF5209
Marshwood Dorset	8	SY3899
Marske N York	61	NZ1000
Marske-by-the-Sea Cleve	62	NZ6322
Marston Ches	47	SJ6775
Marston H & W	27	SO3557
Marston Lincs	50	SK8943
Marston Oxon	29	SP5208
Marston Staffs	38	SJ8314
Marston Staffs	38	SJ9227
Marston Warwks	39	SP2195
Marston Wilts	20	ST9656
Marston Green W Mids	39	SP1785
Marston Magna Somset	9	ST5922
Marston Meysey Wilts	20	SU1297
Marston Montgomery Derbys	48	SK1338
Marston Moretaine Beds	30	SP9941
Marston St. Lawrence Nhants	29	SP5342

Place	County	Page	Grid
Marston Stannet *H & W*		27	SO5655
Marston Trussell *Nhants*		40	SP6985
Marston on Dove *Derbys*		39	SK2329
Marstow *H & W*		27	SO5518
Marsworth *Bucks*		30	SP9214
Marten *Wilts*		21	SU2860
Marthall *Ches*		47	SJ8075
Martham *Norfk*		43	TG4518
Martin *Hants*		10	SU0719
Martin *Kent*		15	TR3347
Martin *Lincs*		50	TF1259
Martin *Lincs*		51	TF2366
Martin Dales *Lincs*		50	TF1762
Martin Drove End *Hants*		10	SU0420
Martin Hussingtree *H & W*		28	SO8860
Martinhoe *Devon*		18	SS6648
Martinscroft *Ches*		47	SJ6589
Martinstown *Dorset*		9	SY6488
Martlesham *Suffk*		33	TM2547
Martletwy *Dyfed*		16	SN0310
Martock *Somset*		8	ST4619
Marton *Ches*		47	SJ8568
Marton *Cleve*		62	NZ5115
Marton *Humb*		57	TA1839
Marton *N York*		55	SE4162
Marton *N York*		63	SE7383
Marton *Shrops*		36	SJ2802
Marton *Warwks*		29	SP4069
Marton-le-Moor *N York*		55	SE3670
Marty Worthy *Hants*		11	SU5132
Marty's Green *Surrey*		22	TQ0857
Marwick *Ork*		103	HY2324
Marybank *Highld*		92	NH4853
Maryburgh *Highld*		92	NH5456
Maryculter *Gramp*		89	NO8599
Maryfield *Cnwll*		4	SX4256
Maryhill *Gramp*		95	NJ8245
Maryhill *Strath*		74	NS5669
Marykirk *Gramp*		89	NO6865
Marylebone *Gt Man*		47	SD5807
Marypark *Gramp*		94	NJ1938
Maryport *Cumb*		58	NY0336
Maryport *D & G*		64	NX1434
Marystow *Devon*		4	SX4383
Maryton *Tays*		89	NO6856
Marywell *Gramp*		89	NO9399
Marywell *Gramp*		89	NO6544
Marywell *Tays*		89	NO5896
Masham *N York*		61	SE2280
Masongill *N York*		60	SD6675
Mastin Moor *Derbys*		49	SK4575
Matching *Essex*		31	TL5212
Matching Green *Essex*		31	TL5311
Matching Tye *Essex*		23	TL5111
Matfen *Nthumb*		68	NZ0371
Matfield *Kent*		13	TQ6541
Mathern *Gwent*		19	ST5291
Mathon *H & W*		28	SO7345
Mathry *Dyfed*		16	SM8832
Matlaske *Norfk*		43	TG1534
Matlock *Derbys*		49	SK3060
Matlock Bank *Derbys*		49	SK3060
Matson *Gloucs*		28	SO8515
Matterdale End *Cumb*		59	NY3933
Mattersey Thorpe *Notts*		49	SK6889
Mattingley *Hants*		22	SU7357
Mattishall *Norfk*		42	TG0511
Mattishall Burgh *Norfk*		42	TG0512
Mauchline *Strath*		74	NS4927
Maud *Gramp*		95	NJ9247
Maufant *Jersey*		101	SV0000
Maufant *Jersey*		101	SV0000
Maugersbury *Gloucs*		29	SP1925
Maughold *IOM*		52	SC4991
Mauld *Highld*		92	NH4038
Maulden *Beds*		30	TL0538
Maulds Meaburn *Cumb*		60	NY6216
Maunby *N York*		62	SE3486
Maund Bryan *H & W*		27	SO5650
Maundown *Somset*		7	ST0528
Mautby *Norfk*		43	TG4812
Mavesyn Ridware *Staffs*		38	SK0816
Mavis Enderby *Lincs*		51	TF3666
Maw Green *Ches*		47	SJ7157
Mawbray *Cumb*		66	NY0846
Mawdesley *Lancs*		53	SD4914
Mawdlam *M Glam*		18	SS8081
Mawgan Porth *Cnwll*		3	SW8467
Mawla *Cnwll*		2	SW7045
Mawnan *Cnwll*		2	SW7827
Mawnan Smith *Cnwll*		2	SW7728
Maxstoke *Warwks*		39	SP2386
Maxted Street *Kent*		15	TR1244
Maxton *Border*		76	NT6130
Maxton *Kent*		15	TR3041
Maxwellheugh *Border*		76	NT7333
Maxwelltown *D & G*		66	NX9676
Maxworthy *Cnwll*		4	SX2593
May Bank *Staffs*		47	SJ8547
May's Green *Oxon*		22	SU7580
Mayals *W Glam*		17	SS6090
Maybole *Strath*		73	NS2909
Maybury *Surrey*		22	TQ0158
Mayfield *E Susx*		13	TQ5827
Mayfield *Loth*		75	NT3565
Mayfield *Staffs*		48	SK1545
Mayford *Surrey*		22	SU9956
Maymore *Strath*		80	NR9986
Maynard's Green *E Susx*		13	TQ5818
Maypole *W Mids*		38	SP0878
Maypole Green *Norfk*		43	TM4195
Maypole Green *Suffk*		32	TL9159
Meadgate *Avon*		20	ST6758
Meadle *Bucks*		22	SP8006
Meadowtown *Shrops*		36	SJ3101
Meadwell *Devon*		4	SX4081
Mealrigg *Cumb*		67	NY1345
Mealsgate *Cumb*		58	NY2141
Meanskirk *Strath*		74	NS5455
Meanwood *W York*		55	SE2837
Meare *Somset*		19	ST4541
Meare Green *Somset*		8	ST2922
Mears Ashby *Nhants*		30	SP8366
Measham *Leics*		39	SK3312
Meathop *Cumb*		59	SD4380
Meavy *Devon*		4	SX5467
Med *Avon*		20	ST7358
Medbourne *Leics*		40	SP8093
Meden Vale *Notts*		56	SE5870
Medmenham *Berks*		22	SU8084
Medomsley *Dur*		69	NZ1254
Medstead *Hants*		11	SU6537
Meer End *W Mids*		39	SP2474
Meerbrook *Staffs*		48	SJ9860
Meesden *Herts*		31	TL4322
Meeson *Shrops*		37	SJ6420
Meeth *Devon*		6	SS5408
Meeting Green *Suffk*		32	TL7455
Meeting House Hill *Norfk*		43	TG3028
Meidrim *Dyfed*		17	SN2820
Meifod *Powys*		36	SJ1513
Meigle *Tays*		88	NO2944
Meikle Carco *D & G*		66	NS7813
Meikle Earnock *Strath*		74	NS7053
Meikle Grenach *Strath*		72	NS0760
Meikle Kilmory *Strath*		72	NS0561
Meikle Obney *Tays*		82	NO0337
Meikle Wartle *Gramp*		95	NJ7231
Meikleour *Tays*		82	NO1539
Meinciau *Dyfed*		17	SN4610
Meir *Staffs*		48	SJ9342
Melbourn *Cambs*		31	TL3844
Melbourne *Humb*		56	SE7543
Melbury Abbas *Dorset*		9	ST8820
Melbury Bubb *Dorset*		9	ST5906
Melbury Osmond *Dorset*		8	ST5707
Melchbourne *Beds*		30	TL0365
Melcombe Bingham *Dorset*		9	ST7602
Meldon *Devon*		4	SX5592
Meldon *Devon*		4	SX5692
Meldon *Nthumb*		69	NZ1183
Meldreth *Cambs*		31	TL3746
Meldrum *Cent*		81	NS7199
Melfort *Strath*		79	NM8313
Melgund Castle *Tays*		89	NO5455
Meliden *Clwyd*		45	SJ0580
Melin-y-ddol *Powys*		36	SJ0907
Melin-y-wig *Clwyd*		45	SJ0448
Melkinthorpe *Cumb*		59	NY5525
Melkridge *Nthumb*		68	NY7363
Melksham *Wilts*		20	ST9063
Melldalloch *Strath*		71	NR9375
Mellguards *Cumb*		67	NY4446
Melling *Lancs*		54	SD5970
Melling *Mersyd*		46	SD3800
Mellis *Suffk*		33	TM0974
Mellon Charles *Highld*		91	NG8491
Mellon Udrigle *Highld*		91	NG8895
Mellor *Gt Man*		48	SJ9988
Mellor *Lancs*		54	SD6530
Mellor Brook *Lancs*		54	SD6431
Mells *Somset*		20	ST7249
Melmerby *Gramp*		59	NY6137
Melmerby *N York*		61	SE0785
Melmerby *N York*		62	SE3376
Melness *Highld*		99	NC5661
Melplash *Dorset*		8	SY4797
Melrose *Border*		76	NT5434
Melsetter *Ork*		103	ND2689
Melsonby *N York*		61	NZ1908
Meltham *W York*		55	SE0910
Meltham Mills *W York*		55	SE1010
Melton *Humb*		56	SE9726
Melton *Suffk*		33	TM2850
Melton Constable *Norfk*		42	TG0433
Melton Mowbray *Leics*		40	SK7518
Melton Ross *Humb*		57	TA0610
Melvaig *Highld*		91	NG7486
Melverley *Shrops*		36	SJ3316
Melverley Green *Shrops*		36	NC8784
Melvich *Highld*		99	NC8764
Membury *Devon*		8	ST2703
Memsie *Gramp*		95	NJ9762
Menai Bridge *Gwynd*		44	SH5571
Mendham *Suffk*		33	TM2783
Mendlesham *Suffk*		33	TM1065
Mendlesham Green *Suffk*		33	TM0963
Menethorpe *N York*		56	SE7667
Menheniot *Cnwll*		4	SX2862
Mennock *D & G*		66	NS8008
Menston *W York*		55	SE1743
Menstrie *Cent*		82	NS8596
Menthorpe *N York*		56	SE6934
Mentmore *Bucks*		30	SP9019
Meoble *Highld*		85	NM7987
Meole Brace *Shrops*		37	SJ4810
Meonstoke *Hants*		11	SU6119
Mepal *Cambs*		41	TL4481
Meppershall *Beds*		30	TL1336
Mere *Ches*		47	SJ7281
Mere *Wilts*		9	ST8132
Mere Brow *Lancs*		53	SD4218
Mere Green *W Mids*		38	SP1298
Mereclough *Lancs*		54	SD8730
Mereworth *Kent*		13	TQ6553
Meriden *W Mids*		39	SP2482
Merkadale *Highld*		84	NG3931
Merriott *Somset*		8	ST4412
Merrow *Surrey*		12	TQ0250
Merry Hill *Herts*		22	TQ1394
Merry Hill *W Mids*		38	SO9386
Merryhill *W Mids*		38	SO8897
Merrymeet *Cnwll*		4	SX2766
Mersham *Kent*		15	TR0540
Merstham *Surrey*		12	TQ2953
Merston *W Susx*		11	SU8903
Merstone *IOW*		11	SZ5285
Merther *Cnwll*		3	SW8644
Merthyr Cynog *Powys*		26	SN9837
Merthyr Dyfan *S Glam*		18	ST1169
Merthyr Mawr *M Glam*		18	SS8877
Merthyr Tydfil *M Glam*		26	SO0506
Merthyr Vale *M Glam*		18	ST0799
Merthyr Vale *M Glam*		18	ST0799
Merton *Devon*		6	SS5212
Merton *Gt Lon*		23	TQ2570
Merton *Norfk*		42	TL9098
Merton *Oxon*		29	SP5717
Mervinslaw *Border*		68	NT6713
Meshaw *Devon*		7	SS7519
Messing *Essex*		24	TL8919
Messingham *Humb*		56	SE8904
Metcombe *Devon*		5	SY0791
Metfield *Suffk*		33	TM2980
Metherell *Cnwll*		4	SX4069
Metheringham *Lincs*		50	TF0661
Methil *Fife*		83	NT3799
Methley *W York*		55	SE3826
Methlick *Gramp*		95	NJ8537
Methven *Tays*		82	NO0226
Methwold *Norfk*		42	TL7394
Methwold Hythe *Norfk*		42	TL7195
Mettingham *Suffk*		33	TM3690
Metton *Norfk*		43	TG1937
Mevagissey *Cnwll*		3	SX0144
Mexborough *S York*		49	SE4700
Mey *Highld*		100	ND2872
Meyllteyrn *Gwynd*		44	SH2332
Meyllteyrn *Gwynd*		44	SH2333
Meysey Hampton *Gloucs*		20	SU1199
Miavaig *W Isls*		102	NB0834
Michaelchurch *H & W*		27	SO5125
Michaelchurch Escley *H & W*		27	SO3134
Michaelston-le-Pit *S Glam*		19	ST1573
Michaelstone-y-Fedw *Gwent*		19	ST2484
Michaelstow *Cnwll*		3	SX0878
Michelcombe *Devon*		5	SX6968
Micheldever *Hants*		11	SU5139
Micheldever Station *Hants*		11	SU5143
Michelmersh *Hants*		10	SU3426
Mickfield *Suffk*		33	TM1361
Mickle Trafford *Ches*		46	SJ4469
Micklebring *S York*		49	SK5194
Mickleby *N York*		63	NZ8012
Micklefield *W York*		55	SE4432
Mickleham *Surrey*		12	TQ1753
Mickleover *Derbys*		39	SK3034
Mickleton *Dur*		61	NY9623
Mickleton *Gloucs*		28	SP1643
Mickleton *W York*		55	SE4027
Mickley *Derbys*		49	SK3379
Mickley *N York*		61	SE2576
Mickley Green *Suffk*		32	TL8457
Mickley Square *Nthumb*		68	NZ0762
Mid Ardlaw *Gramp*		95	NJ9464
Mid Beltie *Gramp*		89	NJ6200
Mid Calder *Loth*		75	NT0767
Mid Clyth *Highld*		100	ND2937
Mid Lavant *W Susx*		11	SU8508
Mid Mains *Highld*		92	NH4239
Mid Sannox *Strath*		72	NS0145
Mid Yell *Shet*		103	HU4591
Midbea *Ork*		103	HY4444
Middle Aston *Oxon*		29	SP4726
Middle Chinnock *Somset*		8	ST4713
Middle Claydon *Bucks*		30	SP7225
Middle Duntisbourne *Gloucs*		20	SO9806
Middle Handley *Derbys*		49	SK4077
Middle Kames *Strath*		71	NR9189
Middle Mayfield *Staffs*		48	SK1444
Middle Quarter *Kent*		14	TQ8937
Middle Rasen *Lincs*		50	TF0889
Middle Rocombe *Devon*		5	SX9069
Middle Stoke *Kent*		14	TQ8275
Middle Stoughton *Somset*		19	ST4248
Middle Street *Essex*		23	TL4005
Middle Street *Gloucs*		20	SO7803
Middle Town *IOS*		2	SV8808
Middle Tysoe *Warwks*		29	SP3344
Middle Wallop *Hants*		10	SU2937
Middle Wallop *Hants*		10	SU2938
Middle Winterslow *Wilts*		10	SU2432
Middle Woodford *Wilts*		10	SU1136
Middle Yard *Gloucs*		20	SO8103
Middlebie *D & G*		67	NY2176
Middlegill *D & G*		66	NT0407
Middleham *N York*		61	SE1287
Middlehope *Shrops*		37	SO4988
Middlemarsh *Dorset*		9	ST6707
Middlemore *Devon*		4	SX5073
Middlesbrough *Cleve*		62	NZ4920
Middlesceugh *Cumb*		59	NY3942
Middleshaw *Cumb*		59	SD5589
Middleshaw *D & G*		67	NY1475
Middlesmoor *N York*		61	SE0973
Middlestone *Dur*		61	NZ2531
Middlethird *Border*		76	NT6743
Middleton *Derbys*		48	SK1963
Middleton *Derbys*		49	SK2756
Middleton *Essex*		32	TL8739
Middleton *Gt Man*		47	SD8705
Middleton *H & W*		27	SO5469
Middleton *Hants*		21	SU4244
Middleton *Loth*		76	NT3758
Middleton *N York*		63	SE7885
Middleton *Nhants*		40	SP8489
Middleton *Norfk*		42	TF6616
Middleton *Nthumb*		68	NZ0584
Middleton *Nthumb*		77	NU0024
Middleton *Shrops*		37	SO5477
Middleton *Shrops*		36	SJ3012
Middleton *Strath*		78	NL9443
Middleton *Strath*		73	NS3952
Middleton *Suffk*		33	TM4267
Middleton *Tays*		82	NO1206
Middleton *W Glam*		17	SS4287
Middleton *W York*		55	SE3027
Middleton *W York*		55	SE1249
Middleton *Warwks*		38	SP1798
Middleton Cheney *Nhants*		29	SP4941
Middleton Moor *Suffk*		33	TM4167
Middleton Quernhow *N York*		62	SE3378
Middleton Scriven *Shrops*		37	SO6887
Middleton St. George *Dur*		62	NZ3412
Middleton Stoney *Oxon*		29	SP5323
Middleton one Tow *Dur*		62	NZ2512
Middleton Tyas *N York*		61	NZ2205
Middleton-in-Teesdale *Dur*		61	NY9425
Middleton-on-the-Hill *H & W*		27	SO5364
Middleton-on-the-Wolds *Humb*		56	SE9449
Middleton *Avon*		19	ST4571
Middletown *Powys*		36	SJ3012
Middlewich *Ches*		47	SJ7066
Middlewood *Cnwll*		4	SX2775
Middlewood *H & W*		27	SO2844
Middlewood Green *Suffk*		33	TM0961
Middleyard *Strath*		74	NS5132
Middlezoy *Somset*		8	ST3733
Middridge *Dur*		61	NZ2526
Midford *Avon*		20	ST7660
Midge Hall *Lancs*		53	SD5123
Midgham *Berks*		21	SU5567
Midgley *W York*		55	SE0226
Midgley *W York*		55	SE2714
Midhopestones *S York*		48	SK2399
Midhurst *W Susx*		11	SU8821
Midlem *Border*		76	NT5227
Midpark *Strath*		72	NS0259
Midsomer Norton *Avon*		20	ST6654
Midtown *Highld*		91	NG8285
Midtown *Highld*		99	NC5861
Midway *Ches*		48	SJ9282
Migvie *Gramp*		88	NJ4306
Milarrochy *Cent*		80	NS4092
Milborne Port *Somset*		9	ST6718
Milborne St. Andrew *Dorset*		9	SY8097
Milborne Wick *Somset*		9	ST6620
Milbourne *Nthumb*		69	NZ1175
Milbourne *Wilts*		20	ST9587
Milburn *Cumb*		60	NY6529
Milbury Heath *Avon*		20	ST6790
Milby *N York*		55	SE4067
Milcombe *Oxon*		29	SP4134
Milden *Suffk*		32	TL9546
Mildenhall *Suffk*		32	TL7174
Mildenhall *Wilts*		21	SU2069
Mile End *Gloucs*		27	SO5911
Mile End *Gloucs*		27	SO5911
Mile Head *Lancs*		53	SD4970
Mile Oak *E Susx*		12	TQ2407
Mile Town *Kent*		14	TQ9274
Mileham *Norfk*		42	TF9119
Milehead *Highld*		91	NH8406
Miles Hope *H & W*		27	SO5764
Miles Platting *Gt Man*		47	SJ8599
Milesmark *Fife*		82	NT0688
Milfield *Nthumb*		77	NT9333
Milford *Derbys*		49	SK3545
Milford *Staffs*		38	SJ9721
Milford *Surrey*		12	SU9442
Milford Haven *Dyfed*		16	SM9006
Milford on Sea *Hants*		10	SZ2891
Milkwall *Gloucs*		27	SO5809
Mill Bank *W York*		55	SE0321
Mill Brow *Gt Man*		48	SJ9889
Mill Common *Norfk*		43	TG3301
Mill Common *Suffk*		33	TM4082
Mill Cross *Devon*		5	SX7361
Mill End *Bucks*		22	SU7885
Mill End *Cambs*		41	TL3180
Mill End *Herts*		31	TL3332
Mill Green *Cambs*		32	TL6245
Mill Green *Essex*		24	TL6301
Mill Green *Lincs*		41	TF2223
Mill Green *Suffk*		32	TL9542
Mill Green *Suffk*		32	TL9957
Mill Green *Suffk*		33	TM1360
Mill Hill *E Susx*		13	TQ6104
Mill Hill *Gt Lon*		23	TQ2292
Mill Meece *Staffs*		38	SJ8333
Mill of Cammie *Gramp*		89	NO6993
Mill of Drummond *Tays*		82	NN8315
Mill of Grange *Gramp*		93	NJ0460
Mill of Haldane *Strath*		80	NS4083
Mill of Uras *Gramp*		89	NO8680
Millais *Jersey*		101	SV0000
Millbeck *Cumb*		58	NY2526
Millbreck *Gramp*		95	NK0044
Millbrex *Gramp*		95	NJ8144
Millbrook *Beds*		30	TL0138
Millbrook *Hants*		10	SU3813
Millbrook *Jersey*		101	SV0000
Millbrook *Jersey*		101	SV0000
Millburn *Gramp*		95	NJ7909
Millcombe *Devon*		5	SX8050
Millcorner *E Susx*		14	TQ8223
Millcraig *Highld*		93	NH6571
Milldale *Staffs*		48	SK1354
Millend *Gloucs*		27	SO5608
Miller's Dale *Derbys*		48	SK1373
Millerhill *Loth*		75	NT3269
Millers Green *Derbys*		49	SK2752
Millerston *Strath*		74	NS6467
Millhalf *H & W*		27	SO2847
Millheugh *Strath*		74	NS7450
Millholme *Cumb*		59	SD5690
Millhouse *Cumb*		59	NR9570
Millhouse Green *S York*		55	SE2203
Millhousebridge *D & G*		67	NY1085
Millhouses *S York*		49	SK3484
Millikenpark *Strath*		73	NS4162
Millington *Humb*		56	SE8351
Millness *Cumb*		59	SD5383
Millom *Cumb*		58	SD1780
Millport *Strath*		73	NS1655
Millthrop *Cumb*		60	SD6691
Milltimber *Gramp*		89	NJ8601
Milltown *D & G*		67	NY3375
Milltown *Devon*		6	SS5539
Milltown *Gramp*		94	NJ2609
Milltown *Gramp*		94	NJ3462
Milltown of Campfield *Gramp*		89	NJ6500
Milltown of Edinvillie *Gramp*		94	NJ2639
Milltown of Learney *Gramp*		89	NJ6303
Milnathort *Tays*		82	NO1204
Milngavie *Strath*		74	NS5574
Milnmark *D & G*		65	NX6582
Milnrow *Gt Man*		54	SD9212
Milnthorpe *Cumb*		59	SD4981
Milovaig *Highld*		90	NG1550
Milson *Shrops*		37	SO6472
Milstead *Kent*		14	TQ9058
Milsthorpe *Nhants*		29	SP5946
Milston *Wilts*		20	SU1645
Milton *Avon*		19	ST3462
Milton *Cambs*		31	TL4762
Milton *Cent*		81	NS4490
Milton *Cent*		81	NN5001
Milton *Cumb*		67	NY5560
Milton *D & G*		64	NX3154
Milton *D & G*		66	NX8470
Milton *Derbys*		39	SK3126
Milton *Dyfed*		16	SN0303
Milton *Gramp*		94	NJ5163
Milton *Gwent*		19	ST3688
Milton *Highld*		85	NG7134
Milton *Highld*		92	NH4930
Milton *Highld*		92	NH5030
Milton *Highld*		92	NH5749
Milton *Highld*		97	NH7674
Milton *Highld*		100	ND3451
Milton *Kent*		14	TQ6573
Milton *Notts*		49	SK7173
Milton *Oxon*		21	SU4892
Milton *Somset*		8	ST4621
Milton *Staffs*		48	SJ9050
Milton *Strath*		73	NS3468
Milton *Strath*		81	NS4274
Milton *Tays*		88	NO1357
Milton Abbas *Dorset*		9	ST8001
Milton Abbot *Devon*		4	SX4079
Milton Bridge *Fife*		75	NT2562
Milton Bryan *Beds*		30	SP9730
Milton Clevedon *Somset*		20	ST6637
Milton Combe *Devon*		4	SX4866
Milton Damerel *Devon*		6	SS3810
Milton End *Gloucs*		20	SP1401
Milton Ernest *Beds*		30	TL0156
Milton Green *Ches*		46	SJ4658
Milton Hill *Devon*		5	SX9278
Milton Hill *Oxon*		21	SU4790
Milton Keynes *Bucks*		30	SP8537
Milton Lilbourne *Wilts*		21	SU1860
Milton Malsor *Nhants*		30	SP7355
Milton Morenish *Tays*		81	NN6136
Milton Regis *Kent*		14	TQ9064
Milton of Auchinhove *Gramp*		89	NJ5503
Milton of Balgonie *Fife*		83	NO3200
Milton of Campsie *Strath*		74	NS6576
Milton of Cushnie *Gramp*		94	NJ5111
Milton of Tullich *Gramp*		88	NO3897
Milton on Stour *Dorset*		9	ST7828
Milton-under-Wychwood *Oxon*		29	SP2618
Milverton *Somset*		8	ST1226
Milverton *Warwks*		29	SP3066
Milwich *Staffs*		38	SJ9632
Minard *Strath*		71	NR9796
Minchinhampton *Gloucs*		20	SO8700
Mindrum *Nthumb*		77	NT8332
Minehead *Somset*		7	SS9746
Minera *Clwyd*		46	SJ2651
Minffordd *Gwynd*		44	SH5938
Mingarry Park *Highld*		79	NM6869
Mingary *W Isls*		102	NF7426
Miningsby *Lincs*		51	TF3264
Minions *Cnwll*		4	SX2671
Minishant *Strath*		73	NS3314
Minllyn *Gwynd*		35	SH8514
Minmore Hotel *Gramp*		94	NJ1929
Minnigaff *D & G*		64	NX4166
Minnonie *Gramp*		95	NJ7760
Minskip *N York*		55	SE3864
Minstead *Hants*		10	SU2811
Minstead *Hants*		10	SU2811
Minster *W Susx*		11	SU8520
Minster *Kent*		14	TQ9572
Minster *Kent*		15	TR3064
Minster Lovell *Oxon*		29	SP3111
Minsterley *Shrops*		36	SJ3705
Minsterworth *Gloucs*		28	SO7816
Minterne Magna *Dorset*		9	ST6504
Minting *Lincs*		50	TF1873
Mintlaw *Gramp*		95	NJ9948
Minto *Border*		76	NT5620
Minton *Shrops*		36	SO4390
Minworth *W Mids*		38	SP1692
Mirehouse *Cumb*		58	NX9715
Mireland *Highld*		100	ND3160
Mirfield *W York*		55	SE2019
Miskin *M Glam*		18	ST0481
Misson *Notts*		49	SK6895
Misterton *Leics*		39	SP5584
Misterton *Notts*		50	SK7694
Misterton *Somset*		8	ST4508
Mistley *Essex*		25	TM1231
Mitcham *Gt Lon*		23	TQ2768
Mitcham *Gt Lon*		23	TQ2768
Mitchel Troy *Gwent*		27	SO4910
Mitcheldean *Gloucs*		28	SO6618
Mitchell *Cnwll*		3	SW8654
Mitchellslacks *D & G*		66	NX9696
Mitchelltroy Common *Gwent*		27	SO4909
Mitford *Nthumb*		69	NZ1786
Mithian *Cnwll*		2	SW7450
Mixbury *Oxon*		29	SP6033
Mobberley *Ches*		47	SJ7879
Mobberley *Staffs*		48	SK0041
Moccas *H & W*		27	SO3543
Mochdre *Powys*		36	SO0788
Mochrum *D & G*		64	NX3446
Mockbeggar *Kent*		14	TQ7246
Mockerkin *Cumb*		58	NY0923
Modbury *Devon*		5	SX6852
Moddershall *Staffs*		38	SJ9236
Modsary *Gramp*		99	NC6562
Moelfre *Clwyd*		36	SJ1828
Moelfre *Gwynd*		44	SH5186
Moffat *D & G*		66	NT0805
Mogerhanger *Beds*		30	TL1439
Mogworthy *Devon*		7	SS8517
Moira *Leics*		39	SK3215
Mol-Chlach *Highld*		84	NG4513
Molash *Kent*		15	TR0251
Mold *Clwyd*		46	SJ2363
Moldgreen *W York*		55	SE1516
Molehill Green *Essex*		31	TL6624
Molescroft *Humb*		56	TA0140
Molesworth *Cambs*		30	TL0775
Molland *Devon*		7	SS8028
Mollington *Ches*		46	SJ3870
Mollington *Oxon*		29	SP4347
Mollinsburn *Strath*		74	NS7171
Monachty *Dyfed*		34	SN5062
Monachylemore *Cent*		81	NN4719
Monboddo *Gramp*		89	NO7478
Mondynes *Gramp*		89	NO7779
Monewden *Suffk*		33	TM2458
Moneydie *Tays*		82	NO0629
Moneygrow Green *Berks*		22	SU8977
Moniaive *D & G*		66	NX7791
Monifieth *Tays*		83	NO4932
Monikie *Tays*		83	NO4938
Monimail *Fife*		83	NO2914
Monk Fryston *N York*		55	SE5029
Monk Hesleden *Dur*		62	NZ4536
Monk Sherborne *Hants*		21	SU6056
Monk Soham *Suffk*		33	TM2165
Monk Street *Essex*		24	TL6128
Monk's Gate *W Susx*		12	TQ2027
Monken Hadley *Gt Lon*		23	TQ2497
Monkhide *H & W*		27	SO6144
Monkhill *Cumb*		67	NY3458
Monkhopton *Shrops*		37	SO6293
Monkland *H & W*		27	SO4557
Monkleigh *Devon*		6	SS4520
Monknash *S Glam*		18	SS9170
Monkokehampton *Devon*		6	SS5805
Monks Eleigh *Suffk*		32	TL9647
Monks Heath *Ches*		47	SJ8474
Monksilver *Somset*		7	ST0737
Monkspath *W Mids*		38	SP1516
Monksthorpe *Lincs*		51	TF4465
Monkswood *Gwent*		19	SO3402
Monkton *E Susx*		8	ST1803
Monkton *Kent*		15	TR2864
Monkton *S Glam*		18	SS9271
Monkton *Strath*		73	NS3527
Monkton *T & W*		69	NZ3463
Monkton Combe *Avon*		20	ST7762
Monkton Deverill *Wilts*		20	ST8537
Monkton Farleigh *Wilts*		20	ST8065
Monkton Heathfield *Somset*		8	ST2526
Monkton Wyld *Dorset*		8	SY3396
Monkwear-Mouth *T & W*		69	NZ4058
Monkwood *Hants*		11	SU6730
Monmore Green *W Mids*		38	SO9297
Monnington on Wye *H & W*		27	SO3743
Monreith *D & G*		64	NX3641
Mont Saint *Guern*		101	SV0000
Montacute *Somset*		8	ST4916
Montcliffe *Gt Man*		54	SD6511
Montford *Shrops*		36	SJ4114
Montford Bridge *Shrops*		36	SJ4215

Montgarrie Gramp 94 NJ5717
Montgarswood Strath 74 NS5227
Montgomery Powys 36 SO2296
Montgreenan Strath 73 NS3343
Montrave Fife 83 NO3806
Montrose Tays 89 NO7157
Monxton Hants 21 SU3144
Monyash Derbs 48 SK1566
Monybachach Strath 71 NR9058
Monymusk Gramp 95 NJ6815
Monzie Tays 82 NN8725
Moodiesburn Strath 74 NS6970
Moonzie Fife 83 NO3317
Moor Allerton W York 55 SE3038
Moor Crichel Dorset 9 ST9908
Moor End Devon 7 SS6608
Moor End N York 56 SE5938
Moor End W York 55 SE0528
Moor Green Herts 31 TL3226
Moor Head W York 55 SE1337
Moor Monkton N York 55 SE5156
Moor Row Cumb 60 NY0114
Moor Street W Mids 38 SP0083
Moor The Kent 14 TQ7529
Moorby Lincs 51 TF2964
Moorcock Inn N York 60 SD8092
Moordown Dorset 10 SZ0994
Moore Ches 47 SJ5884
Moorend Gloucs 20 SO7303
Moorhall Derbys 49 SK3174
Moorhouse Notts 50 SK7566
Moorhouse W York 55 SE4311
Moorhouse Bank Surrey 13 TQ4253
Moorlinch Somset 19 ST3936
Moorsgreen Notts 49 SK4847
Moorsholm Cleve 62 NZ6814
Moorside Dorset 9 ST7919
Moorside Gt Man 54 SD9507
Moorside Gt Man 54 SD9507
Moorswater Cnwll 4 SX2364
Moorthorpe W York 55 SE4511
Moortown Hants 10 SU1504
Moortown Lincs 50 TF0699
Morangie Highld 97 NH7683
Murar Highld 85 NM6793
Morborne Cambs 40 TL1391
Morchard Bishop Devon 7 SS7707
Morcombelake Dorset 8 SY4093
Morcott Leics 40 SK9200
Morda Shrops 36 SJ2827
Morden Dorset 9 SY9195
Morden Gt Lon 23 TQ2567
Mordiford H & W 27 SO5737
Mordon Dur 62 NZ3226
More Shrops 36 SO3491
Morebath Devon 7 SS9525
Morebattle Border 76 NT7724
Morecambe Lancs 53 SD4364
Moredon Wilts 20 SU1387
Morefield Highld 96 NH1195
Morehall Kent 15 TR2137
Moreleigh Devon 5 SX7652
Morenish Tays 81 NN6035
Moresby Parks Cumb 58 NV0019
Morestead Hants 10 SU6025
Moreton Dorset 9 SY8089
Moreton Essex 23 TL5307
Moreton H & W 27 SO5164
Moreton Mersyd 46 SJ2690
Moreton Oxon 22 SP6904
Moreton Corbet Shrops 37 SJ5523
Moreton Jeffries H & W 27 SO6048
Moreton Mill Shrops 37 SJ5823
Moreton Morrell Warwks 29 SP3155
Moreton Paddox Warwks 29 SP3054
Moreton Pinkney Nhants 29 SP5749
Moreton Say Shrops 37 SJ6234
Moreton Valence Gloucs 28 SO7609
Moreton on Lugg H & W 27 SO5045
Moreton-in-Marsh Gloucs 29 SP2032
Moretonhampstead Devon 5 SX7586
Morfa Glas W Glam 26 SN8706
Morfa Nefyn Gwynd 44 SH2840
Morgan's Vale Wilts 10 SU1921
Morham Loth 76 NT5571
Morland Cumb 59 NY6022
Morley Ches 47 SJ8282
Morley Derbys 49 SK3941
Morley W York 55 SE2627
Morley Green Ches 47 SJ8281
Morley St. Botolph Norfk 42 TM0799
Mornick Cnwll 4 SX3172
Morningside Loth 75 NT2470
Morningside Strath 74 NS8355
Morningthorpe Norfk 33 TM2192
Morpeth Nthumb 69 NZ2085
Morphie Gramp 89 NO7164
Morrey Staffs 38 SK1218
Morriston W Glam 18 SS6697
Morston Norfk 42 TG0043
Mortehoe Devon 6 SS4545
Morthen S York 49 SK4789
Mortimer Berks 21 SU6564
Mortimer West End Hants 21 SU6363
Mortimer's Cross H & W 27 SO4263
Mortlake Gt Lon 23 TQ2075
Morton Cumb 67 NY3855
Morton Derbys 49 SK4060
Morton IOW 11 SZ6086
Morton Lincs 40 TF0923
Morton Lincs 50 SK8091
Morton Norfk 43 TG1217
Morton Notts 50 SK7262
Morton Shrops 36 SJ2924
Morton Bagot Warwks 28 SP1164
Morton-on-Swale N York 62 SE3292
Morvah Cnwll 2 SW4035
Morval Cnwll 4 SX2656
Morvich Highld 85 NG9621
Morville Shrops 37 SO6794
Morwenstow Cnwll 6 SS2015
Mosborough S York 49 SK4281
Moscow Strath 73 NS4840
Moseley H & W 28 SO8159
Moseley W Mids 38 SO0398
Moseley W Mids 38 SP0783
Moss S York 56 SE5914
Moss Strath 78 NL9644
Moss Bank Mersyd 46 SJ5198
Moss Nook Gt Man 47 SJ8385
Moss-Side Highld 93 NH8554
Mossat Gramp 94 NJ4719
Mossbank Shet 103 HU4575
Mossbay Cumb 58 NX9927
Mossblown Strath 73 NS3925
Mossbrow Gt Man 47 SJ7189
Mossburnford Border 76 NT6616
Mossdale D & G 65 NX6570
Mossdale Strath 73 NS4904
Mossend Strath 74 NS7360
Mossgiel Strath 73 NS4828
Mossknowe D & G 67 NY2769
Mossy Gt Man 47 SD9702
Mosspaul Hotel Border 67 NY4099
Mosstodloch Gramp 94 NJ3259
Mossy Lea Lancs 53 SD5312
Mossyard D & G 65 NX5551
Mosterton Dorset 8 ST4505
Moston Gt Man 47 SD8701
Motcombe Dorset 9 ST8425
Mothecombe Devon 5 SX6147
Motherwell Strath 74 NS7457
Motspur Park Gt Lon 23 TQ2267
Mottingham Gt Lon 23 TQ4272
Mottistone IOW 10 SZ4083
Mottram in Longendale Gt Man 48 SJ9995
Mottram in Longendale Gt Man 48 SJ9995
Mouilpied Guern 101 SV0000
Mouldsworth Ches 46 SJ5071
Moulin Tays 87 NN9459
Moulsecoomb E Susx 12 TQ3307
Moulsford Oxon 21 SU5084
Moulsoe Bucks 30 SP9041
Moultavie Highld 92 NH6371
Moulton Ches 47 SJ6569
Moulton Lincs 41 TF3023
Moulton N York 61 NZ2303

Moulton Nhants 30 SP7866
Moulton S Glam 18 ST0770
Moulton Suffk 32 TL6964
Moulton Chapel Lincs 41 TF2918
Moulton Seas End Lincs 41 TF3227
Moulton St. Mary Norfk 43 TG3907
Mount Cnwll 3 SX1468
Mount W York 55 SE0918
Mount Ambrose Cnwll 2 SW7143
Mount Bures Essex 24 TL9032
Mount Hawke Cnwll 2 SW7147
Mount Lothian Loth 75 NT2757
Mount Pleasant Derbys 49 SK3448
Mount Pleasant E Susx 13 TQ4216
Mount Pleasant Suffk 32 TL7347
Mount Tabor W York 55 SE0527
Mountain Ash M Glam 18 ST0499
Mountain Cross Border 75 NT1547
Mountblairy Gramp 95 NJ6954
Mountfield E Susx 14 TQ7320
Mountgerald House Highld 92 NH5661
Mountjoy Cnwll 3 SW8760
Mountnessing Essex 24 TQ6297
Mounton Gwent 19 ST5193
Mountsorrel Leics 39 SK5814
Mountstuart Strath 73 NS1159
Mousehail Surrey 12 SU9441
Mouswald D & G 66 NY0672
Mowacre Hill Leics 39 SK5707
Mowhaugh Border 76 NT8120
Mowsley Leics 39 SP6489
Mowtie Gramp 89 NO8388
Moxby N York 56 SE5966
Moy Highld 86 NN4282
Moy Highld 93 NH7634
Moye Highld 86 NG8818
Moylgrove Dyfed 16 SN1144
Muasdale Strath 72 NR6840
Much Birch H & W 27 SO5030
Much Cowarne H & W 27 SO6147
Much Dewchurch H & W 27 SO4831
Much Hadham Herts 31 TL4219
Much Hoole Lancs 53 SD4723
Much Marcle H & W 27 SO6533
Much Wenlock Shrops 37 SO6299
Muchalls Gramp 89 NO9092
Muchelney Somset 8 ST4224
Muchelney Ham Somset 8 ST4323
Muchlarnick Cnwll 4 SX2156
Muckingford Essex 24 TQ6779
Muckleford Dorset 9 SY6393
Mucklestone Staffs 37 SJ7237
Muckton Lincs 51 TF3781
Mucomir Highld 86 NN1884
Mudale Highld 99 NC5335
Muddiford Devon 6 SS5638
Muddlebridge Devon 6 SS5132
Muddles Green E Susx 13 TQ5413
Mudeford Dorset 10 SZ1892
Mudford Somset 8 ST5719
Mudford Sock Somset 8 ST5519
Mudgley Somset 19 ST4445
Mugdock Cent 74 NS5577
Mugeary Highld 84 NG4438
Mugginton Derbys 49 SK2843
Muggleswick Dur 68 NZ0449
Muie Highld 97 NC6704
Muir of Fowlis Gramp 94 NJ5612
Muir of Miltonduff Gramp 94 NJ1859
Muir of Ord Highld 92 NH5250
Muir of Thorn Tays 82 NO0637
Muirden Gramp 95 NJ7054
Muirdrum Tays 83 NO6637
Muiresk Gramp 95 NJ6948
Muirhead Fife 83 NO2805
Muirhead Strath 45 NS6869
Muirhead Tays 83 NO3434
Muirhouselaw Border 76 NT6328
Muirhouses Cent 82 NT0180
Muirkirk Strath 74 NS6927
Muirmill Cent 81 NS72B3
Muirshearlich Highld 86 NN1380
Muirtack Gramp 95 NJ9937
Muirton Mains Highld 92 NH3553
Muirton of Ardblair Tays 88 NO1643
Muirtown Tays 82 NN9211
Muker N York 60 SD9098
Mulbarton Norfk 43 TG1901
Mulben Gramp 94 NJ3550
Mulfra Cnwll 2 SW4534
Mulindry Strath 70 NR3659
Mullion Cnwll 2 SW6719
Mumby Lincs 51 TF5174
Muncher's Green Herts 31 TL3126
Munderfield Row H & W 27 SO6451
Munderfield Stocks H & W 27 SO6550
Mundesley Norfk 43 TG3136
Mundford Norfk 42 TL8093
Mundham Norfk 43 TM3397
Mundon Hill Essex 24 TL8602
Munerigie Highld 86 NH2602
Mungrisdale Cumb 59 NY3630
Munlochy Highld 92 NH6453
Munnoch Strath 73 NS2548
Munsley H & W 28 SO6641
Munslow Shrops 37 SO5287
Munslow Aston Shrops 37 SO5186
Munslow Aston Shrops 37 SO5187
Murchington Devon 5 SX6888
Murcott Oxon 29 SP5815
Murkle Highld 100 ND1668
Murlaggan Highld 85 NN0192
Murroes Tays 83 NO4635
Murrow Cambs 41 TF3707
Mursley Bucks 30 SP8128
Murthill Tays 89 NO4657
Murthly Tays 82 NO1038
Murton Cumb 60 NY7221
Murton Dur 69 NZ3947
Murton N York 56 SE6452
Murton N York 56 SE6452
Murton Nthumb 77 NT9748
Musbury Devon 8 SY2794
Muston Leics 40 SK8237
Muston N York 63 TA0979
Mustow Green H & W 38 SO8774
Muswell Hill Gt Lon 23 TQ2889
Mutehill D & G 65 NX6848
Mutford Suffk 33 TM4688
Muthill Tays 82 NN8616
Mutterton Devon 8 ST0305
Muxton Shrops 37 SJ7114
Mybster Highld 100 ND1652
Myddfai Dyfed 26 SN7730
Myddle Shrops 36 SJ4623
Mydroilyn Dyfed 34 SN4585
Mylor Bridge Cnwll 2 SW8036
Mynachlog-ddu Dyfed 16 SN1430
Myndtown Shrops 36 SO3999
Mynydd Isa Clwyd 46 SJ2363
Mynydd-bach Gwent 19 ST4894
Mynydd-bach W Glam 18 SS6597
Myrebird Gramp 89 NO7398
Myredykes Border 67 NY5998
Mytchett Surrey 22 SU8855
Mytholm W York 54 SD9827
Mytholmroyd W York 55 SE0126
Myton-on-Swale N York 55 SE4466

N

Naast Highld 91 NG8283
Nab's Head Lancs 54 SD6229
Naburn N York 56 SE5945
Nackington Kent 15 TR1554
Nacton Suffk 25 TM2240
Nafferton Humb 57 TA0559
Nag's Head Gloucs 20 ST8898
Nailbridge Gloucs 27 SO6416
Nailsbourne Somset 8 ST2128
Nailsea Avon 19 ST4770

Nailstone Leics 39 SK4107
Nailsworth Gloucs 20 ST8499
Nairn Highld 93 NH8756
Nalderswood Surrey 12 TQ2345
Nannerch Clwyd 46 SJ1669
Nanpantan Leics 39 SK5017
Nanpean Cnwll 3 SW9656
Nant Peris Gwynd 44 SH6658
Nant-ddu Powys 26 SO0015
Nant-y-gollen Shrops 36 SJ2429
Nant-y-pandy Gwynd 45 SH6974
Nanternis Dyfed 34 SN3756
Nantgaredig Dyfed 17 SN4921
Nantglyn Clwyd 45 SJ0061
Nantle Gwynd 44 SH5053
Nantmel Powys 26 SO0366
Nantmor Gwynd 44 SH6046
Nantwich Ches 47 SJ6552
Nantyffyllon M Glam 18 SS8592
Nantyglo Gwent 27 SO1910
Naphill Bucks 22 SU8496
Napleton H & W 28 SO8648
Napton on the Hill Warwks 29 SP4661
Narberth Dyfed 16 SN1114
Narborough Leics 39 SP5497
Narborough Norfk 42 TF7412
Nasareth Gwynd 44 SH4749
Naseby Nhants 30 SP6978
Nash Bucks 30 SP7833
Nash Gwent 19 ST3483
Nash Shrops 37 SO6071
Nash's Green Hants 22 SU6745
Nassington Nhants 40 TL0696
Nateby Cumb 60 NY7706
Nateby Lancs 53 SD4644
Natland Cumb 59 SD5289
Naughton Suffk 32 TM0249
Naunton Gloucs 28 SP1123
Naunton H & W 28 SO8645
Naunton H & W 28 SO8739
Naunton Beauchamp H & W 28 SO9652
Navenby Lincs 50 SK9857
Navestock Essex 23 TQ5397
Navestock Side Essex 24 TQ5697
Navidale Highld 97 ND0316
Navity Highld 93 NH7864
Nawton N York 62 SE6584
Nayland Suffk 25 TL9734
Nazeing Essex 23 TL4106
Neacroft Hants 10 SZ1897
Neap Shet 103 HU5058
Near Cotton Staffs 48 SK0646
Near Sawry Cumb 59 SD3795
Nearsden Gt Lon 23 TQ2185
Neasham Dur 62 NZ3210
Neath W Glam 18 SS7597
Neatham Hants 11 SU7440
Neatishead Norfk 43 TG3421
Nebo Gwynd 44 SH4750
Nebo Gwynd 45 SH8356
Necton Norfk 42 TF8709
Nedd Highld 98 NC1331
Nedging Suffk 32 TM0048
Nedging Tye Suffk 32 TM0250
Needham Norfk 33 TM2281
Needham Market Suffk 32 TM0855
Needingworth Cambs 31 TL3472
Neen Savage Shrops 37 SO6777
Neen Sollars Shrops 37 SO6572
Neenton Shrops 37 SO6388
Nefyn Gwynd 44 SH3040
Neilston Strath 73 NS4857
Nelson Lancs 54 SD8638
Nelson M Glam 18 ST1195
Nemphlar Strath 74 NS8544
Nempnett Thrubwell Avon 19 ST5260
Nenthead Cumb 68 NY7743
Nenthorn Border 76 NT6637
Neopardy Devon 7 SX7998
Nercwys Clwyd 46 SJ2360
Nereabolls Strath 70 NR2255
Nerston Strath 74 NS6457
Nesbit Nthumb 77 NT9833
Nesfield N York 55 SE0949
Nesscliffe Shrops 36 SJ3819
Neston Ches 46 SJ2977
Neston Wilts 20 ST8667
Netchwood Shrops 37 SO6291
Nether Alderley Ches 47 SJ8476
Nether Blainslie Border 76 NT5443
Nether Broughton Notts 40 SK6925
Nether Burrow Lancs 59 SD6174
Nether Cassock D & G 67 NT2303
Nether Cerne Dorset 9 SY6698
Nether Compton Dorset 9 ST5917
Nether Crimond Gramp 95 NJ8222
Nether Dallachy Gramp 94 NJ3664
Nether Exe Devon 7 SS9300
Nether Fingland Strath 66 NS9310
Nether Handwick Tays 88 NO3641
Nether Haugh S York 49 SK4196
Nether Headon Notts 50 SK7477
Nether Heage Derbys 49 SK3650
Nether Heyford Nhants 30 SP6658
Nether Howcleveh Strath 66 NT0312
Nether Kellet Lancs 53 SD5067
Nether Kinmundy Gramp 95 NK0543
Nether Moor Derbys 49 SK3866
Nether Newton Cumb 59 SD4082
Nether Poppleton N York 56 SE5654
Nether Row Cumb 58 NY3238
Nether Silton N York 62 SE4592
Nether Skyberry Shrops 36 SO2273
Nether Stowey Somset 19 ST1939
Nether Wallop Hants 10 SU3036
Nether Wasdale Cumb 58 NY1204
Nether Wellwood Strath 74 NS6526
Nether Westcote Oxon 29 SP2220
Nether Whitacre Warwks 39 SP2392
Nether Whitecleuch Strath 74 NS8319
Netheravon Wilts 20 SU1448
Netherbrae Gramp 95 NJ7959
Netherburn Strath 74 NS7947
Netherbury Dorset 8 SY4799
Nethercleuch D & G 67 NY1186
Netherend Gloucs 19 SO5900
Netherfield E Susx 14 TQ7019
Netherfield Road E Susx 14 TQ7417
Netherhampton Wilts 10 SU1029
Netherlaw D & G 65 NX7445
Netherley Gramp 89 NO8493
Nethermill D & G 66 NY0487
Nethermuir Gramp 95 NJ9144
Netherplace Strath 74 NS5255
Netherseal Derbys 39 SK2813
Netherstreet Wilts 20 ST9764
Netherthong W York 55 SE1309
Netherthorpe Derbys 49 SK4574
Netherton Cent 81 NS5579
Netherton Devon 5 SX8971
Netherton H & W 28 SO5126
Netherton Nthumb 69 NZ2382
Netherton Nthumb 68 NT9807
Netherton Oxon 19 ST4199
Netherton Shrops 37 SO7382
Netherton Strath 74 NS7854
Netherton Tays 88 NO1452
Netherton Tays 88 NO2273
Netherton W Mids 38 SO9488
Netherton W York 55 SE2716
Netherton Cumb 58 NX9807
Netherton Highld 100 ND3578
Netherton Staffs 38 SK1017
Netherwitton Nthumb 68 NZ0390
Nethy Bridge Highld 93 NJ0020
Netley Hants 10 SU4508
Netley Marsh Hants 10 SU3313
Nettacott Devon 7 SX9099
Nettlebed Oxon 22 SU6986
Nettlebridge Somset 19 ST6448
Nettlecombe Dorset 8 SY5195
Nettleden Herts 22 TL0110
Nettleham Lincs 50 TF0075
Nettlestead Kent 14 TQ6852
Nettlestead Green Kent 14 TQ6850
Nettlestone IOW 11 SZ6290
Nettlesworth Dur 69 NZ2547

Nettleton Lincs 50 TA1100
Nettleton Wilts 20 ST8278
Netton Wilts
Neuadd Fawr Dyfed
Neuadd-ddu Powys
Nevern Dyfed 1
Nevill Holt Leics 40
New Abbey D & G 66 N
New Aberdour Gramp 95 NJ
New Addington Gt Lon 23 TQ
New Alresford Hants 11 SU5B
New Alyth Tays 88 NO244
New Ash Green Kent 14 TQ6064
New Balderton Notts 50 SK8152
New Barn Kent 14 TQ6168
New Barnet Gt Lon 23 TQ2695
New Bewick Nthumb 77 NU0620
New Bilton Warwks 39 SP4975
New Bolingbroke Lincs 51 TF3057
New Bradwell Bucks 30 SP8341
New Brampton Derbys 49 SK3671
New Brighton Mersyd 46 SJ3193
New Brinsley Notts 49 SK4650
New Brotton Cleve 62 NZ6820
New Buckenham Norfk 32 TM0890
New Bury Gt Man 47 SD7305
New Byth Gramp 95 NJ8254
New Clipstone Notts 49 SK5863
New Costessey Norfk 43 TG1810
New Crofton W York 55 SE3817
New Cross Gt Lon 23 TQ3676
New Cross Somset 8 ST4219
New Cumnock Strath 66 NS6113
New Cut E Susx 14 TO8115
New Deer Gramp 95 NJ8847
New Denham Bucks 22 TQ0485
New Duston Nhants 30 SP7162
New Eastwood Notts 49 SK4646
New Edlington S York 49 SK5399
New Elgin Gramp 94 NJ2261
New Ellerby Humb 57 TA1639
New Eltham Gt Lon 23 TQ4472
New End H & W 28 SP0560
New England Notts 50 SE5163
New Farnley W York 55 SE2431
New Fletton Cambs 40 TL1997
New Galloway D & G 65 NX6377
New Gilston Fife 83 NO4208
New Grimsby IOS 2 SV8915
New Hedges Dyfed 16 SN1302
New Holkham Norfk 42 TF8839
New Holland Humb 57 TA0823
New Houghton Derbys 49 SK5065
New Houghton Norfk 42 TF7927
New Hutton Cumb 59 SD5691
New Inn Devon 6 SS4408
New Inn Dyfed 17 SN4736
New Inn Gwent 19 SO4800
New Inn Gwent 19 ST3099
New Inn N York 55 SD8072
New Invention Shrops 36 SO2976
New Kelso Highld 91 NG9442
New Lakenham Norfk 43 TG2308
New Lanark Strath 74 NS8842
New Langholm D & G 67 NY3584
New Leake Lincs 51 TF4057
New Leeds Gramp 95 NJ9954
New Luce D & G 64 NX1764
New Machar Gramp 95 NJ8919
New Malden Gt Lon 23 TQ2168
New Marske Cleve 62 NZ6110
New Marston Oxon 29 SP5307
New Mill Gramp 89 NO7883
New Mill W York 55 SE1608
New Mills Powys 36 SJ0901
New Milton Hants 10 SZ2495
New Mistley Essex 25 TM1131
New Moat Dyfed 16 SN0626
New Ollerton Notts 49 SK6668
New Pitsligo Gramp 95 NJ8855
New Prestwick Strath 73 NS3424
New Quay Dyfed 34 SN3859
New Rackheath Norfk 43 TG2812
New Radnor Powys 27 SO2161
New Ridley Nthumb 68 NZ0559
New Romney Kent 15 TR0624
New Rossington Notts 49 SK6198
New Sauchie Cent 82 NS8994
New Scone Tays 82 NO1326
New Sharlston W York 55 SE3820
New Silksworth T & W 69 NZ3863
New Somerby Lincs 40 SK9235
New Spilsby Lincs 51 TF4165
New Stevenston Strath 74 NS7659
New Town Dorset 9 ST8318
New Town Dorset 9 ST9515
New Town Dorset 9 ST9620
New Town E Susx 13 TQ4720
New Town Loth 76 NT4470
New Tredegar M Glam 18 SO1403
New Trows Strath 74 NS8038
New Ulva Strath 71 NR7080
New Village Humb 56 SE8530
New Walsoken Cambs 41 TF4609
New Waltham Humb 51 TA2904
New Whittington Derbys 49 SK4075
New Wimpole Cambs 31 TL3449
New Wimpole Cambs 31 TL3640
New Winton Loth 76 NT4271
New York Lincs 51 TF2455
New York N York 55 SE1962
New Zealand Derbys 39 SK3336
Newall W York 55 SE1946
Newark D & G 66 NS7809
Newark-on-Trent Notts 50 SK7953
Newarthill Strath 74 NS7859
Newbattle Loth 75 NT3365
Newbie D & G 67 NY1764
Newbiggin Cumb 58 SD0993
Newbiggin Cumb 59 NY4729
Newbiggin Cumb 59 NY5549
Newbiggin Cumb 60 NY6228
Newbiggin Dur 68 NY9127
Newbiggin Nthumb 61 SE0085
Newbiggin Nthumb 69 NY9461
Newbiggin Nthumb 69 NZ3087
Newbiggin-by-the-Sea Nthumb 69 NT0145
Newbigging Strath 75 NT0142
Newbigging Tays 88 NO2842
Newbigging Tays 83 NO4237
Newbold Pacey Warwks 29 SP2957
Newbold Verdon Leics 39 SK4403
Newbold on Avon Warwks 39 SP4977
Newbold on Stour Warwks 29 SP2446
Newborough Cambs 41 TF2006
Newborough Gwynd 44 SH4265
Newborough Staffs 38 SK1325
Newbourn Suffk 33 TM2743
Newbridge Cnwll 2 SW4231
Newbridge D & G 66 NX9579
Newbridge Hants 10 SU2915
Newbridge Hants 10 SU2915
Newbridge IOW 10 SZ4187
Newbridge Loth 75 NT1272
Newbridge Green H & W 28 SO8439
Newbridge on Wye Powys 26 SO0158
Newbrough Nthumb 68 NY8767
Newbuildings Devon 7 SS7903
Newburgh Gramp 95 NJ9659
Newburgh Gramp 95 NK0030
Newburgh Lancs 53 SD4810
Newburgh Priory N York 56 SE5476
Newburn T & W 69 NZ1665
Newbury Berks 21 SU4666
Newbury Somset 20 ST6950
Newbury Wilts 20 ST8241
Newby Lancs 54 NY5921
Newby Lancs 54 SD7269
Newby N York 62 NZ5012
Newby N York 62 TA0190
Newby N York 54 SD7169
Newby Bridge Cumb 59 SD3686
Newby East Cumb 67 NY4758
Newby West Cumb 67 NY3854
Newby Wiske N York 62 SE3687

SO4417
SO2482
SN3040
NZ2464
SJ8445
NY4887
SN2239
TQ3642
SO1710
ST4597
SZ5685
TR0531
SO2150
SK1423
ST2309
IT2973
Q1942
U8771
D8327
O7226

50 TA1100
ST8178
10 SU1236
26
SN9275
SP8663

Newfield Highld 61 NZ2033
Newfield Highld 97 NH7877
Newgale Dyfed 16 SM8422
Newgate Street Herts 23 TL3005
Newhall Ches 47 SJ6145
Newhall Derbys 38 SK2821
Newham Gt Lon 23 TQ4081
Newhaven E Susx 13 TQ4401
Newholm N York 63 NZ8610
Newhouse Strath 74 NS7961
Newick E Susx 13 TQ4121
Newington Kent 14 TQ8564
Newington Kent 15 TR1837
Newington Oxon 21 SU6096
Newington Shrops 36 SO4283
Newland Cumb 67 NY2979
Newland Gloucs 27 SO5409
Newland H & W 28 SO7948
Newland Humb 57 TA0631
Newland N York 56 SE6824
Newland Somset 7 SS8338
Newlandrig Loth 76 NT3762
Newlands Border 67 NY5194
Newlands Nthumb 68 NZ0855
Newlands of Dundurlas Gramp 94 NJ2950
Newlyn Cnwll 2 SW4628
Newlyn East Cnwll 2 SW8266
Newmains Strath 74 NS8256
Newman's Green Suffk 32 TL8843
Newmarket Cumb 59 NY3338
Newmarket Suffk 32 TL6463
Newmill Border 67 NT4510
Newmill Gramp 94 NJ4352
Newmill of Inshewan Tays 88 NO4260
Newmillerdam W York 55 SE3215
Newmills Fife 82 NT0186
Newmills Gwent 27 SO5107
Newmills Loth 75 NT1667
Newmiln Tays 82 NO1230
Newmilns Strath 74 NS5337
Newney Green Essex 24 TL6507
Newnham Gloucs 28 SO6911
Newnham H & W 27 SO6469
Newnham Hants 22 SU7054
Newnham Herts 31 TL2437
Newnham Kent 14 TQ9557
Newnham Paddox Warwks 39 SP4783
Newport Devon 6 SS5631
Newport Essex 31 TL5234
Newport Gloucs 20 ST7097
Newport Gwent 19 ST3188
Newport Highld 100 ND1324
Newport IOW 10 SZ4989
Newport Norfk 43 TG5016
Newport Shrops 37 SJ7419
Newport Bagnell Bucks 30 SP8743
Newport-on-Tay Fife 83 NO4228
Newquay Cnwll 2 SW8161
Newseat Gramp 95 NJ7033
Newsham Lancs 53 SD5136
Newsham N York 61 NZ1010
Newsham N York 62 SE3884
Newsham Nthumb 69 NZ3080
Newsholme Humb 56 SE7129
Newstead Border 76 NT5634
Newstead Notts 49 SK5152
Newstead Nthumb 77 NU1527
Newtack Gramp 94 NJ4446
Newthorpe N York 55 SE4632
Newton Beds 31 TL2344
Newton Border 76 NT6020
Newton Cambs 31 TL4349
Newton Cambs 41 TF4314
Newton Ches 46 SJ4167
Newton Ches 46 SJ5059
Newton Cumb 53 SD2271
Newton D & G 67 NY1194
Newton Derbys 49 SK4459
Newton Gramp 94 NJ1663
Newton Gramp 94 NJ3362
Newton H & W 27 SO3432
Newton H & W 27 SO5153
Newton Highld 92 NH5850
Newton Highld 88 NH7448
Newton Highld 93 NH7866
Newton Highld 100 ND3449
Newton Lancs 53 SD3436
Newton Lancs 53 SD4430
Newton Lancs 59 SD5974
Newton Lancs 54 SD6950
Newton Lincs 40 TF0436
Newton Loth 75 NT0977
Newton M Glam 18 SS8377
Newton Nhants 40 SP8883
Newton Norfk 42 TF8315
Newton Notts 49 SK6841
Newton Nthumb 68 NZ0364
Newton Nthumb 68 NU9407
Newton S Glam 19 ST2378
Newton Staffs 38 SK0325
Newton Strath 74 NS6560
Newton Strath 75 NS9331
Newton Strath 80 NS0498
Newton Suffk 32 TL9240
Newton W Isls 17 SS6088
Newton W Isls 102 NF8877
Newton W York 55 SE4427
Newton Warwks 39 SP5378
Newton Abbot Devon 5 SX8671
Newton Arlosh Cumb 67 NY2055
Newton Aycliffe Dur 62 NZ2724
Newton Bewley Cleve 62 NZ4626
Newton Blossomville Bucks 30 SP9251
Newton Bromswold Beds 30 SP9996
Newton Burgoland Leics 39 SK3709
Newton Ferrers Devon 4 SX5447
Newton Ferrers M Glam 4 SX3466
Newton Flotman Norfk 43 TM2198
Newton Harcourt Leics 39 SP6497
Newton Heath Gt Man 47 SD8700
Newton Kyme Highld 89 NO9193
Newton Kyme N York 55 SE4644
Newton Longville Bucks 30 SP8431
Newton Mearns Strath 74 NS5355
Newton Morrel N York 61 NZ2309
Newton Mountain Dyfed 16 SM9807
Newton Poppleford Devon 5 SY0089
Newton Purcell Oxon 29 SP6230
Newton Regis Warwks 39 SK2707
Newton Reigny Cumb 59 NY4731
Newton Solney Derbys 39 SK2825
Newton St. Cyres Devon 7 SX8797
Newton St. Faith Norfk 43 TG2217
Newton St. Loe Avon 20 ST7064
Newton St. Petrock Devon 6 SS4112
Newton Stacey Hants 21 SU4140
Newton Stewart D & G 64 NX4165
Newton Toney Wilts 21 SU2140
Newton Tracey Devon 6 SS5226
Newton Valence Hants 11 SU7232
Newton by Toft Lincs 50 TF0487
Newton of Balcanquhal Tays 82 NO1610
Newton on Ouse N York 55 SE5159
Newton on Trent Lincs 50 SK8374
Newton under Roseberry Cleve 62 NZ5613
Newton upon Derwent Humb 56 SE7149
Newton-le-Willows Mersyd 47 SJ5995
Newton-le-Willows N York 61 SE2189

Newton-on-the-Moor Nthumb 69 NU1705
Newtonairds D & G 66 NX8880
Newtongarry Croft Gramp 94 NJ5735
Newtongrange Loth 75 NT3364
Newtonloan Loth 75 NT3362
Newtonmill Tays 89 NO6064
Newtonmore Highld 87 NN7198
Newtown Beds 31 TL1945
Newtown Ches 46 SJ5374
Newtown Ches 48 SJ9060
Newtown Cnwll 4 SX2978
Newtown Cumb 67 NY0948
Newtown Cumb 67 NY5262
Newtown D & G 66 NS7710
Newtown Devon 4 SX0699
Newtown Devon 7 SS7625
Newtown Dorset 8 ST4701
Newtown Dorset 8 SZ0393
Newtown Gloucs 20 SO6702
Newtown Gt Man 47 SD5605
Newtown H & W 27 SO5533
Newtown H & W 27 SO6145
Newtown H & W 28 SO7037
Newtown H & W 28 SO8655
Newtown Hants 10 SU2710
Newtown Hants 11 SU6113
Newtown Highld 86 NH3504
Newtown IOW 52 SC3273
Newtown IOW 10 SZ4290
Newtown Nthumb 68 NU0300
Newtown Powys 36 SO1091
Newtown Shrops 36 SJ4222
Newtown Shrops 37 SJ4631
Newtown Somset 8 ST2712
Newtown Wilts 9 ST9128
Newtown Linford Leics 39 SK5110
Newtown St. Boswells Border 76 NT5732
Newtown of Beltrees Strath 73 NS3758
Newtyle Tays 88 NO2941
Newydd Strath 80 NM9611
Neyland Dyfed 16 SM9605
Nibley Green Gloucs 20 ST7296
Nicholashayne Devon 8 ST1016
Nicholaston W Glam 17 SS5288
Nickies Hill Cumb 67 NY5467
Nidd N York 55 SE3060
Nigg Gramp 89 NJ9402
Nigg Highld 93 NH8071
Nightcott Devon 7 SS8925
Nine Ashes Essex 24 TL5902
Nine Elms Wilts 20 SU1085
Nine Elms Wilts 10 SU1236
Nine Wells Dyfed 16 SM7824
Ninebanks Nthumb 68 NY7853
Ninemile Bar or Crocketford D & G 66 NX8373
Nineveh H & W 27 SO6265
Ningwood IOW 10 SZ3989
Nisbet Border 76 NT6725
Nisbet Hill Border 76 NT7850
Niton IOW 10 SZ5076
Nitshill Strath 74 NS5260
No Man's Heath Ches 46 SJ5148
No Man's Heath Warwks 39 SK2909
Nocton Lincs 50 TF0564
Noke Oxon 29 SP5413
Nolton Dyfed 16 SM8718
Nolton Haven Dyfed 16 SM8618
Nomansland Devon 7 SS8313
Nomansland Wilts 10 SU2517
Noneley Shrops 37 SJ4728
Nonington Kent 15 TR2552
Nook Cumb 59 SD5482
Norbiton Common Gt Lon 23 TQ2167
Norbury Ches 47 SJ5547
Norbury Derbys 48 SK1241
Norbury Gt Lon 23 TQ3069
Norbury Shrops 36 SO3693
Norbury Staffs 37 SJ7823
Norby N York 62 SE4381
Norchard H & W 28 SO8568
Norcott Brook Ches 47 SJ6180
Nordelph Norfk 41 TF5501
Nordley Shrops 37 SO6997
Norham Nthumb 77 NT9047
Norland Town W York 55 SE0622
Norley Ches 47 SJ5772
Norley Devon 6 SS4900
Norleywood Hants 10 SZ3597
Norman Cross Cambs 40 TL1691
Norman's Green Devon 7 ST0503
Normanby Cleve 62 NZ5518
Normanby Humb 56 SE8716
Normanby Lincs 50 TF0088
Normanby N York 63 SE7381
Normanby le Wold Lincs 50 TF1295
Normansland Wilts 10 SU2517
Normanton Derbys 39 SK3433
Normanton Leics 50 SK8140
Normanton Lincs 50 SK9446
Normanton Notts 49 SK7054
Normanton W York 55 SE3822
Normanton le Heath Leics 39 SK3712
Normanton on Soar Notts 39 SK5123
Normanton on Trent Notts 50 SK7868
Normanton on the Wolds Notts 39 SK6232
Normoss Lancs 53 SD3437
Norney Surrey 12 SU9444
Norristhorpe W York 55 SE2123
North Anston S York 49 SK5184
North Aston Oxon 29 SP4728
North Baddesley Hants 10 SU3920
North Ballchulish Highld 86 NN0580
North Barrow Somset 9 ST6029
North Barsham Norfk 42 TF9135
North Benfleet Essex 24 TQ7690
North Bersted W Susx 11 SU9200
North Berwick Loth 83 NT5485
North Biddick T & W 69 NZ5153
North Bitchburn Dur 61 NZ1733
North Boarhunt Hants 11 SU6010
North Bovey Devon 5 SX7483
North Bradley Wilts 20 ST8554
North Brentor Devon 4 SX4881
North Brewham Somset 20 ST7236
North Brook End Cambs 31 TL2844
North Buckland Devon 6 SS4840
North Burlingham Norfk 43 TG3610
North Cadbury Somset 9 ST6327
North Cairn D & G 64 NW9770
North Carlton Lincs 50 SK9477
North Carlton Notts 49 SK5885
North Cave Humb 56 SE8832
North Cerney Gloucs 28 SP0208
North Charford Hants 10 SU1919
North Charlton Nthumb 77 NU1622
North Cheam Gt Lon 23 TQ2365
North Cheriton Somset 9 ST6825
North Chideock Dorset 8 SY4294
North Cliffe Humb 56 SE8737
North Clifton Notts 50 SK8272
North Cockerington Lincs 51 TF3790
North Collingham Notts 50 SK8362
North Common E Susx 13 TQ3921
North Connel Strath 80 NM9135
North Cornelly M Glam 18 SS8281
North Corner Cnwll 2 SW7818
North Corry Highld 79 NM8353
North Cotes Lincs 51 TA3400
North Cottingham Notts 50 SK8061
North Cove Suffk 33 TM4689
North Cowton N York 61 NZ2803
North Creake Norfk 42 TF8538
North Curry Somset 8 ST3125
North Dalton Humb 56 SE9352
North Deighton N York 55 SE3951
North Duffield N York 56 SE6837
North Elham Kent 15 TR1844
North Elmham Norfk 42 TF9820
North Elmsall W York 55 SE4712
North End Avon 19 ST4267
North End Essex 24 TL6619
North End Hants 10 SU1016
North End Hants 11 SU5829
North End Hants 11 SU6502
North End Humb 57 TA2931
North End Humb 57 TA3007
North End Nhants 30 SP9668
North End Nthumb 67 NT1301

North End W Susx 12 SU9804
North End W Susx 12 TQ1209
North Erradale Highld 91 NG7481
North Evington Leics 39 SK6204
North Fambridge Essex 24 TQ8597
North Feorline Strath 72 NR8129
North Ferriby Humb 56 SE9826
North Frodingham Humb 57 TA1053
North Gorley Hants 10 SU1611
North Green Suffk 33 TM3162
North Grimston N York 56 SE8467
North Hayling Hants 11 SU7303
North Hill Cnwll 4 SX2776
North Hillington Gt Lon 22 TQ0784
North Hinksey Oxon 29 SP4805
North Huish Devon 5 SX7156
North Hykeham Lincs 50 SK9466
North Kelsey Humb 50 TA0401
North Kessock Highld 93 NH6548
North Killingholme Humb 57 TA1417
North Kilvington N York 62 SE4284
North Kilworth Leics 39 SP6183
North Kingston Hants 10 SU1603
North Kyme Lincs 50 TF1552
North Lee Bucks 22 SP8308
North Lees N York 61 SE3073
North Leigh Oxon 15 TR1447
North Leigh Oxon 29 SP3813
North Leverton with Habblesthorpe Notts 50 SK7882
North Lopham Norfk 32 TM0383
North Luffenham Leics 40 SK9303
North Marden W Susx 11 SU8016
North Marston Bucks 30 SP7722
North Middleton Loth 75 NT3559
North Milmain D & G 64 NX0952
North Molton Devon 7 SS7329
North Moreton Oxon 21 SU5689
North Mundham W Susx 11 SU8702
North Muskham Notts 50 SK7958
North Newbald Humb 56 SE9136
North Newington Oxon 29 SP4139
North Newnton Wilts 20 SU1257
North Newton Somset 8 ST3031
North Nibley Gloucs 20 ST7395
North Ormsby Lincs 51 TF2893
North Otterington N York 62 SE3689
North Owersby Lincs 50 TF0594
North Perrott Somset 8 ST4709
North Petherton Somset 8 ST2832
North Petherwin Cnwll 4 SX2889
North Pickenham Norfk 42 TF8607
North Piddle H & W 28 SO9654
North Pool Devon 5 SX7741
North Poorton Dorset 8 SY5197
North Queensferry Fife 82 NT1380
North Radworthy Devon 7 SS7534
North Rauceby Lincs 50 TF0246
North Reston Lincs 51 TF3883
North Rigton N York 55 SE2749
North Runcton Norfk 42 TF6416
North Scarle Lincs 50 SK8466
North Shian Strath 79 NM9143
North Shields T & W 69 NZ3568
North Shoebury Essex 24 TQ9286
North Shore Lancs 53 SD3037
North Side Cambs 41 TL2799
North Side Cumb 58 NY0029
North Skirlaugh Humb 57 TA1439
North Somercotes Lincs 51 TF4296
North Stainley N York 61 SE2876
North Stainmore Cumb 60 NY8215
North Stifford Essex 24 TQ6080
North Stoke Avon 20 ST7068
North Stoke Oxon 21 SU6186
North Stoke W Susx 12 TQ0210
North Street Berks 21 SU6371
North Street Kent 15 TR0157
North Sunderland Nthumb 77 NU2131
North Tamerton Cnwll 6 SX3197
North Tawton Devon 7 SS6601
North Third Cent 81 NS7589
North Tidworth Wilts 21 SU2248
North Town Berks 22 SU8882
North Town Devon 6 SS5109
North Town Somset 19 ST5642
North Tuddenham Norfk 42 TG0414
North Walsham Norfk 43 TG2830
North Waltham Hants 21 SU5646
North Warnborough Hants 22 SU7351
North Weald Bassett Essex 23 TL4904
North Weston Avon 19 ST4674
North Wheatley Notts 50 SK7685
North Widcombe Somset 19 ST5758
North Willingham Lincs 50 TF1688
North Wingfield Derbys 49 SK4064
North Witham Lincs 40 SK9221
North Wootton Dorset 9 ST6614
North Wootton Norfk 42 TF6424
North Wootton Somset 19 ST5641
North Wraxall Wilts 20 ST8175
Northall Bucks 30 SP9520
Northall Green Norfk 42 TF9915
Northallerton N York 62 SE3793
Northam Devon 6 SS4429
Northam Hants 10 SU4312
Northampton H & W 28 SO8365
Northampton Nhants 30 SP7560
Northaw Herts 23 TL2702
Northay Somset 8 ST2811
Northborough Cambs 41 TF1507
Northbourne Kent 15 TR3352
Northbridge Street E Susx 14 TQ7423
Northbrook Hants 11 SU5139
Northchapel W Susx 12 SU9529
Northchurch Herts 22 SP9708
Northcott Devon 4 SX3392
Northcott Devon 8 ST1109
Northcourt Oxon 21 SU5098
Northdown Kent 15 TR3170
Northedge Derbys 49 SK3565
Northend Warwks 29 SP3852
Northenden Gt Man 47 SJ8290
Northfield Gramp 95 NJ9008
Northfield Humb 56 TA0328
Northfield W Mids 38 SP0279
Northfields Lincs 40 TF0208
Northfleet Essex 14 TQ6274
Northiam E Susx 14 TQ8324
Northill Beds 30 TL1446
Northington Hants 11 SU5637
Northlands Lincs 51 TF3453
Northleach Gloucs 28 SP1114
Northleigh Devon 8 SS6034
Northleigh Devon 8 SY1195
Northlew Devon 6 SX5099
Northmoor Oxon 21 SP4202
Northmoor Green or Moorland Somset 8 ST3332
Northmuir Tays 88 NO3854
Northney Hants 11 SU7303
Northolt Gt Lon 22 TQ1384
Northop Clwyd 46 SJ2468
Northop Hall Clwyd 46 SJ2667
Northorpe Lincs 50 SK8996
Northorpe Lincs 41 TF2036
Northorpe Lincs 50 SE2121
Northorwram W York 55 SE1127
Northport Dorset 9 SY9288
Northrepps Norfk 43 TG2439
Northton W Isls 102 NF9889
Northway Somset 8 ST1329
Northway W Glam 17 SS6889
Northwich Ches 47 SJ6673
Northwick H & W 28 SO8458
Northwold Norfk 42 TL7597
Northwood Gt Lon 22 TQ0990
Northwood IOW 10 SZ4893
Northwood Shrops 36 SJ4633
Northwood Staffs 48 SJ8948
Northwood End Beds 30 TL0941
Northwood Green Gloucs 28 SO7216
Norton Ches 47 SJ5582
Norton Cleve 62 NZ4421
Norton E Susx 13 TQ4601
Norton Gloucs 28 SO8524
Norton H & W 28 SO8751

Norton H & W 28 SP0448
Norton IOW 10 SZ3489
Norton N York 56 SE7971
Norton Nhants 29 SP5963
Norton Notts 49 SK5772
Norton Powys 27 SO3087
Norton S York 56 SE5415
Norton S York 49 SK3561
Norton Shrops 37 SJ7200
Norton Shrops 37 SO6482
Norton Suffk 32 TL9565
Norton W Glam 17 SS6188
Norton Wilts 11 SU9306
Norton Wilts 20 ST9884
Norton Bavant Wilts 20 ST9043
Norton Bridge Staffs 38 SJ8730
Norton Brook Staffs 48 SJ9052
Norton Canon H & W 27 SO3847
Norton Disney Lincs 50 SK8859
Norton Fitzwarren Somset 8 ST1925
Norton Green IOW 10 SZ3388
Norton Green Staffs 38 SK0107
Norton Hawkfield Avon 19 ST5964
Norton Heath Essex 24 TL6004
Norton Lindsey Warwks 29 SP2263
Norton Little Green Suffk 32 TL9766
Norton Malreward Avon 19 ST6065
Norton St. Philip Somset 20 ST7755
Norton Subcourse Norfk 43 TM4198
Norton Wood H & W 27 SO3648
Norton in Hales Shrops 37 SJ7038
Norton sub Hamdon Somset 8 ST4415
Norton-Juxta-Twycross Leics 39 SK3207
Norton-le-Clay N York 55 SE4071
Norwell Notts 50 SK7661
Norwell Woodhouse Notts 50 SK7362
Norwich Norfk 43 TG2308
Norwick Shet 103 HP6514
Norwood Cent 82 NS8793
Norwood Kent 15 TR0430
Norwood Green Gt Lon 22 TQ1378
Norwood Green W York 55 SE1427
Norwood Hill Surrey 12 TQ2443
Noseley Leics 40 SP7398
Noss Mayo Devon 4 SX5447
Nosterfield N York 61 SE2780
Nostie Highld 85 NG8527
Notgrove Gloucs 28 SP1020
Nottage M Glam 18 SS8278
Notter M Glam 4 SX3961
Nottingham Notts 49 SK5739
Nottington Dorset 9 SY6582
Notton W York 55 SE3413
Notton Wilts 20 ST9169
Noutard's Green H & W 28 SO8066
Nox Shrops 36 SJ4110
Nuffield Oxon 22 SU6687
Nun Monkton N York 55 SE5057
Nuneaton Warwks 39 SP3692
Nuneham Courtenay Oxon 21 SU5599
Nunhead Gt Lon 23 TQ3475
Nunkeeling Humb 57 TA1449
Nunnerie Strath 66 NS9612
Nunney Somset 20 ST7345
Nunnington N York 62 SE6679
Nunsthorpe Humb 57 TA2508
Nunthorpe N York 56 SE6050
Nunthorpe Village Cleve 62 NZ5313
Nunton W Isls 102 NF7653
Nunton Wilts 10 SU1525
Nunwick N York 62 SE3274
Nupend Gloucs 28 SO7806
Nuptow Berks 22 SU8873
Nursling Hants 10 SU3616
Nursted Hants 11 SU7621
Nutbourne W Susx 11 SU7805
Nutbourne W Susx 12 TQ0718
Nutfield Surrey 12 TQ3050
Nuthall Notts 49 SK5144
Nuthampstead Herts 31 TL4034
Nuthurst W Susx 12 TQ1926
Nutley E Susx 13 TQ4427
Nutley Hants 21 SU6144
Nybster Highld 100 ND3663
Nyetimber W Susx 11 SZ8998
Nyewood W Susx 11 SU8021
Nymet Rowland Devon 7 SS7108
Nymet Tracey Devon 7 SS7200
Nympsfield Gloucs 20 SO8000
Nynehead Somset 8 ST1423
Nyton W Susx 11 SU9322

O

Oad Street Kent 14 TQ8662
Oadby Leics 39 SK6200
Oak Cross Devon 6 SX5399
Oakamoor Staffs 48 SK0544
Oakbank Loth 75 NT0766
Oakdale Gwent 19 ST1898
Oake Somset 8 ST1525
Oaken Staffs 38 SJ8502
Oakenclough Lancs 53 SD5447
Oakengates Shrops 37 SJ7010
Oakenshaw Dur 61 NZ1937
Oakenshaw W York 55 SE1728
Oaker Side Derbys 49 SK2761
Oakford Devon 7 SS9021
Oakford Dyfed 34 SN4558
Oakfordbridge Devon 7 SS9122
Oakham Leics 40 SK8608
Oakhanger Ches 47 SJ7654
Oakhanger Hants 11 SU7635
Oakhill Somset 19 ST6347
Oakhurst Kent 13 TQ5450
Oakington Cambs 31 TL4164
Oakle Street Gloucs 28 SO7517
Oakley Suffk 33 TM1678
Oakley Beds 30 TL0053
Oakley Bucks 29 SP6412
Oakley Hants 21 SU5650
Oakley Oxon 22 SP7400
Oakridge Gloucs 20 SO9103
Oaks Dur 61 NZ1526
Oaks Lancs 54 SD6733
Oaksey Wilts 20 ST9893
Oakshaw Cumb 67 NY5076
Oakthorpe Leics 39 SK3213
Oakwood Border 76 NT4225
Oakwoodhill Surrey 12 TQ1337
Oakworth W York 55 SE0339
Oape Highld 96 NC4101
Oare Kent 15 TR0063
Oare Somset 18 SS8047
Oare Wilts 20 SU1163
Oasby Lincs 40 TF0039
Oath Somset 8 ST3827
Oathlaw Tays 89 NO4756
Oatlands Park Surrey 22 TQ0865
Oban Strath 79 NM8630
Obinan Highld 91 NG8796
Obney Tays 82 NO0237
Oborne Dorset 9 ST6518
Obthorpe Lincs 40 TF0915
Occlestone Green Ches 47 SJ6962
Occold Suffk 33 TM1570
Ochertyre Tays 81 NN8323
Ochiltree Strath 74 NS5121
Ockbrook Derbys 49 SK4235
Ockle Highld 79 NM5570
Ockley Surrey 12 TQ1440
Ocle Pychard H & W 27 SO5946
Odcombe Somset 8 ST5015
Odd Down Avon 20 ST7462
Oddingley H & W 28 SO9159
Oddington Gloucs 29 SP2225
Oddington Oxon 29 SP5514
Odell Beds 30 SP9657
Odiham Hants 22 SU7451
Odsal W York 55 SE1529

Odsey Herts	31	TL2938
Odstock Wilts	10	SU1426
Odstone Leics	39	SK3907
Offchurch Warwks	29	SP3566
Offenham H & W	28	SP0546
Offham E Susx	13	TQ4012
Offham Kent	14	TQ6557
Offham W Susx	12	TQ0208
Offordmarsh Shrops	37	SJ7829
Offord Cluny Cambs	31	TL2267
Offord Darcy Cambs	31	TL2266
Offton Suffk	32	TM0649
Offwell Devon	8	SY1999
Ogbourne Maizey Wilts	21	SU1871
Ogbourne St. Andrew Wilts	21	SU1872
Ogbourne St. George Wilts	21	SU2074
Ogle Nthumb	69	NZ1378
Oglet Mersyd	46	SJ4481
Ogmore M Glam	18	SS8876
Ogmore Vale M Glam	18	SS9390
Ogmore-by-Sea M Glam	18	SS8675
Okeford Fitzpaine Dorset	9	ST8010
Okehampton Devon	5	SX5895
Okehampton Camp Devon	5	SX5893
Olchard Devon	5	SX8776
Old Nhants	30	SP7873
Old Aberdeen Gramp	95	NJ9407
Old Alresford Hants	10	SU5834
Old Auchenbrack D & G	65	NX7597
Old Basford Notts	49	SK5543
Old Basing Hants	22	SU6652
Old Bewick Nthumb	77	NU0621
Old Bolingbroke Lincs	51	TF3564
Old Bramhope W York	55	SE2343
Old Brampton Derbys	49	SK3371
Old Bridge of Tilt Tays	87	NN8866
Old Bridge of Urr D & G	66	NX7767
Old Buckenham Norfk	32	TM0691
Old Burghclere Hants	21	SU4657
Old Byland N York	62	SE5485
Old Castle M Glam	18	SS9079
Old Church Stoke Powys	36	SO2894
Old Clee Humb	57	TA2808
Old Cleeve Somset	7	ST0342
Old Dailly Strath	64	NX2299
Old Dalby Leics	39	SK6723
Old Dam Derbys	48	SK1179
Old Deer Gramp	95	NJ9747
Old Edington S York	49	SK5397
Old Ellerby Humb	57	TA1637
Old Felixstowe Suffk	25	TM3136
Old Fletton Cambs	40	TL1997
Old Forge H & W	27	SO5518
Old Grimsby IOS	2	SV8915
Old Hall Green Herts	31	TL3622
Old Harlow Essex	23	TL4711
Old Hunstanton Norfk	42	TF6842
Old Hutton Cumb	59	SD5088
Old Hutton Cumb	59	SD5688
Old Kea Cnwll	3	SW8441
Old Kilpatrick Strath	81	NS4673
Old Knebworth Herts	31	TL2320
Old Lakenham Norfk	43	TG2206
Old Leake Lincs	51	TF4050
Old Malton N York	56	SE7972
Old Micklefield W York	55	SE4432
Old Milton Hants	10	SZ2494
Old Milverton Warwks	29	SP2967
Old Newton Suffk	32	TM0662
Old Radnor Powys	27	SO2559
Old Rattray Gramp	95	NK0857
Old Rayne Gramp	95	NJ6728
Old Romney Kent	15	TR0325
Old Scone Tays	82	NO1226
Old Shoreham W Susx	12	TQ2006
Old Shoremore Highld	98	NC2059
Old Soar Kent	14	TQ6154
Old Sodbury Avon	20	ST7581
Old Somerby Lincs	40	SK9633
Old Stratford Nhants	30	SP7741
Old Sunnford W Mids	38	SO9083
Old Thirsk N York	62	SE4382
Old Town Cumb	59	SD5983
Old Town IOS	2	SV9110
Old Trafford Gt Man	47	SJ8196
Old Warden Beds	30	TL1343
Old Weston Cambs	30	TL0977
Old Wick Highld	100	ND3649
Old Windsor Berks	22	SU9874
Old Wives Lees Kent	15	TR0754
Old Woking Surrey	22	TQ0156
Oldany Highld	98	NC0932
Oldberrow Warwks	28	SP1266
Oldborough Devon	7	SS7706
Oldbury Kent	14	TQ5956
Oldbury Shrops	37	SO7192
Oldbury Warwks	39	SP3194
Oldbury on the Hill Gloucs	20	ST8287
Oldbury-on-Severn Avon	19	ST6092
Oldcastle Gwent	27	SO3224
Oldcotes Notts	49	SK5888
Oldfield H & W	28	SO8465
Oldford Somset	20	ST7849
Oldhall Green Suffk	32	TL8956
Oldham Gt Man	54	SD9215
Oldhamstocks Loth	76	NT7470
Oldhurst Cambs	31	TL3077
Oldland Avon	20	ST6771
Oldley Shrops	36	SO3378
Oldmeldrum Gramp	95	NJ8027
Oldmill Cnwll	4	SX3774
Oldmixon Avon	19	ST3358
Oldridge Devon	7	SX8295
Oldstead N York	62	SE5279
Oldwall Cumb	67	NY4761
Oldwalls W Glam	17	SS4891
Oldways End Devon	7	SS8624
Olive Green Staffs	38	SK1118
Oliver Border	75	NT0924
Oliver's Battery Hants	10	SU4527
Olaberry Shet	103	HU3680
Ollach Highld	84	NG5137
Ollerton Ches	47	SJ7776
Ollerton Notts	49	SK6567
Ollerton Shrops	37	SJ6425
Olney Bucks	30	SP8851
Olney Nhants	30	SP6643
Olrig House Highld	100	ND1866
Olveston Avon	19	ST6087
Ombersley H & W	28	SO8463
Onchan IOM	52	SC4078
Onecote Staffs	48	SK0455
Onibury Shrops	36	SO4579
Onich Highld	86	NN0261
Onllwyn W Glam	26	SN8410
Onneley Staffs	47	SJ7543
Onslow Village Surrey	12	SU9849
Onston Ches	47	SJ5973
Opinan Highld	91	NG7472
Orbliston Gramp	94	NJ3057
Orbost Highld	90	NG2543
Orby Lincs	51	TF4967
Orchard Portman Somset	8	ST2421
Orcheston Wilts	20	SU0545
Orcop H & W	27	SO4726
Orcop Hill H & W	27	SO4828
Ord Gramp	94	NJ6259
Ord Highld	84	NG6113
Ordhead Gramp	94	NJ6610
Ordie Gramp	88	NJ4501
Ordiequish Gramp	94	NJ3356
Ordley Nthumb	68	NY9559
Ordsall Notts	49	SK7079
Ore E Susx	14	TQ8311
Oreton Shrops	37	SO6581
Orford Ches	47	SJ6190
Orford Suffk	33	TM4250
Organford Dorset	9	SY9392
Orlestone Kent	15	TR0034
Orleton H & W	27	SO4967
Orleton H & W	28	SO7067
Orlingbury Nhants	30	SP8572
Ormesby Cleve	62	NZ5317
Ormesby St. Margaret Norfk	43	TG4914
Ormesby St. Michael Norfk	43	TG4814
Ormidale Strath	80	NS0081

Ormiscaig Highld	91	NG8590
Ormiston Loth	76	NT4269
Ormsaigmore Highld	79	NM4763
Ormsary Strath	71	NR7472
Ormskirk Lancs	46	SD4108
Oronsay Strath	70	NR3588
Orosay W Isls	90	NB3612
Orphir Ork	103	HY3405
Orpington Gt Lon	23	TQ4666
Orrell Gt Man	46	SD5303
Orrell Mersyd	46	SJ3496
Orrisdale IOM	52	SC3293
Orrisdale Head IOM	52	SC3192
Orsett Essex	24	TQ6482
Orslow Staffs	37	SJ8015
Orston Notts	50	SK7740
Orton Cumb	60	NY6208
Orton Nhants	40	SP8079
Orton Staffs	38	SO8795
Orton Longueville Cambs	40	TL1696
Orton Waterville Cambs	40	TL1596
Orton-on-the-Hill Leics	39	SK3003
Orwell Cambs	31	TL3650
Osbaldeston Lancs	54	SD6431
Osbaldwick N York	56	SE6251
Osbaston Leics	39	SK4204
Osbaston Shrops	36	SJ3222
Osbournby Lincs	40	TF0638
Oscroft Ches	46	SJ5067
Osgathorpe Leics	39	SK4219
Osgodby Lincs	50	TF0792
Osgodby N York	56	SE6433
Osgodby N York	63	TA0584
Oskaig Highld	84	NG5438
Oskamull Strath	79	NM4540
Osmaston Derbys	48	SK1943
Osmington Dorset	9	SY7282
Osmington Mills Dorset	9	SY7381
Osmonthorpe W York	55	SE3333
Osmotherley N York	62	SE4596
Osney Oxon	29	SP5006
Ospringe Kent	15	TR0060
Ossett W York	55	SE2720
Ossington Notts	50	SK7564
Oswaldkirk N York	62	SE6278
Oswaldtwistle Lancs	54	SD7327
Oswestry Shrops	36	SJ2829
Otford Kent	23	TQ5359
Otham Kent	14	TQ7954
Otham Hole Kent	14	TQ7952
Othery Somset	8	ST3831
Otley Suffk	33	TM2055
Otley W York	55	SE2045
Otter Ferry Strath	71	NR9384
Otterbourne Hants	10	SU4523
Otterburn N York	54	SD8857
Otterburn Nthumb	68	NY8893
Otterham Cnwll	4	SX1690
Otterhampton Somset	8	ST2423
Ottershaw Surrey	22	TQ0264
Otterswick Shet	103	HU5185
Otterton Devon	5	SY0785
Ottery Devon	4	SX4475
Ottery St. Mary Devon	7	SY0995
Ottinge Kent	15	TR1642
Ottringham Humb	57	TA2624
Oughtershaw N York	60	SD8781
Oughterside Cumb	58	NY1140
Oughtibridge S York	49	SK3093
Oulston N York	62	SE5474
Oulton Cumb	67	NY2451
Oulton Norfk	43	TG1328
Oulton Staffs	38	SJ9135
Oulton Suffk	33	TM5294
Oulton W York	55	SE3627
Oulton Broad Suffk	33	TM5292
Oulton Street Norfk	43	TG1527
Oundle Nhants	40	TL0488
Ousby Cumb	59	NY6134
Ousden Suffk	32	TL7459
Ousefleet Humb	56	SE8323
Ouston Dur	69	NZ2554
Out Elmstead Kent	12	TQ2050
Out Newton Humb	51	TA3801
Outgate Cumb	59	SD3599
Outhgill Cumb	60	NY7801
Outlands Staffs	38	SP1066
Outlane W York	55	SJ7730
Outwell Norfk	41	TF5104
Outwood Surrey	12	TQ3245
Outwood Surrey	55	SE3223
Outwoods Staffs	37	SJ7818
Ouzlewell Green W York	55	SE3426
Over Avon	19	ST5882
Over Cambs	31	TL3770
Over Ches	47	SJ6466
Over Compton Dorset	9	ST5917
Over End Cambs	40	TL0893
Over Green Warwks	38	SP1694
Over Haddon Derbys	48	SK2066
Over Kellet Lancs	53	SD5169
Over Kiddington Oxon	29	SP4122
Over Monnow Gwent	27	SO4912
Over Norton Oxon	29	SP3128
Over Silton N York	62	SE4593
Over Stenton Fife	83	NT2799
Over Stowey Somset	19	ST1838
Over Stratton Somset	8	ST4315
Over Tabley Ches	47	SJ7280
Over Wallop Hants	10	SU2838
Over Wallop Hants	10	SU2838
Over Whitacre Warwks	39	SP2590
Over Worton Oxon	29	SP4329
Overbury H & W	28	SO9637
Overleigh Somset	8	ST5035
Overpool Ches	46	SJ3877
Overscaig Hotel Highld	96	NC4223
Overseal Derbys	39	SK2915
Oversland Kent	15	TR0557
Overstone Nhants	30	SP8066
Overstrand Norfk	43	TG2440
Overstreet Wilts	10	SU0637
Overthorpe Nhants	29	SP4840
Overton Clwyd	36	SJ3741
Overton Gramp	95	NJ8714
Overton Hants	21	SU5149
Overton Lancs	53	SD4358
Overton N York	56	SE5555
Overton Shrops	37	SO5072
Overton W Glam	17	SS4685
Overton W York	55	SE2516
Overtown Lancs	60	SD6275
Overtown Strath	74	NS8053
Overtown W York	55	SE3516
Overy Oxon	21	SU5894
Overy Staithe Norfk	42	TF8444
Oving Bucks	30	SP7821
Oving W Susx	11	SU9005
Ovingdean E Susx	12	TQ3503
Ovingham Nthumb	68	NZ0863
Ovington Dur	61	NZ1314
Ovington Essex	32	TL7742
Ovington Hants	11	SU5631
Ovington Norfk	42	TF9202
Ovington Nthumb	68	NZ0663
Ower Hants	10	SU3216
Owermoigne Dorset	9	SY7685
Owler Bar Derbys	49	SK2978
Owlerton S York	49	SK3389
Owlsmoor Berks	22	SU8462
Owlswick Bucks	22	SP7806
Owmby Lincs	50	SK0087
Owmby Lincs	57	TA0724
Owmby Lincs	50	TF0087
Owslebury Hants	11	SU5123
Owston Leics	40	SK7707
Owston S York	56	SE5511
Owston Ferry Humb	50	SE8000
Owstwick Humb	57	TA2732
Owthorne Humb	57	TA3327
Owthorpe Notts	39	SK6233
Oxborough Norfk	41	TF7401
Oxcombe Lincs	51	TF3177
Oxen End Essex	24	TL6629
Oxenhope W York	55	SE0335
Oxenpill Somset	19	ST4441

Oxenton Gloucs	28	SO9531
Oxenwood Wilts	21	SU3059
Oxford Oxon	29	SP5305
Oxhey Herts	22	TQ1295
Oxhill Warwks	29	SP3145
Oxley W Mids	38	SJ9001
Oxley Green Essex	24	TL9114
Oxley's Green E Susx	14	TQ6921
Oxlode Cambs	41	TL4886
Oxnam Border	76	NT7018
Oxnead Norfk	43	TG2224
Oxshott Surrey	22	TQ1460
Oxspring S York	49	SE2601
Oxted Surrey	23	TQ3852
Oxton Border	76	NT4953
Oxton N York	55	SE5043
Oxton Notts	49	SK6351
Oxwich W Glam	17	SS4986
Oxwich Green W Glam	17	SS4986
Oykel Bridge Highld	96	NC3801
Oyne Gramp	95	NJ6725

P

Packers hill Dorset	9	ST7011
Packington Leics	39	SK3614
Packmores Warwks	29	SP2865
Padanaram Tays	88	NO4251
Padbury Bucks	30	SP7230
Paddington Gt Lon	23	TQ2681
Paddlesworth Kent	14	TQ6862
Paddlesworth Kent	15	TR1939
Paddock Wood Kent	14	TQ6644
Paddon Devon	6	SS3609
Padfield Derbys	48	SK0396
Padiham Lancs	54	SD7933
Padside N York	56	SE5719
Padstow Cnwll	3	SW9175
Padworth Berks	21	SU6166
Pagham W Susx	11	SZ8897
Paglesham Essex	24	TQ9293
Paible W Isls	102	NF7367
Paible W Isls	102	NG0299
Paignton Devon	5	SX8960
Pailton Warwks	39	SP4781
Paincastle Powys	27	SO1646
Painshawfield Nthumb	68	NZ0560
Painsthorpe Humb	56	SE8158
Painswick Gloucs	28	SO8609
Painter's Forstal Kent	15	TQ9958
Paisley Strath	73	NS4864
Pakefield Suffk	33	TM5390
Pakenham Suffk	32	TL9267
Palestine Hants	21	SU2540
Palfrey W Mids	38	SP0197
Palgrave Suffk	33	TM1178
Pallington Dorset	9	SY7891
Palmers Green Gt Lon	23	TQ3193
Palmerston Strath	74	NS5019
Palnackie D & G	66	NX8257
Palnure D & G	65	NX4563
Palterton Derbys	49	SK4768
Pamber End Hants	21	SU6458
Pamber Green Hants	21	SU6059
Pamber Heath Hants	21	SU6162
Pamington Gloucs	28	SO9333
Pamphill Dorset	9	ST9900
Pampisford Cambs	31	TL4948
Panborough Somset	19	ST4846
Panbride Tays	83	NO5635
Pancrasweek Devon	6	SS2900
Pandy Gwent	27	SO3322
Pandy Gwent	27	SO3322
Pandy Gwent	35	SH6203
Pandy M Glam	19	ST1587
Pandy Tudur Clwyd	45	SH8564
Panfield Essex	24	TL7425
Pangbourne Berks	21	SU6376
Pangdean W Susx	12	TQ2911
Pannal N York	55	SE3051
Pannal Ash N York	55	SE2853
Pannanich Wells Hotel Gramp	88	NO4097
Pant Shrops	36	SJ2722
Pant-glas Gwynd	44	SH4747
Pant-y-dwr Powys	35	SN9874
Pant-y-mwyn Clwyd	46	SJ1964
Pant-yr-awel M Glam	18	SS9287
Pantglas Gwynd	35	SN7797
Panton Lincs	50	TF1778
Pantside Gwent	19	ST2297
Panxworth Norfk	43	TG3513
Papigoe Highld	100	ND3851
Papple Loth	76	NT5972
Papplewick Notts	49	SK5451
Papworth Everard Cambs	31	TL2862
Papworth St. Agnes Cambs	31	TL2664
Par Cnwll	3	SX0753
Paramour Street Kent	23	TQ2861
Parbold Lancs	53	SD4911
Parbrook W Susx	12	TQ0824
Parc Gwynd	45	SH8834
Parc Seymour Gwent	19	ST4091
Pardshaw Cumb	58	NY0925
Parham Suffk	33	TM3060
Park D & G	66	NX909
Park Gramp	89	NO7898
Park Nthumb	68	NY6861
Park Corner Berks	22	SU8583
Park Corner Oxon	22	SU6988
Park Bed Beds	30	SP9853
Park Gate Hants	11	SU5108
Park Gate W York	55	SE1841
Park Head W York	55	SE1907
Park Hill Gloucs	19	ST5699
Park Royal Gt Lon	22	TQ2082
Park Street W Susx	12	TQ1131
Parkend Gloucs	27	SO6108
Parkers Green Kent	13	TQ6138
Parkfield M Glam	4	SX5267
Parkgate D & G	66	NY0288
Parkgate Surrey	12	TQ2043
Parkhall Strath	81	NS4871
Parkham Devon	6	SS3821
Parkhill House Gramp	95	NJ8914
Parkhouse Gwent	19	SO5002
Parkmill W Glam	17	SS5489
Parkside Dur	69	NZ4148
Parkstone Dorset	10	SZ0491
Parlington N York	55	SE4235
Parndon Essex	23	TL4308
Parr Bridge Gt Man	47	SD7001
Parracombe Devon	7	SS6645
Parrog Dyfed	16	SN0439
Parson Drove Cambs	41	TF3708
Parson's Cross S York	49	SK3491
Parson's Heath Essex	25	TM0226
Partick Strath	74	NS5567
Partington Gt Man	47	SJ7191
Partney Lincs	51	TF4168
Parton Cumb	58	NX9720
Parton Cumb	59	NY2715
Parton D & G	65	NX6970
Partridge Green W Susx	12	TQ1919
Parwich Derbys	48	SK1854
Passenham Nhants	30	SP7839
Passfield Hants	11	SU8234
Passingford Bridge Essex	23	TQ5098
Paston Norfk	43	TG3234
Pasturefields Staffs	38	SJ9925
Patcham E Susx	12	TQ3009
Patching W Susx	12	TQ0806
Pathway Avon	19	ST6081
Pateley Bridge N York	55	SE1565
Path of Condie Tays	82	NO0711
Pathhead Gramp	89	NO7263
Pathhead Loth	76	NT3964
Pathhead Strath	66	NS6114
Patna Strath	73	NS4110
Patney Wilts	20	SU0758
Patrick IOM	52	SC2482

Patrick Brompton N York	61	SE2290
Patricroft Gt Man	47	SJ7597
Patrington Humb	57	TA3122
Patrixbourne Kent	15	TR1855
Patterdale Cumb	59	NY3915
Pattingham Staffs	38	SO8299
Pattishall Nhants	30	SP6754
Pattiswick Green Essex	24	TL8224
Paul Cnwll	2	SW4627
Paul's Dene Wilts	10	SU1432
Paulerspury Bucks	30	SP7144
Paull Humb	57	TA1626
Paulton Avon	19	ST6456
Pauperhaugh Nthumb	68	NZ1099
Pave Lane Shrops	37	SJ7516
Pavenham Beds	30	SP9955
Pawlett Somset	19	ST2942
Paxford Gloucs	29	SP1837
Paxton Border	77	NT9353
Payden Street Kent	14	TQ9253
Payhembury Devon	7	ST0801
Paythorne Lincs	54	SD8251
Peacehaven E Susx	13	TQ4101
Peak Hill Lincs	41	TF2614
Peakirk Cambs	40	TF1606
Pean Kent	15	TR1837
Peanmeanach Highld	85	NM7180
Pearsie Tays	88	NO3659
Pease Pottage W Susx	12	TQ2633
Peasedown St. John Avon	20	ST7057
Peaseland Norfk	42	TG0516
Peasemore Berks	21	SU4576
Peasenhall Suffk	33	TM3569
Peaslake Surrey	12	TQ0844
Peasley Cross Mersyd	46	SJ5294
Peasmarsh E Susx	14	TQ8822
Peasmarsh Somset	8	ST3313
Peat Inn Fife	83	NO4509
Peathill Gramp	95	NJ9365
Peatling Magna Leics	39	SP5992
Peatling Parva Leics	39	SP5989
Pebmarsh Essex	24	TL8633
Pebworth H & W	28	SP1347
Pecket Well W York	54	SD9929
Peckforton Ches	46	SJ5356
Peckham Gt Lon	23	TQ3476
Peckleton Leics	39	SK4701
Pedlinge Kent	15	TR1335
Pedmore W Mids	38	SO9182
Pedwell Somset	19	ST4236
Peebles Border	75	NT2540
Peel IOM	52	SC2484
Peel Common Hants	11	SU5804
Pegsdon Beds	30	TL1130
Pegswood Nthumb	69	NZ2287
Pegwell Kent	15	TR3664
Peinchorran Highld	84	NG5233
Peinlich Highld	90	NG4158
Pelaw T & W	69	NZ2962
Peldon Essex	25	TL9817
Pell Green E Susx	14	TQ6736
Pelsall W Mids	38	SK0103
Pelsall Wood W Mids	38	SK0103
Pelton Dur	69	NZ2552
Pelynt Cnwll	4	SX2055
Pemberton Devon	5	SS5300
Pemberton Dyfed	17	SN5500
Pemberton Gt Man	47	SD5503
Pembles Cross Kent	14	TQ8847
Pembrey Dyfed	17	SN4201
Pembridge H & W	27	SO3958
Pembroke Dyfed	16	SM9901
Pembroke Dock Dyfed	16	SM9603
Pembury Kent	13	TQ6240
Pen Rhiwfawr W Glam	26	SN7410
Pen-Sarn Gwynd	44	SH4344
Pen-Sarn Gwynd	44	SH5728
Pen-bont Rhydybeddau Dyfed	35	SN6582
Pen-ffordd Dyfed	16	SN0722
Pen-groes-oped Gwent	27	SO3107
Pen-llyn Gwynd	44	SH3482
Pen-lon Gwynd	44	SH4364
Pen-twyn Gwent	27	SO5209
Pen-y-Gwryd Hotel Gwynd	44	SH6555
Pen-y-bont Clwyd	36	SJ2123
Pen-y-bryn Dyfed	17	SN1743
Pen-y-cae-mawr Gwent	19	ST4095
Pen-y-clawdd Gwent	27	SO4507
Pen-y-coedcae M Glam	18	ST0687
Pen-y-cwm Dyfed	16	SM8423
Pen-y-darren M Glam	28	SO0506
Pen-y-felin Clwyd	46	SJ1569
Pen-y-genffordd Powys	27	SO1730
Pen-y-graig Gwynd	44	SH1933
Pen-y-stryt Clwyd	46	SJ1952
Pen-y-stryt Clwyd	46	SJ2052
Penallt Gwent	27	SO5210
Penally Dyfed	16	SS1199
Penare Cnwll	3	SW9940
Penarth S Glam	19	ST1872
Penbryn Dyfed	17	SN2952
Pencader Dyfed	17	SN4436
Pencaitland Loth	76	NT4468
Pencarnisiog Gwynd	44	SH3573
Pencarreg Dyfed	17	SN5345
Pencelli Powys	26	SO0925
Penclawdd W Glam	17	SS5495
Pencoed M Glam	18	SS9681
Pencombe H & W	27	SO5952
Pencraig H & W	27	SO5620
Pencraig Powys	36	SJ0426
Pendeen Cnwll	2	SW3834
Penderyn M Glam	26	SN9408
Pendine Dyfed	17	SN2308
Pendlebury Gt Man	47	SD7802
Pendleton Lancs	54	SD7539
Pendock H & W	28	SO7832
Pendoggett Cnwll	3	SX0279
Pendomer Somset	8	ST5210
Pendoylan S Glam	18	ST0776
Penegoes Powys	35	SH7701
Pengam Gwent	19	ST1597
Pengam S Glam	19	ST2178
Penge Gt Lon	23	TQ3570
Pengelly Cnwll	3	SX0783
Pengover Green Cnwll	4	SX2865
Pengrugla Cnwll	3	SW9947
Pengwern Clwyd	45	SJ0176
Penhallow Cnwll	2	SW7651
Penhalvean Cnwll	2	SW7037
Penhill Wilts	20	SU1588
Penhow Gwent	19	ST4290
Penifiler Highld	84	NG4841
Peninver Strath	72	NR7524
Penisar Waun Gwynd	44	SH5564
Penistone S York	55	SE2402
Penkill Strath	64	NX2398
Penkridge Staffs	38	SJ9214
Penlean Cnwll	4	SX2098
Penllyn S Glam	18	SS9776
Penmachno Gwynd	45	SH7950
Penmaen Gwent	19	ST1897
Penmaen W Glam	17	SS5388
Penmaenmawr Gwynd	45	SH7176
Penmaenan Gwynd	45	SH7176
Penmaenpool Gwynd	35	SH6918
Penmark S Glam	18	ST0568
Penmon Gwynd	44	SH6381
Penmorfa Gwynd	44	SH5440
Penmynydd Gwynd	44	SH5174
Penn Bucks	22	SU9193
Penn Green Notts	49	SK5735
Penn Street Bucks	22	SU9295
Pennal Gwynd	35	SH6900
Pennan Gramp	95	NJ8465
Pennant Powys	35	SN8897
Pennant W Glam	17	SS5688
Pennerley Shrops	36	SO3599
Pennington Cumb	59	SD2677
Pennington Hants	10	SZ3194
Penntorth Powys	26	SO1125
Penny Bridge Cumb	59	SD3183
Penny Hill Lincs	41	TF3626
Pennycross Strath	79	NM5025
Pennygate Strath	79	NM4525
Pennyghael Strath	79	NM5125
Pennyglen Strath	73	NS2710
Pennygown Strath	79	NM6042

Place	County	Page	Grid
Pennymoor	Devon	7	SS8611
Penparc	Cnwll	17	SN2148
Penperlleni	Gwent	27	SO3204
Penpillick	Cnwll	3	SX0756
Penpoll	Cnwll	3	SX1454
Penponds	Cnwll	2	SW6339
Penpont	D & G	66	NX6494
Penrest	M Glam	4	SX3378
Penrherber	Dyfed	17	SN2839
Penrhiw	Dyfed	17	SN2440
Penrhiwceiber	M Glam	18	ST0597
Penrhiwllan	Dyfed	17	SN3742
Penrhiwpal	Dyfed	17	SN3445
Penrhos	Gwent	27	SO4411
Penrhos	Gwynd	44	SH3433
Penrhyn Bay	Gwynd	45	SH8281
Penrhyncoch	Dyfed	35	SN6384
Penrhyndeudraeth	Gwynd	45	SH6138
Penrice	W Glam	17	SS4987
Penrioch	Strath	72	NR8744
Penrith	Cumb	59	NY5130
Penrose	Cnwll	3	SW8770
Penruddock	Cumb	59	NY4227
Penryn	Cnwll	2	SW7834
Pensarn	Clwyd	45	SH9478
Pensax	H & W	28	SO7269
Penselwood	Somset	9	ST7531
Pensford	Avon	19	ST6263
Pensham	H & W	28	SO9444
Penshurst	Kent	13	TQ5243
Pensilva	Cnwll	4	SX2969
Pentewan	Cnwll	3	SX0147
Pentir	Gwynd	44	SH5767
Pentire	Cnwll	2	SW7961
Pentlow	Essex	32	TL8146
Pentney	Norfk	42	TF7214
Penton Grafton	Hants	21	SU3247
Penton Mewsey	Hants	21	SU3347
Pentraeth	Gwynd	44	SH5278
Pentre	Clwyd	46	SJ3267
Pentre	M Glam	18	SS9796
Pentre	Powys	36	SO0686
Pentre	Shrops	36	SJ3617
Pentre Bach	Clwyd	46	SJ2176
Pentre Berw	Gwynd	44	SH4772
Pentre Hodrey	Shrops	36	SO3277
Pentre Meyrick	S Glam	18	SS9675
Pentre-Cagal	Dyfed	17	SN3440
Pentre-Dolau-Honddu	Powys	26	SN9943
Pentre-Gwenlais	Dyfed	17	SN6116
Pentre-Maw	Powys	35	SH8903
Pentre-bach	Powys	26	SN9133
Pentre-celyn	Clwyd	46	SJ1453
Pentre-celyn	Powys	35	SH8905
Pentre-cwrt	Dyfed	17	SN3838
Pentre-llyn	Dyfed	35	SN6174
Pentre-piod	Gwent	19	SO2602
Pentre-poeth	Gwent	19	ST2687
Pentre-tafarn-y-fedw	Gwynd	45	SH8162
Pentrebach	M Glam	26	SO0604
Pentrebeirdd	Powys	36	SJ1913
Pentredwr	Clwyd	46	SJ1946
Pentrefelin	Gwynd	44	SH5239
Pentrefoelas	Clwyd	45	SH8751
Pentregalar	Dyfed	17	SN1831
Pentregat	Dyfed	17	SN3551
Pentrich	Derbys	49	SK3852
Pentridge Hill	Dorset	9	SU0317
Pentyrch	M Glam	18	ST1081
Penwithick	Cnwll	3	SX0256
Penybanc	Dyfed	17	SN6124
Penybont	Powys	26	SO1164
Penybontfawr	Powys	36	SJ0824
Penybryn	M Glam	18	ST1395
Penycae	Clwyd	46	SJ2745
Penyffordd	Clwyd	46	SJ3061
Penygarneddd	Powys	36	SJ1023
Penygraig	M Glam	18	SS9890
Penygroes	Dyfed	17	SN5813
Penygroes	Gwynd	44	SH4753
Penysarn	Gwynd	44	SH4690
Penywaun	M Glam	26	SN9804
Penzance	Cnwll	2	SW4730
Peopleton	H & W	28	SO9350
Peover Heath	Ches	47	SJ7973
Pepper Harow	Surrey	22	SU9344
Peplow	Shrops	37	SJ6324
Pepper's Green	Essex	24	TL6210
Pepperstock	Beds	30	TL0817
Percie	Gramp	89	NO5991
Percyhorner	Gramp	95	NJ9665
Perelle	Guern	101	SV0000
Periton	Somset	7	SS9645
Perivale	Gt Lon	23	TQ1682
Perkin's Beach	Shrops	36	SJ3600
Perkins Village	Devon	5	SY0291
Perkinsville	Dur	69	NZ2553
Perlethorpe	Notts	49	SK6471
Permanorm	Loth	75	NT2459
Perran Wharf	Cnwll	2	SW7738
Perranporth	Cnwll	2	SW7554
Perranuthnoe	Cnwll	2	SW5329
Perranwell	Cnwll	2	SW7739
Perranwell	Cnwll	2	SW7752
Perry	W Mids	38	SP0792
Perry Barr	W Mids	38	SP0791
Perry Green	Essex	24	TL8122
Perry Green	Somset	19	ST2738
Perry Green	Wilts	20	ST9689
Perry Street	Somset	8	ST3405
Pershall	Staffs	37	SJ8129
Pershore	H & W	28	SO9445
Perth	Tays	82	NO1123
Perthcelyn	M Glam	18	ST0595
Perthy	Shrops	36	SJ3633
Perton	Staffs	38	SO8699
Pertwood	Wilts	20	ST8936
Peter Tavy	Devon	4	SX5177
Peterborough	Cambs	40	TL1989
Peterchurch	H & W	27	SO3438
Peterculter	Gramp	89	NJ8400
Peterhead	Gramp	95	NK1246
Peterlee	Dur	62	NZ4341
Peters Marland	Devon	6	SS4713
Petersfield	Hants	11	SU7423
Petersham	Gt Lon	23	TQ1873
Peterstone Wentlooge	Gwent	19	ST2679
Peterstonsuper-Ely	S Glam	18	ST0876
Peterstow	H & W	27	SO5624
Petham	Kent	15	TR1251
Petherwin Gate	Cnwll	4	SX2889
Petrockstow	Devon	17	SS5190
Pett	E Susx	14	TQ8714
Pettaugh	Suffk	33	TM1659
Petterden	Tays	83	NO4240
Pettinain	Strath	75	NS9542
Pettistree	Suffk	33	TM3055
Petton	Devon	7	ST0024
Petts Wood	Gt Lon	23	TQ4567
Pettycur	Fife	83	NT2686
Pettymuick	Gramp	95	NJ9024
Petworth	W Susx	12	SU9721
Pevensey	E Susx	13	TQ6405
Pewsey	Wilts	20	SU1660
Pheasant's Hill	Bucks	22	SU7887
Phepson	H & W	28	SO9459
Philham	Devon	6	SS2522
Philiphaugh	Border	76	NT4327
Phillack	Cnwll	2	SW5638
Phillleigh	Cnwll	3	SW8739
Philpot End	Essex	24	TL6118
Philpstoun	Loth	75	NT0677
Phocle Green	H & W	27	SO6226
Phoenix Green	Hants	22	SU7555
Phones	Highld	87	NN7093
Pibsbury	Somset	8	ST4326
Pica	Cumb	58	NY0222
Pickering	N York	63	SE7983
Picket Piece	Hants	21	SU3947
Picket Post	Hants	10	SU1905
Pickford	W Mids	39	SP2781
Pickhill	N York	62	SE3483
Picklescott	Shrops	36	SO4399
Pickmere	Ches	47	SJ6977
Pickney	Somset	8	ST2128
Pickup Bank	Lancs	54	SD7122
Pickwell	Devon	6	SS4540
Pickwell	Leics	40	SK7811
Pickworth	Leics	40	SK9913
Pickworth	Lincs	40	TF0433
Pictillum	Gramp	95	NJ7317
Picton	Ches	46	SJ4371
Picton	Clwyd	46	SJ1282
Picton	N York	62	NZ4107
Piddinghoe	E Susx	13	TQ4303
Piddington	Nhants	30	SP8054
Piddington	Oxon	29	SP6317
Piddlehinton	Dorset	9	SY7197
Piddletrenthide	Dorset	9	SY7099
Pidley	Cambs	31	TL3377
Piercebridge	Dur	61	NZ2015
Pierowall	Ork	103	HY4348
Piff's Elm	Gloucs	28	SO8926
Pilgrims Hatch	Essex	24	TQ5895
Pilham	Lincs	50	SK8693
Pillaton	Cnwll	4	SX3664
Pillatonmill	M Glam	4	SX3063
Pilley	Hants	10	SZ3398
Pilley	S York	49	SE3300
Pillgwenlly	Gwent	19	ST3186
Pilling	Lancs	53	SD4048
Pilning	Avon	19	ST5684
Pilsbury	Derbys	48	SK1163
Pilsdon	Dorset	8	SY4199
Pilsley	Derbys	48	SK2471
Pilsley	Derbys	49	SK4262
Pilson Green	Norfk	43	TG3713
Piltdown	E Susx	13	TQ4422
Pilton	Leics	40	SK9102
Pilton	Nhants	40	TL0284
Pilton	Somset	19	ST5940
Pimlico	Lancs	54	SD7543
Pimperne	Dorset	9	ST9009
Pin Green	Herts	31	TL2525
Pinchbeck	Lincs	41	TF2425
Pinchbeck Bars	Lincs	41	TF1905
Pincock	Lancs	53	SD5517
Pinford End	Suffk	32	TL8559
Pinhoe	Devon	7	SX9694
Pinmill	Suffk	25	TM2037
Pinminnoch	Strath	64	NX1993
Pinmore	Strath	64	NX2091
Pinn	Devon	7	SX0986
Pinner	Gt Lon	22	TQ1289
Pinner Green	Gt Lon	22	TQ1290
Pinvin	H & W	28	SO9549
Pinwherry	Strath	64	NX2086
Pinxton	Derbys	49	SK4555
Pipe Gate	Shrops	37	SJ7340
Pipe and Lyde	H & W	27	SO5043
Pipehill	Staffs	38	SK0908
Piperhill	Highld	93	NH8650
Pipewell	Nhants	40	SP8385
Pippin Street	Lancs	54	SD5824
Pirbright	Surrey	22	SU9455
Pirbright Camp	Surrey	22	SU9257
Pirnie	Border	76	NT6528
Pirton	H & W	28	SO8847
Pirton	Herts	30	TL1431
Pishill	Oxon	22	SU7389
Pistyll	Gwynd	44	SH3242
Pitagowan	Tays	87	NN8165
Pitblae	Gramp	95	NJ9864
Pitcairngreen	Tays	82	NO0627
Pitcalnie	Highld	93	NH8172
Pitcaple	Gramp	95	NJ7225
Pitcarity	Tays	88	NO3365
Pitch Green	Bucks	22	SP7703
Pitch Place	Surrey	11	SU8939
Pitchcombe	Gloucs	28	SO8508
Pitchcott	Bucks	30	SP7720
Pitchford	Shrops	37	SJ5303
Pitchroy	Gramp	94	NJ1738
Pitcombe	Somset	9	ST6732
Pitcot	M Glam	18	SS8974
Pitcox	Loth	76	NT6475
Pitcur	Tays	83	NO2437
Pitfichie	Gramp	95	NJ6716
Pitfour Castle	Tays	82	NO1921
Pitglassie	Gramp	95	NJ6943
Pitgrudy	Highld	97	NH7991
Pitkennedy	Tays	89	NO5454
Pitlessie	Fife	83	NO3309
Pitlochry	Tays	87	NN9458
Pitmachie	Gramp	95	NJ6728
Pitmain	Highld	87	NH7400
Pitmedden	Gramp	95	NJ8827
Pitminster	Somset	8	ST2119
Pitmuies	Tays	89	NO5649
Pitmunie	Gramp	94	NJ6615
Pitney	Somset	8	ST4428
Pitroddie	Tays	82	NO2125
Pitscottie	Fife	83	NO4112
Pitsea	Essex	24	TQ7488
Pitsford	Nhants	30	SP7568
Pitsford Hill	Somset	7	ST0930
Pitt	Devon	7	SO0316
Pittarrow	Gramp	89	NO7274
Pittenweem	Fife	83	NO5502
Pittleuchar	Fife	83	NT2899
Pittington	Dur	62	NZ3244
Pitodrie	Gramp	95	NJ6925
Pitton	Wilts	10	SU2131
Pittulie	Gramp	95	NJ9567
Pity Me	Dur	69	NZ2645
Pityme	Cnwll	3	SW9575
Pixham	Surrey	12	TQ1750
Plains	Strath	74	NS7966
Plaish	Shrops	37	SO5296
Plaistow	Derbys	49	SK3556
Plaistow	Gt Lon	23	TQ4082
Plaistow	W Susx	12	TQ0030
Plaitford	Hants	10	SU2719
Plaitford	Hants	10	SU2719
Plas Llanfair	Gwynd	44	SH5371
Plas Llysyn	Powys	35	SN9596
Plastow Green	Hants	21	SU5361
Platt	Kent	14	TQ6257
Plawsworth	Dur	69	NZ2647
Plaxtol	Kent	13	TQ6053
Play Hatch	Oxon	22	SU7376
Playden	E Susx	14	TQ9121
Playford	Suffk	33	TM2147
Playing Place	Cnwll	2	SW8141
Playley Green	Gloucs	28	SO7631
Plealey	Shrops	36	SJ4206
Plean	Cent	82	NS8386
Pleasance	Fife	83	NO2312
Pleasey Hill	Notts	55	SE5064
Pleasington	Lancs	54	SD6426
Pleck	Dorset	9	ST7011
Pleinheaume	Guern	101	SV0000
Plemont	Jersey	101	SV0000
Plemstall	Ches	46	SJ4570
Plenmeller	Nthumb	68	NY7162
Pleshey	Essex	24	TL6614
Plockton	Highld	85	NG8033
Ploughfield	H & W	27	SO3841
Plowden	Shrops	36	SO3888
Ploxgreen	Shrops	36	SJ3604
Pluckley	Kent	14	TQ9245
Pluckley Thorne	Kent	15	TQ9044
Plumley	Ches	47	SJ7275
Plumpton	E Susx	12	TQ3613
Plumpton End	Nhants	30	SP7245
Plumpton Green	E Susx	12	TQ3616
Plumstead	Gt Lon	23	TQ4478
Plumstead	Norfk	43	TG1335
Plumstead Green	Norfk	43	TG1334
Plumtree	Notts	39	SK6133
Plungar	Leics	40	SK7633
Plusenden	Kent	14	TQ9237
Plush	Dorset	9	ST7102
Plwmp	Dyfed	17	SN3652
Plymouth	Devon	4	SX4755
Plympton	Devon	4	SX5356
Plymtree	Devon	7	ST0502
Pockley	N York	62	SE6085
Pocklington	Humb	56	SE8048
Podimore	Somset	8	ST5424
Podington	Beds	30	SP9462
Podmore	Staffs	37	SJ7835
Pointon	Lincs	40	TF1131
Pokesdown	Dorset	10	SZ1292
Polbae	D & G	64	NX2873
Polbain	Highld	91	NB9910
Polbathic	Cnwll	4	SX3456
Polbeth	Loth	75	NT0364
Polchar	Highld	93	NH8909
Pole Elm	H & W	28	SO8450
Polebrook	Nhants	40	TL0687
Polegate	E Susx	13	TQ5804
Polesworth	Warwks	39	SK2602
Polglass	Highld	91	NC0307
Polgooth	Cnwll	3	SW9950
Polgown	D & G	66	NS7104
Poling	W Susx	12	TQ0404
Poling Corner	W Susx	12	TQ0405
Polkerris	Cnwll	3	SX0952
Polla	Highld	98	NC3854
Pollington	Humb	56	SE6119
Polloch	Highld	79	NM7868
Pollokshaws	Strath	74	NS5661
Pollokshields	Strath	74	NS5773
Polmassick	Cnwll	3	SW9745
Polmear	Cent	3	SX0833
Polmont	Cent	82	NS9378
Polnish	Highld	85	NM7582
Polperro	Cnwll	4	SX2051
Polruan	Cnwll	3	SX1250
Polsham	Somset	19	ST5142
Polstead	Suffk	25	TL9938
Poltalloch	Strath	71	NR8196
Poltescoe	Cnwll	2	SW7215
Poltimore	Devon	7	SX9696
Polton	Loth	75	NT2864
Polwarth	Border	76	NT7450
Polyphant	Cnwll	4	SX2682
Polzeath	Cnwll	3	SW9378
Ponders End	Gt Lon	23	TQ3596
Pondersbridge	Cambs	41	TL2692
Ponsanooth	Cnwll	2	SW7537
Ponsworthy	Devon	5	SX7073
Pont Pen-y-bénglog	Gwynd	45	SH6460
Pont Robert	Powys	36	SJ1112
Pontardulais	W Glam	17	SN5903
Pontarsais	Dyfed	17	SN4428
Pontblyddyn	Clwyd	46	SJ2760
Pontefract	W York	55	SE4521
Ponteland	Nthumb	69	NZ1673
Ponterwyd	Dyfed	35	SN7481
Pontesbury	Shrops	36	SJ3906
Pontesbury Hill	Shrops	36	SJ3905
Pontesford	Shrops	36	SJ4106
Pontfadog	Clwyd	36	SJ2338
Pontfaen	Dyfed	16	SN0234
Pontgarreg	Dyfed	34	SN3354
Ponthenry	Dyfed	17	SN4709
Ponthir	Gwent	19	ST3293
Ponthirwaun	Dyfed	17	SN2645
Pontllanfraith	Gwent	19	ST1895
Pontlliw	W Glam	17	SN6101
Pontlyfni	Gwynd	44	SH4352
Pontnewydd	Gwent	19	ST2896
Pontop	Dur	69	NZ1453
Pontrhydfendigaid	Dyfed	35	SN7366
Pontrhydygroes	Dyfed	35	SN7472
Pontrilas	H & W	27	SO3927
Ponts Green	E Susx	14	TQ6716
Pontshaen	Dyfed	17	SN4446
Pontshill	H & W	27	SO6321
Pontsticill	M Glam	26	SO0511
Pontwelly	Dyfed	17	SN4140
Pontyates	Dyfed	17	SN4708
Pontyberem	Dyfed	17	SN5011
Pontybodkin	Clwyd	46	SJ2659
Pontyclun	M Glam	18	ST0381
Pontycymer	M Glam	18	SS9091
Pontypool	Gwent	19	SO2800
Pontypridd	M Glam	18	ST0790
Pontywaun	Gwent	19	ST2292
Pool	Cnwll	2	SW6741
Pool	IOS	2	SV8714
Pool	W York	55	SE2445
Pool O' Muckhart	Cent	82	NO0000
Pool Street	Essex	24	TL7637
Poole	Dorset	9	SZ0190
Poole Keynes	Wilts	20	ST9995
Poolewe	Highld	91	NG8680
Pooley Bridge	Cumb	59	NY4724
Poolfold	Staffs	48	SJ8959
Poolhill	Gloucs	28	SO7329
Poolmill	H & W	27	SO5724
Pooting's	Kent	13	TQ4449
Popham	Hants	21	SU5543
Poplar	Gt Lon	23	TQ3780
Porchfield	IOW	10	SZ4491
Porin	Highld	92	NH3155
Porkellis	Cnwll	2	SW6933
Porlock	Somset	7	SS8846
Porlock Weir	Somset	18	SS8647
Port Akaig	Strath	70	NR4369
Port Appin	Strath	79	NM9045
Port Bannatyne	Strath	73	NS0867
Port Carlisle	Cumb	67	NY2461
Port Charlotte	Strath	70	NR2558
Port Clarence	Cleve	62	NZ5022
Port Cornaa	IOM	52	SC4787
Port Dinorwic	Gwynd	44	SH5267
Port Driseach	Strath	80	NR9973
Port Ellen	Strath	70	NR3645
Port Elphinstone	Gramp	95	NJ7720
Port Erin	IOM	52	SC1969
Port Erroll	Gramp	95	NK0935
Port Glasgow	Strath	80	NS3274
Port Henderson	Highld	91	NG7573
Port Isaac	Cnwll	3	SW9980
Port Logan	D & G	64	NX0940
Port Mor	Highld	84	NM4279
Port Na-Craig	Tays	75	NN9357
Port Quin	Cnwll	3	SW9780
Port Ramsay	Strath	79	NM8845
Port Soderick	IOM	52	SC3472
Port St. Mary	IOM	52	SC2067
Port Talbot	W Glam	18	SS7589
Port Wemyss	Strath	70	NR1751
Port William	D & G	64	NX3343
Port e Vullen	IOM	52	SC4793
Port of Menteith	Cent	81	NN5801
Port of Ness	W Isls	102	NB5363
Portachoillan	Strath	71	NR7557
Portavadie	Strath	71	NR9369
Portbury	Avon	19	ST5075
Portchester	Hants	11	SU6105
Portencalzie	D & G	64	NX0171
Portencross	Strath	73	NS1748
Portesham	Dorset	9	SY6085
Portessie	Gramp	94	NJ4366
Portgate	H & W	27	SX4285
Portgordon	Gramp	94	NJ3964
Portgower	Highld	97	ND0013
Porth	M Glam	18	ST0291
Porth	Cnwll	2	SW6618
Porth Navas	Cnwll	2	SW7527
Porth-y-Waen	Shrops	36	SJ2642
Porthallow	Cnwll	2	SX2251
Porthcawl	M Glam	18	SS8177
Porthcothan	Cnwll	3	SW8572
Porthcurno	Cnwll	2	SW3822
Porthgain	Dyfed	16	SM8132
Porthill	Staffs	47	SJ8448
Porthkerry	S Glam	18	ST0866
Porthleven	Cnwll	2	SW6225
Porthmadog	Gwynd	44	SH5638
Porthmeor	Cnwll	2	SW4337
Porthoustock	Cnwll	3	SW8021
Porthpean	Cnwll	3	SX0250
Porthtowan	Cnwll	2	SW6947
Porthyrhyd	Dyfed	17	SN5215
Porthyrhyd	Dyfed	26	SN7137
Portincaple	Strath	80	NS2393
Portinfer	Jersey	101	SV0000
Portington	Humb	56	SE7830
Portinnisherrich	Strath	80	NM9711
Portinscale	Cumb	58	NY2524
Portishead	Avon	19	ST4675
Portknockie	Gramp	94	NJ4868
Portlethen	Gramp	89	NO9296
Portloe	Cnwll	3	SW9339
Portmahomack	Highld	97	NH9184
Portmeirion	Gwynd	44	SH5937
Portmellon	Cnwll	3	SX0143
Portnacroish	Strath	79	NM9247
Portnaguiran	W Isls	102	NB5537
Portnahaven	Strath	70	NR1652
Portnalong	Highld	84	NG3435
Portnancon	Highld	98	NC4260
Portneora	Highld	85	NG7731
Portobello	Loth	75	NT3073
Portobello	T & W	69	NZ2755
Portobello	W Mids	38	SO9598
Porton	Wilts	10	SU1836
Portpatrick	D & G	64	NX0054
Portreath	Cnwll	2	SW6545
Portreath	Cnwll	2	SW9679
Portree	Highld	90	NG4843
Portrye	Strath	73	NS1757
Portscatho	Cnwll	3	SW8735
Portsea	Hants	11	SU6300
Portskerra	Highld	99	NC8765
Portskewett	Gwent	19	ST4988
Portslade	E Susx	12	TQ2506
Portslade-by-Sea	E Susx	12	TQ2604
Portsmouth	Hants	11	SU6400
Portsmouth	W York	54	SD9026
Portsoy	Gramp	94	NJ5866
Portswood	Hants	10	SU4314
Portuairk	Highld	79	NM4468
Portvasgo	Highld	99	NC5865
Portway	Cnwll	4	SX3553
Portway	H & W	27	SO4844
Portway	H & W	36	SO0872
Portway	W Mids	38	SO9788
Portwrinkle	Cnwll	4	SX3553
Poslingford	Suffk	32	TL7748
Posso	Border	75	NT2033
Post Green	Dorset	9	SY8683
Postbridge	Devon	5	SX6579
Postcombe	Oxon	22	SU7099
Postling	Kent	15	TR1439
Postwick	Norfk	43	TG2907
Pothole	Cnwll	3	SW9750
Potsgrove	Beds	30	SP9529
Pott Shrigley	Ches	48	SJ9479
Potten Street	Kent	23	TQ2567
Potter Brompton	N York	63	SE9776
Potter Heigham	Norfk	43	TG4119
Potter Somersal	Derbys	38	SK1436
Potter's Forstal	Kent	14	TO8946
Potter's Green	Herts	31	TL3520
Pottergate Street	Norfk	33	TM1581
Potterhanworth	Lincs	50	TF0166
Potterhanworth Booths	Lincs	50	TF0767
Potterne	Wilts	20	ST9958
Potterne Wick	Wilts	20	ST9957
Potters Bar	Herts	23	TL2501
Potters Crouch	Herts	22	TL1105
Potters Green	W Mids	39	SP3781
Potters Marston	Leics	39	SP4996
Pottershash	Herts	31	TL2318
Potterspury	Nhants	30	SP7543
Potterton	W York	55	SE4038
Pottle Street	Wilts	20	ST8141
Potto	N York	62	NZ4703
Potton	Beds	31	TL2249
Poughill	Cnwll	6	SS2207
Poughill	Devon	7	SS8508
Poulshot	Wilts	20	ST9659
Poulton	Gloucs	20	SP0900
Poulton-le-Fylde	Lancs	53	SD3439
Pound Green	E Susx	13	TQ5123
Pound Green	Hants	21	SU5759
Pound Street	Hants	21	SU4561
Poundffald	W Glam	17	SS6494
Poundgates	E Susx	13	TQ4918
Poundon	Bucks	29	SP6425
Poundsgate	Devon	5	SX7072
Poundstock	Cnwll	6	SX2099
Povey Cross	Surrey	12	TQ2642
Pow Green	H & W	28	SO7044
Powburn	Nthumb	77	NU0616
Powderham	Devon	5	SX9684
Powerstock	Dorset	8	SY5196
Powfoot	D & G	67	NY1465
Powhill	Cumb	67	NY2355
Powick	H & W	28	SO8351
Powler's Piece	Devon	6	SS3618
Powmill	Tays	82	NT0097
Poxwell	Dorset	9	SY7484
Poynings	W Susx	12	TQ2612
Poynters	Dorset	78	SE7419
Poynton	Ches	48	SJ9283
Poynton Green	Shrops	37	SJ5717
Poynton Green	Shrops	37	SJ5618
Poys Street	Suffk	33	TM3570
Poystreet Green	Suffk	32	TL9858
Praa Sands	Cnwll	2	SW5828
Pratt's Bottom	Gt Lon	23	TQ4762
Prawle Point	Devon	5	SX7734
Praze-an-Beeble	Cnwll	2	SW6336
Prees	Shrops	37	SJ5533
Prees Green	Shrops	37	SJ5531
Prees Higher Heath	Shrops	37	SJ5636
Preesall	Lancs	53	SD3647
Pren-gwyn	Dyfed	17	SN4244
Prendwick	Nthumb	68	NU0012
Prenteg	Gwynd	44	SH5841
Prescot	Mersyd	46	SJ4692
Prescott	Devon	7	ST0814
Presnerb	Tays	88	NO1866
Prestatyn	Clwyd	45	SJ0682
Prestbury	Ches	48	SJ9077
Prestbury	Gloucs	28	SO9723
Presteigne	Powys	27	SO3164
Prestleigh	Somset	19	ST6340
Preston	Border	76	NT7957
Preston	Devon	5	SX7351
Preston	Devon	5	SX8574
Preston	Dorset	9	SY7083
Preston	E Susx	12	TQ3106
Preston	Gloucs	28	SO6734
Preston	Gloucs	20	SP0400
Preston	Herts	31	TL1824
Preston	Kent	15	TR0260
Preston	Lancs	53	SD5329
Preston	Leics	40	SK8602
Preston	Loth	76	NT5977
Preston	Nthumb	77	NU1825
Preston	Shrops	37	SJ5215
Preston	Shrops	18	ST1036
Preston	Suffk	32	TL9450
Preston	Wilts	21	SU2774
Preston Bagot	Warwks	29	SP1766
Preston Bissett	Bucks	29	SP6529
Preston Bowyer	Somset	8	ST1326
Preston Brook	Ches	47	SJ5680
Preston Candover	Hants	21	SU6041
Preston Capes	Nhants	29	SP5754
Preston Gubbals	Shrops	37	SJ4919
Preston Patrick	Cumb	59	SD5483
Preston Plucknett	Somset	8	ST5515
Preston Street	Kent	23	TQ2561
Preston Wynne	H & W	27	SO5648
Preston on Stour	Warwks	29	SP2049
Preston on Wye	H & W	27	SO3842
Preston on the Hill	Ches	47	SJ5780
Preston upon the Weald Moors	Shrops	37	SJ6815
Preston-under-Scar	N York	61	SE0791
Prestonpans	Loth	76	NT3874
Prestwich	Gt Man	47	SD8104
Prestwick	Strath	73	NS3525
Prestwood	Bucks	22	SP8700
Prestwood	Staffs	38	SO8686
Prickwillow	Cambs	31	TL5982
Priddy	Somset	19	ST5250
Priest Hutton	Lancs	59	SD5373
Priestacott	Devon	6	SS4206
Priestcliffe	Derbys	48	SK1471
Priestcliffe Ditch	Derbys	48	SK1271

Priestend *Bucks*	22	SP6906
Priestweston *Shrops*	36	SO2997
Primrose Green *Norfk*	42	TG0616
Primrose Hill *Nthumb*	76	NT7857
Primsidemill *Border*	76	NT8126
Princes Risborough *Bucks*	22	SP8003
Princethorpe *Warwks*	29	SP4070
Princetown *Devon*	5	SX5873
Prinsted *W Susx*	11	SU7605
Priors Hardwick *Warwks*	29	SP4756
Priors Marston *Warwks*	29	SP4957
Priors Norton *Gloucs*	28	SO8624
Priory Wood *H & W*	27	SO2545
Priston *Avon*	20	ST6960
Prittlewell *Essex*	24	TQ8687
Privett *Hants*	11	SU6727
Prixton *Devon*	6	SS5436
Probus *Cnwll*	3	SW8947
Prospect *Cumb*	58	NY1041
Prospidnick *Cnwll*	2	SW6431
Prostonhill *Gramp*	95	NJ8163
Providence *Avon*	19	ST5370
Prowse *Devon*	7	SS8405
Prudhoe *Nthumb*	68	NZ0962
Ptarmigan Lodge *Cent*	80	NN3500
Publow *Avon*	19	ST6264
Puckeridge *Herts*	31	TL3823
Puckington *Somset*	8	ST3718
Pucklechurch *Avon*	20	ST6976
Puddinglake *Ches*	47	SJ7269
Puddington *Ches*	46	SJ3273
Puddington *Devon*	7	SS8310
Puddletown *Dorset*	9	SY7594
Pudleston *H & W*	27	SO5659
Pudsey *W York*	55	SE2232
Pulborough *W Susx*	12	TQ0418
Pulham Market *Norfk*	33	TM1986
Pulham St. Mary *Norfk*	33	TM2185
Pulloxhill *Beds*	30	TL0634
Pumpherston *Loth*	75	NT0669
Pumsaint *Dyfed*	26	SN6540
Puncheston *Dyfed*	16	SN0030
Puncknowle *Dorset*	8	SY5388
Punnett's Town *E Susx*	13	TQ6220
Purbrook Park *Hants*	11	SU6107
Purfleet *Essex*	24	TQ5578
Puriton *Somset*	19	ST3241
Purleigh *Essex*	24	TL8402
Purley *Berks*	22	SU6675
Purley *Gt Lon*	23	TQ3161
Purls Bridge *Cambs*	41	TL4787
Purse Caundle *Dorset*	9	ST6917
Purslow *Shrops*	36	SO3681
Purslow *Shrops*	36	SO3681
Purtington *Somset*	8	ST3808
Purton *Gloucs*	28	SO6705
Purton *Gloucs*	28	SO6904
Purton Stoke *Wilts*	20	SU0990
Pury End *Nhants*	30	SP7045
Pusey *Oxon*	21	SU3596
Putley *H & W*	27	SO6337
Putley Green *H & W*	27	SO6437
Putloe *Gloucs*	28	SO7809
Putney *Gt Lon*	23	TQ2374
Putron Village *Guern*	101	SV0000
Puttenham *Surrey*	22	SU9347
Puttock End *Essex*	32	TL8140
Puttock's End *Essex*	24	TL5619
Putton *Dorset*	9	SY6480
Puxley *Nhants*	30	SP7542
Puxton *Avon*	19	ST4063
Pwll *Dyfed*	17	SN4800
Pwll Trap *Dyfed*	17	SN2616
Pwll-du *Gwent*	27	SO2411
Pwll-y-glaw *W Glam*	18	SS7993
Pwllgloyw *Powys*	26	SO0333
Pwllheli *Gwynd*	44	SH3734
Pwllmeyric *Gwent*	19	ST5192
Pye Bridge *Derbys*	49	SK4452
Pye Corner *Herts*	31	TL4412
Pye Green *Staffs*	38	SJ9814
Pyecombe *W Susx*	12	TQ2912
Pyle *M Glam*	18	SS8282
Pyleigh *Somset*	18	ST1331
Pylle *Somset*	19	ST6038
Pymore *Cambs*	41	TL4986
Pymore *Dorset*	8	SY4694
Pyrford *Surrey*	22	TQ0458
Pyrton *Oxon*	22	SU6896
Pyrton *Oxon*	22	SU6896
Pytchley *Nhants*	30	SP8574
Pyworthy *Devon*	6	SS3002

Q

Quabbs *Shrops*	36	SO2080
Quadring *Lincs*	41	TF2233
Quainton *Bucks*	30	SP7420
Quaker's Yard *M Glam*	18	ST0996
Quarley *Hants*	21	SU2743
Quarley *Hants*	21	SU2743
Quarndon *Derbys*	49	SK3340
Quarr Hill *IOW*	11	SZ5792
Quarrier's Homes *Strath*	73	NS3666
Quarrington *Lincs*	50	TF0544
Quarrington Hill *Dur*	62	NZ3337
Quarry Bank *W Mids*	38	SO9386
Quarrywood *Gramp*	94	NJ1764
Quarter *Strath*	74	NS7251
Quatford *Shrops*	37	SO7391
Quatt *Shrops*	37	SO7588
Quebec *Dur*	69	NZ1743
Quedgeley *Gloucs*	28	SO8113
Queen Adelaide *Cambs*	41	TL5681
Queen Camel *Somset*	9	ST5924
Queen Charlton *Avon*	19	ST6367
Queen Oak *Dorset*	20	ST7840
Queen Street *Kent*	14	TQ6845
Queen's Bower *IOW*	11	SZ5784
Queen's Park *Nhants*	30	SP7662
Queenborough *Kent*	14	TQ9172
Queenborough *Kent*	14	TQ9172
Queenhill *H & W*	28	SO8537
Queensbury *W York*	55	SE1030
Queensferry *Clwyd*	46	SJ3168
Queenzieburn *Strath*	74	NS6977
Quendon *Essex*	31	TL5130
Queniborough *Leics*	39	SK6412
Quenington *Gloucs*	28	SP1404
Quethiock *Cnwll*	4	SX3164
Quidenham *Norfk*	32	TM0287
Quidhampton *Wilts*	10	SU1030
Quina Brook *Shrops*	37	SJ5233
Quine's Hill *IOM*	52	SC3473
Quinish House *Strath*	78	NM4154
Quinton *Nhants*	30	SP7754
Quinton *W Mids*	38	SO9884
Quinton Green *Nhants*	30	SP7852
Quintrell Downs *Cnwll*	2	SW8460
Quither *Devon*	4	SX4481
Quixwood *Border*	76	NT7863
Quoditch *Devon*	6	SX4097
Quorndon *Leics*	39	SK5616
Quothquan *Strath*	75	NS9939
Quoyburray *Ork*	103	HY5005
Quoyloo *Ork*	103	HY2421

R

Rabbit's Cross *Kent*	14	TQ7848
Rableyheath *Herts*	31	TL2319
Rachan Mill *Border*	75	NT1134

Rachub *Gwynd*	45	SH6267
Rackenford *Devon*	7	SS8418
Rackham *W Susx*	12	TQ0513
Rackheath *Norfk*	43	TG2814
Racks *D & G*	66	NY0274
Rackwick *Ork*	103	ND2099
Radbourne *Derbys*	39	SK2836
Radcliffe *Gt Man*	47	SD7807
Radcliffe *Nthumb*	69	NU2602
Radcliffe on Trent *Notts*	49	SK6439
Radclive *Bucks*	30	SP6734
Radernie *Fife*	83	NO4609
Radford Semele *Warwks*	29	SP3464
Radlett *Herts*	23	TL1600
Radley *Oxon*	21	SU5399
Radley Green *Essex*	24	TL6205
Radstock *Avon*	20	ST6854
Radstone *Nhants*	29	SP5840
Radway *Warwks*	29	SP3648
Radwell *Beds*	30	TL0057
Radwell *Herts*	31	TL2335
Radwinter *Essex*	24	TL6037
Radyr *S Glam*	18	ST1380
Raecleugh *D & G*	66	NT0311
Rafford *Gramp*	93	NJ0656
Ragdale *Leics*	39	SK6619
Raglan *Gwent*	27	SO4107
Ragnall *Notts*	50	SK8073
Raigbeg *Highld*	93	NH8128
Rainbow Hill *H & W*	28	SO8656
Rainford *Gt Man*	46	SD4700
Rainham *Gt Lon*	23	TQ5282
Rainham *Kent*	14	TQ8165
Rainhill *Mersyd*	46	SJ4991
Rainhill Stoops *Mersyd*	46	SJ5090
Rainton *N York*	62	SE3775
Rainworth *Notts*	49	SK5958
Raise *Cumb*	68	NY7146
Raisthorpe *N York*	56	SE8661
Rait *Tays*	82	NO2226
Raithby *Lincs*	51	TF3084
Raithby *Lincs*	51	TF3767
Rake *W Susx*	11	SU8027
Ralia *Highld*	87	NN7097
Ramasaig *Highld*	90	NG1644
Rame *Cnwll*	2	SW7233
Rame *Cnwll*	4	SX4249
Rampisham *Dorset*	8	ST5502
Rampside *Cumb*	53	SD2366
Rampton *Cambs*	31	TL4268
Rampton *Notts*	50	SK8078
Ramridge End *Beds*	30	TL1022
Ramsbottom *Gt Man*	54	SD7916
Ramsbury *Wilts*	21	SU2771
Ramscraigs *Highld*	100	ND1427
Ramsdean *Hants*	11	SU7022
Ramsdell *Hants*	21	SU5957
Ramsden *Oxon*	29	SP3515
Ramsden Bellhouse *Essex*	24	TQ7194
Ramsey *Cambs*	41	TL2885
Ramsey *Essex*	25	TM2130
Ramsey *IOM*	52	SC4594
Ramsey Forty Foot *Cambs*	41	TL3087
Ramsey Heights *Cambs*	41	TL2484
Ramsey Island *Essex*	25	TL9506
Ramsey Mereside *Cambs*	41	TL2889
Ramsey St. Mary's *Cambs*	41	TL2588
Ramsgate *Kent*	15	TR3865
Ramsgill *N York*	55	SE1170
Ramshope *Nthumb*	68	NT7304
Ramshorn *Staffs*	48	SK0845
Ramsley *Devon*	5	SX6493
Ramsnest Common *Surrey*	12	SU9533
Ranby *Lincs*	51	TF2278
Ranby *Notts*	49	SK6580
Rand *Lincs*	50	TF1078
Randwick *Gloucs*	28	SO8206
Ranfurly *Strath*	73	NS3864
Rangemore *Staffs*	38	SK1822
Rangeworthy *Avon*	20	ST6986
Rank's Green *Essex*	24	TL7518
Rankinston *Strath*	73	NS4513
Ranksborough *Leics*	40	SK8310
Rann *Lancs*	54	SD7124
Rannoch Station *Tays*	86	NN4257
Ranochan *Highld*	85	NM8282
Ranscombe *Somset*	7	SS9543
Ranskill *Notts*	49	SK6587
Ranton *Staffs*	38	SJ8524
Ranton Green *Staffs*	38	SJ8423
Ranworth *Norfk*	43	TG3514
Raploch *Cent*	81	NS7894
Rapness *Ork*	103	HY5041
Rapps *Somset*	8	ST3316
Rashfield *Strath*	80	NS1483
Rashwood *H & W*	28	SO9165
Raskelf *N York*	55	SE4971
Rassau *Gwent*	26	SO1411
Ratagan *Highld*	85	NG9220
Ratby *Leics*	39	SK5105
Ratcliffe Culey *Leics*	39	SP3299
Ratcliffe on Soar *Notts*	39	SK4928
Ratcliffe on the Wreake *Leics*	39	SK6314
Rathen *Gramp*	95	NJ9960
Rathhead *Fife*	83	NT2992
Rathillet *Fife*	83	NO3620
Rathmell *N York*	54	SD8059
Ratho *Loth*	75	NT1370
Rathven *Gramp*	94	NJ4465
Ratley *Warwks*	29	SP3847
Ratling *Kent*	15	TR2453
Ratlinghope *Shrops*	36	SO4097
Rattar *Highld*	100	ND2673
Ratten Row *Cumb*	58	NY3140
Ratton Village *E Susx*	13	TQ5901
Rattray *Tays*	88	NO1845
Raughton *Cumb*	67	NY3848
Raunds *Nhants*	30	SP9972
Raven Meols *Mersyd*	46	SD2905
Ravenfield *S York*	49	SK4895
Ravenglass *Cumb*	58	SD0896
Raveningham *Norfk*	33	TM3396
Ravenscliffe *Staffs*	47	SJ8452
Ravensden *Beds*	30	TL0754
Ravenshead *Notts*	49	SK5654
Ravensthorpe *Nhants*	30	SP6670
Ravensthorpe *W York*	55	SE2220
Ravenstone *Bucks*	30	SP8450
Ravenstone *Leics*	39	SK4013
Ravenstonedale *Cumb*	60	NY7203
Ravenstruther *Strath*	75	NS9245
Ravensworth *N York*	61	NZ1307
Rawcliffe *N York*	56	SE6822
Rawcliffe *N York*	56	SE5854
Rawcliffe *N York*	56	SE5854
Rawling Street *Kent*	14	TQ9059
Rawmarsh *S York*	49	SK4396
Rawreth *Essex*	24	TQ7893
Rawridge *Devon*	8	ST2006
Rawtenstall *Lancs*	54	SD8123
Raydon *Suffk*	25	TM0438
Rayleigh *Essex*	24	TQ8090
Raymond's Hill *Devon*	8	SY3396
Rayne *Essex*	24	TL7222
Raynes Park *Gt Lon*	23	TL5666
Read *Lancs*	54	SD7734
Reading *Berks*	22	SU7173
Reading Street *Kent*	14	TQ9230
Reading Street *Kent*	15	TR3868
Reagill *Cumb*	59	NY6017
Rearquhar *Highld*	97	NH7492
Rearsby *Leics*	39	SK6514
Reaster *Highld*	100	ND2565
Reay *Highld*	99	NC9664
Reculver *Kent*	15	TR2269
Red Ball *Devon*	7	ST0917
Red Bull *Ches*	47	SJ8255
Red Cross *Cambs*	31	TL4754
Red Cross *Cnwll*	6	SS2605
Red Hill *Dorset*	15	SZ0995
Red Hill *Warwks*	28	SP1355
Red Roses *Dyfed*	17	SN2012
Red Row *T & W*	69	NZ2599
Red Wharf Bay *Gwynd*	44	SH5281
Redberth *Dyfed*	16	SN0804
Redbourn *Herts*	30	TL1012

Redbourne *Lincs*	50	SK9699
Redbrook *Clwyd*	37	SJ5040
Redbrook *Gloucs*	14	SO5309
Redbrook Street *Kent*	14	TQ9336
Redburn *Highld*	93	NH9447
Redcar *Cleve*	62	NZ6024
Redcastle *D & G*	66	NX8165
Redcastle *Highld*	92	NH5849
Redcliff Bay *Avon*	19	ST4475
Redding *Cent*	75	NS9177
Reddingmuirhead *Cent*	75	NS9178
Redditch *H & W*	28	SP0467
Rede *Suffk*	32	TL8056
Redenhall *Norfk*	33	TM2684
Redesmouth *Nthumb*	68	NY8681
Redford *Gramp*	89	NO7570
Redford *Tays*	89	NO5644
Redford *W Susx*	11	SU8626
Redfordgreen *Border*	68	NT3616
Redgate *M Glam*	18	ST0188
Redgorton *Tays*	82	NO0828
Redgrave *Suffk*	32	TM0478
Redhill *Avon*	19	ST4963
Redhill *Surrey*	12	TQ2850
Redisham *Suffk*	33	TM4084
Redland *Avon*	19	ST5775
Redland *Avon*	19	ST5875
Redland *Ork*	103	HY3724
Redlingfield *Suffk*	33	TM1870
Redlingfield Green *Suffk*	33	TM1871
Redlynch *Somset*	20	ST6933
Redlynch *Wilts*	10	SU2020
Redmain *Cumb*	58	NY1434
Redmarley *H & W*	28	SO7666
Redmarley D'Abitot *Gloucs*	28	SO7531
Redmarshall *Cleve*	62	NZ3821
Redmile *Leics*	40	SK7935
Redmire *N York*	61	SE0491
Redmyre *Gramp*	89	NO7575
Rednal *Shrops*	36	SJ3628
Redpath *Border*	76	NT5835
Redruth *Cnwll*	2	SW6941
Redstone *Tays*	82	NO1834
Redwick *Avon*	19	ST5486
Redwick *Gwent*	19	ST4184
Redworth *Dur*	61	NZ2423
Reed *Herts*	31	TL3636
Reedham *Norfk*	43	TG4101
Reedness *Humb*	56	SE7923
Reeds Holme *Lancs*	54	SD8124
Reedy *Devon*	5	SX8189
Reef *W Isls*	102	NB1134
Reepham *Lincs*	50	TF0373
Reepham *Norfk*	43	TG1023
Reeth *N York*	61	SE0499
Reeves Green *W Mids*	39	SP2677
Regaby *IOM*	52	SC4397
Reiff *Highld*	98	NB9614
Reigate *Surrey*	12	TQ2550
Reighton *N York*	63	TA1375
Reinachait *Highld*	98	NC0430
Reisque *Gramp*	95	NJ8820
Reiss *Highld*	100	ND3354
Rejerrah *Cnwll*	2	SW8056
Releath *Cnwll*	2	SW6633
Relubbus *Cnwll*	2	SW5631
Relugas *Gramp*	93	NH9948
Remenham *Berks*	22	SU7783
Remenham Hill *Berks*	22	SU7882
Remony *Tays*	87	NN7643
Rempstone *Notts*	39	SK5724
Rendcomb *Gloucs*	28	SP0209
Rendham *Suffk*	33	TM3464
Renfrew *Strath*	74	NS4967
Renhold *Beds*	30	TL0953
Renishaw *Derbys*	49	SK4477
Rennington *Nthumb*	77	NU2118
Renton *Strath*	80	NS3878
Renwick *Cumb*	67	NY5943
Repps *Norfk*	43	TG4217
Repton *Derbys*	39	SK3026
Resaurie *Highld*	93	NH7045
Rescassa *Cnwll*	3	SW9842
Resipole *Highld*	79	NM7264
Reskadinnick *Cnwll*	2	SW6341
Resolis *Highld*	93	NH6765
Resolven *W Glam*	18	SN8302
Rest and be Thankful *Strath*	80	NN2307
Reston *Border*	77	NT8862
Reswallie *Tays*	89	NO5051
Retew *Cnwll*	3	SW9256
Retford *Notts*	49	SK7081
Rettendon *Essex*	24	TQ7698
Revesby *Lincs*	51	TF2961
Rew Street *IOW*	10	SZ4994
Rewe *Devon*	7	SX9499
Rexon *Devon*	4	SX4188
Reydon *Suffk*	33	TM4977
Reymerston *Norfk*	42	TG0206
Reynalton *Dyfed*	16	SN0908
Reynoldston *W Glam*	17	SS4890
Rezare *Cnwll*	4	SX3677
Rhandirmwyn *Dyfed*	26	SN7843
Rhayader *Powys*	35	SN9768
Rheindown *Highld*	92	NH5147
Rhelonie *Highld*	96	NH5597
Rhes-y-cae *Clwyd*	46	SJ1971
Rhewl *Clwyd*	45	SJ1160
Rhewl *Clwyd*	46	SJ1744
Rhewl Mostyn *Clwyd*	45	SJ1580
Rhicarn *Highld*	98	NC0825
Rhiconich *Highld*	98	NC2552
Rhicullen *Highld*	93	NH6971
Rhifail *Highld*	99	NC7249
Rhigos *M Glam*	26	SN9205
Rhilochan *Highld*	97	NC7407
Rhireavach *Highld*	91	NH0295
Rhives *Highld*	97	NC8200
Rhiwbina *S Glam*	19	ST1682
Rhiwderyn *Gwent*	19	ST2687
Rhiwlas *Gwynd*	44	SH5765
Rhoden Green *Kent*	14	TQ6745
Rhodes Minnis *Kent*	15	TR1542
Rhodesia *Notts*	49	SK5680
Rhodiad-y-brenin *Dyfed*	16	SM7627
Rhonehouse or Kelton Hill *D & G*	65	NX7459
Rhoose *S Glam*	18	ST0666
Rhos *Dyfed*	18	SN3835
Rhos *W Glam*	18	SN7403
Rhos Haminiog *Dyfed*	34	SN5564
Rhos Lligwy *Gwynd*	44	SH4986
Rhos-hill *Dyfed*	17	SN1940
Rhos-on-Sea *Clwyd*	45	SH8480
Rhos-y-gwaliau *Gwynd*	45	SH9434
Rhosaman *Dyfed*	26	SN7214
Rhoscolyn *Gwynd*	44	SH2735
Rhoscrowther *Dyfed*	16	SM9002
Rhosesmor *Clwyd*	46	SJ2168
Rhosgoch *Gwynd*	44	SH4189
Rhosgoch *Powys*	27	SO1847
Rhoshirwaun *Gwynd*	44	SH1930
Rhoslan *Gwynd*	44	SH4841
Rhoslefain *Gwynd*	34	SH5705
Rhosllanerchrugog *Clwyd*	46	SJ2946
Rhosmeirch *Gwynd*	44	SH4677
Rhosneigr *Gwynd*	44	SH3172
Rhosnesni *Clwyd*	46	SJ3450
Rhosrobin *Clwyd*	46	SJ3452
Rhossili *W Glam*	17	SS4188
Rhostryfan *Clwyd*	44	SH4958
Rhostyllen *Clwyd*	46	SJ3148
Rhosybol *Gwynd*	44	SH4288
Rhosymedre *Clwyd*	36	SJ2842
Rhu *Strath*	80	NS2783
Rhuallt *Clwyd*	45	SJ0774
Rhuban *W Isls*	102	NF7811
Rhuddach *Highld*	80	NS0273
Rhuddall Heath *Ches*	47	SJ5562
Rhuddlan *Clwyd*	45	SJ0277
Rhunahaorine *Strath*	72	NR7048
Rhyd *Gwynd*	45	SH6341
Rhyd-Ddu *Gwynd*	44	SH5552
Rhyd-y pennau *Dyfed*	35	SN6386
Rhyd-y-clafdy *Gwynd*	44	SH3234
Rhyd-y-foel *Clwyd*	45	SH9176
Rhyd-y-groes *Gwynd*	44	SH5867

Rhydargaeau *Dyfed*	17	SN4326
Rhydcymerau *Dyfed*	17	SN5738
Rhydding *W Glam*	18	SS7499
Rhydlewis *Dyfed*	17	SN3447
Rhydlios *Gwynd*	44	SH1830
Rhydowen *Dyfed*	17	SN4445
Rhydwyn *Gwynd*	44	SH3188
Rhydycroesau *Shrops*	36	SJ2430
Rhydyfro *W Glam*	26	SN7105
Rhydymwyn *Clwyd*	46	SJ2067
Rhyl *Clwyd*	45	SJ0181
Rhyl *Clwyd*	45	SJ0181
Rhymney *M Glam*	26	SO1107
Rhynd *Tays*	82	NO1520
Rhynie *Gramp*	94	NJ4927
Rhynie *Highld*	97	NH8479
Ribbesford *H & W*	37	SO7874
Ribbleton *Lancs*	53	SD5631
Ribchester *Lancs*	54	SD6535
Ribigill *Highld*	99	NC5854
Riby *Lincs*	57	TA1807
Riccall *N York*	56	SE6237
Riccarton *Strath*	67	NY5496
Riccarton *Strath*	73	NS4236
Richards Castle *H & W*	27	SO4969
Richmond *N York*	61	NZ1701
Richmond *S York*	49	SK4085
Richmond Fort *Guern*	101	SV0000
Richmond upon Thames *Gt Lon*	23	TQ1874
Richs Halford *Somset*	8	ST1534
Rickerscote *Staffs*	38	SJ9220
Rickford *Avon*	19	ST4859
Rickham *Devon*	5	SX7437
Rickham *Devon*	5	SX7437
Rickinghall Inferior *Suffk*	32	TM0475
Rickinghall Superior *Suffk*	32	TM0375
Rickling *Essex*	31	TL4931
Rickling Green *Essex*	31	TL5029
Rickmansworth *Herts*	22	TQ0694
Riddell *Border*	76	NT5124
Riddings *Cumb*	67	NY4075
Riddlecombe *Devon*	6	SS6013
Riddlesden *W York*	55	SE0742
Ridge *Avon*	19	ST5555
Ridge *Dorset*	9	SY9386
Ridge *Herts*	23	TL2100
Ridge *Wilts*	9	ST9531
Ridge Lane *Warwks*	39	SP2994
Ridgehill *Avon*	19	ST5362
Ridgeway *Derbys*	32	TL7340
Ridgewell *Essex*	32	TL7340
Ridgewood *E Susx*	13	TQ4719
Ridgmont *Beds*	30	SP9736
Riding Mill *Nthumb*	68	NZ0161
Ridlington *Leics*	40	SK8402
Ridlington *Norfk*	43	TG3431
Ridsdale *Nthumb*	68	NY9084
Rievaulx *N York*	62	SE5785
Rigg *D & G*	67	NY2966
Rigged *Strath*	74	NS7670
Righoul *Highld*	93	NH8851
Rigmadon Park *Cumb*	59	SD6185
Rigsby *Lincs*	51	TF4375
Rigside *Strath*	74	NS8735
Riley Green *Lancs*	54	SD6225
Rileyhill *Staffs*	38	SK1115
Rilla Mill *Cnwll*	4	SX2973
Rillington *N York*	63	SE8574
Rimington *Lancs*	54	SD8045
Rimpton *Somset*	9	ST6021
Rimswell *Humb*	57	TA3028
Rinaston *Dyfed*	16	SM9826
Ringford *D & G*	65	NX6857
Ringinglow *Derbys*	49	SK2983
Ringland *Norfk*	43	TG1314
Ringmer *E Susx*	13	TQ4412
Ringmore *Devon*	5	SX6545
Ringmore *Devon*	5	SX9272
Ringorm *Gramp*	94	NJ2644
Ringsfield *Suffk*	33	TM4088
Ringsfield Corner *Suffk*	33	TM4087
Ringshall *Bucks*	30	SP9814
Ringshall *Suffk*	32	TM0453
Ringshall Stocks *Suffk*	32	TM0551
Ringstead *Nhants*	30	SP9875
Ringstead *Norfk*	42	TF7040
Ringwood *Hants*	10	SU1405
Ringwould *Kent*	15	TR3548
Rinsey Croft *Cnwll*	2	SW6028
Ripe *E Susx*	13	TQ5110
Ripley *Derbys*	49	SK3950
Ripley *Hants*	10	SZ1698
Ripley *N York*	55	SE2860
Ripley *Surrey*	22	TQ0556
Riplington *Hants*	11	SU6623
Ripon *N York*	55	SE3171
Rippingale *Lincs*	40	TF0927
Ripple *H & W*	28	SO8737
Ripple *Kent*	15	TR3550
Ripponden *W York*	55	SE0319
Risabus *Strath*	70	NR3143
Risbury *H & W*	27	SO5454
Risby *Suffk*	32	TL7966
Risca *Gwent*	19	ST2391
Rise *Humb*	57	TA1542
Riseden *E Susx*	13	TQ6130
Risegate *Lincs*	41	TF2129
Risehow *Cumb*	58	NY0335
Riseley *Beds*	30	TL0462
Riseley *Berks*	22	SU7263
Rishangles *Suffk*	33	TM1668
Rishton *Lancs*	54	SD7230
Rishworth *W York*	55	SE0318
Risley *Derbys*	39	SK4635
Risplith *N York*	55	SE2468
Rivenhall End *Essex*	24	TL8416
River *Kent*	15	TR2943
Riverford *Highld*	92	NH5455
Rivington *Lancs*	54	SD6214
Roa Island *Cumb*	53	SD2364
Roachill *Devon*	7	SS8422
Road Green *Norfk*	43	TM2694
Road Weedon *Nhants*	29	SP6559
Roade *Nhants*	30	SP7551
Roadhead *Cumb*	67	NY5175
Roadmeetings *Strath*	74	NS8649
Roadside *Highld*	100	ND1560
Roadside *Strath*	74	NS5717
Roadside of Catterline *Gramp*	89	NO8678
Roadside of Kinneff *Gramp*	89	NO8477
Roadwater *Somset*	7	ST0238
Roag *Highld*	90	NG2244
Roan of Craigoch *Strath*	73	NS2904
Roast Green *Essex*	31	TL4632
Roath *S Glam*	19	ST1977
Roberton *Border*	67	NT4214
Roberton *Strath*	75	NS9428
Robertsbridge *E Susx*	14	TQ7423
Robertstown *W Glam*	55	SE1922
Roberston Wathen *Dyfed*	16	SN0815
Robgill Tower *D & G*	67	NY2471
Robin Hood's Bay *N York*	63	NZ9505
Roborough *Devon*	6	SS5717
Roby *Mersyd*	46	SJ4390
Rocester *Staffs*	48	SK1039
Roch *Dyfed*	16	SM8821
Rochdale *Gt Man*	54	SD8913
Roche *Cnwll*	3	SW9860
Rochester *Kent*	14	TQ7468
Rochester *Nthumb*	68	NY8298
Rochford *Essex*	24	TQ8790
Rochford *H & W*	27	SO6368
Rochville *Strath*	80	SO2371
Rock *H & W*	37	SO7371
Rock *Nthumb*	77	NU2020
Rock *W Susx*	12	TQ1014
Rock Ferry *Mersyd*	46	SJ3386
Rockbeare *Devon*	7	SY0195
Rockbourne *Hants*	10	SU1118
Rockcliffe *Cumb*	67	NY3561
Rockcliffe *D & G*	66	NX8553
Rockfield *Gwent*	27	SO4814
Rockfield *Highld*	97	NH9283
Rockford *Devon*	18	SS7547
Rockhampton *Gloucs*	19	SO6593
Rockhill *Shrops*	36	SO2879
Rockingham *Nhants*	40	SP8691

S

Rockland All Saints Norfk ... 42 TL9996
Rockland St. Mary Norfk ... 43 TG3104
Rockland St. Peter Norfk ... 42 TL9897
Rockley Notts ... 49 SK7174
Rockley Wilts ... 20 SU1571
Rockwell End Bucks ... 22 SU7988
Rockwell Green Somset ... 8 ST1320
Rodborough Gloucs ... 28 SO8304
Rodbourne Wilts ... 20 SU1485
Rodbourne Wilts ... 20 ST9383
Rodden Dorset ... 9 SY6184
Rode Somset ... 20 ST8053
Rode Heath Ches ... 47 SJ8767
Rodel W Isls ... 102 NG0483
Roden Shrops ... 37 SJ5716
Rodhuish Somset ... 7 ST0139
Rodington Shrops ... 37 SJ5814
Rodington Heath Shrops ... 37 SJ5814
Rodley Gloucs ... 28 SO7411
Rodmarton Gloucs ... 20 ST9497
Rodmell E Susx ... 13 TQ4106
Rodmersham Kent ... 14 TQ9261
Rodmersham Green Kent ... 14 TQ9161
Rodney Stoke Somset ... 19 ST4849
Rodono Border ... 75 NT2321
Rodsley Derbys ... 48 SK2040
Roe Green Herts ... 23 TL2107
Roe Green Herts ... 31 TL3133
Roecliffe N York ... 55 SE3765
Roehampton Gt Lon ... 23 TQ2273
Roewen Gwynd ... 45 SH7571
Roewen Gwynd ... 45 SH7672
Roffey W Susx ... 12 TQ1932
Rogart Highld ... 97 NC7304
Rogate W Susx ... 11 SU8023
Roger Ground Cumb ... 67 NY3597
Rogerstone Gwent ... 19 ST2788
Rogiet Gwent ... 19 ST4587
Roke Oxon ... 21 SU6293
Roker T & W ... 69 NZ4059
Rollesby Norfk ... 43 TG4415
Rolleston Leics ... 40 SK7300
Rolleston Staffs ... 39 SK2327
Rolston Humb ... 57 TA2145
Rolstone Avon ... 19 ST3862
Rolvenden Kent ... 14 TQ8431
Rolvenden Layne Kent ... 14 TQ8530
Romaldkirk Dur ... 61 NY9921
Romanby N York ... 62 SE3693
Romanno Bridge Border ... 75 NT1647
Romansleigh Devon ... 7 SS7220
Romesdal Highld ... 84 NG4033
Romford Dorset ... 10 SU0709
Romford Gt Lon ... 23 TQ5188
Romiley Gt Man ... 48 SJ9490
Romney Street Kent ... 23 TQ5461
Romsey Hants ... 10 SU3521
Romsley H & W ... 38 SO9679
Romsley Shrops ... 37 SO7883
Ronachan Strath ... 71 NR7454
Ronague IOM ... 52 SC2472
Rookhope Dur ... 61 NY9342
Rookley IOW ... 10 SZ5084
Rooks Bridge Somset ... 19 ST3752
Rooks Nest Somset ... 7 ST0339
Rookwith N York ... 61 SE2086
Roos Humb ... 57 TA2830
Roosebeck Cumb ... 67 NY2567
Roothams Green Beds ... 30 TL1057
Ropley Hants ... 11 SU6431
Ropley Dean Hants ... 11 SU6332
Ropsley Lincs ... 40 SK9934
Rora Gramp ... 95 NK0650
Rorrington Shrops ... 36 SJ3000
Rosarie Gramp ... 94 NJ3860
Rose Cnwll ... 2 SW7754
Rose Ash Devon ... 7 SS7821
Rose Green Essex ... 24 TL9028
Rose Green Suffk ... 25 TL9337
Rose Green Suffk ... 32 TL9744
Rose Green W Susx ... 11 SZ9099
Rose Hill Lancs ... 54 SD8231
Rose Lands E Susx ... 13 TQ6200
Rosebank Strath ... 74 NS8049
Rosebush Dyfed ... 16 SN0729
Rosedale Abbey N York ... 63 SE7296
Rosehall Highld ... 96 NC4701
Rosehearty Gramp ... 95 NJ9367
Rosehill Shrops ... 37 SJ4717
Roseisle Gramp ... 93 NJ1466
Rosemarket Dyfed ... 16 SM9508
Rosemarkie Highld ... 93 NH7357
Rosemary Lane Devon ... 8 ST1514
Rosemount Tays ... 88 NO1843
Rosenannon Cnwll ... 3 SW9566
Rosenithon Cnwll ... 3 SW8021
Rosewarne Cnwll ... 2 SW6137
Rosewell Loth ... 75 NT2862
Roseworth Cleve ... 62 NZ4121
Rosgill Cumb ... 59 NY5316
Roshven Highld ... 85 NM7078
Roskhill Highld ... 90 NG2745
Roskorwell Cnwll ... 2 SW7923
Rosley Cumb ... 67 NY3245
Roslin Loth ... 75 NT2763
Rosliston Derbys ... 39 SK2416
Rosneath Strath ... 80 NS2583
Ross D & G ... 65 NX6444
Ross Tays ... 81 NN7621
Ross-on-Wye H & W ... 27 SO6024
Rossett Clwyd ... 46 SJ3657
Rossett Green N York ... 55 SE2952
Rossie Ochill Tays ... 82 NO0912
Rossington Notts ... 49 SK6298
Rosskeen Highld ... 93 NH6869
Rossland Strath ... 73 NS4370
Roster Highld ... 100 ND2839
Rostherne Ches ... 47 SJ7483
Roston Derbys ... 48 SK1241
Rosyth Loth ... 82 NT1182
Rothbury Nthumb ... 68 NU0501
Rotherby Leics ... 39 SK6716
Rotherfield E Susx ... 13 TQ5529
Rotherfield Greys Oxon ... 22 SU7282
Rotherfield Peppard Oxon ... 22 SU7082
Rotherham S York ... 49 SK4392
Rothersthorpe Nhants ... 30 SP7156
Rotherwick Hants ... 22 SU7156
Rothes Gramp ... 94 NJ2749
Rothesay Strath ... 73 NS0864
Rothiebrisbane Gramp ... 95 NJ7437
Rothiemay Gramp ... 94 NJ5448
Rothienorman Gramp ... 95 NJ7235
Rothley Leics ... 39 SK5812
Rothmaise Gramp ... 95 NJ6832
Rothwell Lincs ... 50 TF1499
Rothwell Nhants ... 40 SP8181
Rothwell W York ... 55 SE3428
Rottal Tays ... 88 NO3769
Rottingdean E Susx ... 12 TQ3602
Rottington Cumb ... 58 NX9613
Roucan D & G ... 66 NY0277
Rough Common Kent ... 15 TR1359
Rougham Norfk ... 42 TF8320
Rougham Green Suffk ... 32 TL9061
Roughton Lincs ... 51 TF2364
Roughton Norfk ... 43 TG2237
Roughton Shrops ... 37 SO7594
Round Bush Herts ... 22 TQ1498
Round Green Suffk ... 32 TL7154
Roundham Essex ... 24 TL8601
Roundbush Green Essex ... 24 TL5815
Roundham Somset ... 8 ST4209
Roundhay W York ... 55 SE3235
Rounds Green W Mids ... 38 SO9889
Roundstone Foot D & G ... 67 NT1308
Roundway Wilts ... 20 SU0163
Roundyhill Tays ... 88 NO3750
Rous Lench H & W ... 28 SP0153
Rousdon Devon ... 8 SY2990
Rousham Oxon ... 29 SP4724
Rout's Green Bucks ... 22 SU7899
Routenburn Strath ... 73 NS1961
Routh Humb ... 57 TA0942
Row Cnwll ... 3 SX0976
Row Cumb ... 59 SD4589
Row Cumb ... 60 NY6235
Row Green Essex ... 24 TL7420

Rowanburn D & G ... 67 NY4177
Rowardennan Cent ... 80 NS3698
Rowarth Derbys ... 48 SK0189
Rowberrow Somset ... 19 ST4558
Rowborough IOW ... 10 SZ4685
Rowde Wilts ... 20 ST9762
Rowfield Derbys ... 48 SK1949
Rowfoot Nthumb ... 68 NY6860
Rowhedge Essex ... 25 TM0321
Rowington Warwks ... 29 SP2069
Rowland Derbys ... 48 SK2172
Rowland's Castle Hants ... 11 SU7310
Rowland's Gill T & W ... 69 NZ1658
Rowledge Surrey ... 11 SU8243
Rowley Dur ... 68 NZ0848
Rowley Humb ... 56 SE9732
Rowley Green W Mids ... 39 SP3483
Rowley Hill W York ... 55 SE1915
Rowlstone H & W ... 27 SO3727
Rowly Surrey ... 12 TQ0441
Rowner Hants ... 11 SU5801
Rowney Green H & W ... 38 SP0471
Rownhams Hants ... 10 SU3817
Rowsham Bucks ... 30 SP8418
Rowsley Derbys ... 48 SK2566
Rowstock Oxon ... 21 SU4788
Rowston Lincs ... 50 TF0856
Rowthorne Derbys ... 49 SK4864
Rowton Ches ... 46 SJ4564
Rowton Shrops ... 37 SJ6120
Roxburgh Border ... 76 NT6930
Roxby Humb ... 56 SE9217
Roxton Beds ... 30 TL1554
Roxwell Essex ... 24 TL6408
Roy Bridge Highld ... 86 NN2681
Royal Leamington Spa Warwks ... 29 SP3265
Royal Tunbridge Wells Kent ... 13 TQ5839
Roydon Essex ... 23 TL4009
Roydon Norfk ... 42 TF7023
Roydon Norfk ... 33 TM0980
Roydon Hamlet Essex ... 23 TL4107
Royston Herts ... 31 TL3540
Royston S York ... 55 SE3611
Royton Gt Man ... 54 SD9107
Rozel Jersey ... 101 SV0001
Ruaig Strath ... 78 NM0747
Ruan Lanihorne Cnwll ... 3 SW8942
Ruan Major Cnwll ... 2 SW7016
Ruardean Gloucs ... 27 SO6117
Ruardean Hill Gloucs ... 27 SO6317
Ruardean Woodside Gloucs ... 27 SO6215
Rubery H & W ... 38 SO9877
Ruckinge Kent ... 15 TR0233
Ruckley Shrops ... 37 SJ5300
Rudchester Nthumb ... 69 NZ1167
Ruddington Notts ... 39 SK5733
Rudge Somset ... 20 ST8252
Rudgeway Avon ... 19 ST6386
Rudgwick W Susx ... 12 TQ0833
Rudhall H & W ... 27 SO6225
Rudley Green Essex ... 24 TL8303
Rudry M Glam ... 17 ST2086
Rudston Humb ... 57 TA0967
Rudway Barton Devon ... 7 SS9301
Rudyard Staffs ... 48 SJ9558
Ruecastle Border ... 76 NT6120
Rufford Lancs ... 53 SD4615
Rufforth N York ... 55 SE5251
Rugby Warwks ... 39 SP5075
Rugeley Staffs ... 38 SK0418
Ruggaton Devon ... 6 SS5645
Ruishton Somset ... 8 ST2624
Ruislip Gt Lon ... 22 TQ0987
Ruletown Head Border ... 76 NT6113
Rumbach Gramp ... 94 NJ3852
Rumbling Bridge Tays ... 82 NT0199
Rumburgh Suffk ... 33 TM3481
Rumford Cent ... 75 NS9377
Rumford Cnwll ... 3 SW8970
Rumney S Glam ... 19 ST2179
Runcorn Ches ... 46 SJ5182
Runcton W Susx ... 11 SU8802
Runcton Holme Norfk ... 41 TF6109
Runfold Surrey ... 22 SU8747
Runhall Norfk ... 42 TG0507
Runham Norfk ... 43 TG4610
Running Waters Dur ... 62 NZ3340
Runnington Somset ... 8 ST1121
Runswick N York ... 63 NZ8016
Runtaleave Tays ... 88 NO2867
Runwell Essex ... 24 TQ7594
Ruscombe Berks ... 22 SU8076
Rush Green Essex ... 25 TM1615
Rush Green Gt Lon ... 23 TQ5187
Rushall H & W ... 27 SO6435
Rushall Norfk ... 33 TM1982
Rushall W Mids ... 38 SK0201
Rushall Wilts ... 20 SU1255
Rushbury Shrops ... 37 SO5092
Rushden Herts ... 31 TL3031
Rushden Nhants ... 30 SP9566
Rushford Devon ... 4 SX4476
Rushford Norfk ... 32 TL9281
Rushlake Green E Susx ... 13 TQ6218
Rushmere Suffk ... 33 TM4987
Rushmoor Surrey ... 11 SU8740
Rushock H & W ... 27 SO3058
Rushock H & W ... 28 SO8871
Rusholme Gt Man ... 47 SJ5864
Rushton Ches ... 47 SJ5864
Rushton Nhants ... 40 SP8483
Rushton Spencer Staffs ... 48 SJ9362
Rushwick H & W ... 28 SO8254
Rushyford Dur ... 61 NZ2828
Ruskie Cent ... 81 NN6200
Ruskington Lincs ... 50 TF0850
Rusland Cumb ... 59 SD3488
Rusper W Susx ... 12 TQ2037
Ruspidge Gloucs ... 28 SO6611
Russ Hill Surrey ... 12 TQ2340
Russell's Water Oxon ... 22 SU7089
Rusthall Kent ... 13 TQ5639
Rusthall Kent ... 13 TQ5639
Rustington W Susx ... 12 TQ0502
Ruston N York ... 63 SE9583
Ruston Parva Humb ... 57 TA0661
Ruswarp N York ... 63 NZ8809
Rutherford Border ... 76 NT6430
Rutherglen Strath ... 74 NS6162
Ruthernbridge Cnwll ... 3 SX0166
Ruthin Clwyd ... 46 SJ1258
Ruthrieston Gramp ... 89 NJ9204
Ruthven Gramp ... 94 NJ5046
Ruthven Highld ... 93 NH8132
Ruthven Highld ... 87 NN7699
Ruthven Tays ... 88 NO2848
Ruthven House Tays ... 88 NO3047
Ruthvoes Cnwll ... 3 SW9260
Ruthwell D & G ... 67 NY1067
Ruxley Corner Gt Lon ... 23 TQ4770
Ruyton-XI-Towns Shrops ... 36 SJ3922
Ryal Nthumb ... 68 NZ0174
Ryall Dorset ... 8 SY4094
Ryarsh Kent ... 14 TQ6660
Rydal Cumb ... 59 NY3606
Ryde IOW ... 11 SZ5992
Rye E Susx ... 14 TQ9220
Rye Foreign E Susx ... 14 TQ8922
Rye Street H & W ... 28 SO7835
Ryebank Shrops ... 37 SJ5131
Ryeish Green Nhants ... 21 SU6267
Ryhall Leics ... 40 TF0310
Ryhope T & W ... 69 NZ4152
Ryland Lincs ... 50 TF0179
Rylands Notts ... 39 SK5336
Rylstone N York ... 54 SD9658
Ryme Intrinseca Dorset ... 9 ST5810
Ryther N York ... 55 SE5539
Ryton Shrops ... 37 SJ7602
Ryton T & W ... 69 NZ1564
Ryton Warwks ... 39 SP3986
Ryton-on-Dunsmore Warwks ... 39 SP3874

Sabden Lancs ... 54 SD7837
Sacombe Herts ... 31 TL3319
Sacombe Green Herts ... 31 TL3419
Sacriston T & W ... 69 NZ2447
Sadberge Dur ... 62 NZ3416
Saddell Strath ... 72 NR7832
Saddington Leics ... 39 SP6591
Saddle Bow Norfk ... 41 TF6015
Saddlescombe W Susx ... 12 TQ2711
Saffron Walden Essex ... 24 TL5438
Sageston Dyfed ... 16 SN0503
Saham Hills Norfk ... 42 TF9003
Saham Toney Norfk ... 42 TF9001
Saighton Ches ... 46 SJ4462
Saintbury Gloucs ... 28 SP1139
Salachail Strath ... 86 NN0551
Salcombe Devon ... 5 SX7338
Salcombe Regis Devon ... 8 SY1588
Salcott Essex ... 25 TL9413
Sale Gt Man ... 47 SJ7991
Sale Green H & W ... 28 SO9358
Saleby Lincs ... 51 TF4578
Salehurst E Susx ... 14 TQ7424
Salem Dyfed ... 17 SN6336
Salem Dyfed ... 35 SN6684
Salem Gwynd ... 44 SH5456
Salen Highld ... 79 NM6864
Salen Strath ... 79 NM5743
Salesbury Lancs ... 54 SD6832
Salford Beds ... 30 SP9339
Salford Gt Man ... 47 SJ8198
Salford Oxon ... 29 SP2828
Salford Priors Warwks ... 28 SP0751
Salfords Surrey ... 12 TQ2846
Salhouse Norfk ... 43 TG3013
Saline Fife ... 82 NT0292
Salisbury Wilts ... 10 SU1429
Salkeld Dykes Cumb ... 59 NY5437
Sall Norfk ... 43 TG1025
Sallachy Highld ... 85 NG9130
Sallachy Highld ... 96 NC5408
Salmonby Lincs ... 51 TF3273
Salmond's Muir Tays ... 83 NO5838
Salperton Gloucs ... 28 SP0720
Salsburgh Strath ... 74 NS8262
Salt Staffs ... 38 SJ9527
Saltaire W York ... 55 SE1337
Saltash Cnwll ... 4 SX4258
Saltburn Highld ... 93 NH7270
Saltburn-by-the-Sea Cleve ... 62 NZ6621
Saltby Leics ... 40 SK8526
Saltcoats Strath ... 73 NS2441
Saltdean E Susx ... 13 TQ3802
Salterbeck Cumb ... 58 NX9926
Salterforth IOM ... 54 SD8845
Salterton Wilts ... 10 SU1236
Saltfleet Lincs ... 51 TF4593
Saltfleetby All Saints Lincs ... 51 TF4590
Saltfleetby St. Clements Lincs ... 51 TF4591
Saltfleetby St. Peter Lincs ... 51 TF4489
Saltford Avon ... 20 ST6867
Salthouse Norfk ... 42 TG0743
Saltley W Mids ... 38 SP0987
Saltmarsh Gwent ... 19 ST3483
Saltmarshe Humb ... 56 SE7824
Saltney Ches ... 46 SJ3865
Salton N York ... 63 SE7179
Saltrens Devon ... 6 SS4521
Saltwood Kent ... 15 TR1535
Salvington W Susx ... 12 TQ1305
Salwarpe H & W ... 28 SO8762
Salwayash Dorset ... 8 SY4596
Sambourne Warwks ... 28 SP0662
Sambrook Shrops ... 37 SJ7124
Samlesbury Lancs ... 54 SD5930
Sampford Arundel Somset ... 8 ST1018
Sampford Brett Somset ... 7 ST0941
Sampford Courtenay Devon ... 7 SS6301
Sampford Moor Somset ... 8 ST1118
Sampford Peverell Devon ... 7 ST0214
Sampford Spiney Devon ... 4 SX5372
Samsonlane Ork ... 103 HY6525
Samuelston Loth ... 76 NT4870
Sanaigmore Strath ... 70 NR2370
Sancreed Cnwll ... 2 SW4129
Sancton Humb ... 56 SE8939
Sand Hills W York ... 55 SE3739
Sand Hole Humb ... 56 SE8037
Sand Hutton N York ... 56 SE6958
Sandaig Highld ... 85 NG7102
Sandal Magna W York ... 55 SE3417
Sandavore Highld ... 84 NM4785
Sandbach Ches ... 47 SJ7560
Sandbank Strath ... 80 NS1580
Sandbanks Dorset ... 10 SZ0487
Sandend Gramp ... 94 NJ5566
Sanderstead Gt Lon ... 23 TQ3461
Sandford Avon ... 19 ST4159
Sandford Cumb ... 60 NY7216
Sandford Devon ... 7 SS8202
Sandford Hants ... 10 SU1601
Sandford IOW ... 11 SZ5481
Sandford Shrops ... 37 SJ5834
Sandford Strath ... 74 NS7143
Sandford Batch Avon ... 19 ST4158
Sandford Orcas Dorset ... 9 ST6220
Sandford St. Martin Oxon ... 29 SP4226
Sandford-on-Thames Oxon ... 21 SP5301
Sandgate Kent ... 15 TR2035
Sandhaven Gramp ... 95 NJ9667
Sandhead D & G ... 64 NX0949
Sandhills Surrey ... 12 SU9438
Sandhoe Nthumb ... 68 NY9666
Sandhole Strath ... 80 NS0098
Sandholme Humb ... 56 SE8230
Sandhurst Berks ... 22 SU8361
Sandhurst Gloucs ... 28 SO8223
Sandhurst Kent ... 14 TQ8028
Sandhutton N York ... 62 SE3881
Sandilands Lincs ... 51 TF5280
Sandleheath Hants ... 10 SU1214
Sandley Dorset ... 9 ST7724
Sandness Shet ... 103 HU1957
Sandon Essex ... 24 TL7404
Sandon Herts ... 31 TL3234
Sandon Staffs ... 38 SJ9429
Sandon Bank Staffs ... 38 SJ9428
Sandown IOW ... 11 SZ5984
Sandplace Cnwll ... 4 SX2556
Sandridge Herts ... 23 TL1710
Sandringham Norfk ... 42 TF6928
Sands Bucks ... 22 SU8393
Sandsend N York ... 63 NZ8612
Sandside Moor Highld ... 99 NC9565
Sandtoft Humb ... 56 SE7408
Sandwich Kent ... 15 TR3358
Sandwick Shet ... 103 HU4323
Sandwith Cumb ... 58 NX9615
Sandy Beds ... 31 TL1649
Sandy Bank Lincs ... 51 TF2654
Sandy Lane Clwyd ... 36 SJ4040
Sandy Lane W York ... 55 SE1136
Sandy Lane Wilts ... 20 ST9668
Sandy Park Devon ... 5 SX7189
Sandyford D & G ... 67 NY2093
Sandygate Devon ... 5 SX8674
Sandygate IOM ... 52 SC3797
Sandylands Lancs ... 53 SD4163
Sandystones Border ... 76 NT5926
Sangobeg Highld ... 98 NC4266
Sangomore Highld ... 98 NC4067
Sankyn's Green H & W ... 28 SO7964
Sanna Bay Highld ... 79 NM4469
Santon Bridge Cumb ... 58 NY1101
Santon Downham Suffk ... 32 TL8187
Sapcote Leics ... 39 SP4993

Sapey Common H & W ... 28 SO7064
Sapiston Suffk ... 32 TL9175
Sapperton Gloucs ... 20 SO9403
Sapperton Lincs ... 40 TF0133
Saracen's Head Lincs ... 41 TF3427
Sarclet Highld ... 100 ND3443
Sarisbury Hants ... 10 SU5608
Sarn Gwynd ... 44 SH2432
Sarn Gwynd ... 44 SH2432
Sarn Powys ... 36 SO2091
Sarnau Dyfed ... 17 SN3151
Sarnau Gwynd ... 45 SH9739
Sarnau Powys ... 36 SJ2315
Sarnesfield H & W ... 27 SO3750
Saron Dyfed ... 17 SN6012
Saron Gwynd ... 44 SH5365
Sarratt Herts ... 22 TQ0499
Sarre Kent ... 15 TR2565
Sarsden Oxon ... 29 SP2822
Satley Dur ... 69 NZ1143
Satterleigh Devon ... 7 SS6622
Satterthwaite Cumb ... 59 SD3392
Sauchen Gramp ... 95 NJ7011
Saucher Tays ... 82 NO1933
Sauchieburn Gramp ... 89 NO6669
Saughtree Border ... 67 NY5696
Saul Gloucs ... 28 SO7409
Saundby Notts ... 50 SK7888
Saundersfoot Dyfed ... 16 SN1304
Saunderton Bucks ... 22 SP7901
Saunton Devon ... 6 SS4637
Sausthorpe Lincs ... 51 TF3868
Savile Town W York ... 55 SE2420
Sawbridge Warwks ... 29 SP5065
Sawbridgeworth Herts ... 31 TL4814
Sawdon N York ... 63 SE9485
Sawley Derbys ... 39 SK4731
Sawley Lancs ... 54 SD7746
Sawley N York ... 55 SE2467
Sawry Cumb ... 59 SD3795
Sawston Cambs ... 31 TL4849
Saxby Leics ... 40 SK8219
Saxby Lincs ... 50 TF0086
Saxby W Susx ... 12 SU9604
Saxby All Saints Humb ... 56 SE9816
Saxelbye Leics ... 40 SK7021
Saxham Street Suffk ... 32 TM0861
Saxilby Lincs ... 50 SK8875
Saxlingham Norfk ... 42 TG0239
Saxlingham Green Norfk ... 43 TM2496
Saxlingham Nethergate Norfk ... 43 TM2397
Saxlingham Thorpe Norfk ... 43 TM2198
Saxmundham Suffk ... 33 TM3863
Saxon Street Cambs ... 32 TL6579
Saxondale Notts ... 49 SK6839
Saxtead Suffk ... 33 TM2665
Saxtead Green Suffk ... 33 TM2564
Saxtead Little Green Suffk ... 33 TM2566
Saxthorpe Norfk ... 43 TG1130
Saxton N York ... 55 SE4736
Sayers Common W Susx ... 12 TQ2618
Scackleton N York ... 56 SE6472
Scadabay W Isls ... 90 NG1792
Scaftworth Notts ... 49 SK6691
Scagglethorpe N York ... 56 SE8372
Scalasaig Strath ... 70 NR3994
Scaldwell Nhants ... 30 SP7672
Scaleby Cumb ... 67 NY4463
Scalebyhill Cumb ... 67 NY4363
Scales Cumb ... 53 SD2772
Scales Cumb ... 59 NY3426
Scales Cumb ... 59 NY3427
Scalesceough Cumb ... 67 NY4450
Scalford Leics ... 40 SK7624
Scaling N York ... 62 NZ7413
Scalloway Shet ... 103 HU4039
Scalpay W Isls ... 90 NG2395
Scambleby Lincs ... 51 TF2778
Scamodala Highld ... 85 NM8373
Scampston N York ... 63 SE8575
Scampton Lincs ... 50 SK9479
Scancroft Hill W York ... 55 SE3741
Scaniport Highld ... 92 NH6239
Scapegoat Hill W York ... 55 SE0916
Scarborough N York ... 63 TA0388
Scarcewater Cnwll ... 3 SW9552
Scarcliffe Derbys ... 49 SK4968
Scarcroft W York ... 55 SE3540
Scarfskerry Highld ... 100 ND2674
Scargill Dur ... 61 NZ0510
Scarinish Strath ... 78 NM0444
Scarness Cumb ... 58 NY2130
Scarning Norfk ... 42 TF9512
Scarrington Notts ... 50 SK7341
Scarthingwell N York ... 55 SE4837
Scartho Humb ... 57 TA2606
Scawby Humb ... 56 SE9605
Scawthorpe S York ... 56 SE5506
Scawton N York ... 62 SE5483
Scayne's Hill W Susx ... 12 TQ3623
Scethrog Powys ... 26 SO1025
Scholes Gt Man ... 47 SD5905
Scholes S York ... 49 SK3896
Scholes W York ... 55 SE1507
Scholes W York ... 55 SE1726
Schoolgreen Berks ... 21 SU6367
Scissett W York ... 55 SE2510
Scleddau Dyfed ... 16 SM9434
Sco Ruston Norfk ... 43 TG2822
Scofton Notts ... 49 SK6280
Scole Norfk ... 33 TM1579
Sconser Highld ... 84 NG5131
Scoonie Fife ... 83 NO3801
Scopwick Lincs ... 50 TF0757
Scoraig Highld ... 91 NH0096
Scorborough Humb ... 56 TA0145
Scorrier Cnwll ... 2 SW7244
Scorton Lancs ... 53 SD5048
Scorton N York ... 61 NZ2500
Scot Hay Staffs ... 47 SJ8047
Scot's Gap Nthumb ... 68 NZ0386
Scotby Cumb ... 67 NY4455
Scotforth Lancs ... 53 SD4859
Scothern Lincs ... 50 TF0377
Scotlandwell Tays ... 82 NO1801
Scotsburn Highld ... 93 NH7275
Scotscalder Highld ... 100 ND0956
Scotscraig Fife ... 83 NO4428
Scotsmill Gramp ... 94 NJ5618
Scotstoun Strath ... 74 NS5367
Scotswood T & W ... 69 NZ2064
Scotter Lincs ... 50 SE8800
Scotterthorpe Lincs ... 50 SE8701
Scotton Lincs ... 50 SK8899
Scotton N York ... 61 SE1895
Scotton N York ... 55 SE3259
Scoughall Loth ... 83 NT6183
Scoulton Norfk ... 42 TF9800
Scourie Highld ... 98 NC1544
Scouriemore Highld ... 98 NC1443
Scousburgh Shet ... 103 HU3717
Scrabster Highld ... 100 ND1070
Scrafield Lincs ... 51 TF3068
Scrane End Lincs ... 51 TF3841
Scraptoft Leics ... 39 SK6405
Scratby Norfk ... 43 TG5115
Scrayingham N York ... 56 SE7359
Scrayingham N York ... 56 SE7359
Scredington Lincs ... 50 TF0940
Screel D & G ... 66 NX7953
Scremby Lincs ... 51 TF4467
Scremerston Nthumb ... 77 NU0148
Screveton Notts ... 50 SK7343
Scriven N York ... 55 SE3458
Scrooby Notts ... 49 SK6590
Scropton Derbys ... 39 SK1930
Scrub Hill Lincs ... 51 TF2355
Scruschloch Tays ... 88 NO2357
Scruton N York ... 61 SE2992
Sculthorpe Norfk ... 42 TF8931
Scunthorpe Humb ... 56 SE8910
Sea Palling Norfk ... 43 TG4226
Seaborough Dorset ... 8 ST4206
Seabrook Kent ... 15 TR1835
Seaburn T & W ... 69 NZ4160
Seacroft W York ... 55 SE3536
Seafield Highld ... 90 NG4743

Place	Page	Grid
Soberton Heath Hants	11	SU6014
Sockbridge Cumb	59	NY5127
Sockburn Nthumb	62	NZ3406
Sodylt Bank Shrops	36	SJ3440
Soham Cambs	31	TL5973
Soham Cotes Cambs	31	TL5774
Soldridge Hants	11	SU6535
Sole Street Kent	15	TR0949
Solihull W Mids	38	SP1679
Solitote Highld	90	NG4274
Sollas W Isls	102	NF8074
Sollers Dilwyn H & W	27	SO4255
Sollers Hope H & W	27	SO6132
Solva Dyfed	16	SM8024
Solwaybank D & G	67	NY3077
Somerby Leics	40	SK7710
Somerby Lincs	57	TA0626
Somercotes Derbys	49	SK4253
Somerford Keynes Gloucs	20	SU0195
Somerley W Susx	11	SZ8198
Somerleyton Suffk	43	TM4897
Somersby Lincs	51	TF3472
Somersham Cambs	31	TL3678
Somersham Suffk	32	TM0848
Somerton Oxon	29	SP4928
Somerton Somset	8	ST4828
Somerton Suffk	32	TL8153
Somerwood Shrops	37	SJ5615
Sonning Berks	22	SU7575
Sonning Common Oxon	22	SU7080
Sonning Eye Oxon	22	SU7576
Sopley Hants	10	SZ1596
Sopworth Wilts	20	ST8286
Sorbie D & G	64	NX4346
Sorbietrees Cumb	67	NY4884
Sordale Highld	100	ND1462
Sorisdale Strath	78	NM2763
Sorn Strath	74	NS5526
Sortat Highld	100	ND2863
Sosgill Cumb	58	NY1024
Sotby Lincs	51	TF2078
Sots Hole Lincs	50	TF1164
Sotterly Suffk	33	TM4585
Sotwell Oxon	21	SU5790
Soulbury Bucks	30	SP8826
Soulby Cumb	60	NY7410
Souldern Oxon	29	SP5231
Souldrop Beds	30	SP9861
Sound Muir Gramp	94	NJ3652
Soundwell Avon	19	ST6575
Sourtergate Cumb	58	SD2281
South Acre Norfk	42	TF8114
South Alkham Kent	15	TR2441
South Allington Devon	5	SX7938
South Alloa Cent	82	NS8791
South Ambersham W Susx	11	SU9120
South Anston S York	49	SK5183
South Ascot Berks	22	SU9268
South Ashford Kent	15	TR0041
South Baddesley Hants	10	SZ3596
South Bank N York	56	NZ5320
South Barrow Somset	9	ST6027
South Benfleet Gt Lon	23	TQ2863
South Benfleet Essex	24	TQ7787
South Bersted W Susx	11	SU9300
South Bockhampton Dorset	10	SZ1796
South Bramwith S York	56	SE6211
South Brent Devon	5	SX6960
South Brewham Somset	20	ST7236
South Broomhill Nthumb	69	NZ2499
South Burlingham Norfk	43	TG3807
South Cadbury Somset	9	ST6325
South Cairn D & G	64	NW9669
South Carlton Lincs	50	SK9476
South Carlton Notts	49	SK8883
South Carrine Strath	72	NR6709
South Cave Humb	56	SE9231
South Cerney Gloucs	20	SU0497
South Charlton Nthumb	77	NU1620
South Cheriton Somset	9	ST6924
South Church Dur	61	NZ2128
South Cleatlam Dur	61	NZ1217
South Cliffe Humb	56	SE8736
South Clifton Notts	50	SK8270
South Cockerington Lincs	50	TF1888
South Collingham Notts	50	SK8260
South Cornelly M Glam	18	SS8280
South Cove Suffk	33	TM4981
South Creake Norfk	42	TF8536
South Croxton Leics	39	SK6810
South Dalton Humb	56	SE9645
South Duffield N York	56	SE6733
South Elkington Lincs	51	TF2988
South Elmsall W York	55	SE4711
South End Berks	21	SU5970
South End Cumb	53	SD2063
South End H & W	28	SO7344
South End Hants	10	SU1015
South Erradale Highld	91	NG7471
South Fambridge Essex	24	TQ8694
South Fawley Berks	21	SU3880
South Feorline Strath	72	NR9027
South Ferriby Humb	56	SE9820
South Field Humb	56	TA0225
South Godstone Surrey	12	TQ3546
South Gorley Hants	10	SU1610
South Gosworth T & W	69	NZ2467
South Green Essex	24	TQ6893
South Green Essex	14	TQ8560
South Green Norfk	42	TG0510
South Hanningfield Essex	24	TQ749?/
South Harting W Susx	11	SU7819
South Hayling Hants	11	SZ7299
South Heath Bucks	22	SP9101
South Heighton E Susx	13	TQ4503
South Hetton Cleve	69	NZ3845
South Hiendley Strath	55	SE3912
South Hiendly W York	55	SE3912
South Hill Cnwll	4	SX3373
South Hill Somset	8	ST4727
South Hinksey Oxon	21	SP5003
South Holmwood Surrey	12	TQ1745
South Hornchurch Gt Lon	23	TQ5283
South Huish Devon	5	SX6941
South Hykeham Lincs	50	SK9364
South Hylton T & W	69	NZ3556
South Kelsey Lincs	50	TF0398
South Kessock Highld	93	NH6547
South Killingholme Humb	57	TA1416
South Kilvington N York	62	SE4283
South Kilworth Nhants	39	SP6081
South Kirkby W York	55	SE4410
South Knighton Devon	5	SX8072
South Kyme Lincs	50	TF1749
South Lambeth Gt Lon	23	TQ3077
South Lawn Oxon	29	SP2814
South Leigh Oxon	29	SP3909
South Leverton Notts	50	SK7881
South Lochboisdale W Isls	102	NF7817
South Lopham Norfk	32	TM0481
South Luffenham Leics	40	SK9401
South Mains D & G	66	NS7808
South Malling E Susx	13	TQ4211
South Marston Wilts	21	SU1987
South Milford N York	55	SE4931
South Milton Devon	5	SX7042
South Mimms Herts	23	TL2210
South Molton Devon	7	SS7125
South Moor Dur	69	NZ1952
South Moreton Oxon	21	SU5688
South Muskham Notts	50	SK7956
South Newbald Humb	56	SE9136
South Newington Oxon	29	SP4033
South Newton Wilts	10	SU0834
South Normanton Derbys	49	SK4456
South Norwood Gt Lon	23	TQ3368
South Ockendon Essex	24	TQ5983
South Ormsby Lincs	51	TF3875
South Otterington N York	62	SE3787
South Owersby Lincs	50	TF0693
South Park Surrey	12	TQ2548
South Perrott Dorset	8	ST4706
South Petherton Somset	8	ST4316
South Pickenham Norfk	42	TF8504
South Pill M Glam	4	SX4259
South Pool Devon	5	SX7740
South Poorton Dorset	8	SY5197
South Port Strath	80	NN0420
South Queensferry Loth	82	NT1378
South Radworthy Devon	7	SS7432
South Rauceby Lincs	50	TF0245
South Raynham Norfk	42	TF8723
South Reddish Gt Man	48	SJ8992
South Reston Lincs	51	TF4083
South Runcton Norfk	41	TF6308
South Scarle Notts	50	SK8463
South Shian Strath	79	NM9042
South Shields T & W	69	NZ3567
South Shore Lancs	53	SD3033
South Skirlaugh Humb	57	TA1438
South Stainley N York	55	SE3063
South Stifford Essex	24	TQ5977
South Stoke Avon	20	ST7461
South Stoke Oxon	21	SU5983
South Stoke Oxon	21	SU6083
South Stoke W Susx	12	TQ0210
South Street E Susx	13	TQ3918
South Street Kent	15	TR0557
South Street Kent	15	TR1265
South Tarbrax Strath	75	NT0353
South Tawton Devon	7	SX6594
South Thoresby Lincs	51	TF4077
South Tidworth Hants	21	SU2347
South Town Devon	5	SX9683
South Walsham Norfk	43	TG3613
South Warnborough Hants	22	SU7247
South Weald Essex	24	TQ5793
South Weston Oxon	22	SU7098
South Wheatley Cnwll	4	SX2492
South Widcombe Somset	19	ST5756
South Wigston Leics	39	SP5897
South Willesborough Kent	15	TR0240
South Willingham Lincs	50	TF1983
South Wingate Dur	62	NZ4135
South Wingfield Derbys	49	SK3755
South Witham Lincs	40	SK8219
South Wonston Hants	10	SU4635
South Woodham Ferrers Essex	24	TQ8097
South Wootton Norfk	42	TF6422
South Wraxall Wilts	20	ST8364
South Yeo Devon	6	SS5100
South Zeal Devon	5	SX6493
Southall Gt Lon	22	TQ1279
Southam Gloucs	28	SO9725
Southam Warwks	29	SP4161
Southampton Hants	10	SU4211
Southborough Gt Lon	23	TQ4267
Southborough Kent	13	TQ5842
Southbourne Dorset	10	SZ1491
Southbourne Norfk	42	TG0004
Southburn Humb	56	SE9954
Southchurch Essex	24	TQ9086
Southcott Cnwll	6	SX1995
Southcott Devon	6	SX5495
Southcott Devon	5	SX7580
Southcourt Bucks	30	SP8112
Southease E Susx	13	TQ4205
Southend Strath	72	NR6908
Southend-on-Sea Essex	24	TQ8886
Southeranby Cumb	59	NY3739
Southernown M Glam	18	SS8873
Southerness D & G	66	NX9754
Southerton Devon	5	SX0790
Southery Norfk	41	TL6294
Southfield Cent	74	NS8472
Southfleet Kent	14	TQ6171
Southgate IOW	11	SZ5178
Southgate Gt Lon	23	TQ2994
Southgate W Glam	17	SS5587
Southill Beds	30	TL1442
Southington Hants	21	SU5049
Southleigh Devon	8	SY2093
Southminster Essex	25	TQ9599
Southmoor Oxon	21	SU3998
Southmuir Tays	88	NO3853
Southoe Cambs	31	TL1864
Southolt Suffk	33	TM1968
Southorpe Cambs	40	TF0803
Southover Dorset	9	SY6294
Southowram W York	55	SE1123
Southport Mersyd	53	SD3317
Southrepps Norfk	43	TG2536
Southrey Lincs	50	TF1366
Southrop Gloucs	21	SP1903
Southrope Hants	22	SU6744
Southsea Clwyd	46	SJ2951
Southsea Hants	11	SZ6498
Southside Dur	61	NZ1026
Southtown Norfk	43	TG5206
Southwark Gt Lon	23	TQ3279
Southwater W Susx	12	TQ1526
Southwater Street W Susx	12	TQ1527
Southwick Hants	11	SU6208
Southwick Nhants	40	TL0192
Southwick Somset	19	ST3546
Southwick T & W	69	NZ3758
Southwick W Susx	12	TQ2405
Southwick Wilts	20	ST8354
Southwold Suffk	33	TM5076
Soutra Mains Loth	76	NT4559
Sowe Common W Mids	39	SP3783
Sowerby N York	62	SE4281
Sowerby Bridge W York	55	SE0523
Sowerby Row Cumb	59	NY3940
Sowley reen Suffk	32	TL7051
Sowood W York	55	SE0818
Sowton Devon	5	SX5065
Sowton Devon	5	SX9792
Soyland Town W York	55	SE0320
Spain's End Essex	24	TL6637
Spalding Lincs	41	TF2422
Spaldington Humb	56	SE7533
Spaldwick Cambs	30	TL1372
Spalford Notts	50	SK8369
Spanish Green Hants	22	SU6959
Sparham Norfk	42	TG0719
Sparhamill Norfk	42	TG0819
Spark Bridge Cumb	58	SD3084
Sparkford Somset	9	ST6026
Sparkhill W Mids	38	SP1083
Sparkwell Devon	4	SX5757
Sparrow Green Norfk	42	TF9514
Sparrowpit Derbys	48	SK0880
Sparrows Green E Susx	13	TQ6332
Sparsholt Hants	10	SU4331
Sparsholt Oxon	21	SU3487
Spaunton N York	63	SE7289
Spaxton Somset	19	ST2236
Spean Bridge Highld	86	NN2281
Spearywell Hants	10	SU3127
Speen Berks	21	SU4568
Speen Bucks	22	SU8399
Speeton N York	63	TA1574
Speke Mersyd	46	SJ4383
Speldhurst Kent	13	TQ5541
Spellbrook Herts	31	TL4817
Spen Green Ches	47	SJ8260
Spencers Wood Berks	22	SU7167
Spennithorne N York	61	SE1489
Spennymoor Dur	61	NZ2533
Spetchley H & W	28	SO8954
Spettisbury Dorset	9	ST9002
Spexhall Suffk	33	TM3780
Spey Bay Gramp	94	NJ3565
Speybridge Highld	93	NJ0326
Speyview Gramp	94	NJ2541
Spilsby Lincs	51	TF4065
Spinkhill Derbys	49	SK4478
Spinningdale Highld	97	NH6789
Spirthill Wilts	20	ST9975
Spital Berks	22	SU9675
Spital Hill Notts	49	SK6193
Spital Dyfed	16	SM9723
Spital Highld	100	ND1654
Spital Loth	76	NT4677
Spital Nthumb	77	NU0051
Spital of Glenmuick Gramp	88	NO3085
Spital of Glenshee Tays	88	NO1069
Spittalfield Tays	88	NO1141
Spittal Rule Border	76	NT5819
Spixworth Norfk	43	TG2415
Splatt Cnwll	3	SW9476
Splatt Devon	6	SS6005
Slayne's Green E Susx	13	TQ4324
Splottlands S Glam	19	ST2077
Spofforth N York	55	SE3650
Spon Green Clwyd	46	SJ2963
Spondon Derbys	39	SK3935
Spooner Row Norfk	43	TM0997
Sporle Norfk	42	TF8411
Spott Loth	76	NT6775
Spottiswoode Border	76	NT6049
Spratton Nhants	30	SP7170
Spreakley Surrey	11	SU8441
Spreyton Devon	7	SX6997
Spriddlestone Devon	4	SX5351
Spridlington Lincs	50	TF0084
Spring Vale S York	55	SE2503
Springburn Strath	74	NS6068
Springfield Essex	24	TL7208
Springfield Fife	83	NO3411
Springhill Staffs	38	SK0706
Springholm D & G	66	NX8070
Springkell D & G	67	NY2575
Springside Strath	73	NS3738
Springthorpe Lincs	50	SK8789
Springwell T & W	69	NZ2958
Sproatley Humb	57	TA1934
Sproston Green Ches	47	SJ7366
Sprotbrough S York	49	SE5301
Sproughton Suffk	33	TM1244
Sprowston Norfk	43	TG2512
Sproxton Leics	40	SK8524
Sproxton N York	62	SE6181
Spurstow Ches	47	SJ5657
Spyway Dorset	8	SY5293
Squirrel's Heath Gt Lon	23	TQ5289
St Giles in the Wood Devon	6	SS5318
St-y-Nyll S Glam	18	ST0978
St. Abbs Border	77	NT9167
St. Aethans Gramp	93	NJ1168
St. Agnes Cnwll	2	SW7250
St. Agnes Loth	76	NT6763
St. Albans Herts	22	TL1407
St. Allen Cnwll	2	SW8250
St. Andrew Guern	101	SV0000
St. Andrew's Major S Glam	18	ST1371
St. Andrews Fife	83	NO5116
St. Andrews Well Dorset	8	SY4793
St. Ann's D & G	66	NY0793
St. Ann's Chapel Devon	5	SX6647
St. Anne's Lancs	53	SD3228
St. Anthony Cnwll	2	SW7825
St. Anthony's Hill E Susx	13	TQ6201
St. Arvans Gwent	19	ST5196
St. Athan S Glam	18	ST0168
St. Aubin Jersey	101	SV0000
St. Austell Cnwll	3	SX0152
St. Bees Cumb	58	NX9611
St. Blazey Cnwll	3	SX0654
St. Boswells Border	76	NT5930
St. Brelade Jersey	101	SV0000
St. Brelades Bay Jersey	101	SV0000
St. Breock Cnwll	3	SW9771
St. Breward Cnwll	3	SX0977
St. Bride's Major M Glam	18	SS8974
St. Brides Dyfed	16	SM8010
St. Brides Netherwent Gwent	19	ST4290
St. Brides Wentlooge Gwent	19	ST2982
St. Budeaux Devon	4	SX4558
St. Buryan Cnwll	2	SW4025
St. Catherine Avon	20	ST7770
St. Catherines Strath	80	NN1207
St. Chloe Gloucs	20	SO8401
St. Clears Dyfed	17	SN2716
St. Cleer Cnwll	4	SX2468
St. Clement Cnwll	3	SW8443
St. Clement Jersey	101	SV0000
St. Clether Cnwll	4	SX2084
St. Colmac Strath	72	NS0467
St. Columb Major Cnwll	3	SW9163
St. Columb Minor Cnwll	3	SW8362
St. Columb Road Cnwll	3	SW9159
St. Combs Gramp	95	NK0563
St. Cross South Elmham Suffk	33	TM2984
St. Cyrus Gramp	89	NO7464
St. David's Tays	82	NN9420
St. Davids Dyfed	16	SM7525
St. Day Cnwll	2	SW7242
St. Decumans Somset	7	ST0642
St. Dennis Cnwll	3	SW9557
St. Dogmaels Dyfed	17	SN1646
St. Dogwells Dyfed	16	SM9728
St. Dominick Cnwll	4	SX3967
St. Donats S Glam	18	SS9368
St. Endellion Cnwll	3	SW9978
St. Enoder Cnwll	3	SW8956
St. Erme Cnwll	3	SW8449
St. Erney Cnwll	4	SX3659
St. Erth Cnwll	2	SW5535
St. Erth Praze Cnwll	2	SW5735
St. Ervan Cnwll	3	SW8970
St. Ewe Cnwll	3	SW9746
St. Fagans S Glam	18	ST1277
St. Fergus Gramp	95	NK0952
St. Fillans Tays	81	NN6924
St. Florence Dyfed	16	SN0801
St. Gennys Cnwll	6	SX1497
St. George Clwyd	45	SH9775
St. George's Glam	18	ST1076
St. Georges Avon	19	ST3762
St. Germans Cnwll	4	SX3657
St. Giles-on-the-Heath Devon	6	SX3690
St. Gluvia's Cnwll	2	SW7834
St. Harmon Powys	35	SN9872
St. Helen Auckland Dur	61	NZ1826
St. Helena Norfk	43	TG1916
St. Helens Cumb	58	NY0132
St. Helens IOW	11	SZ6288
St. Helens Mersyd	46	SJ5195
St. Helier Gt Lon	23	TQ2667
St. Helier Jersey	101	SV0000
St. Hilary Cnwll	2	SW5531
St. Hilary S Glam	18	ST0173
St. Ibbs Herts	31	TL1926
St. Illtyd Gwent	19	SO2102
St. Ishmaels Dyfed	16	SM8307
St. Issey Cnwll	3	SW9271
St. Ives Cambs	31	TL3171
St. Ives Cnwll	2	SW5140
St. Ives Dorset	10	SU1203
St. James's End Nhants	30	SP7460
St. James North Nhants	43	TG2820
St. James South Elmham Suffk	33	TM3281
St. John Cnwll	4	SX4053
St. John Jersey	101	SV0000
St. John's IOM	52	SC2781
St. John's Chapel Devon	6	SS5329
St. John's Chapel Dur	60	NY8837
St. John's Fen End Norfk	41	TF5312
St. John's Kirk Strath	75	NS9836
St. John's Town of Dalry D & G	65	NX6281
St. John's Wood Gt Lon	23	TQ2683
St. Johns Dur	61	NZ0733
St. Johns H & W	28	SO8453
St. Johns Surrey	22	SU9858
St. Johns Surrey	12	SU9956
St. Jude's IOM	52	SC3996
St. Just Cnwll	2	SW3631
St. Just Cnwll	3	SW8435
St. Katherines Gramp	95	NJ7834
St. Keverne Cnwll	2	SW7921
St. Kew Cnwll	3	SX0276
St. Kew Highway Cnwll	3	SX0375
St. Keyne Cnwll	4	SX2461
St. Lawrence Kent	15	TR3665
St. Lawrence Essex	25	TL9604
St. Lawrence IOW	11	SZ5376
St. Lawrence Jersey	101	SV0000
St. Leonards Bucks	22	SP9007
St. Leonards E Susx	14	TQ8009
St. Leonards Street Kent	14	TQ6756
St. Levan Cnwll	2	SW3822
St. Lythans S Glam	18	ST1072
St. Mabyn Cnwll	3	SX0473
St. Margaret South Elmham Suffk	33	TM3184
St. Margaret's at Cliffe Kent	15	TR3544
St. Margarets H & W	27	SO3533
St. Margarets Herts	23	TL3811
St. Margarets Hope Ork	103	ND4493
St. Marks Cnwll	52	SC2974
St. Martin Cnwll	4	SX2655
St. Martin Guern	101	SV0000
St. Martin Jersey	101	SV0000
St. Martin's Tays	82	NO1530
St. Martin's Green Cnwll	2	SW7324
St. Martins Shrops	36	SJ3236
St. Mary Jersey	101	SV0000
St. Mary Bourne Hants	21	SU4250
St. Mary Church S Glam	18	ST0071
St. Mary Cray Gt Lon	23	TQ4767
St. Mary in the Marsh Kent	15	TR0628
St. Mary's Ork	103	HY4701
St. Mary's Bay Kent	15	TR0827
St. Mary's Hoo Kent	14	TQ8076
St. Marylebone Gt Lon	23	TQ2782
St. Marys Bay Devon	5	SX9355
St. Marys Church Devon	5	SX9166
St. Maughans Green Gwent	27	SO4717
St. Mawes Cnwll	3	SW8433
St. Mellion Cnwll	4	SX3865
St. Mellons S Glam	19	ST2281
St. Merryn Cnwll	3	SW8874
St. Mewan Cnwll	3	SW9951
St. Michael Caerhays Cnwll	3	SW9642
St. Michael Church Somset	8	ST3130
St. Michael Penkevil Cnwll	3	SW8542
St. Michael South Elmham Suffk	33	TM3483
St. Michael's on Wyre Lancs	53	SD4641
St. Michaels H & W	27	SO5865
St. Michaels Kent	14	TQ8835
St. Monans Fife	83	NO5201
St. Neots Cambs	31	TL1860
St. Nicholas Dyfed	16	SM9035
St. Nicholas S Glam	18	ST0974
St. Nicholas at Wade Kent	15	TR2666
St. Ninians Cent	81	NS7991
St. Olaves Norfk	43	TM4599
St. Osyth Essex	25	TM1215
St. Ouen Jersey	101	SV0000
St. Owens Cross H & W	27	SO5324
St. Paul's Walden Herts	31	TL1922
St. Pauls Cray Gt Lon	23	TQ4668
St. Peter Jersey	101	SV0000
St. Peter Port Guern	101	SV0000
St. Peter's Guern	101	SV0000
St. Peter's Kent	15	TR3768
St. Peter's Hill Cambs	31	TL2373
St. Pinnock Cnwll	4	SX2063
St. Quivox Strath	73	NS3724
St. Sampson Guern	101	SV0000
St. Saviour Guern	101	SV0000
St. Stephen Cnwll	3	SW9453
St. Stephen Cnwll	3	SW9453
St. Stephens Cnwll	4	SX4158
St. Stephens Cnwll	4	SX3285
St. Teath Cnwll	3	SX0680
St. Tudy Cnwll	3	SX0676
St. Twynnells Dyfed	16	SR9597
St. Veep Cnwll	3	SX1455
St. Vigeans Tays	89	NO6443
St. Wenn Cnwll	3	SW9664
St. Weonards H & W	27	SO4924
Stableford Shrops	37	SO7598
Stacey Bank Derbys	48	SK2890
Stackhouse N York	54	SD8165
Stackpole Dyfed	16	SR9896
Stadbury Devon	5	SX6845
Staddiscombe Devon	4	SX5151
Staddlethorpe Humb	56	SE8428
Staffin Highld	90	NG4967
Stafford Staffs	38	SJ9223
Stag's Head Devon	7	SS6728
Stagsden Beds	30	SP9849
Stainburn Cumb	58	NY0229
Stainburn N York	55	SE2448
Stainby Lincs	40	SK9022
Staincross S York	55	SE3210
Staindrop Dur	61	NZ1220
Staines Surrey	22	TQ0371
Stainfield Lincs	50	TF0724
Stainforth N York	54	SD8267
Stainforth S York	56	SE6411
Stainland W York	55	SE0719
Stainsacre N York	63	NZ9108
Stainsby Derbys	49	SK4465
Stainton Cleve	62	NZ4714
Stainton Cumb	59	SD5285
Stainton Cumb	59	NY4828
Stainton Dur	61	NZ0718
Stainton S York	49	SK5593
Stainton by Langworth Lincs	50	TF0577
Stainton le Vale Lincs	50	TF1794
Stainton with Adgarley Cumb	53	SD2472
Staintondale N York	63	SE9998
Stair Strath	73	NS4323
Stair Haven D & G	64	NX2153
Staithes N York	62	NZ7818
Stakeford Nthumb	69	NZ2785
Stakes Hants	11	SU6808
Stalbridge Dorset	9	ST7317
Stalbridge Weston Dorset	9	ST7216
Stalham Norfk	43	TG3725
Stalisfield Green Kent	14	TQ9552
Stallen Dorset	9	ST6016
Stallingborough Humb	57	TA1911
Stalmine Lancs	53	SD3745
Stalybridge Gt Man	48	SJ9698
Stambourne Green Essex	24	TL6938
Stamford Lincs	40	TF0307
Stamford Nthumb	77	NU2219
Stamford Bridge Ches	46	SJ4667
Stamford Bridge Humb	56	SE7155
Stamford Hill Gt Lon	23	TQ3387
Stamfordham Nthumb	68	NZ0772
Stamnton Lees Derbys	48	SK2562
Stanborough Herts	23	TL2210
Stanbridge Beds	30	SP9624
Stanbridge Dorset	9	SU0003
Stanbury W York	55	SE0137
Stand Strath	74	NS7668
Standburn Cent	75	NS9274
Standeford Staffs	38	SJ9107
Standen Kent	14	TQ8540
Standerwick Somset	20	ST8160
Standford Hants	11	SU8134
Standish Gloucs	28	SO8018
Standish Gt Man	53	SD5610
Standlake Oxon	21	SP3902
Standon Hants	10	SU4226
Standon Herts	31	TL3922
Standon Staffs	37	SJ8135
Standwell Green Suffk	33	TM1370
Stane Strath	74	NS8859
Stanfield Norfk	42	TF9320
Stanford Beds	31	TL1640
Stanford Kent	15	TR1238
Stanford Bishop H & W	28	SO6651
Stanford Bridge H & W	28	SO7165
Stanford Dingley Berks	21	SU5771
Stanford in the Vale Oxon	21	SU3493
Stanford le Hope Essex	24	TQ6882
Stanford on Avon Nhants	39	SP5978
Stanford on Soar Notts	39	SK5422
Stanford on Teme H & W	28	SO7065
Stanford's End Kent	13	TQ4444
Stanfree Derbys	49	SK4774
Stanghow Cleve	62	NZ6715
Stanground Cambs	41	TL2096
Stanhoe Norfk	42	TF8036
Stanhope Border	75	NT1229
Stanhope Dur	40	NY9339
Stanion Nhants	40	SP9186
Stanley Derbys	49	SK4140
Stanley Dur	69	NZ1953
Stanley Notts	49	SK4661
Stanley Shrops	37	SO7583
Stanley Staffs	48	SJ9352
Stanley Tays	88	NO1033
Stanley S York	55	SE3422
Stanley W York	55	SE3422
Stanley Common Derbys	49	SK4142
Stanley Crook Dur	61	NZ1638
Stanley Pontlarge Gloucs	28	SO9930
Stanmer E Susx	13	TQ3309
Stanmore Gt Lon	23	TQ1692
Stanmore Hants	10	SU4628
Stannersburn Nthumb	68	NY7286
Stannington Nthumb	69	NZ2179
Stannington S York	49	SK2988
Stansbatch H & W	27	SO3461

Place	Page	Grid
Stanshope *Staffs*	48	SK1254
Stanstead *Suffk*	32	TL8449
Stanstead Abbots *Herts*	23	TL3811
Stanstead Street *Suffk*	32	TL8448
Stansted *Kent*	14	TQ6062
Stansted Mountfitchet *Essex*	31	TL5125
Stanton *Derbys*	39	SK2719
Stanton *Gloucs*	28	SP0634
Stanton *Nthumb*	69	NZ1390
Stanton *Staffs*	48	SK1246
Stanton *Suffk*	32	TL9673
Stanton Drew *Avon*	19	ST5963
Stanton Fitzwarren *Wilts*	21	SU1790
Stanton Harcourt *Oxon*	29	SP4105
Stanton Lacy *Shrops*	37	SO4979
Stanton Long *Shrops*	37	SO5691
Stanton Prior *Avon*	20	ST6762
Stanton St. Bernard *Wilts*	20	SU0962
Stanton St. John *Oxon*	29	SP5709
Stanton St. Quintin *Wilts*	20	ST9079
Stanton Street *Suffk*	32	TL9566
Stanton Wick *Avon*	19	ST6162
Stanton by Bridge *Derbys*	39	SK3627
Stanton by Dale *Derbys*	49	SK4637
Stanton in Peak *Derbys*	48	SK2464
Stanton on the Wolds *Notts*	39	SK6330
Stanton under Bardon *Leics*	39	SK4610
Stanton upon Hine Heath *Shrops*	37	SJ5624
Stanway *Essex*	25	TL9424
Stanway *Gloucs*	28	SP0632
Stanway Green *Essex*	25	TL9623
Stanwell *Surrey*	22	TQ0574
Stanwick *Nhants*	30	SP9871
Stanwix *Cumb*	67	NY3957
Stape *N York*	63	SE7994
Stapeley *Ches*	47	SJ6749
Stapenhill *Staffs*	39	SK2521
Staple *Kent*	15	TR2756
Staple *Somset*	18	ST1141
Staple Cross *Devon*	7	ST0320
Staple Fitzpaine *Somset*	8	ST2618
Staplefield *W Susx*	12	TQ2728
Stapleford *Cambs*	31	TL4751
Stapleford *Herts*	31	TL3117
Stapleford *Leics*	40	SK8018
Stapleford *Lincs*	50	SK8857
Stapleford *Notts*	49	SK4837
Stapleford Abbotts *Essex*	23	TQ5194
Staplegrove *Somset*	8	ST2126
Staplehay *Somset*	8	ST2121
Staplehurst *Kent*	14	TQ7843
Staplestreet *Kent*	15	TR0660
Stapleton *H & W*	27	SO3265
Stapleton *Leics*	39	SP4398
Stapleton *N York*	61	NZ2612
Stapleton *Shrops*	36	SJ4604
Stapleton *Somset*	8	ST4621
Stapley *Somset*	8	ST1813
Staploe *Beds*	30	TL1560
Staplow *H & W*	28	SO6941
Star *Dyfed*	17	SN2435
Star *Fife*	83	NO3103
Star *Somset*	19	ST4358
Star Hill *Gwent*	19	SO4702
Starbotton *N York*	61	SD9574
Starcross *Devon*	5	SX9781
Stareton *Warwks*	39	SP3371
Starlings Green *Essex*	31	TL4531
Starston *Norfk*	33	TM2384
Start *Devon*	5	SX8144
Start Point *Devon*	5	SX8337
Startforth *Dur*	61	NZ0415
Startley *Wilts*	20	ST9482
Statenborough *Kent*	15	TR3155
Stathe *Somset*	8	ST3728
Stathern *Leics*	40	SK7731
Staughton Green *Cambs*	30	TL1365
Staughton Highway *Cambs*	30	TL1364
Staunton *Gloucs*	27	SO5512
Staunton *Gloucs*	27	SO7929
Staunton Green *H & W*	27	SO3661
Staunton on Arrow *H & W*	27	SO3760
Staunton on Wye *H & W*	27	SO3044
Staveley *Cumb*	59	SD3786
Staveley *Cumb*	59	SD4698
Staveley *Derbys*	49	SK4374
Staveley *N York*	55	SE3662
Staverton *Devon*	5	SX7964
Staverton *Gloucs*	28	SO8923
Staverton *Nhants*	29	SP5461
Staverton *Wilts*	20	ST8560
Stawell *Somset*	19	ST3638
Stawley *Somset*	7	ST0622
Staxigoe *Highld*	100	ND3852
Staxton *N York*	63	TA0179
Staylittle *Powys*	35	SN8892
Staynall *Lancs*	53	SD3643
Stean *N York*	61	SE0973
Steane *Nhants*	29	SP5538
Stearsby *N York*	56	SE6071
Steart *Somset*	19	ST2745
Stebbing *Essex*	24	TL6624
Stebbing Green *Essex*	24	TL6823
Stebbing Park *Essex*	24	TL6524
Stechford *W Mids*	38	SP1387
Stede Quarter *Kent*	14	TQ8737
Stedham *W Susx*	11	SU8622
Steele Road *Border*	67	NY5292
Steen's Bridge *H & W*	27	SO5357
Steep *Hants*	11	SU7425
Steep Lane *W York*	55	SE0223
Steephill *IOW*	11	SZ5477
Steeple *Dorset*	9	SY9080
Steeple *Essex*	25	TL9303
Steeple Ashton *Wilts*	20	ST9056
Steeple Aston *Oxon*	29	SP4725
Steeple Barton *Oxon*	29	SP4424
Steeple Bumpstead *Essex*	32	TL6841
Steeple Claydon *Bucks*	30	SP7026
Steeple Gidding *Cambs*	40	TL1381
Steeple Langford *Wilts*	21	SU0337
Steeple Morden *Cambs*	31	TL2842
Steeton *W York*	55	SE0344
Stein *Highld*	90	NG2656
Stelling Minnis *Kent*	15	TR1447
Stenhouse *D & G*	66	NX7993
Stenhousemuir *Cent*	82	NS8682
Stenigot *Lincs*	51	TF2481
Stenscholl *Highld*	90	NG4767
Stenton *Loth*	76	NT6274
Stepaside *Dyfed*	16	SN1307
Stepney *Gt Lon*	23	TQ3581
Steppingley *Beds*	30	TL0135
Stepps *Strath*	74	NS6568
Sternfield *Suffk*	33	TM3861
Sterridge *Devon*	6	SS5546
Stert *Wilts*	20	SU0259
Stetchworth *Cambs*	32	TL6459
Stevenage *Herts*	31	TL2325
Stevenston *Strath*	73	NS2742
Steventon *Hants*	21	SU5447
Steventon *Oxon*	21	SU4691
Steventon End *Essex*	31	TL5942
Stevington *Beds*	30	SP9853
Stewartby *Beds*	30	TL0142
Stewarton *Strath*	72	NR6919
Stewarton *Strath*	73	NS4246
Stewkley *Bucks*	30	SP8525
Stewley *Somset*	8	ST3118
Steynton *Lincs*	51	TF3687
Steyning *W Susx*	12	TQ1711
Steynton *Dyfed*	16	SM9108
Stibb *Cnwll*	6	SS2210
Stibb Cross *Devon*	6	SS4314
Stibb Green *Wilts*	21	SU2262
Stibbard *Norfk*	42	TF9828
Stibbington *Cambs*	40	TL0998
Stichill *Border*	76	NT7138
Stickford *Lincs*	51	TF3560
Sticklepath *Devon*	7	SX6494
Sticklepath *Somset*	7	ST0435
Stickling Green *Essex*	31	TL4732
Stickney *Lincs*	51	TF3456
Stiffkey *Norfk*	42	TF9743
Stifford's Bridge *H & W*	28	SO7448
Stile Bridge *Kent*	14	TQ7547
Stileway *Somset*	19	ST4640
Stilligarry *W Isls*	102	NF7638
Stillingfleet *N York*	56	SE5940
Stillington *Cleve*	62	NZ3723
Stillington *N York*	56	SE5867
Stilton *Cambs*	40	TL1689
Stinchcombe *Gloucs*	20	ST7398
Stinsford *Dorset*	9	SY7191
Stirchley *Shrops*	37	SJ6906
Stirling *Cent*	81	NS7993
Stirling *Gramp*	95	NK1242
Stirtloe *Cambs*	31	TL1966
Stirton *N York*	54	SD9753
Stisted *Essex*	24	TL8024
Stithians *Cnwll*	2	SW7336
Stittenham *N York*	56	SE6767
Stivichall *W Mids*	39	SP3376
Stixwould *Lincs*	50	TF1765
Stoak *Ches*	46	SJ4273
Stobo *Border*	75	NT1838
Stoborough *Dorset*	9	SY9286
Stoborough Green *Dorset*	9	SY9285
Stobs Castle *Border*	67	NT5008
Stobswood *Nthumb*	69	NZ2195
Stock *Essex*	24	TQ6999
Stock *Avon*	19	ST6279
Stock Green *H & W*	28	SO9859
Stock Wood *H & W*	28	SO9858
Stockbridge *Hants*	10	SU3535
Stockbriggs *Strath*	74	NS7936
Stockbury *Kent*	14	TQ8461
Stockcross *Berks*	21	SU4368
Stockerston *Leics*	40	SP8397
Stocking *H & W*	27	SO6230
Stocking Pelham *Herts*	31	TL4529
Stockingford *Warwks*	39	SP3391
Stockinish *W Isls*	90	NG1391
Stockland *Devon*	8	ST2404
Stockland Bristol *Somset*	19	ST2443
Stockleigh English *Devon*	7	SS8406
Stockleigh Pomeroy *Devon*	7	SS8703
Stockley *Wilts*	20	ST9967
Stocklinch *Somset*	8	ST3817
Stockmoor *H & W*	27	SO3954
Stockport *Gt Man*	48	SJ8990
Stocksbridge *S York*	49	SK2698
Stocksfield *Nthumb*	68	NZ0561
Stockstreet *Essex*	24	TL8322
Stockton *H & W*	27	SO5261
Stockton *Norfk*	43	TM3894
Stockton *Shrops*	37	SJ7716
Stockton *Shrops*	37	SO7299
Stockton *Shrops*	37	SO7399
Stockton *Warwks*	29	SP4364
Stockton *Wilts*	20	ST9738
Stockton Brook *Staffs*	48	SJ9152
Stockton Heath *Ches*	47	SJ6186
Stockton on Teme *H & W*	28	SO7167
Stockton on the Forest *N York*	56	SE6556
Stockton-on-Tees *Cleve*	62	NZ4419
Stockwell End *W Mids*	38	SJ8800
Stockwood *Avon*	19	ST6268
Stockwood *Dorset*	8	ST5806
Stodmarsh *Kent*	15	TR2160
Stody *Norfk*	42	TG0535
Stoer *Highld*	98	NC0428
Stoford *Somset*	8	ST5613
Stoford *Wilts*	10	SU0835
Stogumber *Somset*	7	ST0936
Stogumber *Somset*	7	ST0937
Stogursey *Somset*	19	ST1942
Stogursey *Somset*	19	ST2042
Stoke *Devon*	6	SS2324
Stoke *Hants*	21	SU4051
Stoke *Hants*	11	SU7202
Stoke *Kent*	14	TQ8274
Stoke *W Mids*	39	SP3878
Stoke Abbott *Dorset*	8	ST4500
Stoke Albany *Nhants*	40	SP8088
Stoke Ash *Suffk*	33	TM1170
Stoke Bardolph *Notts*	49	SK6441
Stoke Bliss *H & W*	27	SO6563
Stoke Bruerne *Nhants*	30	SP7449
Stoke Canon *Devon*	7	SX9397
Stoke Charity *Hants*	10	SU4839
Stoke Cross *H & W*	27	SO6250
Stoke D'Abernon *Surrey*	22	TQ1259
Stoke Doyle *Nhants*	40	TL0286
Stoke Dry *Leics*	40	SP8596
Stoke End *Warwks*	38	SP1696
Stoke Farthing *Wilts*	10	SU0525
Stoke Ferry *Norfk*	42	TF7000
Stoke Fleming *Devon*	5	SX8648
Stoke Gabriel *Devon*	5	SX8457
Stoke Gabriel *Devon*	5	SX8557
Stoke Golding *Leics*	39	SP3997
Stoke Goldington *Bucks*	30	SP8348
Stoke Green *Bucks*	22	SU9882
Stoke Hammond *Bucks*	30	SP8829
Stoke Heath *W Mids*	39	SP3580
Stoke Holy Cross *Norfk*	43	TG2301
Stoke Lacy *H & W*	27	SO6149
Stoke Lyne *Oxon*	29	SP5628
Stoke Mandeville *Bucks*	22	SP8310
Stoke Newington *Gt Lon*	23	TQ3386
Stoke Orchard *Gloucs*	28	SO9128
Stoke Poges *Bucks*	22	SU9783
Stoke Prior *H & W*	27	SO5256
Stoke Prior *H & W*	28	SO9467
Stoke Rivers *Devon*	7	SS6335
Stoke Rochford *Lincs*	40	SK9127
Stoke Row *Oxon*	22	SU6884
Stoke St. Gregory *Somset*	8	ST3426
Stoke St. Mary *Somset*	8	ST2622
Stoke St. Michael *Somset*	20	ST6646
Stoke St. Milborough *Shrops*	37	SO5682
Stoke Talmage *Oxon*	22	SU6799
Stoke Trister *Somset*	9	ST7328
Stoke Wake *Dorset*	9	ST7606
Stoke by Clare *Suffk*	32	TL7443
Stoke sub Hamdon *Somset*	8	ST4717
Stoke upon Tern *Shrops*	37	SJ6328
Stoke-by-Nayland *Suffk*	25	TL9836
Stoke-on-Trent *Staffs*	47	SJ8745
Stoke-upon-Trent *Staffs*	47	SJ8745
Stokeford *Dorset*	9	SY8787
Stokeham *Notts*	50	SK7876
Stokeinteignhead *Devon*	5	SX9170
Stokenchurch *Bucks*	22	SU7696
Stokenham *Devon*	5	SX8042
Stokesay *Shrops*	36	SO4381
Stokesby *Norfk*	43	TG4310
Stokesley *N York*	62	NZ5208
Stolford *Somset*	7	ST0332
Stolford *Somset*	19	ST2245
Ston Easton *Somset*	19	ST6253
Stondon Massey *Essex*	24	TL5800
Stone *Bucks*	30	SP7812
Stone *Gloucs*	20	ST6895
Stone *H & W*	38	SO8675
Stone *Kent*	14	TQ9427
Stone *S York*	49	SK5589
Stone *Staffs*	38	SJ9034
Stone Allerton *Somset*	19	ST3950
Stone Cross *E Susx*	13	TQ6431
Stone Cross *Kent*	15	TR3257
Stone House *Cumb*	60	SD7785
Stone Street *Kent*	14	TQ5754
Stone Street *Suffk*	33	TL9639
Stone Street *Suffk*	33	TM3882
Stonea *Cambs*	41	TL4693
Stonebridge *Avon*	19	ST3959
Stonebroom *Derbys*	49	SK4159
Stonebury *Herts*	31	TL3828
Stonechrubie *Highld*	96	NC2419
Stonecrouch *Kent*	14	TQ7033
Stoneferry *Humb*	57	TA1231
Stonegate *E Susx*	14	TQ6627
Stonegate *N York*	63	NZ7709
Stonegrave *N York*	62	SE6577
Stonehall *H & W*	28	SO8848
Stonehaven *Gramp*	89	NO8786
Stonehill Green *Gt Lon*	23	TQ4870
Stonehouse *Ches*	46	SJ5070
Stonehouse *D & G*	66	NX8268
Stonehouse *Devon*	4	SX4653
Stonehouse *Gloucs*	28	SO8005
Stonehouse *Nthumb*	68	NY6958
Stonehouse *Strath*	74	NS7546
Stoneleigh *Warwks*	39	SP3372
Stones Green *Essex*	25	TM1626
Stonesby *Leics*	40	SK8224
Stonesfield *Oxon*	29	SP3917
Stonewells *Gramp*	94	NJ2865
Stoney Cross *Hants*	10	SU2511
Stoney Middleton *Derbys*	48	SK2275
Stoney Stanton *Leics*	39	SP4994
Stoney Stoke *Somset*	9	ST7032
Stoney Stratton *Somset*	19	ST6539
Stoney Stretton *Shrops*	36	SJ3809
Stoneybridge *W Isls*	102	NF7433
Stoneyburn *Loth*	75	NS9862
Stoneykirk *D & G*	64	NX0853
Stoneywood *Cent*	81	NS7982
Stoneywood *Gramp*	95	NJ8811
Stonham Aspal *Suffk*	33	TM1359
Stonnall *Staffs*	38	SK0603
Stonor *Oxon*	22	SU7388
Stonton Wyville *Leics*	40	SP7395
Stony Cross *Devon*	6	SS5125
Stony Cross *H & W*	27	SO5467
Stony Houghton *Derbys*	49	SK4966
Stony Stratford *Bucks*	30	SP7840
Stonywell *Staffs*	38	SK0812
Stoodleigh *Devon*	7	SS6532
Stopham *W Susx*	12	TQ0218
Stopsley *Beds*	30	TL1023
Storeton *Mersyd*	46	SJ3084
Stornoway *W Isls*	102	NB4333
Storrington *W Susx*	12	TQ0814
Storth *Cumb*	59	SD4780
Storwood *Humb*	56	SE7144
Stotfield *Beds*	31	TL2136
Stottesdon *Shrops*	37	SO6782
Stoughton *Leics*	39	SK6402
Stoughton *Surrey*	12	SU9851
Stoughton *W Susx*	11	SU8011
Stoul *Highld*	85	NM7594
Stour Provost *Dorset*	9	ST7921
Stour Row *Dorset*	9	ST8220
Stourbridge *W Mids*	38	SO9084
Stourpaine *Dorset*	9	ST8509
Stourport-on-Severn *H & W*	28	SO8171
Stourton *Staffs*	38	SO8684
Stourton *Warwks*	29	SP3036
Stourton *Wilts*	9	ST7733
Stourton Caundle *Dorset*	9	ST7114
Stove *Shet*	103	HU4224
Stoven *Suffk*	33	TM4481
Stow *Border*	76	NT4644
Stow *Lincs*	50	SK8781
Stow Bardolph *Norfk*	41	TF6206
Stow Bedon *Norfk*	42	TL9596
Stow Longa *Cambs*	30	TL1171
Stow Maries *Essex*	24	TL8399
Stow cum Quy *Cambs*	31	TL5260
Stow-on-the-Wold *Gloucs*	29	SP1926
Stowbridge *Norfk*	41	TF6007
Stowe *Shrops*	36	SO3173
Stowe by Chartley *Staffs*	38	SK0027
Stowell *Somset*	9	ST6822
Stowey *Avon*	19	ST5959
Stowford *Devon*	4	SX4387
Stowford *Devon*	6	SS6541
Stowlangtoft *Suffk*	32	TL9568
Stowmarket *Suffk*	32	TM0458
Stowting *Kent*	15	TR1242
Stowting Common *Kent*	15	TR1242
Stowupland *Suffk*	32	TM0760
Straad *Strath*	72	NS0462
Strachan *Gramp*	89	NO6692
Strachur *Strath*	80	NN0901
Stradbroke *Suffk*	33	TM2374
Stradishall *Wilts*	32	TL7552
Stradsett *Norfk*	42	TF6605
Stragglethorpe *Lincs*	50	SK9152
Straight Soley *Wilts*	21	SU3272
Straiton *Loth*	75	NT2766
Straiton *Strath*	95	NJ8621
Straloch *Gramp*	88	NO0463
Straloch *Tays*	88	NO0463
Stramshall *Staffs*	38	SK0735
Strang *IOM*	52	SC3678
Strangford *H & W*	27	SO5727
Stranraer *D & G*	64	NX0660
Stratfield Mortimer *Berks*	22	SU6664
Stratfield Saye *Hants*	22	SU6861
Stratfield Turgis *Hants*	22	SU6959
Stratford *Gt Lon*	23	TQ3884
Stratford St. Andrew *Suffk*	33	TM3560
Stratford St. Mary *Suffk*	25	TM0434
Stratford Tony *Wilts*	10	SU0926
Stratford sub Castle *Wilts*	10	SU1331
Stratford-upon-Avon *Warwks*	29	SP2055
Strath *Highld*	91	NG7978
Strath *Highld*	100	ND2652
Strathan *Highld*	85	NM9791
Strathan *Highld*	98	NC0821
Strathan *Highld*	99	NC5764
Strathaven *Strath*	74	NS6944
Strathblane *Cent*	81	NS5679
Strathcarron *Highld*	91	NG9442
Strathcoil *Strath*	79	NM6830
Strathdon *Gramp*	94	NJ3512
Strathkanaird *Highld*	96	NC1501
Strathkinness *Fife*	83	NO4616
Strathlene *Gramp*	94	NJ4567
Strathmashie House *Tays*	87	NN5891
Strathmiglo *Fife*	82	NO2109
Strathpeffer *Highld*	92	NH4858
Strathwhillan *Strath*	72	NS0235
Strathy *Highld*	99	NC8464
Strathy Inn *Highld*	99	NC8365
Strathyre *Cent*	81	NN5617
Stratton *Cnwll*	6	SS2206
Stratton *Dorset*	9	SY6593
Stratton *Gloucs*	20	SP0103
Stratton Audley *Oxon*	29	SP6026
Stratton St. Margaret *Wilts*	21	SU1786
Stratton St. Michael *Norfk*	43	TM2093
Stratton Strawless *Norfk*	43	TG2220
Stratton-on-the-Fosse *Somset*	19	ST6550
Stravithie *Fife*	83	NO5313
Stream *Somset*	7	ST0639
Streat *E Susx*	12	TQ3515
Streatham *Gt Lon*	23	TQ3171
Streatley *Beds*	30	TL0728
Streatley *Berks*	21	SU5980
Street *Devon*	5	SX1895
Street *Devon*	8	SY1888
Street *Somset*	19	ST4836
Street Ashton *Warwks*	39	SP4682
Street Dinas *Shrops*	36	SJ3338
Street End *Kent*	15	TR1453
Street Gate *T & W*	69	NZ2159
Street Houses *N York*	56	SE5346
Street of Kincardine *Highld*	93	NH9417
Street on the Fosse *Somset*	19	ST6139
Streethay *Staffs*	38	SK1410
Streetlam *N York*	61	SE3098
Streetly End *Cambs*	32	TL6418
Strelitz *Tays*	88	NO1836
Strelley *Notts*	49	SK5141
Strensall *N York*	56	SE6360
Strete *Devon*	5	SX8447
Stretford *Gt Man*	47	SJ7994
Strethall *Essex*	31	TL4839
Stretham *Cambs*	31	TL5174
Strettington *W Susx*	11	SU8907
Stretton *Ches*	47	SJ6282
Stretton *Derbys*	49	SK3961
Stretton *Leics*	40	SK9415
Stretton *Staffs*	38	SJ8811
Stretton *Staffs*	39	SK2526
Stretton Grandison *H & W*	27	SO6344
Stretton Sugwas *H & W*	27	SO4642
Stretton Westwood *Shrops*	37	SO5998
Stretton en le Field *Leics*	39	SK3012
Stretton on Fosse *Warwks*	29	SP2238
Stretton under Fosse *Warwks*	39	SP4581
Stretton-on-Dunsmore *Warwks*	39	SP4072
Strichen *Gramp*	95	NJ9455
Stringston *Somset*	19	ST1742
Strixton *Nhants*	30	SP9061
Stroat *Gloucs*	19	ST5797
Stromeferry *Highld*	85	NG8634
Stromness *Ork*	103	HY2509
Stronachlachar *Cent*	80	NN4010
Stronafian *Strath*	80	NS0281
Stronchrubie *Highld*	102	NQ0384
Strone *Highld*	86	NH1481
Strone *Highld*	92	NH5428
Strone *Strath*	80	NS1980
Stronenaba *Highld*	86	NN2084
Stronmilchan *Strath*	80	NN1528
Strontian *Highld*	79	NM8161
Strood *Kent*	14	TQ7269
Strood *Kent*	28	SO8605
Stroud *Gloucs*	11	SU7223
Stroud *Hants*	11	SU7223
Stroud Green *Essex*	24	TQ8690
Stroud Green *Gloucs*	28	SO8007
Stroxton *Lincs*	40	SK9030
Struan *Highld*	84	NG3438
Struan *Tays*	87	NN8065
Strumpshaw *Norfk*	43	TG3507
Strutherhill *Strath*	74	NS7649
Struthers *Fife*	83	NO3709
Struy *Highld*	92	NH4039
Stuartfield *Gramp*	95	NJ9745
Stubbington *Hants*	11	SU5503
Stubbington *Hants*	58	SD0892
Stubley *Derbys*	49	SK3372
Stubshaw Cross *Gt Man*	47	SD5800
Stubton *Lincs*	50	SK8748
Stuckgown *Strath*	80	NN3203
Stuckton *Hants*	10	SU1613
Studfold *N York*	54	SD8169
Studham *Beds*	30	TL0215
Studholme *Cumb*	67	NY2656
Studland *Dorset*	9	SZ0382
Studley *Oxon*	29	SP6012
Studley *Warwks*	28	SP0764
Studley *Wilts*	20	ST9671
Studley Common *H & W*	28	SP0665
Studley Roger *N York*	55	SE2969
Studley Royal *N York*	55	SE2770
Stuntney *Cambs*	31	TL5578
Sturgate *Lincs*	50	SK8788
Sturmer *Essex*	32	TL6943
Sturminster Common *Dorset*	9	ST7812
Sturminster Marshall *Dorset*	9	ST9400
Sturminster Newton *Dorset*	9	ST7813
Sturry *Kent*	15	TR1760
Sturton *Humb*	56	SE9704
Sturton by Stow *Lincs*	50	SK8980
Sturton le Steeple *Notts*	50	SK7884
Stuston *Suffk*	33	TM1378
Stutton *N York*	55	SE4741
Styal *Ches*	47	SJ8383
Stynie *Gramp*	94	NJ3360
Styrrup *Notts*	49	SK6090
Succoth *Strath*	80	NN2905
Suckley *H & W*	28	SO7251
Sudborough *Nhants*	40	SP9682
Sudbourne *Suffk*	33	TM4153
Sudbrook *Gwent*	19	ST5087
Sudbrook *Lincs*	50	SK9744
Sudbrooke *Lincs*	50	TF0276
Sudbury *Derbys*	38	SK1632
Sudbury *Gt Lon*	23	TQ1685
Sudbury *Suffk*	32	TL8741
Suddie *Highld*	93	NH6554
Suddington *H & W*	28	SO8563
Sugnall *Gloucs*	28	SO9307
Suffield *N York*	63	SE9890
Suffield *Norfk*	43	TG2332
Sugdon *Shrops*	37	SJ6014
Sugnall *Staffs*	37	SJ7931
Sugwas Pool *H & W*	27	SO4541
Suishnish *Highld*	84	NG5816
Sulaisiadar *W Isls*	102	SC3994
Sulgrave *Nhants*	29	SP5545
Sulham *Berks*	22	SU6474
Sulhamstead Abbots *Berks*	21	SU6467
Sulhamstead Bannister *Berks*	21	SU6368
Sullom *Shet*	103	HU3573
Sullom Voe *Shet*	103	HU4075
Sully *S Glam*	19	ST1568
Summerbridge *N York*	55	SE2062
Summercourt *Cnwll*	3	SW8856
Summerfield *Norfk*	42	TF7538
Summerhouse *Dur*	61	NZ2019
Summerleaze *Gwent*	19	ST4284
Summersdale *W Susx*	11	SU8606
Summerseat *Gt Man*	54	SD7914
Summertown *Oxon*	29	SP5009
Sunadale *Strath*	72	NR8145
Sunbiggin *Cumb*	60	NY6508
Sunbury *Surrey*	22	TQ1169
Sundaywell *D & G*	66	NX8284
Sunderland *Cumb*	58	NY1735
Sunderland *Lancs*	53	SD4255
Sunderland *Strath*	70	NR2464
Sunderland *T & W*	69	NZ3957
Sunderland Bridge *Dur*	61	NZ2637
Sundhope *Border*	75	NT3325
Sundridge *Kent*	23	TQ4855
Sunk Island *Humb*	57	TA2618
Sunningdale *Surrey*	22	SU9567
Sunninghill *Surrey*	22	SU9367
Sunningwell *Oxon*	21	SP4900
Sunniside *Dur*	61	NZ1438
Sunny Bank *Cumb*	58	SD2992
Sunnyhill *Derbys*	39	SK3332
Sunnyhurst *Lancs*	54	SD6722
Sunnylaw *Cent*	81	NS7998
Sunnymead *Oxon*	29	SP5010
Sunwick *Border*	77	NT9052
Surbiton *Gt Lon*	23	TQ1867
Surfleet *Lincs*	41	TF2528
Surlingham *Norfk*	43	TG3106
Surrex *Essex*	24	TL8722
Sustead *Norfk*	43	TG1837
Susworth *Lincs*	50	SE8302
Sutcombe *Devon*	6	SS3412
Sutcombemill *Devon*	6	SS3412
Sutterby *Lincs*	51	TF3872
Sutterton *Lincs*	41	TF2835
Sutton *Beds*	31	TL2247
Sutton *Cambs*	40	TL0998
Sutton *Cambs*	41	TL4479
Sutton *Devon*	5	SX7042
Sutton *Gt Lon*	16	SM9116
Sutton *E Susx*	13	TV4999
Sutton *Gt Lon*	23	TQ2564
Sutton *Kent*	15	TR3349
Sutton *N York*	55	SE4925
Sutton *Norfk*	43	TG3823
Sutton *Notts*	40	SK7637
Sutton *Notts*	49	SK6784
Sutton *Oxon*	29	SP4106
Sutton *Shrops*	37	SJ6632
Sutton *Shrops*	37	SO7286
Sutton *Shrops*	37	SJ7622
Sutton *Suffk*	33	TM3046
Sutton *W Susx*	12	SU9715
Sutton Bassett *Nhants*	40	SP7790
Sutton Benger *Wilts*	20	ST9478
Sutton Bingham *Somset*	8	ST5411
Sutton Bonington *Notts*	39	SK5025
Sutton Bridge *Lincs*	41	TF4821
Sutton Cheney *Leics*	39	SK4100
Sutton Coldfield *W Mids*	38	SP1296
Sutton Courtenay *Oxon*	21	SU5093
Sutton Grange *N York*	61	SE2873
Sutton Green *Surrey*	22	TQ0054
Sutton Howgrave *N York*	55	SE3279
Sutton Maddock *Shrops*	37	SJ7201
Sutton Mallet *Somset*	19	ST3736
Sutton Mandeville *Wilts*	9	ST9828
Sutton Montis *Somset*	9	ST6224
Sutton Scotney *Hants*	10	SU4639
Sutton St. Edmund *Lincs*	41	TF3613
Sutton St. James *Lincs*	41	TF3918
Sutton St. Nicholas *H & W*	27	SO5245
Sutton Street *Kent*	14	TQ8149
Sutton Valence *Kent*	14	TQ8149
Sutton Veny *Wilts*	20	ST9041
Sutton Waldron *Dorset*	9	ST8615
Sutton Weaver *Ches*	47	SJ5479
Sutton Wick *Avon*	19	ST5758

Sutton Wick *Oxon*	21	SU4894
Sutton at Hone *Kent*	23	TQ5569
Sutton in Ashfield *Notts*	49	SK4959
Sutton le Marsh *Lincs*	51	TF5280
Sutton on Sea *Lincs*	51	TF5181
Sutton on Trent *Notts*	50	SK7965
Sutton on the Hill *Derbys*	39	SK2333
Sutton upon Derwent *Humb*	56	SE7046
Sutton-in-Craven *N York*	54	SE0044
Sutton-on-Hull *Humb*	57	TA1113
Sutton-on-Hull *Humb*	57	TA1132
Sutton-on-the-Forest *N York*	56	SE5864
Sutton-under-Brailes *Warwks*	29	SP3037
Sutton-under-Whitestonecliffe *N York*	62	SE4882
Swaby *Lincs*	51	TF3877
Swadlincote *Derbys*	39	SK3019
Swaffham *Norfk*	42	TF8209
Swaffham Bulbeck *Cambs*	31	TL5562
Swaffham Prior *Cambs*	31	TL5764
Swafield *Norfk*	43	TG2832
Swainby *N York*	62	NZ4701
Swainsthorpe *Norfk*	43	TG2201
Swalcliffe *Oxon*	20	SP3438
Swalcliffe *Oxon*	29	SP3737
Swalecliffe *Kent*	15	TR1367
Swallow *Lincs*	57	TA1703
Swallow Beck *Lincs*	50	SK9567
Swallow Nest *S York*	49	SK4584
Swallowcliffe *Wilts*	9	ST9626
Swallowfield *Berks*	22	SU7264
Swallows Cross *Essex*	24	TQ6199
Swan Green *Ches*	47	SJ7373
Swan Village *W Mids*	38	SO9992
Swanage *Dorset*	9	SZ0278
Swanbourne *Bucks*	30	SP8026
Swanland *Humb*	56	SE9827
Swanley *Kent*	23	TQ5168
Swanley Village *Kent*	23	TQ5269
Swanmore *Hants*	11	SU5716
Swannington *Leics*	39	SK4116
Swannington *Norfk*	43	TG1319
Swanpool Garden Suberb *Lincs*	50	SK9569
Swanscombe *Kent*	14	TQ6074
Swansea *W Glam*	18	SS6592
Swanton Abbott *Norfk*	43	TG2625
Swanton Morley *Norfk*	42	TG0117
Swanton Novers *Norfk*	42	TG0231
Swanwick *Derbys*	49	SK4053
Swanwick *Hants*	11	SU5109
Swarby *Lincs*	50	TF0440
Swardeston *Norfk*	43	TG2002
Swarkestone *Derbys*	39	SK3728
Swarland *Nthumb*	69	NU1602
Swarraton *Hants*	11	SU5637
Swarthmoor *Cumb*	58	SD2777
Swaton *Lincs*	40	TF1337
Swavesey *Cambs*	31	TL3668
Sway *Hants*	10	SZ2798
Swayfield *Lincs*	40	SK9922
Swaythling *Hants*	10	SU4315
Sweetham *Devon*	7	SX8899
Sweethaws *E Susx*	13	TQ5028
Sweets *Cnwll*	6	SX1595
Sweetshouse *Cnwll*	3	SX0861
Swefling *Suffk*	33	TM3463
Swepstone *Leics*	39	SK3610
Swerford *Oxon*	29	SP3731
Swettenham *Ches*	47	SJ8067
Swffryd *Gwent*	19	ST2199
Swiftsden *E Susx*	14	TQ7228
Swilland *Suffk*	33	TM1853
Swillington *W York*	55	SE3830
Swimbridge *Devon*	6	SS6330
Swimbridge Newland *Devon*	6	SS6230
Swinbrook *Oxon*	29	SP2812
Swinderby *Lincs*	50	SK8663
Swindon *Gloucs*	28	SO9325
Swindon *Staffs*	38	SO8690
Swindon *Wilts*	20	SU1484
Swine *Humb*	57	TA1335
Swinefleet *Humb*	56	SE7621
Swineford *Avon*	20	ST6968
Swineshead *Beds*	30	TL0565
Swineshead *Lincs*	51	TF2340
Swineshead Bridge *Lincs*	51	TF2142
Swiney *Highld*	100	ND2335
Swinford *Leics*	39	SP5779
Swingfield Minnis *Kent*	15	TR2142
Swingfield Street *Kent*	15	TR2343
Swingleton Green *Suffk*	32	TL9647
Swinhill *Strath*	74	NS7748
Swinhoe *Nthumb*	77	NU2128
Swinithwaite *N York*	61	SE0489
Swinscoe *Staffs*	48	SK1348
Swinside *Cumb*	58	NY2421
Swinstead *Lincs*	40	TF0122
Swinton *Border*	77	NT8447
Swinton *Gt Man*	47	SD7701
Swinton *N York*	61	SE2179
Swinton *N York*	63	SE7573
Swinton *S York*	49	SK4599
Swithland *Leics*	39	SK5413
Swordale *Highld*	92	NH5765
Swordland *Highld*	85	NM7891
Swordly *Highld*	99	NC7463
Sworton Heath *Ches*	47	SJ6984
Swynnerton *Staffs*	38	SJ8535
Sychtyn *Powys*	35	SH8907
Syde *Gloucs*	28	SO9511
Sydenham *Gt Lon*	23	TQ3571
Sydenham *Oxon*	22	SP7301
Sydenham Damerel *Devon*	4	SX4075
Syderstone *Norfk*	42	TF8332
Sydling St. Nicholas *Dorset*	9	SY6399
Sydmonton *Hants*	21	SU4857
Syerston *Notts*	50	SK7447
Sykehouse *S York*	56	SE6216
Symbister *Shet*	103	HU5462
Symington *Strath*	73	NS3831
Symington *Strath*	75	NS9935
Symonds Yat *H & W*	27	SO5515
Symondsbury *Dorset*	8	SY4493
Synton *Border*	76	NT4822
Syre *Highld*	99	NC6943
Syreford *Gloucs*	28	SP0320
Sysham Nhants*	29	SP6241
Syston *Leics*	39	SK6211
Syston *Lincs*	50	SK9240
Sytchampton *H & W*	28	SO8466
Sywell *Nhants*	30	SP8267

T

Tackley *Oxon*	29	SP4720
Tacolneston *Norfk*	43	TM1495
Tadcaster *N York*	55	SE4843
Tadley *Hants*	21	SU6061
Tadlow *Cambs*	31	TL2847
Tadmarton *Oxon*	29	SP3937
Tadworth *Surrey*	23	TQ2356
Tafarnaubach *M Glam*	26	SO1110
Taff Merthyr Garden Villa *M Glam*	18	ST1198
Taff's Well *M Glam*	18	ST1283
Tafolwern *Powys*	35	SH8902
Tai-n-lon *Gwynd*	44	SH4450
Tai'r Bull *Powys*	26	SN9926
Taibach *W Glam*	18	SS7788
Tain *Highld*	97	NH7281
Tain *Highld*	100	ND2286
Takeley *Essex*	24	TL5621
Takeley Street *Essex*	24	TL5421
Tal-y-Bont *Gwynd*	45	SH7668
Tal-y-Bont *Gwynd*	45	SH7668
Tal-y-Waun *Gwent*	27	SO2604
Tal-y-bont *Gwynd*	34	SH5921
Tal-y-bont *Gwynd*	45	SH6070
Tal-y-cafn *Gwynd*	45	SH7971
Tal-y-coed *Gwent*	27	SO4115
Tal-y-garn *M Glam*	18	ST0379

Talachddu *Powys*	26	SO0833
Talacre *Clwyd*	46	SJ1283
Talaton *Devon*	7	SY0699
Talbenny *Dyfed*	16	SM8412
Taleford *Devon*	6	SX0996
Talerddig *Powys*	35	SH9300
Talgarreg *Dyfed*	17	SN4251
Talgarth *Powys*	27	SO1533
Taliesin *Dyfed*	35	SN6591
Talisker *Highld*	84	NG3230
Talke Pits *Staffs*	47	SJ8352
Talkin *Cumb*	67	NY5457
Talla Linnfoots *Border*	75	NT1320
Talladale *Highld*	91	NG9270
Tallaminnoch *Strath*	64	NX4098
Talley *Dyfed*	17	SN6332
Tallington *Lincs*	40	TF0908
Talmine *Highld*	99	NC5863
Talog *Dyfed*	17	SN3325
Talsarn *Dyfed*	34	SN5456
Talsarnau *Gwynd*	45	SH6135
Talskiddy *Cnwll*	3	SW9165
Talwrn *Gwynd*	44	SH4877
Talybont *Dyfed*	35	SN6589
Talybont-on-Usk *Powys*	26	SO1122
Talysarn *Gwynd*	44	SH4852
Tamerton Foliot *Devon*	4	SX4761
Tamworth *Staffs*	39	SK2004
Tan Hill *N York*	60	NY8907
Tan Office Green *Suffk*	32	TL7858
Tan-y-fron *Clwyd*	45	SH9664
Tan-y-groes *Dyfed*	17	SN2849
Tandlemuir *Strath*	73	NS3361
Tandridge *Surrey*	13	TQ3750
Tanfield *Dur*	69	NZ1855
Tanfield Lea *Dur*	69	NZ1854
Tangley *Hants*	21	SU3252
Tangmere *W Susx*	11	SU9006
Tangusdale *W Isls*	102	NF6500
Tankerness *Ork*	103	HY5108
Tankerton *Kent*	15	TR1167
Tannach *Highld*	100	ND3247
Tannachie *Gramp*	89	NO7884
Tannadice *Tays*	89	NO4758
Tanner Green *H & W*	38	SP0874
Tannington *Suffk*	33	TM2467
Tannochside *Strath*	74	NS6962
Tansley *Derbys*	49	SK3259
Tansor *Nhants*	40	TL0590
Tantobie *Dur*	69	NZ1754
Tanton *N York*	62	NZ5210
Tanworth in Arden *Warwks*	28	SP1170
Tanygrisiau *Gwynd*	44	SH4945
Taplow *Bucks*	22	SU9182
Tarbert *Strath*	71	NR6182
Tarbert *Strath*	72	NR6551
Tarbert *Strath*	71	NR8668
Tarbert *W Isls*	90	NB1500
Tarbet *Highld*	85	NM7992
Tarbet *Highld*	98	NC1649
Tarbet *Strath*	80	NN3104
Tarbolton *Strath*	73	NS4327
Tarbrax *Strath*	75	NT0255
Tardebigge *H & W*	28	SO9969
Tardy Gate *Lancs*	53	SD5426
Tarfside *Tays*	89	NO4979
Tarland *Gramp*	89	NJ4804
Tarleton *Lancs*	53	SD4520
Tarlton *Gloucs*	20	ST9599
Tarnock *Somset*	19	ST3852
Tarns *Cumb*	67	NY1247
Tarporley *Ches*	47	SJ5562
Tarr *Somset*	7	SS8632
Tarrant Crawford *Dorset*	9	ST9203
Tarrant Gunville *Dorset*	9	ST9212
Tarrant Hinton *Dorset*	9	ST9310
Tarrant Keynston *Dorset*	9	ST9204
Tarrant Launceston *Dorset*	9	ST9409
Tarrant Monkton *Dorset*	9	ST9408
Tarrant Rawston *Dorset*	9	ST9306
Tarrant Rushton *Dorset*	9	ST9305
Tarring Neville *E Susx*	13	TQ4404
Tarrington *H & W*	27	SO6240
Tarrylin *Strath*	72	NR9621
Tarskavaig *Highld*	84	NG5810
Tarves *Gramp*	95	NJ8631
Tarvie *Tays*	88	NO0164
Tarvin *Ches*	46	SJ4966
Tasburgh *Norfk*	43	TM2096
Taston *Oxon*	29	SP3621
Tatenhill *Staffs*	39	SK2022
Tathwell *Lincs*	51	TF3281
Tatsfield *Surrey*	23	TQ4156
Tattenhall *Ches*	46	SJ4858
Tatterford *Norfk*	42	TF8628
Tattersett *Norfk*	42	TF8429
Tattershall *Lincs*	51	TF2157
Tattershall Thorpe *Lincs*	51	TF2159
Tattingstone *Suffk*	25	TM1337
Tattingstone White Horse *Suffk*	25	TM1338
Tatworth *Somset*	8	ST3205
Tauchers *Gramp*	94	NJ3649
Taunton *Somset*	8	ST2324
Taverham *Norfk*	43	TG1614
Tavernspite *Dyfed*	17	SN1812
Tavistock *Devon*	4	SX4774
Taw green *Devon*	7	SX6597
Taxal *Derbys*	48	SK0079
Taychreggan Hotel *Strath*	80	NN0421
Tayinloan *Strath*	72	NR7044
Taynish *Strath*	71	NR7282
Taynton *Gloucs*	28	SO7222
Taynton *Oxon*	29	SP2313
Taynuilt *Strath*	80	NN0031
Tayport *Fife*	83	NO4628
Tayvallich *Strath*	71	NR7487
Tealby *Lincs*	50	TF1590
Teangue *Highld*	85	NG6609
Teanord *Highld*	92	NH5964
Tebay *Cumb*	59	NY6104
Tebworth *Beds*	30	SP9926
Tedburn St. Mary *Devon*	7	SX8194
Teddington *Gloucs*	28	SO9632
Teddington *Gt Lon*	23	TQ1671
Tedstone Delamere *H & W*	28	SO6958
Tedstone Wafer *H & W*	28	SO6759
Teeton *Nhants*	30	SP6970
Teffont Evias *Wilts*	9	ST9831
Teffont Magna *Wilts*	9	ST9832
Tegryn *Dyfed*	17	SN2233
Teigh *Leics*	40	SK8615
Teign Village *Devon*	5	SX8381
Teigngrace *Devon*	5	SX8474
Teignmouth *Devon*	5	SX9473
Telford *Shrops*	37	SJ6908
Tellisford *Somset*	20	ST8055
Telscombe *E Susx*	13	TQ4003
Tempar *Tays*	87	NN6857
Templand *D & G*	66	NY0886
Temple *Cnwll*	3	SX1473
Temple *Loth*	75	NT3158
Temple *Strath*	74	NS5469
Temple Bar *Dyfed*	34	SN5354
Temple Cloud *Avon*	19	ST6157
Temple Ewell *Kent*	15	TR2844
Temple Grafton *Warwks*	28	SP1255
Temple Guiting *Gloucs*	28	SP0928
Temple Hirst *N York*	56	SE6024
Temple Normanton *Derbys*	49	SK4167
Temple Pier *Highld*	92	NH5330
Temple Sowerby *Cumb*	59	NY6127
Templecombe *Somset*	9	ST7022
Templehall *Tays*	83	NO4936
Templeton *Devon*	7	SS8813
Templeton *Dyfed*	16	SN1111
Templeton Bridge *Devon*	7	SS8714
Tempsford *Beds*	31	TL1653
Ten Mile Bank *Norfk*	41	TL5996
Tenbury Wells *H & W*	27	SO5968
Tenby *Dyfed*	16	SN1300
Tendring *Essex*	25	TM1424
Tendring Green *Essex*	25	TM1326
Tendring Heath *Essex*	25	TM1326
Tenterden *Kent*	14	TQ8833

Terling *Essex*	24	TL7715
Ternhill *Shrops*	37	SJ6332
Terregles *D & G*	66	NX9377
Terrington *N York*	56	SE6670
Terrington St. Clement *Norfk*	41	TF5520
Terrington St. John *Norfk*	41	TF5514
Terry's Cross *W Susx*	12	TQ2314
Teston *Kent*	14	TQ7053
Testwood *Hants*	10	SU3514
Tetbury *Gloucs*	20	ST8993
Tetbury Upton *Gloucs*	20	ST8795
Tetchill *Shrops*	36	SJ3932
Tetcott *Devon*	6	SX3396
Tetney *Lincs*	51	TA3100
Tetsworth *Oxon*	22	SP6801
Tettenhall *W Mids*	38	SJ8800
Tettenhall Wood *W Mids*	38	SO8799
Teversal *Notts*	49	SK4861
Teversham *Cambs*	31	TL4958
Teviothead *Border*	67	NT4005
Tewel *Gramp*	89	NO8085
Tewin *Herts*	23	TL2714
Tewkesbury *Gloucs*	28	SO8933
Teynham *Kent*	14	TQ9562
Thackthwaite *Cumb*	58	NY1524
Thakeham *W Susx*	12	TQ1017
Thame *Oxon*	22	SP7005
Thames Ditton *Surrey*	22	TQ1567
Thamesmead *Gt Lon*	23	TQ4780
Thanington *Kent*	15	TR1356
Tharston *Norfk*	75	NS9737
Tharston *Norfk*	43	TM1894
Thatcham *Berks*	21	SU5167
Thaxted *Essex*	24	TL6131
The Abbey *Gwynd*	45	SH7865
The Beeches *Gloucs*	20	SP0201
The Brunt *Loth*	76	NT6873
The Den *Strath*	73	NS3251
The Bungalow *IOM*	52	SC3987
The Butts *Gloucs*	28	SO8916
The Chart *Surrey*	13	TQ4251
The City *Bucks*	22	SU7896
The Corner *Shrops*	36	SO4387
The Crossways *H & W*	27	SO3538
The Den *Strath*	73	NS3251
The Fence *Gloucs*	27	SO5405
The Forstal *E Susx*	23	TQ5455
The Forstal *Kent*	15	TR0439
The Green *Essex*	24	TL7719
The Grove *H & W*	28	SO8740
The Hirsel *Border*	77	NT8240
The Holt *Berks*	22	SU8078
The Howe *IOM*	52	SC1967
The Lees *Bucks*	22	SP9004
The Lochs *Gramp*	94	NJ3020
The Marsh *Ches*	47	SJ8463
The Mound *Highld*	97	NH7798
The Mumbles *W Glam*	17	SS6187
The Mythe *Gloucs*	28	SO8934
The Nant *Clwyd*	46	SJ2850
The Neuk *Gramp*	89	NO7397
The Pill *Gwent*	19	ST4887
The Quarry *Gloucs*	20	ST7399
The Reddings *Gloucs*	28	SO9021
The Shoe *Wilts*	20	ST8074
The Stair *Kent*	13	TQ6037
The Stocks *Kent*	14	TQ9127
The Wrythe *Gt Lon*	23	TQ2765
The alby *Humb*	56	SE8917
Theale *Berks*	21	SU6471
Theale *Somset*	19	ST4646
Thearne *Humb*	57	TA0736
Theberton *Suffk*	33	TM4365
Theddingworth *Leics*	39	SP6685
Theddlethorpe All Saints *Lincs*	51	TF4688
Theddlethorpe St. Helen *Lincs*	51	TF4788
Thelbridge Barton *Devon*	7	SS7812
Thelbridge Cross *Devon*	7	SS7812
Thelnetham *Suffk*	32	TM0178
Thelveton *Norfk*	33	TM1681
Thelwall *Ches*	47	SJ6587
Themelthorpe *Norfk*	43	TG0524
Thenford *Nhants*	29	SP5241
Theobald's Green *Wilts*	20	SU0268
Therfield *Herts*	31	TL3337
Thetford *Norfk*	32	TL8783
Theydon Bois *Essex*	23	TQ4499
Thickwood *Wilts*	20	ST8272
Thimbleby *Lincs*	51	TF2369
Thimbleby *N York*	62	SE4495
Thingwall *Mersyd*	46	SJ2784
Thirlby *N York*	62	SE4883
Thirlestane *Border*	76	NT5647
Thirlspot *Cumb*	58	NY3118
Thirn *N York*	61	SE2185
Thirsk *N York*	53	SD4037
Thistleton *Lancs*	53	SD4037
Thistleton *Leics*	40	SK9117
Thistley Green *Suffk*	32	TL6176
Thixendale *N York*	56	SE8461
Thockrington *Nthumb*	68	NY9578
Tholomas Drove *Cambs*	41	TF4006
Tholthorpe *N York*	55	SE4766
Thomas Town *Warwks*	26	SO0763
Thomastown *Gramp*	94	NJ5737
Thompson *Norfk*	42	TL9296
Thomshill *Gramp*	94	NJ2157
Thong *Kent*	14	TQ6770
Thongsleigh *Devon*	7	SS9011
Thoralby *N York*	61	SE0086
Thoresthorpe *l incs*	51	TF4578
Thoresway *Lincs*	51	IF1696
Thorganby *Lincs*	51	TF2097
Thorganby *N York*	56	SE6941
Thorgill *N York*	62	SE7096
Thorington *Suffk*	33	TM4174
Thorington Street *Suffk*	25	TM0135
Thorley *Herts*	54	SD9653
Thorley *Herts*	31	TL4719
Thorley *IOW*	10	SZ3688
Thorley Street *IOW*	10	SZ3388
Thormanby *N York*	62	SE4974
Thornage *Norfk*	42	TG0536
Thornborough *Bucks*	30	SP7433
Thornborough *N York*	61	SE3679
Thornbury *Avon*	19	ST6490
Thornbury *Devon*	6	SS3908
Thornbury *Devon*	6	SS4408
Thornbury *H & W*	27	SO6159
Thornbury *W York*	55	SE1933
Thornbury *W York*	55	SE2033
Thornby *Cumb*	67	NY2951
Thornby *Nhants*	39	SP6675
Thorncliff *Staffs*	48	SK0158
Thorncombe Street *Surrey*	12	TQ0042
Thorncott Green *Beds*	30	TL1547
Thorndon *Suffk*	33	TM1469
Thorndon Cross *Devon*	4	SX5293
Thorne *S York*	56	SE6813
Thorne *Somset*	8	ST5217
Thorne St. Margaret *Somset*	7	ST0920
Thorner *W York*	55	SE3740
Thornes *Staffs*	38	SK0703
Thorney *Cambs*	41	TF2804
Thorney *Notts*	50	SK8572
Thorney Hill *Hants*	10	SZ2099
Thornfalcon *Somset*	8	ST2723
Thornford *Dorset*	9	ST6013
Thorngumbald *Humb*	57	TA2026
Thornham *Norfk*	42	TF7343
Thornham Magna *Suffk*	33	TM1071
Thornham Parva *Suffk*	33	TM1072
Thornhaugh *Cambs*	40	TF0600
Thornhill *Cent*	81	NN6600
Thornhill *D & G*	66	NX8795
Thornhill *Derbys*	48	SK1983
Thornhill *Hants*	10	SU4612
Thornhill *W York*	55	SE2418
Thornhills *Humb*	57	TA1163
Thornholme *Humb*	57	TA1163
Thornicombe *Dorset*	9	ST8703
Thornington *Nthumb*	77	NT8833
Thornley *Dur*	61	NZ1137
Thornley *Dur*	62	NZ3639
Thornliebank *Strath*	74	NS5459
Thorns Green *Gt Man*	47	SJ7984
Thornsett *Derbys*	48	SK0187
Thornthwaite *Cumb*	58	NY2225
Thornthwaite *N York*	56	SE5618

Thornthwaite *N York*	55	SE1758
Thornton *Bucks*	30	SP7435
Thornton *Cleve*	62	NZ4713
Thornton *Fife*	83	NT2897
Thornton *Humb*	56	SE7545
Thornton *Lancs*	53	SD3342
Thornton *Leics*	39	SK4607
Thornton *Lincs*	51	TF2467
Thornton *Nthumb*	77	NT9547
Thornton *Tays*	88	NO3946
Thornton *W York*	55	SE0932
Thornton *W York*	55	SE1032
Thornton Curtis *Humb*	57	TA0817
Thornton Dale *N York*	63	SE8383
Thornton Heath *Gt Lon*	23	TO3168
Thornton Hough *Mersyd*	46	SJ3081
Thornton Rust *N York*	61	SD9689
Thornton Steward *N York*	61	SE1786
Thornton Watlass *N York*	61	SE2385
Thornton le Moor *Lincs*	50	TF0496
Thornton-in-Craven *N York*	54	SD9048
Thornton-in-Lonsdale *N York*	60	SD6879
Thornton-le-Beans *N York*	62	SE3990
Thornton-le-Clay *N York*	62	SE6875
Thornton-le-Moor *N York*	62	SE3988
Thornton-le-Moors *Ches*	46	SJ4474
Thornton-le-Street *N York*	62	SE4186
Thorntonhall *Strath*	74	NS5955
Thorntonloch *Loth*	76	NT7574
Thornydyke *Border*	76	NT6148
Thornythwaite *Cumb*	59	NY3922
Thoroton *Notts*	50	SK7642
Thorp Arch *W York*	55	SE4346
Thorpe *Derbys*	48	SK1550
Thorpe *Humb*	56	SE9946
Thorpe *N York*	54	SE0161
Thorpe *Notts*	50	SK7649
Thorpe *Surrey*	22	TO0168
Thorpe Abbotts *Norfk*	33	TM1979
Thorpe Acre *Leics*	39	SK5120
Thorpe Arnold *Leics*	40	SK7720
Thorpe Audlin *W York*	55	SE4715
Thorpe Bassett *N York*	63	SE8673
Thorpe Bay *Essex*	24	TQ9185
Thorpe Constantine *Staffs*	39	SK2608
Thorpe End *Norfk*	43	TG2811
Thorpe Green *Essex*	25	TM1623
Thorpe Green *Lancs*	54	SD5823
Thorpe Green *Suffk*	32	TL9354
Thorpe Hesley *S York*	49	SK3796
Thorpe Langton *Leics*	40	SP7492
Thorpe Lea *Surrey*	22	TQ0270
Thorpe Malsor *Nhants*	30	SP8378
Thorpe Mandeville *Nhants*	29	SP5344
Thorpe Market *Norfk*	43	TG2435
Thorpe Morieux *Suffk*	32	TL9453
Thorpe Perrow *N York*	61	SE2685
Thorpe Salvin *S York*	49	SK5281
Thorpe Satchville *Leics*	40	SK7311
Thorpe St. Andrew *Norfk*	43	TG2608
Thorpe St. Peter *Lincs*	51	TF4860
Thorpe Thewles *Cleve*	62	NZ4023
Thorpe Tilney *Lincs*	50	TF1257
Thorpe Underwood *N York*	55	SE4659
Thorpe Underwood *Nhants*	40	SP7880
Thorpe Waterville *Nhants*	40	TL0281
Thorpe Willoughby *N York*	56	SE5731
Thorpe by Water *Leics*	40	SP8996
Thorpe in Balne *S York*	56	SE5910
Thorpe in the Fallows *Lincs*	50	SK9180
Thorpe le Street *Humb*	56	SE8343
Thorpe on the Hill *Lincs*	50	SK9065
Thorpe on the Hill *W York*	55	SE3125
Thorpe-le-Soken *Essex*	25	TM1722
Thorpeness *Suffk*	33	TM4759
Thorrington *Essex*	25	TM0920
Thorverton *Devon*	7	SS9202
Thrandeston *Suffk*	33	TM1176
Thrapston *Nhants*	30	SP9978
Threapwood *Ches*	46	SJ4344
Threave *Strath*	73	NS3406
Threawood *Staffs*	48	SK1342
Three Ashes *H & W*	27	SO5123
Three Bridges *W Susx*	12	TQ2837
Three Chimneys *Kent*	14	TQ8238
Three Clocks *Powys*	27	SO1737
Three Crosses *W Glam*	17	SS5794
Three Cups Corner *E Susx*	13	TQ6320
Three Hammers *Cnwll*	4	SX2387
Three Leg Cross *E Susx*	14	TQ6831
Three Mile Cross *Berks*	22	SU7167
Three Miletown *Loth*	75	NT0675
Three Oaks *E Susx*	14	TQ8314
Threekingham *Lincs*	40	TF0836
Threepwood *Border*	76	NT5143
Threlkeld *Cumb*	58	NY3125
Threshfield *N York*	54	SD9963
Thrigby *Norfk*	43	TG4612
Thringstone *Leics*	39	SK4217
Thrintoft *N York*	62	SE3193
Thriplow *Cambs*	31	TL4346
Throcking *Herts*	31	TL3330
Throckley *T & W*	69	NZ1566
Throckmorton *H & W*	28	SO9749
Throop *Dorset*	9	SY8292
Throop *Dorset*	10	SZ1294
Throphill *Nthumb*	69	NZ1386
Thropton *Nthumb*	68	NU0202
Throughgate *D & G*	66	NX8784
Throwleigh *Devn*	5	SX6690
Throwley Forstal *Kent*	15	I G9654
Thrumpton *Notts*	39	SK5131
Thrumster *Highld*	100	ND3345
Thrunscoe *Humb*	51	TA3001
Thrup *Oxon*	21	SU2998
Thrupp *Gloucs*	20	SO8603
Thrushesbush *Essex*	23	TL4909
Thrushgill *Lancs*	54	SD6462
Thrussington *Leics*	39	SK6515
Thruxton *H & W*	27	SO4334
Thruxton *Hants*	21	SU2845
Thruxton *Hants*	21	SU2845
Thulston *Derbys*	39	SK4031
Thundergarth Mains *D & G*	67	NY1780
Thundersley *Essex*	24	TQ7988
Thurcaston *Leics*	39	SK5610
Thurcroft *S York*	49	SK4988
Thurdistoft *Highld*	100	ND2167
Thurgarton *Norfk*	43	TG1835
Thurgarton *Notts*	49	SE6949
Thurgoland *S York*	49	SE2801
Thurlaston *Leics*	39	SP5099
Thurlaston *Warwks*	39	SP4671
Thurlbear *Somset*	8	ST2621
Thurlby *Lincs*	40	TF0916
Thurlby *Lincs*	50	SK9061
Thurlby *Lincs*	51	TF4876
Thurlestone *Devon*	5	SX6742
Thurloxton *Somset*	8	ST2730
Thurlstone *S York*	55	SE2303
Thurlton *Norfk*	43	TM4198
Thurlwood *Ches*	47	SJ8057
Thurmaston *Leics*	39	SK6403
Thurnby *Leics*	39	SK6404
Thurne *Norfk*	43	TG4015
Thurnham *Kent*	14	TQ8057
Thurning *Nhants*	40	TL0883
Thurning *Norfk*	42	TG0829
Thurnscoe *S York*	55	SE4605
Thursby *Cumb*	67	NY3250
Thursden *Lancs*	54	SD9035
Thursford *Norfk*	42	TF9833
Thursley *Surrey*	11	SU9039
Thurso *Highld*	100	ND1168
Thurstaston *Mersyd*	46	SJ2484
Thurston *Suffk*	32	TL9365
Thurstonfield *Cumb*	67	NY3156
Thurstonland *W York*	55	SE1610
Thurton *Norfk*	43	TG3200
Thuvaston *Derbys*	48	SK2437
Thuxton *Norfk*	42	TG0307
Thwaite *N York*	60	SD8998
Thwaite *Suffk*	33	TM1168
Thwaite Head *Cumb*	67	NY3490
Thwaite St. Mary *Norfk*	43	TM3395

243

Tydd Gote Lincs	41	TF4518
Tydd St. Giles Cambs	41	TF4216
Tydd St. Mary Lincs	41	TF4418
Tye Green Essex	24	TL5424
Tye Green Essex	24	TL5935
Tyldesley Gt Man	47	SD6802
Tyler Hill Kent	15	TR1461
Tylorstown M Glam	18	ST0095
Tyn-y-graig Powys	26	SO0149
Tyn-y-nant M Glam	18	ST0685
Tynant M Glam	18	ST0684
Tyndrum Cent	80	NN3330
Tynemouth T & W	69	NZ3669
Tynewydd Loth	18	SS9399
Tyninghame Loth	83	NT6179
Tynron D & G	66	NX8093
Tyntesfield Avon	19	ST5071
Tynygongl Gwynd	44	SH5182
Tynygraig Dyfed	35	SN6969
Tyringham Bucks	30	SP8546
Tythecott Devon	6	SS4117
Tythegston M Glam	18	SS8578
Tytherington Avon	20	ST6788
Tytherington Ches	48	SJ9175
Tytherington Somset	20	ST7744
Tytherington Wilts	20	ST9140
Tytherleigh Devon	8	ST3203
Tywardreath Cnwll	3	SX0854
Tywyn Gwynd	44	SH5790
Tywyn Gwynd	45	SH7978

U

Uachdar W Isls	102	NF7955
Ubbeston Green Suffk	33	TM3272
Ubley Avon	19	ST5257
Uckerby N York	61	NZ2402
Uckfield E Susx	13	TQ4721
Uckinghall H & W	28	SO8637
Uckington Gloucs	28	SO9224
Uckington Shrops	37	SJ5709
Uddingston Strath	74	NS6960
Uddington Strath	74	NS8633
Udimore E Susx	17	TQ8719
Udny Green Gramp	95	NJ8726
Uffculme Devon	7	ST0620
Uffington Oxon	21	SU3089
Uffington Shrops	37	SJ5314
Ufford Cambs	40	TF0904
Ufton Warwks	29	SP3762
Ufton Nervet Berks	21	SU6367
Ugadale Strath	72	NR7828
Ugborough Devon	5	SX6755
Uggeshall Suffk	33	TM4480
Ugglebarnby N York	63	NZ8807
Ughill Derbys	48	SK2590
Ugley Essex	31	TL5228
Ugley Green Essex	31	TL5227
Ugthorpe N York	63	NZ7911
Uig Highld	90	NG1952
Uig Highld	90	NG3963
Uig Strath	78	NM1754
Uig W Isls	102	NB0534
Uigshader Highld	90	NG4346
Uisken Strath	78	NM3919
Ulbster Highld	100	ND3241
Ulcat Row Cumb	59	NY4022
Ulceby Humb	57	TA1014
Ulceby Lincs	51	TF4272
Ulceby Skitter Humb	57	TA1014
Uldale Cumb	58	NY2437
Uley Gloucs	20	ST7898
Ulgham Nthumb	69	NZ2392
Ullapool Highld	96	NH1294
Ullenhall Warwks	28	SP1267
Ulleskelf N York	55	SE5139
Ullesthorpe Leics	39	SP5087
Ulley S York	49	SK4687
Ullingswick H & W	27	SO5950
Ullinish Highld	84	NG3237
Ullock Cumb	58	NY0724
Ulpha Cumb	58	SD1993
Ulpha Cumb	59	SD3581
Ulrome Humb	57	TA1656
Ulsta Shet	103	HU4680
Ulverley Green W Mids	38	SP1381
Ulverston Cumb	58	SD2878
Umachan Highld	90	NG6150
Umberleigh Devon	6	SS6023
Under Burnmouth D & G	67	NY4783
Under River Kent	13	TQ5552
Underbarrow Cumb	59	SD4692
Undercliffe W York	55	SE1834
Underdale Shrops	37	SJ5013
Underwood Gwent	19	ST3888
Undy Gwent	19	ST4486
Union Mills IOM	52	SC3578
Unstone Derbys	49	SK3777
Unthank Cumb	68	NY6050
Up Cerne Dorset	9	ST6502
Up Exe Devon	7	SS9302
Up Holland Lancs	46	SD5105
Up Marden W Susx	11	SU7914
Up Mudford Somset	8	ST5718
Up Nately Hants	22	SU6951
Up Somborne Hants	10	SU3932
Up Sydling Dorset	9	ST6201
Upavon Wilts	20	SU1354
Upchurch Kent	14	TQ8467
Upcott Devon	6	SS5739
Upcott Devon	7	SS7529
Upcott Somset	7	SS9025
Upgate Norfk	43	TG1418
Uphall Dorset	8	ST5502
Uphall Loth	75	NT0671
Upham Devon	7	SS8808
Upham Hants	11	SU5320
Uphampton H & W	27	SO3963
Uphampton H & W	28	SO8364
Uphill Avon	19	ST3158
Uplawmoor Strath	73	NS4355
Upleadon Gloucs	28	SO7527
Upleatham Cleve	62	NZ6319
Uplees Kent	15	TR0004
Uploders Dorset	8	SY5093
Uplowman Devon	7	ST0115
Uplyme Devon	8	SY3293
Upminster Gt Lon	24	TQ5686
Upottery Devon	8	ST2007
Upparthong W York	55	SE1208
Uppat House Highld	97	NC8702
Upper Affcot Shrops	36	SO4486
Upper Ardchronie Highld	97	NH6188
Upper Arley H & W	37	SO7680
Upper Arncott Oxon	29	SP6017
Upper Basildon Berks	21	SU5976
Upper Batley W York	55	SE2325
Upper Beeding W Susx	12	TQ1910
Upper Benefield Nhants	40	SP9789
Upper Bentley H & W	28	SO9966
Upper Bighouse Highld	99	NC8857
Upper Boat M Glam	18	ST1087
Upper Boddington Nhants	29	SP4853
Upper Brailes Warwks	29	SP3040
Upper Breakish Highld	85	NG6823
Upper Broadheath H & W	28	SO8056
Upper Broughton Notts	39	SK6826
Upper Bucklebury Berks	21	SU5468
Upper Burgate Hants	10	SU1516
Upper Cairnie Tays	72	NS0319
Upper Cairn D & G	66	NS6912
Upper Caldecote Beds	31	TL1645
Upper Canada Avon	19	ST3658
Upper Catesby Nhants	29	SP5259
Upper Chapel Powys	26	SO0040
Upper Cheddon Somset	8	ST2328
Upper Chickgrove Wilts	9	ST9730
Upper Chute Wilts	21	SU2953
Upper Chute Wilts	21	SU2953
Upper Clapton Gt Lon	23	TQ3487

Upper Clatford Hants	21	SU3543
Upper Clynnog Gwynd	44	SH4746
Upper Coberley Gloucs	28	SO9815
Upper Cokeham W Susx	12	TQ1705
Upper Cound Shrops	37	SJ5505
Upper Cudworth W York	55	SE3908
Upper Cumberworth W York	55	SE2008
Upper Cumberworth W York	55	SE2108
Upper Cwmtwrch Powys	26	SN7611
Upper Dallachy Gramp	94	NJ3662
Upper Deal Kent	15	TR3651
Upper Dean Beds	30	TL0467
Upper Dicker E Susx	13	TQ5509
Upper Dovercourt Essex	25	TM2331
Upper Drumbane Cent	81	NN6606
Upper Dunsforth N York	55	SE4463
Upper Eashing Surrey	12	SU9543
Upper Egleton H & W	27	SO6345
Upper Elkstone Staffs	48	SK0559
Upper Ellastone Staffs	48	SK1143
Upper Elmers End Gt Lon	23	TQ3667
Upper End Derbys	48	SK0876
Upper Enham Hants	21	SU3649
Upper Ethrie Highld	93	NH7662
Upper Farmcote Shrops	37	SO7792
Upper Farringdon Hants	11	SU7135
Upper Framilode Gloucs	28	SO7510
Upper Froyle Hants	11	SU7542
Upper Godney Somset	19	ST4842
Upper Gravenhurst Beds	30	TL1136
Upper Green Essex	24	TL5935
Upper Hackney Derbys	48	SK2961
Upper Hale Surrey	22	SU8449
Upper Halliford Surrey	22	TQ0968
Upper Hambleton Leics	40	SK9007
Upper Harbledown Kent	15	TR1158
Upper Hatherley Gloucs	28	SO9221
Upper Hatton Staffs	38	SJ8337
Upper Hayton Shrops	37	SO5281
Upper Heaton W York	55	SE1719
Upper Helmsley N York	56	SE6956
Upper Hergest H & W	27	SO2654
Upper Heyford Nhants	30	SP6659
Upper Hill H & W	27	SO4753
Upper Hopton W York	55	SE1918
Upper Howsell H & W	28	SO7748
Upper Hulme Staffs	48	SK0160
Upper Inglesham Wilts	21	SU2096
Upper Keith Loth	76	NT4562
Upper Killay W Glam	17	SS5892
Upper Kinchrackine Strath	80	NN1627
Upper Lambourn Berks	21	SU3180
Upper Langford Avon	19	ST4659
Upper Langwith Derbys	49	SK5169
Upper Largo Fife	83	NO4203
Upper Leigh Staffs	38	SK0136
Upper Lochton Gramp	89	NO6997
Upper Longdon Staffs	38	SK0614
Upper Lybster Highld	100	ND2537
Upper Lydbrook Gloucs	27	SO6015
Upper Lye H & W	27	SO3965
Upper Milton H & W	27	SO8072
Upper Minety Wilts	20	SU0091
Upper Moor H & W	28	SO9747
Upper Mulben Gramp	94	NJ2551
Upper Nesbet Border	76	NT6727
Upper Netchwood Shrops	37	SO6192
Upper Nobut Staffs	38	SK0435
Upper Norwood W Susx	11	SU9317
Upper Ollach Highld	84	NG5137
Upper Padley Derbys	48	SK2478
Upper Pond Street Essex	31	TL4536
Upper Poppleton N York	56	SE5554
Upper Pulley Shrops	37	SJ4808
Upper Quinton Warwks	29	SP1846
Upper Ratley Hants	10	SU3223
Upper Rochford H & W	27	SO6367
Upper Ruscoe D & G	65	NX5661
Upper Sapey H & W	28	SO6863
Upper Shelton Beds	30	SP9843
Upper Sheringham Norfk	43	TG1441
Upper Shuckburgh Warwks	29	SP4961
Upper Slaughter Gloucs	29	SP1523
Upper Soudley Gloucs	27	SO6510
Upper Spond H & W	27	SO3153
Upper Standen Kent	15	TR2240
Upper Stepford D & G	66	NX8681
Upper Stoke Norfk	43	TG2502
Upper Stondon Beds	30	TL1535
Upper Stowe Nhants	29	SP6456
Upper Street Hants	10	SU1418
Upper Street Norfk	43	TG3217
Upper Street Norfk	43	TG3617
Upper Street Suffk	32	TL7851
Upper Street Suffk	33	TM1051
Upper Street Suffk	25	TM1434
Upper Sundon Beds	30	TL0427
Upper Swell Gloucs	29	SP1726
Upper Tankersley S York	49	SK3399
Upper Tasburgh Norfk	43	TM2095
Upper Tean Staffs	48	SK0139
Upper Town Avon	19	ST5265
Upper Town Derbys	48	SK2462
Upper Town H & W	27	SO5848
Upper Town Suffk	32	TL9267
Upper Tysoe Warwks	29	SP3343
Upper Ufford Suffk	33	TM2953
Upper Victoria Tays	83	NO5336
Upper Wardington Oxon	29	SP4945
Upper Weedon Nhants	29	SP6158
Upper Wellingham E Susx	13	TQ4313
Upper Weston Avon	20	ST7266
Upper Weybread Suffk	33	TM2379
Upper Whiston S York	49	SK4588
Upper Wield Hants	11	SU6238
Upper Winchendon Bucks	30	SP7414
Upper Witton W Mids	38	SP0892
Upper Woodford Wilts	10	SU1237
Upper Wootton Hants	21	SU5854
Upperby Cumb	67	NY4153
Upperglen Highld	90	NG3151
Uppermill Gt Man	54	SD9905
Upperthorpe Derbys	49	SK4580
Upperton W Susx	11	SU9522
Uppertown Highld	100	ND3576
Uppington Gloucs	20	SU0396
Uppingham Leics	40	SP8699
Uppington Shrops	37	SJ5909
Upsall N York	62	SE4586
Upsettlington Border	77	NT8846
Upshire Essex	23	TL4100
Upstreet Kent	15	TR2263
Upton Berks	22	SU9779
Upton Bucks	22	SP7711
Upton Cambs	40	TF1000
Upton Cambs	31	TL1778
Upton Cnwll	5	SX7042
Upton Devon	7	ST0902
Upton Devon	8	ST1002
Upton Dorset	9	SY7483
Upton Dorset	9	SY9893
Upton Hants	21	SU3555
Upton Hants	10	SU3717
Upton Leics	39	SP3699
Upton Lincs	50	SK8686
Upton Mersyd	46	SJ2788
Upton Norfk	43	TG3912
Upton Notts	50	SK7354
Upton Notts	50	SK7480
Upton Oxon	21	SU5186
Upton Somset	7	SS9928
Upton Somset	8	ST4526
Upton W York	55	SE4713
Upton Bishop H & W	27	SO6527
Upton Cheyney H & W	20	ST6970
Upton Cressett Shrops	37	SO6592
Upton Crews H & W	27	SO6527
Upton Cross Cnwll	4	SX2872
Upton Grey Hants	22	SU6948
Upton Heath Ches	46	SJ4169
Upton Hellions Devon	7	SS8303
Upton Lovell Wilts	20	ST9440
Upton Magna Shrops	37	SJ5512
Upton Noble Somset	20	ST7139
Upton Pyne Devon	7	SX9197

Upton Scudamore Wilts	20	ST8647
Upton Snodsbury H & W	28	SO9454
Upton St. Leonards Gloucs	28	SO8615
Upton Warren H & W	28	SO9367
Upton upon Severn H & W	28	SO8540
Upwaltham W Susx	11	SU9413
Upwell Norfk	41	TF5002
Upwey Dorset	9	SY6684
Upwick Green Herts	31	TL4524
Upwood Cambs	41	TL2582
Urchany Highld	93	NH8849
Urchfont Wilts	20	SU0356
Urlay Nook Cleve	62	NZ3816
Urmston Gt Man	47	SJ7694
Urquhart Gramp	94	NJ2862
Urra N York	62	NZ5601
Urray Highld	92	NH5052
Ushaw Moor Dur	61	NZ2242
Usk Gwent	19	SO3700
Usselby Lincs	50	TF0993
Uton Devon	7	SX8298
Utterby Lincs	51	TF3093
Uttoxeter Staffs	38	SK0933
Uxbridge Gt Lon	22	TQ0584
Uyeasound Shet	103	HP5901
Uzmaston Dyfed	16	SM9714

V

Vale Guern	101	SV0000
Valley End Surrey	22	SU9564
Valtos Highld	90	NG5163
Valtos W Isls	102	NB0936
Vange Essex	24	TQ7187
Vardre W Glam	18	SN6902
Vatsetter Shet	103	HU5389
Vatten Highld	90	NG2843
Vaynor M Glam	26	SO0410
Velindre Dyfed	16	SN1039
Velindre Dyfed	17	SN3538
Velindre Powys	27	SO1836
Venn Cnwll	3	SX2608
Venn Devon	5	SX8550
Venn Ottery Devon	5	SY0791
Venngreen Devon	6	SS3711
Ventnor IOW	11	SZ5677
Venton Devon	5	SX5856
Vernham Dean Hants	21	SU3456
Verwig Dyfed	17	SN1849
Verwood Dorset	10	SU0908
Veryan Cnwll	3	SW9139
Vicarage Devon	8	SY2088
Vickerstown Cumb	53	SD1868
Victoria Cnwll	3	SW9861
Victoria S York	55	SE1605
Vidlin Shet	103	HU4765
Viewfield Gramp	94	NJ2864
Viewpark Strath	74	NS7061
Villavin Devon	6	SS5816
Ville la Bas Jersey	101	SV0000
Villiaze Guern	101	SV0000
Vine's Cross E Susx	13	TQ5917
Virginia Water Surrey	12	TQ0007
Virginstow Devon	4	SX3792
Vobster Somset	20	ST7048
Voe Shet	103	HU4063
Vowchurch H & W	27	SO3636

W

Wackerfield Dur	61	NZ1522
Wacton Norfk	33	TM1791
Wadborough H & W	28	SO9047
Waddesdon Bucks	30	SP7416
Waddeton Devon	5	SX8756
Waddingham Lincs	50	SK9896
Waddington Lancs	54	SD7343
Waddington Lincs	50	SK9764
Waddon Dorset	9	SY6185
Wadebridge Cnwll	3	SW9972
Wadeford Somset	8	ST3110
Wadenhoe Nhants	40	TL0183
Wadesmill Herts	31	TL3517
Wadhurst E Susx	13	TQ6431
Wadshelf Derbys	48	SK3170
Wadworth S York	49	SK5697
Waen Clwyd	45	SJ0062
Waen Powys	36	SJ2320
Wainfleet All Saints Lincs	51	TF4959
Wainhouse Corner Cnwll	6	SX1895
Wainscott Kent	14	TQ7470
Wainstalls W York	55	SE0428
Waitby Cumb	60	NY7508
Waithe Lincs	51	TA2800
Wake Green W Mids	38	SP0882
Wakefield W York	55	SE3320
Wakerley Nhants	40	SP9599
Wakes Colne Essex	24	TL8928
Walberswick Suffk	33	TM4974
Walberton W Susx	12	SU9706
Walbutt D & G	65	NX7468
Walcombe Somset	19	ST5546
Walcot Lincs	40	TF0635
Walcot Lincs	50	TF1356
Walcot Shrops	37	SJ5912
Walcot Wilts	20	SU1684
Walcot Green Norfk	33	TM1280
Walcote Leics	39	SP5783
Walcott Norfk	43	TG3632
Walden Stubbs N York	56	SE5516
Walderslade Kent	14	TQ7663
Walderton W Susx	11	SU7910
Walditch Dorset	8	SY4892
Waldley Derbys	48	SK1237
Waldridge Dur	69	NZ2549
Waldron E Susx	13	TQ5419
Wales S York	49	SK4882
Wales Somset	8	ST6925
Walesby Lincs	50	TF1392
Walesby Notts	49	SK6870
Walford H & W	27	SO5820
Walford Staffs	36	SO3872
Walford Staffs	37	SJ8134
Walford Heath Shrops	36	SJ4519
Walgherton Ches	47	SJ6949
Walgrave Nhants	30	SP8071
Walhampton Hants	10	SZ3395
Walk Mill Lancs	54	SD8729
Walkden Gt Man	47	SD7303
Walker T & W	69	NZ2964
Walkerburn Border	76	NT3637
Walker's Green H & W	27	SO5247
Walkeringham Notts	50	SK7692
Walkerith Notts	50	SK7892
Walkern Herts	31	TL2826
Walkerton Fife	83	NO2301
Walkhampton Devon	4	SX5369
Walkington Humb	56	SE9937
Walkley S York	49	SK3388
Walkwood H & W	28	SP0364
Wall Border	76	NT4623
Wall Nthumb	68	NY9168
Wall Staffs	38	SK0906
Wall End Cumb	67	NY2383
Wallacetown D & G	64	NX8487
Wallacetown Strath	73	NS2703
Wallacetown Strath	73	NS3422
Wallands Park E Susx	13	TQ4010
Wallasey Mersyd	46	SJ2991
Waller's Green H & W	28	SO6738
Wallfield Fife	82	NO1909

Wallhead Cumb	67	NY4661
Wallingford Oxon	21	SU6089
Wallington Gt Lon	23	TQ2864
Wallington Hants	11	SU5806
Wallington Herts	31	TL2933
Wallington Heath W Mids	38	SJ8902
Wallisdown Dorset	10	SZ0694
Walliswood W Susx	12	TQ1238
Walls Shet	103	HU2449
Wallsend T & W	69	NZ2966
Wallyford Loth	76	NT3671
Walmer Kent	15	TR3750
Walmer Bridge Lancs	53	SD4824
Walmley Ash W Mids	38	SP1392
Walpole Somset	19	ST3041
Walpole Suffk	33	TM3674
Walpole Cross Keys Norfk	41	TF5119
Walpole Highway Norfk	41	TF5113
Walpole St. Andrew Norfk	41	TF5017
Walpole St. Peter Norfk	41	TF5016
Walrow Somset	19	ST3347
Walsall W Mids	38	SP0198
Walsden W York	54	SD9321
Walsham le Willows Suffk	32	TM0071
Walshford N York	55	SD9731
Walsoken Norfk	41	TF4710
Walston Strath	75	NT0545
Walsworth Herts	31	TL1930
Waltham Humb	57	TA2503
Waltham Kent	15	TR1048
Waltham Abbey Essex	23	TL3800
Waltham Chase Hants	11	SU5615
Waltham Cross Herts	23	TL3600
Waltham St. Lawrence Berks	22	SU8276
Walthamstow Gt Lon	23	TQ3688
Walton Bucks	30	SP8936
Walton Cumb	67	NY5264
Walton Derbys	49	SK3568
Walton Leics	39	SP5987
Walton Powys	27	SO2559
Walton Shrops	37	SJ5818
Walton Staffs	38	SJ8528
Walton Staffs	38	SJ8933
Walton Suffk	25	TM3935
Walton W Susx	11	SU8104
Walton W York	55	SE4447
Walton Cardiff Gloucs	28	SO9032
Walton East Dyfed	16	SN0223
Walton Elm Dorset	9	ST7717
Walton Lower Street Suffk	25	TM2834
Walton Park Avon	19	ST4472
Walton West Dyfed	16	SM8613
Walton on the Hill Surrey	23	TQ2255
Walton on the Naze Essex	25	TM2622
Walton on the Wolds Leics	39	SK5919
Walton-in-Gordano Avon	19	ST4273
Walton-on-Thames Surrey	22	TQ1066
Walton-on-Trent Derbys	39	SK2118
Walton-on-the-Hill Staffs	38	SJ9520
Walwen Clwyd	46	SJ1771
Walworth Dur	61	NZ2318
Walwyn's Castle Dyfed	16	SM8711
Wambrook Somset	8	ST2907
Wamphray D & G	67	NY1295
Wanborough Surrey	22	SU9348
Wanborough Wilts	21	SU2082
Wandel Strath	75	NS9427
Wangford Suffk	33	TM4679
Wanlip Leics	39	SK5910
Wanlockhead D & G	66	NS8712
Wannock E Susx	13	TQ5703
Wansford Cambs	40	TL0799
Wansford Humb	57	TA0656
Wanshurst Green Kent	14	TQ7645
Wanstead Gt Lon	23	TQ4088
Wanstrow Somset	20	ST7141
Wanswell Gloucs	20	SO6801
Wantage Oxon	21	SU3988
Wapley Avon	20	ST7179
Wappenbury Warwks	29	SP3769
Wappenham Nhants	29	SP6245
Warbleton E Susx	13	TQ6018
Warborough Oxon	21	SU5993
Warboys Cambs	41	TL3089
Warbreck Lancs	53	SD3238
Warbstow Cnwll	4	SX2090
Warcop Cumb	60	NY7415
Ward Green Suffk	32	TM0564
Warden Nthumb	68	NY9166
Wardington Oxon	29	SP4946
Wardle Ches	47	SJ6057
Wardle Gt Man	54	SD9116
Wardley Leics	40	SK8300
Wardlow Derbys	48	SK1874
Wardy Hill Cambs	41	TL4782
Ware Herts	31	TL3514
Wareham Dorset	9	SY9287
Warehorne Kent	15	TQ9832
Warenford Nthumb	77	NU1328
Wareside Herts	31	TL3915
Waresley Cambs	31	TL2454
Warfield Berks	22	SU8872
Warfleet Devon	5	SX8750
Wargrave Berks	22	SU7978
Warham All Saints Norfk	42	TF9441
Warham St. Mary Norfk	42	TF9441
Wark Nthumb	68	NY8576
Wark Nthumb	77	NT8238
Warkleigh Devon	7	SS6422
Warkton Nhants	40	SP8979
Warlaby N York	62	SE3591
Warleggan Cnwll	3	SX1569
Warlingham Surrey	23	TQ3658
Warmanbie D & G	67	NY1968
Warmfield W York	55	SE3720
Warmfield W York	55	SE3720
Warmingham Ches	47	SJ7061
Warmington Nhants	40	TL0791
Warmington Warwks	29	SP4147
Warminster Wilts	20	ST8644
Warmley Avon	20	ST6673
Warmsworth S York	49	SE5400
Warmwell Dorset	9	SY7585
Warnford Hants	11	SU6223
Warnham W Susx	12	TQ1633
Warnham Court W Susx	12	TQ0307
Warningcamp W Susx	12	TQ0307
Warninglid W Susx	12	TQ2526
Warren Ches	47	SJ8870
Warren Dyfed	16	SR9397
Warren Row Berks	22	SU8180
Warren Street Kent	14	TQ9253
Warrenby Cleve	69	NZ5755
Warrenhill Strath	75	NS9439
Warrington Bucks	30	SP8953
Warrington Ches	47	SJ6088
Warriston Loth	68	NT2575
Warsash Hants	10	SU4906
Warslow Staffs	48	SK0858
Warsop Notts	49	SK5667
Warsop Vale Notts	56	SE8750
Warter Humb	56	SE8750
Warthermaske N York	61	SE2076
Warthill N York	56	SE6755
Wartling E Susx	13	TQ6509
Wartnaby Leics	40	SK7123
Warton Lancs	53	SD4128
Warton Lancs	53	SD4972
Warton Nthumb	68	NU0003
Warton Warwks	39	SK2803
Warwick Cumb	67	NY4656
Warwick Warwks	29	SP2865
Warwick Bridge Cumb	67	NY4457
Warwicksland Cumb	67	NY4477
Wasdale Head Cumb	58	NY1808
Wash Devon	5	SX7765
Washbourne Devon	5	SX7954
Washbrook Somset	19	ST4150
Washbrook Suffk	33	TM1142
Washfield Devon	7	SS9314
Washfold N York	61	NZ0502
Washford Somset	7	ST0541
Washford Pyne Devon	7	SS8111
Washingborough Lincs	50	TF0170

Place	County	Page	Grid Ref
Washington	T & W	69	NZ2956
Washington	W Susx	12	TQ1212
Wasperton	Warwks	29	SP2659
Wass	N York	62	SE5579
Watchet	Somset	7	ST0743
Watchfield	Oxon	21	SU2490
Water	Devon	5	SX7580
Water Eaton	Oxon	29	SP5112
Water End	Beds	30	TL1151
Water End	Essex	31	TL6840
Water End	Herts	22	TL0310
Water End	Humb	56	SE7938
Water Fryston	W York	55	SE4626
Water Newton	Cambs	40	TL1097
Water Orton	Warwks	38	SP1791
Water Stratford	Bucks	29	SP6534
Waterbeach	Cambs	31	TL4965
Waterbeach	W Susx	11	SU8908
Waterbeck	D & G	67	NY2477
Watercombe	Dorset	9	SY7585
Waterend	Cumb	58	NY1222
Waterfall	Staffs	48	SK0851
Waterfoot	Strath	74	NS5655
Waterford	Herts	31	TL3114
Watergate	Cnwll	3	SX1181
Waterhead	Cumb	59	NY3804
Waterhead	Strath	73	NS5411
Waterheads	Border	75	NT2451
Waterhouses	Staffs	48	SK0850
Wateringbury	Kent	14	TQ6853
Waterloo	Dorset	9	SZ0194
Waterloo	Dyfed	16	SM9803
Waterloo	Highld	85	NG6623
Waterloo	Mersyd	46	SJ3298
Waterloo	Strath	74	NS8054
Waterloo	Tays	82	NO0537
Waterlooville	Hants	11	SU6809
Watermillock	Cumb	59	NY4422
Waterperry	Oxon	29	SP6206
Waterrow	Somset	7	ST0525
Waters Upton	Shrops	37	SJ6319
Watersfield	W Susx	12	TQ0115
Waterside	Cumb	67	NY2445
Waterside	Lancs	54	SD7123
Waterside	Strath	73	NS4308
Waterside	Strath	73	NS4843
Waterside	Strath	74	NS6773
Waterside	Surrey	13	TQ3945
Waterstock	Oxon	29	SP6305
Waterston	Dyfed	16	SM9306
Watford	Herts	22	TQ1196
Watford	Nhants	29	SP6069
Wath	N York	55	SE1467
Wath	N York	62	SE3276
Wath Upon Dearne	S York	49	SE4300
Watlington	Norfk	41	TF6211
Watlington	Oxon	22	SU6894
Watten	Highld	100	ND2454
Wattisfield	Suffk	32	TM0074
Wattisham	Suffk	32	TM0151
Watton	Dorset	8	SY4592
Watton	Humb	56	TA0150
Watton	Norfk	42	TF9100
Watton Green	Norfk	42	TF9301
Watton Green	Norfk	42	TF9301
Watton-at-Stone	Herts	31	TL3019
Wattsville	Gwent	19	ST2091
Wauldby	Humb	56	SE9629
Waulkmill	Gramp	89	NO6492
Waunarlwydd	W Glam	17	SS6095
Waunfawr	Dyfed	34	SN6081
Waunfawr	Gwynd	44	SH5259
Waunlwyd	Gwent	27	SO1807
Wavendon	Bucks	30	SP9037
Waverbridge	Cumb	67	NY2249
Waverton	Ches	46	SJ4663
Waverton	Cumb	67	NY2247
Wawne	Humb	57	TA0936
Waxham	Norfk	43	TG4426
Way Village	Devon	7	SS8810
Wayford	Somset	8	ST4006
Waytown	Devon	6	SS3622
Waytown	Devon	8	SY4698
Weacombe	Somset	18	ST1140
Weald	Oxon	21	SP3002
Wealdstone	Gt Lon	22	TQ1589
Wear Head	Dur	60	NY8539
Weardley	W York	55	SE2944
Weare Giffard	Devon	6	SS4721
Wearne	Somset	8	ST4228
Weasdale	Cumb	60	NY6904
Weasenham All Saints	Norfk	42	TF8421
Weasenham St. Peter	Norfk	42	TF8522
Weaste	Gt Man	47	SJ8098
Weaverham	Ches	47	SJ6174
Weaverthorpe	N York	56	SE9670
Webheath	H & W	28	SP0266
Wedderlairs	Gramp	95	NJ8532
Wedding Hall Fold	N York	54	SD9446
Weddington	Warwks	39	SP3693
Wedhampton	Wilts	20	SU0557
Wedmore	Somset	19	ST4347
Wednesbury	W Mids	38	SO9895
Weecar	Notts	50	SK8267
Weedon	Bucks	30	SP8118
Weedon Lois	Nhants	29	SP6046
Weeford	Staffs	38	SK1404
Week	Devon	7	SS5726
Week	Somset	7	SS9133
Week St. Mary	Cnwll	6	SX2397
Weeke	Hants	10	SU4631
Weekley	Nhants	40	SP8881
Weel	Humb	56	TA0039
Weeley	Essex	25	TM1422
Weeley Heath	Essex	25	TM1520
Weem	Tays	87	NN8449
Weethley	Norfk	28	SP0555
Weeting	Norfk	32	TL7788
Weeton	Humb	51	TA3600
Weeton	Lancs	53	SD3834
Weeton	W York	55	SE2846
Weetwood	W York	55	SE2737
Weir	Lancs	54	SD8625
Weir Quay	Devon	4	SX4365
Weirbrook	Shrops	36	SJ3524
Welborne	Norfk	42	TG0610
Welbourn	Lincs	50	SK9654
Welburn	N York	56	SE7168
Welbury	N York	62	NZ3902
Welby	Lincs	40	SK9738
Welcombe	Devon	6	SS2218
Welford	Nhants	39	SP6480
Welford-on-Avon	Warwks	28	SP1442
Welham	Leics	40	SP7692
Welham	Notts	50	SK7382
Welham Green	Herts	23	TL2305
Well	Hants	22	SU7646
Well	Lincs	51	TF4473
Well	N York	61	SE2681
Well Head	Herts	31	TL1727
Well Town	Devon	18	SS9050
Welland	H & W	28	SO7940
Wellbank	Tays	83	NO4737
Wellesbourne Mountford	Warwks	29	SP2855
Wellfield	Dur	62	NZ4137
Welling	Gt Lon	23	TQ4575
Wellingborough	Nhants	30	SP8968
Wellingham	Norfk	42	TF8722
Wellingore	Lincs	50	SK9856
Wellington	Cumb	58	NY0704
Wellington	H & W	27	SO4948
Wellington	Shrops	37	SJ6511
Wellington	Somset	7	ST1320
Wellington Heath	H & W	28	SO7140
Wellow	Avon	20	ST7358
Wellow	IOW	10	SZ3887
Wellow	Notts	49	SK6666
Wells	Somset	19	ST5445
Wells Green	Ches	47	SJ6853
Wells of Ythan	Gramp	94	NJ6338
Wells-Next-The-Sea	Norfk	42	TF9143
Wellstye Green	Essex	24	TL6318
Welltree	Tays	76	NS9622
Wellwood	Fife	82	NT0988
Welney	Norfk	41	TL5294
Welsh End	Shrops	37	SJ5035
Welsh Frankton	Shrops	36	SJ3633
Welsh Newton	H & W	27	SO4918
Welsh St. Donats	S Glam	18	ST0276
Welshampton	Shrops	36	SJ4335
Welshpool	Powys	36	SJ2207
Welton	Cumb	67	NY3544
Welton	Humb	56	SE9527
Welton	Lincs	50	TF0079
Welton	Nhants	29	SP5865
Welton le Marsh	Lincs	51	TF4768
Welton le Wold	Lincs	51	TF2787
Welwick	Humb	57	TA3421
Welwyn	Herts	31	TL2316
Welwyn Garden City	Herts	31	TL2312
Wem	Shrops	37	SJ5129
Wembdon	Somset	19	ST2837
Wembley	Gt Lon	23	TQ1885
Wembury	Devon	4	SX5148
Wemyss Bay	Strath	73	NS1969
Wendens Ambo	Essex	31	TL5136
Wendlebury	Oxon	29	SP5519
Wendling	Norfk	42	TF9312
Wendover	Bucks	22	SP8607
Wendron	Cnwll	2	SW6731
Wendy	Cambs	31	TL3247
Wenhaston	Suffk	33	TM4275
Wennington	Cambs	41	TL2379
Wennington	Lancs	54	SD6169
Wensley	Derbys	49	SK2661
Wensley	N York	61	SE0989
Wentbridge	W York	55	SE4817
Wentnor	Shrops	36	SO3892
Wentworth	Cambs	31	TL4878
Wentworth	S York	49	SK3898
Wenvoe	S Glam	18	ST1272
Weobley	H & W	27	SO4051
Weobley Marsh	H & W	27	SO4151
Wepham	W Susx	12	TQ0408
Wereham	Norfk	42	TF6801
Wergs	Staffs	38	SJ8701
Wernrheolydd	Gwent	27	SO3913
Werrington	Cambs	40	TF1603
Werrington	Cnwll	4	SX3287
Wervin	Ches	46	SJ4271
Wesham	Lancs	53	SD4133
Wessington	Derbys	49	SK3757
West Acre	Norfk	42	TF7715
West Alvington	Devon	5	SX7243
West Anstey	Devon	7	SS8527
West Appleton	N York	61	SE2294
West Ashling	W Susx	11	SU8107
West Ashton	Wilts	20	ST8755
West Auckland	Dur	61	NZ1826
West Ayton	N York	63	SE9884
West Bagborough	Somset	8	ST1633
West Bank	Ches	46	SJ5184
West Barkwith	Lincs	50	TF1580
West Barnby	N York	63	NZ8112
West Barns	Loth	83	NT6578
West Barsham	Norfk	42	TF9033
West Bay	Dorset	8	SY4690
West Beckham	Norfk	43	TG1439
West Bedfont	Surrey	22	TQ0674
West Bergholt	Essex	25	TL9527
West Bexington	Dorset	8	SY5386
West Bilney	Norfk	42	TF7115
West Blatchington	E Susx	12	TQ2706
West Boldon	T & W	69	NZ3443
West Bourton	Dorset	9	ST7629
West Bowling	W York	55	SE1630
West Brabourne	Kent	15	TR0742
West Bradenham	Norfk	42	TF9208
West Bradford	Lancs	54	SD7444
West Bradley	Somset	19	ST5536
West Bretton	W York	55	SE2813
West Bridgford	Notts	49	SK5837
West Bromwich	W Mids	38	SP0091
West Buckland	Devon	7	SS6531
West Buckland	Somset	8	ST1720
West Burnside	Gramp	89	NO7070
West Burton	N York	61	SE0186
West Burton	W Susx	12	TQ0014
West Butsfield	Dur	68	NZ0945
West Butterwick	Humb	56	SE8305
West Cairngaan	D & G	64	NX1232
West Caistor	Norfk	43	TG5111
West Calder	Loth	75	NT0163
West Camel	Somset	8	ST5724
West Chaldon	Dorset	9	SY7783
West Challow	Oxon	21	SU3688
West Charleton	Devon	5	SX7542
West Chelborough	Dorset	8	ST5405
West Chevington	Nthumb	69	NZ2297
West Chiltington	W Susx	12	TQ0918
West Chinnock	Somset	8	ST4613
West Chisenbury	Wilts	20	SU1352
West Clandon	Surrey	12	TQ0452
West Cliffe	Kent	15	TR3444
West Coker	Somset	8	ST5113
West Compton	Dorset	8	SY5694
West Compton	Somset	19	ST5942
West Cottingwith	N York	56	SE6942
West Cowick	Humb	56	SE6521
West Craigneuk	Strath	74	NS7765
West Cross	W Glam	17	SS6189
West Curthwaite	Cumb	67	NY3249
West Dean	Hants	10	SU2526
West Dean	W Susx	11	SU8512
West Dean	Wilts	10	SU2526
West Deeping	Lincs	40	TF1008
West Derby	Mersyd	46	SJ3993
West Dereham	Norfk	42	TF6500
West Down	Devon	6	SS5142
West Drayton	Gt Lon	22	TQ0679
West Drayton	Notts	49	SK7074
West Dunnet	Highld	100	ND2171
West Ella	Humb	56	TA0029
West End	Beds	30	SP8853
West End	Berks	22	SU8275
West End	Cambs	31	TL3168
West End	Cumb	67	NY3258
West End	Gwent	19	ST2195
West End	Gwent	19	ST2294
West End	Hants	10	SU4614
West End	Herts	23	TL2608
West End	Herts	23	TL3306
West End	Humb	56	SE9131
West End	Humb	57	TA1830
West End	Humb	57	TA2627
West End	N York	55	SE5140
West End	Norfk	42	TF9109
West End	Norfk	43	TG5011
West End	Oxon	21	SU5886
West End	Somset	9	ST6735
West End	Surrey	22	TQ1364
West End	Surrey	22	SU9461
West End	Wilts	9	ST9123
West End	Wilts	9	ST9824
West End Green	Hants	22	SU6661
West Farleigh	Kent	14	TQ7152
West Farndon	Nhants	29	SP5251
West Felton	Shrops	36	SJ3425
West Firle	E Susx	13	TQ4707
West Garforth	W York	55	SE3833
West Garty	Highld	97	NC9912
West Geirnish	W Isls	102	NF7741
West Grafton	Wilts	21	SU2460
West Green	Hants	22	SU7456
West Grimstead	Wilts	10	SU2026
West Grinstead	W Susx	12	TQ1720
West Haddlesey	N York	56	SE5636
West Haddon	Nhants	39	SP6371
West Hagbourne	Oxon	21	SU5187
West Hagley	H & W	38	SO9080
West Hallam	Derbys	49	SK4341
West Halton	Humb	56	SE9020
West Ham	Gt Lon	23	TQ3983
West Handley	Derbys	49	SK3977
West Hanney	Oxon	21	SU4092
West Hanningfield	Essex	24	TQ7300
West Harnham	Wilts	10	SU1229
West Harting	W Susx	11	SU7821
West Hatch	Somset	8	ST2820
West Hatch	Wilts	9	ST9228
West Heath	W Mids	38	SP0277
West Helmsdale	Highld	97	ND0115
West Hendred	Oxon	21	SU4488
West Heslerton	N York	63	SE9175
West Hewish	Avon	19	ST3964
West Hill	Devon	7	SY0694
West Hoathly	W Susx	12	TQ3632
West Holme	Dorset	9	SY8885
West Horrington	Somset	19	ST5747
West Horsley	Surrey	12	TQ0752
West Hougham	Kent	15	TR2640
West Howe	Dorset	10	SZ0595
West Howetown	Somset	7	SS9135
West Huntspill	Somset	19	ST3044
West Hythe	Kent	15	TR1234
West Isley	Berks	21	SU4782
West Itchenor	W Susx	11	SU7900
West Kennet	Wilts	20	SU1168
West Kilbride	Strath	73	NS2048
West Kingsdown	Kent	14	TQ5763
West Kington	Wilts	20	ST8077
West Kirby	Mersyd	46	SJ2186
West Knapton	N York	63	SE8776
West Knighton	Dorset	9	SY7387
West Knoyle	Wilts	9	ST8532
West Lambrook	Somset	8	ST4118
West Langdon	Kent	15	TR3247
West Langwell	Highld	97	NC6909
West Lavington	W Susx	11	SU8920
West Lavington	Wilts	20	SU0052
West Layton	N York	61	NZ1410
West Leake	Notts	39	SK5226
West Leigh	Devon	7	SS7557
West Leigh	Devon	7	SS6805
West Leigh	Somset	8	ST1231
West Lexham	Norfk	42	TF8417
West Lilling	N York	56	SE6465
West Linton	Border	75	NT1551
West Littleton	Avon	20	ST7675
West Lockinge	Oxon	21	SU4187
West Luccombe	Somset	7	SS8946
West Lulworth	Dorset	9	SY8280
West Lutton	N York	56	SE9369
West Lydford	Somset	8	ST5632
West Lyng	Somset	8	ST3228
West Lynn	Norfk	41	TF6120
West Malling	Kent	14	TQ6857
West Malvern	H & W	28	SO7646
West Marden	W Susx	11	SU7713
West Markham	Notts	49	SK7272
West Marsh	Humb	57	TA2509
West Marton	N York	54	SD8950
West Melta	S York	49	SE4001
West Meon	Hants	11	SU6424
West Meon Hut	Hants	11	SU6526
West Mersea	Essex	25	TM0112
West Milton	Dorset	8	SY5096
West Minster	Kent	14	TQ9073
West Monkton	Somset	8	ST2528
West Moors	Dorset	10	SU0802
West Morden	Dorset	9	SY9095
West Mudford	Somset	8	ST5620
West Ness	N York	62	SE6879
West Newton	Humb	57	TA2037
West Newton	Norfk	42	TF6928
West Newton	Somset	8	ST2829
West Norwood	Gt Lon	23	TQ3171
West Ogwell	Devon	5	SX8170
West Orchard	Dorset	9	ST8216
West Overton	Wilts	20	SU1267
West Parley	Dorset	10	SZ0897
West Peckham	Kent	13	TQ6452
West Pelton	Dur	69	NZ2352
West Pennard	Somset	19	ST5438
West Pentire	Cnwll	2	SW7760
West Perry	Cambs	30	TL1466
West Porlock	Somset	18	SS8797
West Preston	W Susx	12	TQ0602
West Pulham	Dorset	9	ST7008
West Putford	Devon	6	SS3616
West Quantoxhead	Somset	18	ST1142
West Raddon	Devon	7	SS8902
West Rainton	T & W	69	NZ3246
West Rasen	Lincs	50	TF0589
West Raynham	Norfk	42	TF8725
West Rounton	N York	62	NZ4103
West Row	Suffk	32	TL6775
West Rudham	Norfk	42	TF8128
West Runton	Norfk	43	TG1842
West Safford	Dorset	9	SY7289
West Saltoun	Loth	76	NT4667
West Sandford	Devon	7	SS8102
West Sandwick	Shet	103	HU4588
West Scrafton	N York	61	SE0783
West Somerton	Norfk	43	TG4720
West Stoke	W Susx	11	SU8308
West Stonesdale	N York	60	NY8802
West Stour	Dorset	9	ST7822
West Stourmouth	Kent	15	TR2562
West Stow	Suffk	32	TL8171
West Stowell	Wilts	20	SU1362
West Street	Kent	14	TQ7376
West Street	Suffk	32	TL9871
West Tanfield	N York	61	SE2678
West Taphouse	Cnwll	3	SX1463
West Tarbert	Strath	71	NR8467
West Tarring	W Susx	12	TQ1203
West Thorney	W Susx	11	SU7602
West Thorpe	Notts	39	SK6225
West Thurrock	Essex	24	TQ5877
West Tisted	Hants	11	SU6529
West Torrington	Lincs	50	TF1381
West Town	Avon	19	ST4668
West Town	Devon	6	SS3221
West Town	Hants	11	SZ7099
West Town	Somset	20	ST7041
West Tytherley	Hants	10	SU2730
West Tytherley	Hants	10	SU2730
West Tytherton	Wilts	20	ST9474
West Walton	Norfk	41	TF4713
West Walton Highway	Norfk	41	TF4913
West Weetwood	Nthumb	77	NU0029
West Wellow	Hants	10	SU2818
West Wellow	Hants	10	SU2818
West Wembury	Devon	4	SX5249
West Wemyss	Fife	83	NT3294
West Wick	Avon	19	ST3762
West Wickham	Cambs	31	TL6149
West Wickham	Gt Lon	23	TQ3766
West Williamston	Dyfed	16	SN0305
West Winch	Norfk	41	TF6316
West Winterslow	Wilts	10	SU2232
West Wittering	W Susx	11	SZ7898
West Witton	N York	61	SE0588
West Woodburn	Nthumb	68	NY8986
West Woodhay	Berks	21	SU3962
West Worldham	Hants	11	SU7437
West Worthing	W Susx	12	TQ1302
West Wratting	Essex	31	TL6052
West Yoke	Kent	14	TQ5965
West Youlstone	Cnwll	6	SS2615
Westbere	Kent	15	TR1961
Westborough	Lincs	50	SK8544
Westbourne	W Susx	11	SU7507
Westbrook	Berks	21	SU4272
Westbrook	Kent	15	TR3470
Westbury	Bucks	29	SP6235
Westbury	Shrops	36	SJ3509
Westbury	Wilts	20	ST8751
Westbury Leigh	Wilts	20	ST8649
Westbury on Severn	Gloucs	28	SO7114
Westbury-on-trym	Avon	19	ST5877
Westbury-on-Trym	Avon	19	ST5877
Westbury-sub-Mendip	Somset	19	ST5049
Westby	Lancs	53	SD3831
Westcliff-on-Sea	Essex	24	TQ8686
Westcombe	Somset	20	ST6739
Westcote	Gloucs	29	SP2120
Westcott	Bucks	30	SP7117
Westcott	Devon	12	TO1448
Westcott	Surrey	12	TQ1448
Westcott Barton	Oxon	29	SP4325
Westcourt	Wilts	20	SU2261
Westdean	E Susx	13	TV5299
Westdowns	Cnwll	3	SX0582
Wester Causewayend	Loth	75	NT0861
Wester Drumashie	Highld	92	NH6032
Wester Ellister	Strath	70	NR2053
Wester Essenside	Border	76	NT4320
Wester Ochiltree	Loth	75	NT0374
Wester Pitkierie	Fife	83	NO5505
Wester Rarichie	Highld	97	NH8374
Westerdale	Highld	100	ND1251
Westerdale	N York	62	NZ6605
Westerfield	Suffk	33	TM1747
Westergate	W Susx	11	SU9305
Westerham	Kent	23	TQ4454
Westerhope	T & W	69	NZ1966
Westerland	Devon	5	SX8662
Westerleigh	Avon	20	ST6979
Westerloch	Highld	100	ND3258
Westerton	Tays	89	NO6754
Westfield	Loth	75	NS9472
Westfield	Norfk	42	TF9009
Westfields of Rattray	Tays	88	NO1846
Westford	Somset	7	ST1120
Westgate	Dur	60	NY9038
Westgate	Humb	56	SE7707
Westgate	Norfk	42	TF9740
Westgate on Sea	Kent	15	TR3270
Westhall	Gramp	95	NJ6330
Westhall	Suffk	33	TM4280
Westham	Dorset	9	SY6579
Westham	E Susx	13	TQ6404
Westham	Somset	19	ST4046
Westhampnett	W Susx	11	SU8806
Westhay	Somset	19	ST4342
Westhide	H & W	27	SO5843
Westhill	Gramp	95	NJ8307
Westholme	Somset	19	ST5642
Westhope	H & W	27	SO4651
Westhope	Shrops	37	SO4786
Westhorpe	Lincs	41	TF2331
Westhorpe	Suffk	32	TM0568
Westhoughton	Gt Man	47	SD6506
Westhouse	N York	60	SD6673
Westhouses	Derbys	49	SK4257
Westhumble	Surrey	12	TQ1651
Westlake	Devon	5	SX6253
Westleigh	Devon	6	SS4728
Westleigh	Devon	7	ST0517
Westleton	Suffk	33	TM4469
Westley	Suffk	32	TL8264
Westley Heights	Essex	24	TQ6887
Westley Waterless	Cambs	31	TL6156
Westlington	Bucks	22	SP7610
Westlinton	Cumb	67	NY3964
Westmarsh	Kent	15	TR2761
Westmeston	E Susx	12	TQ3313
Westmill	Herts	31	TL3627
Westmoor	T & W	69	NZ2670
Westmuir	Tays	88	NO3953
Westnewton	Cumb	67	NY1344
Westoe	T & W	69	NZ3765
Weston	Avon	20	ST7366
Weston	Berks	21	SU3973
Weston	Ches	47	SJ7252
Weston	Devon	8	ST1500
Weston	Devon	8	SY1688
Weston	Hants	9	SU6871
Weston	Herts	31	TL2530
Weston	Lincs	41	TF2925
Weston	Nhants	29	SP5846
Weston	Notts	50	SK7767
Weston	Shrops	36	SO3373
Weston	Shrops	37	SJ5629
Weston	Shrops	37	SJ2927
Weston	Staffs	38	SJ9727
Weston	W York	55	SE1747
Weston Beggard	H & W	27	SO5841
Weston Colley	Hants	10	SU5039
Weston Colville	Cambs	31	TL6153
Weston Corbett	Hants	22	SU6846
Weston Coyney	Staffs	48	SJ9343
Weston Favell	Nhants	30	SP7962
Weston Favell	Nhants	30	SP7962
Weston Green	Cambs	32	TL6252
Weston Heath	Shrops	37	SJ7624
Weston Jones	Staffs	37	SJ7624
Weston Longville	Norfk	43	TG1115
Weston Lullingfields	Shrops	36	SJ4224
Weston Patrick	Hants	22	SU6946
Weston Rhyn	Shrops	36	SJ2835
Weston Subedge	Gloucs	28	SP1240
Weston Turville	Bucks	22	SP8510
Weston Underwood	Bucks	30	SP8650
Weston Underwood	Derbys	49	SK2942
Weston by Welland	Nhants	40	SP7791
Weston under Penyard	H & W	27	SO6322
Weston under Wetherley	Warwks	29	SP3669
Weston-Super-Mare	Avon	19	ST3261
Weston-in-Gordano	Avon	19	ST4474
Weston-on-Trent	Derbys	39	SK4028
Weston-on-the-Green	Oxon	29	SP5318
Weston-on-the-Lizard	Staffs	37	SJ8010
Westonbirt	Gloucs	20	ST8589
Westoning	Beds	30	TL0332
Westonzoyland	Somset	8	ST3534
Westow	N York	56	SE7565
Westport	Somset	8	ST3820
Westport	Strath	72	NR6526
Westquarter	Cent	82	NS9178
Westra	S Glam	18	ST1471
Westridge Green	Berks	21	SU5679
Westrigg	Loth	74	NS9067
Westrop	Wilts	21	SU1092
Westruther	Border	76	NT6349
Westry	Cambs	41	TL3998
Westward	Cumb	67	NY2744
Westward Ho	Devon	6	SS4329
Westwell	Kent	15	TQ9847
Westwell	Oxon	29	SP2210
Westwell Leacon	Kent	14	TQ9547
Westwick	Cambs	31	TL4265
Westwood	Devon	7	SY0199
Westwood	Kent	15	TR3667
Westwood	Wilts	20	ST8059
Westwoodside	Humb	50	SE7400
Wetham Green	Kent	14	TQ8467
Wetheral	Cumb	67	NY4654
Wetherby	W York	55	SE4048
Wetherden	Suffk	32	TM0062
Wetheringsett	Suffk	33	TM1266
Wethersfield	Essex	24	TL7131
Wetherup Street	Suffk	33	TM1464
Wetley Rocks	Staffs	48	SJ9649
Wettenhall	Ches	47	SJ6261
Wetton	Staffs	48	SK1055
Wetwang	Humb	56	SE9358
Wetwood	Staffs	37	SJ7733
Wexcombe	Wilts	21	SU2658
Weybourne	Norfk	43	TG1143
Weybread	Suffk	33	TM2480
Weybread Street	Suffk	33	TM2479
Weybridge	Surrey	22	TQ0764
Weycroft	Devon	8	SY3099
Weydale	Highld	100	ND1564
Weyhill	Hants	21	SU3146
Weymouth	Dorset	9	SY6778
Whaddon	Bucks	30	SP8034
Whaddon	Cambs	31	TL3546
Whaddon	Gloucs	28	SO8313
Whaddon	Wilts	10	SU1926
Whaley	Derbys	49	SK5171
Whaley Bridge	Derbys	48	SK0180
Whaley Thorns	Notts	55	SK5271
Whaligoe	Highld	100	ND3140
Whalley	Lancs	54	SD7336
Wham	N York	54	SD7762
Whaplode	Lincs	41	TF3224
Whaplode Drove	Lincs	41	TF3113
Wharf	Warwks	29	SP4352
Wharfe	N York	54	SD7869
Wharles	Lancs	53	SD4435
Wharley End	Beds	30	SP9342
Wharncliffe Side	S York	49	SK2995
Wharram le Street	N York	56	SE8665
Wharton	H & W	27	SO5055
Whasset	Cumb	59	SD5181
Whaston	N York	61	NZ1506
Whatcote	Warwks	29	SP2944
Whateley	Warwks	39	SP2299
Whatfield	Suffk	32	TM0246
Whatley	Somset	8	ST3607
Whatley	Somset	20	ST7347

Place		
Whatlington E Susx	14	TQ7618
Whatsole Street Kent	15	TR1144
Whatton Notts	40	SK7439
Whauphill D & G	64	NX4049
Wheal Rose Cnwll	2	SW7244
Wheatacre Norfk	43	TM4694
Wheathampstead Herts	31	TL1714
Wheathill Shrops	37	SO6282
Wheatley Hants	11	SU7840
Wheatley Oxon	29	SP5905
Wheatley Hill Dur	62	NZ3738
Wheatley Hills S York	56	SE6905
Wheaton Aston Staffs	38	SJ8512
Wheddon Cross Somset	7	SS9238
Wheelock Ches	47	SJ7559
Wheelock Heath Ches	47	SJ7457
Wheelton Lancs	54	SD6021
Wheldale W York	55	SE4426
Wheldrake N York	56	SE6844
Whelpley Hill Bucks	22	TL0004
Whelpo Cumb	67	NY3149
Whemstead Herts	31	TL3121
Whenby N York	56	SE6369
Whepstead Suffk	32	TL8358
Wherstead Suffk	33	TM1540
Werwell Hants	21	SU3941
Wheston Derbys	48	SK1376
Whetsted Kent	13	TQ6546
Whetstone Leics	39	SP5597
Whicham Cumb	58	SD1382
Whichford Warwks	29	SP3134
Wickham T & W	69	NZ2061
Whiddon Down Devon	5	SX6992
Whight's Corner Suffk	33	TM1242
Whigstreet Tays	89	NO4844
Whilton Nhants	29	SP6364
Whim Border	75	NT2153
Whimble Devon	6	SS3403
Whimple Devon	5	SY0497
Whimpwell Green Norfk	43	TG3829
Whinburgh Norfk	42	TG0009
Whinnie Liggate D & G	65	NX7152
Whipcott Devon	7	ST0718
Whippingham IOW	11	SZ5193
Whipsnade Beds	22	TL0108
Whipton Devon	5	SX9493
Whisby Lincs	50	SK9067
Whissendine Leics	40	SK8214
Whistley Green Berks	22	SU7974
Whiston Mersyd	46	SJ4791
Whiston Nhants	30	SP8460
Whiston S York	49	SK4490
Whiston Staffs	38	SJ8914
Whiston Staffs	48	SK0347
Whitbeck Cumb	58	SD1184
Whitbourne H & W	28	SO7156
Whitburn Loth	75	NS9464
Whitburn T & W	69	NZ4062
Whitby N York	63	NZ8910
Whitchurch Avon	19	ST6167
Whitchurch Bucks	30	SP8020
Whitchurch Devon	4	SX4972
Whitchurch Dyfed	16	SM8025
Whitchurch H & W	27	SO5417
Whitchurch Hants	21	SU4648
Whitchurch Oxon	21	SU6377
Whitchurch S Glam	19	ST1579
Whitchurch Shrops	37	SJ5441
Whitchurch Canonicorum Dorset	8	SY3395
Whitchurch Hill Oxon	21	SU6378
Whitcombe Dorset	9	SY7188
Whitcot Shrops	36	SO3791
Whitcott Keysett Shrops	36	SO2782
White Chapel Lancs	53	SD5541
White Colne Essex	24	TL8830
White Coppice Lancs	54	SD6119
White Cross Cnwll	2	SW6821
White End H & W	28	SO7834
White Kirkley Dur	68	NZ0255
White Lackington Dorset	9	SY7198
White Ladies Aston H & W	28	SO9252
White Notley Essex	24	TL7818
White Pit Lincs	51	TF3777
White Roding Essex	24	TL5613
White Stake Lancs	53	SD5125
White Stone H & W	27	SO5642
White Stone Cross Devon	5	SX8993
White Waltham Berks	22	SU8577
White-le-Head Dur	69	NZ1754
Whiteacre Heath Warwks	39	SP2292
Whiteash Green Essex	24	TL7931
Whitebridge Highld	92	NH4815
Whitebrook Gwent	27	SO5306
Whitecairns Gramp	95	NJ9218
Whitechapel Gt Lon	23	TQ3381
Whitecraig Loth	75	NT3470
Whitecroft Gloucs	27	SO6106
Whiteface Highld	97	NH7088
Whitefarland Strath	72	NR8642
Whitefield Gt Man	47	SD8006
Whiteford Gramp	95	NJ7126
Whitegate Ches	47	SJ6269
Whitehall Ork	103	HY6528
Whitehaven Cumb	58	NX9718
Whitehill Hants	11	SU7934
Whitehill Kent	15	TR0950
Whitehills Gramp	94	NJ6565
Whitehouse Gramp	94	NJ6114
Whitehouse Strath	71	NR8161
Whitekirk Loth	83	NT5981
Whitelackington Somset	8	ST3815
Whiteley Bank IOW	11	SZ5581
Whiteley Village Surrey	22	TQ0962
Whitemire Gramp	93	NH9854
Whitemoor Cnwll	3	SW9757
Whitemoor Derbys	49	SK3648
Whitemoor Notts	49	SK5442
Whitenap Hants	10	SU3721
Whiteparish Wilts	10	SU2423
Whiterashes Gramp	95	NJ8523
Whiterow Gramp	93	NJ0257
Whiterow Highld	100	ND3648
Whiteshill Gloucs	28	SO8407
Whitesmith E Susx	13	TQ5214
Whitestaunton Somset	8	ST2810
Whitestreet Green Suffk	32	TL9739
Whiteway Avon	20	ST7263
Whitewell Lancs	54	SD6646
Whitewell-on-the-Hill N York	56	SE7265
Whitfield Avon	20	ST6791
Whitfield Kent	15	TR3045
Whitfield Nhants	29	SP6039
Whitfield Nthumb	68	NY7758
Whitford Clwyd	46	SJ1478
Whitford Devon	8	SY2595
Whitgift Humb	56	SE8022
Whitgift Humb	56	SE8122
Whitgreave Staffs	38	SJ8928
Whithorn D & G	64	NX4440
Whiting Bay Strath	72	NS0425
Whitington Norfk	42	TL7199
Whitland Dyfed	17	SN1916
Whitlaw Border	67	NT5012
Whitletts Strath	73	NS3623
Whitley Berks	22	SU7270
Whitley Ches	47	SJ6178
Whitley N York	56	SE5620
Whitley S York	49	SK3494
Whitley Wilts	20	ST8866
Whitley Bay T & W	69	NZ3572
Whitley Chapel Nthumb	68	NY9357
Whitley Lower W York	55	SE2217
Whitlburn Strath	73	NS2163
Whitminster Gloucs	28	SO7708
Whitmore Staffs	37	SJ8041
Whitnage Devon	7	ST0215
Whitnash Warwks	29	SP3263
Whitney H & W	27	SO2647
Whitney H & W	27	SO2747
Whitriggees Cumb	67	NY2457
Whitsbury Hants	10	SU1218
Whitsome Border	77	NT8650
Whitson Gwent	19	ST3883
Whitstable Kent	15	TR1066
Whitstone Cnwll	6	SX2698
Whittingham Nthumb	68	NU0612
Whittingslow Shrops	36	SO4388
Whittington Derbys	49	SK3773
Whittington Derbys	49	SK3875
Whittington Gloucs	28	SP0120
Whittington H & W	28	SO8752
Whittington Lancs	54	SD5976
Whittington Shrops	36	SJ3231
Whittington Staffs	38	SO8682
Whittington Staffs	38	SK1508
Whittington Warwks	39	SP2999
Whittle-le-Woods Lancs	54	SD5821
Whittlebury Nhants	30	SP6943
Whittlesey Cambs	41	TL2697
Whittlesford Cambs	31	TL4748
Whitton Cleve	62	NZ3821
Whitton Humb	56	SE9024
Whitton Powys	27	SO2767
Whitton Shrops	37	SO5772
Whittonstall Nthumb	68	NZ0757
Whitway Hants	21	SU4559
Whitwell Derbys	49	SK5276
Whitwell Herts	31	TL1820
Whitwell IOW	11	SZ5277
Whitwell Leics	40	SK9208
Whitwell N York	61	SE2899
Whitwell Street Norfk	43	TG1022
Whitwick Leics	39	SK4316
Whitwood W York	55	SE4124
Whitworth Lancs	54	SD8818
Whixall Shrops	37	SJ5134
Whixley N York	55	SE4458
Whorlton Dur	61	NZ1014
Whorlton N York	62	NZ4802
Whyle H & W	27	SO5561
Whyteleafe Surrey	23	TQ3358
Wibdon Gloucs	19	ST5797
Wibtoft Warwks	39	SP4887
Wichenford H & W	28	SO7860
Wichling Kent	14	TQ9256
Wick Avon	20	ST7072
Wick Devon	8	ST1604
Wick Dorset	10	SZ1591
Wick H & W	28	SO9645
Wick Highld	100	ND3650
Wick M Glam	18	SS9272
Wick Somset	8	ST4027
Wick W Susx	12	TQ0203
Wick Rissington Gloucs	29	SP1821
Wick St. Lawrence Avon	19	ST3665
Wicken Cambs	31	TL5770
Wicken Nhants	30	SP7439
Wicken Bonhunt Essex	31	TL4933
Wickenby Lincs	50	TF0882
Wicker Street Green Suffk	32	TL9742
Wickersley S York	49	SK4791
Wickford Essex	24	TQ7593
Wickham Berks	21	SU3971
Wickham Hants	11	SU5711
Wickham Bishops Essex	24	TL8412
Wickham Green Berks	21	SU4072
Wickham Green Suffk	33	TM0969
Wickham Market Suffk	33	TM3055
Wickham Skeith Suffk	33	TM0969
Wickham St. Paul Essex	24	TL8336
Wickham Street Suffk	32	TM0869
Wickhambreaux Kent	15	TR2158
Wickhambrook Suffk	32	TL7554
Wickhamford H & W	28	SP0641
Wickhampton Norfk	43	TG4205
Wicklewood Norfk	42	TG0702
Wickmere Norfk	43	TG1733
Wickwar Avon	20	ST7288
Widdington Essex	31	TL5331
Widdop Lancs	54	SD9333
Widdrington T & W	69	NZ2595
Wide Open T & W	69	NZ2372
Widecombe in the Moor Devon	5	SX7176
Widemouth Bay Cnwll	6	SS2002
Widford Essex	24	TL8905
Widford Herts	31	TL4116
Widmer End Bucks	22	SU8796
Widmerpool Notts	39	SK6327
Widmore Gt Lon	23	TQ4268
Widnes Ches	46	SJ5184
Widworthy Devon	8	SX2199
Wigan Gt Man	47	SD5805
Wigborough Somset	8	ST4415
Wiggaton Devon	8	SY1093
Wiggenhall St. Germans Norfk	41	TF5914
Wiggenhall St. Mary Magdalan Norfk	41	TF5914
Wiggenhall St. Mary the Virgin Norfk	41	TF5814
Wiggens Green Essex	32	TL6642
Wigginton Herts	22	SP9310
Wigginton N York	56	SE5958
Wigginton Oxon	29	SP3833
Wigginton Staffs	39	SK2106
Wigglesworth N York	54	SD8157
Wiggold Gloucs	28	SP0404
Wiggonby Cumb	67	NY2953
Wigham Devon	7	SS7508
Wighill N York	55	SE4746
Wighton Norfk	42	TF9439
Wigley Hants	10	SU3217
Wigmore H & W	27	SO4169
Wigsley Notts	50	SK8570
Wigsthorpe Nhants	40	TL0482
Wigston Leics	39	SP6199
Wigston Parva Leics	39	SP4689
Wigthorpe Notts	49	SK5983
Wigtoft Lincs	41	TF2636
Wigton Cumb	67	NY2548
Wigtown D & G	64	NX4355
Wike W York	55	SE3342
Wilbarston Nhants	40	SP8188
Wilberfoss Humb	56	SE7350
Wilburton Cambs	41	TL4785
Wilby Norfk	30	SP8666
Wilby Norfk	33	TM0389
Wilby Suffk	33	TM2472
Wilcot Wilts	20	SU1360
Wilday Green Derbys	48	SK2274
Wildboarclough Ches	48	SJ9868
Wilden Beds	30	TL0955
Wilden H & W	38	SO8272
Wildmanbridge Strath	74	NS8253
Wildmoor H & W	38	SO9575
Wildsworth Lincs	50	SK8097
Wilkesley Ches	37	SJ6241
Wilkhaven Highld	97	NH9486
Wilkieston Fife	75	NT1268
Willand Devon	7	ST0310
Willaston Ches	46	SJ3377
Willaston Ches	47	SJ6752
Willcott Shrops	36	SJ3718
Willen Bucks	30	SP8741
Willenhall W Mids	38	SO9698
Willenhall W Mids	39	SJ3676
Willerby Humb	56	TA0230
Willerby N York	63	TA0079
Willersey Gloucs	28	SP1039
Willersley H & W	27	SO3147
Willesborough Kent	15	TR0441
Willesborough Lees Kent	15	TR0342
Willesden Gt Lon	23	TQ2284
Willesley Wilts	20	ST8588
Willett Somset	8	ST1033
Willey Shrops	37	SO6799
Willey Warwks	39	SP4844
Willey Green Surrey	22	SU9351
Williamscot Oxon	29	SP4745
Willian Herts	31	TL2230
Willingale Essex	24	TL5902
Willingdon E Susx	13	TQ5902
Willingham Cambs	31	TL4070
Willingham Lincs	50	SK8784
Willingham Green Cambs	32	TL6254
Willington Beds	30	TL1150
Willington Derbys	39	SK2928
Willington Dur	61	NZ1935
Willington Kent	14	TQ7853
Willington Warwks	29	SP2638
Willington Corner Ches	46	SJ5366
Willington Quay T & W	69	NZ3167
Willitoft Humb	56	SE7434
Williton Somset	7	ST0740
Willoughby Lincs	51	TF4771
Willoughby Warwks	29	SP5167
Willoughby Waterleys Leics	39	SP5792
Willoughby-on-the-Wolds Notts	39	SK6325
Willoughton Lincs	50	SK9293
Willows Green Essex	24	TL7219
Willtown Somset	8	ST3924
Wilmcote Warwks	28	SP1658
Wilmington Devon	8	SY2199
Wilmington E Susx	13	TQ5404
Wilmington Kent	23	TQ5371
Wilmslow Ches	47	SJ8481
Wilnecote Staffs	39	SK2201
Wilsden W York	55	SE0936
Wilsford Lincs	50	TF0042
Wilsford Wilts	10	SU1057
Wilsford Wilts	10	SU1339
Wilshaw W York	55	SE1109
Wilsill N York	55	SE1864
Wilsley Green Kent	14	TQ7737
Wilson Leics	39	SK4024
Wilsontown Strath	75	NS9455
Wilstead Beds	30	TL0643
Wilsthorpe Lincs	40	TF0913
Wilstone Herts	30	SP9014
Wilton Cleve	62	NZ5819
Wilton Cleve	62	NZ5819
Wilton Cumb	58	NY0411
Wilton H & W	27	SO5824
Wilton N York	63	SE8582
Wilton Wilts	10	SU0931
Wilton Wilts	21	SU2661
Wilton Dean Border	67	NT4914
Wimbish Essex	24	TL5936
Wimbish Green Essex	24	TL6035
Wimbledon Gt Lon	23	TQ2370
Wimblington Cambs	41	TL4192
Wimborne Minster Dorset	9	SZ0199
Wimborne St. Giles Dorset	9	SU0212
Wimbotsham Norfk	41	TF6205
Wimpstone Warwks	29	SP2148
Wincanton Somset	9	ST7128
Winchburgh Loth	75	NT0974
Winchcombe Gloucs	28	SP0228
Winchelsea E Susx	14	TQ9017
Winchelsea Beach E Susx	14	TQ9115
Winchester Hants	10	SU4829
Winchet Hill Kent	14	TQ7340
Winchfield Hants	22	SU7654
Winchmore Hill Bucks	22	SU9395
Winchmore Hill Gt Lon	23	TQ3194
Wincle Ches	48	SJ9666
Wincobank S York	49	SK3891
Windermere Cumb	59	SD4198
Winderton Warwks	29	SP3240
Windhill Highld	92	NH5348
Windlesham Surrey	22	SU9364
Windmill Cnwll	2	SW8975
Windmill Hill E Susx	13	TQ6412
Windmill Hill Somset	8	ST3116
Windrush Gloucs	29	SP1913
Windsole Gramp	94	NJ5560
Windsor Berks	22	SU9576
Windsoredge Gloucs	20	ST8499
Windy Arbour Warwks	39	SP2971
Windygates Fife	83	NO3500
Wineham W Susx	12	TQ2320
Winestead Humb	57	TA2924
Winewall Lancs	54	SD9139
Winfarthing Norfk	33	TM1085
Winford Avon	19	ST5465
Winford IOW	11	SZ5684
Winforton H & W	27	SO2946
Winfrith Newburgh Dorset	9	SY8084
Wing Bucks	30	SP8822
Wing Leics	40	SK8903
Wingate Dur	62	NZ4037
Wingerworth Derbys	49	SK3867
Wingfield Beds	30	SP9926
Wingfield Suffk	33	TL8256
Wingfield Wilts	20	ST8256
Wingham Kent	15	TR2457
Wingmore Kent	15	TR1846
Wingrave Bucks	30	SP8719
Winkburn Notts	49	SK7158
Winkfield Berks	22	SU9072
Winkfield Row Berks	22	SU8971
Winkhill Staffs	48	SK0651
Winkleigh Devon	7	SS6308
Winksley N York	55	SE2571
Winlaton T & W	69	NZ1762
Winless Highld	100	ND3054
Winllan Powys	36	SJ2222
Winmarleigh Lancs	53	SD4747
Winnall Hants	10	SU4929
Winnall Common H & W	27	SO4534
Winnersh Berks	22	SU7870
Winnington Ches	47	SJ6474
Winscombe Avon	19	ST4157
Winsford Ches	47	SJ6566
Winsford Somset	7	SS9034
Winsh-wen W Glam	18	SS6896
Winsham Devon	6	SS5038
Winsham Somset	8	ST3706
Winshill Staffs	39	SK2623
Winskill Cumb	67	NY5745
Winslade Hants	21	SU6548
Winsley N York	55	SE2461
Winsley Wilts	20	ST7960
Winslow Bucks	30	SP7627
Winson Gloucs	28	SP0908
Winster Cumb	59	SD4193
Winster Derbys	48	SK2460
Winston Dur	61	NZ1416
Winston Suffk	33	TM1861
Winstone Gloucs	28	SO9609
Winswell Devon	6	SS4913
Winterborne Came Dorset	9	SY7088
Winterborne Clenston Dorset	9	ST8302
Winterborne Herringston Dorset	9	SY6988
Winterborne Houghton Dorset	9	ST8104
Winterborne Kingston Dorset	9	SY8697
Winterborne Monkton Dorset	9	SY6787
Winterborne Stickland Dorset	9	ST8304
Winterborne Whitechurch Dorset	9	ST8300
Winterborne Zelston Dorset	9	SY8997
Winterbourne Avon	19	ST6580
Winterbourne Berks	21	SU4572
Winterbourne Abbas Dorset	9	SY5990
Winterbourne Bassett Wilts	20	SU0974
Winterbourne Dauntsey Wilts	10	SU1734
Winterbourne Earls Wilts	10	SU1633
Winterbourne Gunner Wilts	10	SU1735
Winterbourne Monkton Wilts	20	SU0971
Winterbourne Steepleton Dorset	9	SY6289
Winterbourne Stoke Wilts	20	SU0740
Winteringham Humb	56	SE9222
Winterley Ches	47	SJ7457
Wintersett W York	55	SE3716
Winterton Humb	56	SE9218
Winterton-on-Sea Norfk	43	TG4919
Winthorpe Notts	50	SK8156
Winton Cumb	60	NY7810
Winton Dorset	10	SZ0894
Winton E Susx	13	TQ5103
Wintringham N York	63	SE8873
Winwick Cambs	40	TL1080
Winwick Ches	47	SJ6092
Winwick Nhants	39	SP6273
Wirksworth Derbys	48	SK2854
Wirswall Ches	47	SJ5444
Wisbech Cambs	41	TF4609
Wisbech St. Mary Cambs	41	TF4208
Wisborough Green W Susx	12	TQ0525
Wiseton Notts	49	SK7189
Wishanger Gloucs	28	SO9009
Wishaw Strath	74	NS7955
Wishaw Warwks	38	SP1794
Wisley Surrey	22	TQ0659
Wispington Lincs	51	TF2071
Wissett Suffk	33	TM3679
Wissington Suffk	24	TL9533
Wistanstow Shrops	36	SO4385
Wistanswick Shrops	37	SJ6629
Wisterfield Ches	47	SJ8271
Wiston Dyfed	16	SN0218
Wiston Strath	75	NS9532
Wiston W Susx	12	TQ1512
Wistow Cambs	41	TL2781
Wistow N York	56	SE5835
Wiswell Lancs	54	SD7437
Witcham Cambs	41	TL4680
Witchampton Dorset	9	ST9806
Witchford Cambs	31	TL5078
Witcombe Somset	8	ST4721
Withacott Devon	6	SS4315
Witham Essex	24	TL8214
Witham Friary Somset	20	ST7440
Witham on the Hill Lincs	40	TF0516
Withcall Lincs	51	TF2883
Withdean E Susx	12	TQ3007
Witherenden Hill E Susx	13	TQ6426
Witheridge Devon	7	SS8014
Witherley Leics	39	SP3297
Withern Lincs	51	TF4282
Withernsea Humb	57	TA3427
Withernwick Humb	57	TA1940
Withersdale Street Suffk	33	TM2681
Withersfield Essex	32	TL6448
Witherslack Cumb	59	SD4384
Witherslack Hall Cumb	59	SD4386
Withiel Cnwll	3	SW9965
Withiel Florey Somset	7	SS9832
Withies H & W	27	SO5642
Withington Ches	47	SJ8169
Withington Gloucs	28	SP0315
Withington Gt Man	47	SJ8593
Withington H & W	27	SO5543
Withington H & W	27	SO5643
Withington Shrops	37	SJ5713
Withington Staffs	38	SK0335
Withleigh Devon	7	SS9012
Withybed Green H & W	38	SP0172
Withybrook Warwks	39	SP4384
Withycombe Somset	7	ST0141
Withyham E Susx	13	TQ4935
Withypool Devon	7	SS8435
Witley Surrey	12	SU9439
Witnesham Suffk	33	TM1751
Witney Oxon	29	SP3509
Wittering Cambs	40	TF0502
Wittersham Kent	14	TQ8927
Witton H & W	28	SO8962
Witton Norfk	43	TG3009
Witton Norfk	43	TG3331
Witton Gilbert Dur	69	NZ2345
Witton Park Dur	61	NZ1730
Witton le Wear Dur	61	NZ1431
Wivelrod Hants	11	SU6738
Wivelsfield E Susx	12	TQ3420
Wivelsfield Green E Susx	12	TQ3520
Wivelsfield Station W Susx	12	TQ3220
Wivenhoe Essex	25	TM0322
Wix Essex	25	TM1628
Wixford Warwks	28	SP0854
Wixhill Shrops	37	SJ5628
Wixoe Essex	32	TL7143
Woburn Beds	30	SP9433
Woburn Sands Bucks	30	SP9235
Woking Surrey	22	TQ0058
Wokingham Berks	22	SU8168
Wold Newton Humb	51	TF2496
Wold Newton Humb	63	TA0473
Woldingham Surrey	23	TQ3755
Wolf Hills Nthumb	68	NY7259
Wolf's Castle Dyfed	16	SM9526
Wolfclyde Strath	75	NT0236
Wolferton Norfk	42	TF6528
Wolfhill Tays	82	NO1533
Wolfsdale Dyfed	16	SM9321
Woll Gramp	94	NJ4622
Wollaston Nhants	30	SP9062
Wollaston Shrops	36	SJ3212
Wollaston Notts	49	SK5239
Wollerton Shrops	37	SJ6230
Wollescote W Mids	38	SO9283
Wolseley Staffs	38	SK0220
Wolston Warwks	39	SP4175
Wolvercote Oxon	29	SP5009
Wolverhampton W Mids	38	SO9198
Wolverley H & W	38	SO8279
Wolverton Bucks	30	SP8141
Wolverton Hants	21	SU5558
Wolverton Wilts	9	ST7831
Wolverton Common Hants	21	SU5659
Wolvesnewton Gwent	19	ST4599
Wolvey Warwks	39	SP4387
Wolvey Heath Warwks	39	SP4388
Wolviston Cleve	62	NZ4525
Wombleton N York	62	SE6683
Wombourne Staffs	38	SO8793
Wombwell S York	49	SE3902
Womenswold Kent	15	TR2250
Womersley N York	56	SE5319
Wonersh Surrey	12	TQ0145
Wonford Devon	5	SX8391
Wonston Hants	10	SU4739
Wooburn Green Bucks	22	SU9188
Wood Bevington Warwks	28	SP0554
Wood Dalling Norfk	42	TG0927
Wood Eaton Staffs	38	SJ8417
Wood End Beds	30	TL0046
Wood End Gt Lon	23	TQ1385
Wood End Herts	31	TL3225
Wood End W Mids	39	SJ9401
Wood End Warwks	38	SP1171
Wood Enderby Lincs	51	TF2764
Wood Green Gt Lon	23	TQ3090
Wood Hayes W Mids	38	SJ9401
Wood Norton Norfk	42	TG0127
Wood Row W York	55	SE3826
Wood Street Norfk	43	TG3722
Wood Street Surrey	12	SU9551
Wood Top Lancs	53	SD5644
Wood Walton Cambs	41	TL2180
Wood's Corner E Susx	14	TQ6619
Wood's Green E Susx	13	TQ6333
Woodacott Cross Devon	5	SS3907
Woodall S York	49	SK4680
Woodbastwick Norfk	43	TG3315
Woodborough Notts	49	SK6347
Woodbridge Devon	6	SX1895
Woodbridge Suffk	33	TM2749
Woodbury Devon	3	SX0087
Woodbury Devon	5	SY0189
Woodbury Salterton Devon	5	SY0189
Woodchester Gloucs	20	SO8302
Woodchurch Kent	15	TQ9434
Woodcombe Somset	7	SS9546
Woodcote Oxon	21	SU6482
Woodcote Shrops	38	SJ7715
Woodcott Gloucs	19	ST5495
Woodditton Cambs	32	TL6559
Woodeaton Oxon	29	SP5312
Woodend Cumb	58	SD1096
Woodend Highld	79	NM7861
Woodend Loth	75	NS9269
Woodend Nhants	29	SP6149
Woodend Highld	11	SU8109
Woodend Green Essex	31	TL5528
Woodford Gloucs	20	ST6996
Woodford Gt Lon	23	TQ4092
Woodford Gt Man	47	SJ8882
Woodford Nhants	30	SP9676
Woodford Bridge Gt Lon	23	TQ4291
Woodford Halse Nhants	29	SP5452
Woodford Wells Gt Lon	23	TQ4093
Woodgate Devon	8	ST1015
Woodgate H & W	28	SO9666
Woodgate Norfk	42	TG0216
Woodgate Norfk	42	TG0216
Woodgreen Green W Susx	11	SU9304
Woodgreen Hants	10	SU1717
Woodgreen Oxon	29	SP3610
Woodhall N York	61	SD9790
Woodhall Hill W York	55	SE1935
Woodhall Spa Lincs	51	TF1962
Woodham Bucks	30	SP7018
Woodham Ferrers Essex	24	TQ7999
Woodham Mortimer Essex	24	TL8104
Woodham Walter Essex	24	TL8107
Woodhaven Fife	83	NO4126
Woodhead Gramp	95	NJ7938
Woodhill Shrops	37	SO7384
Woodhill Somset	8	ST3527

Y

Z

Local radio

SCOTLAND
BBC
1 RADIO SCOTLAND 92.5–94.7 810/370. North-west Scotland 97.7–99.3 810/370

IBA
2 MORAY FIRTH RADIO Inverness 97.4 1107/271
3 NORTHSOUND RADIO Aberdeen 96.9 1035/290
4 RADIO CLYDE Glasgow 102.5 1152/261
5 RADIO FORTH Edinburgh 97.3 1548/194
6 RADIO TAY Dundee, Perth 102.8 1161/258
7 WEST SOUND Ayr 96.7 1035/290. Girvan 97.5 1035/290

THE NORTH
BBC
8 GREATER MANCHESTER RADIO 95.1 1458/206
9 RADIO CLEVELAND 95.0 1548/194. Whitby 95.8 1548/194
10 RADIO CUMBRIA North Cumbria 95.6 756/397. Whitehaven 95.6 1458/206
11 RADIO FURNESS South Cumbria 96.1 837/358. Kendal 95.2 837/358. Windermere 104.2 837/358
12 RADIO HUMBERSIDE 95.9 1485/202
13 RADIO LANCASHIRE 95.5 855/351. Lancaster 104.5 1557/193. South Lancashire 103.9 855/351
14 RADIO LEEDS 92.4 774/388. Ilkley, Otley 95.3 774/388
15 RADIO MERSEYSIDE 95.8 1485/202
16 RADIO NEWCASTLE 95.4 1458/206. N.E. Northumberland 96.0 1458/206. Newcastle & Gateshead 104.4 1458/206
17 RADIO SHEFFIELD 104.1 1035/290. Sheffield 88.6 1035/290
18 RADIO YORK 103.7 666/450. Scarborough 95.5 1260/238. Central N. Yorks 104.3 666/450

IBA
19 METRO RADIO Tyne & Wear 97.1 1152/261
20 PENNINE RADIO Bradford 97.5 1278/235. Huddersfield/Halifax 102.5 1530/196
21 PICCADILLY RADIO Manchester 103.0 1152/261
22 RADIO AIRE Leeds 96.3 828/362
23 RADIO CITY Liverpool 96.7 1548/194
24 RADIO HALLAM Sheffield 97.4 1548/194. Rotherham 96.1 1548/194. Doncaster 103.4 990/303. Barnsley 102.9 1305/230
25 RED ROSE RADIO Blackpool & Preston 97.4 999/301

26 TFM RADIO Stockton-on-Tees 96.6 1170/257
27 VIKING RADIO Humberside 96.9 1161/258

WALES
BBC
28 RADIO WALES 882/340. Llandrindod Wells/Builth Wells area 1125/267. Radio Cymru (Welsh Language Service) 92.5–94.5 South Wales 96.8

IBA
29 MARCHER SOUND Wrexham & Deeside 103.4 1260/238
30 RED DRAGON RADIO Cardiff 103.2 1359/221. Newport 97.4 1305/230
31 SWANSEA SOUND 96.4 1170/257

THE MIDLANDS
BBC
32 RADIO CAMBRIDGESHIRE 96.0 1026/292. Peterborough & N. Cambs 95.7 1449/207
33 RADIO DERBY 104.5 1116/269. Derby 94.2 1116/269. Bakewell & Matlock 95.3
34 RADIO HEREFORD & WORCESTER Hereford 94.7 819/336. Worcester 104.0 738/407
35 RADIO LEICESTER 95.1 837/358
36 RADIO LINCOLNSHIRE 94.9 1368/219
37 RADIO NORFOLK East Norfolk 95.1 855/351. West Norfolk 104.4 873/344
38 RADIO NORTHAMPTON 104.2 1107/271. Corby 103.6 1107/271
39 RADIO NOTTINGHAM 103.8 1521/197. Central Notts. 95.5 1584/189
40 RADIO SHROPSHIRE 96.0 1584/189. Ludlow 95.0 1584/189
41 RADIO STOKE-ON-TRENT 94.6 1503/200
42 RADIO W.M. (WEST MIDLANDS) 95.6 1458/206. Wolverhampton 95.6 828/362

IBA
43 BEACON RADIO Wolverhampton 97.2 990/303. Shrewsbury & Telford 103.1 990/303
44 BRMB RADIO Birmingham 96.4 1152/261
45 HEREWARD RADIO Peterborough 102.7 1332/225
46 LEICESTER SOUND 103.2 1260/238
47 MERCIA SOUND Coventry 97.0 1359/220
48 RADIO BROADLAND Gt Yarmouth & Norwich 102.4 1152/260
49 RADIO ORWELL Ipswich 97.1 1170/257
50 RADIO TRENT Nottingham 96.2 999/301. Derby 102.8 945/317
51 RADIO WYVERN Hereford 97.6 954/314. Worcester 102.8 1530/196
52 SAXON RADIO Bury St Edmunds 96.4 1251/240
53 SIGNAL RADIO Stoke-on-Trent 102.6 1170/257

THE SOUTH WEST
BBC
54 BBC WILTSHIRE SOUND Swindon 103.6 1368/219. Salisbury 103.5 North Wilts 104.3 1332
55 RADIO BRISTOL 95.5 1548/194. Bristol 94.9 1548/194. Bath 104.6 1548/194. Central Somerset 95.5 1323/227
56 RADIO CORNWALL East Cornwall 95.2 657/457. West Cornwall 103.9 630/476. Isles of Scilly 96.0 630/476
57 RADIO DEVON Exeter & Devon 95.8 990/303. Torbay 103.4 1458/206. Plymouth 103.4 855/351. Barnstaple 94.8 801/375. North Devon 103.4 801/375. Okehamptom 96.0 801/375
58 RADIO GLOUCESTER 104.7 603/498. Stroud 95.0

IBA
59 DEVONAIR RADIO Exeter 97.0 666/450. Torbay 96.4 954/314
60 GREAT WEST RADIO Bath 103.0 Bristol 96.3 1260/238. Marlborough 96.5 Swindon 97.2 1161/258. West Wilts 102.2 936/321
61 PLYMOUTH SOUND Plymouth 97.0 1152/261. Tavistock 96.6
62 SEVERN SOUND Cheltenham & Gloucester 102.4 774/388. Stroud 103.0
63 2CR (TWO COUNTIES RADIO) Bournemouth 97.2 828/362

THE SOUTH EAST
BBC
64 BBC RADIO ESSEX 103.5 765/392. N. E. Essex 103.5 729/412. S.E. Essex 95.3 1530/196
65 GREATER LONDON RADIO 94.9 1458/206
66 RADIO BEDFORDSHIRE 95.5 630/476. Bedford 95.5. 1161/258. Luton & Dunstable 103.8 630/476
67 RADIO KENT 96.7 1035/290. Tunbridge Wells 96.7 1602/187. East Kent 104.2 774/388
68 RADIO OXFORD 95.2 1485/202
69 RADIO SOLENT 96.1 999/300. Bournemouth 96.1 1359/221
70 RADIO SUSSEX Brighton & Worthing 95.3 1485/202. East Sussex & part of West Sussex 104.5 1161/258. Reigate, Crawley & Horsham 104.0 1368/219. Newhaven FM Frequency to be announced

IBA
71 CAPITAL RADIO London 95.8 1548/194
72 CHILTERN RADIO Bedford 96.9 792/378. Luton 97.6 828/362. Northampton 96.6 1557/193
73 COUNTY SOUND Guildford 96.4 1476/203
74 ESSEX RADIO Chelmsford 102.6 1359/220. Southend 96.3 1431/210
75 INVICTA RADIO Maidstone/Medway 103.1 1242/242. Dover 97.0 603/497. Thanet 95.9 603/497. Canterbury 102.8 603/497. Ashford 96.1 603/497
76 LBC London 97.3 1152/261
77 OCEAN SOUND Southampton 103.2 1557/193. Portsmouth 97.5 1170/257
78 RADIO MERCURY Crawley/Reigate 102.7 1521/197. Horsham 97.5
79 RADIO 210 Thames Valley, Reading & N. Hants 97.0 1431/210. Basingstoke, Andover 102.9 1431/210. Winchester 96.7
80 SOUTHERN SOUND Brighton 103.5 1323/227